▪▪▪ HALLMARK FEATURES: A COMPLETE LEARNING PACKAGE

Through this unique and highly praised set of learning tools, your students come away ready to *understand* the material. Learning objectives set clear expectations, frequent review sections keep students on track, and boxed features engage students in critical thinking.

PREP, CHECK, AND REVIEW

Connecting to... **features** briefly frame the start of each story and connect it to core political science content, preparing students to make important critical thinking connections.

What Have I Learned? **section breaks** offer a brief quiz with an answer key so students can gauge their comprehension, ensure they understand concepts, and know they are making connections between key terms and broader questions.

Chapter Review **sections** offer additional opportunities to review core concepts, connect ideas to stories, think critically about the issues, and master key terms—all conveniently organized around learning objectives.

CONNECTING TO . . .

The Ideas That Drive American Political Culture

As you read the next section, reflect back upon the stories of Bridget Mergens and the Boyd County High GSA. Consider the following:

- What these stories tell us about American political culture
- How very different individuals and groups base their views of a better society on the same foundational ideas
- The ways in which your fellow students have used fundamental ideas in American politics to press for their rights

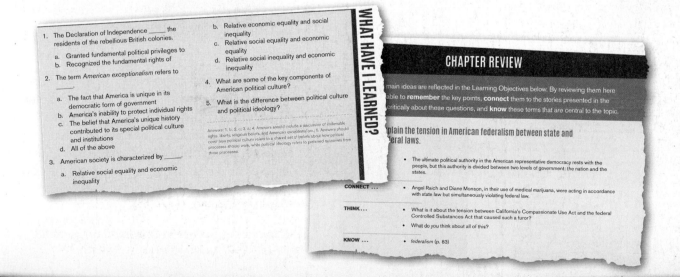

"This feature will help students process the material better, and help them think critically about a topic.**"**

—John Klemanski, *Oakland University*

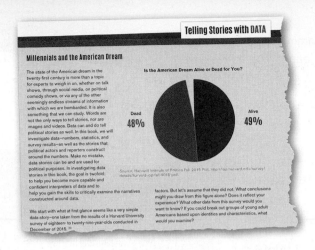

Telling Stories with Data shows students how data can explain—or distort—political phenomona, and improves their ability to interpret facts and figures. **What Do YOU Think? questions** encourage students to challenge the narratives constructed around the data.

Explore this feature in Chapter 1 on page 9.

Telling Stories with Images asks students to take a close look at visuals and the narratives they create. **What Do YOU Think? questions** get students to think more deeply about the impact of imagery on the way we see politics.

Explore this feature in Chapter 10 on p. 347.

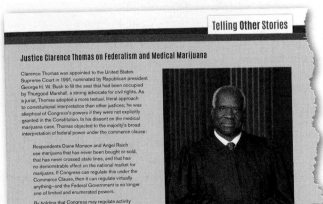

Telling Other Stories introduces counter-narratives to the central voices in each chapter. Students gain a fuller picture of the chapter material and appreciate the importance of alternate perspectives. **What Do YOU Think? questions** get students to think about their own perspectives—how their own stories affect their reading of events.

Explore this feature in Chapter 3 on page 93.

▪▪▪ SAGE COURSEPACKS FOR INSTRUCTORS

OUR CONTENT TAILORED TO YOUR LMS

SAGE **coursepacks** makes it easy to import our quality instructor materials and student resources into your school's learning management system (LMS). Intuitive and simple to use, **SAGE coursepacks** allows you to integrate only the content you need and requires no access code.

A RICH SET OF TEST QUESTIONS

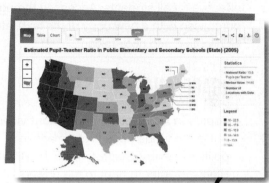

- **The test bank** built on Bloom's Taxonomy (with Bloom's cognitive domain and difficulty level noted for each question) is created specifically for the text, with references to chapter learning objectives (and the page number). It includes **more than 1,500** multiple choice, short answer, essay, fill-in-the blank, and true-false questions.

- **Assessment questions for SAGE Premium Video** in the Interactive eBook offer high-quality video assignments and test students on comprehension as well as analysis and application.

- See more **SAGE coursepacks** features at **sagepub.com/storiesofanation**.

ANALYTIC SKILL-BUILDING

- **Assignable data exercises** in each chapter help students build essential data literacy skills using interactive data visualization tools from **SAGE Stats** and **U.S. Political Stats**. Drawing on key data series ranging from demographic patterns to state budgets to voting behavior, these exercises offer students a dynamic way to analyze real-world data and think critically about the stories behind the numbers.

CUSTOMIZED AND CURATED FOR USE IN:

⑤SAGE coursepacks

For Dylan and Sadie

AMERICAN GOVERNMENT

■■■ **STORIES OF A NATION**
THE ESSENTIALS

SCOTT F. ABERNATHY
University of Minnesota

 |

Los Angeles | London | New Delhi
Singapore | Washington DC | Melbourne

FOR INFORMATION:

CQ Press

An Imprint of SAGE Publications, Inc.

2455 Teller Road

Thousand Oaks, California 91320

E-mail: order@sagepub.com

SAGE Publications Ltd.

1 Oliver's Yard

55 City Road

London, EC1Y 1SP

United Kingdom

SAGE Publications India Pvt. Ltd.

B 1/I 1 Mohan Cooperative Industrial Area

Mathura Road, New Delhi 110 044

India

SAGE Publications Asia-Pacific Pte. Ltd.

3 Church Street

#10-04 Samsung Hub

Singapore 049483

Acquisitions Editor: Michael Kerns

Development Editor: Elise Frasier

eLearning Editor: John Scappini

Editorial Assistant: Zachary Hoskins

Production Editor: Olivia Weber-Stenis

Copy Editor: Shannon Kelly

Typesetter: C&M Digitals (P) Ltd.

Proofreader: Laura Webb

Indexer: Michael Ferreira

Cover and Interior

   Designer: Gail Buschman

Marketing Manager: Amy Whitaker

Printed in Canada

ISBN 978-1-4522-8730-0

This book is printed on acid-free paper.

17 18 19 20 21 10 9 8 7 6 5 4 3 2 1

BRIEF CONTENTS

DETAILED CONTENTS

Equal Access Act   Thomas Jefferson   Martin Luther King Jr.

STORIES OF...

left: Rodger Mallison/Fort Worth Star-Telegram/MCT via Getty Images; *center*: GraphicaArtis/Getty Images; *right*: Birmingham, Ala. Public Library Archives

James Madison

Mercy Otis Warren

Angel Raich

STORIES OF...

left: Ipsumpix/Corbis via Getty Images; *center:* Granger, NYC; *right:* AP Photo/Ben Margot

Schechter Brothers

Edward Snowden

Benjamin Gitlow

STORIES OF...

left: Granger, NYC; *center:* Travis P Ball/Getty Images for SXSW; *right:* Bettmann / Contributor

PART II: POLITICAL BEHAVIOR AND MASS POLITICS

Thea Spyer and Edie Windsor

Judith Heumann

Amanda Collins

left: Neville Elder/Corbis Premium Historical/Getty Images; *center*: Rainer Jensen/picture-alliance/dpa/AP Images; *right*: AP Photo/Lisa J. Tolda

Barack Obama

Michael Brown

Danjel Bout

STORIES OF…

left: Kristoffer Tripplaar/Pool via CNP.; *center*: REUTERS/Whitney Curtis; *right*: Courtesy of Danjel Bout.

Hillary Clinton

Donald Trump

Ted Poe

STORIES OF...

left: Photo by Lars Niki/Corbis via Getty Images.; *center*: BRENDAN SMIALOWSKI/AFP/Getty Images; *right*: Alex Wong/Getty Images.

Latino Outreach  Salud Carbajal  Former Senator Trent Lott

left: AP Photo/David Zalubowski; *center*: Courtesy of Salud Carbajal for Congress; *right*: Photo by Bill Clark/CQ Roll Call.

PART III: INSTITUTIONS

STORIES OF...

Maria Cantwell, Lisa Murkowski

Joseph R. Biden, Ted Kennedy

Schoolhouse Rock

left: Bill Clark/CQ Roll Call; *center*: AP Photo/Greg Gibson, File.; *right*: Kari Rene Hall/Los Angeles Times via Getty Images.

Anwar al-Awlaki

George W. Bush

Attorney General Eric Holder

STORIES OF...

left: Tracy Woodward/The Washington Post via Getty Images; *center*: STEPHEN JAFFE/AFP/Getty Images.; *right*: PAUL J. RICHARDS/AFP/Getty Images.

Andrew Jackson

Sonia Sotomayor

William Marbury

STORIES OF...

left: Library of Congress, Prints and Photographs Division; *center:* Alex Wong/Getty Images.; *right:* The Granger Collection, New York.

Judge Robert Bork   Missionary Samuel Worcester

left: James K. W. Atherton/The Washington Post via Getty Images; *right:* New Echota Historical Site.

PREFACE

REAL PEOPLE, REAL STORIES, REAL POLITICS

Stories are powerful things. They help shape the political world in which we each live. They help define who we are as individuals and as a people. And stories are also excellent teaching tools, making the material relatable, memorable, and real. This book harnesses the full power of narrative to draw students into the study of American politics, highlighting the unpredictable outcomes of people's actions and strategies—both of individuals and groups of individuals acting together.

As you'll soon discover, this textbook is narrative to its core. Stories are not used as marginal introductory elements that serve only as gateways into the main material, nor just as examples that extend the lessons—but as the text itself. I have taught undergraduates for more than fifteen years here at the University of Minnesota, and my experience has been that students read right past the chapter opening vignettes in their textbooks. I'll bet you have had that same, frustrating experience. It's not because those brief intros are poorly written or boring either; it's that students know these supplemental narratives are, by design, peripheral and can be skipped to get to the real testable content. That is a real missed opportunity for them to learn, remember, connect with, and ultimately join in the narratives. In this book, the stories are the main event, the method through which students come to understand American politics and processes, from the founding to current policy implementation.

The Benefit of Real Stories

This textbook tells stories about real people: their strategies, the actions they took, the contingencies surrounding those actions and their outcomes, and the struggles they faced. The topics and scope of coverage are consistent with other introductory American government texts and equally comprehensive. What is different about this approach is that storytelling drives the pedagogy and thematic development in a way that engages students to interact more directly with the material, one of the biggest challenges in any introductory class.

A Richer Understanding of Political Dynamics

With this approach students will better understand that political outcomes are not predetermined but are instead the results of strategic choices made by political actors, usually undertaken in an uncertain environment, often amid unequal relationships of power. The approach in this book is designed to show students how others have wrestled with similar questions of power, action, and change, whether in very different times and circumstances or in situations ripped from today's headlines. How some have succeeded, others failed, but, more importantly, how many have operated in the space between success and failure, adjusting their strategies along the way.

Stronger Connections through Engagement

A second benefit is that your students will actually read the book. In doing so they will be doing much more than skimming for key terms or IDs. By combining the deep dives into one or a few key stories in each chapter with solid research-backed core content, *Stories of a Nation* will guide your students to a genuine engagement with the material, the theories that try to explain political outcomes, and the enduring questions of American representative democracy. And, they will connect the dots between those elements. The first chapter of the book, for example, clearly identifies and explains the founding ideals of American democracy—liberty, equality, natural rights, the American Dream, American exceptionalism. But those ideas are each situated within a set of vivid stories about people and groups coming from different times, places, and experiences who claimed their rights as citizens. Starting on page one, students learn about Bridget Mergens, a high school student who wanted to start a Bible club at her high school. They read about a group of high school students in Kentucky who—using the same set of rights—wanted to start a Gay-Straight Alliance club. Later in the chapter they pick up the narrative thread again to hear how Thomas Jefferson went about arguing for natural rights in drafting the *Declaration of Independence* and the revolution of ideas that followed. As important, they learn what he and others left out. They hear the voices of people like Lemuel Johnson and Esther DeBerdt Reed who spoke on behalf of African-Americans and women in colonial America. Finally, at the chapter's end readers conclude the journey in the 20th century to witness Martin Luther King Jr. take up the language of natural rights to advance rights for African-Americans. Together, these stories help students understand so-called "key terms" in ways no ordinary descriptive text can.

Greater Instructional Flexibility

Third, *American Government: Stories of a Nation* is adaptable to the approach that *you* want to use. This is not a book that pushes a specific perspective or one that envisions a teacher as a repository of fact. These narratives allow for an emphasis on institutions, behavior, or a combination of both. For example, two stories are used to present the core concepts underlying a study of interest groups and social movements—one of the efforts of lobbyists in the wake of the financial crisis of 2008, the other of Occupy Wall Street and its efforts to call attention to economic inequality in the years following. They can be used to highlight the ways in which institutions structure political action, the ways in which individuals make strategic choices in their efforts to solve problems of collective action, or both.

The stories can also be used to focus on American political development, ideas, or an approach that focuses on people, or their efforts to secure their own rights and liberties. In the Presidency chapter, for example, the narrative surrounding President Obama's order to use an unmanned drone to kill an American citizen in Yemen without trial, Anwar Al-Awlaki, could facilitate a deeper conversation about the institutional powers of the modern presidency, of the rights of Americans in times of war, or both.

In addition, the variety of sources used to present the material in the book—textual, visual, and data-based—as well as the self-assessment tools, make the content accessible to students with a variety of learning strengths. As a teacher, that kind of book is what I always wanted, but I never found one that completely fulfilled that promise. That is another reason that I wrote it.

Greater Inclusiveness

The fourth reason is just as important and closely connected to the narrative approach in this book. In spite of efforts by the authors, editors, and publishers of American government textbooks to address the diversity of Americans' lived experiences, the majority of books on the market do not fully embrace that diversity. A mounting body of scholarship analyzing the text, image, content, and context of those works arrives at strikingly similar conclusions: depictions and considerations of members of traditionally marginalized groups are sparse and, when presented, placed in a specific set of chapters and topics. Covering the struggle of African-Americans to achieve civil rights in a chapter on civil rights, for example, makes perfect sense. But it doesn't make sense that that would be the only place we'd hear stories of other political actions taken by African-American people or others with similarly marginalized coverage in texts. An exploration of political campaigns and elections, for example, becomes more immediate through a thoughtful examination of the ways in which political parties are struggling to attract the Latino vote (and questioning the existence of such a monolithic entity), and efforts by Latino candidates themselves, in an era of profound demographic change.

In this book, diversity is not a list of boxes to check off. Americans' diverse identities have powerfully shaped political processes and outcomes even when not successful in any given struggle. It includes a broad vision of the diversity of Americans' lived experiences, including the reality that any one American may have multiple conceptions of their own identities, and that those self-understandings shape their participation in the political process. Through the power of narrative and of stories, my goal is that *all* students—reading and using this book—will find that they are also a part of the American experience, whether or not their voices have been heard.

THE ORGANIZATION OF THE BOOK

By now you've noticed that *American Government: Stories of a Nation* approaches American politics a little bit differently than other introductory textbooks. Still, if you look at the table of contents, you'll see that the text covers everything you'd expect and require in a book that primes your students for future engagement in the political world, or, if we're lucky, future study in the field. You'll also notice that this book covers topics having to do with political participation and behavior before it covers institutions, which is a natural outgrowth of the fact that we highlight the role that real people have played in the development of our government—although the chapters could certainly be assigned out of order to suit your preferences.

In Part I, Chapters 1-5, therefore, cover foundations beginning with an introduction to the central themes in American politics (Chapter 1), then covering the Constitution (Chapter 2), federalism (Chapter 3), civil liberties (Chapter 4), and civil rights (Chapter 5). Chapters 6-10, Part II, Political Behavior and Mass Politics, covers participation (Chapter 6), public opinion (Chapter 7), the media (Chapter 8), parties (Chapter 9), campaigns and elections (Chapter 10), and interest groups and social movements (Chapter 11). The chapters in Part III cover political institutions: Congress (Chapter 12), the presidency (Chapter 13), bureaucracy (Chapter 14), and the judiciary (Chapter 15). The last section covers policy with Chapter 16 on domestic social policy, Chapter 17 on economic policy, and Chapter 18 on foreign policy.

What may be less obvious at a glance is that the organization *within* each chapter differs from your standard textbook. Each chapter in *Stories of a Nation* begins with an extended narrative that sets up and integrates the subject matter that follows, subject matter that is tied to four to six learning objectives. The nuts and bolts sections that follow the initial narrative refer back to that story, with figures, tables, and images chosen to connect the narrative with the subject matter. Each major section concludes with a set of quiz questions (with answers) to reinforce the learning.

In some chapters, one central narrative is sustained throughout. When the core material demands it, two, or occasionally three, narratives contribute, to avoid having to "force" one story to convey what may be a bit more disparate set of concepts. The conclusion ties everything together, helping students to reflect deeply upon the subject matter and the questions raised in each chapter.

How does this approach work in practice? In Chapter 7, for example, on Public Opinion, I focus the narrative on the aftermath of the fatal police shooting of Michael Brown in Ferguson, Missouri in 2014. The basic question is this: has public opinion about the way that African-Americans are treated by police changed since that event and others related to it?

The chapter begins by setting up the story, focusing on the one-year anniversary of the tragic event. Learning objectives guide students to a full set of issues that political scientists consider when presenting the topic of American public opinion--assessing the components and formation of opinions, ways of measuring it, patterns of change in people's attitudes, and the larger meaning and impact of public opinion in American democracy. The nuts and bolts section that follows explores debates over the stability, coherence, and meaning of public opinion. Following a quiz on the material in the previous section, we return to the fallout from Ferguson, only this time with a detailed exploration (including figures with data representing public opinion surveys) of divisions in opinion over the meanings of the event and the protests that followed. After another brief check in on comprehension, we dive into the ways in which public opinion is measured, its importance to representative democracy, and the challenges inherent in scientific polling, followed again, with a short check on comprehension.

A section on political socialization fuses the narrative and the research-based content into one section, with an in-depth consideration (again with figures) of the partisan divides in opinion on the core issues of race and policing. A narrative section on political leaders' responses to the events ties public opinion to democratic representation, again with a quick concept assessment. The chapter concludes with a section that challenges students to continue to explore the meanings of public opinion. Finally, like every chapter, this one also has a comprehensive guide for review that connects the learning objectives, take-home points of the stories, major political science themes, and key terms, to help students confirm that they have fully comprehended the chapter.

As you can see, no political science content gets "lost" at the expense of the narrative—and with plenty of built-in guidance, no student gets lost in the narrative.

PEDAGOGY: DIFFERENT WAYS OF TELLING STORIES

This book acknowledges the challenges of dealing with the political world that students will inevitably have to confront in their own lives. To that end, it also provides students with specific skills with which to bring the deeper understandings that they will develop to bear on their own political realities. Each of the pedagogical features of the book is designed to harness the power of narrative in the service of teaching students to be critical readers of image, data, and text.

Telling Stories with Images

Image literacy is as crucial to the pedagogical objectives of this book as textual literacy. Instead of solely offering images as illustrative enhancements to the text, the book also examines the ways in which images themselves have played and continue to play a role in the development of American government and politics. The feature *Telling Stories with Images* helps students understand how visual narratives have been and are employed in the services of specific political objectives. Political stories are told not only through text, especially in a political space increasingly driven by social media. Through a critical presentation of the use of images, students will gain skills in interpreting images as they gain a deeper understanding of the political world of which they are part, and which they will help to shape.

As an example, Chapter 7's *Telling Stories with Images* feature called *The St. Louis Post-Dispatch Changes its Cover Photo* explores the changes the editors and publishers of that paper made to its front page photograph within a few hours on the one-year anniversary of Michael Brown's shooting and the protests on that day. Because of another shooting of a young African American man on the evening following the peaceful demonstrations, those in charge chose to dramatically alter the next day's front page. The feature concludes with a section called "What Do You Think," which asks students to place themselves in the position of a newspaper editor covering a highly controversial event, to encourage them to think about the social and political ramifications of these decisions that are made every day.

Telling Stories with Data

In an increasingly data-driven world, the ability to act as a critical interpreter of data—and perhaps most importantly—of the stories told based on the sometimes-competing interpretations of those data is a fundamental skill. Data, and their interpretation, constitute an exercise of power. By engaging with *Telling Stories with Data* students will understand that data-stories can be just as important in the political process as any other narrative. Students will critically reflect on how the data were obtained, how they were interpreted, and how political narratives were constructed around them. In doing so, students will engage with the use of data to advance a particular political objective and become more thoughtful and critical readers of the stories constructed around numbers and statistics.

Chapter 7's feature *Change in American Public Opinion after Ferguson* presents data from Pew Research Center on the perceptions of the importance for the nation to make changes to secure equal rights. The data are broken down by respondents' racial identities. Between 2014 and 2015, immediately following Ferguson and related protests, both African American and white public opinion appeared to shift towards an increasing support for needed changes. The "What Do You Think?" section asks students to reflect upon what other kinds of evidence might be useful to confirm that the events of 2014–2015 *caused* the apparent shift in opinion.

Telling Other Stories

When writing a textbook, any author exercises power by the necessary act of writing some stories in and leaving others out. Even as we try to remain neutral or objective, we inevitably impose a particular point of view on events, or even a false coherence to actions and consequences that may in fact be incoherent and messy. Another key feature of the textbook is *Telling Other Stories*, oral and written statements by people, historical and contemporary, in which they reflect on key issues or the impact of their words on their own story and on American political history. These writings, speeches, and communications, have been chosen to challenge any one dominant narrative in the text, rather than to reinforce it. In Chapter 7, *Different Perspectives about the Meaning of Ferguson*, different responses are presented about the protests in Ferguson, through the voices of residents. These perspectives do not follow a neat and clear divide based upon identity but instead convey the need to reflect carefully and thoughtfully about narratives that are constructed around events. As with the others, the feature concludes with a "What Do You Think?" section that asks students to synthesize and evaluate what they have read.

Reinforcing the Fundamentals

Several smaller features of the book also serve to reinforce the nuts and bolts materials and also help students understand why the chosen narratives will help them gain a deeper and more memorable understanding of this material.

- *Learning Objectives* at the start of each chapter guide students' reading of and engagement with the material, signposting the goals and setting clear expectations for what they will master.
- *Connecting To . . .* boxes bridge the narrative and "nuts and bolts" sections, which helps students link core political science lessons to the stories they are engaging with. These concise tools encourage a more robust treatment of the concepts and prepare students to make important critical thinking connections.
- *What Have I Learned?* section breaks offer a brief quiz with an answer key so students can gauge their comprehension, ensure they understand concepts, and know they are making connections between key terms and broader questions.
- *Chapter Review* sections conclude each chapter by offering students additional opportunities to review core concepts, connect them to the stories, think critically about the issues, and master key terms—all helpfully framed around the chapter's learning objectives.

BRINGING IT ALL TOGETHER: TEACHING AND A NARRATIVE APPROACH

I have taught incarcerated youths, homeless adolescents, fourth graders, seventh graders, undergraduates, and graduate students. Across all these experiences I have learned that narrative is a powerful educational tool. People are born to be storytellers and story-hearers; it seems to be in our make-up. We are wired to respond to narrative and its ability to convey the contingency, complexity, and uncertainty of collective human action, and the hopes of what might be accomplished if it succeeds. Our students care about these stories. They are also already talking about them—all the time. My goal, in this book, is to give students both a framework and set of tools with which to discuss the complexities and contradictions of American government and politics.

The stories told within this book will resonate with and engage your students. They are not sugarcoated. This book does not shy away from the difficult issues with which your students are already dealing. As a teacher first considering the text you may have some reservations about covering topics such as police-community relations in predominantly African-American neighborhoods, Edward Snowden's release of documents from the NSA, Occupy Wall Street, or sexual violence on college campuses.

With so much to cover in an introductory course like this, we instructors want to make sure to convey all the important material central to our course goals. You might wonder if students will get "lost" in the narratives and fail to sufficiently attend to the "nuts and bolts," or that conversations in your classes might become sidetracked into debates on the narratives themselves rather than discussions about the underlying political processes and institutions. Though these are reasonable questions, rest assured that we have taken a very thoughtful and proactive approach to this issue, efforts that, based on results from class-testing, work.

Over the last few years, we took the time to ask hundreds of college students to respond to a set of survey questions after conducting a class-test of several draft chapters of the book. Here is what just a handful said about how well they thought the book's approach works. Note that these are unedited—real students' own words:

> Many government and history books can be dry and dull unless the subject is the reader's passion. This chapter held my attention and I was interested the entire time I read.

> I want to keep reading

> I LOVED how I could relate more to the examples or there were more recent issues on public opinion that I saw first hand like the news, such as the Ferguson incident. I would say the biggest strengths of this book are keeping the readers engaged. It does not feel like an ordinary American Government textbook...which is very important if you want your students to actually read.

> It was very easy for me to connect the stories to the overall concepts of the chapter which is critical in a textbook. Student are usually not thrilled about being forced to read chapter after chapter of information on American Government but this approach lightens that burden. Bravo.

> I think this book is more interesting than the book I am using for my course. I actually enjoyed reading it, and did not have to force myself to finish the chapter.

> I was very engaged with this approach. I thought it was extremely helpful and interesting. I agree one hundred percent with the stories and this method because it got my attention.

> This textbook excites me as it speaks of issues that have happened recently that I have actually lived to experience.

> I was very surprised a textbook took this approach, and I enjoyed it very much. It builds a general feeling of rapport with whoever is reading the textbook and made it feel relatable to the topics we dove into. I felt connected with the concepts & felt myself more interested to continue reading.

> The stories (specially as a woman and a minority) most definitely helped me connect the concept to the story. I like the stories that were used because they were interesting and I haven't heard of them before.

> [I] enjoyed this approach. It made this book more pleasurable to read. I could put myself in the shoes of these women at the time and get a better understanding of the mindset of the time. It's encouraging to read the stories and see that though the odds were against them, they didn't give up. They're not made up stories but real women with real issues and had the drive to push forward despite the obstacles.

The book consciously strives to avoid weighing in on one side or another of heated debates but instead guides students to use their own engagement with them to more deeply understand American politics. A set of instructors' resources offer concrete tips on guiding successful and focused class discussions. The pedagogical features within each chapter (see above) have been designed to reinforce the nuts and bolts in a way that preserves the immediacy of the narratives without sacrificing all of the coverage that you expect.

Stories that are devoid of people, their actions, aspirations, and mistakes are not very interesting. Fortunately, as teachers of American government, we rarely encounter stories like that. The political world that we teach our students about is vibrant, fascinating, and charged. The description of the chapter content above and a glance at the table of contents of the book shows that this book takes up stories that emerge directly from that political world, stories that will draw your students in to a *real* understanding of their political worlds, and their places in it.

That is why stories are such powerful things.

SUPPORTING YOUR TEACHING

This textbook comes with a host of resources to help both instructors and students get the most out of this class. For some, the book alone will provide a rich and engaging experience. But, more likely, you may want to avail yourself of some of the following.

⑤SAGE edge

SAGE edge is a robust online environment featuring an impressive array of tools and resources for review, study, and further exploration, keeping both instructors and students on the cutting edge of teaching and learning. SAGE edge content is open access and available on demand. Learning and teaching has never been easier! We gratefully acknowledge Jeneen Hobby, Cleveland State University; Andrew Levin, Harper College; Hyung Lae Park, El Paso Community College; Nick Pyeatt, Penn State Altoona; John Seymour, El Paso Community College; and Theresa Marchant-Shapiro, Southern Connecticut State University for developing the ancillaries on this site.

SAGE edge for Students at **http://edge.sagepub.com/abernathy1e** provides a personalized approach to help students accomplish their coursework goals in an easy-to-use learning environment.

- An online **action plan** includes tips and feedback on progress through the course and materials, which allows students to individualize their learning experience.
- **Chapter summaries** with **learning objectives** reinforce the most important material.
- Mobile-friendly **eFlashcards** strengthen understanding of key terms and concepts, and make it easy to maximize your study time, anywhere, anytime.
- Mobile-friendly practice **quizzes** allow you to assess how much you've learned and where you need to focus your attention.
- Carefully selected **video resources** bring concepts to life, are tied to learning objectives, and make learning easier.
- **Exclusive access to influential SAGE journal and reference content**, ties important research and scholarship to chapter concepts to strengthen learning.

SAGE edge for Instructors at **http://edge.sagepub.com/abernathy1e** supports teaching by making it easy to integrate quality content and create a rich learning environment for students.

- The **Test bank** built on Bloom's taxonomy (with Bloom's cognitive domain and difficulty level noted for each question) is created specifically for this text, with references to chapter learning objectives (and page number) and ExamView test generation. It includes more than 1,500 multiple choice, short answer, essay, fill-in-the-blank, and true-false questions, as well as the opportunity to edit any question and/or insert personalized questions to effectively assess the students' progress and understanding.

- **Sample course syllabi** provide suggested models for structuring one's course.
- Editable, chapter-specific **PowerPoint® slides** offer complete flexibility for creating a multimedia presentation for the course, so you don't have to start from scratch but you can customize to your exact needs.
- An **instructor's manual** features chapter overviews and learning objectives, lecture starters, ideas for class activities, and discussion questions.
- A set of all the **graphics from the text**, including all the maps, tables, and figures in PowerPoint, PDF, and JPG formats for class presentations.
- Carefully selected chapter-by-chapter **video and multimedia content** that enhances classroom-based exploration of key topics.

Enriched Learning through Technology

Students today are connected, wired, and networked in ways previous generations could not have imagined, and they process information in ways that go way beyond reading the printed word on a paper page. To keep up with them and their quickly evolving world, *American Government: Stories of a Nation* is also a full-fledged, integrated media experience. When students purchase a new print copy of the book they receive **FREE access** to an enhanced ebook. This interactive ebook uses the VitalSource Bookshelf®, where students can read the eBook online, on any device, and download it to read offline. They can also share notes and highlights with instructors and classmates, and "follow" friends and instructors as they make their own notes and highlights. Through a series of annotated icons on select pages, students can quickly link to multimedia on the page where a topic is discussed, pointed to articles and background pieces, to audio clips of interviews, to video clips of news stories or satirical commentary, to reference and biography material, to CQ Researcher policy backgrounder reports, to important current data on such topics as approval ratings and public opinion polls.

In addition to the curated multimedia content discussed above, two excited types of **SAGE Premium Video** truly set this ebook apart:

- **Topics in American Government** videos recap the fundamentals of American politics in every chapter—from the Bill of Rights to voter turnout to the powers of the presidency. Each animated video is paired with chapter learning objectives and tied to assessment in our **SAGE coursepacks**, offering a more complete way to **reinforce mastery of key concepts** while meeting your students' diverse learning styles.
- **American Government News Clips** bring extra coverage of current events into the book, connecting multiple, brief 2- to 4-minute news clips to core chapter content. With multiple-choice assessment in **SAGE coursepacks**, these clips offer an ideal way for students to practice using higher level analysis and application skills to apply chapter concepts to recent political events.

Altogether, these resources allow students to explore an important topic or idea while reading—a reinforcing exercise as well as vetted content that provides depth and added context. It's an enhanced, enriching, and interactive learning experience.

SAGE Coursepacks for Instructors

The **SAGE coursepack** for *American Government: Stories of a Nation* makes it easy to import our quality instructor materials and student resources into your school's learning management system (LMS), such as Blackboard, Canvas, Brightspace by D2L, or Moodle. Intuitive and simple to use, **SAGE coursepack** allows you to integrate only the content you need, with minimal effort, and requires no access code. Don't use an LMS platform? You can still access many of the online resources for *Stories of a Nation* via the SAGE edge site.

Available SAGE content through the coursepack includes:

- Pedagogically robust **assessment tools** that foster review, practice, and critical thinking, and offer a more complete way to measure student engagement, including:

  o Diagnostic chapter **pre tests and post tests** that identify opportunities for improvement, track student progress, and ensure mastery of key learning objectives

  o **Test banks** built on Bloom's Taxonomy that provide a diverse range of test items with ExamView test generation

  o **Activity and quiz options** that allow you to choose only the assignments and tests you want

  o **Instructions** on how to use and integrate the comprehensive assessments and resources provided

- **Chapter-specific discussion questions** to help launch engaging classroom interaction while reinforcing important content

- **Assessment questions for SAGE Premium Video** from the Interactive eBook offer high-quality video assignments and test students on comprehension as well as analysis and application.

- **Assignable data exercises** in each chapter help students build essential data literacy skills using interactive data visualization tools from **SAGE Stats** and **U.S. Political Stats**. Drawing on key data series ranging from demographic patterns to state budgets to voting behavior, these exercises offer students a dynamic way to analyze real-world data and think critically about the stories behind the numbers.

- Additional **video resources** that bring concepts to life, are tied to learning objectives and make learning easier

- EXCLUSIVE, influential **SAGE journal and reference content**, built into course materials and assessment tools, that ties important research and scholarship to chapter concepts to strengthen learning

- Editable, chapter-specific **PowerPoint® slides** that offer flexibility when creating multimedia lectures so you don't have to start from scratch but you can customize to your exact needs

- **Integrated links to the FREE interactive eBook** that make it easy for your students to maximize their study time with this "anywhere, anytime" mobile-friendly version of the text. It also offers access to more digital tools and resources, including SAGE Premium Video

- **All tables and figures** from the textbook

A number of instructors helped to guide the development of the above resources. We appreciate the time and thoughts our reviewers put into their feedback, which helped us to refine the material and ensure that we provide content useful to both instructors and students. We offer special thanks to Justin S. Vaughn, Boise State University, and to:

Richard A. Almeida, Francis Marion University

John A. Aughenbaugh, Virginia Commonwealth University

Madelyn P. Bowman, Tarrant County College, South Campus

Marla Brettschneider, University of New Hampshire

Mark A. Cichock, University of Texas at Arlington

Amy Colon, SUNY Sullivan

Victoria Cordova, Sam Houston State University

Kevin Davis, North Central Texas College

Michael J. Faber, Texas State University

Terry Filicko, Clark State Community College

Patrick Gilbert, Lone Star College

Andrew Green, Central College

Sally Hansen, Daytona State College

Alyx D. Mark, North Central College

David F. McClendon, Tyler Junior College

Michael P. McConachie, Collin College

Patrick Moore, Richland College

Tracy Osborn, University of Iowa

Carl Palmer, Illinois State University

Melodie Pickett, Tarleton State University

Daniel E. Ponder, Drury University

Nicholas L. Pyeatt, Penn State Altoona

Paul Rozycki, Mott Community College

Deron T. Schreck, Moraine Valley Community College

Tony Wohlers, Cameron University

ACKNOWLEDGMENTS

There are many, many people who have helped to make this book a reality, some of whom probably have, or have had, no idea that they did so. I am grateful to all of them. Just as the Ninth Amendment makes it clear that Americans' fundamental rights and freedoms can never be fully enumerated, this will be a necessarily incomplete statement of my gratitude.

First, I would like to thank some of my teachers over the years. I owe a great debt to William S. Kilborne Jr. for teaching me how to write and to William Voss and Sharon Foster for inspiring a group of middle-school students to explore the natural and social worlds, and to embrace the wonderful uncertainly of being outside of our comfort zones. I would like to also thank David Schaafsma for teaching me why stories matter and how they can change the world, as well as Sister Luke from the Missionaries of Charity in Calcutta and Ellen Maling of Bridge Over Troubled Waters in Boston who taught me what it means to do service, what it means to be a professional, and what it means to change the world, one very small step at a time. I would also like to thank R. Douglas Arnold, my dissertation advisor, as well as Jennifer Hochschild and Larry Bartels for their mentorship. John J. DiIulio Jr., in a small conference room for an independent study at Princeton, taught me American bureaucratic politics. I owe each of these professors much more than I can repay.

Colleagues at the University of Minnesota, past and present, have offered their knowledge, feedback, and support over the years: Teri Caraway, John Freeman, Paul Goren, Timothy R. Johnson, Andrew Karch, Howard Lavine, Nancy Luxon, Daniel Kelliher, Joanne Miller, C. Daniel Myers, Robert Nichols, August Nimtz, Kathryn Pearson, Wendy Rahn, Martin Sampson, Paul Soper, Joe Soss, Dara Strolovitch, John Sullivan, and Joan Tronto, among many. I owe special thanks to W. Phillips Shively for not trying to talk me out of writing an American government textbook and supporting me throughout the process. Thanks to the many students over the years who inspired and motivated me to write the book. Graduate student teaching assistants offered their own insights and suggestions on the project, in particular: Emily Baer, Adam Dahl, Ashley English, John Greenwood, Daniel Habchi, Serena Laws, Eli Meyerhoff, Zein Murib, Adam Olson, and Paul Snell. Members of the staff in the Department of Political Science have been invaluable over the years, especially Alexis Cuttance, Jessie Eastman, Kyle Edwards, and Rose Miskowiec.

To the many talented, warm, and professional people at SAGE/CQ Press I owe much. The book began with an idea floated to Earl Pingel who then passed it along to Charisse Kiino. Though Charisse has moved on from the role of acquisitions editor to other responsibilities, her stamp is very much on this book, and I am grateful for it. In addition, many thanks to Carrie Brandon, Gail Bushman, Matthew Byrnie, Sarah Calabi, Erica DeLuca, Eric Garner, Jade Henderson, Zachary Hoskins, Jennifer Jones, Nancy Matuszak, Michele Rhoads, John Scappini, Michele Sordi, Rose Storey, and Amy Whitaker. All have made me feel like part of the SAGE/CQ family in addition to doing their jobs superbly. Though not technically part of the SAGE/CQ group, I am indebted to Chuck McCutcheon for collaborating on the Parties chapter.

I would like to thank the many colleagues who very helpfully offered their time, praise, criticisms, and support throughout the process of writing this book. They offered feedback in reviews, surveys, focus groups, and class testing. In addition to several who wish to remain anonymous, they include:

Milan Andrejevich, Ivy Tech Community College

Stephen Anthony, Georgia State University

Juan Arzola, College of the Sequoias

Yan Bai, Grand Rapids Community College

Patricia Bodelson, St. Cloud State University

Seth Bordner, Kent State University

Christopher Borick, Muhlenberg College

Madelyn Bowman, Tarrant County College South

Mark Brewer, University of Maine

Jeffrey Brown, Wayne County Community College

Susan Burgess, Ohio University

Timothy Campbell, Labette Community College

Mary Carver, Longwood College

Kimberly Casey, Northwest Missouri State University

LaTasha Chaffin, College of Charleston

Ben Christ, Harrisburg Area Community College

Dewey Clayton, University of Louisville

Diana Cohen, Central Connecticut State University

Kathleen Cole, Metropolitan State University

Todd Collins, Western Carolina University

Michael Coulter, Grove City College

Kevin Davis, North Central Texas College

Chris Deis, Depaul University, Lincoln Campus

Joseph S. Devaney, East Georgia State College

Richardson Dilworth, Drexel University

Agber Dimah, Chicago State University

Cristina Dragomir, SUNY Oswego

Lauren Elliott-Dorans, Ohio State University

Bond Faulwell, Johnson County Community College

Daniel Franklin, Georgia State University

John Frendreis, Loyola University of Chicago

Maria Garcia-Acevedo, California State University Northridge

Sarah Gershon, Georgia State University

Tobias Gibson, Westminster College

Patrick Gilbert, Lone Star College

Andra Gillespie, Emory University

Frederick Gordon, Columbus State University

George Gordon, Illinois Wesleyan University

Andrea Graff, Lincoln Land Community College

Greg Granger, Northwestern State University of Louisiana

Matthew Gritter, Angelo State University

Gloria Guevara, California State University Northridge

Homer Guevara, Northwest Vista College

Paul Henri Gurian, University of Georgia

Mel Hailey, Abilene Christian University

Therese M. Hammond, Pennsylvania State University Lehigh Valley

Jeneen Hobby, Cleveland State University

Tom Hoffman, Spring Hill College

Michael Hoover, Seminole Community College

Jennifer Hopper, Washington College

JoyAnna Hopper, University of Missouri

Tony Horton, Arkansas State University

Mark Jendrysik, University of North Dakota

Caitlin Jewitt, Virginia Tech

April Johnson, University of Illinois at Chicago

Gabe Jolivet, Ashford University

Jeff Justice, Tarleton State University

Mily Kao, Mesa Community College

Kimberly Keenan, City College of San Francisco

Christopher Kelley, Miami University

Athena King, Eastern Michigan University

John Klemanski, Oakland University

Lisa Krasner, Truckee Meadows Community College

Andrew Levin, Harper College

La Della Levy, College of Southern Nevada Henderson Campus

Eric Lomazoff, Villanova University

Benjamin Lundgren, Santa Clara University

James Malone, Hillsborough Community College

Alyx Mark, North Central College

Mack Mariani, Xavier University

Shane Martin, Fitchburg State University

Wendy Martinek, Binghamton University

Valerie Martinez-Ebers, University of North Texas

Michael McConachie, Collin College

Karen McCurdy, Georgia Southern University

Mary McHugh, Merrimack College

Stephen Meinhold, University of North Carolina, Wilmington

Melissa Merry, University of Louisville

Keesha Middlemass, Trinity University

Mark Miller, Clark University

Patrick Moore, Richland College

Samantha Mosier, Missouri State University

Brian Naples, Panola College

Sharon A. Navarro, University of Texas at San Antonio

Brian Newman, Pepperdine University

Timothy Nokken, Texas Tech University

Hyung Park, El Paso Community College

Sara Parker, Chabot College

Scott Parker, Sierra College

Lisa Perez-Nichols, Austin Community College

Robert Peters, Western Michigan University

Clarissa Peterson, DePauw University

William Pierros, Concordia University Chicago

Blayne Primozich, El Paso Community College

Nicholas Pyeatt, Pennsylvania State University, Altoona

Judd Quarles, Tyler Junior College

Andree Reeves, University of Alabama, Huntsville

Ted Ritter, John Tyler Community College

Joseph Robbins, Shepherd University

Jason Robles, Colorado State University

Michelle Rodriguez, San Diego Mesa College

Jon Ross, City Colleges of Chicago

Paul Rozycki, Mott Community College

Mikhail Rybalko, Texas Tech University

Ray Sandoval, Richland College

Erich Saphir, Pima Community College

Deron Schreck, Moraine Valley Community College

Eric Schwartz, Hagerstown Community College

Allen Settle, California Polytechnic State University

John Seymour, El Paso Community College

Brent Sharp, University of Central Oklahoma

Amy Shriver Dreussi, University of Akron

Abha Singh, Univerisity of Texas, El Paso

Sue Ann Skipworth, University of Mississippi

Gwyn Sutherland, Elizabethtown Community and Technical College

Nate Steffen, Bismarck State College

Bob Switky, Sonoma State

Barry Tadlock, Ohio University

Chris Thuot, SUNY Onondaga Community College

Anip Uppal, Central New Mexico Community College

Troy Vidal, Columbus State University

Danny Vyain, Ivy Tech Community College

Kimball Waites, Big Bend Community College

Adam Warber, Clemson University

Jessica Webb, Kalamazoo Valley Community College

Zach Wilhide, Tidewater Community College

Mark Williams, St Charles Community College

Claire Wofford, College of Charleston

Tony Wohlers, Cameron University

Patrick Wohlfarth, University of Maryland

Laura Wood, Tarrant County College

Tyler Young, Collin College

Kimberly Zagorski, University of Wisconsin-Stout

Penultimately, I am deeply grateful to the other members of our band: Shannon Kelly on copyediting and badger management, Olivia Weber-Stenis on production and keeping the band in tune, Elise Frasier on development editing and llama communications, and Michael Kerns on senior acquisitions editing, project oversight, and punk rock philosophy. This book is theirs as much as it is mine.

Finally, I would like to thank friends and family: Mark Dailey, Erik Ness, and other buttheads. Also, the members of the Knox Block ring. They are my friends; their kids are like cousins to mine, and fire pits rule. My family, Mom, Dad, Julie, and Jeannette, to whom I am deeply thankful, and at times apologetic for randomly-timed phone calls seeking support and discussing the history of central Asia and/or the Dallas Cowboys. Dylan and Sadie, who have grown—too quickly—into wonderful and wonderfully different people. And lastly my wife, Sara: In spite of the hours, days, and weeks away from you and the kids, I am still here, and I am still yours.

Scott
Minneapolis, Minnesota
November 2016

ABOUT THE AUTHOR

Scott F. Abernathy was born and raised in Fort Worth, Texas. While an undergraduate at Dartmouth College he volunteered for three months with Mother Theresa's Missionaries of Charity in Calcutta, India. After graduation, hoping to do service work closer to home, Scott worked as an on-street counselor with homeless adolescents in Boston, MA.

Scott then received a Master of Curriculum and Instruction and taught fourth and seventh grades in Wisconsin public schools. Hoping to learn more about the underlying systems that drove the educational outcomes he was trying to change, Scott completed an M.P.A. in Domestic Policy and then a Ph.D. in Politics from Princeton University. Scott is now an associate professor of political science and a University Distinguished Teaching Professor at the University of Minnesota. He is also the author of *School Choice and the Future of American Democracy* and *No Child Left Behind and the Public Schools*, both from University of Michigan Press.

While Scott says that being a street outreach worker was the most transforming job he ever had, he admits that the chance to teach students, not in a subway stop or a squat, but through the writing of this textbook, is pretty cool as well.

AMERICAN GOVERNMENT

■■■ STORIES OF A NATION

THE ESSENTIALS

1 AMERICAN POLITICAL STORIES
Claiming Rights, Demanding to Be Heard

College and high school students marching in Baltimore, Maryland, in 2015 in protest of the death of Freddie Gray while in police custody. Their call to have others listen to their voices is part of the American political story: people claiming their constitutional rights and demanding to be heard.

Andrew Burton/Getty.

In my undergraduate introduction to American government course here at the University of Minnesota, on the first day of class, I tell my students, "I don't care *what* you think," which does tend to generate some uncomfortable silence. But I mean it. Before things get too out of hand, though, I quickly follow up with, "However, I care very much about *how* you think. That is what this course is about."

This book is no different. My hope is that you will use this book to question what everyone tells you that you *should* know or think, to become more confident in making your own ideas known, and to sharpen your ability to interpret for yourself the political world around you. This book uses stories to help accomplish those goals. As you will quickly realize, these stories are very much a central part of the book's structure and objectives. In each chapter, you will be presented with stories that illustrate big and important concepts in the study of American politics. They are meant to make those ideas come to life—to help you understand that American government is not something that exists apart from you. And because they are *real* stories, in all their messy, complicated glory, they will also force you and your classmates to think in ways that are not either/or and to walk in the shoes of people who may be very different from you.

This book, therefore, is going to be difficult at times, although not in the sense of being difficult to read and follow—far from that, I hope. I mean that many of the stories are not always happy or optimistic. Most don't have clear heroines, heroes, or villains. Hardly any of them have tidy endings. In this book, I will quote individuals whose words or ideas some will strongly disagree with, maybe even find objectionable. This book will not offer any one political, theoretical, or academic perspective. There will be no magic wand waved in the final chapter of this book that announces, "Here! We've got it!" Welcome to the world of American politics and government.

Read the stories; absorb the nuts-and-bolts facts and concepts that emerge along the way in these chapters. Most importantly, however, connect the two. Use the stories to more deeply understand the complexity and contestation of American politics, then and now. Use them to understand the diversity of the voices that have been a part of the national conversation and why some voices have been and continue to be excluded from the dominant conversations in American society. Use the stories to make your own voices stronger, better informed, more politically savvy, and more effective.

In this chapter and in the book generally, we raise fundamental questions when we try to define what we mean by a "good government" or a bad one. Whose rights get protected? Whose get restricted? How do these questions get resolved? Who gets to decide? Well, in a sense, these questions do not get resolved, at least not all at once and for all time. The stories told in this book illustrate how big questions like these are resolved, revisited, and re-resolved through **politics**, the process of influencing the actions and policies of a **government**. Politics and government are closely connected, but they are not the same thing. Politics describes processes; government describes the rules and institutions that arise from political action and conflict and that structure future political action. Throughout the book, we'll hear from people who have engaged with those institutions and who have taken part in those processes.

politics
the process of influencing the actions of officials and the policies of a nation, state, locality, or community.

government
a system of rules and institutions that defines and shapes the contours of public action.

We will begin with two stories: one about a young woman in Nebraska who fought for the right to establish a Christian Bible study group at her school, the other about a group of Kentucky students who claimed their rights to establish a Gay-Straight Alliance. We will then go back in time to the American Revolution and Thomas Jefferson's drafting of the Declaration of Independence and conclude by fast-forwarding to Dr. Martin Luther King Jr.'s "Letter from Birmingham Jail."

What could all of these stories possibly have in common? In them we will witness the efforts of vastly different people who have wrestled with what fundamental rights mean in American democracy and see how they as individuals and groups have tried to answer that question, staking their own claims upon their rights.

LEARNING OBJECTIVES

By connecting to those stories about the foundations of American government, you will be able to:

1.1 Explain how diverse Americans have been able to use the same political tools to achieve their own distinct visions of good government

1.2 Define the key elements of American political culture

1.3 Examine the ways in which natural rights and the theory of the social contract helped to shape the ideas expressed in the Declaration of Independence

1.4 Identify the factors that gave rise to the American Revolution and discuss the war's legacy, both in what was and what was not achieved

1.5 Describe the core features of American political institutions

1.6 Compare Dr. Martin Luther King Jr.'s "Letter from Birmingham Jail" to Thomas Jefferson's draft of the Declaration of Independence in terms of their ideas and the political strategies of their authors

AMERICAN STUDENTS CLAIM THEIR RIGHTS

NEWS CLIP
Transgender student rights

Bridget Mergens walked into the office of her school principal in Omaha, Nebraska, with a request. She wanted to start a student group—a Christian Bible study club.

"I thought he liked me and I was sure he'd say yes," Mergens later recounted.[1] As one reporter noted, "Principal James Findley did like her . . . but he didn't say yes. 'An informal get-together over lunch at the cafeteria would be fine,' Findley [recalled] saying, 'but a school-sponsored club? Don't ask me that, Bridget, because I have a problem with that.'"[2]

Mergens's high school sponsored many other extracurricular clubs, including a chess club, a photography club, and a scuba diving club. Was her proposal fundamentally different from these sanctioned student groups? This became a question with which her principal and her local school board had to wrestle, and they ultimately denied her request. To Mergens, the school board's arguments were fundamentally flawed.

The legal basis of Mergens's claim was a national law, the Equal Access Act of 1984 (EAA), passed during the administration of Republican president Ronald Reagan. Though there are some details in the EAA about the ways in which schools must treat clubs in general, the law's primary intent is to restrict the ability of public high schools to exclude faith-based religious extracurricular clubs. The act states, "It shall be unlawful for any public secondary school which receives Federal financial assistance . . . to deny equal access or a fair

Liz Loverde, a sophomore at Wantagh High School in Long Island, New York, in 2014. Loverde successfully pressured her school to allow a Christian Bible study club, thus following in the footsteps of others, such as Bridget Mergens, in claiming rights under the Equal Access Act of 1984.

First Liberty Institute

opportunity to, or discriminate against, any students who wish to conduct a meeting . . . on the basis of the religious, political, philosophical, or other content of the speech at such meetings."[3]

In 1981, prior to the act's passage, the United States Supreme Court had already affirmed these rights for students at public colleges and universities, but it had not yet done so for those in public high schools. In that decision, the Court ruled in favor of a student religious group that had been denied access to facilities at the University of Missouri at Kansas City even though other, non faith-based groups had been granted the use of university facilities.[4]

As Mergens's case proceeded, it was far from certain that the Court would now affirm those same rights for high school students. The reason was the potential "impressionability of high school" students, compared to those in college and beyond.[5] Would high school students be mature enough to distinguish between their school's efforts to provide an open and vibrant forum for voices and the possibility that the school itself endorsed the club members' beliefs? As one observer wondered, "How mature are high school students? Do they feel pressured to join school-sponsored clubs, or will they feel ostracized if their views differ?"[6]

In June 1990, five years after Bridget Mergens tried to start the Bible club, the Supreme Court ruled in her favor. By this point, she was Bridget Mergens Mayhew, married and with a young child. The Court upheld high school students' rights to have the same access for their faith-based extracurricular clubs as that granted to other student groups. It also upheld the constitutionality of the EAA. In her majority opinion in *Board of Education of Westside Community Schools v. Mergens*, Supreme Court justice Sandra Day O'Connor wrote, "There is a crucial difference between government and private speech endorsing religion, and, as Congress recognized in passing the Act, high school students are mature enough and are likely to understand that a school does not endorse or support student speech that it merely permits on a nondiscriminatory basis."[7]

To some, Mergens Mayhew's efforts harkened back to the civil rights movement, in which African Americans claimed their own rights. The director of the Christian-based National Legal Foundation said so explicitly: "Just as officials in the 1950s shut the doors of the schoolhouse to black children, some school officials of the 1980s have attempted to keep out Christians who want to form a Bible club. Such arbitrary censorship is anti-religious discrimination, pure and simple."[8]

To others, including some of the members of the Supreme Court, the worry was more about the limits of Mergens Mayhew's claims on her rights. Who else might make a claim based upon her efforts? In his contribution to the Court's decision in *Board v. Mergens*, Justice Anthony Kennedy added another concern about the constitutionality of the EAA: that other students with other voices might also use the act to gain access for their student clubs, even if some of their issues of interest might make school administrators uncomfortable.[9] While the EAA opened the doors for student groups such as Bible study groups, its free speech provisions might also guarantee access for student groups with much more controversial agendas. It was this possibility that especially worried school administrators.

Reflecting back upon his decision to deny Mergens Mayhew's request and the Supreme Court's ruling, Omaha principal James Findley recounted, "I didn't have a concern about the five or six kids having a Bible study club. I was concerned about what and who it opens the doors to. I've had students say they'll start a Satanist club or a skinheads group."[10]

As it turned out, other groups of high school students *did* test the system, but perhaps not in the ways that Congress intended when it passed the EAA in the first place, or in the ways that Principal Findley or members of the Supreme Court worried about. These groups were not Satanists or skinheads. One was a collection of young people in Boyd County, Kentucky, who wanted to start a Gay-Straight Alliance (GSA). In 2002 they circulated a petition declaring their intent. Driving the formation of GSAs was the desire not only to create solidarity between high school students with diverse sexual identities but also to provide a safe space for students who had not yet chosen to make public their own sexual identities, perhaps because of the potential of harassment by their fellow students.

School officials turned down the student's request to form the GSA. Of twenty-one student group applications, theirs was the only one denied. Requests from groups such as the Future Business Leaders of America and the Fellowship of Christian Athletes were approved.[11] The students then contacted the American Civil Liberties Union (ACLU) for help. One month after the ACLU sent a letter to the school board in which it referred to the Equal Access Act, the board reversed itself and approved the formation of the GSA.[12]

But that didn't fully settle the case. Back at Boyd County High, GSA club founders' fears of harassment turned out to be valid. According to testimony from the school's principal, at the first official meeting of the GSA following the announcement of the group's approval, a crowd "directly confronted the GSA supporters 'with facial expressions, hand gestures . . . some very uncivil body language . . . people were using loud voices and angry voices.'"[13] Two days later, a group of students protesting outside the school "shouted at [GSA] students as they arrived, 'We don't want something like that in our school.'"[14]

In an emergency meeting held in December, the school board, following the recommendation of the district superintendent, decided to "ban all noncurricular clubs for the remainder of the 2002–03 school year."[15] After the decision, members of the GSA stopped using school facilities to meet, but other groups, including the school's drama and Bible clubs, continued to use the high school's facilities. The members of the GSA went to court.

Their case did not make it to the Supreme Court; it did not have to. In 2004 the ACLU announced a settlement with the Boyd County public schools and claimed victory: "The settlement requires that the district treat all student clubs equally and conduct an anti-harassment training for all district staff as well as all students in high school and middle school."[16] The GSA's was not the first or the only case brought by student groups focused on challenging discrimination based on a student's sexual identity, but the efforts of these students highlight the ways in which individuals have used the political tools available to them to secure their own rights.

Decades after the Mergens and Boyd County cases, Jennifer Villasana, president of the Gay-Straight Alliance at Richland High School, holds a badge she wears at the White House LGBT Conference on Safe Schools and Communities at the University of Texas at Arlington on March 20, 2012.

Rodger Mallison/Fort Worth Star-Telegram/MCT via Getty Images

NEWS CLIP
Oklahoma students protest

NEWS CLIP
First African American Kentucky Lieutenant Governor talks about good governance

In filing her lawsuit and pursuing her claims all the way to the Supreme Court, Bridget Mergens had help from the National Legal Foundation, a Christian public interest law firm.[17] The Boyd County High GSA had the help of the ACLU. Posting to its Web site in December 2002 while it considered legal action on the GSA's behalf, the ACLU attacked the decision of the Boyd County school board to shut down all student clubs rather than allowing members of the GSA to meet. In doing so, attorneys from the ACLU referred back to the civil rights movement, just as Mergens's attorneys had done in claiming her right to start a Bible study club, saying, "This decision is frightfully similar to the days when many cities chose to shut down public swimming pools rather than let African Americans use them."[18]

Both groups' efforts were undertaken with knowledge of the complicated ways in which laws and policies are enacted in the United States and a strategic understanding of the political process. In this book, we will consider those dynamics in detail. We will also dive into the stories of many other individuals and groups who have sought to claim their rights and reshape the laws of the land. In a very deep sense, however, whether or not any of the others whose stories you will read "won" or "lost" is not the most important consideration. By adding their voices to the American conversation, they mattered.

> **Their efforts demonstrated that people really do matter in the development of American politics.**

While Bridget Mergens and the members of the Boyd County High GSA differed in the particular rights of freedom and speech that they asserted, they shared much in common. They both staked their claims on the same federal law, the Equal Access Act. With help, they harnessed the power of the American judicial system to realize their goals. Their efforts demonstrated that people really do matter in the development of American politics.

The Equal Access Act is just one of many political instruments that individuals have used to claim their rights. Underpinning all of these instruments are the political ideals drawn from thinkers throughout history, expressed in the Declaration of Independence and affirmed as rights by the framers of the Constitution of the United States. These rights form the basis for the story of this evolving thing we call American democracy, whether or not the framers fully envisioned how others would use their ideas and the institutions that they created. These efforts are central to the subjects and approach of this chapter and of this book.

WHAT HAVE I LEARNED?

1. Why have high schools, colleges, and universities struggled with the expression of student voices in cases as diverse as those involving Christian Bible study clubs and Gay-Straight Alliances?

2. How did Bridget Mergens and the members of the Boyd County High GSA make use of the same law, the Equal Access Act, to claim their rights?

3. What other rights might students in high schools, colleges, and universities claim?

Answer Key: 1. Students might reflect upon the rights of all students to have their voices made present in their educational institutions, as well as on concerns of school officials that groups might form promoting unpopular, or even hateful, ideas.; 2. Answers should focus on fundamental ideas such as freedom of expression.; 3. Answers will vary and might focus on speech, safety, or many other areas.

PEOPLE MATTER! BUT SO DO IDEAS

When they asserted their rights, Bridget Mergens and members of the Boyd County High GSA did so on the basis of a handful of ideas that form the foundation of the American Republic itself. Indeed, these ideas were first affirmed in the Declaration of Independence in 1776, making them part of the country's basic DNA: "We hold these truths to be self-evident, that all men are created equal, that they are endowed by their Creator with certain unalienable Rights, that among these are Life, Liberty, and the pursuit of Happiness." In this passage, the author of the Declaration, Thomas Jefferson, captured many of the ideas that shape **American political culture** even today. Americans have long argued about what these words mean, and for good reason, as the American experiment continues to be shaped by the people who try to bring its promises to fruition. As they do so, they draw upon the ideas that helped to define it. As with all things that people build, American political culture is constructed from individual building blocks, which we need to explore in more detail.

CONNECTING TO . . .

The Ideas That Drive American Political Culture

As you read the next section, reflect back upon the stories of Bridget Mergens and the Boyd County High GSA. Consider the following:

- What these stories tell us about American political culture
- How very different individuals and groups base their views of a better society on the same foundational ideas
- The ways in which your fellow students have used fundamental ideas in American politics to press for their rights

Equality

Central to all of this, and the first key idea expressed in the Declaration of Independence, is a commitment to equality, to having the same rights and status. This might involve **social equality**, in which no individuals have an inherently higher social status than others. Unlike Europe, with its nobility and royalty, America was founded on the idea that all individuals could reach the social status that they sought based on their own efforts. **Political equality** exists when members of a society possess the same rights under the laws of the nation. Finally, **economic equality** refers to a situation in which wealth is relatively evenly distributed across society. America does not have economic equality. In fact, differences in wealth and incomes are as stark today as they have ever been in the nation's history. Rather than emphasizing equality of economic *outcomes*, American political ideas tend to focus on ensuring equality of economic *opportunity*.

These are two very different concepts. For example, think about American public education in high schools. Equality of opportunity would point to a right to attend equally good public high schools. Equality of outcomes, however, might point to the right to achieve the same educational success, in, say, graduation rates or test scores. Americans weigh the differences between opportunity and outcomes all the time when we seek to resolve many important civil rights issues and make choices about domestic public policy options.

American political culture
a shared set of beliefs, customs, traditions, and values that define the relationship of Americans to their government and to other American citizens.

social equality
when no individual's social status is inherently higher than another's.

political equality
when members of a society possess the same rights under the laws of the nation.

economic equality
when wealth is relatively evenly distributed across society.

Inalienable Rights

The thinking behind the Declaration of Independence and the government that was eventually based upon it is that some truths and some rights are *self-evident*. These are called **inalienable rights** in the sense that they exist before and above any government

inalienable rights
rights that exist before and above any government or its power.

> *The thinking behind the Declaration of Independence is that some rights exist before and above any government or its powers.*

or its powers. Thomas Jefferson names "life, liberty, and the pursuit of happiness" as among those inherent, self-evident rights. Since they—unlike *privileges* that a government might grant—may not rightly be taken away by a government, a just system of political rule must be constructed in such a way as to protect rights and their expression. The desire to safeguard individuals' rights led to the complex structure of American political institutions in the Constitution, which we will explore in the next chapter.

liberty
social, political, and economic freedoms.

the American dream
The idea that individuals should be able to achieve prosperity through hard work, sacrifice, and their own talents.

Children of the Aldabbi family in the Kentucky Science Center in 2015, after a four-year trek from the violence, chaos, and civil war in Syria, settled in the United States with the help of the Kentucky Refugee Ministries. At its most basic level, the American dream promises hope and opportunity for all.

Jabin Botsford/Washington Post/Getty Images

Liberty

Another foundational American ideal expressed in the Declaration is a commitment to **liberty**, to social, political, and economic freedoms. That liberty might involve freedom *from* interference by a government or a freedom *to* pursue one's dreams. The degree to which the government should focus on freedom *from* or freedom *to* remains a hotly debated topic in American politics. There is often also a tension between these two visions of liberty. In the case of the public school Bible study club with which we began this chapter, the tension between these two freedoms came into sharp relief. Bridget Mergens and her fellow students claimed the freedom *to* explore their faith in an extracurricular club. By allowing the group, however, Omaha public school officials risked violating other students' freedoms *from* having a government endorse a particular religious faith, or endorse religious over nonreligious beliefs.

The Pursuit of Happiness: The American Dream

When Thomas Jefferson wrote about "the pursuit of Happiness," he was tapping into another core American political value: the belief that individuals should be able to achieve prosperity through hard work, sacrifice, and their own talents. The idea of **the American dream** has drawn immigrants to the nation's shores and borders since its founding, and it continues to do so today. Some observers, however, question whether the American dream remains alive and well in an era of such profound economic inequality.

Millennials and the American Dream

The state of the American dream in the twenty-first century is more than a topic for experts to weigh in on, whether on talk shows, through social media, on political comedy shows, or via any of the other seemingly endless streams of information with which we are bombarded. It is also something that we can study. Words are not the only ways to tell stories, nor are images and videos. Data can and do tell political stories as well. In this book, we will investigate data—numbers, statistics, and survey results—as well as the stories that political actors and reporters construct around the numbers. Make no mistake, data stories can be and are used for political purposes. In investigating data stories in this book, the goal is twofold: to help you become more capable and confident interpreters of data and to help you gain the skills to critically examine the narratives constructed around data.

We start with what at first glance seems like a very simple data story—one taken from the results of a Harvard University survey of eighteen- to twenty-nine-year-olds conducted in December of 2015.[19]

In the 2015 Harvard survey, Americans between the ages of eighteen and twenty-nine were just about equally split between those who believed that the American dream was still alive (49 percent) and those who did not (48 percent).

WHAT DO YOU THINK?

To be fair, the authors of the survey report placed these results in context and went into much more detail about other

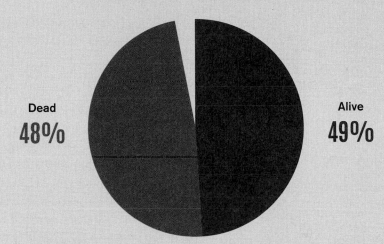

Is the American Dream Alive or Dead for You?

Dead
48%

Alive
49%

Source: Harvard Institute of Politics Fall 2015 Poll, http://iop.harvard.edu/survey/details/harvard-iop-fall-2015-poll.

factors. But let's assume that they did not. What conclusions might you draw from this figure alone? Does it reflect your experience? What other data from this survey would you want to know? If you could break out groups of young adult Americans based upon identities and characteristics, what would you examine?

As it turns out, in the Harvard survey, college graduates (58 percent) were more likely than those who had not graduated or ever enrolled (42 percent) to say the American dream was still alive. Young adult Americans in the survey who said that they were supporters of Democratic presidential candidate Bernie Sanders (56 percent) or Republican Party candidate Donald Trump (61 percent) reported that they felt the American dream was dead. What might these results mean for your understanding of the political attitudes of young adult Americans in 2016?

Religious Beliefs

America's religious traditions have also helped shape American political culture, in ways more significant than in many modern democratic governments. Some of the very first British colonies were founded by groups of individuals fleeing persecution for their religious beliefs and hoping to practice their faiths without interference. While the diversity of religious faiths represented in American society continues to expand, America was, and is, a nation partly defined by religious faith and expression. In this book, we will continue to explore the theme of how a nation founded upon liberty, especially religious liberty, wrestles with decisions about if, or how, to place boundaries on religious expression.

In 2016, questions about the proper role of religion in the nation endured. What kinds of holiday displays are acceptable for a community to officially sponsor? Would a ban on immigration by members of specific religious faiths—one that had been called for by then-presidential candidate Donald Trump—be constitutional?

America the Different?

Finally, when Americans tell stories about themselves, their politics, and their histories, they often refer to the ways in which the nation is different because of the historical patterns of the nation's development. The term **American exceptionalism** refers to these historical and cultural differences, shaped in many ways by the voices of those who have contributed to the national chorus but also by the fact that America was an experiment, starting anew, without the legacy of the European monarchies to constrain its promise.[20] The idea of an exceptional America is not a new one. In 1630 Puritan leader John Winthrop delivered a sermon to a group of immigrants from Britain onboard their ship as they waited to land in what would later be known as New England. In it he exhorted, "We must Consider that we shall be as a City upon a Hill, the eyes of all people are upon us."[21]

Is there such a thing as a shared American political culture in the twenty-first century? In 2016, especially as the presidential campaign unfolded, it was not too far-fetched to wonder if it did still exist. We will explore the deep divisions in American politics today throughout this book and encounter the often harsh and divisive language employed by candidates, citizens, and other political activists. American political culture, however, is only part of the framework of American politics. The questions and debates are not only about *how* differences are resolved but also about *what* those differences are.

American Political Ideologies

Americans may not always agree on a set of foundational concepts that constitute a shared political culture, and they also may disagree sharply about what the desired outcomes of the political processes should be. A person or group's **political ideology** is a set of beliefs about *what* should happen as the result of the process of governance. Individuals' political ideologies may differ on, for example, the degree to which government should regulate economic activity, how deeply government should be involved in individuals' decisions in their private lives, how much government should act to ensure equality of opportunity, or an almost endless list of other policies and issues. As with questions about religious faith, in 2016 debates based upon competing American political ideologies endured, with some observers and scholars arguing that the nation had become deeply divided. In this book, we will explore these debates and discussions in detail.

DRAFTING THE DECLARATION OF INDEPENDENCE

Affirming and Demanding Fundamental Rights

For two and a half weeks in June of 1776, Thomas Jefferson "closeted himself in his rooms in the boarding house" at the corner of Seventh and Market Streets in Philadelphia, Pennsylvania.[22] He was writing a draft of the Declaration of Independence. Sitting at the

---

American exceptionalism
the belief in the special character of the United States as a uniquely free nation based on its history and its commitment to democratic ideals and personal liberty.

political ideology
a set of beliefs about the desired goals and outcomes of a process of governance.

TOPICS IN AMERICAN GOVERNMENT
Declaration of Independence

1. The Declaration of Independence _____ the residents of the rebellious British colonies.

   a. Granted fundamental political privileges to
   b. Recognized the fundamental rights of

2. The term *American exceptionalism* refers to
   _____.

   a. The fact that America is unique in its democratic form of government
   b. America's inability to protect individual rights
   c. The belief that America's unique history contributed to its special political culture and institutions
   d. All of the above

3. American society is characterized by _____.

   a. Relative social equality and economic inequality

   b. Relative economic equality and social inequality
   c. Relative social equality and economic equality
   d. Relative social inequality and economic inequality

4. What are some of the key components of American political culture?

5. What is the difference between political culture and political ideology?

Answers: 1. b; 2. c; 3. a; 4. Answers should include a discussion of inalienable rights, liberty, religious beliefs, and American exceptionalism.; 5. Answers should cover how political culture refers to a shared set of beliefs about how political processes should work, while political ideology refers to preferred outcomes from those processes.

"little portable writing table built to his own design," Jefferson, using quill and ink, penned the first draft of one of the most important statements in American political history.[23] Most of the document was a list of accusations—charges of bad government. Though the indictments were against George III, king of Great Britain, the document's real audience was much larger. The Declaration was meant for the people in the thirteen rebellious American colonies, and for the world. It was a public statement of high treason but one that also tried to express why the representatives of the British colonies in the Second Continental Congress felt that they had no other choice but to break from Great Britain and seek their independence. Before independence could be achieved, however, the colonists needed to explain why they were willing to undertake such a radical, and probably hopeless, course of action.

Jefferson's draft was a very political document. That it named King George III was intentional and significant. For years the American colonies had complained that Parliament, Great Britain's legislative body, was going beyond its authority in the policies that it had imposed on the colonies, but they had nonetheless consistently affirmed their loyalty to the king. By levelling their charges against the king in 1776, the colonies were crossing a line that could not be uncrossed. There would be no going back.

Thomas Jefferson on Natural Rights: Capturing the "American Mind"

Thomas Jefferson did not write the Declaration of Independence alone. He had been appointed to lead a committee of five men to draft a document that would announce and justify the decision of the Second Continental Congress to declare the independence of the thirteen American colonies from Great Britain. Like most members of the Congress, Jefferson had known very few of his fellow delegates before he came to Philadelphia. Two of the members of his committee, John Adams and Benjamin Franklin, became his close friends. Jefferson's draft was edited and revised by his fellow committee members and then by the Second Continental Congress, which upset Jefferson greatly: "The more alterations Congress made on his draft, the more miserable Jefferson became."[24]

Jefferson's Declaration was not an original take on the question of independence. It was not supposed to be. His task was to persuade colonists and European powers of the rightness

Thomas Jefferson in an 1800 painting by Rembrandt Peale.

GraphicaArtis/Getty Images.

of their course of action. To do so, Jefferson drew on arguments and ideas with which people were already familiar. Otherwise, his arguments would not have had the impact that they needed to have. Jefferson saw his own role in this way. In a letter written in 1825, he reflected on the document that he had drafted, pointing to his efforts to use "common sense" and "plain" terms in capturing the "American mind." He wrote, "Neither aiming at originality of principle or sentiment, nor yet copied from any particular and previous writing, it was intended to be an expression of the American mind, and to give to that expression the proper tone and spirit called for by the occasion."[25]

Jefferson drew on his own earlier writings, on lessons from history, and on ideas about liberty and government widely known in the colonies and Great Britain. The American revolutionaries were well familiar with the histories and writings of ancient Greece and Rome. **Democracy** (from the Greek *demos*, meaning "people," and *kratos*, or "power"), whereby power is held by the people, had been instituted in the city-states of ancient Greece, Athens in particular. Democracy in Athens, however, was far from universal. Full citizenship was restricted to free males who owned property. These citizens were allowed to vote on matters of public policy.

Also central to the philosophy of the American Revolution were the ideas of the Enlightenment, a period in Europe in which

In this reproduction of the original draft of the Declaration of Independence it is possible to see the editing marks left by Jefferson and others, a testament to the ways in which the ideas contained within it remain "under construction" even today.

Courtesy of the Library of Congress, Prints and Photographs Division reason and science were applied to better understand the physical and social worlds. From the British Enlightenment, the revolutionaries drew on the works of John Locke, who had argued against the divine, or God-given, right of kings to rule with absolute power. Instead, Locke argued that people are born with **natural rights** that kings cannot give or take away. A legitimate government, to Locke, is one that involves a **social contract**, in which people give to their governments the ability to rule over them to ensure an orderly and functioning society. If a government breaks that social contract— by violating people's natural rights—then the people have the right to replace that unjust government with a just one. Locke was himself a political writer. His works sought to defend the authority and legitimacy of British Parliament against excessive power of the British monarch.

> If a government breaks that social contract—by violating people's natural rights—then the people have the right to replace that unjust government with a just one.

From the French Enlightenment, Jefferson and other revolutionary thinkers drew on the works of Charles-Louis de Secondat, Baron de Montesquieu, who had affirmed the ideas of natural rights and the social contract and also helped to give these goals an institutional form. Montesquieu proposed that power in government should be divided between different branches so that no one branch could become too powerful. He also argued that slavery violated the principles of natural law.

Jefferson also drew upon Scottish Enlightenment thinkers such as David Hume, who explored the idea that there could be a science of politics just as there was a developing science of the natural world. Given the historical tendency of leaders to abuse political power, Hume believed a just government should be carefully designed and the lessons of science and history carefully applied to its structure to keep the greedy and ambitious from using political power to their own advantage. In applying scientific principals from studies of the natural world to human political action and interaction, Hume and others like him made major contributions to the modern study of **political science**.

Is political science really a science? That is a very good question, and one that still gets debated. In one sense, it is often not a science, at least not in the ways in which we often think about science. Say that you are a researcher in a lab trying to find a cure for a disease. You will assign your test subjects randomly; some will receive the treatment and some will not. While political scientists can and do try for random assignment, especially those who study individual political behavior, more often than not, they cannot actually achieve this. Voters, for example, are not randomly assigned. Educational policymakers could never sell a trial program in which parents are told, "Your student has an equal chance of being assigned to an excellent school or one with poor outcomes." On the other hand, political scientists do bring scientific techniques to bear upon important questions of power and representation, efforts that we will explore throughout this book.

democracy
a system of government where power is held and political decisions made by the people in that society.

natural rights
rights that people have inherently that are not granted by any government.

social contract
an agreement in which people give to their governments the ability to rule over them to ensure an orderly and functioning society.

political science
the systematic study of the ways in which ideas, individuals, and institutions shape political outcomes.

Natural Law and the Declaration of Independence: The Case against Bad Government

The opening paragraphs of the Declaration of Independence, as finally revised (see Appendix), lay out the philosophy of natural rights that forms the basis for the justification for pursuing independence. According to the ideas on which Jefferson and his contemporaries were drawing, it is not enough to point to the existence of natural rights and then declare independence. One must also lay out, in detail, the ways in which a government has violated these rights. Lawyer that he was, Jefferson followed his appeal to natural law by laying out a long list of charges against King George III. In fact, most of the text of the document consists of charges of bad government against the king: "The history of the present King of Great Britain is a history of repeated injuries and usurpations, all having in direct object the establishment of an absolute Tyranny over these States. To prove this, let Facts be submitted to a candid world."

Jefferson and the members of the Second Continental Congress were being literal when they spoke of submitting the facts to a "candid world." The document was intended to be read by the governments of Britain's European rivals, whom the colonial radicals hoped to ally with or gain assistance from. Without a formal statement of independence, backed by solid evidence, the colonies would not be able to secure assistance from outside powers. Without that assistance, defeating the greatest military power in the world was almost certain to end in failure and in execution for Jefferson and his co-conspirators.

After a long list of charges against the king, Jefferson and the members of the Second Continental Congress formally announced their break from Great Britain, declaring, "We, therefore, the Representatives of the United States of America, in General Congress, Assembled, appealing to the Supreme Judge of the world for rectitude of our intentions, do, in the Name and by the Authority of the good People of these Colonies, solemnly publish and declare, That these United Colonies are, and of Right ought to be Free and Independent States; that they are Absolved from all Allegiance to the British Crown."

Of all of the changes that members of the Second Continental Congress made to Jefferson's first draft, none were more significant than the deletion of his charges against the king on the issue of slavery. The first section of the deleted charges accused the king of violating natural rights by allowing the slave trade to continue. It read, "He has waged cruel war against human nature itself, violating its most sacred rights of life & liberty in the persons of distant people who never offended him, captivating & carrying them into slavery in another hemisphere, or to incur miserable death in their transportation thither."[26]

Thomas Jefferson was a slave owner, one of the largest in Virginia. His lifestyle depended on the capture, sale, and oppression of other human beings. It appears that Jefferson did privately wrestle with the contradiction of asserting the rights of a new nation that continued to preserve and protect slavery. Why he chose to include this charge in the original draft is subject to some historical debate.

The second deleted section, in which Jefferson charged the king with trying to incite slave rebellions in the colonies, spoke directly to the fears of many southern plantation owners. British officials had recently made offers of freedom to colonial slaves who would join the British against the American revolutionaries. Many eventually did. The logic of this charge would have been very well understood by Jefferson's fellow southerners. The charge read, "He is now exciting those very people to rise in arms among us, and to purchase that liberty of which *he* has deprived them, by murdering the people upon whom *he* also obtruded them; thus paying off former crimes committed against the *liberties* of one people, with crimes which he urges them to commit against the *lives* of another."[27]

In the end, Jefferson's charges against the king on the issue of slavery were deleted, partly due to opposition from Southern state delegates. The contradiction—of a new nation announcing its birth on the foundation of freedom while holding hundreds of thousands of people in slavery—remained.

An advertisement taken out in the *Virginia Gazette* by Thomas Jefferson for the return of a runaway slave from his plantation in 1769.

Virginia Historical Society.

The Declaration of Independence did not fall out of the sky or emerge spontaneously from the minds of Thomas Jefferson or the members of the Second Continental Congress. Its creation was shaped by politics and history. It was the product of actions, strategies, calculations, and miscalculations of countless individuals, many of whose stories are unremembered and untold. The events leading up to the drafting of the Declaration offer important lessons in the history and development of American government. To begin to explore these lessons, we have to jump back in time, over a century and a half before Jefferson sat down at his homemade desk in Philadelphia, to a set of events that took place both in the Americas and globally: the establishment of the British colonies in North America and the legacy of war between the European powers in the years leading up to the American Revolution.

THE AMERICAN REVOLUTION
Ideals and Strategic Politics

In April of 1607, three British ships made their way up what would later become known as the James River in Virginia. After deciding on a spot far enough up the river to avoid Spanish warships, these individuals created the settlement of Jamestown, the first permanent British settlement in the modern-day United States of America.[28] The eventual expansion of what became the thirteen colonies of British America forever altered the lives of the native peoples whose societies covered the lands of North America as well as those of the enslaved Africans who later found themselves there as well. The lived experiences of both groups of individuals reverberated throughout American history and had profound effects that many did not, or could not have, predicted.

Indigenous Peoples in North America

To the Europeans, the Western Hemisphere was known as the "New World." To the millions of indigenous peoples spread out across two continents, it was the Europeans who were new. The arrival of the Europeans proved utterly destructive to indigenous societies. Throughout this centuries-long process, however, indigenous peoples challenged this disruption, either outright through diplomacy or armed conflict, or less visibly by trying to maintain centuries-old traditions in the face of constant threats to them.

The indigenous peoples, called "Indians" by the Europeans, were not passive inhabitants of a wild paradise. They had already shaped many North American ecologies and landscapes to suit their own diverse social and economic systems, often with significant environmental impact. The British colonists, in turn, attempted to reshape the landscapes of North America to suit their own purposes and lifestyles, which caused profound disruption of the traditional ways of life of the indigenous peoples.

The social, cultural, and linguistic diversity of the native peoples in North America was staggering. At the time of first contact with the European invaders, perhaps a quarter of "all human languages in the world were North American Indian."[29] Initially, British colonists depended on the adaptive technologies and agricultural advances of the native peoples for their own survival. As the British colonies grew in size and confidence, however, they began to assert their ideas about land ownership more aggressively, provoking resistance by native peoples who had not agreed to such terms. The violence that this clash led to was often horrific, including massacres of entire indigenous local communities and reprisals against individual British colonials.

By the time Thomas Jefferson sat down to draft the Declaration of Independence, the population of the indigenous peoples in the thirteen British colonies had been reduced to a fraction of its level before first contact with the Europeans. Diseases, against which indigenous peoples had little or no immunity, were perhaps the largest factor. Death from armed conflict also played a role. However, the disruption in the traditional ways of life of native peoples that arose from European settlement, including the cascading effects of losing their land—which upset agreements and boundaries between other native peoples—also had an effect. The impact of British colonization on traditional native ways of life was comprehensive and total. The habitats upon which the indigenous peoples depended were altered and depleted. The traditional social and economic systems that had been developed before the British colonists arrived often broke down.

Indigenous peoples, however, did not sit idly by and allow this to happen. They resisted—at times militarily, and often quite successfully. Many indigenous peoples also practiced diplomacy among and between European powers and other native peoples. Sometimes this approach bore fruit, but sometimes it had disastrous outcomes, especially as the European powers were often quite willing to abandon their promises to their "allies" among the native peoples once European objectives had been met. Resistance for most indigenous peoples probably took personal, nonviolent, and largely unrecorded and unremembered forms as they tried to maintain the survival of their families and kinship networks, their spiritual traditions, and their economic and social structures in the presence of powerfully destabilizing forces.[30]

Slavery in the British Colonies

The first group of twenty Africans arrived in Jamestown, Virginia, in 1619 aboard a Dutch ship. They were not the first people of African descent to come to the Western Hemisphere; Spanish explorers had brought with them slaves as well as soldiers and scouts of African descent.[31] Like the native peoples whose lands had been occupied by British settlers, the African peoples who followed this small group came from diverse cultures, nations, and kinship groups. Initially, some were given the status of indentured servants—people who still possessed the ability to pay off their "debts" though labor and achieve their freedom. Throughout the seventeenth and eighteenth centuries, whites arrived in numbers from Europe who also carried the status of indentured servitude. As the plantation economies of colonial America developed, however, African slaves and their descendants confronted legal systems designed more and more to strip African captives and their descendants of any legal or political rights or any hope of freedom under that legal order.

By the time Virginia's government fully codified the status of slaves in the eighteenth century, "no black, free or slave, could own arms, strike a white man, or employ a white servant. Any white person could apprehend any black to demand a certificate of freedom or a pass from the owner giving permission to be off the plantation."[32] Like the indigenous peoples, slaves and their descendants struggled to maintain their ways of life, spiritual and cultural traditions, kinship networks, families, and dignity over the coming centuries.

At times, slaves in Virginia and other slave-holding colonies organized and rose up against their oppression. In at least one uprising, slaves seized on the language of the American revolutionaries, shouting "Liberty!" while they rebelled.[33] Armed uprisings by slaves, however, were put down mercilessly with the goal of sending a message to any who would challenge the white order, and "the great majority of those [slaves] convicted of capital crimes were either hanged or burned alive, their bodies often dismembered or hung in chains for public display."[34]

A diagram from around 1750 showing how slaves were packed into the hull of a ship, some standing and some sitting. The plantation economies of colonial America were dependent upon their forced labor, and the legal and political systems of the time were designed to deny them rights and freedoms enjoyed by most other colonists.

Henry Guttman/Getty Images.

Colonial Independence and Autonomy

The colonists who established Jamestown did not set out on their own. They were backed, funded, and supported by the Virginia Company, chartered in 1606 to exploit the resources of North America for the benefit of Great Britain and the company's investors. They hoped to find gold, harvest forest products, and maybe find a valuable trade route.[35] In terms of the subsequent development of the thirteen British colonies, the initial political and economic structure of the colonies proved to be as important as any other factor. From the beginning, the British colonies in North America were used to doing things for themselves, without much oversight or interference from the British government.

In 1619 the Virginia colony developed its own legislative assembly, the House of Burgesses, which was the first elected assembly in colonial America.[36] Each of the other thirteen colonies eventually did the same. These assemblies instilled in their colonies a tradition of self-governance and a resistance to being told what to do by Great Britain, especially by Parliament. In addition, unlike France and Spain, Great Britain initially lacked a coherent colonial policy. Later, in the face of significant national debts incurred in part to protect its colonies from its European rivals, Great Britain tried to exert more centralized control over what it saw as ungrateful and entitled colonies and get them to pay their fair share of the costs of their own protection.[37] This move likely came too late, however; colonial governments were not about to give up the independence that they had enjoyed for so long.

Global War and Its Aftermath

The Treaty of Paris in 1763 ended the fourth major military conflict between two global powers, France and Great Britain, in less than seventy-five years. In Europe, this conflict was known as the **Seven Years' War**.[38] In the American colonies, it was known as the French and Indian War. It was a global war; fighting took place in North America, the Mediterranean Sea, the Indian Ocean, the West Indies, and the Philippines and involved most of the European powers of the time, including Great Britain, France, Austria, Prussia, Spain, and Sweden.

The North American part of the war began when members of the Ohio Company, a land speculation company established by a group of wealthy Virginians, pushed Virginia's claims

Seven Years' War
a war principally between France and Great Britain and other European nations that was fought across the globe.

Benjamin Franklin's skill in strategic politics as a representative of the would-be Republic abroad proved to be crucial to American independence.

Courtesy of the Library of Congress, Prints and Photographs Division.

Albany Plan
a proposal for a union of British colonies in North America in which colonial legislatures would choose delegates to form an assembly under the leadership of a chief executive appointed by Great Britain.

Sugar Act
a law passed by Great Britain in 1764 that taxed sugar and molasses and angered New England merchants.

on Native American lands in the Ohio River Valley into lands claimed by France. In 1754 a young officer named George Washington was sent to the territory to challenge French control and assert colonial claims. After an initial attack, Washington retreated to a hastily constructed fort, called Fort Necessity, in western Pennsylvania. Washington was later forced to surrender to the French but was allowed to withdraw with his surviving men.

Hoping to coordinate alliances with Native American peoples—and to keep them from allying with the French—Great Britain requested that its colonies meet at a conference in Albany, New York, in the summer of 1754. Seven colonies sent representatives there.[39] The so-called Albany Congress accomplished very little. However, one of its delegates, Benjamin Franklin, who later became America's first international celebrity, presented to the Congress a plan for closer coordination between the colonies. The **Albany Plan** called for a "Plan of Union," in which colonial legislatures would choose delegates to form an assembly under the leadership of a chief executive appointed by Great Britain.[40] This governing body would have power over dealings with Native American peoples and collective self-defense. And, in a premonition of an issue that would return again in debates over governance of the victorious United States, it would have the power to tax the colonies to pay for their collective defense.

Benjamin Franklin's proposal for a unified legislative body was not adopted by the colonial governments. It was not an idea whose time had come. Great Britain was better off dealing with its North American colonies individually rather than as a potentially powerful unified legislature. For their part, many colonies did not want to give up their own sovereignty, especially when it involved land claims that might make a lucky few colonies (especially Virginia) grow even larger and more powerful than they already were at the expense of the small coastal colonies, such as Rhode Island and Delaware, whose boundaries were constricted by the ocean and those of neighboring colonies.

Benjamin Franklin may not have expected his plan to be adopted. He was a very savvy politician. But his plan did plant the seeds for an American union. Writing four years later, Franklin discussed the "impossibility" of an American union at that time, stating, "When I say such a union is impossible, I mean without the most grievous tyranny and oppression."[41] In the minds of many American revolutionaries, they would get just that.

The Treaty of Paris left Great Britain as the unquestioned European power in North America, in Canada, and in the modern United States east of the Mississippi River. Spain gained territories from France as well. With victory, however, came problems: Great Britain had to now confront increasingly assertive colonies. It had acquired a vast new territory that now had to be administered, defended, and paid for. But money was scarce. War had left Great Britain with a significant amount of debt. With bankruptcy a possibility, the British government fully expected its thirteen colonies to pay for their own costs to the British Crown, so as not to make the debt problem even worse.[42]

Beginning in 1763, a series of acts and proclamations began to enlarge the scope of Great Britain's involvement in colonial affairs, producing a backlash from colonists who felt that Great Britain was going too far. The Revenue Act of 1764, also called the **Sugar Act**, was designed to assert tighter control over trade, especially to reduce smuggling and bribes, which were costing Great Britain money. In addition, the act sought to raise money

FIGURE 1.1

European Territorial Claims before and after the Seven Years' War

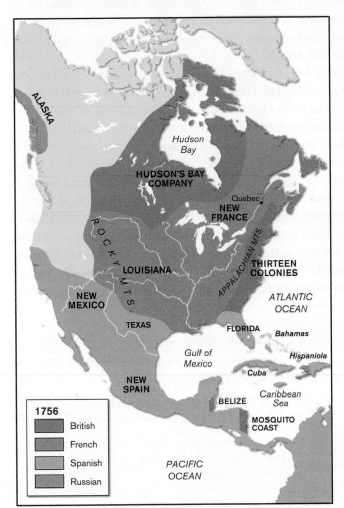

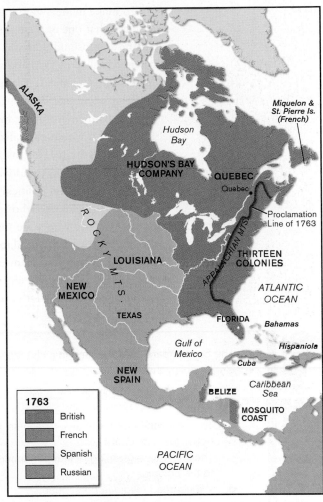

Following the Seven Years' War, Britain laid claim to much of the territory once held by the French, thus consolidating its power in the eastern portion of North America. Administering those colonies and finding ways to fund expansion was enormously difficult.

to pay for the administration and defense of the colonies by collecting a tax on sugar and molasses (used for making rum), which had already existed but had often been ignored.

For its part, Parliament felt that it was "just and necessary that a revenue be raised in [its] Majesty's said dominions in America for defraying the expenses of defending, protecting, and securing the same."[43] The Sugar Act actually reduced the tax on molasses, but it ended up favoring planters in the West Indies over New England rum merchants, and it introduced taxes on other imported goods into the colonies, such as coffee, wine, and imported cloth. The Townshend Acts of 1767 taxed goods that were imported from Great Britain and were also unpopular in the colonies.

One of the most controversial of these laws was the **Stamp Act of 1765**, which attempted to raise money through direct taxes—not just tariffs on trade—by requiring the purchase of a stamp for nearly anything that involved trade, publication, or legal transactions, including

Stamp Act of 1765
a highly unpopular law designed to raise revenue by requiring the purchase of stamps for newspapers, legal papers, and other documents.

"newspapers, pamphlets, cards, dice . . . wills, certificates, [and] academic degrees."[44] The Stamp Act had its opponents in Parliament, mostly those worried how it might affect profits from the colonies. Even these opponents in Great Britain, however, felt that Parliament was justified in using its legislative power to get the colonists to share in the burden of their defense and support. Colonists, though, saw things differently. What else, many wondered, might be taxed next?

To make matters worse, these acts were instituted during an economic depression in the colonies. That one of these acts forbade colonial printing of money to help pay off debt and that the stamps and duties had to be bought and paid for in hard money (gold, silver, and currency backed by gold and silver) only made things worse, especially for the New England merchants.[45] Colonial legislatures became increasingly resistant to having Parliament interfere in areas of economic life that the colonies, not Great Britain, had been in charge of for decades.

It was an environment full of misunderstanding and anxiety, vulnerable to the efforts of those who would capitalize on these fears to promote their own ideas about relations with Great Britain. This instability was made worse by the inability or refusal of Great Britain to fully understand what was happening in its thirteen North American colonies.

In this uncertain political environment, there were a few who advocated for resistance to Great Britain, some who remained loyal to Great Britain throughout the coming crisis, and many more who were undecided and afraid of actions that might lead to a hopeless war against the greatest military power in the world. It was this last group of colonists, the undecided, who found themselves in the crosshairs of a radical few. Those few had a powerful, cheap, and flexible technology on their side. It was called the printing press, and the American radicals used it very well.

WHAT HAVE I LEARNED?

1. The Seven Years' War resulted in a change in British policy that involved _____.

   a. A large transfer of British land claims to France
   b. The decision to be more assertive in its policy towards colonists
   c. The immediate granting of independence to the colonies
   d. Widespread religious persecution

2. The Albany Plan called for _____.

   a. Closer cooperation between colonies
   b. Independence from Great Britain
   c. New forms of taxation
   d. Trade policy reform

3. How did European colonization of North America impact the indigenous peoples?

4. Why was opposition to the Stamp Act on the part of residents of the British colonies in North America so strong?

Answer Key: 1. b; 2. a; 3. Answers might include both the devastation to societies and populations and actions of resistance and survival.; 4. Answers might include the fact that it was a direct tax and fears of what other forms of commerce might be taxed at later date.

THE AMERICAN RADICALS

From Ideas to Strategic Action to Political Institutions

Words and ideas, as the pamphleteers knew well, could also constitute strategic political action.

They were the viral videos of colonial America. Cheap, adaptable, quick to produce, able to reach large numbers of people in a short period of time, and with no central control over their content, they were perfectly suited to the tumultuous times of pre-revolutionary America. They were called pamphlets; their creators, pamphleteers. They consisted of a few printer's sheets stitched together with thread. They were produced on printing presses, roughly 6 x 6 contraptions of metal, screws, wood, and ink. It was hardly a new technology; the printing press was over three hundred years old by the time of the American pamphleteers. But the technology had become cheaper. Enough people had access to it and the ability to read its products to make the pamphlet a potentially revolutionary technological innovation.[46] According to Bernard Bailyn, "It was in this form that much of the most important and characteristic writing of the American Revolution appeared."[47]

The pamphleteers were engaged in **political propaganda**, "which is simply the attempt to control the actions of people indirectly by controlling their attitudes."[48] Their goal was to change public opinion—the distribution of people's attitudes and preferences on the issues of the day. Unlike their British counterparts, who had taken the pamphlet and refined it into something like a witty play or parlor game, the American pamphleteers were mostly amateurs. They were not trying to show their intelligence or literary skill. They were trying to mobilize people in support of their cause. Words and ideas, as the pamphleteers knew well, could also constitute strategic political action.

political propaganda
attempts to shape governmental actions and laws by changing people's beliefs and opinions.

The Idea of Independence: Thomas Paine's *Common Sense*

Of all of the American pamphleteers, the most widely read was ~~Thomas Paine~~. His 1776 pamphlet, *Common Sense*, sold perhaps more than one hundred thousand copies in its first year alone, rivaling in terms of its reach any modern bestseller or viral video. He was, according to one historian, "the greatest pamphleteer of the Age of Revolution."[49] Paine was also one of a relatively small number of white pamphleteers to point out the contradiction of calling for liberty in a society that allowed slavery. In a 1775 newspaper article, he wondered how the colonists could "complain so loudly of attempts to enslave them, while they hold so many hundred thousand in slavery."[50]

Paine was a recent arrival in the colonies, having come to Philadelphia from England in 1774 to establish a school for young women. In this endeavour, he was aided by enough money from a separation settlement with his wife to avoid indentured servitude, plus he possessed letters of introduction from Benjamin Franklin.[51] Many American pamphleteers did not like Paine's work. They thought it too emotional, not reasoned enough. While Paine's contemporaries may have had problems with his style, the people who bought his pamphlet did not. *Common Sense* ultimately "had more influence in focusing the spirit of revolt than the writings of all the intellectuals taken together."[52]

Calling ~~King George III the "royal brute of England,"~~ Paine challenged the legitimacy of the British monarchy, refuted arguments in favor of reconciling differences with Great Britain, and announced that "the period of debate is closed."[53] He used the dreaded *I* word, *independence*, writing that independence from Great Britain was not only possible but that it was sure to come to pass.[54] Drawing on the idea that the American colonists had a unique destiny in the world and in history, Paine called the colonists into action at just the time when many were ready to receive his message.

The cover of Thomas Paine's pamphlet *Common Sense* (1776). Library of Congress.

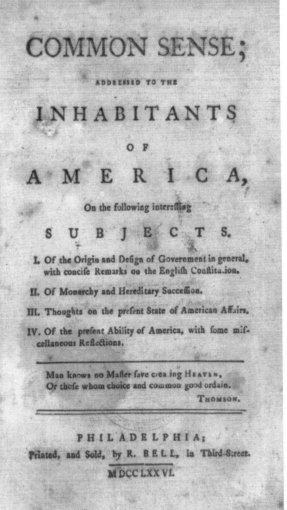

COMMON SENSE;

ADDRESSED TO THE

INHABITANTS

OF

AMERICA,

On the following interesting

SUBJECTS.

I. Of the Origin and Design of Government in general, with concise Remarks on the English Constitution.

II. Of Monarchy and Hereditary Succession.

III. Thoughts on the present State of American Affairs.

IV. Of the present Ability of America, with some miscellaneous Reflections.

Man knows no Master save creating HEAVEN,
Or those whom choice and common good ordain.
THOMSON.

PHILADELPHIA;
Printed, and Sold, by R. BELL, in Third-Street.
MDCCLXXVI.

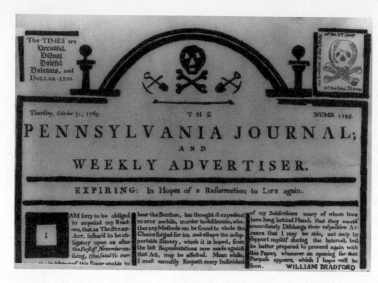

The front page of the *Pennsylvania Journal and Weekly Advertiser* on October 31, 1765. The skull and crossbones is placed where the required stamp is supposed to be, as an act of protest.

Courtesy of the Library of Congress, Prints and Photographs Division

Radical Action and the British Response

Words alone, however powerful, were not enough to mobilize the colonists to make a final break from Great Britain. The strategies of radical leaders in the colonies and the responses of the British government to these actions also played a key role. Adjusting their strategies along the way, the radicals helped drive the uncommitted colonists away from the possibility of reconciliation with Great Britain.

After passage of the Stamp Act and other unpopular policies, colonial radicals began a planned strategy of resistance, one that involved propaganda, organization, and, occasionally, violence. A common phrase associated with resistance to British tax policy was, "No taxation without representation!" While it was used at the time, the phrase did not fully capture the struggle between colonial governments and Great Britain. American radicals generally did not want to be represented in Parliament in Great Britain. Representatives would have been out of communication with the colonies during debates and consistently outvoted in Parliament even if some arrangement for their representation could be worked out. Instead, the colonists argued that the power of taxation should be held by colonial legislatures, not British Parliament. In many ways, colonial opposition to British policies was conservative. Its adherents wanted to go back to the way things had been prior to the Seven Years' War, when British colonial policy was more hands-off. Economic and political realities, however, made this an unrealistic goal.

The Sons of Liberty

Sons of Liberty
a group initially formed of merchants and workingmen in response to the Stamp Act that resisted Great Britain and its tax policies.

In 1765, in response to the Stamp Act, a group of merchants and workingmen, including Sam Adams, formed the "Loyall Nine," a group that later expanded into the **Sons of Liberty**. Through rallies, sermons, protests, and heavy use of the newspapers, the Sons and similar groups tried to mobilize public opinion in support of resistance to Great Britain and its tax policies. It was a working-class organization, with a potentially much larger appeal to the general public than the revolutionary elites. That potential made the Sons both attractive and scary to the wealthy elites in the revolutionary movement. Their fear was that they might not be able to control the actions of the Sons. Acts of violence in response to British policy only reinforced this fear, causing "some conservative American political leaders . . . to worry more about the danger of mobs than they did about British policies."[55]

On August 26, 1765, in a "scene of riot, drunkenness, profaneness, and robbery,"[56] a Boston mob associated with the Sons of Liberty ransacked the house of Thomas Hutchinson, then lieutenant governor of Massachusetts, "splintered the furniture, beat down the inner walls, tore up the garden, and carried off into the night, besides £900 sterling in cash, all of the plate, decorations, and clothes that had survived, and destroyed or scattered in the mud all of Hutchinson's books and papers."[57]

As a strategy of political mobilization the group's actions backfired. Uncommitted colonists looked on the mob violence fearfully, wondering how bad things might get if the crisis were to deepen. In response, radicals changed their strategy. They planned and organized boycotts of British goods, pressuring fellow colonists to comply.

In October 1765, at the invitation of Massachusetts's colonial legislatures, nine of thirteen colonies sent representatives who met in New York to debate and prepare a colonial response to Britain's policies.[58] This Stamp Act Congress issued a "Declaration of Rights and Statement of Grievances," which was, in many ways, quite mild. It affirmed colonial loyalty to the Crown. It did, however, protest against the imposition of taxes without colonial consent. Most importantly, the Stamp Act Congress was an early assembly of representatives across, not just within, the British colonies. In 1766 Great Britain repealed the Stamp Act, mostly due to the pressure of British merchants concerned about its effects on their profits. In fact, the Stamp Act had never been effectively enforced.

The Crisis Accelerates

In spite of continuing tensions, the years following the repeal of the Stamp Act were relatively quiet politically, with radicals losing power and influence and moderates able to keep them in check. Beginning in 1770, however, radical responses to British policies—and British responses to these radical responses—began to shift power and support away from the moderates and into the radical camp.

The exact sequence of events leading up to the Boston Massacre in 1770 is not entirely clear, nor is the exact role of radicals in escalating the situation. It involved a confrontation between a mob of Bostonians and a small group of British soldiers, beginning with taunts and snowballs and ending in the deaths of five American colonials. One of those killed was Crispus Attucks, a young man of African and Native American descent. Sam Adams and other radicals quickly mobilized to use the press to rally support for their cause, describing "the blood of our fellow citizens running like water through King Street."[59]

The Boston Tea Party

In 1773 the Boston Sons of Liberty seized upon an even greater crisis, one partly of their own making, to push away the possibility of reconciliation with Great Britain: the Boston Tea Party. It began over a corporate bailout of the East India Tea Company by the government of Great Britain. The British company was nearly bankrupt, and it had large stocks of unsold tea. Though corrupt and poorly managed, the East India Tea Company was no ordinary company. It ruled much of India with its own private army. It could count among its investors some of the wealthiest and most powerful men in Great Britain. It was—in modern terms—too big to fail.

It needed a bailout, and it got one with the Tea Act, passed by Great Britain in 1773. The act gave the East India Tea Company a tax-free monopoly on the tea trade to the colonies. Britain may have thought that the colonists would be happy to have cheaper tea. If so, they guessed wrong. New England merchants, some of whom were profiting handsomely by smuggling tea from Netherlands merchants into the colonies, were not pleased. The Tea Act cut out the middlemen in the colonial tea trade—the New England merchants—who saw "ruin staring them in the face, for not only were they threatened with the loss of their profits on tea, but they were confronted also with the possibility that the same company or other companies would be granted monopolies in such commodities as silks, drugs, and spices, all of which were essential articles of colonial life."[60]

It was the fear of what Great Britain might do next as much as what it actually *had* done that drove many merchants into the radical camp. In November 1773, the *Dartmouth* entered Boston Harbor loaded with tea. Two other ships soon followed. With the merchants increasingly on their side, the Sons of Liberty provoked a crisis, dumping the tea from the ships into the harbor.

Not everyone in the American colonies cheered the actions of the radicals. That it was an act of lawlessness worried many. The violence that accompanied the protest seemed to some completely unjustifiable. Historians debate Sam Adams's precise role in the Tea Party; some have argued that he helped to plan it. Adams certainly was, however, quick to jump on the crisis, defend the principles behind it, and publicize the events to radicals in other American colonies. The strategic actions of the Boston radicals placed the British government in a very difficult situation. It could not ignore the attack on British property and commerce. Asserting control, however, risked driving moderate colonials into the radical camp.

Parliament, with the support of King George III, clamped down. Hard. In a series of actions in 1774, known in the colonies as the **Intolerable Acts**, Britain sought to make an example of Massachusetts and its radicals. If Parliament and the Crown thought that this show of resolve, backed if necessary by force, would quiet the colonies, they were wrong. Writing many years after the Revolution, John Adams observed, "The colonies had grown up under constitutions of government so different, there was so great a variety of their religions, they were composed of so many different nations . . . that to unite them in the same principles in theory and the same system of action, was certainly a very difficult enterprise. . . . Thirteen clocks were made to strike together—a perfection of mechanism which no artist had ever before effected."[61] The actions of the British government and the Boston radicals had both helped to synchronize these thirteen clocks.

The Natural Rights of African Americans in Colonial America

As colonial America moved towards a revolution based on individual liberty, it was far from an equal society. To many Europeans, the prospect of individual advancement made America more equal than their class-stratified societies, with the exception of the almost feudal southern plantation societies.[62] In New England, working-class colonials had achieved a political status that few of their counterparts in Great Britain could. However, wealth was rapidly accumulating in the hands of a small number of colonial elites.[63]

The revolutionary philosophy of colonial America did not include women, many religious minorities, indigenous peoples, and African Americans in the register of those capable of full citizenship and the rights associated with it. The willingness of white colonial Americans to attack Great Britain for assaults on their liberty while allowing the enslavement of Africans did not go unnoticed by British officials. Thomas Hutchinson, governor of Massachusetts before the war, questioned how the American revolutionaries could "justify the depriving

Intolerable Acts
a term used in the American colonies to refer to a series of laws enacted by Great Britain in response to the Boston Tea Party.

Lemuel Haynes on Natural Rights and Slavery

In 1776 Lemuel Haynes, a Massachusetts minister, wrote an unpublished pamphlet titled *Liberty Further Extended.* The son of an African father and a white mother, Haynes became a servant to a religious white farming family in the backcountry of Massachusetts. Haynes educated himself in Puritan theology and on the pamphlets of colonial America. He volunteered as a minuteman in Boston in 1774 and for the Continental Army in 1776.

In his pamphlet, Haynes anchored his arguments about the injustice of slavery in the principle of natural rights and the Christian theology with which he and colonials were very familiar: "Liberty is a Jewel which was handed Down to man from the cabinet of heaven, and is Coaeval with his Existence. And as it proceed from the Supreme Legislature of the univers, so it is he which hath a sole right to take away; therefore, he that would take away a mans Liberty assumes a prerogative that Belongs to another, and acts out of his own domain."[67]

In the tradition of and expectations for such appeals to natural rights in the face of oppression, Haynes's pamphlet documented the injustices of the institution of slavery. In this passage, he addressed the slave trade:

> Let us go on to consider the great hardships, and sufferings those Slaves are put to, in order to be transported into these plantations. There are generally many hundred slaves put on board a vessel, and they are Shackkled together, two by two, wors than Criminals going to the place of Execution; and they are Crouded together as close as posable, and almost naked; and their sufferings are so great, as I have Been Credibly informed, that it often Carries off one third of them on their passage; yea, many have put an End to their own Lives for very anguish; And as some have manifested a Disposition to rise in their Defense, they have been put to the most Cruel torters, and Deaths.[68]

Lemuel Haynes, a Massachusetts minister who challenged slavery based on its violation of natural rights.
Interim Archives/Getty Images

WHAT DO YOU THINK?

Lemuel Haynes's pamphlet used the ideas of the American revolutionaries to point out the incompleteness of their project at the time. In your own experience, have you encountered situations, publications, or political communications in which others have done the same thing today? If you were to write a pamphlet or post a video, how might you base your own goals for a more complete realization of the promise of American democracy upon an argument for fundamental rights?

of more than a hundred thousand Africans of their rights to liberty, and the same *pursuit of happiness,* and in some degree to their lives, if these rights are so absolutely inalienable."[64]

This contradiction did not go unnoticed by slaves and free peoples of African descent either. Nor did some of these individuals ignore the potential social and political gains that might be made by pointing out the unfulfilled expression of liberty. In April 1773, a group of African Americans in Massachusetts petitioned the government for a redress of their grievances, drawing "a straight line between their own condition as chattel slaves and the conditions colonists were then objecting to as virtual slavery."[65] They asked that the same principles be applied to their own condition in colonial America.

"We expect great things," they wrote, "from men who have made such a noble stand against the designs of their *fellow men* to enslave them. . . . As the people of this province seem to be actuated by the principles of equity and justice, we cannot but expect your house will again take our deplorable case into serious consideration, and give us that ample relief which, *as men*, we have a natural right to."[66]

Institutionalizing Independence

By the time the delegates to a second congress convened in Philadelphia in May 1775, the "war of pamphlets and protests was giving way to the war of rifles and cannon."[69] In April British general Thomas Gage ordered troops to move on Lexington, Massachusetts—to arrest some radical leaders, including Sam Adams—and on Concord, Massachusetts, to seize some weapons. He failed to do both, and the battles of Lexington and Concord, though small, handed the radical pamphleteers the best ammunition that they could hope for. They immediately published exaggerated reports of British atrocities against colonial citizens, especially women and children. Individual colonies began to organize or expand colonial militias and organize their manufacturers for war.

Second Continental Congress

an assembly of delegates from the thirteen British colonies in America that drafted and approved the Declaration of Independence, conducted the Revolutionary War, and created the governmental structure that followed the war.

Though few could probably have imagined it that May, the **Second Continental Congress** remained the government of the United States until 1781, when a new American government, one designed by the Congress, took its place.[70] The Second Continental Congress was perpetually in crisis, trying to fight a war in the face of what seemed like unending military defeats, inadequate supplies, troops, and hard money. Its capital even had to be moved in the face of advancing British troops.

When the Second Continental Congress first assembled, the colonies were not yet united in the cause of war. A group of wealthy elites with personal, political, or financial ties to Great Britain opposed independence. A second group, the radicals, set their sights on armed conflict with Great Britain. A third group, the moderates, agreed that a show of force might be necessary but only to serve the ultimate end of a negotiated solution. There were other divisions, between slave and non slave-holding states, large and small colonies, and urban and rural colonists. These divisions would become more important once independence had actually been achieved.

Richard Henry Lee of Virginia offered a motion in Congress declaring that "these united colonies are, and of right ought to be, free and independent states."

Opponents of independence had many arguments on their side. First, in a full war, they would probably lose. They were almost hopelessly outclassed militarily. Failure, as all knew, would mean execution for treason. Many elites also worried that independence, even if it could be obtained, would lead to chaos and anarchy. The actions of the mobs of Boston had not been forgotten.

Radicals, for their part, could point to the fact that they were already in armed conflict with Great Britain, and successfully, though these early successes were soon to be followed by defeat after defeat. Public opinion was moving their way and was powerfully impacted by the publication of Thomas Paine's *Common Sense*. Perhaps most importantly, radicals had the actions of the British government and its administrators to thank for shifting the balance of power their way.

In the early months of 1776, events began to accelerate towards independence. *Common Sense* had given a clear voice to the cause, and British actions had given ammunition to the radicals. Individual colonies began to pass resolutions authorizing their delegates in Congress (often at the request of those delegates) to move for independence from Great Britain. On June 7, Richard Henry Lee of Virginia offered a motion in Congress declaring "that these united colonies are, and of right ought to be, free and independent states, that they are absolved from all allegiance to the British Crown, and that all political connection between them and the state of Great Britain is, and ought to be, totally dissolved."[71]

Congress was not quite ready to act on the Lee Resolution. The vote was postponed for three weeks in order to allow for more instructions to arrive from some of the colonies and to coerce reluctant colonies and their delegates on board. In the meantime, a committee was appointed to draft a basic structure for a government in the event of independence. A second committee was charged with trying to secure foreign aid. Another committee, consisting of Thomas Jefferson, John Adams, Benjamin Franklin, Roger Sherman, and Robert R. Livingston, was charged with writing a declaration, a justification, for American independence. On July 2, 1776, the Second Continental Congress approved the Lee Resolution, marking, perhaps, the actual date of America's formal declaration of independence from Great Britain. Two days later, on July 4, Congress approved Thomas Jefferson's revised Declaration of Independence, which justified its previous actions to the colonies and to the world.

Revolutionary Women: Invisibility, Exclusion, and Building Other Institutions

In many ways, women in revolutionary America were legally and politically invisible. In spite of commonalities in their legal standing, however, *colonial women* as an all-encompassing term fails to capture significant differences in the status, economic class, and religious orientation of the women in question.[72] Women who were slaves, of African descent, or of Native American ancestry struggled against multiple forms of oppression. While sexual and physical abuse was a danger for all colonial women, those who were slaves or indentured servants faced a higher risk.[73] War only heightened these risks; during the conflict, sexual assault was sometimes practiced systematically. In 1776 in Staten Island, New York, and New Jersey, British troops repeatedly raped women in the area.[74]

White women, unless they had acquired property through widowhood, generally had no legal identity or ability to secure their personal and economic rights in a court of law. For those women who did not struggle against the destruction of their families, traditions, and ways of life—either as slaves or members of Native American communities—theirs was a "protective oppression," designed to keep them out of involvement in government and public life. Because of more restricted educational opportunities and, therefore, lower literacy rates than men, fewer women's voices were expressed in print. In spite of these challenges, however, many women did speak, write, and act against the restrictions on their own rights and liberties in colonial America.

Because of their general exclusion from public life, women had fewer opportunities to adopt leadership roles in revolutionary America. Religious organizations proved an important exception as women could act as leaders in them without the same risk of social approbation as they would face if acting in the male-dominated political space. Maintaining the boycotts of British goods in the years before revolution also "politicized women and the domestic arena," especially in the production of substitutes for those goods.[75] The replacement of British textiles, in particular, brought many colonial women together as **Daughters of Liberty** in spinning events. While these meetings still remained in the "acceptable" realm of home production in the view of the male-dominated white colonial society, they did provide an experience in collective organization—an act of public "joining" that was itself a departure from and challenge to traditional gendered roles.[76]

Daughters of Liberty
a group of colonial-era women who participated in the boycotting of British goods.

Efforts to support the Revolutionary War effort led Esther de Berdt Reed, Sarah Franklin Bache (daughter of Benjamin Franklin), and other colonial women to work to create a women's organization across, not just within, the United States. The Ladies Association was "the biggest

A portrait of Esther de Berdt Reed by Charles Wilson Peale done some time before 1780.

The Print Collector/Getty Images

domestic fundraising campaign of the war,"[77] in part because women and girls who were not wealthy could still participate: "No contribution, however small, would be rejected,"[78] though the women who canvassed door to door for donations "attempted to pass over the homes of women known to be indigent or without funds to spare."[79]

Reed's pamphlet, *The Sentiments of an American Woman*, published in June 1780, laid out the necessity for colonial women to organize to aid the revolutionary cause. The collection, accounting, and delivery of these donations required the development of an organizational and administrative structure. A leader from the local "pooling group" collected and recorded the donations. "The treasuress would then send the register and the money to the wife of the governor of the state, and she in turn would forward the money to 'Mistress Washington'" to deliver the funds to her husband, George.[80] These fund-raising efforts were extremely successful, and this was perhaps the first truly national American women's organization. Though the members focused on activities considered acceptable for white women in colonial America, the act of organizing and institution building was itself revolutionary.

The language in Reed's pamphlet was constructed with colonial conventions in mind. In justifying the women's actions, Reed used the language of gendered differences that served to exclude women from political life at the time, but she used it to her own purpose. She wrote, "They [the women] aspire to render themselves more really useful, and this sentiment is universal from the north to the south of the Thirteen United States. Our ambition is kindled by the fame of those heroines of antiquity, who have rendered their sex illustrious and have proved to the universe that if the weakness of our Constitution, if opinion and manners did not forbid us to march to glory by the same paths as the Men, we should at least equal and sometimes surpass them in our love for the public good."[81]

> It was a revolution of ideas. Though imperfectly and incompletely, the idea of a government based upon natural rights and individual liberty had been given form.

A Revolution Still under Construction

From the start, the Revolutionary War went poorly for the Americans. Successive defeats, disease, and logistical problems all plagued the colonials and their general, George Washington. By adapting their tactics to suit their strengths—knowledge of the terrain and support among many of the locals—the colonials managed to use hit and run tactics to harass Britain and attack its long supply lines. With the help of Britain's rivals, especially France and its powerful navy, the Americans defeated Great Britain at the Battle of Yorktown in 1781. The Treaty of Paris, signed in 1783 and ratified by Congress in 1784, secured the independence of the United States of America.

Militarily and politically, the American Revolution wasn't technically a revolution. King George III was not overthrown; the British Empire remained intact. George would go on to become the longest reigning British monarch until Queen Victoria in the nineteenth century. He survived his historic defeat at the hands of the American revolutionaries to oversee the unification of Ireland and England, thus forming the United Kingdom. The conflict in America is more properly called a secession, in which a group of citizens break off from the larger government to form one of their own. In the backcountry, it was frequently a civil war, with members of the same communities fighting each other, often brutally.

It was, however, very much a revolution of ideas. Though imperfectly and incompletely, the idea of a government based upon natural rights and individual liberty had been given political and institutional form. Later American revolutionaries would undertake their own wars of ideas and political strategies to try to make the government live up to its promises. As part of their efforts, they would build, rebuild, and reshape the political institutions that protect and express Americans' natural rights in a representative democracy.

NEWS CLIP
Burmese government
releases dissidents

1. The American pamphleteers were mostly trying to show their literary skills.

   a. True
   b. False

2. Many colonial American elites worried about some of the actions of the Sons of Liberty because they _____.

   a. Were supporting Great Britain and its policies
   b. Failed to repeal the Stamp Act
   c. Were advocating for the rights of indigenous peoples
   d. Threatened mob rule

3. Lemuel Haynes and Esther de Berdt Reed both acted during the revolutionary period. How were their efforts similar? How were they different?

4. What political institutions did Esther de Berdt Reed help build? Why does this matter?

Answer Key: 1. b; 2. d; 3. Answers might focus on similarities between their appeals to natural rights but also on differences between their specific tactics.; 4. Answers should focus on the transcolonial nature of women's cooperation.

INSTITUTIONS MATTER, TOO

As we have seen in the stories above, while the actions of people and their ideas matter to American government, the **political institutions** that structure how citizens may be involved matter as well. To a great extent, institutions determine how conflicts over political power are resolved, and they can also shape the ideas of people acting within them.

In devising a system of government, two basic questions need to be resolved: how much power that government will claim, and how political power will be distributed or withheld. Different forms of governments distribute power in very different ways. Totalitarian governments admit no limitations on their own power or competing centers of political power. Similarly, authoritarian governments suppress the voices of their citizens to maintain a grip on power; however, unlike totalitarian systems, authoritarian systems may have some economic or social institutions not under governmental control that may serve to moderate the government's power. Governments that admit no external challenge to their claims on power might be monarchies, ruled by royal figures; theocracies, ruled by religious elites; or oligarchies, ruled by a small group of powerful elites. At the other end of the spectrum of power is a **direct democracy**, in which citizens vote directly on public policies. (See Figure 1.2.)

The United States is none of these extremes. While the nation does have elements of direct democracy—in, for example, local votes to approve or reject public school budgets or property tax increases—the vast majority of conflicts over power in America are handled through a system of **representative democracy**, in which voters select representatives who then vote on matters of public policy. In doing so, voters in a representative democracy are confronted with a serious challenge: How can they be sure that their

CONNECTING TO . . .

American Political Institutions

As you read about American political institutions, reflect on the foundational ideas of the American Revolution as well as strategic political action undertaken in the support of the war. Consider the following:

- The ways in which political institutions structure political representation

- How these institutions may serve to protect or restrict individuals' rights

- How individuals may use or reshape these institutions to protect their own rights and the rights of others

political institutions
the rules, laws, and structures that channel and shape political action.

direct democracy
a political system in which citizens vote directly on public policies.

representative democracy
a political system in which voters select representatives who then vote on matters of public policy.

> *Voters in a representative democracy are confronted with a serious challenge: How can they be sure that their representatives are carrying out their wishes?*

representatives are carrying out their wishes? This is a question that we will examine in some detail in this book.

The number of political institutions in America today is almost too long to list, comprised of bodies at the local, state, and national levels. The most important institution in American political life, however, is the United States Constitution. This document forms the basis of the nation's government and, in turn, creates a host of political institutions through which conflicts over political power are resolved. It places textual limits on the power of the national government in order to protect Americans' fundamental rights. It also constitutes, or creates, a people with its first seven words, "We the People of the United States."

constitutional republic
a form of government in which people vote for elected representatives to make laws and policies and in which limits on the ability of that government to restrict individual rights are placed in a constituting document that is recognized as the highest law of the land.

How does a society structure political institutions in such a way that the social contract is upheld? By ceding some of the expression of their natural rights to a government, Americans have tried to create institutions that ensure an orderly and prosperous society. In doing so, however, they run the risk of creating institutions that oppress instead of uplift. The United States of America is, institutionally and fundamentally, a **constitutional republic**. In it, Americans elect representatives to make most of the laws and policies in the nation, rather than voting on them directly, which would be unwieldy in a nation of more than 300 million people. In addition, and crucially, limits are placed upon the power of

FIGURE 1.2

Types of Governments

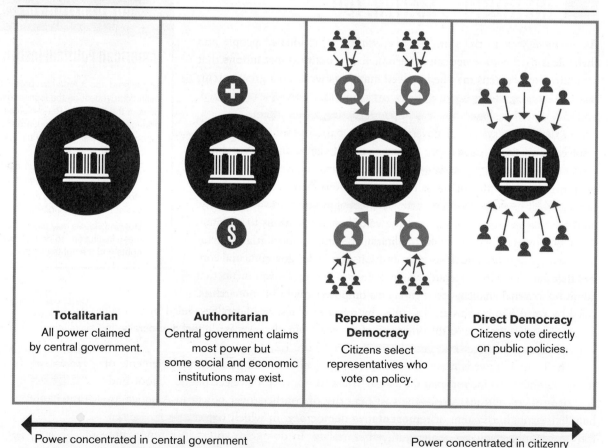

Totalitarian
All power claimed by central government.

Authoritarian
Central government claims most power but some social and economic institutions may exist.

Representative Democracy
Citizens select representatives who vote on policy.

Direct Democracy
Citizens vote directly on public policies.

Power concentrated in central government ← → Power concentrated in citizenry government to infringe upon people's rights in a constituting document that is recognized as the highest and most supreme law of the nation.

The institutions and rules of a government do not only structure the politics of a nation, they also may serve to structure its **economy**, or the ways in which goods and services are produced and distributed within a society.

When comparing different economic systems, the key thing to focus on is how much power a government has to regulate the production and distribution of goods and services. In **communist systems**, a government acting on behalf of all workers in a society controls the means of production and distribution. In **socialist systems**, private firms are allowed to operate but with significant intervention by the government, which may include governmental control of sectors of the economy, in the service of ensuring economic equality. In a **capitalist system**, private ownership of the means of production and distribution of a society's resources is emphasized and protected under the laws of that society. Capitalism emphasizes the efficiency of the marketplace in optimally allocating a society's resources. A completely unregulated capitalist system is called *laissez-faire* (from the French "let go," or "let be") and allows individuals and private firms to operate without regulation or oversight. No representative democracies currently practice laissez-faire capitalism. Instead, even nations like the United States that emphasize private economic action practice regulated capitalism, in which firms are allowed to control much of their own decision making but are also subject to governmental rules and regulations (Figure 1.3).

economy
the systems and organizations through which a society produces and distributes goods and services.

communist system
a way of structuring economic activity in which a government exerts complete control over the production and distribution of goods and services.

socialist system
a way of structuring economic activity in which private firms are allowed to operate and make decisions over production and distribution but with significant governmental involvement to ensure economic equality.

capitalist system
a way of structuring economic activity in which private firms are allowed to make most or all of the decisions involving the production and distribution of goods and services.

FIGURE 1.3

Types of Economic Systems

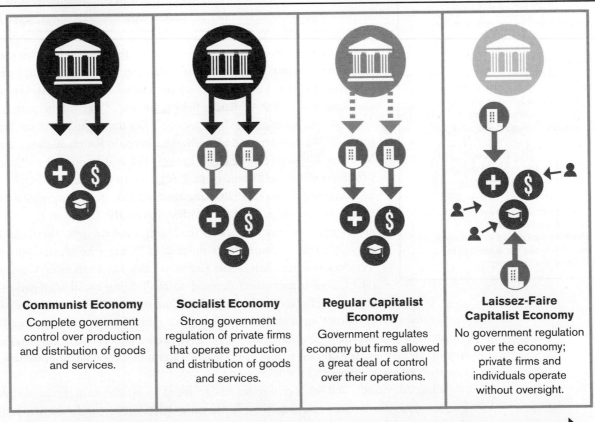

Communist Economy
Complete government control over production and distribution of goods and services.

Socialist Economy
Strong government regulation of private firms that operate production and distribution of goods and services.

Regular Capitalist Economy
Government regulates economy but firms allowed a great deal of control over their operations.

Laissez-Faire Capitalist Economy
No government regulation over the economy; private firms and individuals operate without oversight.

Stronger government control   Stronger private control

1. American political decisions are made primarily through the practice of direct democracy.

   a. True
   b. False

2. In a republic, citizens _____.

   a. Have little say in the formation of laws and policies
   b. Vote directly on laws and policies
   c. Elect representatives who then formulate laws and policies

   d. Place their rights in the hands of unelected officials

3. What is the primary difference between capitalist and socialist economic systems?

....

Answer Key: 1. b; 2. c; 3. Answers should emphasize the role of government in regulating the markets.

DR. MARTIN LUTHER KING JR.'S LETTER FROM BIRMINGHAM JAIL

CONNECTING TO . . .

"Letter from Birmingham Jail"

As you read the final narrative of the chapter, try to tie the story of Dr. Martin Luther King Jr.'s "Letter from Birmingham Jail" to the concepts explored in the other stories in the chapter—students using the Equal Access Act to assert their rights and the ways in which Jefferson's Declaration of Independence defined a vision of rights but was itself challenged. Consider the following:

- The similarities between the structure and language of King's letter and the Declaration

- Similarities and differences between individuals undertaking civil disobedience during the civil rights movement and the actions of the colonial revolutionaries

As they led about forty protesters from the Sixteenth Street Baptist Church in Birmingham, Alabama, Reverend Martin Luther King Jr. and his close friend, Reverend Ralph David Abernathy, were dressed for jail. Wearing work shirts and jeans, carrying coats to ward off the cold and damp of Birmingham City Jail, King and Abernathy walked past hundreds of spectators, witnesses, and supporters. Some "sang freedom songs, some knelt in silence."[82] A few cried.

Despite the seriousness of the situation, the two leaders had tried to show calmness and strength. Prior to leaving for Birmingham, one evening King lightened the mood of all present when, looking at Abernathy and knowing well his friend's habits, he said, "Let me be sure to get arrested with people who don't snore."[83] On the night before the march, King told the planners and supporters gathered in Room 30 of the Gaston Motel in Birmingham, "I don't know what will happen. I don't know where the money will come from. But I have to make a faith act."[84]

Born in Atlanta in 1929, King received a doctorate in theology from Boston University and, like his father, joined the Christian clergy. After university, King moved back to the South, even though "there had been offers of jobs in safe northern universities."[85] Later he became one of the founders and president of the Southern Christian Leadership Conference (SCLC), an organization devoted to challenging racial segregation and advocating for civil rights. In its founding statement, the conference's leaders pointed to the violence against those struggling for racial justice and announced that "we have no moral choice, before God, but to delve deeper into the struggle—and to do so with greater reliance on non-violence and with greater unity, coordination, sharing and Christian understanding."[86]

King, Abernathy, and other civil rights leaders faced a near-constant threat of violence for their opposition to racial segregation, as did many other women and men who took on the white racial order in the American South. King's own home in Montgomery, Alabama, had been bombed in 1956, though both King and his wife escaped harm. Prior to that act of racial violence, King had also been verbally threatened in an anonymous phone call—a clear attempt to intimidate him. It didn't work. King, as well as other leaders, members, and supporters of the SCLC, pressed ahead.

That they were marching in Birmingham in 1963 was no accident. The city was a bastion of segregation and threats of violence to anyone who resisted were pervasive. The protests were designed to conduct acts of civil disobedience in which one defied a law seen as unjust and accepted the consequences of that defiance, as King put it, "openly, lovingly."[87]

For breaking a prohibition on their marching or protesting, King, Abernathy, and about fifty others were arrested and taken to Birmingham City Jail. King was thrown into solitary confinement—"the hole," as it was called—with only a cot with metal slats to sleep on. "You will never know the meaning of utter darkness," he recalled, "until you have lain in such a dungeon."[88]

Southern Christian Leadership Conference leaders marching in Birmingham, Alabama, in April 1963. Fred Shuttlesworth, left, is not carrying a coat. The plan was for Shuttlesworth to join in the march to show solidarity but then break off to organize and raise funds for the conference. However, he was arrested with the others. Reverend Ralph Abernathy, center, with an extra layer of clothing and a coat in preparation for imprisonment, appears relaxed. Reverend Martin Luther King Jr., right, also clothed in preparation for arrest, appears to be much more concerned and contemplative.

Birmingham, Ala. Public Library Archives.

White Clergy Members Urge Moderation

The morning after King's arrest, a copy of an article from the *Birmingham News* was "slipped in to" his cell.[89] Titled "White Clergymen Urge Local Negroes to Withdraw from Demonstrations," the letter, written by eight white members of the Protestant, Catholic, and Jewish clergies, admonished King and the other leaders of the SCLC to slow down, to stop protesting, to end the strategy of civil disobedience in Birmingham.[90]

Calling the demonstrations "unwise and untimely" and "directed and led in part by outsiders," the eight clergy members argued that "honest convictions in racial matters could properly be pursued in the courts." They "commend[ed] the [Birmingham] community as a whole and the local news media and law enforcement officials in particular, on the calm manner in which these demonstrations have been handled." (However, a photograph taken less than a month later and published in the *New York Times* showing a young African American man being attacked by a police dog under the direction of a Birmingham police officer led millions of Americans to question claims of police restraint.) In closing, the clergy members urged Birmingham's "Negro community to withdraw support from these demonstrations."

King's Affirmation of Natural Rights

Writing in the margins of the smuggled newspaper, Martin Luther King Jr. penned a response from jail to the clergymen's accusations and advice.[91] His notes were smuggled out of the jail, typed up, and eventually published by a group of Quakers as the "Letter from Birmingham Jail." Though it did not have the benefit of King's powerful speaking voice to increase its impact, it is one of the most important documents of the American civil rights movement.

The Power of the Media

AP Photo/Bill Hudson.

African American activists in the civil rights movement of the 1960s used a variety of strategies to bring about social change, including holding sit-ins in whites-only areas, such as lunch counters and on public transportation, and organizing marches and demonstrations across the South. The white clergy who urged "moderation" said that those types of protests were unwise and argued that protesters should pursue institutional avenues, such as the courts, for change.

This photograph of a student activist being attacked by a police dog in Birmingham, Alabama, appeared on the front page of the *New York Times* in 1963. President John F. Kennedy is reported to have viewed it and said it sickened him. He also is said to have registered that it would make the United States look bad across the world, as Birmingham was "a dangerous situation for our image abroad." Shortly afterwards, Kennedy delivered his own famous civil rights speech, vindicating Martin Luther King Jr.'s statements in "Letter from Birmingham Jail."

WHAT DO YOU THINK?

What role do you think images like this may have played in shaping American public opinion on civil rights? Might this role be similar or different in the era of cell phone cameras and YouTube?

....

Source: Quoted from Jonathan Rieder, "The Day President Kennedy Embraced Civil Rights—and the Story behind It," *The Atlantic*, June 11, 2013, http://www.theatlantic.com/national/archive/2013/06/the-day-president-kennedy-embraced-civil-rights-and-the-story-behind-it/276749/.

In the letter, King begins by offering his reply as a sincere response to the white clergymen's concerns, calling them "men of genuine goodwill." Then he defends his presence in Birmingham professionally, as president of the Southern Christian Leadership Conference. However, he also lays out a much more fundamental basis for his involvement. He declares, "I am in Birmingham because injustice is here."

King defends his and his movement's tactics on the basis of natural rights, drawing a distinction between just and unjust laws: "A just law is a man-made code that squares with the moral law or the law of God. An unjust law is a code that is out of harmony with the natural law." Racial oppression, he asserts, in all of its legal manifestations, is unjust. Individuals, therefore, have the right to break these unjust laws, but, he adds, "One who breaks an unjust law must do so openly, lovingly."

In a single sentence more than three hundred words long, King lists the grievances, the injustices, and the evidence that led to his and many others' revolutionary acts. In its use of language, logic, and the principles of natural rights, "Letter from Birmingham Jail" knows no superior as an American revolutionary pamphlet. Politically, one of the most important passages in the letter pointed to the white moderate as a severe obstacle to justice: "I have almost reached the regrettable conclusion that the Negro's great stumbling block in the stride toward freedom is not the White citizens' 'Councilor' or the Ku Klux Klanner, but the white moderate who is more devoted to 'order' than justice; who prefers a negative peace which is the absence of tension to a positive peace which is the presence of justice."

Doyle Brunson, one of the greatest Texas No Limit Hold 'Em poker players of all time, said of his poker strategy, "I want to put my opponent to a decision for all his chips."[92] The radicals of the American Revolution meant to present the colonial moderates with exactly the same decision. Through their actions—and with help from British reactions to their strategies—the radicals took away the possibility of a comfortable, moderate, middle ground. By creating a crisis and a confrontation, King and his fellow protesters sought to force white moderates to make a choice, to decide if racial segregation and the oppression of African Americans was consistent with the ideals of the Unites States or not. In their own ways, Bridget Mergens and the members of the Boyd County High Gay-Straight Alliance did the same thing.

CONCLUSION

The American Experiment, Continued, and You Are Part of It

A study of American government requires understanding the ideas upon which it is based. It requires an understanding of the ways in which political institutions promote, shape, or hinder the fulfilment of these fundamental ideas. It requires a study of the past and the present. However, and most importantly, a deep study of American government requires that you think, and perhaps act, as a strategic player in the political space, which is rarely, if ever, neat and clean.

Should you choose to act in American politics—should you choose to stake your own claims for your rights—you will want to be well informed, both about your own positions on critical issues and the positions of those with whom you disagree. You will want to have developed your skills in analyzing the words, images, and data that will serve as your tools along the way. And you will need to question. What is American political culture? Is there such a thing? How do the institutions of American government make "good government" more or less likely?

At the beginning of the chapter, I stated that this book would be centered on stories, and it is. But why? How is it useful to begin a book that teaches American government and politics with stories about a high school student trying to start a Christian Bible study club, a group of high school students trying to start a Gay-Straight Alliance, Thomas Jefferson drafting the Declaration of Independence, Dr. Martin Luther King Jr. writing "Letter from Birmingham Jail," and many other smaller stories about individuals who used the written and spoken word, political action, and protest to claim their own rights? Why read the stories? Why not just skim the definitions for the "important" content? Because the stories and, most importantly, your engagement with them, have the potential to capture what definitions and lists might not:

- The understanding that American political institutions did not fall out of the sky. They were created through conscious action and contestation, sometimes based upon success, sometimes based upon failure, and sometimes based upon pure chance.
- The comprehension that in the world of American government and politics, there is rarely, if ever, an either/or solution to major problems but instead a complex interplay between ideals, actions, time, and place.
- The understanding that the development of American government and politics has always involved the experiences of individuals and groups whose lives were written out of conventional narratives.
- The realization that people matter, even if they did not succeed.
- The knowledge that your own voices matter—that your own opinions, thoughtfully constructed and respectfully offered, matter, even if these ideas and opinions may seem to be outside of some perception of what you are supposed to think or what others tell you to think.

Want a better grade?

Get the tools you need to sharpen your study skills. **SAGE edge** offers a robust online environment featuring an impressive array of free tools and resources. Access practice quizzes, eFlashcards, video, and multimedia at **edge.sagepub.com/abernathy1e.**

As you read, engage with, and discuss the material in this book and in your courses, there are only two things of which I will try to convince you: People like you matter. And your stories matter as well, even if nobody ever retells them in a book.

The American experiment always was a complicated and incomplete thing. It still is. At its heart, it poses one difficult and basic question: Can a people design and maintain a government that uplifts and energizes its citizens rather than oppressing them? The answer to that question is not up to other people. It is up to you.

CHAPTER REVIEW

This chapter's main ideas are reflected in the Learning Objectives below. By reviewing them here you should be able to **remember** the key points, **connect** them to the stories presented in the chapter, **think** critically about these questions, and **know** these terms that are central to the topic.

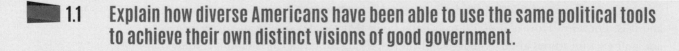

1.1 Explain how diverse Americans have been able to use the same political tools to achieve their own distinct visions of good government.

REMEMBER . . .
- The American political system is designed so that different individuals and groups of people, regardless of their points of view and backgrounds, are able to access the same political tools, such as federal and state laws and different forms of political action, in order to bring about change.

CONNECT...
- Bridget Mergens and the Boyd County High GSA used a federal law, the Equal Access Act to give voice to their political beliefs.

THINK...
- Americans with very different political goals and perspectives have based their efforts on many of the same fundamental ideas. Why do you think this is possible?

KNOW...
- *politics* (p. 2)
- *government* (p. 2)

■ 1.2 Define the key elements of American political culture.

REMEMBER ...
- The American political system was founded on a set of shared ideas and values that together are called political culture.
- The most important aspects of American political culture are the commitments to equality, rights, liberty, the pursuit of happiness, and religious freedom, and the idea that America is unique in the ways it has developed.
- Those ideas and values define the relationship of Americans to their government and to each other.

CONNECT...
- The rights claimed by Bridget Mergens and the Boyd County High GSA, though seemingly opposed to one another, come from the same set of shared ideas and values that make up American political culture.

THINK...
- What are some of the key ideas that define American political culture?
- To what extent do your experiences inform you of the degree to which these ideas have been realized?

KNOW...
- *American political culture* (p. 7)
- *social equality* (p. 7)
- *political equality* (p. 7)
- *economic equality* (p. 7)
- *inalienable rights* (p. 7)
- *liberty* (p. 8)
- *the American dream* (p. 8)
- *American exceptionalism* (p. 10)
- *political ideology* (p. 10)

■ 1.3 Examine the ways in which natural rights and the theory of the social contract helped to shape the ideas expressed in the Declaration of Independence.

REMEMBER ...
- The Declaration of Independence was drafted primarily by Thomas Jefferson in connection with the Second Continental Congress in 1776.
- Jefferson and his colleagues in the Continental Congress made a series of strategic decisions in incorporating key ideas from history into a document that successfully laid out the justification for independence.
- The Declaration was shaped by the politics and historical context of American colonies trying to assert themselves in the face of tyranny.
- Jefferson drew on ideas of democracy from ancient Greece and Rome as well as on ideas from Enlightenment philosophers, such as John Locke, Montesquieu, and David Hume.
- The drafters left out some important ideas that would have had serious implications for the country and its people. In practice, natural rights have been unevenly applied.

CONNECT...
- The roles of Thomas Jefferson as a Virginian, a student of politics and history, and a slave owner played an important part in shaping the Declaration of Independence.
- The cases of Bridget Mergens and the Boyd County High GSA were both enabled by the idea of natural rights and in some ways constrained by a social contract.

THINK...
- What were the main ideas behind the Declaration of Independence?
- Do you think the ideals in the Declaration have been achieved in today's United States?

KNOW...
- *democracy* (p. 13)
- *natural rights* (p. 13)
- *social contract* (p. 13)
- *political science* (p. 13)

1.4 Identify the factors that gave rise to the American Revolution and discuss the war's legacy, both in what was and what was not achieved.

REMEMBER ...
- The British colonists depended upon American Indians for their survival. As the colonial population grew and demands for territories increased, colonists came into violent conflict with native peoples.
- Colonial economies depended upon slavery and slave labor. Slaves, the descendants of slaves, and native peoples were not extended rights under the Declaration of Independence.
- Colonists began to establish forms of state government for the purpose of representation and administration and increasingly asserted their authority and autonomy from Great Britain.
- The political, social, and economic ideas that circulated in political pamphlets, especially Paine's *Common Sense,* contributed greatly to the rationale for independence and revolution in the face of increasing British taxation.
- Women played a role in the economy and affairs of the colonies but were not extended full rights.

CONNECT...
- The stories of Bridget Mergens and the Boyd County High GSA show us that the struggle to extend rights to certain people and groups is ongoing.
- The ideas Jefferson brought the Declaration of Independence were a direct result of the political and historical context of his time.
- Many of the same ideals fought for in the American Revolution had gone unfulfilled for other groups throughout much of American history
- The ideas and actions of the civil rights movement in the mid-twentieth century responded to these unfulfilled promises given voice in the revolutionary period.

THINK...
- How did the history of the American colonial experience shape the drive towards independence?
- What role did political propaganda play in mobilizing American public opinion leading up to the American Revolution? What role do you think it plays today?

KNOW...
- *Seven Years' War* (p. 17)
- *Albany Plan* (p. 18)
- *Sugar Act* (p. 18)
- *Stamp Act of 1765* (p. 19)
- *political propaganda* (p. 21)
- *Sons of Liberty* (p. 22)
- *Intolerable Acts* (p. 24)
- *Second Continental Congress* (p. 26)
- *Daughters of Liberty* (p. 27)

1.5 Describe the core features of American political institutions.

REMEMBER ...
- In the American model of representative democracy, the forms our political institutions take affect how people are represented.
- The institutional structure of the United States is that of a constitutional republic, in which the people elect representatives to make most of the laws and policies in the nation rather than voting on them directly.
- Institutions can both protect and restrict rights, and people may use and change them to protect their own rights or those of others.
- America's political institutions also structure the country's economy.

CONNECT ...
- Bridget Mergens and the Boyd County High GSA used a variety of political institutions to advance their rights.
- In rejecting British rule, Jefferson knew that America would need to create its own political institutions that protected the ideals expressed in the Declaration of Independence.

THINK ...
- What form of government does America have?
- How are political decisions in America made?
- What kind of economic system does America have?

KNOW ...
- *political institutions* (p. 29)
- *direct democracy* (p. 29)
- *representative democracy* (p. 29)
- *constitutional republic* (p. 30)

- *economy* (p. 31)
- *communist systems* (p. 31)
- *socialist system* (p. 31)
- *capitalist system* (p. 31)

1.6 Compare Dr. Martin Luther King Jr.'s "Letter from Birmingham Jail" to Thomas Jefferson's draft of the Declaration of Independence in terms of their ideas and the political strategies of their authors.

REMEMBER ...
- Dr. Martin Luther King Jr.'s "Letter from Birmingham Jail" (1963), one of the most important documents of the civil rights movement, directly echoes the claims for rights made by Thomas Jefferson over 150 years prior.
- Even today, claims for natural rights—rights that cannot be denied by governments—must be made.

CONNECT ...
- Hundreds of years after the drafting of the Declaration of Independence, King based his claim for full rights for African Americans upon the idea of natural rights.

THINK ...
- In what ways is King's "Letter from Birmingham Jail" similar to the Declaration of Independence? In what ways do they differ?

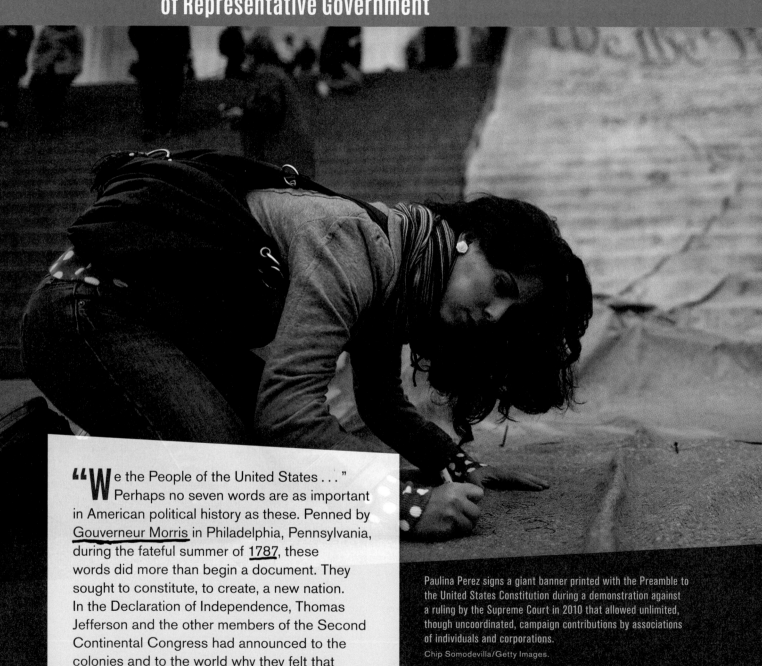

2 THE CONSTITUTION OF THE UNITED STATES

Practical Politics and a New Vision of Representative Government

"We the People of the United States . . . " Perhaps no seven words are as important in American political history as these. Penned by Gouverneur Morris in Philadelphia, Pennsylvania, during the fateful summer of 1787, these words did more than begin a document. They sought to constitute, to create, a new nation. In the Declaration of Independence, Thomas Jefferson and the other members of the Second Continental Congress had announced to the colonies and to the world why they felt that separation from Great Britain was justified and necessary. Following the American Revolution, that goal was achieved . . . but then what?

In the years following the Revolution, the American states and the government that

Paulina Perez signs a giant banner printed with the Preamble to the United States Constitution during a demonstration against a ruling by the Supreme Court in 2010 that allowed unlimited, though uncoordinated, campaign contributions by associations of individuals and corporations.

Chip Somodevilla/Getty Images.

they had collectively agreed to form struggled against the realities of financial crises, the possibility of foreign invasion, and the threat of internal discord and even revolution. Against this backdrop, a group of delegates convened in Philadelphia in 1787 to create a new government—a new *kind* of government—although they were not technically authorized to do so.

The delegates to what we now call the Constitutional Convention drafted—and then tried to sell to skeptical individuals in the thirteen American states—a blueprint for a new government, though the delegates themselves were often divided about what this government should be, how it should be structured, and how much power it should have. In spite of all of these divisions and challenges, they produced a **constitution**, a document that simultaneously creates a people, sets out fundamental principles on which these people agree to be governed, and establishes the rules and institutions through which this governing will take place.

> **constitution**
> A document that defines and creates a people politically, sets out the fundamental principles of governance, and creates the rules and institutions through which a people choose to self-govern.

In this chapter, we will explore the stories of the events leading up to the Constitutional Convention, the political debates within the convention, and the debates surrounding the ratification process. We will focus primarily on one person: James Madison of Virginia. Though he was hardly the most powerful political figure of the time, Madison's efforts were instrumental in shaping the Constitution of the United States.

LEARNING OBJECTIVES

After reading this chapter, you will be able to:

2.1 Explain how the historical context of post-Revolutionary America led to the proposal for a new, stronger national government

2.2 Describe how the Constitution was shaped by the strategic political choices of those involved in its drafting

2.3 Identify the ideas behind the structure of the government under the Constitution

2.4 Compare and contrast the arguments put forth by the Federalists and Antifederalists during the ratification debates

2.5 Consider the different perspectives on the effects of the Constitution in American life today

JAMES MADISON'S RESEARCH PROJECT

"The Fathers Were Practical Men"[1]

In the spring of 1786, thirty-five-year-old James Madison Jr. settled into his home in Montpelier, Virginia, with two trunks full of books. They had been collected and sent over from Europe by his good friend, Thomas Jefferson. Madison, for his part, kept detailed weather readings for Jefferson, looked after the education of his nephew, and occasionally sent him samples of plants and animals from the "New World" that Jefferson could use to enlighten and entertain his hosts and friends in Europe. Madison had successfully collected "Paccan [pecan] Nuts & the seed of the Sugar [Maple] Tree" but had less luck with his attempts to raise native animals. "I lately had on hand a female opossum, with 7 young ones," he wrote to Jefferson, "which I intended to have reared, for the purpose of partly of experiments myself and partly of being able to forward some of them to you, in case of an opporty [opportunity] and your desiring it. Unfortunately they have all died."[2]

Madison was one of America's first political scientists, as much an engineer as a philosopher, and an avid researcher of the most pressing political questions of his era. The subject of Madison's studies that spring of 1786 was death, but of governments, not of opossums. Kingdoms and empires had endured, sometimes for centuries, under the rule of monarchs and emperors. But **republics**, governments ruled by representatives of the people, without exception had eventually died. Madison wanted to know how a people could create a republic that lasted—a republic that could avoid being taken over by a small group of men or descending into civil war or anarchy. Madison poured himself into this project systematically, scientifically, and with a great deal of energy.

To those who knew James Madison, or "Jemmy" as his friends called him, this would probably not have been a surprise. Though he was shy, often sick, and a quiet public speaker, he was smart, and he did his homework. Madison "persuaded others by having the facts and ideas, the knowledge and the thought, already worked out more deeply and thoroughly than anyone else present."[3] Madison had been a dedicated student at the College of New Jersey, which later became Princeton University. While there, he studied political thought from the Greeks to the Enlightenment. In 1786, as the American government of the time came under increasingly harsh criticism and calls to fix or replace it grew louder, Madison's years of preparation proved to be more than a good character trait. It allowed him to help shape the agenda of the debates taking place in his newly independent country and to get others to talk about his ideas, whether they agreed with him or not.

In the tumultuous years that followed American independence, there was no shortage of voices arguing for change. Economic disruption, the threat of European powers, and the threat of rebellion within the thirteen states all gave ammunition to those who wanted change. The question, of course, was what kind of change. On that there was no consensus. Madison's research played a critical role in designing a new American government, selling it to a skeptical public, and laying out the logic of the constitutional republic for subsequent generations of Americans.[4]

Madison's immediate concern that spring was to prepare for a conference set to take place in Annapolis, Maryland, later that fall. Officially, the Annapolis Convention had been called to address trade and navigation disputes between states. Unofficially, at least in the minds of Madison and those who shared his views, the hope was that the outcome of the convention might lead to significant changes in the fundamental structure of the government of the United States. Though Madison wanted to see major reforms, he was not optimistic about the prospect for real change. "Tho' my wishes are in favor of such

republics
governments ruled by representatives of the people.

An engraving of James Madison, American statesman and political theorist. His study of republics led him to investigate how to create a form of government led by people that was capable of enduring.

Ipsumpix/Corbis via Getty Images.

an event," he wrote to Thomas Jefferson in August, "yet I despair so much of its accomplishment at the present crisis that I do not extend my views beyond a Commercial Reform. To speak the truth *I almost despair even of this.*"[5]

Madison's lack of optimism turned out to be well founded. Participation at the convention was weak. Only five of the thirteen states sent representatives; the other states either did not appoint anyone or did not do so in time to make it to the meeting. Maryland itself did not send any delegates, even though the convention was in Annapolis and the state was directly involved in the disputes. Despite the poor attendance, delegates to the convention kept the dialogue of reform moving by calling for a convention in Philadelphia the following spring to discuss how to make the American government more effective in dealing with issues of trade and other pressing needs of the nation.

Madison, as always, showed up in Philadelphia in 1787 having done his homework. Together with a group of similarly practical men, he attempted to create a republic that would last, one that would be strong enough to govern but not so strong as to trample on the rights and liberties of its citizens. Madison and his compatriots sought practical, institutional solutions for the seemingly timeless tendency of political leaders to pursue power, prestige, and riches, even when this meant the downfall of their own republics. That Madison and his comrades were pragmatic politicians was no surprise; most of them had already been involved in the real-world politics of their own colonies and, later, states. Writing in 1923, Robert Livingston Schuyler captured this essential fact about those who shaped the new American Republic better than anyone since. "The Fathers," he declared, "were practical men."[6] Ideas and ideals are certainly part of America's constitutional heritage, but so are politics. Yet as we

> Madison attempted to create a republic that would last, one that would be strong enough to govern but not so strong as to trample on the rights and liberties of its citizens.

The Maryland State House, where the Annapolis Convention took place in 1786.

MPI/Getty Images.

will see, not all Americans wanted changes, and political leaders and citizens in several states, especially the smaller ones, did not trust what Madison and many of his fellow delegates might be up to.

Madison's research, preparation, intellect, and understated political skill played perhaps the most important role in the creation of the Constitution of the United States. The American Republic that he helped shape was based on the premise that liberty is something with which people are born, something that cannot be given or taken away by governments. This concept was expressed powerfully in the Declaration of Independence in its timeless affirmation, "We hold these truths to be self-evident, that all men are created equal." As we have explored in Chapter 1, however, this American liberty was not originally meant for all. Like Jefferson and George Washington—the most respected person in America during this period—Madison owned slaves. Though his own writings show that Madison struggled personally against the institution of slavery and that he realized how the practice had corrupted past republics, Madison's Virginia plantation had more than a hundred slaves. Under Virginia's laws of the time, Madison, or any other slave owner, could "correct" a slave for any offence. If that slave died under such a correction, the master would likely not be punished at all. He could take child from his or her family and sell the child into an unknown future for profit.[7] As the delegates convened in Philadelphia, they had to struggle with these contradictions.

AMERICAN GOVERNMENT BEFORE THE CONSTITUTION

The Articles of Confederation, Problems of National Authority, and Differences between the States

Articles of Confederation and Perpetual Union

a constituting document calling for the creation of a union of thirteen sovereign states in which the states, not the union, were supreme.

The government that James Madison and his like-minded colleagues hoped to change was the first government of the United States. It was a confederation: a union of thirteen sovereign states in which the states, not the union, were supreme. It had been created by the **Articles of Confederation and Perpetual Union**. Adopted by the Second Continental

Congress in 1777 and formally ratified in 1781, the articles created a union of sovereign states that depended on cooperation for its survival. While they had successfully guided the country through war and the accompanying economic and material devastation, the articles had few carrots or sticks to make member states work together to make and carry out national policy. By 1786 the American confederation was showing its limitations, at least in the minds of those who wanted a stronger union.

Uniting Separate States While Preserving Their Authority

When they created the Articles of Confederation, the delegates to the Second Continental Congress had to confront two related issues, both of which dominated the debates surrounding adoption of the articles as well as the debates surrounding the Constitution that eventually replaced them. Both of these issues involved mistrust. Colonists in one state did not always trust the motives of the governments of the other states. They also did not trust any government that would rule over them from far away, whether it be that of Great Britain before the war or of the new American nation after victory had been achieved. These two issues affected politics in the rebellious colonies, in the victorious but unsure confederation of American states, and in the creation of the American Republic in 1787.

Though it may be difficult now to imagine a United States in which states were strong and the nation was weak, the idea that the states were the real centers of power was not at all unnatural for Americans at the time. Long after the Constitution was ratified, many Americans still referred to "these United States" instead of "the United States." Since their inception as business enterprises, plantations, or religious communities, the British colonies were used to being self-sufficient and left alone. While France had a much more centralized approach to its colonies, Great Britain's less coherent policy resulted in a firm tradition of self-governance in the American colonies. Colonists often viewed members of other colonies as foreigners. They also reacted strongly against Britain's tardy attempt to create a more centralized colonial policy in the decades before the American Revolution.[8]

During the debates over the Articles of Confederation, mistrust of other colonies crystallized in conflicts over land, representation, and sovereignty. Some colonies had land claims on parts of other colonies. Small coastal colonies, such as Delaware and Rhode Island, whose size was fixed by their location, viewed the western states' claims on Native American land with worry and suspicion. How big would Virginia, whose charter had land claims extending to the "South Sea," eventually become?[9] "The most acrimonious disagreements," according to one historian, "were over control of western lands."[10] The views of the indigenous peoples on questions of ownership did not factor into these calculations.

Representation and the Sovereignty of States

Because of concerns over land rights, the Articles of Confederation provided states with protections against the possibility of any other state claiming disputed territory on its own, without the approval of the confederal government. In the face of the prospect of large,

FIGURE 2.1

The Original Thirteen Colonies and the Western Territories

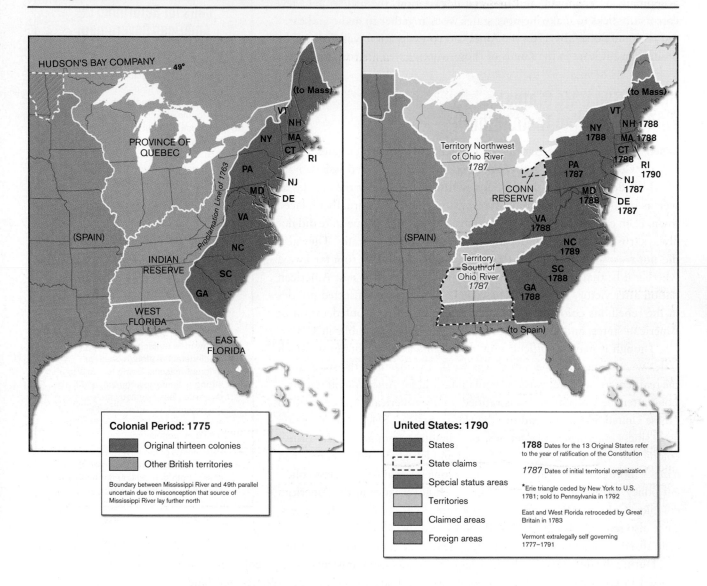

Colonial Period: 1775

- Original thirteen colonies
- Other British territories

Boundary between Mississippi River and 49th parallel uncertain due to misconception that source of Mississippi River lay further north

United States: 1790

- States
- State claims
- Special status areas
- Territories
- Claimed areas
- Foreign areas

1788 Dates for the 13 Original States refer to the year of ratification of the Constitution

1787 Dates of initial territorial organization

*Erie triangle ceded by New York to U.S. 1781; sold to Pennsylvania in 1792

East and West Florida retroceded by Great Britain in 1783

Vermont extralegally self governing 1777–1791

These two maps show the original thirteen British colonies in 1775 and the American states and territories in 1790. Note the vast areas of land bordered by powerful states such as Virginia. Smaller coastal states feared the growth in size and power of these larger states.

populous, and ever-growing neighbors, smaller states demanded, and received, equal representation in the new government. Each state had one vote in the new Congress. This Confederal Congress was unicameral, meaning it had only one chamber. States selected their representatives to the legislature and could choose the number of representatives that they sent, though each state's delegation had to agree on these decisions, and each state received only one vote. Finally, states and not the new union would be sovereign, a right that was firmly established in the document: "Each state retains its sovereignty, freedom, and independence, and every Power, Jurisdiction, and right, which is not by this confederation expressly delegated to the United States, in Congress assembled."[11]

Leading up to the Revolutionary War, the relationship between the colonies and Great Britain was one of a mutual lack of understanding and mistrust. The colonies failed to see how they played a part in Britain's role in global politics and struggles against other empires. For its part, Great Britain failed to understand that what had been plantations, business enterprises, and religious outposts "had grown up and become states in the making—self-conscious and self-reliant political communities."[12] This did not, however, mean naturally united colonies or, later, naturally united states. Each state had its own interests and fears, and each worried that it might lose control over its future to other states or to a national government with its own agendas and desires—a government that might come to display the tyranny of Great Britain over time.

Limitations on the Power of the Confederal Government

The confederal government under the Articles of Confederation was intentionally made to be weak. Colonists were experiencing the tyranny of British rule, and they did not want to recreate it in a new American version. The confederal government could not tax its citizens, and it could not force states to carry out its policies. States could recall their representatives at will, and limits were placed on how long a representative could serve.[13] There was no independent judicial branch; one existed primarily to resolve differences between states but had no real way of enforcing these decisions. The president of the Confederal Congress was even less powerful than the delegates and was there mostly to keep order and count votes.

The confederal government did have certain powers. Only it could declare war and conduct foreign policy, though it had to rely on states to pay for these activities. In practice, the confederal government continually faced the challenge of getting states to contribute to the national effort. Sometimes the states had good reason not to comply with these requests. During the war, colonies had been reluctant to send away scarce troops or supplies when they might be desperately needed close to home. Lack of money was a constant problem, and the Continental Army was continuously without adequate supplies and occasionally faced starvation. Due to the difficulties of collecting contributions from the states or getting loans from European governments, Congress made its own currency, called the continental, which was backed only by the promise of the government to make good on its debts, assuming it won and survived the war intact. The currency later collapsed, creating financial chaos, which only added to calls for reform.

A United States continental currency sixty-five dollar banknote from 1779. The collapse in the value of the currency caused severe economic disruption and unrest in the years leading up to the Constitutional Convention.

Granger Collection.

Unrest and the Danger of Rebellion

To ensure that the agreements made during their creation would hold, the Articles of Confederation placed a tall hurdle in the path of potential reformers: changing or amending the articles required the approval of all thirteen of the states. In spite of what many saw as problems with the articles, many Americans did not want to amend, much less replace, them. Some in the southern states feared that slavery, which was allowed and unregulated under the confederal government, might be

> When their attempts at political solutions failed, citizens began to take the kind of action that they had against King George III and the British Parliament. They rebelled.

restricted or outlawed. Citizens of smaller states feared losing their equal representation in Congress and seeing it replaced by representation based on population, a change that would drastically weaken their position. And many worried that something worse than the problems with the articles might come out of a process of revising them. When a small group of people takes it upon themselves to overturn a political order, there is no guarantee that what they create will not be worse, maybe much worse, than what came before.

Politicians in many states were still mistrustful of the actions and motives of their counterparts in other states. Many were also still nervous about the idea of a strong national government. Since the American Revolution the political landscape had altered: "The vital change which took place between 1776 and 1787 was not in ideas nor in attitudes, but in the balance of political power."[14] State legislative elections in 1786 and 1787 handed strong victories to nationalist candidates, who were in favor of a stronger national government. These nationalist-controlled legislatures would be selecting the delegates to the Philadelphia convention. The nationalists had won partly because of dissatisfaction with the behavior of the state legislators that were in office. Self-interested politicians had managed to use the democratic power of the new state legislatures to try to make themselves rich. Rapid turnover in the composition of some state legislatures had made for sudden and unpredictable changes in state policies.[15] The nationalists had also won because of foreign policy and economic failures by the confederal government and because of the threat of rebellion within the United States—a threat that flared up just as states were preparing to choose and send delegates to Philadelphia.[16]

Shays' Rebellion
a grassroots popular uprising against the government of Massachusetts.

Shays' Rebellion, named after Daniel Shays, one of its military leaders, was a grassroots popular uprising against a state government that, in the minds of many of its citizens, had grown too powerful, too distant, too much like that of Great Britain. The rebellion took place in Massachusetts, but the conditions that caused it and the popular anger that fueled it were also present in other states. This crisis added to the sense of urgency in the American confederation, and it provided ammunition to those who tried to replace the structure of government under the articles. Some, like James Madison, wanted a stronger nation, a different kind of republic than had ever been tried before. Others sought a return to monarchy and the British Empire.

Debt and Economic Crisis in Post-Revolutionary America

The roots of Shays' Rebellion were both economic and political. In the difficult economic times that followed the Revolutionary War, there was a shortage of "hard money," of gold and silver and money backed by gold and silver. What there was no shortage of was debt. Citizens and governments throughout the confederation found themselves unable to pay debts that had been incurred during the war or during the tough economic times that followed. Shopkeepers demanded that their customers pay debts in hard currency. Cash-strapped state governments raised taxes and demanded hard money from their citizens to pay their own sizeable debts. Foreclosures—the taking of property to pay outstanding debts backed by that property—were widespread.

The first responses of citizens in Massachusetts and other states were political. Towns asked state governments to issue paper money to help citizens settle their debts. Local citizens formed "Committees of Correspondence" to petition their governments to take action to help them. Some towns in Massachusetts called for a new state constitutional convention.

Much of the debt, however, was owed to wealthy elites, and those elites wanted to be paid back in real money, not paper promises created by state governments to help out indebted farmers and shopkeepers. Some states were sympathetic to the people's demands. The government of Rhode Island issued paper money, and the state did not see widespread civil unrest, though many elites came to view the "paper money" politicians as dangerous and undependable. Rhode Islanders, for their part, refused to send delegates to the Constitutional Convention and continued to resist the push for a stronger national government.

The government of Massachusetts held the line, siding with the banking interests. Many of the state's citizens began to feel that they had successfully broken with an oppressive government in London only to replace it with one nearly as bad in Boston. When their attempts at political solutions failed, citizens—especially in the western part of the state—began to take the kind of action they had against King George III and the British Parliament. They rebelled.

Civil Unrest and Military Conflict

To each other, the members of Shays' Rebellion were "Regulators," a label used by the American rebels in the struggle against Great Britain. They wore a sprig of hemlock as a badge, just as the revolutionaries had done.[17] Many were Revolutionary War veterans with sufficient military skills and popular support to provide a genuine challenge to the Massachusetts government. The Regulators organized themselves by town and family, and they made a point of trying not to antagonize the local population. Instead, they focused on the courts, as had been done before the Revolution, closing them down in the hopes of stalling the foreclosure process until a solution to the debt crisis could be achieved in the state legislature. Although many were committed by rebels carrying weapons, some of these closures "were peaceful, even jocular, reaching a high point when debtors were turned out of jail."[18]

The rebellion and Massachusetts's response to it began to follow a script similar to that of the American Revolution. Citizens took action. The government (this time of Massachusetts, not Great Britain) clamped down, which only made the population more radical. In October 1786, the Massachusetts legislature passed the Riot Act, which absolved sheriffs and other officials from prosecution for killing rioters. With fears of standing armies fresh in the minds of its members, the resistance grew and became more radical, though never as radical as it was portrayed in the Boston newspapers, which accused the Regulators of wanting to redistribute private property[19] or hoping to reunite with Great Britain.[20] Both claims were untrue but served to increase the level of fear and concern within and beyond the state's borders.

The Massachusetts state militia was unable to put down the rebellion. Many militia members, themselves Revolutionary War veterans, sided with the rebels. The government of the United States, the Confederal Congress, could not raise an army; its requests to the states for money were refused by every state except Virginia. The wealthy elites in Boston ultimately paid for an army on their

An engraving depicts the British colonial governor of North Carolina, center, suppressing the Regulators' revolt in 1771. Daniel Shays and other members of the rebellion in Massachusetts patterned their protests against the state government on the actions of the Revolutionary War Regulators.

Granger Collection.

own, loaning money to Massachusetts for the purposes of suppressing the rebellion. Referring to the Massachusetts elites, General Baron von Stueben, who had helped train the Continental Army, publicly wondered why "would Congress dare to support such an abominable oligarchy?"[21]

Shays' Rebellion: A Crisis and an Opportunity

Daniel Shays, a former captain in the Revolutionary War, joined the Regulators later than many but became a commander of its largest regiment, partly due to his notable service in the war. In January 1787, Shays' regiment and two others moved on the state armory at Springfield. If they had been successful, according to one historian, "they would have been better armed than the state of Massachusetts."[22] Major General William Shepard, commanding the newly raised state militia and in possession of artillery that the Regulators lacked, defeated Shays and the rebels, who were forced to withdraw. Two rebel leaders were hanged, and most of the other rebels eventually returned to their farms and towns. Shays escaped to Vermont and was later pardoned, though he never returned to Massachusetts. With the help of the Boston newspapers, Daniel Shays became the personification of anarchy in the U.S. In reality, most of the Regulators only wanted to keep their farms and keep their family and friends out of foreclosure or debtors' jail.

After the Revolutionary War, George Washington had, as promised, stayed away from public life and retired to his slave-holding plantation in Mount Vernon to focus on agriculture and breeding animals. But upon receiving what turned out to be exaggerated reports of the strength of Shays' militia from one of his most trusted former generals, Washington grew fearful of what would become of the country. In a letter to James Madison in November of 1786, Washington wrote,

> What stronger evidence can be given of the want of energy in our government than these disorders? If there exists not a power to check them, what security has a man of life, liberty, or property? To you, I am sure I need not add aught on this subject, the consequences of a lax, or inefficient government, are too obvious to be dwelt on. Thirteen sovereignties pulling against each other, and all tugging at the foederal head will soon bring ruin to the whole; whereas a liberal, and energetic Constitution, well guarded & closely watched, to prevent incroachments, might restore us to that degree of respectability & consequence, to which we had fair claim, & the brightest prospect of attaining.[23]

Madison may have sensed, or at least hoped, that Shays' Rebellion would be enough to lure Washington out of retirement and place his unequalled status among Americans behind the effort to create a new political order. Though initially reluctant to attend the Philadelphia conference, Washington eventually agreed; the Philadelphia Convention would have the most famous and respected American there to give it legitimacy.[24]

Rebellion was not the only worry among the new states. Great Britain had been defeated but hardly destroyed. The nation had merely been pushed back into Canada, and that was only due to the help of Great Britain's other rivals, who themselves might not always be helpful to the young United States. According to political scientist Keith Dougherty, "By the summer of 1787, the federal government had no funds to protect American shipping from the Barbary [North African] states, it couldn't dislodge the British from their garrisons along the Canadian border, and it could not breach the Spanish blockade of the Mississippi—let alone suppress a domestic insurrection."[25] As states sent their delegates to Philadelphia in the spring of 1787, the world powers were watching, expecting, and perhaps hoping for, failure.

Two Portrayals of Shays' Rebellion

Consider these two depictions of Shays' Rebellion. Though they aim to depict the same broad set of events, they do so in very different ways. In the top image, the Regulators are seen calmly assembled on the steps of a Massachusetts courthouse.

The bottom image depicts violence and discord.

Recall the ways in which advocates for a stronger national government, such as James Madison, and those in favor of maintaining the Articles of Confederation disagreed with the most severe dangers facing the young nation. While these particular images were not used during the debates over amending or replacing the Articles, they do point to differences between the two groups.

WHAT DO YOU THINK?

What stories are these images telling? Which of these images corresponds better with the view of Shays' Rebellion held by those who wanted a stronger national government? Which might correspond better with the view of those who were wary of a strong national government? Can you think of images that you have seen of modern-day controversial events that try to shape the viewer's perception of those events?

The Granger Collection.

The Granger Collection.

1. The Articles of Confederation produced a national government that was supreme to those of the states.

   a. True
   b. False

2. Key provisions in the articles designed to protect states against the power of other states included _____.

   a. A requirement that states could change their boundaries without approval
   b. A supreme court to adjudicate claims between states

   c. A unicameral legislature that gave each state one vote
   d. All of the above

3. What problems in the new nation did Shays' Rebellion highlight? How did people like James Madison capitalize on the crisis to pursue their political goals?

....

Answer Key: 1. b; 2. c; 3. Answers should discuss the inability of the national government to suppress the rebellion as well as how those in favor of a stronger national government highlighted this weakness.

TOPICS IN AMERICAN GOVERNMENT
Constitutional Convention

THE CONSTITUTIONAL CONVENTION IN PHILADELPHIA

"Experience Must Be Our Only Guide" [26]

In May 1787, fifty-five delegates from twelve of the thirteen states began to arrive in Philadelphia. Rhode Island and its "paper money" men had refused to participate. By some reports, it was a hot, humid summer. It could not have been very comfortable in the Pennsylvania State House where they met. It probably did not smell very good either. Southern delegates, dressed in cotton, fared better than the New Englanders in their wool suits. The windows were shut to ensure secrecy. This secrecy was partly to allow the delegates to say what they wanted, partly because none were sure how citizens in the various states would react to their deliberations. At the time, the meeting was called the Grand Convention or the Foederal Convention, not the **Constitutional Convention** as it is called today. The delegates had not been sent to Philadelphia to write a new constitution, only to fix the Articles of Confederation as necessary. Writing a new constitution would have been thought of as a revolutionary act, which it was.

Constitutional Convention
a meeting held in Philadelphia in 1787 at which state delegates met to fix the Articles of Confederation.

The delegates had not been sent to Philadelphia to write a new constitution, only to fix the Articles of Confederation as necessary. Writing a new constitution would have been thought of as a revolutionary act, which it was.

James Madison was the first delegate to arrive—eleven days early—with his research in hand. Though he would become perhaps the most influential person at the convention, Madison was not the only delegate who shaped the final document. And he was certainly not the most famous person there. George Washington served as the president of the proceedings. Most delegates expected that he would be the leader of whatever government emerged, if the convention could agree on one. Once in Philadelphia, the tall and handsome Washington found no shortage of requests for his presence at tea with prominent ladies in the city. His first call, though, was to his friend Benjamin Franklin, possibly the second most famous person in America, "who had laid in a cask of porter against the occasion"[27] of Washington's visit. Because of poor health, four prisoners from a city jail carried Franklin through the streets of Philadelphia in a chair on his way to and from the convention. He remained a shrewd politician, however, and used his many skills at important moments in the debate.

Other delegates, many of whom had done their own reading and study in preparation for the proceedings, also guided and shaped the debates and outcomes. Alexander Hamilton, who had served as Washington's aide in the war, emerged as one of the leading proponents of a strong national government. James Wilson of Pennsylvania, who, like Madison, had been a student of the Scottish Enlightenment, made important, often unheralded, intellectual contributions to the convention. Wilson served as an intellectual ally of Madison's during and after the convention. Also from Pennsylvania, Gouveneur Morris assembled the various resolutions passed by the convention into a whole document, adding his own literary style and crafting the declaration at its beginning, "We the People, of the United States."

Many important leaders from the Revolution could not or would not attend. Thomas Jefferson and John Adams, both future presidents and supporters of the Constitution, were out of the country in service of the American government. Others, like Samuel Adams and Patrick Henry, both vocal revolutionaries and opponents of a national constitution, were not selected as delegates or refused to go, sensing that the delegates planned to do much more than merely revise the Articles of Confederation. Their suspicions were correct. For his part, Samuel Adams was skeptical of what might emerge from the convention, wary of the dangers to liberty that a strong central government might pose and concerned that such a government could not adequately address the diverse needs of the states.[28] Patrick Henry became one of the most effective opponents to the document once it had been submitted to the states. "Here is a revolution as radical as that which separated us from Great Britain," he wrote.[29]

The delegates who assembled in Philadelphia certainly did not represent a snapshot of the people living in the thirteen states. All were men. Most were well educated. None were slaves, former slaves, or Native Americans. Roughly one-third were slave owners. Not all were wealthy, but they were all elites. Unlike the revolutionaries who would soon lead France into chaos in the name of democracy, however, most of the founders of the American Republic had previous practical political experience to guide them and temper their revolutionary ideals, Madison included. The solutions that the delegates came up with were pragmatic, political, and strategic, for better and for worse.

America's State Constitutions: Models, Good and Bad

In the time between the Declaration of Independence and the Philadelphia convention, individual states had drafted their own constitutions. They were often very different from each other. The Philadelphia delegates looked to the experiences of individual states under their own governments for lessons, sometimes with unease. Pennsylvania's state constitution was the most democratic. All real power rested in a unicameral legislature whose legislators served one-year terms. To many elites, the Pennsylvania constitution represented nothing more than institutionalized mob rule,[30] sometimes at the expense of religious minorities. Massachusetts's constitution was much less democratic, with a much more powerful governor and property requirements to serve in the government. To the Regulators and those who sympathized with them, Massachusetts had replaced Great Britain's royal aristocracy with Boston's constitutional aristocracy. As they convened in Philadelphia, the delegates drew from the experiences of the various states as they tried to fashion a new form of government. Some worried about democracy, others about aristocracy. Most worried about failure.

The Convention Begins:
Debates about Representation and Power

By Friday, May 25, 1787, enough delegates had made it over the muddy Pennsylvania roads to begin the deliberations. Their first order of business was to unanimously select Washington as president of the convention. Madison, though not selected (or paid) as the official reporter for the convention, took a seat up front and assumed the role informally. The other delegates were agreeable to this and made sure he got copies of their speeches to be entered into this unofficial record.[31] Much of what we know about what happened in Philadelphia comes from his notes.

The delegates adopted a set of rules to guide themselves. They called for absolute secrecy, "that nothing spoken in the House be printed, or otherwise published, or communicated without leave of the House."[32] They knew that the enormous task of coming to an agreement would only be made more difficult if the details of their discussions were leaked, either deliberately or unintentionally. It was said that a member of the convention was assigned to attend dinners with Franklin, who was fond of alcoholic beverages, to change the conversation if Franklin began to talk too loosely.[33] The delegates agreed not to record their individual votes so that they would not feel bound by previous votes if the same issues came up again, giving themselves the ability to compromise and change their positions as needed.

As they settled into the business at hand, the primary issues of contention were the same ones that had dominated the debates surrounding the creation and adoption of the Articles of Confederation: the representation of states in the national government and the powers of that national government. Most other issues, and many of the details that had to be worked out, were tied to these central questions. Most debates centered on practicalities. With some important exceptions, speeches and discussions about slavery in the convention focused not on its immorality but on how it would affect representation of states and the power of the national government over trade and commerce.

George Washington presiding at the Constitutional Convention at Philadelphia in 1787. Considerable measures were taken to ensure the secrecy of the proceedings at the convention.

The Granger Collection.

The Question of States' Representation

As part of the formalities of the opening days of the convention, each state's delegates introduced themselves. Making its presentation, the Delaware delegation stated to the group that its state legislature had forbade it from changing the provision of the Articles of Confederation that gave each state one equal vote in the national legislature. How states were to be represented in the new government—the most contentious issue of the convention and the one that determined so many other outcomes—had been put on the table. No other question so dominated the convention during the early weeks and months of deliberations or threatened to tear it apart. How would states be represented in a new government? Would it be the same one state, one vote formula as under the Articles of Confederation? Or would states be represented on the basis of their population or wealth?

The Virginia Plan: A New Method for Determining Representation

On just the third day of the convention, the delegation from Virginia, led by the state's most senior delegate, Edmund Randolph, presented a set of proposals for the rest of the members to consider. But the ideas behind what came to be known as the **Virginia Plan** were James Madison's. Madison had been building their foundations for more than a year and had coached the rest of the Virginia delegation in the days before their presentation.[34] The Virginia Plan was much more than a modification of the Articles of Confederation. Its proposals described a new, national, form of government, although Madison and his allies used the less controversial word *federal* when presenting and defending it.

In a typically Madisonian way, the Virginia Plan began by laying out the failures of the American confederation: weakness in national defense and the conduct of foreign policy, conflicts between states, and the failure to suppress internal rebellion. Giving credit to the authors of the articles for doing the best job that they could "in then the infancy of the science, of constitutions, & of confederacies,"[35] the plan laid out an answer to those defects: The national government would be strong. Its constitution would be "paramount to the state constitutions."[36] It would consist of three branches: a legislative branch to make laws, an executive branch to carry the laws out, and a judicial branch to resolve disputes between the states and between the national government and the states. The national legislature would be bicameral, consisting of two houses. Members of the lower house would be elected directly by the people. The upper house would consist of representatives nominated by state legislatures and chosen by members of the lower house. The executive and some members of the judiciary would compose a "council of revision" that could veto—or overturn—acts of the legislature, which could, in turn, override that veto. The supremacy of the national government would be unmistakable. It could make laws as needed to govern the country as a whole and use military force against states if necessary.

Many details were vague or literally left blank, such as the length of terms of members of Congress, the frequency of elections, and the number of votes needed to override a veto by the Council of Revision. The change in representation of states, however, was clear. The Virginia Plan proposed to overturn the one state, one vote structure of the Articles of Confederation. Instead there would be a system of proportional representation in which more populous states would have more members in both houses of the legislature. The answer to the question, "Proportional to what?" was left somewhat vague: "Legislature ought to be proportioned to the Quotas of contribution, or to the number of

Virginia Plan
a plan of government calling for a strong national government with three branches of government and a bicameral legislature, with legislators elected using proportional representation.

A profile portrait of Irish-born American jurist William Paterson. Paterson presented what became known as the New Jersey Plan, which preserved most of the structure of the government as established under the Articles of Confederation.

Stock Montage/Getty Images.

New Jersey Plan

a plan of government that preserved many of the provisions in the Articles of Confederation, including the unicameral legislature with equal votes for each states, but that strengthened the confederal government.

free inhabitants, as the one or the other rule may seem best in different cases."[37] "Quotas of contribution" referred to property or tax revenue. But by property, did this mean slaves? The Virginia Plan was not clear.

Delegates from smaller states reacted immediately and strongly to the Virginia Plan's suggestion of proportional representation. They had successfully fought it off in the Second Continental Congress, when the articles were drafted, and they continued to fight against it. Under the Virginia Plan, Virginia would have sixteen votes to South Carolina's one, plus all there knew that Virginia's boundaries were far from settled. They seemed limitless. New Jersey's William Paterson flatly stated, according to Madison's notes, that "N. Jersey will never confederate on the plan before the Committee. She would be swallowed up. He [Paterson] had rather submit to a monarch, to a despot, than to such a fate."[38]

For the next two weeks, however, the convention discussed the Virginia Plan and little else. Within days of its introduction, several provisions of the plan—a government of three branches and a bicameral legislature—had already been approved. Madison and his fellow nationalists had won the first victory in the strategic political struggle over the Constitution. They had set the agenda. They had forced the opposition to respond to their ideas.

The New Jersey Plan: Less Populous States Respond

Two weeks later, Paterson presented the small states' response to the Virginia Plan. Known as the **New Jersey Plan**, it proposed to strengthen the power of the confederal government but make relatively few changes to the Articles of Confederation. There would only be one house in the legislature, just as under the articles. Each state delegation (chosen by state legislatures) would still get one equal vote in that legislature. That legislature would get new powers, mostly over taxation and the economy, though it would still depend on the states for some revenue. The executive and judicial branches were much less well envisoned than under the Virginia Plan. Paterson correctly argued that his state's plan was consistent with the purpose of the meeting in Philadelphia; the idea of only making some changes to the articles was the original mandate of the convention. However, delegates had already been debating almost nothing except the Virginia Plan, the framework of which centered on a strong national government and provisions that would essentially replace the current form of government.

After Paterson had presented his plan, Madison proceeded to "tear the New Jersey plan to pieces, coldly, logically, point by point, with each phrased as a question."[39] Madison argued the New Jersey Plan would leave the nation with all of the problems that motivated the convention in the first place: "Will the militia march from one State to another to collect the arrears of taxes from the delinquent members of the Republic?"[40] Madison warned that rebellions such as the one Massachusetts had just barely put down would continue to plague the Republic under Paterson's plan: "A certain point of military force is absolutely necessary in large communities. Massts. is now feeling this necessity & making provision for it."[41]

Madison and James Wilson grew frustrated over the less populous states' objections to the Virginia Plan. To these two men, neither the states nor the national government were or should be supreme; the people were supreme to both. How their numbers were apportioned was beside the point. To allow equal representation in Congress for states would allow the political divisions between and within states to infect national politics. Delegates from smaller states did not see it this way. To them, equal representation was not open for negotiation; it was essential to their sovereignty. At one point, Gunning Bedford from Delaware threatened that the small states might have to break off, form their own union, and "find some foreign ally of more honor and good faith, who will take them [the small states] by the hand and do them justice."[42] This was, in modern political terms, the "nuclear option" for the small states. There would be no going back if it were used. All knew it was a possibility, even if unlikely, but to have the idea raised so boldly and so publicly shocked the convention and highlighted for all present the stakes with which they were playing and the possible consequences should they fail to reach an agreement.

> To Madison and Wilson, neither the states nor the national government were or should be supreme; the people were supreme to both.

The Great Compromise

With the issue of how states would be represented threatening to break apart the convention, the question was sent to a committee. While the young nation celebrated the Fourth of July, delegates to the convention were unsure if their work would succeed, or even continue. The stakes were very high. Elbridge Gerry of Massachusetts warned, "If

TABLE 2.1 Legislative Structures under the Virginia Plan, New Jersey Plan, and the Great Compromise

	Virginia Plan	New Jersey Plan	Great Compromise
Structure of Legislature	**Bicameral** (two chamber)	**Unicameral** (single chamber)	**Bicameral** (two chamber)
Apportionment	**Lower House** • Number of seats apportioned by state population (or "quotas of contribution"). • Members directly elected by citizens.	**Legislature** • Equal representation for states regardless of state population. • Members appointed by the states.	**House of Representatives** • States represented according to population. • Members directly elected by citizens.
	Upper House • Number of seats apportioned by state population. • Members elected by lower house (from list supplied by state legislatures).		**Senate** • States represented equally (two senators per state). • Members appointed by state legislatures.
Powers	• Legislature has strong powers, including the ability to veto state laws.	• Legislature has similar power as under the Articles of Confederation but can also levy taxes and regulate commerce.	• Legislature has broad powers over commerce and the ability to make laws as necessary. • House of Representatives has power to levy taxes.

we do nothing, it appears we must have war and confusion."[43] On July 5, the committee responded with a proposal to give something to each side. The new national legislature would be bicameral; it would have two chambers. Representation in the lower house would follow the Virginia Plan, and representation in the upper house, the New Jersey Plan. Compromise having been put on the table, the mood of the convention began to shift. Bedford of Delaware—who had threatened the possibility that small states might seek an alliance with a foreign power—insisted that he had been misunderstood.[44]

On July 16, by a vote of 5–4, the delegates agreed to what would be called the **Great Compromise.**[45] Under this agreement, much like the committee's recommendations, the national legislature would be bicameral. States would be represented in the House of Representatives according to their populations. The people would directly elect these representatives. States would be represented equally in the upper chamber, the Senate. Two senators would be chosen from each state by their state legislatures. Not all of the small-state delegates were satisfied with the agreement; two left in protest. But the rest felt that having the Senate was protection enough, and they became much more cooperative in the weeks that followed. Delaware, for all its threats and opposition early in the convention, was the first state to later ratify the Constitution that was being hammered out in Philadelphia.

Great Compromise

An agreement for a plan of government that drew upon both the Virginia and New Jersey Plans; it settled issues of state representation by calling for a bicameral legislature with a House of Representatives apportioned proportionately and a Senate apportioned equally.

That the question of representation in Congress was settled first is important as this shaped the political strategies of the delegates going forward. Having secured equal representation in the Senate, small states offered less opposition to a strong national government. They were now less afraid of Congress, even seeing it as a defense against the power of their larger neighbors. Madison, who had wanted popular representation in both houses, began to push to strengthen the other two branches to act as a counter to the Congress that he had proposed but now mistrusted due to the equal state representation in the Senate.[46] The Constitution did not fall out of the sky. It was the result of compromise. But it was also the result of adaptation to earlier compromises and to changes in the political landscape in which the delegates pursued their goals and those of the states that they had been chosen to represent.

◼ DETAILS OF THE NEW GOVERNMENT

With the bicameral legislature having resolved the first and largest issue of the convention—the distribution of power between the states—the convention moved on to the structure of the rest of the government and the specific powers of each branch. In doing so, it confronted the second major issue of the convention: the question of national power. Many of the details of the new government were worked out in two committees over the rest of the summer and then presented to the full convention for approval. The Committee of Detail presented its recommendations on the structure of government and the relationships between the three branches. The Committee on Unfinished Parts took up issues that had not been resolved and generally tried to tie up loose ends in the structure of the new government.

CONNECTING TO...

Working Out the Details of Government

While the Great Compromise settled the question of states' representation in the new national legislature, much else still had to be worked out. As you read ahead, reflect upon how delegates such as James Madison acted strategically to pursue their own political objectives. Consider the following:

- The delegates to the Constitutional Convention had much in common, but there were also deep divisions, especially between small and large states, slave and non slave-holding states, and states who wanted a powerful central government and those that did not.

- Through a series of political compromises made during those months in Philadelphia in 1787, the proposed national government was set up to divide power between three branches—the legislative, executive, and judicial—and to also divide power between the national government and the governments of the states.

- One fateful compromise made during the Constitutional Convention involved the issue of slavery.

The Legislative Branch

While representation in Congress had been settled, its powers still had to be worked out. To do so, delegates looked to the powers of the Confederal Congress under the Articles of Confederation as well as to state legislatures under the various state constitutions. As the **legislative branch** of government, Congress's purpose was to legislate—to make laws. Both houses had to work together to pass laws, but because of how congressional members were chosen, each house had a slightly different purpose. Members of the House of Representatives, who were elected directly by the people and had to run for reelection every two years, were meant to be more responsive to the people, to directly represent—or stand for—their constituents. Senators, who were chosen by state legislatures and served six-year terms, were there to check the passions of the people. Senators' terms were staggered in two-year shifts so that only about a third of senators would be up for reelection in any given election year, making it more difficult for any swift change in mood among citizens to quickly affect national policy.

Congress, as expected, was made more powerful than the unicameral legislature under the Articles of Confederation, especially with regard to issues of money and the economy. Congress was given the power to borrow money, collect taxes, and "regulate Commerce with foreign Nations, and among the several states." This commerce clause has enabled Congress to become involved in large areas of the American economy, even within states. Debates over the power of and limits to the commerce clause continue today, especially between states and the federal government.

In order to preserve its flexibility, Congress was also given the ability "to make all Laws which shall be necessary and proper for carrying into Execution the foregoing Powers, and all the other Powers vested by this Constitution in the Government of the United States." The necessary and proper clause, combined with the commerce clause, paved the way for a dramatic expansion in Congress's power over national policy in the centuries following ratification.

legislative branch
in a divided government, the institution responsible for making laws.

executive branch
the institution responsible for carrying out laws passed by the legislative branch.

Shown here arriving at Congress Hall in Philadelphia on March 4, 1793, for his second inauguration, George Washington chose to retire after his second term despite the fact that the Constitution would have permitted him to run for reelection for an unlimited number of terms.
The Granger Collection, New York.

The Executive Branch

Neither the Virginia nor the New Jersey Plan had been very specific about the **executive branch** of government. Madison had not given it as much thought as he had Congress—at least until he decided he needed to build in more protections against equal state representation in the Senate. Initially there was not even a consensus over how many chief executives the country should have, much less over how powerful the branch should be. Alexander Hamilton, young, ambitious, self-made, and not trusted by many delegates, proposed a powerful president who would be elected for life. His plan made the Virginia Plan look moderate. Though it was not voted on, Hamilton's

suggestion of an "American king"[47] followed him for the rest of his political career. Most delegates expected Washington would serve as an, if not *the*, executive of the country. Some wrote that confidence in Washington reduced anxiety about how powerful the executive would become.

In the end, the delegates settled on a single executive—a president—who would serve for four-year terms. As head of the executive branch, the president was there to "execute," or carry out, the laws that had been passed by Congress. The president was given some, but not unlimited, power over Congress with the ability to veto a piece of legislation that Congress had passed. Congress could, however, override the veto with a two-thirds vote in each of the two houses. The president was named commander in chief of the army and navy. Again, though, power was to be shared. Congress, not the president, was given the power to declare (and raise money for) war. Presidents were given power to oversee the people working in the executive branch and to obtain from them the information needed to govern the country, which has led to the growth of a large and influential federal bureaucracy. Finally, the president was given the power to make foreign policy, though, again, this responsibility was to be shared with the Senate.

More controversial than what powers the executive would have was how the president would be elected, raising once again the question of how states would be represented in the new government. In the end, delegates settled on a complicated compromise for electing the president, one that had been suggested by James Wilson of Pennsylvania and one that is still not fully understood by many Americans. Citizens would not vote directly for the president. Instead, an Electoral College consisting of electors awarded to states based on their representation in Congress would select the president. Each state received two electors (for their senators) plus one each for their members of the House of Representatives. States would decide how these electors were to be chosen, and successful candidates would need to win a majority of electors to become president. The system of the Electoral College continues to incite criticism and suggestions for reform. In the minds of the delegates, however, the complicated structure managed to avoid reigniting the disagreements between small and large states over representation.

The Judiciary

judicial branch
the institution responsible for hearing and deciding cases via a system of federal courts.

The Virginia and New Jersey Plans were even less specific about the **judicial branch** of the government, the system of federal courts. Delegates decided on one Supreme Court to be the highest in the land and a system of lower federal courts whose structure and composition would be determined by Congress. Unlike the judiciary under the articles, the federal courts would have jurisdiction—the authority to hear and decide cases—over all disputes between states and the national government, between two or more states, and between citizens of different states. Combined with the supremacy clause of the Constitution, which declared that national treaties and laws "shall be the supreme law of the Land," the federal court emerged as superior to state courts and laws.

Not included in the Constitution was an explicit description of the power of judicial review, which gives the judicial branch of government the authority to determine if a law, part of a law, or an act of government is or is not in violation of the highest law of the land and, if it *is* in conflict, if it is thus invalid. In the United States, that supreme law is the Constitution, and the power of judicial review rests ultimately with the United States Supreme Court. While state supreme courts may exercise judicial review on state laws and actions, the supremacy clause of the Constitution ensures that the exercise of judicial review by the Supreme

NEWS CLIP
Kagan's Supreme Court hearing opening statement

Court includes the authority to use that power over both national and state laws and actions.

In exercising this power, the Supreme Court does not claim to be above the executive or legislative branch. Instead, the Constitution and the people are above all three branches, and it is the role of the Court to act as the interpreter of conflict between the Constitution and governmental action. This power has been retained throughout history by shrewd political action and the conscious preservation of it by Supreme Court justices. We will examine the concept of judicial review, its foundations, and controversies surrounding its use in much more detail in our chapter on the judiciary.

The power of judicial review, combined with the supremacy clause, became crucial in later battles to protect civil liberties and secure civil rights, many of which were waged by citizens who because of their identity had been ignored by the original document or had their rights restricted by it. As with the other two branches, the judiciary was not to exist in isolation. Congress, not the Supreme Court, had the authority to create the lower federal courts. Congress would determine the number of Supreme Court justices, and the Senate had the power to confirm justices (with a majority vote), who first had to be nominated by the president.

> **"Ambition," wrote James Madison in defense of the Constitution, "must be made to counteract ambition."**

Separation of Powers

In drawing up the powers of each of the three branches, the delegates tried to make sure that no one branch could become too powerful on its own. The idea of **separation of powers** was widely supported by delegates at the convention and well known to those who had studied the writings of Baron de Montesquieu. Under this system, branches are not meant to preside over their own spheres. Rather, a system of "separated institutions *sharing* powers" was created.[48] Each branch, whose members tended to represent a different group of people, has to work with the other branches to make things happen, though not on every issue all of the time (see Table 2.2). "Ambition," wrote James Madison in defense of the Constitution "must be made to counteract ambition."[49] This was the central blueprint around which the national government was structured. Popularly known as the system of checks and balances, the idea of overlapping (but not perfectly overlapping) spheres of influence also applies to relations between the states and the federal government. Federalism, or the sharing of power over some aspects of governance between the states and the nation, is as central to American government as checks and balances, and it has been the source of much conflict and controversy throughout its history. While federalism may seem like a somewhat dry topic, as we will explore in the next chapter, many of the most important issues in America in the twenty-first century involve defining the boundaries between the authority of the nation and that of the states.

separation of powers
a design of government that distributes powers across institutions in order to avoid making one branch too powerful on its own.

NEWS CLIP
Senate leadership discuss
Supreme Court nominee

"Unfinished Parts": More Details to Work Out

At the beginning of September 1787, the Committee on Unfinished Parts[50] reported back to the convention on its efforts to address issues that had been left unresolved. Not all of these issues were ironed out, and the question of slavery threatened to break up the proceedings.

In an attempt to clear up commercial relationships between states, the delegates decided that "full faith and credit shall be given in each State to the public Acts, Records, and judicial Proceedings of every other State." The full faith and credit clause was

TABLE 2.2 Separated Institutions Sharing Powers

	INSTITUTIONS		
	Executive Branch	**Legislative Branch**	**Judicial Branch**
Lawmaking Authority	• Executes laws • Veto power • Nominates judges to the federal judiciary and key executive branch officials • Works to shape legislative agenda	• Writes nation's laws • Veto override • Senate confirms judicial nominees and key executive branch officials • Determines number of Supreme Court justices • Creates lower courts	• Interprets contested laws • Can declare both federal and state laws unconstitutional
National Security and Foreign Policy Responsibilities	• President acts as commander in chief of the military • Sets foreign policy agenda	• Declares war • Senate ratifies treaties with other nations	
Oversight Responsibilities	• Oversees federal bureaucracy	• Power of impeachment (over president, executive branch officials, and federal judges) • Budget authority and oversight over executive branch agencies	• May declare laws or executive branch actions in conflict with the Constitution
Sovereignty	Sovereignty rests with the people. The Constitution is the supreme law of the nation.		

designed to ensure that each state recognized contracts and other legal proceedings from other states. It has become an important constitutional element in the question of same-sex marriage and marriage equality in the United States (see Chapter 4). The structure of the Electoral College was finalized, as was the office of vice president of the United States, whose constitutional powers are quite limited but who plays an important role in presidential elections.

In important ways, however, the Constitution remained unfinished even after the delegates completed their deliberations in September. This was partly by design, partly due to political compromises made during the convention itself. By making provisions for changing the Constitution through a process of **amendment**, the framers acknowledged that it would always be unfinished, that it would need to be adaptable if it were to endure. By *adaptable*, however, the delegates did not mean easily changed. They purposefully designed a system for amending the Constitution that made this very difficult to achieve. Once again, divisions over representation of states emerged, with small states arguing that states should have the power to approve amendments and the nationalists arguing that it should be left to the people to decide.

In the end, another complicated compromise emerged, with both the people—through official proposal in Congress—and the states—through the process of final ratification—necessary to alter the Constitution. Amending the document is a two-stage process, with two possible routes to completion of each of the two stages needed for amendment. First, the amendment has to be officially proposed, which involves much more than someone just suggesting an idea. Proposal can happen in one of two ways, only the first of which has ever been used: (1) passage by a two-thirds vote in both the House and the Senate,

amendment
a constitutional provision for a process by which changes may be made to the Constitution.

or (2) passage in a national convention called at the request of two-thirds of the states. After formal proposal, the proposed amendment must be ratified, either by (1) a majority vote in three-fourths of the state legislatures, or (2) acceptance by ratifying conventions in three-fourths of the states. The second method for ratification has only been used once.

Of the thousands of suggestions for amending the Constitution presented in Congress since its founding, only twenty-seven amendments have been formally ratified. The first ten of these, which make up the Bill of Rights, became part of the debate over ratification itself and are often thought of as part of the "original" Constitution. Two others—an amendment prohibiting the sale and consumption of alcoholic beverages and one repealing that prohibition—cancelled each other out. Since the passage of the Bill of Rights, therefore, the Constitution has only had fifteen lasting changes. Though the Constitution has rarely been amended, some scholars argue that important decisions by the Supreme Court and major changes in how the American people view themselves have at critical times in history led to changes in government just as significant as formal amendments.[51]

Slavery: A Fateful Compromise

At the time of the convention, nearly one out of every six individuals living in the thirteen states was a slave. Most, but not all, lived in the southern states. Southern plantation owners, many of whom were politically powerful in their state legislatures and some of whom were delegates to the Philadelphia convention, had no intention of seeing their institution outlawed or heavily regulated. Plantation owners were not the only interests who benefitted from slavery. The slave trade and the trade in goods made by slaves benefitted some powerful shipping interests as well, especially in the Northeast. About one-third of the delegates to the convention, including Madison and Washington, were slave owners. A few others, however, saw the preservation of slavery as a moral failure and spoke out at the convention about the hypocrisy of trying to preserve liberty in a document that allowed slavery.

It was an issue that could have easily torn apart the convention—or the country—at the time. It spoke to the core values of a people who were trying to constitute themselves in a republic. In spite of a few speeches on the floor of the convention, however, the question of slavery was not generally debated in terms of morality or of liberty but rather in terms of states' representation, the same issue that affected so many others at the convention: Would slaves count when it came time to tally a state's population? In the end, the question of slavery was settled not according to high ideals but on practical, political considerations.

The final document dealt with slavery in three ways. The word *slavery* never appears—a minor tactical victory for those who did not want the Constitution to appear to approve of it. On the question of slavery and representation in Congress, the **Three-fifths Compromise** ensured that a slave—called an "other person" in the Constitution—would count as three-fifths of a person for a state's representation.[52] Slaves could not vote or be represented, but their numbers would boost the influence of the slave states in which they were held because since slaves were counted among the population, slave-holding states would be allotted more members of Congress. In a second facet of the compromise, Congress would not be allowed to restrict the slave trade until 1808 at the earliest. Third, slaves who had successfully escaped would have to be "delivered up on a Claim of the Party to whom such Service or Labour may be due." They would have to be returned to their owners, regardless of the laws of individual states.

Three-fifths Compromise
an agreement reached by delegates at the Constitutional Convention that ensured that a slave would count as three-fifths of a person for a state's representation.

Slavery, Population, and the Balance of Power between Southern and Northern States

One of the most important divisions between the states during the Constitutional Convention was on the issue of slavery. In addition to being a moral issue, how slavery was handled during the proceedings, as all delegates knew, would have serious implications for the balance of political power in the federal government, especially in the House of Representatives. While states would be equally represented in the Senate, their representation in the House would depend upon their population. Did that population include slaves?

Figure A shows the percentage of each state's population that was enslaved in 1790, three years after the drafting of the Constitution. The divisions between northern and southern states are striking. What might this mean for representation in the House?

Figure B presents the same data, but it does so in a way that breaks down the population—free, slave, and total—of each state and the two regions. Note the light blue bars, which represent the total population of the states and regions. Looked

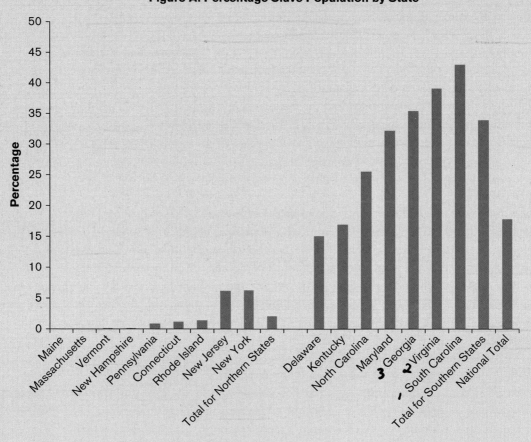

Figure A: Percentage Slave Population by State

at this way, the balance of population between the northern and southern states is roughly equal, with just under two million individuals in each region. However, when one separates out the slave population (the green bars), the northern states have a population advantage of more than six hundred thousand people (the dark blue bars). It was this math that drove much of the bargaining over slavery and representation in the convention.

WHAT DO YOU THINK?

What information does Figure B convey that Figure A does not? Have you encountered different charts and tables that present the same or similar data in different ways, thus allowing you to draw different conclusions?

Figure B: Free and Slave Population Totals by State

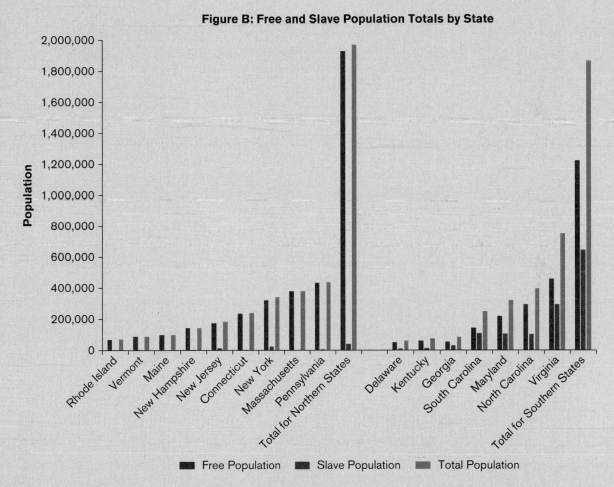

Source: Data are from United States Census Bureau, http://www.census.gov/census-sis/index/teach/history-activities/American-Revolution/1790-census-and-apportionment---analyzing-the-three-fifths-compr.html, accessed June 8, 2016.

Historians and political scientists have debated how the delegates could have agreed to preserve slavery when some observed that it went against the very idea of natural rights upon which the Constitution is based, and at a time when some states were beginning to restrict or outlaw it on their own. There are probably several reasons, and they are not necessarily mutually exclusive. The first reason, perhaps obviously, is that slaves had not voted for their state legislators. Some delegates did oppose slavery, but slaves had no direct representation in the Constitutional Convention. While slaves were not represented, however, slave owners were, and their delegates used the threat of leaving the convention to secure their interests. William Richardson Davie from North Carolina had threatened that if slaves were not included in states' representation, "the business [of the Convention] was at an end."[53] Had the southern states pulled out, the Articles of Confederation, which contained no restrictions on slavery, would have remained the law of the land. Politics during the convention also played a large role. The question of slavery had been handed to the Committee of Detail, chaired by John Rutledge of South Carolina. Not surprisingly, Rutledge's committee proposed to give the slave states everything that they demanded. In his notes, Madison commented on the political implications of this slave-state delegate being in charge of the committee that would set the agenda for debate on the issue of slavery.

logroll

an exchange of political favors, such as when legislators trade votes to support one another's proposed legislation.

Others have argued that the preservation of slavery was the result of a **logroll**, or a trading of votes, between the slave states and the northeastern commercial states. Northeastern states received the strong commercial policy that they wanted in return for protections on slavery for the southern states. Evidence from the records of the convention supports the idea of a logroll, though probably through a deal made in private. On August 29, General Pinckney from South Carolina stated that although strong commercial policy was not in his state's best interests, he would not oppose the eastern states' proposals, given their "liberal conduct towards the views of South Carolina" on the issue of importing slaves. It appears from Madison's notes that a deal had been struck, though the records offer no "smoking gun" evidence.[54]

Regardless of the reasons, the question of slavery was temporarily handled but fundamentally unsettled. Not until the country was literally torn apart in the Civil War eighty years later would the issue of slavery be ultimately decided. It would take nearly another century and a great deal of sacrifice and strategic political activity to make equality for African Americans a reality, or at least more of a reality, on the ground rather than just in words. Even today, the question of whether Americans are all truly equal in the Republic endures.

James Madison on Slavery

Although his views on slavery evolved over time, James Madison was never able to completely resolve the contradictions inherent in a Constitution and government that, although based on natural rights and liberties, permitted slavery. In an essay published following the drafting of the Constitution, Madison acknowledges this contradiction, raising a hypothetical argument with which he later agrees:

> But we must deny the fact, that slaves are considered merely as property, and in no respect whatsoever as persons. The true state of the case is, that they partake of both of these qualities; being considered by our laws, in some respects, as persons, and in other respects as property. In being compelled to labour, not for himself, but for a master; in being vendible [able to be sold] by one master to another master; and in being subject at all times to be restrained in his liberty, and chastised in his body, by the capricious will of another, the slave may appear to be degraded from the human rank, and classed with those irrational animals

which fall under the legal denomination of property. In being protected, on the other hand, in his life and in his limbs, against the violence of all others, even the master of his labour and his liberty; and in being punishable himself for all violence committed against others; the slave is no less evidently regarded by the law as a member of society.[55]

In a letter to a colleague later in his life, Madison discussed a plan for ending slavery that involved a separate treatment for African Americans, whether in returning freed slaves to Africa or settling them in the Western territories:

> Sir,–I have rec. [received] your letter of the 3d instant, requesting such hints as may have occurred to me on the subject of an eventual extinguishment of slavery in the U.S.
>
> A general emancipation of slaves ought to be 1. gradual. 2. equitable & satisfactory for the individuals immediately concerned. 3. consistent with the existing & durable prejudices of the nation.
>
> To be equitable & satisfactory, the consent of both the Master & the slave should be obtained. That of the Master will require a provision in the plan for compensating a loss of what he held as property guarantied by the laws, and recognized by the Constitution. That of the slave, requires that his condition in a state of freedom, be preferable in his own estimation, to his actual one in a state of bondage.
>
> To be consistent with existing and probably unalterable prejudices in the U. S. the freed blacks ought to be permanently removed beyond the region occupied by or allotted to a White population.[56]

The members of the Liberian senate of 1893, mostly made up of freed African American slaves. The Republic of Liberia began as a settlement for freed slaves, similar to Madison's call to remove blacks from the regions populated by whites. But the motivation for the settlement was not always benign: white slaveholders thought that freed slaves in their midst would threaten slave societies in the South.

Library of Congress/Corbis/VCG via Getty Images.

Madison never did free his own slaves or provide for their freedom upon his death, as his colleague George Washington would do.

A Document Finished, But Not the Law of the Land

By proposing a system of amendments, the framers ensured that the Constitution would always be unfinished so that it could adapt over time. More immediately, however, the Constitution was unfinished because the states had yet to approve it. The document that emerged from Philadelphia was just a proposal. It carried no force until the states chose to adopt it. That would be determined by the battle over ratification.

A skillful move by Benjamin Franklin at the convention's conclusion required only that delegates sign their names as witnesses to their states' endorsement, which allowed some delegates to sign the Constitution even knowing that they would soon speak out against it. Franklin's move, and the departure over the summer of delegates who did not approve of the outcomes, made the delegates appear to be in greater agreement than they really were. In fact, many did have strong reservations, and three refused to sign.

The delegates also used a bit of trickery to get around another issue. The Articles of Confederation required that amendments to the articles required the approval of all thirteen state delegations in Congress. This, members of the Constitutional Convention knew, was going to be very difficult. Rhode Island never sent any delegates, and many states were closely divided. So the delegates declared that the Constitution would become the law of the land if ratifying conventions in nine out of thirteen states approved it, bypassing the state legislatures. Even with this somewhat unconventional ploy—breaking the spirit if not the law of the articles—it was still far from certain that the Constitution would be adopted.

RATIFICATION

Federalists versus Antifederalists

It was America's first national political campaign. It was also its first *negative* national political campaign. The fight between those in favour of the Constitution and those opposed to it was characterized by dire premonitions of what might happen if the Constitution was or was not ratified. The debate was carried out through the printing presses, which had become widespread enough to allow both sides to carry their messages to the people. Some wrote under their own names. Others adopted the names of Roman figures or used simple descriptors such as "landowner." Both sides flooded the country with pamphlets and letters to newspapers. The campaign was sometimes personal, with attacks on the character of members of the other side.

Tactically, the first victory in the battle to lodge a favorable image in the minds of citizens went to the supporters of the proposed Constitution. They successfully claimed the name **Federalists** for their group. In fact, the proposed government was strongly national, whereas the term *federalist* generally meant more of a balance between the power of states and the national government. Those arguing against the document could more properly claim the title Federalist. Nonetheless, they would be tagged as **Antifederalists** for the next year's political campaign.

For the Antifederalists, part of the negativity associated with their name and their political campaign was perhaps inevitable. They were, after all, forced to argue against a proposal, and basing their argument only on what was good about the Articles of Confederation was a tough sell. So they turned negative. They raised fears in the minds of Americans about what this new—many would say radical—change in the government would bring. Mostly, they argued, it would trample on the rights of the people and the states in which they lived, perhaps not immediately, but at some point in the nation's future.

For their part, the Federalists also campaigned partly on fear. They pointed to the problems that plagued the government under the articles—the inability to deal with

Federalists
the name taken by supporters of the proposed Constitution; the Federalists called for a strong national government.

Antifederalists
the name taken by those opposed to the proposed Constitution; the Antifederalists favored stronger state governments.

foreign powers, economic challenges, and, especially, the threat of anarchy—and warned citizens that the only way to avoid these dangers was through the new Constitution. The Federalists had celebrity on their side in the figures of Washington and Franklin. A personal appeal by Washington in which he argued, "There is *no Alternative* between the *Adoption* of it [the Constitution] and *Anarchy*," was reprinted fifty-one times during the campaign.[57] The Antifederalists, with the exception of a few misguided attempts to counter the celebrity endorsements of Washington and Franklin, stayed away from the issue of famous endorsements in this, America's first political campaign.

In some ways, the Federalists and Antifederalists split along distinctions of class. Many wealthy merchants favored the strong economic policy that the Constitution would allow, and many wealthy southern plantation owners supported the agreements that had been struck. On the other side, a large number of Antifederalists came from rural areas and mistrusted powerful elites in their states' capitals. To say that the Federalists were wealthy elites and the Antifederalists small farmers and shopkeepers is, however, too

The fate of the Constitution was decided in the state ratifying conventions (nine states had to ratify for the Constitution to take effect), but it was the subject of intense debates everywhere—in homes, taverns, coffeehouses, and newspapers.

The Granger Collection, New York.

TABLE 2.3 Federalists and Antifederalists

Both Federalists and Antifederalists were interested in a politically and economically secure nation, but they differed in how they thought that would best be achieved.

Differed in Terms of...	Federalists	Antifederalists
View of proposed Constitution	Supporters	Opponents
Proponents of...	A strong national government	Stronger state government
Concerned about...	The tyranny of the majority	The tyranny of the minority
Proposed...	The idea of an extended republic to limit the problem of faction and help to resolve the tyranny of the majority	Strong restrictions be placed on branches of government to help solve the problem of too-strong national government
Supporters included...	More wealthy merchants and southern plantation owners George Washington, Benjamin Franklin, Alexander Hamilton, James Madison, John Jay	More people in rural areas, more farmers and shopkeepers Fewer well-known supporters, but leadership included educated elites, Revolutionary War heroes, and convention delegates

strong a simplification. Many Antifederalist leaders were educated elites; some of the most prominent had been heroes in the Revolutionary War, delegates to the convention itself, or important members in state politics.

Though the Federalists tried to associate the threat of anarchy and Shays' Rebellion with their opponents, the Antifederalists were just as concerned as their opponents with securing a stable future for the country. Instead, the divisions between the two sides represented fundamentally different visions for how to do so. Three main issues divided the Antifederalists and the Federalists on a vision of this future: (1) the very possibility of creating a workable republic in such a large nation that would protect individual liberties against **tyranny** (the suppression of the rights of a people by those holding power), (2) the relative power of states and the nation, and (3) the lack of a bill of rights (a list of rights and liberties which people possess and which governments cannot take away) in the Constitution. Each of these issues was closely related to the others.

tyranny
the suppression of the rights of a people by those holding power.

The Dangers of Power in a Large Republic

As the debate over ratification got under way, the factions for and against the Constitution disagreed on the very possibility of a republic in a country as large as the United States. Many of the Enlightenment writers that Madison had drawn his ideas from had argued republics had to be small to work properly, and all expected this one to grow even larger over time, making the challenges even worse. The national government, the Antifederalists argued, would grow more distant from the people over time and would eventually begin to oppress them. Congress having the power to tax would only make this danger greater, they claimed. As the national government grew more powerful and more distant from the citizens, states would grow weaker and provide citizens with less and less of a check on the power of the national government. Therefore, the Antifederalists asserted, more restrictions needed to be placed on the national government now, while it was still possible. They proposed, for example, to narrow the set of cases that the Supreme Court could hear and to limit the power of the president and the nation in military affairs, preserving a larger role for state militias in the country's defense.

These challenges required more than a tactical shift on the part of the Federalists. They spoke to the very viability of an effective republic in the United States and required the Federalists to also go positive in their campaign. They had to lay out for skeptical Americans how a large republic could be constructed in a way that would prevent it from growing so self-interested and powerful that it would trample on the rights of states and their citizens. The Federalists made their strongest theoretical case for the new American Republic in a collection of eighty-five essays written for the New York papers from the fall of 1787 to the spring of 1788. Published under the collective name "Publius," these **Federalist Papers**, which were actually written by Alexander Hamilton, James Madison, and John Jay, are now considered some of the most important writings in American political history. They laid out the theory behind the Constitution, which itself does not directly speak to the reasons behind its own provisions.

Federalist Papers
a series of eighty-five essays written by Alexander Hamilton, James Madison, and John Jay and published between 1787 and 1788 that lay out the theory behind the Constitution.

James Madison was not initially selected to be one of the authors; Alexander Hamilton chose to bring him onto the project as a replacement Federalist. Madison's research allowed him to respond thoughtfully and quickly to the Antifederalist charges against the proposed Constitution. At the time, the *Federalist Papers* were intended to influence the ratification debate, especially in the contested state of New York. Hamilton had the "idea of laying down this propaganda barrage on the still undecided minds of New Yorkers."[58] The *Federalist Papers* were an example of political propaganda—the framing and discussion of a political issue in a way that tries to influence people's views of that issue.

Though "Publius" managed to get wide coverage simply by producing so many essays, "nearly a thousand words a day,"[59] individually the essays may not have been decisive in swaying

Federalist poster circa 1800.

In this political cartoon, George Washington (shown in heaven) tells partisans to keep the pillars of Federalism, Republicanism, and Democracy, warning party men to let all three stand to hold up Peace and Plenty, Liberty and Independence. At the left a Democrat says, "This Pillar shall not stand I am determin'd to support a just and necessary War," and at the right a Federalist claims, "This Pillar must come down I am a friend of Peace."

public opinion in the debates at the time. They were complicated and intellectual, and this was, after all, a political campaign. Their importance to the theory of the American Constitution, however, is unmistakable. Many of Madison's essays are now considered to be the most important in the collection. Two essays in particular, *Federalist* No. 10 and No. 51 (see Appendix), tackle the Antifederalist critiques by laying out the reasons behind the proposed constitutional republic. Though Madison was not entirely happy with the results of the Great Compromise, he now defended the proposed Constitution, seeing its adoption, even with its imperfections, as a far better outcome than failure to secure ratification.

From his research, Madison knew that those who would engineer a republic must not assume that people will always act in noble ways, putting their own needs behind what is best for the republic. Instead, he proposed that the American Republic must be constructed to account for self-interest and selfish motives. In *Federalist* No. 51 he wrote, "If men were angels, no government would be necessary. If angels were to govern men, neither external nor internal controls on government would be necessary. In framing a government which is to be administered by men over men, the great difficulty lies in this: you must first enable to the government to control the governed; and in the next place oblige it to control itself."[60]

The Problem of Faction

The danger was not only that people would act according to their self-interest, it was that they might do so in concert with others who had the same motives. Collectively, this group of people, however large or small, could try to use the government to get what it wanted, trampling the rights of others in the process. Such a group of self-interested individuals would constitute what Madison called a **faction**, and it would present, and has always presented, the most dangerous challenge to a republic. In *Federalist* No. 10, he describes the problem of faction and offers his solution to it, which, he argues, is the basis on which the current Constitution is built. "By faction," Madison wrote, "I understand a number

faction
a group of self-interested people who use the government to get what they want, trampling the rights of others in the process.

> The most common and durable source of factions has been the various and unequal distribution of property. "Those who hold and those who are without property have ever formed distinct interests in society."

of citizens, whether amounting to a majority or minority of the whole, who are united and actuated by a common impulse of passion, or of interest, adverse to the rights of other citizens, or to the permanent and aggregate interests of the community."[61] As we will explore in this book, factions are part of the American political fabric. Political parties and interest groups are both examples of factions that operate today.

Long before Karl Marx wrote about the inevitability of class conflict in capitalist societies, Madison made it clear in *Federalist* No. 10 that inequality of wealth is the primary driver of factionalization, asserting that "those who hold and those who are without property have ever formed distinct interests in society."[62] Madison included slave ownership as a source of faction, as slaves were considered a form of property during the discussions in the Constitutional Convention. However, this issue was not addressed in *Federalist* No. 10.

Factions could be eliminated but, Madison argued, only through unacceptable means. A tyrannical government that suppressed the liberties of its citizens could prevent factions from organizing. "Liberty," Madison argued, "is to faction, what air is to fire."[63] Suppress liberty, and factions cannot survive. Factions also cannot form or survive in societies where everyone has "the same opinions, the same passions, and the same interests."[64] This second preventative measure is as unrealistic as the first is unthinkable, especially in a large republic like the United States. Therefore, Madison concludes that a nation cannot avoid the problem of faction, only try to check its dangers. American history has proven Madison correct. The American Republic has had factions since its origin. Political parties can be thought of as factions, as can interest groups. The question is how a republic can keep them in check.

extended republic
a republic so large and diverse, with so many factions vying for power, that no one faction is able to assert its will over all of the others.

The superior way to check their power, Madison argued in *Federalist* No. 10, is through an **extended republic**: a republic so large and diverse, with so many factions vying for power, that no one faction is able to assert its will over all of the others. Tactically, this was a clever argument. With it, Madison countered the Antifederalist charge that the American republic would be too large to govern effectively by arguing that the only solution to the dangers of faction was precisely to have such a large republic. Madison, however, was no populist; much of the structure of the government that he had helped design was there to place brakes on popular passions, to insulate representatives from the desires of their citizens.

Two Forms of Tyranny

The notion that there are many reasons to mistrust government is not one with which the Antifederalists would have disagreed. Rather, the debate between the Federalists and Antifederalists was over the forms that the danger of self-interest would take and the best solution to the imperfections of those who would hope to govern. Both sides acknowledged that tyranny could take two forms. In a **tyranny of the minority**, a small number of citizens tramples on the rights of the rest of the larger population. In a **tyranny of the majority**, a large number of citizens use the power of their majority to trample on the rights of a smaller group. The two sides disagreed on which was the greater danger and, therefore, on how a republic should be structured.

tyranny of the minority
when a small number of citizens tramples on the rights of the larger population.

tyranny of the majority
when a large number of citizens use the power of their majority to trample on the rights of a smaller group.

The Antifederalists focused more on the dangers of a tyranny of the minority. The Regulators had viewed the government of Massachusetts as becoming dangerously disconnected from the people and controlled by wealthy elites; the Antifederalists feared the government of the United States would follow a similar path. While acknowledging the dangers of minority tyranny, Madison and the Federalists focused more on the dangers of majority rule and its necessary counters. A majority of people, if in control of all of the levers of power, might use that power to oppress a minority of citizens. Slavery could be thought of as a tyranny of the majority, though in fact slaves outnumbered whites in many areas of the country. Given Madison's earlier observations about property and the panic associated with Shays' Rebellion, one of the dangers the Federalists saw was a majority of poorer people using their power to redistribute wealth in a more equal way. In *Federalist* No. 10, Madison did not argue for direct democracy, in which citizens vote directly on policies. Viewing democracies throughout history as "spectacles of turbulence and contention... incompatible with personal security or the rights of property," Madison argued for the Republican remedy to the dangers of tyranny.[65]

Delegation of power to representatives of the people is central to the republican remedy, as is the way in which power is divided within this republican form of government. In *Federalist* No. 51, Madison laid out the blueprints of such a structure. Separation of powers is the guiding principle, with power divided and parsed between the states and nation, between the three branches of the national government, and within each branch.

> Separation of powers is the guiding principle, with power divided and parsed between the states and nation, between the three branches of the national government, and within each branch.

The Power of the National Government and the States

Debates over the relative power of the states and the nation were central to the political battles over ratification of the Constitution. The Federalists tried to convince American citizens that the proposed form of government was necessary to preserve their rights and liberties. The Antifederalists argued against the proposed increase in national power and warned Americans of what might come to pass over time as the advantages given to the national government in the Constitution might allow it to infringe more and more on the authority of the states.

Federalist Arguments for a Strong National Government

In their campaign to defend the proposed Constitution, the Federalists highlighted the problems and dangers of a government in which the states were strong and the nation was weak, pointing out failures of past republics as well as the problems experienced under the Articles of Confederation. In *Federalist* No. 9, Alexander Hamilton claimed that the principle of confederacy, in which smaller sovereign governments unite in a limited union, "has been the cause of incurable disorder and imbecility in the government."[66] In *Federalist* No. 16, Hamilton advocated for a national army, playing on the fears brought about by Shays' Rebellion. He warned that if the national government in a confederacy were ever forced to use military might against one of its members, "The first war of this kind would probably terminate in a dissolution of the union [and end] in the violent death of the confederacy."[67]

In his contributions to the *Federalist Papers*, Madison took a more moderate approach, emphasizing the balance between state and national power in the proposed Constitution. The difference between Hamilton's and Madison's views was more than

NEWS CLIP
Senator Rubio asks federal government to fund Zika prevention

a matter of words. In the coming years these two founders (along with their intellectual and political allies) would split into two different factions, giving rise to the nation's first political parties along with some very personal and negative campaign tactics.

In *Federalist* No. 39, Madison argued that the Constitution divided the people's sovereignty in such a way as to preserve the integrity of both states and nation. The House of Representatives, its members elected directly by Americans and its number determined in proportion to state population, "is *national* not *federal*." The Senate, with its members elected by state legislatures and its numbers apportioned equally, "is *federal*, not *national*." The office of the president, elected under the complicated system of the Electoral College, was similarly compound. Madison concluded that "the proposed constitution, therefore . . . is, in strictness, neither a national nor a federal constitution; but a composition of both."[68]

In *Federalist* No. 45, Madison reassured the states that the list of specific powers given to the national government and the reservation of all other powers to the states provided an important check on the power of the proposed national government: "The powers delegated by the proposed constitution to the federal government, are few and defined. Those which are to remain in the state governments, are numerous and indefinite."[69]

Finally, in *Federalist* No. 51, Madison argued that the separation of powers between the two levels of government would provide an important defense against the dangers of faction: "In the compound republic of America, the power surrendered by the people, is first divided between two distinct governments, and then the portion allotted to each subdivided among the distinct and separate departments. Hence a double security arises to the rights of the people. The different governments will control each other; at the same time that each will be controlled by itself."[70]

Antifederalist Concerns

The Antifederalists were not convinced by the arguments in the *Federalist Papers*. They feared what they saw as a radical increase in national power, not only in the proposed Constitution but in how the government might evolve over time. They feared the distant future as much as the immediate present. They were, in many ways, conservative, trying to preserve the power of the states as enjoyed under the Articles of Confederation. In American political history, there is no one work that encapsulates Antifederalist thought in the same way that the *Federalist Papers* did for Federalists. There are no *Antifederalist Papers*; rather, as scholars have pointed out, "the Antifederalist literature is immense and heterogeneous, encompassing speeches, pamphlets, essays and letters."[71]

Many Antifederalist concerns centered on how representation of the people's interests could be maintained as the country grew in size, population, and power. They "feared that, once elected and comfortable in their jobs, the representatives would not relinquish power. Being some distance away from the [congressional district] would alienate the representatives from their constituent's wishes," creating the possibility of a new, elected, American aristocracy.[72] This "democratic" aristocracy, an Antifederalist essay warned, would be accompanied by an irresistible trend toward a large and complex national government, driven by the demands of a growing nation: "It would be difficult to prove, that anything short of despotism could not bind so great a country under one government; and that whatever plan you might at the first setting out establish, it would issue [end up] in a despotism."[73]

The economic power of the national government to tax and regulate interstate commerce was one of the Antifederalists' greatest worries, and it was only made worse by the necessary and proper clause of the proposed constitution. The author of one Antifederalist essay, writing under the name "Brutus," argued that "this power, given [to] the federal legislature, directly annihilates all the powers of the state legislatures."[74] Over time, when individual states attempted to reassert their authority, "it will be found that the power retained by individual states, small as is it is, will be a clog upon the wheels of government of the United States; the latter therefore will be naturally inclined to remove it out of the way."[75]

A Bill of Rights

Strategically, the most effective Antifederalist charge against the Constitution was that it lacked a bill of rights—a list of rights and liberties with which people are born and which governments cannot take away. Many state constitutions already had them, and the idea of inserting a statement protecting specific rights and liberties into the Constitution had come up during the convention. Motions to include these statements, however, did not pass, though the delegates did place some restrictions on government in scattered sections of the Constitution (see Chapter 4). To Madison and other opponents of a bill of rights, such a statement was simply not necessary. In the republic that the delegates had fashioned, the people were already sovereign, and the government was already limited. There was no need to limit Congress's power over things that the Constitution gave it no control over in the first place. John Dickinson of Delaware asked other delegates rhetorically, "Do we want to be reminded that the sun enlightens, warms, and cheers?"[76] In addition, according to the Federalists, bills of rights had traditionally been associated with agreements between kings and subjects, not constitutions of a free people. Finally, some questioned if it was possible or even desirable to try to make a complete list of rights and liberties. What about the ones that were left out? Would Congress respect rights if they were not part of the official list?

Some however, both during the convention and after, remained strongly in favor of a bill of rights. A bill of rights, they argued, was necessary to check the tendency of government to infringe on the rights and liberties of citizens over time. They pointed out that one should be concerned with what the government might become in the future, not just what it was in the present: "It is of the opinion of the greatest writers that a very extensive country cannot be governed on democratic principles . . . whatever plan you might at the first setting out establish, it would issue into despotism."[77] In addition, the Antifederalists argued that a bill of rights served an important educational function in a

Shown is a draft of the Bill of Rights from September 9, 1789.

New York City celebrates the ratification of the federal Constitution on July 26, 1788.

The Granger Collection, New York.

republic.[78] It would serve to remind citizens of their natural rights and remind them to assert those rights when governments might, often slowly, try to take them away.

In the final days of the Constitutional Convention, two delegates proposed a clause that would guarantee liberty of the press. Their motion lost, but by only one vote, a potential harbinger of future political realities of which, according to one political scientist, the nationalists should have taken heed.[79] As it turned out, the lack of a bill of rights proved to be the most effective argument that the Antifederalists would make in the ratification campaign. Many Americans were suspicious of centralized power and wanted specific protections against it.

In February 1788, the Federalists won a narrow victory in Massachusetts, the sixth of nine states needed for ratification, but only after the pro-constitutional forces agreed to propose a bill of rights once the original document had itself been ratified. Three months later, South Carolina also ratified, also contingent on a set of amendments that would be offered in the first national Congress. On June 21, 1788, with the help of some shrewd procedural tactics on the part of Federalists in the state convention, New Hampshire became the ninth state to ratify.[80] The Constitution of the United States would become the supreme law of the land the following year.

Even after New Hampshire, James Madison continued to worry. It was not North Carolina's reluctance or Rhode Island's rejection that worried him. If Virginia and New York failed to ratify, it might lead to deep divisions within the new country. Virginia ratified in June, and New York followed in July. North Carolina and, finally, Rhode Island ratified within a year. During the campaign, sensing the realities of the political landscape, Madison had shifted course and promised to introduce a bill of rights as proposed amendments during the first session of the new Congress once the Constitution had been ratified. Madison kept his word, and in 1791 ten of the amendments that he proposed became part of the Constitution.

WHAT HAVE I LEARNED?

1. The Federalists were opposed to the Constitution as drafted in Philadelphia in 1787.

   a. True
   b. False

2. James Madison's theory of the extended republic argued that _____.

   a. Members of a republic should be wary of the growth of national power
   b. The greatest safeguard against faction is a people with closely similar ideas and goals

   c. Competition between factions will serve as a safeguard against tyranny
   d. To guard against factions, significant restrictions will need to be placed on citizens' liberties

3. What were some of the points of disagreement between Federalists and Antifederalists?

Answer Key: 1. b; 2. c; 3. Answers may include support for or opposition to the Constitution, differing opinions on the dangers of national power, and/or the need for a bill of rights.

Mercy Otis Warren on the Dangers of the Constitution and the Need for a Bill of Rights

Mercy Otis Warren was born in 1728 "into one of Massachusetts' most prominent, wealthy families."[1] She displayed her strong support of colonial resistance to British rule before and during the American Revolution in her letters, plays, poems, and pamphlets. During the ratification debates, Warren wrote in opposition to the proposed form of government, arguing that it constituted "the abandonment of old republicanism and a betrayal of the revolution."[2] For a woman to engage in politics so publicly was itself a major act, as women during the time were excluded from political dialogue. Although she published anonymously (and, therefore, was assumed to be a man by most readers), she corresponded with many of the nation's leaders, who were well aware of her intellectual contributions to the founding.

Like other Antifederalist writers, Warren warned against the creeping aristocracy among the young nation's political leaders. According to her,

> Man is not immediately corrupted, but power without limitation, or amenability, may endanger the brightest virtue—whereas frequent return to the bar of their Constituents is the strongest check against the corruptions to which men are liable. . . . There is no security in the profered system, either for the rights of conscience or the liberty of the Press: Despotism usually while it is gaining ground, will suffer men to think, say, or write what they please; but when once established, if it is thought necessary to subserve the purposes, of arbitrary power, the most unjust restrictions may take place.

Warren was one of the strongest advocates for the need to include a bill of rights in the Constitution, and her arguments contributed to its eventual inclusion. She claimed that "there is no provision by a bill of rights to guard against dangerous encroachments of power in too many instances to be named. . . . We are told by a gentleman of too much virtue and real probity to suspect he has a design to deceive—'that the whole constitution is a declaration of rights,'—but mankind must think for themselves, and to many very judicious and discerning characters, the whole constitution with very few exceptions appears a perversion of the rights of particular states, and of private citizens."

A nineteenth-century steel engraving depicting Mercy Otis Warren. The Granger Collection, New York.

Warren believed the rights of individuals ought to be the primary object of all government and cannot be too securely guarded by the most explicit declarations in their favor.[3]

WHAT DO YOU THINK?

What are Warren's main critiques against the proposed Constitution? In what ways are her views of human nature similar to or different from those of James Madison?

....

[1] Kate Davies, *Catherine Macaulay and Mercy Otis Warren: The Revolutionary Atlantic and the Politics of Gender* (New York: Oxford University Press, 2005), 7–8.
[2] Ibid., 261.
[3] Mercy Otis Warren, *Observations on the New Constitution, and on the Federal and State Conventions, by a Columbian Patriot* (Library of Congress, 1788).

CONCLUSION

What Is the Constitution?

While the delegates to the Constitutional Convention were debating and negotiating behind the closed windows of the Pennsylvania State House, many Americans wondered what they were really up to. And we still do. The stories surrounding the framers' efforts have shifted over time and will probably continue to do so, and juries of generations have weighed in on the motives of the founders and on the consequences of those motives for Americans then and now.

The founders of the American Republic have been described as being guided by their own privilege and accused of crafting a government that preserved distinctions of wealth and class. According to this critique, wealthy elites supported the proposed Constitution because it would protect private property from attempts at redistribution and confiscation.[81] These men certainly *did* consider their own financial futures, though the argument against them focuses more on protecting elite interests in general than enriching any one individual. If Madison or any of the other founders were motivated primarily by personal gain, however, they were not very good at it. Several of them died bankrupt, had to sell off property, or had to have property sold off upon their deaths.

Some scholars have argued that the founders were motivated not necessarily by their own economic motives but by those of their states.[82] That the delegates would advance the interests of their states is not surprising. They had been chosen, after all, to attend the Constitutional Convention by their state legislatures. The founders were also motivated by a sense of the importance of what they were doing and of their place in history, becoming "fantastically concerned with posterity's judgment of their behavior."[83]

The founders have also been accused of being antidemocratic.[84] This was certainly true of most of the men at the convention. They saw pure democracy as dangerous. During the convention, Madison noted that Roger Sherman of Connecticut "opposed the election [of national legislators] by the people, insisting that it ought to be by the [state] Legislatures. The people, he said, should have as little to do as may be about the Government. They [lack] information and are constantly liable to be misled."[85] Elbridge Gerry of Massachusetts agreed, saying, "The evils we experience flow from the excess of democracy. The people do not want virtue; but are the dupes of pretended patriots."[86] The mistrust of pure democracy was not a controversial opinion at the time. The founders had watched democratic state legislatures with unease. These institutions had often trampled on the rights of minorities, especially members of religious minorities and former supporters of Great Britain, whose wealth they eyed. The framers intentionally placed obstacles in the path of those who would use the government to accede to popular demands.

No one of these explanations likely accounts for the motives of all of the framers as they sought to create a new government. Many probably had mixed motives. What did the founders create? What is the Constitution? Why do Americans follow this fading document, written by educated white men who might have as difficult a time relating to modern Americans as we have understanding their reality? These questions defy simple answers, partly because the Constitution is still evolving and partly because no one answer seems sufficient.

To some scholars, constitutions give order to disorder. They make progress in a society possible, but only if the people place in them credible, enforceable restrictions on the power of those who would abuse such power.[87] The Constitution creates a space for strategic action, a place of contestation. The Constitution drew from the religious traditions and individual constitutions of the colonies. It is a document that creates—or constitutes—a people.[88] It sets out who those people are and why they are doing what they are doing.

To other scholars, the American reverence for the Constitution is a dangerous thing. Faith in the Constitution as a symbol of liberty misdirects citizens from the fact that some persons, past and present, have been able to enrich themselves under its protections at the expense of others.[89] Inequality in all of its forms has survived, and at times thrived, in the American Republic. Is the Constitution antidemocratic? Does it go against or restrain the will of the majority of the people? Yes, sometimes it is, and sometimes it does. The Constitution was intentionally designed to put brakes on popular desire to change public policy quickly. The result—incrementalism in public policy development whereby policy changes tend to be small and come slowly—has important implications for the United States.

James Madison's studies of the untimely deaths of republics helped to shape the longest-lived written national constitution in the history of human experience. That document did not ban slavery or the trade in slaves. It did not affirm or institutionalize the natural-born rights and liberties of women, Native Americans, slaves, former slaves, or many other outsiders, "dangerous" individuals, or invisible people. It did, however, affirm the rights of citizens to worship as they saw fit, to speak out and organize against tyranny, and to expect that their government would exist to protect and promote their rights and liberties. It created mechanisms to enforce these expectations, should those in power forget whom they were there to represent. And, intentionally or not, it provided a platform and a path for those ignored or oppressed by the original document to change it, to make it acknowledge their natural rights and liberties as well.

The founders of the American Republic were practical, tactical, strategic men. Their compromises may have been necessary, but they had enormous consequences for people's lives. The document that emerged from the Pennsylvania State House was unfinished and imperfect. Would it allow for a remedy of its defects? Would it create, as Madison had hoped, a republic that would last? The answers to these questions cannot be found in studies of the motives of the founders or even of the document itself. The answers have come not from words penned in quill and ink but from the efforts of political actors—sometimes generations later—using their own skills in strategic politics, developing their own ideas, and making their own compromises and mistakes. And having done their own homework.

Want a better grade?

Get the tools you need to sharpen your study skills. **SAGE edge** offers a robust online environment featuring an impressive array of free tools and resources. Access practice quizzes, eFlashcards, video, and multimedia at **edge.sagepub.com/abernathy1e.**

CHAPTER REVIEW

This chapter's main ideas are reflected in the Learning Objectives below. By reviewing them here you should be able to **remember** the key points, **connect** them to the stories presented in the chapter, **think** critically about these questions, and **know** these terms that are central to the topic.

2.1 Explain how the historical context of post-Revolutionary America led to the proposal for a new, stronger national government.

REMEMBER ...

- James Madison wanted to form a republic that would last. He and other delegates to the Constitutional Convention met and debated how best to strengthen their union and avoid significant political and economic problems.

CONNECT ...	• Madison was interested in, but not optimistic about, the possibility of making major changes to the government under the Articles of Confederation.
	• Divisions between states, economic problems, and the danger of rebellion all played a role in the path to the Constitutional Convention.

THINK ...	• Why were some Americans worried about amending or replacing the Articles of Confederation?
	• Why were some in favor of the idea?

KNOW ...	• *Articles of Confederation and Perpetual Union* (p. 44)	• *republics* (p. 42)
	• *constitution* (p. 41)	

2.2 Describe how the Constitution was shaped by the strategic political choices of those involved in its drafting.

REMEMBER ...	• The delegates to the Constitutional Convention were not charged with drafting a new Constitution but only with proposing possible changes to the Articles of Confederation.

CONNECT ...	• By placing what became known as the Virginia Plan on the agenda, James Madison forced the opposition to respond to his ideas.

THINK ...	• What issues dominated the early weeks of the convention?
	• What other issues arose as the convention progressed?

KNOW ...	• *Constitutional Convention* (p. 52)	• *Shays' Rebellion* (p. 48)
	• *Great Compromise* (p. 58)	• *Virginia Plan* (p. 55)
	• *New Jersey Plan* (p. 56)	

2.3 Identify the ideas behind the structure of the government under the Constitution.

REMEMBER ...	• The idea of separation of powers influenced the decision to create three separate but connected branches of the federal government.

THINK ...	• What role did the issue of slavery play in the deliberations during the convention and in the document that finally emerged from it?

KNOW ...	• *amendment* (p. 62)	• *logroll* (p. 66)
	• *executive branch* (p. 59)	• *separation of powers* (p. 61)
	• *judicial branch* (p. 60)	• *Three-fifths Compromise* (p. 63)
	• *legislative branch* (p. 59)	

◤ 2.4 Compare and contrast the arguments put forth by the Federalists and the Antifederalists during the ratification campaign.

REMEMBER ...
- The proposed Constitution had to be ratified by nine of the thirteen states in order to replace the Articles of Confederation.
- Proponents and opponents of the Constitution tried to rally others to their side and convince individuals of their position.

CONNECT ...
- The ratification campaigns in the states played upon people's fears, but they also sought to make convincing arguments about the proper structure of government.
- Uncertainty about how powerful the proposed federal government would eventually become informed many of the debates between Federalists and Antifederalists.

THINK ...
- What were the primary points of disagreement between the Federalists and Antifederalists?
- Which side eventually prevailed?

KNOW ...
- *Antifederalists* (p. 68)
- *extended republic* (p. 72)
- *faction* (p. 71)
- *Federalists* (p. 68)
- *Federalist Papers* (p. 70)
- *tyranny* (p. 70)
- *tyranny of the majority* (p. 72)
- *tyranny of the minority* (p. 72)

◤ 2.5 Consider the different perspectives on the effects of the Constitution in American life today.

REMEMBER ...
- Americans still debate the degree to which the Constitution protects individual rights and liberties, the degree to which it preserves inequality, and how democratic the American Republic was and is.

THINK ...
- What are the different functions that a constitution fulfills?

3 FEDERALISM
The Changing Boundaries between the Nation and the States

On one fundamental issue the Constitution of the United States is absolutely clear: who is in charge. In its opening words, "We the People of the United States," the Constitution establishes that ultimate political authority rests with the people and not in any government that those people might create to maintain an orderly, prosperous, and secure nation. The people, and not the government, are sovereign and have supreme political authority.

What the Constitution is far less clear on, however, are the precise mechanisms and structures through which this supreme authority is vested in the government Americans chose to create and maintain. Under the Articles of Confederation, the vast majority of the people's authority

Angel Raich inhales vaporized marijuana in her home in Oakland, California. Her use is legal under the laws of her state but illegal under federal law, thus illustrating the tensions inherent in federalist systems of government.[1]

AP Photo/Ben Margot.

had been placed in state governments, which left the Confederal Congress constantly struggling to secure cooperation from these multiple governments. That changed with the ratification of the Constitution, but the issue was not settled once and for all. The new system of government divided the people's authority between two levels of government—the nation and the states—with some powers exercised by one level alone, some powers denied to both levels, and some powers shared by both levels. In doing so, a system of **federalism** was created.

> **federalism**
> a structure of governance that places the people's authority in two or more levels of government.

As we will explore, the Constitution created much of the basic framework of this division but did not perfectly delineate the boundaries between the specific powers of the national government and those of the state governments. Setting these boundaries would be a process, one that continues even today. While at first glance American federalism may seem like a dry and academic topic, the truth is far different. Many of the most important and controversial issues in our representative democracy involve difficult questions of American federalism.

In this chapter, we will engage with the stories of Angel Raich and Diane Monson, who sought to secure access to medical marijuana; President Roosevelt's response to the Great Depression; and the Schechter brothers' attempts to protect their rights to commerce under threat from Roosevelt's New Deal. In doing so, we will explore the tensions inherent in American federalism, how this federalism has changed over time, and where it stands in the twenty-first century.

LEARNING OBJECTIVES

After reading this chapter, you will be able to:

3.1 Explain the tension in American federalism between state and federal laws

3.2 Identify the elements of the United States Constitution that shape American federalism and evaluate arguments about the proper limits of congressional power under their authority

3.3 Trace the development of American federalism over time

3.4 Describe the impact of economic crisis in the changes to American federalism during the New Deal era

3.5 List changes to American federalism in the post–New Deal era

3.6 Discuss the current status of American federalism and how it might continue to evolve

◼ BETWEEN STATE AND FEDERAL LAW

Fighting for Access to Medical Marijuana

In 2002 Angel McClary Raich and Diane Monson filed suit in a California federal court against the government of the United States, arguing that their use of medical marijuana—legal under the laws of California and eight other states at the time but illegal under federal law—was protected by the laws of their state and by the Constitution of the United States.

Both women were trying to cope with significant health issues, the treatment of which, they argued, was helped by the use of cannabis. Raich, a thirty-six-year-old mother of two, was struggling against an "inoperable brain tumor, seizures, endometriosis, scoliosis and a wasting disorder. She [weighed] only 97 pounds and said without pot she'd starve to death."[2] "I am not a criminal," Raich declared. "I do not deserve to be behind bars."[3] Diane Monson used cannabis as part of her treatment for chronic back pain and spasms and grew her own plants to provide her medication: "Without cannabis, these spasms would be tortuous and unbearable no matter what other medications were available," she testified in federal court.[4]

Both women were using marijuana under the supervision of their physicians and in compliance with California's Compassionate Use Act of 1996. This act made the use and cultivation of marijuana for medical purposes legal if undertaken under the supervision of a licensed physician and in accordance with state regulations. However, Raich and Monson feared that the federal government might restrict their future ability to obtain medical cannabis. The reason for their fears was the unavoidable fact that the use, cultivation, or possession of marijuana was illegal under federal law. Raich and Monson were caught between the laws of their state and those of the nation. As such, they found themselves front and center in one of the most enduring debates in American political life—that of federalism.

The acts of growing, possessing, or using medical marijuana were all legal (with some restrictions) under California law, but illegal under federal law, specifically the Controlled Substances Act of 1970 (CSA).[5] The CSA consolidated existing federal laws governing substance use into a single statue. Under that new law, marijuana was classified as a Schedule I drug, among the most dangerous substances, such as heroin and LSD, due to its "high potential for abuse, lack of any accepted medical use, and absence of any accepted safety for use in medically supervised treatment."[6]

In August 2002, "county deputy sheriffs and agents from the federal Drug Enforcement Administration (DEA) came to Monson's home. After a thorough investigation, the county officials concluded that her cultivation and use of marijuana was entirely lawful as a matter of California law. Nevertheless, after a 3-hour standoff, the federal agents seized and destroyed all six of her cannabis plants."[7] "As I stood by and watched," Monson later testified, "the DEA agents chopped down my medicinal plants. I was crying and my back began to tighten up; for the rest of the week I experienced debilitating back spasms. . . . We do not feel safe; we have had our civil rights and our rights under California law taken from us in our own back yard."[8]

As California law allowed the use and cultivation of marijuana for medicinal purposes, but federal law made both the acts illegal, Raich and Monson found themselves in a federalist limbo. Facing a threat to their continued access to medical marijuana, the two women filed suit, and their case eventually made its way to the United States Supreme Court. In their case, Raich and Monson based their claims upon the laws of California and the Constitution of the United States. In restricting access to marijuana, they argued, the federal government was in violation of several amendments to the Constitution as well as of certain specific powers granted to Congress in the founding document.

For their part, representatives of the federal government and the DEA insisted that they were rightfully upholding federal law and federal authority. "Everything we're doing is according to the law," said Richard Meyer, a San Francisco–based DEA spokesman. "Our job is to enforce the laws enacted by Congress and upheld by the Supreme Court."[9] By enforcing federal law, however, the DEA agents were restricting actions that were legal under California state laws, which begs the central question, when it comes to pot and patients, does federal or state law rule?[10] Upon learning that the Supreme Court would

Diane Monson at her California home with her marijuana plants on the day that the Supreme Court ruled the federal government does have the authority to prohibit marijuana, despite state laws allowing it.

AP Photo/Max Whittaker.

hear her case, Raich indicated how personal, and critical, the outcome was: "It's about whether the federal government has the right to decide who in this country may live and who may die. . . . I've never had a speeding ticket. I'm a law-abiding citizen, and I do not deserve to be sentenced to death just because cannabis is the only medicine for me."[11]

How, one might ask, did the federal government claim the authority to override the laws of a state? The short answer is the Constitution. The long answer is a bit more complicated, which is why we began our exploration of American federalism with an examination of medical marijuana. At the center of Raich and Monson's challenge is one basic question: Where, precisely, does the boundary between the powers of the federal government and those of the states lie? From its beginnings, American federalism has been a messy, complicated, and contested thing. It still is.

WHAT HAVE I LEARNED?

1. The American federalist system _____.

   a. Places the people's power in the national government
   b. Places the people's power in the state governments
   c. Divdes power between national, state, and local governments
   d. Divdes power between national and state governments

2. What laws were in conflict in the case of Angel Raich and Diane Monson?

3. What deeper challenges to the placement of Americans' sovereignty does their case highlight?

Answer Key: 1. d; 2. Answers should focus on the conflict between California law and those of the nation.; 3. Answers should discuss the challenge of defining boundaries in the American federalist system.

AMERICAN FEDERALISM AND THE CONSTITUTION

The form of government that emerged from the Constitutional Convention in Philadelphia in 1787 was new in many ways. One of the most important innovations was the division of

TOPICS IN AMERICAN GOVERNMENT
Powers under Federalism

Angel Raich and Diane Monson's Constitutional Claims

As you read about the construction of American federalism in the United States Constitution, reflect upon the questions raised by Angel Raich and Diane Monson's claims. Specifically, consider the following:

- The conflicts between federal and state laws over the issue of medical marijuana
- The difficulties in drawing boundaries between state and federal authority

the people's sovereignty between two levels of government: the national government and the states. Each level retained some exclusive powers and had some powers denied to it, and in some areas both levels were empowered to act on behalf of the people.

As the delegates convened in Philadelphia, they were far from united on how to resolve the need for a strong national government. A powerful central government would be better poised to address their economic crisis, defend against the threat of foreign powers, and calm the possibility of rebellion. But many also wanted to preserve the tradition of state authority that had been the basis for the Articles of Confederation and Perpetual Union. Under the articles, states were supreme, and the national government had to rely on the cooperation of the state governments to act in most areas of public policy, which consists of the laws or regulations made by government officials that define and describe a proper response to a particular public issue or problem.

Distributing Power between the Levels of Government

What the delegates ended up producing was an entirely new system of government, although not all of the details were finalized. The federal republic created by the Constitution is only one of several possible ways of working out the relationship between different levels of government. The difference between these models is the way in which the people's sovereignty is divided between different governmental units (Figure 3.1). In **unitary systems**, citizens place their power in one central government that then exercises authority over the subnational governments (such as states and provinces). Most policies are then actually carried out by these subnational governments that derive their power from the national government. Great Britain, France, and Japan are examples of democratic governments operating as unitary systems.

At the opposite end of the spectrum are **confederal systems.** Here, citizens limit the authority of the national government, instead placing most of their sovereignty in the subnational governments, which then grant power and authority to the national government. In confederal systems, national governments are heavily dependent upon the states to carry out and pay for public policies. The United States under the Articles of Confederation was an example of a confederal system.

Finally, in **federal systems**, citizens divide their sovereignty between two or more levels of government, each of which may have exclusive authority to act in certain areas of policy, be denied from acting in an area of policy, or be required to share authority with another level in some areas. Key to a true federal system is the existence of constitutional protections for each level against encroachment on its powers by the other level(s). The United States, Canada, and India are examples of countries with federal systems.

Instead of laying out a precise theory of federalism, the Constitutional Convention delegates debated a series of constitutional provisions that would shape the relative authority of the state and national governments, but they did so perhaps without a clear vision of how the system would actually work. In the words of one writer, they failed "to make clear what should be the precise relationship between [the two levels] or how either level might relate to local and private sources of power."[12] In a sense, Americans had already practiced a form of federalism while still part of the British Empire before the Revolutionary War. Though not officially acknowledged by the British government, the American colonies often acted as if much of the people's sovereignty was placed in the hands of colonial governments rather than the British Parliament or Crown.

unitary systems
structures of governance that place the people's sovereignty in a national government, with subnational governments deriving their authority from it.

confederal systems
structures of governance in which the subnational governments retain the majority of the granted authority.

federal systems
structures of governance that divide a people's sovereignty between two or more levels of government.

FIGURE 3.1

The Division of Power under Different Systems of Governance

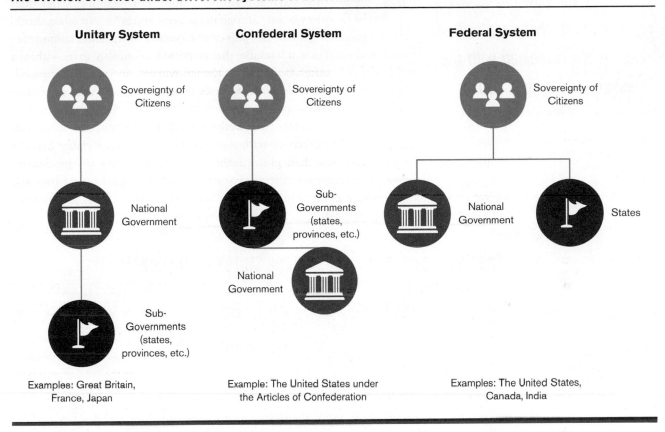

Unitary System

Sovereignty of Citizens

National Government

Sub-Governments (states, provinces, etc.)

Examples: Great Britain, France, Japan

Confederal System

Sovereignty of Citizens

Sub-Governments (states, provinces, etc.)

National Government

Example: The United States under the Articles of Confederation

Federal System

Sovereignty of Citizens

National Government

States

Examples: The United States, Canada, India

Three Key Clauses: Supremacy, Necessary and Proper, and Commerce

One of the Constitution's most important statements about where the people's sovereignty is located is the **supremacy clause**, which reads, "This Constitution, and the Laws of the United States . . . shall be the supreme Law of the Land."[13] The supremacy clause is a powerful statement of national power, one that worried the Antifederalists considerably. It means that the laws that Congress passes—provided that they are passed in accordance with the powers granted to the federal government by the Constitution itself—must be executed by the states, even if state constitutional provisions conflict with them. It means that states must abide by national treaties, and it also binds state courts to the Constitution.

In another key clause, Congress is given the power to "make all Laws which shall be necessary and proper for carrying into Execution . . . Powers vested by this Constitution in the Government of the United States."[14] This **necessary and proper clause**, also called the elastic clause, is a critical source of power for the national government, granting Congress the authority to legislate as necessary for carrying out constitutionally granted powers.

In addition to these two clauses, there is a third that powerfully shapes modern American federalism: the **commerce clause**. In the language of the Constitution, this clause grants Congress the power to "regulate Commerce with foreign Nations, and among the several States, and with the Indian Tribes."[15]

supremacy clause
a part of the Constitution that establishes the Constitution and the laws of the nation passed under its authority as the highest laws of the nation.

necessary and proper clause
a part of the Constitution that grants the federal government the authority to pass laws required to carry out its enumerated powers. Also called the elastic clause.

commerce clause
a part of the Constitution that grants Congress the authority to regulate business and commercial activity.

Vagueness in the language regarding the specific powers of the national government has contributed to the growth of national power when combined with the necessary and proper clause. For example, what does the phrase "among the several States" mean when thinking about the power of Congress to regulate commerce? Does it include the provision of health care within a state's borders? Or the cultivation of marijuana for medical or recreational uses if that marijuana does not travel across state lines?

Under the authority of the commerce clause—in combination with the necessary and proper clause and the supremacy clause—Congress has claimed the authority to define nearly any productive activity as "Commerce . . . among the several States." Even though Diane Monson's homegrown marijuana was never sold or left her home state, the federal government claimed the authority to regulate it as interstate commerce.

The Powers of the Nation and the States in the Constitution

The word *federalism* does not appear in the Constitution. Nor is there any one section that clearly lays out how the framers intended the people's sovereignty to be divided between the states and the national government. Instead, in various sections in the document, powers are given or denied to each level or allowed to be shared by both.

The National Government

In general, the powers of the national government are explicitly listed and described by the Constitution. With a few exceptions, those of the state governments are assumed to encompass those powers not explicitly given to the national government. **Enumerated powers** refer to those powers granted to the national, or federal, government in the Constitution, and especially to Congress. These include the power to tax, coin money, declare war, raise and support an army and navy, make treaties, provide for the naturalization of American citizens, and to "regulate Commerce with foreign Nations, and among the several States, and with Indian Tribes."[16] Most of the enumerated powers in the Constitution are granted to the legislative branch.

Implied powers are those not textually granted to the federal government but which are assumed to be given to it as a result of its need to make all laws "necessary and proper." For example, the Constitution does not give the national government the authority to create an air force (though the world had witnessed the first hot air balloon flight by the time of the drafting of the Constitution so might have anticipated combat in the air). That authority, however, is assumed as part of its power to raise and support a military.

In addition to describing the enumerated and implied (or delegated) powers of the national government, the Constitution denies certain powers to it, especially if consent has not been given by the residents of the states, who usually act through their own state legislatures. The national government may not pass laws that violate the rights and liberties expressed in the Bill of Rights (or other later amendments). The national government may not admit new states to the Union, nor can it change state boundaries without the consent

NEWS CLIP
States use their police powers to adjust their laws, post-Ferguson

enumerated powers
powers explicitly granted to the government via the Constitution.

implied powers
powers not textually granted to a government but considered valid in order to carry out the enumerated powers.

NEWS CLIP
Attorney General launches federal investigation into police practices

of the state's citizens. It also cannot impose taxes on goods and services exported and imported between states.

State Governments

The Constitution is much less specific on the powers allocated to the states. As the document was drafted at a time when states were supreme under the Articles of Confederation, perhaps the framers saw less of a need to lay out state powers in detail. Much of the protection for state authority comes from the Tenth Amendment to the Constitution, which states, "The powers not delegated to the United States by the Constitution, nor prohibited by it to the States, are reserved to the States respectively, or to the people."

Called **reserved powers** because of the text of the Tenth Amendment, these are powers that were not given to the national government and are, therefore, reserved to the states. Among the most important of these are **police powers**, which state governments use to protect residents and provide for their safety, health, and general welfare. States are also authorized to conduct elections, including those for national office.[17] No amendments may be made to the Constitution without the consent of three-fourths of the states, either by their legislatures or by ratification conventions in the states.[18] States are also empowered to establish local, town, county, and regional governmental bodies.

The Constitution also denies certain powers to state governments. States are prevented from entering into treaties or alliances with foreign powers—a real concern to the framers who saw the potential for the European powers to divide the states for their own economic or political gain. States may not print their own money, tax imports or exports, or declare war.[19]

Finally, in the system of federalism that emerged from the early Constitution, both nation and states are given the authority to act in certain areas of public policy. These **concurrent powers** allow national and state authority to overlap—an example of the concept of "separated institutions sharing power" discussed in Chapter 2.[20] The power to tax, already given to states under the Articles of Confederation, was extended to the new national government. Both levels are allowed to borrow money, though states have imposed more restrictions on their own ability to go into debt than the federal government has. Nation and states may both pass and enforce laws, create and operate a system of courts, and charter banks and corporations (Figure 3.2).

Regional and Local Governments

The Constitution does not describe the powers of the levels of government below the states—the cities, towns, counties, and districts. Generally, relationships between American states and their subgovernments are unitary, with the authority of the smaller units dependent upon and subordinate to the power and authority of the states. For example, state governments can change the boundaries of school districts or combine two school districts into one larger one if they choose to. If the relationship between these two levels of government were truly federal, this would not be possible without the consent of both the state and its school districts.

Graduation celebrations at the United States Air Force Academy in 2015. The Constitution gives the national government the implied power to create such an institution as the U.S. Air Force as part of its power to raise and support a military.

RJ Sangosti/The Denver Post via Getty Images.

reserved powers
powers reserved to the states if not textually granted to the federal government.

police powers
a category of reserved powers that includes the protection of people's health, safety, and welfare.

concurrent powers
powers granted to both states and the federal government in the Constitution.

FIGURE 3.2

Enumerated, Concurrent, and Reserved Powers in American Federalism

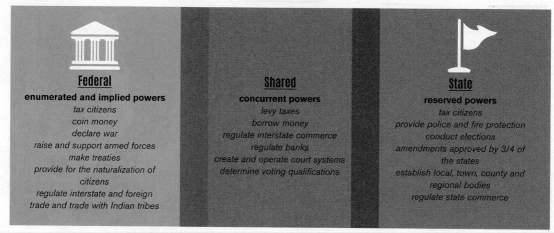

POWERS GRANTED

Federal
enumerated and implied powers
tax citizens
coin money
declare war
raise and support armed forces
make treaties
provide for the naturalization of citizens
regulate interstate and foreign trade and trade with Indian tribes

Shared
concurrent powers
levy taxes
borrow money
regulate interstate commerce
regulate banks
create and operate court systems
determine voting qualifications

State
reserved powers
tax citizens
provide police and fire protection
conduct elections
amendments approved by 3/4 of the states
establish local, town, county and regional bodies
regulate state commerce

POWERS DENIED

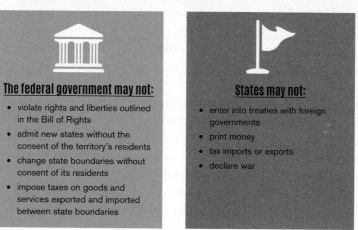

The federal government may not:

- violate rights and liberties outlined in the Bill of Rights
- admit new states without the consent of the territory's residents
- change state boundaries without consent of its residents
- impose taxes on goods and services exported and imported between state boundaries

States may not:

- enter into treaties with foreign governments
- print money
- tax imports or exports
- declare war

Therefore, while we often talk about three levels of government in the United States—national, state, and local—from the point of view of American federalism there are only two—national and state. Dependence upon state authority is often a source of frustration for mayors, school board members, and other local officials, who have sometimes argued for something more like a three-level federalist system. Local officials are not powerless, however. According to political scientist Daniel Elazar, "The largest metropolitan centers, the so-called 'big city bloc,' do possess the political power needed to go directly to Washington."[21]

As Angel Raich and Diane Monson pursued their claims through the American legal system, they did so against a politically murky background. The boundaries between states and nation were not clearly and definitively settled, and local governments—though not explicitly part of the federalist structure—might also act in the political space to protect their own interests.

1. The Constitution structures the relationship between the national government and the states in a section known as the federalism clause.

   a. True
   b. False

2. The necessary and proper clause _____.

   a. Preserves necessary powers at the state level
   b. Allows Congress to pass laws needed to carry out enumerated powers

   c. Has since been ruled unconstitutional
   d. Reserves unenumerated powers for the federal government

3. What are reserved powers?

   ....

   Answer Key: 1. b; 2. b; 3. Answers should address the Tenth Amendment and discuss the lack of enumeration of most state powers.

THE SUPREME COURT WEIGHS IN: MEDICAL MARIJUANA AND AMERICAN FEDERALISM

The United States Supreme Court decided to take up the case of Angel Raich and Diane Monson, weighing their rights against the authority of the federal government under the Controlled Substances Act and the commerce clause of the Constitution. The politics of this case proved to be as complicated as the constitutional issues that it called into question. For Supreme Court watchers and odds-makers, predicting how the Court would rule was not an easy call. Conservative justices were confronted with a state law that might run counter to their own opinions about substance use and personal behavior. However, they might also have misgivings about the federal government dictating public policy against the expressed wishes of voters in the states. For their part, the liberal justices might be more likely to support the Compassionate Use Act on policy grounds, but they might also be worried about nullifying federal law or restricting federal power in the face of state actions that contradicted national policy.

To Raich, the case was about maintaining access to a substance that kept her alive, not about its cultivation or sale. "Going to the Supreme Court makes it a final decision on whether I get to live or die," Raich said in November 2004, "I'm not trying to legalize marijuana. I'm simply trying to stay alive."[22] Reporting that she used cannabis about every two hours, Raich defended her use and the provision of the cannabis by two unnamed providers. She said, "Believe me, if I could take a pill I would. If I stop using cannabis, we know what would happen. I would die."[23]

In his skeptical questioning of the women's attorneys, Justice Antonin Scalia, a conservative, challenged their assertion that growing and distributing cannabis—even if it stayed within California's borders—would not contribute to the nationally problematic underground market in marijuana. Justice Stephen Breyer, considered one of the liberal members of the Court, suggested that a better course of action for medical cannabis advocates was to change federal law itself, as California had done with the Compassionate Use Act, rather than using a state referendum to challenge federal policy. "Medicine by regulation," Breyer said during oral arguments before the Court, "is better than medicine by referendum."[24]

In its decision in *Gonzales v. Raich* (2005), by a 6–3 vote the Court sided with the power of the federal government—and that of Congress under the commerce and supremacy clauses of the Constitution—and ruled against Raich and Monson. In explaining the logic of the Court's decision in his majority opinion, Justice John Paul Stevens hearkened back to the Great Depression and a case that involved the federal government's policies designed to lift the economy out of it.[25] The defendant in that case was Roscoe Filburn, an Ohio farmer raising dairy cattle and poultry, who happened also to cultivate a small crop of winter wheat, some of which he used to feed his livestock and some of which he used to feed his family. Under the regulations of Depression-fighting federal policies, Filburn was required to restrict his wheat acreage. Filburn, however, cultivated roughly double the allowed quota amount but, according to his testimony, only for use on his farm, not for sale.

Filburn argued that the federal government was exceeding its constitutional authority under the commerce clause since his activities were "local in character and their effects upon interstate commerce [were], at most, 'indirect.'"[26] The Supreme Court, in a unanimous decision in *Wickard v. Filburn* (1942), disagreed. The Court found that even though the products in question never left the farm or the state, the quotas were a constitutional use of Congress's power under the commerce clause. According to one scholar of American federalism, "With such a definition of interstate commerce, nothing was local."[27] The Court's decision in *Wickard*, Justice Stevens concluded, established "that Congress can regulate purely intrastate activity that is not itself 'commercial,' in that it is not produced for sale, if it concludes that failure to regulate that class of activity would undercut the regulation of the interstate market in that commodity."[28]

FIGURE 3.3

Marijuana Legalization Today

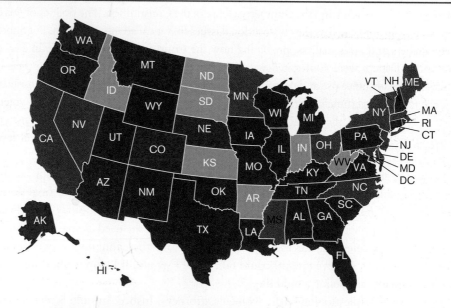

■ Personal posession and consumption of marijuana is legal for recreational and medicinal purposes

■ Marijuana use and/or posession has been decriminalized to some extent, and medicinal marijuana laws have been enacted

■ Medicinal marijuana laws have been enacted, with some states permitting only CBD versions of the drug

■ Marijuana use and/or posession has been decriminalized to some extent

■ No laws legalizing marijuana

Source: Map created with information from NORML.org, http://norml.org/. Accessed November 18, 2016.

Some recent changes to state laws are being phased in.

Justice Clarence Thomas on Federalism and Medical Marijuana

Clarence Thomas was appointed to the United States Supreme Court in 1991, nominated by Republican president George H. W. Bush to fill the seat that had been occupied by Thurgood Marshall, a strong advocate for civil rights. As a jurist, Thomas adopted a more textual, literal approach to constitutional interpretation than other justices; he was skeptical of Congress's powers if they were not explicitly granted in the Constitution. In his dissent on the medical marijuana case, Thomas objected to the majority's broad interpretation of federal power under the commerce clause:

> Respondents Diane Monson and Angel Raich use marijuana that has never been bought or sold, that has never crossed state lines, and that has no demonstrable effect on the national market for marijuana. If Congress can regulate this under the Commerce Clause, then it can regulate virtually anything—and the Federal Government is no longer one of limited and enumerated powers.
>
> By holding that Congress may regulate activity that is neither interstate nor commerce under the Interstate Commerce Clause, the Court abandons any attempt to enforce the Constitution's limits on federal power. . . . In the early days of the Republic, it would have been unthinkable that Congress could prohibit the local cultivation, possession, and consumption of marijuana. . . . Our federalist system, properly understood, allows California and a growing number of other States to decide for themselves how to safeguard the health and welfare of their citizens.[29]

Justice Clarence Thomas, a conservative Supreme Court justice, broke with majority opinion in *Gonzales v. Raich* to express skepticism of powers claimed by Congress but not expressly stated in the Constitution.
The Collection of the Supreme Court of the United States/MCT via Getty Images.

WHAT DO YOU THINK?

Thomas argued that the majority of justices overstepped the authority granted to the federal government under the commerce clause, as the marijuana that Raich and Monson used was not part of commerce "among the several States." On which side of the legal debate do you stand? Are there forms of economic activity that occur within a state that you think should not be subject to federal regulation?

If a product grown on a local farm for local consumption or marijuana grown at home for use in the home can be considered interstate commerce, then what *can't* be? In the debates over American federalism—in America and even between Supreme Court justices—defining the proper limits of the commerce clause remains a hotly contested issue.

By 2016 the landscape had changed. More than half of the states had passed laws allowing the use of marijuana for certain medical conditions, though these laws varied considerably both in terms of the medical conditions covered and in the restrictions placed upon its use. Others had decriminalized the possession of small amounts of marijuana, substituting civil fines for criminal penalties. In addition, eight states and the District of Columbia had legalized marijuana for recreational use. (See Figure 3.3.) Federal law, however had not changed, nor had the Supreme Court reversed its upholding of Congress's power to prohibit the growth, use, or possession of marijuana under the authority of the commerce clause.

President Barack Obama and the Justice Department were in a very difficult spot. Fully enforcing the Controlled Substances Act in the states had become impossible. In December 2015, in a federal suit brought by neighboring states against Colorado—one of the four states in which recreational use had been made legal—Obama's solicitor general argued in a brief presented to the Supreme Court that it should not decide to hear the case. To some observers, the administration's position, though based on specific legal grounds, implied a position "that marijuana should be federally legalized—even for recreational use."[30] The Justice Department, under the president's direction, however, retained authority to prosecute the CSA, though it was to focus on drug trafficking and not on prosecuting "individuals who were in 'unambiguous compliance with existing state laws.'"[31]

THE DEVELOPMENT OF AMERICAN FEDERALISM

Federalism is not one clean and unchanging concept, and there is no one set way to divide the people's sovereignty between levels of government. Defining the relative power of the two levels, as well as deciding how closely they will be intertwined, happens through the political process, and this has changed over the course of American history. In this section, we will look at different types of federalism and see how those relate to specific eras of American political history. We will begin with early attempts by the Supreme Court, under Chief Justice John Marshall, to carve out national power while also trying to not go too far, lest the individual states push back against what they might see as national overreach. Then we move to an era defined by a relative separation of political authority between the nation and the states. Following one of the gravest crises in American economic history, the policies of President Franklin D. Roosevelt led the country into a period in which the national government took on much more responsibility in policy areas traditionally handled by the states. Finally, we turn to the modern era of American federalism, defined by attempts to roll back some of the gains in national power or to assert more state authority, though without fundamentally altering the growth in national power during the twentieth century.

Early Attempts to Carve Out National Power: Three Decisions by the Marshall Court

The void left by the framers of the Constitution in precisely defining the boundaries of American federalism was quickly filled by the Supreme Court—a role that it continues to pursue actively today. Perhaps the most important figure in shaping American federalism after the ratification of the Constitution was John Marshall, chief justice of the Supreme Court from 1801 to 1835, and the longest-serving chief justice in American history.

During his tenure as chief justice, Marshall secured and issued several of the most important decisions in the area of American federalism. The first of these major decisions was in *McCulloch v. Maryland* (1819).[32] The case involved the Second Bank of the United States, a national bank chartered by Congress. Several states, including Maryland, passed laws to tax the state branches of the Second Bank for various reasons, such as to try to kill the branches, to defend their own state's banks, or just to raise money. The case centered on two questions: Did Congress have the authority to establish the bank in the first place? And did individual states have the authority to tax the bank's branches operating within their borders? Marshall, speaking for a unanimous Supreme Court, came down firmly on the side of the authority of the national government in both questions. Citing the necessary and proper clause of the Constitution, Marshall affirmed the right of Congress to establish the bank and denied the right of Maryland and other states to tax the bank's state branches.

In *Gibbons v. Ogden* (1824), the Marshall Court weighed in on the powers of Congress under the commerce clause of the Constitution.[33] As with the *McCulloch* decision, in *Gibbons* the Court affirmed national power, defining that power "as if it were vested in a single government rather than in a federal one."[34] Known as the "steamboat monopoly case," *Gibbons v. Ogden* arose from a battle between two powerful businessmen in the steamboat industry in New York and New Jersey. Aaron Ogden had been granted a monopoly by a New York state law that protected his routes within New York and between New York and New Jersey. Thomas Gibbons filed suit to block the monopoly.

Marshall's decision in the case reaffirmed national power but on a different constitutional principle. While *McCulloch* involved the necessary and proper clause, *Gibbons* focused on the power of Congress to regulate trade "among the several States" as part of its authority under the commerce clause. Marshall also cited the power of the national government under the supremacy clause of the Constitution. Marshall and the Court, again unanimously, struck down the steamboat monopoly between the two states and the part of the New York law that had made the monopoly possible. In doing so, Marshall affirmed the exclusive authority of Congress to regulate interstate commerce, defining commerce "among the several States" as including "the deep streams which penetrate our country in every direction [and] pass through the interior of almost every state in the Union."[35]

The third major federalism case decided by the Marshall Court was *Barron v. Baltimore* (1833).[36] *Barron* dealt with yet another part of the Constitution, in this case the portion of the Fifth Amendment's protections

Chief Justice John Marshall's decisions are widely held to be among the most important for shaping the powers and limits of federalism even today.

The Granger Collection, New York.

called the due process clause, which states. "No person shall . . . be deprived of life, liberty, or property, without due process of law; nor shall private property be taken for public use, without just compensation." John Barron, the owner of a wharf in Baltimore, sued the city for the cost to his business caused by sand that had accumulated in the waters off his wharf as a result of the city's development policies, thus depriving him of property without "just compensation." The Marshall Court issued another unanimous decision; however, in this case, it limited rather than expanded the power of the national government. The court ruled that the Fifth Amendment's protections were aimed exclusively at restraining the power of the national government and were not intended to apply to the states.[37]

The Marshall Court affirmed national power, especially in relation to the necessary and proper clause and the commerce clause. However, Marshall handed down his decisions with an eye toward public opinion and tempered the expansion of national authority with an acknowledgement of state authority.

Lurking in the background during this time were the interconnected and unresolved problems of slavery, states' rights, and American federalism. The delegates to the Constitutional Convention had given in to the demands of the slave states to preserve their institution, in spite of the fact that slavery violated the essential principles of natural rights upon which the Constitution was based. In the nineteenth century, as the American Republic expanded to fill the continent, the question of slavery and its implications for the relationship between the nation and the states could no longer be ignored.

The Era of Dual Federalism: Divided Powers in the Nineteenth Century

dual federalism
a view of American federalism in which the states and the nation operate independently in their own areas of public policy.

For much of the history of the American Republic the model of the relationship between states and nation was one of **dual federalism**, which divided the people's sovereignty between the nation and the states—they were coequals in power, each able to check the power and the growth of power of the other. Dual federalism presumes a distinct, though not complete, separation between the two levels of authority, as if both operate side by side with relatively little interaction between the two. Dual federalism, according to an observer of American government in 1888, "is like a great factory wherein two sets of machinery are at work, their revolving wheels apparently intermixed, their bands crossing one another, yet each set doing its own work without touching or hampering the other."[38] (See Figure 3.4.)

The Supreme Court articulated a similar image of two separate systems in the nineteenth century: "The government of the United States and the government of a state are distinct and independent of each other within their respective spheres of action, although existing and exercising their powers within the same territorial limits. Neither government can intrude within the jurisdiction, or authorize any interference therein by its judicial officers with the action of the other."[39] In fact, however, the division of authority between states and nation has never been this clean and neat. Even in areas of public policy that have been traditionally handled by the states, such as education, the federal government has been involved.[40] Driving much of the politics in the first half of the nineteenth century and heightening tensions between the states and the national government was the institution of slavery and the fears of southerners that it might be restricted or banned outright.

The Era of States' Rights: The Civil War and Reconstruction

The expansion of national power under the Marshall Court did not mean that this new balance of power would be permanent or go unchallenged. Efforts to assert the authority of states continued during the middle decades of the nineteenth century. As the original Federalist justices retired or passed away, many of their replacements held a stronger view of state authority. Increasingly, the question of federalism also became linked with the issues of slavery, **states' rights**, and the threat of secession. In the 1830s, South Carolina senator John Calhoun argued for the right of states to "nullify" federal laws that were in conflict with those of the states.

In December 1860, South Carolina seceded from the nation. Within six months, eleven southern states had followed to form the Confederate States of America. When the American Civil War finally ended in 1865, more than six hundred thousand soldiers had died, and an unknown number of civilians had been killed.

The Civil War and the process of reconstruction had settled the issues of secession and of legalized slavery; however, the question of how forcefully the national government would act to preserve the civil rights (the personal rights guaranteed to citizens or residents) of former slaves and their descendants was far from decided. As the government of the United States began to turn its attention to the expansion of the nation's empire toward the Pacific Ocean, the rights of African Americans received less and less consideration and protection.

states' rights
the idea that American states have the authority to self-govern, even when in conflict with national laws.

Dual Federalism and the Restriction of African Americans' Rights: The Supreme Court and Civil Rights after the Civil War

Following the Civil War, the Supreme Court did not emerge as a defender of African American civil rights, a move that would have provided uniform protection for African Americans at the national level. Instead, it affirmed a vision of federalism that recognized state authority, even if that authority was used to restrict the rights of state citizens based only on their racial identity.

In the *Slaughterhouse Cases* (1873), the Supreme Court weighed in for the first time on the protections offered by the Fourteenth Amendment.[41] Like *Gibbons v. Ogden*, these cases involved a monopoly, this time of the slaughter of animals under a Louisiana state law. Butchers had challenged the monopoly as a violation of their rights under the Fourteenth Amendment. Ruling against the butchers, a closely divided Supreme Court drew a sharp distinction between the rights guaranteed under state and national citizenship.

Narrowly interpreting the equal protection clause of the Fourteenth Amendment to restrict discrimination only against African Americans (the butchers were white), the Court also placed limits on the privileges and immunities clause of the same amendment, stating that its protections apply only to national, not state, citizenship. In doing so, the Court upheld the authority of states to exercise their police powers.[42]

Plessy v. Ferguson (1896) was another landmark case in restricting the rights of African Americans following the Civil War and asserting states' rights.

African American school children at a segregated school in 1896 following the "separate but equal" ruling in *Plessy v. Ferguson*.

Afro American Newspapers/ Gado/Getty Images.

FIGURE 3.4

Dual Federalism

The state and federal levels of government operated under an arrangement of dual federalism for much of the history of the American republic. In this model, federal and state government have distinct powers and function independently of one another, addressing their own areas of policy.

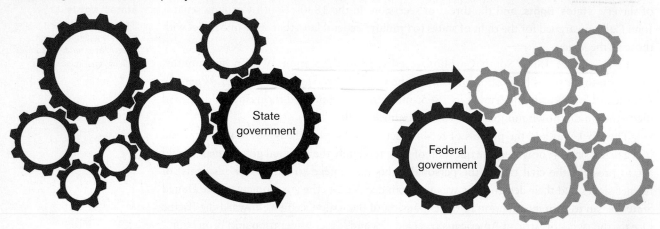

In this case, the Supreme Court upheld the constitutionality of legalized racial segregation (the separation of individuals based on their racial identity) and the ability of states to pass such laws.[43] *Plessy* was a test case, organized by the African American community in New Orleans to challenge Louisiana's segregation laws. Homer Plessy, "a light-skinned man who described himself as 'seven-eighths Caucasian,'" had been arrested and fined for violating a state law requiring separate railroad facilities for whites and African Americans.[44]

In the decision in *Plessy*, Justice Henry Billings Brown declared that Louisiana's law did not violate the Fourteenth Amendment. Arguing that "[s]ocial prejudices cannot be overcome by legislation," Brown upheld Plessy's conviction and declared that "separate but equal" did not violate the Constitution. Justice John Marshall Harlan, the lone dissenter on the Court, countered, "Our Constitution is color-blind, and neither knows nor tolerates classes among citizens. In respect of civil rights, all citizens are equal before the law." Harlan, correctly, as it would turn out, saw *Plessy* as a dangerous and damaging ruling. Brown's majority opinion, however, set policy. The ruling that racial segregation could be constitutionally permissible endured for almost sixty years. We will explore the efforts—first in the states, later in the Supreme Court—of individuals to overturn this doctrine in detail in Chapter 5.

The Era of Big Business and Commerce:
Federalism in the Age of Industry and National Expansion

During the latter part of the nineteenth century and the early decades of the twentieth, the Supreme Court adopted a complex role toward the growing economy. On the one hand, important decisions during this time restricted the power of state and local governments to regulate businesses. On the other hand, however, the Supreme Court pursued a general philosophy of letting American businesses pursue their interests without regulation by the national or state governments.

FIGURE 3.5

Cooperative Federalism

Beginning in the late 19th century and extending into the early 20th, state and federal governments forged a relationship of cooperative federalism in which they worked together to shape public policy. Notice that in cooperative federalism the gears are more closely interlinked, while they work more separately in the dual federalism system.

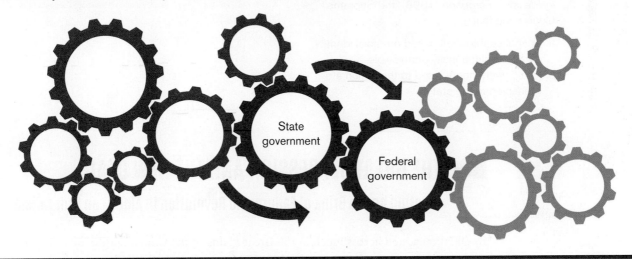

In many cases, states were happy to have the federal government take more of a leading role in regulating increasingly large and powerful corporations. As American corporations grew in size and power, states began to realize that they could not, on their own, "mobilize sufficient power to regulate wealthy railroads that could cut them off from the rest of the country in retaliation [for regulations], or deal with great industrial combines that could pull up and go elsewhere."[45]

Confronting the challenges and opportunities of economic growth together, states and the nation began to forge what is called **cooperative federalism**, in which both levels work together in the same areas of public policy. Under this type of federalism, the two levels do not generally play the same roles. Instead, the national government tends to be "responsible for raising revenues and setting standards," while state and local governments remain "primarily responsible for administering the programs."[46] (See Figure 3.5.)

While both national and state governments began to build the foundations for cooperative federalism in the late nineteenth century, the dominant theme was one of not interfering with American business and the economy, at either the national or state level. Under this approach, government took little action to regulate or restrain private economic activity, even if it resulted in serious inequalities. In decisions that restricted the ability of the national government to regulate economic activity, the Supreme Court supported the philosophy of noninterference in the economy.[47]

While some of the seeds of the later growth in national power were planted during the era of big business, it would take a massive economic crisis, the inability of state governments to cope with the crisis, and the response of the national government to the crisis's challenges to fully realize this growth. To fully understand how major these changes would be, we need to understand the crisis itself: the Great Depression.

cooperative federalism
a vision of American federalism in which the states and the national government work together to shape public policy.

1. Dual federalism is so-named because it refers to the fact that both the House of Representatives and the Senate work to shape it.

   a. True
   b. False

2. In *Plessy v. Ferguson* (1896), the Supreme Court ruled that _____.

   a. Legal segregation based on racial identity was constitutionally permissible
   b. All powers not granted to the nation are reserved to the states

   c. The federal government had the authority to forbid racial segregation
   d. Railroad corporations should be free to pursue westward expansion

3. What is cooperative federalism?

....

Answer Key: 1. b; 2. a.; 3. Answers should discuss the sharing of power between states and the nation.

THE GREAT DEPRESSION AND THE NEW DEAL
A Nation on the Brink of Failure and Revolution in American Federalism

In Oklahoma, and across much of the Great Plains of the United States, the rain stopped. For nearly the entire decade of the 1930s, America's agricultural heartland experienced the worst drought in its history. Though actually a series of several drought episodes, to the farmers of more than half of the nation it seemed like one long, unending nightmare.[48]

In the place of rain came dust. In the place of abundance came crisis. The 1920s had been good to the farmers of the Great Plains. Plentiful rains had enticed many farmers to move onto and plow lands that their parents and grandparents had left untilled because they were too dry, too risky. When the droughts came, the newly plowed topsoil turned into dust, swept up into great dust storms that turned day into night, seeped through cracks in and around windows and doors.

In the boom times of the 1920s it had rained more than water. It had also rained money. Cheap and easy credit, the ability to borrow money to buy farmland or homes, to speculate in stocks and bonds, or to invest in businesses, flowed throughout the American economy. In the 1930s, the easy money dried up along with the land, but the debts taken on during the boom times remained. The decade was a period of prolonged deflation during which money became scarce, loans were hard to come by or pay back, and prices fell. Economic problems in Europe only made things worse for American farmers, who saw the prices they could get for whatever crops they could coax out of the parched soil fall by more than 60 percent between 1929 and 1933. The country could still grow food, but many Americans could not afford to buy it: "In the Great Plains, bread lines snaked past grain elevators bulging with wheat."[49]

Faced with the simultaneous disasters of drought, falling prices, and unpayable debts, millions of famers faced foreclosure as banks repossessed their farms to pay off the debts taken on to purchase land or supplies. The collapse in farm prices was especially hard on tenant farmers, large numbers of whom were members of racial and ethnic minorities and whose for-hire labor was no longer needed.

In one of the largest migrations in American history, millions of displaced farmers and their families left what would become known

A young Oklahoma mother stranded in California's Imperial Valley in 1937. She and her family were among the millions displaced during the Dust Bowl era and ensuing Great Depression. Those events precipitated major structural changes in the federalist system under President Franklin D. Roosevelt.

Courtesy of the Library of Congress, Prints and Photographs Division.

as the Dust Bowl. Many of them headed for the West Coast in search of whatever work that they could find. Waves of hungry, poor, and desperate "Oakies" and "Arkies" loaded up their families and their vehicles, hoping they would make it to California. But not all farmers migrated; some organized, and a few threatened violence. In the Midwest, they formed the Farmers' Holiday movement to protest the foreclosures on their farms and threatened to stop producing crops if necessary. In Nebraska, Holiday movement leaders threatened, "'If we don't get beneficial service from this [state] legislature, 200,000 of us are coming to Lincoln and we'll tear that new State Capitol Building to pieces.'"[50] In January 1933, the head of the nation's Farm Bureau Federation testified before the Senate, claiming, "Unless something is done for the American farmer we will have revolution in the countryside within less than twelve months." It was a national crisis, a threat as serious to the American Republic as any in its history. According to biographer Jean Edward Smith, "In a scene reminiscent of Shays' Rebellion in 1787, U.S. District Court Judge Charles C. Bradley was dragged from the bench in Le Mars, Iowa, by angry farmers, beaten, thrown into a truck, and driven out of town, where he was nearly lynched [hung] for refusing to suspend mortgage foreclosures."[51]

What came to be known as the **Great Depression** was the most significant economic crisis in the nation's history. It went far beyond America's farmers and its agricultural industry. While sunk in its depths, many wondered if the American Republic would even survive, or if the federal government had the power to keep the people free and stave off revolution.

During the Depression, things were no better in the cities than they were in the plains. In October 1929, America's stock market crashed. Though the country's economic growth had actually peaked months earlier, the collapse of the stock market was a very visible signal of an industrial economy grinding to a halt. The same easy credit that had allowed speculation on farmland had also turbocharged the prices of stocks. When the prices of these investments fell, banks and brokerages that had loaned money to investors called in those loans. Indebted investors, desperate to sell their stocks to pay off the loans at any price, contributed to the vicious cycle of collapsing prices in the stock market.

The Great Depression
a period defined by the most significant economic crisis in American history.

The nation's banking system was frozen, on the verge of permanent failure. Banks across the country locked their doors to keep out lines of depositors as they did not have enough money to redeem accounts. By the end of 1932, more than nine million savings accounts were gone. Industrial production also collapsed, idling workers who produced industrial products or the energy sources to power American factories. Firms laid off employees and cut wages for those they kept on the payrolls. The wave of foreclosures swept through cities, driving families into homelessness and hunger, evicted by the banks or their landlords. The Depression was especially hard on the most vulnerable members of the American economy: children, women, and members of racial and ethnic minorities.

> Faced with challenges that they could not meet and citizens whose needs they could not assist, state and local governments appealed to Washington for help. There they hoped to find a new president willing to listen.

During the boom times of the 1920s, states had increased their spending, especially to expand the highways for the nation's growing fleet of automobiles. To do so, states had borrowed large amounts of money. When the economic crisis took hold, many state governments themselves faced shortfalls and were unable to respond to the demands of their residents for action. Local governments were similarly overwhelmed, unable to care for millions of unemployed workers or deal with the increasing homelessness, hunger, desperation, and anger. Faced with challenges that they could not meet and citizens whose needs they could not assist, state and local governments appealed to Washington for help. There they hoped

Franklin Delano Roosevelt's inaugural address, March 4, 1933. In the address, President Roosevelt asserted, "This great Nation will endure as it has endured, will revive and will prosper. So, first of all, let me assert my firm belief that the only thing we have to fear is fear itself—nameless, unreasoning, unjustified terror which paralyzes needed efforts to convert retreat into advance."

Franklin D. Roosevelt Presidential Library & Museum.

to find a new president willing to listen. In 1932 the governor of Oregon appealed to then president Herbert Hoover, saying, "We must have help from the federal government if we are to avert suffering . . . and possible uprisings."[52]

President Franklin Delano Roosevelt's Revolution

The weather in Washington, D.C., on Saturday, March 4, 1933, was as gloomy as the national mood, reflecting a feeling of mounting fear and panic in the country. Unable to walk on his own because of a polio infection earlier in his life, "Franklin [Delano] Roosevelt, braced on the arm of his eldest son, James, began his laborious walk to the rostrum, 146 feet away" to be inaugurated as America's thirty-second president.[53] Roosevelt placed his hand on an ancient family bible and was sworn in by Charles Evans Hughes, the chief justice of the Supreme Court. In the years that followed that day in March, Hughes and the Supreme Court battled the new president, his revolution, and his view of a very different role for the national government in the country's economic life.

Roosevelt's inaugural address lasted perhaps fifteen minutes but conveyed to a worried nation the same sense of calm confidence that he had shown after an attempt on his life a month earlier. Although the new president used his words to reassure the American public, he also made it clear that he was prepared to bring the full power of the executive branch to bear on the Great Depression: "But in the event that Congress shall fail to take [proper action] . . . I shall ask Congress for the one remaining instrument to meet the crisis—broad Executive power to wage a war against the emergency, as great as the power that would be given to me if we were in fact invaded by a foreign foe."[54]

Roosevelt meant what he said, and he would back up those promises and threats as one of the most powerful presidents in United States history and the only to serve more than two terms. Although during Roosevelt's twelve years in office only one amendment to the Constitution was ratified—a repeal of the Eighteenth Amendment's prohibition of alcoholic beverages[55]—to some scholars of constitutional history, his presidency was as revolutionary as if the Constitution had been heavily amended or even rewritten.[56]

What Roosevelt's policies changed above all else was the character of American federalism. That Roosevelt's revolution in American federalism happened during a time of economic crisis is no coincidence. Major changes in American federalism have often been brought about by changes in the nation's economic life.

The "Hundred Days" and the New Deal

Crises have certainly played a role in the development of American federalism. But so has the handling of those crises and challenges by strategic political actors. Within his first few months in office, Roosevelt secured the passage of fifteen major laws covering large areas of the nation's economy. Called the "Hundred Days," this period in Roosevelt's administration resulted in the creation of a host of agencies, thousands of pages of regulations and rules, and a new, stronger role for the national government. It was part of **the New Deal**, Roosevelt's plan for tackling the Great Depression.

The New Deal
a set of policies passed during the administration of President Franklin Roosevelt in order to combat the Great Depression.

Roosevelt was able to use his uncanny sensibilities as a strategic political actor to exert a powerful influence on the country in a short amount of time. Understanding well the sense of helplessness among the state governments, Roosevelt knew they simply did not have the resources on their own to handle the massive poverty, homelessness, and unemployment they faced. State governments were in no position to refuse the massive amount of federal aid that Roosevelt offered, even if accepting the aid meant trading away state authority. Scholars and historians continue to debate the degree to which Roosevelt's policies rescued America from the depths of the Great Depression. However, one fact that is not debated is that his policies fundamentally changed the relationship between the states and the national government; they dramatically strengthened the role of the national government in the economy. In terms of American federalism, it was a true revolution.

Roosevelt's first priority was the nation's crumbling banking system.[57] He officially closed the country's banks, calling it a "banking holiday" in his typically optimistic language. He also introduced a series of bills to regulate the nation's economy and create a set of federal organizations to carry out and enforce these policies.[58] The Hundred Days also saw action to address the problems facing American farmers and the growing discontent brought about by their desperation. The Agricultural Adjustment Act (AAA) paid farmers to reduce production of a host of agricultural products in an attempt to support prices for these commodities.[59] Paid for by taxes on processors of the raw commodities, the AAA was a radical expansion of the role of the national government in farming. For his part, "Roosevelt saw the farm program as the centerpiece of the New Deal."[60]

In 1933 more than six million pigs were slaughtered as part of the AAA—this at a time when many Americans were struggling to feed their families. In response to these concerns, the federal government began a program to distribute surplus agricultural products to Americans. By reducing farm output, the AAA also reduced the need for workers to harvest these products, an outcome that hurt the migrant and tenant farm laborers. As one historian noted, "The program was especially hard on African-Americans, who formed a large proportion of the landless farmers in the South and [who] had less political leverage than their white counterparts."[61] In addition to trying to support farm prices, the New Deal also included legislation to help farmers who had fallen behind on their mortgage payments.[62]

The Civilian Conservation Corps (CCC), which became one of the New Deal's most popular programs, focused on hiring young men to work on national

A political cartoon highlighting the "remedies" that President Roosevelt and Congress introduced to combat the Great Depression. Uncle Sam is seated next to the medicines, which are depicted by the acronyms of the laws and federal agencies.
MPI/Getty Images.

FDR's Blue Eagle

In 1933 President Roosevelt launched a national campaign to increase support for the National Recovery Administration. Business owners were encouraged to show support for the administration's policies by placing Blue Eagle posters in their storefronts and places of employment. Owners, employees, and even customers were encouraged to wear Blue Eagle pins to show their support.

The image shows the eagle holding a gear in its right talon, symbolizing industry, and a lightning bolt in its left talon, symbolizing power.

WHAT DO YOU THINK?

In its refutation of the NRA, the Supreme Court held that Roosevelt's administration had overstepped its constitutional authority. Do you think that the administration's enlistment of businesses to promote its policies represented too much federal involvement with business? Can you think of any modern examples of the

Franklin D. Roosevelt Presidential Library & Museum.

federal government trying to enlist private support for its policies through images?

---

improvement projects, "planting trees, thinning saplings, cutting firebreaks, building bridges, digging reservoirs."[63] The CCC, though popular, was not particularly beneficial to the economic conditions of African American men. While allowed to participate in the CCC's projects, they were generally allowed to do so "only in segregated units and often with lower pay scales" than white workers.[64]

One of the most important, and controversial, results of the Hundred Days was the National Industrial Recovery Act (NIRA). Its purpose was to "drive prices up and put people back to work."[65] To do so, the act created an administrative agency, the National Recovery Administration (NRA), which became involved in regulating the American economy in ways few would have thought possible before the economic crisis hit. The primary tool of the NRA was a code (or set of rules) created by the NIRA governing prices, outputs, wages, working hours and conditions, management-labor relations, and the employment of children that American businesses pledged to follow.

The code was detailed. It "determined the precise components of macaroni; [it] determined what tailors could and could not sew. In the poultry industry the relevant line of code had banned customers from picking their own chickens."[66] The NRA used social pressure as one of the tools used to enforce the code. Its symbol was the Blue Eagle, "a clear invocation of war; it would inspire the economy to march."[67] Business owners who were in compliance with the NRA's code could display a poster of the Blue Eagle in their window. Those who fell out of compliance had to take it down. The purchasers of a bankrupt Philadelphia professional football team renamed their organization in honor of Roosevelt's NRA, calling the new team the Eagles.

From its beginnings, the NIRA was controversial. The implementation of the code created political opposition both from business owners who were frustrated by their inability to raise prices and by workers and labor leaders who felt that the law's protections for workers' rights did not go far enough.[68] The complexity of the code also entangled government in the smallest of details of businesses, about which individual code inspectors often had little or no knowledge. Roosevelt was himself said to be nervous about wading so forcefully into workers' rights, but he later became more enthusiastic "in part because it strengthened workers' loyalty to the New Deal and the Democratic Party."[69]

As the nation sank into the depths of the Great Depression, many Americans wondered if there would be revolution. As it turns out, there was, but with legislation, not with arms. Most fundamentally, the revolution involved redefining American federalism, and it was led by Roosevelt.

NEW DEAL EXPANSION

In 1934 Martin Schechter and his three brothers, operators of two kosher Jewish butcheries in New York, found themselves the target of federal government regulators. The Schechter brothers, immigrants to the United States, conducted their Brooklyn butchery operations according to the Laws of Kashrut, which "involves both how humans are to treat animals they kill (humanely, as kosher butchers must follow specific rules about how animals are killed) as well as how they must treat their customers. For observant Jews such as the Schechter's, the Laws of Kashrut were both a matter of religious observance and good business."[70]

One of the practices in which the Schechter brothers engaged was ensuring that their slaughtered chickens were "glatt kosher," meaning that the lungs of the carcasses were smooth and, therefore, free of tuberculosis, a very serious health issue in America at the time. As part of their observance of kosher practices, the Schechter brothers allowed customers to select and inspect poultry prior to sale. These practices, which the Schechter brothers had been employing for years and which had earned them a loyal customer base, placed the Schechter brothers at odds with the administration of President Franklin Delano Roosevelt.[71]

The brothers were charged with violating the NIRA federal code, including one charge that centered on the sale of "unfit chickens" not suitable for human consumption. As it turned out, only one inspected chicken from their butcheries turned out to be unfit: "It was an 'egg-bound' chicken—eggs—upon its slaughter, were discovered to have been lodged inside it, something that would have been hard for the Schechter's to detect

CONNECTING TO . . .

The Supreme Court's Challenge to President Roosevelt's Revolution

As you engage with the story of the Schechter brothers and their Supreme Court case, reflect upon the ways Roosevelt's Depression-fighting policies fundamentally transformed American federalism. Consider the following:

- The degree to which the New Deal involved the federal government in the details of business practices

- The political battles between the president and the Supreme Court during the early years of the New Deal

- The ways in which New Deal policies may not have been fully inclusive of Americans with diverse lived experiences and how the battles between the president and Court spoke to this

The Schechter brothers celebrate with their attorney, Joseph Heller, center, in his law offices in New York on May 27, 1935, upon learning of the Supreme Court's ruling in their favor in the case of *Schechter Poultry Corp. v. United States*. In this case, the National Industrial Recovery Act was determined to be unconstitutional.

The Granger Collection, New York.

before sale. That they had knowingly planned to sell an unfit chicken was hard to prove."[72]

None of that mattered, at least according to federal law and the power of the federal government introduced to respond to the nation's economic crisis. All four brothers were indicted for violating the new laws, and all four were convicted and imprisoned. Instead of backing down, however, the Schechter brothers sued, and their case made it all the way to the Supreme Court. Their case, *Schechter Poultry Corp. v. U.S.* (1935), shook the foundations of Roosevelt's plan to fight the Great Depression. Though the Schechters probably could not have imagined it, their seemingly unimportant case surrounding the butchery of chickens would play a major role in defining a nation's future and the ways in which power was divided between the states and the nation.

The policy at the center of the battle was the code that the NIRA created and that the NRA was tasked to implement. To the Schechter brothers, the code may have initially seemed to be a distant federal regulation, their only human connection to it being the inspectors, none of whom knew much, if anything, about poultry. Some of the federal inspectors, one of the brothers later recalled, were willing to learn the details of the brothers' craft. Others, not so much. One witness to the initial confrontation between the Schechter brothers and the code inspectors reported that the inspector said, "I am the Code Authority, and I got a right to do anything I want."[73] The power of the NRA, its code inspectors, and the federal government was strong and relentless.

To the brothers, "the NRA code did not make sense."[74] The code required them to change their business practices in such a way as to endanger their relationships with their customers and to violate their own codes of slaughter and sale. Their lawyers began to formulate a counterattack that was premised on the idea that the federal government overstepped its powers in granting Congress and the president authority over commerce that neither had possessed under the Constitution. The Schechter brothers were fined $7,425—a very large amount of money at the time—and each was sentenced to jail for one to three months. They appealed.

By the time the Schechter brothers' case made it to the Supreme Court, even members of Roosevelt's administration had begun to realize that the regulation of the slaughter and sale of chickens was an endeavor that could only produce political opposition without any larger political benefit. The "top-down culture of the NRA" began to take political fire,[75] and even the mainstream political establishment began to turn against it.

So did the Supreme Court.[76] In the early years of the New Deal, the Supreme Court was in no mood to allow the new president to expand federal authority in such an unprecedented way. In its opinion in *Schechter Poultry Corp. v. United States* (1935), in what would become known as the "sick chicken case," the Supreme Court struck at the heart of Roosevelt's New Deal, arguing that his administration's policies had gone far beyond the authority granted by the Constitution and especially by the commerce clause. How, a majority of justices asked critically, could the butchery of chickens in New York City be considered "Commerce . . . among the several States?"

On May 2, 1935, lawyers for both sides presented their arguments before the justices of the Supreme Court. Joseph Heller, the chief litigator on behalf of the Schechter brothers, challenged the fundamental authority of the federal government to regulate his clients' business practices. Front and center was the commerce clause. How far did Congress's power extend to "regulate Commerce . . . among the several States?" More pointedly, how much power did a president with firm partisan control over the legislative branch have to regulate the business activity of American businesses and entrepreneurs?

In his arguments before the Supreme Court, Heller argued that the federal government had exceeded its delegated, or implied, powers, specifically in its expansion of the commerce clause. In its regulation of the slaughter and sale of chickens in Brooklyn, the federal government, Heller asserted, had gone far beyond any reasonable interpretation of the word *among*. Almost all of the chickens, he argued, had been purchased in New York, processed in New York, and sold in New York. Since no state boundary was crossed, the commerce clause could not have been violated. "The whole Code must fall," Heller declared.[77]

Lawyers for the government argued that "extraordinary conditions may call for extraordinary remedies."[78] Many of the lawyers and policy advisors to Roosevelt saw the crisis as an opportunity, offering, perhaps, "a good chance of ramming the case through and vindicating the New Deal."[79] Some pro-Roosevelt columnists in the media tried to play on anti-Jewish sentiment within the nation. One offered an account of the case under the title "Joseph and His Brethren"; the article described a situation in which "the Kosher butchers of the city work in filth, blood and chicken feathers, they operated jointly a prosperous pair of smelly chicken companies."[80]

Roosevelt no doubt knew that the justices of the Supreme Court would be looking very carefully at his radical policies—Republican presidents had appointed most of the justices. For decades the Court had tended to uphold the idea of freedom of contract, which viewed the relationships between employees and employers as private matters not subject to governmental interference. Public opinion had been on the justices' side as well. In his work on the Court, Robert Mayer noted that "the Americans in the 1920's viewed the function of their government as an essentially negative one. The Constitution and the governmental agencies existed only to ensure that laissez-faire economics would work smoothly."[81]

> The Supreme Court overturned the convictions of the Schechter brothers and, by implication, the National Industrial Recovery Act and perhaps the entire New Deal.

In 1935 the Supreme Court returned its decision on *Schechter Poultry Corp v. United States*, striking a potentially fatal blow to Roosevelt's entire New Deal project and to the power of the executive and legislative branches to push the boundaries of American federalism to its constitutional limits in the war against the Depression.[82] In a unanimous opinion, Chief Justice Charles Evans Hughes—the man who had sworn in Roosevelt as president in 1933—sided with the Schechter brothers. In enacting and enforcing the code, Hughes argued, the NRA had exceeded its constitutional authority: "When the poultry had reached the defendants' slaughterhouses, the interstate commerce had ended."[83]

In setting out the "codes of fair competition," Hughes wrote in his opinion, the actions of Congress and the Roosevelt administration consisted of "assertions of extra constitutional authority," an overreach that Hughes argued "[was] anticipated and precluded by the explicit terms of the Tenth Amendment" to the Constitution, which states that "the powers not delegated to the United States by the Constitution, nor prohibited to it by the States, are reserved to the States respective, or to the people." Expanding on the logic of a prior case, the *Panama Refining* decision, the Hughes Court also rejected the power of the president to formulate the code as an "unconstitutional delegation of legislative power."[84]

On both of these counts—exceeding the delegated power of the commerce clause and the excessive delegation of power to the president by Congress to formulate and enforce the code—the Supreme Court overturned the convictions of the Schechter brothers and, by implication, the National Industrial Recovery Act and perhaps the entire New Deal.

Dismissing arguments that the nation's extraordinary economic crisis called for extraordinary measures, Hughes reaffirmed case precedent that in drafting the NIRA, Congress had granted the executive branch unconstitutional authority. In *Schechter*, however, Hughes went farther, finding that "the authority of the federal government may not be pushed to such an extreme as to destroy the distinction, which the commerce clause itself establishes, between commerce 'among the Several' states' and the internal concerns of a State."[85] The code-making and enforcing authority of the NRA, the Court found, violated the commerce clause and was therefore invalid. Without such authority, the NIRA was powerless.

Some members of Roosevelt's administration were quietly relieved at the Court's decision, as "live poultry was precisely the sort of petty trade which NRA officials now generally wished they had never gotten into."[86] Others were "furious at decisions that seemed to deny the country's elected officials the right to govern. Not since *Dred Scott* had judicial review been in such disrepute."[87] To Frances Perkins, Roosevelt's secretary of labor, the first women to serve as a cabinet head in American history, the president was reported to have remarked, "You know the whole thing has been a mess."[88] Roosevelt was, according to some observers, "relieved [that] the Court bailed him out of a program that was increasingly unpopular."[89] It was, however, a stunning blow: "The case did indeed mean death for the NRA."[90] Justice Hughes was far from done, and "between 1933 and 1936, the Court overturned acts of Congress at ten times the traditional rate," actions that "created an atmosphere of crisis in Washington."[91]

Roosevelt Strikes Back

The challenge to the president's authority would not go unanswered, however. In the months surrounding the Supreme Court's invalidation of the core of his New Deal, Roosevelt pushed ahead with his legislative agenda, called the Second New Deal. This period in Roosevelt's presidency saw passage of some of the most important New Deal programs.

The Social Security Act of 1935 created a set of programs to support vulnerable groups of Americans. It established unemployment insurance for American workers. It set up old age insurance and old age assistance programs, which were later supplemented with disability insurance. In addition, it established Aid to Dependent Children.[92] These programs were designed to be self-funding so as not to force the government to raise taxes and further depress the economy.

Passing more laws was not Roosevelt's only response to the Supreme Court's challenge to his power. Roosevelt was as popular as ever. The election of 1936 had handed him a victory even more impressive than that of the election of 1932. Roosevelt won forty-six of the forty-eight states and secured 523 of 531 Electoral College votes.

Speaking at his inauguration on January 20, 1937, in weather just as gloomy as it had been four years earlier, the president was defiant. Though he did not mention the Supreme Court in his inaugural address, he promised to challenge his opponents, stating, "I should like it to be said of my second Administration that in it these forces have met their match."[93] Roosevelt rejected his advisors' suggestions that he try to amend the Constitution to expand the authority of Congress and the national government in regulating the economy, arguing that it would take too long and would be too easy to defeat. "Give me ten million dollars," he said, "and I can prevent any amendment to the Constitution from being ratified by the necessary number of states."[94]

Instead, in a move that alarmed even his closest advisors, Roosevelt decided to take on the Supreme Court directly—"his most implacable opponent, which he saw as the biggest impediment to social and economic progress in America."[95] The president sought to use Congress's constitutional authority to increase the number of justices on the Court from nine to as many as fifteen, thus allowing him to appoint enough pro-New Deal justices to tip the balance of power decisively in his favor. Known as the "court-packing plan," Roosevelt's gambit was constitutional but very bold and very risky. He kept his plan a secret even from his own advisors "until the last possible moment."[96]

In the end, Roosevelt's bill died in the Democratic Congress, "humiliating the president in the process."[97] It divided his own party, driving many conservative Democrats to side with Republicans in Congress, especially over issues of civil rights for African Americans. Most of the justices remained publicly quiet about Roosevelt's proposals. Others, however, were not so polite. Justice James McReynolds vowed "never [to] retire as long as that crippled son-of-a-bitch is in the White house."[98] Roosevelt eventually nominated replacements for most of the justices but only because his unprecedented four terms in office allowed him to outlast the tenure of most of them.

In the end, the Court did change its opinions, reversing in several key rulings its previous opposition to the constitutionality of Roosevelt's New Deal and similar state measures to regulate businesses and the economy. The New Deal survived, and it fundamentally altered the boundaries between the activities of the federal government and those of the states.

A poster from 1935 informing Americans aged sixty-five and older of their entitled benefits under the Social Security program and how to obtain them.

GraphicaArtis/Getty Images.

The Legacy of the New Deal

The expansion of national power under Roosevelt's New Deal—especially Congress's authority to regulate interstate commerce—permanently altered the relationship between the states and the nation. Cooperative federalism, in which both levels of government are involved in setting policy, firmly replaced earlier models of dual federalism and made the national government at least a coequal in many areas of public policy traditionally handled by the states. According to one scholar, "The New Deal constituted the decisive break of the American polity with the old regime of dual federalism, and the transformation toward a more centralized administrative state whose reach extended into the lives of ordinary citizens."[99]

This change did not just happen. Nor was it necessarily inevitable. Roosevelt's popularity, political skill, and miscalculations all played a role. So did the decisions and the shifting opinions of the members of the Supreme Court. However, the revolution was also made possible by the severe economic crisis facing the nation and the inability of states to handle its fallout. States did not always fight Roosevelt's policies, desperate as they were for help in handling the impact of the Great Depression.

Not all Americans benefited equally from the New Deal. Although Roosevelt's administration made strides in hiring women and members of racial and ethnic minorities, his policies did not always benefit these groups. At times, these policies were actively discriminatory. One of the New Deal's early accomplishments, the National Recovery Act, failed to include occupations that employed relatively large numbers of women and African Americans, such as domestic service and temporary farm labor. The program's agricultural policies, which helped farm owners by paying them not to produce as many crops, reduced the need for temporary farm laborers, leaving migrant farmers, who were often members of minority groups, to struggle even harder to find employment.

Roosevelt's relief programs "were designed primarily to employ jobless men," and those that did focus on retraining women for employment "tended to reinforce their traditional roles in the domestic sphere."[100] According to one scholar of the New Deal, "Men, particularly white men, were endowed with national citizenship" and the protections of the national government. Women and members of racial and ethnic minorities, however, "were more likely to remain state citizens," facing discrimination as states were left to regulate the industries in which they worked and the policies under which they strove to improve their lives.[101]

WHAT HAVE I LEARNED?

1. In its decision in, *Schechter Poultry Corp. v. United States* (1935), the Supreme Court challenged President Roosevelt's authority to regulate interstate commerce.

    a. True
    b. False

2. In writing the opinion in *Schechter Poultry Corp. v. United States*, Justice Hughes focused especially on _____.

    a. The Second Amendment
    b. The First Amendment
    c. The Tenth Amendment
    d. The Fourteenth Amendment

3. What are some criticisms of the interpretation of the commerce clause in Roosevelt's New Deal?

4. For what reasons have some scholars criticized the social legacy of the New Deal?

Answer Key: 1. a.; 2. c; 3. Answers should focus on the broad definition of federal power and involvement in individuals' personal economic activity.; 4. Answers should focus on the exclusion of many individuals with diverse identities from the benefits of the New Deal.

MODERN AMERICAN FEDERALISM
Expansion, Restriction, and State Resistance

During the second half of the twentieth century, the expansion of national involvement in the American economy initiated by Roosevelt continued and was in fact strengthened and expanded. Many federal agencies created during the New Deal stayed in place, and some grew larger. As the American economy recovered from the Great Depression and World War II, the conclusion of which left the United States as a global superpower, cooperative federalism remained the dominant model. The dual federalism of the nineteenth and early twentieth centuries was long gone—and, barring a major economic or social crisis, it is not coming back.

One of the primary tools that the federal government can use to achieve its policy objectives within the states is the **grant-in-aid**, money provided to states by the federal government in order to carry out a policy that the national government has decided is important. Though the use of grants-in-aid goes back to the early days of the Republic—especially in grants of land to support public education in the states and territories—they became a common tool in a variety of policy areas during and after the New Deal.

The main form of a grant-in-aid during this period was the **categorical grant**, a grant provided to states or to local or regional governments for specific policy objectives and with certain conditions attached to receiving or spending the funds. (See the left-hand column of Figure 3.6.) These conditions might involve the requirement that the state, local, or regional authority provide matching funds in order to receive the federal monies. They might also include specific instructions on how the grant funds are to be used. Sometimes categorical grants are awarded based on formulas that allocate federal money according to factors such as population, income, and need.

Categorical grants-in-aid are an important source of national power. Though state, local, and regional governmental authorities are often not required to accept these funds, once they do they accept the national regulation that goes along with taking the money. Once a state establishes a program based on the receipt of a categorical grant-in-aid, it depends on the continued provision of those funds by the national government, along with

grants-in-aid
federal money provided to states to implement public policy objectives.

categorical grants
grants-in-aid provided to states with specific provisions on their use.

FIGURE 3.6
Grants-in-Aid

Categorical Grant

Money provided by the national government to state, local, or regional governments that is tied to specific policy objectives and that carries certain conditions for receipt or expenditure.

- National government controls purse strings.
- Once a program is established, states depend upon national government for continuation of that program
- Can mean that wealthier states "subsidize" poorer ones; but can also mean that inequalities between states are reduced and citizens in poorer states have access to benefits they might not otherwise have.
- Can make it harder for states to control their own budgets.
- Can lead to expansion in size of national and state government.

Block Grant

Money proved to state, local, or regional governments over which sub-national governments have greater control.

- State, local, or regional governments have greater say in how funds are spent.
- Sub-national governments given greater flexibility in long term budget planning.
- States can have more authority in setting and enforcing welfare rules.
- Can mean that states decide what priorities to select for their population and are more "in touch" with their needs; but also can mean that federal oversight is reduced and the ability to compare outcomes across states is more limited.
- Can mean that localities with greater need lose out to localities with greater political clout in the allocation of funds.

"In Two Words, Yes And No"

A 1949 political cartoon depicting the uneasy relationship between state governments and the federal government in the post–New Deal era. States are shown to want the federal aid but not the increase in federal authority that comes with it.

© The Herb Block Foundation.

▶ NEWS CLIP

Regulators force coal plant to close despite local government opposition

any attached strings, to avoid a potentially serious disruption of the provision of services to its citizens and residents.

In this way, categorical grants act as both a carrot—to encourage states to carry out national policy objectives—and as a stick—to threaten states with the withholding of funds if they fail to carry out the federal government's policy objectives. According to critics of national power, categorical grants pose several problems for American federalism. They may act as "bribes to induce subnational governments to execute national policies" at the expense of their own authority.[102] Officials and citizens of wealthier states may feel that their taxes are being used to subsidize lower-spending state governments. The uncertainty surrounding the continued provision of the grants can make it harder for states to plan their own budgets. Finally, the administration of these programs requires a further expansion of the size of both national and state government.

Those who argue in favor of the use of categorical grants as a tool of national policymaking emphasize the degree to which the redistribution of monies between states can act to reduce inequality between the states. Also, these monies can help state, local, and regional governments improve the lives of their citizens in ways that might not be possible without the help of the federal government.[103]

Lyndon Johnson's "Great Society" and the Expansion of Cooperative Federalism

The most significant expansion of national power through the use of categorical grants-in-aid in the post–New Deal era occurred during the presidency of Lyndon Baines Johnson. His "Great Society" program created a new set of administrative agencies aimed at improving social welfare in the United States. Social welfare involves the health, safety, education, and opportunities for citizens. Under the old system of dual federalism, social welfare policies were typically thought of as lying within the scope of the police powers of the states and, therefore, mostly under state control.

Although Roosevelt's policies had already involved the federal government in the provision of social welfare policy—for example, by addressing working conditions, unemployment relief, and income security—Johnson's policies expanded this role, aided by strong Democratic Party majorities in both the House and the Senate. The first two years of Johnson's term following the election of 1964 have been described as "the most productive congressional session since the 1930's, and most of the legislative initiatives took the form of grants-in-aid to states and communities."[104]

The Medicare program (1965) supplemented the Social Security program by providing health insurance coverage to individuals aged sixty-five and older. The Medicaid program (1965) provided health care assistance to individuals receiving other forms of aid as well as to those "who were medically indigent but not on welfare."[105] As with many Great Society programs, Medicaid was set up to be funded partly by the federal government and partly by the states. The Elementary and Secondary Education Act of 1965 (ESEA) "provided for the first time, general federal support for public elementary and secondary education."[106] Title I of the ESEA provided federal assistance to children from low-income families in both public and private schools.

"New Federalism," Devolution, and Attempts to Roll Back National Power

Johnson's Great Society programs and the expansion of national authority that they produced were not instituted without opposition, and they eventually produced a backlash from Republicans and many state and local politicians. When Richard Nixon was elected president in 1968, he promised to roll back the expansion of national authority and return at least some of the power back to the states. He called his project "new federalism."

One of Nixon's main tools to try to reduce national authority was the **block grant**. Though they are still a type of grant-in-aid, block grants provide federal money for public policies in a way that tries to increase state, local, and regional authority in how that money is spent and decrease national authority in deciding which states, localities, or regions receive those funds. (Look back at Figure 3.6 on p. 111, right-hand column.)

Efforts to restore more authority to the states continued under the presidency of Ronald Reagan, who, in his speech accepting the Republican Party's nomination in 1980, promised, "Everything that can be run more effectively by state and local government we shall turn over to state and local government, along with the funding sources to pay for it. We are going to put an end to the money merry-go-round where our money becomes Washington's money, to be spent by the states and cities exactly the way the federal bureaucrats tell them to."[107] As part of his program, Reagan reduced funding for several social welfare programs and increased the use of block grants for those that continued to be funded.

The goal of returning authority for federal programs back to the states is called **devolution**, in the sense that authority is devolved, or returned to, the states. Efforts at devolution involved trying to increase states' autonomy in economic and social policy by decentralizing control and administration of programs. One of the most important of these efforts focused on social welfare policies. With the Personal Responsibility and Work Opportunity Reconciliation Act of 1996 (PRWORA), Democratic president Bill Clinton signed into law the principles of devolution to social welfare programs. The outlines of PRWORA had been part of the Republican Party's "Contract with America," a set of campaign promises made during the congressional elections of 1994, in which Republicans took control of both the House and the Senate.[108] PRWORA replaced Aid to Families with Dependent Children (AFDC)—a legacy of Roosevelt's New Deal—with Temporary Assistance for Needy Families (TANF), which placed time limits on receipt of welfare assistance and added work requirements. In addition, block grants and other changes to the administration of the program gave states more authority in setting and enforcing the rules of welfare programs.

Johnson's Great Society expanded the role of the national government and the vision of cooperative federalism that had been firmly established during Roosevelt's New Deal. The Republican administrations of Nixon and Reagan attempted to roll back some of the growth in national power that had occurred during and after the New Deal. Democratic president Clinton—confronted with firm Republican Party control in Congress—applied the principle of devolution to social welfare policy.

Pediatrician Lanre Falusi examining an infant patient in a Maryland community health clinic in 2015. With powerful lobbying efforts behind them, members of the American Medical Association pressured Congress to revamp physician reimbursement under Medicare.

Andrew Harrer/Bloomberg via Getty Images.

block grant
a type of grant-in-aid that gives state officials more authority in the disbursement of the federal funds.

devolution
a national policy goal of returning more authority to state or local governments.

As the United States confronts a new set of challenges in the twenty-first century, calls for a fundamental reexamination of American federalism have gained more and more attention.

In terms of returning America to the dual federalism of its early history, however, none of the policies of the twentieth-century presidents even came close. At this point in American political history, there has been no going back to the stricter separation between state and national authority that operated prior to Roosevelt's revolution. However, as the United States confronts a new set of challenges in the twenty-first century, calls for a fundamental reexamination of American federalism have gained more and more attention.

American Federalism in the Twenty-First Century: Where Do We Go from Here?

In spite of efforts to restrain the power of the national government during the periods of new federalism and devolution, the New Deal legacy of national involvement in state policy has not fundamentally changed, nor is it likely to. For states to opt out of the involvement of the federal government that comes with accepting federal funds would require opting out of the funds themselves and either replacing them or explaining to that state's citizens why certain services will no longer be provided. While individual states may do this in regard to individual programs, a national, wholesale withdrawal is almost unthinkable.

State and local governments, however, have not necessarily been passive players in cooperative federalism, and strategic political actors at the various levels have played a role in trying to shape the balance of power between the two levels of the American federalist system. That is likely to continue and may result in an increased use of tools to assert state power, even confrontationally.

One area where states are beginning to try to set policy in the absence of a comprehensive federal policy is e-commerce taxation. When state residents are able to purchase items over the Internet from companies outside of their states, state governments can lose out on sales tax revenue for those products. In many ways, the e-commerce giants, such as eBay and Amazon.com, present similar challenges to state governments as did the railroads of the nineteenth century, with individual states facing difficulties in regulating businesses that transcend state boundaries. In response, states are increasingly setting policies to collect tax revenues from products purchased online and are coordinating their policies with other state governments.

Another tactic that state and local governments use is to try to influence the content of federal legislation as it is being written and voted on. **Intergovernmental lobbying**, which is often carried out by state or local governmental staff in Washington, involves attempts to influence the national policymaking process to protect state and local interests. In this way, these governments themselves become part of the national legislative process. Examples of intergovernmental lobbying organizations include the National Governors' Association, the National Conference of State Legislatures, and the National League of Cities.

Even when the federal government passes laws that govern state actions, the state governments are typically responsible for implementing these policies, giving them the opportunity to use the process of implementation "to enforce federal policies in a way that promotes their interests."[109]

Although the federal government often has considerable power in crafting laws and creating administrative agencies, the fact that states actually carry out many of these policies provides an important source of state power. In *Federalist* No. 46, James Madison argued that states would have considerable power to resist the carrying out of an "unwarrantable

intergovernmental lobbying

efforts by state and local governments to act in Washington on behalf of their own interests.

measure of the federal government" by making it difficult, if not impossible, for those unpopular policies to actually be carried out.[110] In fact, according to one scholar of American federalism, "state governments have indeed succeeded tremendously in resisting, delaying, or altering the implementation of federal policies at the state level."[111]

While the modern system of cooperative federalism allows states opportunities to try to preserve their authority and influence over policymaking, the relationship between states and the national government is not always cooperative. At times, state governments have objected to federal regulations that, from the point of view of the states, are attempts to make the states pay for federal policies. Such unpaid, or underpaid, requirements are called **unfunded mandates** or, sometimes, underfunded mandates.

From the point of view of Congress, there are strong incentives to make policies whose costs have to be carried by the states: "The legislator gets the credit for benefitting needy constituents, but the cost is paid by a lower governmental tier."[112] State, local, and regional governments have complained to Washington about the imposition of unfunded mandates in a variety of policy areas, including environmental policy, education policy, and the provision of health and social welfare benefits for low-income and disabled Americans. In March 2008, the governor of Montana complained, "We are putting up with the federal government on so many fronts, and nearly every month they come up with another harebrained scheme, an unfunded mandate to tell us that our life is going to be better if we'll just buckle under on some other kind of rule or regulation."[113]

One strategy that states use to try to reduce the impact of unfunded mandates is to pressure the federal government for waivers from certain provisions of a given law. Coordinated state pressure on the federal government can lead to exemptions from implementing—and paying for—certain unpopular provisions of a law.

As the American Republic enters the first decades of the twenty-first century, new state challenges to federal authority are emerging. One tool that many states have used to do this is the **sovereignty resolution**. Passed by state legislatures, sovereignty resolutions affirm the sovereignty of states under the Tenth Amendment to the Constitution. Variations of these resolutions have been passed or considered in response to a variety of federal laws, including those covering education, immigration, and health care. They are often a result of state claims of unfunded mandates. They are typically only statements of protest, stopping short of actually nullifying a law, but asserting the rights of states to do so in the future if necessary.

Another tactic that states have occasionally used, and may continue to use in the future, is to pass a state law that is in direct violation of a federal law or policy, perhaps amending the state constitution in order to do so. During the election of 2012, several states passed laws or amendments to their constitutions that placed state policy in direct violation of

Store owner Justin Wilson III and his son in Wilson's store in Virginia in 2014. Wilson was supporting state tax legislation that would tax online sales similar to how sales at his TennisServ shop were taxed. Like many retail business owners, Wilson expressed concerns that individuals would browse merchandise in his store and then order it more cheaply online, without having to pay state sales tax.

Linda Davidson / The Washington Post via Getty Images.

unfunded mandates
federal regulations that must be followed by the states but whose costs must also be shouldered by the states.

state sovereignty resolutions
state legislative measures that affirm the sovereignty of states under the Tenth Amendment.

federal policy. Three states—Montana, Alabama, and Wyoming—passed initiatives exempting state citizens from some of the provisions or penalties under President Obama's recent health care overhaul, the Patient Protection and Affordable Care Act of 2010. And, as we have explored, more than half of the states have now passed laws legalizing the medical or even recreational use of marijuana, in violation of federal law.

WHAT HAVE I LEARNED?

1. The term *devolution* refers to returning powers over social welfare policy back to the states.

   a. True
   b. False

2. Categorical grants _____.

   a. Are provided with specific provisions on their distribution
   b. Allow state governments great flexibility in their use
   c. Have been nullified as they support a policy of "separate but equal"
   d. Require state constitutional amendments to accept

3. An example of a way that state governments try to assert their own authority is _____.

   a. Nullification
   b. Intergovernmental lobbying
   c. Secession
   d. All of the above

4. How would you describe the current state of American federalism?

....

Answer Key: 1. a; 2. a; 3. c; 4. Answers will vary and should be backed up with arguments. Some may focus on national power. Others may focus on cooperative federalism. Still others may point to increasing state resistance.

 CONCLUSION

American Federalism Challenged, in Progress, and Undecided

Angel Raich visiting a Colorado medical cannabis cultivation site in February 2016.

Courtesy of Angel Raich.

By 2016 Angel Raich was "living very happily with her loving husband" and working as a consultant and advocate for individuals' rights to use medical cannabis.[114] Raich, with the help of medical marijuana, was able to maintain her health, pursue her goals, and express her voice as a political advocate.

However, the issue of the boundary between state and federal laws governing medical and recreational marijuana use remains far from settled. By 2016 more than half of the states had passed legislation legalizing medical cannabis. Eight other states had also passed ballot initiatives legalizing the recreational use of marijuana.[115] However, the Controlled Substances Act still controlled federal law and policy.

According to the Office of National Drug Control Policy, "It is important to recognize that these state marijuana laws do not change the fact that using marijuana continues to be an offense under federal law. Nor do these state laws change the criteria or process for FDA [United States Food and Drug Administration] approval of safe and effective medications."[116] By federal law, any current user of marijuana, even if legal under their own state laws, is violating the Controlled Substances Act and is subject to federal prosecution.

There is no possible—or practical—way that this situation can continue. By 2016 the Controlled Substances Act could not be effectively and totally enforced as federal law since that would have entailed putting more than a million, perhaps millions, of state-law-abiding citizens in federal prison, not to mention the unimaginable political fallout from fully executing the law.[117] Officials with the federal government and the Obama administration were well aware of this situation. In a 2013 memorandum, the Department of Justice affirmed the legality and supremacy of the CSA but also acknowledged the impossibility of enforcing the law in the states in totality. It stated, "The Department is also committed to using its limited investigative and executorial resources to address the most significant threats in the most effective, consistent and rational way."[118] In the memorandum, the Justice Department declared that instead it would focus on preventing access to marijuana by youths, transport of marijuana from a state in which it is legal to states in which it is not, and the use of firearms in connection with the production or distribution of marijuana.

How to deal with the fact that an individual might be complying with the laws of her or his state but at the same time breaking federal law is a fundamental question of federalism that is still unanswered. American federalism has never been a well-defined thing. In the twenty-first century, it remains just as contested as it been for most of the nation's history.

Want a better grade?

Get the tools you need to sharpen your study skills. **SAGE edge** offers a robust online environment featuring an impressive array of free tools and resources. Access practice quizzes, eFlashcards, video, and multimedia at **edge.sagepub.com/abernathy1e.**

CHAPTER REVIEW

This chapter's main ideas are reflected in the Learning Objectives below. By reviewing them here you should be able to **remember** the key points, **connect** them to the stories presented in the chapter, **think** critically about these questions, and **know** these terms that are central to the topic.

3.1 Explain the tension in American federalism between state and federal laws.

REMEMBER ...
- The ultimate political authority in the American representative democracy rests with the people, but this authority is divided between two levels of government: the nation and the states.

CONNECT ...
- Angel Raich and Diane Monson, in their use of medical marijuana, were acting in accordance with state law but simultaneously violating federal law.

THINK ...
- What is it about the tension between California's Compassionate Use Act and the federal Controlled Substances Act that caused such a furor?
- What do you think about all of this?

KNOW ...
- *federalism* (p. 83)

3.2 Identify the elements of the United States Constitution that shape American federalism and evaluate arguments about the proper limits of congressional power under their authority.

REMEMBER ...
- The Constitution lays out much of the framework of American federalism but not in one clear, neatly defined section. Instead, multiple clauses and sections attempt to define its basic boundaries.

CONNECT ...
- In *Gonzales v. Raich*, the Supreme Court upheld the supremacy of federal law in issues involving interstate commerce, broadly interpreted, even when state laws provide for policies such as legalized use of marijuana.

THINK ...
- How does the Constitution structure American federalism?
- In what ways are the boundaries of federalism not very clear, and what are the implications of that ambiguity?

KNOW ...
- *commerce clause* (p. 87)
- *concurrent powers* (p. 89)
- *confederal systems* (p. 86)
- *enumerated powers* (p. 88)
- *federal systems* (p. 86)
- *implied powers* (p. 88)

- *necessary and proper clause* (p. 87)
- *police powers* (p. 89)
- *reserved powers* (p. 89)
- *supremacy clause* (p. 87)
- *unitary systems* (p. 86)

3.3 Trace the development of American federalism over time.

REMEMBER ...
- The boundaries between the authority of national and state governments have changed over time. Many of these changes have come about as a result of Supreme Court decisions in interpreting the Constitution.

CONNECT ...
- What political concerns did Chief Justice John Marshall have to contend with in issuing early decisions that shaped American federalism?

THINK ...
- How has American federalism changed and developed? What factors have helped to drive this change?
- How did nineteenth-century interpretations of American federalism serve to deny some Americans their fundamental rights?

KNOW ...
- *cooperative federalism* (p. 99)
- *dual federalism* (p. 96)

- *states' rights* (p. 97)

3.4 Describe the impact of economic crisis in the changes to American federalism during the New Deal era.

REMEMBER ...
- The New Deal fundamentally reshaped American federalism, but the program was not without challenges, especially by the Supreme Court.

CONNECT ...
- The Great Depression posed a critical test to the United States. In response to this crisis, President Roosevelt and Congress passed a host of laws. To the Schechter brothers, these new regulations threatened their longstanding ways of doing business and serving their customers. Their case presented a fundamental challenge to Roosevelt's New Deal.

THINK ...
- What are the legacies of the New Deal? In what ways did the New Deal fail to achieve full inclusion of Americans with diverse lived experiences?

KNOW ...
- *The Great Depression* (p. 101)
- *The New Deal* (p. 102)

3.5 List changes to American federalism in the post New Deal era.

REMEMBER ...
- Subsequent administrations, especially that of President Lyndon Johnson, expanded upon the promises and programs of the New Deal. However, later presidents, such as Ronald Reagan, attempted to restrict the power of the federal government and turn over more administrative authority to the states.

THINK ...
- What tools have opponents of national power used to transfer more authority in policymaking back to the states and local governments?

KNOW ...
- *block grants* (p. 113)
- *categorical grants* (p. 111)
- *devolution* (p. 113)
- *grants-in-aid* (p. 111)

3.6 Discuss the current status of American federalism and how it might continue to evolve.

REMEMBER ...
- State and local governments continue to be active in asserting their governmental authority.

CONNECT ...
- What challenges to American federalism are posed by medical and recreational marijuana laws in the United States in the twenty-first century? What issues remain unresolved?

THINK ...
- Where do you think American federalism stands in the second decade of the twenty-first century?

KNOW ...
- *intergovernmental lobbying* (p. 114)
- *state sovereignty resolutions* (p. 115)
- *unfunded mandates* (p. 115)

4 CIVIL LIBERTIES
Building and Defending Fences

Google+

The American Republic was founded upon the idea that people are born with certain fundamental rights and freedoms—though, as we have discussed, this idea was far from completely or equitably applied at the time of the founding. According to the foundational principles of American representative democracy, citizens enter into a compact with their government. They willingly allow some restrictions upon their actions and expression of their rights in order to create a functioning political body, provided that government acts in such a way as to preserve and protect citizens' innate rights and liberties. This has always been an uneasy and shifting bargain, with the boundaries delimiting the scope of individual freedoms and the acceptable restrictions placed upon those freedoms constantly in contestation.

Edward Snowden, currently on the run from American authorities for leaking sensitive documents in protest over the government's monitoring of Americans' communications and activities, has become a hero to some but a traitor to others.
Travis P Ball/Getty Images for SXSW.

The fundamental rights and freedoms that citizens possess and that are protected from unreasonable governmental restriction are referred to as **civil liberties**. In contrast, the term *civil rights* refers to the treatment of citizens by their governments as members of particular groups, especially in the equality of their treatment and their access to opportunities.

Civil liberties are often called **negative freedoms**, not because they are not good things, but because protecting them involves restricting–*not* allowing–government actions. Consider that the First Amendment to the Constitution begins, "Congress shall make no law. . . ." It is this affirmation of the *limits* on the proper powers of government that defines the fundamental freedoms of Americans as established by the Constitution. In contrast, civil rights are often referred to as *positive freedoms* since their protection generally implies positive action, either on the part of citizens to exercise them or on the part of a government to secure them. We will explore civil rights and the challenges present in their protection and establishment in the next chapter.

In this chapter, we will read stories about struggles to define and protect fundamental liberties. The stories of Edward Snowden, Benjamin Gitlow, Edie Windsor, and James Obergefell are stories about building fences, especially around the power of government to restrict their expression.

> **civil liberties**
> fundamental rights and freedoms of citizens the protection of which involves restricting the power of a government.
>
> **negative freedoms**
> fundamental liberties the protection of which is ensured by restricting governmental action and authority.

After reading this chapter, you will be able to:

4.1 Outline the controversies surrounding civil liberties and the need to ensure a safe and orderly society

4.2 List the civil liberties protected by the Constitution and amendments to it

4.3 Trace the history of incorporating the Bill of Rights in order to restrict state governmental actions

4.4 Discuss the challenges to constitutional law posed by the establishment and free exercise clauses of the First Amendment

4.5 Assess the special protections of political speech and press affirmed in the First Amendment as well as restrictions subsequently placed upon those protections

4.6 Summarize the protections placed within the Bill of Rights for those accused of, investigated for, tried for, and convicted of crimes

4.7 Discuss the Supreme Court's affirmation of the right to privacy

LEARNING OBJECTIVES

"FROM RUSSIA WITH LOVE"

Edward Snowden: Traitor, Hero, or None of the Above

He has been called "the most wanted man in the world."[1] His name is Edward Joseph Snowden. To some, especially officials from the United States government, Snowden is a traitor, an individual who has fundamentally compromised national security. To others, he is a hero, an advocate for the rights and freedoms of Americans, an individual who made public the fact that citizens' private conversations and postings have been unconstitutionally collected and analyzed by a government gone off the rails.

Edward Snowden is on the run. If he wants to remain a free man, he likely will be on the run for the rest of his life. His cause is the American government's use of technology to spy on its own citizens without authority granted to it by a court, without evidence, without cause. To his potential prosecutors, Snowden leaked valuable and sensitive national security secrets in violation of federal law, placing Americans involved in intelligence gathering at grave risk. Should the documents that Snowden leaked reveal the identities of Americans operating undercover in other nations, this could result in the imprisonment or execution of women and men who have devoted their careers to protecting Americans whom they have never met. That is a very real possibility that cannot be ignored or dismissed.

In May 2013, Snowden, a contractor for the National Security Administration (NSA) and a former employee of the Central Intelligence Agency (CIA), flew to Hong Kong from Hawaii, where he had been working at an NSA facility. He took with him over a million classified files he'd downloaded from government databases. In June Snowden leaked thousands of pages of those classified documents, first to the British newspaper the *Guardian* and then to other outlets including the *Washington Post* and the *New York Times*.

In an interview with the *Guardian* released on June 9, Snowden revealed himself as the leaker and defended what he had done. Part of Snowden's reason for his decision was the

The *Guardian's* Web site hosts a section called "NSA Files: Decoded," which helps clarify the relevance of Snowden's leaks to the public. Here they explain the scope of the surveillance the National Security Agency undertook using their "three hops" rule, which ultimately allowed them to gather enormous amounts of metadata on U.S. citizens. As the *Guardian* reported, the NSA argued that it "collected only a tiny proportion of the world's internet traffic, roughly equivalent to a 'dime on a basketball court.'" But as Congresswoman Zoe Lofgren put it, "Here's the deal. If you couldn't learn anything from that data, they wouldn't be collecting it."

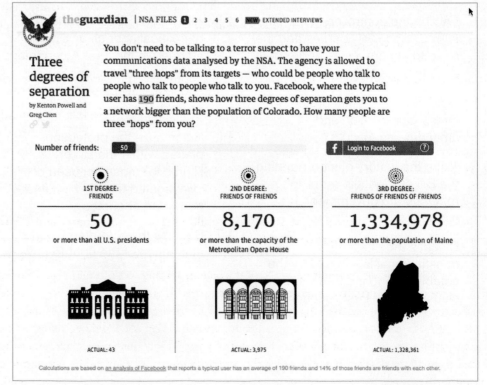

theguardian | NSA FILES 1 2 3 4 5 6 NEW EXTENDED INTERVIEWS

Three degrees of separation
by Kenton Powell and Greg Chen

You don't need to be talking to a terror suspect to have your communications data analysed by the NSA. The agency is allowed to travel "three hops" from its targets — who could be people who talk to people who talk to people who talk to you. Facebook, where the typical user has 190 friends, shows how three degrees of separation gets you to a network bigger than the population of Colorado. How many people are three "hops" from you?

Number of friends: 50

Login to Facebook

1ST DEGREE: FRIENDS
50
or more than all U.S. presidents

ACTUAL: 43

2ND DEGREE: FRIENDS OF FRIENDS
8,170
or more than the capacity of the Metropolitan Opera House

ACTUAL: 3,975

3RD DEGREE: FRIENDS OF FRIENDS OF FRIENDS
1,334,978
or more than the population of Maine

ACTUAL: 1,328,361

Calculations are based on an analysis of Facebook that reports a typical user has an average of 190 friends and 14% of those friends are friends with each other.

The Guardian

immense power of the NSA to monitor Americans' telephone records, texts, e-mails, and browsing history without their knowledge and without a court order. "The NSA has built an infrastructure that allows it to intercept almost everything," Snowden said. "With this capability, the vast majority of human communications are automatically ingested without targeting. If I wanted to see your emails or your wife's phone, all I have to do is use intercepts. I can get your emails, passwords, phone records, credit cards."[2]

Another factor in Snowden's decision, he told the reporter, was what he saw as a reckless abuse of this power by the NSA. The leaked documents, he said, revealed that "the NSA routinely lies in response to Congressional inquiries about the scope of surveillance in America. . . . We collect more digital communications from America than we do from the Russians."[3] One of the leaked documents, from the NSA director himself, was a reference to the agency's practice of "spying on the pornography-viewing habits of political radicals. The memo suggested that the Agency could use these 'personal vulnerabilities' to destroy the reputations of government critics who were not in fact accused of plotting terrorism."[4]

In the interview, Snowden expressed no illusions about the seriousness of what he had done. He said, "My primary fear is that they will come after my family, my friends, my partner. Anyone I have a relationship with. . . . I have to live with that for the rest of my life. I am not going to be able to communicate with them. They [the authorities] will act aggressively against anyone who has known me. That keeps me up at night."[5] In an article written for *Wired* magazine in 2014, James Bamford, a former member of the American intelligence bureaucracy and the journalist assigned to find the elusive rebel, described the extent to which he went to interview Snowden. By then Snowden was living in Russia, with that nation's permission. The cloak and dagger techniques Snowden had adopted to protect his anonymity could have come out of a James Bond movie.

In a 2013 interview, billionaire Donald Trump, who would go on to win the presidential election in 2016, said of Snowden, "I think Snowden is a terrible threat, I think he's a terrible traitor, and you know what we used to do in the good old days when we were a strong country—you know what we used to do to traitors, right?"[6] Trump was alluding to executing Snowden for treason, although Trump did not say so outright in the interview. The point, however, was clear: Trump considered Snowden a threat to national security.

If captured by American officials, Snowden would likely face prosecution under The Espionage Act of 1917, passed two months after the United States declared war on Germany and entered the nation into the cauldron of World War I. The Espionage Act makes a high crime the possession or distribution of "any document, writing, code book, signal book, sketch, photographic negative, blue print, plan, map, model, instrument, appliance, or note relating to the national defense" that the possessor or distributor knows might pose a threat to the nation. In time of war, according to the act, certain violations could be "punished by death or by imprisonment for not more than thirty years."[7] If Snowden ever returns to the United States or gets on a plane over which the American government or its allies or partners has authority, he will most certainly be arrested and tried and could potentially be executed.

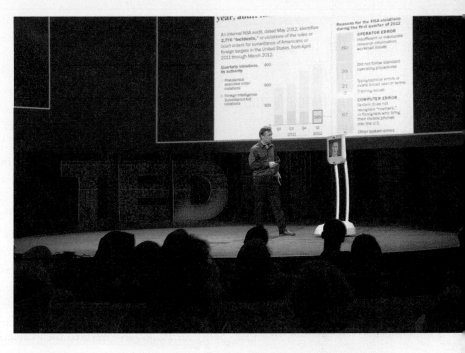

Edward Snowden, right, "appeared" in a 2014 TED Talk via a small screen bearing a live image of his face. The screen was attached to two leg-like poles mounted onto a set of remote-controlled wheels, giving him the ability to "walk" around the event, talk to people, and even pose for selfies.

Steven Rosenbaum/Getty Images

> One of the toughest issues in American constitutional law is the tension between protecting fundamental rights and freedoms and the need to ensure national security. Edward Snowden walked right into the middle of that dilemma.

In an interview in May 2016, however, former U.S. attorney general Eric H. Holder Jr., who served in President Barack Obama's administration, reaffirmed the administration's position that Snowden's actions were "inappropriate and illegal" but added, "We can certainly argue about the way in which Snowden did what he did, but I think that he actually performed a public service by raising the debate that we engaged in."[8]

Not all of the documents Snowden took have been released, much to the worry of American national security officials. Snowden asserts that he no longer possesses them, that he passed them along to a variety of news outlets and organizations. If true, there may be more bombshells out there.

In his defense, Snowden claimed that he was acting out of the need to protect Americans' privacy and their fundamental rights and freedoms—to expose the power of the NSA in hopes it could be reined in. His opponents, however, assert that his actions recklessly endangered the nation. One of the toughest issues in American constitutional law is the tension between protecting fundamental rights and freedoms and the need to ensure national security. Edward Snowden walked right into the middle of that dilemma.

Two questions in particular emerge when thinking about the complexities involving the expression and protection of civil liberties: What exactly are the fundamental rights and freedoms that individuals possess? And, under what circumstances can a government legitimately restrict the expression of these rights and freedoms? As we will explore, the Supreme Court plays a pivotal role in attempting to answer these questions. In doing so, undertakes the difficult task of defining where liberties began and end.

In their essence, questions about civil liberties are questions about boundaries between the rights and freedoms of individuals and governmental authority as well as between individuals as they claim their fundamental freedoms. One of the longest-running struggles in this area involves the tension between the need to have a safe and orderly society and the need to protect Americans' civil liberties, which is precisely what Edward Snowden was challenging. As we will explore in this chapter, the property lines between the rights and freedoms of individuals and the power of the United States government and its states are far from clear, fixed, or even agreed upon.

WHAT HAVE I LEARNED?

1. Civil liberties are called negative freedoms because they _____.

   a. Are not good things
   b. Reject elements of the Declaration of Independence
   c. Place restrictions upon governmental action
   d. Place restrictions upon individual action

2. Edward Snowden's actions highlight the tensions between _____.

   a. Economic growth and governmental regulation
   b. Privacy and national security
   c. Military intervention and foreign aid
   d. Religious expression and governmental action

3. What were the controversies surrounding Edward Snowden's decision to release classified documents?

....

Answer Key: 1. c; 2. b; 3. Answers should discuss the tension between Snowden's desire to protect Americans' privacy versus the need to protect national security. Answers might also include criticisms of his release of personal information.

A Conservative Legal Expert Accuses Edward Snowden of Violating Civil Liberties

In an article for the blog site *Lawfare*, Benjamin Wittes, a senior fellow at the conservative Brookings Institution, offered a contrasting opinion of Edward Snowden's leaked documents and their publication by the *Washington Post*.[9] To Wittes, Snowden was not a whistle-blower. Instead, Wittes claimed Snowden's actions constituted a violation of individuals' civil liberties:

> A government contractor steals tens of thousands of highly-sensitive communications intercepts. The communications have national security implications, yes, but put that aside for now. They also involve the most intimate details of the lives of thousands of people: their love letters, their pictures of their kids, their pictures of themselves in lingerie, records reflecting their domestic and personal struggles. The contractor gives a cache of 160,000 conversations—some of them very lengthy—to a third party [the *Washington Post*]. He does so apparently indiscriminately, and he leaves to nothing more than trust that the recipient will use the material properly . . . .
>
> If the contractor in question were anyone other than Edward Snowden, we would immediately recognize this disclosure for what it is: a massive civil liberties violation of precisely the type we put intelligence under the rule of law to try to prevent. . . . Many civil libertarians don't seem to mind this particularly

Benjamin Wittes, left, shown with FBI director James Comey, right.

Paul Morigi/Getty Images

gross abuse of signals intelligence content in pursuit of Snowden's individual politics.

WHAT DO YOU THINK?

Do you find this argument convincing? Does the fact that Snowden was releasing private, personal information that he did not himself collect alter your assessment of his actions? Does his larger goal of laying bare the scope of federal government surveillance justify the release of personal information or not?

THE CONSTITUTION AND THE BILL OF RIGHTS

The Foundations for the Protections for Americans' Civil Liberties

As they assembled in Philadelphia in the spring of 1787, the delegates to the Constitutional Convention brought with them lessons learned and fears nurtured in their experiences under British colonial rule, the nascent state governments, and the loose union of the Articles of Confederation. One of their main concerns was to secure the protection of individual rights.

The idea that a constituting document should include a list of protections for the rights of individuals was not invented in 1787. Studying the centuries of struggle in Great Britain to rein in the power of the monarchs was a standard part of the education that many of the delegates had received, especially those who were lawyers.[10] The suppression of individual rights by the increasingly assertive British Parliament and Crown leading up to the American Revolution also loomed large in the minds of

CONNECTING TO . . .

Constitutional Protections of Civil Liberties

As you read about the inclusion of textual protections for Americans' civil liberties in the Bill of Rights, reflect upon the controversies surrounding Edward Snowden's action. Consider the following:

- Why he might have felt that his actions were necessary
- Why some criticized his actions as violating, rather than protecting, Americans' civil liberties

bill of rights
a list of fundamental rights
and freedoms that individuals
possess. The first ten
amendments to the United
States Constitution are referred
to as the Bill of Rights.

the delegates. Charges laid against King George III for his unjust restriction of rights and freedoms form the bulk of the text of the Declaration of Independence.

Following independence, most of the state governments had included some protections for individual rights in their own constitutions.[11] However, the protections varied considerably and often lacked key components that Americans today typically think of as fundamental rights, such as freedom of the press or religion. For example, as one scholar noted, "North Carolina's 1776 Constitution declared 'That the freedom of the press is one of the great bulwarks of liberty, and therefore ought never to be restrained.' But the article on freedom of religion ended with this proviso, 'That nothing herin contained shall be construed to exempt preachers of treasonable or seditious discourses, from legal trial and punishment.'"[12] Persecution of religious minorities by state legislatures and religious qualifications for holding office were not uncommon. Moreover, the use of the phrase "ought not" was common in lists of state declarations of rights rather than the phrase "shall not." While it may seem like a small detail in language, the second phrasing, as expressed in the fundamental law of a nation, provides a much stronger foundation for protecting individual rights and freedoms than the first.

Well aware of the need to protect individual rights, the delegates agreed to place within the original document certain protections, such as a strict limit on the definition of treason as well as restrictions on punishments available for those convicted of it.[13] The delegates did not, however, include a **bill of rights**—a list of fundamental individual rights that a government cannot restrict or intrude upon except under specific circumstances and then only according to defined procedures (which themselves may be included in the list).

The delegates did debate the idea of a bill of rights, however. In the final days of the Constitutional Convention, two of the delegates moved to include one in the document, saying it "would give great quiet to the people," and to form a committee to draft one. The motion was defeated unanimously.[14] Two days later, another motion was offered "to insert a declaration 'that the liberty of the Press should be inviolably observed.'"[15] That motion also failed; however, delegations from four states—Massachusetts, Maryland, Virginia, and South Carolina—voted in favor. The narrowness of the defeat might have served as a wake-up call to the proponents of the Constitution. It might have alerted them to the fact that a failure to include a comprehensive list of restrictions on the power of the federal government in relation to individual rights would resonate with the American people and serve as a powerful argument against ratification in the hands of the Antifederalists.

Federalists versus Antifederalists, Ratification, and the Bill of Rights

During the ratification campaign following the Constitutional Convention, the Antifederalists seized upon the lack of a bill of rights in the proposed document. They were far from an organized, uniform group, and their motives for highlighting the issue were likely diverse. Some most likely used the lack of a bill of rights as a tactical weapon, hoping to defeat the Constitution entirely or push for a second convention during which they might secure a more favorable outcome. Some were largely opposed to the federal powers of taxation and regulation of commerce and wanted to see more protections for the rights of states, few of which were listed in the document.[16] Others argued that such a list of fundamental rights was a necessary protection against what they feared would be the inexorable growth of centralized power in what was sure to become a large republic.

To counter the Antifederalists' charges, the Federalists offered several counterarguments, most concisely summed up in Alexander Hamilton's *Federalist* No. 84. Noting that several state constitutions—some in states where opposition to the proposed Constitution was strongest—lacked a bill of rights, Hamilton made two fundamental arguments against the inclusion of such a list in the proposed Constitution. The first was that one was unnecessary. The proposed document, he argued, already contained provisions guaranteeing specific rights, especially in Article III's treatment of the judiciary. More broadly, according to Hamilton, "the constitution is itself, in every rational sense, and to every useful purpose, A BILL OF RIGHTS"; to Hamilton, the plan itself, the design of its government constituted an affirmation and securing of individual rights.[17]

Second, Hamilton argued that including a bill of rights would be dangerous to individual liberty, not supportive of it. Reminding readers that bills of rights were traditionally "stipulations between kings and their subjects, abridgments of prerogative in favor of privilege," Hamilton cautioned against the main danger of providing a list of individual rights in a constituting document: that the list would necessarily be incomplete. What about those rights not enumerated? Might the lack of their textual protections encourage those who would impose tyranny to deny them? Hamilton warned that having "various exceptions to powers not granted, would afford a colourable pretext to claim more than were granted."[18] As we will discuss later in the chapter, the question of protections for rights not specifically enumerated remains one of the most important topics in the study and application of American civil liberties today.

Regardless of their diverse motives, the Antifederalists' strategy was one that proved to have legs. Biographer Catherine Drinker Bowen wrote that "when the Constitution was published in the newspapers after the Convention rose, and the Antifederalists gathered their strength for opposition, nothing created such an uproar as the lack of a bill of rights."[19] As the ratification campaign progressed, the Federalists shifted their tactics. In Massachusetts, several of them proposed a series of nine amendments, not as a prerequisite to ratification but as modifications to be presented to Congress once ratification had been completed and the new government assembled. Similar promises were made in other state ratification debates.

As promised, on Monday, June 8, 1789, during the first session of Congress, James Madison "rose, and reminded the House that this was the day that he had heretofore named for bringing forward amendments to the constitution."[20] After reworking and revising his proposed list, Congress formally proposed twelve amendments to the Constitution and sent them to the states for ratification. Of these, ten were formally ratified on December 15, 1791.[21] The Bill of Rights had become part of the Constitution.

Ten Amendments, Proposed and Ratified

In a variety of clauses, the First Amendment—in much stronger language than the "ought not" so common in state constitutions at the time—prevents the legislative branch from passing laws restricting a variety of individual rights, including religion, speech, the press, and assembly. The next two amendments deal with powers generally under the authority of the executive branch involving firearms, state militias, and the quartering of soldiers in people's homes and on their property. Of course, given the theory of separation of powers underlying the Constitution, these two amendments, like the others, also implicated all of the branches. For example, a law governing the quartering of soldiers in people's houses would have to be passed by Congress; those accused of violating such a law would be tried within the judicial branch.

Federalist Alexander Hamilton, who opposed the inclusion of a bill of rights during the ratification debates.

The Granger Collection, New York.

TABLE 4.1 An Overview of Protections Contained within the Bill of Rights

AMENDMENT	PROTECTION
First Amendment	Restricts the lawmaking powers of Congress in the areas of religion, speech, the press, assembly, and petitioning the government
Second Amendment	The right to keep and bear arms
Third Amendment	No forced quartering of troops in homes
Fourth Amendment	Protects against unreasonable search and seizure and establishes the right to have warrants issued prior to arrest or search
Fifth Amendment	Right to a grand jury indictment in criminal cases, protection against double jeopardy and self-incrimination, the right to due process of law, and the right to just compensation when private property is taken for public use
Sixth Amendment	Protections during criminal prosecutions for a speedy and public trial by an impartial jury, the right to confront witnesses, the right to compel favorable witnesses to testify in one's defense, and the right to the assistance of defense counsel
Seventh Amendment	Right to a trial by jury in certain civil suits
Eighth Amendment	Protections against excessive bail, excessive fines, and cruel and unusual punishment
Ninth Amendment	Nonexclusion of rights not listed in the Constitution
Tenth Amendment	Powers not delegated to the federal government, nor prohibited by it to the states, are reserved to the states or to the people.

Amendments four through eight guarantee rights of Americans involved with the judicial system: those accused of, arrested for, tried for, and convicted of crimes, as well as certain noncriminal cases. The Ninth Amendment arose from concerns that any list of individual rights might be thought of as exhaustive. Therefore, it specifies that the list in the Bill of Rights does not presume or imply the protection of rights not enumerated. Finally, the Tenth Amendment declares that those powers not specifically delegated to the federal government are "reserved to the States," or, in a curious and confounding addendum, "to the people." We will explore specific amendments in detail throughout this chapter. Table 4.1 summarizes the main provisions of the Bill of Rights.

WHAT HAVE I LEARNED?

1. The delegates to the Constitutional Convention did not consider the inclusion of a list of fundamental rights and liberties in the document.

   a. True
   b. False

2. The Bill of Rights affirms the fundamental rights and freedoms of _____.

   a. The federal government
   b. The state governments
   c. Both the federal and state governments
   d. Individual citizens

3. What were Alexander Hamilton's two main arguments against the need to include a bill of rights in the proposed Constitution?

Answer Key: 1. b; 2. d; 3. Answers should include Hamilton's argument that such a list was unnecessary, as the Constitution itself protected rights, and that he warned about the lack of protections for rights and freedoms not listed.

ANOTHER OUTLAW

Another Charge against the Government's Infringements upon Civil Liberties

He was considered a very dangerous man in 1919. His name was Benjamin Gitlow. He was speaking about, writing on, and protesting against American involvement in World War I, and what he saw as a fundamentally unjust economic system that had driven the nation into global war.

Gitlow, breaking from his more moderate colleagues in the Socialist Party, oversaw the printing of a journal, *The Revolutionary Age: Devoted to Communist Struggle*, and also submitted articles to it. In an issue published in July 1919, Gitlow and his colleagues included "The Left Wing Manifesto," which decried American involvement in World War I, capitalism, and American imperialism. The manifesto proclaimed,

> The world is in crisis. Capitalism, the prevailing system of society, is in process of disintegration and collapse. . . . The predatory "war for democracy" dominated the world. But now it is the revolutionary proletariat in action that dominates, conquering power in some nations, mobilizing to conquer power in others, and calling upon the proletariat of all nations to prepare for the final struggle against Capitalism. . . . Revolutionary Socialism does not propose to "capture" the bourgeois parliamentary state, but to conquer and destroy it. . . . The old machinery of the state cannot be used by the revolutionary proletariat. It must be destroyed.[22]

In November of that year, Gitlow and an associate were arrested under the New York State Criminal Anarchy Act, which had been passed in 1902 in response to the assassination of President William McKinley by anarchist Leon Frank Czolgosz. New York's law made it a felony to advocate for "the doctrine that organized government should be overthrown by force or violence."[23]

Gitlow had one of the most notable attorneys in the history of American civil liberties law arguing his defense at his criminal trial: Clarence Darrow. In his closing arguments, Darrow asked the jury, "Should I not advocate a change, because somebody is going to get hurt? Why gentlemen, if that had been the law down through the ages and had been strictly enforced, you would all be living in caves now. Because the civilization of today is made up of an infinite number of revolutions, one after the other, all through the history of the world."[24] In spite of his attorney's impassioned pleas, Gitlow was convicted and sentenced to between five and ten years of hard labor at New York's Sing Sing prison, the maximum sentence allowable. He was assigned to shovel coal.[25]

Appealing his conviction all the way to the Supreme Court, though with different counsel, Gitlow argued that the New York law had violated

The cover of the July 1919 publication of *The Revolutionary Age*, which featured Benjamin Gitlow's "Left Wing Manifesto." Archive.org.

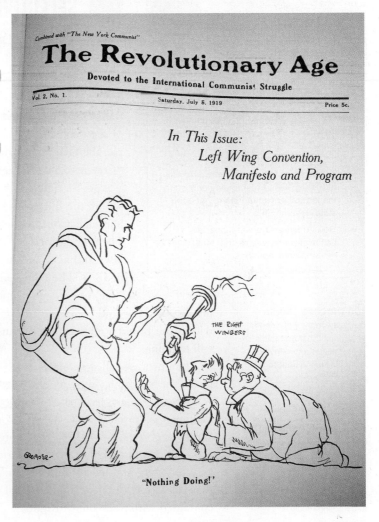

his rights of due process under the Fourteenth Amendment. Gitlow lost his appeal. In his majority opinion, Justice Edward Terry Sanford affirmed that there are restrictions on speech and of the press that are legitimate if such expression sufficiently threatens the public welfare or safety, which, the Court found, Gitlow's revolutionary exhortations did. The New York law, as applied in this case, was not unconstitutional. The opinion stated, "It is a fundamental principle, long established, that the freedom of speech and of the press which is secured by the Constitution does not confer an absolute right to speak or publish, without responsibility, whatever one may choose, or an unrestricted and unbridled license that gives immunity for every possible use of language and prevents the punishment of those who abuse this freedom."[26]

Though separated in time by nearly a century, the stories of Benjamin Gitlow and Edward Snowden share some things in common. Both individuals knowingly broke a national or state law based upon their own convictions and their right to speak and act against war or national security policy. Each knew the likely consequences of his actions. Both were also considered traitors. Gitlow's story turned out somewhat differently, however, partly because Snowden's story is still being written, but mostly because Gitlow helped to change American constitutional law. As originally drafted, the restrictions on power in the Bill of Rights applied only to the federal government and not the state governments. Gitlow's case was one in a long process where that began to change.

CONNECTING TO . . .

Civil Liberties and the States

As you read about the Supreme Court's decision in Gitlow's case, reflect upon the fact that Gitlow had been arrested under a *state law* and not a federal law. Consider the following:

- The fact that the protections in the Bill of Rights placed restrictions only upon the federal government and not upon state governments

- How American constitutional law has evolved to also restrict state governmental action

due process clause
the clause in the Fourteenth Amendment that restricts state governments from denying their citizens the right to due process of law.

selective incorporation
the piecemeal process through which the Supreme Court has affirmed that almost all of the protections within the Bill of Rights also apply to state governments.

◼ SELECTIVE INCORPORATION

Applying the Bill of Rights to State Laws and Actions

The text of the Bill of Rights does not declare restrictions upon the actions of state governments and their officials. Instead, it acts to restrain the powers of the federal government—the perceived need for such protections being one of the main reasons Antifederalists advocated for its inclusion. For example, the First Amendment begins, "Congress shall make no law" and not, "Congress and the Legislatures of the several States shall make no laws."

So, for much of the nation's history, the explicit protections contained within the Bill of Rights did not apply to state laws and actions, and the Supreme Court upheld this strict, textual reading of the Constitution. The foundation for extending the protections of the Bill of Rights to state laws and actions was laid down in the Fourteenth Amendment, ratified in 1868. The Fourteenth Amendment's guarantee against the deprivation by any state of "life, liberty, or property without due process of law"—called the **due process clause**—laid the constitutional foundations for the extensions of the protections within the Bill of Rights to the actions and laws of the states. This process, however, is still ongoing.[27]

In a process called **selective incorporation** because of its selective, piecemeal development, the Supreme Court has, over time, used the due process clause of the Fourteenth Amendment to expand the protections within the Bill of Rights to also cover state laws and actions. Initially, however, the Court refused to do so when given the chance. In *The Slaughterhouse Cases* (1873), the Supreme Court interpreted the Fourteenth Amendment's protections as applying only to African Americans and reaffirmed sharp distinctions between state and federal citizenship.[28] It was not until 1925 with *Gitlow v. New York* that the Court began to make use of the due process clause to incorporate protections contained within the Bill of Rights.[29]

In its decision in *Gitlow v. New York* (1925), the Supreme Court formally incorporated one of the amendments in the Bill of Rights—in this case the First Amendment—through the Fourteenth Amendment. In doing so, it signaled to the states that there were limits on their ability to restrict expression and that the freedoms of speech and the press constituted *fundamental freedoms* that were beyond the legitimate restriction by state actions in the absence of a compelling reason to do so. The decision stated that "for present purposes, we may and do assume that freedom of speech and of the press which are protected by the First Amendment from abridgment by Congress are among the fundamental personal rights and 'liberties' protected by the due process clause of the Fourteenth Amendment from impairment by the States."[30]

Following the decision in *Gitlow*, over the next two decades the Supreme Court began to issue a series of decisions incorporating most of the First Amendment's protections for speech, the press, assembly, and religion. Several decades later, in another burst of activity, the Court incorporated the protections for those accused of, arrested for, tried for, and convicted of crimes under state laws.

Benjamin Gitlow, right, running as a vice presidential candidate for the Workers Party in 1928.
Bettmann/Contributor.

Most recently, in 2010 the Court incorporated the Second Amendment's affirmation of the right "to keep and bear arms" through the due process clause of the Fourteenth Amendment.[31] As of 2016, most, but not all, of the protections within the Bill of Rights had been incorporated. We will explore many of these cases in detail in this chapter as we consider specific amendments, the protections that they affirm, and the tensions and controversies arising from trying to delimit the boundaries of their promises.

After being pardoned by the governor in 1925, Benjamin Gitlow continued to organize, travelling several times to Soviet Russia. He later renounced communism and continued to write and publish, only this time *against* the revolutionary organizations of which he had been a part.[32] His case has become one of the most important in the history of the Supreme Court. *Gitlow v. New York* was the first in a long and punctuated series of decisions by the Court that incorporated the amendments within the Bill of Rights (see Table 4.2).

The process of selective incorporation has cleared up one question about civil liberties: Are state governments also restricted in their ability to infringe upon Americans' fundamental rights and freedoms? They are. Within the long list of protections contained within the Bill of Rights are many other questions, however, all revolving around where the boundaries of these protections lie. To investigate these issues, we will consider the amendments and the liberties affirmed within them in turn.

THE FIRST AMENDMENT: "CONGRESS SHALL MAKE NO LAW"

The third suggested amendment in James Madison's list of seventeen ended up as the First Amendment to the Constitution. The First Amendment restricts the power of what most

TABLE 4.2 Selective Incorporation of the Bill of Rights

Amendment	Right Incorporated	Supreme Court Decision
First	Freedom from establishment of religion	*Everson v. Board of Education*, 330 U.S. 1 (1947)
	Freedom of religious expression	*Cantwell v. Connecticut*, 310 U.S. 296 (1940)
	Freedom of speech	*Gitlow v. New York*, 268 U.S. 652 (1925)
	Freedom of the press	*Near v. Minnesota ex rel. Olson*, 283 U.S. 697 (1931)
	Right to peaceably assemble	*De Jonge v. Oregon*, 299 U.S. 353 (1937)
Second	Right to keep and bear arms	*McDonald v. Chicago*, 561 U.S. 742 (2010)
Third	Right not to have soldiers quartered in homes	Not incorporated
Fourth	Protection against unreasonable searches and seizures	*Wolf v. Colorado*, 338 U.S. 25 (1949) (Illegally obtained evidence is still permissible in trial, however.)
	Warrant needed for search and seizure	*Mapp v. Ohio*, 367 U.S. 643 (1961) (Illegally obtained evidence cannot be used in trial.)
Fifth	Right to indictment by grand jury in cases involving a serious crime	Not incorporated
	Protection against double jeopardy	*Benton v. Maryland*, 395 U.S. 784 (1969)
	Protection against self-incrimination	*Malloy v. Hogan*, 378 U.S. 1 (1964)
	Right of just compensation for private property taken	*Chicago, Burlington, and Quincy Railroad v. City of Chicago*, 166 U.S. 226 (1897)
Sixth	Right to a speedy and public trial	*In re Oliver*, 333 U.S. 257 (1948); *Klopfer v. North Carolina*, 386 U.S. 213 (1967)
	Right to trial by an impartial jury	*Parker v. Gladden*, 385 U.S. 363 (1966)
	Right to confront witnesses	*Pointer v. Texas*, 380 U.S. 400 (1965)
	Right to compel witnesses to testify in the defendant's favor	*Washington v. Texas*, 388 U.S. 14 (1967)
	Right to counsel in cases involving capital punishment	*Powell v. Alabama*, 287 U.S. 45 (1932)
	Right to counsel in felony cases	*Gideon v. Wainwright*, 372 U.S. 335 (1963)
Seventh	Right to trial by jury in civil cases	Not incorporated
Eighth	Protection against excessive bail or fines	Not incorporated*
	Protection against cruel and unusual punishment	*Robinson v. California*, 370 U.S. 660 (1962)

Note: Some constitutional scholars disagree on whether this right has been formally incorporated. See *Schilb v. Kuebel*, 404 U.S. 357 (1971).

delegates to the Constitutional Convention thought would be the most powerful, and potentially the most dangerous, entity of the government: Congress, the legislative branch.

Religion: Establishment and Free Exercise

Of the list of civil liberties affirmed and protected in the Bill of Rights, the first two involve religion. The First Amendment begins, "Congress shall make no law respecting an establishment of religion, or prohibiting the free exercise thereof." These two statements, or clauses, form the constitutional bases for protections of religious freedom and expression in America. The first is called the establishment clause as it protects individuals from governmental establishment of, or support for, religion. The second statement is referred to as the free exercise clause because it guards the rights of individuals to exercise and express their religious beliefs.

> "Congress shall make no law respecting an establishment of religion, or prohibiting the free exercise thereof."

Recall our discussion of Bridget Mergens in Chapter 1. Her case involved questions about the boundaries of establishment protections and those of free exercise. As with so many other areas of civil liberties, these clauses involve situations that are clear-cut as well as those that are not so easy to evaluate. For example, any attempt by the federal government or one of the states to declare an official religion would be a clear violation of the establishment clause. Similarly, any attempt to prohibit Americans' expressions of their religious faiths in their own homes, provided they did not violate others' fundamental rights and freedoms, would also be unconstitutional.

What about the more difficult cases, however? Consider a student who wants to say a prayer in her valedictory address at her public high school's graduation ceremonies. For the school to appear to condone her prayer implies a violation of the establishment clause. For it to restrict her right to say a prayer, however, implies a violation of the free exercise clause. How should this situation be handled? It is in difficult cases like this one that the Supreme Court has had to decide what is and what is not constitutionally permissible.

Wariness about governmental power over religious practice is deep-rooted in the American experience. The desire to avoid religious persecution had fueled the establishment of several of the original colonial settlements. This history, however, did not mean that the colonies—or the later independent states—universally respected religious freedoms or separated the process of governing from the expression of faith. Members of certain faiths found themselves subject to state-imposed restrictions, including religious tests for the holding of office. For part of history, the phrase "In God We Trust" has appeared on the national currency.

The goal of separating governmental power and action from religious faith and expression, however, also has deep roots within the American experience. In his original seventeen suggested amendments, James Madison included a guarantee that "the civil rights of none shall be abridged on account of religious belief or worship, nor shall any national religion be established, nor shall the full and equal rights of conscience be in any manner, or on any pretext, infringed."[33] That Madison used the phrase "rights of conscience" rather than something like religious "toleration" was very intentional. That a government would tolerate religious faith and expression, to Madison, assumed that the government had the authority *to* tolerate it or not, that it could dispense or withdraw such power.

Madison's goals in establishing constitutional protections for the "rights of conscience" were twofold. First, he wanted to ensure protections of people's rights from the fusion of a particular faith with the coercive power of government, a concern that was very real and one against which he struggled his entire life. But there was more to it than this. Madison was not trying to weaken or undermine religion. Far from it. He also wanted to protect the adherence to and expression of religious faith from governmental interference, especially from the factions that always seemed to arise in republics. While

An engraving portraying the whipping of Baptist minister Obadiah Holmes in Massachusetts in 1651. The framers of the Constitution were well aware of religious persecution in the American colonies, even in the Puritan colonies that had been established to preserve their own religious practices.

The Granger Collection, New York.

the promotion of a religious faith could be dangerous to individual liberties, a government might also pose a danger to religious faith and expression.

Another key early statement of religious freedom, and one cited by later Supreme Court justices in their opinions, was Thomas Jefferson's "Letter to the Danbury Baptists," written in 1802. The Danbury Baptists were a religious minority in Connecticut, and they complained that in their state, the religious liberties they enjoyed were not seen as immutable rights but as privileges allocated by the legislature as "favors granted"—favors that could just as readily be taken away. In his letter, Jefferson stated, "I contemplate with sovereign reverence that act of the whole American people which declared that their legislature should make no law respecting an establishment of religion, or prohibiting the free exercise thereof, thus building 'a wall of separation between church and state.'"[34] The metaphor of a "wall of separation" is quite powerful, but how workable is it in the messy world of American politics? Supreme Court justices have had to wrestle with this very question, just as school officials in Bridget Mergens's case had to do.

The Establishment Clause and the Supreme Court

While Madison and Jefferson had been instrumental in laying the foundations of civil liberties in the area of religious freedoms, selective incorporation of these fundamental rights occurred over several decades in the twentieth century. We will begin our exploration of this with the Supreme Court's evolving treatment of establishment questions and then move on to free exercise.

Taxpayer Funds and Private Religious Schools

One of the most important Supreme Court decisions dealing with government support for or involvement with religion, and the one that incorporated the establishment clause, was *Everson v. Board of Education* (1947). The case considered a New Jersey law that authorized payment by local school boards of the costs of transportation to and from private schools, including Catholic ones. A New Jersey taxpayer filed suit claiming the taxpayer support constituted impermissible government support for religion. In its decision, a divided Court ruled that the program, though "on the verge" of offering impermissible aid, was acceptable as it was a "general program to help parents get their children, regardless of their religion, safely and expeditiously to and from accredited schools."[35] In his opinion, however, Justice Hugo Black affirmed the principle of separation, stating, "In the words of Jefferson, the clause against establishment of religion by law was intended to erect 'a wall of separation between Church and State.'"[36]

In *Board of Education v. Allen* (1968), the Supreme Court again affirmed the principle that there could be some permissible forms of taxpayer support for private religious schools. Divided 6–3, the Court ruled in favor of a New York law that provided free textbooks to middle and high school students, including those in private religiously affiliated schools. In his dissenting opinion, Black critiqued the majority's reasoning and warned that it set a dangerous precedent: "It is true, of course, that the New York law does not, as yet, formally adopt or establish a state religion. But it takes a great stride in that direction. . . . And it nearly always is by insidious approaches that the citadels of liberty are most successfully attacked."[37]

Prayer in Schools

Perhaps no establishment clause issue has been more vexing to the Supreme Court than that of prayer in public schools. In 1962, in *Engle v. Vitale*, the Court ruled unconstitutional the voluntary reading in New York's public schools of the prayer, "Almighty God, we acknowledge our dependence upon Thee, and we beg Thy blessings upon us, our parents, our teachers and our Country."[38] Although the policy's supporters argued that the prayer was nondenominational and permitted students to remain silent or be excused from the classroom during the reading, the Court found that it violated the establishment clause. The next year, in *Abington School District v. Schempp*, the Court struck down a program that involved the reading of ten verses from the Bible and a recitation of the Lord's Prayer at the beginning of each day in Pennsylvania's public schools.[39] In his opinion, Justice Tom C. Clark quoted Madison's warnings about the dangers of enmeshing government and religion, even in seemingly small ways, noting that "it is proper to take alarm at the first experiment on our liberties."[40]

Current Status of Prayer in Schools

Supreme Court justices are not the only individuals who have had to try to balance the separation of government and religion against the need to protect the rights of individuals to express their own faiths. Administrators and teachers in the nation's public schools and universities have also had to navigate this complicated constitutional tension.

According to guidelines produced for public schools and districts by the United States Department of Education, students may not pray during instructional time but may do so (on their own volition) during noninstructional time, such as before school or during lunch. They may also, again on their own volition only, pray during "moments of silence" in schools, provided that the school makes it clear that such moments are not set aside to encourage prayer. Students may be excused from instruction "to remove a significant burden on their religious exercise . . . where doing so would not impose material burdens on other students," and they may participate in organized religious student groups and clubs under the same rules as the school sets for nonreligious groups. Students may express their religious beliefs in their homework and other assignments, but their work must be evaluated solely on its academic merits.

Teachers and administrators may not encourage or discourage prayer in their official capacity but may participate in religious activities when not in their official capacity, such as a Bible study group with other teachers that meets outside of instructional time. While schools may not

Students at Royal High School in Simi Valley, California–a public school–in prayer during a lunchtime meeting. As long as such meetings occur outside of instructional time and are both initiated and led by students, they are constitutionally permissible.

Anne Cusack/Los Angeles Times via Getty Images.

offer organized prayers during assemblies and extracurricular events, individual students may—of their own volition, and assuming they have been chosen as speakers based on nonreligious criteria—express their own faith. Schools, however, are free to "make appropriate, neutral disclaimers to clarify that such speech (whether religious or nonreligious) is the speaker's and not the school's."[41] If all of this sounds complicated, that's because it is, for students, parents, school officials, and Supreme Court justices.

Supreme Court Tests for Governmental Involvement with Religion

In trying to set guidelines for what is and is not permissible under the establishment clause, the Court has at different times employed various litmus tests for federal and state laws and actions. Proponents of a strict separationist approach to deciding the issue argue for a close textual reading of the establishment clause and say no forms of government support for religious institutions are permissible. However, given the history of religion in American political life and policy objectives—such as in helping students receive a good education—strict separation can be difficult to achieve in the real world. For example, in its decision in *Everson v. Board of Education*, in which it cited Jefferson's metaphor of a "wall of separation," the Court allowed taxpayer funds to be used for transporting students to and from religious schools.

Lemon test
A three-pronged test developed by the Supreme Court to determine whether a law or action by the federal or a state government violates the establishment clause.

One of the most important tools that the Court has used is the **Lemon test**, named after the Court decision in which it was formally laid out: *Lemon v. Kurtzman* (1971).[42] The case dealt with Rhode Island and Pennsylvania programs that supplemented the salaries of teachers and provided educational materials (though only the same ones used in the public schools) in religiously based private schools for the purpose of teaching nonreligious subjects. The Court struck down both programs as violating the establishment clause. In doing so, it set out a three-pronged test for permissible government involvement. First, the underlying statute must have a "secular legislative purpose." Second, its effect "must be one that neither advances nor inhibits religion." Third, it must not foster "excessive entanglement between government and religion."

The Lemon test has its critics. Many scholars, as well as some Supreme Court justices, have argued that the test is too subjective, requiring justices to ascertain the motives of the legislators who passed the laws in the first place. Others have argued that the test sets too high a wall of separation between church and state, one that is difficult to consistently apply. Since *Lemon*, the Court has been more willing to relax the standards of the test and instead has often followed a logic that emphasizes the principle of religious neutrality, examining the degree to which the law or policy in question provides benefits to a broad class of individuals and if the provision of public funds to religious institutions arises from individual choice without coercion on the part of the government.[43]

neutrality test
a Supreme Court test for examining questions of free expression that allows restrictions upon religious expression, provided that laws doing so not single out one faith, or faith over nonfaith.

Free Exercise and the Supreme Court

While Americans are free to hold any religious beliefs, they are not always free to act on them.

As we examined in the discussion of prayer in schools, important cases concerning religious establishment often involve the second of the First Amendment's two guarantees on religious freedom: freedom of religious expression. While Americans are free to hold any religious beliefs, they are not always free to act on them. As is the case with the establishment clause, the Supreme Court has had to wrestle with the boundaries of free exercise.

The free exercise clause was incorporated through the due process clause of the Fourteenth Amendment in *Cantwell v. Connecticut* (1940). The case involved the distribution of religious materials and playing of religious messages on a phonograph by two members of the Jehovah's Witnesses in a predominantly Catholic neighborhood. The two men, Jesse Cantwell and his son, were arrested under a town ordinance that gave local government officials the authority to decide if such solicitation was legal or not. In its decision, the Supreme Court distinguished between "freedom to believe and freedom to act. The first [the Court noted] is absolute, but, in the nature of things, the second cannot be."[44] While the Court upheld the principal that the state might have a valid interest in restricting the actions involved in religious expression—to maintain safety and public order, for example—in this case the Cantwells' actions posed no threat other than being offensive to some. Their convictions were overturned.

More recently, in *Employment Division v. Smith* (1990), the Court adopted a neutrality test in deciding on conflicts between religious expression and legitimate state action. In that case, two individuals had been fired from their jobs as rehabilitation counselors for using the sacramental religious drug peyote in violation of Oregon State law. They were also denied unemployment benefits as a result of their termination. The two men argued that the use of peyote was within their First Amendment rights of free expression as members of the Native American Church.[45] In its opinion, the Court ruled that the state law banning the use and possession of peyote was not targeted toward individuals as a result of their beliefs but that it represented a valid, compelling state interest and was religiously neutral, even if it restricted the religious expression of individuals.

Supporters of Paul Skyhorse Durant and Buzz Berry gather outside Ventura County court in California where they prayed and beat a drum in support of the men's efforts to have 10,000 Peyote buttons that were seized by the county sheriff's department returned to them. The two men had argued that the use of peyote, a hallucinogen, was a constitutionally protected part of their exercise of their First Amendment rights of free exercise of religion in spite of it's classification as an illegal substance.

Steve Osman/Los Angeles Times via Getty Images.

freedom of expression
a fundamental right affirmed in the First Amendment to speak, publish, and act in the political space.

The Alien and Sedition Acts
four separate laws passed under the administration of President John Adams that, among other things, restricted the freedom of speech and the press.

A 1798 engraving depicting a fight in Congress over the Sedition Act of 1798.

The Granger Collection, New York.

OTHER FIRST AMENDMENT PROTECTIONS

Speech, Press, Assembly, and Petition

Although they come after the two clauses about religion in the text, those parts of the First Amendment that deal with freedom of expression are often considered the most fundamental affirmations of Americans' rights and liberties. They involve the expression of political beliefs and opinions. The right to express one's thoughts, especially in being critical of those in power, is one of the cornerstones of American civil liberties. Thomas Jefferson's draft of the Declaration of Independence, Thomas Paine's *Common Sense*, the *Federalist Papers*, Antifederalist writings, Benjamin Gitlow's essays on the need to overthrow the United States government, and Edward Snowden's release of classified documents all involved or questioned the rights of individuals to speak, to publish, and to peaceably assemble without fear of retribution or imprisonment.

Early Challenges to Expression: The Alien and Sedition Acts

Those who argued for the importance of freedom of expression had good reason to want to protect it. Shortly after the new nation was founded it was confronted with the question of how far a government could go to restrict these rights. Like many other cases since, this one revolved around questions of national security. The situation involved laws known as the **Alien and Sedition Acts**, which were passed by Congress—controlled by the Federalist Party—and signed into law by Federalist president John Adams in 1798. Consisting of four separate acts, these laws attempted to suppress Antifederalist opposition of the policies of the president and Congress. Among other provisions, the acts authorized severe restrictions on the rights of free speech and the free press. Any behavior that was judged by a federal court (which were usually controlled by Federalist Party judges) to be part of a conspiracy against the government of the United States, or any publication or speech that was deemed to be "false, scandalous, [or] malicious. . . . against the government of the United States, or either house of the Congress of the United States, or the President of the United States," was punishable by fines and imprisonment.[46] Under the power of these acts, newspaper editors opposing Adams and the Federalists "were quickly indicted, and ten were brought to trial and convicted by juries under the influence of Federalist judges."[47]

Congressional pugilists.

1. *Jona Dayton, Speaker.* 2. *Jno W. Condy, Clerk.*

He in a trice struck Lyon thrice
Upon his head, enrag'd, sir.

Who seiz'd the tongs to ease his wrongs,
And Grifwold thus engag'd, sir.

Congress Hall,
in Philad.ª Feb. 15. 1798.
S.E. Cor. 6.ᵗʰ & Chesnut S.

National Security and Political Expression

One of the most difficult issues in the protection of political expression is balancing that fundamental right with the needs of national security. Benjamin Gitlow—the radical socialist whose conviction by the New York State judicial system was upheld by the Supreme Court—was not the first American to press his free expression claims following the nation's involvement in World War I. He was also not the first to lose his claim.

In 1917 Charles Schenck and Elizabeth Baer oversaw the printing and distribution of antiwar leaflets encouraging young men not to comply with the military draft. They were convicted under the Espionage Act of 1917, which, among other things, made it a crime to interfere with military recruiting. In *Schenck v. United States* (1919), a unanimous Court ruled against the defendants, arguing that the restrictions on expression under the Espionage Act were permissible.

"The most stringent protection of free speech," Justice Oliver Wendell Holmes wrote in the unanimous decision, "would not protect a man falsely shouting fire in a theatre and causing a panic. . . . The question in every case is whether the words used are used in such circumstances and are of such a nature as to create a clear and present danger that they will bring about the substantive evils that Congress has a right to prevent."[48] In its decision, the Court established the **clear and present danger test** to evaluate legitimate and illegitimate restrictions on political speech, in which, as Holmes noted, the context of that expression must be taken into account.

The danger, so to speak, with the clear and present danger test is its subjectivity. If a government can restrict urgings not to comply with a draft, then the scope of restricted speech might be interpreted quite widely. That is precisely what happened. In 1918, near the end of World War I, a group of Russian-born anarchists distributed pamphlets in which they criticized President Woodrow Wilson, calling him a coward and a hypocrite, and denounced the United States' actions against the communist revolutionaries in the country.

The anarchists were convicted under the Sedition Act of 1918, which made it a criminal offense to "willfully utter, print, write or publish any disloyal, profane, scurrilous, or abusive language about the form of government of the United States or the Constitution of the United States, or the military or naval forces of the United States, or the flag of the United States." In *Abrams v. United States* (1919), the Supreme Court, citing the logic of *Schenck v. United States*, upheld their convictions.[49]

Unlike the decision in *Schenck*, however, that of *Abrams* was not unanimous; two justices opposed the majority. In his dissenting opinion, Holmes—who had established the clear and present danger test in *Schenck*—stood by the ruling in that case but claimed the conviction and twenty-year sentence were not justified by "the surreptitious publishing of a silly leaflet by an unknown man." Failing to be convinced that Abrams's words and those of his colleagues constituted an "imminent threat," Holmes went on to establish the idea that ideas should compete, as in a marketplace. He wrote, "The best test

clear and present danger test
a Supreme Court tool to evaluate whether or not forms of political expression constitute such a threat to national security as to warrant restriction.

Associate Justice Oliver Wendell Holmes, one of the most influential legal minds in American jurisprudence. He participated in some of the most important cases that defined the boundaries of civil liberties.
Bettmann/Contributor.

of truth is the power of the thought to get itself accepted in the competition of the market."[50] As with all dissenting opinions, Holmes's words did not reflect the mindset of the majority, but his language endured and has been cited by justices in future Courts as they wrestled with the need to balance free political expression with national security.

World War II and the years following it also saw efforts to restrict political speech in the name of national security. In 1940, as war raged across the globe, Congress passed the Smith Act, which, among other provisions, made it a federal crime to advocate for the overthrow of the national government.[51] Following World War II, the United States found itself in an ideological and military struggle with the Soviet Union, though one that never resulted in all-out global conflict. During the late 1940s and early 1950s, America experienced what is known as the "Red Scare," in which fears of Communist Party infiltration of the United States government—stoked in part by Wisconsin senator Joseph McCarthy—resulted in investigations and accusations of suspected communist activity from Hollywood to Washington, D.C. It was a time of widespread fear, not only of communists but also of being accused of being one. According to writer Irving Brant, "On July 4, 1951, the Madison Wisconsin *Capital Times* sent out two reporters to ask people encountered at random to sign a petition saying that they believed in the Declaration of Independence. Out of the 112 persons interviewed, all but one refused to sign. The common ground of refusal was not the obvious fact that such a petition was useless. 'They were afraid,' the newspaper reported, 'that it

Clarence Brandenburg, left, a Ku Klux Klan leader, with Richard Hanna, an admitted member of the American Nazi Party, in Cincinnati, Ohio, in August 1964. Brandenburg's case established a high standard of permissible speech, up to advocating for the legitimacy of violent action, but not organizing for it.

AP Photo.

was some kind of subversive document and that they would lose their jobs or be called Communists.'"[52]

The modern standard for restrictions on political speech was set in 1969 in *Brandenburg v. Ohio.* In that case, a leader of the American white supremacist group the Ku Klux Klan was convicted under an Ohio law for advocating "crime, sabotage, violence, or unlawful methods of terrorism as a means of accomplishing industrial or political reform." At issue was a speech at a filmed rally in which a cross was burned and Brandenburg threatened, "if our President, our Congress, our Supreme Court, continues to suppress the white, Caucasian race, it's possible that there might have to be some vengeance taken."[53] The Supreme Court overturned Brandenburg's conviction and established a two-pronged test of acceptable restrictions on such political speech: It must be "directed to inciting or producing imminent lawless action and [must be] likely to incite or produce such action."[54] The test that the Court developed placed a much higher standard on permissible restrictions of political speech, even speech which advocates for the legitimacy of violent action, though it must not actually organize for it.

The Press and National Security

The tension between national security and limits on free expression does not only apply to individuals and organizations, it also applies to the press. As we discussed earlier in the chapter, one of the goals of the Alien and Sedition Acts was to restrict the ability of the press to criticize the federal government. When such restriction happens before an article is published—as opposed to after the fact—it is known as **prior restraint**. The Democratic-Republican victories in the election of 1800 resulted in the repeal or expiration of the Alien and Sedition Acts, but the Supreme Court did not weigh in on the issue of prior restraint until the twentieth century.

The question of the permissibility of prior restraint during wartime came up during the Vietnam conflict and centered on attempts by the Nixon administration to prevent the *New York Times* and the *Washington Post* from publishing classified materials describing—often unflatteringly—high-level decision making on the part of U.S. officials in conducting the war. In *New York Times v. United States* (1971), which was also known as the "Pentagon Papers case," the Supreme Court, in a highly divided opinion, ruled that the government did not demonstrate a sufficiently pressing interest to justify such prior restraint; this set a very high bar for the ability of government to prevent publication.[55]

prior restraint
the suppression of material prior to publication on the grounds that it might endanger national security.

Symbolic Speech

The Supreme Court has not restricted its protection of political expression to spoken and printed words but has also extended it to **symbolic speech**, such as images, signs, and symbols used as forms of political expression. These protections—like those for other forms of political expression—are not, however, absolute.

symbolic speech
protected expression in the form of images, signs, and other symbols.

In 1968, in *United States v. O'Brien*, the Court ruled against David Paul O'Brien and three other individuals in Boston who had burned their draft cards and encouraged others to do so as well in protest against the Vietnam War. In doing so, it set out a three-pronged test of acceptable restriction of symbolic speech under such circumstances: (1) the government must have a substantial interest in doing do, (2) the restriction must not be for the purposes of restricting speech, and (3) the "incidental restriction" of the First Amendment rights should be "no greater than is essential to the furtherance of that interest."[56] In this case, the Supreme Court held that the government's need to have young men register for the selective service passed such a test.

In 1969, in *Tinker v. Des Moines Independent Community School District*, however, the Court upheld the right of three public school students in Des Moines, Iowa, to wear black armbands in protest of the war, an act for which they had been suspended from school. The Court argued that such restrictions were not necessary to preserve the school's ability to carry out its academic mission.[57] As with other forms of political expression, though, the rights of students to express their political beliefs—through speech, writing, or symbols—is not absolute. In yet another closely divided opinion, the Court ruled in *Morse v. Frederick* (2007) that school officials can restrict students' rights of expression if that conduct occurs on school grounds or under school supervision and if it violates or disrupts the mission of the school. The case involved a banner displayed by a group of students in Alaska during a school-supervised event featuring the carrying of the Olympic torch through Juneau. The banner read, "BONG HITS 4 JESUS," which school officials concluded promoted drug use, which was a violation of school rules and conduct.[58] The Court agreed.

Protesters burn an American flag in Central Park in opposition to the Vietnam War in 1967. The Supreme Court has made the symbolic act of flag burning a form of protected speech.

Leonard Detrick/NY Daily News Archive via Getty Images.

libel

expression in written form or similarly published media that defames a person's character.

slander

expression in spoken form that defames a person's character.

hate speech

speech that has no other purpose but to express hatred, particularly toward members of a group identified by racial or ethnic identity, gender, or sexual orientation.

The burning, alteration, or destruction of the American flag in protest—though controversial among the American public—has also received Supreme Court protection as a form of symbolic political expression. In *Texas v. Johnson* (1989), a closely divided Court overturned the conviction of a man who had burned the American flag during the 1984 Republican National Convention in protest of the policies of the administration of President Ronald Reagan. "The Government," the Court held, "may not prohibit the verbal or nonverbal expression of an idea merely because society finds the idea offensive or disagreeable, even where our flag is involved."[59]

Less Protected Forms of Expression

While political expression (in speech, writing, symbols, and of the press) has secured considerable protection, the Supreme Court has ruled that other types and forms of speech and publications do not have the same privilege, though it has often set a high bar for restrictions on them.

Expression that defames a person's character—whether in writing or similarly published media (**libel**) or in spoken form (**slander**)—is not protected in the same way as political expression and may leave the actor responsible for such statements in legal trouble.[60] To win a case based on libel or slander in the United States, an aggrieved party must show that the statements or publications were made with the knowledge that they were untrue, which is rather difficult to prove. For public figures, the standard is even higher, though there is often an unclear line dividing those who qualify as public figures from those who do not.

In 1964, in *New York Times v. Sullivan*, the Supreme Court placed significant hurdles on the ability of public officials to successfully sue for libel. In that case, a Montgomery, Alabama, official had won a $500,000 lawsuit against the *New York Times* for a full-page advertisement that the newspaper had published that had been written and paid for by civil rights activists and that accused Alabama officials of acting excessively during student protests. Even though some of the content of the advertisement was false, the Court, in a unanimous ruling, held that factual inaccuracies were not themselves sufficient to win a libel suit against a public official unless it could be demonstrated that they were published with "actual malice," meaning that the publishers had knowledge that the statements were untrue, or that they were published with "reckless disregard of the truth."[61]

Hate speech is another form of damaging expression upon which limits have been placed and for which the Court has struggled to define the proper boundaries. Hate speech is speech that has no other purpose but to express hatred, particularly toward members of a group identified by racial or ethnic identity, gender, or sexual orientation. One of the most charged forms of hate speech is the burning of crosses—sometimes even in people's yards—by white supremacist groups such as the Ku Klux Klan. In response to these acts, many communities have passed ordinances prohibiting such expression.

In 1990 a group of teenagers was arrested in St. Paul, Minnesota, for burning a cross made out of broken chair legs that had been taped together in the yard of an African American family who lived across the street from one of the members of the group. The teens were charged under a city ordinance that made it a misdemeanor to place "on public or private property" a symbol or object "including but not limited to, a burning cross or Nazi swastika," knowing that such an action might arouse "anger, alarm, or resentment in others on the basis of race, color, creed, religion or gender."[62]

While the Supreme Court agreed that the members of the group could have been legitimately arrested, tried, and prosecuted for committing other crimes—such as arson or making terroristic threats—it unanimously overturned their conviction under the hate speech ordinance and ruled the ordinance itself unconstitutional, stating, "The point of the First Amendment is that majority preferences must be expressed in some fashion other than silencing speech on the basis of its content."[63] Today, many college campuses have instituted hate speech codes for student conduct. While some of these policies have been challenged in federal court, the Supreme Court has yet to issue a decision on their constitutionality.

Another form of expression that receives weaker protection under the First Amendment is the issuance of fighting words—expression (spoken, written, or symbolic) that is likely to incite violence or disrupt the peace. Again, it is a tricky issue of definition. The same words spoken in one context might lead to a violent altercation but not do so in another context. In *Chaplinsky v. State of New Hampshire* (1942), the Court upheld restrictions on words that "by their very utterance, inflict injury or tend to incite an immediate breach of the peace," but it also affirmed that such restrictions must be narrowly targeted so as not to constitute an undue restriction of First Amendment rights.[64]

Finally, The Supreme Court has upheld restrictions on **obscenity and pornography**, though, as with other forms of expression, it has not always been clear just what constitutes an obscene statement or publication. In *Roth v. United States* (1957), the Court defined the standard for judging obscenity—and, therefore, constitutionally permissible restrictions on its expression—as "whether, to the average person, applying contemporary community standards, the dominant theme of the material, taken as a whole, appeals to prurient interest."[65] Marking the boundaries this way raises another challenge, however. What, exactly, are "contemporary community standards" and who gets to delimit them?

In *Miller v. California* (1973), the Supreme Court attempted to present a clearer definition of obscenity. Called the Miller test—in reference to the case name—it sets out three criteria that all must be met for material to be considered obscene and, therefore, legitimately subject to restriction. First, the material must be "patently offensive." It must also be "utterly without redeeming social value." Finally, in determining the applicability of the first two parts of the test, "contemporary community standards" must be applied, meaning that different locales may have different standards.[66]

When one considers material published over the Internet, things become even more challenging. For example, how does one define "community" when considering online material? In 1997 the Court struck down provisions of the 1996 Communications Decency Act, which had been designed to protect minors from viewing obscene or pornographic material on the Internet. The Court held that the restrictions in the act were too vague and restrictive and that they carried the danger of having a "chilling effect on free speech."[67] Depictions of sexual material involving minors, however, have carried no similar First Amendment protections and are subject to full restriction and criminalization.

Freedom of Assembly

The final two rights within the First Amendment—the right to peaceably assemble and to petition the government—have received relatively little Supreme Court attention. When the Court has ruled on them, however, it has generally done so in a way similar to how it has treated political expression, regarding them as cornerstones of civil liberties and rights that should be broadly protected.

obscenity and pornography
text, images, or video that depicts sexual activity in ways offensive to the broader community and that lacks any artistic merit.

The right to peacefully assemble was incorporated in 1937 in *De Jonge v. Oregon*. In that case, the Court overturned an Oregon law under which a member of the Communist Party had been convicted and sentenced to seven years in prison for holding a public meeting. In his opinion, quoting an earlier case, Chief Justice Charles Hughes noted, "The very idea of a government, republican in form, implies a right on the part of citizens to meet peaceably for consultation in respect to public affairs and to petition for a redress of grievances."[68]

As is probably clear by now, there has been a great deal of struggle, controversy, and Supreme Court action throughout American history with regard to freedom of religion, speech, the press, and assembly—and these all involve only the First Amendment.[69] In the Bill of Rights, there are nine other liberties that are also addressed.

NEWS CLIP
McDonald v. Chicago

THE SECOND AMENDMENT: FIREARMS

Although firearms ownership by Americans has become a highly charged topic of debate in politics today, for most of its history the Supreme Court said very little about the issue. In 1939 the Court upheld restrictions on private ownership of certain types of weapons—sawed-off shotguns and machine guns—as a result of gangland violence during the era of prohibition.[70] In his opinion in *United States v. Miller*, Justice James McReynolds stated that "in the absence of any evidence tending to show that possession or use of a 'shotgun having a barrel of less than eighteen inches in length' at this time has some reasonable relationship to the preservation or efficiency of a well regulated militia, we cannot say that the Second Amendment guarantees the right to keep and bear such an instrument."[71]

Not until 2008 did the Court rule directly on laws prohibiting personal possession of firearms generally, as opposed to specific types of them. In a 5–4 decision in *District of Columbia v. Heller*, the Court overturned a District of Columbia ban on handgun ownership for the purpose of self-defense within an individual's home.[72] As the *Heller* case involved Washington, D.C., and not a state, it was decided based on the Second Amendment directly. Incorporation, however, happened two years later, in *McDonald v. Chicago*. In this case, the Court—again splitting 5–4—overturned a Chicago ban on handgun ownership.[73]

"Philosoraptor" and Second Amendment Memes

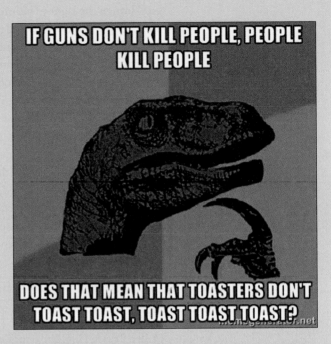

Philosoraptor © LonelyDinosaur.com/CC BY-NC-SA, https://creativecommons.org/licenses/by-nc-sa/3.0/.

In 2008 Sam Smith, a T-shirt designer, introduced to the world his image of "Philosoraptor," a dinosaur appearing to be engaged in deep contemplation. The image quickly became the subject of countless Internet memes, some of which alluded to debates over the Second Amendment.

Proponents of the right of Americans to carry firearms used the meme to challenge arguments that the Second Amendment referred to times past and did not apply in the twenty-first century.

Proponents of restrictions on firearms ownership used the same meme to challenge arguments that people, and not firearms, are the ultimate source of the problem of gun violence in America.

WHAT DO YOU THINK?

Regardless of your own views on the Second Amendment and firearms ownership, how effective do you think the use of a meme such as "Philosoraptor" can be when trying to shape opinion on issues as hotly debated as gun ownership? Can the humor lead people to reflect, or might it undercut the seriousness of the underlying issues and debates? On what other issues have you encountered the use of memes to shape political opinion? Do you think they were successful?

■ CRIMINAL RIGHTS

As its defenders pointed out during the ratification debates, one area in which the proposed Constitution (prior to the adding of the Bill of Rights) did address civil liberties was in protecting the rights of the accused and convicted. Article I, which lays out the powers of Congress, prohibits that branch from passing laws—called *ex post facto* laws—that make illegal, and therefore punishable, conduct that was legal prior to the passage of a new law. It also prohibits bills of attainder, which are acts that punish individuals without a trial.[74]

writ of habeas corpus

a statement demanding that authorities in charge of a person's detention establish the reasons for that detention.

Article I also establishes the right of an individual to demand a **writ of habeas corpus** upon his or her arrest or detention (except in the case of rebellion or invasion). Such a writ, if granted by a court, demands that authorities in charge of the person's detention establish the reasons for that detention. If the authorities fail to do so, the person is free to go. Though the right to petition for a writ of habeas corpus may seem like an obscure legal issue, as we will explore in depth in Chapter 13, it has become one of the central issues in defining and debating the limits on presidential power as America engages in the war on terror in the twenty-first century.

All these protections, however, were not sufficient for many of the opponents of the proposed Constitution, who feared that the federal government would use its power to upend, violate, or ignore the actions of the courts within the states or of the individuals residing in the states. Their worries found support during the ratification debates, and fully half of the ten amendments in the Bill of Rights set boundaries for federal governmental action in dealing with the breaking of and enforcing of the laws. Central to the protections for those accused, tried, and/or convicted of a crime is the idea of **procedural justice**, in which the standard of fairness is applied to all participants equally.[75] Most, but not all, of these standards have since been applied to the actions of the states themselves through the process of incorporation.

procedural justice

a judicial standard requiring that fairness be applied to all participants equally.

NEWS CLIP
California pier shooting

The Fourth Amendment:
Search, Seizure, Warrants, and Evidence

Under British rule, the American colonists had gained a vivid understanding of the potential dangers of allowing a government to stop or inspect individuals or to search citizens' homes without oversight or procedural protections for those who were targeted. Under what conditions can a government legitimately search a person or persons? Even at the time of the adoption of the Bill of Rights, this was not an easy question to answer. With the development of modern technology, the question has only grown more complicated.

In *Katz v. United States* (1967), the Supreme Court established a standard for procedures for obtaining evidence of a crime and wrestled with the challenges that technology poses to setting such boundaries.[76] The case involved an individual, Katz, who had been convicted of operating a gambling operation based on evidence obtained from a police wiretap of a phone booth that he had been using. While the Court found there was ample reason for a judge to issue a **warrant**—a writ issued by a judge authorizing some activity, such as tapping a phone line or searching an apartment—the officers had not done so in this case. The Court overturned Katz's conviction and established the need for officers to obtain a warrant from a judge based on **probable cause**, or reasonable suspicion that a crime has been committed or that there is evidence indicating so. In his decision in *Katz*, Justice Potter Stewart mentioned, however, that police in "hot pursuit" of a suspect were exempt from this requirement since such a delay might endanger their safety or that of others.[77]

A closely related issue is whether or not evidence that has been obtained without following proper procedures can be used in a trial. The **exclusionary rule** governs the inadmissibility of evidence obtained without a proper warrant.

The case through which the Fourth Amendment's protections were extended to the states, *Mapp v. Ohio* (1961), dealt with just such an issue. It also happened to involve pornography. While investigating a different crime (a recent bombing), police obtained in the dwelling of Dollree Mapp—without possessing a warrant—"certain lewd and lascivious books, pictures, and photographs," placing her in violation of an Ohio

warrant

a writ issued by a judge authorizing some activity.

probable cause

reasonable belief that a crime has been committed or that there is evidence indicating so.

exclusionary rule

a rule governing the inadmissibility of evidence obtained without a proper warrant.

anti-obscenity law.[78] The Court threw out her conviction and declared, "All evidence obtained by searches and seizures in violation of the Federal Constitution is inadmissible in a criminal trial in a state court."

As it has wrestled with the trickier issues in interpreting the exclusionary rule, such as electronic communications and transportation, the Court has ruled that the Fourth Amendment's protections are not absolute. In 1989 the Court upheld the conviction of a suspected drug dealer whose luggage had been searched without a warrant based on his behavior—he had paid cash for his ticket, checked no bags, and appeared nervous, among other "tells." The Court found that the DEA agents conducting the search had "reasonable suspicion" of criminal activity "based on the totality of circumstances."[79]

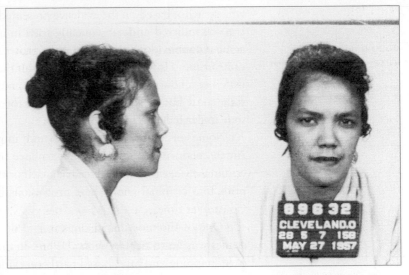

Dollree Mapp at the time of her arrest in 1957. The case of *Mapp v. Ohio* extended Fourth Amendment protections to the states by establishing that evidence gathered via illegal search and seizure is inadmissible in criminal trials in a state court.

AP Photo.

The Court has also upheld the use of evidence connected with a crime (such as a weapon) that was not named in the warrant but that was discovered in plain sight while lawfully searching for a different type of evidence (the stolen property).[80] In 1996 the Court upheld the introduction of illegal drugs as evidence, though the drugs had been obtained as a result of a traffic stop in which the officers were found to have had a "reasonable cause" to believe that a traffic violation had occurred.[81]

However, the Court has placed some restrictions on the use of evidence when modern surveillance or communications technologies are involved. In 2001 a closely divided Court invalidated the use of a thermal imaging scan done—without the suspect's knowledge or consent—to obtain evidence of the cultivation of marijuana in the suspect's private property. Such use of technology "that is not in general public use, to explore details of a private home that would previously have been unknowable without physical intrusion, the surveillance is a 4th Amendment 'search,' and is presumptively unreasonable without a warrant."[82] In 2014 the Court declared inadmissible evidence obtained from a suspect's cell phone without a warrant, though it allowed for some exceptions in certain emergencies.[83]

Testing individuals for the use of drugs is a specific, but controversial, aspect of procedural justice in searches. Private businesses may conduct drug testing of employees, but the Court has placed some limits on the use of drug testing as evidence of a criminal activity. For example, such testing is not permissible for patients in public hospitals without their consent.[84] Students in public schools enjoy a less robust interpretation of personal security, given the governmental interest in preserving the school's mission and student safety. In 1995 the Court upheld random drug testing of student athletes[85] and in 2002 drug testing of students involved in extracurricular activities.[86]

The Fifth Amendment: The Grand Jury, Double Jeopardy, and Self-Incrimination

The Fifth Amendment also provides protections for those accused of crimes, especially in guaranteeing processes and procedures for their defense. Those suspected of having committed serious crimes must have an indictment handed down by a **grand jury**—a group of

grand jury
a group of citizens who, based on the evidence presented to them, conclude whether or not a person is to be indicted and subsequently tried in a court of law.

double jeopardy
the prosecution of an individual more than once for the same crime.

citizens who, based on the evidence presented to them, conclude whether or not the person is to be indicted and subsequently tried in a court of law. It also establishes protections against **double jeopardy**, which is the prosecution of an individual more than once for the same crime. However, while an individual cannot be acquitted of a crime and then convicted in a court in the same jurisdiction, individuals can be acquitted for an offence in a state court but then tried and convicted for the same incident in a federal court, but this time under federal charges.

Some of the most sweeping and important protections described in the Fifth Amendment involve the right not to have to testify or bear witness against oneself in a criminal case, either during the trial itself or during the introduction of testimony obtained prior to a criminal trial. These protections have been extended and strengthened by the Court over time.

One of the most important cases in delineating the protections of those accused of crimes was *Miranda v. Arizona* (1966). In that case, Ernesto Miranda had been convicted of kidnapping and rape, based partly on evidence obtained while he was being questioned by officers without an attorney present. During this questioning, he signed a confession. In its ruling, the Supreme Court overturned Miranda's conviction, declaring, "Prior to any questioning, the person must be warned that he has a right to remain silent, that any statement he does make may be used as evidence against him, and that he has a right to the presence of an attorney, either retained or appointed. The defendant may waive effectuation of these rights, provided the waiver is made voluntarily, knowingly and intelligently."[87] Police officers now routinely inform individuals suspected of criminal activity that they have the right not to speak and to have an attorney present during questioning; these rights are commonly referred to as **Miranda rights**.

Miranda rights
the right not to speak and to have an attorney present during questioning; these rights must be given by police to individuals suspected of criminal activity.

The Sixth Amendment: Trials, Juries, and Attorneys

The Bill of Rights guarantees those accused of committing crimes the right to a speedy trial—a right that was extended to the states in 1963.[88] It also ensures the right to be tried in front of an impartial jury, which is more and more of a challenge given the instantaneous spread of news and opinion with modern technology. These protections, however, may not be of much use to a defendant if he or she does not have access to a qualified attorney during the complex legal process. While the Sixth Amendment guarantees the right to have counsel present at trial, for most of the nation's history that meant the right to hire an attorney only if you could afford one.

In 1932 the Court extended this right to include the provision of attorneys in federal capital murder cases that carried the possibility of the death penalty if conviction was reached.[89] In 1938 the Court extended these protections to all federal criminal cases.[90] It was not until 1963—in one of the most famous cases in Supreme Court history—that the Court extended the guarantee of counsel for those unable to afford it to state criminal cases. That decision, in *Gideon v. Wainwright*, involved the conviction for robbery of Clarence Gideon, who had resorted to defending himself in a Florida court when his request to the judge for an attorney was denied.[91] More recently, the Court has strengthened these protections to try to ensure that criminal defendants receive "effective" legal representation and not just legal representation.[92]

bail
an amount of money posted as a security to allow the charged individual to be freed while awaiting trial.

The Eighth Amendment: Bail and Punishment

While a criminal defendant is awaiting a speedy trial before a jury, he or she may be able to post **bail**—an amount of money posted as a security to allow the charged individual to be freed while awaiting trial. Although the Eighth Amendment protects against "excessive bail," not every criminal defendant is entitled to bail at all. Those who are deemed to pose a sufficient risk of flight or further criminal activity may legitimately be denied the ability to post bail.

Much more contentious is the question of "cruel and unusual punishment," especially as it applies to the imposition of the death penalty. The death penalty was allowed at the time of ratification of the Constitution and the Bill of Rights, and the Fifth Amendment to the Constitution refers to circumstances in which individuals are "deprived of life." Proponents of its use argue that the death penalty can be an effective deterrent against the most heinous crimes. Opponents point to the potential for errors in conviction, discriminatory sentencing, and the movement away from its use in other democracies. While the Supreme Court has not declared the death penalty to be inherently in violation of the Eighth Amendment, it has imposed restrictions on its imposition.[93] For example, the Court has prohibited its use on convicted defendants with significant cognitive disabilities[94] and on juveniles.[95]

In Clarence Gideon's case, *Gideon v. Wainwright*, the Court extended the guarantee of counsel for those unable to afford it to state criminal cases.

Bettmann/Contributor.

THE LAST TWO AMENDMENTS IN THE BILL OF RIGHTS

Setting the Larger Boundaries around the Power of the Federal Government

Each of the first eight amendments in the Bill of Rights places literal, textual limits on the power of the federal government. The final two do not. Instead, the Ninth and Tenth Amendments more broadly structure the inclusion and exclusion of rights as well as powers of national and state governments.

The Ninth Amendment: Rights Not Specified

One of the concerns raised by opponents of including a list of rights in the Constitution was that such a list would be necessarily incomplete. What about those rights assumed but not specified? Would future federal government officials recognize or try to restrict them? The Ninth Amendment was included to address these fears as well as general concerns by Antifederalists about the future growth of federal governmental power. Its purpose was to put into writing one of the main worries about a bill of rights expressed during the ratification debates: that those fundamental rights and freedoms not textually listed might not be protected. The Ninth Amendment was ratified to make sure that American governments in the future would not be able to take advantage of the incompleteness of the listing of fundamental rights and freedoms to encroach on Americans' civil liberties.

The Tenth Amendment: Powers Reserved to the States

The inclusion of the Tenth Amendment was a direct response to the fears and demands of the Antifederalists during the ratification debates. Many of them wanted a direct statement of the limitation of national power to those powers textually listed, those enumerated, in the original document. All other powers were to be reserved to the several states, which is why we call most state powers under the Constitution "reserved powers." As it has turned

> "The powers not delegated to the United States by the Constitution, nor prohibited by it to the States, are reserved to the States respectively, or to the people."

out, however, and as we have already explored in our discussion of the development of American federalism, the Tenth Amendment has not proven to be as strong a protector of state power as some might have thought. That is not to say that it is irrelevant, however. States and their legislatures are increasingly protesting the power of the federal government—especially when they feel that it is requiring them to enact policies without fully funding their implementation—using the Tenth Amendment as their constitutional justification for doing so.

WHAT HAVE I LEARNED?

1. A writ of habeas corpus is a statement demanding authorities to produce justification for a person's detention.

   a. True
   b. False

2. Miranda rights offer protections _____.

   a. For protest
   b. During arrest
   c. Against being tried twice for the same incident
   d. In carrying out the death penalty

3. For what groups of individuals has the Supreme Court prohibited the use of the death penalty?

4. How are the Ninth and Tenth Amendments different from the first eight?

Answer Key: 1. a; 2. b; 3. Answers should include individuals with cognitive disabilities and juveniles.; 4. Answers should include a discussion of rights not specified (Ninth) and powers reserved to the states (Tenth).

CONNECTING TO . . .

The Right to Marry

As you read about the struggles to obtain marriage equality, consider the role of the Ninth Amendment in these efforts. Reflect upon the following:

- Rights enumerated in the other amendments that point to a right to privacy
- The challenges associated with a necessarily limited enumeration of fundamental rights and freedoms

AMERICANS CLAIM THEIR RIGHTS TO MARRIAGE EQUALITY

In 2009 Edith Windsor's wife, Thea C. Spyer, passed away from a progressive neurological disease. They had been married in Canada two years before, and their same-sex marriage had been recognized as valid by New York, their state of residence at the time of Spyer's passing.

In her biography, Windsor recalled the moment when they decided to commit to each other; it was in the 1960s, when Windsor answered Spyer's question about where the relationship was going. Windsor's answer, as she recalled decades later, was "I think I'd like to be engaged, say for a year. And if it still feels this goofy joyous, I'd like us to spend the rest of our lives together."[96] In 2007, after a nearly lifelong relationship, Windsor and Spyer married in Canada, a nation that recognized marriage equality.

Windsor and Spyer's marriage, however, was not considered legal under U.S. federal law. As such, after her wife's passing, Windsor was not entitled to the same federal tax provisions granted to surviving spouses in opposite-sex, federally recognized marriages. Therefore, Windsor had to pay more than $350,000 in federal estate taxes. With help, especially from the Lesbian, Gay, Bisexual, and Transgender (LGBT) Community Center in New York City, she sued the federal government, claiming her right to have her marriage recognized as legal under federal law and to "the equal protection

principles that the Court has found in the Fifth Amendment's Due Process clause."[97] In an interview in 2015, after Windsor had made constitutional history, she stated, "Honey, you've got to be loud and proud."[98]

At issue were a federal law and a right that Windsor claimed. The law was the Defense of Marriage Act (DOMA), passed by Congress during the presidency of Bill Clinton in 1996 by opponents of marriage equality. It was a reaction to an increasing belief that some states and state courts were likely to legalize same-sex marriages in the coming years. DOMA had two substantive sections. One section stated that for purposes of federal law, marriage meant a legal union between a man and a woman: "In determining the meaning of any Act of Congress, or of any ruling, regulation, or interpretation of the various administrative bureaus and agencies of the United States, the word 'marriage' means only a legal union between one man and one woman as husband and wife, and the word 'spouse' refers only to a person of the opposite sex who is a husband or a wife."

Another section reaffirmed the power of the states to make their own decisions about marriage: "No State, territory, or possession of the United States, or Indian tribe, shall be required to give effect to any public act, record, or judicial proceeding of any other State, territory, possession, or tribe respecting a relationship between persons of the same sex that is treated as a marriage under the laws of such other State, territory, possession, or tribe, or a right or claim arising from such relationship." This section of DOMA tried to clarify, or delimit, the Constitution of the United States, specifically the **full faith and credit clause**, which states, "Full faith and credit shall be given in each state to the public acts, records, and judicial proceedings of every other state. And the Congress may by general laws prescribe the manner in which such acts, records, and proceedings shall be proved, and the effect thereof."[99]

Under the full faith and credit clause, a state is generally required to recognize and honor the public laws of other states unless those laws are contrary to the strong public policy of that state. Full faith and credit is why, for example, you only need a driver's license from one state.

In a 5–4 decision in *United States v. Windsor* (2013), the Supreme Court ruled that the section of DOMA classifying only opposite-sex marriages as legal under federal law was unconstitutional.[100] In his majority opinion, Justice Anthony Kennedy decried the intent of DOMA, stating, "The history of DOMA's enactment and its own text demonstrate that interference with the equal dignity of same-sex marriages, a dignity conferred by the States in the exercise of their sovereign power, was more than an incidental effect of the federal statute. It was its essence."[101] In his dissent, one of several written by the

The photo on the left shows Thea Spyer, left, and Edie Windsor, right, whose same sex marriage was legally recognized by the State of New York but not by the federal government. Following the passing of her wife, Windsor successfully fought to overturn a portion of a federal law that defined marriage as only between opposite-sex couples.

left: Neville Elder/Corbis via Getty Images; right: Jennifer S. Altman/Contour by Getty Images.

full faith and credit clause
a portion of the Constitution that generally requires states to honor licenses and judicial outcomes of other states.

members of the minority, Justice Samuel Alito, joined in part by Justice Clarence Thomas, challenged the foundations of the majority's logic, claiming, "Same-sex marriage presents a highly emotional and important question of public policy—but not a difficult question of constitutional law. The Constitution does not guarantee the right to enter into a same-sex marriage. Indeed, no provision of the Constitution speaks to the issue."[102] One of the most consequential results of the Court's decision in *Windsor* was the provision of the same rights to immigration procedures to same-sex married couples that are granted to opposite-sex married couples when one spouse is not an American citizen.

Two years after her landmark case, Windsor continued to work for LGBT causes and had turned her focus to transgender identity and at-risk youth. She stated, "I think we have a lot to do. A lot. There are a million things to still be done to make it equal. . . . First of all, I have a lot of feeling for trans people. They are making gorgeous progress, but it's a very painful progress. . . .We also have somewhere between 40 and 50% of kids living on the street who are gay. This is a whole chunk of us who also took the courage to come out but were thrown out of their homes and forced to live in the street.[103]

While the Supreme Court in *Windsor* had validated state-recognized same-sex marriages for *federal* purposes, it did not strike down the other substantive clause of DOMA, which allowed states to not give full faith and credit to same-sex marriage licenses from other states. Many Americans wondered when, or if, it ever would.

The Supreme Court and the Right to Privacy

Part of Windsor's constitutional claims rested on a right not enumerated in the Bill of Rights: **privacy**. Because of this, Windsor was also resting her claim upon previous cases in American constitutional law. In its decisions in these cases, the Supreme Court had affirmed the right to privacy and applied it to several areas of Americans' private lives, such as birth control, abortion, and sexuality.

The Use of Contraceptives

The foundational case regarding privacy was *Griswold v. Connecticut* (1965).[104] In it, the Court overturned a Connecticut law that prohibited the provision of contraceptives and medical advice about contraceptive techniques to married couples. In striking down the law, Justice William O. Douglas cited affirmations of privacy in several amendments to the Constitution, including the First, which "has a penumbra where privacy is protected from governmental intrusion."[105]

Sexual Conduct between Consenting Adults

In later decades, the Supreme Court clarified that the right to privacy extended beyond the use of contraception. One area in which the Court affirmed privacy in the "penumbras" created by the Constitution's other protections was the right of consenting adults to express their sexuality. In 2003, in *Lawrence*

privacy
a right not enumerated in the Constitution but affirmed by Supreme Court decisions that covers individuals' decisions in their private lives, including decisions regarding reproductive rights and sexuality.

NEWS CLIP
Sotomayor discusses the right to privacy

Tyron Garner, left, and John Lawrence greet supporters at Houston City Hall where people had gathered to celebrate the landmark Supreme Court decision in the *Lawrence v. Texas* case on June 26, 2003. The court struck down a Texas sodomy law, a decision applauded by gay rights advocates as a historic ruling that overturned sodomy laws in thirteen states.

Reuters/Richard Carson.

v. Texas, the Court struck down a Texas law making same-sex sexual conduct illegal.[106] In his decision, Justice Kennedy stated, "Liberty presumes an autonomy of self that includes freedom of thought, belief, expression, and certain intimate conduct."[107]

A Woman's Decision to Terminate a Pregnancy

In a series of decisions, the Court has also affirmed and upheld the right of a woman to terminate a pregnancy. In this area of privacy, the foundational case was *Roe v. Wade* (1973).[108] In that case, the Court struck down a Texas law that made abortion illegal. In affirming the right of a woman to obtain an abortion during the first three months of pregnancy, Justice Harry Blackmun drew on the Court's previous ruling in *Griswold*, stating, "This right of privacy, whether it be founded in the Fourteenth Amendment's concept of personal liberty and restrictions upon state action, as we feel it is, or . . . in the Ninth Amendment's reservation of rights to the people, is broad enough to encompass a woman's decision whether or not to terminate her pregnancy."[109]

In subsequent decisions, the Court has continued to uphold the fundamental right of a woman to have an abortion, but it has also allowed state legislatures to place certain limits upon this right. Examples of this are state laws requiring minors to obtain parental consent, assuming those laws do not place an "undue burden" on the woman, and certain restrictions upon late-term abortions.[110] Despite the Court's rulings, the abortion issue remains a very contentious one in American politics. Since *Roe v. Wade*, trying to assess a nominee's future rulings on abortion has become a key factor in the Senate's application of its power of advice and consent in confirming justices to the Supreme Court and judges to the lower levels of the federal judiciary.

Marriage Equality and the Final Blow to DOMA

While the Supreme Court's decision in *Windsor v. United States* required the federal government to recognize state-recognized same-sex marriages, striking down one of DOMA's two provisions against marriage equality, it had not required states to give full faith and credit to same-sex marriage licenses from other states. Nor had it legalized same-sex marriages generally. One person who would change that was James Obergefell. Though the actual Court decision bundled several cases together, Obergefell's was listed first, which placed his name on the decision. The facts of his case were, sadly, somewhat similar to those of Edith Windsor's.

In 2011, after a decades-long commitment to each other, Obergefell married John Arthur on the tarmac of a Maryland airport. The two men were residents of the state of Ohio, which did not recognize marriage equality, so they flew to Maryland, which did. Arthur was struggling with amyotrophic lateral sclerosis (ALS), a progressive neurological degenerative disease. ALS is often called Lou Gehrig's disease after the famous and widely respected baseball player who died from it in 1941. The disease has no known cure, though recently some medications have shown promise in slowing its progression.[111] The two men flew to Maryland in a medical transport plane, seeking to get married while they still could. In an interview for BuzzFeed News a few months before the Court's decision in his case, Obergefell described their ceremony: "We landed at Baltimore, sat on the tarmac for a little bit, said 'I do,' and 10 minutes later were in the air on the way home."[112] John Arthur passed away in 2013.

Obergefell and Arthur's state of residence did not recognize their marriage. According to the case decision, "Ohio law does not permit Obergefell to be listed as the surviving spouse on Arthur's death certificate. By statute they must remain strangers even in death, a state-imposed separation Obergefell deems 'hurtful for the rest of time.'"[113] Rather

James Obergefell in 2015, two and a half months prior to the Supreme Court decision that would guarantee marriage equality for all Americans.

Maddie McGarvey/For The Washington Post via Getty Images.

than accept Ohio's refusal to recognize their marriage, Obergefell sued. "This case," he said, "was another way to take care of him and to respect him and to respect our relationship."[114]

In 2015, in its decision in *Obergefell v. Hodges*, the Supreme Court, in yet another 5–4 vote, affirmed the legality of Obergefell and Arthur's marriage and guaranteed the right of all couples to marry. Citing many of the cases that we have discussed, constitutional protections of fundamental civil liberties, and the right to privacy, Justice Kennedy, in his majority opinion, affirmed that "the right to marry is a fundamental right inherent in the liberty of the person." The second major section of DOMA had been declared unconstitutional. More fundamentally, marriage equality had become the law of both the nation and the states.

Reflecting on his case in an interview with *USA Today* two months before the Court's decision, Obergefell recalled how he felt about having to fly, given his husband's serious medical issues, to another state just to get married: "All I thought was, 'This isn't right, I'm p---ed off.'"[115] In the same interview, on a much lighter note, he added, "I chuckle about law students and other people just having to learn how to pronounce Obergefell."[116]

▮ CONCLUSION

Fences Still under Construction

The stories regarding civil liberties in the United States are stories about tensions—tensions between one individual's fundamental rights and freedoms and those of another and between individual freedoms and the evolving needs of a society. They are stories about courage and political action. They are controversial, as they should be. They are also evolving, as generations of activists, Supreme Court justices, and politicians have weighed in on the proper boundaries of American rights and freedoms. While initially the restrictions upon governmental action found in the Bill of Rights applied only to the federal government, through the process of selective incorporation, most now apply to state governments as well. Not all of the civil liberties enumerated in the Bill of Rights have received the same level of protection, however. Political speech and expression, for example, has been privileged as fundamental to the ability to secure all other rights and freedoms.

During the ratification debates, one of the most powerful arguments that the Federalists made against a bill of rights was that it would be necessarily incomplete, which might provide the federal government with an excuse to restrict those fundamental freedoms not enumerated. While the Ninth Amendment explicitly states that Americans possess fundamental freedoms not listed in the other amendments, protecting those freedoms has been left to the Supreme Court and to individuals willing to fight for them.

Edward Snowden, Edie Windsor, and Jim Obergefell may not have known where their actions would finally lead, but it is very likely that each knew the controversy that his or her actions would stir up and the risks being taken. Defining and defending civil liberties in American democracy has always been and will always be controversial and challenging; that is why it is so essential to the nation.

CHAPTER REVIEW

This chapter's main ideas are reflected in the Learning Objectives below. By reviewing them here you should be able to **remember** the key points, **connect** them to the stories presented in the chapter, **think** critically about these questions, and **know** these terms that are central to the topic.

4.1 Outline the controversies surrounding civil liberties and the need to ensure a safe and orderly society.

REMEMBER...
- Protecting civil liberties involves placing restrictions upon the ability of government to limit them.
- The need to ensure a safe and orderly society often results in conflict between governmental action and the protection of civil liberties.

CONNECT...
- Edward Snowden, now on the run from U.S. authorities, leaked classified materials in protest of what he saw as excessive governmental surveillance.

THINK...
- What are sources of tension between political expression and national security?
- How do these tensions continue to be debated today?

KNOW...
- *civil liberties* (p. 121)
- *negative freedoms* (p. 121)

4.2 List the civil liberties protected by the Constitution and amendments to it.

REMEMBER...
- The Bill of Rights enumerates a list of fundamental freedoms that the federal government cannot infringe upon.

THINK...
- What are the broad categories of fundamental liberties guaranteed by the Constitution and the Bill of Rights?

KNOW...
- *Bill of Rights* (p. 126)

4.3 Trace the history of incorporating the Bill of Rights in order to restrict state governmental actions.

REMEMBER...

- The protections set out in the Bill of Rights as written applied to the actions of the federal government and not of the state governments. A decades-long process, in which the Supreme Court played a key role, changed this.

CONNECT...

- Benjamin Gitlow, like Edward Snowden nearly a century later, was accused of violating federal law in his protests over national policies. His case was an important watershed in incorporating the protections of the Bill of Rights to the actions of state governments.

THINK...

- Why was the process of selective incorporation important?

KNOW...

- *due process clause of the Fourteenth Amendment* (p. 130)
- *selective incorporation* (p. 130)

4.4 Discuss the challenges to constitutional law posed by the establishment and free exercise clauses of the First Amendment.

REMEMBER...

- The first two clauses in the First Amendment to the Constitution both involve religion; they prevent the federal government from establishing religion and protect Americans' rights to exercise their religious freedoms.

CONNECT...

- The Supreme Court continues to struggle with defining the boundaries surrounding the establishment and free exercise clauses.
- Issues such as prayer in public schools also illustrate tensions *between* these two fundamental freedoms.

THINK...

- What are the tensions between the free exercise and establishment clauses of the First Amendment?

KNOW...

- *Lemon test* (p. 136)
- *neutrality test* (p. 136)

4.5 Assess the special protections of political speech and press affirmed in the First Amendment as well as restrictions subsequently placed upon those protections.

REMEMBER...

- Political speech and expression are considered particularly important fundamental freedoms.
- Since the early years of the American Republic, the federal government has struggled with protecting these freedoms while also ensuring a secure and orderly society.

CONNECT...

- In the early decades of the twentieth century, the Supreme Court struggled with protecting political speech and expression while also protecting national security.

THINK...

- How should government weigh the tensions between political expression and national security concerns?

4.6 Summarize the protections placed within the Bill of Rights for those accused of, investigated for, tried for, and convicted of crimes.

REMEMBER...
- The Bill of Rights guarantees a set of protections for those accused of, investigated for, tried for, and convicted of crimes.

CONNECT...
- Cases involving Dollree Mapp and Clarence Gideon led to more robust protections for Americans involved with the criminal justice system.

THINK...
- What are some of the protections for Americans involved in the criminal justice system?
- Do you think these protections are sufficient?

4.7 Discuss the Supreme Court's affirmation of the right to privacy.

REMEMBER...
- The Supreme Court, drawing upon the Ninth Amendment, which states that the Bill of Rights does not contain an exhaustive list of fundamental liberties, has affirmed a right of privacy in areas such as reproductive rights, sexuality, and marriage.

CONNECT...
- Edith Windsor and James Obergefell, drawing upon early Supreme Court precedent, successfully fought to overturn a federal law and establish marriage equality in the United States in the twenty-first century.

THINK...
- What are the implications of the Supreme Court's identification of a right to privacy?

5 CIVIL RIGHTS
How Equal Is Equal?[1]

Judith Heumann, U.S. State Department special advisor for international disability rights, left, meets with German officials in Berlin to discuss a set of measures to improve inclusion of people with disabilities. A disabled American herself, Heumann has spent a lifetime advocating for the rights of people with disabilities in America and across the globe.

Rainer Jensen/picture-alliance/dpa/AP Images.

The preamble to the Declaration of Independence makes clear a central purpose of a representative government: to guard and protect the fundamental rights and freedoms of its citizens. However, it does not offer many specifics on the processes and structures needed to make this happen. The rules and institutions set out in the Constitution and later amendments to it have given detailed form to a federal government that would help to secure these rights. Even so, the institutions of American government do not run on autopilot. They require both the actions of those within the government to carry out their responsibilities and the actions of Americans to define, advocate for, and protect their **civil rights**—the fundamental rights of individuals to be treated equally under the laws and policies of governments, regardless of their identities and lived experiences.

Civil rights are not binary things. In a sense, one has them or not; however, in practice it is much more complicated than that. Recall the discussion of civil liberties from Chapter 4. As a rule, the protection of civil liberties requires that a government does not do certain things—does not pass laws that might restrict the expression of civil rights. As with civil liberties, the framers of the Constitution assumed that citizens possessed civil rights upon birth, though many Americans were excluded or ignored at that point in history. Unlike civil liberties, however, civil rights require positive action, both by individuals acting to secure them and by governments in taking action to ensure their expression. For this reason, civil rights are sometimes called **positive freedoms**.

The challenge with civil rights comes from deciding how vigorously a government should act to protect them. How much action does a government need to take? How strongly does government have to act? How equal is equal? There is no single answer to these questions. Americans have always disagreed on how strongly government should act to protect the civil rights of its citizens. In this chapter, we will examine the efforts of individuals such as Judith Heumann, Thurgood Marshall, and members of the National Association for the Advancement of Colored People (NAACP), as well as a host of other people acting alone or in concert to achieve a broader, more robust, vision of Americans' civil rights.

> **civil rights**
> fundamental guarantees ensuring equal treatment and protecting against discrimination under the laws of a nation.
>
> **positive freedoms**
> fundamental rights and freedoms that require action by individuals to express and by governments to secure.

After reading this chapter, you will be able to:

5.1 Analyze the challenges associated with defining how strongly a government should act to help secure civil rights

5.2 Trace the struggles to secure civil rights for people with disabilities, African Americans, and women

5.3 Explain the dangers associated with the NAACP's decision to use the courts to make social change

5.4 Evaluate the role of all three branches of the federal government in changing policy on the ground to desegregate America's public schools

5.5 Contrast the tactics employed by individuals working to secure civil rights in the area of racial equality to the tactics of those acting to secure gender and sexual equality

5.6 Evaluate the ways the diversity of Americans' identities shapes efforts to secure civil rights in the twenty-first century

LEARNING OBJECTIVES

SECURING RIGHTS FOR THOSE WITH DISABILITIES
Refusing to Be Called a "Fire Hazard"

In January 2016, writing in celebration of the American holiday devoted to Dr. Martin Luther King Jr., Judith Heumann, a special advisor for international disability rights with the United States Department of State, posted an article to the State Department's official blog. In it, she looked both to the past and to the present:

> A stable, prosperous democracy succeeds when individuals can fully participate in political and public life. As we celebrate MLK Day and reflect on past struggles fought by Americans determined to uphold their individual rights, Dr. King's message of inclusion lives on. Dr. King encouraged everyone to participate when he said, "It is not possible to be in favor of justice for some people and not be in favor of justice for all people."
>
> While change takes time, we must take action to: establish disabled people's organizations; adopt and enforce strong laws; create and enforce standards that advance inclusion of disabled people; and remove barriers—physical and attitudinal in all areas of life.[2]

In writing about the struggles to secure rights and freedoms for persons with disabilities, Heumann knows what she is talking about. She has spent a lifetime advocating for, protesting, and changing American laws that affect those with disabilities.

> "We demonstrated to the entire nation that disabled people could take control over our own lives and take leadership in the struggle for equality."

As a very young child in 1949, Heumann contracted polio, which required her to use a wheelchair for mobility for the rest of her life. In the 1950s, administrators at her local public elementary school in Brooklyn, New York, refused her attendance. They cited her inability to access the building since it had no ramps, which was pretty much universal at the time. They refused to relent even when her mother offered to carry her up and down the school's steps. "I was considered to be a fire hazard," Heumann recalled.[3]

In spite of these obstacles—imposed not by her disability but by others' actions— Heumann earned two degrees, including a Master of Arts from the University of California at Berkeley in 1975. After graduation she applied to become a teacher with the New York City schools but was rejected based on her disability. Instead of backing down, however, "she filed suit against them and won."[4]

Heumann was far from done. In 1977 she helped to organize a series of rallies and sit-ins across the nation to protest the slowness of the federal government's implementation of an important law regarding disability rights, Section 504 of the Rehabilitation Act of 1973. This was the first federal law to prohibit discrimination against Americans with disabilities, but it was not being enforced. Officials in the executive branch had not signed key regulations of the act, likely because of how much it would cost to do so.

In response, individuals across the nation protested; in San Francisco, supporters of the act took over a federal office building. The protests were called the "504 sit-ins" after the section of the law the protesters demanded be fully, immediately, and effectively implemented. According to one news account, "By the late '70s, Americans were used to seeing civil rights marches. But this one was something new: people in wheelchairs, people on portable respirators, deaf people, people with mental retardation. And most were fighting mad."[5]

The protesters won. Four weeks into the San Francisco sit-in, the secretary of the Department of Health, Education, and Welfare endorsed the regulations contained within the law. Reflecting back on the time, Heumann recalled the personal risks that the activists were willing to take: "People weren't going to work, people were willing to risk arrest, people were risking their own health. Everybody was risking something. . . . Through the sit-in, we turned ourselves from being oppressed individuals into being empowered people. We demonstrated to the entire nation that disabled people could take control over our own lives and take leadership in the struggle for equality."[6]

A later piece of legislation on which Heumann also worked tirelessly was the Americans with Disabilities Act (ADA), signed into law in 1990. Among its provisions, the ADA offered protections for Americans with disabilities against discrimination in the workplace and improved their access to public transportation, public services, and other areas of public and commercial life.[7] "The ADA was like the Emancipation Proclamation for disabled individuals," Heumann said in 2015, referring to the Civil War proclamation by President Abraham Lincoln that freed the slaves in the states that had rebelled.[8]

Demonstrators converge on the offices of the Department of Health, Education, and Welfare in San Francisco in April 1977. They were part of a "504 sit-in" to urge civil rights law for disabled Americans be fully implemented. In the center, a woman briefs the group in American Sign Language.
AP Photo/JP.

In her remarks on Martin Luther King Jr. Day in 2016, Heumann referred to the words of Supreme Court justice Thurgood Marshall—the first African American appointed to the highest Court in the land—in an opinion that he wrote in 1985. The case involved the denial of a permit to build a facility to house and serve people with cognitive disabilities in Cleburne, Texas. The Court unanimously ruled against the city's actions, saying that the permit denial violated those individuals' constitutional rights.[9] In his opinion, Marshall directly connected the struggles to secure civil rights for the disabled to those of African Americans. The "mentally retarded," Marshall noted, "have been subject to a 'lengthy and tragic history' . . . of segregation and discrimination that can only be called grotesque."[10]

When he used the word *grotesque*, Marshall was not exaggerating. Throughout much of its history, the nation has discriminated against people with disabilities in restrictive, even violent ways. In addition to being excluded from the workplace, schools, transportation, and other forms of public and private life, Americans with disabilities—especially those with cognitive disabilities—have been forcibly institutionalized, and even sterilized.[11]

Many advocates for the rights of Americans with disabilities drew connections between their struggles and those of African Americans decades before. A 1999 position paper for the American Civil Liberties Union—which noted that "people with disabilities are the poorest, least employed, and least educated minority in America"—pointed to a long history of discrimination against Americans with disabilities.[12] "Finally" the report noted, "thanks in part to the inspiration provided by the civil rights struggles of the 1960's, disability rights advocates began to press for full legal equality and access to mainstream society. Through lobbying and litigation, laws were passed and rights established; public education and advocacy were used to promote reason and inclusiveness rather than fear and pity."[13] Heumann had helped to lead that charge.

When he commented on the similarity between the securing of civil rights for Americans with disabilities and African Americans, Justice Marshall had a personal connection to the subject. He knew the history of the struggle for civil rights very well. To find out how well, we will have to jump back in time several decades, when Thurgood Marshall was arguing before the Supreme Court rather than sitting on its bench.

"EQUAL JUSTICE UNDER LAW"

Confronting a History of Segregation and Oppression

By the morning of December 9, 1952, hundreds of Americans—far more than the chamber could hold—had already lined up outside the Supreme Court of the United States. Those lucky enough to get seats would not give them up lightly; the better prepared had brought food, knowing someone else would take their place if they left. The line of people standing under the motto of the Supreme Court, "Equal Justice under Law," was integrated. African Americans and whites stood together for a chance to witness history. Though the line was integrated, the public schools of the District of Columbia where they were gathered were not. By law, African American and white children in the nation's capital and in the American South attended separate schools. On this day, those laws would be challenged.

The proceedings themselves were often not that dramatic. Instead of fireworks and grand speeches, members of the audience mostly saw lawyers state their arguments and nine white men in black robes ask them questions. But it was nonetheless historic, and everyone knew it at the time. The events of that day were not just occurring by happenstance, and they had not been inevitable. They had been a long time coming, and it would still be a long road ahead.

In the audience was the president of Howard University, a predominantly African American university whose law school had trained a generation of civil rights lawyers, including the man who would lead his legal team in its attempt to challenge segregated education: Thurgood Marshall. Marshall was the chief litigator for the Legal Defense Fund of the NAACP, and he and his team of lawyers were arguing five cases in front of the Court.[14] These five cases had been gathered together under the name of the first one on the list, *Brown v. Board of Education of Topeka*. Though differing in their details and pathways through the legal system, together the cases dealt with the same question—whether or not **legal segregation**, or the separation by law of African American and white children in the public schools based only on their race, was constitutionally permissible.

It had been a long journey through the courts for Marshall and the NAACP. They had been waging a legal attack on segregation in the United States for decades. The individuals who had filed the lawsuits, those who helped organize them, and the lawyers who had prepared and argued the cases had often done so in the face of genuine personal danger. Some were threatened and assaulted. Many lost their jobs. Some had been shot at. In some cases their homes and churches had been burned.

Marshall had showed up in Washington ten days before the trial began to coordinate his team and make sure that they were as prepared as they possibly could be. Their main concern was that the Supreme Court might agree that the African American children in the five cases had been treated unfairly but only because their schools were not equal to the schools of the white children, not because they were segregated. It was not enough to have the Court declare that the educations of the African American children in the cases were unequal. That ruling would have forced the NAACP to try for remedies on a case-by-case basis, to sue to force thousands of school districts to equalize their educational facilities, with districts, counties, and states digging in their heels and trying to slow things down all along the way. According to a member of Marshall's legal team, if they won, "there would be momentous changes in the lives of black people, indeed of all Americans," and if they lost, "we would have spent our best chance and would face a long, dismal future of quibbling over the equality of school buildings, books, libraries, gyms, playgrounds."[15]

Marshall's legal team needed the Court to overturn itself—something that it rarely does—and declare that segregation itself was unequal. Merely showing that the educational facilities in the areas named in the cases were not equal for white and African American children might be a small tactical victory, but it would be a major strategic defeat. To anyone who had seen the evidence, it was clear that many public educational facilities were far from equal, at least in the Deep South. What Marshall and his team were trying to prove was that there was no possibility for equality in the presence of segregated education. They needed the Court to declare that segregation based on racial identity was *inherently* unequal and that it violated the Constitution of the United States.

The fact that Marshall and his team were fighting segregation in the courts—indeed, that they were fighting segregation at all—was its own accomplishment. Given the history of the Supreme Court with respect to the rights of African Americans, the NAACP's strategy was not promising. On several occasions in its history the Court had issued rulings that severely restricted the rights of African Americans.

There were other possible strategies. Marshall and his team could try to get laws passed rather than overturned by focusing their efforts on Congress or the state legislatures. Some voices within the NAACP and in many African American communities felt that the scarce resources available would be better spent on economic development, on

Thurgood Marshall, center, special counsel for the NAACP in *Brown v. Board of Education*, and two other members of his legal team in front of the Supreme Court following their landmark victory in 1954.
Bettmann/Contributor.

building communities and businesses, rather than on the courts or the legislatures. They believed this would mean African Americans would not have to be dependent upon whites for their jobs and opportunities. In the end, however, the NAACP decided to focus much of its resource base on attacking segregation through the courts, especially the Supreme Court, with the hope of making lasting social change. Thus, it adopted a judicial strategy.

The NAACP's choice to base much of its strategy on winning in the Supreme Court was a risky move. Even if its lawyers succeeded, they had to confront the fact that the judicial branch of the United States was not designed to be a strong instrument of public policy. Though no one branch was supposed to be too powerful on its own, the founders generally regarded the judiciary as the weakest of the three. In *Federalist* No. 78, Alexander Hamilton wrote that the "judiciary is beyond comparison the weakest of the three departments of power; that it can never attack with success either of the other two; and that all possible care is requisite to enable it to defend itself against their attacks."[16] In part, Hamilton was trying to reassure the American public in the face of Antifederalist charges that the federal courts would trample on people's rights. Additionally, the founders had not given the judiciary powers to enforce its decisions. Justice Tom Clark, commenting on the decision in *Brown v. Board of Education*, cautioned that "we don't have money at the Court for an army and we can't take ads in the newspapers, and we don't want to go out on a picket line in our robes. We have to convince the nation by the force of our opinions."[17]

The American Civil War and Its Aftermath

Another risk of trying to use the Supreme Court to break the hold of segregation was the Court itself, or, more accurately, its history. The Court had at times issued decisions that severely restricted the rights of African Americans. In 1857, in *Dred Scott v. Sandford*, the Supreme Court ruled that Scott, former slaves, and the descendants of slaves were not citizens of the United States, even if they were residents of free states or territories. The natural rights proclaimed in the Declaration of Independence and protected in the Constitution, Justice Roger Taney wrote in his opinion, did not extend to individuals "whose ancestors were negroes of the African race," who, at the time of the founding, were considered an "inferior class of beings who had been subjugated by the dominant race, and, whether emancipated or not, yet remained subject to their authority, and had no rights or privileges but such as those who held the power and the Government might choose to grant them."[18] Natural rights, according to the Court, had been selectively bestowed.

Scott's inability to sue for his freedom or that of his family was not the only effect of Taney's majority opinion in *Dred Scott*. In addition, the Court—five of whose nine members were from the South—ruled that the Missouri Compromise, which was a plan that had been created by Congress in 1820 to maintain a balance of slave and nonslave states in the Senate, was unconstitutional. In practice, the balance between slave and nonslave states had already been upended. The Court's ruling in *Dred Scott*, though, threatened the constitutionality of any state laws against slavery, as slaves were considered property subject to the Constitution's protections. The Court's decision served to further polarize public opinion on the question of slavery and galvanize both pro-slavery and antislavery forces in the United States.

The threat that states might secede from the Union was not a new one. During the constitutional convention, a delegate from Delaware had raised it is an implicit threat against the American confederation during the Constitutional Convention, though in the context of state representation in Congress rather than over the regulation of slavery. To the southern states in the convention, however, the preservation of slavery in their states had been a precondition to their ratification of the Constitution.

In December 1860, South Carolina made the long-simmering threat of secession a reality. Within six months, eleven southern states had seceded from the United States to form the Confederate States of America. In April they fired on a federal fort in Charleston Harbor. To reunite the Union, President Abraham Lincoln had to take what remained of the American Republic to war. Like many times before and since, leaders, soldiers, and citizens on both sides thought that the war would be over quickly. And like many times before and since, they were all wrong—tragically wrong.

When the American Civil War finally ended in 1865, more than six hundred thousand soldiers had died. An unknown number of civilians were killed as well. In some ways it was similar to other wars of the nineteenth century; disease and infection were just as deadly as bullets. In other ways, however, it was a "modern" war, foreshadowing the terrible devastation of the industrial wars of the twentieth century. Technology, modern transportation, and mass production of weapons led to massive casualties in the presence of traditional fighting techniques, such as mass charges of soldiers into prepared fighting positions. Toward the end of the war, some battlefields—with their trenches and emplaced gun works—looked like those of Europe would during World War I fifty years later. It was total war, and it did not end until the Union armies had literally destroyed the ability of the Confederacy to support and conduct war.

Historians continue to debate the relative roles of slavery, politics, and economics as causes of the Civil War. In many ways it is difficult to disentangle these causes from each other. Similarly, stories of the Reconstruction—the years after the Civil War when the rebellious southern states were brought back into the Union—have shifted in their focus over time. Early histories of the period told stories of vengeful Republicans taking out their wrath on a South wanting nothing but to be brought back into the fold. In the 1930s, W. E. B Du Bois, an African American scholar and political activist, reminded historians of the important contributions of African Americans to the securing of their own rights in the postwar South, including the fact that many African American men ran for, and won, seats in state legislatures and Congress.[19] More recent scholars of the period have also

Members of Company E., 4th United States Colored Infantry in Washington, D.C., in 1865. Many African American veterans followed their service in the Civil War with political activism after its conclusion.

The Granger Collection, New York.

emphasized the pragmatism and caution exercised on the part of the northern Republicans, whose own political goals were not necessarily aligned with full equality for the freed men and women of the South.

During the war, President Lincoln had signed the Emancipation Proclamation, which in 1863 declared that all slaves in the states under rebellion were "henceforward and forever free." However, it took the actions of Union troops and slaves themselves to make that proclamation a reality on the ground. Excluded from the proclamation were slaves in the border states still loyal to the Union and territories in the South already under federal control. This was a political move, designed to preserve the loyalty of the border states while also putting pressure on Europe not to come to the aid of the Confederacy.

As the war dragged on, African Americans were increasingly brought into the Union war effort. Although forced to serve in segregated units and often assigned to labor detachments, many of the nearly two hundred thousand African Americans who served in the Union Army used their experiences to gain education, advancement, and a claim of equal status as citizens in the victorious Union. African American combat units quickly gained a reputation for effectiveness and bravery under fire. "From the army," according to one historian, "would come many of the black political leaders of the Reconstruction, including at least forty-one delegates to state constitutional conventions, sixty legislators, three lieutenant governors, and four Congressmen."[20]

At the conclusion of the war, southern states began to pass laws to preserve the pre-defeat status quo between whites and African Americans. Known as the black codes, these pieces of legislation attempted to restrict the economic and political rights of freedmen, to "make Negroes slaves in everything but name."[21] Some of these laws required former slaves to leave their former master's property to make new labor contracts but had them arrested for vagrancy when they did so—with punishment consisting of a return to servitude. Other laws restricted African Americans' rights in the courts or at the polls, prevented them from owning firearms, or made self-employment all but impossible through heavy taxes or obscure licensing requirements.

President Andrew Johnson, who succeeded Lincoln upon his assassination, pushed for quick readmission of the southern states with relatively little regard for the preservation of African American political rights. One historian noted that Johnson's "hatred of slave owners was as intense as his hatred of blacks."[22] The Republican-controlled Congress, however, was more assertive. In some cases, Republicans were staunch abolitionists on moral grounds; in other cases, on strategic political grounds. Making sure that African American men could vote—and, it was expected, vote Republican—was seen as a way to avoid an unbreakable and dominant political alliance of northern and southern Democrats.

Within five years of the conclusion of the Civil War, three amendments had been added to the Constitution, although not without considerable opposition. In 1865 the **Thirteenth Amendment** to the Constitution prohibited slavery within the United States.

Thirteenth Amendment
an amendment to the Constitution passed in 1865 prohibiting slavery within the United States.

To ensure the power of the national government to make this provision a reality, and to prevent a Supreme Court from overturning antislavery laws at it had done in *Dred Scott*, Section 2 of the amendment stated that "Congress shall have the power to enforce this article by appropriate legislation." In 1868 the **Fourteenth Amendment** affirmed the citizenship of all persons "born or naturalized in the United States" and, for the first time in the history of the Constitution, placed explicit restrictions on the laws of states: "No State shall make or enforce any law which shall abridge the privileges and immunities of citizens of the United States; nor shall any State deprive any person of life, liberty, or property, without due process of law; nor deny to any person within its jurisdiction the equal protection of the laws."

The **equal protection clause** of the Fourteenth Amendment served as the constitutional basis for the assault on educational segregation in the courts and for the assertion of civil rights for Americans of many different identities in many different areas of public and private life. In addition to addressing issues of state debts and office holding for former Confederate leaders, the Fourteenth Amendment also overturned the three-fifths rule for representation in the original Constitution.

Faced with southern resistance to the Fourteenth Amendment—southern states rejected or ratified modified versions of it—the Republican Congress, having won major victories in the 1866 elections, passed the First Reconstruction Act of 1867. This act disbanded southern governments, thus voiding their rejection of the Fourteenth Amendment, and replaced them with military rule. It gave freedmen the right to vote and took that right away from Confederate veterans, and it made ratification of the Fourteenth Amendment a necessary condition of readmission to the United States. The **Fifteenth Amendment**, ratified in 1870, went beyond threats against states for restricting voting rights and affirmed the voting rights of all freedmen, again giving Congress the power to make necessary laws: "The right of citizens of the United States to vote shall not be denied or abridged by the United States or by any State on account of race, color, or previous condition of servitude."

In addition to these Reconstruction amendments, Congress in this period passed several pieces of legislation aimed at securing the civil rights of African Americans. In 1865 Congress created the Freedmen's Bureau, which took steps to provide former slaves with the two things that they desired most: land and education. This was not always done in the interests of freedmen, however. The bureau sometimes forced African Americans to work for whites.[23] "Free then, with a desire for land and a frenzy for schools," according to W. E. B. Du Bois, "the Negro lurched into the new day."[24] Throughout the South, former slaves organized for the purpose of building communities, churches, and especially schools, and they attempted to reconstruct families that had been sold into fragmentation. The Civil Rights Act of 1866 affirmed the legal and property rights of former slaves, while the Civil Rights Act of 1875 affirmed "the equality of all men before the law" and the duty of government to enforce that equality. The latter also acknowledged the rights of all to "the full and equal enjoyment of the accommodations, advantages, facilities, and privileges of inns, public conveyances on land or water, theaters, and other places of public amusement" regardless of race or "previous condition of servitude."

These efforts did not go unopposed. As the Democratic Party gained political power in the southern states and the will of the Republican Party to make civil rights a reality

Fourteenth Amendment
an amendment to the Constitution passed in 1868 affirming the citizenship of all persons born or naturalized in the United States and, for the first time in the history of the Constitution, placing explicit restrictions on the laws of states that sought to abridge the privileges and immunities of citizens of the United States.

equal protection clause
a clause of the Fourteenth Amendment that serves as the constitutional basis for the assault on educational segregation in the courts and for the assertion of civil rights for Americans of many different identities in many different areas of public and private life.

Fifteenth Amendment
an amendment to the Constitution passed in 1870 affirming the voting rights of all freedmen.

> At one point, Thurgood Marshall brought it to the attention of the Justice Department that a Mississippi registrar was asking black voters, "How many bubbles in a bar of soap?"

A young African American man drinks from a segregated water fountain in Oklahoma City, Oklahoma, in 1939. Jim Crow laws persisted across the United States long after the civil rights acts of the late nineteenth century were passed.

The Granger Collection, New York.

on the ground faded, the early gains made by African Americans began to disappear. Southern states passed laws to preserve segregation and prevent African American men from exercising their Fifteenth Amendment right to vote. Known as Jim Crow laws, these efforts enforced segregation across all aspects of daily life, including transportation, entertainment, business, and education. While legal segregation had been enforced in the North before the Civil War, by the time of Reconstruction it had largely disappeared there but remained deeply entrenched in the post–Civil War South. Selective enforcement of poll taxes, which required voters to pay a tax at the polling place, and literacy tests, which were used by registrars to determine whether voters were "qualified" to vote, combined to prevent African American men from voting. At one point, Thurgood Marshall brought it to the attention of the Justice Department that "a Mississippi registrar was asking black voters, 'How many bubbles in a bar of soap?'"[25]

Backing up the laws and statutes were violence and the persistent threat of violence against African Americans who tried to exercise their rights and against whites who tried to help them. The violence against African Americans, especially former soldiers, was often organized, sometimes random, and sometimes continued against a person's body after they had already died: "In Texas, one woman reported that it was a common sight to see the bodies of freedmen floating down a river."[26] Schools that educated former slaves were seen as especially dangerous to the white order. Many were burned; their white teachers were beaten and ostracized. Across the South, the Ku Klux Klan terrorized and murdered African American politicians and civic leaders. Thousands of African Americans were murdered, often to send a message that the racial order was not to be challenged. Terrorism in the postwar South was, as it has always been, a political weapon.

In a speech before the Republican Party National Convention in 1872, Frederick Douglass, a former slave, abolitionist leader, and noted orator, highlighted the incompleteness of efforts on behalf of African American civil rights and the dangers many continued to face. He declared, "You say you have emancipated us. You have; and I thank you for it. You say you have enfranchised us. You have; and I thank you for it. But what is your emancipation?—what is your enfranchisement? What does it all amount to, if the black man, after having been made free by the letter of your law, is unable to exercise that freedom, and, after having been freed from the slaveholder's lash, he is subject to the slaveholder's shot-gun?"[27]

Using the Federal Judiciary to Challenge Jim Crow, and Failing

Plessy v. Ferguson
a Supreme Court case in 1896 that upheld legal racial segregation.

In the decades following the Civil War, the Supreme Court proved to be an enabler of racial oppression rather than a protector against it. In 1896 it upheld the constitutionality of legalized racial segregation, dealing a further blow to fading reconstructionist dreams.[28] *Plessy v. Ferguson* was a test case organized by the African American community in New

Orleans to challenge Louisiana's Jim Crow laws.[29] Homer Plessy, "a light-skinned man who described himself as 'seven-eighths Caucasian,'"[30] had been arrested and fined for violating a state law requiring separate railroad facilities for whites and African Americans. In the racialized math of the time, his ancestry placed Plessy just over the legal boundary between white and African American in Louisiana. After losing in the state courts, he appealed his case to the Supreme Court.

In the decision in *Plessy*, Justice Henry Billings Brown declared that Louisiana's law did not violate the Fourteenth Amendment to the Constitution. Arguing that "social prejudices cannot be overcome by legislation," Brown upheld Plessy's conviction and declared that "**separate but equal**" did not violate the Constitution. Justice John Marshall Harlan, the lone dissenter on the Court, countered, "Our Constitution is color-blind, and neither knows nor tolerates classes among citizens. In respect of civil rights, all citizens are equal before the law." Harlan, correctly, as it turned out, saw *Plessy* as a dangerous and damaging ruling, one that would "prove to be quite as pernicious as the decision made by this tribunal in the *Dred Scott* case." His charge, however, was only a dissent; Brown's majority opinion set policy. The doctrine of "separate but equal" remained constitutional for almost sixty years.

As Thurgood Marshall and the Legal Defense Fund of the NAACP launched their attack on legal segregation in the courts in the twentieth century, they had to confront the issue of precedent, or the fact that the Supreme Court looks to past decisions on similar cases for guidance on how to rule on current ones. Precedent is not always binding; however, breaking from it is something that the Court does not do lightly, in part to preserve its legitimacy in the eyes of the American people. *Plessy*, along with some later related cases, was precedent. For the Court to declare that segregated education was *inherently* in violation of the Fourteenth Amendment, it would have to break from its own precedent. The members of the NAACP's legal team were also well aware of the fact that *Plessy* was a test case that had failed. Rather than overturning the Louisiana segregationist laws, the efforts of members of the New Orleans African American community resulted in the laws being declared constitutional. As they had no guarantee of success, the NAACP was risking the same fate for the segregated schools of twentieth-century America. Marshall and his team pushed ahead anyway.

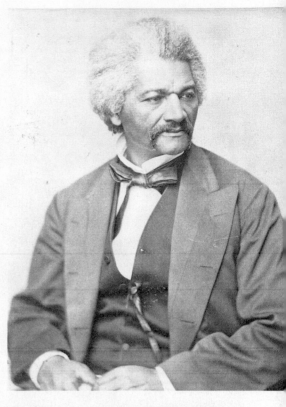

A portrait of Frederick Douglass in 1850. Douglass was a noted orator, writer, activist, staunch opponent of slavery, and supporter of women's suffrage.

Courtesy of the Library of Congress, Prints and Photographs Division.

separate but equal
the doctrine that racial segregation was constitutional so long as the facilities for blacks and whites were roughly equal.

1. *Dred Scott v. Sandford* (1857) negated _____.

   a. The Fourteenth Amendment
   b. Equal protection of the laws
   c. The Missouri Compromise
   d. Slavery

2. The Thirteenth Amendment _____.

   a. Abolished slavery
   b. Affirmed equal protection of the laws
   c. Guaranteed the right of African American men to vote
   d. Guaranteed the right of women to vote

3. In *Plessy v. Ferguson* (1896), the Supreme Court _____.

   a. Overturned legal segregation
   b. Upheld legal segregation
   c. Overturned restrictions on voting
   d. Upheld restrictions on voting

4. Why do you think the Court ruled the way that it did in *Plessy*?

Answer Key: 1. c; 2. a; 3. b; 4. Answers might mention public opinion or social prejudices.

Charles Hamilton Houston, lawyer, former dean of the Howard University School of Law, and an early leader in the NAACP's efforts to overturn legal segregation in the United States.

The Granger Collection, New York.

TOPICS IN AMERICAN GOVERNMENT
Civil rights movements

THE NAACP'S JUDICIAL ASSAULT ON LEGAL SEGREGATION

The African Americans and whites who formed the NAACP in 1909 did so largely in response to white violence against African Americans. However, the organization's founders—including W. E. B Du Bois, who published *The Crisis* magazine to educate, organize, and promote civil rights—did not always share the same vision of how to most effectively confront white racism. Its decision to push for integrated schools as a main effort in the first half of the twentieth century only came about after serious discussions and disagreements within the organization itself— disagreements that reflected a dialogue taking place within many African American communities at the time. A central question was whether the organization should push for integration or if it should focus on building up the African American community internally, especially economically, so that it would be able to confront the white establishment on a more equal footing when it chose to do so. This debate—of integration or self-development—continues to this day within many African American communities and other minority American communities.

Part of the NAACP's focus on educational segregation was by chance; early donors had requested that the organization do some research into disparities in funding between white and African American schools in the South, and this disparity did indeed prove to be quite substantial. The decision was also strategic. It was hoped that equalizing the salaries of African American and white teachers—which was part of the educational strategy— would generate interest in, and therefore membership and donations from, the African American professional community. Part of the focus on education also resulted from individual effort, choices, and strategic action.

Another debate centered on strategy. Given that legal segregation was made possible by laws passed by state legislatures, one option was to focus on getting the laws changed by electing African Americans and allied opponents of segregation to the state governments. While these efforts did bring about some victories, they proved not to be durable. Segregationists countermobilized to undo these legislative gains. A second tactic was to focus on the courts. Although it entailed its own risks, being able to secure judicial rulings against legal segregation offered the promise of more enduring gains.

Charles Hamilton Houston had been an officer in an African American artillery regiment in World War I and, as a law student, was the first African American editor of the *Harvard Law Review*. As its dean, he reorganized the law school of Howard University to make it a center of African American legal thinking, training a new generation of civil rights lawyers. After joining the NAACP, Houston oversaw the organization's early efforts in guiding educational segregation cases through the courts, a complicated and lengthy process even when things went well. Many of the cases brought by the NAACP in the 1930s focused on segregation in graduate schools. One reason for this was that "plaintiffs were more readily available in these cases than in cases involving elementary and secondary education, where becoming a plaintiff mean putting one's job or one's children at substantial risk."[31]

One important success in these graduate school cases came in 1938 in *Missouri ex rel Gaines v. Canada*.[32] Lloyd Gaines had applied for admission to Missouri's only, and all-white, law school. The state refused Gaines admission and instead offered him the choice of either accepting a scholarship to a law school in another state or applying to an all-black school in the state that would have to construct a law program for him as one did not exist. The Supreme Court in *Missouri* ruled that the scholarship option was unconstitutional and that Missouri had to provide an equal law school program for Gaines and other African American law school students. While the Court did not rule against segregated legal education within the state, it did take a close look at the equality of legal segregation in higher education. This case was followed by other, more sweeping, decisions in the coming decades.

There were also setbacks for the NAACP in these years from which the organization learned and used to adjust its strategy. There were problems coordinating so many cases in different states. In some cases, the NAACP's lack of knowledge of local laws had provided loopholes for the segregationists that they successfully exploited. The NAACP also realized that success was more likely in the border states, where it was easier to organize the cases and judges might not be as hostile as many were in the Deep South.[33] Another important step during this time was the appointment of Thurgood Marshall as chief counsel for the desegregation cases. A star student of Houston's, Marshall was a skilled litigator and adept at coordinating many different cases. Perhaps most importantly, Marshall was very thorough in his preparation, attending to all of the details of the cases himself, knowing that much could be won or lost over what might seem at the time to be a small point. Marshall showed up early and prepared, just as James Madison had done at the Constitutional Convention nearly two centuries before.

Using what had been learned, Marshall and the NAACP won two important legal victories in 1950, one originating in Texas, the other in Oklahoma. *Sweatt v. Painter* was the Texas case.[34] Under pressure from Marshall, who threatened them with the possibility of Oklahoma beating them in the race to make legal history,[35] Texas's NAACP staff recruited Heman Sweatt, an African American applicant to the all-white University of Texas Law School. Trying to comply with the ruling in *Missouri*, Texas quickly put together an all-black law school and told Sweatt that he should apply there because of his race. Key to the NAACP's case in *Sweatt* was the sociological argument that Marshall put forward. It stated that one could not look only at the physical facilities when evaluating educational equality. Things like job networks, contacts, career support, and reputation could never be equal in segregated graduate schools. Intangibles mattered just as much as buildings and books. In its decision, the Supreme Court did not directly weigh in on "separate but equal"; however, it agreed that the intangible aspects of segregated education were destructive and impermissible, and it ordered the state to admit Sweatt to its larger, more established, all-white law school.

> **Marshall showed up early and prepared, just as James Madison had done at the Constitutional Convention nearly two centuries before.**

On the same day that the Supreme Court ruled in *Sweatt*, it handed down a similar decision on the Oklahoma case, *McLaurin v. Oklahoma State Regents for Higher Education*. Though admitted to the state's graduate school, George McLaurin "was made to sit at a desk by himself in an anteroom outside the regular classrooms where his course work was given. In the library, he was assigned a segregated desk in the mezzanine behind half a carload of newspapers. In the cafeteria, he was required to eat in a dingy alcove by himself and at a different hour from the whites."[36] Again, the Court refused to directly address "separate but equal," but it did rule that separate treatment within Oklahoma's graduate school violated McLaurin's civil rights. Removing legal restrictions on McLaurin's education might not overcome social prejudices, Chief Justice Fred Vinson noted in his opinion,

Can Separate Ever Be Equal?

George McLaurin, the plaintiff in one of the two major graduate school cases, sits in a room apart from the main lecture room at the University of Oklahoma. Consider the sociological argument advanced by the NAACP in relation to this photograph. Thurgood Marshall and his team argued that intangible effects of segregation were damaging even when the physical facilities were identical.

WHAT DO YOU THINK?

In this photograph, what kinds of intangible consequences might Mr. McLaurin be subject to even though he is able to hear the lecture?

Bettmann/Contributor.

"but at the very least, the state will not be depriving appellant of the opportunity to secure acceptance by his fellow students on his own merits."

These were the victories Marshall and the NAACP needed, but they were incomplete. Now armed with precedent and the sociological argument, Marshall and his team were ready to take on segregated elementary and secondary public education in the United States. In doing so, they sought to overturn *Plessy v. Ferguson*, "separate but equal," and Jim Crow itself.

Brown v. Board of Education and Southern Resistance to the End of Legal Segregation: "Separate But Equal Has No Place"

Oliver Brown of Topeka, Kansas, was a railroad welder, a part-time minister, and a reluctant symbol for desegregation.[37] He had attempted to enroll one of his three daughters, Linda, in an all-white elementary school that was both closer to their house than the all-black school and that did not require Linda to walk amongst the busy and dangerous Rock Island railroad yards in order to get there. Brown's request was denied, so, with the help of the local NAACP, he and seven other parents sued. After losing in the state courts, they appealed all the way to the Supreme Court. The Kansas case was joined with four others, and they collectively bore the name ***Brown v. Board of Education***.

This, of course, was not Marshall's first appearance before the Supreme Court. Marshall was well respected in the halls of the Court, but he was not always riveting in his presentation. At times he had seemed "a bit on the dull side."[38] Not this day. Arguing one of the five cases, the one from South Carolina, Marshall got to the heart of the NAACP's arguments. All evidence, including evidence that had been accepted by the Court in earlier cases, had showed that black and white children were equal in their educational potential. Educational

Brown v. Board of Education

a landmark 1954 Supreme Court ruling that overturned *Plessy v. Ferguson* and declared legal segregation in public education to be in conflict with the equal protection clause of the Fourteenth Amendment.

segregation, therefore, had no legitimate basis. Moreover, it violated the Fourteenth Amendment to the Constitution, which had been made part of the Constitution specifically to protect freed slaves from violations of the state legislatures.

As in the two graduate school cases, psychological evidence was a part of the NAACP's strategy. One piece of evidence introduced was a set of earlier research findings by psychologists Kenneth Clark and Mamie Clark. In those studies, the Clarks presented young African American and white children with a set of brown and white dolls. A majority of children stated that they preferred the white dolls over the brown dolls, and many had negative comments about the brown dolls. The Clarks' evidence of psychological damage from segregation was introduced into three of the five cases in *Brown*. After Marshall had presented his arguments, John W. Davis presented South Carolina's side. Davis highlighted the importance of local control in education: "Is it not a fact that the very strength and fiber of our federal system is local self-government in those matters for which local action is competent?"[39]

It was far from certain that Chief Justice Vinson would rule in favor of the NAACP. He had already delayed the case once to ask for more evidence, and he had avoided taking on "separate but equal" in the two earlier law school cases. However, in one of those instances when chance plays a role in political development, Vinson passed away suddenly from a heart attack before a decision could be reached. Felix Frankfurter, one of Vinson's fellow justices and a sharp critic of his refusal to be more active in protecting rights, commented upon hearing the news of his passing, "This is the first indication I have ever heard that there is a God."[40]

Vinson's replacement as chief justice was California governor Earl Warren, chosen by President Dwight D. Eisenhower as much for his political skill and the fact that he was from California, which would be crucial in the next election, as for his judicial experience. Warren's own record on civil rights was not promising. As attorney general of California, he had supported the internment of Japanese Americans during World War II. He had never served as a judge—"not even," according to the press, "for five minutes in a police court."[41] Warren was, however, a skillful politician, and he used those skills to wrangle some of the most important votes in American constitutional history: those of the nine men on the United States Supreme Court.

On May 17, 1954, the last day of the Supreme Court's term, Warren read the Court's decision on *Brown*, years after the case first came before the Court: "Does segregation in public schools solely on the basis of race, even though the physical facilities and other 'tangible' factors may be equal, deprive the children of the minority groups of equal educational opportunities? We believe that it does."[42] Arguing that the premise of *Plessy*—that separation based on race caused no harm in those so separated—was flawed, Warren overturned the 1896 decision, saying, "We conclude that in the field of public education the doctrine of 'separate but equal' has no place. Separate educational facilities are inherently unequal. . . . We have now announced that such segregation is a denial of the equal protection of the laws." The Court was unanimous, a point that Warren inserted into his reading of the official decision.[43] It had to be; a deeply divided Court would not have had the legitimacy that it needed to take on segregation. The unanimous verdict, however, had taken Warren a long time and several compromises within the Court to achieve.

The "doll study" research of Dr. Kenneth B. Clark (shown here in a photo from 1969) and his wife Dr. Mamie Clark demonstrated the psychological harm of segregation and was used as evidence in *Brown v. Board of Education*.

AP Photo.

The reaction of the nation was strong and immediate, but not uniform. Many cheered the moral stance the court had taken. "What the Justices have done," declared a Cincinnati newspaper, "is simply to act as the conscience of the American nation."[44] Many voices in the African American community were supportive but measured; history had shown that white support for their cause had not always been sustained. "As Charles [Hamilton] Houston had said years earlier, 'Nobody needs to explain to a Negro the difference between the law in books and the law in action.'"[45] In the South, there was discussion among moderates on how to make the required adjustments. The Court, after all, had not set a firm date for when "separate but equal" had to be abolished. But there was also anger. Mobs blocked schools and universities. South Carolina governor James F. Byrnes proclaimed, "Ending segregation [will] mark the beginning of the end of civilization in the South as we have known it."[46]

Southern Resistance, and a Lack of Progress on the Ground

Legal segregation began to disappear in the border states, with Washington, D.C., the first of the five defendants in *Brown* to move to comply with the Supreme Court's ruling. Southern states, however, actively resisted. In 1956 Virginia's legislators passed a Resolution of Interposition, which argued that the state was "duty bound" to impose itself between children's education and the Supreme Court decision. Several other state legislatures also forbade their state officials from enforcing **desegregation**—the intentional reversal of segregated educational facilities based on children's race or ethnicity.

desegregation
the act of eliminating laws or practices that separate individuals based upon racial identity.

The Court's decision in *Brown* had intentionally avoided setting a strict timeline on achieving integration. In response to resistance to its efforts, the Court issued a follow-up decision the next year, in 1955. In what is now known as *Brown v. Board of Education of Topeka II,* the Warren Court urged compliance with *Brown I* "with all deliberate speed," a curious choice of words, hardly inflammatory, likely crafted out of political necessity. In addition, the Court dealt with questions of implementation, or making a policy a reality on the ground, by placing the federal district court judges in charge of actual desegregation efforts. Some southern district court judges were not sympathetic to the Court's ruling and tried to slow down compliance with it.[47] In general, in spite of the urging in the second *Brown* decision, compliance across the South was slow at best. Fears on the part of Supreme Court justices that their decision would not be obeyed proved to be well founded. In 1964, ten years after the Court's ruling in *Brown v. Board of Education*, 98 percent of African American children still attended completely segregated schools.

Other Actors Join the Struggle

The decisions of the Supreme Court did not by themselves end the practice of segregation in the South. As was discussed in Chapter 2, the Constitution set up the American system of government to prevent one branch from having that kind of power. And, for a time, the Court found itself acting alone. According to law professor Gerald Rosenberg, "For ten years the Court spoke forcefully while Congress and the executive did little."[48] There were a few exceptions to this, however. In 1957 President Eisenhower sent federal troops to Little Rock, Arkansas, to enforce a Supreme Court order to segregate the schools against the will of the state's governor. The troops escorted nine African American students through an angry white mob. Also that year, Lyndon Johnson, senator and future president, sponsored the Civil Rights Act of 1957, the first piece of civil rights legislation to pass since Reconstruction. Its primary purpose was to put pressure on the states through

Can the Supreme Court Effect Social Change?

Recall how Alexander Hamilton, in *Federalist* No. 78, argued that the Supreme Court had little power acting on its own "and must ultimately depend upon the aid of the executive arm even for the efficacy of its judgments." One scholar has collected data on the pace of integration in the South following *Brown v. Board* to make a similar argument: The Supreme Court cannot, acting on its own, produce social change on the ground. His data are displayed in the chart below.

It was not until 1970 that more than half of African American children in the South were attending integrated schools (and many of these were far from fully integrated). During this period, citizens took action through events such as the Montgomery bus boycott, in which African Americans in Montgomery, Alabama, refused to ride city buses in protest over segregated seating; the executive and legislative branches became more involved in the desegregation process; and the Court issued more related rulings. The data in the graph indicate that the decision of *Brown v. Board* did not immediately

result in desegregation of schools in the South. To say that the Supreme Court is powerless, however, might be too strong a statement to make based on these data alone.

First, the branches were not designed to act alone, but in concert with (and sometimes in opposition to) each other. This is the principle of separation of powers discussed in Chapter 2. Second, *Brown* was only the first of a string of decisions on school desegregation handed down by the Court–decisions that became stronger and stronger during the time period covered in the graph.

WHAT DO YOU THINK?

For ten years after *Brown*, southern public schools remained segregated. Considering all that you have read so far, why might this have been unsurprising? Do these data confirm that the Supreme Court cannot effect social change? Was the NAACP's decision to adopt a judicial strategy a wise one? Why or why not?

Percentage of African American Children Attending Integrated Schools in the South

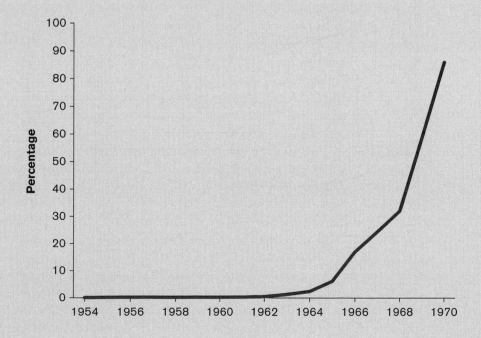

Source: Data are from Table 2.1 in Gerald N. Rosenberg, *The Hollow Hope* (Chicago: University of Chicago Press: 2008), 50–51.

By refusing to give up her seat on the bus, Rosa Parks became a Civil Rights icon. This one woman's civil disobedience has had a strong impact on political culture the world over and she is memorialized in countless ways, even today.

Mark Wilson/Getty Images.

civil disobedience
the intentional refusal to obey a law in order to call attention to its injustice.

the cost of litigation by supporting the lawsuits of African Americans who had been denied the right to vote. Though it did not effect significant policy change, it showed that civil rights legislation could make it past the southern Democrats in Congress.

Citizens themselves took increasingly strong action to end segregation in schools, workplaces, and the community. African American community leaders organized boycotts, in which people refused to buy services or products from an organization in order to force policy changes. Notable among these was the Montgomery bus boycott, which sought to put economic pressure on the city of Montgomery, Alabama, to end its policy of segregating bus passengers based on their race. At first, Montgomery community leaders tried to pressure the city into changing its policy, but this had no effect. In 1955 Claudette Colvin, an African American high school student, refused to move to the "Negro section" of a Montgomery bus. She was not sitting in the "white section," but in "no man's land," a vaguely defined buffer between the two sections that, according to segregationists, was created "to give the driver some discretion to keep the races out of each others' way."[49] Colvin refused to move and was handcuffed and placed under arrest. That year, other African American women in Montgomery were arrested for the same act of protest. Their case eventually resulted in the bus segregation law being declared unconstitutional.[50]

In December, Rosa Parks also refused to give up her bus seat and was later arrested. The decisions of Colvin and Parks were not taken lightly; they faced the prospect of criticism within their own communities and physical violence at the hands of whites. "When she [Rosa] was allowed to call home," one historian has noted, "her mother's first response was to groan and ask, 'Did they beat you?'"[51] Upon word of Parks's arrest, English professor Jo Ann Robinson and other community leaders organized a boycott, getting the word out with the help of African American churches in the city. They printed fliers in secret in the middle of the night at Alabama State College, where Robinson taught. Dr. Martin Luther King Jr. was selected to lead the boycott. Addressing the community in a Montgomery church, King captured the simple, courageous reason behind the actions of the women of the city: "And you know, my friends, there comes a time when people get tired of being trampled over by the iron feet of oppression. . . . We are here—we are here because we are tired now."[52] After lasting for more than a year, the boycott ended with the Supreme Court's 1956 decision in the case of Colvin and three others that declared the bus law unconstitutional. Not only had they won in the Court, but it was a public victory—a citizens' victory.

There were many other acts of **civil disobedience** in the struggle against segregation. Individuals chose to disobey segregation laws despite the dangers they faced in order to point out the injustice inherent in those laws. In 1960 four African American college students sat down at a lunch counter reserved for whites at a Woolworth's in Greensboro, North Carolina, and requested service. They were denied. They returned the next day, and their numbers began to grow. College students, both African American and white, continued the sit-ins. Over the next months, with the organizational help of the Student Nonviolent Coordinating Committee (SNCC), similar protests occurred across the

American South. Some protesters met with arrest, others with violence and intimidation.

In 1961 a group of African Americans and whites undertook another series of protests, these aimed at pressuring the administration of President John F. Kennedy to enforce Supreme Court decisions banning segregation in public facilities involved with interstate travel. These so-called Freedom Riders also faced arrest and violence. In one case, a bus was firebombed, and many protesters were beaten with baseball bats and iron pipes.

The actions of these activists—and their often harsh treatment at the hands of local law enforcement, which was broadcast to Americans on their televisions—began to change public opinion towards the civil rights struggle. By voting in larger and larger numbers, African Americans also began to make their presence felt in Washington, D.C. Close elections during the period highlighted to politicians the importance of securing the African American vote, which might tip an election in their favor.

Aware of changing political realities, Congress, under intense pressure from President Johnson, passed two major pieces of civil rights legislation, finally giving its support to efforts that had begun in the Supreme Court and on the streets. A version of the Civil Rights Act of 1964 had been part of President Kennedy's civil rights efforts prior to his assassination in 1963. The legislation that Congress passed in 1964 authorized the federal government to withhold grants from districts that did not integrate their schools. The act outlawed racial segregation in schools and public places and authorized the attorney general of the United States, and therefore the federal government, to sue individual school districts that failed to desegregate. In addition, the act outlawed employment discrimination based on race or ethnicity and also on religion, national origin, or gender. The provisions of the Civil Rights Act of 1964 proved to be as valuable to women and members of other minority groups in their efforts as the civil rights decisions in the Supreme Court. The Voting Rights Act of 1965 outlawed literacy tests for voters and authorized the Justice Department to send federal officers to register voters in uncooperative cities, counties, and states. The effects on African American voter registration were immediate and significant.

During this period, the Supreme Court also became more active in its rulings. In a series of decisions over the next decade and a half, the Court spoke with a firmer and firmer voice and began to take education policy into its own hands. When outright resistance failed, many southern states and districts tried more creative ways to get around the ruling in *Brown* without appearing to openly defy it. In 1959 the Board of Supervisors in Prince Edward County, Virginia, cut off all funding for the county's public schools; for four years African American students received no public education. In place of the school funding, the county set up a foundation to provide funds for students to attend private

A black student protests outside of a Woolworth's in Greensboro, North Carolina, in 1960. A white counterdemonstrator follows him. The efforts of those involved in the lunch counter protests helped call attention to the injustices of segregation in the American South.

The Granger Collection, New York.

> The debate over civil rights had moved on from laws to policies, to how strongly government should act to contest segregation.

schools, none of which accepted African American children. In 1964, in only its third educational segregation decision since *Brown*, the Court acted to put a stop to such end-around tactics. In *Griffin v. Prince Edward County*, the Court ordered Prince Edward County to reopen its public schools on an integrated basis. "The time for mere 'deliberate speed,'" Justice Hugo Black wrote in the opinion, "has run out."[53]

New Kent County, Virginia, adopted a "freedom of choice" plan, which, in theory, promoted desegregation by allowing students to choose between two high schools that prior to *Brown* had been strictly segregated by race. Three years after this plan was enacted, however, no African American children had been enrolled in the all-white high school. In *Green v. County School Board of New Kent County, Virginia*, the Court ruled that while New Kent County's plan was not unconstitutional, it was not enough. The district had an affirmative duty to comply; the burden of proof was on districts to show that they were desegregating in practice, on the ground. And the Court said that it would be watching.[54]

Two more decisions constituted the high-water mark for the Supreme Court's efforts in desegregation. In 1969, after Thurgood Marshall had joined the Court, Justice Black ruled in *Alexander v. Holmes County Board of Education* that "'all deliberate speed' for desegregation is no longer constitutionally permissible." Southern school districts were ordered to desegregate immediately.[55] In 1971 the Court ruled in *Swann v. Charlotte-Mecklenburg Board of Education* that busing—the use of transportation to desegregate public schools, even if it meant sending students to schools farther away from their homes—was constitutionally permissible.[56] Often unpopular with parents, busing efforts stirred up considerable political opposition in both the North and the South. Those in favor argued that such efforts were necessary given the deepness of the roots of segregation. Those opposed argued that the role of government in securing equal protection was only to strike down unjust laws, not to produce integration on the ground. The debate over civil rights had moved on from laws to policies, to how strongly government should act to contest segregation that exists even when there are no laws that support or maintain it.

Testing the Limits of Equal Protection for African Americans

The southern segregation that Thurgood Marshall and the NAACP had challenged in the courts was written into law—sometimes even into state constitutions. In many cases, these laws did not just allow segregation, they required it. This type of segregation is called **de jure segregation**, meaning that it is written into law. The efforts of activists and citizens had largely eliminated racially based de jure segregation by the end of the 1960s. Attention now focused on **de facto segregation**, segregation based not on law but on private choices, sometimes-private acts of discrimination, or the lingering social consequences of legal segregation even after those laws were no longer on the books. Addressing de facto segregation has proven to be even more complicated than addressing de jure segregation.

The Supreme Court has been more cautious in addressing de facto segregation than legal segregation. In 1974, in *Milliken v. Bradley*, the Court considered a case of educational segregation that had been caused not by law but by residential housing patterns in and around Detroit, Michigan.[57] The sizeable move of citizens to the suburbs in the middle of the twentieth century was made possible by the automobile and the interstate highway; this move was often described by the term *white flight* because of the demographics of the

de jure segregation
the separation of individuals based on their characteristics, such as race, intentionally and by law.

de facto segregation
a separation of individuals based on identity that arises not by law but because of other factors, such as residential housing patterns.

change. Large numbers of whites moved outside the central cities, leaving the urban cores with high percentages of African American residents. Segregation had gone from within school districts, as it had been in the South, to between districts. This pattern repeated across the industrial North. The question in *Milliken* was of responsibility. How much action should be taken, and who should be required to take it, when there was no law to point to? In this case, the Court ruled that there was no requirement to try to desegregate the region's schools since the district boundaries had not been drawn up to segregate them in the first place. The suburban districts did not have to participate in a plan that would move students across school district boundaries. Limits on busing or any other remedy that required action between school districts had been set.

Questions about how far the Court is willing to go to secure equality in the absence of discriminatory laws have arisen in other aspects of political and economic life as well. **Affirmative action**—a policy designed to address the consequences of previous discrimination by providing advantages to individuals based upon their identities— continues to be a subject of debate in American political life. The Court has issued a much less clear set of guidelines on the use of affirmative action than it has with legal segregation. Many of these cases have involved admissions practices at American colleges and universities that have sought to boost the enrollment of African Americans and members of other racial and ethnic minorities. Again, it boils down to what one means by "equal." To those who argue for less government intervention, "equal" only means removing any legal barriers to college admissions for members of racial and ethnic minorities. To those who argue for stronger government involvement, it means taking steps to ensure equality of representation that might selectively benefit certain individuals based on their identity, whether in schools or workplaces. In recent years, the Court has tried to navigate among these approaches, but it has not always done so in a clear-cut way.

A 1978 Supreme Court decision in *Regents of the University of California v. Bakke* concerned the use of quotas, or the setting aside of a number of school slots, contracts with the government, or job opportunities for groups who have suffered past discrimination.[58] In the case, Allan Bakke, who identified himself as white, had sued the regents of the University of California at Davis after having been denied admission to its medical school. Bakke argued that his academic record was superior to the group of sixteen minority applicants for whom seats had been set aside. He brought his suit under the Fourteenth Amendment, claiming that the quota system violated his rights under the equal protection clause of the Constitution. In its ruling, the Court agreed that the quota system had violated Bakke's rights and those of other white applicants and instructed the school to admit him. However, the Court also affirmed the worthiness of the goal of increasing minority student enrollment, leaving open the possibility for plans that did not involve strict quotas.

In the years after *Bakke*, the Court issued several rulings that attempted to define the limits of permissible affirmative action. In 2003 the Court issued two rulings on the same day that tried to clarify its position. In *Gratz v. Bollinger*, the Court considered the use of a points system in undergraduate admissions decisions.[59] Like Alan Bakke, Jennifer Gratz had been denied admission to a university, in this case the University of Michigan at Ann Arbor, and sued on the basis of discrimination. Rather than using a strict quota system, the university ranked applicants on a points system, much of which focused on academics. Some points, however, were awarded for having parents who attended the University of Michigan, being a state resident, having shown a commitment to public service, or having strong athletic ability. Forty of the 150 points were awarded on the basis of "other

affirmative action
a policy designed to address the consequences of previous discrimination by providing advantages to individuals based upon their identities.

factors." One of these factors was membership in a traditionally underrepresented racial or ethnic group. The university argued that having a diverse student body was of educational benefit to the entire learning community. In *Gratz*, the Court ruled that the points system was unconstitutional, but it did not strike down the use of racial or ethnic identity as a consideration for admissions decisions.

In *Grutter v. Bollinger*, also decided in 2003, the Court affirmed the possibility of using racial and ethnic identity in admissions decisions.[60] Barbara Grutter had also sued the University of Michigan, though in this case, its law school. Unlike the admissions system at the undergraduate level, the law school did not use a points system, but it did include racial identity in a group of factors considered in the application decision. By a 5–4 vote, the Court ruled that the university could use race as a factor as long as it could show that it had a "compelling interest" to do so. Ensuring a diverse student body, the Court concluded, does demonstrate such an interest. In June 2016, the Court, in a 4–3 ruling in *Fisher v. University of Texas at Austin*, upheld the constitutionality of considering racial identity in college admissions. President Obama said of the decision, "We are not a country that guarantees equal outcomes, but we do strive to provide an equal shot to everybody."[61]

WHAT HAVE I LEARNED?

1. Key to the NAACP's legal strategy was the goal of demonstrating unequal spending in America's public schools.

   a. True
   b. False

2. The Supreme Court's decision in *Brown v. Board of Education* was met with widespread resistance.

   a. True
   b. False

3. The Civil Rights Act of 1964 _____.

   a. Authorized the Justice Department to sue segregated school districts

   b. Outlawed employment discrimination based on racial identity
   c. Outlawed employment discrimination based on gender
   d. All of the above

4. Do you think the NAACP's decision to focus much of its energy and resources on using the judiciary to end legal segregation was the correct one?

   Answer Key: 1. b; 2. a; 3. d; 4. Answers should discuss the power of the federal judiciary in making broader social change as well as limitations on that power.

SECURING CIVIL RIGHTS FOR AMERICAN WOMEN

Though they constitute a slight majority of the American population, women have also struggled to secure their civil rights throughout the nation's history. Scholars often frame these efforts as having taken place in two waves. The first wave, the effort to secure the right to vote, was closely tied to the efforts of nineteenth-century American women to secure their rights in education and to end the practice of slavery. The second wave, which began in the middle of the twentieth century, extended the scope of civil rights protections to women's participation in the classroom and the workplace, their freedom from sexual harassment, and their control over their bodies and their sexuality.

Enfranchisement: Voting, Education, and Ending Slavery

Early efforts by women to secure their rights often focused on education, which was considered an acceptable political space for a nineteenth-century white woman to inhabit. Many early activists for women's rights were also active in the **abolitionist movement**—the movement to end the practice of slavery.

Prudence Crandall was a white educator whose political activism in the 1830s demonstrates the close link between education, opposition to slavery, and political activism on the part of early advocates for women's rights. In 1832 Crandall admitted Sarah Harris, an African American girl, to her school for ladies in Canterbury, Connecticut, so that Harris might herself become a teacher.[62] At a time when "progressive" white thinking on race generally involved plans to recolonize African Americans to the West Indies or Africa, the actions of Crandall and Harris were considered extraordinarily radical. Many in Canterbury voiced their disapproval of the situation.

Rather than cave in to the strong community pressure that she was facing to expel Harris, Crandall closed her school. Two months later, she opened another school exclusively for African American girls and soon had seventeen students. Crandall was arrested and briefly jailed, her school vandalized, "pupils and teachers . . . were stoned as they went for walks; manure was dropped in the well; local shopkeepers refused to sell food, and doctors denied their services."[63] With the help of some supportive community members and funds from abolitionists, the school remained open for a year and a half. However, after masked men attacked and vandalized the school using battering rams and attempted to burn it to the ground, Crandall feared for the physical safety of her students and closed her school for good in 1834.

The suppression of women's rights was often justified by claims that women needed to be protected from, and therefore shut out of, elements of public life. This "protection" had legal aspects. Rights of women were severely restricted in the public space, and married women had no legal identity outside of their marriage. For the purposes of the courts, they did not exist. The restriction of women's rights was as much social as it was legal. Part of the effort to secure women's rights, therefore, involved redefining what was considered acceptable behavior for a woman. Taking action in the public space—by speaking out, organizing, and mobilizing public opinion—was as political in its challenge to the boundaries of acceptable behavior as was the act of actually changing laws.

The efforts of sisters Sarah and Angelina Grimké to organize and speak out against slavery in the 1830s challenged both the institution of slavery and the less visible institution of protection of women from public life. Daughters of a prominent South Carolina

abolitionist movement
a political struggle to end slavery and free all slaves.

An engraving depicting an attack on Prudence Crandall's school for "young ladies of color" in Connecticut in 1834. This, and previous threats against students and teachers, forced Crandall to close her school.

The Granger Collection, New York.

> Taking action in the public space—by speaking out, organizing, and mobilizing public opinion—was as political in its challenge to the boundaries of acceptable behavior as was the act of actually changing laws.

slaveholding family, the Grimké sisters set out in 1837 on an anti-slavery speaking tour in New England. In doing so, they helped to change public perception about a woman's proper role in public life. As children, Sarah and Angelina had been educated personally about the horrors of slavery, and they drew from these experiences in their speeches and writings. Their campaign drew much of its strength from their own Christianity—and drew much of its opposition from Christian churches. Their audiences included women and men, African Americans and whites. Their speeches highlighted the cruelty at the heart of the institution of slavery, and they expressed solidarity with women slaves. At a national convention of antislavery women in 1837, which the sisters had helped organize, Angelina presented a pamphlet that she had written, *An Appeal to the Women of the Nominally Free States*. She wrote,

And dear sisters, in a country where women are degraded and brutalized, and where their exposed persons bleed under the lash—where they are sold in the shambles of "negro brokers"—robbed of their hard earnings—torn from their husbands, and forcibly plundered of their virtue and their offspring; surely, in *such* a country, it is very natural that *women* should wish to know "the reason why"—especially when these outrages of blood and nameless horror are practiced in violation of the principles of our national Bill of Rights and the Preamble of our Constitution.[64]

A few of the male leaders of the abolitionist movement supported an active role for women as co-participants along with their push for equal rights. Frederick Douglass published on the masthead of the newspaper that he edited, "Right is of no sex—Truth is of no color."[65] Others urged these advocates to drop their push for "a woman's rights," as it was called, fearful that the controversy might detract from the goal of abolition, but the proponents refused. However, the male-dominated abolitionist movement continued to prevent women from assuming public roles as leaders. Sometimes women were only allowed to join antislavery conferences as observers in segregated seating, without the right to speak or vote.

Shut out of prominent antislavery conventions in the mid-nineteenth century, abolitionist women organized their own. Lucretia Mott and Elizabeth Cady Stanton met at an antislavery convention in London in 1840 and on their way back to the United States began to plan a separate conference on women's rights. The conference met in a Methodist church in Seneca Falls, New York, over two days in July 1848. On the first day of what would come to be known as the Seneca Falls Convention, Stanton read a list of eleven resolutions, known as the Declaration of Sentiments. These resolutions derived their legitimacy from an appeal to higher law, just as the Declaration of Independence had done seventy-two years earlier and Dr. Martin Luther King Jr.'s "Letter from Birmingham Jail" would do 115 years later: "Resolved, That all laws which prevent woman from occupying such a station in society as her conscience shall dictate, or which place her in a position inferior to that of man, are contrary to the great precept of nature, and therefore of no force or authority. Resolved, That woman is man's equal—was intended to be so by the Creator, and the highest good of the race demands that she should be recognized as such."[66]

Support for the women's declaration was not universal. Only one-third of the delegates to the convention signed it. Some, including Mott, thought that it was too bold, especially in its call for suffrage (the right to vote) for women. The convention, however, had given energy to the movement. In the years following Seneca Falls, "a cascade of women's rights conventions . . . carried the movement into towns and villages throughout the Northeast and the Midwest."[67]

Frances Ellen Watkins Harper on Women's Rights, Racism, and American Society

In an 1866 speech before the eleventh Woman's Rights Convention in New York, Frances Ellen Watkins Harper, a prominent African American activist and writer, challenged the most optimistic attendees, who argued that white women's suffrage would improve the situation of African Americans:

> I do not believe that giving the woman the ballot is immediately going to cure all the ills of life. I do not believe that white women are dewdrops just exhaled from the skies. I think that like men they may be divided into three classes, the good, the bad, and the indifferent. The good would vote according to their convictions and principle; the bad, as dictated by prejudice or malice; and the indifferent will vote on the strongest side of the question, with the winning party.
>
> You white women speak here of rights. I speak of wrongs. I, as a colored woman, have had in this country an education which has made me feel as if I were in the situation of Ishmael, my hand against every man, and every man's hand against me. Let me go to-morrow morning and take my seat in one of your street cars—I do not know that they will do it in New York, but they will in Philadelphia—and the conductor will put up his hand and stop the car there rather than let me ride . . . .
>
> While there exists this brutal element in society which tramples upon the feeble and treads down the weak, I tell you that if there is any class of people who need to be lifted out of their airy nothings and selfishness, it is the white women of America.[69]

Frances E. W. Harper in a nineteenth-century engraving. Harper challenged the idea that the efforts of white women political activists would inevitably lead to gains for African American women.
The Granger Collection, New York.

WHAT DO YOU THINK?

Harper's accusations were controversial in 1866, and they still are. They speak to divisions *between* Americans fighting for civil rights for different groups of excluded citizens. In 2016 we are still confronted with this challenge. In struggles for civil rights in the twenty-first century, what are your perceptions about the solidarity between, or divisions among, different groups of civil rights advocates?

Unlike the efforts to secure the civil rights of African Americans, women's rights activists, especially in the first wave, pursued a mostly, though not solely, legislative strategy, attempting to change state and federal laws to guarantee they received equal protection in them. The legislative strategy was seen as necessary. Similar to the struggle for African American rights, the women's movement did not speak with a unified voice. Debates over goals and strategy led to sharp divisions within it. In the last national convention held before the Civil War, Stanton spoke out against marriage laws and in favor of new resolutions making it easier for a woman to obtain a divorce. Many reformers felt that she "had gone too far."[68]

These divisions continued after the Civil War, when giving the right to vote to freed African American men came onto the national agenda. Some women's rights activists wanted to include suffrage for women in the Fifteenth Amendment. Others feared that trying to obtain the right to vote for African Americans and women at the same time might stir up too much opposition. There was often a stated racial bias against African Americans on the part of white women's rights advocates, and far less attention was paid to the rights of African American women than either those of African American men or white women. According to one historian, the issue of suffrage was often portrayed as "a choice between black men and educated white women."[70]

Divisions within the women's rights movement crystallized in the formation of two separate organizations that agreed on the need for suffrage but disagreed over the importance of trying to secure a broader commitment to women's equality. In 1869 Stanton and Susan B. Anthony formed the National Woman's Suffrage Association to try to secure civil rights for women beyond only the right to vote. Also in 1869, Lucy Stone helped to organize the American Women's Suffrage Association, which focused on suffrage, pursuing its goals at the level of state and territory.

Nineteenth Amendment
a 1920 amendment to the Constitution that prevented states from denying the right to vote based on sex.

Wyoming Territory granted the women the right to vote in 1869. When Wyoming joined the Union in 1890, it became the first state to grant women the right to vote. By 1918 fifteen states had passed laws allowing women's suffrage. The right was secured at the national level in 1920 with the ratification of the **Nineteenth Amendment** to the Constitution, which had been drafted by Anthony and Stanton more than forty years earlier. The amendment stated, "The right of citizens of the United States to vote shall not be denied or abridged by the United States or by any State on account of sex. Congress shall have power to enforce this article by appropriate legislation."

Though the constitutional right to vote came later for women than it did for African American men, women did not face the same kind of tactics of resistance aimed to keep the legal right from becoming a practical right. As they began to exercise their right to vote, however, the broader vision of equality that many of the pioneers in the American women's movement hoped for was far from secured.

Beyond the Vote: The Second Wave

The second wave of the movement to secure the civil rights of women in the United States began in the 1960s. Like the first wave, much of the strategy involved changing laws. However, the focus went far beyond the voting booth and addressed inequalities at work and in the home as well as protection from violence and sexual harassment.

> The focus went far beyond the voting booth and addressed inequalities at work and in the home as well as protection from violence and sexual harassment.

Crucial to these legislative and legal efforts was the Civil Rights Act of 1964. Title VII of the act prohibits discrimination in employment based on race, color, religion, national origin, or sex. While some scholars have argued that women were added to the act as an attempt to mobilize enough opposition to kill it, the southern congressman who introduced the amendment to add women to the legislation claimed that his motives were sincere.[71] Regardless of the truth, Title VII has proved to be an important element of equal rights for women and the basis for several rulings about gender discrimination by the Supreme Court.

One of the early leaders of this second wave was Betty Friedan. Her 1963 book, *The Feminine Mystique*, highlighted the ways in which American society assumed that domestic roles for women were "natural" and argued for a "dramatic reshaping of the cultural image of femininity that will permit women to reach maturity, identity, completeness of self, without conflict with sexual fulfillment."[72] Friedan also served as the first president of the National Organization for Women (NOW), a women's rights advocacy group that pushed for change in both the legislature and the Supreme Court. NOW initially organized largely to pressure the federal government to enforce the antidiscrimination provisions of Title VII. The organization's goals, however, became much more sweeping: "The purpose of NOW is to take action to bring women into full participation in the mainstream of American society now, exercising all the privileges and responsibilities thereof in truly equal partnership with men."[73]

In the 1960s and 1970s, women's rights activists secured several important pieces of legislation. They also lobbied to ensure that these laws were vigorously enforced—to make sure that equal meant equal in the workplaces and schools and not just in the laws. Through these pieces of legislation, women secured the legal right to receive equal pay for equal work in the same workplace and protections against discrimination based on gender, pregnancy, or childbirth. Many of these laws contain language that makes it illegal to retaliate against employees who file or participate in the filing of discrimination claims. The threat of retaliation can be a powerful disincentive for individuals to file discrimination claims, and, therefore, a powerful tool to preserve discrimination.

Protections against gender discrimination apply not just to workplaces but also to schools, states, and local governments. One of the most notable provisions is contained in a set of amendments to the Higher Education Act passed in 1972. Title IX of these amendments states, "No person in the United States shall, on the basis of sex, be excluded from participation in, or denied the benefits of, or subjected to discrimination under any educational program or activity receiving federal aid."[74] While its provisions apply equally to curriculum, health care, and residential life, Title IX has had a public impact on the provision of athletic programs and, more recently, on the efforts of LGBT students to overcome harassment based on sexual identity.

One of the most important elements of the legislative campaign for women's rights was an attempt to secure ratification of the **Equal Rights Amendment (ERA)** to the United States Constitution. The proposed amendment read, "Section 1: Equality of rights under the law shall not be denied or abridged by the United States or by any state on account of sex."

Activist Alice Paul had written the original version of the amendment in 1923, and it had been submitted to Congress for official acceptance (the first stage of the two-stage amendment process) every year since. Partly due to the help of NOW, the proposed amendment easily cleared the two-thirds vote requirement of the House of Representatives in 1971 and the Senate in 1972. Submitted to the states for ratification, the ERA got off to a quick and successful beginning, outpacing other recent amendments with its speed of state ratifications. By 1977 thirty-five of the needed thirty-eight states

Betty Friedan in a 1970 protest march commemorating the fiftieth anniversary of the ratification of the Nineteenth Amendment. Friedan was a writer, an activist in efforts to secure equal rights for American women, and the first president of the National Organization for Women.

Fred W. McDarrah/Getty Images.

Equal Rights Amendment
a proposed but not ratified amendment to the Constitution that sought to guarantee equality of rights based upon sex.

had ratified the ERA. No more states, however, would ratify. In spite of having its ratification deadline extended by Congress, the clock ran out on the ERA in 1982, and the amendment died.

Scholars continue to debate why the ERA failed. Part of the reason is that the framers designed the amendment process in such a way that most proposals to amend it do fail. The Constitution was designed to be amendable, but the two-stage process for ratification is a very high hurdle. Other explanations have focused on the possibility that proponents did not mobilize as successfully at the state level as they had done in Congress during the first stage of the process. Additionally, the controversy surrounding the Supreme Court's decision on abortion in *Roe v. Wade* (see Chapter 4) may have mobilized opponents to the proposed amendment.[75] The fact that so many states ratified early on also allowed opponents to concentrate their resources on a smaller number of remaining states than if they had to wage a counterstrategy in a larger number of states.[76]

Though the Equal Rights Amendment was not ratified, the debate over its ratification did help increase the visibility of women's rights issues and place them on the national agenda. And, as it turns out, the Fourteenth Amendment to the Constitution and Title VII of the Civil Rights Act of 1964 provided a sufficient basis for the Supreme Court to act in the absence of the Equal Rights Amendment.

Supreme Court Decisions on Gender Discrimination and Sexual Harassment

Although part of the strategy for women's rights advocates was to use the Supreme Court, as African American rights activists had done, they did so under a slightly different standard. Due to the nation's history of slavery, the Court has treated protection of civil rights based on race and ethnicity differently than protection for other groups. Historically, the Court has used three different standards to decide if a law or policy that treats people differently based on some aspect of their identity is allowable or not. Race has been considered a suspect classification for the purposes of this decision. It's not the people who are suspect, or their race. It's the treatment of people differently on the basis of race that is suspect. In cases involving racial identity, the Court applies a standard of strict scrutiny to any attempt to provide different or separate treatment. Under such scrutiny, a government has to show a "compelling interest" to justify the unequal treatment, a high standard that is difficult to meet.

At the other end of the spectrum is the reasonableness standard, in which differential treatment must be shown to be reasonable and not arbitrary. It is also called the rational basis standard as one merely has to show that there is a rational reason for the distinction.[77] This is a much lower bar legally. Under the application of the reasonableness standard, for example, government may tax people at different rates based on their incomes or impose a curfew on minors that does not apply to adults.

Cases involving the rights of women have generally been considered by applying a standard in between these two extremes, one of intermediate scrutiny. While the Court has not yet placed gender on the same level as race in its critical view of justifications for differential treatment, it has placed gender on a higher standard than, for example, age or disability. In general, the Court has found most forms of differential treatment for men and women to be unconstitutional, except when such treatment can be justified as serving important objectives or necessities. This standard has evolved in recent years and continues to be a source of conflict and disagreement between the justices themselves.

Cases involving sexual harassment have generally been evaluated on the basis of the discrimination provisions of Title VII of the Civil Rights Act of 1964 rather than the Fourteenth Amendment. Though Title VII does not specifically mention sexual harassment, the Court has ruled in several recent cases that sexual, or gender-based, harassment does violate the act's antidiscrimination provisions. The Court has identified two types of harassment. *Quid pro quo* harassment occurs when employers request or demand sexual favors in return for advancement or employment. A *hostile working environment* involves actions, statements, or conditions that unreasonably interfere with the ability of employees to do their jobs. In cases of quid pro quo harassment, employers can be found liable for the behavior of their offending employees, even if that behavior was not known at the time it occurred. In cases involving hostile working environments, employers are generally held liable only if they knew about the offending behavior but did nothing to stop it. As with other forms of gender-based discrimination, the Court's treatment of sexual harassment is still evolving and is the source of considerable disagreements within the Court itself.

COMPLEXITY AND CHANGE IN AMERICANS' EFFORTS TO SECURE THEIR CIVIL RIGHTS

In 1851 Sojourner Truth, an orator, activist, and former slave, addressed a women's rights convention in Akron, Ohio. Her speech, only a few paragraphs long, drew from her own experiences as a person confronting more than one form of oppression:

> I have plowed and reaped and husked and chopped and mowed, and can any man do more than that? I have heard much about the sexes being equal; I can carry as much as any man, and eat as much too, if I can get it. I am as strong as any man that is now. . . .
> But the women are coming up bless be God and a few of the men are coming up with them. But man is in a tight place, the poor slave is on him, woman is coming on him, and he is surely between a hawk and a buzzard.[78]

Other African American women's rights activists had been hard at work in the decades before Truth's speech. For example, Maria W. Stewart, an African American essayist,

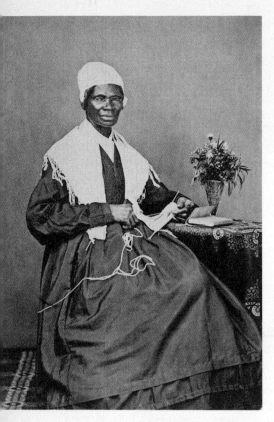

A portrait of Sojourner Truth. Her efforts to call attention to the multiple forms of oppression facing African American women in the nineteenth century highlighted what scholars now call challenges of intersectionality.

Time Life Pictures/Timepix/The LIFE Picture Collection/Getty Images.

NEWS CLIP

Controversy regarding Arizona bill's possible anti-Latino profiling

activist, and orator from Boston, was the "first American woman to speak in public to a mixed audience of men and women, addressing a gathering at Boston's Franklin Hall in 1832."[79]

Truth's speech, however, has resonated throughout the history of civil rights and succinctly and eloquently captures the reality that many Americans have been confronting more than one form of inequality in their lived experiences. Scholars of identity and politics call the presence of multiple and overlapping identities and inequalities *intersectionality*.[80] This approach recognizes that multiple forms of oppression are not just additive; they interact with each other to present individuals with complex challenges to the assertion of their own rights and liberties.

This concept is more than the subject of academic study. Intersectionality and the responses to it have shaped activists' own strategic choices in the political space. Confronting inequalities based on both race and gender shaped the choices and strategies of early African American women activists. Some chose to focus their efforts primarily on abolition, confronting the very different expectations of "proper" behavior for white and African American women. Others focused their efforts within their own communities, challenging realities of poverty and poor education at the local level.[81] In the slave states, many African American women focused on keeping their families together and alive. This complex set of choices and challenges continues to present itself to Americans working to secure equal rights against multiple and overlapping forms of discrimination.

Civil Rights and the Diversity of Lived Experiences in American History

In this chapter, we have focused on efforts to secure civil rights for Americans with disabilities, African Americans, and women. Throughout the nation's history, however, members of many other groups have acted to secure their own rights. Some of these struggles also go back to the early decades of the American Republic. To give proper attention to all of these efforts would require an entire book at least; therefore, we have focused on only some of them. The guiding principle of this necessary omission is that we cover many of these issues in other parts of this book.

Native Americans, as we discussed in Chapter 1, have worked to preserve their traditions and identities since the first arrival of the European colonists. Drawing upon lessons from the American civil rights movement, in 1969 a group of Native American activists occupied Alcatraz Island in protest of American policy. The last of the protestors were removed nineteen months after the protest began, but the occupation had helped call national attention to historical and current grievances against the federal government. Similarly, many Latinos and Latinas have and continue to employ tactics of protest, organization, education, and mobilization to challenge discrimination against members of their communities, especially on issues such as immigration and labor policy. As they are the fastest growing group of Americans, issues of concern to Latino/a Americans are quickly becoming issues of concern to politicians and the major political parties, a subject to which we will return later in the book. Individuals and groups have also mobilized to secure the rights of gay, lesbian, transgendered, and transsexual Americans. While we explored the issue of marriage equality in the previous chapter, it is important to note that these efforts involved civil rights as much as civil liberties. The Supreme Court decision

Thurgood Marshall on the Nation's Progress, or Lack of It, toward Racial Equality

In a speech given by Justice Thurgood Marshall on the occasion of his friend, Wiley Branton, being installed as the new dean of Howard University Law School in 1978, Marshall reflected on the progress that African Americans had made on achieving racial equality:

> But today, you know, we have reached the place where people say, "We've come a long way". But so have other people come a long way. And so have other schools come a long way.

> Has the gap been getting smaller? It's getting bigger. Everybody's been doing better.

> And so, as you look at the Howard University Law School today, that's what we have to remember. You look back, and people say we are better off today. *Better than what*?

> You know, I used to be amazed at people who would say that, "the poorest Negro kid in the South was better off than the kid in South Africa." So what! We are not in South Africa. We are here.

> I'm also amazed by people who say, "You ought to go around the country and show yourself to Negroes; and give them inspiration." For what?

> These Negro kids are not fools. They know to tell them there is a possibility that someday you'll have a chance to be the O-N-L-Y Negro on the Supreme Court, those odds aren't too good.

> When I do get around the country . . . I still get the same problems. You know, like "Years ago, you told us things were going to get better. But they are not a darn bit better for me. I am still having trouble getting to work. I have trouble eating."

> And guess what I am hearing now:

> "You not only told me that; you told my father that. And he's no better off; and neither am I. And can you tell me my children will be better off?"

> Well, all I am trying to tell you . . . there's a lot more to be done.[82]

WHAT DO YOU THINK?

In his words, Marshall pointed to a movement powerful and successful but still incomplete. Consider issues of civil rights that you might be involved with or interested in. What have been the gains to secure civil rights in these areas? What remains to be accomplished? How might you add your own voice to those efforts?

that established marriage equality, *Obergefell v. Hodges* (2015), did so based upon the Fourteenth Amendment's guarantee of equal protection of the laws.

In the United States in the twenty-first century, the concept of racial identity is becoming complicated as well. Multiracial Americans, or those with more than one distinctive racial heritage, have increasingly been carving out a space for themselves in discourse and policies involving race and ethnicity. In 2000 the United States Census allowed, for the first time, individuals to select more than one racial category. Slightly more than 2 percent chose to do so. By 2010 the number of Americans self-identifying as multiracial increased by 32 percent, to about nine million Americans. Where the most common combination in 2000 was "white and some other race," by 2010 the most common combination was "black and white." In addition, over the same ten-year period, the population of multiracial children increased by 50 percent, "making it the fastest growing youth group in the country."[83]

The increase in Americans who self-identify as multiracial is more than an issue of numbers. Traditional racial and ethnic identifications have been used as the basis for evaluating compliance with Title VII of the Civil Rights Act of 1964, the Voting Rights Act,

NEWS CLIP
Supreme Court affirms the right to same-sex marriage

and educational desegregation policies. Broadening the categories will impact all of these regulations, and some African American rights advocates have expressed concern that it might take away from gains in equality that have been achieved since the civil rights era.[84] Proponents of having multiracial classification argue that it more accurately reflects the changing realities of racial identity in the United States. Testifying before Congress, one parent of a multiracial child stated, "In my opinion, the most traumatic experience related to racial identification for the multiracial child occurs when he/she is asked to deny racial connectedness with one parent."[85]

CONCLUSION

Have Americans' Civil Rights Been Secured?

On March 18, 2008, Illinois senator and presidential candidate Barack Obama delivered a campaign speech at the Philadelphia Convention Center in which he candidly addressed his own multiracial identity and his views on race in modern American politics:

> I am the son of a black man from Kenya and a white woman from Kansas. I was raised with the help of a white grandfather who survived a Depression to serve in Patton's Army during World War II and a white grandmother who worked on a bomber assembly line at Fort Leavenworth while he was overseas. I've gone to some of the best schools in America and lived in one of the world's poorest nations. I am married to a black American who carries within her the blood of slaves and slave owners—an inheritance we pass on to our two precious daughters. I have brothers, sisters, nieces, nephews, uncles and cousins of every race and every hue, scattered across three continents, and for as long as I live, I will never forget that in no other country on Earth is my story even possible. . . .
>
> Contrary to the claims of some of my critics, black and white, I have never been so naïve as to believe that we can get beyond our racial divisions in a single election cycle, or with a single candidacy—particularly a candidacy as imperfect as my own.
>
> But I have asserted a firm conviction—a conviction rooted in my faith in God and my faith in the American people—that, working together, we can move beyond some of our old racial wounds, and that in fact we have no choice if we are to continue on the path of a more perfect union.[86]

In spite of all of the progress made in securing rights for all Americans—progress often earned in the face of considerable personal danger—it is not yet possible to state that America has entered a postracial, postgendered, or post"other" phase in its political history. Women and men shaped by their lived experiences of race, ethnicity, gender, disability, age, or sexual orientation continue to try to make equality a reality on the ground rather than under the law alone. And many legal efforts are still underway on issues such as immigration, voting, and recognition of the diversity of sexual identities. The twenty-first century is a time of major change in American civil rights policies, laws, and perceptions.

The struggle to achieve equality under the laws of the United States has never been simple or clear, and it has only grown more complex. Whatever future attempts to secure civil rights in the United States bring, however, this much is certain: Those attempts will require drawing upon the lessons of past struggles, well-planned action, and courage.

CHAPTER REVIEW

This chapter's main ideas are reflected in the Learning Objectives below. By reviewing them here you should be able to **remember** the key points, **connect** them to the stories presented in the chapter, **think** critically about these questions, and **know** these terms that are central to the topic.

5.1 Analyze the challenges associated with defining how strongly a government should act to help secure civil rights.

REMEMBER...
- Securing civil rights requires action, both on the part of individuals to advocate for their rights and on the part of government to secure and protect those rights.

CONNECT...
- In describing efforts to secure civil rights for Americans with disabilities, Judith Heumann highlighted the need to take action, to call attention to injustices, and to make changes to laws and policies.

THINK...
- How strongly should the American government act to secure civil rights?

KNOW...
- *civil rights* (p. 159)
- *positive freedoms* (p. 159)

5.2 Trace the struggles to secure civil rights for people with disabilities, African Americans, and women.

REMEMBER...
- While the conclusion of the Civil War settled the question of secession, struggles to secure rights for African Americans continued, often under threats of economic and physical violence.

CONNECT...
- When Thurgood Marshall and fellow litigators with the NAACP presented their arguments before the Supreme Court in 1952, they did so against the background of a history of discrimination, segregation, slavery, and violence against African Americans.

THINK...
- What are the similarities and differences between the tactics and goals employed by individuals in trying to secure civil rights for Americans with disabilities, African Americans, and women?

KNOW...
- *Thirteenth Amendment* (p. 166)
- *Fourteenth Amendment* (p. 167)
- *Fifteenth Amendment* (p. 167)
- *Nineteenth Amendment* (p. 184)
- *legal segregation* (p. 163)

5.3 Explain the dangers associated with the NAACP's decision to use the courts to make social change.

REMEMBER...
- The NAACP's choice to focus its efforts on ending legal segregation was not preordained, nor was the strategy of using the courts instead of focusing on changing the laws in the states.

CONNECT...
- Charles Hamilton Houston, Thurgood Marshall, and members of the NAACP's legal teams knew that they had to establish that separate could never be equal and was in fundamental conflict with the equal protection clause of the Fourteenth Amendment.

THINK...
- What were the risks faced by Marshall and the NAACP in using the federal judiciary to end legal segregation?

KNOW...
- Brown v. Board of Education (p. 172)
- *equal protection clause* (p. 167)
- Plessy v. Ferguson (p. 168)
- *separate but equal* (p. 169)

5.4 Evaluate the role of all three branches of the federal government in changing policy on the ground to desegrate America's public schools.

REMEMBER...
- The federal judiciary is only one of three branches and faces many challenges in changing public policy on the ground.

CONNECT...
- In the wake of the Supreme Court's ruling in *Brown v. Board of Education*, segregationists fought the implementation of the ruling, and many other individuals undertook acts of protest and civil disobedience.

THINK...
- What role can the Supreme Court play in effecting change on the ground? What are some limitations on its ability to do so?

KNOW...
- *civil disobedience* (p. 176)
- *de facto segregation* (p. 178)
- *de jure segregation* (p. 178)
- *desegregation* (p. 174)

5.5 Contrast the tactics employed by individuals working to secure civil rights in the area of racial equality to the tactics of those acting to secure gender and sexual equality.

REMEMBER...
- Early efforts to secure civil rights for African Americans and those to secure civil rights for American women often overlapped but with differences in their goals and tactics.

CONNECT...
- While efforts to secure civil rights for American women did involve the courts, they also involved legislative and administrative strategies.

THINK...

THINK...

- How did advocates for gender equality overcome the failure to secure ratification of the Equal Rights Amendment?

KNOW ...

- *abolitionist movement* (p. 181)
- *affirmative action* (p. 179)
- *Equal Rights Amendment (ERA)* (p. 185)

5.6 Evaluate the ways the diversity of Americans' identities shapes efforts to secure civil rights in the twenty-first century.

REMEMBER...

- Americans may face multiple forms of discrimination that may act to reinforce each other.

THINK...

- In what ways do changes in the diversity and complexity of American society expand our understanding of efforts to secure civil rights?

6 POLITICAL PARTICIPATION

Carry That Weight[1]

Amanda Collins, a student at the University of Nevada, Reno, became an activist for campus carry legislation and a spokesperson for gun rights after being sexually assaulted on campus. Here she urges the Nevada legislature to support a bill that would allow individuals with concealed carry permits to bring weapons onto state university and college campuses.

AP Photo/Cathleen Allison

By its nature, representative democracy requires action. It cannot survive without it. Representatives act in the space of government to enact their constituents' concerns and preferences in the laws and policies of a nation. For their part, citizens must act to make their wishes known. They must find candidates they feel good about supporting and help those candidates achieve political office; they must also hold those representatives accountable after they are elected. In addition, individuals must also rally others to their causes and speak as a member of a group rather than as a lone voice in the political wilderness. But how? What tools can people use to accomplish all of these weighty goals? That is where **political participation** comes in. Through its many avenues, people act to shape the laws and policies of the nation.

◼ SHAPING THE POLITICAL AGENDA
Testifying on the Problem of Sexual Violence and Firearms on College Campuses

In March 2012, Amanda Collins offered her testimony before the Michigan State Senate. It was not the first time that Collins had testified, nor would it be the last. In her statement, Collins claimed the right for women to legally carry firearms on

LEARNING OBJECTIVES

After reading this chapter you will be able to:

6.1 Understand how student political activism on the issue of campus sexual violence illustrates the many ways that political participation can bring about policy change

6.2 Describe the traditional and nontraditional forms of political participation in American representative democracy

6.3 Identify individual factors affecting voter turnout

6.4 Discuss institutional, legal, and election-specific contributors and obstacles to voter turnout

6.5 Explain the potential power of political protest as a tool to effect political change

6.6 Assess the current and future political power of young adult Americans

Political participation in a representative democracy can take many forms. One of them is voting in an election, which may seem kind of obvious. Participating as a voter is critical to the health of a representative democracy and acts, as James Madison noted, as a counterweight to the dangers of faction. As we will explore, however, many Americans do not vote. The decision to go to the polling place (or not) is often connected to a set of individual factors and lived experiences. Level of educational attainment, racial and ethnic identity, economic background, political beliefs, sex, and age play a big role in who votes. Institutional factors matter as well; some states make it easier to vote than others, some make it harder.

Young adult Americans are one group that is consistently underrepresented at the voting booth, for reasons that are both individual and institutional.

But does this nonparticipation in the voting booth *have* to mean that young adult Americans are consistently underrepresented in American government? Not necessarily. While it is true that members of this generation vote at lower rates than members of older generations, they also participate in government through other methods, such as volunteering, protesting, organizing, and other means made possible by modern communications technologies.

There is a universe of potential stories through which we might examine American political participation in the twenty-first century. In this chapter, we will engage with difficult stories told by survivors of sexual violence on college campuses and their allies, and we will examine the different ways they have harnessed the American political process in order to make real change.

political participation
the different ways in which individuals take action to shape the laws and policies of a government.

college and university campuses for their own protection. Collins stated, "My name is Amanda Collins. . . . I am going to share with you my experience of being denied my right to participate in my own self-defense, how my situation could have had a drastically different outcome, and why I have such strong convictions regarding this particular legislation."[2]

In her written remarks, Collins described her rape at gunpoint in a campus parking garage in 2007, while she was a student at the University of Nevada, Reno: "Heading towards my car I surveyed under and around my vehicle to make sure it was safe to approach. . . . I was confident I had just aced my exam and anxious to call my boyfriend who I knew would be my fiancé in a matter of days. . . . The terror I felt in those moments continued to haunt me for the next thirteen months, while my attacker remained at large, in ways that only other rape survivors can understand."[3]

The rapist was later arrested and convicted for his attack on Collins and two other women. He had raped and kidnapped another woman after his assault on Collins and raped and murdered another woman after that.

Collins's testimony was in support of a state bill that would allow individuals with concealed carry weapons (CCW) permits to carry their licensed firearms in areas in which they are typically prohibited, such as on college campuses. Collins had undergone the training, certification, and background checks necessary to obtain a CCW license. Her rapist had not. By law, Collins could not carry on campus.[4] She was unarmed when she was assaulted. According to Collins,

I was raped less than 100 feet away from their campus police office, on the same floor where they park their cruisers. I was twenty-two-years-old when I faced my worst fear, defenseless. I never thought in my wildest dreams I would find myself in such a situation. Allowing law abiding adults to carry their permitted concealed weapons in all areas on campus can protect other potential victims from experiencing the loss and heartbreak that both my family and I have endured.

All I wanted was a chance to be able to defend myself and being able to carry that right would have given me that chance. I believe the choice to participate in one's own defense should be left to the individual. . . . I obeyed the law and left my firearm at home in order to avoid possible expulsion from school and losing my CCW permit. . . . I view concealed carry as, "the ultimate choice" for a woman. Women talk about not allowing the government to mandate what goes on inside their bodies, but then some women are willing to allow their self-protection to be arbitrated by a third party. I am not one of those women who is comfortable entrusting my protection to another person.[5]

Collins's political action did not stop with newspaper editorials and testimony before state legislatures. "After her assault," Collins "helped found the group, Women for Concealed Carry, which frames concealed carry as a victim's rights issue."[6] She is also featured on the Web site of a major national gun rights interest group, the National Rifle Association (NRA), on their page titled "NRA Women: Refuse to Be a Victim."

Other concealed carry advocacy groups have found ways to encourage young women to participate as well. As part of their Campus Leadership Program, members of the conservative Washington, D.C.–based nonprofit Leadership Institute posted an instructional video on YouTube called "Strong Women Fight Back." In it the video's creators give campus concealed carry proponents advice on how to host a self-defense or concealed carry activism event on campus, including suggestions to invite "other like-minded groups," to participate in the event and to "always have a camera ready," as "this project will be highly controversial."[7]

CLP Activism: Strong Women

LeadershipInst
Subscribe 329

292 views

CLP Activism: Strong Women

LeadershipInst
Subscribe 329

292 vie

The efforts of Collins and other CCW activists have met with some success in recent years. In 2015 ten state legislatures were considering changing their laws to permit campus carry. Nevada assemblywoman Michele Fiore, who was sponsoring a campus carry bill in her state, argued, "The sexual assaults that are occurring would go down once these sexual predators get a bullet in their head."[8] Texas began allowing concealed carry on its college campuses in August 2016. (See Figure 6.1.)

Advocating for CCW laws isn't the only possible avenue that politically motivated people can take towards solving the problem of sexual assault on campus. Indeed, some believe that carrying a concealed weapon could potentially do more to harm women than to help them, and there is some evidence to support that view. In a study reviewing survey data covering more than four thousand incidents of the use of firearms in self-defense in crimes in the nation between 2007 and 2011, two researchers from the Harvard School of Public Health challenged the effectiveness of self-defense gun use (SDGU). They concluded that "[c]ompared to other protective actions, the National Crime Victimization Surveys provide little evidence that SDGU is uniquely beneficial in reducing the likelihood of injury or property loss."[9]

Others challenged the effectiveness of campus carry as a deterrent to campus sexual violence. Collins herself was subjected to intense questioning about this issue during her testimony in support of a proposed CWW measure in Colorado in 2013. State senator Evie Hudack (D-Westminister) told Collins that "chances are that if you would have had a gun, then he would have been able to get that from you and possibly use it against you." To Collins, these comments were extremely disturbing. She said, "I had a hard time falling asleep because I couldn't stop thinking about what she said to me."[10]

Researchers point to other factors in campus sexual violence that potentially make CCW a problematic solution. Most campus sexual assaults occur between individuals who know each other and in situations where access to a firearm might not be a realistic option once an assault has begun. According to John D. Foubert, Oklahoma State University professor and president of One in Four, an organization devoted to raising awareness of and combatting campus sexual violence, "If you have a rape situation, usually it starts with some sort of consensual behavior, and by the time it switches to nonconsensual, it would be nearly impossible to run for a gun."[11] There is also the concern that college students, "with high rates of binge drinking and other recklessness, would be particularly prone to gun accidents."[12] To some opponents of CCW,

FIGURE 6.1

Campus Concealed Carry Policies by State

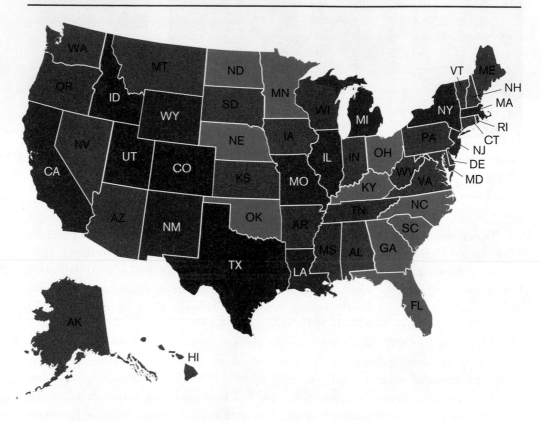

- ■ Concealed guns allowed by law
- ■ Concealed guns allowed by law, but schools limit locations/who carries
- ■ Concealed guns on campus prohibited by law
- ■ Schools decide weapons policy
- ■ Concealed guns allowed only in locked cars in parking lots

Source: "Guns on Campus' Laws for Public Colleges and Universities," Armed Campuses, www.armedcampuses.org. Courtesy of the Campaign to Keep Guns Off Campus (www .keepgunsoffcampus.org).

preventing sexual violence on campuses is more effectively carried out through campus awareness training and campus security personnel.

One point of view shared by both CCW opponents and supporters, however, is that the American higher educational system is failing students on college campuses in its handling of sexual assault. Schools are failing to take adequate steps to prevent sexual violence in the first place, failing to adequately report incidents, and failing to handle the long-term consequences for those affected. According to Katherine Whitney, director of Women for Concealed Carry, "There seems to be kind of a dichotomy in this discussion where people assume either campus carry should be legalized or college campuses should take steps to reduce campus assault. . . . It should be both. We need colleges to acknowledge that campus assault happens, and we need administrators to do everything they can to prevent victimization."[13]

In 2013 Landen Gambill, a student at University of North Carolina at Chapel Hill, filed a federal civil rights complaint against her university over its handling of her sexual assault complaint. The university's adjudication process found her rapist guilty of harassment rather than sexual misconduct—a much less serious offense—and he was allowed to return to campus after a suspension.[14] Gambill later asserted that part of the university's decision to go with the lesser charge was based on the fact that she and her rapist had been in a relationship.

Gambill was threatened with expulsion for making public her experience, though she did so without naming her alleged rapist directly. She had chosen to have the university adjudicate her sexual assault complaint rather than filing a criminal or civil complaint in court, a decision she later regretted. As she told the crowd at a 2013 rally, "I have been treated with great injustice, but there are so many other survivors who have been treated just as poorly as I have and even worse. . . . I have so many heartbreaking stories. Stories of survivors who have been blamed, shamed, ignored, and silenced by this university. . . . I refuse to step back and watch survivors be called crazy sluts and liars."[15]

We will return to the efforts of Gambill and other survivors to use the legal system to force schools to change how they handle and adjudicate sexual assault complaints later in the chapter. Legal action, however, was not the only way in which Gambill chose to participate in the American political process. She also circulated a petition to multiple state legislatures arguing against allowing campus carry. For Gambill, the fact that her attacker repeatedly harassed and attacked her would have made her much less safe had he been allowed to carry a firearm on campus:

> Recently, lawmakers in thirteen states have introduced bills to overturn bans on guns in college campuses. They claim arming students is the key to curbing the epidemic of rape on campus.
>
> As a survivor, I know the opposite to be true. The rationale behind these bills rests on the myth that most people are raped by strangers; however, the vast majority of survivors of sexual assault, including myself, know their rapist. In fact the presence of guns is proven to exacerbate violence against victims, not prevent it.
>
> If my rapist had a gun at school, I have no doubt I would be dead. That's why I started this petition asking legislators in these states not to allow guns on campuses and put survivors like me in even more danger.[16]

In this section, we have studied the political action taken by survivors of campus sexual violence, all acting in the political space to make college campuses safer. They advocated very different policy positions on the right of college students to carry a firearm. As we will explore, the right to carry is only one of the many issues associated with sexual safety on college campuses. Unfortunately, the testimonies of Amanda Collins and Landen Gambill will not be the last we will have to thoughtfully consider. Should campus carry be allowed or not? Will it reduce sexual assaults or might it increase them or lead to a rise in gun-related deaths and accidental discharges? As these policies are so new, we cannot answer these questions with complete certainty,

Landen Gambill, a sophomore at the University of North Carolina at Chapel Hill, speaks to reporters at a campus rally in 2013. In addition to speaking out about university policy on handling campus sexual assault incidents, Gambill also opposed the policy of allowing campus carry of firearms.

Travis Long/Raleigh News & Observer/MCT via Getty Images.

Protestors at the University of Texas gather to oppose the passage of a new state law that in August 2016 expanded the rights of concealed handgun license holders to carry their weapons on public college campuses. Schools can, however, designate limited gun-free zones.

Ralph Barrera/Austin American-Statesman via AP.

and this book will not attempt to do so. Instead, the goal will once again be to help provide students with the tools to critically examine the issues surrounding campus sexual assault policies and the ways in which those issues might be successfully addressed.

The efforts of these women and their supporters—all of which are examples of political participation—represent only a few of the many ways individuals undertake action to shape the laws and public policies of the nation. In this chapter, we will engage with the critical and difficult issue of political participation to end sexual violence on college campuses. In doing so, we will come to understand that political participation can and does extend far beyond the voting booth and that its many possible forms are often not separate and distinct things. One form of participation may lead an individual to act in other political spaces, or it may shape the actions of actors in other venues. We will also learn from strong individuals whose efforts to call attention to the crisis of sexual violence and make lasting political change are helping to carry the necessary weight of political participation in a representative democracy.

WHAT HAVE I LEARNED?

1. Opponents of campus carry cite the following as arguments against the policy _____.

   a. The fact that many assaults begin with consensual behavior
   b. The impracticability of using firearms to prevent assaults among individuals who know each other
   c. The dangers of firearms in an environment where alcohol may be present
   d. All of the above

2. What forms of political participation did Amanda Collins and Landen Gambill use to advance their different beliefs about carrying a concealed weapon on campus? Can you envision other methods they could have used?

3. What other forms of political participation might individuals employ to address the problem of campus sexual violence?

Answer Key: 1. d; 2. Answers might include newspaper editorials, speaking in public and to reporters, and testifying before state legislative bodies or using the legal system to force change.; 3. Answers might include supporting candidates focusing on the issue in their campaigns, educating peers, or using social media to help organize for change.

THE MANY FORMS
OF POLITICAL PARTICIPATION

While Americans often equate political participation with voting, and for good reason, casting a ballot is only one of many forms that political participation can take. While voting serves to choose elected representatives, other forms of participation may serve to influence the choices of those in office and the attitudes and actions of other citizens. Some believe these other forms may not have received enough attention from scholars of American politics. According to political scientists Sidney Verba, Kay Lehman Schlozman, and Henry E. Brady, "Studies of political participation traditionally have begun with—and too often ended with—the vote. Although voting is an important mode of citizen involvement in political life, it is but one of many political acts."[17]

Most fundamentally, when participating in any of the diverse forms of political action, Americans express their commitment to **civic engagement**, which is working to make society better through political and nonpolitical action. Civic engagement can take many forms. In their foundational study of American political participation, Sidney Verba and Norman H. Nie sorted acts of political engagement into four categories: (1) voting, (2) supporting or participating in political campaigns, (3) contacting

CONNECTING TO . . .

The Forms of Political Participation

As you read this chapter and explore the degree to which young adult Americans are participating in the political process, reflect back upon the testimonies of Amanda Collins and Landen Gambill. Consider the following:

- The ways in which their chosen forms of political participation did or did not depart from traditionally defined forms
- The many ways in which Americans can contribute to the political process

civic engagement
working to improve society through political and nonpolitical action.

NEWS CLIP
Moms come out in favor of marijuana legalization in Colorado

FIGURE 6.2

The Categories of Political Participation

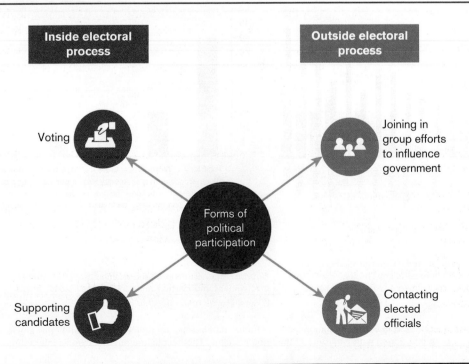

Inside electoral process

Outside electoral process

Voting

Joining in group efforts to influence government

Forms of political participation

Supporting candidates

Contacting elected officials

> "Studies of political participation traditionally have begun with—and too often ended with—the vote. Although voting is an important mode of citizen involvement in political life, it is but one of many political acts."

or pressuring politicians in office, and (4) acting outside of the electoral process—for example, by volunteering or organizing in concert with fellow citizens.[18] The first two of these forms of participation take place within the electoral process; the second two take place after its outcomes have been determined or outside of it. (See Figure 6.2.)

Within the electoral process, individuals may choose to vote. They may also act to support the candidacies of those vying for political office, whether through working on campaigns, donating money, or convincing others to support their chosen candidate.

Once the elections are over, citizens may choose to initiate contact with elected officials to make their preferences known about issues being discussed in government. In the twenty-first century, individuals have many tools with which to initiate contact with their elected representatives. Individuals might join together to work cooperatively for a shared set of political goals. They may, for example, undertake volunteer work, help to organize members of their community,

FIGURE 6.3

Participation in Campaigns

Questions: Which if any did you do during the most recent election?

... talk to other people to persuade them to vote for a particular party or candidate?

... show your support for a particular party or candidate by, for example, attending a meeting, putting up a poster, or in some other way?

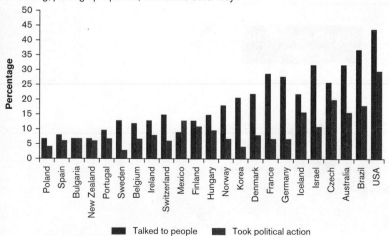

■ Talked to people   ■ Took political action

Source: Data from Steven Weldon and Russell Dalton, "Democratic Structures and Democratic Participation: The Limits of Consensualism Theory," *Elections and Democracy*, ed. Jacques Thomassen, Oxford University Press, 2014: Table 7.1, "Levels of Political Participation."

FIGURE 6.4

Americans' Participation in Elections outside of the Voting Booth

Percent of respondents who reported having been involved in the following activities during the past year.

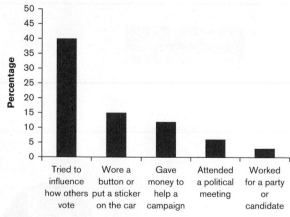

Source: American National Election Study, "Political Involvement and Participation in Politics," 2012, http://electionstudies.org/nesguide/gd-index.htm.

While Americans of voting age participate in elections at lower rates than members of other democratic societies, they remain highly active in participatory activities, such as volunteer work or interacting with members of their communities. These activities tend to involve interacting with others to influence votes.

or work with members of their religious communities. While Americans participate at the voting booth at lower rates than individuals in other democracies, their rates of nonelectoral participation are equal to or higher than their counterparts in other nations.[19] (See Figures 6.3 and 6.4.)

One way that individuals might join together is by taking part in a social movement, which occurs when a group of people come together to make social and political change and place ideas and issues on the political agenda.

As members of social movements, individuals may participate in political protests, attend political meetings, contact elected officials, or reach out to other citizens to educate them about the need to participate to make social and political change. Whether acting as a member of a social movement or on their own, individuals may also work on political campaigns, donate time and money to candidates, work in their communities, or contact their elected representatives. In all of these activities, individuals try to make their voices heard.

In the next section, we will return to the issue of campus sexual violence and explore how students have participated in political protest in order to call attention to the problem, mobilize others in support of change, and pressure elected officials to act.

WHAT HAVE I LEARNED?

1. Americans vote at rates equal to citizens of other representative democracies.

   a. True
   b. False

2. Working to make society better through political and nonpolitical action is often called _____.

   a. Direct political contact
   b. Civic engagement
   c. Protest
   d. Political recruitment

3. What are some examples of forms of political participation outside of the voting booth?

Answer Key: 1. b; 2. b; 3. Answers might include volunteering, communicating with officials, or participating in protests or social movements.

MOBILIZATION AND PRESSURE
Art and Protest as Tools of Social and Political Change

At first, she chose to remain anonymous. One of three Columbia University undergraduates interviewed for a two-part article in the school's newspaper, Emma Sulkowicz shared her experiences without attribution as a survivor of a campus sexual assault in 2012. She also related her criticisms of what she saw as an inadequate, even traumatizing, university response to her reporting of the assault.[20] Later, partly out of frustration with this response, Sulkowicz went public. In an interview conducted with the *New York Times* in 2014, she recounted the assault and Columbia University's actions—or lack thereof. According to the article, "The accused, as is often the case in college, was someone she considered a friend, a man with whom she had had consensual sex

Columbia University senior Emma Sulkowicz carrying a mattress in protest of the university's response to her report of a sexual assault on campus during her sophomore year. Sulkowicz's protest was part of her senior thesis and was undertaken to pressure campus officials to reform school policies.

Andrew Burton/Getty Images

twice the previous school year. The university's adjudication process, she said, left her feeling even more traumatized and unsafe. 'I've never felt more shoved under the rug in my life.'"[21]

After conducting its adjudication process, the university found the accused man "not responsible." After receiving an e-mail informing her of the school's decision, Sulkowicz recalled, "I didn't even cry at first. I don't know. Has anything ever happened to you that was just so bad that you felt like you became a shell of a human being?"[22]

Sulkowicz didn't remain numb for long, however. She took action to protest both the lack of attention paid to sexual assault incidents on college campuses and the mishandling of cases that were reported. For her senior thesis at Columbia University in 2015, Sulkowicz made her voice heard by combining protest and art. She created a performance art piece, *Carry That Weight*, in which she chose to carry "a dorm bed mattress around with her wherever she goes. She'll carry it for as long as she attends the same school as her [alleged] rapist, which, as she told the *Columbia Spectator*, 'could potentially take a day . . . or it could go on until I graduate.'"[23]

Sulkowicz's protest sparked others to act. In October, as part of "Carry That Weight Day," students across the country demonstrated in support of Sulkowicz and other sexual violence survivors and in protest of how school administration officials were dealing with the crisis. Caroline DeCunzo, a student and protester at the University of Vermont, summed up one of the protesters' major goals: "I think that it's important for UVM to acknowledge that we have a sexual assault problem."[24]

In November 2014, "Columbia students carried twenty-eight mattresses around campus with messages of protest against rape and sexual assault, words of support for survivors, and demands for change to the University's sexual assault policy."[25] They called their action "Carry That Weight Day." In response, Columbia University officials announced that the students involved would be charged up to $1,500 for clean-up fees after the mattresses were dumped on the lawn of the university's president.

As part of her protest, Sulkowicz composed an installation piece in her studio on campus. In an interview for the *Washington Post*, Nato Thompson, chief curator at the New York–based arts organization Creative Time, said, "What's happening here is unique. . . . I can't think of another instance where a work of art has triggered a movement in this way."[26]

Elected officials took notice of the efforts of Sulkowicz and other protestors during that year. In April 2014, at Columbia University, "student activists with red tape over their mouths tried to enter an event for prospective freshmen, to hand out letters encouraging the students to press university officials for details about resources available to victims of sexual assault. The next day, Senator Kirsten Gillibrand, Democrat of New York, visited Columbia to call for federal funding to improve handling of college sexual assault cases."[27]

In February 2015, Senator Claire McCaskill (D-MO) introduced the Campus Accountability and Safety Act. She was joined by eleven other senators, including Gillibrand, in a bipartisan coalition. McCaskill had previously and successfully joined with other senators to address national policies on the handling of sexual assault claims in the United States Armed Forces. In a press release posted to her official Web site,

The Use of Images in Political Protest and Mobilization

A Facebook announcement for a 2015 protest by Carry the Weight Together calling for a national day of action.

In February 2015, the group Carry the Weight Together shared their event on Facebook: "Join us for the second national Day of Action to stand with students around the country to demand better policies to prevent and respond to gender-based violence on your campus! Hold a rally, speak out, protest, or collective carry on your campus and call on administrators to help #carrythatweight!" The image that they chose for the announcement was a simple graphic.

WHAT DO YOU THINK?

The organizers of the protest chose a very stark and simple graphic to convey their goals and objectives. Do you think the image was effective? If you were to choose an image for organizing political action or a protest on an issue of importance to you, what images might you use?

McCaskill described the bill's intent: "With added input from survivors, students, colleges and universities, law enforcement and advocates, the bill would flip the current incentives of a broken system to provide real accountability and transparency from higher education institutions. The legislation would professionalize the response to and reporting of sexual assaults that occur on campuses to better protect and empower students, while also protecting the rights of accused students."[28]

The bill would require colleges and universities to designate "confidential advisors" for student sexual violence survivors, enhance training of school personnel, make more transparent the extent of sexual violence incidents on campuses, increase coordination and uniformity of how sexual assault allegations on campuses are treated, and increase penalties for institutions that failed to uphold the new requirements.[29]

The actions of college students themselves helped to call lawmakers' attention to the issue of university treatment of sexual assaults. According to McCaskill, "Students across the U.S. have filed complaints alleging that their universities have violated Title IX, which prohibits gender discrimination in education, by failing to prevent and

Emma Sulkowicz with her installation piece, *Rules of Engagement*, in 2014.

respond to sexual assaults. Many administrators may be incorrectly telling female students that they're unlikely to obtain rape convictions in cases whether there's a dispute over whether sex was consensual."[30] Sulkowicz was one of many students who had filed suit under Title IX and other federal regulations. In response to the increased focus on campus assault, many schools are now training faculty and staff on Title IX's provisions regarding sexual harassment.

Landen Gambill, whose stance against campus carry we discussed earlier in the chapter, also based her legal action against the University of North Carolina at Chapel Hill on claims under Title IX. Returning to campus for her sophomore year "with a sense of dread," Gambill began to connect with other survivors who felt that the university administration mishandled their cases as well. She wrote, "I also learned that you can file a Title IX complaint with the government when schools mishandle reports of sexual violence. Later that semester, I got together with some fellow students and filed a complaint with the Department of Education's Office for Civil Rights. An assistant dean of students joined us in the complaint—she said the school had encouraged her to under-report cases of sexual assault to the government."[31]

To Gambill, however, speaking out is not the only way that survivors can act and make change. In an interview she said, "I always try to be clear that those who speak out are not the only heroes: Many survivors are not able to speak up for legal reasons, or due to physical or emotional threats. Surviving in and of itself is heroic."[32]

In September 2014, the issue of sexual assault on campuses received national attention when President Barack Obama and Vice President Joe Biden announced the formation of the It's On Us campaign, which urges men and women to commit to helping solve the problem of campus sexual assault. They addressed the topic in blunt and unequivocal terms. "Society still does not sufficiently value women," the president said.[33]

As the issue of sexual violence on college campuses began to take a more prominent place on the national political agenda, contrasting voices weighed in. In responding to accusations of gender-based violence, some male college students have argued that their rights have been violated by school sexual assault procedures on the basis of Title IX. Other groups have expressed concern that the due process rights of the accused have been undermined by some overreaching university sexual harassment and assault policies.[34]

In December 2014, Senator Gillibrand offered her testimony before the Senate Judiciary Committee in support of the Campus Accountability and Safety Act. She stated, "Young women like Emma Sulkowicz, who was raped by a fellow student at Columbia University in 2012, reported her rape to police in 2014. . . . The detective responded by telling Emma that the encounter was consensual because she'd had previous consensual sex with this individual. The officer repeatedly stated that the perpetrator just 'got a little weird that night, right?' and told her that a defense attorney would rip her story apart."[35]

In 2015 the man accused in the assault of Emma Sulkowicz and two other women on campus filed a lawsuit against Columbia University trustees, administrators, and the professor who had supervised Sulkowicz's art installation, arguing that he was "defamed and faced gender-based discrimination, and that Columbia was negligent and breached contracts."[36] Responding to the lawsuit, especially with regard to the professor involved, Sulkowicz replied, "If artists are not allowed to make art that reflect on our experiences, then how are we to heal?"[37] Columbia University officials declined to comment.[38]

Senators Kirsten Gillibrand (D-NY), left, and Claire McCaskill (D-MO), right, led a bipartisan group of senators supporting the Campus Safety and Accountability Act aimed at curbing rape on campus. The proposed legislation came after a Senate subcommittee survey revealed that 41 percent of 236 American colleges had conducted no investigations of alleged assaults in the last five years.
Brooks Kraft LLC/Corbis via Getty Images

Although it is useful to categorize political participation into its various forms, as we did earlier in the chapter, the participatory actions of Sulkowicz and others—as well as elected officials' responses to them—highlight the reality that such activities are often not neatly categorized and often flow together or trigger others. Tying all of these activities together is the idea of political voice and the tactics used to make that voice heard. Individual political actors may undertake action outside of the electoral process in order to effect change within the structures of government. They may also, of course, participate within the electoral process by voting or working on campaigns. It is to these activities—voting and working on campaigns—and individual decisions of whether or not to be active *within* electoral politics that we now turn.

WHAT HAVE I LEARNED?

1. Emma Sulkowicz's protest and senior project were designed to call attention to _____.

   a. The need for legal access to firearms on college campuses

   b. Increased dialogue with those accused of sexual assault

   c. The handling of sexual assault claims by university officials

   d. All of the above

2. What role did Title IX play in the efforts of survivors to force change in their colleges and universities?

3. In what ways were the efforts of survivors to protest and call attention to campus policy on investigating sexual assaults connected to other forms of political action?

Answer Key: 1. c; 2. Answers might focus on the connection between gender equality in the law and efforts to reform college and university processes.; 3. Answers might connect protests, testimony, filing lawsuits, and responses by elected officials to these actions.

VOTING

Factors That Shape Electoral Participation

When Americans consider the concept of political participation, they often think about voting, and for many good reasons. Participation in the electoral process is an essential component of a representative democracy. Voting gives expression to individuals' voices and serves to hold elected representatives accountable for their promises and actions. It is foundational to what James Madison called the "Democratic Remedy" to the dangers of faction and the tyranny of the minority that we examined in Chapter 2.

The fact, however, is that large percentages of Americans do not vote. In 2016, a presidential election year, only an estimated 58 percent of eligible voters showed up at the polls, placing the U.S. near the bottom of democratic nations based on **voter turnout** (see the Telling Stories with Data, page 210). Turnout in midterm elections is even lower. In 2014, roughly 36 percent of eligible voters cast ballots, continuing a trend of decline decades in the making and marking the lowest level of voter turnout since 1942, when the nation was involved in a global war.[39] The trend is unmistakable. Americans' relative lack of voting participation raises two immediate questions: Why? And, does it matter?

voter turnout
the number of eligible voters who actually participate in an election versus the total number of eligible voters.

> In the view of democratic theorists, however, should all potential voters make a rational calculation not to vote, then the mechanism of representation would be endangered.

For Anthony Downs, writing in 1957, the decision not to vote might very well be a rational one, given the costs of voting in terms of an individual's time and intellectual effort and the infinitesimally small probability that any one vote will prove to be decisive, especially in national elections. According to Downs, "It may be rational for a [person] to delegate part or all of his political decision-making to others, no matter how important it is that [they] make correct decisions,"[40] a conclusion with which other political scientists have agreed. In the view of democratic theorists, however, should all potential voters make a rational calculation not to vote, then the mechanism of representation would be endangered.

Individual Factors and the Decision to Vote

Many factors shape a person's decision of whether or not to vote. Some contributors to voter turnout are institutional, shaped by the laws and procedures surrounding the electoral process. Others depend upon the particulars of an election—for example, whether or not it takes place during a presidential election year. A third category of contributors centers on the potential voters themselves, their characteristics and lived experiences. Later in the book, we will examine how individual characteristics impact *how* people vote and *who* they choose to support. Now, we will consider how these characteristics shape *whether or not* people vote. Political scientists count a set of individual factors as among the most important determinants for voting: level of economic status, level of education, age, race or ethnicity, sex, and partisan attachment.

NEWS CLIP
Citizen explains rationale for participating in protest

Socioeconomic Status and Educational Attainment

Voting is costly. It takes time, commitment, and intellectual engagement. Not all voting-eligible Americans have the same resources with which to engage in the process of voting.[41]

A key factor in voter turnout is an individual's **socioeconomic status (SES)**, which is a measure of an individual's wealth, income, occupation, and educational attainment.

A clear and consistent pattern in electoral participation is that Americans with higher levels of SES participate in electoral activities. There are several reasons for this, but the central idea is that individuals with higher incomes might have more money to donate to a political campaign. Also, certain occupations might be associated with networks in which political issues are more likely to be discussed and acted upon.

The most important contributor to the measure of an individual's SES, and one of the most important determinants of the decision to vote, is the level of educational attainment by a potential voter (Figure 6.5). Not only are higher levels of educational attainment associated with higher incomes, they also reduce the "costs" of voting, in the sense of making it easier to navigate the issues involved in an election and the process of becoming a voter itself.

Political Efficacy

Education also plays a role in shaping how individuals think about themselves as political actors and potential voters. The intellectual resources and skills that higher levels of education produce also increase an individual's sense of **political efficacy**, or one's confidence that she or he can make effective political change.

Age

Another trend is also clear: Young adult voting-eligible Americans vote at lower rates than members of older generations (Figure 6.6).[42] Why? Again, like income and education, age is connected to many other factors. Older Americans are more likely to have higher levels of

socioeconomic status (SES)
a measure that captures an individual's wealth, income, occupation, and educational attainment.

NEWS CLIP
Activists and police leaders on their discussions with President Obama

political efficacy
a person's belief that she or he can make effective political change.

FIGURE 6.5

Voting and Registration by Educational Attainment in United States, 2014

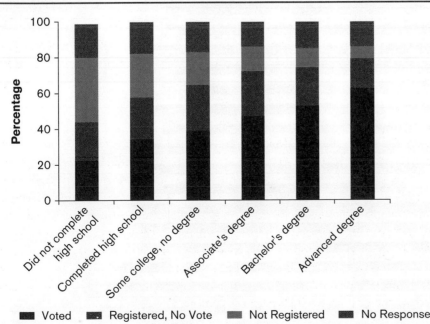

■ Voted   ■ Registered, No Vote   ■ Not Registered   ■ No Response

Source: United States Census Bureau, "Voting and Registration," http://thedataweb.rm.census.gov/TheDataWeb_HotReport2/voting/voting.hrml, accessed February 16, 2016.

Americans Are Exceptional at Not Voting, but Why?

Votes Cast in OECD Countries' Recent National Elections as a Percentage of Registered Voters and Voting Age Population . . .

Percentage

■ % of registered voters   ▨ % of voting age population

Source: "U.S. voter turnout trails most developed countries" Pew Research Center, Washington, DC (August, 2016) http://www.pewresearch.org/fact-tank/2016/08/02/u-s-voter-turnout-trails-most-developed-countries/.

In May 2015, the Pew Research Center published a graphic depicting voter turnout in national elections in member nations of the Organization for Economic Co-operation and Development (OECD) since 2010. As is clear, voter turnout in the United States lagged behind that of almost all of its peer nations.[43]

Clearly, in terms of national voter turnout, the percentage of the voting-age population that voted in recent national elections (the green bars) in the United States is far below that of most other members of the OECD. What is going on? We will examine many of the contributors to this gap in this chapter. For now, however, notice the blue bars, which depict voter turnout as a percentage of registered voters. By that measure, voter turnout in the United States does not appear to be so different from the others and in fact leads most nations.

Voting age and *registered voters* are two very different terms. Large numbers of voting-age Americans are not voting eligible. Undocumented Americans as well as Americans convicted of felonies (in many states) are not allowed to vote. The numbers of individuals who are not allowed to vote because of a felony conviction—a large percentage of whom have been convicted for drug offenses—have grown dramatically in recent decades. In 2010 it was estimated that nearly six million Americans were denied the right to vote because of felony convictions.[44]

WHAT DO YOU THINK?

Are you registered to vote? Are your friends and fellow students? If not, what are the barriers to registration that you or those close to you face in doing so? What policies might be enacted to make it easier for unregistered voting-age Americans to register for the vote?

income and wealth. Another factor may be the challenges of learning about voter registration requirements, especially if the young adult voter is in college or has recently moved to a new state. For college students living in a different state, voter identification laws may add another hurdle to their decision to participate at the polling place. While a 1979 Supreme Court ruling affirmed the right of college students to vote in their states of school attendance,[45] state voting laws and local practices "often make students travel a rocky road."[46]

Racial and Ethnic Identities

The turnout of voting-age Americans is also highly correlated with racial and ethnic identity (Figure 6.7), which, again, is often connected to SES. While turnout rates between white and African American potential voters have narrowed in recent years, Latina and Latino American turnout rates lag far behind those of Americans with other racial and ethnic identities. While some Latino/a Americans are undocumented immigrants and therefore ineligible to vote, they are also as a group younger, and, as we have discussed, younger voting-eligible Americans vote in far fewer numbers than their older counterparts. As we will explore in Chapter 10, as Latino/a eligible voters grow older, and grow in numbers, the political landscape is going to shift dramatically.

Sex and Voter Turnout

Since the presidential election of 1980, women have voted at a slightly higher rate than men—typically a difference of a few percentage points.[47] Prior to 1980, voting-eligible men voted at higher rates than women. The differences between men's and women's modern voting patterns hold true across racial and ethnic identities, with the largest percentage difference between black men and women, which was more than 9 percent in the 2102 presidential election. Differences in voter turnout in recent elections between men and women are also connected with age, as a higher percentage of women ages eighteen to forty-four voted than men in the same age cohort, while men seventy-five and up voted at higher rates than women within the same age group.

FIGURE 6.6

FIGURE 6.6

Historical Patterns of Voter Turnout, by Age

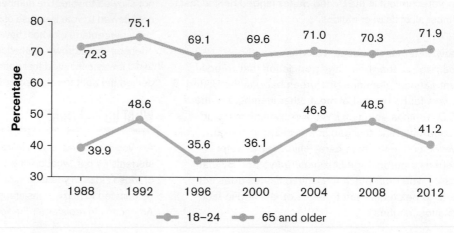

Voter Turnout Rates by Age in Presidential Elections, 1988–2012

Note: Data for those ages 25 to 64 not shown.

Source: "Six take-aways from the Census Bureau's voting report" Pew Research Center, Washington, DC (May, 2013) http://www.pewresearch.org/fact-tank/2013/05/08/six-take-aways-from-the-census-bureaus-voting-report/.

FIGURE 6.7

American Voter Turnout in Midterm Elections by Racial and Ethnic Identity

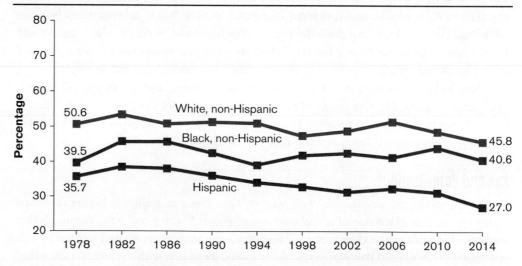

Source: Thom File, "Who Votes? Congressional Elections and the American Electorate: 1978–2014," U.S. Census Bureau, Washington, D.C., 2015, https://www.census.gov/content/dam/Census/library/publications/2015/demo/p20-577.pdf.

Hey Older Americans, It's the Economy: Young Adult Americans on the Elections of 2016

While it is true that Americans aged eighteen to thirty-four vote at lower rates than older Americans, this does not mean that they are disconnected from the political process. As the 2016 presidential nomination process was underway, researchers, reporters, and political pundits all weighed in on the potential impact of this generation's individual and collective decisions about whether or not to vote and who to vote for. One of the clearest themes that emerged was the effect of the economy on voting decisions. This factor had a profound impact on a generation maturing after the financial crisis of 2008 and saddled with levels of student debt unimaginable to earlier generations.

In an interview with *International Business Times*, Tori Hall, a student at The Ohio State University and a board member of her school's Students for Bernie [Sanders] Club, countered criticisms that young adult Americans were disinterested in the elections, saying that she and her peers were constantly discussing the election. To Hall, her primary reason for this interest was economic inequality in twenty-first-century America. According to the article,

> One of Hall's personal political interests is income inequality, because "something's obviously wrong and needs to be fixed," she said. She finds evidence for that in her own upbringing: Hall is paying for college herself. Her parents live paycheck to paycheck despite both having masters' degrees.

> "We went a winter without heat because we couldn't afford the gas bill," she said. "In the U.S., one of the wealthiest countries in the world, there shouldn't be anybody going through that. . . . I'm 20. When I was 6, that's when 9/11 occurred. Then we entered two wars before I was even 8 years old. By 2008, we were in a financial crisis. . . . We're coming to terms with that and [looking for] the best candidate we can find who's not part of the establishment."[1]

For the most part, polls seemed to indicate that Sanders's supporters would likely gravitate towards Hillary Clinton after she won the Democratic Party's nomination. According to a report by *PBS NewsHour*, however, Donald Trump's message of economic insecurity swayed some millennials to his side, given the way it dovetailed with Sanders's talk of a "rigged system":

. . . young voters are united in their anger and disillusionment, having come of age during the Great Recession. Trump has tapped into that subset of those voters in the same way as Sanders, despite their radically different policy proposals, said Morley Winograd, a senior fellow at the University of Southern California who has authored books on millennials.

> Young voters think: "'The system is rigged, I need somebody to totally overthrow the system' and that's what Trump says he's going to do," he said. "You can understand where there might be those commonalities."[2]

That same concern was echoed by student Jeremy Wiggins, a junior at the University of Missouri and a delegate to the Republican National Convention, who supported Trump,

> ". . . for somebody my age you're going to be in the job market very soon, starting your first job, getting health insurance and . . . we want the jobs to be there."[3]

On election day, roughly 37 percent of the millennial vote went to Trump, a larger segment of that population than expected. In a post-election analysis, one reporter surmised that one of the main reasons may have been that 1 out of 5 men ages 21 to 30 was unemployed in 2015.[4]

WHAT DO YOU THINK?

How important to you are issues such as student debt and economic inequality? Have these issues led you to become more aware of or involved in the political process?

Notes:

[1] Julia Glum, "Young Voters Don't Like Hillary Clinton or Donald Trump: What That Means for November," *International Business Times*, March 29, 2016, http://www.ibtimes.com/young-voters-dont-hillary-clinton-or-donald-trump-what-means-november-2342879, accessed June 7, 2016.

[2] Gillian Flaccus, "Why Some Millennial Voters Are Turning to Trump," *PBS NewsHour*, May 27, 2016, http://www.pbs.org/newshour/rundown/why-some-millennial-voters-are-turning-to-trump/.

[3] Ibid.

[4] Jean M. Twenge, "Five Reasons Why Millennials Helped Elect Donald Trump," *Psychology Today*, November 16, 2016. https://www.psychologytoday.com/blog/our-changing-culture/201611/five-reasons-why-millennials-helped-elect-donald-trump.

FIGURE 6.8

Registration Requirements: Voter Identification and Forms of Registration, by State

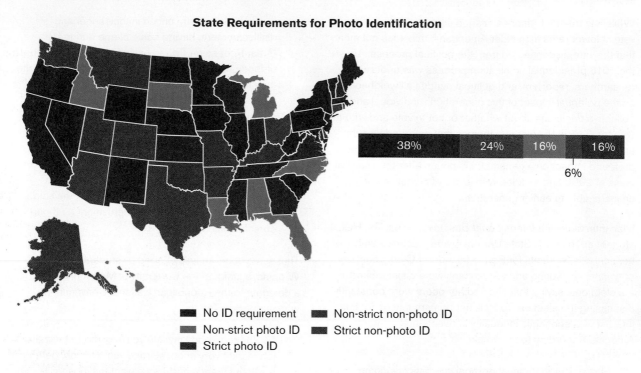

State Requirements for Photo Identification

38%	24%	16%	16%

6%

- No ID requirement
- Non-strict photo ID
- Strict photo ID
- Non-strict non-photo ID
- Strict non-photo ID

States Allowing Online Voter Registration

Available   Unavailable

States Allowing Same-Day Voter Registration

Available   Unavailable

Source: Ballotpedia.org, "Voter Identification Laws by State," 2016, https://ballotpedia.org/Voter_identification_laws_by_state; "Same-Day Voter Registration," 2016, https://ballotpedia.org/Same-day_voter_registration; and "Online Voter Registration," 2016, https://ballotpedia.org/Online_voter_registration.

Partisan Attachment

The degree to which an individual identifies with a political party also factors into not only the vote choices that individual makes but also the decision of whether to vote or not. Individuals with a stronger attachment to a political party are more likely to vote than those without one.[48] Efforts by members of American political parties to turn out the vote matter as well, and individuals with strong partisan attachment may find themselves more likely to be on the receiving end of party activities. **Political mobilization**, such as efforts to "get out the vote" (GOTV), can be decisive in an election. These efforts may be direct—recruitment, sponsorship of meetings, or requests for contributions—or indirect, such as in the building of social networks through which potential voters engage with their friends and associates.[49]

Legal and Institutional Contributors and Barriers to Voter Turnout

Other factors that affect voter turnout are not individual but rather systemic or institutional. Since the ratification of the Twenty-sixth Amendment to the Constitution in 1971, all American citizens eighteen years old or older are guaranteed the right of **suffrage**. The practical exercise of this basic right, however, is complicated. As noted above, undocumented American immigrants are not granted the right of suffrage, and, in most states, otherwise eligible voters who have been convicted of felonies are also denied the right to vote in what is called **felon disenfranchisement**, though the time of their loss of this right varies according to state laws.

State **registration requirements** may also help or hinder the ability of voting-age Americans to participate in the electoral process. Voting actually involves two actions. The second is the casting of a ballot on an Election Day. But the first is the act of registering to vote. In some states, a voter may register on Election Day. In most states, however, would-be voters need to register prior to the election, often as much as thirty days before, otherwise they will not be allowed to vote.[50]

In addition, in order to register to vote, Americans need to show identification and/or proof of residency in their state. About 16 percent of states require a photo identification in order to vote. Others require another form of documentation of residency, and some accept a vouching of residency by another registered voter. Even in states that allow same-day registration, however, residency requirements may serve to disenfranchise certain Americans, such as the homeless, who may lack documentation such as utility bills that can serve to document state residency. (See Figure 6.8 for voter registration requirements by state.)

As state legislatures debate bills requiring identification at the polling place, college students are one, but not the only, group of voting-eligible Americans potentially disenfranchised by these current and proposed laws. Across the nation, state lawmakers continue to debate whether or not a college student should be able to use her or his ID as proof of residency in voter registration, especially if he or she attends a private college or university. When such policies were being debated in Texas, Natalie Butler, a graduate and former student government president of the University of Texas at Austin, spoke out against a state law that prohibited the use of school IDs as proof of residence. She especially noted the law's impact on participation in local elections, stating, "If we're going to make it even harder for students to impact city politics, that's a huge problem."[51]

NEWS CLIP
Bernie Sanders addresses barriers to voting

political mobilization
efforts by members of American political parties to turn out the vote and encourage their members to get others to do so.

suffrage
the right to vote in political elections.

felon disenfranchisement
the denial of voting rights to Americans who have been convicted of felonies.

registration requirements
the set of rules that govern who can vote and how, when, and where they vote.

Natalie Butler, former University of Texas student and advocate for the use of school IDs as acceptable proof of residency in voter registration.

absentee ballots

votes completed and submitted by a voter prior to the day of an election.

Motor Voter Law

a law allowing Americans to register to vote when applying for or renewing their driver's licenses and making it easier for Americans with disabilities to register to vote.

The scheduling of national presidential and congressional elections, by tradition held on the first Tuesday after the first Monday of November, may also serve to discourage participation as work schedules may make it more challenging for some Americans to make it to the polling place. Although states are increasingly allowing voters to cast **absentee ballots**, some reformers have proposed that national elections be held on weekends or that Election Day be declared a national holiday.

Finally, some advocates of electoral reform have focused on the process of registration itself, hoping to make it easier and less costly in terms of time and energy. In contrast to most modern representative democracies, in the United States the burden of registering to vote falls entirely on the potential voter, and there is no governmental action to register them automatically. The National Voter Registration Act of 1993, commonly called the **Motor Voter Law**, tried to make voter registration less difficult by allowing Americans to register to vote when applying for or renewing their driver's licenses and making it easier for Americans with disabilities to register to vote. As of 2016, thirty-one states and the District of Columbia had established systems of online voter registration, with six more having passed but not yet fully implemented them.[52] While effective online registration requires efforts to make the process secure and free from fraud, it offers the promise of increasing turnout.

FIGURE 6.9

Comparing Voter Turnout in Presidential and Midterm Election Years

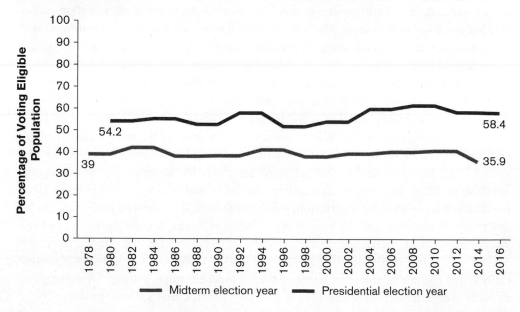

Source: United States Elections Project, http://www.electproject.org/home/voter-turnout/voter-turnout-data. Accessed November 20, 2016.

Election-Specific Factors

Also contributing to the level of voter turnout in a given election are factors surrounding the election itself. If it is a presidential election year, then voters will turn out in higher numbers than if it is not (Figure 6.9).

Finally, an "election" is not really one election. It is many. When Americans go to the polls, they are often confronted with a long list of choices that, depending on the election parameters, can include the president, members of Congress, state legislature positions, state judges, county supervisors, and members of a water resource board. **Ballot roll-off** refers to the fact that voters may often not complete the entire ballot; they may stop once they reach a set of races with which they are not familiar and for which they may not have traditional cues, such as partisan affiliation.

ballot roll-off
when voters do not cast votes for a set of races with which they are not familiar and for which they may not have traditional cues.

1. Political participation refers only to voting.
   a. True
   b. False

2. Factors that contribute to Americans' relatively lower levels of voter turnout among representative democracies include _____.
   a. Felon disenfranchisement
   b. Registration requirements
   c. Mobilization
   d. All of the above

3. Election-specific factors that affect voter turnout include _____.
   a. Presidential or nonpresidential election years
   b. Age
   c. Level of education
   d. All of the above

4. Why do you think Americans choose to vote or not vote?

Answer Key: 1. b; 2. d; 3. a; 4. Answers might focus on demographic characteristics, election-specific factors, or thoughts about why people might feel that their voices do not matter.

WHAT HAVE I LEARNED?

ACTING AT A VERY LOCAL LEVEL

Preventing Campus Sexual Assaults through Education and Distraction

In this chapter, we have examined many traditional and nontraditional forms of political participation through the lens of efforts to address sexual violence on college campuses. We have encountered stories of strong individuals choosing to testify, advocate, and mobilize in support of diverse policies in the hopes of addressing and eliminating this serious issue.

These individuals are not acting alone. On many college campuses, men and women are organizing to educate and promote a tactic called *bystander intervention*, in which individuals act to diffuse potentially abusive situations before they happen. One of the largest campus bystander intervention initiatives is Green Dot. The initiative's name refers to the replacement of a red dot on a map indicating where a campus sexual assault happened with a green dot indicating where an assault did *not* happen.

Protestors in New York City in 2011, calling attention to the need to end the shaming of rape survivors and reframe policy debates to focus on the requirement for active consent.
© Charlotte Cooper /CC-BY-2.0

Green Dot's founder, psychologist Dorothy Edwards, recounted that her research-based strategy grew out of frustration with what was not working. On the initiative's Web site, she wrote, "Conference after conference we sat and listened to each other present on yet another clever poster campaign, another creative one-time-only mandatory program, and another date-rape skit. There seemed to be an unspoken agreement that we would resist the urge to cry out in the middle of the presentation, 'Are you frickin' kidding me? Isn't this the exact same thing I heard 10 years ago, just with a different slogan slapped on the front?'"[53]

Central to Green Dot's strategy, as well as those of other bystander intervention programs, are education and intervention. Students are trained to spot a potentially abusive situation—say at a college party—and then step in to diffuse it, often by distracting the potential assailant. According to Greg Liautaud, a junior at Connecticut College and a member of the men's hockey team when interviewed in 2016, "You step in like that and it kind of just ends the situation. It's not really about calling someone a bad person, it's just diffusing the situation."[54] For proponents of bystander intervention, one of its greatest strengths is that "rather than treating everyone as a potential rapist or rape victim, students are treated like allies who are empowered to step in."[55]

While a friend, teammate, or fraternity brother seeing the potential for a sexual assault and offering to take a person out for mozzarella sticks to diffuse a potentially devastating situation might not seem like an act of political participation, it is. Bystander intervention is a central part of the White House's It's On Us campaign, supported and promoted by Vice President Joe Biden. Research on the effectiveness of bystander intervention has shown some promise, though more study is needed. Bystander intervention by itself, however, will not end sexual violence on college campuses. Many sexual assaults happen when there are no observers present.

 CONNECTING TO . . .

Patterns of Young Adult Political Participation

As you read about different perspectives regarding political participation and nonparticipation by young adult Americans, reflect upon the political activities of Amanda Collins, Emma Sulkowicz, Landen Gambill, and members and supporters of Green Dot. Consider the following:

- How their forms of participation were similar to or different from one another
- How their activities impacted the electoral process
- How elected representatives have responded to some of their efforts

YOUNG AMERICANS

Political Participation and Nonparticipation in the Twenty-First Century

As we explored earlier in this chapter, young voting-age Americans remain chronically underrepresented in elections. Voter turnout by young adult voters has been the lowest of any age group since at least 1971, the year the Twenty-sixth Amendment to the Constitution was ratified, guaranteeing suffrage for Americans ages eighteen to twenty-one. Preliminary results from the 2016 presidential election point to a continuation of this pattern, especially in key battleground states.[56] But why? "The bottom line," according to one political science professor, "is that people generally agree that the extent to which young adults feel they have a stake in the establishment is less than the older voter."[57]

We have explored legal and institutional barriers that work against young adult voting, including state voter registration requirements, especially for students enrolled in colleges and universities outside of their home states. Dissatisfaction and disassociation from the political process also likely play a role. The new generation of young adult Americans, often called *millennials*, now constitute a massive group of potential voters—the nation's largest living generation. While the specific ages that qualify as being

FIGURE 6.10

American Student Activism 2014-2015

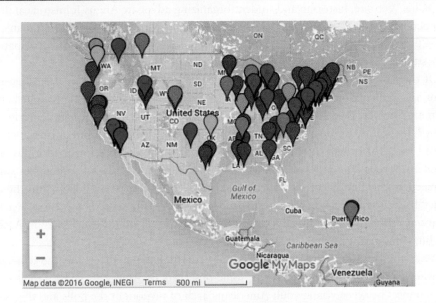

A screenshot from historian Angus Johnston's "American Student Protest Timeline, 2014–15," which is a snapshot in map form of student activism across the United States. The colored pinpoints correspond to different types of events: Red indicates activism targeting racism and police violence, blue corresponds to protests against sexual assault and sexism, green dots represent actions on tuition and funding, and yellow indicates activism regarding governance and student rights.

Source: Angus Johnston, "American Student Protest Timeline, 2014–15," Student Activism, https://studentactivism.net/2014/12/04/american-student-protest-timeline-2014-15/.

millennial often depend on who is describing the generation, as of 2016 there were more than 75 million Americans between the ages of eighteen and thirty-four.[58]

Currently, millennials don't vote, at least not at rates comparable to members of older generations. Of course, as we have explored, members of this generation are likely to increase their levels of electoral participation as they age. However, young adult Americans constitute a potentially very powerful voting bloc should they choose to use that nascent power.[59] The big question, however, is how, or if, this bloc will use the power of its numbers to effect political change. The jury is still out on this.

Young adult Americans today constitute a complicated generation. They are, according to a 2014 study by the Pew Research Center, "America's most racially diverse generation," and "they are relatively unattached to organized politics and religion, linked by social media, burdened by debt, distrustful of people, in no rush to marry—and optimistic about the future."[60] Half of the millennials in the survey self-identified as "political independents," a political reality that was expected to have an impact on the 2016 presidential and congressional elections (Chapter 9).[61]

Their patterns of political participation are also complicated. While it is true that young adult Americans vote in lower numbers than other generations, as we have seen, they do take part in many other forms of political participation. As we will explore later in this book, students and young adult Americans have often taken the lead in protests against the treatment of African American men by law enforcement officers in political movements such as Black Lives Matter. As we will also see, members of the millennial generation have also spearheaded protests against the persistent and growing income and wealth inequality in the nation through movements such as Occupy Wall Street and by supporting outsiders in the presidential election of 2016.

On his Web site, historian and student-organizing advocate Angus Johnston catalogued and documented 160 college and university student protests during the academic year 2014–2015. (See Figure 6.10.) His data also display the different forms of participation in which students were engaged and the issues they chose to address.

Of the campus protests that Johnston documented, the majority were "focused on racism and police violence," with "about half" of the remainder "evenly split between two main themes: sexism/sexual assault and university governance/student rights."[62] Some of the points on the map highlighted Emma Sulkowicz's Columbia University protest and those of others in support of her efforts to bring attention to campus sexual violence. Another icon pointed to a walkout of Georgia high school students in support of a teacher who had been put on leave for bringing his Christian beliefs into the classroom. "I teach world history," the suspended teacher commented, "so there is a lot of talk about religion and really all I want is equality to talk about everything in America, including Christianity."[63]

While the specific topics of these campus protests were as diverse as the women and men who led and participated in them, some observers of American politics took note of the disconnect between young adult Americans' lack of turnout at the polls and their efforts to mobilize and protest over social issues. "Young Americans are often characterized as politically apathetic and ignorant," noted Alia Wong in an essay for *The Atlantic* in 2014. "It's true that they vote at exceptionally low rates, but some say that's because they don't believe going to the polls makes much of a difference. . . . Sometimes students demonstrate precisely because they *don't* have political power."[64] According to researchers from Harvard University's Institute of Politics, "Although millennials may be souring on both political parties and Washington politics in general, our polling and other research also bear strong evidence that they care deeply about their country and are willing to work—with or without government—to improve the quality of life in their communities through public service programs and activities."[65]

For political scientist Russell J. Dalton, the burden is not on young adults to vote more but on members of other generations to come to grips with what political participation means to young people: "American youth thus have a different image of government and a different relationship to politics. . . . So the current challenge for American democracy is not to convince young people to act like their grandparents, but for us to understand their changing values and norms and respond in ways that integrate them into the political process—and potentially change the process to better match this new electorate."[66]

> "The current challenge for American democracy is not to convince young people to act like their grandparents, but for us to understand their changing values and norms and respond in ways that integrate them into the political process."

1. Young adult Americans vote at higher rates than members of older generations.

    a. True
    b. False

2. In recent years, young adult Americans have been acting and protesting over issues such as _____.

    a. The treatment of African American men by law enforcement officials
    b. Economic inequality
    c. Sexual assault on college and university campuses
    d. All of the above

3. Why do you think young adult Americans choose to participate in the ways that they do?

Answer Key: 1. b; 2. d; 3. Answers may focus on feeling disconnected from traditional forms of participation or feeling more connected to ways of participating outside of the voting booth.

CONCLUSION

Are Young Adult Americans Really Disconnected from the Political Process?

We know that young adult Americans continue to participate as voters at much lower rates than members of older generations. We also know, however, that something is happening among young adult Americans and the forms of political participation that they are choosing to engage in, though the impact of this engagement is not yet entirely clear. What is clear, however, is this: Many are speaking out with courage and determination.

Throughout this chapter and the stories in it, we have sustained one metaphor—that of "carrying." The decision to do so was intentional. Its use refers to the claim by Amanda Collins of the right to carry a licensed firearm to protect against sexual violence on campuses. It refers to Landen Gambill's activism to prevent campus carry. It refers to Emma Sulkowicz's protests and her art, in which she carried a mattress to call attention to how school administrators address campus sexual violence. It refers to the efforts of college students to act to diffuse potentially violent situations and educate their peers about the reality of campus sexual assault.

Most fundamentally, however, the idea of "carrying" highlights the difficult but necessary reality that all members of a representative democracy are tasked with carrying the weight of self-governance. In many ways that defy traditional notions of what it means to participate in the political process in a representative democracy, young adult Americans are carrying that weight. Even if their lived experiences, opinions, and political preferences have not yet been attended to by members of older generations in positions of political power, young adult Americans are speaking and acting, and they demand to be heard.

Want a better grade?

Get the tools you need to sharpen your study skills. **SAGE edge** offers a robust online environment featuring an impressive array of free tools and resources. Access practice quizzes, eFlashcards, video, and multimedia at **edge.sagepub.com/abernathy1e.**

CHAPTER REVIEW

This chapter's main ideas are reflected in the Learning Objectives below. By reviewing them here you should be able to **remember** the key points, **connect** them to the stories presented in the chapter, **think** critically about these questions, and **know** these terms that are central to the topic.

6.1 Understand how student political activism on the issue of campus sexual violence illustrates the many ways that political participation can bring about policy change.

REMEMBER ...

- Individuals and groups undertake many different kinds of political activities to shape America's laws and public policies.

- One form of participation may lead an individual to act in other political spaces, or it may shape the actions of actors in other venues.

CONNECT ...

- The stories of Amanda Collins, Landen Gambill, Emma Sulkowicz, Green Dot, and others show that individuals and groups can take many different kinds of political action, both within and outside of formal political institutions.

THINK ...

- In what ways have many young adult Americans tried to call attention to sexual violence on college and university campuses?

6.2 Describe the traditional and nontraditional forms of political participation in American representative democracy.

REMEMBER ...

- By participating politically, either in traditional or nontraditional ways, Americans express their commitment to civic engagement—to making society better.

- Political scientists think of participation as taking place either inside or outside the electoral process.

- Within the electoral process, people can vote or take a variety of actions to support candidates for office.

- Outside of the electoral process, people can volunteer or help organize for causes or take other actions to persuade peers and pressure representatives.

- Americans participate at the voting booth at lower rates than individuals in other democracies, but their rates of nonelectoral participation are equal to or higher than those of their counterparts in other nations.

- In joining social movements, people act collectively to make social and political change and place ideas and issues on the political agenda.

- Amanda Collins acted outside the electoral process by testifying before state representatives to influence CCW legislation and by using various kinds of media platforms to reach a broader audience.

- The actions of Collins and others have resulted in more pro-CCW legislation in some states.

- Landen Gambill also acted outside the electoral process by taking legal action to pressure her university to change how it handled and adjucated sexual assault complaints. She also took part in campus rallies and protests.

- Emma Sulkowicz acted outside the electoral process by using a performance art project and by inspiring allies to protest to draw attention to the mishandling of her rape case.

- The actions of Sulkowicz, Gambill, and others caught the attention of legislators at the federal level who responded by drawing up legislation to improve how colleges and universities handle and monitor campus sexual violence.

THINK . . .

- What forms can political participation take?

- How do Americans' patterns of political participation compare to those in other representative democracies?

KNOW . . .

- *political participation* (p. 195)

- *civic engagement* (p. 201)

6.3 Identify individual factors affecting voter turnout.

REMEMBER . . .

- Voting in elections is a core component of a representative democracy and is a mechanism by which elected officials may be held accountable to the people and by which the people's views may be heard.

- Many Americans do not vote. For any given election, the number of people who do vote is called voter turnout.

- Political scientists have described how not voting may be considered a rational act: Voting is costly in terms of time and effort, and individual votes rarely matter. Others point out that this important mechanism of representation would be endangered if all potential voters chose not to vote.

- Voter turnout is affected by several factors, some of which are individual-level ones.

- Individual factors include socioeconomic status, level of educational attainment, age, race or ethnicity, sex, and partisan attachment.

- Members of American political parties engage in political mobilization to turn out the vote. Those efforts are often focused on reaching people with strong partisan attachment.

CONNECT . . .

- Elected officials such as Michele Fiore, Claire McCaskill, and Kirsten Gillibrand responded to the efforts of people like Collins, Gambill, and Sulkowicz, helping to advance their causes legislatively. Representatives are accountable to activists because they must seek their support at the ballot box if they want to stay in office.

THINK . . .

- What demographic factors shape an individual's decision to vote or not?

KNOW...

- *voter turnout* (p. 208)
- *political mobilization* (p. 215)
- *socioeconomic status* (p. 209)
- *political efficacy* (p. 209)

6.4 Discuss institutional, legal, and election-specific contributors and obstacles to voter turnout.

REMEMBER ...

- Other factors that affect voter turnout are not individual but rather systemic or institutional.
- All American citizens eighteen years old or older are guaranteed the right to vote, which is known as suffrage.
- However, there are limitations to the guarantee of suffrage; undocumented American immigrants and, in many states, convicted felons may not vote.
- Some states have registration requirements that make it harder to vote; others have requirements that make it easier.
- The traditional scheduling of national presidential and congressional elections may serve to discourage participation.
- Some states' registration processes encourage participation.
- Factors surrounding an election itself—especially whether it is a presidential election year—also affect voter turnout.
- Sometimes voters do not cast votes for a set of races with which they are not familiar and for which they may not have traditional cues.

THINK...

- What institutional, legal, and election-specific factors contribute to an individual's decision to vote or not?

KNOW...

- *suffrage* (p. 215)
- *felon disenfranchisement* (p. 215)
- *registration requirements* (p. 215)
- *absentee ballots* (p. 216)
- *Motor Voter Law* (p. 216)
- *ballot roll-off* (p. 217)

6.5 Explain the potential power of political protest as a tool to effect political change.

REMEMBER ...

- As members of social movements, individuals may participate in political protests, attend political meetings, contact elected officials, or reach out to other citizens to educate them about the need to participate to make social and political change.

CONNECT...

- Emma Sulkowicz's highly visible piece of performance art inspired students across the country to demonstrate in support of sexual violence survivors and in protest of how college and university administration officials were dealing with the crisis. Those protests caught the attention of lawmakers on the national level.

THINK...

- How might protest impact electoral politics?

6.6 Assess the current and future political power of young adult Americans.

REMEMBER ...

- Young voting-aged Americans remain chronically underrepresented in American elections, largely because they do not feel they have a stake in the political establishment.

- However, young adult Americans do take part in many other forms of political participation.

CONNECT ...

- Collins, Gambill, and Sulkowicz all took political action outside of the electoral cycle and were able to make important changes.

THINK ...

- What are the patterns of political participation by young adult Americans? What effect do you think this participation has had or will have in the future?

7 PUBLIC OPINION
How Are Americans' Voices Measured?
Does It Matter?

A protester holds up a sign during a demonstration in Ferguson, Missouri. Eighteen-year-old Michael Brown was killed in a confrontation with a police officer, sparking a series of protests that led to a nationwide conversation about the treatment of blacks by law enforcement officials and that possibly influenced the public's view of the issue.

Bilgin Sasmaz/Anadolu Agency/Getty Images

Information is necessary to representative government. Citizens must have some knowledge of what their elected representatives are up to in order to keep watch on their activities, hold them accountable, and potentially punish them at the voting booth if those representatives are no longer serving their interests. On the other side of the equation, elected representatives need to know what citizens' preferences are in order to convince voters to send them into office and to carry out their wishes once there.

As we will explore in this chapter, and later in this book, neither half of the equation is a given. We will start with the foundation of the second concern: citizens' preferences on issues and policies. Though it may seem obvious, the act of conveying opinions and preferences to candidates or elected officials requires that people have preferences on issues in the first place and that these preferences are coherent and meaningful, both on the individual level and when individuals' preferences are combined with others to present potential or elected representatives with useful information.

These are the central challenges of **public opinion**, which is the sum of individual attitudes about government, policies, and issues. Do people have individually coherent and meaningful opinions about the issues with which government deals? If so, when these individual bits of information are aggregated into the collective thing that we call public opinion, does it constitute a meaningful communication, or is it just noise?

> **public opinion**
> the sum of individual attitudes about government, policies, and issues.

In this chapter, we will focus on American public opinion in one specific area: the treatment of young African American men by law enforcement officials. We will deal with the difficult story of the shooting death of Michael Brown by a police officer in Ferguson, Missouri, as well as the aftermath of the shooting and the protests that erupted in response to this and other similar events. We will question whether or not these events have produced meaningful changes in American public opinion on the topic of police-community relations.

After reading this chapter, you will be able to:

7.1 Discuss differing theories about public opinion formation and expression and the degree to which it is meaningful

7.2 Describe the issues involved in surveying American public opinion and the construction of the instruments used to do so

7.3 Examine the sources of individual political attitudes and preferences

7.4 Assess patterns of American public opinion over time and between different groups

7.5 Reflect upon the role, possibilities, and dangers of modern public opinion gathering in the United States

7.6 Debate the power of individuals, events, and people's interpretations of events to make lasting change in American politics

LEARNING OBJECTIVES

 ## THE "FERGUSONS" OF AMERICA

Differing Views on a Tragic Event

NEWS CLIP
Reporter discusses the protests in Ferguson

On August 9, 2015, a group of demonstrators made their way to West Florissant Avenue in Ferguson, Missouri, shouting, "Hands up, don't shoot!"[1] This protest marked the one-year anniversary of the shooting of Michael Brown—an unarmed eighteen-year-old African American—by white law enforcement officer Darren Wilson during a police stop on Florissant Avenue on August 9, 2014. In the confrontation, Wilson shot Brown six times, killing him. Brown had graduated from high school just eight days earlier and

The Black Lives Matter movement began after the death of Trayvon Martin, an unarmed black Florida teenager who was shot to death by a white neighborhood watch volunteer in 2012. The group continued protesting in Ferguson after Michael Brown's death.

NICHOLAS KAMM/AFP/ Getty Images

was planning on attending college that fall. Some eyewitness accounts asserted that Brown had his hands raised in surrender when he was shot.[2]

The day after Brown's death protesters gathered peacefully in Ferguson. "Tension," however, "flared off and on through the evening. A calm settled over the area after mourners gathered at a prayer circle—watched over by a St. Louis County police officer sitting atop a SWAT vehicle—and then a candlelight vigil as darkness fell. The acrimony briefly resurfaced about 8:30 p.m. as demonstrators again swarmed the street chanting, 'We are Michael Brown' as wary police officers stood nearby with assault rifles."[3]

By nightfall, there was violence: "After a candlelight vigil, people smash[ed] car windows, carr[ied] away armloads of looted goods from stores and burn[ed] down a Quick Trip."[4] Early the next morning, police issued warnings that the crowd needed "to disperse or police could use 'chemical munitions' against them. Smoke bombs appeared to be fired around 2 a.m."[5] By the time the first wave of violence ended, "more than two dozen businesses in Ferguson and neighboring Dellwood were damaged or looted."[6] The protests, some peaceful and some violent, continued for weeks.

In the weeks following Brown's death, many of the protestors and other residents of Ferguson called for the arrest and prosecution of the officer who had shot Brown. Some chanted. One of their common refrains was "black life matters." The social movement to which the protesters were referring existed before Ferguson. It had begun with the Twitter hashtag #BlackLivesMatter, which sprang into use following the 2013 acquittal of George Zimmerman in the shooting death of Trayvon Martin in Florida. After Ferguson, however, Black Lives Matter became part of the national conversation in ways it had never been before. *Time* magazine included the protestors of Ferguson in its list of candidates for "Person of the Year."[7]

In an interview with ABC News in fall 2014, Darren Wilson, who had announced his resignation from the Ferguson Police Department, argued that he acted in self-defense in killing Brown: "I had to. If I don't, he [Brown] will kill me if he gets to me."[8] Ferguson police chief Thomas Jackson relayed to the public Wilson's suspicions that Brown and a friend were suspects in a convenience store robbery that had occurred shortly before the encounter.[9]

Michael Brown was not the only unarmed African American man killed by police officers during the summer and fall of 2014. On August 5 near Dayton, Ohio, police shot and killed twenty-one-year-old John Crawford inside a Walmart. Crawford was handling an air rifle, which officers thought was a firearm.[10] Roughly three weeks before Brown was killed, Eric Garner "died from a police chokehold in Staten Island, N.Y., after telling the arresting officers that he could not breathe."[11]

By 2015 the national conversation had changed. Maybe this was due to one specific tragic event or to the cluster of deaths of young African American men during police stops and arrests in 2014. Perhaps it was due to a complicated mixture of events, media coverage, elite messages, and the use of social media that followed these deaths. Regardless of the exact reason, public opinion on the issue of police-citizen interactions, especially in predominantly African American communities, appeared to be shifting. To many Americans, especially whites, the protesters' anger over the events in Ferguson came as a surprise. To large percentages of African Americans, however, the death of Brown was not unique, only another tragedy in a long history of tragedies when young African American men came face to face with the American law enforcement system:

> "To a lot of people, Mike Brown was a big shock," said Carlotta Bussey, a St. Louis resident who attended [a memorial] march with her 7-year-old son. "But to the black community, it wasn't a big shock because it happens all the time." Ms. Bussey said she went to a few protests last August in the days after Mr. Brown's death, but had not been involved in the rallies that have continued on a smaller scale since then. She planned to attend several weekend events, she said, to "show my son that he does have a voice."[12]

To individuals within African American communities across the country, the only surprising thing about the fallout from Ferguson was that the issue had not been more debated, more talked about. According to Representative John Conyers of Michigan, the dean of the Congressional Black Caucus, "There are virtually no African-American males— including congressmen, actors, athletes and office workers, who have not been stopped at one time or another for driving while black."[13]

Less than two weeks following Brown's death, the Pew Research Center published the results of a public opinion survey of Americans' responses to what Ferguson and racial identity meant in the larger national conversation. To conduct the survey, researchers had contacted a random sample of one thousand American adults, half via landlines and half via cell phones. The divisions between African Americans and whites on what Ferguson meant were clear. A full 80 percent of blacks said that Brown's shooting raised "important issues about race." Only 37 percent of white respondents agreed. A full 47 percent of whites said that "race [was] getting more attention than it deserves" (see Figure 7.1).

FIGURE 7.1

Opinion about Ferguson Divided by Racial Identity

Thinking about the police shooting of an African American teen in Ferguson, Missouri, percent saying . . .

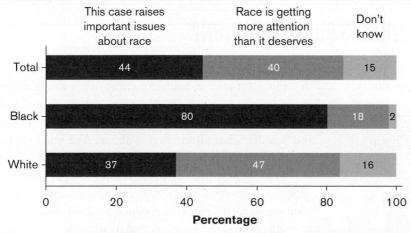

Note: Survey conducted August 14–17, 2014. Whites and blacks include only those who are not Hispanic. Figures may not add to 100% because of rounding.

Source: Pew Research Center, "Stark Racial Divisions in Reactions to Ferguson Police Shooting," August 18, 2014, http://www.people-press.org/2014/08/18/stark-racial-divisions-in-reactions-to-ferguson-police-shooting/.

Clearly Americans were deeply split about whether Brown's death reflected important issues about the state of race in America. The idea that there were two Fergusons, one African American and one white, seemed to extend beyond the city limits and apply to the whole of the American public.

By 2015 the word *Ferguson* had taken on meanings beyond what many of its residents might have previously imagined. Of all of the critical questions that arose from the events in that city, these are the ones that we will explore: Did the events in Ferguson meaningfully shape American public opinion? If these events *did* have an impact on American public opinion, what effect did the resulting change in attitudes have on representation and the American political process? Did these changes endure, or did the national conversation go back to the way it was before, divided sharply by racial identity? Did leaders and government officials pay attention to these shifts in the opinion landscape?

Once again we return to the question of representation. This time, however, the focus is on the voices of those who are represented in American democracy, their coherence, their meaning, and their effect on American political life.

WHAT IS PUBLIC OPINION?

One of the most interesting and important debates about American public opinion is whether or not there is such a thing. Of course, many Americans *have* thoughts and ideas about politics and policies, but many others do not have well-formed views on these topics. Some people might not care at all and wonder what all the fuss is about. And what do we really learn by asking Americans what they think? Recall the definition of public opinion presented above: the sum of individual attitudes about government, policies, and issues. Public opinion, by definition, involves two components: an individual's own beliefs and attitudes, and the accumulation of all of these individual preferences into something that we then call *public opinion*. Either of these two pieces—individual attitudes and the aggregation of individual attitudes—can make American public opinion difficult to understand. This is because individuals may not actually have meaningful preferences on any given issue, and, even if they do, the

> Individuals may not actually have meaningful preferences on any given issue, and, even if they do, the aggregation of these individual preferences might not yield meaningful and useful information.

aggregation of these individual preferences might not yield meaningful and useful information.

These are more than just academic concerns. A representative democracy cannot function without meaningful public opinion. If our elected representatives do not know what we want, then how can they hope to represent us? Later in this book we will explore the role that constituents play in shaping the behavior of their elected senators and representatives. Inherent in the role of constituency, however, are two assumptions: that constituents have preferences and that they can meaningfully communicate those preferences to their members of Congress. In this chapter, we will consider both these assumptions.

What Does Public Opinion Really Tell Us?

Arguments about the meaning of public opinion in American political life fall into two general camps. One perspective holds that the average citizen either doesn't have or is unable to express meaningful opinions on the vast array of issues with which he or she is confronted. Maybe there are simply too many issues for any of us to have well-informed and meaningful opinions about all of them. Another perspective holds that even though individuals sometimes lack the information they need to form opinions, they can find ways to overcome or work around these challenges by, for example, making inferences based on their attitudes about other policies and questions, responding to messages from political parties, and/or relying on friends. Perhaps these cues help us arrive at an opinion. Aggregating individual opinions—even if they are individually unclear or inconsistent—can send a useful and impactful signal to elected representatives and government officials.

Stereotypes and Nonattitudes:
A Pessimistic View of What the Public Knows and Thinks

Proponents of what political scientists have called the **minimalist paradigm** emphasize how most people fall short of what we expect them to know, think about, and pay attention to in the complicated world of politics and policy.[14] Most people, according to this perspective, pay minimum attention to issues and have minimal information about them. Additionally, the opinions that they *do* have are minimally stable; they change over time or in response to attempts to control or shape them.

One of the earliest and most influential expressions of the minimalist argument was Walter Lippmann's *Public Opinion* (1922). A prominent journalist and political observer, Lippmann was concerned about how malleable (or flexible) and receptive Americans' attitudes appeared to be under the pressure of political propaganda leading up to the nation's involvement in World War I. If, in the mind of many observers of American public opinion, a nation could be led to a war most felt had nothing to do with American interests, then what *couldn't* the American people be talked into?

For Lippmann, a key concept was the **stereotype**, a preconceived, often oversimplified idea about something that people apply as a filter to the world. Stereotypes do not filter based upon a rational consideration of the issues but upon emotions, and in the world of

minimalist paradigm
a theory of public opinion that emphasizes how most people fall short of what we expect them to know, think about, and pay attention to in the complicated world of politics and policy.

TOPICS IN AMERICAN GOVERNMENT
Influences on political opinions

stereotype
a preconceived, often oversimplified idea about something that people apply as a filter to the world.

The Uncle Sam recruitment poster for the U.S. Army was originally published in 1916. The image was an effective piece of propaganda, and more than four million copies were printed in the years leading up to the United States' entry into World War I in 1919. DeAgostini/Getty Images.

elites
a small number of individuals (who tend to have well-informed and well-reasoned opinions).

masses
the majority of individuals (who tend to be less well informed).

nonattitudes
a term referring to the lack of stable and coherent opinions on political issues and candidates.

public opinion surveys
systematic attempts to make inferences about the opinions of large numbers of individuals by carefully sampling and asking questions of a small, randomly assigned sample of the larger population.

politics they are easily manipulated by those who seek to shape American public opinion for their own political purposes.

Lippmann described a public that is dangerously unreflective and vulnerable to attempts to shape its opinions: "In the great blooming, buzzing confusion of the outer world we pick out what our culture has already defined for us, and we tend to perceive that which we have picked out in the form stereotyped for us by our culture."[15] For Lippmann, part of the reason why the framers of the Constitution instituted so many checks and balances in the federal government, so many roadblocks to making major policy change, was mistrust of individuals' haphazard, shifting, and malleable stereotypes.

Inherent in the minimalist critique is the idea that not all Americans have the same amount of political information. A small number of individuals, the **elites**, may have well-informed and well-reasoned opinions, but the majority of individuals, the **masses,** do not. In their 1960 study, *The American Voter*, Campbell, Converse, Miller, and Stokes, using large sample surveys, painted a grim picture of the majority of American voters: "The average citizen is very much less involved in politics than is often imagined. His awareness of political events is limited and his concern with ideological problems is only rudimentary."[16] Instead, voters often rely on their identification with a political party—an identification that itself might not be the result of careful, thoughtful, conscious deliberation.

In 1964 Philip E. Converse, one of the authors of *The American Voter*, extended this critique to question whether masses can and do learn from elites, become more informed and produce responses to surveys that are stable over time. Generally, Converse found, masses do not learn from elites: "Very little information 'trickles down' very far."[17] Instead, most voters have **nonattitudes**. The opinions that most people express in, for example, a public opinion survey, might be vulnerable to the efforts of propagandists, as Lippmann feared, and, frankly, might just be random.

It is not only the lack of meaningful opinions that has concerned scholars in this tradition. Many have also considered that even if such a thing exists, we might not be able to measure it in a meaningful way. Later in this chapter we will explore the science behind the design and use of **public opinion surveys**—systematic attempts to make inferences about the opinions of large numbers of individuals by carefully sampling and asking questions of a small, randomly assigned sample of the larger population.

In 1975 a study by political scientist Christopher Achen questioned Converse's conclusion that mass publics do not have meaningful opinions.[18] Achen focused on the tools of measurement used by Converse and based his critique upon the lack of coherence and stability in individuals' survey responses. In doing so, Achen posed another challenge: that the scientific poll, the tool that forms the basis of so much of what we think we know about American public opinion, may itself contribute to the measured results. Though Achen focused on the problems of social scientific research methods, his conclusions raise another important concern: the possibility that a survey of American public opinion might be used to actually shape public opinion rather than just reporting it as a consequence of the partisan or policy preferences of those conducting or paying for the polls. In this way, according to political scientists John Zaller and Stanley Feldman, "survey questions do not simply *measure* public opinion. They also shape and channel it by the manner in which they frame issues, order the alternatives, and otherwise set the context of the question."[19]

What Do Americans Know, or Not Know, about Politics, and Does It Matter?

Concerns about a lack of coherent opinions in the American electorate and the challenges that this poses to American representative democracy have not gone away. In their 1996 book, *What Americans Know about Politics and Why It Matters*, two researchers examined decades of historical surveys of Americans' political knowledge. They also posed a series of political knowledge questions to a large sample of Americans.[20] To the authors, the findings were troubling. Significant percentages of Americans were not able to answer basic questions about American government, such as being able to name one or more branches of the federal government or name constitutional protections in the Bill of Rights.

As or more problematic was that political knowledge was predictably and unequally distributed. Younger Americans, women, lower-income Americans, and members of racial and ethnic minorities consistently fared worse in their answers to such factual political knowledge questions. These gaps have not narrowed over the past few decades. Researchers with the Pew Center periodically administer a "News IQ" quiz to a random sample of Americans. The test contains questions regarding political figures, knowledge of current issues in domestic and international politics, and geography (Figure 7.2). While the number of Americans who can correctly answer a question varies within and across these knowledge tests, significant amounts are unable to answer the questions correctly. To what extent does this information gap matter? Can Americans with unequal knowledge of, or access to, information about American politics express their desires with voices as impactful as those of informed Americans?

An editorial cartoon by Tom Toles critiquing the lack of influence of the American public voice following the financial crisis of 2008.
TOLES © 2009 The Washington Post. Reprinted with permission of UNIVERSAL UCLICK.

Cues, Information Shortcuts, and Aggregation: A More Optimistic View of American Public Opinion

While more recent scholarship acknowledges the challenges posed by proponents of the minimalist paradigm, it also emphasizes the ways in which the public can still make sense of their opinions and transmit those opinions to their representatives, both collectively and individually. On the most basic point—that Americans often lack opinions on many issues in politics and policy—these scholars agree. Where they disagree is on the need for any one person to have an encyclopedic set of policy preferences to be able to offer an opinion. The aggregation of individuals' opinions, according to some scholars, can produce useful information even in the presence of noise at the individual level.

FIGURE 7.2

A Sample Question from Pew's Political Knowledge Test

The News IQ Quiz

What is the name of this person?

Thurgood Marshall

Malcolm X

Jesse Jackson

Martin Luther King, Jr.

Ninety-one percent of respondents to Pew's "News IQ" quiz were able to correctly identify this image of Dr. Martin Luther King Jr. Far fewer were able to identify images of 2014 Nobel Peace Prize winner Malala Yousafzai or Massachusetts senator Elizabeth Warren. Only about 33 percent knew there were three female Supreme Court justices.

Source: Pew Research Center, "The News IQ Quiz," http://www.pewresearch.org/quiz/the-news-iq-quiz/

How do individuals answer survey questions? Do they act as file cabinets, carrying around preformed opinions and waiting to pull out the relevant opinion when prompted? Or do they construct at least some of their opinions when asked to do so—opinions that are based on their own understandings but also perhaps shaped by the survey and the context in which they answered the survey's questions? If that is how individual opinions might be "formed," then one might reasonably expect to see changes in answers to surveys over time and in different situations since the administration of the survey will vary. By incorporating findings from studies of cognition and political psychology, scholars have emphasized this more dynamic process and, though they acknowledge gaps in knowledge and understanding, present a more complex picture of the public's ability to make sense of the political world. For Zaller, a basic concept in attitude construction is **consideration**, a combination of cognition and affect that contributes to any one answer to any one question or evaluation.[21] It's not as complicated a concept as it may seem. Basically, Zaller's theory says that our knowledge and our emotions both come into play when we form and express an opinion. We are not file cabinets, but we are also not the modeling clay that Lippmann worried about. We are something in between.[22]

Other research focuses on the ability of voters with low levels of specific political knowledge to make effective use of cues and information shortcuts to form meaningful opinions. These informational helpers may come from a variety of sources. Individuals' own personal experiences and interactions with government, accumulated over a lifetime, can help them make sense of an issue or problem. This "gut rationality" may not help on a political knowledge

consideration
a combination of cognition and affect that contributes to any one answer to any one question or evaluation.

quiz, but it can assist people in making meaningful political choices.[23] In addition, individuals might rely on advice from friends and colleagues.[24]

Identification with a particular political party is another powerful informational shortcut that voters frequently use when evaluating candidates and forming opinions about specific issues.[25] If I identify as a Republican, I'm likely to be more favorable toward the Republican candidate rather than the Democratic candidate, even without knowing anything other than their party affiliations. Or if I identify as a Democrat, I am more likely to oppose a policy option that Republicans endorse than one Democrats endorse.

> We are not file cabinets, but we are also not the modeling clay that Lippmann worried about. We are something in between.

Finally, some political scientists have emphasized the possibility of the "wisdom of crowds,"[26] in which individuals, imperfectly informed, can come up with a meaningful assessment of a problem or situation. Writing in 1954, a group of political scientists highlighted what they called the "paradox" of individual capabilities and system capability: "*Individual voters* today seem unable to satisfy the requirements for a democratic system of government outlined by political theorists. But the *system of democracy* does meet certain requirements for a going political organization."[27]

More recently, Benjamin Page and Robert Shapiro emphasized the possibility for a public to be collectively rational even in the presence of individually inconsistent and shapeable opinions: "While we grant the rational ignorance of most individuals, and the possibility that their policy preferences are shallow and unstable, we maintain that public opinion as a *collective* phenomenon is nonetheless stable (though not immovable), meaningful, and indeed rational in a higher, if somewhat looser sense: it is able to make distinctions; it is organized in coherent patterns; it is reasonable, based on the best available information; and it is adaptive to new information or changed circumstances, responding in similar ways to similar stimuli."[28]

The Components of Individual Opinions

When political scientists and scholars of political psychology and mass communication describe an individual's opinion, they break it down into distinct components. The first is the **direction** of the opinion, which is what we commonly focus on. Is the person for an issue, against it, or neutral? Does the person think favorably about a political candidate, unfavorably, or neutral? A second dimension of an opinion is the **intensity**, or strength of involvement and preference, with which an individual holds that opinion. Another component describes the **stability** of the opinion. Stable opinions tend not to change over time, in different contexts, or in response to differently worded survey questions. Some opinions, such as which political party one prefers, tend to be stable, while others, such as a preference over a specific water or transportation policy, tend to be much more variable over time and across different surveys, if the individuals have opinions at all. These two parts of an opinion are related. Intense opinions are more likely to be stable than those held with less intensity. Finally, there is the **salience** (or centrality) of an opinion, in the sense that some strongly held opinions shape expressed opinions on other issues or candidate evaluations. For example, a strongly held belief about the need for an active and involved government might shape a person's opinions about specific government policies. Salient opinions tend to be more intense and stable.

One area of representation in American government that continues to evoke intense, stable, and salient opinions is the equality of treatment of individuals by law enforcement

direction
the focus of an individual's opinion.

intensity
the strength of involvement and preference of an individual's opinion.

stability
the degree of change over time, in different contexts, or in response to differently worded survey questions of a particular opinion.

salience
the centrality of an individual's opinion in the sense of the opinion's ability to shape the individual's views on other issues or candidates.

officers and the relationship between that treatment and the racial and ethnic identity of those who interact with law enforcement and the criminal justice system. As residents of Ferguson and other communities in which young men of color had been killed by law enforcement officers reacted, protested, and expressed their anger, it quickly became clear that opinions about race and treatment by law enforcement officials were often highly intense and salient. These opinions, however, were sharply divided by race, ethnicity, age, and partisan affiliation.

A political cartoon highlighting racial divisions in public opinion about the treatment of young African American men by law enforcement officials. The figure representing "Black America" is referring to the choking death of Eric Garner while in police custody in 2014. The figure representing "White America" is alleging that white Americans are not sufficiently aware of the underlying issues.

SHAPING PUBLIC OPINION
The Battle over the "Fergusons"

In the days and weeks that followed the shooting of Michael Brown, deep divisions emerged, with events divided by the time of day, and with Americans' views on the shooting divided by racial and ethnic identity. Ferguson, Missouri, was quickly becoming many Fergusons. According to reporter Chuck Raasch, "Mostly peaceful protesters march hand-in-hand by day. At night, people splinter, defiance and lawlessness take a firmer grip, and expressions and intentions move into the shadows."[29] A *New York Times* article stated that "where once there was only one Ferguson—an anonymous suburb of St. Louis—now there is another: a small city whose name has become known for civil unrest, racial division and police harassment. Few of the deep grievances that divide the city have been resolved. Anger, despair and resentment have been driven to the surface, and many here are unsure when, or if, Ferguson will recover."[30]

It was not only the shooting that caused controversy. The different "Fergusons," did not exist only in the streets of the city. The opinions of the community's reactions were as divided as the opinions over the event itself. To some, the reactions represented a justifiable expression of inequalities and injustices too long ignored; to others, they were nothing more than violence and anarchy.

To many of the protesters in Ferguson, the treatment of young African American men by the American political and legal system had been a critical issue for a very long time. One of the many tasks of the president is to act as a "communicator in chief"—to focus attention on specific issues and events and to make sense of tragedies and challenges. In this role, President Barack Obama addressed the shooting of Brown in a speech at the White House, saying, "In too many communities around the country, a gulf of mistrust exists between local residents and law enforcement. . . . In too many communities, too many young men of color are left behind and seen only as objects of fear."[31]

Assuming the mantle of "communicator in chief," President Barack Obama delivered remarks on the Michael Brown shooting from the White House in November 2014. The president was responding to the announcement that the Ferguson, Missouri, grand jury had decided no charges would be filed against police officer Darren Wilson in the shooting.
Kristoffer Tripplaar / Pool via CNP.

To many Americans not involved with the protests, relations between police agencies and African American men had been far from the top of the national agenda. The events in Ferguson, however, led some to reflect. As one newspaper article put it, "Some Ferguson residents—most of them white, but not all—insisted that Mr. Brown's death had revealed racial tensions that they had not realized were there."[32]

The battle over Ferguson quickly became a battle over public opinion—a battle to tell the story from a particular point of view. Some criticized Michael Brown and pointed to incidents in his past. Responding to these accusations, journalist Touré questioned the motives, and the power, behind those who tried to make Brown's history relevant: "But it doesn't matter whether Brown was an angel. He was a young and growing human, and he made mistakes. That's okay. The real question is not: Was Brown a good kid? The real question is: How are police officers supposed to treat citizens?"[36]

In November 2014, a grand jury announced that Officer Wilson would not be indicted for the shooting. In preparation for the announcement, "boards covered block after block of windows along West Florissant Avenue. Workers had pasted shatter-proof film on windows at the county jail. At least one school district canceled classes early. . . . Workers wrapped statues in Clayton to prevent graffiti. Firefighters screwed plywood around the Clayton firehouse bell. QuickTrip closed four gas stations in and near Ferguson. . . . Two of the region's major malls . . . closed early."[37] These precautions proved to be warranted as the community erupted in protest again after the announcement. "Buildings in Ferguson and Dellwood [were] burned; dozens more there and on South Grand Avenue in St. Louis [were] damaged."[38] A separate investigation conducted later by the Justice Department also declined to prosecute Wilson, concluding that the officer had reason to believe that his own life was in danger during the stop.

Nearly a year after the death of Michael Brown, William Lacy Clay (D-MO), a representative from St. Louis, related to a gathering of supporters of Open Society Foundations some troubling lessons that he had learned about American public opinion: "I have gained a profound and staggering new understanding of just how deep the divisions really are in this country. . . . Between white Americans and other Americans. Between police and the citizens in urban communities whom they are sworn to serve and protect. And even

FIGURE 7.3

Widespread Support for the Use of Body Cameras by Law Enforcement Officers

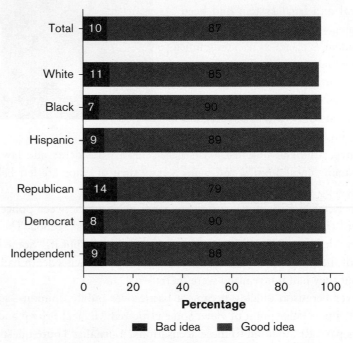

More police officers wearing body cameras to record interactions would be a . . . (%)

	Bad idea	Good idea
Total	10	87
White	11	85
Black	7	90
Hispanic	9	89
Republican	14	79
Democrat	8	90
Independent	9	88

Note: Survey conducted Dec. 3–7, 2014. Don't know responses not shown. Whites and blacks include only non-Hispanics; Hispanics are of any race.

Source: Pew Research Center, "Sharp Racial Divisions in Reactions to Brown, Garner Decisions: Many Blacks Expect Police-Minority Relations to Worsen," December 8, 2014, http://www.people-press. org/2014/12/08/sharp-racial-divisions-in-reactions-to-brown-garner-decisions/.

between the generations."[39] In his prepared remarks, Clay also mentioned legislation that he was cosponsoring with Senator Claire McCaskill (D-MO) that would heighten scrutiny and place restrictions on the distribution of surplus military equipment to local law enforcement agencies.

Public opinion polls conducted in the weeks and months following the deaths of Brown and Garner backed up Clay's observations. A poll conducted several months after Brown's shooting found that a large majority of Americans, regardless of racial or ethnic identity or political party affiliation, expressed support for the use of body cameras by law enforcement officers to record their interactions with the public (see Figure 7.3).

Commenting on the cluster of lethal shootings of young African American men in 2014, a sociologist at George Washington University claimed that while one single event might not move American public opinion, several might: "Once a critical mass of these incidents occur in real time it can certainly shift public opinion even among those . . . who might have thought the police could do no wrong."[40]

1. The officer involved in the shooting death of Michael Brown was indicted by a grand jury.

   a. True
   b. False

2. In the days and weeks following the shooting death of Michael Brown, what divisions emerged in the community?

3. How did individuals with different agendas try to shape the interpretation of the shooting?

....

Answer Key: 1. b; 2. Answers might include a discussion of peaceful protests and violent resistance, of different portrayals of the community's reactions, or of the degree to which police-community relations were or were not given sufficient attention in the national debate.; 3. Answers might include a discussion of the portrayal of Brown himself.

MEASURING AND TRANSMITTING PUBLIC OPINION

The act of representation in a republican form of government has two basic, and crucial, informational requirements. First, voters must have opinions and preferences that can be communicated to their elected representatives. Second, elected officials must respond to, or be forced to respond to, these expressed preferences. We have already considered the debates about whether or not Americans have meaningful opinions. The second part of the equation is just as important. How can Americans effectively communicate their preferences to their government? How do elected representatives learn about the preferences of their constituents?

One method that citizens use is to directly communicate with their elected officials through phone calls or e-mails. The challenge with direct communication as a tool of representation is that elected officials know that those who call or write do not represent their constituents as a whole but only a motivated subset of people who are often unhappy about something. While direct communication can signal to an elected official the intense preferences of a small group of individuals, it does not convey a sense of the overall preferences of the citizens as a whole.

A tool that *does* give elected officials this broader knowledge is an election. While we may not often think about an election as a tool for measuring public opinion, that is precisely what it is. However, in this regard, elections have their own limitations. First, many eligible voters do not vote. The decision of whether or not to vote can be affected by efforts to mobilize potential voters, to "get out the vote" (see Chapter 6). In terms of measuring the preferences of constituents, the greater challenge with elections is that they tend to revolve around a small set of issues, albeit ones for which voters have intense preferences. For the majority of public policy issues with which elected officials will have to contend, elections are too broad a tool to reveal useful information.

Therefore, rather than waiting for individuals to contact them or trying to decipher the results of an election, prospective and elected officials go directly to the citizens to find out what they think and want. One tool sometimes used for this is the **focus group**,

CONNECTING TO . . .

The Role of Public Opinion in a Representative Democracy

As you learn about the methods used to measure American public opinion and transmit it to elected representatives, reflect upon the ways in which public opinion might have changed in response to the events of Ferguson, Missouri, and news media and social media coverage of those events. Consider the following:

- The various tools that Americans use to communicate their policy preferences to elected officials

- The challenges of trying to understand the opinions of millions of Americans while only sampling 1,500 of them

focus group
a small group of individuals assembled for a directed conversation during which one hopes to uncover patterns of thinking about issues and individuals.

Telling Other Stories

Different Perspectives about the Meaning of Ferguson

Not all residents of Ferguson supported the activities of those who vented their anger and frustration at the shooting of Brown. Many of these residents, both African Americans and whites, may have agreed with the need to see justice, but they based their disapproval of the protest activities on fear of what might happen to their communities. Chantea Arthur, an African American nurse's aide interviewed by the *New York Times* about the protests, said, "What they're doing is bringing down everything. I think the cop should get in trouble for what he did. But I'm getting tired of it all."[33]

The *Times* also interviewed Doug Hindle, a white man who had lived in Ferguson for thirty years at the time of the protests. Hindle said the shooting had changed relations between whites and African Americans in the community. "Everything was fine before," he said. "People are making this look like a bad place to live. People are chanting at night. You can't leave, you can't open your windows at night. People are shooting their guns off. It's never been like that. If they let Wilson go, all

Hell's going to break loose. I really hope he goes to jail, just so people can get their justice. This has got to stop."[34]

Linda Hensiek, who runs a beauty shop in Ferguson, talked not about the past or present but about the future. "We're hoping that two years from now, we can say that this was given to us for a reason and something good will have come out of it," she said. "Right now, it's hell."[35]

WHAT DO YOU THINK?

Controversial events and issues, and the ways that communities deal with them, often produce difficult conversations in which some may feel that their voices are not being heard. Have you been a part of a political or social discussion in which you felt some voices and viewpoints were not helpful? Have you been a part of one in which you felt that a voice, story, or point of view was not being included when it might have been useful?

---

in which a small group of individuals is assembled for a directed conversation during which one hopes to uncover patterns of thinking about issues and individuals. Focus groups can be useful in understanding how individuals come to understand the political issues with which they are contending. However, by their nature, focus groups cannot paint a picture of the constituency as a whole and are therefore limited in their utility.

There is another, deeper, concern about focus groups and other tools for measuring public opinion that we will examine shortly: Much of their development and use is tied to the history of product marketing, in which companies use these tools to try to get a sense of which products will sell best and why. This textbook, in fact, as well as most others, involved the use of focus groups in its development. The challenge for representative democracy is whether or not we want our elected officials to think of us like breakfast cereals. In one sense, we might. We want our elected representatives to care enough about our opinions to find out what they are. On the other hand, there is a danger that our elected representatives might be too concerned with taking the nation's pulse, too hesitant to make difficult decisions that might be unpopular but are necessary. The framers most certainly did not intend for elected representatives to consistently bend to the will of voters. That is part of the reason why they set up so many roadblocks to making major and sweeping changes to American public policy.

Even so, a candidate whose eyes are on election (or reelection) will use any tools that she or he has to gauge the opinions of the voters. The most effective of these—although it comes with its own issues and challenges—is the **scientific poll.** With this tool, pollsters try to gain an understanding of a large group of individuals by obtaining the opinions of a carefully chosen small sample of the group, although they are aware of the limitations of the effort.

scientific poll
when pollsters try to gain an understanding of a large group of individuals by obtaining the opinions of a carefully chosen small sample of the group, although they are aware of the limitations of the effort.

The Foundations of Scientific Polling

In theory, scientific polling is simple. Given the impossibility and the unfeasibly expensive prospect of asking everyone in a House district, a state, or the nation what they think, one instead selects a smaller representative subset of that constituency and asks its members what they think. In practice, this is impossible to do with 100 percent certainty. The problem is one of the **sample**, the subgroup of individuals from the larger population one wants to measure the opinions of. For some political polls, the population may be the entire voting-age population of the United States or of an individual state or congressional district. However, there are many other possible populations of interest in a survey, such as individuals with specific racial or ethnic identities or the student population of a college or university.

A key challenge in sampling is **random selection**. For the sample to be useful, it must represent the larger population as best as possible, with no systematic errors. Some errors in sampling are not a problem. If your **respondents**, or those individuals who respond to your survey, are more likely to choose blue over green socks, that is probably not an issue. If, however, a poll systematically oversamples or undersamples individuals based on characteristics that are relevant to what the poll is trying to measure—for example, support for a presidential candidate from the Democratic or Republican Party—then you have a problem. Pollsters are well aware of these challenges. Often they may use the technique of **weighting** to adjust the results of a survey. Weighting is done based on differences between the percentages of specific groups participating in the survey and what is known about the proportion of their representation in the larger population.

Unless one can survey every single person in a population, community, or nation, no researcher can ever know what the "true" opinion of that population is. The goal is to minimize the uncertainty as much as possible while also conducting a poll that does not cost vast sums of money or take an unacceptable amount of time to conduct. When pollsters present their results, they include a measure of the **sampling error** (or margin of error) in their surveys. In larger national polls, which typically aim for about 1,500 respondents, the sampling error is often plus or minus three points, meaning that they can assert that about 95 percent of the time the true number—which is never known—lies within three points on either side of the measured number. In American politics, the number of citizens on either side of an issue might be closely divided. If, for example, an opinion survey with a margin of error of three points finds that one party's candidate for president has the support of 49 percent of Americans and the other party's candidate the support of 47 percent, then one could not confidently say that the first candidate would win in a national election. Increasing the size of the sample decreases the error, but it also increases the cost. In addition, the greater the variation in the population that one samples, the larger the sampling error.

Types of Surveys

In choosing how to administer a survey, a researcher has several options. The degree of confidence that one can place in the findings, however, depends critically upon the ways in which the sample is selected. One popular type of survey is a **straw poll**—an unofficial tally of opinion or support at a meeting or event, such as a political party meeting or caucus. While straw polls can be useful in exploring which individuals support a candidate and why, their target population is not randomly selected. The fact that people have chosen to attend the event at which the straw poll is conducted means that the sample was not

sample
the subgroup of individuals from the larger population one wants to measure the opinions of.

random selection
how participants are selected from the population for inclusion in the study.

respondents
individuals who answer a survey.

weighting
a procedure in which the observed results of a survey are adjusted according to what is known about specific proportions in the larger population.

sampling error
error in a statistical analysis arising from the unrepresentativeness of the sample taken.

straw poll
an unofficial tally of opinion or support at a meeting or event.

Two versions of straw polls are shown here. At left, a visitor to the 2015 Iowa State Fair casts a vote for presidential candidate Carly Fiorina with a kernel of corn. At right, attendees at the 2015 Conservative Political Action Conference (CPAC) vote in an electronic straw poll in National Harbor, Maryland.

Left Photo: AP Photo/Paul Sancya

Right Photo: AP Photo/Alex Brandon

self-selected listener opinion polls (or SLOP polls)
a survey in which respondents choose to respond to a survey prompt on their own.

exit poll
a survey conducted outside of a polling place in which individuals are asked who or what they just voted for and why.

random digit dialing
when potential survey respondents are selected by computer-generated random numbers.

randomly chosen and, therefore, cannot be relied upon to draw conclusions about general public opinion.

Self-selected listener opinion polls, also called SLOP polls, in which respondents choose to respond to a survey prompt on their own, suffer from the same disadvantage. SLOP polls are quite common. When individuals respond to a radio talk show host's requests to call in, or when a person fills out a quick survey after reading an article or watching a video on the Internet, he or she is participating in a SLOP poll. Because more involved and motivated individuals choose to participate, and these individuals do not represent a randomly selected subset of the overall population, one cannot confidently say that their opinions reflect the distribution of them in the larger population.

An **exit poll** is a survey conducted outside of a polling place in which individuals are asked who or what they just voted for and why. While there is much to be gained for a news organization that can call a race before other news outlets based on its exit poll results, there are risks as well. Individuals do not vote at random times, and an exit poll may unintentionally be sampling from a group that over- or underrepresents overall public opinion on an issue or candidate. Also, announcing the results of exit polls while polls are still open runs the risk of influencing an election. Learning that one candidate is supposedly winning may discourage another candidate's supporters from turning out to vote because they believe their votes would not matter. To avoid that problem, news networks have voluntarily committed to not releasing exit poll results until all of a state's polling places have closed. Exit polls can be useful, though, in understanding patterns of voting—for example, what issue was most on the minds of voters who voted for one candidate or another.

Because of the challenges posed by nonrandom selection, news organizations, media outlets, and research organizations rely primarily on the telephone when trying to gauge American public opinion. They may draw from lists of phone numbers or employ **random digit dialing**, in which phone numbers are selected randomly by computer. That has the added advantage of potentially including unlisted numbers or those generally not in pollsters' (or marketers') databases, such as numbers for cell phones. Even with random digit dialing, however, there are always risks that a sample is not truly representative of the overall population. Are some of those whom one calls more likely to answer the survey than others? Might patterns of willingness or unwillingness to answer the survey bias the findings? Though pollsters are aware of and try to account for these issues, it is always a potential problem.

Are Public Opinion Surveys Valid?
How Surveys Themselves May Shape Their Findings

In addition to sample selection, pollsters must confront other issues that are important for informed consumers of public opinion surveys—such as the students reading this book—to note. We have explored the challenge that Americans may have nonattitudes on some issues, and there is also the risk that individuals may be unwilling to admit a lack of information or opinion and make up responses on the spot. In one survey of Americans, political scientist George Bishop asked respondents about their opinions of the Public Affairs Act of 1975. The trick was that the act never existed. In spite of this small fact, significant percentages of respondents offered an opinion on the piece of fictitious legislation, casting doubt on the reliability of results of surveys of Americans on specific public policies and policy proposals.[41] In order to try to prevent this, well-constructed survey questions should try to focus on issues with which their respondents will be familiar and have opinions about.

Even on issues for which respondents have actual preferences, other factors may shape the results of a public opinion survey. First, the **question order** might affect the results. Consider a question about whether or not individuals should be permitted to burn an American flag in protest. The same question might produce substantially different results if it were preceded by other questions that included the expressed opinions of other individuals.[42] Perhaps the flag-burning question was preceded by a question about the importance of patriotism, which might produce more opinions against allowing flag burning. Alternatively, the flag-burning question might have followed a question on the importance of free speech in American democracy, priming a different pattern of responses.

Similarly, the **question wording** might, intentionally or not, guide respondents to a specific answer. For example, in a 2003 Pew Research Center Survey about attitudes towards military action in Iraq, 68 percent of respondents said that they favored action when asked if they would "favor or oppose taking military action in Iraq to end Saddam Hussein's rule." However, when asked if they would "favor or oppose taking military action in Iraq to end Saddam Hussein's rule *even if it meant that U.S. forces might suffer thousands of casualties*," only 43 percent of respondents favored military action.[43]

Finally, the interviewers themselves may affect the results of a survey, especially one conducted in person. Political scientists have, for example, documented **race of interviewer effects**, in which the outcomes of surveys, even on questions only asking for political knowledge and information, may depend partly upon the racial identities of respondents and surveyors.[44]

question order
a concern in measuring public opinion having to do with how the sequencing of questions affects responses.

question wording
a concern in measuring public opinion having to do with how the way a question is phrased affects responses.

race of interviewer effects
the shaping of survey responses due to the racial identities of respondents and interviewers.

How Are Polls Used?

Many different individuals and groups make use of public opinion polls. Media outlets work with major polling organizations when covering topics such as Americans' support or opposition to a candidate or policy proposal. Academic researchers rely on more in-depth polls to test theories about politics and public opinion. One tool that political scientists and other researchers may employ is the survey experiment, in which individuals are randomly assigned different surveys, perhaps with different question wording or framing. The goal here is not to try to measure the opinions of a larger population but to use the randomized experiments to better understand how people form opinions.

The *St. Louis Post-Dispatch* Changes Its Cover Photo

Lynden Steele/Twitter

On the one-year anniversary of the death of Michael Brown, and over the space of a few hours, the editors and publishers of the *St. Louis Post-Dispatch* chose to replace the lead photograph for the next day's paper. The reason was another tragic event. The planned image was of a peaceful protest in which at least one thousand marchers commemorated

the tragic events of one-year prior and sought to keep public attention on the issue of the treatment of young African American men by law enforcement officials.

At night, however, police shot and critically wounded another young African American man, eighteen-year-old Tyrone Harris. St. Louis County police officials stated that prior to the shooting two groups of men had been involved in a gunfight with each other and one had fired on four plain-clothed police officers in an unmarked car.

In his tweet, Lynden Steele, director of photography for the newspaper, contrasted the two images, and the two headlines, highlighting yet another heartbreak. Notice the differences in tone and mood of the two images. In the first, the upside down American flag. Officially, it is only displayed as such in times of distress. In this case the protesters used their First Amendment right to display the flag this way to signal the distress that they felt surrounding this issue. Notice the somber tone of the second image and the image itself—one of police officers surrounding a wounded young man—one with which Ferguson residents were well familiar.

WHAT DO YOU THINK?

The decision of the editors and publishers of the *St. Louis Post-Dispatch* to change their lead image highlights both the power of image in political storytelling and the speed with which coverage responds to events. To someone unfamiliar with the news article or the protest controversy, how do these two images frame the stories of the anniversary protests? As an editor of a newspaper, what might you consider when choosing a cover story image of protests in Ferguson or other cities?

Polls also play key roles in political campaigns. The media may use tools such as exit polls to predict the outcomes of political races or to better understand why people voted one way or another in a given election. Candidates themselves may employ polls to better understand voters' interests and concerns or to gauge public support for themselves or their opponents as a campaign progresses. One controversial tool that candidates or those supporting them may employ is a **push poll**, which is not really a poll but a negative campaign tactic. Disguised as surveys, push polls try to present voters with negative or damaging portrayals of opposing candidates, sometimes with false or exaggerated information.

push poll
a negative campaign tactic disguised as a survey in which a candidates' opponent or opponents are portrayed in an unfavorable way.

1. The disadvantage in measuring public opinion that SLOP polls and straw polls both share is _____.

   a. They are too expensive to conduct nationally

   b. They tend to only survey conservative public opinion

   c. Their respondents are not chosen randomly

   d. They tend to only survey liberal public opinion

2. Random selection of survey respondents is challenged by _____.

   a. The communications technology used to contact potential respondents

   b. The time of day in which a respondent is contacted

   c. The decisions of potential respondents to answer or not answer the survey

   d. All of the above

3. If you were to try to sample American public opinion on an issue that you care about, how might you go about trying to assemble a random sample? What challenges might you face?

Answer Key: 1. c; 2. d; 3. Answers will vary but should discuss the challenges of sampling from a given population.

THE FORMATION OF POLITICAL ATTITUDES

Exploring Political Socialization

Did Ferguson matter? Did the shooting, the protests following the shooting, and the national coverage of the controversy actually change the national conversation in a way that affected American public policy? We will return to this question. Before that, however, we need to step back a bit and consider what political scientists know or do not know about how political attitudes are formed in the first place.

Political Socialization: The Sources of Political Knowledge and Opinion

The first step is to explore the formation of these things that we call political attitudes and opinions. The formation and modification of opinions and attitudes towards politics, public policy, and political figures is a lifelong process. **Political socialization** refers to the variety of experiences and factors that shape our political values, attitudes, and behaviors.

political socialization
the variety of experiences and factors that shape our political values, attitudes, and behaviors.

Families, Schools, and Peers: Early Shapers of Information and Opinion

The first and most important contributor to the process of political socialization is the family, especially when it comes to shaping children's views about political figures and political authority.[45] **Party identification**—the degree to which an individual identifies with and supports a particular political party—is highly transmitted through families. Families provide, after all, the first source of political information for those who are seeking out information.[46]

    Schools often intentionally play a role in political socialization through processes of **civic education** that aim to introduce students to politics and help them develop the ability to interpret and make sense of this knowledge.[47] Civic education can also transmit civic norms, such as the importance of being civically involved.[48] As spaces of learning and community, schools are also important for their ability to create a political climate, introduce students to opportunities for political participation, and introduce political

party identification
the degree to which an individual identifies with and supports a particular political party.

civic education
the transmission of information about the political world and civic norms to learners.

In an exercise in civic education, students at Koch Elementary School in St. Louis, Missouri, participate in a vote on the lunch menu in November 2014.

AP Photo/St. Louis Post-Dispatch, Robert Cohen

learners to other students whose diverse lived experiences might reinforce or challenge the civic understandings that students bring into the classroom.[49] Families inform political learners first, then schools and educational experiences leave their mark. As such, an individual's civic education does not occur on a blank canvas but one that has already been at least partially painted by his or her upbringing.

Personal Experience and Lived Events

Individual political opinions are never set in stone. While families, schools, and peers play important but different roles in our political socialization, so do later experiences in life. Our interactions in daily life may also shape our opinions on both individual and national levels, especially in times of crisis.

The effects of national events and crises on opinions and attitudes work on a very individual level and are filtered by the lenses and lived experiences through which people make sense of things. In the weeks and months following the shooting of Michael Brown, individuals across the nation began to take a greater interest in politics and policy and became more informed and involved. One of the individuals attending a protest march at the end of August was forty-four-year-old Ian Buchanan. According to a reporter for the *St. Louis Post-Dispatch*, Buchanan, "a former principal in the St. Louis and Normandy school districts, drove to Ferguson from his home in Memphis, Tenn., to attend Saturday's march. 'I came here because I want to be part of the spirit of the movement,' he said. He spent part of the day talking to his former students about how to voice their concerns about injustice. 'The older generation usually wants to write off the younger generation, but to effect change, it comes from the young people,' Buchanan said."[50]

On Election Day, November 4, 2014, McCluer High School senior Victor Sy woke up before dawn to volunteer at the polling place at the First Presbyterian Church of Ferguson. The Brown shooting had inspired Sy and other students studying government to become more involved in the election process. "I wanted to have the experience," Sy said.[51] Another article in the *Post-Dispatch* quoted teacher Mike Baxter as saying, "In previous years when the St. Louis County Election Board has asked for student volunteers, a handful of students would sign up. This year, 26 participated, some because of recent events in Ferguson."[52]

New Perspectives, Technologies, and the Shaping of Public Opinion

American public opinion, the tools with which it is measured, and the technologies through which it is expressed and understood are not frozen in time. In many ways, political scientists are always trying to keep up with change in how we understand, think about, and measure public opinion. Technology and research continually change the ways in which social scientists have theorized about the sources of American public opinion—for example, one group of political scientists has even found evidence that genetically inherited characteristics play a role in shaping political attitudes and ideologies.[53] Advancements in technology have also changed the ways in which opinion is measured, analyzed, and understood. In the interconnected, live, and unfiltered world of social media, Ferguson made this clear.

After Michael Brown's death, Ferguson police chief Thomas Jackson was concerned how social media might influence future events. Recounting his arrival at the scene of the shooting, Jackson noted that a large crowd was gathering and that people were filming the scene with their cell phones. "One reason I thought this might light up is social media," he said. "It's like poison."[54]

On this, at least, Jackson was correct: Following the death of Brown and the decision of the grand jury not to indict Wilson, social media did indeed light up. According to an article in the *Washington Post*, "'Black Twitter' . . . emerged as a powerful forum for activism and debate regarding Ferguson, helping sway public opinion by challenging racially biased interpretations of Brown's killing."[55] In defending the decision of the Ferguson Police Department not to initially release Wilson's name to the public, a lawyer who had represented other officers in police shootings cited the risks posed by social media and the Internet: "If you have any social media presence, I can get a picture of you. I can find out where you live. . . . I can follow you home. This threat now extends to whoever you live with. And that's why these things don't get released."[56]

On August 12, 2014, Ferguson City Hall's Web site went dark and the phones died. A hacker group, Anonymous, took credit and made a threat via a video posted on Twitter: "We're watching you very closely. If you abuse, harass or harm the protesters in Ferguson we will take every Web-based asset of your departments and federal agencies offline."[57] Demanding the release of Wilson's name, which had not happened at that point, Anonymous "posted a photo of [St. Louis County police chief] Belmar's house. . . . Then came the photos, all allegedly portraying his family: His son, asleep on a couch. His wife and daughter, arm-in-arm. He and his wife together. 'Nice photo, Jon,' TheAnonMessage added. 'Your wife actually looks good for her age.'"[58]

American public opinion in the twenty-first century is more instantaneously shapeable than has ever been possible. Social media allows, in theory, a national conversation between people of very different lived experiences and political attitudes. After Ferguson, however, it became quickly clear that social media did not have the power to change the divide, to change the national conversation.

Badges, including one proclaiming "Justice for Michael Brown," worn by a voter in Ferguson, Missouri, on Election Day, November 4, 2014.
REUTERS/Whitney Curtis

Patterns of American Public Opinion: Partisan Identification, Individual and Group Identities, and Elites

As we have seen, families, schools, and events (either over the course of a lifetime or extraordinary and focusing ones) play a major role in shaping public opinion. But other factors play important roles as well. How we identify politically, as well as how we define ourselves in term of gender, race, or ethnicity, can form clear, consistent, and persistent patterns of similarity and division in American public opinion.

Partisan Identification

One of the single most effective predictors of public opinion is an individual's identification with a political party. Americans' response to Ferguson was no different. On the question of whether or not local law enforcement agencies could be trusted to administer the

NEWS CLIP
Debate regarding gay marriage in Florida

laws of the nation impartially and without regard to racial and ethnic identity, Americans were sharply divided according to the political parties to which they attached themselves.

An ongoing debate among political scientists who study American political parties and elections has been about the sources of **partisan polarization** in Congress. Members of Congress are increasingly voting with members of their own party. Why? It is not clear if this trend represents an increasingly polarized environment among political elites, political masses, or both, or if some other factor or factors are at play.[59]

Of all of the questions that Ferguson raised, one central one was this: Is America a nation divided? For many Americans this was not the first time this question had arisen, but for many others it was something new.

Patterns of division between Americans over Brown's death and the protests that followed became clear very quickly. One of those splits, not surprisingly, was related to respondents' party identification. In a survey of one thousand adults in the week following the shooting, the Pew Research Center observed that while 61 percent of respondents who self-identified as Republicans thought that race was getting too much attention in the media coverage, 68 percent of Democrats thought that the shooting raised important issues about race in American society (Figure 7.4).[60]

partisan polarization

when an individual's stance on a given issue, policy, or person is more likely to be strictly defined by their identification with a particular political party (e.g., Democrat or Republican) or ideology (e.g., liberal or conservative).

FIGURE 7.4

Partisan Divisions in Public Opinion about Ferguson

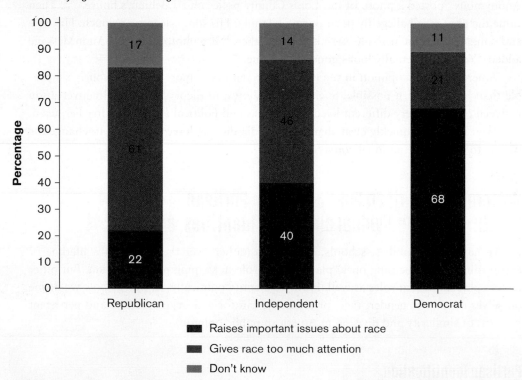

Percent Saying Police Shooting of African-American Teen . . .

- Raises important issues about race
- Gives race too much attention
- Don't know

Source: Data are from Pew Research Center, "Stark Racial Divisions in Reactions to Ferguson Police Shooting," August 18, 2014, http://www.people-press.org/files/2014/08/8-18-14-Ferguson-Release.pdf.

Gender

American public opinion is also often divided along gender lines. On many issues, such as comparative levels of spending on social welfare programs versus national defense, polls have consistently found differences between men and women. These differences in opinion are translated into differences in support for American political parties. The term **gender gap** refers to the fact that American women are more likely to identify with and vote for Democratic Party candidates than men, who are more likely to vote for Republican Party candidates (Figure 7.5).

gender gap
a term that refers to the fact American women are more likely to identify with and vote for Democratic Party candidates than men, who are more likely to vote for Republican Party candidates.

Racial and Ethnic Identity

American public opinion is also often divided on the basis of racial and ethnic identity. Members of American racial and ethnic minorities emphasize the importance of social justice and equality of opportunity more than white Americans,[61] patterns that are correlated with the fact that racial and ethnic minorities are more likely to experience economic challenges and poverty.[62] In addition, scholars of race and gender in American politics have found evidence to support the notion of **linked fate**, in which individuals accept "the belief that [their own] life chances are inextricably tied to the group as a whole."[63]

In the days following the shooting in Ferguson, public opinion surveys revealed sharp racial divisions on the event. African Americans overwhelmingly felt that Brown's

linked fate
a theory of group identification that describes ways in which individuals tie their own life chances to those of a group.

FIGURE 7.5

The Gender Gap in American Politics

Percent identifying as Democratic or leaning Democratic in Pew Research Center polls.

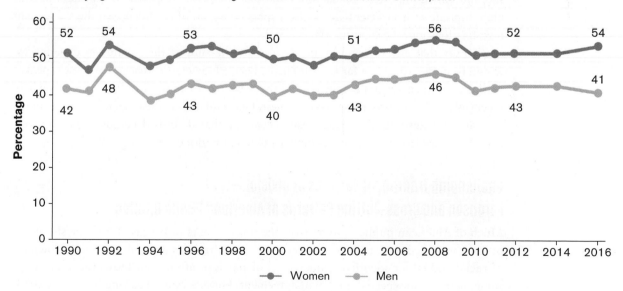

Note: Annual totals based on registered voters.

Source: Pew Research Center, "The Gender Gap: Three Decades Old, as Wide as Ever," March 29, 2012, http://www.people-press.org/2012/03/29/the-gender-gap-three-decades-old-as-wide-as-ever/. Pew Research Center, "Party Identification Trends," 1992-2016, http://www.people-press.org/2016/09/13/party-identification-trends-1992-2016/.

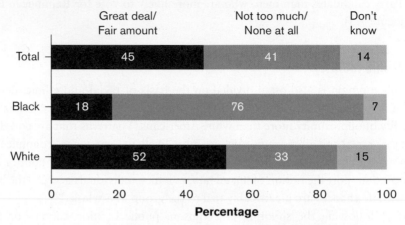

FIGURE 7.6

Racial and Ethnic Divisions in Opinions of Authorities' Handling of the Ferguson Investigation

How much confidence in shooting investigations . . .

	Great deal/Fair amount	Not too much/None at all	Don't know
Total	45	41	14
Black	18	76	7
White	52	33	15

Note: Survey conducted August 14–17, 2014. Whites and blacks include only those who are not Hispanic. Figures may not add to 100% because of rounding.

Source: Pew Research Center, "Stark Racial Divisions in Reactions to Ferguson Police Shooting," August 18, 2014, http://www.people-press.org/files/2014/08/8-18-14-Ferguson-Release.pdf

shooting raised important racial issues and that the police response to the shooting was inappropriate or insufficient. They also expressed a lack of confidence in the subsequent investigations into the shooting (Figure 7.6).[64]

To say that any community (as defined by the sum of their common experiences) would be united would be far too simplistic. Bernie Frazier, an African American speaker and career strategist from Ferguson, told the *New York Times*, "I've had moments where I feel violated by the protesters. To be honest, I feel violated by the media. I read a headline that said, 'Ferguson under siege.' I saw an article that described Ferguson as 'impoverished.' I've just stopped reading comments online. I'm done."[65]

Challenging Traditional Patterns of Division: Ferguson and Cross-Cutting Patterns of American Public Opinion

Much of American public opinion over the tragic events in Ferguson and the shootings of other unarmed African American men in the country was divided, whether along lines of racial and ethnic identity, gender, age, or partisan affiliation. However, there were some, perhaps unexpected, points of agreement. For example, speaking in August 2014, Senator Rand Paul (R-KY) criticized the changes in local law enforcement techniques, equipment, and mentality as surplus weapons from America's wars in the Middle East found their way back home: "Washington has incentivized the militarization of local police precincts by using federal dollars to help municipal governments build what are essentially small armies—where police departments compete to acquire military gear that goes far beyond what most Americans think of as law enforcement."[66] In his efforts to scale back the provision of surplus military equipment to local law enforcement agencies, Paul, a Republican, was joined by Representative Hank Johnson of Georgia, a Democrat.

Some surveys of American public opinion complicated the debate over police community relations. A 2012 survey by the Pew Research Center concluded that 48 percent of Americans agreed with the statement "Guns do more to protect people than place them at risk." In a similar survey in December 2014, the number of Americans agreeing with that statement had increased to 57 percent. Most strikingly, "The shift [in agreement] was even more substantial among African-Americans, going from 29 percent in early 2013 to 54 percent [in 2014] (though with a margin of error of almost 10 percent due to small sample size)."[67] Critics of the poll, however, questioned the wording of the survey items, suggesting that the pollsters may have shaped their findings by the way in which they posed the questions. Reverend Kenn Blanchard, author of *Black Man with a Gun: Reloaded,* countered critiques of the Pew findings by claiming the emergence of "a generational shift in the black community, where all of the old heads say this [pro-gun] stuff is the devil [but] the new guys are, like, 'I don't think so.' . . . There's a racial divide, too, that the anti-gun people have been using to suggest that white people don't want black people to have firearms. But what I see are my white brothers, the old geezers, who are saying to the younger black generation, 'Here's a gun, I'll show you how to shoot it.'"[68]

In spite of these cross-cutting trends, many divisions remained. In a survey conducted in December 2014 following the grand jury decisions in the prosecutions of the police officers involved in the shooting deaths of Brown and Garner, analysts with the Pew Research Center found sharp divisions between white and African American respondents on their agreement with the assertion that race had played a factor in the grand juries' decisions not to charge the officers.[69]

WHAT HAVE I LEARNED?

1. Partisan polarization has decreased in Congress in recent decades.

   a. True
   b. False

2. The *gender gap* in American politics refers to the fact that _____.

   a. Republican Party voters outnumber Democratic Party voters
   b. The number of women representatives and senators has been decreasing in recent decades
   c. Women voters in American elections tend to support candidates from the Democratic Party in state and national elections
   d. Women voters in American elections tend to support candidates from the Republican Party in state and national elections

3. Contributors to the processes of political socialization include _____.

   a. Families
   b. Schools
   c. Lived experiences
   d. All of the above

4. When you reflect upon the events of Ferguson, what divisions in American public opinion do you observe? What might be some issues or perspectives not apparent from these divisions?

   Answer Key: 1. b; 2. c; 3. d; 4. Answers will vary. Students might focus on ideas such as linked fate or differences in opinion about police-community relations.

FERGUSON AND THE EFFECTS OF PUBLIC OPINION ON DEMOCRATIC REPRESENTATION

In 2015, on the one-year anniversary of Michael Brown's death, the city of Ferguson was once again witness to protest and then violence. New reports noted, "A peaceful day of protest and remembrance dissolved into chaos late Sunday after shots were fired and one person was hit by gunfire."[70] In that sense, the two Fergusons, the day and night Fergusons, had not changed in the year since Brown's tragic death.

The police response *had* changed, however. As reported by the *New York Times*, "No police officers in riot gear emerged Friday night when protesters arrived, a tactic that has drawn criticism. Rather, a small handful of officers calmly walked out and spoke with demonstrators. Many of the Ferguson police on the scene wore white polo shirts rather than their regular uniforms."[71]

Political leaders and candidates for the 2016 presidential election were paying attention to the protests. They began to talk about Ferguson and what it meant for the nation going forward. During the first Democratic Party presidential candidate debate in October 2015, one of the invited members of the public asked, "My question for the candidates is, do black lives matter, or do all lives matter?" Senator Bernie Sanders (I-VT) immediately replied, "Black lives matter," and the crowd applauded.[72] When pressed by a moderator, Maryland governor Martin O'Malley "expressed solidarity with the phrase."[73] Both Sanders and O'Malley had been confronted with public disruptions on the campaign trail challenging them to be more outspoken in their support for criminal justice reform.[74]

Though moderator Anderson Cooper had changed the topic when he interacted with former Secretary of State and former Senator Hillary Clinton, she brought the conversation back to criminal justice reform, saying, "What we need to be doing is not only reforming criminal justice—I have talked about that at some length, including things like body cameras. . . . But I believe that the debate, and the discussion has to go further. . . . We need a New Deal for communities of color."[75] Following the debate, members of Black Lives Matter were encouraged by the attention and conversation but wanted more specifics about how each candidate would make the words a reality.

Members of Congress were paying attention as well. In January 2015, as reported by the *St. Louis Post-Dispatch*, "On the eve of the Martin Luther King holiday, leading black members of Congress squeezed into a packed Ferguson church to deliver a specific message: We've got your backs. . . . There, they vowed to push for criminal justice reform."[76] The article quoted Representative Andrew Carson (D-IN), who said, "We're not here to tell you what to do . . . (but) just to let you know you've got some firepower in Washington, D.C. Ferguson is a clarion call. Ferguson is the new Selma."[77] In August the *St. Louis Post-Dispatch* reported that "prominent Ferguson protesters announced on

Protestors prepared to march in downtown St. Louis on August 10, 2015, to mark the one-year anniversary of Michael Brown's death. The police response to the march was markedly different from previous protests and was much more measured and low key.
REUTERS/Rick Wilking

Friday Campaign Zero, a policy platform to end killings by the police in the United States, and a website to help voters keep track of where political candidates stand on police brutality."[78] Political science professor Terry Jones, an expert on urban politics and policies interviewed for the article, said, "This is an effort to put some policy meat on the protest bones and say, 'We're not simply for or against that, but here's what our policies would look like.' . . . It's an appropriate evolutionary step. Anyone who says 'I don't think the world is right as it is' should be prepared to answer the question, 'Well, what do you want to do about it?'"[79]

WHAT HAVE I LEARNED?

1. One year after the first protests in Ferguson, national political candidates were paying more attention to the treatment of African American men by law enforcement officials.

   a. True
   b. False

2. On the one-year anniversary of Michael Brown's death, Ferguson police responded to protests by:

   a. Banning further demonstrations.
   b. Keeping a lower profile.
   c. Trying to intimidate the crowd.
   d. Refusing to keep order.

3. On the one-year anniversary of Michael Brown's death, what appeared to have changed? What may not have changed?

4. What do the results of public opinion surveys tell us about these potential changes?

Answer Key: 1. a; 2. b; 3. Answers might emphasize the fact that the underlying issue had not gone away but that attitudes had changed and people now felt the need to pay more attention to the concerns raised by the protesters.; 4. Answers should focus on an apparent break in trend, both in black and white opinion.

Change in American Public Opinion after Ferguson

In public opinion polls conducted by the Pew Research Center and the *Washington Post* in 2009, 2011, and March 2014, the percentage of Americans who agreed that the nation had "made the changes needed to give blacks equal rights with whites" did not change much. In each poll, a slight majority of Americans expressed the opinion that the nation had made these changes. Individual attitudes, however, diverged sharply by racial identity. A majority of white Americans felt that the nation had made the necessary changes, but the vast majority of African American survey respondents felt that it had not.

Majority Says Nation Needs to Make Changes to Give Blacks Equal Rights

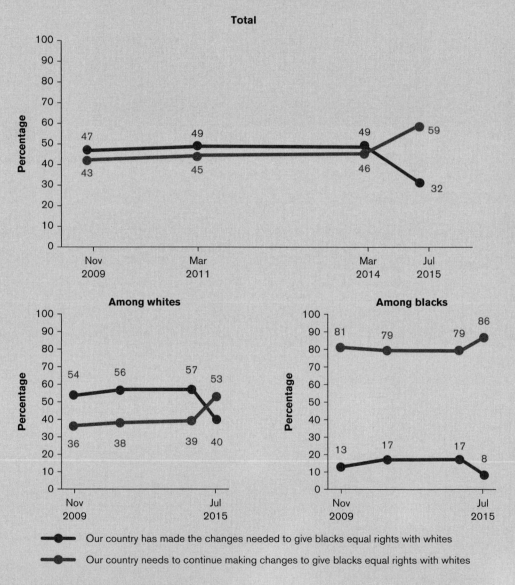

Our country has made the changes needed to give blacks equal rights with whites

Our country needs to continue making changes to give blacks equal rights with whites

Note: Survey conducted July 14–20, 2015. Whites and blacks include only those who are not Hispanic.

Source: Pew Research Center, "Across Racial Lines, More Say Nation Needs to Make Changes to Achieve Racial Equality," August 5, 2015, http://www.people-press.org/2015/08/05/across-racial-lines-more-say-nation-needs-to-make-changes-to-achieve-racial-equality/.

By the late summer of 2015, however, something appeared to have changed.[80] Between the polls conducted in March 2014, six months before Brown's shooting, and July 2015, nearly a year after, there was what political scientists call a *break in trend*, and a sharp one at that. In the 2015 survey, the percentages of Americans surveyed who felt that the nation had done enough to achieve equal rights had changed overall and for both groups of Americans.

However, when drawing conclusions about the causes of this change in public opinion—including if Ferguson caused this change—some caution is warranted. Other events between the 2014 and 2015 surveys may have contributed to the observed findings. A debate about the display of Confederate flags, for example, also made it onto the national political agenda during this time, as did more shootings and tragic events. We cannot, based on these data alone, confirm that Ferguson *caused* this change, only that there is a potentially meaningful *correlation* between the two. That said, this change in American public opinion, how quickly it happened, and how substantial it was are not things to be quickly dismissed.

WHAT DO YOU THINK?

Do these results lead you to conclude that the shooting deaths in Ferguson and other cities and the protests in response actually changed American public opinion? What other evidence might you want to make a firmer conclusion?

 # CONCLUSION
The Meanings of Public Opinion

NEWS CLIP
Opinions regarding release of prisoners held by Iran

Political scientist John W. Kingdon once asked, "But what makes an idea's time come?"[81] That is a very good question, and one to which individuals must attend if they are trying to shape laws and policies, to get their voices heard. In terms of public opinion, we might rephrase Professor Kingdon's question: But what makes *a change of public opinion's* time come? And, we might add, does it even matter if public opinion changes at all?

Reflecting upon Ferguson and other protests inspired by Black Lives Matter, one thing has changed, and that is the list of issues on the national political agenda. To that list has been added the treatment of African Americans, especially young African American men, by the American law enforcement system: "'I live in one of the poorest ZIP codes in Missouri,' said Ferguson protestor Tory Russell in a conference call with reporters . . . adding that fellow African-Americans in the area experience high rates of mortality and murder. 'I never heard any of my elected officials declare those things a state of emergency,' said Mr. Russell, who started the group Hands Up United after Mr. Brown's death to seek justice in Ferguson and beyond."[82]

In this chapter, we have explored debates over the coherence and impact of what we call American public opinion by focusing on one tragic event. While the ultimate effects of the tragedy—as well as the protests and efforts at political mobilization that followed—are not yet certain, at the very least the nation's political conversation has been altered.

In October 2014, "Lesley McSpadden, Mr. Brown's mother, made one of her regular visits to the place where her son was killed. . . . She comes to the memorial all the time, she said, even though visits to the site of her son's death deepen her pain. . . . Gazing down at the memorial, Ms. McSpadden pondered the question of how long it should stay in place. 'Forever,' she said."[83]

Want a better grade?

Get the tools you need to sharpen your study skills. **SAGE edge** offers a robust online environment featuring an impressive array of free tools and resources. Access practice quizzes, eFlashcards, video, and multimedia at **edge.sagepub.com/abernathy1e.**

CHAPTER REVIEW

This chapter's main ideas are reflected in the Learning Objectives below. By reviewing them here you should be able to **remember** the key points, **connect** them to the stories presented in the chapter, **think** about these questions, and **know** these terms that are central to the topic.

7.1 Discuss differing theories about public opinion formation and expression and the degree to which it is meaningful.

REMEMBER...

- Public opinion is characterized as the aggregation of individual beliefs and attitudes.

- Representative democracy depends upon individuals having meaningful preferences on issues. Only when constituents are able to convey meaningful opinions can they can be adequately represented by public officials.

- The minimalist paradigm emphasizes that most people pay minimal attention to issues and have minimal information about them. Additionally, the opinions that they *do* have are minimally stable; they change over time or in response to attempts to control or shape them.

- Other scholars emphasize the ways in which the public can still make sense of and transmit their opinions to their representatives, both collectively and individually. No single individual needs to have fully formed policy preferences and political views because when taken in the aggregate, public opinion is meaningful.

- Still others have emphasized the possibility for a public to be collectively rational even in the presence of individually inconsistent and shapeable opinions.

CONNECT...

- The 2014 fatal shooting of Michael Brown, a young unarmed African American man, by white police officer Darren Wilson galvanized the community of Ferguson, Missouri—and communities across the nation—to protest the treatment of African Americans by law enforcement agencies.

THINK...

- What are some of the challenges in identifying what we can meaningfully conclude from measures of public opinion?

- What are some contrasting perspectives on the coherence of mass public opinion?

KNOW...

- *consideration* (p. 234)
- *elites* (p. 232)
- *masses* (p. 232)
- *minimalist paradigm* (p. 231)
- *nonattitudes* (p. 232)
- *public opinion* (p. 227)
- *stereotype* (p. 231)

7.2 Describe the issues involved in surveying American public opinion and constructing the instruments used to do so.

REMEMBER...

- Even when people's opinions are well informed or when enough opinions are sampled to make them meaningful in aggregate, the instruments used to measure opinion can themselves be flawed, making survey results not meaningful.

- When poorly constructed or deliberately flawed, public opinion surveys can shape survey results and thus deliver misleading findings.

- In some cases, people are unwilling to admit a lack of information or opinion and so make up responses to survey questions.

- The way questions are ordered and worded can also affect survey results.

CONNECT...

- As residents of Ferguson and other communities in which young men of color were killed by law enforcement officers reacted, protested, and expressed their anger, it quickly became clear that opinions about treatment of racial minorities by law enforcement officials were often intense and salient. These opinions, however, were sharply divided by race, ethnicity, age, and partisan affiliation.

THINK...

- What are different methods used to gauge public opinion?

- What issues might arise when designing surveys and questionnaires?

KNOW...

- *public opinion surveys* (p. 232)
- *direction* (p. 235)
- *intensity* (p. 235)
- *stability* (p. 235)
- *salience* (p. 235)

- *push poll* (p. 244)
- *question order* (p. 243)
- *race of interviewer effects* (p. 243)
- *question wording* (p. 243)

 7.3 Examine the sources of individual political attitudes and preferences.

REMEMBER...

- Forming and changing political opinions and attitudes is a lifelong process. The process by which our experiences and other personal factors shape our attitudes towards political issues and public policies is called political socialization.

- There are many sources of political socialization.

- Families convey political attitudes and shape party identification.

- Schools deliver political information and values via civic education.

- People's personal life experiences affect their views.

- Gender, race, and ethnic identity also affect people's attitudes.

- On some issues we see opinions that cut across identities.

CONNECT...

- Public opinion polling revealed sharp racial divisions in perceptions of Michael Brown's killing and the protests that followed.

THINK...

- What factors contribute to the formation of individual political attitudes and preferences?

- How have new communications tools, such as social media, altered the ways in which individuals form political attitudes and preferences?

KNOW...

- *political socialization* (p. 245)
- *party identification* (p. 245)

- *civic education* (p. 245)

7.4 Assess patterns of American public opinion over time and between different groups.

REMEMBER...

- Political knowledge is predictably and unequally distributed. Younger Americans, women, lower-income Americans, and members of racial and ethnic minorities have consistently fared worse in their answers to factual political knowledge questions.

- How we identify politically, as well as how we define ourselves in term of gender, race, or ethnicity, can form clear, consistent, and persistent patterns of similarity and division in American public opinion.

CONNECT...

- Patterns of division emerged in public opinion polling following the events in Ferguson, showing divisions based on party identification.

THINK...

- What are some traditional patterns in the connection between political attitudes and individuals' lived experiences?

KNOW...

- *gender* gap (p. 249)
- *linked fate* (p. 249)
- *partisan polarization* (p. 248)

7.5 Reflect upon the role, possibilities, and dangers of modern public opinion gathering in the United States.

REMEMBER...

- Americans need to be able to communicate their preferences to government, and their representatives need mechanisms that allow them to learn what those preferences are.

- Individuals can communicate directly with representatives, but people who do so tend to represent subgroups with intense preferences rather than the constituency as a whole.

- Elections give representatives information about the public's views. But since not all eligible voters do vote, that information is imperfect.

- Sometimes elected officials solicit the public's views directly through mechanisms such as focus groups.

- Types of surveys include straw polls, self-selected listener opinion polls, and exit polls.

- In order to achieve random selection in polling, surveyors often reach individuals via telephone using random digit dialing.

THINK...

- What are the advantages and disadvantages of different tools used to assess individuals' opinions and attitudes?

- Why is random sampling so important when constructing a survey?

KNOW...

- *focus group* (p. 239)
- *scientific poll* (p. 240)
- *sample* (p. 241)
- *random selection* (p. 241)
- *respondents* (p. 241)
- *sampling error* (p. 241)
- *straw poll* (p. 241)
- *self-selected listener opinion polls* (SLOP polls) (p. 242)
- *exit poll* (p. 242)
- *random digit dialing* (p. 242)
- *weighting* (p. 241)

7.6 Debate the power of individuals, events, and people's interpretations of events to make lasting change in American politics.

REMEMBER...

- Important events can shape public opinion.

- Individuals may filter their interpretation of these events through lenses such as partisan identification, gender, or racial or ethnic identity.

- How the media portray these events may also play a role in opinion formation and change.

CONNECT...

- The protests in Ferguson appear to have forced the 2016 presidential candidates to take positions on race relations in the United States and put the issue on their agendas.

- Public opinion seemed to have shifted after Ferguson as well.

THINK...

- Did the events in Ferguson lead to meaningful change in American public opinion on the treatment of young African American men by law enforcement officials?

- How might we know if it did or did not?

8 THE MEDIA
New Technologies, Enduring Issues

Americans' knowledge of the political world may be directly learned by going to a school board meeting, talking with a political candidate, or attending a rally or protest. More often, however, it is mediated, filtered through all of the outlets that inform us of political issues. Collectively, this group of news providers is called the **news media,** a broad term that includes newspapers, magazines, radio, television, Internet sources, blogs, and social media postings, all in service of informing or persuading. The word *media* is plural as it refers to a universe of venues and outlets. As we will see, the way those outlets are funded, who their audiences are, and what technological capabilities they possess all shape the presentation, reception, effect, and even the definition of the news.

Modern communications technologies have allowed members of the armed forces to share their experiences with a speed and immediacy never before possible.

Tim Rue/Corbis via Getty Images.

So, what exactly is "the news?" Who are "the journalists?" What do we mean by "the media?" What do changes in the media landscape mean for political representation and participation in the twenty-first century? Today, the pace of change seems mind-bending. Americans are simultaneously witnessing a major decline in daily newspaper readership, the rise of social media, increasingly divisive language in political talk shows, and, in the face of pressure to make themselves heard above all of the noise, the blurring of reporter with entertainer and celebrity.

news media
the variety of sources providing information and covering events, including newspapers, television, radio, the Internet, and social media.

It is hardly newsworthy to state that the American news media is in a period of radical flux. The themes of technology-driven change, partisan politics, capitalism, ownership, trustworthiness, bias, and objectivity are as old as the American media itself. Aren't the changes currently taking place just another step in the news media's evolution? Maybe not. This time, things may just be different.

Underlying all of these changes is one central question: How effective are the news media in shaping Americans' political understandings? Our stories in this chapter, all of which involve coverage of the nation's involvement in the wars in Afghanistan and Iraq in the twenty-first century, will help us come to terms with the implications of these profound changes. We will first read about American soldiers blogging directly from war. Then we will examine a scandal surrounding national television news anchor Brian Williams and his changing accounts of covering the Iraq War. Finally, we will explore comedian Jon Stewart's commentary on what the Williams scandal meant.

By reading this chapter, you will be able to:

8.1 Contrast different political news media sources in the twenty-first century

8.2 Trace the historical development of the American news media

8.3 Discuss changes in the regulation of media ownership and media content

8.4 Evaluate the consequences of the pressure on traditional news outlets to compete for an audience

8.5 Contrast different perspectives on bias in the media and the power of the media to shape political understanding and behaviors

LEARNING OBJECTIVES

 BLOGGING FROM WAR

Soldiers as Journalists

In October 2006, American serviceman Mike Guzman posted an entry to a blog, *The Sandbox,* founded and hosted by *Doonesbury* cartoonist Gary Trudeau. Guzman was posting from a forward operating base (FOB) in Iraq. He wrote,

I wonder if anyone back home in the US has any idea what is really going on here in Iraq. For some reason the media has to change everything to suit someone's interests, and I wonder if they even care about us over here. On this past Memorial Day, one journalist and her cameraman died. CNN ran the story and did about a five-minute piece on her. What made me so mad was that in that same incident a soldier also died, but I guess CNN only had 10 seconds left at the end of the story to say that a soldier had died. I wish they would actually do what they say they are doing and report what is actually happening.[1]

Guzman's blog entry was only one of thousands of blogs, e-mails, messages, and photographs sent from Iraq and Afghanistan by members of the American armed forces. He was posting to what is called a milblog, a weblog through which servicemen, servicewomen, their families, friends, and supporters stay in touch and become informed. Milblog posts inform others what life in the theatre of war is like—boring, maddening, confusing, inspiring, and, at times, terrifying. As one journalist put it, "Milblogs . . . have become a phenomenon of modern warfare. Computer-savvy Americans thrown into combat find solace in sharing their travails and victories, as well as hooking up with similar-minded writers to comment on army life, war, politics and much-missed families. . . . Often ungrammatical and peppered with rough language, the soldiers' accounts challenge reports in the regular media, which many see as over-negative. But others question the positive spin given by their comrades."[2]

Since the beginning of the American Republic, members of the American armed forces have sent word home, their letters traditionally censored by military superiors. What has changed is technology. Telecommunications, the Internet, and social media have provided Americans in combat with instantaneous and interactive communications technologies unprecedented in the nation's history. Their blog entries are not just a new form of "letters from the front." They have become part of a revolution. As we will explore in depth in this chapter, the ways in which the Internet and **social media** have changed coverage of combat is only one part of a redefinition of the American news media itself.

Much of the news content transmitted through social media is generated in traditional ways—previously produced stories, videos, and commentaries linked to on Facebook, posted on YouTube, or tweeted to members of one's social network. Other content, however, is generated by **citizen journalists**, nonprofessionals who cover events, say, through filming them on their cell phones or by providing their own commentaries and analysis. The Internet and modern communications technologies did not create the idea of citizen journalism, but they did provide the ability to capture, report on, and transmit citizen-generated news content more quickly and cheaply than has ever been possible. While citizen journalists operate in a variety of contexts, one of the most extreme is combat and military operations abroad. Some scholars of the news media point to the benefits of its democratization, but others worry that citizen journalists lack the ability to fact-check that large news organizations possess.

Does this type of citizen journalism matter? Take the case of Captain Danjel Bout. After having lost three of his fellow servicemen in combat on one day in 2005 in Baghdad, Iraq, Bout "stifled his grief and remained focused on what seemed to be the longest day of his life. The next day, he let it out. He went to his computer and wrote a detailed and emotional account of the losses in his blog, '365 and a Wakeup.'"[3] To Ward Carroll, the editor of the Web site Military.com, the contributions of Bout and other milbloggers went far beyond personal accounts. He saw them as essential reading for understanding the war: "If you are going to be informed, especially with something so controversial and polarizing as the Iraq War, you need to read one of these blogs along with the *Washington Post* and the *New York Times*."[4]

The provision of news covering combat operations has always been treated differently than that covering a political campaign or other more routine political story. American armed forces personnel have censored soldiers' letters in an effort to prevent the disclosure

social media
forms of electronic communication that enable users to create and share content or to participate in social networking.

citizen journalists
nonprofessionals who cover or document news and events or offer their own analyses of them.

Danjel Bout, known in the blogosphere as "thunder6," shown here in dress uniform. Bout's weblog *365 and a Wakeup* is considered "essential reading" for understanding the Iraq War. An excerpt from February 20, 2005, describes a night raid on Baghdad. U.S. Marines raid a house during a similar action in an area near Baghdad. U.S. and Iraqi soldiers scan Baghdad as they patrol the city.

Courtesy of Danjel Bout.

365 and a Wakeup
BAGHDAD BEFORE THE SURGE

thunder6
I'm a husband, a father, a son, a brother, and a Soldier.

1 FOLLOWING   2 FOLLOWERS   Follow

Search

My Other Accounts
Facebook 835050692

Midnight Caller

When this year started I told myself that I would chronicle this entire year, but every so often making a daily journal becomes difficult. Like today for instance. Yesterday I had to move between 4 bases, help plan some ongoing operations, arrange for the smooth transfer of a big chunk of tax payer funded equipment and conduct a raid. The chain of back to back missions started at 6 am 2 days ago, and ended this morning at just before sunrise. Ouch. As we prepare to take over there are tons and tons of equipment that has to be inventoried, counted and collected. And I am not just talking about budgets, bullets, and vehicles. If it was that easy I would have been done long ago. No, the problem is everything has to be inventoried. Everything. Even stupid useless things that are better off in the trash are counted. I can't even begin to remember how many widgets I have seen that I have no earthly clue how to use. I managed, ith the help of the company XOs (eXecutive Officers), to make sure we are tracking but it took a huge portion of my day. When I finally crashed at 11pm I was pretty much down for the count. So of course Massengale tasked me with an immediate mission that would take all night. I crawled out of bed and reluctantly went to work on something he had failed to do and finished just as the sun was breaking the dusky horizon. As soon as I tried to lay down I was asked to serve as the Battalion representative at a Brigade meeting. I had enough time to shave before stumbling off to a excruciatingly boring meeting. By time I finished the meeting I had to move to several different bases to spot check the XO's work.

I was settling in for a much needed rest when I was asked to take part in a raid. For obvious reasons I can't get into specifics, but I can tell you a little about how they usually play out. After gaining credible evidence that the insurgents are operating in a certain area we gather amplifying information to confirm or deny the validity of the report. If it is valid we do a "cordon and knock" mission. If you've seen the movie Blackhawk Down you have the basic idea. One team isolates the area, one team goes in to check for bad guys in the target zone. The only difference is we always have to hit several houses, and we know some of them are innocent. So instead of kicking in the doors guns blazing, we ask for permission to search the area. But if the owner did disagree and we believed it was suspicious we would probably just go in anyway. I spent the next several hours preparing my gear for mission. It was black as midnight when we left and the slums of Baghdad looked especially menacing as we shuttled down dimly lit alleys and cratered streets. There was enough light to see by, but our view of the road was limited to how far our headlights could reach. The architecture in most of Baghdad climbs upward 3 to 4 stories, which can make for some very dark alleys and streets. The asphalt seemed like it was cloaking itself in a veil of murkiness in the wilderness beyond our lights. I kept wondering if we would stumble across an IED (Improvised

of information that may endanger operations or place soldiers at risk. Like everything else in the twenty-first century, however, technology has overtaken longstanding policies, forcing military and political leaders to balance the benefits to morale brought by milbloggers with potential threats to operational security should details of operations be unintentionally released.

At the outset of the Iraq War, military commanders "originally gave deployed soldiers access to the Internet in the combat zone in an effort to boost morale."[5] As posts by service personnel to milblogs and other outlets expanded, however, the Department of Defense began to question the limits on expression by these personnel. In April 2005, Lieutenant General John R. Vines issued a policy memorandum that required soldiers to register their Web sites with unit commanders for monitoring, including the posting of photographs.[6] Some legal and constitutional scholars questioned both the constitutionality and appropriateness of these restrictions: "The Department of Defense's milblogging regulations contain several elements that will potentially chill speech. The requirement that milbloggers and website hosts register their blogs with unit commanders has the chilling effect of removing the Internet's anonymity. Milbloggers now know that their unit, location, webmaster name, telephone number and IP address of their blog or website are all on file with their commanders."[7]

Parts of the American armed services tried to embrace the new media reality, acknowledging and complying with army regulations. A captain in the army described the tension between free speech, morale, and operational security, saying, "We don't want to impede soldiers' ability to express themselves, but we must maintain operational security . . . . These are young, Web-savvy soldiers . . . and they blog to release their emotions. It's a huge morale factor. It's also a great benefit to the Army: We know that soldiers are our best spokesmen. People want to hear the story from troops on the ground."[8]

One of the primary complaints made by milbloggers has been of the coverage of the wars in Iraq and Afghanistan by the mainstream media, all of which tend to toe the

Doonesbury and Milbloggers

In his compilation blog, *The Sandbox*, cartoonist Gary Trudeau, the creator of *Doonesbury*, published a comic strip devoted to milblogs and milbloggers.

Read the cartoon above carefully, and pay attention to the turn the cartoon takes in the final panel.

WHAT DO YOU THINK?

What do you think Trudeau is trying to convey about milbloggers? How does he use humor to reinforce deeper points about blogging from combat or the wars in Iraq and Afghanistan?

same line and convey the same sellable narrative. For example, in the run-up to the first Iraqi elections, most of the major media outlets were skeptical that the elections would be successful and occur without widespread violence. In contrast, milbloggers such as Captain Jason Van Steenwyk were "pretty optimistic. The people who weren't surprised when the elections went off as well as they did were the soldiers and the Iraqi people."[9] Many milbloggers at the time asserted that they were filling a gap in the mainstream press coverage of the wars. To John Upperman, a milblogger and officer in the Texas Army National Guard, posting in 2005, "There is no way the media can cover the story to the same extent that bloggers do, We live it every day and therefore bring a very unique perspective."[10]

Comments and posts by Upperman and others at the time reflected more than just dissatisfaction with the mainstream media's coverage of their efforts and challenges— dissatisfaction with *how* their stories were being told on the other side of the world. Many also spoke to dissatisfaction with *what* stories were or were not being told. And so they took advantage of the technologies available to them in order to change this.

As the wars progressed, the American military chain of command changed its stance on milbloggers once again, opening up opportunities for soldiers to blog but with close supervision to ensure operational security: "Only a few short years ago, the Pentagon seemed unnerved by what its creatively inspired young service members were posting online, citing concerns about operational security and the rough and uncensored reality of combat stories. But the military has altered course . . . and now it offers bloggers regular access for interviews with top officials, reflecting the changing role of both 'new media' and public affairs."[11] Adapting to the techniques of enemy combatants in the theatre was not the only challenge facing American policymakers and leaders of the armed forces. Their service personnel had become journalists and, in many cases, widely followed ones at that.

Much of the power of social media lies in the immediacy and interactivity of the experience. Not only does social media allow instantaneous or near-instantaneous coverage, it also allows individuals to "report" on events in a very personal way. Perhaps nothing can illustrate the immediate impact of social media in reporting and responding as much as a post by Sergeant Dan Gazelka from Minnesota, writing from Iraq's Anbar Province on his blog, *Bleeding the Valve* (as reported by the *Minneapolis Star Tribune*):

> "We were on bridge sweep yesterday (going under and around the bridge to check for anything that goes boom). I was on top of the bridge in the gunner seat."
>
> A car approached. Gazelka waved a warning flag, but the intruder didn't slow.
>
> "I picked up my flare and fired. . . . Misfire. I fired again and it shot towards the car. The car sped up!
>
> He's not stopping! I pulled up my M-16 and shot three rounds. Left, Right-Right, 'Pop, Pop, POP!' Last round kicked up dirt 5 feet to the front-right of his tire! He still wasn't stopping. . . . I've gotta kill him!
>
> Squeezing trigger . . .
>
> SCREEEEEEEEECH!!!
>
> At the very last possible second the driver locked up his brakes, leaving two streaks of smoking black rubber. Thank God for both our sakes that he stopped just in time."
>
> *Soon after that post goes up, a reader in Bemidji [Minnesota] posts a response, her shaky fingers fumbling her spelling:*
>
> "Thank you, Jesus.
>
> -Mom."[12]

In the history of the American news media and in the history of American combat, communication like this has never been possible until now. A mother has typically not been looped in on her child's very recent brush with death in combat. For some milbloggers, the goal was to connect to family, friends, and fellow members of the armed forces. For others, it was an attempt to bypass the mainstream news outlets, to get their stories out in ways that they felt were not happening through other media outlets. Technology made all of this possible; their drive made it real. There is no doubt that the twenty-first century revolution in communications technologies has changed the landscape of the delivery of political news and opinion. What is still being figured out, however, is what all of these changes mean to representation in the American Republic.

We often hear that Americans' attention spans are incredibly short. Certainly the stories we are covering in this chapter might seem far in the past by the standards of today's social media. At the time of this writing, the vast majority of American soldiers have left Iraq and Afghanistan, their milblogs shuttered. The major controversy we will discuss surrounding the coverage of the wars by a major television news network has faded into the background, also lost in the seemingly endless stream of data, image, text, and analysis. And one of the most successful television hosts of the twenty-first century has retired, his departure having been treated in many ways as the loss of a respected news anchor rather than that of a comedian. The fleeting nature of news media today is itself an important point to hold on to. However, the questions that the stories in this chapter raise in terms of the American political news media are timeless: Where do we get the information that we need to act in representative democracy? Can we trust our sources? And trust them to do what—provide us with unbiased coverage of the "news?" Get our attention so that we will consume their news products? And who controls all of this? Journalists, corporations, government, consumers? To get a better read on the present, once again, we first go back to the past.

CONNECTING TO . . .

The American News Media Past and Present

As you read about the development of the American news media, reflect back upon the efforts of milbloggers in Iraq and Afghanistan in the twenty-first century. Consider the following:

*   The ways in which technological innovation has driven changes in American news media coverage, content, and delivery

*   The changing relationship between the American news media, partisan politics, and the concept of objectivity

THE DEVELOPMENT OF THE AMERICAN NEWS MEDIA

From before the country's founding to today, the news media have played an important role in shaping American political culture and Americans' attitudes towards their political leaders and institutions. Throughout this history, the connection between the nation's media and American politics has also been shaped in important ways by technological change, politics, and the tension between the rights of a free press and other demands, especially the desire to preserve national security.

The Print Media, Revolution, and a New Nation

As we explored in Chapter 1, the pamphlet, a loosely stitched booklet made on a hand-cranked printing press, played an important role in shaping colonial public opinion and mobilizing Americans to support the cause of independence from Great Britain. While printing had become cheaper and more widespread in the years leading up to the Revolutionary

War, publishing was far from easy; the British colonial administration recognized the pamphlet for what it was, a potentially powerful and revolutionary tool. According to Patrick Novotny, "Some printers had their presses confiscated by the British while still others hid their presses or fled their homes with their families, taking their presses with them. Others closed their shops before the British could."[13]

With the growth of weekly, and then daily, newspapers in the years following the Revolutionary War, during the time in which the Articles of Confederation united the newly independent states, the newspaper took its place as the primary source for news and coverage of politics. First published in 1783, the *Pennsylvania Evening Post and Daily Advertiser* was the nation's first daily newspaper; its young salesmen instructed to shout out to passersby, "All the news for two coppers."[14] Like the pamphlets, early newspapers were a form of the print media. Like the pamphlets as well, early newspapers were hand printed, one sheet at a time, which made them expensive and restricted their access, even among those who could read them.

Four years later, the nation's second daily newspaper, the *Pennsylvania Packet and Daily Advertiser*, published just blocks away from where the *Evening Post* had started out, was the first to print the full text of the proposed Constitution of the United States. The delegates to the Constitutional Convention, as we explored in Chapter 2, had been very careful to prevent any leaks during the proceedings, thus starving the weeklies and dailies of raw materials for their stories. With the publication of the proposed Constitution, which spurred a flood of editorials for and against the document, newspapers took their place front and center in American political life in the late 1780s.

Freedom of the Press, the Constitution, and the Ratification Debates

With memories of British colonial suppression of freedoms of speech and of the press fresh in their minds, the delegates to the Constitutional Convention were well aware of the need to preserve and protect these freedoms. On August 20, 1787, Charles Pinckney from South Carolina proposed to one of the committees the inclusion of the guarantee, "The liberty of the Press shall be inviolably preserved."[15] While a guarantee of freedom of the press did not end up in the original Constitution, Pinckney's proposal signaled support for including specific rights and liberties in the constituting document. As the ratification debates began, the argument to include such a list became one of the most convincing arguments that the Antifederalists presented.

While the Bill of Rights was not part of the original document, a promise to introduce a set of amendments during the session of Congress in 1789 proved crucial to securing the ratification of the Constitution. Included in the first of the ten ratified amendments was language very close to Pinckney's initial proposal: "Congress shall make no law . . . abridging the freedom of speech, or of the press." This provided the foundation for press freedoms.

The press also played a pivotal role in the ratification debates themselves, as proponents and opponents of the document made their cases through the nation's newspapers, often writing under pseudonyms. The *Federalist Papers*, the classic statement of the theory behind

> *Included in the first of the ten ratified amendments was language very close to Pinckney's initial proposal: "Congress shall make no law . . . abridging the freedom of speech, or of the press."*

A newsboy carrying inexpensive newspapers called penny press runs along a train platform selling papers to passengers. As the cost of printing decreased with technological advances in the process, the price of newspapers also decreased, and readership dramatically increased.

World History Archive/Alamy Stock Photo.

partisan press
media outlets or organizations that promote a particular political ideology or support a political party.

penny press
nineteenth-century American newspapers that sold for only one cent each, thus increasing the size of the audience that could afford to purchase them.

mass media
sources of information that appeal to a wide audience, including newspapers, radio, television, and Internet outlets.

the Constitution, authored by Alexander Hamilton, James Madison, and John Jay, first appeared as a series of essays written under the pseudonym "Publius" in the New York newspapers. For their part, the Antifederalists produced essays warning of the dangers to liberty presented by the proposed Constitution.

The Media Go "Mass": Penny Presses, Partisanship, and Scandal

In the late eighteenth and early nineteenth century, however, the dailies and weeklies only reached a relatively small part of the population, in large part due to the fact that they were expensive and often only available through an annual subscription, which required putting down a large sum of money all at once rather than for each issue. Political and financial elites were the main consumers, not the mass public. Much of the space in newspapers was taken up by advertisements, and the stories' content was often overtly political, a fact that was hardly hidden or a point of controversy. Political parties and candidates often supported the presses financially in addition to providing them with essays, stories, and content.[16] By taking political positions and supporting candidates and parties, these papers were acting as a **partisan press**. The nation's first political parties were backed by partisan press. James Madison and Thomas Jefferson supported the founding of the *National Gazette* in 1791 in response to the partisan coverage presented by the Federalist *Gazette of the United States*.

As the cost to produce, and, therefore, buy a newspaper fell during the 1830s, readership grew rapidly. The **penny press**, so labeled because an individual paper cost one penny, could be purchased on the street from newsboys hawking their products. Within just a few months of its introduction as the nation's first penny press, the *New York Sun* was the city's top-selling paper; by 1834 the *Sun* "was selling 15,000 copies a day."[17] The penny press was truly an example of the **mass media**—sources of information and entertainment (including newspapers, television and radio broadcasts, and Internet content) designed to reach large audiences.

Their content was sometimes overtly political; however, the penny papers depended far less on political parties for funding or support. They had a new boss: the public. Instead of relying on parties, candidates, or politicians for their content, the penny papers had to make their own. To do so, they hired reporters to dig up the kind of stories that would lure readers and advertisers. Newspapers depended on sales and on providing an audience for the advertisers, and so they often focused on dramatic stories of crime, riots, and scandalous behavior.[18] **Yellow journalism**, or the use of sensational headlines, cartoons and graphics, and emotional language, had a very commercial reason behind its emergence. It worked, boosting sales and profits.

Sensationalism was not confined only to stories of crime, misdeeds, and moral failures. In skilled hands, bold headlines, enticing leads, and emotional language could also be put to political purposes. William Randolph Hearst, publisher of the *New York Journal*, harnessed yellow journalism to advocate for war with Spain in the late 1890s. While the Spanish-American War had many causes, Hearst's efforts helped to shape public opinion about the prospect for war. This example of the potential power of the press to influence public opinion raised the specter of a malleable American public at the mercy of presses and publishers with their own political agendas.

Journalists as Investigators and Activists

A faster and cheaper printing press was not the only technological development that shaped the newspaper in the nineteenth century. The telegraph allowed news to travel instantaneously over distances that might have taken days or weeks otherwise. The papers benefitted tremendously from the technology and helped to finance and spread it. In 1846 New York newspapers combined their efforts to fund a pony express route to more quickly deliver news of the Mexican-American War, thus creating the Associated Press.[19] Though the technology that they were originally funding ran on four legs, the Associated Press took advantage of the telegraph to create a **wire service**, an organization that gathers the news and offers it for sale to other media outlets. The nineteenth century also witnessed a new approach to news coverage, **investigative journalism**, in which journalists actively dug up and dug into stories rather than simply conveying the speeches and opinions of political leaders. During the Progressive Era, an important group of investigative reporters became known as *muckrakers*; the name was a reference to a tool used to collect manure. Muckrakers used their investigative tactics to bring to light corruption and scandal and also to shape public opinion in support of business or governmental reforms.[20]

Direct to Americans' Homes: Radio and Television

Technological advances during the twentieth century brought political figures into Americans' lives and homes in a direct way, first providing their voices with the advent and widespread adoption of radio and then adding their faces and actions with television. Radio and television, which are examples of **broadcast media**, offered political news to citizens directly and immediately. Its consumption was often a shared experience, with only one radio or television set in the home or in the neighborhood, and the news could be consumed while doing other things, such as driving, doing chores, working, or eating a meal. These forms of media were also truly mass in the sense of a shared media experience by their consumers. In breaking down geographic barriers, the broadcast media were truly national in scope.

As an instrument of conveying political news, radio really came into its own in the 1930s, and no public official was more adept in its use than President Franklin Delano Roosevelt. Beginning

yellow journalism
an approach to reporting employed in the nineteenth century that relied on sensational headlines and emotional language to persuade readers and sell newspapers.

wire service
an organization that gathers and reports on news and then sells the stories to other outlets.

investigative journalism
an approach to newsgathering in which reporters dig into stories, often looking for instances of corruption or failures to uphold the interests of citizens.

An example of yellow journalism, the sensationalistic coverage by Hearst of the destruction of the USS *Maine* contributed to public support for the decision to declare war on Spain.
The Granger Collection, New York.

President Franklin Delano Roosevelt at a Fireside Chat in 1936. Roosevelt's broadcasts to the nation during times of crisis helped calm a worried population and enabled him to successfully pitch his policies.

Courtesy of the Library of Congress, Prints and Photographs Division.

broadcast media
outlets for news and other content that rely on mass communications technology to bring stories directly into people's homes; these media sources are subject to stricter content regulations than cable television outlets and alternative sources of information.

in March 1933, Roosevelt began broadcasting speeches to the American public; these speeches became known as "Fireside Chats," a term coined by a bureau chief with CBS News, even though there was no fireplace.[21] The broadcasts were designed to calm anxious Americans during the depths of the Great Depression, present Roosevelt's Depression-fighting policies, and, later, guide citizens through the travails of World War II.

Today the nation's radios crackle with political commentary and critiques of the views of the other side of the aisle. Many of these shows lean Republican, such as *The Rush Limbaugh Show*, but there are liberal examples as well. These talk radio broadcasts have been criticized for their efforts to "provoke emotional responses (e.g., anger, fear, moral indignation) from the audience through the use of overgeneralizations, sensationalism, misleading or patently inaccurate information, ad hominem attacks, and belittling ridicule of opponents."[22]

If the 1930s signaled the emergence of radio as a powerful new force in political news, the late 1950s did the same for television. Television's version of Roosevelt was also a president: John F. Kennedy. Even though most American homes had a television set by the 1950s (Figure 8.1), newspapers remained the primary source of news and coverage of political events. In September 1960, candidates Kennedy and Richard Nixon participated in the first of a series of the first televised presidential debates in American history. While experts and radio listeners did not declare a clear winner, Kennedy's image on television came across as robust and energetic, while Nixon, who had been fighting the flu, appeared pallid and sweaty. In 1961 Kennedy, having won the presidency, gave the first live televised news conference.

As television news broadcasts lengthened and more and more Americans relied upon the major networks for their news and coverage of political events, television news anchors became trusted figures in relaying, describing, and interpreting these events. As the Vietnam War progressed, American casualties mounted, and protests against American involvement spread and grew, trusted television journalist Walter Cronkite questioned if the war had become unwinnable. It was widely reported that President Lyndon Johnson observed, "If I've lost Cronkite, I've lost Middle America"—or some variation thereof.[23] Though this response may be apocryphal, the idea that a trusted news anchor could so strongly affect American public opinion in an area as vital as foreign policy speaks to the power that many attributed to television news anchors during the heyday of network news.

The 1990s witnessed the rise of a new outlet for television and television news, and its emergence as a major player came about during wartime. First broadcasting in 1980, CNN, the Cable News Network, presented Americans with twenty-four-hour coverage of the news. CNN had gained prominence for its coverage of the 1986 space shuttle *Challenger* disaster, which killed all seven crewmembers aboard, but it was the network's coverage of the Persian Gulf War that truly placed it on the news media map. In 1991 CNN broadcast video coverage of the bombing of Baghdad by American and coalition forces during the war live, in real time, and unconstrained by a set news broadcast schedule such as those typically employed by the major broadcast networks.

The American political news media had broken the clock. They had gone 24/7, and America tuned in. Later that decade, in 1996, Australian media entrepreneur Rupert Murdoch launched Fox News, which provided a self-consciously conservative interpretation of the nation's news and political events. Americans who felt that network news coverage was too liberal tuned in.

Cable television news changed more than just the schedule of coverage; it changed the form itself. Operating under looser regulatory constraints than the broadcast networks, and in a time when those constraints were being relaxed (see below), television news became more avowedly partisan, less "objective." To some, this overt partisanship seemed like a new and dangerous thing. In fact, it was not new at all—questions of the objectivity of network news had long been a common source of commentary and conversation. Cable television news coverage became more like what newspapers had been during much of the nation's history: unapologetically partisan.

A screenshot of CNN correspondent Bernard Shaw reporting on the bombing of Baghdad, Iraq, via satellite phone on the first night of the Gulf War, January 16, 1991. The network's strategy for round-the-clock news coverage established a new pattern for how the news was covered.

CNN via Getty Images.

The New Media: "The Revolution Will Be Posted"[24]

And then there was the Internet, broadband and wireless delivery, and the rise of social media. Quite possibly, there is some Web site or blog out there that asserts that the Internet was created by cats in a secret conspiracy to dethrone dogs as the house pet of choice. While there are literally an uncounted number of cat videos and photoshopped cat pictures peppering the new technology, the Internet was in fact developed and deployed though a collaboration between the United States Defense Department's Advanced Research Projects Agency (DARPA) and research universities.

The adoption of broadband reception, the Internet, and other communications technologies enabled Americans to receive and send text, sound, and video at increasingly fast speeds and in increasingly large volumes. Broadband and wireless technology has followed an accelerating pattern of adoption of new technologies not entirely different from that of radio and television (Figure 8.1).

These new forms of media communication have revolutionized far more than the speed of delivery, or even the content, of political news available to consumers of the news and politics. In the era of 24/7 news coverage and the merging of entertainment and social media, individuals can be journalists, citizens can be editors and commentators, and members of the media can be—and are often pressured to be—celebrities. Throughout much of the nation's history, most Americans had a limited number of choices in their news media outlets—generally, one or two daily newspapers, several radio stations, and a few major television broadcast networks. The rise of cable television expanded the number of options, then the Internet increased these options even further. The rise of social media put these trends into hyperdrive. However, the story was not only about the rise of *new* media outlets, it was also about the need for *old* media outlets, such as broadcast television, to stay relevant. One strategy was to create a greater presence of traditional network broadcast journalists in other venues and highlight their visibility, even celebrity, in order to reach larger audiences in an age of intense competition.

FIGURE 8.1

Patterns of Adoption of Communications Technologies

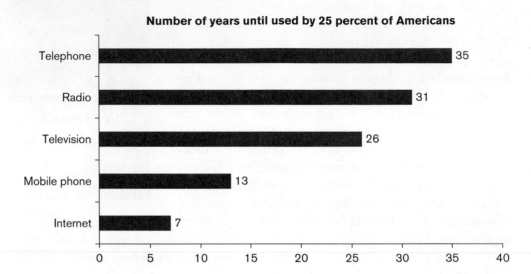

Number of years until used by 25 percent of Americans

Telephone	35
Radio	31
Television	26
Mobile phone	13
Internet	7

Source: Data are from *The Economist*, http://www.economist.com/blogs/graphicdetail/2014/03/daily-chart-7?%3Ffsrc%3Dscn%2F=tw%2Fdc.

The term *new media* is used to refer to all of the various digital platforms through which individuals receive, share, and produce content. In one sense, the new media are examples of mass media. They often reach large audiences, and in many cases do so with startling speed. In another sense, however, there are also aspects to the new media that are very old. They often do not have mass appeal, but cater to a group of individuals with shared perspectives, similar to many cable news channels but even more so. They shatter geographic boundaries, like the mass media but create their own form of fragmentation, providing an opportunity for individuals to self-select into narrow political and informational enclaves. This type of journalism is known as **niche journalism.**

niche journalism
media that caters to fragmented and specialized audiences.

WHAT HAVE I LEARNED?

1. The attempts of media providers to persuade Americans of a particular political point of view is a relatively new phenomenon.

    a. True
    b. False

2. The penny press was important because _____.

    a. It gave equal time to all political viewpoints
    b. It focused only on economic issues, hence the word *penny*
    c. It was financed primarily by political parties
    d. It brought the news to a much larger audience

3. In what ways did radio and television change Americans' reception of the news?

4. How have the new media changed coverage of political news?

Answer Key: 1. b; 2. d; 3. Answers might include a discussion of the role that these media played in standardizing coverage and bringing it directly into Americans' homes.; 4. Answers might include the speed and immediacy of coverage and also the pressure new media has put upon broadcast media outlets to compete and survive in the new media landscape.

REGULATING THE MEDIA
Ownership and Content

Although the media serve, in part, to try to exercise control over elected officials and government employees, the media are themselves subject to regulation and control by the government. While the challenges to effective and fair regulation have often been specific to certain times, places, and technologies, the desire for elected officials to shape the landscape of media coverage has been present for a long time. These efforts have focused primarily on regulating two things: media ownership and media content.

Regulation, Consolidation of Ownership, and Changes in Patterns of Consumption

NEWS CLIP
Expert discusses ethical lapses in Rupert Murdoch's *Wall Street Journal*

With the technological revolutions of radio and television in the twentieth century came demands from both citizens and content providers themselves for the federal government to regulate the broadcast media. The business logic behind these regulations was based on the fact that the nation's radio and television frequencies were finite, like rivers, canals, and grazing lands.[25] Demands to use them, however, were not. From the point of view of publishers and broadcasters, regulations were necessary to prevent "overgrazing," or, in this case, radio stations from wandering onto the electronic lands of others, which happened all too frequently. There were also calls to regulate the morality of the content of the material that beamed directly into American's homes. And there were calls to regulate the political content of radio and television broadcasts to ensure that multiple political viewpoints were all represented.

The Federal Radio Act (1927) established the Federal Radio Commission and required broadcasters to obtain a license to broadcast on specific frequencies in an attempt to try to bring order to "the utter confusion within the broadcasting band" brought about by the technological reality that "the physical capacity of the available channels, or wave lengths, [were] already far exceeded by the number of stations actually in operation."[26] The Communications Act of 1934 expanded the federal role in governing the nation's broadcast media, creating the Federal Communications Commission (FCC) to oversee the implementation of its provisions. National defense was cited as one of the reasons that the FCC was needed as a matter of public policy.

In the latter half of the twentieth century, spiking demand from content providers and marketplace competition, as well as changes in the ways news stories were created and distributed, forced government to rethink the rules governing telecommunications. New legislation was needed to help overcome what was an increasingly messy traffic jam in the nation's telecommunications systems. The Telecommunications Act of 1996 was passed by Congress in order "to let anyone enter any communications business—to let any communications business compete in any market against any other."[27] The act essentially brought deregulation to media ownership, setting in motion a process that led to massive consolidation of media ownership (Figure 8.2). While deregulation might have been expected to increase the diversity of the nation's major news outlets, it had the opposite effect. It led to increasing consolidation as news firms tried to maximize their profits in the face of declining sales on things like printed classified advertisements, long a mainstay of traditional newspaper revenue, made obsolete by the Internet.

The concentration of ownership of major media outlets is not only due to relaxation of regulations. There is also a logic to it. Media outlets largely fund their operations

FIGURE 8.2

Consolidation of Media Ownership

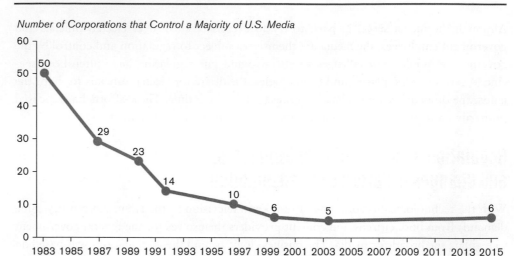

Number of Corporations that Control a Majority of U.S. Media

Source: Modified from Ben H. Bagdikan, *The New Media Monopoly* (Boston: Beacon Press, 2004). Available online at http://www.corporations.org/media/.

through advertising revenue. Advertisers, for their part, want to reach as many consumers as possible. Therefore, media outlets try to expand their reach as far as they can, whether by attracting the largest audiences possible or by purchasing smaller content providers. This has consequences for the content of media coverage as well. Providers may shape their coverage to attract as wide an audience as possible. We will explore the effects of these pressures on news content—and the potential dangers that they pose—later in the chapter.

The twenty-first century has also witnessed a marked decline in consumption of printed newspapers (Figure 8.3). Does that mean overall consumption of *news* has declined? The story is more complicated than that. Traditional papers have gone online, sometimes for free and with advertisements, sometimes behind firewalls that require registration and/or a subscription fee. Nontraditional Internet news sources often get their stories from a process called **aggregating**. In this process, they still rely on the basic reporting that newspaper journalists do, but then they disseminate and comment on the original coverage.

During this era of proliferation of media outlets and the federal government's relaxation of many of the regulations first introduced during the days of radio, and later, television, the question of "who owns the grazing lands?" has not gone away. In fact, with the issue of **net neutrality**, it is still here, only in a somewhat different form. Should companies that provide the highways of the Internet and broadband age be able to charge more to content providers whose "livestock" chew up more bandwidth? The companies say that they should be able to. Critics say that allowing firms to price discriminate based on bandwidth use will stifle the expression of multiple and diverse views.

President Barack Obama has been a vocal advocate for net neutrality, and in June 2016, the D.C. Circuit Court of Appeals, in a 2–1 vote, upheld the FCC's net neutrality rules. Several major telecommunications companies promised to appeal the decision. Net

aggregating

a process through which Internet and other news providers relay the news as reported by journalists and other sources.

net neutrality

a Federal Communications Commission (FCC) rule that requires Internet service providers to treat all data and content providers equally and not discriminate based upon content or bandwidth demands.

FIGURE 8.3

Changes in American Political News Consumption

Main Source for News

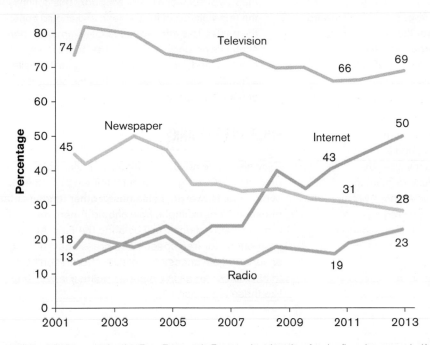

The results of a 2013 survey by the Pew Research Center showing that for the first time, over half of Americans cited the Internet as one of their major sources for national and international news. Respondents were allowed to name up to two sources.

Sources: Andrea Caumot, "12 Trends Shaping Digital News," Pew Research Center, October 16, 2013, http://www.pewresearch.org/fact-tank/2013/10/16/12-trends-shaping-digital-news/, accessed May 12, 2016. "Amid Criticism, Support for Media's 'Watchdog' Role Stands Out" Pew Research Center, Washington, DC (August, 2013) http://www.people-press.org/2013/08/08/amid-criticism-support-for-medias-watchdog-role-stands-out/.

neutrality also came up in the 2016 presidential election. Following the Court's decision, Democratic Party candidate Bernie Sanders tweeted that the ruling "will help ensure we don't turn over our democracy to the highest bidder," while Republican senator Ted Cruz labeled net neutrality "Obamacare for the Internet," referring to the Affordable Care Act's major changes to American health care policy.[28]

Regulating Content: Another Changing Landscape

While the federal government plays only a small role in providing media content—with exceptions such the Corporation for Public Broadcasting, created by Congress in 1967—it has played an important role in regulating its content. The Federal Communications Act (1934) led to the establishment of several rules designed to shape news media content to serve the public at large. On of these, the **equal time rule**, requires licensees to guarantee political candidates equal time to present their views and opinions.

One of the more controversial aspects of the equal time provision is an implicit, and perhaps unintended, incentive for broadcasters to avoid presenting the platforms of candidates at all, for fear of running afoul of the law. According to media and politics scholar Doris A. Graber,

Equal time rule
a regulation that requires American radio and television broadcast networks to provide equal time for political candidates to present their views on issues.

In Defense of Deregulation

In a 2003 article, Wayne Crews from the politically conservative Cato Institute argued in favor of the trend toward deregulation and against concerns over the consolidation of news media that it has led to. His arguments focused on the free flow of information and the limiting effects of governmental effort to shape the media landscape:

> Absent government censorship, there is no fundamental scarcity of information. More information can always be created, and in a free society, nobody can silence anybody else. The most that big media can do is refuse to share their megaphones and soapboxes, which is not a violation of anybody's rights. Real suppression requires governmental censorship, or the actual prohibition of the airing of alternative views.
>
> Ironically, opponents of deregulation feel entitled to commandeer someone else's resources, to limit the size of someone else's soapbox. This action is the true violation of free speech and should concern the public. This effective constraint imposed upon another's property is regarded as acceptable, however, and even laudatory, as long as it is called a "media ownership rule" and has the support of enough politicians.[29]

WHAT DO YOU THINK?

Crews's article advocates for a particular political position: reduced governmental influence on media ownership. However, it also raises other fundamental questions. For example, how should American representative democracy balance the First Amendment's protections for free speech and press against the goal of ensuring equal access to political information? Can you think of other areas in American politics in which tensions like these are present?

---

the equal time provision may act to restrict rather than expand political information as a station may choose not to cover candidates at all, especially those in local races where many candidates are vying for office. She wrote, "This keeps many viable candidates off the air and has led to widespread dissatisfaction with the equal time rule and demands to abandon it."[30]

The rise of social media has also challenged the ability to ensure equal coverage. Political candidates who are also celebrities, for example, can obtain disproportionate attention based on their celebrity status alone. In the 2016 presidential campaign, Republican candidate Donald Trump used his large following on Twitter to obtain coverage without having to purchase as much airtime as other candidates. During the transition period after the election, Trump remained active on Twitter, raising questions about how he would use social media during his presidency.

fairness doctrine
a federal rule that expanded regulations for American political news coverage beyond just the provision of time for candidates to the content of the coverage itself.

The **fairness doctrine**, introduced in 1949, expanded regulations for American political news coverage beyond just the provision of time for candidates to the content of the coverage itself. It required "that every licensee devote a reasonable portion of broadcast time to the discussion and consideration of controversial issues of public importance" and that broadcasters must "affirmatively endeavor to make . . . facilities available for the expression of contrasting viewpoints held by responsible elements with respect to the controversial issues presented."[31] Again, scholars and broadcasters have questioned the unintended consequences of the fairness doctrine. In trying to avoid the appearance of being unfair, political news media providers might decide to play it safe, "to shy away from programs dealing with controversial public issues to avoid demands to air opposing views, in place of regular revenue-producing programs."[32] The fairness doctrine has ceased to be rigorously enforced, partly due to the proliferation of cable television channels and shows, which allow for a wide variety of political viewpoints and coverage.

1. The primary motivation behind the Federal Radio Act (1927) and the Federal Communications Act (1934) was to ensure that _____.

   a. All political viewpoints were equally represented
   b. Broadcasters could be sure that others could not encroach on their channels
   c. Americans of different racial and ethnic backgrounds were included in news coverage
   d. The federal government would receive revenue from broadcasters

2. The primary effect of the Telecommunications Act of 1996 was _____.

   a. A consolidation of ownership of media outlets
   b. The prevention of many cable television outlets from entering the marketplace
   c. Ensuring equal treatment of outlets in access to bandwidth
   d. All of the above

3. What challenges has technological change presented to the relevance and enforcement of the equal time rule and the fairness doctrine?

....

Answer Key: 1. b; 2. a; 3. Answers should discuss the challenges presented by cable television and the Internet to rules originally designed to cover the activities of broadcast media outlets.

MERGING NEWS AND ENTERTAINMENT

Journalists as Celebrities

On March 26, 2003, at the beginning of the Iraq War, *NBC Nightly News* anchor Tom Brokaw introduced a report from the field: "Our colleague, Brian Williams is back in Kuwait City tonight after a close call in the skies over Iraq. Brian, tell us about what you got yourself into."[33]

Williams had accompanied the Bravo 159th Army Aviation Regiment as it lifted sections of steel bridge to a location near Najaf. As footage of the helicopter in which Williams and his film crew were riding appeared, Williams commented in a voice-over, "We're going along for the ride. We are one of four Chinook helicopters flying north this morning, third in line." They passed over a "convoy of American troop carriers" and some civilians, "seemingly happy to see us. . . . But these soldiers have heard reports of Iraqis in civilian clothes firing on American troops. . . . Indeed, just before we're able to make our drop, radio traffic makes clear that this routine mission is running into trouble. . . . On the ground we learn the Chinook ahead of us was almost blown out of the sky," hit by a rocket-propelled grenade (RPG) "fired from the ground . . . though, amazingly, it didn't detonate. . . . The chopper pilots are too shaken to let us interview them."[34] As a sandstorm moved in, members of the 3rd Infantry stayed with Williams and his crew for two nights.

Brian Williams and David Letterman talk about the killing of Osama bin Laden on the *Late Show with David Letterman* on May 2, 2011.
Jeffrey R. Staab/CBS via Getty Images.

Ten years later, the story appeared to have changed. Appearing on *Late Night with David Letterman*, Williams, by then anchor and managing editor of *NBC Nightly News*, offered Letterman a different account: "We were the northernmost Americans in Iraq. We were going to drop some bridge positions across the Euphrates so the 3rd Infantry could cross them. Uh, two of our four helicopters were hit by ground fire including the one I was in. . . . We got hit, and I came away with just more respect, uh, for these men and women. We just got to make sure they get everything they deserve when they come home."[35]

Two years later, a human interest segment at the end of that night's broadcast of *NBC Nightly News* showed Williams reunited with a member of the 3rd Infantry, Command Sergeant Tim Terpack, at a New York Rangers game the night before. "We want to share with you a great moment that took place here in New York last night," Williams said. "The story actually started with a terrible moment a dozen years back during the invasion of Iraq, when the helicopter we were travelling in was forced down after being hit by an RPG. . . . We got to return to our homes and families thanks to him and his men."[36]

When NBC posted the video clip of the Rangers event to Facebook, flight engineer Lance Reynolds, who asserted that he was on the helicopter that got hit—a helicopter travelling far ahead of the one Williams was in—posted his response.

In the controversy surrounding Williams's comments, it was a traditional newspaper that played a key role in breaking the story. *Stars and Stripes*, a paper dedicated to stories of interest to members of the armed forces, their families, and others, posted an interview of Williams conducted by reporter Travis Tritten in which Williams admitted to having changed the facts—an interview that, to the horror of *NBC News* executives, was on the record. According to a *Vanity Fair* article, "Williams was supposed to talk to him [Tritten] off the record in an effort to determine what the reporter planned to write. Instead, to the dismay of NBC's P.R. [public relations] staff, Williams had gone on the record and admitted he hadn't been telling the truth, not only on a *Nightly News* broadcast the previous week but also over the years at public appearances and on talk shows."[37]

Asked if he had any regrets that the controversy may have taken away from the service accomplishments of Tim Terpack, the veteran whom Williams had honored at the New York Rangers game, Williams expressed that he did: "I have expressed my frustration that this is in some way going to soil what I attempted to do for him. Yes, I am very frustrated by this. . . . I'm the son of a U.S. Army captain in the World War II era—and I just, anything that takes attention away from him [Terpack], anything that ends up not honoring the veterans is a failure on my part."[38]

The backlash against Williams was as swift as the social media that spawned it. Facebook, blogs, and Twitter had played a key role in breaking the story, and they lit up with accusations of exaggeration and discussions about journalistic credibility. The controversy, however, went far beyond Williams's actions. It raised deeper questions about what Americans expected from journalists. A *Los Angeles Times* article stated, "Indeed, we now expect our journalists to be personalities, to exist outside the confines of their day jobs in exciting and entertaining ways. It's not enough to deliver the news; star journalists need to tweet humorously and/or with special insight. They need to make cameos in comedies, appear on talk shows and in magazines, to share their style secrets and personal lives, and offer across-the-board commentary."[39]

To many, the exaggerations made by Williams permanently damaged the most important thing a journalist has: credibility. A *USA Today* reporter claimed that "an anchor's

No. 1 requirement is that he or she has credibility. If we don't believe what an anchor tells us, what's the point?"[40] Trying to preserve the credibility of the network and its journalistic brand, "a day after the popular 'Nightly News' anchor's war story lie was exposed, the network entered damage control."[41] Though Williams apologized on the air, it was not enough. Later that month, NBC suspended Williams for six months while it investigated the controversy and planned its next moves. Some

REPORTING LIVE FROM THE MOON. I'M BRIAN WILLIAMS.

A sarcastic image posted in the wake of the scandal over Brian Williams's changing accounts of the events in Iraq years before, questioning his veracity and trustworthiness.

observers and insiders projected that he could never again return as the anchor of *NBC News*. The *New York Times* reported, "Six months is a long time to disappear from the television landscape, and analysts said it would be difficult for him to re-establish himself as a viable nightly presence. . . . A friend who spoke to Williams on Tuesday described him as 'shattered.'"[42] Others, like reporter Brian Moylan, were not so sure. Moylan wrote, "But Williams is likely to be fine. Why? NBC has always positioned him less as a journalist and more as an entertainer."[43]

Williams was not the first major television news personality to have questions raised about his journalistic credibility. For example, in 2004, news anchor and *60 Minutes* contributor Dan Rather came under sharp criticism surrounding the veracity of documents allegedly showing preferential treatment of President George W. Bush during the Vietnam War. Rather and CBS later retracted claims based upon these documents after more research questioned the documents' origin. That controversy became known as "Rathergate."

Defenders of Williams placed much of the blame on the drive for *NBC News*, under its new corporate ownership, to get ratings. *Vanity Fair*'s Bryan Burrough wrote, "The irony is that the very things people are criticizing Brian for now were the things they [the executives] loved most about him at the time, the fact that by going on all these shows, with their young audiences, he was building bridges to the younger people who weren't watching network news anymore."[44]

It was not only about celebrity, though. It was about ratings and revenue. Competition with new media forms and outlets and the drive for audiences changed the role of the news anchor, the lead journalist, itself. "Williams," according to one reporter, "belongs to this new generation of anchors, expected to keep us entertained as well as informed."[45] Celebrity, however, is double-edged sword. "Particularly on Twitter—the weapon of choice when a public figure is disgraced—Williams was subjected to an endless stream of ridicule all day, and even calls for his resignation."[46] His reputation was publicly and mercilessly attacked, he had "become the butt of late night comedy TV and social media."[47]

Social media played a key role in breaking the story; indeed, it was the Facebook post by Lance Reynolds that instigated the furor. Social media also acted as a forum for the subsequent analysis and apportioning of blame. Some of the tweets and posts were sent by other journalists, such as this from David Kenner, Middle East editor for *Foreign*

Policy magazine: "This Brian Williams story is crazy. You don't 'misremember' whether your helicopter was shot down by an RPG in Iraq."[48] As reported in the *Contra Costa Times*, "The Internet, of course, pounced, with a number of people going after Williams, both for lying and saying he misremembered the whole thing. A number of people inserted Williams' face in historical photos, including the moon landing and the JFK assassination."[49] In the image on the previous page, you can see several components of a meme: the juxtaposition of images, the use of irony, and an intentionally absurd caption.

The frenzy of media consolidation following the Telecommunications Act of 1996 placed many news organizations and their employees under new ownership that did not always demonstrate a clear understanding of the news business. According to some reporters and industry insiders, the process of consolidation was one of the contributing causes of the scandal that enveloped *NBC Nightly News* and Brian Williams. Mass media giant Comcast had taken over NBCUniversal several years before Williams's alleged misrepresentations of his war experiences, making it the parent company of *NBC Nightly News*, "the network's news division—famously termed Comcast's 'crown jewel'" by its chief executive officer.[50]

"You have to understand something about Comcast," Bryan Burrough wrote in 2015, citing an unnamed former NBC executive. "If you're going to be made the head of the shoe business, you need to actually know that shoes need to be sourced and designed. In the big corporate vision of NBCU, there's almost no regard for that line of thinking."[51] According to this inside source, there had been a failure to understand the product: "There is also a sense that the newsroom has been adrift since Comcast Cable took over NBCUniversal in 2011. NBC journalists said editors who once kept a close watch over the broadcast have departed, leaving Williams to operate with few meaningful checks and balances."[52]

The blurring of the line between news and entertainment and the demands placed upon the news to attract a commercial audience have pressured reporters to be more entertaining. "Since the advent of television," according to an article in *The Hollywood Reporter*, "no network news anchor has so fervently courted celebrity quite like NBC's Brian Williams. . . . Underlying Williams' many appearances on David Letterman's *Late Show* or NBC's *The Tonight Show* or *The Daily Show with Jon Stewart* or any number of events he has hosted or cameos he has made [including hosting *Saturday Night Live*], which appear to have increased exponentially in recent years, is a seemingly undeniable drive to be not just a 'famous news anchor' known for appearances on Nightly News but a 'cool celebrity' who is a mainstay of NBC's brand."[53]

In 2016 MSNBC announced that Williams would be returning to the network, covering breaking news stories to compete with rival cable channels such as CNN. The controversy surrounding Williams's accounts of the events in Iraq during his initial coverage had largely faded from public discussion. It had become "old news," which is itself revealing. The notion of 24/7 coverage of the news had become, in many ways, too slow a description, with stories breaking, being discussed, and being discarded in minutes and seconds rather than hours or days. The pressures to inform and entertain have only grown more intense. The degree to which any of this matters, however, is very much related to one basic question: How powerful are the news media? It is to this question that we now turn.

1. Questions about Brian Williams's accounts of his time as reporter in Iraq in 2003 focused on _____.

   a. Trust in journalists' coverage
   b. Net neutrality
   c. Political partisanship in modern journalism
   d. All of the above

2. How does the controversy surrounding Williams's accounts of the incident in Iraq highlight deeper issues about the news media in the twenty-first century?

3. What tensions, if any, do you observe between the desires of news media providers to be objective and entertaining at the same time?

Answer Key: 1. a; 2. Answers should include a discussion of the Telecommunications Act of 1996, consolidation of media ownership, and pressures to attract viewership in an age of competing outlets.; 3. Answers will vary and might include a discussion of the role of consumers in any tension between these two goals.

HOW THE MEDIA SHAPE AMERICAN POLITICS TODAY
Bias, Campaign Coverage, and the Power of the Media

Earlier in the chapter we explored historical attempts to regulate the American news media and how those efforts were driven in part by the need to respond to changes in technology, which, in turn, drove changes in patterns of media consumption and the structure of news organizations themselves. Today is no different. Why all of this matters, however, comes down to one central question: How powerful are the media in shaping individuals' attitudes and understandings? The more power that the media have, then the more one needs to be concerned with who is providing political news and if they are doing so in a fair and unbiased way.

> **CONNECTING TO . . .**
>
> ### The Media and Politics
>
> As you read this section, reflect upon the concerns raised by the controversy surrounding Williams's accounts of his involvement in Iraq. Consider the following:
>
> - Questions about the degree to which specific media outlets are or are not politically biased
> - The competing pressures faced by media outlets to entertain as well as inform
> - The possible power of media outlets to shape political understandings and behaviors

The Rise of New Media

One of the most important developments in the Internet age has been the rise of social media outlets, such as Facebook and Twitter. These interactive media environments allow individuals to create or share text, image, and video as well as comment on the content and forward it to other members of their own personal networks. We have already discussed the effects of new technologies in supporting citizen journalism and addressed concerns about the ability to verify such reports for accuracy. For politicians, however, there is another worry. As they are often acting and speaking amidst a sea of cell phone cameras, they must always be aware that any spontaneous, off-the-cuff remarks might find their way onto YouTube or Facebook within minutes. While the use of social media as the primary source of political news has grown tremendously in recent years, these trends are very much divided by generational differences (Figure 8.4).

NEWS CLIP
White House discusses development program in Cuba

The News as Entertainment

Commercial demands upon mainstream news providers have changed the approach with which many network executives treat not just their anchors and reporters but the news

NEWS CLIP
Q&A with outgoing CEO of Associated Press regarding changing media landscape

FIGURE 8.4

Generational Differences in Primary Sources for Political News

Percentage who got news about politics and government in the previous week from . . .

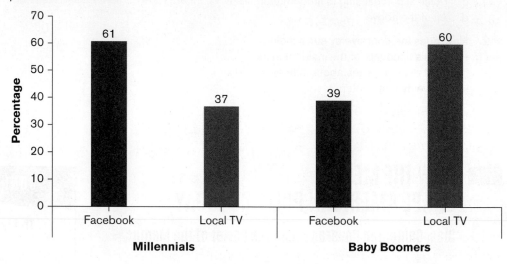

Source: Amy Mitchell, Jeffrey Gottfried, and Katrina Eva Matsa, "Millennials and Political News: Social Media—the Local TV for the Next Generation?," Pew Research Center, http://www.journalism .org/2015/06/01/millennials-political-news/, accessed June 19, 2015.

divisions themselves. According to one communications scholar, "Once upon a time, news was a money loser, but was kept separate from the other divisions of the networks so that the journalists in their employ could operate without much attention to the bottom line. No more."[54]

The pressure of attracting an audience in a marketplace with so many easily accessible alternatives has led news outlets to focus on **infotainment**, which is a merging of information and entertainment in a way designed to attract viewers and gain market share. This dynamic includes pressures to provide **soft news**, stories that focus on celebrities, personalities, and entertaining events rather than on events of local, national, or international political or economic significance.

Scholars continue to debate the effects of soft news on Americans' political knowledge and understanding. Candidate appearances on talk shows might engage viewers who otherwise would not have been exposed to their candidacy or the campaign in general,[55] an engagement that can increase the likelihood that voters will select candidates that more closely resemble citizens' political preferences.[56]

Soft news can act to engage individuals with foreign policy issues.[57] On the other hand, scholars have found that viewership of political comedy shows, such as *The Daily Show*, may decrease individuals' support for and engagement with political institutions, exposing them to political issues but increasing cynicism in the process.[58] There are also concerns that soft news may decrease the amount of knowledge about public affairs—knowledge that is necessary for effective democratic governance.[59]

infotainment

a merging of information and entertainment in a way designed to attract viewers and gain market share.

soft news

stories that focus on celebrity and personality rather than political or economic issues.

Bias and Coverage of the News

A perennial critique of the American news media is that it is biased. Typically, the charge, especially against the nation's largest newspapers and mainstream television news outlets, is that a **partisan bias** is demonstrated, and a liberal one at that. Many studies and critiques of journalists have focused on the fact that a majority of them self-identify as liberal.[60] So *are* the media politically biased? This is actually a very complicated question.[61] Journalists are more likely to self-identify as liberal than members of the general population, but they also tend to have higher levels of educational attainment, which may contribute to these patterns.

Presidential candidate Hillary Clinton appears with DJ tWitch on the Ellen DeGeneres Show. Reaching audiences through talk shows has long been a way for candidates to gain exposure to viewers who might not otherwise be tuned into political news.

Photo by Lars Niki/Corbis via Getty Images.

partisan bias
the slanting of political news coverage in support of a particular political party or ideology.

However, journalists also operate under norms and professional expectations that reward objectivity. Finally, the perception that the media are politically biased might itself be partly shaped by certain media outlets that run stories on the "biased media," thereby encouraging their readers, listeners, or viewers to believe a bias exists.[62] Perhaps unsurprisingly, whether or not an individual believes the news media are politically biased depends upon that person's own political viewpoints. The percentage of Americans who feel that there is a "great deal" of political bias in the news has risen recently (Figure 8.5).

FIGURE 8.5

Do Americans Think the News Media Are Biased?

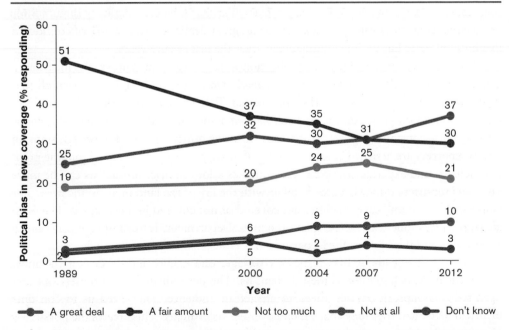

Source: Pew Research Center, "Perceptions of Bias, News Knowledge," February 7, 2012, http://www.people-press.org/2012/02/07/section-3-perceptions-of-bias-news-knowledge/?src=prc-number.

The Decline in Confidence in Television News

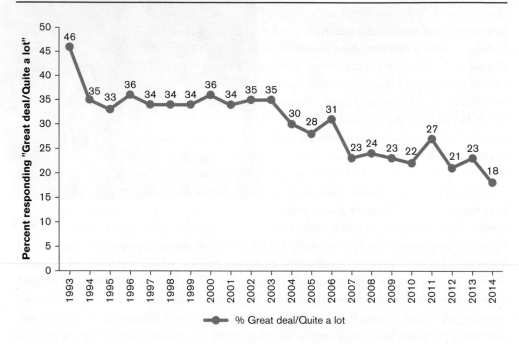

Source: Frank Newport, "Brian Williams Situation Plays Out in Context of Already Low Trust in Mass Media," Gallup, February 11, 2015, http://www.gallup.com/opinion/polling-matters/181544/brian-williams-situation-plays-context-already-low-trust-mass-media, accessed May 12, 2016.[63]

Concerns about bias in the media has been accompanied by a lack of trust in the news sources. Confidence in television news, in particular, has fallen dramatically (Figure 8.6).

The percentage of Americans expressing a "great deal" or "quite a lot" of confidence in television news has declined dramatically over the last twenty years.

To the reader of a penny press publication in the nineteenth century, the idea that a particular news outlet pursued a partisan agenda would probably not have been all that surprising; it was an accepted part of the format. Factors other than the political orientation of the journalists, editors, or publishers of a specific media outlet may also shape coverage in important ways. Most mainstream news outlets employ the **beat system**, in which reporters are assigned to specific types of news, policies, and events. From the point of efficiency and expertise, the beat system makes a lot of sense. Journalists can be more informed reporters if they become familiar with the lay of the land in a specific area. The worry is that certain beats are either not covered or not covered in much detail. The president, the Department of Defense, and the State Department, for example, receive much attention under this system; the Department of Transportation, not so much.

When thinking about bias in news coverage, one cannot ignore one of the most important potential sources of the problem: us. The news media—even outlets that are operated as nonprofit entities—need to attract an audience. They need us to consume their products, and they may shape their coverage accordingly. This creates the possibility of **commercial bias**, in which some news outlets might pursue inflammatory, sensational coverage to secure their niche of the marketplace, while others might choose to play it safe for fear of upsetting their audience.

commercial bias
the shaping of the content and focus of news based upon the desire to capture news consumers.

Commercial bias may shape not just *how* stories are covered but also *which* stories are covered. Stories, for example, about government regulation or public policies are often far from the compelling narratives that will attract a large audience, unless, of course, a major disaster or event shines a spotlight on some underlying problem. In a competitive marketplace, news, including political news, is based on providing compelling narratives—stories that we want to read, hear, watch, and re-tweet. It is easy, and often useful, to critique the American news media for failing to report on the "important stories." However, one might also ask if we would tune into the "Federal Bureaucracy Channel" with any regularity.

The Media and Political Campaigns and Elections

The drive to attract an audience also shapes how media outlets cover political campaigns and elections, and it affects how candidates try to present themselves. When covering political campaigns, news outlets may focus on the drama of the race rather than on the policy differences between candidates, a tendency often called the **horse race phenomenon**. Scandals also sell, as we have explored, tempting media outlets to focus on them and often crowding out discussions of policy, a pattern that political scientist Larry Sabato has called a "feeding frenzy."[64]

Candidates and politicians are not bystanders in the coverage of politics; they actively try to shape the news agenda and the content of the stories covered. Politicians and their staff members try to get their message out and shape its reception. The goal is to control the message, sometimes seemingly obsessively, by focusing on one message per news cycle, per day. Allowing or restricting access by journalists is also a strategic decision, made according to which choice seems most likely to "spin" a story in the desired way.

The Power of the News Media

None of the topics that we have explored in this chapter matter, at least for democratic representation, unless one thing is true: The media *can* actually shape individuals' political knowledge and understanding. If the media don't have that power, then the themes of technological change, corporate consolidation, and the rise of social media are only of interest to the scholars who study them. If, however, the media can shape political beliefs and understanding, then the story is very different.

Are media outlets powerful? Are they major players in the national political drama or just commentators on it? As with so much else about the American news media, the answers to these questions are evolving. Scholars' views of **media effects**—the power of the news media in shaping individuals' political knowledge, understanding, and preferences—have evolved along with the media itself.

In the early decades of the twentieth century, many observers of American political life considered the media a powerful and potentially dangerous force. The effectiveness of World War I propaganda posters and efforts, which helped to mobilize the nation in support for intervention in a European conflict about which many Americans were ambivalent, seemed to indicate that the public was like political Play-Dough: shapeable and malleable. Journalist Walter Lippmann, writing in 1922, captured the vulnerable American public, stating, "In the great blooming, buzzing confusion of the outer world, we pick out what our culture has already defined for us, and we tend to perceive that which we have picked out in the form stereotyped for us."[65] In this view, media were thought to have a direct effect on a public.

This model of the direct effects of the media began to fall out of favor in later decades as scholars employing empirical techniques and focusing primarily on the effects of the media in vote choices found important but limited effects of the media on political outcomes. Though playing an important role in citizen information about candidates and

NEWS CLIP
Behind the scenes with the media during Illinois primary

horse race phenomenon
coverage of political campaigns that focuses more on the drama of the campaign than on policy issues.

media effects
the power of the news media in shaping individuals' political knowledge, preferences, and political behavior.

their policy positions, the media were found to be only one factor in an individual's ultimate choice about which candidates to vote for in a given election.[66]

The current view of most scholars of the relationship between the media and American politics lies somewhere in between those of the direct and limited effects models. The model of subtle effects focuses not so much on how the media may or may not change, for example, the partisan affiliation or vote choice of a given individual, but on the ways in which the media may shape the overall conversation taking place in the public sphere.

How the media place a story in a larger context—the textual or visual cues that they present along with a story—may cause individuals to focus on particular considerations when consuming a media product, an effect known as **framing**. According to political scientists James Druckman and Kjersten Nelson, "For example, if a speaker describes a hate-group rally in terms of free speech, then the audience will subsequently base their opinions about the rally on free speech considerations and, perhaps, support the right to rally. In contrast, if the speaker uses a public-safety frame, the audience will base their opinions on public-safety considerations and oppose the rally."[67] Similarly, a particular media source's coverage of a candidate or issue may highlight specific contextual details in providing the coverage, thereby **priming** individuals to draw on those details when forming opinions.

The power of the media to select which stories are covered cannot be understated. In the choice of coverage, the media may exert an **agenda setting** role by highlighting which issues are worthy of coverage and, as a consequence, worthy of the public's attention. The question of agenda setting gets to the very purpose of the role of the media in a representative democracy. According to political scientist Harold Lasswell, the media perform three important and interconnected functions: to survey and report on political events and outcomes, to interpret those events and outcomes to the public, and to educate citizens.[68] To these three, media and politics scholar Doris Graber added a fourth function: to deliberately manipulate the political process.[69]

Lasswell's assertion that the media survey and report on the political world is often what we think about when we consider the media's role in American representative democracy—hard-hitting journalists asking hard-hitting questions and acting as a watchdog for, or, perhaps more accurately, a watchtower over, American politics. The role of watchdog is well entrenched in Americans' understanding of the role of journalists, editors, and anchors. Objective, aggressive interviews designed to get to the truth are very much a part of the ideal of the American news media. The tricky questions, however, are these: On what issues does the watchtower shine its light? Corruption? Scandal? Cats? Infrastructure? Who controls its aim and focus? To whom does the watchtower's controller answer? Corporate interests, powerful politicians, fellow journalists, or the American consumer? Important questions, with no easy answers. A watchtower cannot, by design, focus on the entire ocean, only a very small part of it at one time. Who decides where the light is to shine, and what are the consequences of those decisions?

The challenge of interpreting the dynamics behind these findings illustrates an important concept in empirical political science research: that correlation does not, by itself, establish causation. As you consume stories that show a relationship between variables, be careful not to assume that this relationship demonstrates that one factor is causing another.

A Digital Divide?

At first glance, the proliferation of news sources in the twenty-first century might provide scholars of the news media with a source of optimism. Perhaps, through infotainment, the diversity of perspectives on cable stations, and the spread of social media, Americans who were previously disconnected from the political process might be brought into it and

framing
influencing people's interpretations of news, events, or issues through the presentation of the context.

priming
shaping individuals' interpretations of news or events by highlighting certain details or contexts.

agenda setting
the media's ability to highlight certain issues and bring them to the attention of the public.

Do the Media Make Us Smart (or Not So Smart)? Or Do We Make Them Look Good (or Not So Good)?

In a study published in 2007, the Pew Research Center reported the findings of a study of Americans' political knowledge and media usage.[70] Part of the study was a political knowledge quiz, in which the roughly 1,500 respondents were asked to identify individuals and answer questions about American government.

Based on how well they did answering these questions, researchers divided the respondents into three groups, high knowledge, moderate knowledge, and low knowledge. Another part of the survey asked respondents to identify which sources of political news they regularly consumed, including print, radio, television, cable, and Internet sources. The sources themselves were then "scored" based on how knowledgeable their regular consumers were. While no one technology emerged as being more or less consumed by more or less knowledgeable individuals, there were some considerable differences between specific sources.

The Daily Show and *The Colbert Report*, along with newspaper Web sites, had the most knowledgeable consumers. The conservative Rush Limbaugh radio show and *O'Reilly Factor* also had relatively knowledgeable consumers. Fox News Channel and the network morning shows had the least knowledgeable consumers.

WHAT DO YOU THINK?

What kind of a "story" can one write about these findings? This is where it is important to be careful. It may be that *The Daily Show* is very educational, making its consumers more informed. On the other hand, it may be that it attracts more informed consumers, as much of the show's humor is not that funny without some background information. Or it may be a combination of these two factors.

Source: "What Americans Know: 1989-2007" Pew Research Center, Washington, DC (April, 2007) http://www.people-press.org/files/legacy-pdf/319.pdf.

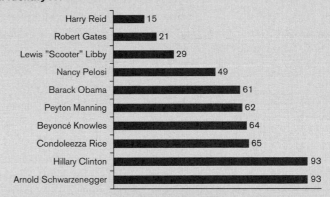

Percentage of Survey Respondents Who Can Identify . . .

Harry Reid	15
Robert Gates	21
Lewis "Scooter" Libby	29
Nancy Pelosi	49
Barack Obama	61
Peyton Manning	62
Beyoncé Knowles	64
Condoleezza Rice	65
Hillary Clinton	93
Arnold Schwarzenegger	93

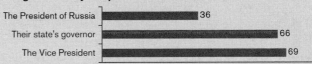

Percentage of Survey Respondents Who Can Recall the Name of . . .

The President of Russia	36
Their state's governor	66
The Vice President	69

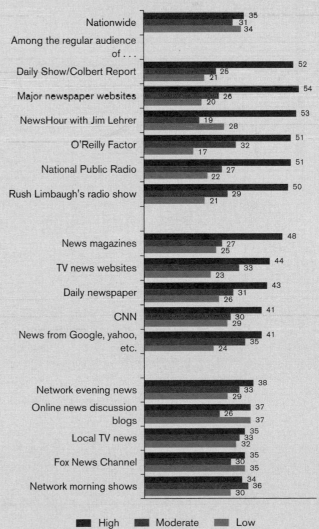

Knowledge Levels by News Source

	High	Moderate	Low
Nationwide	35	31	34
Among the regular audience of . . .			
Daily Show/Colbert Report	52	25	21
Major newspaper websites	54	26	20
NewsHour with Jim Lehrer	53	19	28
O'Reilly Factor	51	32	17
National Public Radio	51	27	22
Rush Limbaugh's radio show	50	29	21
News magazines	48	27	25
TV news websites	44	33	23
Daily newspaper	43	31	26
CNN	41	30	29
News from Google, yahoo, etc.	41	35	24
Network evening news	38	33	29
Online news discussion blogs	37	26	37
Local TV news	35	33	32
Fox News Channel	35	30	35
Network morning shows	34	36	30

■ High ■ Moderate ■ Low

prompted to think about issues and to connect friends and family in their social networks to American politics. Again, it may not be that simple; the story might not be so neat and inspiring. All Americans do not make use of the new technologies and outlets in the same way. According to the work of political scientist Markus Prior, the new technologies and media avenues may be dividing Americans, making them more partisan.[71] We call this gap, and others discussed below, the **digital divide**.

Perhaps more worrisome, Americans with the skills to navigate this "Brave New World"[72] of multiple options and unclear editorial standards may benefit tremendously, but those who cannot, or choose not to, may be left behind. The Internet, according to Prior, "has widened gaps in news exposure, political knowledge, and turnout between those who like news and those who prefer entertainment."[73] These gaps are not independent of Americans' identities and lived experiences. Older, low-income, rural, Spanish-speaking, and disabled Americans are less likely to make use of the Internet, as are those with lower levels of educational attainment.[74]

digital divide

divisions in society that are driven by access to and knowledge about technologies; these gaps often fall along the lines of partisanship, class, race, and ethnicity.

WHAT HAVE I LEARNED?

1. The question of political bias in political news has been largely settled.

   a. True
   b. False

2. Commercial bias refers to _____.

   a. The increase of commercials in television news
   b. The role that journalists play in trying to push a certain political perspective

   c. The way in which the media shape their coverage to attract an audience
   d. All of the above

3. How have scholars' views of the power of the media changed over time?

4. Why are scholars worried about an increasing digital divide?

Answer Key: 1. a; 2. c; 3. Answers should include a discussion of the direct effects, limited effects, and subtle effects models.; 4. Answers should include the connection between access to news sources and individuals' identities and lived experiences.

CONCLUSION

Comedians as Respected Journalists

In the days following the breaking of the Brian Williams scandal, Jon Stewart, host of *The Daily Show with Jon Stewart* on Comedy Central, a show on which Williams had appeared, weighed in on the downfall of one of the nation's most respected journalists:

"Bri?" Stewart queried.

"Why?"

"Why, Bri?"

"Why Bri lie?"

"Sigh."

"Were you Bri high?"

"Cause if they keep finding ****, Bri bye."[75]

Taking a dig at the demographic makeup of the network television news audience, as opposed to that of Comedy Central, Stewart offered, "A quick recap in case you're under seventy and don't religiously turn on the network news every night at 6:30 . . . demo slam!"[76] In recapping the events of the scandal, Stewart provided his diagnosis of the dangers of merging news and entertainment: "See, I see the problem. We got us a case here of infotainment-confusion-syndrome. It occurs when the celebrity cortex gets its wires crossed with the medulla-anchordala."[77]

The focus of Stewart's fake-anchor critique, however, went far deeper than criticizing and lampooning a real anchor and, according to some reports, a good friend.[78] Stewart compared the outrage and media circus over one reporter's account of his own personal experiences with the mainstream media's uncritical coverage of the events leading up to the war itself. He called out its lack of diligence in challenging the claims used to justify the invasion in 2003, especially claims made by the administration of George W. Bush that Saddam Hussein had weapons of mass destruction that he might use against American allies in the region, American forces stationed nearby, or on America itself.

With obvious sarcasm and to enthusiastic and escalating audience applause, Stewart placed the NBC controversy in a very different context, declaring, "The media is ON IT! Now, this may seem like overkill, but, for me, no it's not overkill, because I'm happy. Finally someone is being held to account for misleading America about the Iraq War. . . . But never again will Brian Williams mislead this great nation about being shot at in a war we probably wouldn't have ended up in if the media had applied this level of scrutiny to the actual ****ing war."[79]

Stewart then showed clips from statements by members of the administration making accusations against the regime of Saddam Hussein that proved to be unsupported. He said, "Imagine, if you let lies slip into news stories, like a huge pile of them that was disseminated in, say, the *New York Times* and *Meet the Press*, and sometimes in the *New York Times*, just so the administration could then go on *Meet the Press*.... The run-up to the Iraq War was kind of beautiful in the evil efficiency of its media manipulation."[80]

As the investigation into Williams's alleged exaggerations continued in the days following the original Facebook post, reporters focused on inconsistencies in statements made by Williams regarding Hurricane Katrina, of being mugged while selling Christmas trees in New Jersey to help out a local charity, and how many puppies he had claimed to rescue in a fire. "Dammit, Brian Williams!" Stewart shouted with sarcastic fury. "One puppy or two! Don't you ****ing lie to me! I want the truth!"[81] In that segment, a cable comedy show host pretending to be a real journalist had just called out the mainstream news media, not just for inaccuracies but for being, at best, irrelevant and focused on ratings and, at worst, for being complicit in falsehoods that helped lead the nation into war. But it was just a comedy show after all, right?

In the same month that the Williams scandal broke, Stewart announced that he would be stepping down from *The Daily Show* within the year, "leaving his phony anchor desk and ending his reign as a phony newsman, and the loss is to real news."[82] Other comedian commentators, however, had entered the space by this point. John Oliver took over hosting *The Daily Show* and then later moved to his own show, *Last Week Tonight*, and Samantha Bee was hosting TBS's *Full Frontal*.

What was so surprising about the media's approach to Stewart's announced retirement was that Stewart was treated as one of the country's premier journalists rather than one of America's most popular comedians. According to one journalist,

For a segment of the audience that had lost its faith in broadcast and print news outlets or never regarded them as sacrosanct in the first place, Mr. Stewart emerged a figure as trusted as Walter Cronkite or Edward R. Murrow. . . . Mr. Stewart proved that nightly humor could be not only hilarious but as incisive and passionate as the best news organizations. . . . Every time a political scandal exploded or a candidate made headlines or a cable fight went viral, the first thought for many viewers was: I can't wait to see what Jon Stewart will say about this.[83]

Welcome to the twenty-first century.

CHAPTER REVIEW

This chapter's main ideas are reflected in the Learning Objectives below. By reviewing them here you should be able to **remember** the key points, **connect** them to the stories presented in the chapter, **think** critically about these questions, and **know** these terms that are central to the topic.

8.1   Contrast different political news media sources in the twenty-first century.

REMEMBER . . .
- Most of the time, people learn about politics indirectly via the news media, including newspapers, magazines, radio, television, online sources, and social media.
- New technologies have profoundly affected how Americans receive and spread news and information.

CONNECT . . .
- Servicemen and servicewomen can now report their experiences directly from the front lines and connect to friends and family members via a type of blog called a milblog.

THINK . . .
- How have the sources of Americans' political news changed in the twenty-first century? What do these changes mean?
- Has the rise of social media increased the ability of Americans to have their voices heard?

KNOW . . .
- *citizen journalists* (p. 262)
- *news media* (p. 261)
- *social media* (p. 262)

8.2   Trace the historical development of the American news media.

REMEMBER . . .
- Since the founding, there has been tension between the constitutional right to freedom of speech and of the press and constraints on those rights.
- Pamphlets and later weekly and daily newspapers were among the first print media in the United States.

- As time went on, costs to produce newspapers decreased, making the news more affordable and available and able to reach a mass audience.

- For much of the history of the American media, the press has been partisan—funded by and disseminating the point of view of particular political factions.

- Sensationalism was also used to sell news, a practice that continues today.

- The nineteenth and twentieth centuries saw the rise of other technologies, such as the telegraph (which brought us wire services) and radio and television (which brought us broadcast news).

- Cable news offers round-the-clock news coverage, often with a partisan slant.

- Newer technologies, such as the Internet, broadband, and social media, have not only increased the pace and volume of news content but have also blurred the lines between information and entertainment, citizens and journalists.

THINK...

- How did technological changes in the eighteenth and nineteenth centuries drive changes in the news media?

- How did the print media in the nineteenth century deal with political partisanship? Has the rise in social media increased the ability of Americans to have their voices heard?

KNOW...

- *broadcast media* (p. 270)
- *investigative journalism* (p. 269)
- *mass media* (p. 268)
- *niche journalism* (p. 272)

- *partisan press* (p. 268)
- *penny press* (p. 268)
- *yellow journalism* (p. 269)
- *wire service* (p. 269)

8.3 Discuss changes in the regulation of media ownership and media content.

REMEMBER...

- Some efforts to regulate the news media have focused on ownership; others have focused on content.

- The Federal Radio Act of 1927 established the Federal Communications Commission (FCC) and required broadcasters to obtain licenses.

- The Telecommunications Act of 1996 modified regulations on media ownership and led to a period of consolidation.

- The rule of net neutrality requires Internet service providers to treat data streams equally. A recent federal court ruling upheld this rule.

- The equal time rule and fairness doctrine seek to ensure a level playing field for political candidates; however, recent regulatory and technological changes have reduced their impact and raised questions about their relevance.

THINK...

- How has the federal government tried to regulate the news media throughout the nation's history?

- What challenges do new communications technologies pose to the government's ability to do this?

KNOW...

- *aggregating* (p. 274)
- *equal time rule* (p. 275)

- *fairness doctrine* (p. 276)
- *net neutrality* (p. 274)

8.4 Evaluate the consequences of the pressure on traditional news outlets to compete for an audience.

REMEMBER...

- With the proliferation of news sources, media outlets are under pressure to cast their reporters as celebrities in order to draw audiences, which is critical for increasing ratings and raising revenue for the network and its owners.

- Having to act as a celebrity, however, can put the core duties of accurate reporting into conflict with the temptation to sensationalize the news.

CONNECT...

- *NBC Nightly News* anchor Brian Williams was found to have misreported an incident he was involved in while covering military operations in Iraq. This ultimately tarnished his reputation and that of the network.

THINK...

- What role does the desire of consumers to be entertained play in decisions to focus stories on sensational and entertaining topics?

KNOW...

- *commercial bias* (p. 284)
- *digital divide* (p. 288)
- *infotainment* (p. 282)
- *soft news* (p. 282)

8.5 Contrast different perspectives on bias in the media and the power of the media to shape political understanding and behaviors.

REMEMBER...

- Americans increasingly perceive the media as politically biased and less trustworthy.

- Coverage of political campaigns and elections is often sensationalized.

- Scholars' views of the power of the media to shape political understanding and behaviors have changed over time.

- The current view focuses on the agenda-setting power of media coverage.

- A growing digital divide separates Americans along partisan lines as well as by race, class, and ethnicity.

CONNECT...

- Jon Stewart of Comedy Central's *The Daily Show with Jon Stewart* emerged not just as an admired comedian but also as a trusted source of political news.

THINK...

- How has the need to attract an audience shaped the coverage of political news?

- What are possible sources of bias in coverage of political news? Which of these do you think are the most significant?

- Can the media shape Americans' political understandings?

KNOW...

- *agenda setting* (p. 286)
- *beat system* (p. 284)
- *framing* (p. 286)
- *horse race phenomenon* (p. 285)
- *media effects* (p. 285)
- *partisan bias* (p. 283)
- *priming* (p. 286)

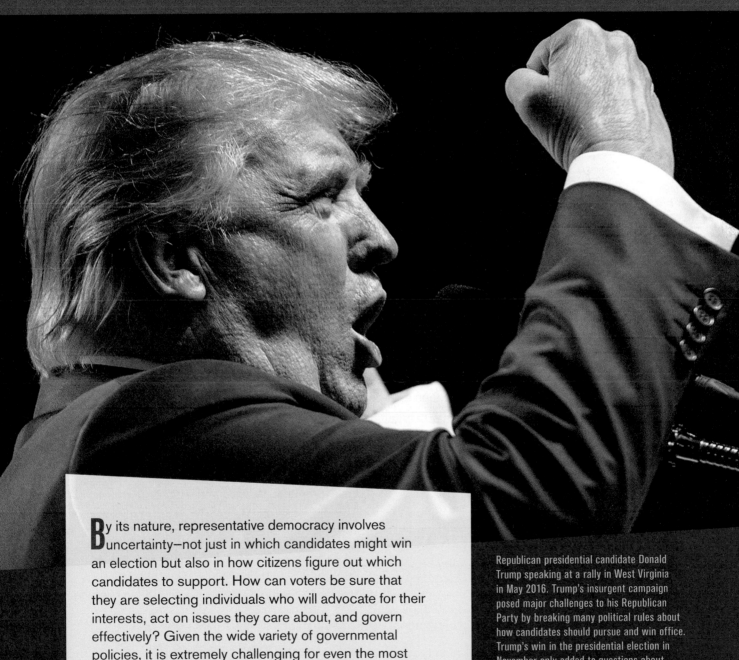

9 POLITICAL PARTIES
The Insurgents versus the Establishment

By its nature, representative democracy involves uncertainty—not just in which candidates might win an election but also in how citizens figure out which candidates to support. How can voters be sure that they are selecting individuals who will advocate for their interests, act on issues they care about, and govern effectively? Given the wide variety of governmental policies, it is extremely challenging for even the most attentive voters to know all of the details about what a candidate stands for or hopes to accomplish once in office.

Enter the **political party.** By organizing and supporting candidates running for office, parties provide labels to those candidates—shortcuts for voters, really—that cut through the noise and signal to voters that this is a candidate who

Republican presidential candidate Donald Trump speaking at a rally in West Virginia in May 2016. Trump's insurgent campaign posed major challenges to his Republican Party by breaking many political rules about how candidates should pursue and win office. Trump's win in the presidential election in November only added to questions about whether traditional wisdom about political parties still applies.

BRENDAN SMIALOWSKI/AFP/Getty Images.

political party

an organized group of candidates, officeholders, voters, and activists that work together to elect candidates to political office.

deserves their support. Once in office, those candidates work with the support of other party members to advance a set of policies.

Party leaders face another challenge: creating an attractive and consistent message that gets their candidates elected and maintains party cohesion. American political parties have often been successful in doing this, but not always. Once in a while, maybe every several decades or so, a party finds itself challenged not by another party but by members within its own ranks who have felt that their voices are being ignored by party leaders.

In 2016 both of America's dominant parties, the Democrats and the Republicans, found themselves confronting just such a situation. Two candidates, Senator Bernie Sanders of Vermont and entrepreneur and television celebrity Donald Trump—as far apart on the traditional American political spectrum as one could diagram—emerged as major forces in their respective parties. Sanders and Trump, regardless of how far they would make it in their respective campaigns, changed the national conversation. Despite their differences, both men were outsiders and insurgents, and a lot of Americans responded to their campaigns.

So much conventional wisdom turned on its head, so many experts in American politics forced to admit that they had gotten it wrong, and so many of the established leaders in America's dominant political parties left scrambling to figure out what was going on and what to do about it. This was the presidential election of 2016.

This election may very well be studied by future political scientists as one of the most critical in the nation's history. How did this all come to pass? And what will it mean for the future of America's political parties? Was it just a circus? Or could it result in a reshaping of party politics or even the destruction of one or both of America's major political parties? We do not yet know the answers to any of these questions. However, trying to get a bead on the election of 2016 provides a chance to do much more than analyze one presidential election. It also offers the chance to better understand the role that parties play in American representative democracy.

LEARNING OBJECTIVES

Through an exploration of the presidential election of 2016 and the challenges that Bernie Sanders and Donald Trump posed to their own party establishment, you will be able to:

9.1 Understand why Sanders and Trump posed such a challenge to their parties as well as why their messages resonated with large numbers of voters

9.2 Identify the roles that parties play in American representative democracy

9.3 Evaluate the ways in which the structure of the nomination process can affect both the outcomes of the process and the representation of party members

9.4 Explain how American party systems have evolved over time

9.5 Examine theories behind two-party dominance in American political history

9.6 Debate the prospects for third parties in American politics

TWO PRESIDENTIAL CANDIDATES SHAKE UP THE FIELD

American presidential elections are often filled with drama. However, traditionally, most of the drama is between the parties or between candidates trying to stake their claim as the best person to represent the goals of their party. To put it mildly, 2016 was different. Two of the leading candidates in the election, Republican multimillionaire Donald Trump and Vermont senator Bernie Sanders, an independent running as a Democrat, in different times would probably have been regarded as too extreme to pose a legitimate threat to party status quo. Trump's highly unconventional and controversial campaign in particular upended many widely accepted political rules and challenged the belief that political party leaders are powerful.

In 2016 Trump and Sanders advanced far in the electoral process due to voters' profound disgust with "politics as usual." Both made statements or adopted policy positions that were on the fringes of party platforms or far out of touch with the mainstream. And, unlike many presidential contenders, neither of them concentrated on courting the best-known activists and leaders in their parties—the so-called party establishment or party elites, who are the most powerful insiders in party politics. In fact, their campaigns went out of their way to alienate those elites.

Other presidential candidates have run similar campaigns. The emphasis on criticizing elites and the establishment has a long tradition and has taken many forms, some of which are generally referred to as *populism*. America has witnessed several powerful populist movements in its history, many of which tied their critique of the establishment to perceptions of racial, ethnic, or cultural superiority or to strong anti-immigrant views, a charge frequently leveled against Trump. What made Trump and Sanders more noteworthy was that their criticisms struck such a deep chord with so many voters; each kept winning state nomination contests long after many political observers were certain they would fade. To the astonishment of both Republican and Democratic loyalists in their respective parties, Trump would eventually go on to win the general election.

The success of the campaigns of Trump and Sanders came in part because Americans have become less attached to political parties in recent years. At the same time, the country has grown increasingly more polarized by political ideology. More conservatives hold strongly conservative views than in the past, and more liberals strongly liberal views. The party organizations have shouldered much of the blame for creating and fostering an environment in which the two sides seem forever locked in combat. Despite this ongoing battle, the parties haven't become any stronger. According to journalist Jonathan Rauch, "Here is the reigning political paradox of our era: Partisanship is strong, but parties are weak."[1] To many Democratic and Republican stalwarts, the presidential campaigns of Sanders and Trump represented the opposite of what parties should present to voters—an umbrella of interests, linked by a shared goal, forming a larger, unified system.

> What made Trump and Sanders more noteworthy was that their criticisms struck such a deep chord with voters.

Sanders didn't even belong to the Democratic Party when he announced he was running for that party's nomination. Instead, he described himself as an "independent socialist," strongly in favor of the idea that government and society should meet the needs of the public, even if that means rich people can't earn as much as they normally would. He was known for criticizing so-called corporate welfare—government benefits, such as special provisions in the tax code, provided to businesses in the hopes of enabling them to succeed and keep workers on their payrolls. As public resentment rose toward financial companies in 2011 and gave rise to the Occupy

An attendee holds up a sign in support of Democratic presidential candidate Bernie Sanders at a rally in Brooklyn, New York, in April 2016. Sanders's call for a "political revolution" was an effective rallying cry, especially among young voters.

Victor J. Blue/Bloomberg via Getty Images.

Wall Street movement, Sanders endorsed the movement's widespread demonstrations. Though Sanders was not the first, or only, candidate to call attention to wealth inequality in the country in the twenty-first century, his message that the playing field was unacceptably tilted towards the top 1 percent of Americans resonated with many voters, especially young adults struggling with student loan debt or seeking to stake their claim on the American dream.

Many Democrats also supported the Occupy Wall Street protests. Yet some of them, unlike Sanders, nonetheless accepted generous campaign donations from the same Wall Street companies and employees that were the targets of the Occupy movement. Sanders often made an issue of how much his main Democratic opponent, Hillary Clinton, received from such firms—more than $15 million as of early 2016, according to the nonpartisan watchdog group Center for Responsive Politics.[2]

In 2010 President Barack Obama proposed extending tax cuts that were set to expire and that would mostly benefit the wealthiest Americans. Some Democrats joined the president in supporting the extension. But Sanders was upset with the idea—so upset that he spoke against it on the floor of the Senate for more than eight hours without once taking a break. He said the cuts would make already-rich people even richer and called for a proposal that "better reflects the needs of the middle class and working families of our country and to me, most importantly, the children of our country."[3]

The speech catapulted Sanders into the national spotlight. His stances made him popular with many liberals, especially young ones. They agreed with his calls to substantially raise taxes on the wealthy, expand the reach of health care beyond Obama's Patient Protection and Affordable Care Act (better known as Obamacare), and make college education free. Sanders said his campaign involved creating a "political revolution" that could serve "millions of Americans, working people who have given up on the political process."[4]

But Clinton and many others in the mainstream of the Democratic Party said Sanders's proposals were unrealistic. They were concerned those ideas might lead many voters to think that the Democratic Party wanted to raise everyone's taxes and have the federal government run everything. That perception, they worried, could drive away people who otherwise might support Democrats in other races. Clinton criticized Sanders for wanting the United States to resemble Denmark, a country that offers its citizens free health care and free tuition—but where taxes are more than 26 percent of the country's gross domestic product, compared to less than 10 percent in the United States.[5] Many Americans, especially young American voters disagreed. "I really like Bernie Sanders for his consistency, authenticity and relative independence from corporate interests," said Anton Terrell, a twenty-three-year-old recent college graduate in Austin, Texas, summing up why many liberal millennial voters positively regarded Sanders.[6]

Like Sanders, Trump was very much an outsider in his party. Unlike Sanders and most other presidential candidates, though, he had never held elected office. That disturbed some in the GOP ("Grand Old Party" or Republican Party) as they believed those seeking the nation's highest legislative post should have at least some prior political experience. Also, long before he ran for president, Trump was an outspoken proponent of "birtherism"—a movement questioning whether Obama was born in the United States and thus eligible to be elected president. That offended even Republicans who intensely disliked Obama's policies.

Trump became famous in the 1980s as a real estate and casino developer in New York and for hosting a reality TV show starting in 2008. He was a Democrat until 1987, then a

Republican from 1987 to 1999. After that, he was a member of a third party called the Independence Party. He became a Democrat again in 2001, a Republican once more in 2009, then a registered independent for several months until he became a Republican again in 2012.[7] His switching led many conservative Republicans to question whether Trump would remain faithful to the party. He made them even more uncomfortable when he boasted he would use his business acumen to cut deals to benefit the U.S. economy. Many Republicans blasted that approach as contradicting their philosophy of limited government; the conservative magazine *National Review* devoted an entire issue to arguing why its readers shouldn't support Trump for that reason. Trump acknowledged, "I identify with some things as a Democrat."[8]

Donald Trump addresses contestants on the NBC reality show *The Apprentice*. Trump's unconventional candidacy, including his criticisms of many of his own party's leaders, resonated with many in the electorate.

Trump's extreme statements on immigration caused a further uproar. He called for building a massive wall on the U.S.-Mexico border to keep out those coming into the country illegally. After the 2015 terrorist attacks in San Bernardino, California, and overseas, Trump called for a ban on Muslims being allowed to enter the United States. His positions enraged Hispanics and Muslims, and a number of Republicans said he had gone too far. He also offended many voters by making disparaging remarks about women and people with disabilities. Mitt Romney, the 2012 Republican presidential nominee, was outspoken in his criticism of Trump. According to him, "There is a contest between Trumpism and Republicanism. Through the calculated statements of its leader, Trumpism has become associated with racism, misogyny, bigotry, xenophobia, vulgarity and, most recently, threats and violence. I am repulsed by each and every one of these."[9]

While many party elites were horrified by some of Trump's inflammatory statements, his messages did resonate with voters. Trump campaigned on a theme of "Make America Great Again," which he said involved replacing "stupid" decision makers with smart ones. His blaming of all politicians—not just Democratic ones—for what he called their inability to solve problems irked many Republicans. That included the GOP's establishment, which he bluntly described as ineffectual, and his fellow Republicans seeking the presidential nomination. He accused them of outright lying and of being, among other things, too beholden to what he said were the party's narrow interests and unresponsive to the public's massive hostility toward government. "People are angry . . . I just know it can be turned around. It can be turned around quickly," Trump said.[10]

Trump didn't have to rely on the party because of his celebrity and his ability to command significant news media attention without buying advertisements. Unlike other Republicans, he feuded with Fox News, whose audience consisted largely of hard-core GOP loyalists. One study in March 2016 estimated that he had essentially been given $2 billion in free media coverage in newspapers, television, and other journalistic sources. That was two-and-a-half times more than Democratic Party candidate Hillary Clinton and many times greater that of any of his Republican rivals.[11] Trump made frequent use of Twitter, regularly tweeting out 140-character statements, often condemning his opponents, that drew even more media attention. "I do a tweet on something, something not even significant, and they break into their news within seconds," he said of other media outlets.[12]

Many of Trump's supporters professed to care little about any of the criticisms leveled against him. He tapped into their deep frustration with politics and, in turn, the parties.

Bernie Sanders speaking at a rally at Pennsylvania State University in April 2016. Both Sanders and Trump drew large crowds at their rallies, presenting themselves as candidates who weren't beholden to the political establishment.

Ricky Carioti/The Washington Post via Getty Images.

They said they agreed with Trump's call to upend the entire system and described him as refreshingly authentic and blunt—qualities they said mattered more to them than his sometimes-vague policy stances. "He disrupts a broken political process and beats establishment candidates who've long ignored their interests," a lawyer in a poor, rural North Carolina town wrote in explaining Trump's widespread appeal there. "When you're earning $32,000 a year and haven't had a decent vacation in over a decade, it doesn't matter who Trump appoints to the [United Nations], or if he poisons America's standing in the world—you just want to win again, whoever the victim, whatever the price."[13]

Trump and Sanders had completely different styles and messages, but they shared some things in common. One was a refusal to rely on large outside campaign contributions, which gave them an image among their supporters that they "couldn't be bought." Another trait they shared was a message of economic pessimism. Both drew strong support from voters who were found to be the most anxious about where the economy was headed.[14] In particular, both actively criticized their parties' mainstream beliefs on trade with other countries. They accused the parties of supporting trade deals that had led to thousands of American jobs being outsourced to foreign competitors. Trade is an issue that splits Americans less along lines of party than of economic class, especially in states with a lot of factories and blue-collar industrial workers. The senior ranks of the Democratic and, especially, the Republican Party tend to strongly support trade deals as being essential to the U.S. economy because they open up new markets for goods and services. They argue that the creation of jobs by those new markets more than offsets the losses in manufacturing to other countries and that companies are unlikely to bring back jobs that have moved overseas.[15] The public has been split over these ideas: More people support trade agreements than oppose them, but more people also say they believe that they lower, rather than raise, U.S. wages.[16]

In a normal presidential election campaign, Sanders and Trump might have made a splash, but neither would probably have had a real chance at securing the nomination, especially Trump, with his incendiary statements. 2016 was not such a year. "We have something happening that makes the Republican Party probably the biggest political story in the world," Trump said early in 2016. "Millions of people are coming into vote. . . . Democrats are coming in, independents are coming in, and—very, very important —

people who have never voted before. It's an incredible thing."[17] While Trump's opponents repeatedly questioned his interpretations of polls, Trump stood by his claims that he was sparking a revolution in Republican Party politics. For his part, Sanders emphasized the resonance of his message of ensuring economic opportunities for Americans by taking on Wall Street and promising to enact legislation providing free college education.

WHAT ARE PARTIES, AND WHAT DO THEY DO?

We began this chapter with a brief overview of the roles that parties play in representative government. Before going into much more detail about these roles, it is important to note that understanding what role parties *do play* in American democracy is only part of the story. It is also important to consider what roles they *should play* in order to help citizens and society and *how effective* parties are. Both of these issues continue to be the subject of research and debate in political science.

While the Constitution of the United States does not mention parties, many of the framers and early leaders of the young Republic feared the potential consequences from parties grown too powerful. The parties have "baneful effects," President George Washington warned in 1796, because they are rooted "in the strongest passions of the human mind," causing splits that lead to political conflict and stagnation.[18] Parties are, after all, factions, with all of the dangers that a group of like-minded citizens can inflict upon others that factions entail.

Political parties, however, have long been central to democracy and serve several functions. A healthy party serves as a credible check on the opposition, promoting ideas and candidates that differ from the other party's so that voters can choose how they want to be represented. In 1950 a committee composed of members of the American Political Science Association reflected upon the importance of parties for most Americans, noting that "the most valuable opportunity to influence the course of public affairs is the choice they are able to make between the parties in the principal elections."[19]

In developing what is now called the **responsible party model**, the report's authors called for changes in the organization and function of America's political parties. They

CONNECTING TO . . .

Challenging the Status Quo

As you read ahead, reflect upon the presidential candidacies of Bernie Sanders and Donald Trump. Consider the following:

- The consequences of conflicts between the candidates and their respective party organizations
- The power of political party leaders to select nominees
- The power of voters to select nominees

responsible party model
a proposal for party reform that emphasized cohesive party positions that presents voters with a clear set of choices and allows members' voices to be effectively incorporated into party positions on issues.

highlighted the need for parties to present their members with clear positions to which the parties are strongly committed (allowing for reasoned and lively debate between their members), party cohesion both in the party in power and in the party in opposition, an ability to resist pressures from interest groups, and the deliverance to their members of the promises that they make. Party members, for their part, should also act strongly to hold their party leadership accountable in fulfilling those promises.[20]

The Roles That Parties Play

Political scientist V. O. Key Jr. identified three primary roles that political parties play in American representative democracy:[21]

1. As organizations, political parties recruit, nominate, and support candidates for political office.

2. In the electorate, parties act as labels that are provided to candidates and office holders and that voters can use as shortcuts in identifying candidates closer to their own political ideologies and advocating similar policy positions.

3. In government, a party enacts the policy positions of its members and acts as an opposition to the majority party when it is in the minority.

Parties as Organizations

A political party seeks to unite people under a shared banner of social, economic, and ideological goals. It finds and supports candidates to run for federal, state, and local offices, which includes mobilizing voters and potential voters to support its candidates. Parties raise money to fund campaigns and provide other forms of help to try to get their candidates elected. If those candidates win, the parties then try to make sure the politicians stay in office. The parties also come up with themes and principles that they want their candidates to follow in appealing for votes.

Federalism and Political Parties

When some people think of political parties, they think of big shots in Washington, D.C., commanding armies of supporters who wait for their marching orders from above. The reality is that parties are decentralized. They're basically a large collection of state organizations that, in turn, are loose collections of local groups. This is because of federalism, the system dictating that power should not just be concentrated at the top. As *Los Angeles Times* reporter Jonathan Rauch explains it, "State parties play a key role. They recruit and cultivate political talent, building a farm team of candidates for higher office. They coordinate campaigns up and down the ballot, connecting politicians to each other and discouraging rogue behavior. They build networks of volunteers, connecting leaders with the party base. They gather voter data and make it available to all candidates, building a library of knowledge about the electorate."[22] (See Figure 9.1).

Today, however, many state party organizations are struggling. That's partly because of the ability of nonparty groups to legally raise and spend large amounts of money on behalf of political causes. This has overshadowed not just state parties but the federal ones as well. Another problem facing state parties is the complexity of the campaign finance system. Its rules restrict the ability of the state parties to raise and spend money and to coordinate campaigns so that candidates of the same party can pool their expenses. "Even when they use state money to promote state (and local) candidacies, the state parties must follow restrictive federal rules that only a team of lawyers can understand," Rauch reported.[23]

FIGURE 9.1

The Organizational Structure of Missouri's Republican Party

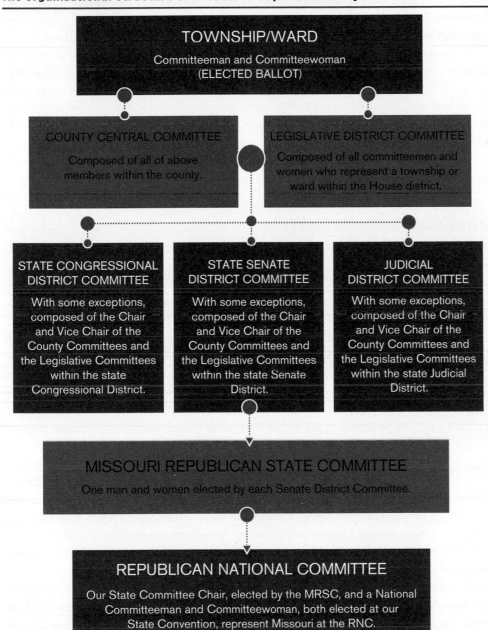

TOWNSHIP/WARD

Committeeman and Committeewoman
(ELECTED BALLOT)

COUNTY CENTRAL COMMITTEE

Composed of all of above
members within the county.

LEGISLATIVE DISTRICT COMMITTEE

Composed of all committeemen and
women who represent a township or
ward within the House district.

**STATE CONGRESSIONAL
DISTRICT COMMITTEE**

With some exceptions,
composed of the Chair
and Vice Chair of the
County Committees and
the Legislative Committees
within the state
Congressional District.

**STATE SENATE
DISTRICT COMMITTEE**

With some exceptions,
composed of the Chair
and Vice Chair of the
County Committees and
the Legislative Committees
within the state Senate
District.

**JUDICIAL
DISTRICT COMMITTEE**

With some exceptions,
composed of the Chair
and Vice Chair of the
County Committees and
the Legislative Committees
within the state Judicial
District.

MISSOURI REPUBLICAN STATE COMMITTEE

One man and women elected by each Senate District Committee.

REPUBLICAN NATIONAL COMMITTEE

Our State Committee Chair, elected by the MRSC, and a National
Committeeman and Committeewoman, both elected at our
State Convention, represent Missouri at the RNC.

A sample party organization chart from the Missouri Republican Party.

Source: The Missouri Republican Party, "Republican Party Organizational Structure," https://www
.missouri.gop/wp-content/uploads/2015/07/Org-Flowchart-Transparent-e1438705456327.png,
accessed August 15, 2016.

Party Leadership

The president generally chooses the chair of his or her national party. The national party chair
raises money and serves as a prominent spokesperson on television and other media. But the
national party organization's power over the state and local parties is advisory; it can't tell

them what to do. In fact, the state parties can put pressure on national parties. In 2014, as public opinion in the United States shifted rapidly toward greater acceptance of same-sex marriage, some Republican Party officials in Illinois replaced six party officials who disagreed with a former state party chair's support for same-sex marriage. At the same time, Nevada's Republican Party dropped language from its party platform opposing the idea.[24] The national committee later rejected proposed resolutions that were critical of same-sex marriage.[25]

Each state has a central committee made up of men and women from that state's counties and legislative districts who run for office and are elected to terms just like regular politicians. They help shape the national party's governance, or how it manages its money and runs its operations. In 2009 members of the Republican National Committee (RNC) got into a highly publicized fight with Michael Steele, the RNC chair at the time, over guidelines dictating how the party's money was spent. Some of the members wanted strict limits over how Steele controlled spending. Steele and his supporters called those moves an attempt to weaken his authority but ultimately agreed to some controls.[26]

Recruiting and Supporting Candidates

recruitment
the process through which political parties identify potential candidates.

One way a party tries to shape elections is through **recruitment**, which is considered one of its central tasks. The parties seek candidates who best reflect the party's philosophy and who can attract the voters the parties seek to mobilize. Party officials often recruit by finding people who can appeal to specific groups with high concentrations of voters, such as African Americans or Latinos. The parties also look for people who can contrast sharply with their opponents.

Parties discourage prospective candidates within their own ranks who aren't seen as having a good chance of winning.

While parties often recruit candidates who are similar to the person they seek to replace, this is not always the case. In Iowa, for example, Republicans recruited Joni Ernst to run for the Senate in 2014 after long-time Democratic senator Tom Harkin announced his retirement. Ernst was very different from Harkin, a liberal who was in his mid-seventies and who had been in Congress for four decades. The Republican Party wanted to demonstrate the state was ready for a new type of senator. In addition to holding more conservative views than Harkin, Ernst was in her mid-forties and female. She had served as a lieutenant colonel in the Iowa Army National Guard and won election to become the Senate's first female veteran.[27]

In recruiting, parties also try to discourage prospective candidates within their own ranks who aren't seen as having a good chance of winning. They fear that those candidates could end up drawing votes away from their preferred choice.

When Hillary Clinton resigned from representing New York in the U.S. Senate to become secretary of State in 2009, multiple Democratic politicians—many from the New York City region—wanted the state's governor to appoint them to fill Clinton's unexpired term, then they intended to run for the position in the election the next year. But New York's Democratic leaders wanted another woman in the seat who could appeal to supporters in areas outside New York City that weren't as liberal. They backed Kirsten Gillibrand, who represented an area of upstate New York and who was known for taking middle-of-the-road stances on some issues. After her appointment to the seat, Gillibrand won the election in 2010 without any serious Democratic competition.[28]

Parties and Political Campaigns

Parties play a key role in national, state, and local political campaigns. While we often talk about one candidate's "campaign," in fact there are several phases to a campaign, each with its own dynamics. First, candidates have to decide to run, which often invovles the help of party leaders and activists. Second, parties establish a process through which they will nominate their chosen candidates. Finally, parties act to support their nominees in the elections themselves. We will examine the decision to run for national office (Chapter 12) and the dynamics of political campaigns (Chapter 10) later in this book. Here the focus will be on the process of nomination.

The Nomination Process

After recruiting and supporting candidates, parties shape the process of **nomination**, in which a party officially selects one candidate to run for one office against the nominees from other parties. In some races and in some

Exploratory presidential candidate Bobby Jindal, Republican governor of Louisiana, speaking to reporters at a sponsored event in May 2015.
Richard Ellis/Getty Images.

states, the electoral process may pit members of the same party against each other in the general election. We will explore this in more detail in the next chapter when we consider the race to become the newest member of California's Twenty-Fourth District in the House of Representatives.

Once the official presidential campaign process kicks off, declared candidates vie with others in their own party for that party's nomination. Beginning early in the election year, candidates seek to get the support of party **delegates**, whose votes they will later need to secure the party's nomination. While many of the rules governing the nomination process are set by federal and state laws, most of the details about *how* things actually work are hammered out by the parties themselves. There remain key differences across states and between the parties themselves.

Most states hold **presidential primary elections**, in which a state's voters choose delegates who support a particular candidate (see Figure 9.2). In some states, these elections may be **open primaries**, in which all eligible voters may vote in a party's primary election, regardless of that voter's partisan affiliation. Others may hold **closed primaries**, open only to registered voters from a particular political party. While open primaries encourage undecided and independent voters to participate in a way that closed primaries do not, they also open up the possibility for strategic voting. Feeling confident in the chances of the presumed nominee in their own party, voters may then use their votes to sabotage the candidate in the opposing party whom they see as the biggest threat to their own preferred candidate.

Advocates of holding more open primaries say they help make elections more competitive while taking the gatekeeper role away from senior party officials. "The problem [with politics] isn't the money. The problem is the parties themselves," said John Opdycke, the president of Open Primaries, a group seeking to implement the process nationwide.[29] But critics of open primaries in presidential races say the importance of registered voters choosing a party's candidate is diluted because members of the other party and independents can cast ballots. Advocates say this system produces candidates who are in line with what that party's voters want. But critics say that it radicalizes candidates by making them appeal to the party's hard-core extremists, leading to nominees who are too far outside the mainstream.

nomination
the formal process through which parties choose their candidates for political office.

delegates
people who act as voters' representatives at a convention to select their party's presidential nominee.

presidential primaries
elections in which a state's voters choose delegates who support a particular candidate for nomination.

open primary
a primary election in which all eligible voters may vote, regardless of their partisan affiliation.

closed primary
a primary election in which only registered voters from a particular political party may vote.

NEWS CLIP
Democratic Convention delegates respond to anti-Sanders emails

FIGURE 9.2

Presidential Primary Systems by State, 2016

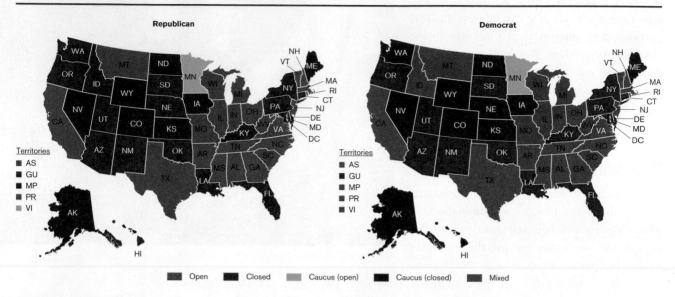

Republican

Democrat

| Open | Closed | Caucus (open) | Caucus (closed) | Mixed |

Source: Information about the 2016 primary calendar is from 2016 Election Central, "2016 Primary Schedule," http://www
.uspresidentialelectionnews.com/2016-presidential-primary-schedule-calendar/.

caucus

a process through which
a state's eligible voters
gather to discuss candidates
and issues and select
delegates to represent their
preferences in later stages of
the nomination process.

Some states hold **caucuses**, in which eligible voters gather to discuss candidates and issues and to select delegates to represent their preferences in later stages of the nomination process. Caucuses differ from primaries because the voting may be public instead of being done by secret ballot. The rules for taking part in a caucus also are more complicated as they involve more than simply marking a ballot to record the selection of a candidate.

At their most basic level, the caucuses are organized by voting precincts within cities and towns. At a typical precinct caucus meeting, supporters from various campaigns give speeches about why they back their candidate. Then participants break into groups depending on which candidate they support, or they indicate that they are still undecided. Before any delegates can be elected, a group needs to meet a certain threshold of all of those present—usually at least 15 percent. If that requirement is not met, groups can try to persuade people to join them to increase their size.[30] Because of their complexity, caucuses tend to draw fewer participants than primaries, typically attracting those who are more committed to a candidate or cause. In Iowa's first-in-the-nation presidential caucuses in February 2016, more than 186,000 Republicans and 171,000 Democrats took part, a turnout rate among those eligible to vote of just under 16 percent.[31] In the first twelve presidential primary election contests that followed that year, the combined turnout rate was 29 percent (17.3 percent for Republicans and 11.7 percent for Democrats).[32]

Why do some states have primaries while other have caucuses, and still others have mixed systems? There are a variety of reasons, but they generally center on how much control the state seeks to exercise. If a state holds a primary, the state government—and not the state party—has to finance it. But in return, the party has to abide by the state laws governing the process, such as the date of the primary and who can participate. Holding a caucus gives a state party more flexibility on the date.

The two major political parties have differed in how they award delegates based on primary elections and caucus results. The rules continue to change and evolve, but the

Democratic Party has tended to award delegates through a proportional system in which delegates are divided based upon total vote share, though with a few twists and wrinkles. One of these is the existence of **superdelegates**. Superdelegates are members of the Democratic Party—usually elected officials or party activists—who are not pledged to any certain candidate based on the outcomes of their state's primary or caucus. They can support any candidate they choose (Figure 9.3). The Republican Party, on the other hand, has tended toward more of a winner-take-all (or winner-take-most) system of awarding delegates, in which a state's committed delegates are awarded either to the winning candidate statewide or, more commonly, split between winners in the state overall and winners in the individual congressional districts.

There are risks with either approach. Awarding delegates through a proportional system tends to push back the date by which any one candidate wins enough delegates to secure the nomination; awarding them based on a winner-take-all system tends to speed it up. A quicker conclusion to a nomination season benefits a party by allowing it to focus its efforts on the general election to follow and avoid the narratives of a divided party. On the other hand, a rapid conclusion to the process may end things before some potentially viable candidates—especially those favored by party elites and insiders—have a chance to gain traction among regular voters in the nomination season.

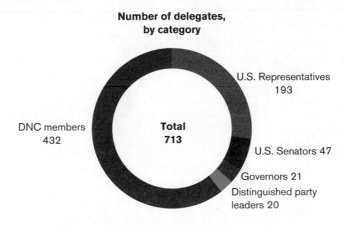

Alan Nelson, a caucus chair for the Bernie Sanders campaign, counts caucus attendees at a Democratic caucus at Jackson Township Fire Station in Keokuk, Iowa, in February 2016.
Michael B. Thomas/AFP/Getty Images.

superdelegates
members of the Democratic Party—usually leaders or members of note—who are not pledged to any certain candidate based on the outcomes of their state's primary or caucus.

FIGURE 9.3

Who Are the Democratic Party's Superdelegates?

Number of delegates, by category

- DNC members 432
- Total 713
- U.S. Representatives 193
- U.S. Senators 47
- Governors 21
- Distinguished party leaders 20

A breakdown of Democratic Party superdelegates, by position.

Notes: Four vacant Democratic National Convention (DNC) positions not shown. Twelve governors, senators, and representatives also are DNC members; they are categorized by elective office only.

Source: "Who Are the Democratic Superdelegates" Pew Research Center, Washington, DC (May, 2016) http://www.pewresearch.org/fact-tank/2016/05/05/who-are-the-democratic-superdelegates/.

Using Maps to Explore the Consequences of Primary and Caucus Schedules

Geographical representations of data can be useful tools in exploring important topics in political science. We have discussed the fact that the schedule of state caucuses and primaries can and does have important political consequences. One of the issues with this scheduling involves the degree to which voters in states that participate early in the cycle may be advantaged in selecting eventual nominees. Figure A displays the month of a state's primary or caucus in the 2016 presidential elections.

Keeping Figure A in mind, consider Figure B, which displays counties in which racial or ethnic minorities constituted a majority of voters in 2014. While the data are county based, focus on the patterns between states, connecting these population patterns to the data presented in Figure A.

WHAT DO YOU THINK?

One of the criticisms of the current caucus and primary schedule is that it disadvantages members of racial and ethnic minorities by bringing states with larger minority populations into the nomination process later in the process, when many campaign narratives have already been constructed or reconstructed. Do you think these data support that argument? What other data might you want to investigate this issue further?

Figure A: Frontloading: Presidential Primary and Caucus Scheduling by State, 2016

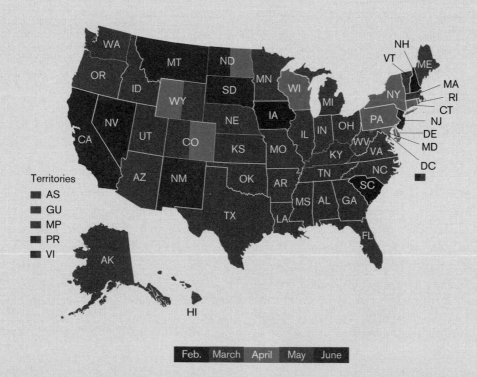

Territories
- AS
- GU
- MP
- PR
- VI

Feb. March April May June

Note: In states where Democrats and Republicans hold primaries and caucuses in different months, the timing of the Democratic elections is shown on the left and the timing of the Republican elections is shown on the right.

Source: Data are from "Presidential Primaries and Caucuses by Month (2016)," FrontloadingHQ, January 31, 2016, http://frontloading .blogspot.com/p/2016-presidential-primary-calendar.html, accessed June 15, 2016.

Figure B: The Distribution of Counties in Which Racial and Ethnic Minorities Constitute a Majority of the Population

Legend:
- Hispanic (94 counties)
- Black (93 counties)
- American Indian/ Alaskan Native (26 counties)
- No single racial/ ethnic majority (151 counties)
- Non-Hispanic white majority

Source: Map is from Drew DeSilver, "Share of Counties Where Whites Are a Minority Has Doubled since 1980," Pew Research Center, July 1, 2015, http://www.pewresearch.org/fact-tank/2015/07/01/share-of-counties-where-whites-are-a-minority-has-doubled-since-1980/, accessed June 30, 2016.

The schedule of primary elections and caucuses also matters to the ultimate outcomes of the nomination process. Party leaders in a state have a strong incentive to hold their primary election as early as possible in order to garner media attention as well as candidate attention. A win in an early state helps party candidates establish momentum, and issues that are important to specific states may translate later into policy attention should one of the party's candidates win the presidency. To take advantage of this, states try to engage in a process of **front-loading**—pushing their primaries or caucuses as early in the season as possible. Of course, party leaders know of this problem and have even threatened to punish states that jump the line and push their primaries or caucuses forward with a loss of delegates, a threat that the RNC made real in 2012, for example, when Florida moved its primary to January.

By tradition, the Iowa caucuses and then the New Hampshire primary have been the first two on the schedule. While neither state's nomination process results in a large number of delegates awarded, their early position creates a problem of perception and demographics. Since both states have larger white, non-Hispanic voting populations than much of the rest of the nation, there is a concern that the diversity of American voices will not be heard until the narrative of the nomination campaign has already been established.

front-loading
when a state pushes its primary or caucus to a date as early in the season as possible to become more instrumental in the nomination process.

national convention
a meeting where delegates officially select their party's nominee for the presidency.

The final phase of the nomination process takes place in the **national conventions** held by the parties in the summer of the presidential election year. During the conventions, delegates vote to select the party's nominee. While for much of American history national conventions were sources of high drama, with many rounds of delegate voting required to select a nominee, in recent decades the final outcome is already known or expected. In modern conventions, the drama comes from the selection of the vice presidential nominee—typically done by the presumptive presidential nominee and (usually) without much drama—and from speakers and the order in which they speak at the convention. For failed candidates, a key speaking spot at a national convention can be a useful consolation prize or a stepping stone to future prominence on the national stage. In 2004 Barack Obama, then an Illinois state senator and candidate for the U.S. Senate, was selected to give the keynote address at the Democratic National Convention (DNC), which both signaled and fueled his status as a rising star within the party.

At the national convention, most, but not all, delegates are "bound" to vote for the candidate that voters have chosen in their state or district during at least the first round of balloting. But if no candidate gets the delegates needed to win, subsequent rounds of votes are held until someone does. This process features a lot of behind-the-scenes courting of delegates to switch their votes and is known as a "brokered" or "contested" convention.

Questions about what parties do and how they should go about it both involve a third consideration: how effective parties are in going about their activities. When it comes to the power of the national parties in deciding on presidential nominees, that question remains the subject of considerable debate in political science. In 2008 four political scientists argued in an influential book titled *The Party Decides* that party leaders serve as powerful gatekeepers. The parties—whom the political scientists defined not just as senior party officials but the organized advocacy and interest groups that make them up—"scrutinize and winnow the field before voters get involved, attempt to build coalitions behind a single preferred candidate, and sway voters to ratify their choice."[33]

It is a complicated relationship between candidates and their parties. Politicians rely on their parties to help them get elected or stave off challengers, but in doing so they grant power to party leaders. According to political scientist John Aldrich, when things get really interesting, though, is when candidates no longer feel that the parties and party

Parties typically select their nominees for president at their national conventions amidst much fanfare but without much drama. In 2016, both the Republican National Convention in Cleveland, OH (left) and the Democratic National Convention in Philadelphia, PA (right) had more drama than usual. At the Republican Convention, some Republican Party leaders refused to endorse Trump, and Sanders supporters disrupted the proceedings in Philadelphia at several points. Eventually, however, both Donald Trump and Hillary Clinton received their party's nod.

Jim Watson/AFP/Getty Images; Ricky Carioti/The Washington Post via Getty Images.

leadership are serving their goals. Aldrich says, "In such cases politicians turn elsewhere to seek the means to win."[34] Does the party decide, steering the nomination process towards selecting the most "electable" candidates in the general election, or can voters in primaries and caucuses impose their will should they feel that party leaders are not responding to the issues that voters want addressed? If there ever was a presidential election to put this question to the test, it was 2016.

> **Does the party decide, steering the nomination process towards selecting the most "electable" candidates in the general election?**

The Party in the Electorate

Parties shape American politics not only through their organizational capabilities but also through their ability to connect with voters. In their efforts to do this, parties rely on a variety of methods. One is **party identification**, or the degree to which voters are connected to a particular party.

We have already explored the individual contributors to Americans' political beliefs (Chapter 7). Later we will explore how individuals' identities and lived experiences affect their vote choices and whether or not they vote in the first place (Chapter 10). Parties, however, are not passive actors in this relationship. One of the most important things that parties do is to signal that they will advance the agendas associated with a particular set of political beliefs, which is key to their role in providing candidates with labels and voters with cues and shortcuts. **Party ideology** refers to the consistent set of stances on major issues shaped by an underlying philosophy about the proper role of government in society and then communicated to voters.

In the United States, the two major parties identify with the key political ideologies that we discussed earlier. In recent decades, the Democratic Party has told voters that it will pursue policies connected with liberalism; the Republican Party, with conservatism (Figure 9.4). It is important to remember that party ideology and party identification are not the same thing. Parties do try to appeal to potential members by focusing on issues, policies, and solutions that might appeal to individuals with particular ideologies. As we discussed in Chapter 6, however, individuals' political beliefs, including partisan identification, have many contributors and sources, including family, education, and life experiences.

Since the 1980s, more people have identified themselves as Democrats than as Republicans. But one frustration for both parties is that larger numbers of people consistently have not identified with either party (Figure 9.5). In fact, a Gallup poll taken in 2015 showed that just 29 percent of those surveyed called themselves Democrats—the lowest figure in the past twenty-seven years and probably the lowest since the early 1950s. Meanwhile, 26 percent of those questioned for the survey considered themselves Republican—just one percentage point above the historically low figure of 25 percent recorded two years earlier.[35] In contrast, the percentage of Americans self-identifying as independent has grown sharply. Why? A big part of it is Americans' deep frustration with the inability of the federal government to enact policies. A separate Gallup poll published in January 2016 asked Americans what they felt was the nation's top problem. Government came in first, several percentage points ahead of the economy.[36]

However, it is more complicated than that. As we discussed in Chapter 7, the wording of surveys matters. How might a researcher deal with individuals who do not identify

party identification
an individual's attachment to a particular party.

party ideology
a set of stances shaped by an underlying philosophy about key issues and the proper role of government in society and then communicated to voters.

FIGURE 9.4

Party Ideology: How Democrats and Republicans Differ

Democrat		Republican
Pro-choice	*Abortion*	Pro-life
Maintain race-based preferences	*Affirmative action*	Against race-based preferences
Protect the rights of the accused	*Crime*	Strong punishment for offenders and protect the rights of the victim
Increased regulation and worker protection	*Business*	Ease regulation and keep government out of business
Ban	*Death penalty*	Maintain
Decrease or maintain	*Defense spending*	Increase
More regulation	*Gun control*	Protect gun ownership
Maintain or expand the Affordable Care Act	*Health care*	Repeal the Affordable Care Act
Amnesty for undocumented immigrants, allow undocumented people to obtain drivers' licenses	*Immigration*	Prevent amnesty, no drivers' licenses, create a national ID card, add border fences
Increase	*Minimum wage*	Lower or eliminate
Legalize	*Same-sex marriage*	Ban
End	*School vouchers*	Expand
Increase taxes, especially for wealthy	*Taxes*	Cut taxes, especially for businesses

Liberalism ← → *Conservatism*

with a major party but say that they do "lean" towards one? In the same survey that measured party identification, Gallup presented the data of those who leaned toward the Democratic or Republican Party. Based on those results, the landscape looks a bit different. In 2016 will those who lean towards a party vote with that party or choose a third party? Based upon what we know, most will vote for candidates from the party that they are closest to, though this is not a lock.

Although Americans often say they want politicians to compromise, some experts have found that in reality, they generally prefer the other side to accede to their wishes. That's because consistency has been shown to be very important to people, no matter what their ideology. The parties reflect those attitudes. As one scholar of political beliefs stated, "Few people march under a banner that says, 'We may be right, we may be wrong, let's compromise!' You know, that's not good politics."[37]

In general, the parties try to make their case to the public by offering sharp contrasts to each other. Both the Republican and Democratic national committees make daily assertions and put out dozens of news releases, videos, tweets, and other social media presentations that seek to further a single larger point: The other side is wrong. In this sense, both parties have a partisan agenda—they are less interested in fostering cooperation than they are in criticizing their opponents. After the terrorist shootings in San Bernardino, California, in 2015, RNC chair

> "Few people march under a banner that says, 'We may be right, we may be wrong, let's compromise!' You know, that's not good politics."

FIGURE 9.5

Americans' Party Identification over Time: Two Perspectives, with and without "Leaners"

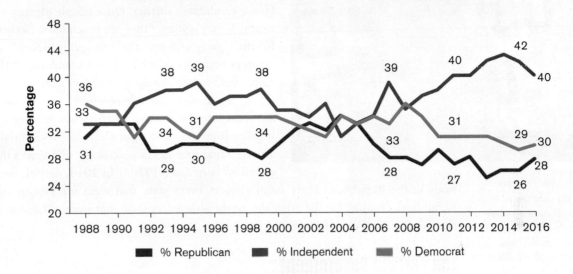

U.S. Party Identification, Yearly Averages, 1988–2016

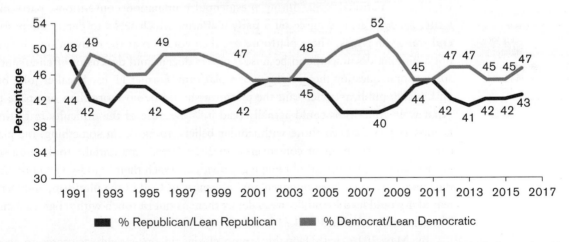

U.S. Party Identification (Including Independent Leanings), Annual Averages, Gallup Polls, 1991–2016

Note: Gallup began regularly measuring independent' party learnings in 1991. Data for 2016 are current through September 18, 2016.

Source: Jeffrey M. Jones, "Democratic, Republican Identification near Historical Lows," Gallup, January 11, 2016, http://www.gallup.com/poll/188096/democratic-republican-identification-near-historical-lows.aspx?g_source=Politics&g_medium=lead&g_campaign=tiles and Gallup, "Party Affiliation," http://www.gallup.com/poll/15370/party-affiliation.aspx. Copyright © 2016 Gallup, Inc. All rights reserved. The content is used with permission; however, Gallup retains all rights of republication.

Reince Priebus issued a statement saying that it proved Democrats "cannot be trusted to keep America safe from radical Islamic terrorists."[38] Meanwhile, DNC chair Debbie Wasserman Schultz said her reelection to the House of Representatives was preferable to voters choosing "a bunch of radical Republicans who act like children. Actually, sorry. That's insulting to children."[39]

Colorado Republican voters gather at the state capitol to protest the delegate selection process when GOP officials decided not to hold a straw poll in March 2016 and denied them their vote.

Joe Amon/The Denver Post via Getty Images.

split-ticket voting
when a voter chooses a candidate from one party for one office and a candidate from a different party for another position on the ballot.

party platform
a set of positions and policy objectives that members of a political party agree to.

polarization
a sharp ideological distance between political parties.

gridlock
an inability to compromise and enact legislation that is driven by political polarization.

Voters have shown less inclination in recent decades to back candidates of different parties in a single election, a practice known as **split-ticket voting.** From 1964 until 1988, as many as one-third of House elections featured a candidate of one party winning even though a presidential candidate of the other party got the most votes in that House candidate's district. Once people identify a group to which they belong, "they are much more likely to vote for their party and less likely to split a ticket," according to political scientist Matthew Levendusky. "They are more likely to become devoted cheerleaders."[40]

In 2012 only twenty-six out of the House's 435 members won elections in districts where someone who was not from their party got the most presidential votes. The resulting split-ticket percentage of 5.7 was the lowest it had been since 1920.[41] In 2016, despite deep divisions in the Republican Party establishment, every state that went for Trump elected a Republican senator. On the other side of the aisle, every state that went in Clinton's favor elected a Democrat to the Senate.

The Party in Government

If they have been successful in mobilizing citizens to vote for the candidates they have selected and supported, a party's members take office and begin the process of governing. At the national level, during presidential nomination conventions, party members write, argue over, and agree on a **party platform,** which seeks to define the party's general stance on issues. These platforms are then voted on at the conventions. Because it is not a binding document, and because it covers dozens and dozens of often-arcane issues, some people question the usefulness of a platform. Former House Speaker John Boehner, an Ohio Republican, once said the platform should be no more than one page because "that way, Americans could actually read it."[42] Because of the difficulty in getting large groups of people, even those with similar beliefs, to agree on something, the platforms can be the source of great controversy. In 2012 Democrats initially took out a sentence in their party's platform about helping individuals reach their "God-given potential." But that removal would have removed any references to God in the platform, and Democrats feared it would lead Republicans to depict them as out of touch with religious Americans. The sentence was added back.[43]

By May 2016, with Donald Trump closing in on enough delegates to secure the Republican nomination outright, there was less talk about what a Trump platform might look like than about his battles with the party establishment, which were partly because of his refusal to present detailed policy positions on many issues. According to a *Los Angeles Times* reporter, "One cannot even agree with Trump in his 'policies,' because that is like committing to the blob in a lava lamp."[44] As Bernie Sanders continued to perform well in the Democratic primaries and caucuses, however—though the delegate math was turning against him—many observers looked ahead to a Sanders-influenced Democratic Party platform in the summer conventions with Hillary Clinton as the presumptive nominee.

The pressures that parties face to point out sharp differences between their positions and those of the opposition have led to increasing political **polarization.** Polarization isn't the result of a flaw in our constitutional system, but the Constitution's separation of powers has made it worse. In Washington, increased polarization has led to **gridlock,**

The Two Parties Rethink Their National Strategies

After Mitt Romney lost the 2012 presidential election, the Republican National Committee appointed a task force of long-time party activists called the Growth and Opportunity Project to make recommendations on how the party needed to change. In 2013 it issued its report, claiming, "It is time to smartly change course, modernize the party, and learn once again how to appeal to more people, including those who share some but not all of our conservative principles."[45]

The report talked about the enduring influence of former president Ronald Reagan but warned that the party seemed too dependent on invoking Reagan's legacy without trying to appeal to younger voters who did not remember Reagan's 1981–1989 tenure. It stated,

> Our party knows how to appeal to older voters, but we have lost our way with younger ones. We sound increasingly out of touch. The Republican Party needs to stop talking to itself. . . . Devastatingly we have lost the ability to be persuasive with, or welcoming to, those who do not agree with us on every issue. Instead of driving around in circles on an ideological cul-de-sac, we need a Party whose brand of conservatism invites and inspires new people to visit us. We need to remain America's conservative alternative to big-government, redistribution-to-extremes liberalism, while building a route into our party that a non-traditional Republican will want to travel.[46]

Overwhelming Republican gains in the 2014 midterm elections, in which Democrats lost majority control of the Senate, led Democratic National Convention officials to form their own task force in 2015 to examine how their party could improve. The task force specifically pointed to how poorly Democrats have done in contrast to the Republicans in recruiting talented young candidates who can rise through the ranks. Democratic Party task force members also said the party had not communicated its message effectively. Their report stated that the party would create a National Narrative Project to better articulate what the party stands for: "One of the most striking findings of the Task Force's initial conversations was the difficulty faced by candidates, elected officials, activists and others in concisely, consistently answering the question, 'What does it mean to be a Democrat?' The beauty of the Democratic Party lies in the very fact that we are not one-size-fits-all. We are enriched by our diversity."[47]

WHAT DO YOU THINK?

Both of America's two major parties have undertaken serious reflection about what they need to do to appeal to more voters. What does the fact that two outsiders, Bernie Sanders and Donald Trump, managed to secure so much support, and with one of them—Donald Trump—winning the presidential election, say about the parties' success in achieving the goals the parties laid out in the statements above?

which occurs when parties are unable to find any common ground to work together, an increasingly common occurrence over the last few decades. When separation of powers is combined with extreme positions, the result is deadlock, according to political scientist Jane Mansbridge. "Deadlock was less of a problem in the early days of the republic, when today's interdependence in commerce, law and order could not even have been imagined, and the national legislature did not have to pass many laws. Today that deadlock is a disaster."[48]

All members of a political party do not hold the same beliefs. Each party contains factions within it that try to pressure the party to adopt its positions. Labor unions are one important faction within the Democratic Party; they push the party to raise the minimum wage and pass other bills aimed at improving working conditions. In the Republican Party, the Tea Party has become an influential faction within the last decade. It is not a formal party but a loosely organized collection of groups that demands steep cuts in government spending, extremely limited regulation of private companies, and more accountability from government employees.

1. The responsible party model focuses on the need for party leaders to be less cohesive and offer a variety of perspectives to voters.

   a. True
   b. False

2. How do state caucuses and primaries differ?

3. How has party identification by the American electorate changed in recent decades?

4. What challenge to the theory that "the party decides" did the Sanders and Trump campaigns pose?

Answer Key: 1. b; 2. Answers should focus both on the different mechanics of the processes and on the differences between participants; 3. Answers should emphasize the fact that while most Americans still identify as either Democratic or Republican, the percentage of those who identify as independents has risen.; 5. Answers should focus on the candidates' different challenges to the party establishment.

THE PRESIDENTIAL ELECTION OF 2016

Bye Bye, Conventional Wisdom

As the presidential nomination season of 2016 progressed, both Bernie Sanders and Donald Trump surprised political scientists, political pundits, and their own party leaders with their success, although, in Sanders's case, Hillary Clinton was still seen as the almost inevitable nominee for the Democratic Party. On the Republican side, several mainstream candidates, such as former Florida governor Jeb Bush, Florida senator Marco Rubio, and New Jersey governor Chris Christie, all vied for their party's endorsement, along with more than a dozen other candidates. "Successful political parties unite interests under a broadly shared policy agenda," social scientist Joel Kotkin observed.[49] Under Clinton, Kotkin said, Democrats "share basic positions on many core issues and a unifying belief in federal power as the favored instrument for change. In contrast, the Republican Party consists of interest groups that so broadly dislike each other that they share little common ground."[50]

The Democratic Party's rules worked in Clinton's favor. Even though Sanders thoroughly defeated her, 60 percent to 38 percent, in the New Hampshire primary, the party's delegate-allocation rules neutralized his victory. The win earned Sanders fifteen delegates, while Clinton earned nine. But she also had won the earlier endorsement of six of the state's eight superdelegates—the party's elected officials and party activists—earning her essentially a tie in the state. Sanders's supporters cried foul, but the process in place wasn't a new one. The Democratic Party had developed the superdelegates because it wanted to be able to pick presidential nominees strategically. Party members believed that long-term party members would have an interest in backing the strongest possible candidates and that giving those officials the power to switch their votes could avoid messy fights over the nomination.[51]

Sanders alienated many in the Democratic Party establishment over a controversy involving access to computerized voter data. Employees working for Sanders were accused of improperly obtaining information from Clinton's data files after a firewall between the two campaigns' information was inadvertently dropped. The DNC retaliated by cutting off the Sanders campaign's access to the committee's own voter file information, leading the senator's supporters to accuse the party of blatantly favoring Clinton, even though Sanders himself apologized to Clinton at a debate over the incident. His campaign later filed a lawsuit against the committee.[52]

The Sanders campaign also bickered with the DNC about the number and timing of debates during the primary season. Underdog candidates always vastly prefer as many debates as possible because it gives them great visibility without having to spend any campaign dollars. The committee had scheduled some debates on Saturday nights, when the senator said fewer people would be watching. In one instance, an Iowa debate ran at the same time as a big University of Iowa football game. The party said that was a coincidence, but Sanders said it was done deliberately to draw attention away from the debate.[53]

In the early voting states, Sanders did better than Clinton at caucuses than in primaries. That is because caucuses tend to favor candidates who have extremely enthusiastic supporters, which Bernie Sanders often had. In caucuses, participants get to make speeches to try to persuade others to support their candidates, and there are sometimes multiple rounds of voting, neither of which occurs in a primary, where a voter casts a private ballot alone.

The Democratic Party provided Clinton with other advantages over Sanders. The most obvious was that she actually belonged to the party; he did not. That gave her a broad network of prominent supporters who coalesced ahead of primary voting to warn of what they saw as the danger of a Sanders candidacy affecting other races in which Democrats were running. "Here in the heartland, we like our politicians in the mainstream, and [Sanders] is not—he's a socialist," said Democratic Missouri governor Jay Nixon two months before his state's primary. "He's entitled to his positions, and it's a big-tent party. But as far as having him at the top of the ticket, it would be a meltdown all the way down the ballot."[54]

Sanders's message, however, had gotten through. Sanders succeeded in forcing Clinton to take positions similar to his on trade and jobs. For example, when she first declared her candidacy, Clinton vowed to be "president for the struggling, the striving and the successful."[55] But after losing the Michigan primary, she said, "I don't want to be the president for those who are already successful—they don't need me. I want to be the president for the struggling and the striving."[56] She also expressed a greater willingness to raise taxes on the wealthy to keep Social Security from going broke.[57] After her loss to Sanders in the Michigan primary, Clinton won primaries in other states, such as Ohio and Missouri, where trade and job losses to foreign countries were big concerns.

In his campaign, Donald Trump took positions that were so extreme—and made statements considered so outrageous and off-putting—that fewer than usual Republican Party loyalists were willing to join him, even though his stances and pugnacious style attracted public support. Few senior party officials took Trump seriously in the early months after he announced his candidacy. But as he gained strength in the polls and began winning primaries, those party officials were caught in a difficult bind. Many of them were appalled by Trump, yet the RNC had created the rules that enabled Trump to prevail in the early primaries. RNC chair Priebus insisted that the party would support whoever emerged as its nominee, boasting in January that he was "100 percent" confident of that fact.[58]

Trump's candidacy exposed the Republican Party's weaknesses in several ways. Republicans could not, as they had in some past elections, unify around a consensus candidate. Several candidates who were popular with the party's establishment all plunged into the race, including Jeb Bush and Marco Rubio. None of the consensus mainstream candidates succeeded in captivating broad swaths of voters, however, and all eventually dropped out.

Democratic presidential candidates Hillary Clinton and Bernie Sanders at a CNN debate in 2016. Clinton's "insider" status within the Democratic party was a significant factor in her ultimately securing the nomination.

Louise Wateridge/Pacific Press/LightRocket via Getty Images.

Part of the reason for this was that the RNC, in drawing up the rules for 2016, ended up providing Trump with significant institutional advantages. The RNC had come under criticism within the party for the primary process in 2012, which dragged on for months before Romney emerged as the nominee. Thus, for 2016 it moved up its schedule with the hope that a front-runner could emerge more quickly. The result was that many states that year voted in March, a month or two earlier than they had in 2012. Another change intended to help cement an early frontrunner was that a majority of the Republican delegates at stake were awarded by states' congressional districts—the winner of each district received two delegates, the runner-up received one, and none of the other finishers received any. In making those changes, the RNC was trying to placate both the party's establishment, which wanted a shorter calendar, and its conservative activists, who had advocated for proportional delegate selection. But it did not anticipate that Trump would get more votes than candidates from either of those groups. As journalist Trip Gabriel put it, "It's right in line with what the folks designing these rules wanted. It's just not the candidate they preferred."[59]

> "It's right in line with what the folks designing these rules wanted. It's just not the candidate they preferred."

Trump's campaign rallies, in which several demonstrators were attacked and Trump offered to pay his supporters' legal fees, made party officials even more uneasy, leading the RNC chair to issue a public call for calm. By March some prominent Republicans said it was impossible for them to support Trump. "If our party is no longer working for the things we believe in . . . then people of good conscience should stop supporting that party until it is reformed," said Republican senator Ben Sasse of Nebraska.[60] The result was that many Republican officials switched their endorsements to Texas senator Ted Cruz, a man whom many of them loathed for his disdain for working with colleagues in his party and for likening the Republican establishment to a "cartel," or drug mafia. Cruz also picked up some of the delegates from other candidates who had abandoned their campaigns. In Louisiana, for example, Trump beat Cruz by four percentage points, but Cruz picked up several of Marco Rubio's delegates.[61]

Cruz and Trump became locked in a race filled with a nastiness never before seen in modern presidential politics. Trump repeatedly referred to Cruz as "Lyin' Ted." When the supermarket tabloid *National Enquirer* subsequently alleged that Cruz had had multiple extramarital affairs, the Texas senator blamed "Trump and his henchmen" for spreading a story he said was "garbage" and "complete and utter lies."[62] As the bickering raged, the Republican Party's image nosedived. A CNN poll in late March found the party's unfavorable rating at its highest level since the partial government shutdown in 2013, when it had notched its worst ratings in polling dating back to 1992. Just 34 percent of adults said they had a positive view of the party, with 61 percent saying they had a negative one. Even among registered Republicans, the favorability rating plunged from 73 percent in January to 66 percent.[63]

The RNC had anticipated acrimony among the large field of candidates. In 2015 the committee asked all of them to sign a formal public pledge that they would support the party's eventual nominee. Initially, the candidates agreed during several debates—even

The field of contenders for the Republican presidential ticket in 2016 was extensive. In an early debate in October 2015, ten of the top candidates participated in a prime-time event (another group had debated earlier). Shown are, from left to right, John Kasich, Mike Huckabee, Jeb Bush, Marco Rubio, Donald Trump, Ben Carson, Carly Fiorina, Ted Cruz, Chris Christie, and Rand Paul.

Jason Bahr/CNBC/NBCU Photo Bank via Getty Images.

Bernie Sanders and the Superdelegates

In June of 2016, Hillary Clinton secured the magic number of 2,383 pledged delegates to the Democratic Party's national convention in July. It was not a primary or caucus that carried her over the hurdle, but commitments by previously uncommitted superdelegates (composed of members of Congress, governors, and other party leaders). During the early months of 2016 many supporters of Bernie Sanders criticized the fact that a large number of superdelegates had already pledged to support Clinton, even while the nomination campaign was just getting under way. Activists with MoveOn.org started a petition to require that superdelegates wait to pledge until after results of the caucuses and primaries were in. Following Clinton's nomination, however, MoveOn.org poured its energies into defeating Donald Trump in the General election.

In May, prior to the official nomination, political cartoonist Mike Keefe created the image above right.

WHAT DO YOU THINK?

What themes do you think Keefe is trying to portray with this image? What do you make of the portrayal of Bernie Sanders and Hillary Clinton in this image? Which of the two candidates do you think is pictured in a more positive way? In a more negative way?

---

those laden with personal attacks—that they would stick to it. But at a town hall meeting in March 2016, Cruz backed away from the pledge, followed by Ohio governor John Kasich and Trump.[64] Trump's campaign accused senior party officials and the news media of conspiring against Trump. "The press is printing the narrative that the Republican establishment is setting," said Barry Bennett, a senior adviser to Trump's campaign.[65]

1. In the 2016 presidential campaigns, Donald Trump and Bernie Sanders agreed on _____.

   a. The need to restrict immigration
   b. A more robust role for the American military in world affairs
   c. A dissatisfaction with political insiders and elites
   d. The need for a more robust national social welfare policy

2. As the presidential nomination campaigns of 2016 progressed, how did the parties' establishments respond?

3. What issues that we have explored in terms of party cohesion and the challenges of insurgents did Trump's success—despite establishment opposition—illustrate?

Answer Key: 1. c; 2. Answers should include party establishment worries about the policies and statements by Trump and Sanders.; 3. Answers should discuss the desire of party elites to maintain party cohesion and also respond to challenges by those on the extreme ends of party goals.

WHAT HAVE I LEARNED?

THE DEVELOPMENT OF AMERICAN POLITICAL PARTIES

As you read about how the system of American political parties has mostly remained stable except for a small number of major shifts, reflect upon why the candidacies of Sanders and Trump posed a challenge to their own parties. Consider the following:

- What factors contribute to elections that redefine the party landscape

- How the presidential election of 2016 might or might not signal a shift in American politics

- The role and power of third parties in American elections

For about the last 150 years, most politicians have belonged to either the Democratic or Republican Party. Since then, control of government has shifted back and forth between the parties in periods of **realignment**, which occur when public support shifts substantially from one party to the other. Periods of realignment may be ushered in by **critical elections** (or critical eras), which, according to political scientist John H. Aldrich, describe what some evolutionary biologists refer to as a phenomenon of punctuated equilibrium, in which a short event or era leads to a "new period of relative stability."[66]

While party realignments and critical elections may be related, they are not necessarily the same thing. Nor do they have to go together. A party realignment may be signaled or brought on rapidly by a critical election, but many important realignments, such as the movement from Democratic Party dominance to Republican Party allegiance in the American South during the civil rights era, occur over a longer period of time. Political scientists disagree over how well realignment theory accurately describes the modern landscape.

realignment
a major shift in allegiance to the political parties that is often driven by changes in the issues that unite or divide voters.

critical election
a major national election that signals a change either in the balance of power between two major parties or the emergence of a new party system.

party systems
periods of stability of the composition of political parties and the issues around which they coalesce, brought on by shorter periods of intense change.

The Party Systems

While political scientists continue to debate the boundaries of major eras in party control and how decisive a particular election was in signaling a change in those boundaries, they often refer to the underlying phenomenon to which Aldrich was referring: periods of stability punctuated by periods of rapid change. They call the more-or-less stable eras **party systems**. Political scientists often divide American political history into six party systems, though, again, there is still debate about their boundaries and when precisely the shifts between them happened (see Figure 9.6).

The First Party System, 1790-1828: Factions and the Creation of America's First Political Parties

America's first president, George Washington, was not a member of a political party and indeed had warned the nation about the dangers partisanship posed to the young Republic. However, during his tenure, Washington's administration split into two factions. On one side were Treasury Secretary Alexander Hamilton and Vice President John Adams. They supported a strong federal government, especially in the area of national economic policy. On the other side were Secretary of State Thomas Jefferson and James Madison. Jefferson and Madison worried about national power and believed that individual states should be given more authority over their own affairs. As these individuals tried to gain support for their policies in Congress and in the state legislatures, they coalesced into two parties: the Democratic-Republicans (Jefferson and Madison) and the Federalists (Adams and Hamilton).

The Second Party System, 1828-1856: The Roots of Mass Politics

The Democratic-Republican Party had largely dissolved by 1824, with many of its members moving to form what became known as the Whig Party. This era also saw the decline of the Federalist Party. Due to the granting of suffrage to large numbers of white men who had previously been excluded because of their lack of wealth or property, this era saw the rise of the Democratic Party and the election of Andrew Jackson as president in 1828. The Democratic Party remained the dominant party in Congress for the next three decades. The politics of national campaigns evolved into how we now think about them, featuring broad appeals to voters and strengthening party organizations.

The Third Party System, 1856-1892:
The Issue of Slavery Upends the Party System

The issue of slavery, present but unresolved at the Constitutional Convention, led to a major realignment, with members of both parties divided among themselves. This led to the forming of two new parties. "Free Soil" Democrats joined with Whigs in arguing that slavery should be kept out of the rapidly expanding southwestern territories in the United States. They stressed a belief in the potential of the individual and argued against slavery on moral grounds, saying slaves "cannot choose if they are coerced by their so-called masters, and if slaves have no moral choices, they cannot develop."[67] The antislavery Whigs and Democrats formed the Republican Party. The new Republican Party won control of the House of Representatives but then lost it two years later. That led the party to broaden its appeal to owners of small farms and businesses, and it succeeded in recapturing control of the House in 1858. Two years later, it also took control of the Senate and elected Abraham Lincoln as president.[68] After the Civil War, the United States entered the period of two-party dominance by the Democratic and Republicans. Party identification became sharply regional, with Republicans dominating the Northeast and Democrats the South. Support for the parties was divided in the Midwestern states.

The Fourth Party System, 1892-1932:
New Divisions in the American Party System

During this era, Democrats and Republicans continued to dominate national politics, though not without occasional challenges by third parties. Slavery had ended, but the two parties were divided by the politics of Reconstruction and differences of opinion about how strongly the federal government should act to secure civil rights. In addition, divisions between urban and rural voters as well as debates over immigration and federal policy in an era of massive industrialization shaped politics and party success and failure.

The Fifth Party System, 1932-1968:
Economic Crisis and a New Party System

The Civil War caused a tectonic shift in the American party system; in 1932 it was an economic catastrophe that ushered in another major change: the Great Depression. The election of Franklin Roosevelt in 1932 and in three subsequent elections led to a period of Democratic Party dominance. Between 1930 and 1994, the Democrats lost their majority in the House just twice, in 1946 and 1952, and they quickly regained control two years later both times.[69] The Democratic Party emphasized a commitment to a strong federal government in the service of social welfare policies. Republicans emphasized a smaller role for the federal government and less involvement in and regulation of the economy.

FIGURE 9.6

American Party Systems

1790–1828

FIRST PARTY SYSTEM
- Hamilton and Adams's Federalist Party: strong federal government
- Jefferson and Madison's Democratic-Republicans: more power to states

1828–1856

SECOND PARTY SYSTEM
- Demise of the Democratic-Republican Party, replaced largely by the Whig Party
- Decline of the Federalist Party; rise of the Democratic Party

1856–1892

THIRD PARTY SYSTEM
- Disputes about slavery precipitate realignment. Party identification becomes regionally divided
- "Free Soil" Democrats join Whigs, together form Republican Party: opposed to slavery

1892–1932

FOURTH PARTY SYSTEM
- Democrats and Republicans dominate with some third party challenges.
- Electorate divided by urban/rural splits and other policy issues

1932–1968

FIFTH PARTY SYSTEM
- Depression Era Democratic Party focuses on strong federal government
- Republican Party fights for smaller federal role

1968–present

SIXTH PARTY SYSTEM
- Democratic and Republican Parties remain divided about role of government but constituency changes with Nixon's "Southern Strategy."

The Sixth Party System, 1968-Present Day: Shaping Modern Contours of American Party Politics

During the sixth party system, the Democratic Party remained focused on a vigorous federal government in the service of securing civil rights and support for affirmative action and a woman's right to choose. Republicans remained focused on a smaller federal government, advocating conservative views on social issues, lower taxes, and fewer restrictions on American businesses. What changed were the coalitions of voters supporting the parties, especially with regard to the geography of partisan support in the nation.

The underpinnings of today's Republican Party were laid half a century ago with the resounding defeat of Arizona senator Barry Goldwater, its 1964 presidential nominee. Incumbent Democratic president Lyndon B. Johnson took forty-four states against Goldwater, but the senator energized the political right by running as an uncompromising conservative in opposition to federal civil rights legislation. He declared, "Extremism in the defense of liberty is no vice." His campaign received more than one million contributions, or twenty-five times the number that Richard Nixon got in his ill-fated run for president in 1960 against Democrat John F. Kennedy.[70]

The Republican Party's base began shifting away from the Northeast and toward the rapidly growing South and West, enabling Nixon to win the presidency in 1968 and even more decisively in the 1972 election. Much of this had been driven by the realignment of large numbers of southern white voters from the Democratic Party to the Republican Party during the civil rights era. Nixon strategist Kevin Phillips had urged the president to pursue a "southern strategy" and play on whites' negative reaction to the Civil Rights Act of 1964. Nixon also capitalized on the backlash to the anti-Vietnam War movement, calling on "the great silent majority of my fellow Americans" to support Republican policies.[71]

The Republican Party's fortunes declined temporarily as a result of the Watergate scandal, which led to Nixon's resignation in 1974. But Ronald Reagan reinvigorated the party with his landslide critical-election win in 1980 against Democrat Jimmy Carter. Reagan's message of lower taxes, smaller government, and a strong defense remains highly influential in the GOP today, even though Reagan made compromises on issues such as taxes and immigration that now might not win widespread support for a Republican candidate in 2016. "Anybody who did those things today would be pilloried by conservatives," said historian James H. Broussard, the author of a biography of Reagan.[72]

In 1992 Bill Clinton became the first Democrat since Carter to occupy the White House, partly by prodding his party toward the ideological center after years of being depicted as being too captive to its most liberal factions. But two years later, Republican representative Newt Gingrich of Georgia emerged with a sharply partisan approach that focused on intensifying public resentment of Washington politicians. He unveiled a manifesto, the "Contract with America," that called for tax cuts, an overhaul of the welfare system, and a balanced budget. Gingrich's moves helped his party break the Democrats' forty-year hold on the House and also regain control of the Senate. But continued warring between the parties helped propel Clinton to reelection in 1996.

With Republicans in search of someone who could unite the party, Texas governor George W. Bush campaigned in 2000 as a "compassionate conservative." He lost the popular vote to Vice President Al Gore but carried every southern state while drawing 83 percent of the Evangelical Christian vote, or nine percentage points more than former Kansas senator Bob Dole had received four years earlier in losing to Bill Clinton.[73]

Throughout this period, other changes in the South led to a dwindling in the number of conservative Democrats serving in Congress and a corresponding number of conservative Republicans. At the state level, the Republican Party began using the congressional redistricting process to redraw districts to move greater numbers of Democrats into cities, making the Republican Party more competitive in suburban areas. Meanwhile, northeastern states became less Republican as large numbers of people migrated to the South and West and the mostly moderate and liberal Republicans who remained were overshadowed by what had become a southern-anchored party.

Over the last decade, party control has swung wildly back and forth. Democrats won back control of the House and Senate in 2006. But Republicans castigated the Democratic Party's leader, Nancy Pelosi, the first female Speaker of the House, as a "San Francisco liberal" who was out of touch with the rest of the country. By this time, the Republicans had several conservative mass-media networks that transmitted and amplified their anti-government messages, including Fox News. Also, the Internet had become an entrenched part of Americans' lives. One major consequence of these shifting electoral fortunes was a closely divided Supreme Court.

In 2008 Republicans hoped that Arizona senator John McCain could muster enthusiasm among voters with his national security credentials and heroic story of survival as a prisoner of war in Vietnam. But his selection of Alaska governor Sarah Palin as his vice presidential nominee alarmed even some Republicans as she held extreme positions on issues and often resorted to personal attacks that pleased hard-core conservatives but alienated those not as far to the right.[74] Obama took 53 percent of the popular vote, the best Democratic percentage since 1964. Democrats also kept control of the House and Senate and eventually had a sixty-vote majority in the latter chamber to give them even more clout.

Nevertheless, the party's dominance was extremely short-lived. President Obama pushed several measures to stem the economic downturn, including hundreds of billions of dollars in federal spending and extensions of bailouts of the banking, investment, and automobile industries that Bush had initiated. But these actions led to a political backlash that gave rise to the Tea Party movement. Members of the Tea Party were not hostile to all government programs, however. A Harvard University study found that their opposition to Obama's health care overhaul came even as members liked programs such as Social Security and Medicare, "to which Tea Partiers feel legitimately entitled. Opposition is concentrated on resentment of perceived federal government 'handouts' to 'undeserving' groups," which it said were influenced by racial and ethnic stereotypes.[75]

The Tea Party was credited with helping Republicans regain control of the House in the 2010 elections, though some political scientists said traditional factors such as high unemployment and favorably drawn legislative districts were more responsible.[76] Nevertheless, in the months following the election, the Tea Party's—and the Republican Party's—reputation sustained considerable public damage. A protracted stalemate over passing a budget in 2011, followed by an even tenser showdown over raising the federal government's ability to borrow money, led Democrats to brand Tea Party followers as stubborn obstructionists.

Representative Ted Poe (R-TX) speaks during a Tea Party Patriots rally against the Affordable Care Act in front of the Supreme Court in March 2015.

Alex Wong/Getty Images.

The weakened economy, with an unemployment rate stuck at around 8 percent, led Republicans to confidently predict they could recapture the White House in 2012. But the party did not coalesce quickly around its candidate, Romney, as it had with Bush in 2000. Romney and other Republicans sought to make the elections a referendum on the president's handling of the economy, but Democrats portrayed Romney as a wealthy corporate executive with an inability to understand average Americans. Not only did Obama win, Democrats kept their majority status in the Senate.

After the election, the Republican Party decided to take a hard look at how it could do better. The RNC formed a panel of veteran activists that made numerous criticisms and a series of recommendations, including putting out a positive message and creating a diverse, nationwide operation of local activists. But what drew

FIGURE 9.7

Changes in Party Control, 2000-2016

Election	Presidency	House	Senate
2000	Republican George W. Bush	Republican	Democrat
2002		Republican	Republican
2004	Republican George W. Bush	Republican	Republican
2006		Democrat	Democrat
2008	Democrat Barack Obama	Democrat	Democrat
2010		Republican	Democrat
2012	Democrat Barack Obama	Republican	Democrat
2014		Republican	Republican
2016	Republican Donald Trump	Republican	Republican

the most attention was its call for the party to support passage in Congress of a comprehensive immigration reform bill to help attract the rapidly growing number of Hispanic voters. The panel noted that while Bush drew 44 percent of Hispanic votes in 2004, Romney had won just 27 percent.[77]

The Senate passed an immigration bill in 2013 that won bipartisan support. But the measure stalled in the more conservative House, and the issue became a major concern among those on the political right. They insisted on tougher border security, such as Trump's call for building a wall between the United States and Mexico, and denounced as "amnesty" any attempt to grant those illegally in the country a path to becoming U.S. citizens.

Republicans turned out in much greater numbers than Democrats in the 2014 midterms, swinging control of the Senate back to their party. That led the DNC to do its own postelection assessment of how to improve. It called for a better long-term strategy for winning state elections that could help the party redraw future congressional districts. But most of its report said the party should continue its existing goals of protecting voting rights and recruiting a diverse set of candidates.[78]

A Seventh Party System?

The sixth party system has been one of the longest in the nation's history. However, it is unclear how much longer it will last. The Democratic and Republican parties are trying to stay relevant in an age of intense polarization. That polarization has grown and has led some voters to become engaged not just because they support their party but out of an intense dislike of the other side. Decades ago, party loyalty was based on broad factors. "You could be a Southern Democrat voting for a candidate who loved segregation and hated government health care, or a Northern Republican voting for a candidate who hated segregation and supported Medicare," noted Ezra Klein, editor in chief of the political Web site Vox.com.[79] Although the parties clearly hold very different views from each

NEWS CLIP
Growing impact of Latinos on the 2012 presidential elections

other, political scientist Corwin D. Smidt has argued that "polarization has not strengthened [voters'] sense of partisan loyalty."[80]

It remains to be seen what this means for the parties. Robert Reich, an economist and liberal activist who served as secretary of labor under President Clinton, predicted an anti-establishment "People's Party" made up of disaffected Democrats and Republicans could take root as soon as 2020.[81] Others say such a shift could occur but that it's also possible the parties could absorb elements that are currently in the other party, such as urban corporate interests switching their allegiance from the Republicans to the Democrats. Even though that won't end the partisanship, they say, it might perhaps cool it. The candidacies of Trump and Sanders, in spite of critical differences between them, did share the anti-establishment theme that Reich predicted.

In the 2016 election, both party establishments witnessed major challenges to their parties' status quo. Sanders, though ultimately unsuccessful in his pursuit of the nomination, challenged the Democratic Party to focus more on issues of economic inequality and the power of Wall Street and the nation's financial institutions. Trump threw verbal grenades into the debate seemingly at every turn. According to an RNC official, "Donald Trump has done to the Republican Party what the killer comet did to the dinosaurs."[82] In terms of conventional wisdom, Trump's extreme statements should have doomed his candidacy. Yet they did not.

Democrats, and even some Republicans, said Trump was the culmination of a Republican Party that encouraged extremism and anger within its ranks but had not harnessed it into a broader vision of what it wanted to accomplish.[83] That caused a deep rupture between the party's corporate-backed wealthier donors and its less affluent blue-collar supporters. Historian Robert Kagan, an adviser to both Republican and Democratic politicians, said Republican voters were taught during the Obama years "that government, institutions, political traditions, party leadership and even parties themselves were things to be overthrown, evaded, ignored, insulted [and] laughed at."[84] Trump voters seemed to agree, electing the insurgent to the presidency. At the same time, voters returned even those Congressional Republicans who did not embrace Trump to the House and Senate. Even party loyalist Paul Ryan, who managed to hold onto his job as Speaker of the House, bent towards Trump, saying, "We are eager to work hand-in-hand with the new administration to advance an agenda to improve the lives of the American people."[85]

> Communicating their messages to Latino voters in the coming decades will determine their strength and relevance in American national politics.

The Democratic Party, however, has had its own problems. Even though Obama easily won election in both 2008 and 2012, Democrats were unable to translate support for him into broader enthusiasm for the party and unable to recruit successful candidates for many lower political offices. As a result, during Obama's two terms, the Democrats lost many seats in the House, Senate, and state legislatures as well as more state governorships. By 2016 Democrats controlled fewer elected offices nationwide than at any time since the 1920s.[86] Part of the reason was Republicans' ability in many states to redraw congressional districts after the 2010 census to make it easier for members of their party to win and remain in office. Democrats tend to cluster in cities, where they can win local elections, but they have less success in congressional or statewide offices. Another reason was the continued inability of Democrats to turn out their most loyal supporters in midterm elections, when a presidential candidate isn't on the ballot.

In the cases of both the Democratic and Republican parties, many experts agree: They are institutions formed in a different era that now must deal with a host of obstacles—including the impatience of society in the twenty-first century—in maintaining the social conditions that help parties thrive. And the landscape is changing dramatically. As we will

FIGURE 9.8

Differences across Countries in the Number of Major Political Parties

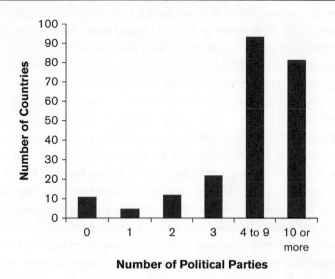

Source: Data are from CIA World Factbook, "Political Parties and Leaders," https://www.cia.gov/library/publications/the-world-factbook/fields/2118.html, accessed June 15, 2016.

explore in the next chapter, America is in the midst of a massive demographic shift, with Latino voters rapidly growing as a share of the electorate. How well the major parties do in communicating their messages to Latino voters in the coming decades will, in no small part, determine their strength and relevance in American national politics.

In 2016 both parties were under siege, especially the Republicans. Some wondered if the Republican Party was about to break up, like a planet hit by a comet or an asteroid. The deeper story, however, was not the possibility of one of the two major parties imploding but why the potential for this was such a big deal. In most democracies, parties often rise and fall without fireworks. Why might 2016 be a critical election for parties in the United States? It turns out the answer to this, the ultimate question in the universe of partisan politics, is—to misquote science fiction writer Douglas Adams—two.[87]

Two-Party Dominance

There is no law requiring that American national politics be dominated by two major political parties. Other countries have none, one, two, or many political parties dominating national politics, with the existence of more than two being the norm (Figure 9.8). With a few very important exceptions, a two-party system has been dominant for most of America's political history. Why? Political scientists have long debated and researched this question. One set of explanations focuses on American political ideology and the historical legacy of conflicts over issues with two sides or between two sets of interests. The problem with this set of explanations is that many other modern democracies wrestle with similar issues and yet have more than two major parties vying for representation.

Instead, scholars usually point to institutional explanations for America's two-party dominance, specifically the ways in which candidates are elected to national office, especially Congress. The United States' method of voting—a **single-member plurality system**, in which voters have a single vote for one candidate and the candidate with the votes

TOPICS IN AMERICAN GOVERNMENT
Two-party system

single-member plurality system
a structure of electoral representation in which a candidate and the party that he or she represents must win the most votes in a state or district in order to be represented in government.

wins—encourages this. Other countries have **proportional representation systems**, in which the rules discourage a two-party system. Although there are many differences between nations in the details, proportional representation systems award party representation in legislative bodies based upon percentage of votes overall.

In the American winner-take-all single-member plurality system, the candidate who gets the most votes in a state or congressional district wins the election. This extends to presidential elections, in which the candidate who wins the popular vote in a state wins all of that state's electoral votes. (Maine and Nebraska are the only two states that don't do it this way; they award one vote to the winner of each of the state's congressional districts then give two additional electoral votes to the winner of the popular vote.)

The winner-take-all system allows the largest politically cohesive groups—the Democrats or Republicans—to elect almost every office in a jurisdiction. Proponents of the system say this promotes stability; if people are happy with the job that a representative from one of those parties is doing, they can keep on voting for that representative's party even after he or she leaves office. They also say that it makes for better representation at the local level; unlike other democracies in which voters get to make second or third choices, the people who want their first choice can mobilize support behind that candidate.

But the system has critics. Some say it doesn't do much to help people who are stuck in an area in which one party dominates, such as Republicans in cities and Democrats in rural states. They say that this can be a significant barrier to encouraging greater numbers of people, including minority groups and young people, to take part in politics. Instead, candidates can run divisive campaigns aimed at turning out only the most partisan voters since the winner-take-all system provides little incentive to reach out to opponents.

The Prospect for Minor Parties in the Twenty-First Century

The Democratic and Republican parties have occasionally had some competition. More than a hundred years ago, it came from the Populists, who called for loosening control over the amount of money in the U.S. economy. In 1896 that party was able to win seven Senate seats and thirty House seats. Many of its initiatives, however, were folded into the Democratic agenda. Another independent party of the era was the Progressive Party, which sought to open the political system and end corruption. Former Republican president Theodore Roosevelt became a leader of the movement, and the so-called Bull Moose-Progressives (named for Roosevelt's admiration of the animal's strength and vigor) succeeded in placing some controls on congressional power. But it eventually evaporated after Roosevelt challenged Republican William Howard Taft for the presidency in 1912; both of them lost to Democrat Woodrow Wilson.

Third-party candidates usually focus on a single issue that they don't think the major parties are emphasizing enough. "What happens is, third parties act as a gadfly," said Sean Wilentz, director of the American Studies program at Princeton University. "There'll be an issue that's being neglected or that is being purposely excluded from national debate because neither party wants to face the political criticism that it would bring."[88]

In 1968 George Wallace, a onetime Democrat, ran for president as an independent candidate on a platform in favor of segregating blacks and whites. (Many commentators have compared Trump to Wallace due to Wallace's fiery, outspoken rhetoric.) Wallace took nearly 14 percent of the vote.[89] Twelve years later, John Anderson, an Illinois GOP congressman, ran under the banner of the National Unity Party as a moderate alternative to Democratic president Jimmy Carter and the more conservative Republican Ronald Reagan and received 6.6 percent.[90]

Third-party candidates have made even bigger splashes since then. In 1992 billionaire businessman H. Ross Perot ran as an independent with the Reform Party on a platform of cutting the federal budget deficit. He captured nearly 19 percent of the vote.[91] And eight years later, consumer activist Ralph Nader captivated many liberals when he ran for president under the Green Party banner. He won 2.74 percent of the popular vote—just enough, many Democrats continue to believe, to deny the presidency to Al Gore.[92] The backlash against Perot in 1992 and Nader in 2000 helped prevent them from leading successful third-party movements. This tendency among some voters to conclude that a vote for a third-party candidate essentially is a vote helping someone they oppose has made it difficult for third-party candidates to win national elections.

The Democratic and Republican parties have worked to discourage third-party candidacies. One way is to prevent those candidates from taking part in presidential debates. Another is having local officials set stringent requirements for candidates to collect a certain number of signatures before they can appear on a ballot, which can be difficult for many third-party hopefuls.

During the general election, as the Clinton and Trump campaigns both struggled against heavily negative perceptions, third party challengers emerged, drawing votes from both. Gary Johnson, candidate for the Libertarian Party, Jill Stein, the Green Party candidate, and Independent Party candidate Evan McMullin all vied to establish their respective parties as credible challengers to the Democratic and Republican parties. Prior to the election, many observers expected third-party presidential candidates to do well, Johnson and Stein in particular. While Johnson won around 3.3 percent of the national vote, and while Stein won roughly 1 percent, neither presented a serious challenge to Hillary Clinton or Donald Trump.[93]

FIGURE 9.9

Americans' Opinions of the Need for Third Parties in the United States

In your view, do the Republican and Democratic parties do an adequate job of representing the American people, or do they do such a poor job that a third major party is needed?

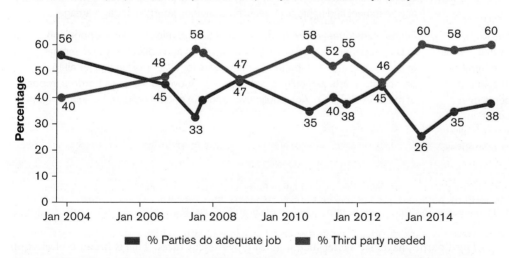

■ % Parties do adequate job   ■ % Third party needed

TABLE 9.1 Third Parties Compared: A Selection

Party	Platform
Constitution Party: "The sole purpose of government, as stated in the Declaration of Independence, is to secure our inalienable rights give us by our Creator. When Government grows beyond this scope, it is usurpation, and liberty is compromised."	Pro: life, state's rights, Second Amendment, limited government Against: illegal immigration and amnesty, influence of the United Nations and other globalist organizations on the United States, undeclared wars, free trade
Green Party: "An independent political party that is connected to American social movements, and is part of a global Green movement."	Democracy, social justice, ecological sustainability, economic justice and sustainability
Libertarian Party: "Minimum government, maximum freedom."	Personal liberty, economic liberty, securing liberty
Peace and Freedom Party: "California's feminist socialist political party."	Double the minimum wage and index it to the cost of living; global disarmament of nuclear, chemical, and biological weapons; defend and extend liberties guaranteed in the Bill of Rights; full and free high-quality public education from pre-K to graduate school; lifelong learning and retraining; cancellation of student debt; free high-quality health care; restore and protect the environment
Prohibition Party: "Charactered leadership driven by hope for a return to traditional values."	Loyalty to the Constitution and especially the Bill of Rights, U.S. sovereignty, no relations with countries that do not practice humanitarian treatment of all people and no aid to unfriendly nations, no wars without consent of Congress, legislation to nullify judicial decisions based on foreign or international law, nine-year term limits to Supreme Court justices, no lawyers may hold legislative or executive branch office, abolish the Federal Reserve system, all-volunteer army
Reform Party: "A moderate, centrist and populist party that sits in the center of the political spectrum."	Fiscal responsibility and accountability; fair taxation without special interest exceptions; an "America first" position on job creation; affordable, accessible health care based on decision making between doctors and patients; reforms at the federal level to enforce the highest ethical standards and effective oversight; protection of natural resources while addressing needs for economic development; energy independence; border security; upholding of Constitution to define scope of government and rights of citizens; no stance on abortion or gay marriage
Socialist Party USA: "Strives to establish a radical democracy that places people's lives under their own control—a non-racist, classless, feminist socialist society . . . where working people own and control the means of production and distribution through democratically-controlled public agencies, cooperatives, or other collective groups."	Global transformation from capitalism to democratic socialism, opposition to U.S. imperialism, workers' rights to organize and collectively own means of production and distribution, human rights for all, opportunities for all to participate in arts and cultural activities, free movement across borders, repeal of the USA PATRIOT Act, public ownership of natural resources, animal rights

Sources: Quotes and other information are from the party Web sites: Constitution Party, http://www.constitutionparty.com/; Green Party, http://www.gp.org/; Libertarian Party, http://www.lp.org/; Peace and Freedom Party, http://www.peaceandfreedom.org/home/; Prohibition Party, http://www.prohibitionparty.org/; Reform Party, http://reformparty.org/; Socialist Party, http://socialistparty-usa.net/.

Third parties have had better luck in local government races. This is because of election rules that help them compete in those races, such as ranked choice voting, which allows voters to rank the candidates in order of preference instead of voting for a single candidate. Proponents of the idea say that it provides voters with more choices and prevents having to hold runoff elections. They point to Cambridge, Massachusetts, a city outside Boston where Harvard is located. Cambridge has used the system since 1941 to elect its city council and school board members, and proponents say it has resulted in greater representation by minority groups and women and has increased voter turnout.[94] Critics of the approach, however, say that the system can be confusing for voters. And they claim it actually discriminates against minorities, non-English speakers, and people without much education. When the city of San Francisco used the system in 2011, turnout was the lowest it had been in thirty-six years.[95]

CONCLUSION
The Fallout

There is a somewhat obscure 1950s science fiction movie called *Attack of the Crab Monsters*. Thanks to, I think, radiation, giant mutant crabs on an island evolve, eat people, and absorb their unfortunate victims' voices, personalities, and knowledge to grow stronger, more powerful, and more dangerous. The mutant crabs use the voices and identities they've stolen to lure other unsuspecting humans to their doom. In the "words" of one of the crab monsters, impersonating a human and trying to lure a group of people into the caves, "It is almost exhilarating! Will you come?"[96]

This is what the two dominant American political parties in American political history have always tried to do with insurgents—without the eating people part, of course. An internal revolution is often a signal that the party has to adapt, to bring the voices of those insurgents back into the fold, to keep the party viable, relevant, and strong. Or, if that fails, to put an end to the insurgency, once and for all.

To say that the presidential election of 2016 was full of drama, controversy, and conflict would be a massive understatement. It was perhaps one of, if not the, most divisive elections in American history. Its consequences are still being digested and debated.

After having finally endorsed and supported nominee Hillary Clinton during the summer's Democratic Party Convention, Bernie Sanders continued to campaign on her behalf. Some observers, however, wondered if Sanders could have beaten Donald Trump in the general election, drawing out voters who might have ended up staying home on the day of the general election. Donald Trump's candidacy, though ultimately successful, struggled against opposition from the Republican Party establishment. For example, former Republican Presidents George H. W. Bush and George W. Bush refused to endorse Trump.

In the weeks leading up to the general election, the situation continued to heat up for both candidates. In October, a 2005 taped conversation between Donald Trump and a reporter from *Access Hollywood* emerged, recording statements in which Trump made derogatory, hostile, and demeaning comments about women. Eleven days before the general election, FBI Director James Comey sent a letter to Congress alerting members that he was reviewing possible new evidence related to the investigation into Secretary Clinton's use of a private email server while she was in office. Two days before the election, Director Comey announced that the reopened inquiry was being closed.

In the end, Donald Trump defeated Hillary Clinton in the only vote that matters for the presidency: the Electoral College. While Secretary Clinton won the popular vote by over 2 million votes (as of November of 2016), Trump defeated Clinton 306 to 232 in the Electoral College. To many observers' surprise, Trump managed to breach what had been called the "blue wall" of solidly Democratic states, including Pennsylvania, Michigan, and Wisconsin. In the days following Donald Trump's win, protests erupted around the nation; some of them turning violent. A few posts on Facebook and Twitter called for his assassination.

While political scientists will no doubt be talking about the election of 2016 for years, one of the main questions will be this: what impact will the candidacies of Bernie Sanders and Donald Trump have on their respective political parties? Sanders attempted to push the Democratic Party to embrace the need to address economic inequality, issues that nominee Clinton began to address more frequently as her campaign progressed. Donald Trump's populist rhetoric alienated many Republican leaders, yet, in 2017, the Republican Party will control the White House, Congress, and the majority of state governorships and legislatures.

In this chapter, we have explored the challenge that Bernie Sanders and Donald Trump presented to their own parties' establishment. That turned out to be very true; however, the larger story about the election of 2016 may not be only about divisions within political parties, but about deeper divisions within the American republic itself.

CHAPTER REVIEW

This chapter's main ideas are reflected in the Learning Objectives below. By reviewing them here you should be able to **remember** the key points, **connect** them to the stories presented in the chapter, **think** critically about these questions, and **know** these terms that are central to the topic.

9.1 Understand why Sanders and Trump posed such a challenge to their parties as well as why their messages resonated with large numbers of voters.

REMEMBER...

- Political parties help citizens figure out which candidates to vote for, send cues about policy positions, and help translate platforms into policy.
- There is increasing partisanship in the U.S. electorate, and parties are more polarized than ever.
- At the same time, parties themselves are becoming weaker and less able to enact their preferred policies.

CONNECT...
- In the election of 2016, Trump and Sanders both challenged their parties' leadership and platforms, claiming to be speaking for citizens whose interests weren't actually being represented by their parties.

THINK...
- What was so unusual about the presidential candidacies of Sanders and Trump?

KNOW...
- *political party* (p. 294)

▶ 9.2 Identify the roles that parties play in American representative democracy.

REMEMBER...
- Ideally, political parties provide clear positions on issues the parties are strongly committed to, demonstrate internal cohesion both while in power and when in opposition, and have the ability to resist interest group pressure.
- Parties are organizations with leaders who work to promote the candidates and issues they support. They unite people under a set of common ideas and goals.
- Parties are reflected in the electorate by citizens who express solidarity with their views.
- In government, elected officials work to enact their parties' policies.

THINK...
- Do you think parties are helpful or harmful to American democracy?

KNOW...
- *responsible party model* (p. 299)

▶ 9.3 Evaluate the ways in which the structure of the nomination process can affect both the outcomes of the process and the representation of party members.

REMEMBER...
- Parties recruit candidates to run for offices at all levels, selecting people who reflect the ideas of the party and who would make strong challengers for office.
- Parties shape the nomination process by setting rules for how candidates are picked and selecting candidates to run on their tickets.
- Parties support potential candidates by fund-raising, helping them determine their viability and raise their visibility, and other kinds of outreach.
- Candidates for the presidency must seek the support of delegates who will later vote for their nomination.
- In conjunction with federal and state laws, state parties establish the rules by which their candidates are nominated for the presidency, including what type of primary election process that state will have and when it will be held.
- At their national convention, most state delegates are bound to vote for the candidate voters have chosen for their state, but in a brokered convention their votes may change.
- Political scientists have argued that parties often play the deciding role in candidate selection.
- Parties signal to voters their support for a particular set of political beliefs. Consistent party ideology provides candidates with labels and voters with cues and shortcuts.
- Fewer Americans are identifying with the Republican and Democratic parties, which has consequences for voting behavior.
- Once in office, parties advocate for issues that align with their platform; the party out of power does what it can to resist policy changes at odds with its views. Pressure to maintain contrasts between the parties has led to increased polarization. Inability to compromise has led to gridlock.

- Both the Democratic and Republican races for the presidency in 2016 presented a major challenge to the idea that the parties, and not voters themselves, ultimately decide who the candidate will be.

- Trump's candidacy exposed some important weaknesses within the Republican Party in terms of its cohesion, problems that were further complicated by some of the rules the party implemented prior to the election that gave Trump certain institutional advantages.

THINK...

- How powerful are parties?

KNOW...

- *recruitment* (p. 302)
- *nomination* (p. 303)
- *delegates* (p. 303)
- *presidential primary elections* (p. 303)
- *open primary* (p. 303)
- *closed primary* (p. 303)
- *caucus* (p. 304)
- *superdelegates* (p. 305)

- *front-loading* (p. 307)
- *national convention* (p. 308)
- *party identification* (p. 309)
- *party ideology* (p. 309)
- *split-ticket voting* (p. 312)
- *party platform* (p. 312)
- *polarization* (p. 312)
- *gridlock* (p. 312)

9.4 Explain how American party systems have evolved over time.

REMEMBER...

- Control of government has shifted back and forth between the parties during periods of realignment, which occur when public support shifts substantially from one party to the other, often following critical elections.

- Coherent party systems exist during periods of stability between episodes of realignment. Major parties are then identified with a clear set of issues and compete for voter support based on stable distinctions.

- Scholars generally have divided American political history into six party systems.

CONNECT...

- Trump's success as a disruptor candidate—one who at least threatened to usher in a new party system—may have been the result of a Republican Party that had over time encouraged extremism and anger within its ranks without having connected it to a broader vision.

THINK...

- Why have American party systems been relatively stable throughout the nation's history? What has led to change?

KNOW...

- *realignment* (p. 318)
- *critical elections* (p. 318)

- *party systems* (p. 318)

9.5 Examine theories behind two-party dominance in American political history.

REMEMBER...

- Unlike most countries in the world, the United States has for most of its history had just two major parties. For the last 150 years, those have been the Democratic and Republican parties.

- The United States uses a single-member plurality system (or winner-take-all system), which typically means that the largest politically cohesive groups—the Democrats or Republicans—are able to elect every office in a jurisdiction.

KNOW...
- *single-member plurality system* (p. 325)
- *proportional representation system* (p. 326)

▰ 9.6   Debate the prospects for third parties in American politics.

REMEMBER...

- Competition for the two main parties in the United States has sometimes come from third (or minor) parties, which tend to focus on a single issue their members think the other parties are not emphasizing enough. The major parties generally try to squelch their efforts.

- Third parties tend to have more success at the local level, where different electoral rules give them more space.

THINK...

- Do you think a new major third party might emerge in the near future? If so, what might its core beliefs be?

KNOW...

- *third party* (p. 326)

10 CAMPAIGNS AND ELECTIONS
Candidates and Voters in an Era of Demographic Change

National elections are the tools with which the American political system chooses its representatives—its presidents and members of Congress. National campaigns are the tools that would-be representatives use to connect to American voters. Candidates use them to introduce themselves and to convince voters that they—and not any of their opponents—are the best choice for making the people's wishes known in Washington and enacting these wishes in legislation and policies.

As we will explore, however, campaigns and elections are both composed of many moving parts. The rules governing them, the people who choose to run, and the composition of the electorate all may shift over time, sometimes with profound and long-lasting consequences. Candidates, even those who have been in elected

Nomey Pacheco welcomes people to a Latino voting rally on the campus of the University of Colorado in advance of the Republican Party's presidential debate in October 2015. Both Republicans and Democrats knew that courting the Latino vote and encouraging turnout would be critical to success in the 2016 elections.

AP Photo/David Zalubowski.

office for years, need to be aware and adaptable, ready to change message or strategy if necessary. American political campaigns are no place for dinosaurs . . . not in the long run.

In this chapter, we will focus on the stories of presidential and congressional candidates in the election of 2016 and, especially, on their efforts to capture the votes of Latina and Latino voters. Candidates sought to mobilize these voters to turn out in the elections and to convince members of these communities that they were the ones best suited to make the Latino voice heard in the national government. This is not always an easy task. Even the term that candidates, political scientists, and others use to describe these voters is up for discussion and contestation. Some sources refer to them as Latino or Latino/a, others as Hispanic.[1] In this chapter we will generally use the term *Latino*, though with occasional references to *Hispanic* when quoting others or referring to census data and other official categorizations.

After reading this chapter, you will be able to:

10.1 Discuss the challenges facing the candidates for the 2016 presidential election as they sought to reach out to the growing Latino population

10.2 Describe the role of campaign contributions in national elections and discuss efforts to regulate them

10.3 Understand the rules surrounding national elections as well as the structure and stages of presidential campaigns

10.4 Evaluate the main issues in congressional campaigns, including the roles of constituency and incumbency

10.5 Appraise the degree to which Americans' diverse voices are heard in national political campaigns and elections

LEARNING OBJECTIVES

LATINO OUTREACH IN THE 2016 ELECTION

NEWS CLIP
Trump's controversial immigration comments

As the 2016 presidential and congressional elections moved from debates and commercials to the parties' nomination campaigns in caucuses and primaries, one reality was becoming impossible to ignore: the American Latino vote, especially the young adult Latino vote, was going to be critical. Latinos have become the fastest growing ethnic group in the United States, a trend that is very likely to continue for decades. Should these potential voters speak with a coordinated voice and cast ballots in an election, this could fundamentally reshape American national elections, and candidates ignore this possibility at tremendous political risk. However, in 2016 the group's nascent electoral power was far from fully realized, in large part because their presence at the polls was not guaranteed.

Candidates and leaders within both major parties took notice of the seemingly inevitable demographic ascendency of Latinos in American national politics and tried to convince these potential voters that if elected they would truly represent the diverse interests of members of Latino American communities. However, as the 2016 presidential campaign kicked into high gear, many leading candidates in both parties were struggling with these attempts to connect.

On the Republican side, two of the would-be presidential nominees highlighted their Latino ancestry and the fact that none of the likely Democratic Party nominees shared that ancestry. Both Republican Party hopefuls were U.S. senators of Cuban American descent—two of only three Latino Americans serving in the Senate.[2] During the nomination campaign, Ted Cruz of Texas and Marco Rubio of Florida both sought to portray their candidacies as the one best able to represent Latino voters and siphon support from the eventual Democratic Party nominee in the fall. Both also focused on the issues many Latino voters said they cared about.

When announcing his candidacy for the Republican Party's nomination in Miami in April 2015, Rubio alluded to his ancestry and family history. He took a subtle jab at his opponent, Republican governor Jeb Bush, the son of one former president and the brother of another, when he stated, "I live in an exceptional country where the son of a bartender and a maid can have the same dreams and the same future as those who come from power and privilege."[3] Cruz and his supporters also tried to highlight the benefits for the Republican Party's prospects should it nominate a Hispanic candidate. "Ted has a history of connecting with Hispanic voters. In his run for Texas Senator he garnered 40 percent of the Hispanic vote," proclaimed a Web page run by powerful backers. "To win a swing state like Florida, Ted would need to receive 66 percent of the Cuban vote. Considering Ted himself is of Cuban descent, winning key swing states with large Hispanic populations is feasible."[4]

As Cruz and Rubio reached out to Latino voters, however, they faced two challenges. The first was the diversity of lived experiences of individuals described by the term *Hispanic*. As Cuban Americans, Cruz and Rubio share ancestry with only one of many nationalities of origin of Americans who self-describe as Hispanic or Latino. This diversity of origin is accompanied by a diversity of views and policy preferences, with many Latino voters expressing connections to their nation of ancestry rather than to an umbrella term like *Hispanic*. For example, Maria Herrera, a retired housekeeper in Las Vegas interviewed for the *Washington Post* in 2016, expressed "no affinity for Marco Rubio even as he aims to make history as the first Hispanic president of the United States. As she explained: 'He's Cuban. I'm Mexican. . . . I would never vote for him just because he's Latino.'"[5]

Another challenge involved the issues at play in politics in 2016. To many critics, some within the Republican Party itself, solutions were to be found in policies, not the identities of candidates. In the words of J. C. Watts, an African American and former member of Congress (R-OK), "Where are our solutions to deal with incarceration reform, unemployment, the trouble blacks and Hispanics have getting home mortgages? Republicans who ignore Ferguson and Baltimore and Black Lives Matter are refusing to hear the depths of what people are experiencing."[6] College senior Jessica Carrera summed up the feelings of many young Latinos when she stated, "Certain candidates in the Republican party just don't embody any of the qualities that I want to see in the future president. . . . They're just so closed off to the possibility that immigrants can have a positive effect on the country."[7]

During a series of Republican Party debates, Cruz and Rubio both tried to portray

Republican candidates Marco Rubio, left, and Ted Cruz take part in debates at the Reagan Library in Simi Valley, California.

Justin Sullivan/Getty Images.

the other as "a major flip-flopper on immigration."[8] Political advertisements made in support of two of Rubio's opponents—Cruz and Jeb Bush—"cast him [Rubio] as cozy with President Obama and Democratic Sen[ator] Chuck Schumer" in devising a failed 2013 effort to pass immigration reform in Congress.[9] For his part, Rubio took on Cruz as well. In an appearance on ABC's *This Week*, Rubio said of Cruz, "When it comes to Ted, he has changed his position on immigration all over the place."[10]

In December 2015, Hispanic leaders within the Democratic Party organized a gathering in Nevada. A major part of its focus was to strategize about how to take on Cruz and Rubio. Democratic Party activists launched a series of attacks through social media, radio, and television ads. Members of these Democratic Party–affiliated groups called the two men "traitors to their own culture."[11] To some, the decision to use such harsh language against fellow Americans of Latino ancestry was not an easy one to make: "It's not comfortable for us to do this, to call out members of our own community who don't reflect our community values, but we have no choice," said Cristóbal Alex, president of the Latino Victory Project.[12]

The groups' decision to call out Rubio and Cruz for what they saw as a failure to listen to the voices of Latino Americans was based both upon policy and politics. On the public policy side, to those leveling the charges the core issue was clear. It was about the two Republican hopefuls' positions and statements on immigration policy. Democratic Party activist attacks on Rubio and Cruz, however, were also about political strategy. Should either win the Republican Party nomination, he might draw Latino voters, who traditionally have tended to vote Democrat, away from that political party and away from that party's presidential nominee. One conservative Hispanic activist said "the attacks represent an acknowledgement by pro-Democratic activists that either Cruz or Rubio could alter the landscape of the Hispanic vote."[13] According to Daniel Garza, executive director of the Libre Initiative, "They [Cruz and Rubio] are a huge threat to the Latino left . . . . Oh, man, you are going to see the aggressiveness ramp up because they are a genuine threat to increasing the percentage of the Latino vote if they win."[14] Garza said Rubio "especially would have tremendous appeal as he taps into the aspirational struggle of many Latinos and talks about his own rise as the son of a bartender and a maid."[15]

Of the leading Republican candidates for that party's nomination, Rubio and Cruz were not the only ones singled out for their policy proposals and statements on American immigration policy. In a news release issued in December 2015, Latino Democratic Party activists also targeted Donald Trump, who was leading national polls of Republican Party candidates. But the *Washington Post* reported that "while Trump continues to grab headlines with his hateful anti-Latino, anti-immigrant language, the positions of the two Latino presidential candidates in the race are equally dangerous for Nevada communities."[16]

> The coming decades will mark the first time in the nation's history that white non-Hispanics will not have constituted a majority of Americans and eligible voters.

On the other side of the political aisle, however, things were not going entirely smoothly either. In December 2015, Democratic Party front-runner Hillary Clinton posted to her official campaign Web site, "7 Things Hillary Clinton Has in Common with Your *Abuela* [Grandmother]."[17] The post led with a picture of Clinton and her husband, former president Bill Clinton, with their new granddaughter. Its goal was to reach out to Latino voters and potential voters and to connect Clinton's goals, experiences, and policy positions to issues of concern to them.

In the post, Clinton highlighted the fact that "she isn't afraid to talk about the importance of *el respeto*" [respect].[18] She also voiced her concerns for children throughout the nation, saying, "You shouldn't have to be the granddaughter of a former president to live

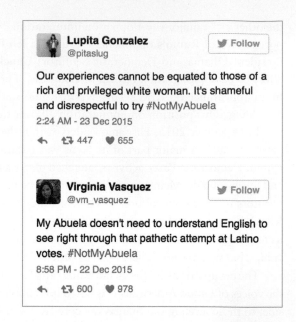

Lupita Gonzalez
@pitaslug
🐦 Follow

Our experiences cannot be equated to those of a rich and privileged white woman. It's shameful and disrespectful to try #NotMyAbuela

2:24 AM - 23 Dec 2015

↩ ⟲ 447   ♥ 655

Virginia Vasquez
@vm_vasquez
🐦 Follow

My Abuela doesn't need to understand English to see right through that pathetic attempt at Latino votes. #NotMyAbuela

8:58 PM - 22 Dec 2015

↩ ⟲ 600   ♥ 978

Left: A 2015 photo from Hillary Clinton's official campaign Web site in which she tries to reach out to Latino voters. *Right:* Tweets to #NotMyAbuela in which these Latina posters sharply criticized Hillary Clinton's strategy.

Left photo: Hillary Clinton for President 2016.
Right photo: Twitter.

demographics
the grouping of individuals based on shared characteristics, such as ancestry, race, ethnicity, and gender.

up to your God-given potential in America. You should be able to be the granddaughter of a factory worker or the grandson of a truck-driver—and every day as your president, I'm going to get up trying to figure out what more I can do to make sure every person, and particularly every child, has a chance to do just that."[19]

Clinton's efforts to reach out to Latino voters did not go completely as planned; some "criticized the list as pandering to Hispanics, while others pushed back against Clinton's economic privileges and advantages."[20] Some Twitter followers and political commentators called these efforts "Hispandering"[21] and said they were not backed up by a stronger call for a basic, and substantial, overhaul of American immigration policy.

At the beginning of 2016, the presidential election campaigns kicked into high gear. The leading contenders in both parties faced their own struggles in convincing Latino voters that they were best qualified to represent the diverse interests of these communities. Every candidate realized this was a political effort that had to be made. It was a battle for votes that had to be won, both in this election and those that would follow. The reason for this is math.

In the future, American political campaigns will be heavily driven by **demographics**, which are groupings of individuals based on shared characteristics. The composition of the American electorate will be changing over the next several decades. Candidates, parties, and political activists are already very familiar with what is coming down the pike in terms of this future composition of the nation. The ways in which American parties and candidates respond to these changes will, to a very large degree, determine their electoral successes and failures and, perhaps, their very survival in their current form.

Driving all of this is the growth in the number of Latino Americans via immigration, birth rates, and generational change. By 2043, according to analysts with the United States Census Bureau, America will be a plural nation, with members of no single traditional racial or ethnic group constituting an absolute majority of the population. This will mark the first time in the nation's history that white non-Hispanics will not have constituted a majority of Americans and eligible voters.[22]

The force behind these changes is the massive growth of the population of Hispanic Americans. By 2060 Hispanics are projected to make up over 30 percent of the nation's population—nearly doubling the percentage of just a few decades prior. In contrast, the percentage of white, non-Hispanic Americans in the nation's population is projected to decline from more than 60 percent in 2013 to roughly 43 percent (Figure 10.1).

FIGURE 10.1

Projected Changes in the Racial and Ethnic Makeup of the United States

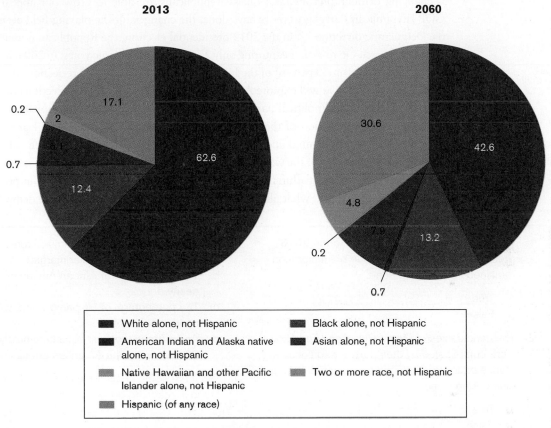

2013

0.2

2

5.1

0.7

12.4

17.1

62.6

2060

30.6

42.6

4.8

7.9

13.2

0.2

0.7

■ White alone, not Hispanic	■ Black alone, not Hispanic
■ American Indian and Alaska native alone, not Hispanic	■ Asian alone, not Hispanic
■ Native Hawaiian and other Pacific Islander alone, not Hispanic	■ Two or more race, not Hispanic
■ Hispanic (of any race)	

Source: Data are from United States Census Bureau.

While the math may be very clear, however, the political changes due to this shift in demographics are not. The political consequences will be profound if—and this is a big *if*—eligible voters from Latino communities exercise the power of their collective numbers by voting and by mobilizing other potential voters within their communities. That big *if* is very much part of the political calculi of candidates and political parties. In the coming decades, in the political battles between America's two major political parties—or any hopeful third party—much of the fight will center on capturing and energizing Latino votes.

In Chapter 9, we discussed the issue of party realignments in American political history, noting that many political scientists challenge the theory. The future demographic changes in the American electorate might have the potential to produce a major shift in the party system, depending upon the participation rates of Latino voters as well as their support for one political party or another. Consider Texas, for example. In 2016 the state had thirty-eight electoral votes, second only to California's fifty-five (we will explore what electoral votes are later in the chapter). Traditionally a safe Republican state in modern presidential elections, Texas is undergoing a profound demographic change. By 2020 Hispanic Texans are expected to outnumber whites; by 2042 they are expected to make up a majority of the state's population.[23] Should these changes tip the state to the Democratic Party in future presidential elections, it would be very difficult for any Republican candidate to secure the presidency.

Republican Party officials are well aware of these challenges. In a 2012 report by the Republican National Committee's Growth and Opportunity Project, often referred to as the "autopsy report," party officials and strategists concluded, "The nation's demographic changes add to the urgency of recognizing how precarious our position has become. America is changing demographically, and unless Republicans are able to grow our appeal the way GOP [Republican Party] governors have done, the changes tilt the playing field even more in the Democratic direction."[24] In the 2012 presidential election, the Republican nominee lost to President Barack Obama after capturing only 27 percent of Hispanic votes. In 2004, in contrast, George W. Bush won 40 percent of the Hispanic vote in his successful reelection campaign.[25]

In this chapter, we will explore American national campaigns and elections through the lens of candidates and political parties confronting, successfully or not, a profound coming change in the composition of the nation's electorate. In doing so, we will learn about the nuts and bolts of presidential and congressional campaigns and elections. We will also gain a deeper understanding of the ways in which the electoral process does, or does not, respond to the diversity of voices within the electorate. Once again, the stories are about people, how their choices matter, and what all of this means for American representative democracy.

WHAT HAVE I LEARNED?

1. During the campaign leading up to the 2016 presidential elections, the issue of immigration remained in the background.

   a. True
   b. False

2. The candidacies of Marco Rubio and Ted Cruz were complicated by their party's traditional stance on immigration and their own identity as Latino Americans.

   a. True
   b. False

3. Projections of the future composition of the American electorate in the twenty-first century predicted that by 2060 _____.

   a. White, non-Hispanic voters will remain a majority but by a smaller margin
   b. The percentage of African Americans will nearly double
   c. The percentage of Hispanic voters will nearly double
   d. Asian Americans will constitute nearly 20 percent of the American population

4. What are some challenges that Cruz and Rubio faced in reaching out to Latino voters?

Answer Key: 1. b; 2. a; 3. c; 4. Answers may mention the diversity of the experiences and ancestry of Latino voters as well as Republican Party stances on issues such as immigration, which remain problematic to many Latinos.

ELECTIONS AND DEMOCRATIC REPRESENTATION

The framers of the Constitution did not want the system they created to be *too* democratic; they feared the potential mischief of faction and the dangers of tyranny of the majority. Therefore, they built in roadblocks to slow down the transmission of the "passions of the people" into public policy. Senators, for example, were originally chosen by state legislatures rather than by the people and, as we will explore later in the chapter, the process of electing presidents was a complicated and perhaps convoluted one.

Another safeguard against faction is the system of American federalism, which divides sovereignty between the nation and the states, with each level checking the other and the two often having to come together to enact major policy change. One consequence of American federalism, as provided for in the Constitution, is that "The Times, Places and Manner of holding Elections for Senators and Representatives, shall be prescribed in each State by the Legislature thereof."[26] The effects of this clause have been consequential. For example, prior to the ratification of the Nineteenth Amendment, women could vote in some states but not others. And today its language ensures that states can devise their own voting technologies, whether electronic or paper based, and have different policies on whether or not those convicted of felonies are allowed to vote.[27]

Compared to other democracies in the world, Americans get to exercise their right to vote with a frequency that is rather unique. If one includes local, county, state, and national officials, Americans, in the aggregate, have the chance to decide how more than half a million governmental posts are filled. As we explored in Chapter 6, however, many Americans do not vote, sometimes because they choose not to do so or in some cases because they are shut out of the process. The latter may occur because of immigration status, small but significant barriers to registering as voters and making it to the polling place during a workday, or previous involvement with the criminal justice system.

American elections are also notable for the fact that they occur on fixed and predictable schedules. Unlike in parliamentary systems, in which the chief national executive has the choice of when to "call" an election (subject to specific rules and constraints), in the United States, voters weigh in on their president every four years, regardless of what is happening in the nation or world, through economic depressions and even war.

Protestors outside Republican Party headquarters in Chicago, Illinois, hold signs calling for immigration reform and a new focus on domestic policies such as education, which is one of the most important issues to many Latino voters.
Scott Olson/Getty Images.

The Functions of Elections

In a representative democracy, elections serve other important purposes besides selecting individuals for a specific office or position in government. Elections are the key way Americans can keep their elected officials in line. Voters achieve this by using the threat of voting an **incumbent** out of office and voting in a **challenger** if they decide the incumbent's performance has not been in line with their goals and policy preferences. This reflecting back on an incumbent's past performance in an election is called **retrospective voting**.[28] Elections also serve as a signal—a way of transmitting information to elected officials about voters' preferences and priorities.

Elections help define or change the national agenda, especially when candidates respond to the growing electoral and political power of voters whose agenda-setting preferences may not have been well-addressed in the past. Trying to assess the top issues for Latino voters is not always an easy task. It is a diverse group, and many surveys are not conducted in Spanish. However, a 2014 Pew Research Center survey concluded that the top five issues for Latino registered voters were—in order of perceived importance—education, jobs and the economy, health care, immigration, and conflicts in the Middle East.[29]

Elections also confer legitimacy on the laws and public policies enacted. Finally, participation in the electoral system may serve to remind Americans of their rights and liberties and the need to protect those rights; thus, they are educative.

incumbent
a current officeholder.

challenger
a candidate for office who does not currently hold office.

retrospective voting
reflecting back on an incumbent's past performance in an election.

One of many things that money buys in a campaign is the ability to reach voters, in this case by financing travel to get to them.

Brendan Hoffman/Getty Images.

Money in Political Campaigns

So you want to be president. Do you have a billion dollars? Or, more precisely, can you come up with a billion dollars or encourage others to spend a good chunk of that sum on behalf of your efforts? You will probably need it. In the 2012 presidential campaign, roughly $1 billion in total was spent in support of each of the campaigns of Democratic candidate Barack Obama and Republican candidate Mitt Romney, a figure that includes candidate spending, national party spending, and money spent by others in support of their respective campaigns.[30]

Adding in total candidate and outside spending on the other national elections that year, the total spent was about $7 billion, a "total number of dollars [that] exceeded the number of people on this planet."[31] Early estimates of total spending in the 2016 election campaigns pointed to a similarly massive expenditure, perhaps more than $6.9 billion when finally counted.

What Money Buys

What do candidates get for all of this money; where does it go? Certainly, money is used to purchase goods and services, but it is a bit more complicated and strategic than that. First and foremost, money buys media time, on television and radio, in print, and in social media outlets. Some campaign advertisements focus on the candidate's qualities and creating a positive image. Others focus on policy differences between the candidate and his or her opponents. Finally, **negative campaign advertisements** attack an opponent or opponents and try to raise doubts in voters' minds about them. While negative campaigning, which has been part of presidential politics since the election of 1800, is pervasive and often uncomfortable, not all scholars agree that it is a bad thing. Political scientists John Geer has argued that negative campaign ads may actually "increase the quality of information available to voters as they make choices in elections."[32]

negative campaign advertisements
campaign ads that attack an opponent or opponents and try to raise doubts in voters' minds about them.

Money also allows a candidate to hire campaign staff, help manage the campaign message, coordinate a campaign and media strategy, arrange public appearances, and conduct public opinion polls. Efforts to mobilize voters or potential voters, called **get out the vote (GOTV)** efforts, also cost money. Finally, having a sizeable war chest, especially early in a campaign, might discourage potential challengers from entering a race in the first place. In this way, money is also a strategic weapon. For all of these reasons, the cost of winning the presidency has only gone up (Figure 10.2).

Get out the vote (GOTV)
efforts to mobilize voters or potential voters.

Can Campaign Contributions Be Effectively Regulated?

Given the power of money, several sources, including activists, the Supreme Court, and the federal government, have long struggled to control the dangers of campaign finance. In the 1970s, following the Watergate scandal, Congress passed the Federal Election Campaign Act, which created the Federal Election Commission (FEC), a bureaucratic entity charged with overseeing and implementing national campaign finance laws. The act also set rules for the disclosure of the source of campaign funds, placed limits on

FIGURE 10.2

Comparing the Cost of Presidential Campaigns, American Gross Domestic Product (GDP), and Gold

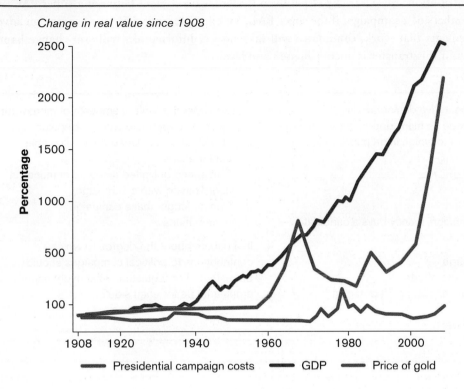

Change in real value since 1908

Source: Dave Gilson, "The Crazy Cost of Becoming President, from Lincoln to Obama," Mother Jones, February 20, 2012, http://www.motherjones.com/mojo/2012/02/historic-price-cost-presidential-elections.

campaign contributions, and instituted a system for public financing of presidential elections. In 1976, in *Buckley v. Valeo*, the Supreme Court upheld the constitutionality of restrictions on campaign contributions by individuals, though not on monies spent independently, monies spent by the candidates themselves, or the total amount of contributions.[33]

When it comes to money and elections, however, controlling the influence of money has often been like handling a balloon—squeeze it in one place and it seems to pop up somewhere else. In 2002, in an effort to more effectively control the balloon, Congress passed the Bipartisan Campaign Reform Act (BCRA), which placed stricter limits on campaign contributions. Since then, however, the Supreme Court has limited these regulations. In *Citizens United v. Federal Election Commission* (2010), in a divided 5–4 decision, the Court struck down portions of the BCRA, ruling that independent, uncoordinated political contributions by corporations during political campaigns is protected by the First Amendment.[34]

The "new world" of campaign finance in the United States is a fluid and complicated one. Although limits on individual campaign donations remain in place, groups of individuals may contribute, but the rules are complicated. **Political action committees** (PACs) are groups of at least fifty individuals that seek to raise money to elect and

NEWS CLIP
Citizens United impact

political action committees
organizations that raise money to support chosen candidates and defeat others.

super PACs

political action committees permitted to spend unlimited amounts of money in a campaign, though these actions must not be coordinated with that campaign.

defeat candidates. PACs may contribute higher dollar amounts than individuals, though, again, there are limits. In the wake of the Court's decision in *Citizens United*, certain types of PACs called **super PACs** are allowed to spend unlimited amounts on a political campaign; however, that spending must not be coordinated with that campaign. These contributions raise a tricky issue. Even if there is no contact between a super PAC and members of a campaign, if the super PAC, for example, runs a series of campaign advertisements that work, candidates will take notice. Information will still change hands, even if this transfer is uncoordinated and legal.

WHAT HAVE I LEARNED?

1. American representative democracy is designed to provide as many opportunities as possible for voters to weigh in on public policy directly.

   a. True
   b. False

2. In a political campaign, money buys a candidate _____.

   a. Media coverage
   b. Get out the vote efforts
   c. The possibility of scaring off potential challengers
   d. All of the above

3. A super PAC _____.

   a. Can spend unlimited amounts of money but must not coordinate with a campaign
   b. Has strict limits placed on its allowable contributions
   c. Can spend unlimited amounts of money in coordination with a campaign
   d. Can no longer make campaign contributions

4. In a debate about the degree to which contributions to political campaigns should be restricted or regulated, what might some arguments be for each side?

Answer Key: 1. b; 2. d; 3. a; 4. Answers for restrictions may focus on wealth inequality or factions. Answers against might focus on free speech and the First Amendment.

NEWS CLIP
Stephen Colbert forms a super PAC

COMPETING FOR LATINO VOTES IN A PRESIDENTIAL CAMPAIGN
Capturing an Unrealized Potential

As Marco Rubio, Ted Cruz, Donald Trump, Hillary Clinton, Bernie Sanders, and other candidates sought the presidential nomination in 2016, they all realized that the Latino vote had the potential to impact the outcomes of their nomination campaigns. In that year, 27.3 million Latinos were eligible voters—a national record. However, the growth in this demographic has been, and is likely to continue to be, concentrated in the West and Southwest (Figure 10.3).[35] This uneven distribution has had significant consequences, as we will explore later.

The candidates' calculations and strategies were also informed by another fact: Latino voters, in spite of their growing *potential* electoral power, were not voting, at least not in comparison to white and African American voters. According to Kate Linthicum of the *Los Angeles Times*,

> For all the talk of the growing Latino electorate and the pivotal role it is expected to play in the 2016 presidential race, there is another often overlooked demographic reality: Latinos, along with Asian Americans, remain dramatically underrepresented in most U.S. elections. Half a century after the passage of the Voting Rights Act, which ended legal barriers to voting for blacks across the South, blacks and whites now vote at roughly equal rates, especially in presidential elections. But Latinos and Asians lag far behind in all races, even when noncitizen immigrants are accounted for.[36]

FIGURE 10.3

Distribution of the Latino Population in the United States in 2016

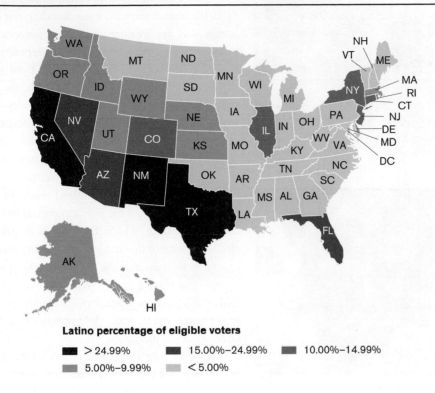

Latino percentage of eligible voters

- ■ > 24.99%
- ■ 15.00%–24.99%
- ■ 10.00%–14.99%
- ■ 5.00%–9.99%
- ■ < 5.00%

Source: Pew Research Center, "Mapping the Latino Electorate by State," January 19, 2016, http://www.pewhispanic.org/interactives/mapping-the-latino-electorate-by-state/, accessed January 30, 2016.

The reasons for the comparative lack of turnout by Latino voters are complicated. Part of the answer is age. Latino Americans tend to be younger than members of other racial and ethnic groups, and young voting-eligible Americans vote at lower rates than older ones. In addition, the fact that Latino voters tend to cluster in states such as California and Texas—states that tend to lean heavily to either the Democratic or Republican Party—has led to an unintentional, but rational, neglect. Since neither is a swing state, these two states get relatively less attention than those that are seen to be "in play" during an election. "Organizations and political parties aren't focused enough on this segment of the population," says Marcela Ruiz, the deputy director of California Rural Legal Assistance.[37] As the percentage of Latino voters grows in **swing states**—states such as Nevada where no one political party tends to dominate national elections—that will almost certainly change.

Candidate strategies to highlight issues of interest to Latino voters are complicated by the fact that the patterns of issue preferences within members of these communities are themselves complicated. While a majority of registered Latino voters supported candidates from the Democratic Party in 2014, that party's advantage had been slipping.[38] In 2014 the Pew Research Center surveyed Latino voters on the issue of immigration, which two-thirds of respondents said was either an extremely important or a very important issue to them. The respondents placed more blame on the nation's lack of progress on immigration matters on congressional Republicans (40 percent) than on President Obama (24 percent) or congressional Democrats (15 percent).[39] However, on other issues, such as

swing states
states where no one political party tends to dominate national elections.

Top: Voters cast their ballots at the House of Mercy in Los Angeles in November 2012. Latino voters made up almost 25 percent of all registered voters in California during that election cycle. *Bottom:* A chalkboard sign at a mock caucus event in Des Moines, Iowa, held by LULAC, the League of United Latin American Citizens.

Top photo: Brian van der Brug/ Los Angeles Times; bottom photo: Courtesy of Emily Aitken/ Think Progress

abortion, Latino public opinion is much more closely divided, minimizing the Democratic advantage.[40]

On the eve of the Iowa caucuses on February 1, 2016, one of the stories surrounding the campaigns was the weather, with a snowstorm projected to move across much of the state, potentially lowering turnout for the caucuses.[41] Even when there is no snowstorm to contend with, the process in Iowa is complicated. Caucus participants in Iowa's 1,774 voting precincts choose delegates to county conventions, who then choose delegates to state party conventions, who then in turn choose delegates to the national party conventions. Some of the caucuses are held in people's homes "or even machine sheds."[42] As the political parties bear the cost of caucusing, which they do not in primary elections, "one of the first activities of any precinct caucus is to 'pass the hat' to raise funds for the county and state party."[43] We will take a closer look at the mechanisms that political parties in different states use to select their nominees in detail later in this chapter.

Another story involved speculation about how much of a challenge Democratic Party hopeful Senator Bernie Sanders would actually pose to Hillary Clinton, a former senator and secretary of State. Although Sanders had enjoyed a surge in the polls in the months and weeks prior to the caucus, according to political analyst Nate Silver, if Sanders did not win, "It's probably over."[44] Silver made this prediction based on the fact that Iowa's demographics favored Sanders much more than they would in primaries to follow, especially in the South.

A third story revolved around the Republican Party hopefuls. Polls prior to the caucus had Donald Trump in the lead by seven to eight percentage points in the state, with Senator Ted Cruz and Senator Marco Rubio polling in second and third place, respectively. Part of the discussion focused on the potential turnout of Latino participants in the Republican and Democratic Party caucuses. While, according to the State Data Center of Iowa, in 2014 Latino Iowans made up the state's largest racial and ethnic minority, they still only constituted 5.6 percent of the state's population.[45] Prior to the caucuses, officials with the League of United Latin American Citizens [LULAC] "set a lofty goal: Turn out 10,000 Latino Iowans, more than the state has had in its history."[46] Two weeks later, estimates pointed to thirteen thousand Latino voters having joined in. In the end, Cruz won the Republican Iowa caucuses, besting Trump and Rubio, though likely mostly because of his appeal to white, non-Hispanic, conservative and evangelical Iowans.

Just days before the Iowa caucuses, Fox News cohosted a Republican Party debate, the seventh one in the seemingly endless series of debates. One of the questioners selected—chosen from a group of influential YouTube video creators—was Dulce Candy Tejeda Ruiz, who had served with the army in Iraq as a mechanic. While in service, she began to create and post videos featuring cosmetics tips. By the time of the Republican Party debate in January 2016, she had become a successful social media entrepreneur.

"My Story | Dulce Candy"

In a video posted to her YouTube account, titled "My Story | Dulce Candy," entrepreneur, author, and former member of the U.S. Army Dulce Candy shared with her audience her goals for her growing and very successful business:

> My success is OUR success and together, we can achieve our dreams, and make the world a more creative and loving place. Beauty and Fashion are our forms of expression, but the true beauty lies from within. Your beauty inspires me everyday, so I thank each and every one of you from the bottom of my heart! And a big thank you to YouTube for creating this amazing video about me. I'm humbled ☺ Always remember, happiness is now! xo, Dulce[48]

Included in the video were photographs from her service with the army in Iraq.[49]

In an interview conducted after the 2015 Hispanicize event, at which Candy received the first Latinovator award, she directly related her service in Iraq—during which she and her fellow soldiers came under attack with rocket-propelled grenades—to her entrepreneurship. She stated, "You're restricted from wearing makeup and expressing your individuality. For 15 months I had to blend in like everyone else."[50]

Another video posted to her YouTube account presents a very different image, one that focuses on her business, expertise, and entrepreneurship.

WHAT DO YOU THINK?

In his presidential campaign in 2016, candidate Donald Trump assailed American immigration policy and promised if elected to build a wall across the entirety of the U.S-Mexico border, which was to be paid for by Mexico. In justifying the policy proposal, Trump portrayed undocumented immigrants as dangerous to American democracy and security. In what ways does Dulce Candy's use of image challenge these accusations? If you were to present counterstereotypical images of an issue of importance to you, what might they be?

Courtesy of Dulce Candy Ruiz

Courtesy of Dulce Candy Ruiz

In 2013 Dulce Candy had stated that she came to America as an undocumented immigrant from Mexico with her mother and three sisters when she was six years old. In the opinion of a commentator from the highly conservative Web site Breitbart.com, the decision to include her as a questioner "was likely intended to hit Donald Trump" on the issue of immigration, given his highly controversial proposals and, to many, inflammatory statements.[47]

Donald Trump never got Dulce Candy's question. As it turned out, the candidate—feeling that Fox News had not treated him fairly in its campaign coverage—skipped the debate and instead hosted a simultaneous event focused on raising money for American veterans. The event was successful and Trump raised more than six million dollars, "$1 million from his own checkbook."[51] During the event, Trump once again brought up the issue of immigration. "Our vets are being mistreated," he told his enthusiastic audience. "Illegal immigrants are treated better in many cases than our vets and it's not going to happen any more. It's not going to happen."[52]

At the Republican debate, however, Trump's opponents *did* get Dulce Candy's question. "There are many immigrants who contribute positively to the American economy," she asked, "but some of the comments in the campaign make us question our place in this country. If America does not seem like a welcoming place for immigrant entrepreneurs, will the American economy suffer?"[53] When the debate moderator handed the question to Dr. Ben Carson, his initial response was, "Oh, great."[54]

As the results of the 2016 election came in, in spite of early exit polling results, it appeared that Donald Trump had failed to capture more than 20 percent of the Latino vote. In the presidential election Latinos had cast, perhaps, more than three million more votes than they had in the presidential election of 2012, though these estimates remained just that, estimates.[55]

CONNECTING TO . . .

The 2016 Latino Vote

As you engage with the next section, which describes the nuts and bolts of presidential campaigns and elections, keep in mind the stories that you have read about efforts to reach out to Latino voters as well as the challenges and failures faced by many candidates in doing so. Reflect upon the following:

- The ways in which the nomination process may or may not be responsive to all Americans' voices
- The ways in which the Electoral College may affect the attention candidates pay to states with large Latino populations

THE POLITICS OF PRESIDENTIAL ELECTIONS

The basics of presidential elections are, unsurprisingly, laid out in the United States Constitution and subsequent amendments, including the frequency of these elections (every four years) and the general rules defining what it takes to run for the presidency. However, many important structures and processes are also influenced by two other sets of actors: the states and the political parties.

The Stages of Presidential Campaigns

Presidential elections have two official campaign phases: the nomination campaign, in which candidates try to secure the nomination of their political party, and the general election campaign, in which successful nominees compete for the presidency. While the ways in which parties structure their nomination processes have changed, the general trend in modern campaigns has been one of increasing openness, of taking some of the power away from party elites and placing it in the hands of party activists and average Americans. This is not to say that party leaders do not matter, however. They still have more power to shape the nomination than the average American voter.

Before the Official Campaign

Nomination campaigns begin long before the actual events through which the nominees are picked. Presidential hopefuls may work on laying the foundations for their bids years before the official process begins. They begin raising money and set up an **exploratory committee**, which is subject to different federal campaign finance rules than a campaign committee. An exploratory committee allows a potential candidate to "test the waters," to travel around the country in order to conduct public opinion polls, make outreach phone calls, and raise money to pay for all of this. In addition, a candidate's announcement that he or she has formed an exploratory committee may gain a bit of a bump in media coverage.

If a candidate decides to press ahead, his or her campaign will become official, a status that can be triggered through a potential candidate's statements and fund-raising or other activities. According to Chris Good of *The Atlantic*, "Once any of those things happen, the campaign is officially on. The candidate must register with the FEC, transfer all of his/her exploratory-committee money into a campaign account, disclose all of it to the FEC, and start filing regular disclosures."[56]

The Nomination Process

Once the official campaign process kicks off, declared candidates vie with others in their own party for that party's nomination. Beginning early in the election year, candidates seek to get the support of party delegates, whose votes they will later need to secure the party's nomination. While many of the rules governing the nomination process are set by federal and state laws, most of the details about *how* things actually work are hammered out by the parties themselves. Key differences exist across states and between the parties themselves.

As we discussed in detail in Chapter 9, most states hold presidential primary elections, in which a state's voters choose delegates who support a particular candidate. In some states, these elections may be open primaries; all eligible voters may vote in an open primary, regardless of partisan affiliation. Other states may hold closed primaries, which are open only to registered voters from a particular political party. Some states hold caucuses, in which eligible voters gather to discuss candidates and issues and to select delegates to represent them in later stages of the nomination process. The concluding phase of the nomination process takes place in the national conventions held by the parties late in the summer of the presidential election year.

The General Election

Once selected by their parties, the nominees then proceed to the general election campaign. By then, the nominees are likely seasoned campaigners, having polished their talking points and dealings with the media. The problem is that now, instead of speaking mainly to their base of core supporters, nominees also have to appeal to independent and undecided voters—something they did not have to do much of during the nomination campaign. This can be a trap. Voters who participate during the nomination campaigns trend towards the wings of their parties, and there are fewer of them.

It is a delicate dance—maintaining the energy of core party voters while also appealing to the undecided middle. The worry is not that

NEWS CLIP
Romney creates exploratory committee in 2012

exploratory committee
a group that helps determine whether a potential candidate should run for office and that helps lay the groundwork for the campaign.

NEWS CLIP
Florida 2000 Supreme Court decision and the Electoral College

Senator Marco Rubio announces his bid for the American presidency in a tweet.

@marcorubio, Twitter.

Marco Rubio @marcorubio · 13 Apr 2015
I'm **running** for **President** of the United States.

Become a Day One Supporter at tinyurl.com/ofl2kk8

VISIT MARCORUBIO.COM

GIF

619   746

voters who represent the wings of a nominee's party will vote for a candidate from the other party. The worry is that if core partisan voters think their nominee has moved too far to the center and abandoned core party goals, they will not make phone calls, knock on doors, and mobilize undecided voters to their nominee's campaign. On the other hand, if a candidate has survived the nomination campaign by appealing primarily to the extremes of the party, then he or she may be seen as too far left or too far right to be the best person for governing the nation in the views of independents and undecided voters.

In addition to this challenge, a would-be president has another problem to deal with: When they go to the polls in November every four years, American voters are not technically voting for the president. Instead, they are voting for a slate of electors pledged to vote for a nominee in the presidential election. These electors are chosen by party leaders within their respective states, and they constitute what we call the **Electoral College**. It is their vote just over a month after the general election that actually chooses the president.

It is an odd arrangement, established in the original Constitution and modified since the founding. Its roots lie partly in the framers' mistrust of direct democracy but also in concerns of convention delegates from less populous states; these delegates feared Virginians would always be elected since theirs was the most populous and powerful state at the time.

If you want to be president, the number of Electoral College votes you need is clear: 270. Each of the fifty states is allocated its number of electoral votes based on its representation in Congress—one for each of its two senators and one for each of its members of the House of Representatives, guaranteeing each state at least three electoral votes. Adding the three electoral votes allocated to the District of Columbia brings the total to 538. In all but two states, electoral votes are awarded in a winner-take-all system. In Maine and Nebraska, the two electoral votes connected to senatorial representation are awarded for winning a plurality across the state, and each electoral vote allocated to that state based on representation in the House is awarded based on winning a plurality of votes within each of the state's congressional districts.

Electors are chosen from party leaders and loyal activists. Although they have pledged to vote for their party's candidate, there is a risk that they may change their minds in between the general election and the electors' vote, which happens in the state capitals. These **faithless electors** act sometimes out of protest but more commonly because the candidate to whom they had pledged their vote passed away before the Electoral College was able to cast a vote. Faithless electors, however, have never changed the outcome of a presidential election. Many states have laws to prohibit faithless electoral voting. In the days following Donald Trump's victory in the general election, some called for the electors of his states' victories to become "faithless" and vote instead for Secretary Clinton, though that possibility seemed highly unlikely.

If no nominee wins a majority of electoral votes, then the presidential election goes to Congress, with the House of Representatives choosing among the top three electoral vote winners. There, each state's group of representatives casts one vote for the president, and the candidate with a majority of votes wins. The Senate chooses the vice president. This process has been called upon twice in the nation's history, but not since the election of 1824.

There are significant consequences from this somewhat odd system. Theoretically, it is possible to become president by winning in only the eleven most populous states. In reality, however, given that this would entail winning both Texas and California, which tend heavily towards candidates from different parties, this possibility remains unlikely. More significantly, a presidential candidate can win the presidency without actually winning the popular vote, an outcome that may come about because a third-party candidate made a serious challenge, which contributed to President Bill Clinton's victory in 1992, or because a candidate

Electoral College
a process for electing the president that involves the voting population choosing a slate of electors who are pledged to vote for a nominee in the presidential election.

faithless elector
a party elector who changes his or her mind in between the general election and the Electoral College vote.

It is a delicate dance—maintaining the energy of core party voters while also appealing to the undecided middle.

FIGURE 10.4

Electoral College Results, 2016

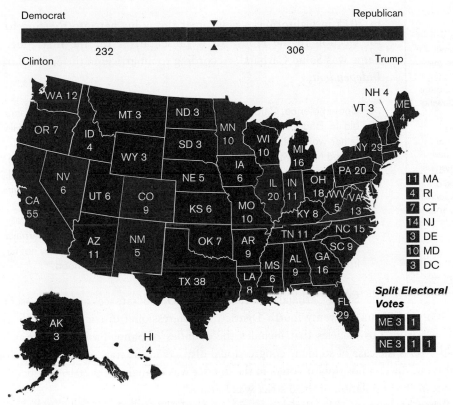

Note: Voting outcomes as of November 29, 2016, pending possible recounts.

won a majority of the popular vote but lost in the Electoral College, which happened in 2000 when George W. Bush defeated Al Gore, and again in 2016 when Donald Trump defeated Hillary Clinton.

The system of electors shapes candidate strategies. Given that all but two states award their electoral votes in a block, candidates tend to focus their campaigns on states with a large number of electoral votes and those whose electoral votes seem to be in play, largely ignoring other states.

1. Party leaders choose the timing of presidential general elections.

   a. True
   b. False

2. The nuts and bolts of the nomination process are mostly the same across states and between political parties.

   a. True
   b. False

3. How might the timing of state caucuses and primaries structure the ways in which the diversity of Americans' lived experiences is made present in the nomination process?

4. What are some of the potential problems raised by the Electoral College?

Answer Key: 1. b; 2. b; 3. Students may want to focus on the demographic makeup of Iowa and New Hampshire and how that might shape opinions of candidates before voters in more diverse states have had a chance to weigh in; 4. Answers may include the possibility, which happened again in 2016, of winning the popular vote but failing to secure the presidency. Answers might also include how the system alters presidential campaign strategies.

WHAT HAVE I LEARNED?

The Politics of Congressional Elections

In the next section of this chapter, we will move from presidential to congressional electoral campaigns. We will continue our theme of American electoral politics in an era of demographic change. As you engage with this material, reflect upon the following:

- The ways in which the differences between running in a congressional district and running for the American presidency shape candidate strategies
- The ways in which the boundaries of congressional representation, especially in the House of Representatives, shape both the politics of House elections and candidate strategies
- The effects of the incumbency advantage on the decisions of potential first-time candidates for Congress

CALIFORNIA'S TWENTY-FOURTH CONGRESSIONAL DISTRICT: A FIRST-TIMER RUNS FOR THE HOUSE OF REPRESENTATIVES

In 2015 in California, a newcomer threw his hat into the ring to run for election to the House of Representatives for the first time. His name was Salud Carbajal. According to an article in the *Santa Barbara Independent*,

> Born in Mexico, Carbajal moved with his family when he was five years old to Bagdad, a small copper mining town in western Arizona. His father worked the mines while his mother, who suffered from arthritis, stayed home with their eight children. When Carbajal was in sixth grade, the copper mine closed and the family moved to Oxnard [California], where Carbajal spent his junior high and high school years while his father worked in the fields.
>
> In Oxnard, the Carbajals lived in the projects of an economically depressed neighbourhood. . . . "The police were there constantly," Carbajal said over lunch [in 2008] at El Zarape, a Westside Mexican eatery not far from his West Islay Street home. "It was a tough neighborhood."[57]

Salud Carbajal was running as a Democrat, seeking to represent the voters of California's Twenty-fourth District, a congressional district just north along the coast from Los Angeles that includes the counties of Santa Barbara and San Luis Obispo. As is the case of so many congressional districts in the state and in the American Southwest, the composition of voters in the district was changing. By 2016 just below 35 percent of the population of the district was Latino.[58]

When he announced his decision to run in April 2015, Carbajal presented to voters his reasons for standing for national office:

> Our region has been well represented by Congresswoman Capps for the past 17 years and I am privileged to have had the opportunity to work collaboratively with her to improve our local communities.
>
> Following her recent announcement that she would not run for reelection, I have decided to run for Congress to be an effective voice in Washington for the issues that people care about on the Central Coast—creating jobs, educational opportunity for all, preserving essential safety net services, improving our infrastructure and protecting the environment.
>
> I have a proven track record of working in a bipartisan way to get results on these issues in my service as County Supervisor and want to bring the same effective and collaborative approach to Congress.[59]

While Carbajal's announcement described to potential voters his policy objectives, politically, one of the most telling parts of his statement was this: "Our region has been well represented by Congresswoman Capps for the past 17 years." Carbajal was giving respect to Democratic congresswoman Lois Capps, who was retiring from Congress. Her retirement probably was one of the key factors in Carbajal's decision to run for Congress for the first time.

The decision to stand for national legislative office, though a monumental one, is only the first step in the long journey towards election to Congress. For first-timers such as Carbajal, this initial decision is made knowing that each new step along the way is just another in a very steep climb. The odds are usually stacked against them.

Due to the retirement of Capps, there was no **incumbent**, no sitting member of the House running for reelection in the Twenty-fourth District. The election was an **open seat election**, with no incumbent defending her or his seat. That, as we will soon explore, is extremely important. In congressional elections, the most important determinant of who will win is incumbency. Stated simply, incumbents usually win, and those with serious aspirations to enter Congress are often, and wisely, very wary of challenging an incumbent representative or senator. Losing looks bad; serious contenders do not like to lose.

In terms of political experience, Carbajal was no rookie. He announced his bid while serving as a member of the Santa Barbara County Board of Supervisors. In terms of Congress, however, Carbajal was an outsider. His victory was far from assured. He faced other qualified candidates, including the Democratic mayor of Santa Barbara, Helene Schneider, and Katcho Achadjian, a Republican state assemblyman.

The dynamics of the 2016 race were profoundly shaped by Capps's decision to retire. When incumbents run for reelection, they are often opposed by, frankly, amateurs, or those candidates who only want to make a statement but expect to lose. In open seat elections, the serious potential challengers like Carbajal often take their shot. Capps's decision may have been partly affected by the changing makeup of the Twenty-fourth District, changes brought about by shifting demographics and a redistricting following the 2010 census (Table 10.1)

Unlike how the majority of states do things, Carbajal was running under California's **top-two primary system** (also called a nonpartisan blanket primary), in which statewide and federal candidates, regardless of party, compete in the primary elections and are listed on the same ballot.[60] The top two vote-getters then move on to the general election. In some forms of blanket primaries, such as the one used in Louisiana, there is only a second round of voting if no one candidate receives a majority of votes in the first round. In California's top-two system, in contrast, the top two vote-getters in the

An image of candidate Salud Carbajal from his campaign Web site. The description reads, "Salud Carbajal tiene un historial efectivo y comprobado en unir personas para trabajar juntos en fortalecer nuestra comunidad." (In English, "Salud Carbajal has an effective and proven track record in bringing people to work together to strengthen our community.")

Courtesy of Salud Carbajal for Congress.

incumbent
a political official who is currently in office.

open seat election
an election in which no incumbent is seeking reelection.

top-two primary system
an electoral system in which candidates, regardless of party, compete in the primary elections, with the top two vote-getters, regardless of party, advancing to the general election.

TABLE 10.1 A Difference Redistricting Makes: California's Twenty-Fourth District before and after Redistricting

	111th Congress (2009–2010)	113th Congress (2013–2014)
Population	681,622	526,519
Gender	49.5% Male 50.5% Female	50.2% Male 49.8% Female
Race and Ethnicity	75.9% White 28.8% Hispanic 6.3% Asian 1.7% Black	79.6% White 34.7% Hispanic 4.6% Asian 2.0% Black
Median Household Income	$79,562	$56,943
High School Graduate	88.2%	83.4%
Bachelor's Degree or Higher	33.70%	31.70%

Source: Data are from United States Census Bureau.

first round face off in the general election. The result is that two potential nominees from the same political party might very well face off against each other in the general election, especially in a congressional district whose voters are predominantly Democrat or Republican.

California's Independent Voter Project wrote and supported the proposition to implement a top-two primary system, which passed in 2010. "You know what, you get a little lazy sometimes, with a closed primary system, where you keep independents from voting, let me tell you something, you can be lazy," noted Abel Maldonado, a state senator and key player in the politics of presenting the top-two system to California. "With this open primary, you have to work for the taxpayers."[61] California's system stands in contrast to how most states conduct their congressional primary elections; in most states voters choose potential nominees within a party. As we discussed in the previous chapter in the context of presidential nominations, the structure of a party's nomination process can and does lead to strategic voting choices.

For Salud Carbajal, California's primary system meant that if he moved on from the primary, he might well have faced a fellow Democrat, given the fact that California's Twenty-fourth District tends to lean slightly Democratic. In 2016, however, there were a lot of "probables" that no longer seemed as close to certain. A Republican Party surge in the national elections, especially the surge of a Republican presidential nominee, could have meant a Democrat running in California's Twenty-fourth District might face additional headwinds. This phenomenon—when a presidential nominee's popularity surges, energizing support for his or her party and its policies—is called the **coattail effect.**

coattail effect

a phenomenon that occurs when a presidential candidate's increasing popularity results in increased support for congressional candidates of the same party.

Carbajal and his opponents were not only confronting the changes to California's electoral system, they also had to deal with the fact that the boundaries defining the people they were trying to represent had also shifted. In elections to the House of Representatives, as we will discuss, the boundaries of the House districts are not set in stone. Drawing these lines is often—and for very practical reasons—a contested and political process. After the 2010 census and the redrawing of district boundaries that followed (see below), the boundaries that defined California's Twenty-fourth District had changed. The *Los Angeles Times* reported that "Capps' district, once derided as the 'ribbon of shame' because of its blatantly gerrymandered boundaries, was redrawn into a politically balanced 'swing district' that could be won by a candidate of either major party. Registration [in late 2015 was] nearly even—37 percent Democratic, 34 percent Republican—with more than 23 percent of voters unaffiliated" with either major party.[62]

In the 2014 general election, Capps won a narrow victory, defeating her Republican Party opponent by a hardly comfortable margin of 52 to 48 percent, down considerably from her ten-point victory in the election before that. This slimmer margin can partly be attributed to redistricting. After the 2010 census, Capps's congressional district lost "heavily Democratic Oxnard while adding the conservative interiors of Santa Barbara and San Luis Obispo counties."[63] Latino voters then comprised 34 percent of the Twenty-fourth District's eligible voters. According to an April 2015 analysis by Politico, "Republicans view the seat as a potential pickup opportunity in the 2016 election cycle."[64] According to a political scientist from Claremont McKenna College, "The Capps seat leans Democratic, but could be within reach for Republicans if everything goes right for them."[65]

In what was playing out as a potentially hotly contested election, Carbajal and his opponents, Democrat and Republican alike, had a lot of work to do. The battle for votes would be fought in the shadow of two other contests: the battle for money and the battle for endorsements from influential politicians, business leaders, community activists, and other key players in California politics.

By both measures, as 2015 turned into 2016, Carbajal's campaign was doing very well. Mayor Schneider received support from "women's groups,"[66] but Carbajal picked up an early and key endorsement from retiring incumbent Capps. After that, House minority leader and former House majority leader Nancy Pelosi added her endorsement to his campaign, "a rare pick in a contested Democratic primary."[67] In an interview with The Hill.com, former state assemblyman Pedro Nava said, "It's shaping up as though Carbajal is essentially the institutional Democratic candidate."[68] Pelosi's endorsement, though extremely helpful, did not come without its own risks, however. It exposed Carbajal to charges that he was running as part of the establishment—an establishment that many voters felt was in need of change.

By December 2015, Carbajal was also doing very well in the fund-raising battle. His campaign hit the $1 million mark, far outpacing his rivals from either party. "I continue to be amazed by the tremendous support I have received in the past few months and am grateful to the many individual [sic] who have contributed to our campaign," said Carbajal. "We are building a movement for a stronger middle class and the broad support we have received demonstrates the momentum that we are building."[69] (See Figure 10.4.)

FIGURE 10.5

Reported Donations to Candidates in California's Twenty-Fourth District House Race as of June 2016

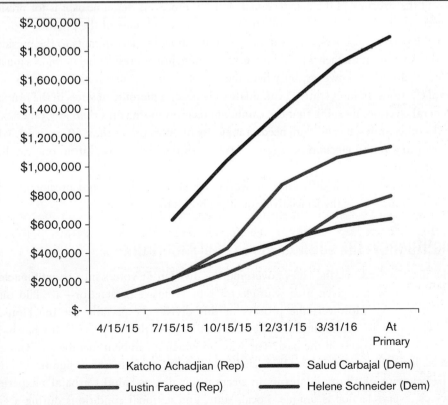

Legend:
— Katcho Achadjian (Rep) — Salud Carbajal (Dem)
— Justin Fareed (Rep) — Helene Schneider (Dem)

Source: Federal Election Commission.

Momentum, or "Big Mo" as political scientist Larry Bartels describes it in his book, *Presidential Primaries and the Dynamics of Public Choice*, may be the most important and hard to obtain resource that a candidate for national office can hope to have.[70] At the beginning of 2016, Carbajal appeared to have it.

TOPICS IN AMERICAN GOVERNMENT
Congress

THE POLITICS OF CONGRESSIONAL ELECTIONS

Much of the structure of the congressional electoral process is the same as it is for presidential elections. For example, states still structure the nuts and bolts of the process. Would-be national legislators also seek out their party's nomination, just as aspirants to the presidency must do. And they must then win in the general election, just as presidential nominees must do.

States do differ, however, on where the bar is set for congressional nominees in the general elections. In most states, a candidate only needs a **plurality** of votes in the primaries or general election, meaning that the candidate receives more votes than any other candidate. In other states, a candidate needs a **majority** of votes (more than 50 percent), which may lead to a **runoff election** between the two with the highest total if no one candidate scores a majority.

The most important difference, however, between legislative and presidential elections is defining whom the legislative candidate hopes to represent.

Constituency: The Boundaries of Representation

At the most basic level, the rules governing the division of voters into **constituencies**—bodies of voters in a given area who elect a representative or senator—are laid out in the Constitution. However, the process of this division, especially for the House of Representatives, is often political and controversial. Even the Supreme Court has had to weigh in on the process in the past. The ways in which incumbent members of Congress use their incumbency to enhance their chances of getting reelected have significant effects on the behavior of all candidates in an election. Finally, as Salud Carbajal's experience shows us, every election is unique. Local, state, and national conditions during a given election matter as well, and there are always unanticipated events that can powerfully shape a given candidate's electoral chances.

plurality
when a candidate receives more votes than any other candidate.

majority
when a candidate receives more than 50 percent of the vote.

runoff election
an election that is held between the two candidates with the highest total votes if no one candidate scores a majority.

constituencies
bodies of voters in a given area who elect a representative or senator.

Constituency and the Senate

The size of the Senate depends only on the number of states in the Union since two senators represent each state. Since the admission of Hawaii as the fiftieth state in 1959, therefore, the Senate has been composed of one hundred members, each representing the entire state from which they were elected. Because the Senate was divided into three "classes" in order to stagger the elections of senators, no two senate seats from the same state will be up for grabs in the same election, unless a retirement or other event has opened up one of the seats.

Like many other aspects of the basic structure of the federal government, the guarantee of equal state representation in the Senate came about as a result of conflicts and bargaining between less populous and more populous states as well as between slave-holding and non slave-holding states during the Constitutional Convention. The result of equal *state* representation is that individual *voters* are unequally represented in the Senate. The 586,107 citizens of Wyoming get two senators; so do the 39,144,818 citizens of California.

Constituency and the House of Representatives

In spite of the potential repercussions of equal state representation in the Senate, determining one's potential constituents is a very simple matter for that chamber. When it comes to the House of Representatives however, things are a bit more complicated—and political.

Apportionment

While initially the size of the House was allowed to grow with the population, it is now fixed at 435 members.[71] The size of a state's representation in the House depends upon its population. The process of determining the number of representatives for each state is called **apportionment**; through this process the number of representatives is allocated based on the results of the census that is conducted every ten years. (See Figure 10.5.) As part of the process of apportionment, each state is divided into one or more congressional districts, with one seat in the House representing each district and each state guaranteed one representative, no matter how small its population.

Given the fact that the size of the House is capped, changes in population can produce "winners and losers" among the states following each census. Trends in population growth and distribution in recent decades have produced a clear pattern of gains in House seats for states in the South and the West and losses for states in the Northeast and Midwest.

Redistricting and Gerrymandering

While the process of apportionment has important consequences for the representation of states in the House, it also has important consequences for the boundaries of constituency. Following each census, states enter into the process of **redistricting**, in which they redraw the electoral district boundaries. Seven states have only one representative; therefore, their district boundaries are the same as the boundaries of the state. Some states have undertaken redistricting *between* censuses, especially when a political party gains control over the state's legislative and executive branches, though many states have constitutional or legislative prohibitions against this practice.

CONNECTING TO . . .

One Candidate's Campaign and the Structure of Congressional Elections

As you read the next section, which describes the nuts and bolts of American congressional elections, reflect upon the story of Salud Carbajal's campaign in California's Twenty-fourth District. Consider the following:

- Why Carbajal might have chosen the 2016 election to run for Congress for the first time

- How the redistricting and the changing constituency of the congressional district that he hoped to represent could have influenced his chances

- What characteristics a serious congressional candidate needs in order to have a chance at winning

---

apportionment
the process of determining the number of representatives for each state using census data; states are divided into congressional districts that have at least one representative each.

TOPICS IN AMERICAN GOVERNMENT
Redistricting and gerrymandering

redistricting
states' redrawing of the electoral district boundaries following each census.

FIGURE 10.6

Apportionment Gains and Losses after the 2010 Census

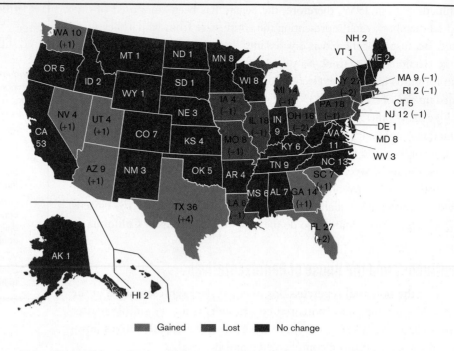

Gained   Lost   No change

Source: United States Census Bureau, "Congressional Apportionment," November 2011, https://www
.census.gov/prod/cen2010/briefs/c2010br-08.pdf, accessed February 28, 2016.

Note: Numbers to the right of the state names show the total number of representatives allocated to the
state. Numbers below show the change as either a gain (+) or a loss (−).

The stakes involved in redistricting are high, and the process is often very political and controversial. In most states, the legislature appoints the members of a commission to draw the district boundaries. In others, a bipartisan or nonpartisan commission handles the process to try to make it less political, though the state legislatures typically still have to approve these plans.

The intentional use of redistricting to benefit a specific interest or group of voters is referred to as **gerrymandering**. The term comes from state legislative districts that were oddly drawn in 1812 under Massachusetts governor Elbridge Gerry to benefit his Democratic-Republican Party. Federalists complained that one district looked like a monster or a salamander, and the term created by the fusion of salamander with the governor's last name stuck.

In California, an independent commission creates the district boundaries. Established by Proposition 20 in 2010, the Citizens Redistricting Commission "gave hope to reformers around the country that there is a way out of the cycle of endless gerrymandering."[72] While some evidence suggested that these efforts did lead to more competition and higher incumbent turnover, "the polarization of the American electorate makes achieving competitive single-member districts effectively impossible on a large scale."[73]

Partisan Gerrymandering

Gerry's redistricting gambit, which was designed to help his political party, is one of three types of gerrymandering: partisan, racial and ethnic, and incumbent. Partisan gerrymandering aims to increase the representation of one political party at the expense of another.

gerrymandering
the intentional use of
redistricting to benefit a
specific interest or group
of voters.

"Congressman L" and the Consequences of Redistricting

From 1970 to 1977, political scientist Richard F. Fenno Jr. followed members of Congress around as they visited their home districts in what he called "an exploration of the relationship between members of the House of Representatives and their constituents about which the Founding Fathers philosophized."[1] The actions of members in their districts, the choices that they make, and the relationships that they cultivate constitute, for Fenno, their *home style*, which is expressed not just in speeches but also in conversations, meetings, and countless chicken dinners.

One of the members interviewed by Fenno was "Congressman L," so identified to protect research confidentiality. After many years in the House, Congressman L found himself on the wrong side of a redistricting in which his urban district—which had declined in population—was augmented with suburban voters. "And that change," according to Fenno, "after many years, had made him uneasy about constituency relationships. He did not feel at home in the suburbs."[2]

According to Congressman L., "My old district was easier to run in. I don't feel comfortable in suburbia. They have so many local jealousies and rivalries. I wasn't prepared for their pettiness and petulance, for the dozen different city councils

and all those government districts of one kind or another. I'm used to dealing with a city. It has problems, but if you have a reasonable solution to those problems, people listen to you and you can accomplish something. Not in suburbia."[3]

After many years of service, "Congressman L's ambition had clearly waned—or perhaps peaked," and he questioned running again for his seat. "We'll see," the congressman said. "I don't care if I lose. I seriously considered not running at this time."[4]

WHAT DO YOU THINK?

Reflect on where you live or grew up and then think about the communities that bordered your city, town, or neighborhood. If your community was suddenly redistricted into a neighboring one, how might that change the concerns and behavior of your representative? How might it change the results of the election itself?

[1] Richard F. Fenno Jr., *Home Style: House Members in Their Districts* (New York: Longman, 2003), xi.
[2] Ibid., 187.
[3] Ibid.
[4] Ibid.

The idea is to concentrate the opposing party's supporters in a small number of districts, which that party will win easily. The party in control then tries to maximize the number of districts that its candidates will win comfortably but not by huge margins. By doing so, the party in charge of redistricting is able to "waste" many of the votes of its opposition since there is no more of an advantage—in terms of the number of House seats a party has—of winning 90 percent of the votes in any one district than there is by winning 55 percent. Redistricting can put incumbents at risk by changing the composition of their constituencies or by forcing two incumbents to run for the same seat.

One of the most heated recent examples of partisan gerrymandering occurred in Texas following the 2002 elections, which placed the Texas state government firmly in the hands of the Republican Party for the first time in 130 years. It was a between-censuses redistricting, as the state had just completed redistricting following the 2000 census, which also had its own share of drama and controversy. At the urging of House majority leader Tom Delay and Texas governor Rick Perry, the Republicans attempted to use their control of the legislature and the governorship to "thoroughly dismantle several House Democrat's districts," either by changing the makeup of their constituencies or placing them in the same congressional districts.[74]

Democrats in the Texas state legislature resisted, twice fleeing the state "en masse (once to Oklahoma once to New Mexico) to prevent action by denying legislative quorums while avoiding arrest under a Texas statue aimed at preventing just this tactic."[75] The Texas Democrats' strategy of holing up in hotel rooms across the state's borders delayed but did not ultimately defeat the Republicans' partisan gerrymander. As political

AP Photo/LM Otero.

scientist Gary Jacobson observed, "Only one targeted Democrat . . . managed to survive" the redistricting and win reelection in 2004.[76] Delay was later admonished by the House Ethics Committee for attempting to use federal law enforcement resources to track down the elusive Texas Democrats.[77]

Racial and Ethnic Gerrymandering

A second form of gerrymandering aims to increase the likelihood of electing members of racial and ethnic minorities as representatives by concentrating voters of minority ethnicity within specific congressional districts. Racial and ethnic gerrymandering results in **majority-minority**

Texas state representative Gabi Canales (D-Alice), left, holds a Texas flag as Representative Jose Menendez (D-San Antonio), center, and Representative Mark Homer (D-Paris), right, stand arm in arm during a news conference at a hotel in Ardmore, Oklahoma, in May 2013.

districts, in which voters of *minority* ethnicity constitute an electoral *majority* within the electoral district. Racial and ethnic gerrymandering has led to some oddly shaped congressional districts, some of the most notable of which were drawn after the 1990 census. The Twelfth District in North Carolina, for example, "stitched together African American communities in several of the state's larger cities, using Interstate 85 . . . as the thread."[78]

Incumbent Gerrymandering

The third form of strategic redistricting is incumbent gerrymandering, in which district lines are drawn to protect the reelection prospects of an incumbent representative. It is often less compelling for a party in power in state government to undertake incumbent gerrymandering, as it does not necessarily improve the prospects of the party overall. In addition, ambitious members of a state legislature may themselves be eyeing a seat in the House, giving them a strong incentive to ensure their party's victory in their home district but few incentives to protect the electoral fortunes of a potential rival.

majority-minority district

a district in which voters of a minority ethnicity constitute an electoral majority within that electoral district.

The Supreme Court and Congressional District Boundaries

In recent decades, the Supreme Court has become more active in ruling on congressional district boundaries, the drawing of which had generally been left up to the states and the political process. Affirming the "one person, one vote" rule of representation, the Court in two cases ruled that **malapportionment**—where the population is distributed in uneven numbers between legislative districts—is unconstitutional as it violates the equal protection clause of the Fourteenth Amendment.[79]

malapportionment

the uneven distribution of the population between legislative districts.

While the Court has highlighted potential problems with partisan gerrymandering in several recent cases, it has not gone so far as to declare the practice inherently unconstitutional. The Court has held that voters in these districts are still represented but by members from different political parties. *Davis v. Bandemer* (1986) involved an Indiana redistricting plan. The Court upheld the plan, ruling that the partisan gerrymander did not violate the Fourteenth Amendment's equal protection clause.[80] *Vieth v. Jubelirer* (2004) involved a Pennsylvania partisan gerrymander. In this case, the

FIGURE 10.7

North Carolina's Twelfth Congressional District: The "I-85 District"

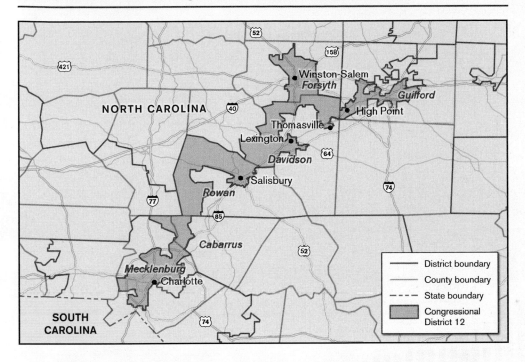

The Twelfth Congressional District in North Carolina was put in place for the 1992 elections and was one of the primary districts at issue in *Shaw v. Reno*. It was designed with the aid of computer technology to merge predominantly African American communities. The narrow parts of the district followed Interstate I-85. According to the Redistricting Task Force for the National Conference of State Legislatures, "The laboratory that made this birth possible was the computer technology that became available for the 1990s redistricting cycle. The progeny won no Beautiful Baby contests. A *Wall Street Journal* editorial described the 12th as 'political pornography.' Known as the 'I-85 district,' the12th stretched 160 miles across the central Piedmont region of the State, for part of its length no wider than the freeway right-of-way."

Court overturned the Republican-controlled gerrymander, but it did so on the grounds that the plan created districts with unequal numbers of voters, not because it was an attempt to favor one political party.[81] In 2006, in *League of United Latin American Citizens v. Perry*, the Court upheld most of the Texas redistricting plan from 2003 but required that one district's lines be redrawn to protect the voting rights of Hispanic Americans.[82]

The Court has also weighed in on the proper role of racial and ethnic considerations in drawing district boundaries. In *Thornburg v. Gingles* (1986), the Court overturned a state's legislative district boundaries on the basis that they diluted the electoral power of African American voters and violated their voting rights.[83] In *Shaw v. Reno* (1993), the Court rejected a North Carolina reapportionment plan designed to produce majority-minority districts because it resulted in a bizarrely shaped district and used race to such a degree in drawing these boundaries that it could "only be understood as an effort to segregate voters into separate districts on the basis of race."[84] (See Figure 10.6.) Since *Shaw v. Reno*, states are allowed to use race as a consideration but not as the predominant factor in drawing district boundaries.

The Representational Consequences of the Great Compromise

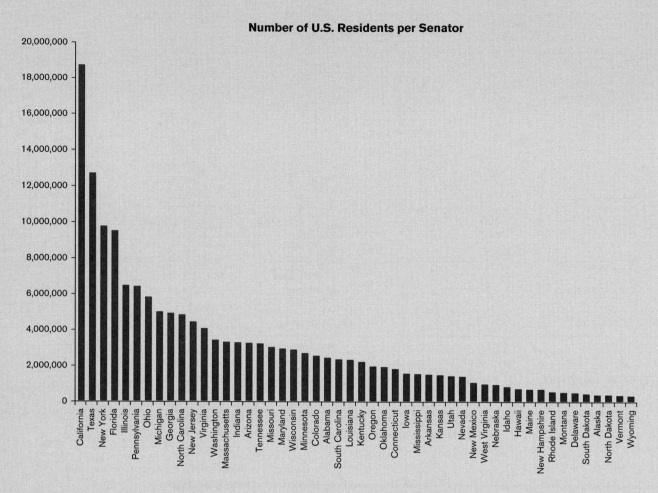

Number of U.S. Residents per Senator

Source: Data are from "2012–2020 Federal Representation by People per House Seat, Senate Seat, and Electors," The Green Papers, January 5, 2011, http://www.thegreenpapers.com/Census10/FedRep.phtml?sort=Sena#table.

As we explored in Chapter 2, one of the most contentious battles in the Constitutional Convention, especially during the early weeks, was over changing the "one state, one vote" structure of state representation in the Confederal Congress (under the Articles of Confederation). Less populous states, such as New Jersey, Delaware, and Connecticut, were not about to consent to the formation of a new congress in which states received votes based on their populations. The Great Compromise settled this question, with the House of Representatives apportioning seats based on population and the Senate allotting seats equally, two to each state.

While the compromise avoided what many feared was a fight that would tear the Constitutional Convention, and perhaps the young nation, apart, it did so with representational consequences. Although each state is guaranteed at least one representative in the House, there are variations between states in the number of representatives per resident, which range from about six hundred thousand residents per representative to nearly a million, with an average of about 710,000 residents per representative.

These variations, however, are very small in comparison to those in the Senate, where each resident of each state is represented by two senators regardless of the state's population. Given the sizeable differences between state populations, the number of state residents per senator varies dramatically.

As they come from the most populous state in the Union, each of California's two senators must represent more than sixty-five times the number of citizens as a senator from Wyoming, the nation's least populous state.[85] This means California's senators are spread much more thinly when trying to address the concerns of individual constituents.

There is also evidence that the least populous states benefit more from congressional spending than they would if the Constitution did not guarantee them equal representation in the Senate.[86]

WHAT DO YOU THINK?

Say that you are a researcher exploring whether or not citizens from less populous states receive better senatorial representation than those from the most populous states. How might you define *better*? What evidence would you look for to form your hypothesis?

Institutional Factors: The Advantages of Congressional Incumbents

While the boundaries of constituency have important consequences for congressional elections, the institutional advantages held by congressional incumbents matter a great deal as well. Making full use of the resources available to them, incumbent representatives and senators possess many advantages over any candidate who might challenge them. This **Incumbency advantage** is very strong, and it has only grown stronger in recent decades.

The fact is that the vast majority of congressional incumbents who seek reelection succeed. Even in years noted for major change in Congress, 85 or even 90 percent of House incumbents are successful. Reelection rates for incumbent senators, though lower than for the House, are still commonly at or above 80 percent. By the 1970s, the high reelection rates for congressional incumbents had become so pronounced that the incumbency advantage dominated much of the research of political scientists studying congressional elections.[87] Given the fact that incumbents enjoy such an advantage, "nearly everything pertaining to candidates and campaigns for Congress is profoundly influenced by whether a candidate is already an incumbent, is challenging an incumbent, or is pursuing an open seat."[88] Scholars continue to debate why incumbents enjoy such a marked advantage as well as why that advantage appears to only be growing stronger. Two of the explanations that have been offered both involve strategic political behavior—in one case on the part of incumbents, in the other case on the part of those who decide whether or not to challenge them.

incumbency advantage
institutional advantages held by those already in office who are trying to fend off challengers in an election.

The Logic of Incumbency

Political scientist David Mayhew articulated the strategic logic of incumbents and how they use their institutional advantages to maximize their chances of reelection. For Mayhew, legislators are "single-minded seekers of re-election" and use their institutional advantages to the fullest.[89] These advantages include advertising their efforts on behalf of their constituents; this is made easier and cheaper by the use of franking, which is

A photo of Salud Carbajal taken during his service with the American armed forces, posted to his official candidate Facebook page, "Carbajal for Congress." The photo signals to voters that he has military experience and is likely meant to convey personal characteristics like patriotism, trustworthiness, and an orientation towards public service.

free use of the mail for communication with constituents. Incumbents usually enjoy higher levels of name recognition than their challengers, which is increased by more media coverage than any potential challengers. In media coverage and public events, incumbents will claim credit for what they have done in Washington and announce their positions on key pieces of legislation of interest to their constituents.[90] Finally, incumbents perform casework for individual constituents, especially in helping them deal with the federal and state bureaucracy.

If incumbents are usually in no danger, then why do they spend so much time and energy trying to secure reelection? The second strategic explanation involves decisions made by potential challengers. Not all challengers are equally credible, and incumbents maximize their resources to try to ensure that they will not face qualified challengers. Knowing the odds, credible challengers often wait for their chance to run in an open seat election, in which there is no incumbent to face: "Experienced candidates are much more likely to be found in races for open seats, regardless of the election year."[91]

What makes for a high-quality challenger? Characteristics "that enable them to garner votes: [being able to] kiss babies without being awkward, speak effectively in public, look good on TV, figure out the appropriate issue positions to take for their constituency [and] run an effective campaign."[92] Successful challengers are skillful with the media and public events, using them to present a focused message that resonates with voters. They also have political information, both about the issues and about where their constituents stand on those issues.

To do all of these things, however, challengers need two things above all else: experience and money. Experience is hard earned, usually gained by moving up through the layers of local and state politics to become professional, polished, and respected. Congressional elections are usually no place for amateurs, who often lack the knowledge, political organization, and well-honed political skills needed for success in the high-stakes enterprise of a national campaign.

Money matters as well. It buys more than airtime, advertising, and campaign events, though those things are important in getting a new candidate's message out. Money also buys information; by hiring pollsters a candidate can better understand her or his constituents' preferences. Money, especially early in a campaign, is also a weapon to scare off potential opponents and a signal to potential donors that this is a campaign with a legitimate shot at success. Challengers face a difficult "chicken and egg problem": to be legitimate, they need money, but to get money, they need to show that they are legitimate. The fact is that most challengers lack the financial resources to wage effective campaigns.[93]

Because of the significant advantages that congressional incumbents possess, high-quality challengers often wait for just the right time, just the right set of circumstances, just the right election to make their bid. If they are successful, rookie congressmen and congresswomen quickly realize what their incumbent colleagues have known since they first joined the institution: The pressures of fund-raising in the modern Congress are relentless, and the process of trying to make sure that they stay in office begins from day one.

By February 2016, Salud Carbajal was continuing to secure money and endorsements. In addition to those of Capps and Peloisi, Carbajal had picked up endorsements from ten other current or former members of the House of Representatives, a long list of county and state political figures, and key interest groups, including teachers and the Latino Victory Fund.

CONCLUSION

From Candidate to Officeholder

As the 2016 presidential and congressional elections kicked into high gear, so much of what was happening was surprising to American voters and political scientists alike. The rise and resiliency of the insurgent presidential campaigns of Democratic candidate Bernie Sanders and Republican candidate Donald Trump stumped the predictions of experts and academics.

However, not everything came out of the blue. The fact that presidential candidates, Democratic and Republican alike, needed to address the potential of the Latino vote was not news. That many of the candidates were struggling in doing so was not news either. What had, perhaps, flown under the radar of national coverage were efforts of Latino candidates themselves—although not necessarily those on the presidential stage—to forge paths to congressional politics. These efforts point to an uncontested and unalterable fact about Latino political participation in American politics and government: It is growing and it continues to grow.

In June 2016, Salud Carbajal won the CA-24 district primary by a large margin, in a prelude to facing off against Republican businessman Justin Fareed in the general election.

But come November, President-elect Donald Trump's Republican coattails were not long enough to carry Fareed to what would have been a mildly surprising

Donald Trump's 2016 electoral victory is announced against the backdrop of a Manhattan skyscraper.

Vanessa Carvalho/Brazil Photo Press/LatinContent/Getty Images.

victory, based on fall polls. Carbajal secured the open seat, winning roughly 55 percent of the vote. However, Representative-elect Carbajal will no doubt be looking two years ahead, when he will have to defend his seat.

Carbajal would not be the only Latino heading off to Congress for the first time in January 2017. Among others, Darren Soto (D-FL) would be "the first Puerto Rican to represent Florida in the House of Representatives and Adrinao Espaillat (D-NY) was elected the first Dominican American to Congress."[94] In January of 2017, a record 38 Latinos and Latinas will be a part of the 115th Congress.[95]

In addition, former state Attorney General Catherine Cortez Masto (D-NV) won the seat of retiring Democrat Harry Reid (D-NV), becoming the nation's first Latina senator: "As the results came in, Cortez Masto tweeted, 'I'm proud to be Nevada's 1st female and our nation's 1st Latina senator. It's about time our government mirrors the diversity of our nation.'"[96]

While the Latino vote may not have proved decisive in the 2016 presidential race, there were several lessons to be learned. First, the concept of a singular "Latino vote," as we have explored, masks a great deal of complexity within Latino communities. While the majority of Latinos voted for Clinton, for example, Trump appeared to do well with Cuban Americans, helping him win Florida. In addition, the inevitability of demographic change will continue to press candidates to try to connect with these growing communities.

CHAPTER REVIEW

This chapter's main ideas are reflected in the Learning Objectives below. By reviewing them here you should be able to **remember** the key points, **connect** them to the stories presented in the chapter, **think** critically about these questions, and **know** these terms that are central to the topic.

10.1 Discuss the challenges facing the candidates for the 2016 presidential and congressional elections as they sought to reach out to the growing Latino population.

REMEMBER...

- The continuing growth of the American Latino voting-age population presents the political parties and their candidates with significant opportunities and challenges as they try to reach out to voters in these communities.

CONNECT...

- During the 2016 presidential campaign, candidates in both major parties tried to convince Latino voters that their candidacies were worth supporting, though all faced challenges in doing so.

- What challenges did the leading candidates for nomination in the 2016 presidential elections face in reaching out to Latino voters?

- How were these political challenges shaped by the parties that the candidates sought to represent?

- What effects do you think the expected massive growth in the percentage of Latinos of voting age will have on national electoral outcomes?

- What might limit the impact of this demographic change?

- Do you think the diversity of Americans' lived experiences is represented in national electoral outcomes? Why or why not?

KNOW...

- *demographics* (p. 338)

- *swing states* (p. 345)

10.2 Describe the role of campaign contributions in national elections and discuss efforts to regulate them.

REMEMBER...

- American national elections are somewhat unique among democratic nations in that they occur on fixed and regular schedules.

- In national campaigns, money can be used to purchase advertising, mobilize voters and supporters, and discourage potential challengers from entering a race.

- Certain federal efforts to control or restrain campaign finance have been found to be constitutionally permissible, while others have been modified or rejected.

THINK...

- Does money matter?

- Should campaign contributions be limited? Why or why not?

KNOW...

- *challenger* (p. 341)
- *get out the vote (GOTV)* (p. 342)
- *incumbent* (p. 341)
- *negative campaign advertisements* (p. 342)

- *political action committees (PACs)* (p. 343)
- *retrospective voting* (p. 341)
- *super PACs* (p. 344)

10.3 Understand the rules surrounding national elections as well as the structure and stages of presidential campaigns.

REMEMBER...

- The presidential campaign involves two formal stages: the nomination campaign and the general elections.

- Prior to the formal campaign, would-be presidential candidates lay the groundwork for their eventual campaigns.

- Political parties have constructed different systems and sets of rules for selecting their nominees.

- In the general election, the system of the Electoral College determines the winner, with states awarded electoral votes according to their representation in Congress.

- Why did the framers mistrust direct democracy? What do you think have been the implications of this mistrust?

- What challenges do presidential candidates face from the different groups of voters who turn out in the nomination phase of the campaigns as opposed to the general elections?

KNOW...

- *Electoral College* (p. 350)

- *exploratory committee* (p. 349)

- *faithless elector* (p. 350)

10.4 Understand the main issues in congressional campaigns, including the roles of constituency and incumbency.

REMEMBER...

- Congressional newcomers face many challenges in seeking election against entrenched incumbents, which often drives credible challengers to wait for an open seat election.

- The rules of congressional elections vary by state, and these differences can affect candidate strategies.

- The redrawing of congressional district lines, typically done following a census, can be a very political process in state politics and can have significant electoral consequences.

- In some cases, the process of redistricting is designed to benefit certain groups of voters, such as those of minority racial or ethnic identity.

CONNECT...

- Salud Carbajal entered the race for the House of Representatives in California's Twenty-fourth Congressional District.

- Carbajal's decision to do so was likely influenced by the fact that he would not be facing an incumbent.

- Carbajal, who faced a recently redrawn district and a new congressional electoral system, sought to convince voters that he was the candidate best suited to represent his constituents' interests.

THINK...

- In what ways do the differences of constituency shape the strategies of congressional candidates as opposed to presidential candidates?

KNOW...

- *apportionment* (p. 357)
- *coattail effect* (p. 354)
- *constituencies* (p. 356)
- *gerrymandering* (p. 358)
- *incumbent* (p. 353)
- *incumbency advantage* (p. 363)
- *majority* (p. 356)

- *majority-minority district* (p. 360)
- *malapportionment* (p. 360)
- *open seat election* (p. 353)
- *plurality* (p. 356)
- *redistricting* (p. 357)
- *runoff election* (p. 356)
- *top-two primary system* (p. 353)

11 INTEREST GROUPS AND SOCIAL MOVEMENTS
Collective Action, Power, and Representation

In the American political system, many of the people who formally represent the interests of citizens in government are the leaders that those citizens have elected: the mayors, governors, members of Congress, and presidents. These individuals are tasked with speaking on behalf of the people, and if the people don't like the policies they put into place, they have a powerful tool to shape the officials' behavior: elections. Elected officials, however, are not the only people who try to represent American interests. The people themselves come together to shape policy or to call attention to issues. They form voluntary associations—groups and communities who join with each other in pursuit of collective interests and common goals.

Former senator Trent Lott, now senior counsel at lobbying firm Squire Patton Boggs in downtown Washington D.C., meets with Senator Bill Nelson (D-FL) at the Capitol. Between 2008 and 2011, financial firm Goldman Sachs spent over $15 million dollars lobbying Congress on its behalf. Squire Patton Boggs was among the lobbying firms hired by Goldman in the wake of the financial collapse of 2008.

Photo by Bill Clark/CQ Roll Call.

In the twenty-first century, there has been no shortage of individuals and groups determined to use the American political process to advance their own interests and goals, and there has been no shortage of crises and controversies to focus the nation's attention on their diverse causes. In this chapter, we will dive into two stories: the first is of lobbyists acting on behalf of America's banks and financial firms; the other, of a group of protesters who came together under the name Occupy Wall Street (OWS) to call attention to, among other things, the growing gap between the ultrawealthy and everyone else. Who were these different groups of people? Why and how did they come together? How did the political landscapes in which they operated shape their options, tools, and tactics?

Both of these two groups were acting on behalf of someone and representing that someone's interests, at least as they perceived those interests. Both groups came together because they chose to; however, there were important differences between them. The financial firms and their representatives in Washington acted as **interest groups**, which are voluntary associations of people who come together with an agreed-upon set of political and policy objectives and who attempt to pull the levers of political power in service of these defined goals. **Social movements** (sometimes referred to as political movements) are associations of individuals who also come together to change things or keep things from changing, but they often do so by calling attention to a set of injustices or wrongs in order to get policymakers to act and to educate the public about the issue. Whether or not OWS formed a successful social movement is still a topic of debate and discussion, as we will explore.

interest groups
voluntary associations of people who come together with an agreed-upon set of political and policy objectives and who attempt to pull the levers of political power in service of these defined goals.

social movements
voluntary associations of individuals who come together to change things or keep things from changing, but they often do so by calling attention to a set of injustices or wrongs in order to get policymakers to act and to educate the public about the issue.

If the distinction between an interest group and a social movement seems fuzzy, this is because it is not a neat and clean one. A social movement may spawn one, or many, interest groups over the course of its development and expression. We have explored this phenomenon already, though not using the same language. For example, the National Association for the Advancement of Colored People (NAACP), in its efforts to end legal segregation, was acting as an interest group but also as part of a larger social movement in the struggle for civil rights. What typically distinguishes these types of associations are questions of power and tactics. Members of interest groups and social movements often resort to different tactics to achieve their goals. They have to; they depend upon a rational determination of what will work to achieve their objectives and of what tools they can bring to bear.

However, there is always a danger inherent with interest groups and social movements: faction. How can one be sure that a group or movement does not trample on the rights of others? As the stories you will explore show, some voices do get heard more clearly than others.

After reading this chapter, you will be able to:

11.1 Identify the constitutional foundations of voluntary association in the American political process

11.2 Summarize the challenges interest groups and social movements confront in recruiting, mobilizing, and organizing the activities of their members

11.3 Discuss the types of interest groups in the American political landscape and the different tactics that they use

11.4 Analyze and contrast the tactics that interest groups and social movements use in order to advocate on their members' behalf

LEARNING OBJECTIVES

BLOWING BUBBLES WITH HOUSES
The Roots of a Financial Crisis

Fueled by cheap money, rampant financial speculation, and a global binge on debt, a financial free-for-all began in the early 2000s, making a very small number of individuals almost unimaginably rich, especially those in powerful positions in the financial industry. At the center of the wealth-making machine was what had been a very ordinary product: the home mortgage. Mortgages are a type of loan issued by a financial firm to cover the purchase of a home. They traditionally were granted by a local bank whose loan officers knew the community and could gauge their customers' ability to repay the loan. But during this new era, lenders started to issue loans to people who would not have qualified for them under older rules, and with terms that were very dicey.

Far from the skyscrapers of Wall Street, then, with new loans in hand, Middle America got in on the action. An entire genre of reality TV emerged to feed expanding appetites to get in on the housing boom, with shows like *Flipping Vegas* dramatizing the buying, renovating, and selling of houses as a way to finance the sort of things that secure bragging rights at the neighborhood potluck: vacation getaways, big-screen TVs, the newest car on the block. Even Americans with very low incomes enjoyed much easier access to home loans, envisioning them as springboards for sending their children to college and moving their families a few rungs up the economic ladder. These types of mortgage loans are called *subprime*, and, despite the increased risk, banks issued them with full confidence that the government had their backs should things go south.

As if that were not enough, the nation's financial firms found yet another fountain of profits in the housing market. Mathematical whiz kids hired by prominent banks and investment firms created investment products that turned out to be some of the most lucrative innovations of the early twenty-first century. To create them, local banks would sell their subprime and other mortgages to larger financial firms, who would then chop the loans into little bits (the process is really complicated) and reconstitute them into increasingly abstract financial products called a mortgage-backed securities (MBSs). They

Blowing Bubbles With Houses **371**

Scenes from the financial crisis: selling the attraction of flipping houses for profits; mountains of bad loans resulted in sprawling developments full of abandoned homes; stadiums full of borrowers seeking help in hopes of avoiding foreclosure or an auction sale of their home.

AP Photo/The Las Vegas Sun, Christopher DeVargas (top); Ethan Miller/Getty Images (center); Justin Sullivan/Getty Images (bottom).

couldn't be traced back to the assets that secured them in the first place, and the relationship between the borrower and the holder of the loan was by that point totally disconnected. Think of the difference between a cup of hand-pressed cider one buys at a local orchard and an "apple beverage," the contents of which probably include some form of apples from some place, or many places. While MBSs had been invented decades prior, during the housing boom of the early 2000s, firms began to find ever more creative, lucrative, and riskier variations on them, and investors gobbled them up.

Mortgage-backed securities became the financial equivalent of junk food: even though they came with assurances from the banks that they were safe, and even though they were very appealing, one could not always be sure exactly what was in them. In fact, they were so complex that not even the banks themselves fully understood the risks they posed. What they *did* know was that there was a lot of money to be made from buying, slicing, and selling these new financial Frankenfoods to a seemingly unending stream of willing buyers. Investors binged on MBSs because they offered a higher rate of return on their money than many other financial products available at that time. Appetite for these products grew so fierce that the banks could hardly produce enough loans to turn into MBSs fast enough. So banks started to take bigger and bigger risks and issue more and more loans, including some loans to people who obviously could not repay them. Between 2000 and 2005, those risks seemed to be paying off.

For all of this to keep going, however, home prices had to keep going up, and homeowners had to keep making their payments. Eventually, however, those people who were the least likely to be able to repay their loans *did not* repay those loans, and the housing market began to crash. The housing bubble was popping.

Things went south, slowly at first, and then very quickly. In 2006 home sales peaked and prices began to decline; foreclosure rates began to spike. By 2007 one of the main lenders, Freddie Mac, announced that it was going to stop buying the riskiest subprime mortgages and MBSs, sending shockwaves through the markets. Other banks that had issued those loans started failing. Some analysts started to suspect that the party was going to end, possibly rather quickly and probably rather badly. Still, others saw less cause for concern. Testifying before the Joint Economic Committee of Congress in March 2007, Ben Bernanke, chair of the Federal Reserve, reassured the committee's members that things would not get out of hand and that losses would be restricted to only the riskiest mortgages and the securities that they were backing. He stated, "At this juncture . . . the impact on the broader economy and financial markets of the problems in the subprime market seems likely to be contained."[1]

Bernanke's reassurances proved to be incorrect. By late 2008, the party came crashing to an end. A total of nine major U.S. banks were teetering on the brink of ruin, and nearly $20 trillion of Americans' wealth had been vaporized (Figure 11.1).[2] The Wall Streeters behind the mess plunged into a panic as global markets imploded. "It was," to one observer, "the end of an era, and the demise of the Master of the Universe."[3] The

FIGURE 11.1

The Crash of the American Housing Market

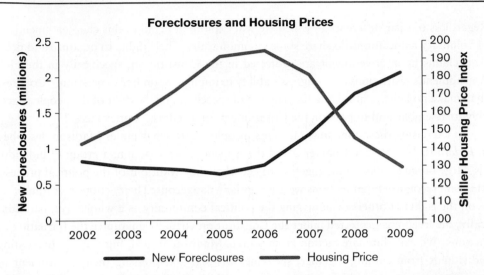

Foreclosures and Housing Prices

Source: Ben Beachy, "A Financial Crisis Manual: Causes, Consequences, and Lessons of the Financial Crisis," Global Development and Environment Institute Working Paper N0. 12-06, Figure 2, Tufts University, December 2012, http://www.ase.tufts.edu/gdae/Pubs/wp/12-06BeachyFinancialCrisis.pdf.

federal government, facing the prospect of the collapse of the nation's and possibly the world's economy as a whole, was about to confront some of the most frightening decisions it would ever have to make.

Powerful interest groups stepped in immediately. Wall Street insiders and the interest groups acting on their behalf quickly realized that it was time to scramble for seats on whatever financial lifeboat the U.S. government might launch, and they grabbed any available ear in Washington that might help them secure a spot for their institution. It appears that Washington was listening. Henry ("Hank") M. Paulson Jr., then Treasury secretary, recounted the steps he took when things began breaking badly: "I immediately started making phone calls to see how Wall Street was responding: Dick Fuld at Lehman, Stan O'Neal at Merrill Lynch, Steve Schwarzman at Blackstone, and Lloyd Blankfein at Goldman Sachs. All these CEOs were on edge."[4] They wanted a bailout—a big one.

1. In contrast to interest groups, members of social movements _____.

   a. Generally have more access to political insiders
   b. Can contribute more money to political campaigns
   c. Focus more on calling public attention to issues
   d. Avoid the dangers of faction

2. In the wake of the financial crisis, what kinds of goals might the financial firms have been trying to advance?

3. What other groups of Americans might have had an interest in the government's response to the crisis?

Answer Key: 1. c; 2. Answers might include efforts to secure the assistance of the federal government in bailing out endangered firms. 3. Answers might include homeowners or individuals threatened with unemployment as the crisis unfolded.

WHAT HAVE I LEARNED?

A NATION OF JOINERS

Acting Collectively in American Representative Democracy

Regardless of their differences—which we will explore in detail in this chapter—members of voluntary associations do share some common traits. Their rights to organize and press their claims upon government are protected in the Constitution, specifically in the First Amendment's restrictions on Congress's ability to impinge upon free expression: "Congress shall make no law . . . abridging the freedom of speech . . . or the right of the people peaceably to assemble, and to petition the Government for a redress of grievances."

In exercising these fundamental rights, people create what James Madison described in *Federalist* No. 10 (see Chapter 2 and the Appendix) as a faction: a group of individuals, large or small, who come together to get what they want out of the political process. Madison recognized that factions were potentially dangerous. Their actions risk trampling upon the rights of others or damaging the political community as a whole. Yet, paradoxically, the freedoms protected under the Constitution virtually guarantee the formation of factions. We can eliminate faction at its source, Madison argued, but only by preventing individuals from coming together, speaking, writing, and pressing their government to address their concerns. While effective, such restrictions upon liberty go against the very principles of a representative democracy. If you have freedom, Madison concluded, you will have faction. The challenge is not how to eliminate it but how to make sure that no one faction can do too much damage.

> "The most common and durable source of factions has been the various and unequal distribution of property."

In the absence of an acceptable way to eliminate faction, Madison developed a theory as to how its effects would be moderated in an extended republic. He believed many factions would compete with each other in the political space that the large American Republic would occupy, making any one faction less of a danger to the nation as a whole. As Madison stated, "Extend the sphere, and you take in a greater variety of parties and interests; you make it less probable that a majority of the whole will have a common motive to invade the rights of other citizens; or if such a common motive exists, it will be more difficult for all who feel it to discover their own strength, and to act in unison with each other."[5] In other words, factions will form, but if there are many competing factions all vying to achieve their goals in a system that allows each a voice, then the most dangerous consequences of their inevitable formation can be contained.

But . . . can they *really* be contained? In the history of the American Republic and, for certain, with regard to the financial crisis of the twenty-first century and the federal government's response to it, no question has been more important or more controversial.

Theories of Interest Group Formation

For one twenty-five-year-old French observer of American life, travelling in the nation in 1831–1832, there was something different about this young country and its people, something that made them want to join together. America and its "equality of conditions" bedazzled Alexis de Tocqueville, whose *Democracy in America* became one of the earliest and most influential expositions on American political life and culture.[6] He was struck by Americans' passion for joining: "Better use has been made of association and this powerful instrument of action has been applied to more varied aims in America than anywhere else in the world."[7] The idea of a "nation of joiners" is a compelling one; however, it does not directly address some key questions. Who joins? What does it mean to join? What do people get from joining? And, most crucially, are the opportunities to join—and the results of doing so—equally effective for all Americans?[8]

As we explored in Chapter 6, Americans' decisions about whether or not to participate in the political process, and how to do so if they so choose, involve a variety of ways in which to make their voices heard. Joining voluntary associations is no different (Figure 11.2).

Although individuals might unite in factions over innumerable shared causes and mutual interests, it was inequality of wealth that posed the greatest danger to James Madison. He wrote, "But the most common and durable source of factions, has been the various and unequal distribution of property. Those who hold, and those who are without property, have ever formed distinct interests in society."[9]

Nearly two centuries later, political scientist Robert Dahl confronted the same basic question that Madison had grappled with: "How does a 'democratic' system work amid an inequality of resources?"[10] Drawing upon Madison's theory of the extended republic, Dahl explored the theory of **pluralism**, in which the distribution of political power—unequal as it may be—among many competing groups serves to keep any one of them in check. Such a widely contested and competitive political space also provides an entry into the political process by groups that might otherwise be excluded, helping to ensure the representation of the interests of the less powerful—although not their success. In this analysis, even though the members of OWS did not enjoy the same level of insider access as the leaders of the nation's financial firms, their participation in the political process allowed them to have a voice in the system and act as a viable counterweight to those with money and all of the political power that money buys.

Not all of Dahl's contemporaries agreed with his pluralist framework or its optimistic conclusion that democratic societies can function effectively despite the presence of inequality of resources and wealth. The debate continues today. In contrast to pluralist perspectives, **elitist theory** focuses on the advantages that certain interests have in the political process based on the unequal distribution of economic and political power. For C. Wright Mills, writing in 1956, a **power elite** composed of the top echelons of people in the business world, government, and military could "look down upon, so to speak, and by their decisions mightily affect, the everyday worlds of ordinary men and women. . . . They rule the big corporations. They run the machinery of the state and claim its prerogatives. They direct the military establishment. They occupy the strategic command posts of the social structure, in which are now centered the effective means of the power and the wealth and the celebrity which they enjoy."[11]

For Mills, it was the nation's defense industry and its allies in government that posed a great danger. Many Americans in the twenty-first century would add the nation's financial firms to a list of power elites. The leaders and members of OWS, whether or not they were aware of the scholarly debates, most certainly did.

In his study, Mills also noted that the exercise of power may be seen not only in those actions that are taken but also in inaction or in preventing actions to which the elites are opposed. A few years later, E. E. Schattschneider also agreed that "the pressure system has an upper-class bias," and he explored the ways in which power can be used.[12] These ways ranged from preventing organization from happening in the first place, to preventing ideas from being discussed at all, to exercising power to keep certain ideas off of the **policy agenda**, which is the set of issues to which policymakers attend.[13] These debates were not

pluralism
a theory of governmental influence that views the distribution of political power among many competing groups as serving to keep any one of them in check.

elitist theory
a theory of governmental influence that focuses on the advantages that certain interests have in the political process based on the unequal distribution of economic and political power.

power elite
a group composed of the top echelons of people in the business world, government, and military.

policy agenda
the set of issues to which government officials, voters, and the public attend.

FIGURE 11.2

Where Americans Join

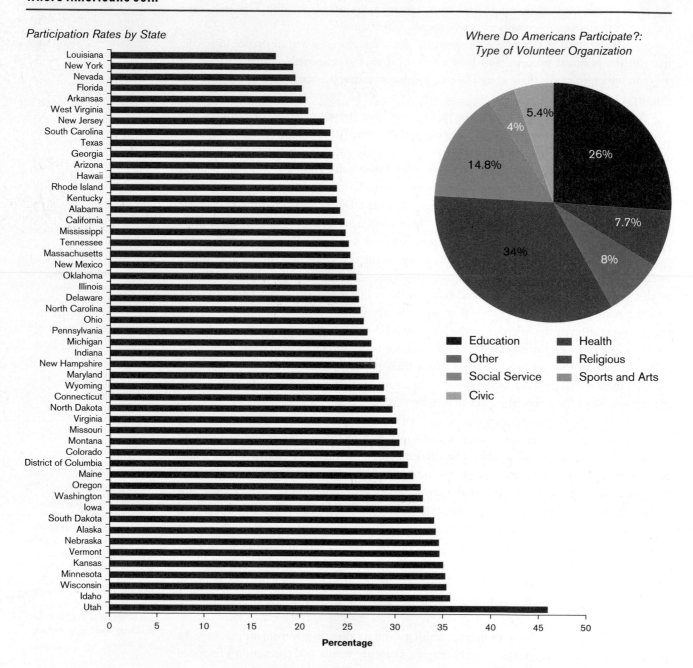

Participation Rates by State

Where Do Americans Participate?:
Type of Volunteer Organization

Legend:
- Education
- Other
- Social Service
- Civic
- Health
- Religious
- Sports and Arts

Source: Data are from the Corporation for National and Community Service, https://www.volunteeringinamerica.gov/data.cfm, accessed September 8, 2016.

settled in the 1960s, and they still have not been. While some scholars point to the dominance of business- and corporate-focused interest groups in campaign contributions (as we will see below), others point out that elite-oriented interest groups are often competing against each other.

Challenges to Group Formation and Activity

David Truman's 1962 *The Governmental Process* is one of the most important early works that systematically explored the dynamics of interest groups in American political life, which were widely referred to at the time as "pressure groups." In his book, Truman noted one of the most telling ironies about Madison and his fellow Federalists— an irony that speaks to the absolute pervasiveness of organized group activity. In advocating for the proposed Constitution, Madison was himself acting in the way that members of interest groups act. According to Truman, "The entire effort of which *The Federalist* was a part was one of the most skillful and important examples of pressure group activity in American history."[14] While the *Federalist Papers*, as we discussed in Chapter 2, are now viewed as one of the most important expositions on the theory of the Constitution, at the time the essays were also pieces of political propaganda, designed to push the pro-Constitution goals forward in opposition to the Antifederalists and their vision of the American Republic.

A businessman, likely someone Mills would have characterized as a member of the power elite, walks by the Bank of New York in Midtown Manhattan, which is home to many of the world's banks, in April 2009.
Jeff Hutchens/Getty Images.

While exploring the pluralist theory of interest group operation, Truman's study also highlighted the fact that interest groups can wield a considerable amount of power in American political life. How each group wields that power—and how much power it has—depends upon organization within the group itself. Interest groups, after all, are not monolithic entities but collections of individuals, each with his or her own goals and desires. Successful interest groups harness those energies and direct them towards the group's goals. In trying to do so, however, leaders and members of voluntary associations—interest groups and social movements alike—have to overcome challenges to successful organization and coordination.

In getting organized and acting for the interests of their members, advocates for American financial firms and the members of OWS both had to contend with one similar basic challenge, that of **collective action**—getting individuals to contribute their energy, time, or money to a larger group goal. However, the members of these two voluntary associations did not necessarily solve this problem in the same way. Differences in size, wealth, and political power all shape the strategies available to the leaders of voluntary associations as they try to overcome the challenges of collective action.

Economist Mancur Olson developed one of the most influential theories of the logic of interest group participation, or, more precisely, the logic of choosing *not* to participate. According to Olson, "Rational, self-interested individuals will not act to achieve their common or group interests . . . unless there is coercion to force them to do so, or unless some separate incentive, distinct from the achievement of the common or group interest, is offered to the members of the group individually on the condition that they help bear the costs or burdens involved in the achievement of group objectives."[15]

A key concept in this framework is the **collective good** (also called a public good), which is some benefit or desirable outcome that individuals can enjoy or profit from even if they do not help achieve or secure it.[16] The problem with collective goods comes from the fact that people can enjoy their benefits without contributing to their

collective action
political action that occurs when individuals contribute their energy, time, or money to a larger group goal.

collective good
also called a public good; some benefit or desirable outcome that individuals can enjoy or profit from even if they do not help achieve or secure it.

provision. Since, in this framework, individuals are completely rational with how they allocate their time, energy, and resources, there is no incentive for them to help out as they know they will receive the benefits of others' efforts. A strong national defense, clean air, or a really nice fireworks display may all be thought of as examples of collective goods. Those individuals who enjoy collective goods without help to secure them are called **free riders**, and they pose a serious challenge to the efforts of any voluntary association to work toward collective goals. Note that free riders are acting rationally in this framework. Based upon a pure cost-benefit logic, individuals should "free ride" and devote their energies elsewhere, knowing that others will make up for their inaction.

In the absence of some way to force individuals to contribute, therefore, public goods will be underprovided. Taxes, laws, and other forms of coercion are tools that governments use to overcome the challenges of public goods provision.[17] Voluntary associations of individuals, however, do not generally have the coercive power of government behind them, yet people still join and contribute, even at great personal cost and risk—as we have explored in the context of securing civil rights and civil liberties. Why? Scholars and observers of American politics have wrestled with this question for a long time and have come up with a variety of reasons and explanations. One explanation, which Olson discussed, is that a given group might be small and homogenous enough that the payoffs for individual participation and the collective risks of nonparticipation are obviously clear and compelling.

free riders
individuals who enjoy collective goods without help to secure them.

A political cartoon illustrating the concept of free riding. The character who is hitchhiking is taking advantage of the character creating the wheel.

Mike Baldwin/CartoonStock.com.

The activities of the leaders of American financial firms during the economic crisis of 2008 might very well have been motivated by such an understanding. Even among the tight-knit group of Wall Street executives, however, it was never that easy. In September of that year, Dick Fuld, head of venerable investment form Lehman Brothers, learned that his firm would be allowed to fail. According to one senior executive at Lehman, it was unbelievable: "Letting Lehman Brothers go was a bit like taking an aeroplane at 40,000 feet, turning the engines off and letting it crash to the city. Then being surprised that it caused mass destruction."[18] Lehman's failure illustrates both the advantages and disadvantages of joining in a collective action effort among a small and homogenous group of similar powerful interests. It is certainly easier to agree upon larger goals in such a group than it is for a more sizeable and diverse protest movement. However, there are no guarantees that any one member will be served, or saved. At the time of Lehman's failure, there were whispers that the failure had been a payback for previous actions by the firm when it did not seem to be acting "on script." Regardless, when swimming with fellow sharks, it is always useful to remember that one is still swimming with sharks.

Other explanations for the ability of interest groups to overcome the challenges of collective action focus on actions by the interest groups themselves, especially in providing incentives for individuals to join or contribute.[19] These inducements may include **selective benefits**, which are made available only to those who join or contribute to the group. One set of selective benefits are **material rewards**, which may include discounts on goods and services, access to group publications and information, special offers, travel opportunities, or a host of other tangible benefits available only to members and contributors. AARP (formerly known as the American Association of Retired Persons) is widely known for the material benefits that it provides for its members. Professional associations or trade unions may provide their members with the credentials needed to operate in their profession, as is the case for state bar associations and regulation of the practice of law, or achieve for their members higher wages or better benefits, as may be the case for trade unions.

Other rewards that may be available only as a result of participation are **social benefits**, which might allow members to network with other individuals with similar interests and goals. Social benefits may come in the form of personal relationships and the benefits individuals attach to forming such relationships for their own sake, or they may take the form of job opportunities and other avenues for personal advancement. A third set of selective benefits arises from the satisfaction of working with others to achieve a common goal or purpose. For this reason, these inducements are referred to as **purposive benefits**.

selective benefits
goods that are made available only to those who join or contribute to a group.

material rewards
a type of tangible benefit made available to members and contributors of a group.

social benefits
rewards in the form of new connections or access to networks that members of a group receive through their participation.

purposive benefits
rewards in the form of satisfaction from working with others to achieve a common goal or purpose.

WHAT HAVE I LEARNED?

1. James Madison formulated the theory of _____, whereby many factions would compete with each other in the large political space of the American Republic.

    a. The extended republic
    b. Elitist politics
    c. Representative democracy
    d. The policy agenda

2. Collective action is _____.

    a. When individuals contribute their time and energy to an effort
    b. Rarely successful
    c. When opposing sides agree on a middle ground
    d. Easier when the group has diverse goals

3. Pluralism occurs when the distribution of political power among many competing groups becomes imbalanced and one group gains more power than the others, emerging as a clear winner.

    a. True
    b. False

4. What kinds of things do interest groups do to overcome the challenges of collective action?

Answer Key: 1. a; 2. a; 3. b; 4. Answers should include concepts such as selective, material, social, and purposive benefits.

INTEREST GROUPS ACT ON THEIR MEMBERS' BEHALF
Responding to the Financial Crisis, Part I

In September 2008, Secretary Henry Paulson and other individuals who controlled the levers of the American financial system came together to preach one message: doom. Both the nation's and the world's financial systems, they warned, were on the brink.

House Speaker Nancy Pelosi of California, center right, and House Democratic leaders meet with Treasury Secretary Henry Paulson, center left, and Federal Reserve Chair Ben Bernanke, second from left, in Pelosi's office on Capitol Hill to discuss the financial crisis.

AP Photo/Manuel Balce Ceneta.

The most powerful financial firms were on the verge of failure, endangering the entire American way of life. Appearing on the Sunday morning political news talk show circuit that month, Paulson warned "of an economic doomsday if Congress [did not] immediately okay a colossal Wall Street bailout, and he resisted Democratic calls to include help for taxpayers and homeowners."[20]

Behind closed doors, the warnings of Paulson, along with those of Ben Bernanke, chair of the Federal Reserve, were even scarier. The two men spoke to members of Congress "in such apocalyptic terms that lawmakers were struck dumb with horror," according to sources who attended the private meetings.[21] "Bernanke warned the credit system was 'a matter of days' away from drying up—and with it, the whole economy. 'The air came out of the room. It was that startling,' said Sen. Chris Dodd (D-Conn.), chairman of the Banking Committee."[22]

There was only one solution, these two powerful men warned: money, taxpayer money, to backstop the arterial bleeding by the most powerful banks and financial firms in the country. The tab, they calculated, involved numbers nearly impossible to comprehend: $700 billion in loan guarantees and funds set aside to purchase the MBSs that were going rancid as quickly as a chicken salad at a summer picnic in Texas. That transaction would transfer these riskiest loans out of the hands of the suddenly imperiled financial giants and place them firmly in the hands of American taxpayers.

In his visits to the Sunday news shows that weekend in September 2008 and in his subsequent appeals to the American electorate, Paulson added two more conditions. He needed the money, the $700 billion, *right away*, within the week at the latest, or extremely bad things would happen. And he requested that there be almost no oversight over how he was going to spend it, in order to allocate these funds quickly and efficiently and preserve the enormously complicated and interconnected financial system. Under fire from skeptical members of Congress, Paulson defended his actions as fundamental to representing the interests of Americans during a time of unprecedented financial crisis. Reviewing the details—or lack thereof—of the proposal during congressional hearings, Senator Christopher Dodd (D-CT) lashed out at the Treasury secretary, declaring, "After reading this proposal, I can only conclude that it is not only our economy that is at risk, Mr. Secretary, but our Constitution as well."[23] Paulson stood his ground and based his defense on the need to protect the American people, arguing that his plan was "the single most effective thing we can do to help homeowners, the American people, and stimulate our economy."[24]

Paulson and his supporters argued that his previous experience on and connections to Wall Street provided him with firsthand insight into how things worked in the industry and the kinds of personal connections necessary to make things happen as he ran this enormous, unprecedented, one-man ATM. This was no place for amateurs.

Senator Elizabeth Warren on Wall Street, Bailouts, Influence, and Representation (or a Lack of It)

In December 2014, Congress was considering, as part of a larger bill, weakening legislation restricting the activities and risk-taking behavior of the nation's financial firms. Senator Elizabeth Warren (D-MA) took to the floor of the Senate to challenge President Barack Obama and her legislative colleagues over Congress's role in bailing out the nation's powerful financial firms during the financial collapse and ignoring the needs of average Americans. In her speech, Warren called out for criticism one of the nation's most powerful financial firms, Citigroup:

> Today I'm coming to the floor not to talk about Democrats or Republicans, but about a third group that also wields tremendous power in Washington: Citigroup. Mr. President, in recent years, many Wall Street institutions have exerted tremendous power in Washington's corridors of power, but Citigroup has risen above the others. Its grip over economic policymaking in the executive branch is unprecedented.
>
> Citigroup has also spent millions trying to influence the political process in ways that are far more subtle—and hidden from public view. Last year, I wrote Citigroup and other big banks a letter asking them to disclose the amount of shareholder money they have been diverting to think tanks to influence public policy. Citigroup's response to my letter? Stonewalling. A year has gone by, and Citigroup didn't even acknowledge receiving the letter. . . .
>
> Washington already works really well for the billionaires and big corporations and the lawyers and lobbyists. But what about the families who lost their homes or their jobs or their retirement savings

Senator Elizabeth Warren (D-MA) speaks at a banking subcommittee hearing in Washington, D.C.
Andrew Harrer/Bloomberg via Getty Images.

> the last time Citi bet big on derivatives and lost? What about the families who are living paycheck to paycheck and saw their tax dollars go to bail out Citi just six years ago? We were sent here to fight for those families, and it's time—it's past time—for Washington to start working for them.[27]

WHAT DO YOU THINK?

How have you and those around you experienced the financial crisis and the efforts to contain it? In the mania that led up to the crisis, both powerful financial firms and many individual homeowners made decisions that went wrong. Is it the role of the federal government to try to alleviate the effects of both of these sets of poor decisions? Neither of them? Or something in between?

One might have wondered if Paulson really represented Americans' interests. He was most certainly an insider. Prior to being tapped to lead the Department of the Treasury in 2006, Paulson had served as chair and chief executive officer of the investment banking titan Goldman Sachs & Co., one of the most powerful players on the American financial scene. And he had led Goldman during "the Gold Rush that [had] brought the global financial system to the brink of collapse."[25] Paulson reassured Americans wary of an insider bailing out insiders that he was only reluctantly "using $700 billion of taxpayers' money to bail out his former colleagues on Wall Street," an unasked for responsibility that, the secretary assured the nation, "sticks in my craw."[26]

In 2008, as the debates of a potential bailout began to take real shape, the titans of Wall Street hardly disappeared into the shadows. As the Senate considered how, or whether, to bail out distressed homeowners—those who owed more on the mortgages taken out on their homes than what those homes could be sold for on the open market—the lobbyists from America's financial firms were hard at work. One proposal was to have the federal government backstop distressed mortgages, allowing underwater homeowners to refinance those mortgages with government guarantees. According to a reporter for the *Washington Post*, this idea became known as the "'Credit Suisse plan'" among congressional staffers and lobbyists. It was named after a powerful financial institution that had benefitted considerably from the sale of MBSs and was advocating for the plan. As related in the *Post* article, "During the first week of January, three officials from Credit Suisse—two from Washington and one from the mortgage-trading desk in New York—spent a day on Capitol Hill briefing the staffs of the committees that oversee housing. They gave a brief PowerPoint presentation to the House Financial Services Committee in the morning and to the Senate Banking Committee in the afternoon."[28]

Their efforts, along with those of other financial firms, appeared to have paid off. "As recently as Saturday morning," a report in the *New York Times* noted on a Monday during the peak of the crisis that September, "the Bush administration's proposal called for Treasury to buy residential or commercial mortgages and related securities. By that evening, the proposal was broadened to give Treasury discretion to buy 'any other financial instrument.' . . . Over the weekend, the Securities Industry and Financial Markets Association, Wall Street's main trade and lobbying group, held conference calls to discuss 'your firms' views and priorities related to Treasury's proposal,' according to an e-mail message sent to members."[29]

As members of Congress assembled, bargained, and assessed their own electoral futures in the fall of 2008, one fact became quite clear: Large numbers of Americans were wary of using taxpayer dollars to backstop or bail out the same financial firms that seemed responsible for the mess in the first place. One of their main concerns was a bailout of the lenders that did not include help for average homeowners facing foreclosure on homes purchased at the height of the mania, homes that were now worth much less than when purchased and often less than the amount owed on the mortgages.

As the congressional negotiations reached a critical point in September 2008, calls to include help for average homeowners grew louder. "We will not simply hand over a $700 billion blank check to Wall Street and hope of a better outcome. Democrats will act responsibly to insulate Main Street from Wall Street," House Speaker Nancy Pelosi (D-CA) promised.[30] The Speaker's promise was made, no doubt, partly because "rank-and-file members were getting an earful from their constituents—and showing signs of a populist revolt."[31] Pelosi's Republican colleagues across the aisle were getting a similar volume of calls and e-mails.

As the vote loomed, "blogs and radio phone-ins were inundated with Americans voicing their exasperation and rage at the proposals. Richard from Anchorage, Alaska, was typical of many when he wrote on CNNMoney.com: 'NO NO NO. Not just no, but HELL NO.'"[32] Messages to members of Congress were clear and came in heavy volume. "The phone calls into the district office are about 75 percent saying: Don't do this. They think this is about Wall Street," reported a Republican member of the House.[33] The results of a Bloomberg/*Los Angeles Times* poll released that week confirmed Americans' widespread opposition: "By a whopping 55 percent to 31 percent margin," respondents agreed that "taxpayers should not be burdened with the costs of resuscitating private companies."[34] In addition to average Americans, organized interest groups joined the chorus of voices expressing concerns about the possible effects of the proposals on struggling Americans. Groups representing farmers, senior citizens, and undocumented Americans as well as civil rights advocates began to put pressure on Washington.[35]

The stock market was about to send its own message. As the House of Representatives voted down the proposed bailout on September 29, the Standard and Poor's 500 (a broad measure of companies in the American economy) suffered its worst one-day loss in more than twenty years. The Dow Jones Industrial Average dropped 777 points, its largest point loss in history. The *New York Daily News* reported that "some traders could be seen shaking their heads sadly. Others grimaced and reached for their phones."[36]

As Congress began to negotiate, cut deals, and generally engage in the some-times-unsightly production of legislation, much of the real work happened out of the public eye, before any vote took place on the floors of the House and the Senate. Members of Congress had to act quickly due to the threat of an imminent global financial meltdown hanging over their heads. The majority of their constituents were sending a clear message: *Let Wall Street fail.* Other players, however, powerful ones, were sending a very different message to Congress: *If you let this happen, the whole ship is going down, and it will take your political career with it.*

A few days later, the Senate passed a bailout bill, one that had been "packed . . . with scores of lavish goodies to please favored groups and win support from opponents" in the House.[37] Included in the "goodies" were tax breaks for consumers to purchase energy efficient appliances, $500 million in tax breaks for film producers, breaks for rum producers and Alaskan fishermen, and a "$10 million credit to help employers defray the costs of storing the bicycles of their employees who commute to work."[38] The strategy, which was designed to peel off enough of the "No" votes in the House, worked; Congress passed the bailout and sent it to President George W. Bush's desk, where it became law. Along the way, however, the tab had grown to $850 billion, inflated by last minute additions, negotiations, and successful efforts on the part of lawmakers to extract concessions for their constituents and interest groups important to their electoral fortunes.

Wall Street breathed a sigh of relief; the stock market stabilized.

In the aftermath of the financial crisis and the Wall Street bailout, many Americans clamored for financial reforms to make sure that what many saw as a taxpayer-backed reward for excessive risk-taking by financial firms would not be repeated. In May 2009, President Obama urged Congress to act on legislation that would provide for more oversight over the riskiest of Wall Street's complex financial instruments, called swaps and derivatives. As the *New York Times* noted, however, lobbyists were already on the move to curtail reforms that would limit their group's interests: "Hinting at a lobbying campaign

Stock traders watch the financial markets plummet as they work on the floor of the New York Stock Exchange on September 29, 2008.
REUTERS/Brendan McDermid.

to come . . . the chief executive of the International Swaps and Derivatives Association, a trade group, said his organization 'looked forward to working with policy makers to ensure these reforms help preserve the widespread availability of swaps and other important risk management tools.'"[39]

To some, preserving the availability to freely market with insufficient oversight the very securities whose collapse had nearly brought the global financial system to a dead stop seemed worrisome. A study published in 2011 by the National Bureau of Economic Research concluded that those firms involved in the greatest risk-taking leading up to the crisis were among the most active in lobbying for the bailout program Congress passed and benefitted the most from it.[40]

As Congress continued to hammer out the details of financial reform, according to a Politico report in 2010, "Wall Street has dramatically expanded its influence on Capitol Hill over the past year, using a lobbying army that includes nearly 1,500 former federal employees and 73 former members of Congress who have been deployed during debate on financial reform legislation."[41] This "army" included "former Speaker of the House Dennis Hastert (R-Ill.), former Senate Majority Leaders Bob Dole (R-Kan.) and Trent Lott (R-Miss.) and former House Majority Leaders Dick Armey (R-Texas) and Dick Gephardt (D-Mo.). One former member, Rep. Vin Weber (R-Minn.) has a whopping 13 financial sector clients. . . . 'Wall Street hires former members of Congress and their staff for a reason,' said Public Citizen Congress Watch Director David Arkush, 'These people are influential because they have personal relationships with current members and staff. It's hard to say no to your friends.'"[42]

> "These people are influential because they have personal relationships with current members and staff. It's hard to say no to your friends."

While representatives from Wall Street firms mobilized in force during and after the financial crisis, they were not the only ones acting. Other interest groups advocated as well, although many of their members were less connected to the corridors of political power than the titans of the American financial services industry. AARP, for example, argued that in the wake of the crisis, "the social safety net needs to strengthened and extended. Workers should not have to worry about losing their health and pension benefits when they lose a job."[43] In the next section, we will explore the landscape of interest groups in the United States and the varied tactics that they use in order to advance their members' goals.

WHAT HAVE I LEARNED?

1. In the wake of the financial crisis of 2008, Treasury Secretary Hank Paulson argued that the nation's most powerful financial firms needed to be allowed to fail and be dismantled.

   a. True
   b. False

2. How did financial executives and members of government use the potential for serious economic consequences to advance their agendas?

3. Why were many ordinary Americans unhappy with the government's response to the financial crisis?

Answer Key: 1. b; 2. Answers might include justifying aid to financial firms for the larger purpose of protecting the American economy.; 3. Many Americans felt that it was unfair to use taxpayer money to bail out financial firms in crisis due to their own mistakes and greed.

THE INTEREST GROUP LANDSCAPE
Types and Tactics

Americans with a wide variety of political goals join, hire, or support interest groups in order to make their wishes known. Interest groups are often categorized and analyzed according to the broader goals that they set out to achieve and for whom they are advocating. Though scholars differ on specific classification schemes, the central idea is to examine what kinds of benefits the groups are seeking.

Economic interest groups, as their name implies, advocate on behalf of the economic interests of their members. These groups form the largest category of interest groups and are responsible for the largest amount of campaign donations. Within the category of economic interest groups, the largest and generally most influential subcategory consists of business groups, which advocate for the policies that favor their particular firms or industries. Labor groups, such as trade unions, advocate on behalf of the workers that they represent. Finally, farm groups have a long historical tradition of acting in American politics on behalf of farmers.

In contrast, **public interest groups** act on behalf of the collective interests of a broad group of individuals, many of who may not be members or contributors to the organization. Groups advocating in the areas of civil rights, civil liberties, social welfare, education, or the environment are all examples of public interest groups. Many of these associations focus on one specific area of public policy and are, therefore, often called single-issue groups. A key subcategory of public interest groups advocate for their members with regard to issues of identity and lived experiences. The actions of the National Association for the Advancement of Colored People (NAACP) in challenging legal segregation, of the National Organization for Women (NOW) on behalf of gender equality, and of groups acting to secure marriage equality are all examples of public interest groups whose efforts we have already examined in the book.

Finally, **government interest groups** act on behalf of state, regional, local, or even foreign governments to keep their members apprised of policy discussions, weigh in on the regulatory process, and generally act on behalf of the relevant government, especially during the appropriations process in Congress.

Acting on the Inside: Lobbying by Interest Groups

All interest groups share the same ultimate goal: to influence public policy on the ground. To do so, they may try to influence any one stage of the policymaking process at the federal, state, or local level. Though we will focus only on efforts directed towards the federal government, even that single piece of the puzzle is quite complicated.

When one pictures organized interest group activity, one of the first things that often comes to mind is the act of **lobbying**, or interacting with government officials in order to advance a group's goals in the area of public policy. Lobbying in America is as old as the Republic itself, although there is some debate about the origin of the term.

CONNECTING TO . . .

The Story of Wall Street Lobbying

As you reflect upon the actions of Wall Street just presented, try to make connections between this story and the terms and concepts that describe lobbying and its tactics, goals, and controversies. Consider the following:

- The financial firms, as an economic interest group, were part of the largest single category of interest groups—and the type that spends the most money

- The financial firms did not only lobby Congress. The executive branch—especially the Department of Treasury—also received their attention.

- In spite of widespread popular opposition to the bailout, it passed, highlighting concerns that powerful interest groups may undermine the ability of average citizens to be represented

economic interest groups
groups that organize to advocate on behalf of the economic interests of their members.

public interest groups
groups that act on behalf of the collective interests of a broad group of individuals, many of who may not be members or contributors to the organization.

government interest groups
organizations that act to secure the interests of local, state, or foreign governments in the political process.

lobbying
interacting with government officials in order to advance a group's goals in the area of public policy.

TOPICS IN AMERICAN GOVERNMENT
Types of interest group activities

The stereotypical idea of lobbying might very well be an image of powerful interest group members contacting members of Congress and pressuring them to act on the group's behalf. Though that may be part of the story, lobbying is actually a much more complex and nuanced process than this image evokes. In the first place, interest group members lobby all three branches of the federal government, not just Congress, though the tactics that they use may vary depending on which branch is being lobbied. Second, even when they do approach Congress, lobbyists' tactics are varied and complicated and often focus as much on providing information to representatives, senators, and congressional staff members as they do on pushing for a specific position directly.

NEWS CLIP
Examples of the lobbying revolving door in the Obama administration

Rather than as a single effort, lobbying is most accurately thought of as an ongoing process, in which a lobbyist "seldom does only one specific thing at one specific time . . . but multiple things over a period of time."[44] It may involve efforts to shape policy across all three branches; legislative lobbying seeks to influence how legislation is written, executive branch lobbying focuses on how these laws are implemented, and judicial lobbying centers on how the laws are interpreted.

FIGURE 11.3

Lobbying by the Numbers

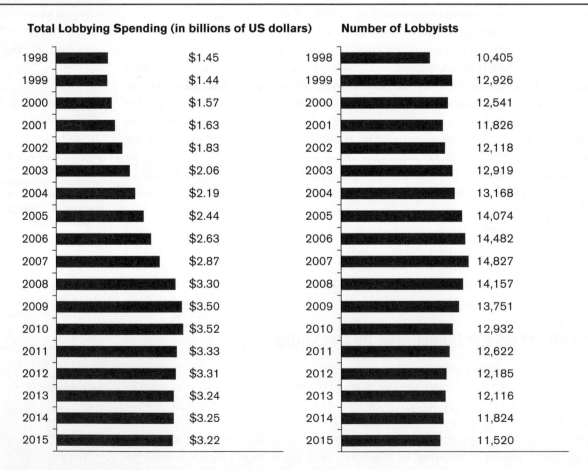

Total Lobbying Spending (in billions of US dollars)	Number of Lobbyists
1998 — $1.45	1998 — 10,405
1999 — $1.44	1999 — 12,926
2000 — $1.57	2000 — 12,541
2001 — $1.63	2001 — 11,826
2002 — $1.83	2002 — 12,118
2003 — $2.06	2003 — 12,919
2004 — $2.19	2004 — 13,168
2005 — $2.44	2005 — 14,074
2006 — $2.63	2006 — 14,482
2007 — $2.87	2007 — 14,827
2008 — $3.30	2008 — 14,157
2009 — $3.50	2009 — 13,751
2010 — $3.52	2010 — 12,932
2011 — $3.33	2011 — 12,622
2012 — $3.31	2012 — 12,185
2013 — $3.24	2013 — 12,116
2014 — $3.25	2014 — 11,824
2015 — $3.22	2015 — 11,520

Source: Center for Responsive Politics, Lobbying Database, OpenSecrets.org, https://www.opensecrets.org/lobby/.

The Lobbyists

The First Amendment to the Constitution guarantees the right of any citizen to lobby—"to petition the Government for a redress of grievances." Modern lobbying, however, is very much a professional undertaking. It involves large numbers of people and a lot of money. The Center for Responsive Politics calculated that in 2015 more than 11,500 paid lobbyists spent a total of $3.22 billion lobbying Congress and federal agencies.[45] As these figures are based only on registered lobbyist activities, however, they understate the actual numbers of total activity, both in the number of lobbyists and the amount of money they spent (Figure 11.3).

Successful lobbyists must be able to provide a service to their clients—the people and firms that hire and pay them. To do so effectively, lobbyists need solid, useful knowledge about the particular policy area and the ability to be heard by those in government. For this reason, former government officials are often in high demand by lobbying firms. And government agencies themselves may recruit individuals from lobbying firms and the private sector for their experience and expertise. The movement of individuals between government and lobbying positions is called the **revolving door phenomenon**. Those who argue that the revolving door is a good thing point to benefits that agencies receive from the experience of former lobbyists and argue that effective lobbying depends on the kind of knowledge and experience that former government officials can bring to the table (Table 11.1). Others, however, have raised concerns about the degree to which those groups capable of paying high prices for well-connected lobbyists tilt public policy in favor of the wealthy and powerful.

Members of interest groups know that their organizations are not all created equally with regard to their wealth, political clout, and access to powerful governmental officials. As such, they may modify their particular lobbying strategies to make the best use of the resources and advantages that they have. Consideration of whether or not all these strategies are equally effective, however, also raises questions about the degree to which Americans are fairly and competently represented . . . or represented at all.

revolving door phenomenon
the movement of individuals between government and lobbying positions.

inside lobbying
when lobbyists contact members of Congress or their staff directly to advocate for their group's position.

This political cartoon depicts the perception that Wall Street's contributions to the federal government give its members undue political influence. The title "Occupy D.C." is a reference to the Occupy Wall Street movement.

Lobbying Congress: Influencing Legislation

Because it writes the nation's laws, Congress is a natural target for lobbyists, who employ several strategies in their efforts to influence legislation. One method, and the one that many people think of when they think of the term *lobbying*, is when lobbyists contact members of Congress or their staff directly to advocate for their group's position. This kind of direct contact is an example of **inside lobbying**, and it takes many forms, which is not surprising given how complex the legislative process is.

In addition to direct contact with representatives, senators, and congressional

TABLE 11.1 Where Do "Revolving Door" People Go after Working for Government?

One of the databases maintained and published by the Center for Responsive Politics is "The Revolving Door," a door, the Web site's editors note, "that shuttles former federal employees into jobs as lobbyists, consultants and strategists just as the door pulls former hired guns into government careers."

Profiling what they call "revolving door people," the table shows the top organizations hiring people who have come from government, excluding lobbying firms themselves.

Organization	Number of "Revolving Door" Employees
U.S. Chamber of Commerce	104
Pharmaceutical Research & Manufacturers of America	56
National Association of Manufacturers	52
General Electric	43
Lockheed Martin	42
Center for American Progress	42
Boeing Co.	40
Goldman Sachs	40
National Federation of Independent Business	38
Citigroup Management Corp	37
AT&T Inc.	37
Biotechnology Industry Organization	34
Fannie Mae	32
George Washington University	31
Mortgage Bankers Association	31
American Petroleum Institute	30
American Medical Association	30
Microsoft Corp	30
JPMorgan Chase & Co	29
Burson-Marsteller	29

Of the top twenty firms listed, note that five are financial firms or organizations involved in the mortgage industry (Goldman Sachs, Citigroup, Fannie Mae, the Mortgage Bankers Association and JPMorgan Chase).

Source: Center for Responsive Politics, "Top Lobbying Firms," OpenSecrets.org, http://www.opensecrets.org/revolving/top.php?display=F, accessed June 23, 2016.

staff members, lobbyists may prepare research reports and briefs, work to shape the legislative agenda by bringing more attention to their issues of interest, or help coordinate a legislative strategy on an issue.[46] These efforts may focus on the content of a piece of legislation and also on the levels of funding for agencies and programs though the appropriations process. Lobbyists may try to influence the total amount of funding available to an agency, spending priorities within that agency, earmarks for specific projects, or riders to appropriations bills, which may specify how money *cannot* be spent and are often a powerful weapon in shaping the implementation of the laws that Congress passes.[47]

Successful inside lobbying often depends on personal relationships, access to decision makers, and financial resources—something not all interest groups possess. Much of the power of inside lobbying, however, also relies on the provision of useful and timely information, such as research that might save a congressional staff valuable time, specific language or wording that may shape or find its way into a bill, or studies that convincingly portray the group's position as one that a member's constituents care about and agree with. Testifying at committee or subcommittee hearings and providing members of Congress with research reports and summaries are two common ways interest groups use information to try to advance their positions.

Lobbying the Executive Branch: Influencing Implementation

From the point of view of interest groups and their lobbyists, winning or losing the battle in Congress is only part of the war. As it is tasked with executing the laws that Congress writes—shaping legislation through the process of implementation—the executive branch also finds itself the target of lobbying efforts. Congress cannot account for every detail within the policy areas covered by its laws. Some flexibility needs to be built in to allow for effective implementation, and legislators eyeing reelection may prefer not to specify certain provisions in too much detail. In trying to influence the appropriations process in Congress, members of organized interest groups try to shape the implementation of the laws by the executive branch. In some cases, they do so directly by lobbying the president (or, more realistically, members of his or her executive staff) or members of the federal bureaucracy.

Federal law requires executive branch agencies to notify the public and solicit its input when establishing rules and procedures, an opening into which organized interests happily step.[48] The detailed nature of most proposed legislation provides an advantage to interest groups armed with data and knowledge of the minutia of the legislation and the affected policy.[49] Interest groups may work to increase the prominence of their goals in the executive branch agenda, and they may also use the courts to challenge federal rules to which they are opposed.

Closely connected to the idea of the revolving door is the risk of **agency capture** (also called regulatory capture), in which those agencies tasked with regulating businesses, industries, or other interest groups are populated by individuals with close ties to the very firms that they are supposed to regulate. This can result in ineffective oversight or regulatory actions that favor the firms over the general interests of society or those not so strongly represented.[50]

agency capture
when agencies tasked with regulating businesses, industries, or other interest groups are populated by individuals with close ties to the very firms that they are supposed to regulate.

Lobbying the Judiciary: Influencing Interpretation

Interest groups and their lobbyists may also try to shape how the nation's laws are interpreted by targeting the federal judiciary. As the thought of a lobbyist badgering an individual member of the Supreme Court about a group's position seems somehow unseemly and, depending on the justice, might actually backfire, groups generally use other methods to try to shape the activities of the federal judiciary, especially the Supreme Court.

Interest groups may try to influence judicial appointments, either through the presidential nomination or Senate confirmation process. Given the importance of the federal judiciary and its influence over a host of issues, interest groups often have a very strong desire to shape the appointment process. In 2016, as Judge Merrick Garland—President Obama's nominee to fill the Supreme Court seat left vacant by the passing of Justice Antonin Scalia—awaited Senate action, interest groups such as the National Federation of Business, the National Rifle Association, Planned Parenthood, and many others acted to support or oppose his confirmation.

The Supreme Court has two decisions to make on each case that comes before it: whether or not to hear the case (to grant *cert*) and how to rule should it decide to hear it. Interest groups may try to influence each of these decisions, typically by filing amicus curiae briefs, which describe a group's position and the arguments for it. As one scholar put it, "Although they were originally envisioned as a 'friend of the Court' and neutral toward the parties, amici are now more appropriately viewed as friends of the participants to the litigation."[51] There is evidence that a high number of amici can increase the chances that justices will hear a case,[52] though some scholars have pointed out that this does not necessarily mean that interest groups have any particular advantage when it comes time for the Court to rule on the merits of the case.[53]

Interest groups may sponsor litigation, guiding a case through the judiciary, but this is an expensive and time-consuming task, even when it goes well. As we explored in Chapter 5, the Legal Defense Fund of the NAACP undertook a lengthy, expensive, and risky strategy in trying to use the federal judiciary to bring an end to legal segregation in the United States. To do so, the group had to find individuals willing to bring suits in court, which could, and did, subject many of them to physical and economic violence. The litigators and staff of the Legal Defense Fund also had to conduct the research and legal analysis that formed the bases of these lawsuits, which was also a personally risky undertaking.

Regulating Lobbying Activities

Given the potential influence of lobbyists on shaping public policy, it is not surprising that attempts have been made over the years to regulate their activities. This is not, however, a simple task. First, the Constitution protects the fundamental rights of interest groups to act on their members' behalf, which includes lobbying activities. Second, there are

FIGURE 11.4

Regulations on Lobbying: A Timeline

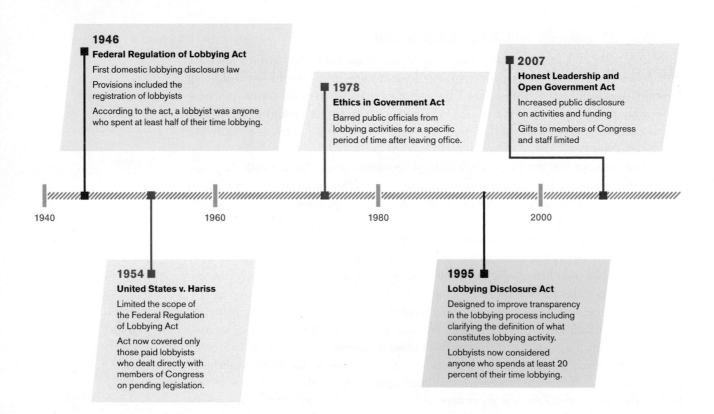

Source: Information compiled from Center for Responsive Politics, "Lobbying History: Timeline," OpenSecrets.org, http://www.opensecrets.org/resources/learn/lobbying_timeline.php; and Elizabeth Dwoskin, "A Brief History of Lobbying," Bloomberg Business, June 7, 2012, http://www.bloomberg.com/bw/articles/2012-06-07/a-brief-history-of-lobbying.

incentives for members of Congress not to overregulate these activities since representatives and senators may benefit from the information and campaign support that interest groups provide. Most recent efforts to regulate lobbying have focused on making the process more transparent (Figure 11.4).

Webs and Networks of Interest Group Influence

One of the classic, and worrisome, depictions of the connections between interest groups and government is the **iron triangle** (Figure 11.5). As the term suggests, the iron triangle consists of three parts—interest groups, Congress, and the bureaucracy—each of which works with the other two to achieve their shared policy goals, even if achieving those goals runs counter to the general interests of society or specific groups within it. In doing so, the members of the triangle act as factions, each helping the other two members and receiving benefits from doing so.

Interest groups provide electoral support to members of Congress, who use their influence, especially on committees and subcommittees, to advance legislation favorable to the interest groups and reduce oversight of interest group activities. These same interest groups lobby on behalf of the relevant bureaucratic agencies to secure the agencies' desired funding and policy goals. In return, the agencies conduct their job of regulation in ways favorable to interest group objectives. Finally, members of Congress determine funding levels and pass legislation desired by the bureaucratic

NEWS CLIP
Former congressman advocates for brain science research funding

iron triangle
the coordinated (and mutually beneficial) activities of interest groups, Congress, and the bureaucracy to achieve shared policy goals, sometimes against the general interests of society or specific groups within it.

FIGURE 11.5

The Iron Triangle

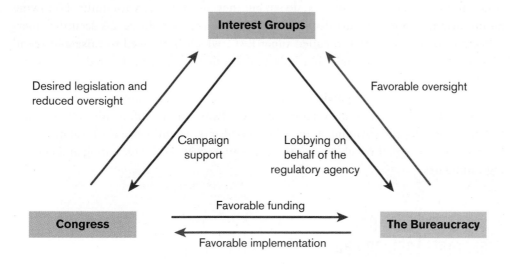

The iron triangle illustrates the linkage of benefits that each of the three members provide to the other two. While all members help each other, it is their common interest in the overall policy goal that drives individual decisions.

agencies, which, in turn, implement the laws passed by Congress in ways desired by those members of Congress.

Due to the growth in the number of interest groups and an increasingly fluid and complex policy landscape in recent decades, political scientists have employed the concept of the **issue network** to describe the webs of influence between interest groups, policymakers, and policy advocates. In contrast to iron triangles, issue networks are often temporary, arising to address a specific policy problem. Any one issue may give rise to competing issue networks, each of which advocates on a different side of the issue. In this way, issue networks are closer to the idea of pluralism than iron triangles.

issue network
the webs of influence between interest groups, policymakers, and policy advocates.

Election-Related Activities

Interest groups are often heavily involved in the electoral process. First, and perhaps foremost, their participation revolves around the targeted distribution of financial resources. Money is a powerful strategic tool as it can fund media coverage, a solid ground campaign, and research. Money can also act as a weapon to discourage others from even running for election. Campaigns are often won or lost long before the actual vote. If a candidate can signal to potential opponents that they will be facing a formidable and well-funded foe, then savvy would-be competitors may very well wait until conditions are more favorable for a realistic run; no serious potential challenger wants to wage a hopeless campaign. Serious challengers are smart and patient; they wait if they have to.

How and under what conditions interest groups contribute to political campaigns is often determined by the status under which they file with the Internal Revenue Service (IRS). Those classified, for example, as 501(c) organizations, whose contributions are tax deductible, face defined rules on the amounts that they may contribute and on the activities towards which those funds may be deployed. Political action committees (PACs) may spend more money on campaigns than individuals and may solicit funds from their members to do so, but they also operate with limits. Following an important Supreme Court decision in 2010, American politics has seen the emergence and rapid rise of the so-called super PAC, which is allowed to raise and spend money without financial limits but only in ways that are uncoordinated with a campaign itself.[54]

As we discussed in the previous chapter, efforts to regulate interest group spending on campaigns and elections are ongoing and not always successful. In addition to financial contributions and spending, interest groups also try to influence electoral outcomes by mobilizing voters through get out the vote campaigns and by recruiting and endorsing candidates.

Acting from Outside: Grassroots Lobbying and Political Protest

Interest groups that attempt to represent less powerful constituencies often have to use a different set of tactics than those available to the more well-funded and well-connected groups. They also aim to change public policy, but they often face different challenges and have to adjust accordingly. Their members generally consist of a diverse group of previously unmobilized and possibly unorganized individuals.

2016 Campaign Contributions by Economic Sector

The OpenSecrets.org project by the independent nonprofit Center for Responsive Politics collects, analyzes, and shares data on money, lobbying, politics, and elections. The center focuses a considerable amount of its efforts on tracking reportable campaign contributions. The figure below presents the total amounts of campaign contributions in the 2016 election cycle reported to the Federal Election Commission as of June 21, 2016, broken down by sector of the economy. It includes contributions from individuals (of $200 or more) and PACs as well as contributions given to super PACs and other groups.

As is clear in the figure, the finance/insurance/real estate sector accounted for the single largest group of contributions. Contributions were dominated by economic sectors; however, interest groups and individuals within

the labor sector as well as those representing single-issue groups also made significant campaign contributions. Note also that the relative allocation of sector donations to Democratic and Republican candidates varied considerably.

WHAT DO YOU THINK?

Why might these groups and individuals have allocated their contributions across the two major political parties in the way that they did? What strategic choices might have been involved in these decisions? What other campaign contribution data would you like to analyze in order to assess the landscape of interest group involvement in American campaigns and elections?

Reportable Campaign Contributions by Economic Sector, 2016

Rank	Sector	Amount	To Cands/ Parties	Dems	Repubs	■ To DEMS ■ To REPUBS
1	Finance/Insur/RealEst	$912,350,256	$465,411,328	42.20%	57.60%	
2	Other	$593,872,619	$494,067,188	58.30%	41.30%	
3	Ideology/Single-Issue	$411,670,519	$271,757,477	61.20%	38.70%	
4	Misc Business	$374,585,616	$267,396,042	43.20%	56.50%	
5	Communic/Electronics	$254,271,572	$159,533,487	67.30%	32.50%	
6	Health	$222,951,892	$165,365,804	49.70%	50.10%	
7	Lawyers & Lobbyists	$198,008,151	$184,822,173	68.40%	31.30%	
8	Energy/Nat Resource	$149,794,510	$97,886,669	22.20%	77.70%	
9	Labor	$142,121,291	$63,252,831	86.90%	12.90%	
10	Agribusiness	$93,418,018	$68,528,589	26.70%	72.80%	
11	Construction	$88,793,884	$66,993,474	31.20%	68.50%	
12	Transportation	$79,237,183	$63,393,786	30.10%	69.70%	
13	Defense	$25,873,898	$25,605,610	38.20%	61.60%	

Source: Center for Responsive Politics, "Totals by Sector," OpenSecrets.org, https://www.opensecrets.org/overview/sectors .php?cycle=2016, accessed November 14, 2016.

Note: Percentages may not add up to 100% as money can be given to third party candidates and party committees.

Problems associated with collective action and the dangers of free-riding are often of more concern to such groups.

These less powerful groups may engage in **outside lobbying**, which focuses on reaching constituents and mobilizing them to pressure their representatives rather than pressuring the representatives directly. A group may decide that outside lobbying is its best course of action, or it may have no other choice and have to use this tactic "out of desperation when an 'inside' strategy has failed."[55] Using outside lobbying tactics is also referred to as **grassroots lobbying**.

In some cases, when grassroots support does not really exist, or would not exist if it hadn't been "purchased" by a lobbying firm, an interest group will present the façade of grassroots support. This is referred to as **Astroturf lobbying**; the term alludes to the fact that the "grassroots" drawn upon are made out of fake grass and thus do not reflect genuine public support. While Astroturf lobbying is widely criticized, the lines between genuine grassroots support and Astroturf lobbying may not always be entirely clear. As political scientist Ken Kollman has questioned, "If two interest groups mobilize the same number of people to contact Congress, but one of them relies on volunteers and its own members and the other pays a consulting house to generate telephone calls and letters, who is to say which is real and which is artificial?"[56] Astroturf lobbying can be effective, and, according to political scientist Kenneth M. Goldstein, its increasing use may be contributing to a new wave of citizen participation that would not exist if not for the fact that "interest groups and lobbying firms inside the beltway are increasingly utilizing new and sophisticated techniques to water the grass roots outside the beltway."[57]

Interest Groups and Representation

Writing in the 1960s, Grant McConnell pointed out that corporations and private interest groups do not rule themselves democratically and that there are far fewer protections provided within them that are afforded to citizens. He stated, "Unfortunately, the governing systems of most private associations do not have the checks upon power or the protections for individuals that have developed out of long experience in the constitutional order of the United States."[58] McConnell's critique of the exercise of power within interest groups also raises questions about representation within social movements themselves—even those that attempt to speak for the less powerful.

In recent decades, political scientists have come back to the questions of power and representation raised by scholars such as Robert Dahl, C. Wright Mills, and E. E. Schattschneider. They have done so often empirically, using the tools of quantitative analysis to get a better understanding of the dynamics of representation among and within interest groups. In general, in spite of a proliferation of groups and movements devoted to the less well-represented members of society, such as minorities, women, and the elderly, much of the evidence points to a continuation of overrepresentation of the elite, powerful, and wealthy.

Exploring data involving nearly seven thousand interest groups, political scientist Kay Lehman Schlozman concluded that in spite of the growth of public interest groups since the 1960s, business and commerce interest groups still account for the majority of associations, a fact that she attributes to their staying power in the face of all of the pressures on a group to maintain its membership and influence.[59] Political scientist Dara Strolovitch concluded that even in interest groups devoted to representing more marginalized members of American society, the relatively better-advantaged members within those groups receive more attention and political effort.[60]

1. Different types of interest groups include _____.

    a. Economic interest groups
    b. Public interest groups
    c. Labor groups
    d. All of the above

2. Lobbying is _____.

    a. Interacting with government officials to secure a group's objectives
    b. Something that only happens in Congress
    c. Rarely a successful strategy
    d. A new development in American politics

3. The "revolving door phenomenon" refers to _____.

    a. Public protests
    b. Individuals moving between government and lobbying positions
    c. Being reelected to Congress
    d. Restrictions on campaign contributions

4. Astroturf lobbying is _____.

    a. The same thing as grassroots lobbying
    b. Conducted by owners of major professional sports teams
    c. When lobbyists go door to door to drum up support for their goals
    d. When firms posing as grassroots groups pay individuals to generate calls and letters

5. The concept of the iron triangle is often illustrated using defense spending and the defense industry. If you were to apply the concept to the financial industry in the twenty-first century, what might the three parts of the triangle be?

Answer Key: 1. d; 2. a; 3. b; 4. d; 5. Answers might include financial firms, members of Congress, and officials with the Department of Treasury.

THE ORIGINS OF A SOCIAL MOVEMENT?
Responding to the Financial Crisis, Part II

NEWS CLIP
Occupy Wall Street protesters use violence in Oakland

In September 2011, almost three years after Secretary Paulson stood in front of the nation and Congress with his $700 billion tab in hand and prognostications of the most doom-ish kind, about eighty individuals were arrested in New York's Zuccotti Park, just blocks from Wall Street and the New York Stock Exchange in lower Manhattan. They had been protesting against the concentration of wealth at the very top of American society and

The Occupy Wall Street movement gets underway in September 2011.
AP Photo/Louis Lanzano.

what they saw as a deep and structural lack of fairness, made far worse by the bailout of Wall Street. This disparate and evolving group of protesters became known as Occupy Wall Street; the movement's message, one fueled by disillusionment and frustration, eventually spread around the globe via strategic use of social media.

Its beginnings, like so many other things about OWS, are disputed, debated, and often derided. Many observers attribute the movement's origins to a blog entry posted in July 2011 by

the Canadian activist group Adbusters.[61] The entry drew connections between the grievances of American youth and those of the protesters in North Africa; the latter's actions had swept across and ignited change in Egypt and other countries in the region. These protests became known as the Arab Spring. The founder of Adbusters, Kalle Lasn, told the press that "his group originally proposed one demand—to separate money from politics." According to an article in *The Christian Science Monitor*, "When asked . . . why it was such a slow burn for people to finally protest the financial crisis, Mr. Lasn said that it took some time for people to realize that President Obama was not handling the meltdown effectively, going so far as to call him a 'gutless wonder.'"[62]

The arrests of the first demonstrators in New York in September 2011 were mostly for blocking traffic, a relatively minor offense. However, in some cases arrests were accompanied by charges of police brutality. Videos that seemed to support those charges were spread far and wide using platforms such as YouTube. The *Charleston Gazette* reported that "one video appear[ed] to show officers using pepper spray on women who were already cordoned off; another show[ed] officers handcuffing a man after pulling him up off the ground, blood trickling down his face."[63] One protester, Ashley Drzymala, who had taken part in the Tahrir Square protests in Cairo, Egypt, during the Arab Spring, told reporters, "We saw police throw a guy who had a video camera into a car. I remembered a police officer pushed the kid and he was trying to get away he was just videotaping, he was not inciting anything. I was saying 'What are you doing? Stop it, we're peaceful.'"[64] New York police commissioner Ray Kelly promised a full investigation into the police response. A few weeks later, OWS protesters marched across the Brooklyn Bridge, again leading to many arrests, hundreds this time. By this point, however, people were more aware of the movement's existence.

Those who joined OWS did so for a variety of reasons; they were not united by self-interest, as the Wall Street financial firms had been. However, their message that a small faction of the wealthiest Americans was working against the interests of everyone else caught on. According to reporter John Ennis, "'WE ARE THE 99 PERCENT' became the rallying cry of a generation. The simplicity and inclusivity was said to be worthy of Madison Avenue. At once the conversation had shifted, and in that discourse, a word starting coming up that used to seem unspeakable: class. That awareness was more than a narrative, more than a meme, more than a point in a debate. The broad perception was that America wasn't just on the wrong track, it had been held up by railroad bandits."[65]

The communication tactics used by OWS were also different. As loudspeakers were prohibited in Zuccotti Park, OWS members invented a very low tech way of communicating. Referred to as "the people's mic," it involved relaying messages through the crowd person by person: "This is how it works: Someone screams 'mic-check' to grab everyone's attention and get the people's mic started. The speaker will then say something, for instance, 'Thank you for your patience tonight,' which the crown repeats. This goes on until the speaker is finished."[67] This was more than just a novel way to communicate; it embodied the ethos of the movement. According to Sheila Nichols, a protester in Los Angeles, "[The] people's mic forces people to be participatory, to listen, to understand that we're in it together. . . . And it's an active experience that forces people to be a part of something that's a whole."[68]

A few prominent Hollywood actors and directors either joined in the protests or expressed their support for them using social media. Director Michael Moore, noted for

Depicting Income Inequality in the U.S.

Using data on wealth and income concentrations in the United States compiled by academic researchers, individuals with Occupy Wall Street created the following image, which found its way into major media outlets and onto T-shirts and posters.

WHAT DO YOU THINK?

How effective do you think this image is in conveying the inequality of wealth in the United States? Though the figure is based on actual data, the creator acknowledges, "I drew the lines in a somewhat impressionistic manner."[66] Does that use of creative license detract at all from the image's power? What other images might one manipulate in a similar way in order to communicate the central point?

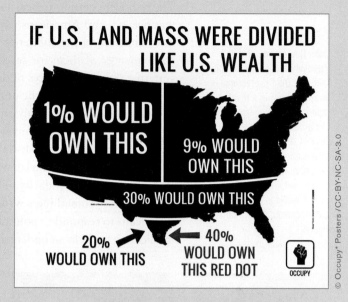

his documentaries criticizing American policy and inequality, said to reporters, "Change has to start somewhere. Why not here?"[69] Yoko Ono, wife of the late John Lennon of the Beatles, tweeted, "I love #OccupyWallStreet. As John said, 'One hero cannot do it. Each one of us have to be heroes.' And you are. Thank you."[70] In October, hip-hop legends Kanye West and Russell Simmons expressed their support, adding "some celebrity glitz to the Occupy Wall Street protest in New York City when they stopped by."[71] MTV posted a casting call for *The Real World* in which it specifically said it was looking for OWS protesters and supporters "to tell their unique stories."[72]

Unlike the round-the-clock media coverage paid to the market crash, the early efforts of OWS barely received a mention in the nation's press. What coverage they did get was condescending and dismissive. The *New York Times* described the protest as "a noble but fractured and airy movement of rightly frustrated young people" who were taking advantage of an "opportunity to air social grievances as carnival."[73] The movement's cause was not terribly well expressed. One activist claimed that his main goal was "to get rid of the combustion engine."[74]

Lucas Brinson takes on the role of a human microphone, relaying information throughout the Occupy Wall Street encampment in New York's Zuccotti Park days before protesters were cleared out by police in mid-November.
AP Photo/Bebeto Matthews.

While the media may have had a hard time figuring out what OWS was all about, the movement's members felt it was clear that something had gone wrong in the nation. The rich were getting richer, and everyone else seemed to be getting left behind. Change was needed, and Americans needed to be woken up. Though members of OWS may not have understood the subtleties of mortgage-backed securities, they had been seeing the consequences of them for several years. The big financial firms had been rescued from suffering the consequences of their risky behavior, thanks to the federal government. On the other hand, many of the unfortunate homeowners involved had lost their homes. The protests saw this as not only an inequality of wealth but also an inequality of justice.

As they struggled to convey their central message to the rest of America, OWS members also struggled to clearly define what that message was. As Rachel Pletz, a participant in the Zuccotti Park protests who helped to organize similar efforts in Philadelphia, put it, "This is about solidarity. This is about getting people together and figuring it out. We just know something's wrong."[75] It is a particular challenge to successfully mobilize Americans to respond to political and economic inequalities since this depends upon communicating to them an understanding of the messy details of the workings of government.

John Hector, one of the relatively few people of color amongst OWS protesters, wraps himself in a blanket against cold temperatures at the group's protest in Zuccotti Park in November 2011. "My concern is the economic situation and particularly police brutality and stop-and-frisk policies in Black and Latino communities," said Hector.

AP Photo/Bebeto Matthews.

"What do you say about a financial crisis where the villains are obscure and the solutions are obscure," wondered a noted British music critic. And one college student who attended a musical performance on behalf of OWS commented, "I have not heard a single song that sums up what we are trying to do here."[76]

On September 29, 2011, the NYC General Assembly adopted a declaration of the goals of the movement. One of many participation-based assemblies across the globe, the New York assembly operated on consensus, trying to invite as many voices as was practical into the conversation. The declaration stated that "as we gather together in solidarity to express a feeling of mass injustice, we must not lose sight of what brought us together. We write so that all people who feel wronged by the corporate forces of the world can know that we are your allies."[77] In spite of the theme of solidarity, the list of grievances in the declaration included charges against such disparate entities as Wall Street and home foreclosures, national agriculture policy, labor conditions, health care, money in politics, the death penalty, and American foreign policy.

Perhaps because its message was so far-reaching, the OWS movement quickly went national, even international. In the first week of October, "smaller-scale protests spread . . . to Los Angeles, Chicago, Boston, Denver, Washington, Albuquerque, Portland, Maine, and several other cities. An 'Occupy Toronto' protest [was] planned in Canada."[78]

As the protests gained energy and global attention, some critics claimed not only did the movement fail to represent the diverse interests of its members but also that it was actively discriminatory, especially towards the American Jewish community. In October 2011, the Republican National Convention issued a memo that "included three videos showing anti-Semitic outbursts by purported Wall Street protestors," though a spokesperson for the Anti-Defamation League countered that these outbursts were "isolated incidents."[79]

The movement was also criticized for failing to sufficiently empower members from traditionally marginalized groups or address their concerns. An article in the *New York Times* in late October 2011, for example, described a sense of alienation felt by a group of organizers from the South Bronx, an area with a high concentration of low-income individuals and those of minority ethnicity. "'Nobody looked like us,' said Rodrigo Venegas, 31, 'It was white, liberal, young people who for the first time in their life are feeling a small percentage of what black and brown communities have been feeling for hundreds of years.'"[80]

Other members of minority groups concluded that a unity of voices—based not on identity but a shared struggle against those in power—might make the social movement stronger. One journalist's account is telling: "Frank Diamond, a 26-year-old-Haitian-American from Jamaica, Queens, who was holding an 'Occupy the Hood' sign at a recent rally, said that many working-class blacks who had originally watched the protests from a distance, were starting to realize they should join. 'It takes a wave to realize that the boat you have been riding is too small,' he said. 'We need to be represented here too. This is about us, too.'"[81]

By November 2011, New York City authorities began to clamp down, stripping the demonstrators in Zuccotti Park of their generators and fuel just as a snowstorm and cold wave "blanketed their tents and tarps with sleet and ice, and left at least one protestor hospitalized for hypothermia."[82] Less than two weeks later, Mayor Michael Bloomberg and city authorities evicted the protestors from Zuccotti Park. Reporter Michelle Nichols described the removal: "Wearing helmets and wielding batons, New York police evicted Occupy Wall Street . . . two months after they set up camp and sparked a national movement against economic inequality. Hundreds of police dismantled the sea of tents, tarps, and outdoor furniture, mattresses and protests signs at Zuccotti Park, arresting 147 people, including about a dozen who had chained themselves to each other and to trees."[83] Other cities removed protestors as well.

By the spring of 2012, the tents had mostly disappeared from New York, Boston, Los Angeles, and other cities. Protests continued, but without the same level of media coverage. Some debated what had been accomplished. A letter to the editor of the *New York Times* framed the question not in terms of what OWS should do but what America should do, asking, "What will they do now? That question misses the point. Whether the 99 percenters retake Zuccotti Park in New York isn't the issue. The question we should be asking ourselves is, What will we do now? The American democracy—our system of capitalism and free markets, the electoral system and tax policies—has been distorted by moneyed interests. Our challenge is to revive America as a land of equal opportunity."[84]

Other observers had a very different set of suggestions for the movement's leaders. According to one reporter, "Many pundits suggest that it's time for the activists to hire political consultants and assemble a list of demands—in short, to become much more involved in electoral politics."[85] It was time, in other words, for OWS to stop trying to form a social movement and become an interest group.

protest
a public demonstration designed to call attention to the need for action or change.

civil disobedience
an intentional breaking of a law for the purpose of calling attention to an injustice.

NEWS CLIP
Study of Occupy Wall Street protesters and the problems of social movements

SOCIAL MOVEMENTS
Pinning Down Their Existence, Success, and Failure

In this book, we have explored the efforts of many social movements in American history, although not through an explicitly theoretical lens. The civil rights movement and the struggle for the rights of women, disabled Americans, and LGBT Americans are all widely acknowledged as social movements that have achieved major policy change. Though their specific goals were different, they often employed similar tactics.

They used **protest**, a public demonstration designed to call attention to the need for action or change. As part of these protests, some members engaged in **civil disobedience**, the intentional breaking of a law for the purpose of calling attention to an injustice. Protest and civil disobedience can be powerful and effective tactics, especially in altering the political agenda—placing an injustice front and center on the national stage and forcing people to confront it. Both of these tactics are risky, however, not only for the individuals involved but also for the movement itself.

In leading or joining an act of protest or civil disobedience, individuals may endanger their freedom, jobs, physical safety, or even their lives. For the movement itself, there is a chance that these activities may alienate rather than mobilize—that they may further isolate the movement from those who its members hope to convince of the importance of the cause. There is also the risk that the protesters will be ignored.

Why Do Some Social Movements Succeed and Others Fail?

As we have explored, small, homogenous, and economically powerful interest groups have many advantages in overcoming the challenges of collective action, though that fact provides no guarantee that any one member might not be sacrificed in the interests of the whole. When broad, diverse, voluntary associations of individuals come together to create a social movement, they lack many of the advantages of the more powerful groups. According to Mancur Olson, there is a logic to the idea that social movements should not come together at all. Yet some do. Why?

This is not an easy question to answer, either for scholars or for participants in the social movements themselves.[86] Part of the problem lies in the inherent differences in observing success and failure between interest groups and social movements.[87] When an interest group tries to influence legislation in Congress, for example, it is much easier to see if its efforts pay off or if they do not. However, what does it mean for a social movement to succeed, and how would we know if it did or did not? Those social movements that fail are difficult to study, like the proverbial tree that falls in the forest with nobody there to observe. To dive a bit deeper into this question, we have to incorporate insights from both political science and sociology, which is a very close relative of political science but which focuses more on social processes than on political institutions, processes, and outcomes.

For social movements, success or failure may be best determined not by the final public policy outcomes or by laws that were or were not passed, but by the fact that the movement came together at all—that it managed to overcome the problems of collective action and engaged others in its efforts to challenge the political dynamics, that it persuaded the uninvolved to become involved, to mobilize, infuriate, and educate. These efforts do not go unopposed, whether by governments, other powerful political players, or the inertia of a public confronted with a new cause or call to combat an injustice.[88] For sociologist Edwin Amenta, some answers, and a better framing of the question itself, may lie in the uneven power relationships that define interest groups and social movements. He claims, "Asking why social movements fail is a little like asking why children do not have backyards full of ponies. Most social movements fail most of the time because they embody a recipe for failure: they combine ambitious goals with severe power deficits."[89]

By some accounts, and not without cause, it is not even clear if OWS had created a social movement at all. By the three-year anniversary of the first Zuccotti Park protests, the movement seemed to be over. In comparison to widely acknowledged twenty-first century movements such as Black Lives Matter, OWS did not appear to have the same staying power or have built the necessary infrastructure to sustain it over the long haul.

However, in our exploration of political parties, we studied the insurgent candidacy of Senator Bernie Sanders, who most certainly highlighted American economic inequality in his campaign. The efforts of Sanders and others to call attention to this issue illustrate one of the primary tools that social movements have: changing the conversation in an effort to influence the political agenda.

Trying to determine whether or not a social movement has been successful by focusing only on what laws were or were not passed might miss this key contribution.[90] The policy agenda is a shifting and evolving thing; nothing is ever settled, and those who wish to influence political outcomes can never let their guard down.[91] The outcome of any one social movement may teach the members of future movements important lessons about what has worked and what has not. The activities of individuals involved with the civil rights movement, for example, served as lessons to members of future movements that sought to call attention to other forms of injustice.[92]

An Occupy Wall Street activist takes part in a protest at Zuccotti Park on July 11, 2012, advocating for the right to form a social movement.
REUTERS/Eduardo Munoz.

"Most social movements fail most of the time because they embody a recipe for failure: they combine ambitious goals with severe power deficits."

1. The difference between social movements and interest groups is that _____.

   a. Social movements tend to focus more on campaign contributions than interest groups
   b. Interest groups tend to reject the idea of collective action
   c. Interest groups tend to have more access to political insiders
   d. Social movements tend to focus on the executive branch

2. Financial industry insiders headed straight to Washington, D.C., when the economy looked like it was about to collapse. Occupy Wall Street headed to Zuccotti Park in lower Manhattan as it mobilized to protest. Why?

3. Was Occupy Wall Street successful? Why or why not?

Answer Key: 1. c; 2. Answers might include a realistic assessment of the tactics most suited to the groups' different resources.; 3. Answers should discuss how one should measure the success or failure of a nascent social movement.

CONCLUSION

Organizing for Change

Separated in space only by city blocks and in time by only three years, the activities of powerful and well-connected American financial firms in 2008 and the protests of Occupy Wall Street in 2011 might seem as far apart as the citizens that they tried to represent. In many ways, they were. The tactics used in these two situations were, to be sure, very different. Insiders—the CEOs of financial institutions and their well-paid lobbyists—worked the levers of the American political system to ensure the survival of the firms that they represented. Outsiders—students, opponents of the American capitalist system, advocates for economic equality, and many others without a well-defined agenda—tried to come together and use tools of protest and action to bring about social change.

These two groups, as different as they were, shared more in common than even they may have realized. Their leaders and members had to assess where they stood strategically in the real world of American economic and political power, and they had to adjust their strategies accordingly. They had to motivate and coerce members to join and contribute. Most fundamentally, they had to decide exactly whose interests they were trying to represent.

The twinned stories of the financial bailout and OWS are united by two strong and interconnected threads: power and inequality. Even within a social movement that hopes to represent the interests of outsiders, the disconnected, and the less powerful, there is no guarantee that all voices within that movement will be heard. When one compares the activities of interest groups and social movements, the challenges are even greater. The concentration of wealth at the very top of the economic strata is as great as it has ever been in the nation's history.

From these two stories one could draw a simple, neat conclusion: One faction ended up tipping the balance of power in its favor, and the other failed. It is an easy, seductive narrative, and one that can be related using a dominant metaphor in American political coverage: sports. One side won, the other lost. The political media often uses this simplistic metaphor in describing political stories to the American electorate. Metaphors, like so many other elements of storytelling in politics, however, can be limited, distracting—even dangerous.

The complex ways in which social movements have been involved in the American political space may be more accurately considered as agriculture than sport. An idea, a cause, a challenge—derided, attacked, or ignored from its beginnings—is more like a seed than a game. Political seeds do not worry about rankings, elections, or media coverage. They worry only about two things: their own potential and the soil upon which that potential falls.

Whether or not OWS had a consistent, clear, saleable message and what effect that message had on the political process in 2011 or in the years since is not the main concern in this view. What matters is whether or not the efforts of OWS sowed the seeds for a true challenge to the power structure of the American political system in the twenty-first century. And did these efforts fall upon a receptive and fertile soil? Did the political dynamics of Americans' confrontation with the inevitable challenge of faction—and the inevitable contribution of economic inequality to the formation of faction in republican forms of government—change? The verdict is still out.

Want a better grade?

Get the tools you need to sharpen your study skills. **SAGE edge** offers a robust online environment featuring an impressive array of free tools and resources. Access practice quizzes, eFlashcards, video, and multimedia at **edge.sagepub.com/abernathy1e.**

CHAPTER REVIEW

This chapter's main ideas are reflected in the Learning Objectives below. By reviewing them here you should be able to **remember** the key points, **connect** them to the stories presented in the chapter, **think** critically about these questions, and **know** these terms that are central to the topic.

11.1 Identify the constitutional foundations of voluntary association in the American political arena.

REMEMBER...
- The constitution of the United States ensures the ability of Americans to form voluntary associations and make their wishes known.

CONNECT...
- In the wake of the financial crisis of 2008, interest groups, including those representing American financial firms, acted to advocate for the goals shared by their members.
- In the presence of increasing economic inequality in the years following the financial bailout, members of Occupy Wall Street attempted to create a social movement.

THINK...
- What are major challenges to successful collective action?
- How do interest groups and social movements attempt to overcome these challenges?

KNOW...
- *elitist theory* (p. 375)
- *interest groups* (p. 370)
- *pluralism* (p. 375)
- *policy agenda* (p. 375)
- *power elite* (p. 375)
- *social movements* (p. 370)

◾ 11.2 Summarize the challenges interest groups and social movements confront in recruiting, mobilizing, and organizing the activities of their members.

REMEMBER...
- Political scientists have offered a variety of explanations for why Americans choose to join or not join voluntary associations in political life.
- When acting collectively, there are often rational incentives for individuals to allow others to carry the burdens of doing so.

CONNECT...
- As was the case with the financial firms in the wake of the 2008 financial crisis, even homogenous interest groups face challenges in organizing the activities of their members.

THINK...
- What methods do interest groups use to encourage potential members to join or support their activities?

KNOW...
- *collective action* (p. 377)
- *collective good (public good)* (p. 377)
- *free riders* (p. 378)
- *material rewards* (p. 379)

- *purposive benefits* (p. 379)
- *selective benefits* (p. 379)
- *social benefits* (p. 379)

◾ 11.3 Discuss the types of interest groups in the American political landscape and the different tactics that they use.

REMEMBER...
- Interest groups may form to advocate for a variety of goals, including those focused on business and the economy, public issues, and the interests of governmental units.
- Interest groups lobby all levels of government.
- When lobbying the federal government, interest groups act to influence the actions of the legislative, executive, and judicial branches.
- Interest groups also act to influence campaigns and elections.

CONNECT...
- In response to the financial crisis of 2008, interest groups representing the financial industry worked the levers of power available to them to shape Congress's response to the crisis.

THINK...
- What have you learned about the different tactics employed by interest groups acting on the "inside" versus those acting on the "outside?"

KNOW...
- *economic interest groups* (p. 385)
- *governmental interest groups* (p. 385)
- *inside lobbying* (p. 387)

- *issue network* (p. 392)
- *lobbying* (p. 385)
- *public interest groups* (p. 385)

11.4 Analyze and contrast the tactics that interest groups and social movements use in order to advocate on their members' behalf.

REMEMBER...
- Close ties between interest groups and governments continue to worry political scientists and observers.
- Interest groups often choose different tactics depending on how well financed or well connected they are.

CONNECT...
- The members of Occupy Wall Street attempted to create a social movement in order to call attention to economic inequality in the United States.

THINK...
- Did Occupy Wall Street create a new social movement?
- Were its tactics successful?
- How open do you think the American political process is?

KNOW...
- *agency capture* (p. 389)
- *astroturf lobbying* (p. 394)
- *civil disobedience* (p. 400)
- *iron triangle* (p. 391)

- *outside lobbying (grassroots lobbying)* (p. 394)
- *protest* (p. 400)
- *revolving door phenomenon* (p. 387)

12 CONGRESS
Representation, Organization, and Legislation

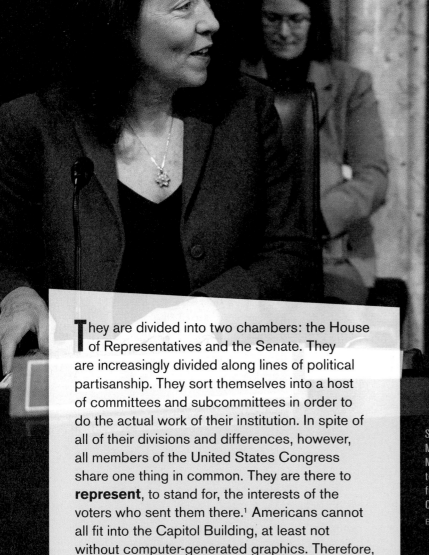

They are divided into two chambers: the House of Representatives and the Senate. They are increasingly divided along lines of political partisanship. They sort themselves into a host of committees and subcommittees in order to do the actual work of their institution. In spite of all of their divisions and differences, however, all members of the United States Congress share one thing in common. They are there to **represent**, to stand for, the interests of the voters who sent them there.[1] Americans cannot all fit into the Capitol Building, at least not without computer-generated graphics. Therefore, Americans elect people to make the laws, raise and spend the nation's money, and watch over other institutions in the federal government, along with a host of activities that shape American public policy in a profound way.

Senator Maria Cantwell (D-WA), left, and Senator Lisa Murkowski (R-AK) talk before the start of a Senate Energy and Natural Resources Committee hearing in early 2016. Compared to just a few decades ago, many more women and people from traditionally underrepresented groups currently serve in Congress.

Bill Clark/CQ Roll Call

In this chapter, we will focus primarily on one particular group of members of Congress: women in the Senate. We will look back on what has been accomplished and ahead to what still needs to be done to achieve more equal representation for women in Congress.

The stories we will consider constitute only one effort to explore and understand congressional organization, action, and representation. Many more stories have been written, are being written, and will be written. Many other groups of Americans have looked and continue to look to Congress to represent their interests and advocate for their preferences and goals. However, the stories in this chapter—many of which happened before some of the readers of this book were born—are far from outdated, irrelevant, or idiosyncratic to one specific group of Americans. They speak to the heart of what representation means in American democracy, what has been accomplished, and what is still under construction.

After reading this chapter, you will be able to:

12.1 Describe the structure of Congress as established in the Constitution, including the differences between the House of Representatives and the Senate and the powers placed in each chamber

12.2 Identify the obstacles to winning a seat in Congress, the factors that influence an individual's decision to run, and the resources and skills that successful candidates need

12.3 List the primary organizational features of Congress and understand the role of chamber leaders, political parties, committees, and congressional norms

12.4 Trace the steps of the legislative process and explain how that process can diverge from traditional "textbook" descriptions

12.5 Connect the issues surrounding the representation of women in Congress to the representation, or lack of it, of other individuals in America, whether based on race, ethnicity, religious beliefs, sexual identity, or other traditionally excluded identities

LEARNING OBJECTIVES

▮ WOMEN IN CONGRESS TODAY

Looking Around, Looking Back, and Looking Ahead

It might have been a record for Washington, D.C. A winter storm referred to as "Snowzilla" slammed the East Coast of the United States on January 22, 2016, prompting governors of eleven states to declare states of emergency. Airlines cancelled more than ten thousand flights, and transportation and commerce ground to a halt.[2] Snowfall records were broken in parts of New Jersey, New York, and Pennsylvania. The nation's capital may have also set a record; meteorologists are unsure because apparently the official measuring device got lost in the snow. Without question, though, D.C. shut

Sen. Susan Collins ✓
@SenatorCollins

Stuck in DC due to blizzard. A real storm. Tough for DC to handle; Maine could!

Jan 23, 2016, 1:53 PM

43 RETWEETS   **83** LIKES

Maine Senator Susan Collins tweeted a photo of herself digging out after "Snowzilla" in January of 2016.

down. Then it began to dig out. Members of Congress were no different. Senator Susan Collins (R-ME), no doubt familiar with snow, got out her shovel and posted a photo to her Twitter account.

That's when things got interesting, at least for one day. On Tuesday morning, after the storm had ended, the Senate convened for a brief morning session. Not much was on the agenda; too many senators were out of town or not able to make it to Capitol Hill. As Senator Lisa Murkowski (R-AK) opened the session, she looked around the chamber and noticed something different, something very, very different: There were no men to be seen. Not one. As Murkowski put it, "You look around the chamber and the presiding officer is female, all of our parliamentarians are female, our floor managers are female, all of our pages are female. . . . Now this was not orchestrated in any way, shape or form. We came in this morning, looked around and thought, something is different this morning. Different in a good way, I might add. But something is genuinely different, and I think it's genuinely fabulous."[3]

The next day, Murkowski introduced a bipartisan energy policy bill cosponsored by Maria Cantwell (D-WA). The men were filing back in, and, when full attendance was achieved, male senators outnumbered women in the Senate five to one.

The 114th session of Congress, which ran from January 2015 to January 2017, was the most diverse in the nation's history. It included twenty women senators, three Latinos, two African Americans, and one Pacific Islander. Serving in the House of Representatives were eighty-five members of racial and ethnic minorities, eighty-four women, and six representatives who self-identified as lesbian, gay, bisexual, or transgender (LGBT).[4] Forty-four African American members were serving in the House and two in the Senate. Thirty-seven representatives identified as Hispanic or Latino/a, thirty-two in the House and four in the Senate, an overall record. Thirteen members, eleven in the House and one in the Senate, identified as Asian or Pacific Islander, another record. Two representatives were Native American. Two members of Congress identified as Buddhist, two as Muslim, and one as Hindu, speaking to, although not perfectly reflecting, the growing religious diversity in the nation as a whole.[5]

The 114th Congress was not the first to set records for representation, however. Many records had already been broken in the preceding two decades. And, with the elections of 2016, the 115th Congress would become more diverse still. The changes occurring in Congress were more than just a question of numbers. Individual members of historically underrepresented groups had also moved up the chain of power within the institution.

Attaining key assignments in congressional leadership depends upon talent, political skill, and seniority. In the Senate, two women, both Democrats, had become especially influential over the years. Patty Murray of Washington was the first woman to chair the powerful Senate Budget Committee, and Barbara Mikulski had served as chair of the Senate Appropriations Committee, one of the most important committees in Congress. These two committees deal with a matter of great concern: money.

As Debbie Walsh, director of the Center for Women and Politics at Rutgers University, put it, "When you are making the decisions and you are controlling the debate around the dollars, that's big. That's what the milestone is here, in having these two women in the positions they currently hold and then to see where that takes them. . . . It's what happens when you get enough women in and they start to have the tenure to move into these positions."[6] Both senators, however, lost their positions of committee leadership when the Republican Party took control of the Senate following the 2014 elections.

Murray and Mikulski, along with other women in Congress who have achieved positions of power and influence, did not end up there by chance, or quickly. To understand what changes, if any, have come about as a result of the electoral gains of women, members of minority groups, or Americans overall, we will have to explore many interconnected topics in the study of Congress: why individuals choose to run for office, how the structure of congressional elections affects the chances of winning, and how the organization of Congress shapes how much power individuals have within the institution. In order to do that, we need to go back in time to 1992, to when many of these women began their journeys as congressional representatives.

1992 was called "the Year of the Woman" because a record number of women ran for and won seats in both the Senate and the House, beginning a trend of record-setting numbers of seats in Congress held by women that continues to this day. Their collective electoral success resulted in the largest number of women in Congress—fifty-three in total—up to that point in American history. After the elections, there were six women senators and forty-seven women representatives, both records at the time.[7] It was, according to scholars of women in American politics, "a turning point for U.S. women's political participation at the national level, with unprecedented attention focused on women running for Congress."[8]

The six women who entered the Senate chamber following the 1992 election were not the first women to do so, though there had not been many before. The first female senator was Rebecca Latimer Felton, who served in 1922 for a single day. Appointed by the governor of Georgia to fill the seat of a senator who had passed away suddenly, Felton was not even expected to travel to Washington, D.C., as the Senate was not in session and an election would take place before it reconvened. She did anyway. Speaking before the chamber, Felton promised, "When the women of this country come in and sit with you, though it may be but a very few in the next few years, I pledge to you that you will get ability, you will get integrity, and you will get unstinted usefulness."[9]

Felton's prediction proved to be true. Between Felton's brief term in office and 1992, only six women were elected to serve full terms in the Senate despite the fact that women make up just over half of the voting-eligible population and

Senators Barbara Mikulski (D-MD), left, and Patty Murray (D-WA) talk politics before a Senate Health, Education, Labor, and Pensions Committee hearing on the health insurance marketplace. Both have been in Congress long enough to have established important leadership positions.
CQ Roll Call via AP Images.

Two percent may be good for milk, but it's not good for the U.S. Senate.

The Senate Women of 1992:
Top, left to right: Patty Murray,
Barbara Mikulski, Barbara Boxer.
Bottom: Carol Moseley Braun,
Dianne Feinstein.
Photo courtesy of Senator Dianne Feinstein.

women "have constituted an absolute majority of voters in presidential elections since 1964."[10] During the 1992 elections, there were only two women in the Senate, prompting candidate Dianne Feinstein to observe, "Two percent may be good for milk, but it's not good for the U.S. Senate."[11]

Stepping into an unfamiliar institution as a first-year student at a new college, each of us has to learn the spoken and unspoken rules that govern the place as we find our way around. With luck, we find mentors to show us the ropes. It is no different in the United States Congress, especially if one is trying to bring a new voice, a new set of lived experiences, to an institution that is not used to paying attention to them. To understand how that group of new members of Congress went about learning the ropes and making their voices heard, we need to learn more about the institution of Congress itself. To do that, we turn once again to the Constitution of the United States.

WHAT HAVE I LEARNED?

1. Men and women have been represented in Congress in about equal numbers for the last twenty-five years.

   a. True
   b. False

2. Representation in Congress means _____.

   a. Advancing one's personal agenda
   b. Running first for a seat in the House and then advancing to the Senate
   c. The act of "standing for" one's constituents in government
   d. Voting according to the majority view

3. What do you think it means for members of Congress to represent the voters' interests?

4. How might the lived experiences of senators and representatives shape their approach to representation?

Answer Key: 1. b; 2. c; 3. Answers might include various aspects of congressional activity and/or speaking for the people.; 4. Answers will vary but should involve an initial reflection about the connection between lived experiences and congressional activity.

◼ THE CONSTITUTION AND CONGRESS

The United States Congress is called the ~~first branch~~ of government, and with good reason. In the Constitution, Congress is dealt with first. The section describing its powers and procedures (Article I) is longer than those dealing with the executive and judicial branches, and its powers are described in more detail. In the confederal government that the Constitution was drafted to replace, nearly all centralized authority had resided within the confederal legislature.

Key Differences between the Chambers

One of the results of compromise between the more populous and less populous states at the Constitutional Convention was the creation of a bicameral legislature composed of two chambers, the House of Representatives and the Senate. While both the House and the Senate are involved in the legislative process, the framers of the Constitution saw their roles differently. These differences were designed partly to add checks and balances *within* Congress and not just between Congress and the other branches. A bicameral legislature, according to James Madison in the *Federalist Papers*, "doubles the security to the people, by requiring the concurrence of two distinct bodies in schemes of usurpation and perfidy."[12] By "usurpation and perfidy" Madison was referring to the dangers of faction, in which a group of individuals, whether constituting a majority of citizens or a minority of them, could damage the rights and liberties of others or the interests of the Republic itself. Federalism and the separation of powers between the three branches were two ways in which the framers tried to contain the dangers of faction. Separating legislative authority within Congress itself was yet another.

The House of Representatives

Directly elected by the eligible voters in their districts, members of the House of Representatives are meant to be close to the people and their wishes. While state legislative terms were as short as six months at the time of the drafting of the Constitution, and one-year terms were quite common, the delegates to the convention agreed upon a term of two years for each representative. It was believed this would keep them close and accountable to the people while also giving them enough time to become competent in their work and familiar with all of the laws and issues in what Madison called "The great theatre of the United States."[13]

The Constitution requires that a representative be at least twenty-five years old, a resident of his or her state, and a citizen of the United States for seven years.[14] Not included in the list of requirements when the Constitution was drafted was the ownership of property or a particular religious affiliation, restrictions imposed by several states for offices in state government. While the Constitution did not textually bar women from holding office, the states did, excluding all but a few (generally widows with property) from participating in public life. By including some, but not all, of the requirements for legislative service present in individual states, Madison argued, "the door to this part of the federal government [meaning the House of Representatives], is open to merit of every description, whether native or adoptive, whether young or old, and without regard to poverty or wealth, or to any particular profession of religious faith."[15] As we have seen elsewhere in this book, certain factors, such as the increasing influence of lobbyists and interest groups and the role of money in campaigns and elections, currently force us to wrestle with the degree to which this "door" is really open to all.

CONNECTING TO. . .

How Representation Is Structured in the American Congress

As you read ahead about how the Constitution structures legislative representation and organization, reflect upon how a member of Congress, or several acting together, can overcome the obstacles involved with policymaking. Consider the following:

- The different expectations placed upon the House of Representatives and the Senate by the framers of the Constitution

- The powers of Congress as enumerated in the Constitution and how a new member to the institution might come to understand and use these powers

NEWS CLIP
Mitch McConnell explains his decision to ban earmarks

The Senate

Senators, in contrast, are meant to be more insulated from the public and any "passions" that might sweep through the populace, adding stability to the legislative branch. Elected for six-year terms, the classes of senators are staggered so that only about a third are up for reelection in a given cycle. Since its members are freed from the need to be reelected every two years, the Senate, Madison argued, should serve "as a defense to the people against their own temporary errors and delusions."[16]

What did Madison mean by "temporary errors and delusions?" This "safeguard" was to protect the Republic from more than just the wayward behavior of members of Congress. Many also feared the combination of direct democracy and an inequality of wealth. With Shays' Rebellion fresh in their minds, many of the delegates to the Constitutional

FIGURE 12.1

The Makeup of the First Federal Congress Compared to Today

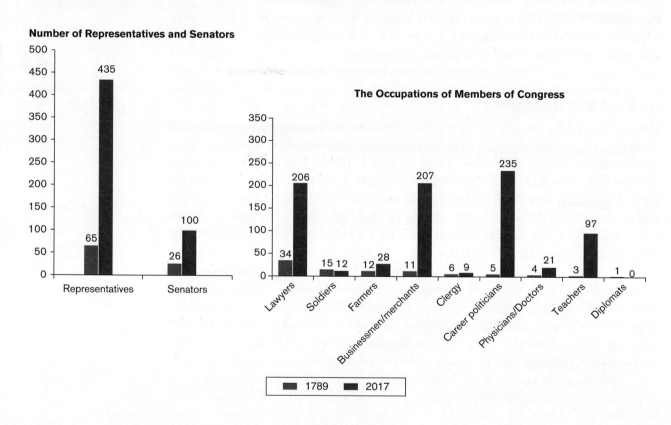

Sources: Kathleen Maher, "By the Numbers: The Jobs of the First Congress vs. the 112th Congress," National Constitution Center, February 16, 2012, http://blog.constitutioncenter.org/2012/02/by-the-numbers-the-jobs-jobs-jobs-of-the-first-congress-vs-the-112th-congress/; and United States Department of Congress, Historical Statistics of the United States: Colonial Times to 1970, https://www.census.gov/history/pdf/histstats-colonial-1970.pdf. Data for the 115th Congress are from CQ, "Guide to the New Congress, Vol. 74, Issue 32. November 9, 2016, p. 60.

Convention were concerned about the ability of the poor majority to vote themselves the wealth of the minority in a pure, direct democracy. Many framers also had deep concerns about the voters themselves. They worried that the passions and prejudices of voters were ripe for manipulation and that Americans' political opinions could be easily shaped by various factions. In anticipation of such possibilities, the framers set up roadblocks to prevent an American electorate from too quickly voting its wishes into policy. The Senate was constructed to help do just this.

Senatorial candidates have to be older than representatives—at least thirty years old—and citizens for at least nine years, and they must live in the state that they seek to represent. In the original Constitution, state legislatures elected senators directly. The Seventeenth Amendment (1913) replaced the election of senators by state legislatures with direct popular election by a state's eligible voters.

Missing from the Constitution was any limitation on how many terms a given representative or senator could serve. A form of what we now call term limits, or restrictions on the length of time an officeholder may serve, had been part of the government under the Articles of Confederation, which stated that "no person shall be capable of being a delegate for more than three years in any term of six years" in the nation's unicameral legislature.[17] The imposition of term limits remains an important and often debated topic in the politics of American elections.

The Powers of Congress

The powers of Congress generally fall into three broad areas: those related to its role as the main lawmaking body, those related to its position at the center of the budgeting process, and those it exerts when exercising oversight of the federal bureaucracy and other public officials.

Legislative Authority

The most important power of Congress is its legislative authority—the ability to pass laws in areas of national policy. The body of law that Congress creates is called statutory law as it is written down in the **statutes** that Congress passes. In the next three chapters, you will also learn about other types of dictates and actions that carry the force of law: presidential executive orders, administrative regulations established by bureaucratic agencies, and constitutional law as defined by courts.

Among legislative bodies in the world's democracies, the United States Congress is the most active and independent in terms of its ability to make national policy. The list of the enumerated powers of Congress is substantial; Congress is authorized to legislate in economic policy, national security, foreign policy, and other policy areas (Table 12.1).

statute
a written law established by a legislative body.

The Budgeting Process

The second major role of Congress involves its central position in setting a federal budget. Many of the rules governing the budgetary process were set in the Congressional Budget Act of 1974, which has since been amended several times. Creating a bureaucratic agency requires two steps: First, congressional action authorizes the department or agency. Second, through the process of **appropriation**, Congress funds the agency's activities.[18] The Budget Act established the process of reconciliation, which instructs relevant congressional committees on the processes of reconciling spending with the overall congressional budget.

appropriation
the process through which congressional committees allocate funds to executive branch agencies, bureaus, and departments.

TABLE 12.1 Legislative Powers of Congress in the Constitution

The constitution grants Congress the power to legislate in the following areas. Unless otherwise noted, these powers are laid out in Article I, Section 8.

	Enumerated Powers		
	Both Chambers	**House**	**Senate**
Economic Policy	Create and collect taxes, coin money, borrow money on the "credit of the United States," regulate the value of currency, borrow money, and regulate "Commerce with foreign Nations, and among the several States, and with the Indian tribes."	All bills to raise revenue must be generated in the House.	Senate may propose or concur with amendments as on other bills. In practice, however, the Senate has become a coequal partner in setting national revenue policy.
Foreign Policy	Regulate trade with other nations.		As an aspect of its role of "advice and consent," the Senate has the power to ratify treaties entered into by a president through a two-thirds majority vote.
National Security	Declare war, raise and support armies and a naval force and make rules for their governance and regulation, power to call up the military "to execute the laws of the Union, suppress Insurrections, and repel Invasions," define and punish piracies and felonies committed on the high seas.		
Other Powers Involving the Executive Branch		Impeach the president, vice president, and other executive branch officers (Article I, Section 2 and Article II, Section 4).	The Senate confirms presidential nominations of executive branch officers (Article II, Section 2) and tries members of the executive branch impeached by the House (Article I, Section 3 and Article II, Section 4).
Powers Involving the Judicial Branch	Create levels of the judicial branch below the Supreme Court, establish the number of Supreme Court justices (Article III, Section 1).	Impeach members of the federal judiciary (Article I, Section 2).	Presidential nominees to the federal judiciary must be confirmed by a majority vote within the Senate (Article II, Section 2), Senate tries members of the federal judiciary who have been impeached (Article I, Section 3).
Via Necessary and Proper Clause			
	"To make all Laws which shall be necessary and proper for carrying into Execution the foregoing Powers, and all other Powers vested by this Constitution in the Government of the United States."		
Via Subsequent Amendments			
	Individual amendments (such as the Thirteenth, Fourteenth, and Fifteenth) grant Congress "the power to enforce, by appropriate legislation," those amendments.		

In Defense of Earmarks

Earmarks—the allocation of money to specific projects in states or congressional districts—are often popular with those who receive them and with the senators and representatives who can claim credit for bringing the money home. Others, however, have criticized them as putting the needs of a few beneficiaries ahead of the needs of the nation as a whole. In the wake of the House's ban on earmarks in 2011, two former members of Congress, Martin Frost (D-TX) and Tom Davis (R-VA) offered their defense of earmarks:

> First, without them, Congress delegates the authority to allocate vast sums of discretionary federal spending to the executive branch. The president submits a budget at the beginning of each year and then Congress decides how much money each department and agency will get for its programs. But then someone in the federal bureaucracy decides which communities and states actually get those dollars. Earmarks reclaim a portion of that power for Congress. . . .

> Second, eliminating earmarks takes away the incentive for the parties to cooperate to pass appropriations bills on time. Instead, for weeks and months after the start of each fiscal year on Oct. 1, much of the government is left operating on a continuing resolution. When a number of representatives and senators have "skin in the game," they'll make sure a spending bill gets passed. . . .

> Third, taking away earmarks removes nearly all the leverage that party leaders have to make Congress run. Already the two parties show little inclination to pass laws simply because they are in the national interest. Removing earmarks took one more arrow out of the party leaders' quivers. [20]

WHAT DO YOU THINK?

Why might the ability of members of Congress to direct monies to projects in their states or districts help representation? How might it be unfair or damaging to the interests of the nation as a whole?

Reconciliation bills are then passed using a more streamlined process than other bills in Congress, making them harder to stop and thus creating a powerful "temptation to use a reconciliation bill as a vehicle for enacting extraneous provisions that have nothing to do with implementing the reconciliation instructions."[19] In 2010 the reconciliation process was used to assist passage of President Obama's major health care overhaul, the Patient Protection and Affordable Care Act. The Budget Act also created the Congressional Budget Office (CBO), the role of which is to provide information and estimates of the likely budgetary consequences of funding the agencies and programs created by Congress.

One of the more controversial ways in which members of Congress have been involved in the budgetary process has been the inclusion of **earmarks** to proposed legislation, through which members allocate and direct monies to projects or groups within their districts or states. Often popular with constituents, earmarks have been criticized for putting particular interests ahead of those of the nation's voters as a whole. In 2011 the House of Representatives, led by Republicans, instituted a ban on earmarks.

earmark
an addition to a piece of legislation that directs specific funds to projects within districts or states.

Oversight

The third major role of Congress in national policymaking is that of **oversight,** in which Congress uses its authority to ensure that laws are implemented in the way that Congress intended when it passed them. Given the growth in the size and complexity of the federal government, this is not an easy task. Congress has oversight responsibilities over the federal bureaucracy as well as over other branches of government and elected and appointed officials.

oversight
efforts by Congress to ensure that executive branch agencies, bureaus, and cabinet departments, as well as their officials, are acting legally and in accordance with congressional goals.

TABLE 12.2 The House of Representatives and the Senate Compared

	House of Representatives	Senate
Requirements for Membership	At least twenty-five years old	At least thirty years old
	Seven years of citizenship	Nine years of citizenship
	Resident of the state	Resident of the state
Service	Two-year terms, with unlimited number of terms	Six-year terms, divided into three classes, with unlimited number of terms
Constituency	District, apportioned to states by population	Entire state
Organization	More governed by rules, more institutionally structured, more power to individual leadership positions	Less governed by rules, more power to individual members, more informal
Goals	To be closer to voters' preferences	To be more insulated from voters' preferences

Congressional committees and subcommittees may conduct hearings and investigations into the actions of the federal bureaucracy to try to ensure that funds appropriated for programs are being spent efficiently, legally, and in accordance with the law's intent. While many committee hearings are routine, some may be called in the event of a perceived breakdown or failure by an executive branch agency, such as the widely criticized federal response to the devastating effects of Hurricane Katrina to New Orleans and the Gulf Coast in 2005.

The calling of hearings in response to a visible crisis is called **fire alarm oversight**, with oversight only being triggered by an alarm call. This kind of oversight is different from **police patrol oversight**, in which Congress continually monitors the actions of a bureaucracy. Because of the difficulty in continuously monitoring the immense federal bureaucracy, fire alarm oversight is more commonly used than police patrol oversight.[21]

In implementing the idea of checks and balances, the Constitution gave each of the branches shared authority over some aspects of governance, which allows a kind of oversight of one branch over the other two. As discussed earlier, Congress is given the authority to declare war, and the Senate to ratify treaties, thus forcing the executive and legislative branches to work together in important aspects of foreign and national security policy.

Congress also has a role in the nation's judicial system as it has the power "to constitute Tribunals inferior to [below] the Supreme Court" (Article I, Section 8) and sets the number of justices on the Supreme Court. The Senate—using its power of advice and consent—confirms presidential nominees to the federal courts by a simple majority. The norm of **senatorial courtesy** generally allows senators to nominate lower-level federal judges to serve in their states with the expectation that they will be confirmed without significant opposition.

In addition to the confirmation of presidential nominees to the federal judiciary, the Senate also exercises the same role of advice and consent in the confirmation of most presidential nominees to important posts in the federal bureaucracy.

Congress is also given the authority to remove federal officials—including the president, vice president, government officials, and federal judges—through the process of

fire alarm oversight
a term that describes congressional oversight procedures primarily in response to problems or complaints.

police patrol oversight
a term that describes congressional oversight as a process of constant monitoring rather than responding to specific crises.

senatorial courtesy
a traditional norm in which presidents consult with senators from the states when considering potential nominees to the lower levels of the federal judiciary.

impeachment. The House of Representatives votes to impeach if a majority of its members feel that an official has committed "Treason, Bribery, or other high Crimes and Misdemeanors" (Article II, Section 4). The vagueness of this language has resulted in debates about just what constitutes an impeachable offense.

If a majority of the members of the House votes to impeach, the trial takes place in the Senate, with a two-thirds majority needed to convict (Article I, Section 3).[22] Impeachment is a power that has rarely been used. Two presidents have faced successful House resolutions to impeach, but neither was removed from office. Andrew Johnson—impeached during the reconstruction era following the Civil War—survived by a single vote in the Senate. Bill Clinton—charged with lying during and obstructing an investigation into his relationship with intern Monica Lewinsky—was acquitted by a vote of 55–45.

STEPPING UP AND CHARTING A PATH TO CONGRESS

Like all senators and representatives, the paths of the women who ran for Congress in 1992 were as diverse as their views, politics, and policy positions. How did they get to Washington? And why did they run?

For many of the women who ran for Congress for the first time during that fateful 1992 election, one moment in congressional history crystalized their commitment to bring about change in Congress. It involved the Senate confirmation hearings of Clarence Thomas to the Supreme Court.

Federal judicial confirmations are often very politically charged. Given Thomas's conservative views, the confirmation proceedings were bound to be heated, as the stakes are so high with Supreme Court confirmations. In an era of such a closely divided Court dealing with highly contentious issues, affecting the makeup of the Court can have profound and enduring consequences. And in the case of the Thomas confirmation hearings, there was an unusual point of controversy. During the confirmation hearings, Thomas's former aide, Professor Anita Hill, asserted that Thomas had sexually harassed her while the two were serving in the federal government.

Though many women were concerned about the specific charges of sexual harassment, it was the skepticism displayed by the members of the all-white, male Senate Judiciary Committee to Hill's testimony—dismissive and condescending in the eyes of many—that galvanized women around the country by "symbolizing the lack of representation for women and their interests on Capitol Hill."[23] In response, "Many voters decided that if given the chance they would vote for a woman candidate, in part because she was a woman. Because of those hearings a number of party and grassroots organizations redoubled their efforts to find and fund women candidates. And because of those hearings a number of women decided that they would put themselves on the line and run for local, state, and national office."[24]

One individual who was outraged by the behavior of the Senate Judiciary Committee was Barbara Boxer, (D-CA), who was serving in the House of Representatives during the Thomas confirmation hearings. Boxer co-led a group of women members of the House to communicate to their fellow Democrats in the Senate their concerns about a lack of consideration, or appreciation, for Hill's charges of sexual harassment in the workplace. The media called their approach to the steps of Capitol Hill to meet with their colleagues "the women's Iwo Jima," conjuring up the iconic image of American servicemen raising the flag during World War II.

For Boxer, "That was an angle tailored by the media. We wanted to try to help the senators rethink their position, and we felt that they might appreciate hearing our perspective. . . . All we were asking was that the Senate take a serious look at Anita Hill's charges."[25] Their efforts, however, were rebuffed. Mikulski later wrote, "We went up to the doors of

Senate Judiciary Committee members Joseph R. Biden, presiding, and Senator Ted Kennedy, right, ask pointed and skeptical questions of Anita Hill during the Clarence Thomas confirmation hearings, 1991.

AP Photo/Greg Gibson, File.

Gender and Metaphors of Power

Barbara Boxer, Nita Lowey, Eleanor Holmes Norton, Pat Schroeder, Jolene Unsoeld, and the late Patsy Mink, the Democratic women members of the House of Representatives in 1991, march to the U.S. Senate to voice their concerns about the treatment of Anita Hill and her charges of sexual harrassment during the Clarence Thomas confirmation hearings. The American press called their action, "the women's Iwo Jima," conjuring up the iconic images of American servicemen during World War II. In the second photo, we see that image. Boxer rejected this label as a media creation.

WHAT DO YOU THINK?

Why do you think a war metaphor was used to portray the efforts of the congresswomen? In what ways might a traditionally male-gendered metaphor shape readers' perceptions of their efforts?

Think about candidates running for Congress. Have you encountered images and portrayals of those you might choose as your representative or senator? How did those depictions reflect your own views of these individuals or your own goals for congressional action? How might they have not?

the room and politely asked if we could have a few minutes to come in and share our views. The senior staff members guarding the doors wouldn't let us in. Did they realize that we were seven congresswomen? Yes, they knew. Did they realize we were colleagues from the Democratic side of the table? Yes they knew that, too. We were turned away, failed supplicants."[26]

Boxer had already decided to run for the Senate, and the poor treatment of herself and her colleagues motivated her to become even more outspoken on the need for Congress to listen to women's voices and concerns. That tactic was not without political risks. As a member of the House, many political observers thought that Boxer "had so aggressively taken feminist positions . . . that the conventional wisdom . . . suggested that she would have difficulty winning" her Senate bid.[27] The energy unleashed by the nationwide reaction to the hearings might have changed the political calculus in Boxer's favor, but this was far from certain.

On the other side of the country, Patty Murray, a state legislator from Washington, "watched in disbelief as the committee members questioned Hill's veracity about Thomas' sexual advances and innuendo. Murray found herself asking 'Who's saying what I would say if I were there?'"[28]

That evening, at a neighborhood party, as others expressed similar frustration, Murray announced, "You know what? I'm going to run for the Senate."[29] Murray's political career had begun in Shoreline, Washington, where she was volunteering in a local cooperative school that her two children attended. The school's funding was suddenly cut off by the state legislature and, according to Murray, "I decided to go to the state capitol in Olympia, to talk to some legislators and convince them of their mistake. I didn't even think twice about it. I put my two kids in the car, and off we went."[30]

Many of the people she approached—state legislators, their staff, and lobbyists—were dismissive. One state representative, she recounted, stunned her: "Lady, that's a really nice story, but you can't get the funding restored," he said. "You can't make a difference. You're just a mom in tennis shoes."[31] Murray said by the time she had driven the seventy miles back to Seattle, she had made the decision to do something about the situation.

The label "a mom in tennis shoes" stuck and became a powerful campaign slogan for Murray's political career. Murray claimed, "I was actually advised to run as *Pat* Murray, so that people might think I was a man. And I said, 'Wait a minute—I'm running *because* I'm a woman. I'm running because we need *women*. . . . We need policymakers who understand what women are going through so these policies work for women."[32] Murray also said, "Almost every woman I've ever met in politics got into it because she was mad about something."[33]

Tammy Baldwin addresses her supporters at her victory party in Madison, Wisconsin, on November 6, 2012.

REUTERS/Sara Stathas.

Many first-time candidates for Congress bring with them a set of policy objectives rather than one specific issue. Fast forward to 2012, when Tammy Baldwin (D-WI) became the first openly gay individual elected to the Senate. It had been a close race and a toughly contested one. Baldwin won with just 51 percent of her state's popular vote, but that was enough. In 1993, as Wisconsin's first openly lesbian Wisconsin State assemblywoman, Baldwin had reflected, "Sometimes I think my most significant contribution is not the legislative initiatives I introduce, but the stereotypes I shatter." According to many political observers, Baldwin won her seat in the Senate on the basis of her policies, her successful fund-raising, her focus on jobs and the economy, and her promise to fight for Wisconsin's workers, students, elderly citizens, and citizens struggling to keep their jobs. In her acceptance speech, Baldwin highlighted not her own story but the concerns of many of her constituents: "I didn't run to make history; I ran to make a difference. . . . A difference in the lives of students worried about debt and seniors worried about their retirement security."[34]

Election-Specific Factors: The Perfect Storm of 1992

While the fallout from the Thomas confirmation hearings energized many women to run for Congress in 1992, several other factors paved the way for newcomers from a wide range of backgrounds to take the plunge and stand for congressional election for the first time. Perhaps most importantly, the 1992 elections saw a post–World War II high in the number of open congressional seats. There were several reasons for this. A scandal involving the overdrawing of accounts in the House Bank broke in 1991 and led to a number of retirements. Redistricting after the 1990 census included efforts to redraw lines to boost the chances of minority candidates and resulted in new district boundaries in which two incumbents were pitted against each other.[35]

Potential challengers who had been waiting for their chance seized on the number of open seat races. According to government professor Clyde Wilcox, "For experienced women politicians who lived in the open districts, 1992 was likely to be their best shot for many years at a House seat."[36]

In addition to the large number of open seat races, the end of the Cold War focused voters' attention away from issues of national security and onto issues of domestic policy, issues on which a number of women candidates had strong track records. Finally, due to Bill Clinton's presidential victory over George H. W. Bush and H. Ross Perot, the electoral strength of the Democratic Party helped other Democratic candidates. Of the twenty-four women elected to the House for the first time in 1992, twenty were Democrats. All five of the newly elected or successfully reelected women in the Senate were Democrats as well.

The opportunity presented in 1992, however, would not have translated into electoral success without a slate of experienced and well-funded candidates. With the political stars aligning in 1992, it was still up to each woman to decide if this was her year to run. One factor affecting this was the willingness of individuals and organizations to contribute money and time to the women's political campaigns, to organize and mobilize voters on their behalf, to vote for them, or to become involved in American politics for the first time.

For political scientists Linda Fowler and Robert McClure, the main factor that sets declared candidates apart from "the unseen candidates—the men and women who could have run for Congress but chose not to" is political ambition.[37] Only those with the strongest personal desire to act in politics decide to face the long odds against success, especially if such a bid would mean "a bruising battle with an incumbent rich in resources."[38] What drives political ambition? Where does it come from? The answers are not always neatly categorized by gender, racial or ethnic identity, or any one simple category. Political ambition is as unique to a potential candidate as it is to the constituents she or he hopes to represent.

For Carol Moseley Braun (D-IL), the Thomas confirmation hearings were most certainly a contributor to her decision to run for the Senate in 1992; however, her path to the chamber was also paved by the hard-earned experience of Chicago politics—as tough a venue as there is in American government. To Moseley Braun, it was about gender, but it was also more than that. Reflecting on the Thomas confirmation hearings and her decision to run, she said, "Women were saying, 'Where are the women? . . . Minorities said, 'Where are the minorities?' workers said, 'Who are these millionaires? These aren't regular Joes.'"[39]

And there was money. Largely because of the fallout from the Thomas confirmation hearings, and partly because of national attention on issues of concern to American women voters, organizations devoted to funding women candidates raised and contributed large amounts of money to their campaigns. Organizations that raise and spend money on behalf of candidates are called political action committees (PACs). In the 1992 elections, women's PACs played a major role in financing and advising the campaigns of women candidates.

Carol Moseley Braun greets constituents in her hometown of Chicago, Ilinois.
Steve Kagan/The LIFE Images Collection/Getty Images.

One of the largest of these was EMILY's List, a pro-choice Democratic women's PAC whose name is an acronym of "early money is like yeast," in the sense that early money grows campaigns like yeast helps bread rise. As political scientist Candice Nelson put it, "Early money enables candidates to do the things necessary to establish credibility: hire a pollster, develop a campaign plan, and be prepared for challenges to her credibility when they occur."[40] EMILY's List was founded in 1985 and was an active player in the 1986 congressional elections, donating $350,000 to Barbara Mikulski's successful Senate bid. By 1992 the PAC had supported the campaigns of thirty-six candidates for the House and eight for the Senate.[41] Not only was EMILY's List the largest collector of contributions among women's PACs in 1992, it was the largest of all PACs in the election.[42] "Ellen Malcolm [then] president of EMILY's List reported that the group's nationwide membership grew from 3,000 before the Thomas-Hill hearings to 24,000 in November 1992."[43] Although Patty Murray's campaign received early support from EMILY's List, Moseley Braun's did not, especially in the Democratic primary because "the PAC did not feel that the early stages of the Moseley Braun campaign had been well-run."[44]

Many of the women congressional candidates in 1992 were both experienced and well funded. Their knowledge, skills, policy positions, and familiarity with the voters had been honed in state, county, and local political offices in the years prior. The contribution of experience and commitment to issues in the decision to run for the first time is not unique to women candidates. First-timers, regardless of political party, gender, racial or ethnic identity, or religious preference, are all driven in part to advance and advocate for a set of policy goals—to change the congressional conversation. Like Baldwin, all congressional candidates have a set of issues they want to focus on. Most, like Murray and Boxer, have had some kind of galvanizing experience that spurs them onto a larger political stage, and most have served in some other political office or gained some other experience necessary for leadership. All candidates have to be familiar with the rules of congressional elections and what successful challengers must do in order to make their voices, and those of their constituents, heard in Congress.

WHAT HAVE I LEARNED?

1. The term *political ambition* refers to _____.

   a. The need for potential candidates to have the commitment necessary to overcome the long odds faced by a challenger running against an incumbent
   b. A willingness on the part of first-time candidates to skirt campaign fund-raising laws
   c. A desire to use a seat in Congress as a springboard to the presidency
   d. The willingness of congressional incumbents to use their advantages to prevent credible challengers

2. Open seat elections tend to attract more first-time challengers in congressional elections.

   a. True
   b. False

3. What were some of the reasons why a record number of women candidates decided to run for Congress in 1992?

4. What qualities do successful first-time candidates for Congress generally need?

Answer Key: 1. a; 2. a; 3. Answers should include the fallout from the Thomas confirmation hearings, the number of open seat elections, and campaign support from outside groups.; 4. Answers should include experience and money and may discuss the challenges of running against incumbents.

THE POLITICS OF CONGRESSIONAL ELECTIONS

The decision to stand for national legislative office, though a monumental one, is only the first step in the long journey towards membership in the United States Congress. The next step is to actually get elected. For first-timers, this involves a very steep climb. The odds are stacked against them. In this process, the first thing a candidate has to assess is whose votes she or he is trying to win.

Constituency and Incumbency

As we explored in our chapter on campaigns and elections, the Constitution sets the framework for the boundaries of constituency. Would-be senators hope to represent the voters of their states. Hopeful candidates for the House strive to secure the votes of the constituents in their congressional districts, the boundaries of which can and do change in response to fluctuations in state population and the often intensely political process of redistricting.

As we have also explored, the power of incumbency—running for reelection as opposed to running for the first time—strongly affects the outcomes of congressional elections. Congressional incumbents possess so many advantages, such as media coverage, a record of providing beneficial service and legislation to a state or district, and name recognition, that qualified challengers often rationally wait until they can run in an open seat election after an incumbent has retired or moved on to another office.

Experience and Money

When challengers do decide to stand for office, they need many things; however, above all else, they need experience and money. Experience is hard earned, usually gained by moving up through the layers of local and state politics and becoming professional, polished, and respected. Congressional elections are usually no place for amateurs, who often lack the knowledge, political organization, and well-honed political skills prerequisite to success in the high-stakes enterprise of a national campaign.

Looking back on her successful campaign for the U.S. Senate in 1992, Dianne Feinstein noted, "If I were advising young women today about becoming involved in public life, I'd tell them, 'Start on the school board, go for a spot on the town council. *Earn your spurs*. That's the key. . . . Don't flit around like a moth. . . . Develop a portfolio of expertise—something you're really good at, so that people will turn to you. Develop your credibility, your integrity, show people they can trust you.'"[45]

Money is inseparable from congressional elections. It buys media spots, funds a ground campaign, and acts to scare off potential opponents. The pressures of fund-raising in the modern Congress are relentless. In March 2015, Senator Barbara Mikulski, one of the most powerful women members of the Senate, who had welcomed her new women colleagues with advice, information, and support in the decades following the 1992 elections, announced her retirement at the end of the 114th Congress. It was not politics or age that Mikulski gave for her decision. According to her, "There's no health problem. I'm not frustrated with the Senate."[46] Instead, the reason she gave was money and the fact that fund-raising was eclipsing her ability to represent: "Do I spend my time raising money or raising hell to meet your day-to-day needs?"[47]

Being in the Right Place at the Right Time . . . or Not

Because of the significant advantages that congressional incumbents possess, high-quality challengers often wait for just the right time, just the right set of circumstances, just the right election to make their bid. 1992 proved to be such an opportunity. Not all of those who ran that year were successful, however. In fact, most women candidates to state and national office lost, as did every woman who ran against a Senate incumbent in the general election. One of these unsuccessful challengers was Lynn Yeakel, although she very nearly succeeded in ousting one of the faces of the Senate Judiciary Committee's alleged poor treatment of Anita Hill, Senator Arlen Specter (R-PA). Motivated in part to run because of the hearings, "Yeakel's campaign ads showed the all-white-male Senate Judiciary Committee, and asked voters, 'Does this make you as mad as it makes me?'"[48]

Lynn Yeakel, campaigning in Philadelphia with presidential candidate Bill Clinton in 1992.
AP Photo/J. Scott Applewhite.

Yeakel was a credible candidate. She had money, much of it her own, and experience. Her "years of non-profit, social service work gave her a squeaky-clean image, an asset in a year in which the state's usual assortment of political scandals had received the usual overdose of media attention."[49] By a narrow margin, however, Specter was able to convince voters to keep him in Washington. Tactical mistakes on the part of the Yeakel campaign probably played a role, but so did efforts on the part of the Specter campaign to counter Yeakel's charges about his ability to effectively represent Pennsylvania's women. He gained support from some key women's groups in the state on the basis of "his seniority [in Congress], his proven political skills, and his voting record on behalf of women's concerns." One of Specter's backers said, "Democrats are pushing female candidates so much it's as if women running for office are saying: 'Here, I've got breasts, vote for me,'" a remark from which the Specter campaign tried to distance itself.[50]

In 1992 the political stars had aligned to make it possible for newcomers to alter the face of the United States Congress: "Change was in the air, and many of these women who came to Washington intended to transform politics as usual."[51] As the 103rd Congress convened in Washington on January 6, 1993, these newcomers would quickly need to learn the complicated rules, procedures, and processes of Congress if they hoped to make their viewpoints manifest in American public policy.

The women who entered Congress confronted an institution that was far from ready to welcome their diverse views and perspectives. Skillfully navigating the complicated high-stakes politics of Cook County, Illinois, Carol Moseley Braun (D-IL) became the nation's first African American woman senator in 1992.[52] Upon arriving on Capitol Hill in 1993, Moseley Braun "sought a congressional identification card, and was initially issued one labeled 'spouse.'"[53] Moseley Braun's response was "Try again."[54]

The gains of women candidates in the 1992 elections were divided sharply by political party: "Almost all of the women who won new seats in the House, and all new women in the Senate, were Democrats. Some Republicans argued that a better phrase would be the 'year of the liberal, Democratic woman.'"[55] During a presidential debate in October of 1992, incumbent Republican president George H. W. Bush, arguing for votes alongside Democratic

"Calling 1992 the Year of the Woman makes it sound like the Year of the Caribou or the Year of the Asparagus. We're not a fad, a fancy, or a year."

challenger Bill Clinton and billionaire independent H. Ross Perot, remarked, "This is supposed to be the year of the women in the Senate. Let's see how they do. I hope a lot of them lose."[56] Conflict between the political parties, especially in recent years, has played an important role in shaping what Congress does or does not do.

As the newly elected or successfully reelected women joined their male colleagues in the 103rd Congress in January of 1993, they brought with them a diversity of beliefs, motivations, skills, and goals.[57] Although the American media highlighted women's electoral accomplishments, to assert that there was one single "woman's voice" arriving in Washington was, as we will see, both incorrect and problematic. And as all new members of Congress quickly learn, translating one's commitments into public policy is very difficult. It is more a marathon than a sprint. As Mikulski remarked at the end of her successful Senate reelection bid in 1992, "Calling 1992 the Year of the Woman makes it sound like the Year of the Caribou or the Year of the Asparagus. We're not a fad, a fancy, or a year."[58]

THE ORGANIZATION OF CONGRESS

The Constitution is much more specific on what Congress does than on how it is supposed to do it. With a few exceptions, the Constitution does not describe most of the day-to-day processes and procedures of Congress. These rules and details have been created by the chambers themselves, with important modifications made over time. Congress includes both formal and informal organizational features. Formally, political parties, party leaders, and the committee system shape much of what happens in the House and Senate. Congressional staff and the congressional bureaucracy are involved as well. Informally, norms and traditional ways of doing things also play a role.

Any like-minded individuals in Congress who come together to advance an agenda must be very familiar with the organizational structure of Congress in order to do so. Groups may form around a shared set of lived experiences, a shared set of policy goals, or a shared desire to reform how Congress works. In addition, as we will explore, members gain power and influence as their congressional careers develop and they establish seniority within the institution.

While rules and procedures may seem like a dry subject of study, they matter a great deal to what legislation does or does not emerge from Congress. Battles over organization or congressional procedure are often just as heated and consequential as battles over specific policies.

Political Parties in Congress

Much of the formal structure of Congress revolves around the role of political parties and party leaders. The majority party, which is the party with the most members in each chamber, and the minority party, which has the second-highest number of members, each control important leadership positions and organize congressional behavior—both to advocate for their preferred policies and to help individual members in their reelection efforts.

IN GOD WE TRUST

Representative Paul Ryan (R-WI) stands next to outgoing House Speaker John Boehner in the House Chamber on Capitol Hill in October 2015. A splintered GOP turned to the relatively young but battle-tested Ryan in hopes of unifying a fractured Republican House.

AP Photo/Andrew Harnik.

Speaker of the House
the leader of the House of Representatives, chosen by an election of its members.

In contrast to most modern representative assemblies, party leaders in the United States Congress often struggle to make sure that their own members act and vote in support of party positions, especially when a member's constituent preferences clash with those of the member's political party. Leaders, however, are not powerless and have a variety of carrots and sticks with which to steer their members in the desired direction. Party leaders work through party caucuses (Democratic Party) and party conferences (Republican Party), in which members of a party meet, set up goals, choose leaders, assign members to committees, and try to present a unified voice to the American electorate through the media.

Party Leadership in the House of Representatives

Larger than the Senate since the founding of Congress, the House of Representatives is, by necessity, more formally structured than the Senate, with rank-and-file House members individually less powerful than their Senate colleagues. The **Speaker of the House**—the only House leadership position described in the Constitution—wields a considerable amount of power, though that power has changed over time in response to demands on the House and strategic political action on the part of its members.

At the beginning of each new Congress (every two years), members of the House elect the Speaker, who has almost always been a member of the majority party. A long history of successful service in the House is usually a prerequisite. Increasingly, the ability to raise money for other members of one's party is considered in selecting a Speaker. These leadership PACs "are designed for two things: to make money and to make friends," and representatives use that money to assist fellow party members' campaigns.[59]

The Speaker is second in the line of succession (behind the vice president) to the presidency in the event of death, resignation, removal from office, or inability to conduct the office's duties. In Congress, the Speaker has considerable power over the House agenda and committee assignments.

Assisting the Speaker is the House **majority leader**, the majority **whip** (and other members of the whip system), and various caucus and conference chairs and vice chairs. Members of the whip system collect information about how individual members are planning to vote, corralling their support on key votes and setting party strategy in Congress. The term comes from British hunting, where the "whipper-in" tried to keep the hounds in some sort of a coherent group. The House **minority party leader** has far less structural influence in the House than the Speaker but works to coordinate minority party activity, opposition to the majority party, and overall strategy. House minority party leadership also includes its own whips and whip systems.

Party Leadership in the Senate

Constitutionally, the official leader of the Senate is the vice president of the United States, though he or she can only cast a vote in the event of a tie. The president pro tempore presides over the chamber's proceedings when the vice president is not present (which is almost all of the time) but wields no real power. Typically, junior senators fill in to oversee the day-to-day proceedings.

The most powerful position in the Senate is the Senate majority leader, who is chosen from the majority party by its members in caucus or conference. Although individual senators retain more power than their colleagues in the House, the Senate majority leader is not as powerful as the Speaker; however, she or he plays a key role in shaping the legislative agenda. The Senate minority leader—chosen by the minority party members—acts as the leader of the opposition in the Senate. Assisting both party leaders are party whips, leadership committees, and party caucuses and conferences.

The Committee System

The work that Congress deals with is considerable and complex. There is no way any one member could be directly involved in each piece of legislation. To divide the workload, both the House and the Senate have established the committee system, a system of committees and subcommittees that do most of the work of Congress. Writing about congressional government in 1885, Princeton professor of politics and future president Woodrow Wilson observed, "It is not far from the truth to say that Congress in session is Congress on public exhibition, whilst Congress in its committee-rooms is Congress at work."[60]

majority party leader
the head of the party with the most seats in Congress, chosen by the party's members.

whip
an individual in the House or Senate, chosen by his or her party members, whose job is to ensure party unity and discipline.

minority party leader
the head of the party with the second-highest number of seats in Congress, chosen by the party's members.

FIGURE 12.2

The Structure of Leadership in Congress

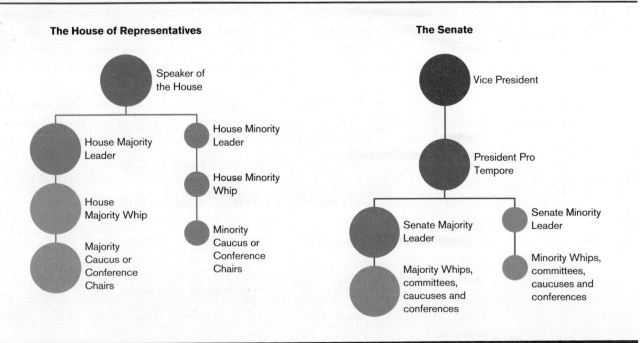

The House of Representatives

- Speaker of the House
- House Majority Leader
- House Majority Whip
- Majority Caucus or Conference Chairs
- House Minority Leader
- House Minority Whip
- Minority Caucus or Conference Chairs

The Senate

- Vice President
- President Pro Tempore
- Senate Majority Leader
- Majority Whips, committees, caucuses and conferences
- Senate Minority Leader
- Minority Whips, committees, caucuses and conferences

Committee Membership and Leadership

committee chairs
leaders of the subunits of
congressional committees
who have authority over the
committee's agenda.

Committee membership is determined and negotiated by party leaders and generally reflects the ratio of party membership in each chamber. Seniority, or the length of consecutive service on the committee, plays a major role in determining **committee chairs**. These chairs have considerable influence over committee processes, especially in setting the committee's agenda. Because of the differences in the size of the chambers, House committees tend to have more members than Senate committees, while individual senators tend to serve on more committees than their colleagues in the House.

New representatives and senators often try to get appointed to committees that deal with issues of interest to their constituents or that provide benefits to their districts and states. That has the added advantage of helping their prospects for reelection along the way. Requests for committee membership, though, may also be driven by genuine policy interests on the part of members of Congress.[61]

Types of Committees

Congress has four types of committees: standing, joint, conference, and select. Standing committees are where most of the work of Congress gets done. They are so named because they continue across Congresses, and members tend to serve on them for multiple terms, developing expertise and working to bring benefits to their districts and states. Standing committees consider legislation and exercise oversight of bureaucratic agencies, usually recommend funding levels for them. They are divided by policy areas, with a given committee having jurisdiction over its area of specialization (Table 12.3). Standing committees are divided into subcommittees, which specialize even further, usually considering parts of legislation under instructions from their parent committees.

Joint committees contain members of both the House and the Senate. In general they do not have a great deal of power but are used to focus public attention on an issue, gather information for Congress, or help party leaders speed things along in the legislative process.

The conference committee is a temporary joint committee that resolves differences between the House and Senate versions of a bill, which is required by the Constitution before a president can sign the bill into law. Party leaders determine conference committee membership, though members who have been centrally involved in a bill are usually included.

The fourth type of committee is the select or special committee. These temporary bodies are usually called upon to investigate an issue, sometimes in response to a crisis or a scandal. Select committees may be given the authority to report legislation, but their role is usually informational only.

Congressional Staff and the Congressional Bureaucracy

The third component of the formal organization of Congress consists of the people and institutions developed to help members represent their constituents. Congressional staff assist representatives and senators in providing casework and give members information about policies, legislation, and constituent preferences. Staff often work closely with members in drafting bills. As the size of the American Republic and the complexity of issues before Congress have both grown, so has the size of the congressional staff.

TABLE 12.3 Standing Committees in the 115th Congress

House of Representatives	Senate
Agriculture	Agriculture, Nutrition, and Forestry
Appropriations	Appropriations
Armed Services	Armed Services
Budget	Banking, Housing, and Urban Affairs
Education and Workforce	Budget
Energy and Commerce	Commerce, Science, and Transportation
Financial Services	Energy and Natural Resources
Foreign Affairs	Environment and Public Works
Homeland Security	Finance
House Administration	Foreign Relations
Judiciary	Health, Education, Labor, and Pensions
Natural Resources	Homeland Security and Governmental Affairs
Rules	Judiciary
Science, Space, and Technology	Rules and Administration
Small Business	Small Business and Entrepreneurship
Transportation and Infrastructure	Veterans' Affairs
Veterans' Affairs	
Ways and Means	

Note: Does not include joint and select committees.

Congress has also developed bureaucratic organizations to assist its members' efforts. These nonpartisan institutions provide members with estimates of the likely impact of laws on the national budget and keep them informed about how well agencies are performing the tasks Congress intended of them. The Congressional Budget Office (CBO) offers estimates of the budgetary consequences of various policy options. The Government Accountability Office (GAO) keeps track of agencies created and funded by Congress.

Norms: Informal Contributors to Congressional Organization

In addition to the formal structures, less formal processes also play a role in congressional action. Norms are unwritten expectations of how members are supposed to act and help members balance representing their constituents and contributing to the smooth functioning of the House and Senate. Members are expected to be respectful toward their colleagues, to reciprocate help from other members, and to specialize in one or more policy areas to assist the overall level of information and expertise in Congress. Animosity between members of the two political parties has challenged the role of norms in constraining member behavior in recent years.

Bill, star of the classic Schoolhouse Rock! Video, sits on the shoulder of a smiling congressperson, sporting his new medal "Law." In the real world, Bill would have faced frowns and frustration. Most bills do not make it through the legislative process to become laws.

Kari Rene Hall/Los Angeles Times via Getty Images.

unorthodox lawmaking
a term that refers to ways in which legislative activity, especially on major bills, is often more fluid than described in a traditional textbook description.

 ## "I'M JUST A BILL"
The Legislative Process

One of the classic *Schoolhouse Rock!* animated educational videos that aired on ABC Saturday mornings in the 1970s and 1980s was "I'm Just a Bill," the story of a "sad little scrap of paper" sitting on the steps of Capitol Hill hoping to become a law someday. Happily, our little cartoon legislative friend, Bill, succeeds in his dream, announcing triumphantly, "Oh! Yes!" when told that the president had just signed him into law.[62]

Though there was quite a bit of useful information in that short cartoon, it could have been a bit more realistic. Bill could have been "surrounded by ninety or so expired comrades scattered about the steps of Capitol Hill. Too disturbing for little kids, of course, but a more accurate picture of the odds against success for any aspiring laws."[63] By design, the legislative process is complicated and multistepped, with each stage offering another chance to kill a prospective law. The framers of the Constitution—having seen the passions of the people sweep through state legislatures and sometimes trample on minority rights—intentionally placed many hurdles in the path of legislation.

There is a second point on the modern legislative process that is just as important: It rarely—especially when the stakes are high—follows the traditional "textbook" way that it is described. Political scientist Barbara Sinclair used the term **unorthodox lawmaking** to describe the realities of the modern legislative process, which are "much more complex and not amenable to a nice, neat diagram," unlike the straightforward textbook version.[64] Unorthodox lawmaking has become increasingly common, especially on major legislation. According to Sinclair, "If the textbook legislative process can be likened to climbing a ladder, the contemporary process is more like climbing a big old tree with many branches. The route to enactment used to be linear and predictable; now it is flexible and varied."[65]

FIGURE 12.3

The Legislative Process

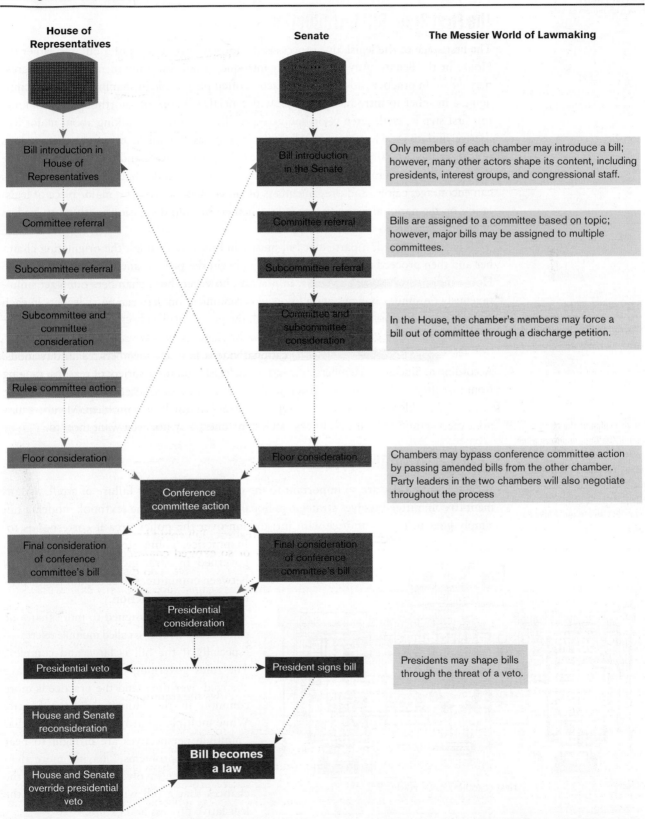

House of Representatives

Senate

The Messier World of Lawmaking

Bill introduction in House of Representatives

Bill introduction in the Senate

Only members of each chamber may introduce a bill; however, many other actors shape its content, including presidents, interest groups, and congressional staff.

Committee referral

Committee referral

Bills are assigned to a committee based on topic; however, major bills may be assigned to multiple committees.

Subcommittee referral

Subcommittee referral

Subcommittee and committee consideration

Committee and subcommittee consideration

In the House, the chamber's members may force a bill out of committee through a discharge petition.

Rules committee action

Floor consideration

Floor consideration

Chambers may bypass conference committee action by passing amended bills from the other chamber. Party leaders in the two chambers will also negotiate throughout the process

Conference committee action

Final consideration of conference committee's bill

Final consideration of conference committee's bill

Presidential consideration

Presidential veto

President signs bill

Presidents may shape bills through the threat of a veto.

House and Senate reconsideration

House and Senate override presidential veto

Bill becomes a law

This reality does not mean that legislators are bypassing constitutional provisions, only that the process is much more fluid, complex, and political than any flowchart can adequately describe (Figure 12.3).

The First Step: Bill Introduction

The first stage of the legislative process is the formal introduction of a bill into either the House or the Senate. Any member may introduce a bill, but only members of Congress may do so. In practice, however, other actors often play a role in shaping a bill or encouraging a member to introduce it. In line with Sinclair's theory of unorthodox lawmaking, this first step is, well, often unorthodox, especially when we are talking about major legislative initiatives. The president of the United States, for all of her or his tremendous power, cannot literally walk into the House of Representatives and place a bill into "the hopper" for consideration; only a member of the House can do that. However, presidents can encourage, cajole, and press members of either chamber to get a major piece of legislation on the national legislative agenda, whether through discussions with party leaders or though appeals to the American public.

Once introduced, a particular bill must wind its way through the originating chamber and then proceed to the other chamber to begin the process anew. Formally, only the House may introduce revenue bills. In practice, however, both chambers often act simultaneously on similar policies, with frequent communication between party leaders in each chamber. In addition, the Senate (along with the president) has become a coequal partner in the overall revenue and spending process.

The vast majority of bills introduced never become law, and members realize these odds. According to Sinclair, "Members may introduce legislation for a variety of reasons, ranging from placating a pesky interest group in their home state or district to publicizing a little recognized problem or an innovative approach to an acknowledged problem. Members may not expect certain of their bills to pass and, sometimes, may not even want them to."[66]

Referral to Committee

Because committees are so important to the ultimate success or failure of a bill, assignment to committee involves strategic political calculations. In the textbook model, a bill simply goes to the committee with jurisdiction over the policy area it corresponds to.

In practice, committee assignment is also governed by strategic politics and battles between committees over expanding or protecting their jurisdiction.

Bills may be assigned to more than one committee—a process called multiple referral—especially if the bill is large and complex. The rules governing multiple referral have changed over time, and the practice is more common in the House than the Senate. While multiple referral can be useful in that "multiple perspectives are brought to bear on complex problems," having more than one committee involved often increases the chances that a bill will get hung up in the legislative process and expire.[67]

The floor plan of the ground level of the Capitol showing the warren of committee chamber rooms. That these rooms are in a lower level is somehow appropriate, as committee rooms are where most bills go to die.

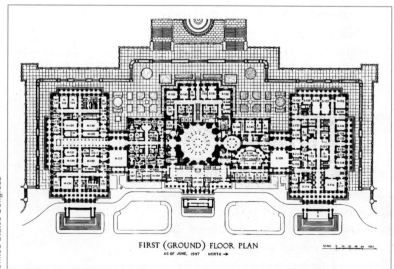

FIRST (GROUND) FLOOR PLAN
AS OF JUNE, 1997   NORTH →

United States Congress

Committee/Subcommittee Action

Once referred to one or more committees, legislation is usually sent to one or more subcommittees—more narrowly focused groups of legislators operating under the guidance of the parent committee of which they are a part. Committees and subcommittees hold hearings to gather information about a bill or issue. Individuals outside of Congress may be brought in to testify and offer their expertise. The **markup** session allows committee members to make changes to a bill before the committee reports it to the floor. The committee report follows the bill from committee to the floor. It acts as a history of the bill and offers guidance to administrative agencies and (if necessary) courts about the committee's intent regarding the bill. Sometimes early cost estimates of the bill's provisions are included in the conference report.

Congressional committees are the graveyards of most bills. Had our cartoon friend, Bill, wanted to visit his deceased comrades to pay his animated respects, congressional committees are the battlegrounds on which he would have found most of their parchment remains. In committee, bills can die from a committee's refusal to report the bill to the full chamber, changes made to them to make them impassable on the House or Senate floor, or simple neglect.

The committee may reject the bill by vote, or it may table the bill with no further action. In the House, a member may file a discharge petition to free a bill from an unfriendly committee and move it to the House floor for a vote if this is agreed to by a majority of representatives. Discharge efforts are rarely successfully used, but they can serve to "pressure a committee and the majority party leadership to bring to the floor measures that they would rather not consider."[68] Often the mere threat of using a procedural maneuver can shape legislative outcomes by signaling to other members that they may face opposition from members of the minority party.

Floor Consideration

Once they have successfully passed out of committee, bills proceed to consideration on the floors of the House and Senate.

Consideration in the House of Representatives

An important difference between the House and the Senate is the role of the **House Rules Committee** in the legislative process, which has no equally powerful analogue in the Senate. A majority of the House Rules Committee's members are chosen by the Speaker. This committee determines when a bill will be subject to debate and vote on the House floor, how long the debate will last, and whether amendments will be allowed on the floor. These special rules can play a major role in whether the bill passes the House or not.

Open rules allow all relevant amendments while closed rules prohibit amendments other than those reported by committee. Most bills are considered under rules that fall in between these extremes, with modified open or modified closed rules. The rules about amendments are important because adding amendments to a bill is yet one more way to kill a piece of legislation. Killer amendments are designed to do just that by peeling away support for a bill by adding unpalatable or indefensible language or provisions. Closed rules can occasionally be used to kill a bill as well, if there are only enough members who would support a bill if key amendments were added, which is not allowed under closed rules.

markup
a process during which a bill is revised prior to a final vote in Congress.

Committee on Rules (House)
a powerful committee that determines when a bill will be subject to debate and vote on the House floor, how long the debate will last, and whether amendments will be allowed on the floor.

If the House approves the rules governing a bill, then floor debate on the bill begins under those rules. A vote to accept or reject the rules reported out of the Rules Committee can be just as consequential to the fate of a piece of legislation as an actual vote on a bill, though in ways that are less visibly clear to most American voters. If allowed, amendments may be offered and, perhaps, amendments to amendments. The time allowed for debate and who controls that time will also have been set by the Rules Committee.

A **roll-call vote** is a vote in which each member of the chamber debating a bill indicates "yea," "nay," or "present." In the House, most votes are electronic. Many interest groups keep track of key votes on issues relevant to them, scoring individual members on how friendly or unfriendly their votes have been to the members of that interest group.

roll-call vote
a recorded vote on a bill.

NEWS CLIP
Senate reduces filibusters against nominees

Consideration in the Senate

In the Senate, individual senators have more ability to shape outcomes on the floor than their House colleagues. Party leadership still matters, however, and the Senate majority leaders schedule the agenda. While the House was first to adopt more formal procedures for bill consideration, the Senate has also become more formalized, though not to the same degree as the House. In the Senate, most procedures are governed by unanimous consent, in which all senators agree to let a motion proceed to a vote. A simple unanimous consent request may be used on noncontroversial measures. A more complex unanimous consent agreement will be worked out between the parties on major legislation to govern the length of debate and the rules governing amendments.

If an individual senator objects to a bill or part of a bill, that senator may place a hold on the legislation and communicate to the majority leader her or his reservations about the bill. In their ability to place holds, offer amendments, and debate issues on the floor, individual senators have the ability to consume Congress's scarcest resource: time. As Sinclair reports, "A single dissatisfied senator, even if she is junior and a minority party member, can cause a great deal of trouble."[69] While the majority leader does not have to honor the hold request, a hold indicates the possibility of a filibuster on the bill.

> "A single dissatisfied senator . . . can cause a great deal of trouble."

A **filibuster** is the use of the power of individual senators to continue to debate issues in order to delay a motion or vote on the floor.[70] Only a successful vote of **cloture**, which requires three-fifths of senators (60), can shut down debate and end a filibuster, allowing the Senate to move on to a vote. Therefore, a determined minority party, provided they have at least forty-one seats and are able to maintain party unity, can delay or kill legislation through the use of the filibuster.

The filibuster has a long and controversial history in the Senate. In 1917, under the urging of President Woodrow Wilson, the Senate adopted the rule of cloture. At the time, ending a filibuster required a two-thirds majority; it was changed to three-fifths in 1975. The placing of holds and threats of a filibuster are increasingly common in a closely split but deeply divided Senate. Because of the increased use of the filibuster threat, votes of cloture have become much more numerous as well. Though there have been frequent calls to eliminate or reform the filibuster, doing so would require changing the rules of the Senate. In addition, individual senators may be reluctant to give up a power that can result in favors for their home states as negotiations to avoid a threatened filibuster take place.

Senators may not only threaten to filibuster a bill that they object to, they may also hold up an unrelated vote or confirmation of a presidential nominee in order to extract

filibuster
a tactic through which an individual senator may postpone action on a piece of legislation.

cloture
a procedure through which senators can end debate on a bill and proceed to action, provided three-fifths of senators agree to it.

concessions on something else, a process referred to as hostage-taking.[71] In March 2013, Rand Paul (R-KY) held up the confirmation of John Brennan as director of the Central Intelligence Agency in order to push the Obama administration to clarify in writing that drone strikes would not be carried out on Americans on American soil in the absence of an imminent threat. "I will speak until I can no longer speak." Paul began. "I will speak as long as it takes, until the alarm is sounded from coast to coast that our Constitution is important, that your rights to trial by jury are precious, that no American should be killed by a drone on American soil without first being charged with a crime, without first being found to be guilty by a court."[72]

Senator Rand Paul (R-KY) filibustering John Brennan's nomination as CIA director, March 6, 2013.
Senate TV via AP.

Paul was joined by colleagues Ted Cruz (R-TX), Mike Lee (R-UT), Ron Wyden (D-OR), and Marco Rubio (R-FL). Paul yielded to their questions—but without yielding the floor, as that would have ended the filibuster—in order to rest his voice. At one point, Cruz read aloud tweets in support of his colleague's efforts. One of the tweets noted, "Rand Paul's filibuster has now lasted longer than the entire Senate's debate on the invasion of Iraq."[73] Another tweet wryly commented, "It turns out that people all over the political spectrum strongly favor the idea of not being murdered by flying robots."[74]

Senator Paul ended his filibuster after nearly thirteen hours—by his own account, defeated by biological necessity.[75] He had, however, used the power of an individual senator to force a discussion about an issue many may have preferred not receive so much attention, and he also earned himself national public attention in the process.

Resolution of Differences between House and Senate Bills

The next step in the legislative process is to resolve differences between House and Senate versions of a bill prior to presidential action. The formal structure for reconciling differences between two versions of a bill is the conference committee. Traditionally bipartisan, the Speaker of the House chooses that chamber's members. Because the Senate operates under unanimous consent, leaders from both parties choose its members to conference. Key players on a bill's progress through Congress are usually included as well.

When the differences are over spending amounts, negotiation is usually more straightforward. When they involve major policy differences—especially if one party controls the House and another the Senate—negotiations may be much more difficult. Because the process of sending a bill to conference from the Senate requires several procedural votes, which are subject to filibuster threat, the modern Congress often bypasses conference, though it still has to produce identical language.

On minor bills, or when the differences are small, one chamber may avoid going to conference by simply accepting the other chamber's version of the bill. This especially happens late in a session when time is scarce and can be used by the political opposition as a weapon.[76] Party leaders may also negotiate informally behind the scenes, with the results of these negotiations offered as amendments. The strategy of ping-ponging (also called amendment exchange) is also designed to avoid having to go to conference. House and Senate versions are amended and sent back and forth between the two chambers until the process has produced a single text.

Floor Reconsideration

Once differences between the two versions have been resolved, the single bill goes back to each chamber for reconsideration, without the possibility of amendment. By this point, on major bills, party leaders have already engaged in lengthy negotiations with their counterparts in the other chamber to avoid any surprises.

Presidential Action

Following successful passage in each chamber, the bill goes to the president for action. The president then has three choices for each bill that lands on her or his desk. The president may sign it, in which case the bill becomes a law. She or he may **veto** it, sending it back to Congress with the objections noted. Bills that are vetoed can still become law if two-thirds of both chambers vote to override the president's veto. Veto overrides are not common and signal a deep disconnect between a president and Congress. One of the most important overrides in recent decades involved a clash between President Richard Nixon and Congress over restricting the president's war-making authority. Just as is the case with a filibuster in the Senate, the power of a presidential veto lies as much with the *threat* of its use as with the actual veto. Veto-bargaining is a negotiation tactic used by presidents to shape the legislation before it lands on his or her desk by using the threat of an eventual veto to gain desired concessions or amendments.[77]

The president's third option is to do nothing, though what happens next depends on how much time is left in that session of Congress. If the president does nothing and there are ten or more days left in session (Sundays excepted), the bill becomes law anyway. This quiet veto does not change the outcome, but it might signal to American voters presidential displeasure with all or part of the law. If Congress has adjourned that year's session during the ten-day period and the president has not signed it, then the law is vetoed, an outcome that is called a pocket veto. A controversial tactic for Congress to avoid a pocket veto is to leave one or more members behind while everyone else goes home.

veto
the power of a president to reject a bill passed by Congress, sending it back to the originating branch with objections noted.

WHAT HAVE I LEARNED?

1. Most bills are defeated on the floors of the House and the Senate.

   a. True
   b. False

2. The threat of a filibuster is used to force members of the _____.

   a. House of Representatives to reconsider or revise a bill
   b. Senate to reconsider or revise a bill
   c. Federal judiciary to reconsider cases before it
   d. State legislatures to sign off on a proposed bill

3. The term *unorthodox lawmaking* refers to the ways in which _____.

   a. Bills representing excluded groups of Americans are introduced into Congress
   b. Interest groups use campaign contributions to influence the legislative process
   c. Possibly illegal ways of passing laws
   d. Standard processes of lawmaking are more fluid than presented in textbooks

4. Why might referral to a particular committee be an effective use of political power?

Answer Key: 1. b; 2. b; 3. d; 4. Answers should include the role of committee chairs and committee makeup in determining the fate of a bill.

THE MEANINGS AND CHALLENGES OF REPRESENTATION

The most difficult question in the study of Congress is what may seem to be the simplest: What does it mean to represent one's constituents in Congress? In *The Concept of Representation*, political theorist Hannah Pitkin provided a foundational exploration of the multiple meanings of representation in Congress.[78] To begin with, Pitkin noted that "representation means, as the word's etymological origins indicate, *re-presentation*, a making present again."[79] What are constituents asking their representatives to "make present" in Washington that was not there before? Part of the answer lies in *acting*—in the sense of what representatives do. In a representative democracy, citizens choose representatives to act on their behalf—to vote on the floor and in committee, to sponsor legislation, to negotiate, and to lead. Another part of the answer lays in *being*—in the sense of who the representatives are.

When voters select representatives, they are choosing people who may or may not reflect and share their policy preferences, identities, interests, and lived experiences. They ask that their representatives transmit information about them—the constituents—to the other members of Congress by adding their voices to the debates and deliberations within the institution. In doing so, according to political scientist Richard F. Fenno Jr., voters are in a sense asking their representatives to take on sometimes competing roles, which he used the term *home style* to denote. Voters want their political representatives to be effective in Washington, which takes them away from home. However, voters also want their members to come home, to present themselves and explain to voters what they have been up to and what they are going to accomplish.[80] More time at home connects representatives and senators to their constituents, while effective representation necessarily involves spending time operating in the intricate machinery of Congress.

Acting in Congress

Passing laws—the legislative function—is Congress's most important task, and voting on the House and Senate floor is the most public legislative act members undertake. However, the process of legislation involves many stages and many less visible acts, such as committee work, bill sponsorship, and negotiation, which can pose a challenge to constituents trying to keep tabs on their elected representatives.

NEWS CLIP
Congress votes to block emissions rules for power plants

Legislators' Voting Decisions

When approaching a vote in Congress, members have several factors to consider.[81] First, they must always at least consider their constituents' interests. Though a senator or representative may ultimately decide to vote against the wishes of those who sent her or him to Washington, no member can ignore voters repeatedly without facing a constituent backlash. If, however, a senator or representative has earned a level of trust from constituents—from long and successful service to them—then she or he may be more willing to act against constituent interests if it feels like the right course of action.[82]

A member's political party also influences how that member will vote. Members may seek input from their colleagues, especially if those colleagues are policy specialists and are known to have a particular expertise relevant to a bill. Input from a member's congressional staff may play a role, as may signals from interest groups, especially if individuals within the interest groups can convince the representative that his or her constituents agree with the group's position. Finally, the president may try to convince representatives to vote a certain way, especially if they are in the same political party.

The Problem of Information in Controlling Representatives' Actions

Elections are the primary tool that voters have to shape the actions of their elected representatives, whether by extracting promises from candidates during the election or by the threat of backlash in the future in the event that those promises are not kept.[83] Both of these mechanisms, however, require some basic level of information on the part of constituents and representatives. Constituents must have policy preferences to begin with and must communicate those preferences to their representatives. They must also have some basic level of information about the actions of their representatives in Congress to know whether to reward or punish those representatives in the next election.

Unfortunately, as we explored in Chapter 7, a long tradition of research in political science has shown that on most issues the majority of constituents are poorly informed, uninterested, or lack any coherent policy preferences. Of course, even the most dedicated congressional observer is challenged to keep track of every issue; however, the fact is some constituents are far better informed than others, especially if they have formed themselves into an interest group for the purpose of influencing congressional action. This inequality of information runs the risk of tilting Congress in the direction of acting only in the interests of its most informed and involved constituents to the detriment of the majority of uninformed ones.

Political scientist R. Douglas Arnold's research explored the ways in which Congress might pass laws that benefit the many even if they impose costs on a well-informed and involved few. But this is not easy.[84] First, representatives must shield themselves as much as possible from the backlash of powerful interests, with as few easily traceable votes as possible. Their leaders must frame failure to act as an unacceptable alternative, making it easier for members to explain individually costly votes.

In addition, there must be a real threat that voters who are not currently paying attention might become aware of and involved in an issue in the future. Interest groups may perform the role of "auditing" on behalf of less informed and less aware voters.[85] Congressional challengers may also play a role, bringing up issues in a campaign that incumbents incorporate into their own agendas.[86] Even the most secure incumbents worry about an issue that might cause their constituents alarm or concern. Successfully worrying about what might happen is part of what has kept them in office in the first place.

The Less Visible Stages of the Legislative Process

There is another challenge to the ability of constituents to control or influence representatives' actions. While votes on the floor or in committee can usually be traced to a particular member, much of the actual work on legislation happens outside of the public eye. The choices that representatives make in allocating their time and energy can have important consequences for the fate of legislation, whether these choices determine how much effort to undertake to steer a bill through the constitutional obstacle course that is Congress or how much energy to devote to blocking a bill's progress.[87] The challenge for constituents is that these individual choices are difficult to observe and, therefore, reward or punish.

Yet members do act, even when the reelectoral math does not add up. Why? Sometimes the decision to act comes from the decision to run for office in the first place. Following the election of 1992, Carol Moseley Braun (D-IL) and Dianne Feinstein (D-CA), two of the newly elected women senators, chose to try to translate their influence into legislation. Primarily because of their experience and qualifications—but also partly because of the public fallout from the Thomas confirmation hearings—these two women joined the powerful Senate Judiciary Committee, whose all-white, all-male membership had been widely criticized for being hostile to and dismissive of Anita Hill's charges of sexual harassment.

Dianne Feinstein, acting mayor of San Francisco, on November 28, 1978, the day after Mayor George Moscone and Supervisor Harvey Milk were assassinated. Feinstein's personal experience later shaped her views on gun control and criminal justice issues.

AP Photo/Walter Zeboski.

Moseley Braun and Feinstein used their positions on the committee to influence one of the most important pieces of legislation taken up by the 103rd Congress: a comprehensive effort to reduce crime and reshape criminal justice policy. According to one article, "Moseley-Braun . . . highlighted racial concerns while Feinstein led a successful floor fight to add an assault weapons ban to the Senate crime bill."[88]

Feinstein brought with her from California a professional and personal commitment to reducing gun violence and improving criminal justice policy. She had served on the California Women's Board of Terms and Parole as well as the state's Crime Commission. In 1978 Feinstein suddenly became acting mayor of San Francisco when Mayor George Moscone and Supervisor Harvey Milk, a noted gay rights advocate and the first openly gay person elected to public office in California, were assassinated by a former city supervisor. Working nearby at the time of the shootings, Feinstein discovered the body of Milk. She "tried to take a pulse, but instead her finger slipped into a bullet hole in his wrist."[89] Even her staunchest political opponents praised Feinstein's strength, calmness, and resolve in the days and weeks following the shootings.

As a member of Congress, Feinstein was instrumental in securing an assault weapons ban that eventually became law. Moseley Braun summed up her colleague's efforts in the Judiciary Committee and in the later stages of the legislative process: "[Senator Feinstein] hounded everyone, she talked to every member, she talked to every member's mother, she talked to everyone, but she worked that bill, she really worked that bill. . . . I'd say that the assault weapons ban is a testimony to her hard work and just doggedness, because at a time when I and every other member of the Committee had concluded that this was a symbolic thing and there was no way we were going to get the votes, Dianne went out and worked and got the votes."[90]

The Problem of Partisanship

Representatives do not act in a vacuum. Their behavior is influenced both by the rules and procedures in Congress and by political parties. Political scientists, congressional observers, and some members themselves have become increasingly concerned about trends in partisan polarization in which members of parties vote and act strongly with their own party and become less likely to cross the aisle and cooperate with each other. While scholars disagree about the causes of polarization in Congress, voting records on the House and Senate floor show a clear trend towards intraparty cohesion (Figure 12.4).[91]

FIGURE 12.4

Visualizing Partisan Polarization

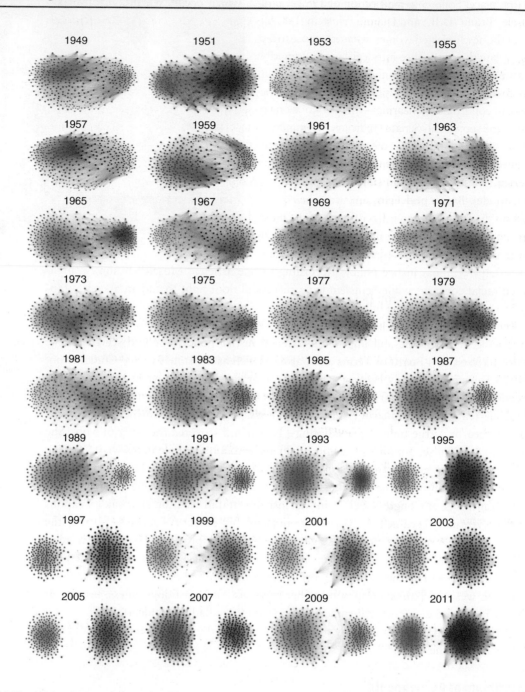

In 2015 a group of researchers mapped the networks of members of the House of Representatives from 1949 to 2011, identifying points of agreement between members on significant issues based on political party. Democratic members are identified in blue and Republicans in red. Each dot represents an individual. The connections represent points of agreement above a specific threshold. Note that over time, the dots have increasingly separated into red and blue groups and are increasingly tightly clustered.

Source: Clio Andris et al., "The Rise of Partisanship and Super-Cooperators in the U.S. House of Representatives," *PloS One* 10, no. 4 (2015), http://journals.plos.org/plosone/article?id=10.1371/journal.pone.0123507.

Intense partisanship can lead to more than ill feelings between members. It may contribute to **gridlock**, a situation in which Congress's ability to legislate is slowed or stopped by its inability to overcome divisions, especially those based on partisanship. Gridlock is made more likely in a period of **divided government**, which occurs when control of the presidency and one or both chambers of Congress is split between the two major parties.

gridlock
a situation in which Congress's ability to legislate is slowed or stopped by its inability to overcome divisions, especially those based on partisanship.

divided government
a situation that occurs when control of the presidency and one or both chambers of Congress is split between the two major parties.

Being in Congress: Who Members Are

Many of the framers and supporters of the United States Constitution expected that Congress would be a reflection of the people in the Republic, though the definition of who had the right to be a represented person was highly restrictive. John Adams wrote that Congress "should be a portrait, in miniature, of the people at large, as it should think, feel, reason and act like them."[92]

Several issues and challenges arise when attempting to view Congress as a portrait of America. The first is that no single member can represent each of his or her constituents' diverse identities, experiences, and interests. Even if somehow possible, this might not be desirable in the extreme. Constituents, for example, might want their legislators to be more knowledgeable about, experienced in, and motivated to act in the messy space of politics than the average American voter.

Descriptive Representation in Congress

Instead, when scholars and observers talk about making Congress a more accurate reflection of America, they are referring to increasing **descriptive representation**, in which members of Congress "mirror some of the more frequent experiences and outward manifestations of belonging to the group."[93] Usually a focus on increasing descriptive representation in Congress aims to selectively increase the membership of a particular group or groups who because of other historical and contextual factors remain underrepresented in proportion to their share of the population.[94]

descriptive representation
the degree to which a body of representatives in a legislature does or does not reflect the diversity of that nation's identities and lived experiences.

Looking at the modern Congress, it is clear that the members do not come close to presenting a mirror of the American electorate. While Congress has grown more descriptively representative in recent years, women, lower-income Americans, members of racial and ethnic minorities, members of certain religious faiths, and gay, lesbian, and transgendered Americans remain underrepresented in proportion to their percentage of the American voting-age population.

As a whole, members of Congress tend to be older, whiter, wealthier, and more educated than the American electorate. The lack of descriptive representation raises a complicated set of related questions: Does it matter? Is it necessary for a member of Congress to share the lived experiences of the constituents whom she or he hopes to represent? Can a man represent a woman? Can a wealthy person represent a lower-income person?

Some scholars have posited that there may be benefits to having a descriptively representative legislature apart from what it actually does in Congress. Seeing a diversity of faces in Congress may, in the eyes of the American electorate, confer greater legitimacy to the institution and the policies that it passes. Others have pointed out that legislators who do not descriptively represent groups of their constituents are still under the reelectoral threat of ignoring those constitutents' concerns. In the Pennsylvania senatorial campaign of 1992, Arlen Specter successfully convinced enough voters—with the help of some key women's groups—that he could effectively represent women's interests in Congress. Specter argued that his seniority and clout within the institution made him a more effective advocate for them than Lynn Yeakel, who would have been a Senate rookie.

Another challenge to descriptive representation is that any given legislator may share key attributes with some of her or his constituents, but not others. Does a wealthy African

NEWS CLIP
Challenges faced by women running for Congress

Representing Representation

The United States Congress remains descriptively unrepresentative. Women; lower-income Americans; members of many racial and ethnic minorities; members of certain religious faiths; lesbian, gay, bisexual, and transgendered Americans; and members of other minority groups remain underrepresented in Congress in proportion to their numbers in the American voting-age population.

There has been improvement in recent elections, however. Telling the story of this improvement in pictures and graphs is subject to the way in which these data are presented. As with all data stories told with graphs, how one draws the *scale* of the chart, the vertical or *y*-axis here, can convey very different impressions using the same data. Consider this graph of the percentages of women in the Senate over the past twenty-five Congresses (fifty years).

In this chart, the gains made by women in recent elections look quite impressive. Notice, however, that the *y*-axis (the vertical one) does not go from 0 to 100—the actual number of senators—but from 1 to 25. Consider the same data but with the scale of the *y*-axis showing the full range of the number of senators that might be categorized on the basis of gender, from 0 to 100.

This presentation of the same data in the second graph tells a very different story. With the full scale changed from 0 to 100, recent gains in the descriptive representation of women in the Senate do not look so impressive. The tactic of cutting off, or truncating, the scale of a graph can be used to either present a pessimistic or an optimistic portrait, depending on the data storyteller's objective. In the first presentation of the data, the election of 1992 appears to mark the beginning of a major wave of change, which it did. Looking at the same data in the second figure, however, tells a somewhat different story; there were gains, to be sure, but much less revolutionary ones.

When reading a graph and the story it's telling, pay attention to the ways in which different presentations of the same set of data—in this case the scale—can portray very different narratives depending on which one the data storyteller wishes to present. The presentation of data can be just as political as that of word stories.

Women Senators in the United States Congress

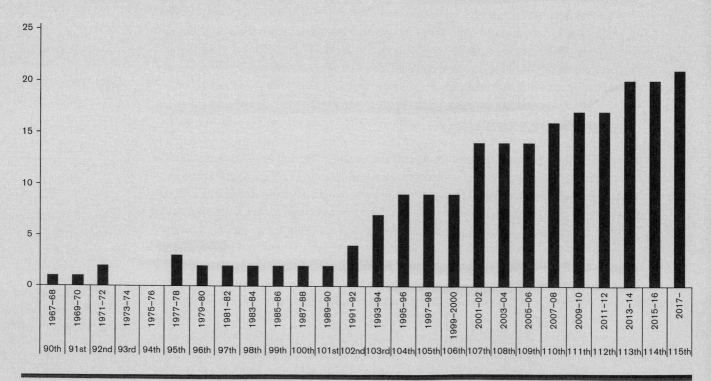

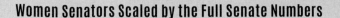

Women Senators Scaled by the Full Senate Numbers

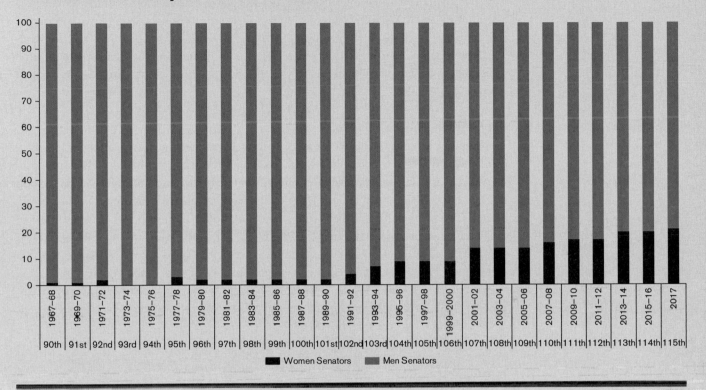

American legislator from an urban district reflect her constituents? In terms of racial and ethnic identity, quite possibly; in terms of income and wealth, perhaps not so much. Similarly, does a white legislator from a Midwestern agricultural district with little experience in farming describe his constituents? Again, in some ways, probably, but maybe not in others.

Increasing Descriptive Representation: Racial and Ethnic Gerrymandering

Actions have been taken to improve the electoral chances of legislators of racial and ethnic minority identities, and therefore the descriptive representation of Congress along these characteristics. This is the racial and ethnic gerrymandering that we explored in Chapter 10. There is, however, a potential contradiction in the logic of such gerrymandering. Recall that in the case of partisan gerrymandering, the logic is to isolate the opposing party into a small number of districts that you know they will win but dilute their votes in a larger number of other districts—to "waste" the opposing party's votes. In the case of racial and ethnic gerrymandering, the tactic is the same, but the goal is different: to concentrate minority voters in a small number of districts but in order to help their overall representation in Congress.

Not all scholars agree that creating these majority-minority districts increases the overall representation of minorities in Congress. Political scientist Carol Swain has argued that while creating such districts increases the probability of electing African Americans within those districts, it does not necessarily improve the representation of African Americans overall. According to her, "More black faces in political office (that is, more descriptive representation for African Americans) will not necessarily lead to more representation of the tangible interests of blacks."[95] Perhaps, Swain argues, it is better to have a larger number of legislators who have to consider the views of their African American constituents than have a small number of descriptively representative legislators who lack enough votes to advocate for their positions. If the creation of majority-minority districts dilutes the degree to which members have to attend to their minority constituents' interests, then there must be something to be gained from increasing the plurality of voices within Congress on its own.

The Problem of Essentialism

essentialism

the risks posed by linking individuals' lived experiences to policy preferences, whether by identifying those individuals by those policies or excluding them from advocating different policy objectives.

Thinking about constituents in terms of specific characteristics poses another challenge, that of **essentialism**, which political theorist Jane Mansbridge defines as "the assumption that members of certain groups have an essential identity that all members of that group share and of which no others can partake."[96] Essentialism risks masking the complexity of views *within* members of that group, sidelining policy disagreements between them in the name of some shared "women's interest" or "African American interest." Second, it also risks cordoning off members' efforts into a few predefined acceptable issues: the idea that women should only talk about "women's issues" or that black people should only talk about "black issues." Such segregation harkens back to the definition of a woman's "proper" role outside of public life against which American women have struggled for much of the nation's political history.

Substantive Representation: The Connection between Acting and Being

substantive representation

the degree to which elected representatives or senators represent the interests and policy preferences of their constituents.

Both the acts that members of Congress undertake and the degree to which they share the lived experiences of their constituents shape representation. While both acting and reflecting, as we have seen, are complicated, it is the connection between the two that holds the promise of sorting out some of the contradictions and challenges in each. While it very well may be important for American voters to feel that their Congress is a legitimate portrait of the nation, what really matters is, according to Hanna Pitkin, "the nature of the activity itself, what goes on during representation, the substance of the content of acting for others."[97] Pitkin calls this **substantive representation**.

Substantive representation is important because it holds the promise of linking constituents' lived experiences not just to the actions of their own legislators but to the actions of the institution itself, to the way that the institution works. It has the potential to improve the way that Congress deliberates by expanding the congressional agenda and by facilitating representation across geographical and partisan boundaries.

Deliberation

legislative deliberation

the considered argument and discussion of the issues by congressional representatives.

As imagined by those who designed it, Congress is supposed to be much more than just a place to count predecided votes and hear preformed arguments. It is also supposed to be a place for **legislative deliberation**, the considered argument and discussion of the issues. Deliberation is discussion of "which policies are good for the polity as a whole, which policies are good for representatives' constituents, and when the interests of various groups within the policy and constituency conflict."[98]

Deliberation is itself a complicated thing. For viewpoints to be discussed, they must first capture the attention of a large enough number of legislators. Second, deliberation is personal, as often are its politics. Individual relationships between members who share interests and experiences can make for a more effective deliberative body. When this occurs, members who share common experiences can work with colleagues in the other party, thereby helping to counter trends in partisan polarization.

> *Substantive representation holds the promise of linking constituent's lived experiences not just to the actions of their own legislators but to the actions of the institution itself, to the way that the institution works.*

In any given session of Congress, there are only so many issues that can be dealt with and discussed, the list of which constitutes the legislative agenda. Why some issues seem to rocket toward the top of the agenda and others languish at the bottom or are ignored is sometimes easily explained—for example, in times of national crisis some concerns are seen as more urgent than others. However, the setting of the congressional agenda is often unpredictable.[99]

By bringing unconsidered issues to Congress's table and making them salient, legislators who share common lived experiences with underrepresented constituents may enlarge the institution's agenda. In doing so, members are acting (in political theorist Jane Mansbridge's analysis) as surrogate representatives—they are representing people who may not live in their district or state but with whom they share common concerns.[100] Presenting information to one's legislative colleagues is an important part of representation, helping to create, in the words of John Stuart Mill, "an arena in which not only the general opinion of the nation, but every section of it, and as far as possible of every eminent individual whom it contains, can produce itself in full light."[101]

After the 2000 election, a reporter asked Senator Kay Bailey Hutchinson (R-TX), "Why can't a male senator do everything a woman senator can do?" Hutchinson's reply was, "Sometimes, from our experience there are issues that men just haven't thought about. . . . Most of the time our colleagues are supportive once we've made the case."[102] In 1993 Carol Moseley Braun—the only African American senator serving at the time—brought to the chamber's attention the larger implications of an issue that may have seemed trivial to many members, if it was on their radar at all. Senator Jesse Helms (R-NC) had offered as an amendment a renewal of the patent for the design of the symbol of the United Daughters of the Confederacy, which included the confederate flag—an image the national sanctioning of which many African Americans find problematic.

Had Moseley Braun been focused only on her reelectoral prospects, this was probably not a battle that needed to be fought. As Mansbridge noted, "Moseley Braun undoubtedly had never mentioned the issue in her election campaign. Nor could Moseley Braun have feared reelection sanctions on this point, since without her intervention the amendment would have passed unnoticed."[103] Moseley Braun successfully killed the amendment and in doing so signaled to her own constituents as well as to African American voters across the nation that she intended to voice their shared concerns in the Senate.

Rarely, however, can one legislator reshape the congressional agenda on his or her own. It requires, in the analysis of Mansbridge, "a critical mass for their own members to become willing to enunciate minority positions."[104] And, as we have seen, the importance of committee action (or inaction) suggests that effective substantive representation requires enough members with shared experiences to make present these voices not just on the floor but in "a variety of committees and subcommittees in whose deliberative spaces the most important features of policy are often hammered out."[105] Equally important is going beyond just getting a "woman's issue" or an "African American issue" on the congressional agenda—having enough voices to reveal the conflicts and tensions *within* members of these groups and presenting the full range of opinion on the issues.

Mentorship

One important, but not frequently discussed, way that legislators can represent their own constituents—as well as those in other states and districts—is to act as mentors to newly elected colleagues. Mentorship builds the kinds of personal connections that a legislator needs to advance the interests of her or his constituents and also helps build a more effective legislative body.

After successfully defending her Senate seat in 1992, Barbara Mikulski took it upon herself to mentor her four new women colleagues. She called this "Getting Started in the Senate." As related in the book *Nine and Counting*, "When the women arrived in Washington, Mikulski invited them to her office and conducted two separate seminars, during which she explained the complex workings of the Senate. In addition, she complied thick notebooks for each of them containing all of the key details concerning committee assignments and procedures. . . . The Senate had a long tradition of 'every man for himself.' Mikulski was determined that it would not be every woman for herself while she was in the Senate."[106] About her senior colleague's assistance, Senator Patty Murray reflected, "Barbara Mikulski was a godsend. She brought all of us together and laid it all out. She explained, 'Here's how you can be successful.' She explained everything—how to get an incorporation into a bill, what you had to do to steer yourself onto a good committee, how to set up a mailroom."[107]

In a Congress often defined by partisanship, substantive representation holds the potential to make James Madison's vision of the extended republic more of a reality, though not in the sense of a united "women's bloc," or any other bloc based solely on identity. "There was," according to Mikulski, "never any thought of forming a women's voting bloc. There was a clear understanding that each senator was independent. The fact that they were women certainly didn't mean that they held the same views on issues—even those seen as traditional women's issues."[108]

In 1993 Republican Kay Bailey Hutchinson defeated a Democratic incumbent for a seat in the Senate. Like the incoming women senators in Mikulski's own Democratic Party, Hutchinson was greeted with offers of mentorship and advice from Mikulski, along with her guidebook. In the years that followed, other Republican women senators also benefitted from Mikulski's mentorship efforts. On July 26, 2000, a group of Republican and Democratic women senators appearing on the show *Larry King Live*—including Mikulski, Hutchinson, Feinstein, Boxer, and Murray—stunned their host by announcing that they were not going to campaign against each other in the upcoming election, regardless of party affiliation and even if asked to by their party's leaders. "We are going to duke it out in the Senate," Mikulski said. "We have different issues, different parties. But I think we all feel that every one of us has made a difference, and we want to support that. When we have been together, we have brought about change. And we are proud of each other."[109]

Senator Barbara Mikulski (D-MD), right, was well known for her mentoring of other women in the Senate. Here, Mikulski plays host to fellow women senators, including new senator-elect Joni Ernst (R-IA), left, at a meeting at the U.S. Capitol in Washington on November 13, 2014. Also pictured are Senator Patty Murray (D-WA), second from left; Senator Jeanne Shaheen (D-NH); and Senator Kirsten Gillibrand (D-NY).

REUTERS/Jonathan Ernst.

1. Representation in Congress involves both acting on behalf of constituents and understanding their concerns.

   a. True
   b. False

2. When members of Congress consider how to vote on a bill, they take into consideration _____.

   a. Constituent interests
   b. Their own reelectoral considerations
   c. Information from staffers and fellow members of Congress
   d. All of the above

3. The difference between descriptive and substantive representation is _____.

   a. That descriptive representation focuses more on what members of Congress do than who they are
   b. That descriptive representation focuses on making present the lived experiences of members
   c. That descriptive representation focuses on creating a portrait of America in Congress
   d. All of the above

4. What do you think it means to truly represent one's constituents in Congress?

Answer Key: 1. a; 2. d; 3. c; 4. Answers should focus on the relationship between descriptive and substantive representation.

CONCLUSION

The Complexity of Representation

By 2015, as the 114th Congress convened, much had changed in the representation of women in the Senate and with regard to women senators' ability to pull the levers of congressional power at the highest level. Patty Murray (D-WA), for example, had risen to one of the most powerful positions in the Senate hierarchy, partly because of her skill and partly because of her survivorship; as we have discussed, seniority is an important component of senatorial power in committee leadership and in key party positions. Tammy Baldwin (D-WI) was elected in 2012 as the first openly gay, lesbian, transsexual, or transgender member of the Senate. Mazie Hirono (D-HI) had been the first Asian-American women elected to Congress when she won a House seat in 2006, and in 2012 she became the first Asian American woman, as well as the first Buddhist, to serve in the Senate.

Notice, however, all the *D*s in the paragraph above, meaning that each of these women was elected as a candidate from the Democratic Party, a pattern that has had consequences both for electoral outcomes and leadership assignments (see below). Given that (1) descriptive representation is now very much tied to party affiliation, (2) the Republican Party took control of the Senate in the election of 2014, and (3) committee leadership positions in 2016 were occupied by members of the majority party, the 114th Congress saw the number of women leading Senate committees drop from nine to zero. As a *New York Times* article put it, "When Democrats lost control, women lost top jobs."[110]

One of those powerful woman senators who found herself no longer serving as committee chair was Barbara Mikulski. Mikulski had been chair of the powerful Senate Appropriations Committee before the Republican takeover but then relegated to the ranking Democratic member of that committee. Well aware of the future electoral risks of appearing to be a party of men in a nation in which women outnumber men in terms of eligible voters, the Republican leadership scrambled to present a more representative face on the party. Majority Whip John Cornyn, the second-highest ranking Republican in the Senate, noted, "I think it helps to have a Senate leadership that looks more like the rest of America."[111] As we explored in Chapter 10, the electoral need to reach out to the diversity of American voters in the twenty-first century has become a critical goal of American political parties. For her part, Mikulski was undeterred: "While I've been in the minority before, I've never been on the sidelines."[112]

Mikulski, the longest serving woman in the history of the United States Congress, as she had announced, chose not to run for reelection in 2016. Her successor will be a man, former

Representative Chris Van Hollen (D-MD), whom Mikulski supported in the general election. Others will have to step up and maintain Senator Mikulski's mentorship program.

In the final weeks of the 114th Congress, Senator Barbara Boxer, also retiring, introduced a bill in Congress to abolish the Electoral College in the wake of Secretary Hillary Clinton's popular vote victory but electoral defeat in the 2016 presidential election. "The presidency," Boxer tweeted, "is the only office where you can win more votes & still lose. It's time to end the Electoral College."[113] Given the intense partisan divisions in Congress and the American republic—as well as the hurdles placed upon the process of constitutional amendment—Boxer's proposal will, in all likelihood, not move forward.

The 115th Congress, which will convene in January of 2017, will include 21 women, one more than the outgoing 114th Congress. One of these senators will be Catherine Cortez Masto (D-NV), the first Latina senator in United States history. Patty Murray will likely "move up in leadership," having "garnered the respect of Democrats and Republicans."[114] Senator Murray, however, will remain in the minority party, as Republicans retained control of the Senate.

In 2017, representation in the Senate will involve the same goals, questions, and complications that it always has: standing for constituents, bringing voices and energy to its deliberations and outcomes, and operating within an institution intentionally designed by the framers of the Constitution to place brakes on the pace of political change.

While you were reading this chapter, you may have wondered about the choices of the specific narrative focus: Why 1992? Why women? What about all of the other members of the American Republic not addressed by the stories presented? Don't they matter? By now, I hope you realize that they have, and do, and will. To try to capture, however, the complexity of those who seek to be represented, who expect to be represented, and who are promised representation in the Constitution with any one set of stories—a focus on any one set of lived experiences—is frankly impossible. Whether or not James Madison had any idea how truly "extended" the "extended republic" had become that he described and argued for in Federalist No. 10 is not the point. What matters is who we are now and if—and how—we can make the underlying promise of an inclusive, enduring republic a reality.

The framers of the Constitution did not intend for Congress to be purely and perfectly representative. They mistrusted the ability of *citizens* to avoid the dangers of faction. The meaning of citizen at the time of the founding of the nation was narrowly defined. The enslavement of African Americans and the exclusion of Native Americans, women, and many other individuals from public life was an accepted norm at this time. In recent decades, however, Congress has come to more accurately reflect the American electorate, though it is still far from being perfectly descriptive. These gains have not come about by chance; they are mostly due to the strategic actions of citizens to reshape Congress to better portray the diversity of the nation. It is not a matter of what should have been or has not been; it is a question of what can be and what we are going to do to make it so.

In this chapter we have explored two major themes: representation and lawmaking. We have done so through the lens of women in Congress. The lessons learned and the questions raised are not unique to any one gender, party, or set of lived experiences, however. Most fundamentally, we are left with the issue of the relationship *between* these two themes. How do representation and lawmaking reinforce each other? How might they challenge each other?

Representation and lawmaking in Congress have always been, and still are, complicated, messy, and often uncomfortable. Though the legislative branch is the first branch of government—and viewed as the most powerful by the framers—it is still only one of three. Over the course of American history, strategic political actors in the other two branches—the executive and judicial—have also tried to shape the power of their institutions, to present their own views of representation in the United States, and to stand for the people.

CHAPTER REVIEW

This chapter's main ideas are reflected in the Learning Objectives below. By reviewing them here you should be able to **remember** the key points, **connect** them to the stories presented in the chapter, **think** about these questions, and **know** these terms that are central to the topic.

12.1 Describe the structure of Congress as established in the Constitution, including the differences between the House of Representatives and the Senate and the powers placed in each chamber.

REMEMBER...

- The Constitution called for a bicameral legislature divided between the House of Representatives and the Senate to establish a set of checks and balances within Congress. Members of Congress are meant to represent the interests of the people of the nation.

- Members of the House are meant to be closer to the people. Shorter terms and looser eligibility requirements open the doors wider to potential representatives.

- Senators are meant to be more insulated from the public to ensure greater stability. Longer terms and stricter eligibility requirements make the bar higher for candidates.

- Both the House and Senate have legislative authority as well as budgetary and oversight powers. They have the power to tax, coin money, regulate currency, regulate trade domestically and with foreign nations, declare war, and create lower courts.

- The House may introduce bills to raise revenue and impeach members of the executive and judicial branches.

- The Senate has the power to ratify treaties and confirm executive branch officers and Supreme Court justices. It also tries members of the executive and judicial branches impeached by the House.

CONNECT...

- Despite making up over half of the voting population, women had been dramatically underrepresented in Congress, comprising only two percent of membership when the women of the class of 1992 were originally elected.

THINK...

- What does it mean for representatives and senators to "stand for" the interests of their constituents?

- What were the intended differences that the framers devised in separating legislative representation between the House and the Senate?

- What are the powers of Congress as enumerated in the Constitution?

KNOW...

- *representation* (p. 407)

12.2 Identify the obstacles to winning a seat in Congress, the factors that influence an individual's decision to run, and the resources and skills that successful candidates need.

REMEMBER...

- Factors that contribute to a decision to run for election include election-specific ones, such as whether there is an open seat election and the particular political climate at the time; adequate funding resources; and personal ambition.

- Factors that contribute to winning a seat in Congress include understanding one's constituency, experience, and money. Incumbents enjoy an easier path to reelection, whereas challengers typically try to spot the right circumstances to make a bid.

CONNECT...

- The women running for Congress in 1992 were motivated by a variety of reasons, but many were inspired to run in reaction to Anita Hill's treatment during her congressional testimony and a general sense that no one in Congress was truly representing women's viewpoints.

- The existence of an unusual number of open seat elections, a political climate favoring domestic policy issues, the rise of EMILY's List, and personal ambition all also played a part in the decision of women to run in 1992.

THINK...

- What are the obstacles that first-time candidates for Congress face? What are the political strategies they employ?

KNOW...

- *appropriation* (p. 413)
- *earmark* (p. 415)
- *fire alarm oversight* (p. 416)
- *oversight* (p. 415)
- *police patrol oversight* (p. 416)
- *senatorial courtesy* (p. 416)
- *statute* (p. 413)

12.3 List the primary organizational features of Congress and understand the role of chamber leaders, political parties, committees, and congressional norms.

REMEMBER...

- Political parties exert a good deal of influence in Congress. Both the majority and minority parties in Congress control key leadership positions and work to advance policy goals and get members reelected. The Speaker of the House is especially powerful, and the Senate majority leader also plays a key role.

- Congressional committees do most of the work of Congress and are divided into types with different specializations.

- A large Congressional staff assists with casework, researching and drafting policy and legislation, and constituent preferences. Nonpartisan organizations like the CBO and GAO provide members with information and insight as well.

- Norms and traditional ways of doing things also play a role—albeit a more informal one—in the smooth functioning of Congress.

CONNECT...

- The women elected in the class of 1992 learned the formal rules of Congress and some assumed powerful leadership positions. Informally, they followed existing norms of conduct and also established their own.

THINK...

• How do the rules of congressional organization shape its outcomes?

KNOW...

• *committee chairs* (p. 428)
• *majority party leader* (p. 427)
• *minority party leader* (p. 427)

• *Speaker of the House* (p. 426)
• *whip* (p. 427)

12.4 Trace the steps of the legislative process and explain how that process can diverge from traditional "textbook" descriptions.

REMEMBER...

• Before they can become law, bills must be passed by both the House and Senate and then approved by the president. They are first introduced in either chamber then referred to committee. The committee and/or subcommittee may take various actions, such as holding hearings, marking up the bill, or voting on the bill. The bill then proceeds to the House or Senate floor for a vote. If passed, it is reconciled and then reconsidered. Finally, the bill moves on to the president for consideration.

• Actors other than members of Congress may play a role in influencing whether a bill gets introduced. Some bills go to multiple committees. Bills can be forced out of committees through discharge petition. A chamber may bypass conference committee action by passing an amended bill from the other chamber. Presidents have the ability to shape bills through the threat of a veto vote.

• Most bills are never passed.

CONNECT...

• Senator Rand Paul recently used a filibuster to influence legislation.

THINK...

• What are the stages of getting bills passed in Congress? How do they often differ from "textbook" descriptions of the processes?

KNOW...

• *cloture* (p. 434)
• *Committee on Rules* (p. 433)
• *filibuster* (p. 434)
• *markup* (p. 433)

• *roll-call vote* (p. 434)
• *subcommittees* (p. 445)
• *unorthodox lawmaking* (p. 430)
• *veto* (p. 436)

12.5 Connect the issues surrounding the representation of women in Congress to the representation, or lack of it, of other individuals in America, whether based on race, ethnicity, sexual identity, or other traditionally excluded identities.

REMEMBER...

• When taking action in Congress, members must consider several factors, including how to consider the preferences of their constituents, their party, and other influencers. They must gather information about those preferences and inform their own choices by gathering information from sources such as election results and constituents' communications. Their voting behavior is influenced by congressional rules and procedures and by political parties.

• With regard to congressional representation, we consider both descriptive representation (the degree to which a body of representatives in a legislature reflects the diversity of that nation's identities and lived experiences) and substantive representation (the degree to which elected representatives or senators represent the interests and policy preferences of their constituents).

CONNECT...

- The women who were elected to Congress in 1992 worked individually, as a group, and with other members of Congress to represent their constituents' interests. Congress's potential to be descriptively representative has improved but is not perfect.

THINK...

- Are Americans descriptively represented in Congress? Do you think the answer to this question matters?

- What lessons might we learn from the efforts of women in Congress that could be germane to the struggles of other underrepresented groups to secure substantive representation?

KNOW...

- *descriptive representation* (p. 441)
- *divided government* (p. 441)
- *essentialism* (p. 444)

- *gridlock* (p. 441)
- *legislative deliberation* (p. 444)
- *substantive representation* (p. 444)

13 THE AMERICAN PRESIDENCY
Individuals, Institutions, and Executive Power

It has to be a very lonely job, and maybe the hardest. It is, without question, one of the most powerful positions in the world—perhaps *the* most powerful. If you want to understand the weight of the American presidency, compare photographs or paintings of the heady days of a new president's inauguration to those taken or created in the final days before leaving office. You will observe that each person has aged, often dramatically, and often far beyond what one would expect from what is generally just a few years of time.

The American president stands alone, and not just at a podium or a press conference, but also in comparison to leaders of other democratic nations. However, he or she does not *operate* alone, which is as the framers of the Constitution intended. The president sits atop a massive collection of organizations, agencies, and bureaus. He or she must contend with a Congress whose members have their own political goals, even if the majority of those members are from the president's own political party. If the majority of one or both chambers in Congress is not from the president's party, then things get even tougher. And then there are the American people, to whom a president speaks directly. With the American people on his or her side, a president can be very powerful, especially when dealing with members of Congress. Without this support, presidents are vulnerable. In the American political system, the president acts as the head of the **executive branch** of government, which is charged with executing, or putting into effect, the laws of the nation.

In the stories in this chapter, we will focus primarily on one aspect of presidential power: the making of war. There are many others. Presidents act to shape policy in all areas—economic, social, domestic, and foreign. However, by focusing on this one facet of presidential power, you will confront a fundamental question in American politics: In American representative democracy, how much power should any one person have, even if he or she is the elected president? By engaging with the stories of presidential decisions to imprison or kill citizens suspected of acting against vital national security interests in the nineteenth and twenty-first centuries, you will gain a deeper understanding of the American presidency.

LEARNING OBJECTIVES

After reading this chapter, you will be able to:

13.1 Describe the powers of the presidency as defined in the Constitution, the tensions inherent in those descriptions, and constitutional limitations on presidential power

13.2 Evaluate how presidents have tested the limits of the power of the office during wartime and national crises

13.3 Appraise the impact of individual presidencies in establishing the powers of the office

13.4 Discuss institutional and informal sources of presidential power

THE "BODY" OF ANWAR AL-AWLAKI
Presidential War-Making Power in the Twenty-First Century

On a September morning in 2011, a group of men had just finished eating breakfast in a remote desert in the country of Yemen. One of them was Anwar al-Awlaki, an American citizen who was, to counterterrorism officials, "a rock star propagandist for al-Qaeda's arm in Yemen who recruited followers over the Internet. He posted fiery sermons in idiomatic English and called on all who listened to attack the West."[1] Patrolling the Yemeni skies that day were American drones launched from an airstrip in Saudi Arabia and remotely piloted from far away. Noticing the drones, the men "scrambled to get to their trucks."[2]

They were too late. Two Predator drones marked the men's trucks with lasers, and larger Reaper drones launched three Hellfire missiles. Al-Awlaki's vehicle "was totally torn up into pieces" according to reports from unidentified witnesses to the strike. The missiles "left nothing of the target but small human parts, which were later collected together and buried in one tomb."[3] Also killed in the strike was American Samir Khan, "who had moved to Yemen from North Carolina and was the creative force behind *Inspire*, the militant group's English-language magazine."[4]

For more than a year and a half following the strike, the administration of President Barack Obama remained officially silent on the targets. Under pressure from members of Congress, including some key Democrats, Attorney General Eric Holder formally acknowledged in May 2013 that the 2011 strike had targeted an American citizen: al-Awlaki. According to the *New York Times*, "For what was apparently the first time since the Civil War, the United States government had carried out the deliberate killing of an American citizen as a wartime enemy and without a trial."[5] Al-Awlaki's name had been placed at the top of the Central Intelligence Agency's (CIA) list of individuals to be captured if possible, or killed if not. Many of the details about how individuals made this list were secret. One journalist reported that "officials said that every name added to the list underwent a careful, if secret, legal review. Because of Mr. Awlaki's [American] citizenship, the decision to add him to the target list was approved by the National Security Council as well."[6]

It was the "secret" part of the administration's decision to target al-Awlaki that made many uncomfortable. In a public speech in 2012, Obama's top counterterrorism adviser, John Brennan, reassured his audience that individuals, including Americans, were only targeted for killing if capture was not a realistic option and only after a careful and thorough review. "Of course," he added, "how we identify an individual naturally involves intelligence sources and methods, which I will not discuss."[7]

Two weeks after the killing of al-Awlaki, "his 16-year-old son, Abdulrahman—also an American citizen who had gone to the Yemeni desert in search of his father—was killed in a drone strike meant for someone else. That strike was similarly unacknowledged, although a senior administration official privately characterized it as a 'mistake.'"[8] The actual target, a senior al-Qaeda official, was not at the outdoor eating place at the time of the strike. Abdulrahman, who "liked sports and music and kept his Facebook page regularly updated" was apparently an unintended casualty of the war on terror.[9]

In less than a month, the United States government had killed three American citizens with drone strikes on foreign soil, though the death of one, the younger al-Awlaki, was likely unintentional. In a highly controversial exchange with the Washington press corps, White House press secretary Robert Gibbs responded to a reporter's question about the killing of Abdulrahman. "It's an American citizen that is being targeted without due process, without trial. And he's underage. He's a minor," the reporter charged. "I would suggest that you should have a far more responsible father if they are truly concerned about the well being of their children," Gibbs replied.[10]

Just as many of the details surrounding the decision to target Anwar al-Awlaki were kept secret, the portrait of the man himself also remains murky and disputed. What is known is this: He was born in New Mexico in 1971, while his father was studying agricultural economics. After pursuing Islamic studies in Yemen, al-Awlaki returned to the

American citizen and Muslim cleric Anwar al-Awlaki poses for a photo at Dar al Hijrah Mosque in October 2001 in Falls Church, Virginia. Ten years later, al-Awlaki was killed in a targeted drone strike by the United States in Yemen.

Tracy Woodward/The Washington Post via Getty Images.

United States for undergraduate and graduate education. He was serving as imam of a mosque near Washington, D.C., in 2001 at the time of the 9/11 attacks. In the weeks following, al-Awlaki presented a moderate face to Americans trying to understand what had happened and to many Muslim Americans worried about a backlash against members of their faith. The *New York Times* reported that al-Awlaki "became a go-to Muslim cleric for reporters scrambling to explain Islam. He condemned the mass murder, invited television crews to follow him around and patiently explained the rituals of his religion. 'We came here to build, not to destroy,' [he] said in a sermon. 'We are the bridge between Americans and one billion Muslims worldwide.' . . . Nine years later, from his hide-out in Yemen, [he had] declared war on the United States."[11]

His primary weapon was the Internet. With his blog posts and YouTube videos, "Mr. Awlaki's website became a favorite for English-speaking Muslims who were curious about jihad."[12] With his command of the English language and ability to draw on American social and cultural references in his posts and videos, al-Awlaki became a very effective "recruiter and propagandist."[13] In a video posted in 2010, he declared that "no special clerical ruling is required to kill Americans. Don't consult with anyone in fighting the Americans; fighting the devil doesn't require consultation or prayers or seeking divine guidance."[14] According to one U.S. counterterrorism researcher, "Al-Awlaki condense[d] the Al Qaeda philosophy into digestible, well-written treatises. . . . They may not tell people how to build a bomb or shoot a gun. But he [told] them who to kill, and why."[15]

There is yet no clear answer to the question of how an American citizen and Muslim cleric who preached peace following the 9/11 attacks came to wage war on the country of his birth. Instead, there are competing narratives, depending on who is or was doing the telling.

By al-Awlaki's own account, it was U.S. policy in prosecuting the wars in Iraq and Afghanistan overtly, and in Pakistan, Yemen, and other countries covertly, that drove him to follow "the religious obligation to defend his faith."[16] Another account, though never officially confirmed, claimed that al-Awlaki had always been an al-Qaeda operative, even before the 9/11 attacks.[17] It is known that he met two of the future 9/11 hijackers in his mosque in San Diego, though it was never established that the contact was anything more than all three moving in the same relatively small social and religious circles at the time.

Interviews with people who frequented his mosques and knew him personally portray a complicated, conflicted, and transformed man. Many of those who knew him cited al-Awlaki's eighteen months in a Yemeni prison—much of it in solitary confinement—as the driving force behind his radicalization. He blamed the United States for allowing his detention, and there is some evidence that this was the case. The *New York Times* reported that "John D. Negroponte, then director of national intelligence, told Yemeni officials that the United States did not object to his detention, according to American and Yemeni sources."[18]

On May 22, 2013, Attorney General Holder informed congressional leaders of the decision made by the Obama administration to target and kill al-Awlaki two years earlier. In the memo, Holder laid out the administration's case for why such measures had been necessary to protect the security of the nation. He based the justification not on al-Awlaki's inflammatory rhetoric but on intelligence that al-Awlaki had moved from the role of terrorist propagandist to one of senior leadership in al-Qaeda in the Arabian Peninsula (AQAP). Holder said the decision to target and kill al-Awlaki had been taken only after extensive review "involving top lawyers for the Pentagon, State Department, National Security Council and intelligence agencies" and only after the conclusion that he could not feasibly be captured alive and brought to a court for a hearing.[19]

In its justification for the targeted killing of al-Awlaki, the Obama administration argued that it was left with no other options to protect national security. Al-Awlaki had, in the estimation of officials, become a clear and present danger to the United States. In 2010 an anonymous counterterrorism official in the Obama administration told the *New York Times*, "American citizenship doesn't give you carte blanche to wage war against your own country."[20]

The targeted killing of al-Awlaki and other American citizens in the war on terror is a hotly debated issue in the nation's politics. In this chapter, we will use the targeted killing and imprisonment of Americans without trial as a lens to focus on what is probably the most powerful job in the world: the American presidency. In doing so, the goal will not be to debate the use of drones or the targeted assassination of Americans in other nations—though that is certainly a topic worthy of careful and reasoned discussion. Instead, the goal will be to gain a deeper understanding of the power that American presidents have and reflect upon the proper limits to the exercise of that power in the twenty-first century.

1. The executive branch of government is charged with putting the nation's laws into effect.

   a. True
   b. False

2. Obama administration officials conceded that for the first time since the Civil War, the United States government had _____.

   a. Carried out the deliberate killing of an American citizen as a wartime enemy and without a trial
   b. Found an American citizen guilty of treason and revoked his citizenship

   c. Found a foreign national guilty of being a terrorist and sentenced him to life in prison in the United States
   d. None of the above

3. What justifications did the Obama administration offer for its action against al-Awlaki? What criticisms did it receive?

Answer Key: 1. a; 2. a; 3. Answers might include a discussion of how the administration argued that al-Awlaki had become a member of the organization's leadership as well as concerns that he was an American citizen who was targeted and killed without trial.

THE CONSTITUTION AND THE AMERICAN PRESIDENCY
A Vague Description of the Most Complicated Job in the World

TOPICS IN AMERICAN GOVERNMENT
Presidential power

In the Virginia Plan, even James Madison, who had given more thought to creating a new type of republic than any of the other delegates to the Constitutional Convention, had worked out few specifics for what his proposal called the "National Executive." In fact, both the Virginia Plan and the New Jersey Plan literally left the length of the executive's term blank, to be worked out later. The New Jersey Plan also failed to specify the number of chief executives. Like so many other details involving the office, the agreement that there would be one president was worked out in committee and through individual votes in the convention. Some provisions, especially the method of electing presidents, were sources of intense conflict. The job that the delegates ended up creating had no real

The Constitution

As you read about the American presidency as established in the original Constitution and subsequent amendments, reflect upon the controversy surrounding the proper limits of presidential authority in protecting the nation from terrorism. Consider the following:

- The dilemma of establishing an office that was robust and effective but would not lead to tyranny
- The multiple roles assigned to the American president and how fulfilling all of these roles might present challenges to the officeholder
- The challenges created by the sharing of war-making authority between the president and Congress

precedent, though delegates looked to the constitutions of the individual states and other sources for its formation.

Delegates to the convention were in general agreement that the new government would have to be more powerful than that under the Articles of Confederation. That confederal government had been in perpetual financial crisis, often unable to coerce individual states to contribute sufficient funds to allow it to operate effectively. While the framers of the Constitution knew that the executive needed to be powerful enough to lead, they also feared that the office might become too powerful. They were in no mood to recreate the tyranny of the British monarchy with an elected one on American shores.

The most prominent advocate for a strong and single executive was James Madison's ally, James Wilson of Pennsylvania, whom George Washington considered "one of the strongest men in the convention."[21] According to presidential scholar Clinton Rossiter, "Persistent voices were raised against almost every arrangement that eventually appeared in Article II [which describes the presidency], and Wilson and his colleagues were able to score their final success only after a series of debates, decisions, reconsiderations, references to committees, and private maneuvers that still leave the historian befuddled."[22]

Selection, Qualifications for Office, and Length of Terms

Once they settled on a single president, the most contentious issue facing the delegates was how this person was going to be selected. The factionalized debate between less populous and more populous states that had resulted in the bicameral Congress reared its head once again. Less populous states feared that direct popular election of the president would see their states' interests swallowed up by their more populous neighbors. Most delegates assumed that voters would pick candidates from their own states. Many delegates also mistrusted the ability of Americans to responsibly directly elect a president. In the end, the delegates agreed to a complicated method of presidential selection, one that did not involve direct popular election. Instead, electors, chosen by state legislatures and apportioned to states based on congressional representation, were to choose the president.

Although they debated terms ranging from four to fifteen years for the president—some with and some without the possibility of reelection—the delegates settled on a term of four years with the possibility of reelection. No limits were placed on the number of times a person could be elected president. The nation's first president, George Washington (1789–1797), chose not to seek a third term, however, establishing a precedent that held until Franklin Roosevelt (1933–1945) was elected four times.[23] Proposed and ratified largely in response to Roosevelt's multiple terms, the Twenty-second Amendment (1951) prohibited future presidents from being elected more than twice, and only once if that person had assumed the office (due to a death, resignation, or impeachment) more than two years prior to the end of that partial term.

To be eligible to hold the office of the presidency, the delegates stipulated a candidate had to be "a natural born Citizen, or a Citizen of the United States at the time of the Adoption of this

> The framers were in no mood to recreate the tyranny of the British monarchy with an elected one on American shores.

Constitution" as well as having "attained to the Age of thirty-five years, and been fourteen years a Resident within the United States" (Article II, Section 1). The Constitution did not explicitly prohibit women from holding the office; however, at the time of ratification, women were generally denied the right to vote or hold political office within their states.[24]

Presidential Powers and Roles

One of the main reasons that the method of selecting the president caused so much debate was that as the summer of 1787 progressed, the office grew in power and scope. According to historian Max Farrand, "From an official designed to be, at the outset of the convention, a dependent of the legislature, the executive had developed into an independent figure of importance."[25] The expectation that Washington, trusted and admired throughout the nation, would be the first president may have allayed delegates' concerns about the powerful office that they were creating. Although the convention settled on the simple title of president of the United States, Washington was said to have preferred, "His High Mightiness, the President of the United States and Protector of their Liberties."[26]

When the delegates hammered out the framework of the American presidency, they created an institution that had never been seen on a national scale. In some ways there is still no exact equivalent to its scope and complexity in modern democracies. The powers placed in the president's hands are threefold. Expressed (or enumerated) powers are those given to the president explicitly in the Constitution. Implied powers, though not laid out in the text, are assumed as part of the president's expressed powers as they are necessary to carry out the expressed powers. Delegated powers are those that Congress grants to the president in order to execute, or carry out, the laws that Congress has passed (hence the name the *executive branch*). In wielding these three types of powers, the American president assumes a variety of roles.[27]

A portrait of George Washington, the first president of the United States, circa 1796. That Washington was so respected a figure may have calmed fears that the executive office would be overly powerful.

Universal History Archive/Getty Images.

Chief Executive

As the head of the executive branch, the president is responsible for carrying out the laws of the nation. He or she oversees what has become a large and complex system of agencies and bureaucracies in order to do so. The Constitution, however, does not offer many specifics as to what it means to execute the laws. Article II, which is devoted to the presidency, begins, "The executive Power shall be vested in a President of the United States of America."[28] When taking the oath of office, the president promises to "faithfully execute the Office of the President of the United States" and is later instructed to "take Care that the Laws be faithfully executed."[29]

Other than that, the Constitution does not give much detail on *how* the president is supposed to run the federal government.

Presidents *are* given some help, however. They are authorized to "require the Opinion, in writing, of the principal Office in each of the executive Departments, upon any Subject relating to the Duties of their respective Offices."[30] Though not mentioned by name, the president's cabinet has evolved into a powerful source of information and a point of contact with the nation's sprawling federal bureaucracy. It also provides a way to reward individuals and members of important interest groups for past (and future) support through their appointment to positions within the cabinet.

Modern presidents have the authority to appoint individuals to thousands of administrative positions, from his or her closest advisors and heads of large agencies to lower level administrative staff. Roughly one thousand of these appointments require Senate confirmation. Presidents also nominate individuals to serve as judges in the federal judiciary, with each nomination also requiring Senate confirmation. A president may make a **recess appointment** without Senate confirmation while Congress is not in session, but the term of the recess appointment ends at the conclusion of that congressional term.

Chief Diplomat

The president is also responsible for guiding U.S. foreign policy and interacting with the heads of other nations. The president is authorized "to make Treaties," to "appoint Ambassadors," and to "receive Ambassadors and other public Ministers."[31] This diplomatic power is partly symbolic and ceremonial; it involves elaborate state dinners and parties and, in the case of President Obama's reception of British prime minister David Cameron in 2012, courtside seats to the NCAA men's basketball tournament.

The diplomatic power of the president also helps to shape national foreign policy. While Congress, particularly the Senate, plays a major role in foreign affairs, the fact that the president is one person—and not 100 or 435, as is the case for the Senate and House—gives him or her an advantage over Congress in the ability to act quickly and decisively on the international stage. As Rossiter put it, "Secrecy, dispatch, unity, continuity, and access to information—the ingredients of successful diplomacy—are properties of his office, and Congress . . . possesses none of them."[32]

Chief Legislator

In devising a system where power was to be shared between the three branches, the framers gave the president a limited and mostly negative role in the legislative process. However, this role has since been extended quite far.

The president is directed to "from time to time give Congress Information of the State of the Union" (Article II, Section 3). Constitutionally, a president might possibly get away with just tweeting Congress, reporting with a simple ☺. For much of the nation's history, presidents sent written reports to Congress without actually addressing the legislative branch in person. Today, however, no president would pass on the opportunity provided by the **State of the Union Address** to speak live on television before Congress, members of the Supreme Court, the military, and, most importantly, the entire nation. In the address, a president often encourages or cajoles Congress to pass key pieces of his or her legislative agenda. The real audience, however, is the American people, and presidents use the address to try to mobilize support and pressure members of Congress to act.

The president is also expected to "recommend to their [Congress's] Consideration such Measures as he shall judge necessary and expedient."[33] While, as we saw in Chapter 12,

recess appointment
occurs when Congress is not in session and the president appoints a person to fill a position that would normally require the advice and consent of the Senate. Unless the person is formally confirmed when the Senate reconvenes, the position ends at the conclusion of that session of Congress.

NEWS CLIP
Recap of Obama's last State of the Union Address

State of the Union Address
the annual, constitutionally required transmittal of information from the president to Congress updating that branch on the state of national affairs.

Familiarity and Formality in Presidential Diplomacy

Compare the two images shown here. At top, President Barack Obama chats with British prime minister David Cameron at the NCAA men's basketball tournament on March 13, 2012. In the second photo, Samantha Cameron, First Lady Michelle Obama, Prime Minister Cameron, and President Obama pose for a photo before a state dinner for the prime minister and his wife on March 14, 2012.

WHAT DO YOU THINK?

How might strategic presidents use different settings to receive and entertain foreign leaders and other important individuals? What messages can a president send to audiences at home and abroad through the images of these different kinds of receptions?

only members of Congress can formally introduce bills, presidents work with party leaders in both chambers to shape the legislative agenda. Finally, the president is given the power to veto legislation, although this veto is subject to a potential override by a two-thirds vote in both chambers. Individual presidents have varied considerably in the use (and successful use) of the veto. Overrides are rare; marshalling the required two-thirds vote in both chambers is usually very difficult to do. The mere threat of a presidential veto is often enough to shape a piece of legislation more to a president's liking.[34] Vetoes are more likely during periods of divided government, when one or both chambers of Congress are under the control of a party other than that of the president.

Commander in Chief

Perhaps the most fateful role that the Constitution creates for the president is his or her authority as "Commander in Chief of the Army and Navy of the United States, and of the Militia of the several States."[35] The president is at the top of the entire military chain of command, including the strategic nuclear forces of the nation. No president is ever intentionally far from the so-called nuclear football; the contents of this heavy briefcase are classified but have traditionally included communications equipment and strategic plans and codes for a variety of nuclear combat scenarios. It is an awesome responsibility. Every president "is never for one day allowed to forget that he will be held accountable by

NEWS CLIP
White House Easter Egg Roll celebrates First Lady's initiatives

NEWS CLIP
Obama explains military strategy to defeat ISIL

A military aide carries a briefcase with the classified U.S. nuclear war plan aboard Air Force One to join the president.

AP Photo/Cliff Owen.

people, Congress, and history for the nation's readiness to meet an enemy assault."[36]

For the framers of the Constitution, the war-making power of the presidency was a limited one; it was designed so the president could efficiently lead the American armed forces during a time of war. According to political scientist Edward Corwin, "The war power, as it was known to the framers of the Constitution, embraced . . . three relatively simple elements. . . . Recruiting, which was on a voluntary basis for the most part . . . the problem of supply [and] the power to command the forces."[37] While giving Congress the broader power to "make war" and not just declare it had been discussed during the Constitutional Convention, it was feared that the nation might be unable to respond quickly to threats when Congress was not in session. Therefore, the president was also given a role in national war making, though "the Commander-in-chief clause remained 'the forgotten clause' of the Constitution for the early decades of the nation's history.[38] That would change, however.

Pardons

presidential pardon
the presidential authority to forgive an individual and set aside punishment for a crime.

Another power the Constitution carves out for the president is the ability to issue a **pardon**. The "Power to grant Reprieves and Pardons for Offenses against the United States, except in Cases of Impeachment," allows the president to release individuals convicted of federal crimes from all legal consequences and restore their benefits of citizenship.[39] Presidents often grant pardons in the final days and weeks of office. In cases where it appears that

TABLE 13.1 Powers and Limits to Powers of the President

Enumerated, Implied, and Delegated Powers	Limits to Powers
The President may. . . .	*Congress may. . .*
Execute the nation's laws	Investigate or impeach the president
Submit the annual federal budget	Pass the budget
Appoint and seek the advice of cabinet departments	Confirm, delay, or block nominations
Shape foreign policy by enacting treaties, appointing ambassadors, and conducting diplomacy	Ratify treaties
Provide information and make policy recommendations to Congress; veto congressional legislation	Override vetoes
Act as commander in chief of the armed forces	Declare war and fund the armed forces
Deliver pardons, but may not pardon individuals who have been impeached	Neither the legislature nor the judiciary may override a pardon

pardoned individuals have close personal or professional ties to the president, this practice can be quite controversial.

Limitations on the Powers of the Presidency

The framers also placed limitations on the power of the office, primarily by granting specific powers to Congress and the federal judiciary.[40] In most circumstances, the judicial branch has little involvement with presidential actions and responsibilities. Congress, however, is a different story. Presidents cannot accomplish most of their objectives without at the very least a lack of opposition by Congress, as the Constitution places in Congress's hands several negative checks on presidential action. Presidents need majority support in Congress to pass the laws, create and fund the programs, and confirm the presidential appointments that are necessary to fully realize their policy objectives. The president must obtain from the Senate majority approval to confirm appointments to the federal judiciary as well as to many executive branch offices. Ratification of a treaty requires a two-thirds vote in the Senate.[41] With a two-thirds vote in each chamber, Congress can override a presidential veto, though veto overrides are relatively uncommon given the high vote hurdle needed to succeed.

Congress has the power to impeach the president (as well as "the Vice President and all civil Officers of the United States") for the vaguely defined transgressions of "Treason, Bribery, or other high Crimes and Misdemeanors."[42] A majority vote in the House is needed to pass articles of impeachment. Once an officeholder is impeached, the trial takes place in the Senate. The chief justice of the Supreme Court presides over a presidential impeachment and a two-thirds vote is necessary to convict.[43]

Only two presidents have been impeached, and none have been removed from office. Andrew Johnson barely survived a Senate vote over political battles following the Civil War in 1868, and Bill Clinton avoided conviction over charges of perjury and obstruction of justice during an investigation into his involvement with a White House intern, Monica Lewinsky, in 1998. President Richard Nixon would almost certainly have been impeached and convicted for his role in covering up a break-in at the Democratic Party national headquarters (the so-called Watergate Affair) in 1972. He resigned from office in 1974 before a House vote took place, however, and received a pardon from his successor, President Gerald R. Ford, later that year.

1. The delegates to the Constitutional Convention were in general agreement on the basic structure of the American presidency when they convened.

   a. True
   b. False

2. George Washington's role in the Constitutional Convention helped to shape the American presidency because _____.

   a. He was a forceful advocate for a strong national executive
   b. Most delegates agreed that he would be the first individual to fill the post

   c. He wrote the sections of the Constitution dealing with war-making authority
   d. All of the above

3. The American president serves as the nation's _____.

   a. Chief executive
   b. Chief diplomat
   c. Commander in chief
   d. All of the above

4. Why did the framers divide war-making authority between the president and Congress?

Answer Key: 1. b; 2. b; 3. d; 4. Answers should discuss issues of expediency and separation of powers.

WHAT HAVE I LEARNED?

TESTING THE LIMITS OF PRESIDENTIAL POWER DURING THE AMERICAN CIVIL WAR

When President Obama ordered the targeted killing of Anwar al-Awlaki, he did so with the conviction that he was acting within his constitutional powers as the commander in chief of the United States. Some questioned whether this was in fact true. What is not up for debate, however, is that Obama was not the first American president to challenge the boundaries of war-making authority in the name of national security. He would not likely be the last, as President-elect Donald Trump made several promises on the campaign trail that indicated his willingness to use drone strikes and other tactics against ISIS and other potential targets.

On a Tuesday morning in May 1861, Roger Brooke Taney, then chief justice of the United States Supreme Court, entered a federal courtroom in Baltimore, Maryland. He was about to take on the most powerful man in what remained of the United States: President Abraham Lincoln (1861–1865). The chief justice began reading from a memorandum that he had prepared for that day's hearing. "A huge crowd, estimated by some as large as two thousand had formed on St. Paul Street on the morning of the hearing and the federal courtroom was jammed."[44]

Taney demanded the body—alive and in person—of one John Merryman, a Marylander being held in a federal fort in Baltimore Harbor. Merryman was suspected of burning railroad bridges, cutting telegraph lines, and being in possession of stolen Union rifles. It was believed he committed all these crimes in the aid of the secessionist forces operating in Maryland in the early weeks of the Civil War.

A *New York Times* article published that spring described Merryman as "a man of family, and a gentleman of property and position."[45] He was also a slave owner, sympathetic to the southern states. Merryman's property, Hayfields, which was inherited from his wife's family, "included more than five hundred acres of the best land in Maryland, with a mineral-rich soil that produced prodigious crops of the hay for which the farm was named."[46] The Merrymans had been in Maryland since at least the 1600s and were prominent figures in the state's elite social and political circles.

To many in the American South, Merryman became a symbol of resistance to northern aggression. To the northern military commanders who detained him, he might easily have been thought of (in modern terms) as a terrorist. By the time of Merryman's detention, the United States of America was already at war—with itself. President Abraham Lincoln struggled to hold the Union together in the face of armed conflict and the secession of southern states.

The Civil War remains the bloodiest and costliest conflict in the nation's history. By the war's end, many parts of the South—its plantations, towns, and cities—had been burned to the ground or bombarded into rubble. Some six hundred thousand American soldiers died in the war, or about 2 percent of the nation's population. An unknown number of civilians were killed as well. On one day, at Cold Harbor in 1864, Union forces suffered seven thousand casualties in less than an hour.[47] In 1866, the year following the Union victory, the state of Mississippi spent one-fifth of its budget on artificial limbs.[48]

The "Body" of John Merryman: Presidential Power and the Civil War

Just over a month before Taney sat down in the federal courtroom, a mob had attacked Union soldiers in Baltimore en route to Washington, D.C.; "a perfect shower of paving stones rained on their heads."[49] According to testimony from an observer, a local police officer assaulted one of the Union soldiers "and broke his head with a spontoon, crying, 'You black son of a bitch you came here to fight us white men.'"[50] Someone fired a pistol into the group of soldiers, and the soldiers—frightened and disorganized—fired upon the mob.[51] Four Union soldiers and twelve civilians died in the violence. Reports began to come in that southern sympathizers were tearing up railroad tracks. "Civil War," the *New York Times* reported, "has commenced."[52] Maryland, like the nation, was tearing itself apart.

Four days later, John Merryman, a member of the secessionist Baltimore County Horse Guards—acting, he said, on orders from a former United States Army captain—oversaw and led the burning of at least six railroad bridges and the toppling of telegraph lines along the Northern Central Railroad, one of the key military links between Washington, D.C., and the Union states of the North. According to witnesses,

> Barking orders, repeatedly citing his "authority," Merryman proclaimed his intention to stop Northern troops from invading Maryland. "God damn them," he shouted at one place, "We'll stop them from coming down and stealing our slaves." . . . At another bridge, Merryman ordered his men to cut telegraph lines, then ordered some bystanders to overturn a water cask kept at the bridge to protect it against fire. When the bystanders hesitated, Merryman drew his sword, his men drew their pistols, and the bystanders complied with his orders. Camphene was poured on the bridge and the structure was set afire.[53]

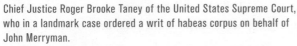

Chief Justice Roger Brooke Taney of the United States Supreme Court, who in a landmark case ordered a writ of habeas corpus on behalf of John Merryman.

The Granger Collection, New York.

John Merryman, prominent Maryland citizen, was accused of acts of treason and held in a Union prison under the authority of President Abraham Lincoln, his writ of habeas corpus having been denied.

Courtesy of Archives of Maryland.

FIGURE 13.1

The United States at the Start of the Civil War

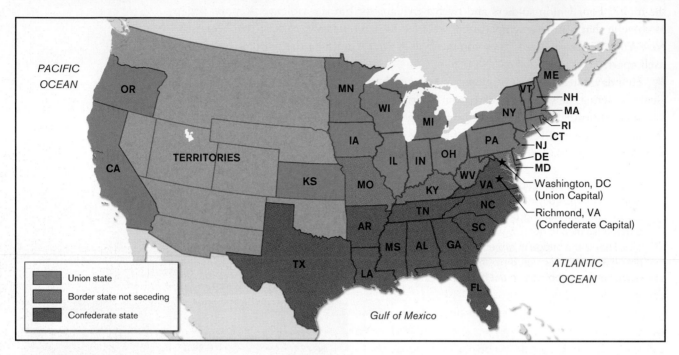

The map in Figure 13.1 shows Union states to the north and Confederate states to the south. Lincoln knew that ensuring the border states (shown in yellow) did not secede was key to winning the war. Maryland, where John Merryman was jailed for treason, was one of the most important of these states: if it joined the Confederacy, the Union's capital in Washington, D.C., would be nearly impossible to defend.

President Lincoln knew that keeping the border states from joining the South was absolutely key to any hope of winning the war and reconstituting the Union, and Maryland was one of the most important of these states. If Maryland were lost, then the Union's capital would be nearly impossible to defend as it would be cut off from supplies and reinforcements by land. In a letter later that year, Lincoln confessed, "Kentucky gone, we can not hold Missouri, nor, as I think, Maryland. These all against us, and the job on our hands is too large for us. We would as well consent to separation at once, including the surrender of this capitol."[54]

Lincoln used the full force of his presidency to ensure the border states remained in the Union. During the eleven weeks between Lincoln's call for Congress to meet in special session and the beginning of the session on July 4, Lincoln called up state militias, blockaded southern ports, expanded the army and the navy, spent $2 million from the U.S. Treasury, "closed the Post Office to 'treasonable correspondence' . . . suspended the writ of habeas corpus in certain localities, [and] caused the arrest and detention of persons who were 'represented to him as being engaged in treasonable practices'—and all this, except for the calls to state militias, without any statutory authorization."[55]

At 2:00 a.m. on the morning of May 25, 1861, federal troops roused Merryman from his bed and took him to Fort McHenry in Baltimore Harbor where, according to Taney, he was "imprisoned by the commanding officer, without warrant from any lawful authority . . . upon charges of treason and rebellion, without proof and without giving the names of the witnesses, or specifying the acts which, in the judgment of the military officer, constituted these crimes."[56]

As he was from a prominent family and had powerful political connections in Maryland, Merryman's detention did not go unnoticed. Within hours of his internment at the federal fort, Merryman's lawyers arrived and prepared a petition for his release.[57] Taney received Merryman's petition and issued a writ of habeas corpus on his behalf, calling on the Union general in charge of the fort to produce "the body of John Merryman"[58] so the charges against him could be examined.[59] Habeas corpus—from the Latin "you [shall] have the body"—defines a procedure through which a person can challenge what they see as unlawful detention. If Taney's writ of habeas corpus in the case of Merryman was honored, either an arrest warrant would be issued for Merryman or Merryman would be free to go.

When he entered the Baltimore courtroom that Tuesday, Taney was almost certainly impatient and angry. The Union commander had refused to honor the writ. Instead, he sent an aide, who showed up in Taney's courtroom without Merryman. "The commanding officer, then, declined to obey the writ?" Taney asked.[60] The general's aide tried to sidestep the direct question, but the answer was clear: Merryman was being held under the authority of President Lincoln and was not to be released, not even upon the demand of the chief justice of the Supreme Court. According to Baltimore mayor George William Brown, "A more important question could hardly have occurred. Where did the president acquire such a power? Was it true that a citizen held his liberty subject to the arbitrary will of any man? In what part of the Constitution could such a power be found?"[61]

Abraham Lincoln, left, shown here with Chief Justice Roger Brooke Taney at Lincoln's inauguration on March 4, 1861. *Ex parte Merryman* pitted the two men against one another in a watershed case that tested the limits of executive power.

ullstein bild via Getty Images.

Taney threatened to arrest the fort's commander if his orders were not followed and directed the aide to have the commander produce Merryman by noon the next day, Tuesday, May 28. Taney's demand, however, was never delivered to the commander; the marshal carrying the writ was not even allowed beyond the fort's gates. Merryman remained imprisoned, without a trial or an arrest warrant, under the authority of the president of the United States.

On that Tuesday morning, having been twice rebuffed, Taney began to prepare to confront the president. He wrote an opinion that he delivered to Lincoln within the week.[62] In that opinion, *Ex parte Merryman* (1861), Taney challenged the president's authority to suspend writs of habeas corpus, even in times of war and rebellion. "The President, under the Constitution and laws of the United States," Taney declared, "cannot suspend the privilege of the writ of *habeas corpus*, nor authorize any military officer to do so."[63]

Taney had just issued a direct challenge to Lincoln and his use of the power of the American presidency in fighting the Civil War. "Never before had a judicial officer—much less the presiding justice of the highest court in the United States—taken so strong and so vehement a stand against executive authority."[64] The confrontation between Taney and Lincoln was much more than a fight between two powerful, intelligent, and—according to some—stubborn lawyers, as both the chief justice and the president were.

Their confrontation spoke to the heart of the Constitution. It spoke to the limitations on the power of the presidency and just how far Americans would, or should, let those limits be pushed during times of national crisis and war.

President Lincoln's Actions to Preserve the Union

Taney issued his challenge to Lincoln after having observed a series of unprecedented presidential actions. What remained of the Union was at war with the seven secessionist states of the American South, which had left the Union and formed the Confederate States of America.[65] At 4:30 a.m. on April 12, 1861, Confederate troops began firing on Fort Sumter in the harbor outside of Charleston, South Carolina. Brigadier General P. G. T. Beauregard, the Confederate officer in charge of the artillery bombardment, had been such a talented student at West Point that his instructor had asked him to stay on for an extra year as an assistant. That instructor, General Robert Anderson, was in command of the fort. Such was the nature of the Civil War. Some thirty-four hours after the southern guns opened up, Anderson surrendered the fort to the Confederate forces.

Abraham Lincoln, shown in a photograph taken in April 1861. This is likely the first photograph of Lincoln as president.

The Granger Collection, New York.

After learning about the fall of Fort Sumter on April 14, Lincoln undertook a series of actions over the next several months that he believed were necessary to preserve the Union. These actions, however, expanded the power of the American presidency, quickly and radically, and set the stage for his battle with Taney.

On April 15, Lincoln issued a proclamation: "I, Abraham Lincoln, President of the United States, in virtue of the power in me vested by the Constitution, and the laws, have thought fit to call forth, and hereby do call forth the, the militia of the several States of the Union, to the aggregate number of seventy-five thousand, in order to suppress said combinations, and to cause the laws to be duly executed."[66] Lincoln also summoned Congress to a special session, which was to begin at noon on July 4, 1861, "to consider and determine, such measures as, in their wisdom, the public safety, and interest may seem to demand."[67] Lincoln's April 15 proclamation had an immediate and incendiary effect in the South. Fearing and expecting a military invasion by the recently called Union militia, four more southern states seceded.[68]

Keeping the railroad lines open between the nation's capital and the rest of the Union was very much a part of the president's overall strategy. The Northern Central Railroad, which ran between Harrisburg, Pennsylvania, and Baltimore, Maryland, was one of these critical military lines and the one that Merryman and his associates had severed on the night of April 19, 1861. To Lincoln, Merryman's actions constituted nothing less than treason against the government of the United States and a direct threat to national security. On April 25,

Lincoln authorized General Winfield Scott to take all necessary action against pro-secessionist mobs in Maryland, including "in the extremist necessity, the suspension of the writ of habeas corpus."[69] Merryman was detained under the authority of these orders without trial.

It was this power that Taney challenged in *Ex parte Merryman*. In his opinion, Taney acknowledged that the federal government had the power to suspend the writ of habeas corpus during times of rebellion or invasion; the Constitution provides for this.[70] However, Taney argued that it is Congress, not the president, who has such authority. The text granting the power, the chief justice noted, lies within Article I of the Constitution, which is devoted to the structure and powers of Congress, not the executive branch. And, Taney continued, it is to the judicial branch that the power to issue arrest warrants is given, not the president or the military under his command. The president, therefore, "has exercised a power which he does not possess under the Constitution."[71]

Taney helped ensure that his opinion in *Ex parte Merryman* was heard across the country. It was printed in pamphlets and circulated in newspapers in both the North and the South. On the key constitutional question of whether the president had the authority to suspend writs of habeas corpus in times of rebellion or invasion, however, the Supreme Court had not decided.

Although Taney accused Lincoln of exceeding his constitutional authority, he did not order the president to release Merryman, acknowledging that his power as a member of the judicial branch "has been resisted by a force too strong for me to overcome." Instead, the chief justice declared, "It will then remain for that high officer [meaning President Lincoln] . . . to determine what measures he will take to cause the civil process of the United States to be respected and enforced."[72] To Taney, the constitutional question was obvious. The political calculations, however, were much more complicated.

Addressing the assembled Congress on July 4, 1861, Lincoln justified to members of Congress and the Union "these actions of dubious constitutionality by reference to the 'war powers' granted to the executive."[73] Congress retroactively approved most of Lincoln's actions taken that year. However, it did not approve the suspension of habeas corpus (with some limits) until 1863, after the president had issued a broader suspension of the privilege the year before.[74]

> "The Constitution is an easily dispensable factor of our war effort . . . transforming it, during wartime, from a *Constitution of Rights* into a *Constitution of Powers*."

Such drastic unilateral presidential action in times of war and national crisis led political scientist Edward S. Corwin to conclude that "the Constitution is an easily dispensable factor of our war effort—perhaps one might say 'expendable' factor," transforming it, during wartime, "from a *Constitution of Rights* into a *Constitution of Powers*."[75]

President Lincoln's Justification for His Wartime Powers: Strong and Temporary Medicine

John Merryman's legal battles continued throughout the Civil War, though he would be freed from the federal fort in the summer of 1861 as it began to fill up. He was indicted for treason in 1861 and again in 1863. Merryman's cases proceeded slowly because Taney, who was in charge of the court where Merryman would be tried, repeatedly delayed the cases and others like them. Charges against Merryman were formally dropped in 1867. "Habeas Corpus John," as his friends and neighbors called him, died in 1881 on his farm at Hayfields, which is now the site of a country club and golf course.[76]

Taney expected to be impeached or even arrested over his confrontation with Lincoln, and Lincoln is said to have contemplated it. In the end, however, the president simply ignored Taney, prosecuting the war with whatever means he saw necessary in order to restore the Union. In a lengthy letter written in 1863—when the outcome of the Civil War was still far from certain—Lincoln defended his suspension of habeas corpus and other measures as valid uses of the constitutional power of the government "when in cases of Rebellion or Invasion the public Safety may require it."[77] Lincoln compared his use of extraordinary measures to those a physician might use for the benefit of a sick patient, claiming,

> I can no more be persuaded that the government can constitutionally take no strong measure in time of rebellion, because it can be shown that the same could not lawfully be taken in time of peace, that I can be persuaded that a particular drug is not good medicine for a sick man, because it can be shown not to be good for a well one. Nor am I able to appreciate the danger . . . that the American people will, by means of military arrests during the rebellion, lose the right of public discussion, the liberty of speech and the press, the law of evidence, trial by jury, and Habeas corpus, throughout the indefinite peaceful future which I trust lies before them, any more than I am able to believe that a man could contract so strong an appetite for emetics during temporary illness, as to persist in feeding upon them through the remainder of his healthful life.[78]

For Lincoln, the powers that he had to assume during the war—like the strong medicine given by a physician—would no longer be necessary once the crisis was successfully resolved. In this prediction, he proved to be correct. Presidential power in the decades following the Union victory in the Civil War did recede, and Congress once again assumed its position as the strongest of the three branches. As America again confronted war in the twentieth and twenty-first centuries, however, future presidents also tested the limits of executive branch power in the face of new threats to national security.

INDIVIDUALS AND THE DEVELOPMENT OF PRESIDENTIAL POWER

Since George Washington was inaugurated as the nation's first president in 1789, the institution of the American presidency has undergone a major transformation, one that would likely seem remarkable to the framers of the Constitution. The office has grown in power, prestige, and complexity, "not smoothly but with great leaps, periods of dormancy, and occasional setbacks."[79] These changes have been affected by the actions, choices, and strategic behavior of the individuals who have held the nation's highest office.

When scholars examine the development of the presidency, they often, and for many good reasons, focus on what some have called the "great presidents"—those individuals who left office having strengthened or transformed the presidency. However, the "forgotten presidents" have mattered as well. Their inaction or stumbles have also contributed to the grand narrative, even if by doing nothing more than helping shift the balance of power toward Congress and away from the Oval Office.

Over the centuries—and across all of the great and small dramas of the national political stage—the presidency has grown more powerful, as has the federal government in general. This has occurred through a process in which individual presidents have, whether out of opportunity or necessity, seized upon crises and key turning points in American political development to redefine the boundaries of their power and influence.

CONNECTING TO . . .

Presidential Power

As you read about how individual presidents have expanded the power of the office, consider the following:

- How the political skills of individual presidents play a part in carving out the powers of the office

- The role that national crises, especially national security crises, have played in the expansion of the power of the American presidency

George Washington (1789-1797).

George Washington helped to shape the office even before becoming the nation's first president. Delegates to the Constitutional Convention—over which Washington presided—generally expected that he would be chosen as the country's first chief executive. Whether the delegates would have been more reluctant to place powers in the office had they not assumed the respected and trusted general would be the first to fill it is difficult to know for sure. However, some of the delegates themselves indicated the calming influence of Washington's likely assumption of the role. In May 1788, delegate Pierce Butler wrote of the presidency that he and his colleagues had created, "I am free to acknowledge that His Powers are full great, and greater than I was disposed to make them. Nor, Entre Nous [between us], do I believe they would have been so great had not many of the members cast their eyes towards General Washington as President; and shaped their Ideas of the Powers to be given to a President, by their opinions of his Virtue."[80]

As he was the first president, everything Washington did set a precedent for his successors, intentionally or not. Whether or not future presidents chose to follow his lead, Washington's decisions cast a shadow over their terms in office. By establishing regular meetings with heads of executive branch departments, Washington laid the foundations of the modern cabinet system. Two major tours, one of the northern states in 1789 and another of the southern states in 1791, linked the office to the people of the entire nation. His suppression of the Whiskey Rebellion in 1794 "helped establish both the idea of the supremacy of federal law and the power of the federal government to levy and collect taxes."[81] Washington retired from office after two terms, though he was not obligated to do so, thus setting a two-term precedent that was followed until Franklin Delano Roosevelt's election for four terms in the twentieth century.

Thomas Jefferson (1801-1809).

Jefferson came to office riding the wave of a major victory of his Democratic-Republic Party over the Federalist Party in the election of 1800. Using this power, Jefferson was "the first president to govern through personal leadership of a political party."[82] In his two terms in office, Jefferson did not veto a single bill. He did not have to. Since his party controlled Congress the president was able to use his influence to shape or kill legislation before it arrived on his desk. Possibly pushing the boundaries of his powers beyond their intended limits, Jefferson doubled—in one deal—the size of the nation with the Louisiana Purchase in 1803.

An image of President Andrew Jackson, seventh president of the United States, who was well known for his populism.

Stock Montage/Getty Images.

Andrew Jackson (1829-1837). Andrew Jackson was a rough and quick-tempered frontier man and a wealthy land and slave owner. Jackson gained the presidency during a period in which the presidential nominating process became more democratic and less under the control of powerful party men. With a power base among the American people—or, more precisely, among white workers, backwoodsmen, Irish immigrants, and farmers—Jackson was able to challenge both Congress and the Supreme Court.

His opponents portrayed him as uncouth and uncivilized and claimed he was supported by uneducated mobs, a charge to which Jackson helped give credence. His 1829 inaugural reception "was a brawl. People poured into the White House through windows as well as doors, upset waiters carrying trays of food, broke china and glassware, overturned tables . . . spilled whiskey and chicken and squirted tobacco juice on the carpets, and stood with muddy boots on the damask-covered chairs in order to get a good look at 'Old Hickory.'"[83]

The legacy of Jackson's connection to the people, however, was a double-edged sword, or, perhaps more appropriately given Jackson's history of duels with pistols, a double-barrelled weapon: "The electoral changes made the presidency more powerful vis-à-vis other branches, and also yet more dependent upon—and controlled by—the public."[84] To a president, Congress may be frustrating and seem obstinate. Party leaders may have their own power bases from which to challenge the chief executive. To rely on popular support for one's power, however, risks seeing that power erode quickly with the shifting and often unpredictable opinions of the American people.

Theodore Roosevelt (1901-1909). "Teddy" Roosevelt took office during a breathtaking period of growth in American industrial power and all of the social upheaval that this transformation brought about. He carried a "big stick" in foreign affairs, using the navy to demonstrate the nation's growing industrial might to both European powers and nations in the Western hemisphere. He intervened in Central and South American political affairs in order to promote and preserve American interests as he saw them. Roosevelt was also a national celebrity, by design: "He went on bear-hunting trips in the west, played tennis and took jujitsu lessons in the White House, and went horseback riding in the afternoon."[85] To Roosevelt, the presidency was a "bully pulpit" that he could use to shape and mobilize public opinion in support of his administration's objectives.

Woodrow Wilson (1913-1921). Woodrow Wilson was, in character and demeanor, as far from Teddy Roosevelt as one could get. To many, he came off as intolerant and arrogant. He was also firmly convinced that his presidency was part of a divine plan. After he was elected president, he told the chair of the Democratic National Committee (who helped get him there), *God ordained that I should be the next President of the United States. Neither you nor any other mortal could have prevented that!*[86]

Wilson took office with the goal of increasing the president's role in legislative affairs. He both succeeded and failed spectacularly in this. A skilled speaker, Wilson was the first president since John Adams (1797–1801) to deliver the State of the Union Address in person. His greatest legislative success was securing from Congress unprecedented control over the nation's economy during America's involvement in World War I (1914–1918).[87] These powers included the authority to "allocate food and fuel, to license trade with the enemy, to censor the mail, to regulate the foreign language press of the country, and to operate railroads, water transportation systems, and telegraph and telephone facilities."[88]

However, Wilson also saw the defeat in the Senate of the Treaty of Versailles—a treaty that he had helped write. The treaty included the League of Nations, which was his vision for an international governing body to prevent future catastrophes like World War I. Many scholars attribute the failed ratification at least partly to Wilson's stubbornness and refusal to compromise. Even though the country's president designed it, the League of Nations would not count the United States among its members.

President Woodrow Wilson (bottom row, center) with his cabinet in 1917.
The Granger Collection, New York.

Franklin Delano Roosevelt (1933–1945). Roosevelt responded to the economic crisis of the Great Depression by greatly expanding the size, scope, and power of the federal government as well as that of the executive branch within it. He sponsored a variety of programs and policies, collectively known as the New Deal, aimed at helping those suffering from the Depression. Responding to the military crisis of World War II (1939–1945), Roosevelt "carried the wartime Presidency to breath-taking heights of authority of the American economy and social order."[89] He created an alphabet of bureaucratic organizations to oversee the mobilization of the American economy in pursuit of military victory. The agencies, which the president claimed were advisory only, "rested on no statutory foundation" but instead on the "President simply by virtue of power which he claimed as Commander-in-Chief."[90] Roosevelt used the power of his voice—carried via the radio into living rooms for his "fireside chats"—to rally support for the war effort. He encouraged Americans to buy war bonds to finance the war and to remain committed to the cause and confident of a victorious outcome.

Lyndon Baines Johnson (1963–1969). Johnson was able to use his perhaps unequalled skill in working with, cajoling, and arm-twisting members of Congress in pursuit of his vision of a Great Society, in which the power of the federal government was put to work in order to eradicate poverty and racial and social injustice. He was an excellent, if sometimes crude, storyteller and a tireless campaigner. In spite of his achievements in domestic policy, however, Johnson's dramatic expansion of the conflict in Vietnam eclipsed all else. The war was becoming increasingly unpopular, and more and more people were saying that it could not be won, Johnson chose not to run for a second term in 1968.[91] To a

President Richard Nixon and Chinese premier Zhou Enlai toast during Nixon's unprecedented trip to China in 1972.

AFP/Getty Images.

War Powers Resolution
A law passed over President Nixon's veto that restricts the power of the president in committing the nation's armed forces into combat or situations of likely combat.

biographer, Johnson later lamented, "I knew from the start that if I left the woman I really loved—the Great Society—in order to fight that bitch of a war . . . then I would lose everything at home. All my hopes . . . my dreams."[92]

Richard Milhous Nixon (1969-1974).

Nixon's presidency is considered one of the most troubled in American history. He is the only president to have resigned from office. He did so because he was facing near-certain impeachment and conviction for his role in covering up illegal activities, including a break-in at the Democratic Party headquarters at the Watergate office complex in 1972. The break-in was part of a misguided and illegal set of strategies for a reelection that Nixon would have won easily. However, Nixon's efforts to build relations with China, which included a visit to that country in 1972, have been credited as an important step in U.S.-Chinese relations. These efforts were important as the United States sought to drive a wedge between China and the Soviet Union during the Cold War.

The **War Powers Resolution (1973),** passed despite Nixon's veto, has been one of the most enduring and controversial legacies of his presidency.[93] Initially intended by its sponsors to reassert congressional authority over the introduction of American armed forces into combat, the resolution is credited by some scholars as being "the high-water mark of congressional reassertion in national security affairs."[94] Passed during the weakening of Nixon's authority as the Watergate investigations unfolded, the resolution was the product of widespread public and congressional dissatisfaction with the prosecution and expansion of the Vietnam conflict as well as unilateral presidential actions carried out by Johnson and Nixon.

Drawing on Congress's authority under the necessary and proper clause of the Constitution, the resolution's stated purpose was "to fulfill the intent of the framers of the Constitution of the United States and insure that the collective judgment of both the Congress and the President will apply to the introduction of United States Armed Forces into hostilities, or into situations where imminent involvement in hostilities is clearly indicated by the circumstances, and to the continued use of such forces in hostilities or in such situations."[95]

Under the terms of the War Powers Resolution, a president may only introduce armed forces into conflict or likely conflict if one of the three following conditions is present:

1. "A declaration of war [by Congress]," a

2. "specific statutory authorization [by Congress]," or

3. "a national emergency created by an attack on the United States, its territories or possessions, or its armed forces."[96]

Once introduced, the president is required within forty-eight hours to notify Congress of "the circumstances necessitating the introduction of United States Armed Forces; . . . the constitutional and legislative authority under which such introduction took place; and . . . the estimated scope and duration of the hostilities or involvement."[97] Unless Congress has declared war, passed specific authorization, extended the notification deadline, or is physically unable to meet, the president must withdraw those forces within sixty days, with a thirty-day extension allowed if necessary to withdraw those forces safely.[98]

The last war officially declared by Congress was World War II in 1941. Since that time, American armed forces have been stationed in more than one hundred countries, though many of these are allies or military partners. Presidents have often held that the War Powers Resolution unconstitutionally restricts their war power, though they have also routinely pursued congressional authorization of the use of military force consistent with the resolution. Some critics of the resolution argue that it actually makes the president more powerful since he or she may feel less constrained during those sixty or ninety days than they would if the resolution did not exist.[99]

Ronald Reagan (1981–1989). Reagan, who earned the nickname "The Great Communicator," drew on his experience in film, television, and radio to connect to the American people and encourage their support of his initiatives, often to the dismay of Congress. Reagan did not only rely on his public voice and personality, however. He assembled an effective communications staff devoted to "managing the message" and controlling the media agenda to shape the national conversation in support of his policy objectives.

Chief of Staff Andrew Card whispers into the ear of President George W. Bush on the morning of the September 11, 2001, attacks during a visit to an elementary school in Sarasota, Florida.
AP Photo/Doug Mills.

George W. Bush (2001–2009). On the morning of September 11, 2001, Bush was reading aloud from an instructional book, *The Pet Goat*, to a second-grade classroom in Sarasota, Florida, when Chief of Staff Andrew Card whispered into his ear, "A second plane hit the second tower. America is under attack." Card was referring to the second of two hijacked planes to hit the World Trade Center buildings in New York City that morning, both of which later collapsed.[100] A third plane hit the Pentagon, and a fourth was brought down over Pennsylvania after passengers resisted its hijackers. Washington, D.C., was likely the hijackers' intended target for the fourth plane. Nearly three thousand people died in these attacks, which national security and military officials concluded had been planned and carried out by al-Qaeda, a radical Islamic terrorist organization, and its leader, Osama bin Laden, who later claimed responsibility for the attacks.

That Bush was in a school that fall was no accident. He had campaigned with the hope, as had his father, President George H. W. Bush (1989–1993), that he would be remembered as "an education president." Prior to the attacks, the president had been working with congressional leaders to pass the No Child Left Behind Act of 2001, a major, if controversial, national effort to reform public education. Instead of being remembered as an education president, however, George W. Bush became a wartime president, serving as commander in chief in two wars, one in Afghanistan (2001) and the other in Iraq

(2002). Neither involved an official declaration of war, though both had congressional authorization.[101]

The resolution that authorized the president to use force in Afghanistan stated "that the President is authorized to use all necessary and appropriate force against those nations, organizations, or persons he determines planned, authorized, committed, or aided the terrorist attacks that occurred on September 11, 2001, or harbored such organizations or persons, in order to prevent any future acts of international terrorism against the United States by such nations, organizations, or persons."[102]

The war on terror had begun. By including "organizations or persons" and not just nations as acceptable targets, the boundaries of this twenty-first century war were much less defined and restricted than those in previous conflicts. The consequences for presidential power of that authorization are still being determined and debated.

THE MODERN PRESIDENCY IN CONTEXT

Institutions and Informal Sources of Power

While the American presidency must feel at times like the loneliest job in the world, no president truly acts alone. Instead, the president operates at the center of multiple organizations and institutions. As with many aspects of the presidency, the size and complexity of the presidential establishment is both a source of presidential power and a constraint on it. The machinery of the presidential establishment allows the president to act in many areas of domestic and foreign policy and provides him or her with large amounts of information, which is an important commodity in dealing with other nations, Congress, and the many actors in American politics. However, the size and complexity of the executive branch establishment—especially the federal bureaucracy—can act as a powerful brake on presidential initiatives, particularly since most lower-level federal bureaucrats keep their jobs long after any one president has come and gone.

The Vice Presidency

While the Constitution's vague language created an ambiguous but ultimately powerful presidency, it also created a very weak second in command: the office of the vice president.

NEWS CLIP
Clinton evaluates potential VPs and their impacts on the election

The Problem of Small Numbers in the Study of the Presidency

How much do the personal characteristics of an individual president matter to his or her performance in office? Can we say anything systematic about the relationship between character and performance?[103]

Originally published in 1972, James David Barber's *The Presidential Character: Predicting Performance in the White House* applied understandings from psychology to try to predict how presidents would behave—and how successful they would be—by categorizing them into four types, based on two separate personality traits: (1) how active or passive they were, in the sense of the energy and innovation that they bought to the office, and (2) how positively or negatively they approached their duties, in the sense of the enjoyment they displayed in managing the ship of state.

Based on these determinations, George Washington, for example, was a passive-negative president in that he reluctantly led the nation and preferred stability over dramatic change. Thomas Jefferson, on the other hand, was an active-positive president who actively engaged in the give-and-take of politics in the service of a grand vision for the young nation.

Though it has been highly influential in political science, Barber's approach has not escaped criticism. Some have argued that the many institutional and political limitations on presidential action overwhelm the ability to define a president's actions. Others have critiqued the validity of the two underlying measures themselves.

There is another challenge in drawing systematic conclusions about individual presidents that goes beyond the issue of character. The reality is that there have not been that many presidents, thus the question is one of sample size. To demonstrate empirical relationships with confidence we need a certain number of observations to better ensure that the patterns we observe are indeed representative of the group under study.

WHAT DO YOU THINK?

How might political scientists get around the problem of the limited number of presidents in making social scientific claims about executive branch politics? One option might be to look at executives across nations, giving us more observations. The problem here is that other systems are typically very different from that of the United States. Another approach might be to look at state governors. The challenge here, though, is that the American federalist system defines very different roles for state and federal executives. This is not to say that such an approach might not be useful, only that we should be careful in using it. What might we learn from examining the behavior of state governors that could translate into a better understanding of the American presidency?

Delegates to the Constitutional Convention were not even sure that the nation needed a vice president. The ultimate inclusion of the position was probably driven by the need to sooth tensions between more populous and less populous states over the presidential election process.[104]

Constitutionally, the vice president has two jobs. He or she is "President of the Senate, but shall have no Vote, unless they be equally divided."[105] Rarely does the vice president actually preside over the Senate. Instead the president pro tempore of the Senate usually presides officially, but junior senators routinely fill in for this role. The logic behind the vice president's leadership role in the Senate was to ensure that no state lost its equal Senate representation by virtue of having one of its two senators serving as president of the chamber.

> *The size and complexity of the executive branch establishment—especially the federal bureaucracy—can act as a powerful brake on presidential initiatives.*

Second, the vice president assumes the office of the presidency should a serving president vacate the office due to death, resignation, or impeachment. The Twenty-fifth Amendment (1967) established the modern rules of succession and also established a process for replacing a vice president who leaves office during his or her term. In this process, the president nominates a replacement and approval is required "by a majority vote of both Houses of Congress."

In 1973 Gerald R. Ford, who was serving in Congress at the time, was approved as vice president in the Nixon administration after the resignation of Spiro T. Agnew over criminal charges surrounding a bribery scandal while Agnew had been governor of Maryland. The following year, Ford became president after Nixon's resignation over the Watergate scandal, and Congress approved Ford's nominee for vice president, Nelson Rockefeller. From 1974 to 1977, therefore, neither the president nor the vice president of the United States had been elected by the people.

In addition to addressing succession, the Twenty-fifth Amendment also established a procedure through which the vice president may temporarily assume the role of acting president in the event "that the President is unable to discharge the powers and duties of his office." During his presidency, George W. Bush twice notified Congress that he would temporarily be unable to fulfill his duties as he underwent sedation for colonoscopies, making Vice President Dick Cheney acting president for about two hours each time.

As noted above, the office of the vice presidency is officially weak. Commenting on his election as the nation's first vice president, John Adams lamented, "My country in its wisdom contrived for me the most insignificant office that ever the invention of man contrived or his imagination conceived."[106] Upon hearing talk of his possible selection as a vice presidential candidate in the 1960 election, John F. Kennedy—who would in fact win the presidential nomination and the presidency—commented wryly, "Let's not talk so much about vice. I'm against vice in any form."[107]

Any vice president knows, however, that he or she is a heartbeat away from one of the most powerful positions in the world. Reflecting on his role, Adams also noted, "I am Vice President. In this I am nothing, but I may be everything."[108] In calling for the abolition of the institution of the vice presidency, Arthur M. Schlesinger Jr. argued, "The Vice President has only one serious thing to do: that is, to wait around for the President to die. This is hardly the basis for a cordial and enduring friendship."[109] In the nation's history, eight vice presidents have assumed the office of the presidency upon the death of the serving president and one upon the president's resignation.

Historically, most vice presidents have had little impact on national policy, but it has recently become more common for vice presidents to have a larger role in White House deliberations. Other than being ready to take over, the main job of the vice president is to help the president get elected. Vice presidential nominees have often been selected to "balance the ticket" with respect to geographical representation, connections to important blocks of voters, or experience.

The Cabinet and the Executive Branch Bureaucracy

The president's cabinet consists of the heads of the fifteen major executive branch departments, the vice president, and the heads of other agencies that the president wishes to assign cabinet-level status. In addition to leading their agencies, cabinet department heads, most of whom are called secretaries, advise the president and act as the link between the president and their own bureaucracies. Unlike the majority of people who work for the federal bureaucracy, heads of the executive branch departments typically come and go with each new administration.

In choosing cabinet members, presidents have to juggle several considerations. Presidents need capable, experienced, and strong appointees to provide useful information

FIGURE 13.2

The Organization of the Executive Office

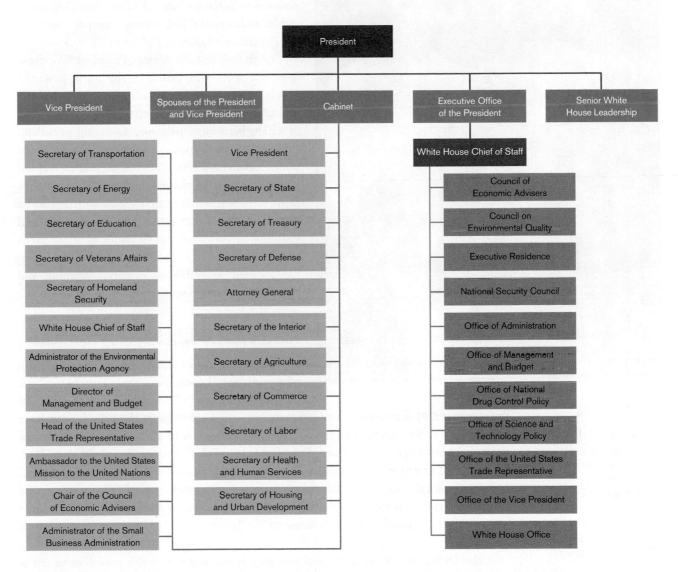

Source: The White House, https://www.whitehouse.gov/administration/cabinet

and to effectively run their departments. However, assertive cabinet secretaries, who often have their own bases of power, can challenge the president or drag their heels if they disagree with a policy objective. Presidents must also consider politics and public opinion in their choices. Cabinet department heads with ties to important interest groups—teachers or members of the business community, for example—can help a president to be informed of the concerns of those groups as policy is shaped. Finally, having a diverse cabinet can communicate to the people a president's commitment to representing all Americans and their interests.

Marian Anderson, renowned opera singer, receives the Spingarn Medal from First Lady Eleanor Roosevelt in Richmond, Virginia, in July 1939. Eleanor Roosevelt's efforts to overcome racial discrimination in the United States were among her most important achievements on behalf of her husband's administration.

Keystone-France/Gamma-Keystone via Getty Images.

Executive Office of the President
a collection of offices within the White House organization designed primarily to provide information to the president.

The First Spouse

The wife or husband of a president occupies no formal role in an administration but is in a unique position to act as an advisor to the president and a public and personal link between the president and the American people.

Edith Bolling Galt Wilson, President Woodrow Wilson's wife, was probably the most powerful first lady. She helped to organize and run the White House after her husband suffered a serious stroke in 1919, becoming, to some, an acting president. Eleanor Roosevelt spoke and wrote frequently about public policy and had a successful and influential career in public life following Franklin Roosevelt's death in 1945. Modern first spouses often choose one or more policy areas and use their influence and visibility to call attention to issues in those areas and promote solutions. Michelle Obama, for example, focused on childhood obesity, nutrition, and physical fitness among young people.

The Executive Office of the President

Established in 1939 upon the recommendation of a presidential commission that concluded "the president needs help," the **Executive Office of the President (EOP)** is a collection of agencies and offices that assist the president in both an advisory and policymaking capacity.[110] The White House chief of staff oversees the EOP and is usually a close, trusted, and politically skilled associate of the president. The chief of staff often acts as a protector of the president's scarcest resource: time. Most individuals who work for the various agencies within the EOP do so "at the pleasure of the president"; they are appointed by a president and not expected to serve past that administration, though some of the larger offices do have permanent staff members.

The Office of Management and Budget advises and assists the president in crafting the national budget and studies various plans and initiatives designed to increase the efficiency of executive branch departments. The National Security Council advises the president on issues of national security, the military, and foreign policy. The Council of Economic Advisors assists the president on issues involving the American economy.

The White House Office (part of the EOP) has grown into an important bureaucracy itself, and its most important members share offices near the president's. The four hundred or so staff members in this office are there to support the president in achieving his or her policy objectives. They achieve this by effectively communicating the president's vision to the American people, building support for goals and polices, and playing the complicated and high-stakes game of Washington politics. In choosing the members of the White House staff, presidents value political skill and loyalty. Many times staff members are individuals who were involved in the campaign or with the president in previous roles. Directors and deputy directors of communication ensure that the president's message is clearly and coherently presented to the American people. The White House press secretary acts as the president's spokesperson to members of the media and conducts daily press briefings, partly to inform but also partly to shape the national conversation in a way that helps the president achieve his or her policy goals.

Parties and Public Opinion

The role that the president plays as "chief of party" is not mentioned in the Constitution. The framers worried privately and publicly about the dangers of faction, of which political parties were viewed as a particularly dangerous example. Parties, however, are nearly as old as the Republic; divisions between President Washington's closest advisors gave rise to the nation's first political parties.

Modern presidents serve as the unofficial, but real, leaders of their own political parties. They often choose the official leadership of their party, or at least have a major say in it. Presidents must contend with partisan politics in Congress, especially if they serve during a period of divided government and the opposing political party is controlling one or both chambers of Congress. Periods of divided government are often associated with legislative gridlock, in which Congress's ability to pass laws is diminished or grinds to a halt completely.[111]

Presidents expect to have to battle and negotiate with members of the opposing party in Congress. However, support from their own party members can never be taken for granted either. Presidents and members of Congress serve different constituencies. The American people demand that their presidents keep them safe and prosperous. Demands on senators and representatives are often more local and address the unique characteristics and needs of their states or districts. No member of Congress can ignore the wishes of her or his constituents without risk, even if the president requests it. Skillful presidents are fully aware of these tensions and—working with party leaders in Congress—often try to accommodate individual defections by members of their own party with the expectation that loyalty will be shown on less locally contentious votes somewhere down the line.

The President and Public Opinion

As the power of the American presidency has evolved, so has the president's relationship to the nation's citizens. Public opinion—the distribution of people's preferences and evaluations of policies and individual political actors—has come to play an important role in expanding or constraining the power of individual presidents. When expertly harnessed, public opinion is a powerful tool in battles with Congress, the judiciary, or too-independent members of a president's own political party. If it is poorly mobilized or understood, however, the unfortunate president, in the words of Clinton Rossiter, "will find himself exposed to all those enemies who multiply like mosquitoes in a [New] Jersey August. The various institutions and centers of power that check the President are inept and often useless without public opinion—and with it are often wondrously armed."[112]

Modern communications technologies and ease of travel have significantly contributed to connecting the president to the American public. But long before the Internet, television, and even radio, individual presidents recognized and tried to harness the latent power of public opinion. Andrew Jackson, who drew on his public support in battles with

Congress and the judiciary, commented, "The President must be accountable at the bar of public opinion for every act of his administration."[113]

Modern presidents attempt to make full use of communications technologies and public appearances in order to mobilize American public opinion in support of their own goals and policies. Political scientist Samuel Kernell used the term **going public** to describe "a strategy whereby a president promotes himself and his policies in Washington by appealing directly to the American public for support."[114] The State of the Union Address, press conferences, and major speeches—this last category often choreographed in front of a dramatic backdrop of a group of adults or children—all provide an opportunity for presidents to go public. They have to be careful, though, as these attempts can later backfire. Public opinion is not set in stone and can turn against a president powerfully and quickly.

Americans' Evaluations of Presidential Performance

Since Franklin Roosevelt's presidency, pollsters have periodically taken the national pulse on Americans' views of how well their presidents are doing. These presidential approval ratings provide more than just a snapshot of the public's views. A president with high approval ratings is in a more powerful position in relation to Congress than one with low or sinking ratings. Sometimes unanticipated events—and the president's response to them—can produce dramatic changes in presidential approval. A national economic or military crisis, if handled successfully in the eyes of the American public, can produce a surge in presidential approval. In the months after the 9/11 attacks, President Bush's approval rating rose to 90 percent, the highest ever recorded, but it later declined as the public became increasingly skeptical of his handling of the war in Iraq and of the nation's economy.

Some patterns of presidential approval are more predictable. A president—especially after a convincing first-term victory—often enjoys a period of strong public approval, called a honeymoon period. For this reason, presidents often try to secure major legislative victories early in their first terms to capture public support and build momentum for future battles with Congress. Presidential approval, however, usually declines over time as the American public begins to assign blame to the president for things that are not going well, whether this is deserved or not. There is also typically some recovery in presidential approval as the term draws to a close.[115]

Unilateral Presidential Action

Scholars' views of the American presidency and the power of the office have, like the institution itself, changed over time and in response to the individual presidents and the times in which they have governed. Increasingly, political scientists have focused on a unilateral model of presidential action, in which presidents attempt to influence both domestic and foreign policy with few or no constraints by Congress or the judiciary. It is, in other words, when presidents try to act alone. Individual presidents have often tried to defend the power of their office or even push the boundaries of that power, but the scope and frequency of unilateral presidential action in recent administrations has raised questions about the degree to which powers truly remain separated among the three branches of the United States government.

Presidents attempt to exercise independent control over information through the assertion of **executive privilege**, in which they try to shield from Congress, the judiciary, and, ultimately, the public the details of debates, discussions, memos, and e-mails

---

going public
a strategy through which presidents reach out directly to the American people with the hope that the people will, in turn, put pressure upon their representatives and senators to press for a president's policy goals.

executive privilege
a right claimed by presidents to keep confidential certain conversations, records, and transcripts from outside scrutiny, especially that of Congress.

The Risks of the Photo-Op

In the photo at right, President George W. Bush delivers a speech aboard the aircraft carrier *USS Abraham Lincoln* on May 1, 2003. The president's speech declared an end to major combat operations in Iraq. Behind him is a banner reading "Mission Accomplished." Administration officials insisted that the banner referred to the specific deployment of the carrier and its crew. As violence within Iraq and attacks on American forces increased in the months following Bush's speech, critics of the war and the Bush administration pointed to the photo opportunity as an indication of the president's unwarranted optimism and lack of candor with the American people about the challenges of a war that would go on for eight more years, claiming more than four thousand American lives and likely resulting in more than one hundred thousand Iraqi deaths.

STEPHEN JAFFE/AFP/Getty Images.

WHAT DO YOU THINK?

What do this photograph and the controversy surrounding it illustrate about the use of the media by presidents trying to win public support for their programs and goals? How might presidents benefit from these major photo opportunities? What might the dangers be?

surrounding presidential decisions and actions. Since the administration of George Washington, presidents have asserted that their ability to control information is essential to their effectiveness.[116]

During the investigation of President Nixon and his role in the Watergate Affair, Nixon refused to hand over to a special prosecutor audio recordings of his conversations with senior aides as well as other documents relating to the investigation, citing the power of executive privilege. In *United States v. Nixon* (1974), the Supreme Court affirmed the power of executive privilege, finding that "a President and those who assist him must be free to explore alternatives in the process of shaping policies and making decisions, and to do so in a way many would be unwilling to express except privately."[117] However, the Court also demanded that the president hand over the recordings and documents, balancing the need for executive privilege with the need for the rule of law in criminal investigations.

In the area of foreign policy, presidents may sign **executive agreements** with foreign nations without the need for Senate ratification, which is needed for treaties. Though they are not binding upon future presidents in the way that treaties are, executive agreements can give a president a way to shape foreign policy that bypasses the Senate's role of advice and consent. Their details are often kept secret from the public and Congress for reasons of national security.

executive agreement
an agreement between a president and another nation that does not have the same durability in the American system as a treaty but that may carry important foreign policy consequences.

signing statements
text written by presidents while signing a bill into law that usually consists of political statements or reasons for signing the bill but that might also include a president's interpretation of the law itself.

In the president's role in the legislative process, the use of **signing statements** has gained increased attention recently. When a president signs a bill into law, he or she may add written comments that convey instructions to the various agencies that will actually carry out the law or that offer the president's interpretation of the law. Sometimes signing statements are far from controversial; they may be offered to try to build a public record of support for an issue, to call attention to an issue, or to offer a slightly different interpretation of a law that a president otherwise supports. However, if the president either interprets the law differently from the way Congress intended or instructs agencies to execute it selectively or differently, then concerns can be raised that the president is taking the lawmaking authority intended for Congress for him- or herself.

executive orders
directions made by presidents to the executive branch departments that often contain nothing more than instructions to be carried out by agencies, bureaus, and departments but that may at times be considered to be acts of presidential lawmaking.

Executive orders are policy directives issued by presidents to the executive branch bureaucracy that do not require congressional approval. Most executive orders are issued under congressional authorization and constitute a set of instructions given by the president to the executive branch agencies informing them of how they are supposed to go about implementing a law or policy. Often they deal with routine administrative procedures. Presidents have also used executive orders, however, to make major changes in public policy.[118]

In 1942 President Roosevelt issued Executive Order 9066, which authorized the secretary of war to declare certain areas in the United States as "military areas . . . from which any or all persons may be excluded, and with respect to which the right of any person to enter, remain in, or leave shall be subject to whatever restrictions the Secretary of War or the appropriate Military Commander may impose in his discretion."[119] Issued for the declared purpose of "protection against espionage and against sabotage to national-defense material," Roosevelt's executive order led to the internment of more than 130,000 individuals, most of whom were Japanese Americans.[120] In *Korematsu v. United States* (1944), the Supreme Court upheld Roosevelt's authority. In a dissent, however, one justice commented about the internment, "I need hardly labor the conclusion that Constitutional rights have been violated."[121]

Following President Roosevelt's Executive Order 9066, two soldiers escort a Japanese American couple during their evacuation from Bainbridge Island, WA, to a relocation center in 1942. More than 130,000 individuals were interned as a result of the order.

Library of Congress/Corbis/VCG via Getty Images.

The Supreme Court, however, has not always upheld presidential use of the executive order, even during wartime. In *Youngstown Sheet & Tube Co. v. Sawyer* (1952), the Court rejected the authority of President Harry S. Truman (1945–1953) to order the seizure of most of the nation's steel mills to avert a strike by steel workers while the nation was at war in Korea.[122] The Court concluded that the president's power did not extend to labor disputes and that he lacked legislative authorization for his actions.

While you have read primarily about unilateral presidential action in the area of national security, questions about its exercise extend to many other political fields. As political scientist William Howell has examined, presidents may act first and alone across a wide variety of policy areas, often by issuing directives to the vast federal bureaucracy without waiting for Congress

FIGURE 13.3

Executive Orders, Washington to Obama

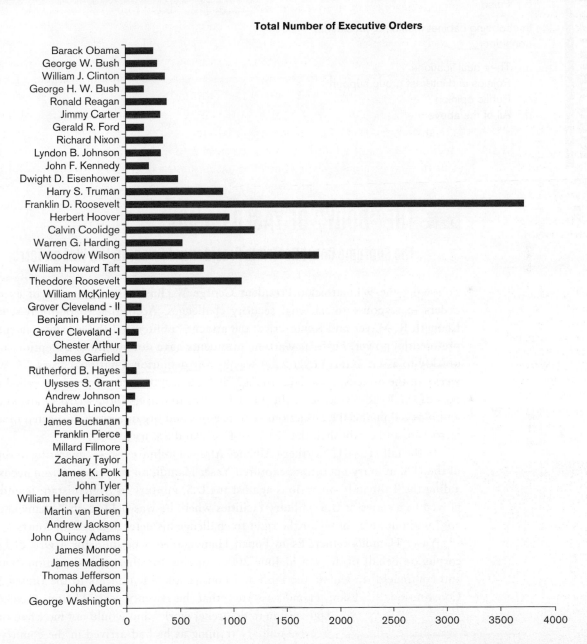

Total Number of Executive Orders

Source: Data for executive orders are from Gerhard Peters, "Executive Orders," in *The American Presidency Project*, ed. John T. Woolley and Gerhard Peters (Santa Barbara: University of California, 1999–2016). Available online at http://www.presidency.ucsb.edu/data/orders.php#orderlist.

Note: Data for the Obama administration are current through October 2016.

to clarify the laws that it has passed (see Chapter 14). In doing so, "the president moves policy first and thereby places upon Congress and the courts the burden of revising a new political landscape."[123] Acting first and acting alone may force the other two branches to react.

1. The office of the vice presidency was created to be an important check on presidential power.

   a. True
   b. False

2. In choosing cabinet members, presidents consider _____.

   a. Their qualifications
   b. Politics and interest group support
   c. Public opinion
   d. All of the above

3. What tools of unilateral action do presidents have at their disposal?

Answer Key: 1. b; 2. d; 3. Answers should include executive orders, executive agreements, and signing statements.

THE "BODY" OF YASER HAMDI

The Supreme Court Restricts Presidential Power in the War on Terror

Following the 9/11 attacks, President George W. Bush issued a series of executive orders in response to national security challenges. According to political scientists Kenneth R. Mayer and Kevin Price, the attacks "obliterated the previous calculus of presidential power. Bush, as wartime presidents have done without exception, moved quickly to assert control over what was by any definition a national crisis."[124] Within weeks of the attacks, Bush had, though the issuance of executive orders, called members of the Ready Reserve of the Armed Forces to active duty, seized financial assets and blocked financial transactions with persons and organizations suspected of aiding terrorism, and established the Office of Homeland Security.[125]

In the fall of 2001, Northern Alliance Afghani military forces, operating in support of the U.S. military operation, captured Yaser Hamdi, an American citizen accused of aiding the Taliban in operations against the U.S. military in Afghanistan. Hamdi was moved to a series of U.S. military facilities where he was held as an "enemy combatant" without an attorney or the right to challenge his detention in U.S. courts.

Yaser Hamdi's father, Esam Fouad Hamdi, filed a petition for a writ of habeas corpus on behalf of his son in June 2002, arguing that his son's detention "violated and continue[d] to violate the Fifth and Fourteenth Amendments to the United States Constitution."[126] Esam Hamdi asserted that his twenty-year-old son travelled to Afghanistan to do "relief work" and would not have had time to receive military training as he had arrived in the country only months before 9/11 attacks.[127] Attorneys for the Bush administration argued that "the Executive possesses plenary authority to detain pursuant to Article II of the Constitution" as part of the office's constitutional war-making authority.[128]

> "A state of war is not a blank check for the President when it comes to the rights of the Nation's citizens."

In a decision in many ways as complicated as the underlying issues, Justice Sandra Day O'Connor delivered the Court's opinion in *Hamdi v. Rumsfeld* (2002), which concluded that "a state of war is not a blank check for the President when it comes to the rights of the Nation's citizens." The decision also asserted that Yaser Hamdi had the right to a hearing "before a neutral decisionmaker."[129]

In the twenty-first century, with the nation involved in combating threats to national security arising from multiple terrorist networks without defined geographic and political boundaries, the question of unilateral presidential power has only grown more complex, more relevant, and more controversial.

Presidential Character

Some political scientists have looked to the character and personality of individual presidents to explain their relative effectiveness in office. That individual presidents—their characters, skills, successes, and failures—have all contributed to the development of the American presidency is a point on which most would agree. For scholars of the presidency, however, the challenge is to figure out just how these traits matter to presidential performance. Some scholars have classified presidents based on personal and psychological characteristics as a way of gaining insight into behavior inside the Oval Office.[130] Successfully predicting presidential behavior based on assessments of character is, however, a difficult thing to do. Separating the person of the president from the times and context in which that president governed is never easy. In addition, sudden, unexpected events can thrust a president into situations that none could have imagined or predicted.

Presidential scholar Richard E. Neustadt painted a strategic, but constrained, portrait of the source of presidential power. For Neustadt, the power of an individual president is not automatic but must be developed, especially through skillful political action. Presidents must be "wise and prudent athletes," orchestrating the high-stakes game of Washington politics from the center of multiple games of power.[131] Neustadt wrote that presidential power is the power of information, of presenting a credible threat to known and potential political enemies, and, finally, of convincing allies and opponents that supporting the president is in their own self-interest. According to him, "The essence of a President's persuasive task is to convince such men that what the White House wants of them is what they ought to do for their sake and on their own authority."[132]

In times of crisis, especially economic or military crises, no single actor in the American political system is able to react to the demands of the situation as quickly and decisively as the president. As political scientist Lester G. Seligman put it, "Under crisis conditions the political system undergoes a drastic change. The White House becomes a command post, Congress and interest groups assume minor roles, the public becomes acutely aware of the threat and looks fervently to the president for authoritative guidance."[133]

As we explored in Chapter 3, President Roosevelt's response to the Great Depression fundamentally altered American federalism and increased the power of the national government and the executive branch. It has been in times of military crises and threats to national security, however, when the nation has witnessed the starkest increase in presidential authority and the transformation of the character, scope, and reach of the American president.

Arguing in favor of a single executive in *Federalist* No. 74, Alexander Hamilton saw the potential of and need for presidential power in wartime. He wrote, "Of all the cares or concerns

Yaser Hamdi in captivity at Guantanamo Bay in 2002. Hamdi's father petitioned for a writ of habeas corpus, but the Bush administration claimed to have the wartime power to hold Hamdi indefinitely without trial.

Photographer's Mate 1st Class (AW) Shawn P. Eklund, United States Navy.

Attorney General Eric Holder on the Use of Lethal Force against U.S. Citizens Abroad

Pressured by members of Congress to disclose more information about the use of lethal force against Americans abroad without trial and away from active combat operations, on May 22, 2013, President Obama's attorney general, Eric H. Holder Jr., released a memorandum to key congressional leaders justifying the administration's actions in the killing of four Americans in the ongoing war on terror.

Although Holder's memo did not explicitly state that any of the four Americans were killed by pilotless drone aircraft, it was widely reported in the media that at least one, Anwar al-Awlaki, had in fact been killed by a drone strike. Holder's memo focused largely on laying out the justification for killing al-Awlaki. In it, Holder stated,

United States Attorney General Eric H. Holder Jr.

PAUL J. RICHARDS/AFP/Getty Images.

Since 2009, the United States, in the conduct of U.S. counterterrorism operations against al-Qa'ida and its associated forces outside of areas of active hostilities, has specifically targeted and killed one U.S. citizen, Anwar al-Aulaqi. The United States is further aware of three other U.S. citizens who have been killed in such U.S. counterterrorism operations over that same time period. . . .

Al-Aulaqi was a senior operational leader of al-Qa'ida in the Arabian Peninsula (AQAP), the most dangerous regional affiliate of al-Qa'ida and a group that has committed numerous terrorist attacks overseas and attempted multiple times to conduct terrorist attacks against the U.S. homeland. Anwar al-Aulaqi was not just a senior leader of AQAP—he was the group's chief of external operations, intimately involved in detailed planning and putting in place plots against U.S. persons.

Moreover, information that remains classified to protect sensitive sources and methods evidences al-Aulaqi's involvement in the planning of numerous *other* plots against U.S.

and Western interests and makes clear he was continuing to plot attacks when killed.

The decision to use lethal force is one of the gravest that our government, at every level, can face. The operation to target Anwar al-Aulaqi was thus subjected to an exceptionally rigorous interagency review. . . . When capture is not feasible, the policy provides that lethal force may be used only when a terrorist target poses a continuing, imminent threat to Americans, and when certain other preconditions, including a requirement that no other reasonable alternatives exist to effectively address the threat, are satisfied.[136]

WHAT DO YOU THINK?

What limits, if any, do you think should be placed upon a president and his or her advisors with regard to the targeting and killing of an American citizen suspected of terrorism against the nation if that citizen is located in a foreign country? Would your evaluations change if you were to consider the same actions on American soil?

of government, the direction of war most peculiarly demands those qualities which distinguish the exercise of power by a single hand."[134] Writing in 1888, noted observer of American political life James Bryce confirmed the transformative power of war and conflict on the American presidency, saying, "In quiet times the power of the President is not great. . . . In troublous times it is otherwise, for immense responsibility is then thrown on one who is both the commander-in-chief and the head of the civil executive."[135] The ability to act first and act alone is a tool unique to the president. Its power is only magnified during times of threat and crisis.

CONCLUSION

The Paradox of Power

No writ of habeas corpus was ever issued for Anwar al-Awlaki. After the U.S. government had acted, there was no live person to bring to a United States court for a hearing. There was likely not even an intact body. Barack Obama was not the first American president to authorize a drone strike that resulted in the death of an American citizen. In 2002, under the administration of President George W. Bush, "the C.I.A. struck a car carrying a group of suspected militants, including an American citizen, who were believed to have Qaeda ties."[137] Nor was Obama or Bush the first president to refuse or negate a writ of habeas corpus for an American citizen in time of military conflict. President Abraham Lincoln never honored Chief Justice Taney's directive, though the president tried to calm a worried public by assuring that his assumption of unprecedented power—his "medicine"—would no longer be needed once the Union had been restored.

The power of the American presidency is not easily defined, nor are its roots and sources easily traced or separated. Many factors—constitutional provisions, institutional and political contexts, individual personality and skill, and responses to crises—have all played a role in its development. As scholars have observed, the office of the presidency is full of paradoxes.[138] The framers wanted a strong and decisive office, yet they were wary of creating an elected monarch. Americans often look to their presidents for leadership above the fray of partisan politics, yet the position is, by design, political and embedded in a system of checks and balances. Americans look to their presidents for leadership yet expect them to follow the will of the people.

The modern presidency is a massively powerful office. As Americans are confronted with a global war on terror in the twenty-first century—a war that features undefined boundaries and no specific nation with which to conclude a peace treaty—the question of the proper limits of presidential power remains as vital as it did in 1861 when Abraham Lincoln expanded his authority to reconstitute a nation divided. Certainly President Trump will face these questions during his term in office; these issues are not going away.

During his campaign in 2016, Donald Trump had argued for "bombing the s—out of ISIS," a militant Islamic group operating and holding ground in Iraq and Syria, and trying to make inroads into other North African and Middle-Eastern nations.[139] As president-elect, however, Trump tagged retired Lt. General Michael Flynn as his prospective nominee for national security advisor, in spite of the fact that Trump had said on the campaign trail that he "will back waterboarding and go even further in questioning suspected terrorists."[140] Trump's prospective NSA advisor, in a speech in 2014, presented a different opinion, questioning the future use of such techniques: "If there's an American strategic advantage," Flynn testified, "it is our values. We must protect our values at all costs."[141]

CHAPTER REVIEW

This chapter's main ideas are reflected in the Learning Objectives below. By reviewing them here you should be able to **remember** the key points, **connect** them to the stories presented in the chapter, **think** critically about these questions, and **know** these terms that are central to the topic.

13.1 Describe the powers of the presidency as defined in the Constitution as well as the tensions inherent in those descriptions.

REMEMBER...

- The framers called for a single executive, the president, with enough power to lead successfully but not so much power to make him susceptible to tyranny.

- As set out in the Constitution, the president serves a four-year term with the possibility of reelection. Candidates must be natural-born citizens, at least thirty-five years old, and a resident of the nation for fourteen years. Women were not expressly prohibited from running in the Constitution but were disenfranchised.

- The office of the presidency is granted a set of expressed, implied, and delegated powers, including the powers to carry out the laws of the nation, guide foreign policy and relations with foreign leaders, provide Congress with information, make policy recommendations to Congress, veto legislation, act as commander in chief of the military, and grant pardons.

- Executive power is constitutionally limited by powers granted to Congress and the judiciary.

CONNECT...

- Though granted power to act as commander in chief of the nation's armed forces, the targeted killing of American citizen Anwar al-Awlaki by President Obama's administration seemed to some to be an overreach of those powers.

THINK...

- What are the powers of the American president as laid out in the Constitution?

- What are the tensions between the president and Congress in making war as established in the Constitution?

- How have those tensions been resolved or changed?

KNOW...

- *executive branch* (p. 454)
- *recess appointment* (p. 460)
- *State of the Union Address* (p. 460)
- *presidential pardons* (p. 462)

13.2 Evaluate how presidents have tested the limits of the power of the office during wartime and national crises.

REMEMBER...

- The Constitution provides that the U.S. government has certain powers to suspend rights during times of rebellion or invasion. The text granting that power is within Article I, which is devoted to the structure and powers of Congress, not the executive branch. However, presidents have sometimes pointed to the "war powers" granted to the executive as justification for their actions.

- President Lincoln suspended habeas corpus during the Civil War on the grounds that the crisis necessitated it.

- When President Lincoln suspended habeas corpus, Chief Justice Taney challenged his action, claiming that Lincoln did not have the constitutional authority, even during wartime, to do so. Lincoln claimed he had the right granted to the executive via the war powers clause to do so.

THINK...

- What was the controversy surrounding President Lincoln's use of executive authority during the Civil War?

- On what basis did Lincoln defend his use of executive authority?

◼ 13.3 Appraise the impact of individual presidencies in establishing the powers of the office.

REMEMBER...

- George Washington laid the foundations for the modern cabinet system, established the supremacy of federal law, and set the precedent for two-term limits of office.

- Thomas Jefferson demonstrated the use of personal influence, via the political party, to shape legislation. Potentially acting outside the boundaries of his powers, he expanded the size of the nation.

- Andrew Jackson accessed the support of the American people to challenge Congress and the Supreme Court.

- Theodore Roosevelt wielded power internationally via foreign intervention and used his office as a bully pulpit.

- Woodrow Wilson expanded the role of the president in legislative affairs.

- Franklin Delano Roosevelt expanded the size, scope, and power of the federal government as well as that of the executive branch within it during the Great Depression.

- Lyndon Baines Johnson used his skill in working with Congress to pursue his vision of a Great Society.

- Richard Nixon attempted to veto the War Powers Resolution, which aimed to restrict the power of the president in committing American armed forces into combat or situations of likely combat.

- Ronald Reagan drew on his prior professional experience in media to connect with the public and gain support for his priorities.

- George W. Bush became a wartime president overseeing two conflicts, neither of which involved an official declaration of war, though both had congressional authorization.

THINK...

- Do individual presidents matter? How? What are the constraints on their ability to reshape the office?

KNOW...

- *War Powers Resolution* (p. 474)

◼ 13.4 Discuss institutional and informal sources of presidential power.

REMEMBER...

- No president truly acts alone. The president operates at the center of multiple organizations and institutions within the executive branch.

- The office of the vice presidency provides stability as the vice president assumes the office of the presidency should a serving president vacate the office due to death, resignation, or impeachment. The vice president also helps get the president get elected.

- The president's cabinet acts as a source of information for the president and also can communicate to the citizens a president's commitment to representing all Americans and their interests.

- The first spouse typically chooses a policy area or areas to focus on and uses his or her influence and visibility to call attention to these issues and promote solutions.

- The Executive Office of the President is a collection of agencies and offices that assist the president in both an advisory and policymaking capacity.

- As chief of his or her political party, presidents often choose or have a major say in the selection of the official leadership of the party.

- Public opinion has come to play an important role in expanding or constraining the power of individual presidents. However, a president's approval ratings tend to decline over time.

- Presidents sometimes attempt to exercise a degree of unilateral authority through the assertion of executive privilege, signing statements, and executive orders.

CONNECT...

- The stories of Anwar al-Awlaki, John Merryman, and Yaser Hamdi all demonstrate instances where a president claimed war power authority and was challenged either by other branches of government or by the population at large.

THINK...

- How is the war on terror different—or not—from previous American crises in terms of presidential authority?

- Is the modern president too powerful? Not powerful enough?

KNOW...

- *Executive Office of the President* (p. 480)

- *going public* (p. 482)

- *executive privilege* (p. 482)

- *executive agreements* (p. 483)

- *signing statements* (p. 484)

- *executive orders* (p. 484)

14 THE FEDERAL BUREAUCRACY
Putting the Nation's Laws into Effect

To many, if not most, Americans, the word *bureaucracy* refers to something that must be dealt with when necessary, complained about at times, and perhaps feared when confronted with its seemingly faceless exercise of power. Formally, the term *bureaucracy* does not carry any positive or negative meanings. A bureaucracy is simply an organization designed to carry out specific tasks according to a prescribed set of rules and procedures. Literally, the word refers to "rule by offices," and it was coined in the nineteenth century. The phenomenon of the bureaucracy, however, goes back much farther, to Rome, Persia, Egypt, the Chinese Empire, Central and South America, Africa, and other large, developed societies in history.[1]

In this chapter, you will learn about the **federal bureaucracy**—what it is, how it is structured, and how it works . . . or doesn't work. You will also be asked to wrestle with the complicated question of what

National Hurricane Center director Max Mayfield prepares for an interview in August 2005, a satellite image of Hurricane Katrina in the background. In his role as director and as part of the national bureaucracy, Mayfield warned the governors of Louisiana and Mississippi, the mayor of New Orleans, and then president George W. Bush about the impending storm and urged them to prepare.

AP Photo/Andy Newman.

Americans want and demand from the part of the federal government that actually impacts their lives in a more personal way than the actions of the president, Congress, or the judiciary typically do—often more than they realize. Formally, the federal bureaucracy is part of the executive branch of the national government, charged with executing, or putting into action, the laws that Congress has written. However, the federal bureaucracy is actually a powerful player in the American political scene in its own right, though one that rarely makes the news unless something goes wrong.

The federal bureaucracy is not always well understood, and Americans often have contradictory views of it. At times, Americans complain that bureaucracy is too powerful, capable of making their lives more difficult or expensive. At other times, they complain that it is powerless to help them, incompetent, wasteful, and inefficient. A tried and true campaign strategy is to promise to reform a bloated and inefficient bureaucracy.

In this chapter, we will examine the American federal bureaucracy through the lens of one of the most destructive natural disasters in the nation's history, Hurricane Katrina, which devastated the Gulf Coast in August 2005. Though it has been more than a decade since Katrina made landfall, its effects are still being felt, not only in New Orleans and other Gulf Coast communities still recovering and rebuilding but also in an ongoing debate about the efficiency of the federal bureaucracy.

LEARNING OBJECTIVES

After reading this chapter, you will be able to:

14.1 Name the key characteristics of bureaucratic organization and the theories that try to explain why bureaucratic organization happens

14.2 Outline the historical development of the American federal bureaucracy

14.3 Describe the structure of the federal bureaucracy, including executive branch agencies, cabinet departments, and regulatory bodies

14.4 Describe the tools of bureaucratic control, oversight, and reform

◼ HURRICANE KATRINA

A National Crisis Places the Federal Bureaucracy under the Microscope

Max Mayfield saw it coming, and he tried to warn as many people as he could. As director of the National Hurricane Center, based in Miami, Florida, Mayfield and the scientists on his team sounded the alarm on August 26, 2005, that a potentially catastrophic hurricane would make landfall on the coast of Louisiana, southeast of New Orleans. In predicting the precise point of impact for the hurricane's eye, they were off by a mere eighteen miles. As one reporter noted, "In the business of hurricane prediction, that's laser-beam accuracy."[2]

That storm was Hurricane Katrina, one of the deadliest, most destructive, and costliest hurricanes in the nation's history. Interviewed immediately after Katrina slammed into the Gulf Coast on August 29, Mayfield's "eyes were puffy, his voice slightly cracked from giving interviews to media outlets around the world. 'I don't even know what day it is,'" he said.[3] Two days prior to landfall, "Mayfield was so worried about Hurricane Katrina that he called the governors of Louisiana and Mississippi and the mayor of New Orleans. On Sunday, he even talked about the force of Katrina during a video conference call to President George W. Bush at his ranch in Crawford, Texas. 'I just wanted to be able to go to sleep that night knowing that I did all I could do.'"[4]

Mayfield and the members of his team were only a few of the thousands of individuals working for only one of hundreds of pieces of the almost unimaginably vast system of the American federal bureaucracy. How did the federal bureaucracy develop? Does it work? Can it be improved? These are the crucial questions that frame our exploration in this chapter.

All along the coast of the Gulf of Mexico in August 2005 and the months that followed, the federal bureaucracy moved from the wings to front and center on the national political stage. Many people felt that something had gone truly wrong, and there was no shortage of blame to go around. Hurricane Katrina did not appear out of nowhere. The storm had made its first landfall in southern Florida on August 25 as a much weaker hurricane.[5] Forecasts from the National Hurricane Center were not as accurate in pinpointing this first landfall, though, leading to criticism from some Floridians who prepared for the storm only to see it veer away at the last minute. Many residents were dismissive of official forecasts. An article that appeared before the storm in the *Palm Beach Post*, "Boca Couldn't Have Ordered a Better Storm Than Katrina," lamented that the wealthy town was "rife with flashy enhancements that get noticed, but in the end, turn out to be a tad oversold."[6] It compared the storm to the glitz and glamour of the town, saying both lacked any real substance. Still, by the time Katrina had passed over Florida, seven people had lost their lives, flooding was widespread, mobile homes were ripped apart, and small airplanes tossed around like toys.[7] Katrina's next landfall would be much, much worse.[8]

As the storm approached Louisiana and the Gulf Coast, officials warned that it could make landfall with winds in excess of 130 mph, pushing ahead of it a storm surge of devastating intensity and volume. "Ladies and gentlemen," New Orleans mayor C. Ray Nagin warned at a news conference prior to landfall, "This is the real deal. Board up your homes, make sure you have enough medicine, make sure the car has enough gas. Do all things you normally do for a hurricane but treat this one differently because it is pointed towards New Orleans."[9]

Of all of the concerns, perhaps the most worrisome was the city's system of levees and pumps, designed by the Army Corps of Engineers to keep the water at bay. With much

The extent of the flooding in New Orleans was devastating, with whole neighborhoods underwater following the failure of the levees that were meant to protect the city.

of the city below sea level, a failure in any one section of the "125 miles of interlocking channels, drainage canals, dikes, levees, walls, dams, and pumps" would cause New Orleans "to fill up like a bathtub."[10] As officials watched the powerful storm roar towards shore, some scientists "predicted that Katrina could easily overtake the city's levee system, swamping the city under a pool of toxic chemicals, human waste and even coffins set adrift from the city's graveyards."[11] Shortly before landfall, Nagin conceded that Katrina's storm surge would "most likely topple our levee system."[12]

By the morning of Sunday, August 28, New Orleans was under evacuation orders. The roads were packed. Inbound lanes of the main highways were redirected to handle outbound traffic. Many residents, however, could not or would not leave. A reporter for the *Atlanta Journal-Constitution* interviewed Harry Hornet, a retired physician whose home was on Lake Pontchartrain. "I knew it was going to hit one day," Hornet said. "But I was just hoping I'd be gone by then."[13] In a press conference, Nagin had acknowledged that one hundred thousand or more of the city's residents lacked the transportation needed to leave the city; a disproportionate number of these residents were elderly, poor, or African American. "The Superdome might be used as a shelter for people with no transportation," Nagin announced.[14] John Martin, a sixty-year-old "druid and voodoo priest" chose to ride out the storm in the city's historic French Quarter, saying that he did not want to leave because he had "four snakes, including a giant Burmese python, Eugene, who ha[d] gone into hiding. The snake sense[d] something coming, Martin said—something horrific."[15] When the Superdome opened to receive those unable to evacuate, "people on walkers, some with oxygen tanks, began checking in." The mayor had advised them to bring "enough food and supplies to last three to five days."[16]

On the morning of August 29, Hurricane Katrina's eyewall made its first Gulf Coast landfall at Plaquemines Parish, Louisiana. Initially, New Orleans and its mayor were hopeful that a disaster had been avoided. The city had been spared the storm's strongest winds and storm surge. "Wall Street breathed a sigh of relief as New Orleans escaped the doomsday scenario many had painted for the city from the big storm."[17] Oil prices backed off from their highs, and stocks held steady.

Within hours, however, it became clear that the levee system was failing. Water overtopped the levees in some areas. In others, leaks developed and the pumps designed to protect the city from the water that entered it began to fail. The "bowl" that included many of the city's poorest neighborhoods began to fill up. Public policy expert Donald Kettl wrote that "some terrified residents clambered up from the ground floor and, as the water continued to rise, retreated to their attics. As the water kept rising, they punched holes in their roofs and found themselves stranded. Some residents did not move fast enough. . . . Soon, the television crews began documenting bodies floating down the city's streets."[18] Although they initially defended the levee system, officials from the Army Corps of Engineers "eventually conceded [that the levees] were breached because of flawed engineering."[19]

More than one thousand residents of Louisiana died in the storm and the flooding that followed. Elderly residents, many unable to evacuate, were particularly vulnerable. A study of the bodies recovered following the storm concluded that "64 percent of the people who died were elderly."[20] The devastation was not limited to New Orleans or Louisiana. Reports of deaths and injuries in Mississippi and parts of Alabama began coming in, most of those caused by the storm's powerful surge of water. According to the *Edmonton Journal*, "Mississippi governor Haley Barbour said the hurricane hit the state 'like a ton of bricks.' In Gulfport, there were reports of storm surges close to six metres high and boats tossed into the sides of buildings."[21] Half of the residents of Mississippi lost power, and entire neighborhoods were flattened. Wildlife disappeared.

FIGURE 14.1

New Orleans' Levee System

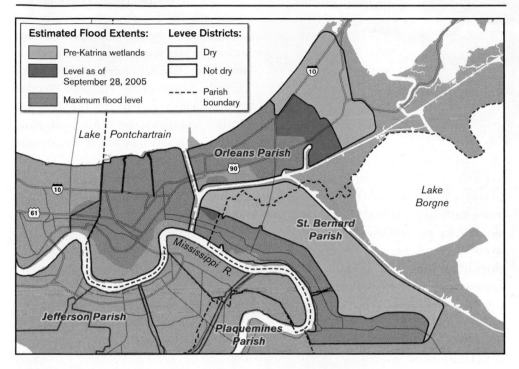

Estimated Flood Extents:
- Pre-Katrina wetlands
- Level as of September 28, 2005
- Maximum flood level

Levee Districts:
- Dry
- Not dry
- ----- Parish boundary

Lake Pontchartrain

Orleans Parish

Lake Borgne

St. Bernard Parish

Mississippi R.

Jefferson Parish

Plaquemines Parish

A map showing the New Orleans levee system following Hurricane Katrina. The areas in blue and red show the extent of flooding following the breaches in the levee system.

Source: R. B. Seed et al., "Figure 1.4: Map Showing Principal Features of the Main Flood Protection Rings or 'Polders' in the New Orleans Area," in *Preliminary Report on the Performance of the New Orleans Levee Systems in Hurricane Katrina on August 9, 2005*, U.S. Senate Committee on Homeland Security and Governmental Affairs, November 17, 2005, http://www.hsgac.senate.gov//imo/media/doc/Katrina/Preliminary_Report.pdf?attempt=2.

Immediately after the scope of the devastation became clear, calls went out for donations to private relief agencies, such as the American Red Cross and the Salvation Army. Money—rather than food, blankets, or other goods—was the main request, which allowed these organizations to respond more quickly and effectively as they saw needs arise. "Please contribute what you can," a Florida newspaper implored, "and be grateful—again—that you are at the giving end."[22]

In the days, weeks, and months that followed, Gulf Coast residents looked to the Federal Emergency Management Agency (FEMA) to step in and lead recovery efforts. A disaster specialist at Colorado University predicted that the agency's response would be significant. "In these large disasters," he said, "the traditional rules of operation get thrown out the window."[23] However, as refugees from New Orleans evacuated to nearby states following the storm, they shared not only stories of loss and devastation but plenty of criticism for how public officials had handled the disaster. Some of the sharpest words came from those who sheltered at the Superdome. The stadium was "like a war zone," according to sisters Maia Brisco and Anysia Nickerson. "It was a total hell hole," Brisco angrily told a reporter.[24]

In the aftermath of Hurricane Katrina, the performance of local, state, and federal officials in predicting, preparing for, and responding to the storm came under intense

The effects of Hurricane Katrina were felt far beyond New Orleans. New Orleans residents, including five-year-old Donte Percy, were evacuated first to the Superdome and then ultimately to places like this shelter for refugees in Houston, Texas.

scrutiny. Figuring prominently in this process was the federal bureaucracy, which is really a small universe of organizations operating across the country. Within this vast system are departments, agencies, and bureaus, which themselves are often divided and subdivided into smaller organizational units. The National Hurricane Center, for example, is part of the National Weather Service, which is part of the National Oceanic and Atmospheric Administration, which, in turn, is part of the Department of Commerce.

As the nation was confronted with scenes of devastation and loss in Katrina's wake, parts of the federal bureaucracy, such as the National Hurricane Center, were singled out for praise. Others, however, such as the Army Corps of Engineers and FEMA, received sharp criticism. How could some parts of the vast machinery of the federal government have gotten things right while others seemed to have gotten them so wrong? As Congress, the White House, and the American people asked this very question, it was concluded that the answers were complicated, just like the vast bureaucracy responsible for preparing for and responding to disasters such as Hurricane Katrina.

▮ THEORIES OF BUREAUCRATIC ORGANIZATION

Americans' ambivalent feelings about the federal bureaucracy may be partly due to the fact that—unlike Congress, the president, or the Supreme Court—Americans actually have contact with it in their personal or professional lives, often without even thinking about it. Before he or she even gets out of bed in the morning, the federal bureaucracy has impacted the life of the average American in ways almost too numerous to list. If a person's mattress, pillows, sheets, and blankets were made in the United States, federal agencies were involved in making sure that the factory was safe for its employees, that it did not discriminate in hiring, that it dealt with labor issues and complaints fairly, and that it did not degrade the environment. If the bedding was not manufactured in the United States, the bureaucracy acted to ensure that the country of origin was following rules of fair trade and labor practices promised in trade agreements. Even the time on the alarm clock has a federal agency overseeing it to make sure that states are in compliance with time zones and Daylight Savings Time.[25]

Driving much of this bureaucratic involvement in daily life are the demands of Americans themselves—for safe products, fair labor practices, and environmentally conscious factories. Ensuring that these demands are met involves the federal bureaucracy in many areas of the nation's economy and private life. The vast majority of the federal bureaucracy lies within the executive branch of the federal government, which is tasked with executing, or carrying out, federal laws.

The many agencies within the federal bureaucracy are only a part of the bureaucratic landscape in which Americans live. In addition to the federal bureaucracy, there is another category of public bureaucracies: **state and local bureaucracies**. These agencies are also involved in the life of our newly awakened American citizen; they make the rules that governed the construction of the house in which the citizen lives; determine the property taxes that he or she pays; provide the school, police station, and firehouse down the street; and supply the water in the glass next to the alarm clock.

But it is more complicated than that. The same products regulated by public bureaucracies—federal, state, and local—have been produced by another category of bureaucratic organizations: **private bureaucracies**. While corporations and companies are not usually called bureaucracies, they in fact are. They share some, though not all, of the characteristics of public bureaucracies. A common critique of public bureaucracies is that they should try to operate more like the makers of mattresses, sheets, and alarm clocks and less like the government, a topic to which we will return later in the chapter. In short, bureaucratic organization is everywhere. It is an elaborate system, but not necessarily a mysterious one.

Before we begin to untangle the complex constellation of federal administrative organizations, we need to consider how bureaucracies operate, which is not an easy task as there does not exist one single, neat summation. The term *bureaucracy* describes an organization or a set of organizations, but it also describes a way of organizing, a way of distributing power. Scholars have offered a variety of theoretical approaches to explaining bureaucratic organization, none of which have to be mutually exclusive. Three approaches, in particular, highlight different aspects of bureaucratic organization: rules, people, and tasks.

Rules and Procedures-Centered Organization

Max Weber (pronounced VAY-ber), a German sociologist, undertook one of the first scholarly attempts to define the boundaries and characteristics of bureaucratic organization. The bureaucracy in Weber's analysis was a large and complex machine. Each individual in this machine—a **bureaucrat**—was "only a single cog in an ever-moving mechanism, which prescribes him to an essentially fixed route of march."[26] For Weber, bureaucratic power rested upon what he called "rational-legal authority," in which citizens accept the authority of organizations, or, more precisely, the rules and organizational structures that define that authority and place limits upon it. Once firmly established, Weber

CONNECTING TO . . .

Theories of Bureaucratic Organization

As you reflect upon the criticism of local, state, and federal officials that followed Hurricane Katrina as well as the theories of bureaucratic organization that we will explore next, consider the following:

- What a bureaucracy is and how prevalent bureaucratic organizations are in everyday life, often in ways that go unnoticed

- How specialization, division of labor, and standard operating procedures shape bureaucratic outcomes and the actions of individuals within them

- How federal, state, and local bureaucratic agencies may all interact in certain policy areas, such as preparation and response to natural disasters

state and local bureaucracies
public organizations below the federal level designed to carry out specific tasks according to a prescribed set of rules and procedures.

private bureaucracies
privately owned corporations and companies that carry out specific tasks according to a prescribed set of rules and procedures.

bureaucrat
an official employed within a government bureaucracy.

An employee performs the first inspection of fresh potatoes at the Campbell Soup Co. plant in Sacramento, California. Campbell's produces up to ten million cans of soup every day. Every can is impacted by the rules and regulations that are administered by federal, state, and local bureaucracies. These regulations cover everything from the soup's production to its distribution, sale, and consumption.

Ken James/Bloomberg via Getty Images.

standard operating procedures
the sets of rules governing the behavior of bureaucrats.

principal-agent problem
the challenge that arises when one actor, the principal, tasks another, the agent, to carry out the principal's wishes in the presence of uncertainty and unequal information.

concluded, "bureaucracy is among those social structures which are hardest to destroy."[27]

The Weberian bureaucracy is characterized by four main organizational traits. First, bureaucrats have defined tasks and rules governing how these tasks should be carried out, creating a clear *division of labor* within the organization. The sets of rules governing the behavior of bureaucrats are commonly referred to as **standard operating procedures.** Second, authority in bureaucracy is *hierarchical*, with "a clearly established system of super- and sub-ordination in which there is a supervision of the lower offices by the higher ones."[28] Third, individual jobs within the organization are *specialized*, with workers increasingly selected for specific jobs based on their technical competence. Finally, the modern bureaucracy is characterized by *impersonal relationships*. Weber's ideal of a bureaucracy was, by design, divorced from politics and personal relationships, its effective functioning made more likely if "it succeeds in eliminating from official business love, hatred, and all purely personal, irrational, and emotional elements which escape calculation."[29]

People-Centered Organization

Chester Barnard drew on decades of experience with the American Telephone and Telegraph Company in the early twentieth century to outline a theory of the bureaucracy in which people—and not just rules and procedures—mattered to the life of a bureaucracy. For Barnard, the essence of a bureaucracy is that it involves "conscious coordination" of the activities of individuals in pursuit of a joint objective.[30] Looked at this way, bureaucracies are literally everywhere.

Consider a married couple whose goal is to enjoy an evening in the city. One spouse organizes the entertainment. Her job is to read the movie reviews and buy the tickets online. Her partner is in charge of dinner. She reads local restaurant reviews and makes the reservation. These two women have consciously coordinated their activities; they have divided their authority and responsibility with a clear set of tasks for each. They have created a kind of bureaucracy, even if a small and temporary one. In doing so, each runs the risk that the other may fail to carry out her assigned task or do so according to her own preferences, failing to take the other's desires into consideration. From this perspective, bureaucracy is not an either/or thing but a continuum between small and temporary efforts at coordination and large, complex, and enduring ones. People are constantly participating in bureaucratic organization, knowingly or not. It is a question of degree and complexity.

Whenever people undertake action in pursuit of a common goal, however, they are taking a risk that others involved might not do what they are supposed to do. Political scientists often describe these risks in terms of the **principal-agent problem**. The "principal" in this model does not have to be a school principal, though he or she could be. Instead, the principal is the actor who asks the agent to carry out a task. The challenge in doing so is twofold. First, the agent may have his or her own goals, which may not be the same as the principal's. Second, the agent may have information that the principal lacks, which opens up the opportunity for the agent to behave in a way that is not in the interests of the principal.

Principal-agent relationships are everywhere. When a person takes his or her car into a repair shop, for example, he or she runs the risk that the mechanic, who may know much more about cars than the customer does, could take advantage of the inequality of information. When voters (the principals) elect members of Congress (the agents), the voters

FIGURE 14.2

Weber's Model Bureaucracy

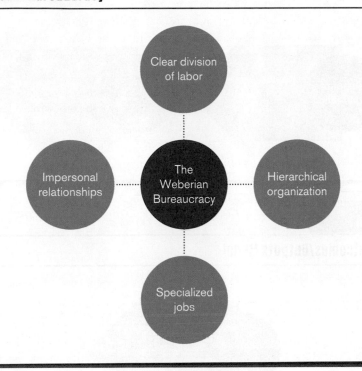

run the risk that their elected representatives will not faithfully carry out their wishes, especially during the parts of the legislative process that are harder to observe and happen out of public view.

According to Barnard, bureaucratic leadership is central to the success of a bureaucracy. The job of the leader is to secure the cooperation of those within the organization: "The vitality of organizations lies in the willingness of individuals to contribute forces to the cooperative system."[31] In this effort, **incentives**—those inducements that the leaders of a bureaucracy can offer to their employees—are key to successful performance. Incentives do not always have to involve money. Power, prestige, a sense of accomplishment, and a shared vision of important work can also act as incentives for successful bureaucratic performance. As we will examine later, however, incentives can act the other way, sending bureaucrats off in directions that Congress, the president, or the American people did not intend for them to go.

incentives
inducements that leaders of a bureaucracy can offer to their employees to spur successful performance.

Tasks: Outputs and Outcomes-Centered Organization

For political scientist James Q. Wilson, rules and procedures mattered, as did individuals. However, his analysis added a third element of bureaucratic organization: tasks, or what different bureaucrats in their organizations actually do. Wilson wrote that "people matter, but organization matters also, and tasks matter most of all."[32] Of special concern in Wilson's analysis was the ability or inability to observe two consequences of bureaucratic action: outputs and outcomes. Outputs are what bureaucratic operators do; outcomes are what changes in the world as a result of their actions. When either outputs or outcomes are difficult to observe with any certainty, problems arise. When both are difficult to discern, "effective management is almost impossible."[33]

FIGURE 14.3

Barnard's People-Centered Model

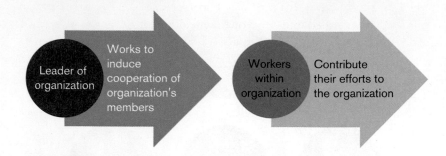

Leader of organization — Works to induce cooperation of organization's members → Workers within organization — Contribute their efforts to the organization

FIGURE 14.4

Wilson's Outcomes/Outputs Model

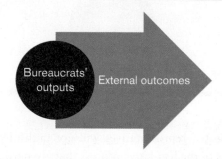

Bureaucrats' outputs — External outcomes

Consider the nation's public schools.[34] When a teacher closes the classroom door, that teacher's outputs are largely unseen except by the students. Sure, the principal can observe the teacher, but both know that the observation day is likely not a typical class. More problematically, especially as America is testing its students like never before, it is very difficult and expensive to try to measure a teacher's outcomes, or what a teacher is adding to the mind of one particular student.[35] In order to be effectively managed, both outputs and outcomes must be "visible."

WHAT HAVE I LEARNED?

1. According to Max Weber, one of the key characteristics of bureaucratic organization is _____.

   a. Its highly political nature
   b. A set of standard operating procedures
   c. The highly personal nature of relationships within it
   d. The ability to vote bureaucrats out of office

2. In a people-centered model of bureaucracy, one of the most important elements is _____.

   a. Strict control of employees based on rules and procedure
   b. Using incentives to encourage better performance
   c. Weak leadership
   d. Routine weekly meetings

3. What is the principal agent problem?

Answer Key: 1. b; 2. b; 3. Answers should discuss the challenges principals face in holding their agents accountable, especially in the presence of unequal levels of information.

THE DEVELOPMENT OF THE AMERICAN FEDERAL BUREAUCRACY

In the early years of its history, the American bureaucracy was absolutely tiny in comparison to what it has developed into, reflecting the reality that the autonomous and mostly agrarian society did not place many demands on the young national government. From its beginnings as a small set of departments employing few people, the bureaucracy has grown enormously and as of 2016 had nearly three million civilian employees working across the country.

This growth has not been steady and gradual, but—like the power of the national government itself—has experienced periods of relatively little growth and periods of intense expansion. The increase in the nation's population and boundaries, the complexity of tasks performed by the federal government, and greater demands for services by citizens have all contributed to this process. In addition, responses to crises— economic, social, and military—have produced some of the most dramatic expansions in the size, scope, and complexity of the federal bureaucracy.

> From its beginnings as a small set of departments employing few people, the American bureaucracy has grown enormously and as of 2016 had nearly three million civilian employees working across the country.

The Constitution and the Early Years of the Republic

Although the delegates to the Constitutional Convention wrestled a great deal with the issue of the power and independence of the chief executive, they spent very little time discussing the administrative apparatus itself, and the "Constitution is virtually silent on the subject."[36] Much of the constitutional basis for the bureaucracy lies in Article II, which lays out the functions and processes of the executive branch of government. In it, the president is authorized to "require the Opinion, in writing, of the principal Officer in each of the executive Departments, upon any Subject relating to the Duties of their respective Offices."[37] This section forms the basis for the executive branch departments, special organizations created by acts of Congress to assist the president in executing the laws of the nation. The heads of these departments are referred to as secretaries. Those secretaries form the president's cabinet, along with the vice president and the heads of other offices given cabinet-level status.

Avoiding Tyranny but Preserving Efficiency

The delegates to the Constitutional Convention brought with them a deep mistrust of administrative power that was born out of experiences under British colonial rule. Many of the charges against King George III in the Declaration of Independence focused on administrative abuses, including the charge that "he . . . erected a multitude of New Offices, and sent hither swarms of new Officers to harass our people, and eat out their substance." The delegates were in no mood to create a home-grown swarm of officers to harass the citizens of the nascent republic and take the fruits of their labor.

On the other hand, the delegates also held the general belief, gained from hard experience, that placing administrative responsibilities entirely in the hands of the legislature would be slow and inefficient. The Continental Congress had done just that, with numerous committees handling the business of fighting a revolution. This arrangement worked poorly, and individual members of the Congress were constantly overworked and overburdened. General George Washington complained that "there is a vital and inherent Principle of Delay incompatible with military service in transacting business thro' such numerous and different channels."[38]

Trying to steer a course between executive tyranny and legislative inefficiency, the delegates agreed to place in the hands of the president the authority to nominate executive branch officials rather than having a council of officers selected by Congress, which had been discussed in the convention. The Senate, though, retained the role of advice and consent in approving presidential nominees by a majority vote.[39] In addition, Congress retained the ability to impeach (in the House) and try (in the Senate) "all civil Officers of the United States" for "Treason, Bribery, or Other high Crimes and Misdemeanors."[40]

Removing Officers: The Unsettled Question

Having settled on how executive branch offers would be selected, the most contentious question facing the delegates was how these people were to be *removed*. Did the president have the authority to remove officers at will, was it Congress's job, or should there be a role for both the president and the Congress? Or were these people to serve for life with no possibility for removal? On this question—other than setting out the rarely used process of impeachment—the Constitution remained silent.

Only weeks after the first national Congress assembled, the issue of the removal of officers came before it in what has become known as the Decision of 1789. According to one historian, "For five days in June [this issue] completely absorbed the attention of the House and precipitated the first major constitutional debate" in the young Republic.[41] The trigger was a bill to create the Department of Foreign Affairs (later the Department of State). The Constitution had already established how the secretary would be selected: presidential nomination and Senate confirmation. But it said nothing about how to go about getting rid of him.[42]

Those who did not want the president to have this power argued that good, qualified men would not seek high administrative posts if the president could remove them for any reason, such as just not liking them. Representative Elbridge Gerry from Massachusetts warned that "perhaps the officer is not good-natured enough; he makes an ungraceful bow. . . . Now because he is so unfortunate as not to be a good dancer and he is a worthy officer, he must be removed."[43] James Madison was the most vocal proponent of the need to give the president removal power, lest the power of the executive branch itself be undermined. "The danger to liberty," Madison argued, "the danger of mal-administration has not yet been found to lay so much in the facility of introducing improper persons into office, as in the difficulty of displacing those who are unworthy of the public trust."[44]

With Vice President John Adams casting the tie-breaking vote in the Senate, Congress left the power of removal in the hands of the president. The question, however, reemerged with the Tenure of Office Act (1867), which—largely because of the tense politics following the Civil War—restricted the president's authority of removal. Only in 1926, in the case of *Myers v. United States*, which held the Tenure of Office Act unconstitutional, was the question settled. Presidents retained the authority to remove officials in the executive branch, a necessary ability in their role of ensuring laws are faithfully executed.[45]

The First Administration and the First Cabinet Departments

President George Washington's cabinet included just four men and three official departments. Secretary of State Thomas Jefferson oversaw the Department of State, handling the young nation's dealings with foreign nations as well as publishing laws and overseeing the hiring of civil officials. The Department of War (later incorporated into the Department of Defense) oversaw the nation's small military with less than one hundred civilian employees. Alexander Hamilton used his position as secretary of the Treasury to advance his goal of expanding the role of the federal government in the nation's economic affairs. Finally, Washington's attorney general (later made the head of the Department of Justice) acted as a legal advisor to the president and members of his cabinet. In the centuries since, Congress has created new departments and reorganized others (Figure 14.5).

In forming his first cabinet, Washington tried to reassure members of the experimental nation that his government was competent and representative of all of the thirteen states. He knew this task would not be easy. A week after his inauguration, the president wrote to a friend, "I anticipate that one of the most difficult and delicate parts of the duty of my Office will be that which relates to nominations for appointments."[46] Three of the members of his small cabinet represented diverse and powerful states: Massachusetts, New York, and Virginia.[47]

Washington was right to be worried. Within the first three years of his administration, "open warfare had broken out" between two powerful members of his cabinet: Alexander Hamilton and Thomas Jefferson.[48] With very different visions of the role of the federal government—especially in the nation's economic life—these men participated in some of the first **turf wars** in the history of the federal bureaucracy, in which each tried to take duties and responsibilities away from the other's department or keep his opponent from doing so. Neither man would serve out the entirety of Washington's two terms in office.

In choosing men to fill out his administration, Washington's primary consideration was what he referred to as "fitness of character," by which he meant integrity, a man's standing in the community, and qualities that would ensure the nation's confidence. Washington's priorities ensured that members of the upper social classes tended to be the ones to fill these positions.[49] Technical competence, except in a few positions, such as those involving legal matters, was not the primary consideration. Washington also viewed his cabinet as very much subordinate to his leadership, sometimes calling on his cabinet secretaries to take dictation.

turf wars
when bureaucrats compete to take duties and responsibilities away from one another's departments or keep their opponents from doing so.

The Jacksonian Era and the Rise of Political Patronage

In the early decades of the nineteenth century, most of the growth of the federal bureaucracy was a result of the geographic expansion of the nation; one particular issue that needed to be addressed was delivery of the mail across the growing territory. The bureaucratic reforms of President Andrew Jackson (1829–1837) sought to separate the person from the office. In his inaugural address in 1829, Jackson railed against the sense of "ownership" of important (and sometimes well-paying) administrative positions on the part of the office-holders, who in some cases unofficially handed the positions down to their heirs, as had been done officially in Britain and other European countries. "In a country where offices are created solely for the benefit of the people," Jackson argued, "no one man has any more intrinsic right to official station than another. Offices were not established to give support to particular men at the public expense. . . . The proposed limitation would destroy the idea of property now so generally connected with official station, and although individual distress may be sometimes produced, it would, by promoting that rotation which constitutes a leading principle in the republican creed, give healthful action to the system."[50]

As part of his reforms, Jackson employed what is called **political patronage**—filling administrative positions as a reward for support, rather than solely on merit. His use of patronage is commonly referred to as the **spoils system**; the name indicates that part of the

political patronage
filling administrative positions as a reward for support, rather than solely on merit.

spoils system
the practice of cleaning house of one's opponents and installing supporters in their place following a successful election.

FIGURE 14.5

Executive Branch Departments: Year of Establishment and Primary Tasks

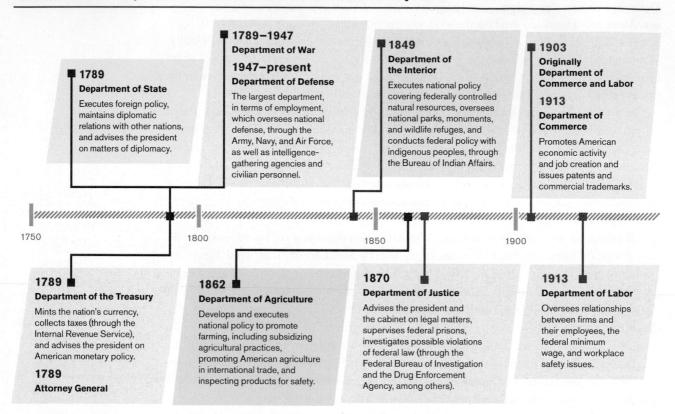

1789
Department of State
Executes foreign policy, maintains diplomatic relations with other nations, and advises the president on matters of diplomacy.

1789–1947
Department of War
1947–present
Department of Defense
The largest department, in terms of employment, which oversees national defense, through the Army, Navy, and Air Force, as well as intelligence-gathering agencies and civilian personnel.

1849
Department of the Interior
Executes national policy covering federally controlled natural resources, oversees national parks, monuments, and wildlife refuges, and conducts federal policy with indigenous peoples, through the Bureau of Indian Affairs.

1903
Originally Department of Commerce and Labor
1913
Department of Commerce
Promotes American economic activity and job creation and issues patents and commercial trademarks.

1750   1800   1850   1900

1789
Department of the Treasury
Mints the nation's currency, collects taxes (through the Internal Revenue Service), and advises the president on American monetary policy.
1789
Attorney General

1862
Department of Agriculture
Develops and executes national policy to promote farming, including subsidizing agricultural practices, promoting American agriculture in international trade, and inspecting products for safety.

1870
Department of Justice
Advises the president and the cabinet on legal matters, supervises federal prisons, investigates possible violations of federal law (through the Federal Bureau of Investigation and the Drug Enforcement Agency, among others).

1913
Department of Labor
Oversees relationships between firms and their employees, the federal minimum wage, and workplace safety issues.

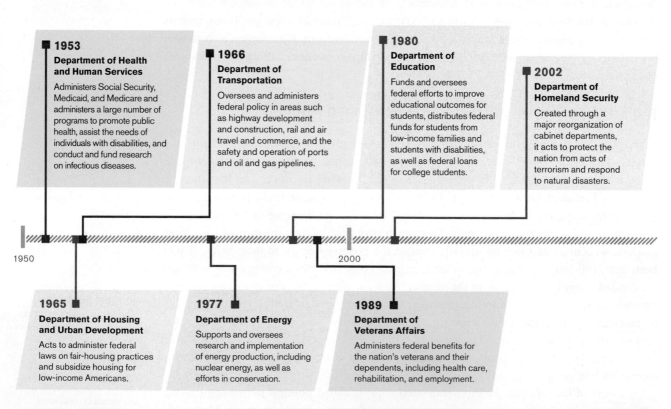

1953
Department of Health and Human Services
Administers Social Security, Medicaid, and Medicare and administers a large number of programs to promote public health, assist the needs of individuals with disabilities, and conduct and fund research on infectious diseases.

1966
Department of Transportation
Oversees and administers federal policy in areas such as highway development and construction, rail and air travel and commerce, and the safety and operation of ports and oil and gas pipelines.

1980
Department of Education
Funds and oversees federal efforts to improve educational outcomes for students, distributes federal funds for students from low-income families and students with disabilities, as well as federal loans for college students.

2002
Department of Homeland Security
Created through a major reorganization of cabinet departments, it acts to protect the nation from acts of terrorism and respond to natural disasters.

1950   2000

1965
Department of Housing and Urban Development
Acts to administer federal laws on fair-housing practices and subsidize housing for low-income Americans.

1977
Department of Energy
Supports and oversees research and implementation of energy production, including nuclear energy, as well as efforts in conservation.

1989
Department of Veterans Affairs
Administers federal benefits for the nation's veterans and their dependents, including health care, rehabilitation, and employment.

"spoils" of a successful election is the ability to clean house of one's opponents and install supporters in their place. Although politics—specifically removing political opponents and installing supporters—played a role in Jackson's reforms, so did a desire to separate a man from the office he held in order to undercut individual power bases as a challenge to Jackson's power and authority.

Ironically, one of the consequences of patronage was to make the federal bureaucracy in some ways closer to what Weber described: impartial, neutral, driven by standard operating procedures and technical expertise. If, after elections, a nation is constantly shuffling people in and out of important administrative positions—people who often have little expertise in the operations of those agencies and departments—then it becomes necessary to standardize procedures. Otherwise, little would get done, or at least done well. Thus, through his practices, Jackson and his supporters laid the foundations for the modern federal bureaucracy. As James Wilson put it, "Far from being enemies of the bureaucracy, the Jacksonians were among its principal architects."[51]

Post-Civil War Expansion

As America emerged from the devastation of the Civil War, the nation found itself engaged in relentless expansion of both the nation's boundaries in the West and of agriculture and industry. In order to cope with the demands placed upon the federal government as a result of this expansion, the bureaucracy grew in size and also in the scope of its involvement with the nation's economy.

As large corporations, such as the railroads, outgrew the ability of individual states to control and regulate them, demands by the public for a more active federal role in supervising businesses and commerce led to the creation of **independent regulatory agencies**, which exist outside of the major cabinet departments and whose job is to monitor and regulate specific sectors of the economy. Congress created the nation's first independent regulatory agency, the Interstate Commerce Commission, in 1887 in order to monitor price setting and other practices by the railroads. Other modes of transportation were added in later decades.

In addition to calls for regulation, the federal bureaucracy found itself confronted with the demands of organized interests, such as farmers, who sought to use the power of the federal government to advance and promote their own endeavors. The result was the development of **clientele agencies**, which, like their name implies, act to serve and promote the interests of their clients. The Department of Agriculture (1862) served the interests of farmers—one of the most powerful clientele groups of the time—by, for example, collecting and distributing data about advancements in agricultural practices.[52]

The development and expansion of the federal bureaucracy happened relatively late in the life of the American democracy, especially when compared to European democracies of the period. For most of these nations, a well-developed bureaucracy existed before they became democracies, having developed under the rule of monarchs. For political scientist

Courtesy of the Library of Congress, Prints and Photographs Division.

"In Memoriam—Our Civil Service as It Was," a cartoon by Thomas Nast, 1877. Nast's depiction highlights the end of the spoils system under civil service reforms.

independent regulatory agencies
organizations that exist outside of the major cabinet departments and whose job is to monitor and regulate specific sectors of the economy.

clientele agencies
organizations that act to serve and promote the interests of their clients.

Stephen Skowronek, the fact that the American bureaucracy had to develop in the shadow of two other, already established, sets of political institutions—the court system and political parties—resulted in a federal bureaucracy that was more fragmented and decentralized than its European counterparts.[53]

Political scientist Theda Skocpol looked to the same period in state development in order to explain why America never developed the kind of comprehensive social welfare state as Europe, even though America introduced some of the earliest social welfare policies in the world with its system of pensions for Civil War veterans and their survivors. For Skocpol, the well-developed system of federal courts was hostile to large-scale government intervention on behalf of citizens, and American political parties did not want to give up the power they gained by providing benefits in return for political patronage.[54]

Both of these studies highlight the idea of American exceptionalism, in which scholars have examined how the unique histories, paths, and development of American political institutions may have led to uniqueness in the nation's representative government itself. In doing so, scholars have also stressed the importance of **path dependence**, in which a set of political choices at one time produces a set of outcomes that shapes the possibilities for future politics and public policies.

path dependence
the way in which a set of political outcomes shapes future possibilities for political action.

The Progressive Era

The period known as the Progressive Era (roughly from 1890 to 1920) is known for the continued expansion of the role of the federal bureaucracy in the nation's economic life and for attempts to take politics out of the bureaucracy itself. The Sherman Antitrust Act of 1890 and the Pure Food and Drug Act of 1906, for example, expanded the role of the federal government in regulating businesses that affected the lives of ordinary Americans. Congress created the Department of Commerce and Labor in 1903 to oversee and regulate workplaces, the rights of employees, and working conditions, which had become the focus of reform-minded journalists called muckrakers.[55] In 1913 the department was split in two, with the Department of Commerce focusing on economic growth and the Department of Labor on employee-employer relations and workplace conditions.

Pendleton Act
(or Civil Service Reform Act of 1883) created the first United States Civil Service Commission to draw up and enforce rules on hiring, promotion, and tenure of office within the civil service.

While the Progressive Era saw the expansion of the federal bureaucracy, it also witnessed attempts to reform it, especially in trying to alleviate the effects of the patronage system of appointment to and within the bureaucracy. The model that these reformers used was one of science and business. Their target was what they saw as a corrupt, inefficient, and too-political bureaucracy. "Reform as we understand it," according to a speaker at the annual meeting of the Civil Service Reform League in 1886, "seeks to take the whole non-political public service out of politics."[56]

A political cartoon depicting President Theodore Roosevelt as a muckraker taking on the meatpacking industry. Muckrakers focused on a variety of abuses in private industry, including working conditions.

President James Garfield (1881) had intended to work on bureaucratic reform in his administration, but his presidency was cut short with his assassination in 1881 by a troubled and unsuccessful office seeker, an act that helped catalyze public opinion in support for reform. The reform taken up by Garfield's successor, Chester A. Arthur (1881–1885), was popular among voters. During Arthur's tenure, Congress passed the Civil Service Reform Act of 1883, commonly known as the **Pendleton Act**

A NAUSEATING JOB, BUT IT MUST BE DONE

in reference to its primary Senate sponsor. The Pendleton Act created the first United States Civil Service Commission. Its three members, appointed by Arthur, were active reformers. Their task was to draw up and enforce rules on hiring, promotion, and tenure of office within the civil service.

Under these new rules, members of the **federal civil service** were hired and promoted on the basis of the **merit system**, in which competitive testing results, educational attainment, and other qualifications formed the basis for hiring and promotion rather than politics and personal connections. Even the test questions themselves were prohibited from calling "for the expression or disclosure of any political or religious opinion or affiliation."[57] In addition, civil service workers' participation in political campaigns was restricted—in particular, they could not be forced or coerced by superiors into donating to or participating in a political campaign.[58] In the early years after the act's passage, only a small percentage of federal bureaucrats were covered by its content; by 2016, more than 90 percent were.

The Great Depression, World War II, and the Cold War

As we discussed in Chapter 3, President Franklin Roosevelt's efforts to combat the crisis of the Great Depression, collectively called the New Deal, resulted in an unprecedented expansion of the size of the federal bureaucracy as well as an equally startling expansion of the role of government and the bureaucracy in the American economy. In enacting his numerous policies, Roosevelt created a host of bureaucratic agencies—though only after a challenge from the Supreme Court. Many of these were clientele agencies, acting on behalf of specific groups of citizens, such as the unemployed. Their purpose was to increase the provision of social services to affected Americans, including senior citizens, low-income and unemployed Americans, and individuals with disabilities.

The Great Depression, however, was only one of two struggles that Roosevelt and the nation faced during his administration. As president, Roosevelt was commander in chief during most of his nation's involvement in World War II. In the fight with U.S. allies (especially Great Britain and the Soviet Union) against what were then known as the axis powers (Germany, Japan, and Italy), Roosevelt and his administration oversaw a massive expansion of the military, the creation of new agencies to prosecute the war, and significant federal intervention in the American economy in order to support and supply the war effort. The Office of Price Administration, for example, had power over the prices of almost all retail goods and oversaw a system of rationing for scarce goods and those crucial to the war effort.[59]

President Abraham Lincoln, at the outbreak of the Civil War in 1861, reassured Americans that the "strong medicine" of his wartime powers would not be needed once the nation was successfully restored, and he was correct in his prediction. When the allies emerged successful in World War II, however, no similar retrenchment occurred. America and its former ally, the Soviet Union, entered a decades-long period of competition for global supremacy known as the Cold War. While no full-scale global war occurred between the two superpowers, they aimed thousands of nuclear weapons at each other and engaged in smaller military confrontations across the globe, supporting opposing sides without directly engaging each other's militaries on a large scale.

To fight the Cold War, the federal bureaucracy saw the creation of new agencies. President Harry S. Truman (1945–1953) signed into law the National Security Act of 1947, which created the National Security Council to advise the president on security matters and the Central Intelligence Agency (CIA) to advise the president on intelligence matters and help coordinate intelligence-gathering activities.[60] Not a formal cabinet department, the CIA is an example of an **independent executive agency**. These agencies resemble cabinet departments in many ways, such as having their top administrators appointed by and reporting to the president, but they

federal civil service
the permanent professional branches of government concerned with administrative functions, excluding the armed forces and political appointments.

merit system
a system of hiring and promotion based on competitive testing results, education, and other qualifications rather than politics and personal connections.

independent executive agency
agencies otherwise similar to cabinet departments but existing outside of the cabinet structure and usually having a narrower focus of mission.

President Barack Obama and members of his National Security Council, an important part of the federal bureaucracy. From left: Director Nicholas Rasmussen of the National Counterterrorism Center, Deputy Secretary of State Tony Blinken, Chairman of the Joint Chiefs of Staff General Joseph Dunford, Defense Secretary Ashton Carter, Secretary of State John Kerry, Obama, National Security Advisor Susan Rice, Attorney General Loretta Lynch, Director John Brennan of the CIA, Director of National Intelligence James Clapper, Deputy National Security Advisor Avril Haines, and Deputy National Security Adviser for Strategic Communication Ben Rhodes.

Mandel Ngan/AFP/Getty Images.

exist outside of the cabinet structure and usually have a narrower focus of mission. The National Aeronautics and Space Administration (NASA) is another example of an independent agency. Created in 1958, it was in many ways another product of the Cold War, spawned to help American efforts in the "space race" with the Soviets after they had won the first round with the launch of the first orbital satellite, Sputnik, in 1957. Fearful of Soviet nuclear weapons raining down from space, the American people demanded action.

The Great Society and the War on Poverty

Postwar economic prosperity allowed the nation to fund a large expansion in the national bureaucracy in the areas of defense and the provision of social services. Under the umbrella of the Great Society, President Lyndon B. Johnson (1963–1969) proposed a series of expansions to the social safety net with the goal of securing opportunity for more Americans. Congress passed these proposals, in no small part to Johnson's knowledge of and skill in dealing with the institution. Some of these programs and goals had already been proposed by President John F. Kennedy (1961–1963) prior to his assassination but had been stuck in Congress.

Health care, education, housing, transit, job training, and urban renewal all became targets for Johnson's programs, and an increase in the size and budgets of federal departments and agencies made it possible to carry these projects out. The Department of Housing and Urban Development was created in 1965 and the Department of Transportation in 1966. Efforts to secure civil rights for Americans and battle discrimination based on sex and race led to the passage of the Civil Rights Act of 1964.[61] The act created the Equal Employment Opportunity Commission, which today acts to enforce prohibitions on discrimination in the workplace based on racial identity, sex, religious preference, national origin, age, or disability.

Retrenchment and Scaling Back

When he was elected president of the United States in 1980, Ronald Reagan (1981–1989) promised to reduce the size of the federal government as well as its impact the daily lives of Americans. As discussed in Chapter 3, efforts at devolution attempted to return power over implementing public policy back to the individual states. Efforts at deregulation aimed to reduce government oversight of and involvement with specific industries, notably transportation, banking, and utilities. Though Reagan, his Republican successor President George H. W. Bush (1989–1993), and his Democratic successor Bill Clinton (1993–2001) all promised some form of bureaucratic reform or improvement, the federal bureaucracy did not undergo a major restructuring during the period. One area in which the federal bureaucracy did see a significant reduction, however, was in defense; this was a result of the end of the Cold War with the collapse of the Soviet Union in 1991 and a re-prioritizing of American military goals and strategy.

1. Reasons for the growth of the federal bureaucracy include _____.

    a. Growth in the nation's population
    b. Demands for services
    c. The complexity of tasks performed by government
    d. All of the above

2. The cabinet includes _____.

    a. The heads of executive branch departments
    b. Members of key congressional committees
    c. Federal justices
    d. All of the above

3. The spoils system refers to _____.

    a. Ruining the chances of one's electoral competition

    b. Rewarding political supporters with political appointments
    c. Restrictions on campaign contributions
    d. Firing bureaucrats for incompetence

4. Clientele agencies _____.

    a. Are found mostly in local bureaucracies
    b. Act as independent regulators of businesses
    c. Undertake mostly technical tasks, such as space exploration
    d. Promote the interests of specific groups or industries

5. What is the theory of path dependence?

Answer Key: 1. d; 2. a; 3. b; 4. d; 5. Answers should describe the ways in which a set of political outcomes shapes future possibilities for political action.

THE STRUCTURE OF THE MODERN FEDERAL BUREAUCRACY

The American federal bureaucracy is not one structure but a complex web of organizations and organizations within organizations. As the head of the executive branch, the president is tasked to ensure that the apparatus of the executive branch bureaucracy faithfully executes the laws of the nation. She or he appoints (with Senate confirmation) people to the top levels of the bureaucracy and directs and advises the departments, bureaus, and agencies on how they should go about putting the laws into effect. The requirements of this task, however, are by no means only technical. They are also political. When the American people feel that the federal bureaucracy has failed, the president acts as a lightning rod for their outrage.

In the weeks and months following Katrina's landfall, President George W. Bush came under intense scrutiny and criticism for his management of the disaster, the preparations for it, and the federal government's handling of rebuilding efforts. Documents that emerged indicated that Bush's administration had been warned in advance about the potential devastation and the potential "collapse of floodwalls along New Orleans's Lake Pontchartrain shoreline, an event that [a] report described as 'the greatest concern.'"[62]

As Hurricane Rita bore down on Texas less than a month after Katrina, Bush flew to his home state to show the nation that his administration was prepared and engaged. The *New York Times* reported that "Mr. Bush, who was photographed strumming a guitar in San Diego on the morning that New Orleans was being flooded . . . appeared intent on ensuring that there would be no off-message pictures this time and no question of where his attention was focused."[63] Briefings held with Texas governor Rick Perry, the heads of federal agencies, and Pentagon officials showed that, according to White House press secretary Scott McClellan, "[Bush] is the president, and he has indicated [that] it is his responsibility when it comes to the federal government's role in these hurricanes."[64]

The primary administrative units in the federal bureaucracy are the fifteen cabinet departments. Congress has the authority to establish and fund the departments, each of which is responsible for a major area of public policy. They are typically divided into subunits based on the policy in which they specialize. The division of tasks between departments does not always follow a clear logic; historical development, politics, and competition between the divisions of the federal bureaucracy over the authority to perform a specific task—and spend the funds Congress has allocated to do so—have all shaped the complicated, and often confusing, division of labor between departments.

FIGURE 14.6

Differences in Size and Funding between Cabinet Departments

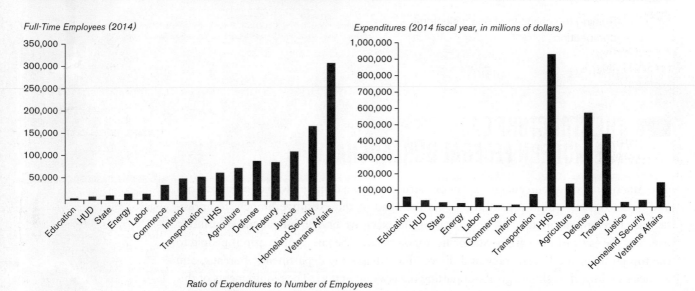

Note: HUD = Housing and Urban Development; HHS = Health and Human Services.

Source: Employment data are from United States Office of Personnel Management, "Sizing Up the Executive Branch, Fiscal Year 2014," August 2015, https://www.opm.gov/policy-data-oversight/data-analysis-documentation/federal-employment-reports/reports-publications/sizing-up-the-executive-branch.pdf. Expenditures are from Office of Management and Budget, "Table 4.1: Outlays by Agency, 1962–2021," Historical Tables, https://www.whitehouse.gov/omb/budget/Historicals.

There is considerable diversity in the size and budgets of the cabinet departments. (See Figure 14.6.) Sizeable budgets do not always mean large numbers of employees. For example, the Department of Health and Human Services (which issues payments for Social Security and Medicare) and the Department of the Treasury (which makes interest payments on the national debt) both have relatively large budgets for the number of employees in them. Prestige also varies between the departments, including one of its most visible markers: face time with the president.

Cabinet departments are headed by cabinet secretaries (or by the attorney general in the case of the Justice Department) who are nominated by the president and confirmed by a majority vote in the Senate. Cabinet secretaries formally work under the president; however, they also depend on Congress for appropriation of funds and for legislation that sets out specific goals and objectives for their departments. In addition, cabinet secretaries often have to contend with pressure from those affected by the actions of their departments, such as citizens or organized interest groups. It is a complicated job; they "are expected to perform an array of what might otherwise be viewed as distinctive tasks— building electoral support, making policy, and managing people and programs—while withstanding intense public scrutiny."[65] Secretaries have deputy secretaries, undersecretaries, and administrative staff to help them with their efforts.[66]

The newest cabinet department, now considered one of the most influential, is the Department of Homeland Security (DHS), formed in 2002 in response to the terrorist attacks the previous September.[67] The DHS pulled together twenty-two agencies from eight cabinet departments to better coordinate preemption of and national responses to terrorist acts as well as oversee general preparedness for other national emergencies.

In the aftermath of Katrina, President Bush was not alone in feeling the wrath of the American public. Secretary of Homeland Security Michael Chertoff shared blame for what was widely perceived as poor preparation and response, having "waited 36 hours after Katrina made landfall to activate the National Response Plan, which unites all federal disaster-response resources."[69] Calls for Chertoff's resignation were widespread.

Independent executive agencies function similarly to departments in many ways but are usually narrower in focus and retain more independence in carrying out their goals. NASA, which is in charge of the nation's space program, and the Environmental Protection Agency (EPA), which is tasked with preserving the quality of the environment, are notable examples of independent executive agencies. FEMA had previously been an independent agency but was folded into the Department of Homeland Security.

FEMA and its director, Michael Brown, came under some of the sharpest criticism. Days after the storm hit the Gulf Coast, Bush praised FEMA, and Brown's leadership, saying, "Brownie, you're doing a heck of a job."[70] Most others were not convinced of this, and some argued that Brown's primary qualification to serve as head of FEMA was that he had close personal ties to the president.[71] The agency was accused of wasting "precious days" in mounting its response.[72] Senator Susan Collins (R-ME)

Three-year-old Aaliyah Blanchard, and eighteen-year-old Shantell Blanchard eat a Thanksgiving meal of gumbo outside the trailers they were calling home in November 2005 in New Orleans. Sixteen Blanchard family members whose residences were destroyed by the flooding were living in three FEMA trailers in the backyard of a family member's home. Criticism of how FEMA handled the disaster ultimately led to the resignation of its director, Michael Brown.

Mario Tama/Getty Images.

critiqued the "lack of coordination and planning and a disconnect between what FEMA officials' perception was and what the reality was facing state and local officials."[73] Two weeks after Katrina struck, and with most of his role in relief efforts assigned to other officials, Brown resigned as director of FEMA.

As relief and rebuilding efforts began, there were widespread charges of inefficiency, waste, and fraud. According to journalist Megan O'Matz, "FEMA signed off on most emergency claims without ever verifying damage and failed to confirm the identities of applicants filing by phone. In at least 1,000 cases, people succeeded in collecting aid by using the social security numbers of dead people."[74] Charges such as this led to widespread calls to dismantle the agency entirely.

Independent regulatory agencies act to oversee and regulate governmental function, especially in economic affairs. Created by Congress to have enough independence to protect them from political partisanship, they are typically headed by appointed boards with fixed and staggered terms of service, making it more difficult to remove their leadership.

government corporations
organizations that act as businesses within the federal government, charging fees for their services but still subject to governmental control and possible financial subsidization.

Government corporations act as businesses within the federal government, charging fees for their services but still subject to governmental control and possible financial subsidization (Figure 14.7). The earliest government corporation was the Federal Deposit Insurance Corporation (FDIC), established as part of the New Deal to avoid a repeat of the bank runs in the Great Depression by insuring deposits in the nation's banks. Congress has since established other government corporations, often to step in and provide services when the private sector does not. The National Railroad Passenger Railroad Corporation, for example, operates commuter railroads under the business name Amtrak to ensure the provision of intercity rail service.

private contractors
nongovernmental workers hired by the federal bureaucracy to provide goods and services in support of federal activity.

Private contractors are not officially a part of the federal bureaucracy, but the government increasingly relies on them to provide goods and services in support of federal activity. The United States military, for example, relies on contractors for logistical support. Proponents of contracting argue that it allows the military and federal agencies to focus on their core missions. Opponents worry about a lack of careful oversight of contractor activities.

WHAT HAVE I LEARNED?

1. Congress plays a major role in how cabinet departments function.

   a. True
   b. False

2. Independent executive agencies are different from cabinet departments because _____.

   a. Cabinet departments are responsible for fewer tasks
   b. Independent executive agencies are narrower in their focus
   c. Independent agencies charge fees for their services
   d. Cabinet heads are hired to lobby the government

3. In this story, DHS stands for the _____.

   a. Department of Housing and Schools
   b. Department of Hospital Services
   c. Department of Homeland Security
   d. Department of Human Services

4. The federal bureaucracy is often criticized for its size and complexity. What examples of this do we see illustrated in the story of Hurricane Katrina?

Answer Key: 1. a; 2. b; 3. c; 4. Answers should include a discussion of multiple agencies with overlapping responsibilities, leading to inefficiency and slowness in responding to crises.

The Department of Homeland Security's Color-Coded Advisory System

In 2002, in the wake of the 9/11 attacks, the Department of Homeland Security created a color-coded advisory system that was designed to alert the American people to the risk of terrorist attacks.

The system was often criticized, partly for its vagueness and partly for the fact that the information underlying a change to the threat level was not made public. Government officials, however, countered that the release of such information would endanger national security. In 2011 the system was replaced with a two-tiered advisory system, consisting of bulletins and alerts. Before this happened, however, many commentators and comedians had a field day lampooning the old system.

Blogger Frank J., for example, created a "guide" for Americans to use to interpret the warning levels:

You see some movement in a nearby tree.

* Green: It's probably a squirrel. Hello squirrel.

* Blue: Better check out what it is to be on the safe side.

* Yellow: Might be the escaped monkey from the zoo. Better contact the authorities.

* Orange: It's a ninja! Fire indiscriminately into the treetops.

* Red: Set fire to the tree and all trees around it. No safe haven for ninjas![68]

WHAT DO YOU THINK?

What kinds of judgments might officials in the Department of Homeland Security make in balancing the need to alert Americans to the risk of terrorism against the need to protect source information? What kinds of information might Americans reasonably demand from such a system?

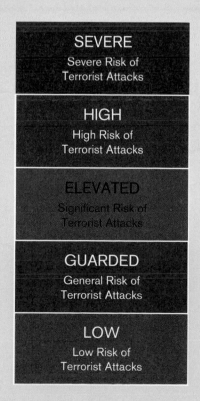

Source: United States Department of Homeland Security, Wikipedia, July 29, 2016, https://en.wikipedia.org/wiki/Homeland_Security_Advisory_System.

The Growth of the Federal Bureaucracy

One of the common concerns about the federal bureaucracy has been its dramatic increase in size, number of regulations, and spending, especially over the last century. This growth has led to charges that the federal government is becoming too powerful, too involved in Americans' lives. Critics often imply that more power—and more money—should be found at the state and local level.

Consider the graph below, which plots the real (inflation-adjusted) per capita federal expenditures from 1947 to 2004 (with and without defense spending included).[1]

Based on the chart above, one might plausibly tell a story about the massive growth in the influence of the federal government in the past fifty years. For example, in the early 1950s, real per capita federal spending was about $2,000. By the early 1980s, it had grown to $6,000 per person, three times as much, even when adjusted for inflation. When reading and interpreting graphs, however, it is often useful to also consider data that are not presented when making an argument—data that might complicate or counter the argument being made. Consider a similar chart that plots

spending by state and local governments during roughly the same period.

Adding this second graph leads to a more complex story. The past fifty years have witnessed increased spending across all levels of the American bureaucracy—federal, state, and local. Again, note that real per capita expenditures by state and local bureaucracies nearly tripled in the same time period (from the early 1950s to the early 1980s), rising from about $1,000 per person to nearly $3,000 per person. While the amounts were smaller than federal spending, the rate of growth was nearly the same.

WHAT DO YOU THINK?

How might these additional data affect your evaluations about the development of bureaucracy in the United States? What other data or graphs might you want to have in order to fully evaluate the growth in the federal bureaucracy?

[1] Thomas A. Garrett and Russell M. Rhine, "On the Size and Growth of Government," *Federal Reserve Bank of St. Louis Review* 88, no. 1 (January/February 2006): 13–30.

Real per Capita Federal Expenditures, 1947-2004

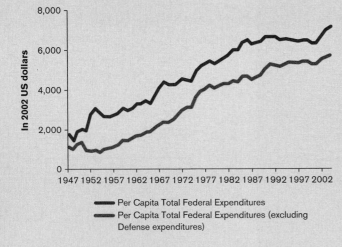

Per Capita Total Federal Expenditures
Per Capita Total Federal Expenditures (excluding Defense expenditures)

Real per Capita State and Local Government Expenditures, 1948-2004

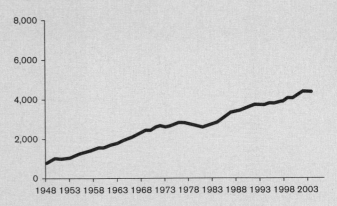

FIGURE 14.7

Examples of Federal Independent Regulatory Agencies and Government Corporations

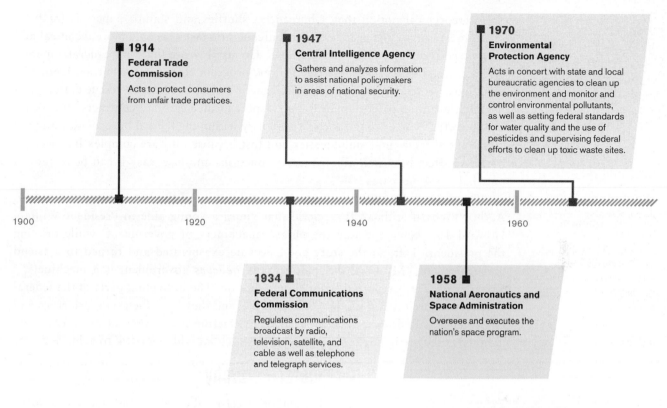

1914
Federal Trade Commission
Acts to protect consumers from unfair trade practices.

1947
Central Intelligence Agency
Gathers and analyzes information to assist national policymakers in areas of national security.

1970
Environmental Protection Agency
Acts in concert with state and local bureaucratic agencies to clean up the environment and monitor and control environmental pollutants, as well as setting federal standards for water quality and the use of pesticides and supervising federal efforts to clean up toxic waste sites.

1900   1920   1940   1960

1934
Federal Communications Commission
Regulates communications broadcast by radio, television, satellite, and cable as well as telephone and telegraph services.

1958
National Aeronautics and Space Administration
Oversees and executes the nation's space program.

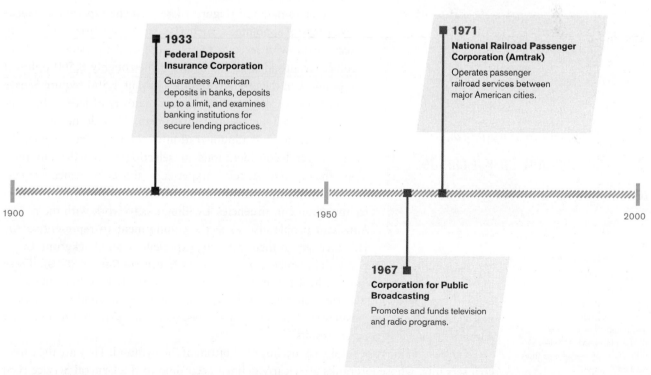

1933
Federal Deposit Insurance Corporation
Guarantees American deposits in banks, deposits up to a limit, and examines banking institutions for secure lending practices.

1971
National Railroad Passenger Corporation (Amtrak)
Operates passenger railroad services between major American cities.

1900   1950   2000

1967
Corporation for Public Broadcasting
Promotes and funds television and radio programs.

■ FEDERAL BUREAUCRATS

Organizations, Tasks, and Oversight

The stereotypical notion that a bureaucrat shuffles and stamps papers is far from accurate and becoming even less so as bureaucratic tasks become more technical and specialized. Professor emeritus Charles T. Goodsell wrote that "bureaucrats operate bridges, investigate crimes, manage forests, program computers, arbitrate labor disputes, counsel teenagers, calculate cost-benefit ratios, operate sea-rescue cutters, run libraries, examine patent applications, inspect meat, negotiate contracts, and so on and so forth."[75] The organization of authority within the federal bureaucracy and the tasks that agencies undertake matter, not just because they are complex but because both can affect how well a bureaucracy functions and how easy it can be to reform one that has gone astray.

The clash between the perception and the reality of the bureaucracy is not new. Author Richard Stillman II reported that "once a young aide to President William Howard Taft kept repeating the phrase 'machinery of government' while briefing the president. Taft, so the story goes, became exasperated and turned to a friend and whispered, 'My God, the man actually *believes* government is a machine!'"[76] True or not, Taft's reported estimation is spot on. The individual parts of the federal bureaucracy are people, not bits of a machine, and they have their own priorities and competencies. Politics, competition, and even faction are as present in bureaucratic action as they are in any other endeavor in which individuals work to achieve goals.

executive political appointees

employees at high levels in the federal bureaucracy who serve at the pleasure of the president and are subject to presidential removal.

The Federal Hierarchy

> The organization of authority within the federal bureaucracy and the tasks that agencies undertake matter . . . because both can affect how well a bureaucracy functions and how easy it can be to reform one that has gone astray.

Formally, authority across the federal bureaucracy is structured like a pyramid (Figure 14.8).[77] At the top are the **executive political appointees**, such as cabinet secretaries and deputy secretaries, who serve at the pleasure of the president and are subject to presidential removal. Of the roughly 6,500 political appointees in the executive branch, about 1,500 require Senate confirmation. Compared to the vast majority of federal bureaucrats, these individuals are short-timers. They do not expect to transition from one administration to the next. Presidents must juggle several considerations in selecting who will lead their departments and agencies. Experience and competence are certainly important, but so are political calculi and a desire to signal to important constituencies a willingness to work with them. The American people also expect a commitment to representing the wide diversity of their interests, experiences, and backgrounds.

Senior Executive Service (SES)

federal employees with higher-level supervisory and administrative responsibilities who are paid and treated more like vice presidents of businesses than political figures.

Below this top level are the members of the **Senior Executive Service (SES)**. These individuals—most of who are drawn from the lower ranks of the federal bureaucracy—enjoy slightly more job security than high-level appointees and are paid and treated more like vice presidents of businesses than political figures. They are expected to use their authority to achieve concrete results.

The vast majority of employees occupy the bottom of the pyramid. They are the career civil servants, whose job ranks are clearly defined according to the General Service (GS)

FIGURE 14.8

The Hierarchy of Labor in the Federal Bureaucracy

The structure of the federal bureaucracy, including the civil service system, is in many ways similar to that described by Max Weber: hierarchical and organized, with clear divisions between the levels. This structure was intentional, designed to insulate the majority of federal bureaucrats from the ebb and flow of party control of the executive branch.

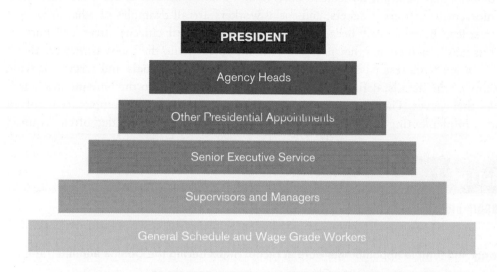

levels. Entrance into and advancement within the federal civil service is governed by the merit system, which relies on competitive examinations, educational qualifications, and performance reviews. Career civil servants enjoy considerable protections from termination, especially for political reasons. This job security is by design, though it presents presidents with a significant challenge. The federal bureaucracy is not a power station in which a president flips a switch and makes things happen automatically. Instead, it is a complex hierarchy of people, most of who will still have their jobs long after the president and political appointees have moved on.

Core Tasks: Implementation, Rulemaking, Advising, and Representation

The primary function of the federal bureaucracy is to implement, or put into action, the laws that Congress has passed. **Implementation** is rarely, if ever, a straightforward process.[78] New policies are not enacted in isolation; they are introduced into a universe of existing policies, sometimes with competing demands. As political scientist Herbert Kaufman observed, "A simple command or a single new statute sometimes has little effect because there is such a large body of existing law and practice . . . that it is not possible for government officers and employees to respond to the latest instruction without violating others and without infringing on the legitimate interests of a good many people."[79]

implementation
the bureaucracy's role in putting into action the laws that Congress has passed.

The technical knowledge required of many federal bureaucrats in order to successfully implement public policies also acts as a brake on the ability of a president or her or his political appointees to shape bureaucrats' actions. High-level executive branch officials may lack the technical expertise necessary to evaluate or challenge the actions of their subordinates. As Herbert Kaufman cautioned, "Against this formidable array . . . of knowledge, outsiders and generalists and politicians whose principle skills are in the realm of partisan battle find they must defer to the technicians."[80]

In addition, many front-line bureaucrats interact directly with citizens in an environment that makes it difficult to observe and control their behavior effectively. Law enforcement officers, teachers, and social workers are all examples of what are called street-level bureaucrats.[81] Because of their close contact with citizens, street-level bureaucrats may conclude that they need to "bend the rules" to do their jobs as they see them.

When Congress passes laws it often only sets general goals and targets, leaving many of the details, definitions, and specific procedures up to the bureaucratic agencies themselves. There is a sound logic behind this decision. The complexity involved with implementing policies, the technical and specialized knowledge often required

FIGURE 14.9

Increasing Diversity in Cabinet Appointments

Minority and female appointments were at record highs during the Obama administration

Across several demographic groups, Obama's appointments have shown an uptick in diversity over previous administrations. African Americans have seen the smallest gains compared with other groups.

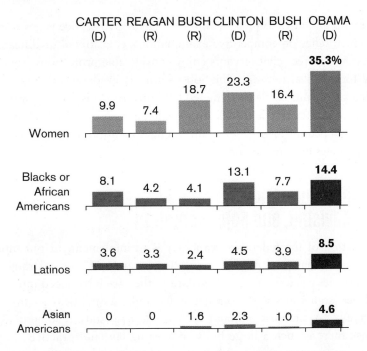

to do so, and the flexibility needed to handle unforeseen circumstances all argue for giving bureaucrats the authority to flesh out parts of the laws in action. By doing so, however, Congress opens up a space for **bureaucratic discretion**, in which the

bureaucratic discretion the power to decide how a law is implemented and, at times, what Congress actually meant when it passed a given law.

FIGURE 14.10

Patterns of Diversity in Cabinet Appointments

Most Cabinet positions are more diverse, but not all

Obama's cabinet has been the most diverse, with 17 of 31 secretaries being minorities or women. Two positions – Defense secretary and Treasury secretary – have been held only by white males. Each appointee is represented by a figure below.

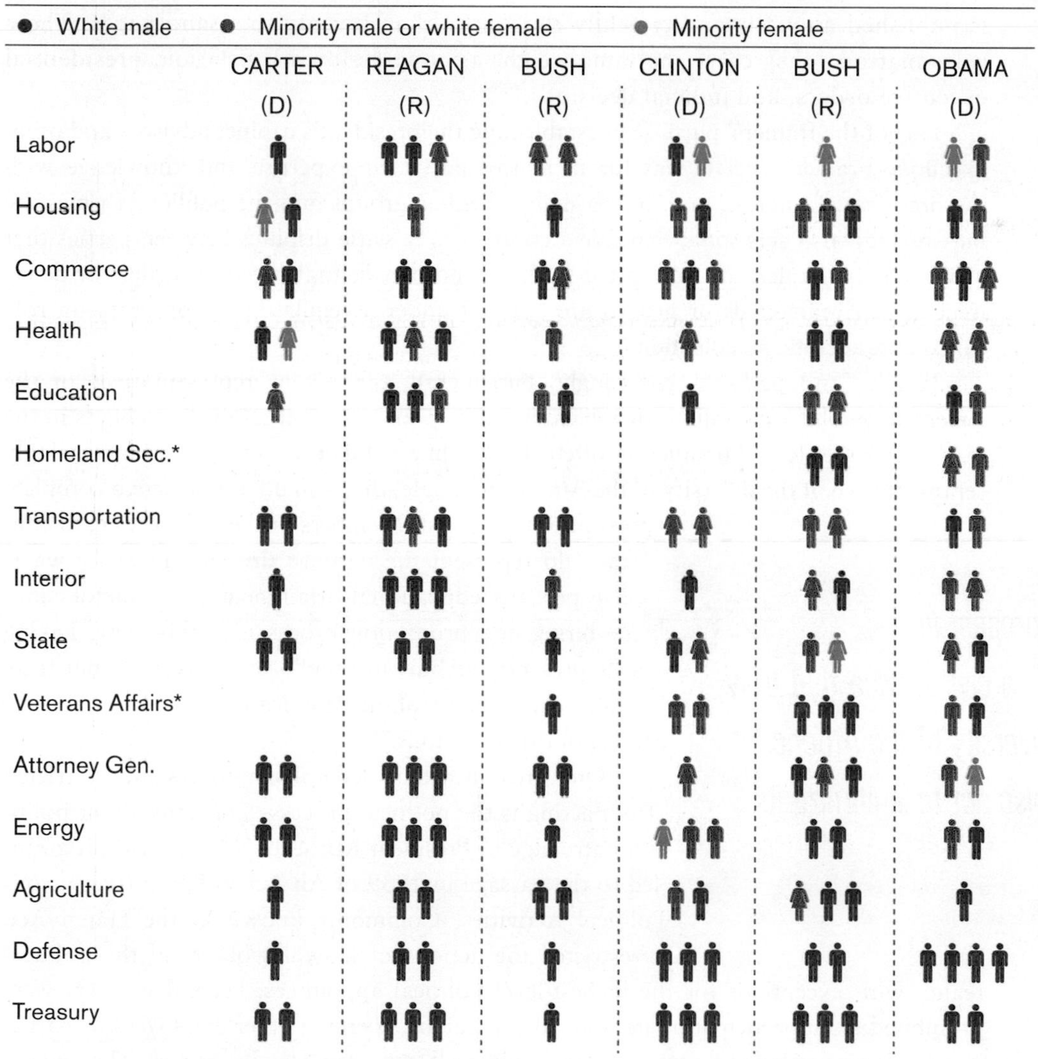
White male
Minority male or white female
Minority female
CARTER (D)
REAGAN (R)
BUSH (R)
CLINTON (D)
BUSH (R)
OBAMA (D)
Labor
Housing
Commerce
Health
Education
Homeland Sec.*
Transportation
Interior
State
Veterans Affairs*
Attorney Gen.
Energy
Agriculture
Defense
Treasury

*The Department of Homeland Security began in 2003. The Department of Veterans Affairs was elevated to cabinet-level agency in 1989.

Source: From The Washington Post, September 10, 2015, © 2015 The Washington Post.

bureaucrats have some power to decide how a law is implemented and, at times, what Congress actually meant when it passed a given law. In addition, individuals, organizations, and businesses affected by legislation cannot go about planning how they are going to respond to a law or set of regulations until they actually know the details of it. How much will it cost to comply? What changes must be made in order to do so? The answers to these important questions more often than not come from the bureaucracy rather than Congress, the president, or the courts.

The process through which the federal bureaucracy fills in critical details of a law is called **rulemaking**. This procedure—which must, by law, follow a specific set of steps—was established in the Administrative Procedure Act of 1946 (APA). Agencies must first announce a proposed set of rules and allow interested parties to weigh in; this process is called *notice and comment*. Agencies may have to notify the president or Congress about the anticipated impact of a proposed rule or set of rules. Finally, the adopted rules must be published in the *Federal Register*, which is published annually and typically runs more than seventy thousand pages. These rules matter; "they carry the same weight as congressional legislation, presidential executive orders, and judicial decisions."[82]

Part of the framers' purpose in establishing the president's cabinet advisors and other executive branch officials was for them to share their expertise and knowledge with the president, Congress, and, increasingly, clientele groups and the public. At times the bureaucracy also acts somewhat like a court. It may settle disputes between parties that arise over the implementation of federal laws and presidential executive orders or determine which individuals or groups are covered under a regulation or program—a role called **bureaucratic adjudication**.

Finally, and perhaps surprisingly, bureaucrats can act as representatives of the American public, especially if they have the ability to act on behalf of their clients in the way that street-level bureaucrats often do.[83] While cabinet secretaries are increasingly representative of the diversity of the American people, they still do not present a complete portrait of the nation. Members of the civil service, in contrast, do represent the nation's diversity in many ways, save perhaps educational attainment (as it factors into the hiring and promotion process). In this view, having a "representative bureaucracy"—a civil service that truly reflects the diversity of the American people—may also act to legitimize its actions.[84]

One area in which federal employees are restricted from acting is the political process. Concerns about political patronage in President Roosevelt's New Deal programs led to the passage in 1939 of An Act to Prevent Pernicious Political Activities. Commonly known as the Hatch Act, it restricted the actions of federal workers in the political realm, with exceptions for the highest-level political appointees. Federal workers were prohibited from participating in political campaigns, coercing other employees to participate, raising funds for a campaign, or holding all but a few elective offices. The Federal Employees Political Activities Act of 1993 relaxed some of the restrictions of the Hatch Act, allowing most federal employees to run in nonpartisan elections and contribute to and to participate in fund-raising for political campaigns, as long as they do not use their official authority to do so.

rulemaking
the process through which the federal bureaucracy fills in critical details of a law.

bureaucratic adjudication
when the federal bureaucracy settles disputes between parties that arise over the implementation of federal laws and presidential executive orders or determine which individuals or groups are covered under a regulation or program.

Having a "representative bureaucracy"—a civil service that truly reflects the diversity of the American people—may also act to legitimize its actions.

1. The top of the federal bureaucratic organizational structure consists of _____.

   a. Executive political appointees
   b. Career civil servants
   c. Members of the Senior Executive Service
   d. Private contractors

2. Implementation is usually a very straightforward process

   a. True
   b. False

3. A process through which many details of laws are filled in is _____.

   a. Rulemaking
   b. Appropriation

   c. Bureaucratic discretion
   d. Bureaucratic adjudication

4. The *Federal Register*, published annually, often runs more than seventy thousand pages. What is in this enormous publication? Why do you think it is so massive?

HANDLING THE BUREAUCRACY
Control, Oversight, and Reform

While complaints about the bureaucracy are as old as the institution itself, recent decades have seen a renewed focus on highlighting its failures and offering reforms to fix them. One set of critiques focuses on the inefficiency of large and complex bureaucracies. The term *red tape*, derived from "the narrow ribbons used at one time in England and America to tie up packets of legal and government documents," conjures up images of bureaucrats mindlessly following rules and standard operating procedures, whether or not it actually helps get things done.[85] Another line of critique emphasizes the tendencies of federal departments, bureaus, and agencies to be budget maximizers—that is, to seek to expand their level of appropriations beyond that necessary for the efficient provision of their services.[86]

Still another accusation points to problems that arise when bureaucracies stray from their established goals and devote their energies and efforts to nonessential tasks, an outcome known as **bureaucratic drift**. Worries about straying from the intended mission may apply to individual bureaucrats as well. Individuals may not do their jobs effectively or responsibly, a failing commonly referred to as shirking. Or they may actively work against the stated mission of their agency, substituting their own evaluations of a proper course of action, which is referred to as sabotage.[87] From the point of view of the bureaucrat, sabotage may be for very good reasons—for example, bending the rules to help out a client confronted with a rigid set of rules and procedures.

Another concern, especially for bureaucrats in regulatory agencies, is that individuals may undermine effective regulation if their own interests are more closely aligned with the targets of regulation than the mission of the agency, a problem known as **agency capture**. If a regulator has close ties to the industry being regulated—either through previous

bureaucratic drift
when bureaucracies stray from their established goals and devote their energies and efforts to peripheral tasks.

agency capture
a problem that occurs when a bureaucrat's own interests are more closely aligned with the targets of regulation than the mission of the agency, thus undermining effective regulation.

employment or, perhaps, expected future employment—then there may be temptations to "look the other way," instruct their subordinates to do so, or conduct their jobs in such a way as to benefit a few preferred clients.[88]

Controlling the Bureaucracy

The system of separation of powers that the framers designed poses a special challenge to controlling the bureaucracy. As authority over the federal bureaucracy is divided between different branches, federal agencies and bureaus often have to answer to more than one overseer. According to political scientist Joel Aberbach, "Since usually no one set of institutional actors has clear control and signals often conflict, it is difficult to hold the bureaucracy, or any other institution, reasonably to account."[89]

A political cartoon depicting octopus-shaped red tape from Washington, D.C., gripping the states with its tentacles.

NEWS CLIP
Committee hearing over ACA website

The President

As head of the executive branch, the president formally controls most of the federal bureaucracy.[90] He or she has the authority to appoint and remove individuals at the top layers of the bureaucracy. Presidents can also shape bureaucratic priorities in the annual budgets that they present to Congress and, with congressional approval, by reorganizing agencies. As discussed in Chapter 13, executive orders carry the force of law and typically instruct departments, agencies, and bureaus on how they are to go about implementing policy.

Presidents, however, often confront restrictions in their control over the day-to-day functions of the bureaucracy. Bureaucratic discretion and the bureaucracy's size and complexity all conspire against achieving quick results. In one of the literally smaller battles of his presidency, Jimmy Carter (1977–1981) discovered one of the obstacles to his power when he confronted a problem that had apparently existed in the White House since the administration of Dwight David Eisenhower (1953–1961): mice. With maintenance personnel unable to control the mouse population, Carter called on the bureaucracy. Unfortunately, the Department of the Interior said that the mice were a problem for the General Services Administration (GSA) since Interior was only responsible for the grounds of the White House and not the building itself. GSA countered that the problem was Interior's "since the mice were obviously migrating from outside." Only after Carter "ordered an immediate meeting in his office of all concerned officials of the GSA, Department of Interior, White House administrators, and others" was progress made.[91]

Congress

Congress plays a key role in controlling and guiding the bureaucracy. The Senate has power over confirmation for the higher levels of the federal service. Congress as a whole

President Barack Obama's cabinet was one of the most diverse in history. Here he meets with them in the Cabinet Room of the White House in May 2015. From left: Education Secretary Arne Duncan, Health and Human Services Secretary Sylvia Mathews Burwell, Interior Secretary Sally Jewell, Secretary of State John Kerry, Obama, Defense Secretary Ash Carter, Commerce Secretary Penny Pritzker, Transportation Secretary Anthony Foxx, and Homeland Security Secretary Jeh Johnson.

can pass legislation creating or terminating agencies and programs and, through the process of appropriation, has control over the resources that departments, bureaus, and agencies receive to carry out their tasks. Congressional committees, especially the House and Senate appropriations committees, are key players in these processes.

While legislation can be a proactive way to shape bureaucratic behavior by setting goals, priorities, and the overall organizational structure, Congress also has the ability to influence what happens when agencies are up and running through the process of oversight. Congress has established its own bureaucracies to keep tabs on executive branch implementation. The Government Accountability Office (GAO) is an example of this type of agency.

In a series of reports based on its investigations on preparedness and response regarding Hurricane Katrina, the GAO detailed a list of evaluations and suggestions for the future. The GAO's reports praised some parts of the bureaucracy, such as the Coast Guard. Much of what the office found, however, was far from flattering, and it called out failed leadership, communication, and coordination within the executive branch. One report stated, "No one was designated in advance to lead the overall federal response in anticipation of the event despite clear warnings from the National Hurricane Center."[92]

When deciding how to oversee the federal bureaucracy, Congress has a choice. By doing field investigations, conducting hearings, or requiring information from the agencies, Congress may exercise police patrol oversight, analogous to a law enforcement official surveying the neighborhood to make sure all is well. The problem with police patrol oversight is that it is expensive, especially in terms of Congress's scarcest resource: time. Therefore, Congress often chooses instead to exercise fire alarm oversight, bringing the machinery of investigation and correction into action only when individuals or interest groups—some formally authorized to acquire information or bring suit in court—sound the alarm that part of the federal bureaucracy has gone astray.[93]

While the GAO conducted its investigations into Katrina, Congress conducted its own hearings into the federal government's performance, at times grilling top officials on their actions or lack of action. Much of the sharpest questioning was directed toward President Bush's top political appointees. Testifying before the Senate in February 2006, Secretary of Homeland Security Michael Chertoff "endured two and a half hours of intense political criticism" and offered an apology to Congress and the American people.[94] "The worst element of this catastrophe personally is not criticism I've received," he said, "but the derision of people who did have their suffering unnecessarily prolonged because this department did not perform."[95] Chertoff also conceded that his trust in former FEMA director Michael Brown was misplaced after Brown, in his own testimony, "all but boasted . . . that he did not respect Mr. Chertoff's authority and circumvented him, leaving the secretary unaware of what was going on in New Orleans."[96]

A report by a bipartisan investigative committee in the House of Representatives was also scathing. It documented, page after page, "a litany of mistakes, misjudgments, lapses, and absurdities all cascading together."[97] The "American people," the report concluded, "don't care about acronyms or organizational charts. They want to know who was supposed to do what, when, and whether the job got done. And if it didn't get done, they want to know how we are going to make sure it does next time."[98]

NEWS CLIP
Army Corps of Engineers
ends up in the middle of
a multistage water war

interagency rivalry

when two or more agencies
are charged with a similar
mandate, an outcome that
becomes more likely in
times of budget cuts and
competition for scarce or
dwindling appropriations.

Other Influences

While infrequently tailored to specific agencies, departments, and bureaus, decisions by the federal judiciary can significantly impact bureaucratic behavior. Judicial control is typically negative—not in the sense that it is bad, but in the sense that judicial decisions on, for example, civil liberties and civil rights, restrict and constrain the scope of accepted bureaucratic action. One part of the federal bureaucracy may also find its actions constrained by other departments, agencies, and bureaus.[100] Bureaucratic jurisdiction—the authority to act in a certain policy area—is often not clearly or cleanly defined. **Interagency rivalry** occurs when two or more agencies are charged with a similar mandate, an outcome that becomes more likely in times of budget cuts and competition for scarce or dwindling appropriations. Clientele groups and businesses affected by federal rules, whether proposed or formalized, will lobby parts of the federal bureaucracy as well as Congress to get a more favorable outcome according to their perceived interests.

As a rule, the media infrequently cover the workings of the federal bureaucracy. Most Americans are understandably not well informed of the day-to-day workings of the vast bureaucracy, and there are no doubt numerous agencies many Americans don't know even exist. As Walter Lippmann, scholar and commenter on American politics, noted, "The public will arrive in the middle of the third act and will leave before the last curtain, having stayed just long enough perhaps to decide who is the hero and who is the villain of the piece."[101] Therefore, public opinion rarely constrains bureaucratic behavior. When, however, the machinery of government is involved in a major crisis or catastrophe—and especially when it appears that it has failed—the federal bureaucracy might find itself center stage in Lippmann's play, with a full and angry audience in attendance.

Such was the case after Katrina. A year after its landfall on the Gulf Cost, thousands of residents were still waiting for federal help, and public opinion had turned against President Bush on his handling of the disaster. A national poll found that only 31 percent of Americans approved of his management of the storm, and 56 percent did not "believe that the country [was] ready for another disaster."[102]

Leah Hodges, Resident of New Orleans, Criticizes the Treatment of Evacuees

In her prepared testimony before the Select Bipartisan Committee to Investigate the Preparation for and Response to Hurricane Katrina in December 2005, New Orleans resident Leah Hodges raised troubling concerns about how she and other individuals who sought refuge were treated.[99] While not all of the witnesses testifying felt that African Americans were treated differently because of their race, Hodges's assessment of the connection between racial identity and equality of treatment echoed the accusations of many others. Hodges testified,

> I come from a family of musicians. Before Hurricane Katrina, we were planning a musical family reunion. I had taken time off from pursuing my law degree to care for my sick granddad. I was also in the process of working with community leaders on setting up music and art workshops for youths. The manual I was writing for the workshops was severely damaged in the flood. I intend to finish it. . . . But I have also started a new project, which is all about my experience as a detainee at the Highway 10 causeway.
>
> My family was ordered to evacuate our home. We were directed to evacuation points. . . . We were then lured to the so-called evacuation points. This was several days after the hurricane had struck. The city was flooded. Soldiers had showed up with M16s and military weapons. They had declared New Orleans and Jefferson Parish a war zone.
>
> We were just three miles from an airport, but we were detained there for several days. Many of those who were there when we arrived had already been there several days. On any given day there were at least ten thousand people in the camp. On my last day there, I would estimate there were still three thousand detainees. By that time, nearly all the white people had been selected to evacuate first. They

New Orleans citizens and evacuees (from left) Terrol Williams, Doreen Keeler, Patricia Thompson, Leah Hodges, and "Mama D" Dyan French testify before Congress in December 2005.

> were put on buses and shipped out, leaving the remaining population 95 percent black.
>
> People died in the camp. We saw the bodies lying there.
>
> They were all about detention, as if it were Iraq, like we were foreigners and they were fighting a war. They implemented war-like conditions. They treated us worse than prisoners of war. Even prisoners of war have rights under the Geneva Convention.

WHAT DO YOU THINK?

Some of the harshest criticism about the response to Hurricane Katrina involved accusations of differential treatment of African Americans. Can you think of other examples where a federal, state, or local agency has been accused of racial and ethnic bias? Have you or people close to you experienced this?

Reform: Devolution, Deregulation, Reinvention, and Privatization

In addition to calls for oversight of bureaucracies and the agencies in which they operate, pushes have been made—especially in recent decades—to shrink, overhaul, or eliminate parts of the federal bureaucracy. Ronald Reagan's petitions to roll back the growth in the size and power of the bureaucracy in his successful presidential bid in 1980 focused public attention on these efforts. As discussed in Chapter 3, **devolution** aimed to transfer power

devolution
the transfer of power over public policy back to the states in order to shrink the size of the federal government and allow states to have more authority to determine how taxpayer dollars should be spent.

deregulation

the reduction or elimination of government power in a particular industry, usually in order to create more competition within the industry.

NEWS CLIP

HHS fixes ACA website with the help of private contractors

privatization

shifting control over the provision of certain governmental functions from the federal bureaucracy to the private sector.

over public policy back to the states and shrink the size of the federal government by allowing states to have more authority to determine how taxpayer dollars should be spent. Proponents of **deregulation** argued that the personnel rules of the civil service, along with excessive red tape, made it difficult to attract "talented energetic potential candidates" to the federal service and restrained their energies once hired.[103] As a result of deregulation efforts beginning in the 1970s, certain federal agencies saw their authority curtailed or they were abolished entirely, particularly in the areas of transportation, commerce, and the provision of utilities.

Another set of reforms sought to make the federal bureaucracy work more efficiently—more like the private sector. President Bill Clinton, shortly after his election in 1992, placed Vice President Al Gore in charge of these efforts. The National Performance Review sought to collect detailed data on bureaucratic efficiency and inefficiency and to propose measures to streamline bureaucratic operations. The review's unofficial title, the "reinventing government initiative," drew its name from a book by David Osborne and Ted Gaebler that became an extreme rarity in studies of the federal bureaucracy—a national bestseller.[104] In this book, *Reinventing Government*, Osborne and Gaebler argued for changing rules and practices to unleash and support the energies of individuals within the federal bureaucracy in order to cut waste, increase efficiency, and innovate, a model that they termed "entrepreneurial government."[105]

Other reform proposals advocate placing control over the provision of certain functions in the hands of the private sector and not the federal bureaucracy. Proponents of **privatization** argue that many tasks currently handled by the federal service can be more efficiently and more cheaply handled by private organizations and businesses. Opponents of privatization argue that reducing or eliminating governmental oversight over the provision of these services might lead to waste or fraud or might undermine the larger policy goals of the national government.

Political scientist James Q. Wilson pointed out that there might be valid reasons for the fact that public bureaucracies often act differently and less efficiently than private bureaucracies. By their very nature, public bureaucracies operate under a different set of constraints. Congress, and not the marketplace, sets the goals for, budgets of, and allocation of resources within the federal service. In addition, the American public often demands a higher standard of fairness in the actions of its public bureaucracies than it does of private ones. Public schools, for example, generally face more binding constraints over admission and expulsion of students than do the nation's private schools.[106]

Following Katrina, investigators and members of Congress began to question both the government's reliance on private contractors in relief efforts and governmental interference with private sector efforts. Concerns included a lack of competition in awarding contracts for cleanup and recovery efforts, a failure to adequately employ local businesses and contractors, and a failure on the part of FEMA to have enough "sufficiently trained procurement professionals" to effectively manage and oversee the contracting process.[107] According to a local official in Louisiana, FEMA had blocked private relief efforts as well: "We had Wal-Mart deliver three trailer trucks of water. FEMA turned them back. They said we didn't need them."[108]

As it became clear that the effects from Katrina would be felt for years, many private organizations and individuals stepped up to help. Habitat for Humanity dispatched thousands of volunteers to the Gulf Coast to rebuild housing for low-income residents. Mary Gray founded MinnesotaHelpers, a "Mississippi-to-Minnesota arts pipeline," to provide opportunities for Gulf Coast artists to display and sell their work as they had few such venues in their own devastated communities.[109]

Not all private responses were viewed so positively, however. Some were accused of running scams to take advantage of the federal dollars that flowed into devastated areas, prompting the government to establish the Hurricane Katrina Fraud Task Force to "thwart and prosecute hurricane-related fraud."[110] Some initiatives, though not illegal, seemed to take advantage of the disaster. In January 2006, a local tour bus company planned to operate a "Hurricane Katrina Tour—America's Worst Catastrophe!" to offer tourists the chance to see the aftermath of the storm from air-conditioned buses, though the company promised a portion of the $35 ticket price would benefit recovery efforts.[111]

Trucks from Walmart with relief supplies for residents of the Gulf Coast. FEMA was widely criticized for hampering private efforts at assistance.
NICHOLAS KAMM/AFP/Getty Images

CONCLUSION

Another Devastating Hurricane, Another Federal Response

In October 2012, Hurricane Sandy spread destruction from the Caribbean to the East Coast of the United States, from Florida to Maine. More than 140 people died as a direct result of the storm. In America, the devastation was the worst in New Jersey and New York, mostly due to flooding. Millions lost power, and tens of thousands of Americans became homeless. According to the National Hurricane Center, Sandy resulted in tens of billions of dollars in damages, ranking it second behind Katrina in total economic costs in the United States from a hurricane or tropical cyclone.

In Sandy's wake, many observers praised the federal government's response, including President Barack Obama's swift action in declaring a state of emergency from Washington, D.C., to New York a day before Sandy made landfall in New Jersey. Enabled by legislation passed in Katrina's wake, Obama was able to quickly instruct "FEMA to create the National Power Restoration Taskforce, which was to minimize red tape, increase coordination among government agencies at all levels and the private sector, and rapidly restore fuel and power."[112] Not all evaluations of the federal bureaucracy's response to Sandy, however, were positive. Three months after Sandy's landfall, when a blast of arctic air hit the Northeast, some critics pointed to families having to rely on space heaters to stave off the cold while still awaiting repairs and rebuilding. Others questioned whether the states, and not the federal government, should pick up more of the tab for disaster prevention and relief.

Americans want the primary instrument of national policy implementation to be effective and strong. When they feel that it is not—such as was the case with Hurricane Katrina—they demand change. However, Americans do not want the federal bureaucracy to be *too* strong. When they feel that it has become too powerful, they worry. Both the separation of powers and the realities of American federalism shape the behaviors of the federal departments, agencies, and bureaus. These organizations are not smoothly running machines but a constellation of teams operating in an often political space; they have multiple constraints on their behavior and also must contend with multiple interests and groups trying to shape that behavior. Such is the complex nature of the American federal bureaucracy.

CHAPTER REVIEW

This chapter's main ideas are reflected in the Learning Objectives below. By reviewing them here you should be able to **remember** the key points, **connect** them to the stories presented in the chapter, **think** critically about these questions, and **know** these terms that are central to the topic.

14.1 Name the key characteristics of bureaucratic organization and the theories that try to explain why bureaucratic organization happens.

REMEMBER...
- Most of the federal bureaucracy lies within the executive branch. State and local bureaucracies also make rules that impact people's daily lives. Private bureaucracies are companies and corporations that also operate like federal, state, and local bureaucracies.

- Bureaucrats are people who work within bureaucracies.

- Various theories of bureaucracies exist to explain how and why they are organized the way they are.

- Max Weber proposed a rules and procedures–centered organizational model in which bureaucratic power was based on rational-legal authority.

- Chester Barnard focused on overcoming problems inherent in principle-agent relationships and in organizations in general and saw bureaucratic leadership as key.

- James Q. Wilson saw tasks—what different bureaucrats in their organizations actually do—as central to the effective functioning of a bureaucracy and to understanding the outcomes of bureaucratic actions.

CONNECT...

- During and after Hurricane Katrina, the bureaucracy at all levels—federal, state and local—had to anticipate and respond to the needs of those affected by the storm. The National Hurricane Center attempted to alert authorities and residents to impending danger.

THINK...

- What is a bureaucracy? What are its defining characteristics?

KNOW...

- *bureaucrat* (p. 499)
- *federal bureaucracy* (p. 494)
- *incentives* (p. 501)
- *principal-agent problem* (p. 500)
- *private bureaucracies* (p. 499)
- *standard operating procedures* (p. 500)
- *state and local bureaucracies* (p. 499)

14.2 Outline the historical development of the American federal bureaucracy.

REMEMBER...

- The federal bureaucracy has grown exponentially over time, as has the complexity of the tasks it must perform and the demands for services placed upon it by the American people.

- The Constitution calls for executive branch departments to assist the president in executing the laws of the nation. To control the power of the executive, Congress was given the power to approve nominees and impeach executive officers.

- There was not initially a set number of cabinet departments, nor were their responsibilities set in stone; they have changed over time according to the needs of the nation.

- Andrew Jackson changed how bureaucratic positions were filled, using political patronage and the spoils system to reward supporters with appointments and remove opponents from office. One effect of his actions was to strengthen the standard operating procedures of the bureaucracy.

- During Reconstruction and up through the Progressive Era, the federal bureaucracy grew. Independent regulatory agencies were created to monitor the bureaucracy and various efforts at reform were undertaken to try to curb corruption and inefficiency in the bureaucracy.

- Following the Pendleton Act, a federal civil service with employees hired and promoted according to a merit system emerged.

- Facing a series of crises in the Great Depression, World War II, and the Cold War, the federal bureaucracy again expanded, adding new clientele agencies to assist with economic and social issues and new agencies focused on national security to fight the wars.

- Scholars see the effects of American exceptionalism in how the federal bureaucracy has developed over time, highlighting the role of path dependency in producing a set of outcomes that shapes future policies.

THINK...

- How has the American federal bureaucracy changed since its creation? Why did it develop and grow in the ways that it has?

14.3 Describe the structure of the federal bureaucracy, including executive branch agencies, cabinet departments, and regulatory bodies.

REMEMBER...

- The federal bureaucracy is a complex web of organizations and organizations within organizations, headed by the president. The president appoints top-level heads of departments who execute the laws of the nation.

- Congress has the authority to establish and fund the departments, each of which is responsible for a major area of public policy. The budget and employment numbers vary from department to department, as does the degree of influence a department holds.

- Independent regulatory agencies act to oversee and regulate governmental function, especially in economic affairs.

- At the top of the bureaucracy are executive political appointees who are often in their positions for short periods of time. Below them are Senior Executive Service employees with supervisory and administrative responsibilities. Career civil servants make up the bulk of the employees.

- Implementing the laws passed by Congress is one of the bureaucracy's core tasks. Bureaucrats typically have some discretion over how the laws are implemented. Agencies also have critical rulemaking responsibilities and they may fill in the details of legislation, sometimes using bureaucratic adjudication to settle disputes that arise during implementation. The bureaucracy also can serve to represent the citizens.

CONNECT...

- FEMA and other federal, state, and local authorities were widely viewed as being slow to understand the scope of the Hurricane Katrina disaster and respond appropriately.

THINK...

- What are cabinet departments? What are their functions?
- Who are federal bureaucrats? How are they organized, hired, and fired?

14.4 Describe the tools of bureaucratic control, oversight, and reform.

REMEMBER...

- The most common complaint about the bureaucracy is its perceived inefficiency. Another has to do with bureaucratic drift, which occurs when bureaucracies stray from their established goals and devote their energies and efforts elsewhere. Agency capture—when individuals undermine effective regulation if their own interests are more closely aligned with the targets of regulation than with the mission of the agency—is also a concern.

- Control over the bureaucracy is challenging given that responsibility and power are shared across the executive, legislative, and judicial branches of government.

- Interagency rivalry occurs when two or more agencies are charged with a similar mandate, an outcome that becomes more likely in times of budget cuts and competition for scarce or dwindling appropriations.

- Efforts to reform the bureaucracy—limit its power, reduce its size, and fix inefficiencies—include devolving responsibilities to the states, deregulation, and privatizing government responsibilities to increase competitiveness.

CONNECT...

- Congress, in investigating failures in the bureaucracy following Katrina, authorized the GAO to evaluate the performance of the relevant agencies and offer recommendations for change and reform. Congress itself also held hearings looking into the federal government's performance.

THINK...

- What are some of the main criticisms leveled against the federal bureaucracy?

- What are some ways in which the federal bureaucracy is controlled? What are some proposals for reforming it?

KNOW...

- *agency capture* (p. 523)
- *bureaucratic drift* (p. 523)
- *deregulation* (p. 528)

- *devolution* (p. 527)
- *interagency rivalry* (p. 526)
- *privatization* (p. 528)

15 THE FEDERAL JUDICIARY
Politics, Power, and the "Least Dangerous" Branch[1]

What is the federal judiciary? Like with many questions you are asked to consider in this book, there are both simple answers and more complicated ones. In this chapter, we will deal with both. In terms of definition, it is simple. The **federal judiciary** is one of the three branches of the nation's government. Its role is to interpret and apply the laws of the nation. Sitting atop the federal judiciary is the **Supreme Court**, which was established in the Constitution and serves as the highest court in the nation.

On a deeper level, however, more difficult questions arise. First, how different is the federal judiciary from the other two branches—or, more precisely, how *political* is it? How political should it be? Also, how *powerful* is it? As we have explored, both Congress and the president have at

At her confirmation hearing in July 2009, Supreme Court nominee Judge Sonia Sotomayor answered questions from Senator Jeff Sessions (R-AL). Because they are appointed to lifetime terms, Supreme Court justices are very influential and their appointment can be a challenging political process. Sotomayor would go on to become the third woman on the Court and the Court's first Hispanic justice.

Alex Wong/Getty Images.

their disposal powerful levers to shape national public policy. Congress writes the laws; it has the power to tax and to fund. The president is the commander in chief of the armed forces and is tasked with executing, or carrying out, the laws of the nation. What power does the federal judiciary have other than the authority to apply the law to the cases brought before it?

These questions are very much interconnected. The power of the federal judiciary implicates how it engages as a political actor. Conversely, the degree to which the federal judiciary chooses to involve itself in political controversies has and will continue to impact its legitimacy with the American public.

In this chapter, you will engage with the stories of the confirmation of Sonia Sotomayor to the Supreme Court, the failed confirmation of Robert Bork, and John Marshall's establishment of judicial review. They are all presented as "trials," though none of the three individuals were actually *on* trial. Their institution, however, was, and it still is.

federal judiciary
the branch of the federal government that interprets and applies the laws of the nation.

Supreme Court
the highest level of the federal judiciary, which was established in the Constitution and serves as the highest court in the nation.

After reading this chapter, you will be able to:

15.1 Describe the structure and powers of the federal judiciary as laid out in the Constitution

15.2 Summarize John Marshall's development of judicial review in the Supreme Court decision in *Marbury v. Madison*

15.3 Be familiar with the structure of the American legal system and the federal judiciary

15.4 Trace the path of most cases through the federal judiciary

15.5 Compare theories of judicial decision making as well as arguments for or against judicial restraint and activism in constitutional review

LEARNING OBJECTIVES

 # THE "TRIAL" OF SONIA SOTOMAYOR

Identity, Politics, and the Supreme Court

NEWS CLIP
Recap of the Sotomayor hearings

In May 2009, President Barack Obama was presented with his first opportunity to nominate an individual to the United States Supreme Court. Although the retiring justice, David H. Souter, had been appointed by a Republican president (George H. W. Bush), his votes on the Court had generally placed him in the liberal bloc of justices. Obama's appointment, therefore, would likely not shift the ideological balance of the Court, which—in the intensely partisan world of the modern federal government—lessened, if only a bit, the tensions surrounding the nomination. Even so, observers and insiders expected an intensely political battle as justices on the Supreme Court are appointed for life.

Although the nomination of a liberal justice was expected, there were other hopes pinned on the president's selection. With only one woman, one African American, and no Latino justices on the bench, many urged the president to use the opportunity to expand the diversity of the Court. Rumored to be on Obama's short list was Sonia Sotomayor, the daughter of Puerto Rican immigrants, a graduate of Yale Law School, a former prosecutor and litigator, and—at the time—a judge with the U.S. Court of Appeals for the Second Circuit. She was, however, according to the *Washington Post*, the "riskiest choice" of the likely nominees, largely because of public remarks that she had made on the importance of identity and personal history in approaching judicial decision making.[2]

When Sotomayor's nomination became official, both sides swung into campaign mode, with each accusing the other of violating norms of propriety in handling a Supreme Court nomination. Comments for and against Sotomayor were issued "off the record," unattributable to any one source. A May 4 article in the *New Republic* quoted an unnamed former law clerk of one of Sotomayor's colleagues as stating that Sotomayor was "not that smart and kind of a bully on the bench." On the other side, an unnamed former clerk praised the judge for being committed to giving "everyone the fair break they deserve, regardless of who they are."[3] Although she was not *literally* on trial as the confirmation proceedings in the Senate began, Sotomayor may very well have felt like she was, and with good reason.

Republicans in the Senate employed a strategy of assailing Sotomayor as a justice who would be "willing to expand constitutional rights beyond the text of the constitution."[4] Given a popular president and a Senate under Democratic control, defeating Sotomayor was unlikely, but Republicans hoped to use the confirmation proceedings to "refill depleted coffers and galvanize a movement demoralized by Republican electoral defeats."[5] With their opposition, however, Republicans risked alienating women voters as well as Latina and Latino voters; the latter make up an increasingly important—and the fastest-growing—group of Americans.

Remarks made by Sotomayor at a public lecture received particular scrutiny from Republicans during the confirmation proceedings. Speaking in 2001 Sotomayor, then an appellate court judge, had highlighted the role that her Latina identity and life experiences had played and would continue to play in her judicial career—a perspective that, to her, helped her make just decisions, especially in cases involving equality and discrimination. Addressing the attendees, Sotomayor said,

> Who am I? I am a "Newyorkrican." For those of you on the West Coast who do not know what the term means: I am a born and bred New Yorker of Puerto Rican-born parents who came to the states during World War II. . . .
>
> No one person, judge or nominee will speak in a female or people of color voice. . . . Yet, because I accept the proposition that, as Judge Resnik describes it, "to judge is an exercise of power" and because as, another former law school classmate, Professor Martha Minnow of Harvard Law School, states "there is no objective stance but only a series of perspectives—no neutrality, no escape from choice in judging," I further accept that our experiences as women and people of color affect our decisions. The aspiration to impartiality is just that—it's an aspiration because it denies the fact that we are by our experiences making different choices than others. . . .
>
> Justice O'Connor has often been cited as saying that a wise old man and a wise old woman will reach the same conclusions in deciding cases. I am not so sure that Justice O'Connor is the author of that line since Professor Resnik attributes that line to Supreme Court Justice Coyle. I am also not so sure that I agree with the statement. First, as Professor Martha Minnow has noted, there can never be a universal declaration of wise. Second, I would hope that a wise Latina woman with the richness of her experiences would more often than not reach a better conclusion than a white male who hasn't lived that life.[6]

With President Obama urging quick action on the nomination, the press began to revisit the failed, and very political, confirmation of Robert Bork in 1987, wondering if a similar ideological showdown was looming.[7] A leading Republican senator summed up his party's planned line of questioning: "Do I want a judge that objectively applies the law to the facts?"[8]

When the Senate Judiciary Committee began its proceedings on the nomination in mid-July, Republicans promised to avoid personal attacks, quite possibly in an attempt to avoid the political fallout that had accompanied the committee's harsh examination of witness Anita Hill during the Clarence Thomas confirmation. (As we explored in Chapter 12, Hill's treatment by the committee led many women to run for Congress for the first time.) Sotomayor rehearsed her testimony and her answers to expected questions in the week before the hearings. At least one surprise witness was offered on the list of those scheduled to testify: David Cone, a former Major League pitcher, was set to offer support for the argument that Sotomayor "saved baseball when she ended the 1995 strike."[9]

This undated family photograph shows Judge Sonia Sotomayor as a child with her mother Celina Sotomayor, left, and father Juan Luis Sotomayor, right. Both of her parents immigrated to the United States from Puerto Rico during World War II. Sonia Sotomayor was born and raised in New York. She has spoken about her experiences as a "NewYorkrican" and the role of identity in judicial decision making.

The White House via Getty Images.

Supporters, some of who had travelled thousands of miles, lined up to get a glimpse of the proceedings. Lynette Oliver, who ran a women's support group in Puerto Rico, told the *Washington Post*, "Her journey is my journey." Oliver had brought a small Puerto Rican flag with her because "I want her to know people from the island are here."[10] Addressing her critics, Sotomayor affirmed her judicial legacy, stating that in her seventeen years on the bench, she had "applied the law to the facts at hand."[11] Sotomayor's record gave little indication as to how she might vote on a case involving the right to terminate a pregnancy, and she avoided being drawn into predictions on how she would vote in hypothetical cases on this and other issues.[12] Prior to the hearings, however, the White House press secretary had sought to reassure pro-choice advocates by stating that the president was comfortable "with her interpretation of the Constitution being similar to his."[13]

In the end, the vote in the Senate Judiciary Committee was without much drama or surprise. In a 13–6 vote, with one Republican joining the unanimous Democrats, the committee approved her nomination and sent it to the full Senate, where an expected filibuster-proof confirmation vote was all but certain. On August 9, the Senate confirmed Sotomayor's appointment to the Supreme Court by a vote of 68–31. Like other supporters gathered at a "vote watch" party nearby, law student Lucy Flores was jubilant, but she offered words of caution for those who might think that Sotomayor's confirmation marked an end, rather than just a step forward. "It shouldn't be a historic moment," she said. "Everyone of all races and all backgrounds should be able to get to where she is based on their ability and their desire."[14]

On Saturday, August 8, Sotomayor took the judicial oath of office, promising to "administer justice without respect to persons, and do equal right to the poor and the rich" as the nation's newest member of the Supreme Court. As a member of the Court, Sotomayor would be carrying the hopes and aspirations of many Americans on her shoulders. She would also be joining an institution that itself carries the burdens of adjudicating Americans' claims upon their rights and defining and protecting the Constitution that established a nation.

CONNECTING TO . . .

The Establishment of the Judicial Branch

As you read about the creation of the federal judiciary in the Constitution and in the early Congress, reflect upon the confirmation of Sonia Sotomayor in 2009. Consider the following:

- The ways in which the politics of Sotomayor's confirmation hearings may or may not have mirrored the framers' expectations for how political the federal judiciary would be

- How these developments relate to the concerns of Antifederalists about the future development of the federal judiciary

THE CONSTITUTION AND THE FEDERAL JUDICIARY

The delegates to the Constitutional Convention spent much less time debating the structure and powers of the federal judiciary than they did hammering out the design of the legislative and executive branches. It may seem odd that a convention populated by so many lawyers would apparently neglect the experimental nation's system of courts. It is quite possible, however, that they did so precisely because they shared so many of the same views about how the judicial system should operate that they did not feel the need to debate its mechanics in detail.

Delegates were in general agreement that the judicial branch would be the weakest of the three, lacking an equivalent to Congress's power of the purse and the president's power as commander in chief. Second, the delegates agreed that the judiciary should retain a degree of independence from the other two branches—especially in the processes of appointment and removal of judges—though the specific details were not worked out until the summer of 1787.[15] That federal judges should have tenure with "good Behavior" was generally agreed upon, as was the need to protect their salaries from efforts to reduce them by an unhappy or vengeful Congress.[16] Both of these protections made it into the final document.[17] The question of appointment, however, remained unresolved until late in the convention, with the delegates finally approving a process through which the president would nominate federal judges and the Senate—through its role of advice and consent—would confirm the nominations.[18]

Finally, a diverse group of delegates agreed that the judiciary should have the power to strike down laws that were in violation of the Constitution. Unfortunately, according to constitutional scholar Forrest McDonald, in "one of several instances of carelessness in constituting the judiciary," the federal "courts were not *expressly* given the power to rule on constitutionality."[19]

Article III: The Federal Judiciary in the Constitution

In "one of several instances of carelessness in constituting the judiciary," the federal "courts were not *expressly* given the power to rule on constitutionality."

This issue of constitutionality and the judiciary is not the only instance in which the text of the Constitution is less than thorough. In the document, the judiciary (Article III) comes in third place, behind Congress (Article I) and the executive branch (Article II), both in terms of position and in amount of coverage. Only the highest level of the federal judiciary—the Supreme Court—is actually described in the document, leaving the establishment of lower federal courts in the hands of Congress: "The judicial Power of the United States, shall be vested in one supreme Court, and in such inferior Courts as the Congress may from time ordain and establish."[20]

On one point the Constitution was clear: the federal judiciary, and the Supreme Court in particular, was to be the highest judicial power in the land: "The judicial power shall extend to all Cases, in Law and Equity, arising under this Constitution, the laws of the United States, and Treaties made, or which shall be made, under their Authority."[21] This judicial power, when combined with the supremacy clause of the Constitution, which declared the "Constitution, and the Laws of the United States" to be "the supreme Law of the Land; and [instructed that] the Judges in every State shall be bound thereby," established the federal judiciary as supreme to those of the states.[22]

In defining the scope of the power of the federal judiciary, the Constitution also (briefly) describes one of the most fundamental characteristics of any court: its jurisdiction, or its authority to hear and decide on specific cases.[23] Although there are many types and classifications of jurisdiction, the two most relevant to the study of the American judicial system are original and appellate jurisdiction. If a court has **original jurisdiction** in a case, then that court acts as the originating court, with the authority to hear the case first and to establish the facts pertaining to it. Courts with original jurisdiction are commonly referred to as trial courts. If a court has **appellate jurisdiction** over a case, then it possesses the authority to review the decision of a lower court and, if it so decides, to revise that decision. Courts operating under appellate jurisdiction generally focus on the lower courts' actions and procedures, without finding facts on their own.

original jurisdiction
the authority of a court to act as the first court to hear a case, which includes the finding of facts in the case.

appellate jurisdiction
the authority of a court to hear and review decisions made by lower courts in that system.

Ratification: Antifederalist Concerns and the Federalist Response

During the ratification debates, opponents of the Constitution raised concerns about potential abuses of power by the proposed federal judiciary. Lawyers were not particularly popular or admired in the states, especially in the backcountry where memories of the foreclosures that had led to Shays' Rebellion were fresh in many people's minds.[24] The Antifederalists—as opponents of ratification became known—had many concerns about the Constitution and the proposed federal judiciary. One was a lack of specific protections for individual liberties in the drafted document. During the ratification debates, many Antifederalists argued for the need to include in the Constitution an enumerated list of such rights and liberties to protect against the encroachment of federal power. This argument proved to be the most resonant and influential made by the Antifederalists and it ultimately produced the Bill of Rights.

Opponents of the proposed Constitution also feared the growth in the power of the national government and an associated subjugation of the rights of states and individuals

The Presentation of the Supreme Court

Periodically, members of the Supreme Court pose for a "class photo," which is posted on the Court's official Web site.

While several of the justices appear to be relaxed, the presentation in this image is a formal, ceremonial one, robes and all. Unlike members of Congress or the president, justices have an official "costume." While there is no requirement for justices to wear robes, some scholars have argued that the ceremony surrounding the Court and its proceedings adds to its legitimacy in the view of the American public.

Compare the 2016 image to a picture taken during the "class photo" shoot in 2006, in which Justice Clarence Thomas, a staunch conservative, interacts with Justice Stephen Breyer, one of the Court's liberal justices.

While Breyer and Thomas are far apart ideologically, the second photo presents an image of camaraderie and fellowship between the two justices—a friendship of two people, not two members of a hallowed institution or two political opponents.

WHAT DO YOU THINK?

Why might the federal judiciary be the only institution that employs a uniform dress code when its officials are presented to the public? How important are the robes, rituals, and formality of the Supreme Court in maintaining its legitimacy in the view of the American public?

The justices of the Supreme Court, 2016. Front row (left to right): Clarence Thomas, Antonin Scalia (deceased), John Roberts (chief justice), Anthony Kennedy, Ruth Bader Ginsburg. Back row (left to right): Sonia Sotomayor, Stephen G. Breyer, Samuel A. Alito, Elena Kagan.

Steve Petteway, Collection of the Supreme Court of the United States.

Supreme Court justices Stephen Breyer, left, and Clarence Thomas.

Paul J. Richards/AFP/Getty Images

by an increasingly powerful federal judiciary. In an essay published in a New York newspaper in December 1787, "Brutus," who is thought to be one of the delegates to the Constitutional Convention, warned against this very possibility. "The judicial power," he argued, "will operate to effect in the most certain, but yet silent and imperceptible manner, what is evidently the tendency of the constitution: an entire subversion of the legislative, executive and judicial powers of the individual states."[25] In granting the power to overturn legislation to the Supreme Court, "Brutus" argued that the nation would run the risk of unconstrained justices imposing their own views of what is constitutional and what is not. He cautioned, "They will give the sense of every article of the constitution that may from time to time come before them. And in their decisions they will not confine themselves to any fixed or established rules, but will determine, according to what appears to them, the reason and spirit of the constitution. The opinions of the supreme court, whatever they may be, will have the force of law, because there is no power provided in the constitution that can correct their errors or control their adjudications."[26]

In *Federalist* No. 78, Alexander Hamilton sought to reassure skeptical Antifederalists and others that the planned federal judiciary would not trample upon their rights and liberties because it would neither want to nor be able to. In the first place, Hamilton argued, members of the federal judiciary—because of the process of their selection and their lifetime tenure—would stand apart from politics and the dangers that politics might pose to liberties and be able to "secure a steady, upright, and impartial administration of the laws."[27] Second, compared to the other two branches, the federal judiciary was weak. According to Hamilton,

> Whoever attentively considers the different departments of power must perceive that, in a government in which they are separated from each other, the judiciary, from the nature of its functions, will always be the least dangerous to the political rights of the constitution; because it will be least in a capacity to annoy or injure them. The executive not only dispenses the honours, but holds the sword of the community; the legislature not only commands the purse, but prescribes the rules by which the duties and rights of every citizen are to be regulated; the judiciary, on the contrary, has no influence over either the sword or the purse; no direction either of the strength or of the wealth of the society; and can take no active resolution whatever. It may truly be said to have neither FORCE nor WILL, but merely judgment; and it must ultimately depend upon the aid of the executive arm even for the efficacy of its judgments.[28]

Compared to the power of the sword and the purse, Hamilton reassured, the federal judiciary—exercising only the power of judgment and located outside of the arena of political struggle—was not to be feared. He argued that it was in fact the judiciary that needed protection from encroachment on its limited powers by the other two branches.

> The federal judiciary—exercising only the power of judgment and located outside of the arena of political struggle—was not to be feared.

Congress Fills in the Blanks

Taking up its constitutional authority to establish "inferior Courts" in the federal judiciary, the first Congress passed the Judiciary Act of 1789 to flesh out "the nature and the organization" of the court system.[29] Only the chief justice of the Supreme Court is mentioned in the Constitution; the document does not specify the number of justices in the Court, instead leaving that decision to Congress. The Judiciary Act added five associate judges to the Supreme Court, bringing the total number of justices to six, and it instructed that the Court was to meet in session twice a year, in February and August. (Although the number of justices has varied throughout the nation's history, it has been set at nine since 1869.) The act also established two lower tiers to the federal judiciary, as only the Supreme Court had been set out in the Constitution, though changes have been made to their organization since.

The Judiciary Act of 1789 also created the office of attorney general "to prosecute and conduct all suits in the Supreme Court in which the United States shall be concerned, and to give his advice and opinion upon questions of law when required to by the president of the United States."[30] Today, the office of the solicitor general represents the president in the Supreme Court, while the attorney general is head of the Justice Department. Finally, the act gave the Supreme Court the power to review and reverse actions of the state courts if it found them to be in conflict with the Constitution—a power tied to both the Constitution's description of the scope of judicial power and the supremacy clause.

TOPICS IN AMERICAN GOVERNMENT
Judicial review

 # THE "TRIAL" OF JOHN MARSHALL
The Establishment of Judicial Review

In 1803, John Marshall faced a most difficult test. He was chief justice of the United States Supreme Court, the highest court in the federal judiciary. Marshall's Court was hearing a case that on its surface might have seemed to be a small one. It was brought by four men who felt that they had been cheated out of their jobs, partly—in one of those too-good-to-be-true ironies in American political history—because of what Marshall had done in his previous job.

Like so many other seemingly "small" cases in the history of the Supreme Court, this one turned out to be much, much bigger. Marshall's handling of it had profound effects on the power and prestige of the federal judiciary. The case was about politics; it placed front and center the question of what this third branch of the federal government really was, or might it might become.

The Election of 1800

It started with a national election, one of the nastiest in American history. According to historian John Ferling, "The winner, Thomas Jefferson, called it the Revolution of 1800."[31] In that year, incumbent president John Adams and his Federalist Party squared off against Thomas Jefferson and the Republican Party.[32] Although the nation's first president, George Washington, was not affiliated with any political party—he had in fact warned against the dangers of party politics—the seeds of America's first parties were planted during his administration. Ironically, the formation of the parties was heavily influenced by divisions between the very people who had warned of faction and defended the proposed Constitution as the best way to deal with it: the authors of the *Federalist Papers* themselves. John Adams, vice president at the time, allied with Washington's secretary of the Treasury, Alexander Hamilton, in order to promote a strong national government, especially in the area of economic policy and banking.[33] Secretary of State James Madison and his good friend and intellectual and political ally, Thomas Jefferson, mistrusted their motives and the reach of Hamilton's economic policies. As each side sought support for its views in Congress and in the state legislatures, America's first parties coalesced, like new planets pulling in more and more supporters into their political gravity.

By 1800, with the parties well formed and organized, many Americans had had enough of President Adams and his Federalists.[34] Fearing that laws such as the Alien and Sedition Acts portended a Federalist drift toward tyranny and suppression of individual liberties, voters were willing to listen to Jefferson and his fellow Republicans.[35]

Adams and Jefferson had once been good friends. In fact, "Abigail Adams called Jefferson, 'the only person' with whom her husband 'could associate with perfect freedom and unreserve.'"[36] As the presidential campaign got underway, however, both campaigns turned negative and personal. Through letters and pamphlets—usually written by supporters of the candidates rather than the men themselves—each side challenged the policies and character of the other. The Republicans accused Adams and the Federalists of trying to bring a British-style monarchy to America. The Federalists accused Jefferson and his fellow Republicans of being too close to France and pointed to the chaos that had unfolded in that country in the wake of the French Revolution. Jefferson was accused of cowardice during the Revolutionary War when, as governor of Virginia, he had fled advancing British troops. His detractors called him an atheist, a revolutionary.[37]

Under the rules of the Constitution at the time, the electors voted "for two Persons, of whom one at least shall not be an inhabitant of the same State with themselves."[38] The parties each nominated two candidates. Assuming a majority of electors voted for a single candidate, that person was elected president, and the vote-getter with the second largest number of votes (assuming no tie) became the vice president. In the case of a tie, or absent a majority vote for any one candidate by the electors, the election of the president went to the House of Representatives, with each state delegation receiving one vote and a majority vote required to secure the presidency.[39]

This scenario is precisely what happened in 1800, with Thomas Jefferson tied not with his opponent, John Adams, but with his presumed vice president, Aaron Burr. With accusations of voting irregularities surrounding the election and no majority vote winner in the Electoral College, some Federalists argued for stalling the process of picking a winner in the House long enough so that no one would be chosen by inauguration day, March 4.[40] According to Ferling, "Reports swirled of a Federalist conspiracy to assassinate Jefferson."[41] There was talk of civil war.

With only weeks to go before the inauguration was supposed to take place, Thomas Jefferson was finally elected president of the United States by the House of Representatives on the thirty-sixth ballot. The Republic had survived a most serious test. Jefferson, in his inaugural address, sought to calm tensions throughout the nation. "We are all republicans," he said. "We are all federalists."[42]

The election had cost John Adams the presidency; it would eventually cost Alexander Hamilton his life. Hamilton was killed in a duel with Aaron Burr in 1804.

A political cartoon criticizing Thomas Jefferson during the presidential campaign of 1800. The American eagle attempts to snatch the Constitution from Jefferson, who is trying to burn it on the "Altar of Gallic Despotism"–an allusion to Jefferson's supposed sympathies to the French revolutionaries.

CARICATURE OF JEFFERSON.

The election of 1800 had far-reaching implications. John Adams lost the election, and the Federalist Party unraveled. In addition, friendships and political alliances were fractured. Here, Alexander Hamilton and Aaron Burr prepare to duel in July 1804. Hamilton was killed in the duel.

Bettmann / Contributor.

The animosity between the two men was fueled in no small part by the election of 1800 and Hamilton's endorsement of former foe Jefferson. The Federalist Party also paid dearly. It had been soundly defeated in both the presidential election and in the congressional elections. Its days in power were numbered.

The Federalist Response to Electoral Defeat: A Judicial Strategy

Trying to preserve their influence within the national government, the Federalists turned to the federal judiciary, the one branch where they might endure, shielded from electoral removal due to the "good Behaviour" clause of the Constitution that gives federal judges lifetime job security providing they do not commit any offences worthy of impeachment.[43] In the waning weeks of Adams's administration, the Federalists sought to cement their position within the federal judiciary by reorganizing it and expanding the number of federal judges.[44] Gouverneur Morris, the author of the preamble to the Constitution, saw the political logic behind their attempts, noting that "the Federalists 'are about to experience a heavy gale of adverse wind; can they be blamed for casting many anchors to hold their ship through the storm?'"[45]

With the Judiciary Act of 1801, the Federalists changed the Supreme Court's schedule, reduced the size of the Court from six to five justices, and reorganized the lower federal courts in such a way as to create sixteen vacancies that were promptly filled by Adams's administration. The reduction in the size of the Supreme Court could not force a justice out; that would have been unconstitutional. What it did do was ensure that incoming president Jefferson would not be able to fill the next vacancy with someone the Federalists presumed would be a Republican, or at least a person sympathetic to Jefferson's political ideology. Once in office, Jefferson saw clearly what his adversaries had done. "The Federalists have retired into the judiciary as a stronghold," Jefferson lamented, "and from that battery all the works of republicanism are to be beaten down and erased."[46]

Just before leaving office, Adams set about filling the vacancies and strengthening the Federalist hold on the judiciary. In addition to the vacancies created by the Judiciary Act of 1801, the business of building up the administration of the nation's new capital in Washington D.C., had to be dealt with (the seat of government had been recently relocated from Philadelphia in 1800). There were many good jobs to fill in "the muddy village of Washington," including justices of the peace.[47] According to historian Kathryn Preyer, "Such an abundance of new offices drew applications from many, some of whom were out of office, or out of money, or both."[48] One of these job seekers was a Mr. William Marbury.

Less than two weeks before he signed the Judiciary Act of 1801 into law, the Senate confirmed Adams's appointment of his secretary of State, John Marshall, to be the new chief justice of the Supreme Court.[49] Born in Virginia in 1755, Marshall had served with distinction in the Revolutionary War, surviving the "starving winter of 1777–78" with George Washington and the Continental Army.[50] His fellow soldiers and officers had given him the nickname "Silver-Heels" because of an incident when he competed in a foot race wearing only a pair of stockings that his mother had knitted for him.[51]

Marshall was a Federalist. He was also an experienced politician. He had been a supporter of the Constitution at Virginia's ratifying convention and was considered "a gregarious [sociable] individual, someone who valued good company, good food, and good wine."[52] He had served in the Virginia General Assembly and, later, in Congress. Marshall served as chief justice of the Supreme Court from 1801 to 1835 and remains the longest-serving chief justice in American history. Over the course of his service as chief justice, Marshall worked to strengthen the power of the national government and the independence of the judicial branch. For the last weeks of the Adams administration, Marshall was both chief justice and secretary of State. He had a lot on his plate. Fatefully, as it turned out, perhaps too much.

The Case: Appointments Signed, Sealed, (but Not) Delivered

Adams's last minute appointments have been called "the midnight judges" because of the hasty nature of their nomination and confirmation. Republicans at the time were not at all pleased with the process, particularly as it seemed Marshall and other Federalists had taken care to see that several of their own relatives were among those appointed.[53] In the scramble to complete the paperwork before the Republicans took the reins of government, some of the commissions signed by Adams, including one for William Marbury, had not been delivered and were still sitting on Secretary of State Marshall's desk when the Adams's term expired at midnight.

While President Jefferson did deliver the commissions to some of the midnight appointees after he took office, William Marbury and several others did not receive theirs. Marbury, along with three other men, brought suit against James Madison, Jefferson's secretary of State, requesting that the Court issue a writ of mandamus ("we command") ordering Madison to deliver their commissions as justices of the peace of the District of Columbia.[54] The men argued that all of the required steps in their appointments had been properly taken: President Adams had nominated them, the Senate had confirmed their nominations, and the commissions had been signed and affixed with the presidential seal. Marshall's failure to deliver the commissions, they insisted, constituted a serious breach of etiquette and tradition.

Chief Justice John Marshall Confronts Politics and the Power of the Supreme Court

As he contemplated how the Court would respond to the demands of Marbury and his fellow would-be justices, Marshall confronted two powerful and related sets of questions about the role of the federal judiciary in the life of the American Republic—the same two questions with which we began this chapter: How powerful is the federal judiciary? And how political is it? In **Marbury v. Madison** (1803), the Court found itself involved in an intense partisan battle between the defeated Federalists and

Marbury v. Madison (1803)
a Supreme Court decision that established judicial review over federal laws.

Judicial nominee William Marbury, whose suit against James Madison in *Marbury v. Madison* established judicial review of federal law.

The Granger Collection, New York.

the victorious Republicans.[55] That Congress and the executive were highly political branches was obvious to everyone, especially after the election of 1800. The judiciary, however, was supposed to be different. It was constrained and defined by law, not politics. How should such an institution handle its role in the larger political life of the nation?

Chief Justice Marshall could not ignore either of these considerations; both had to be addressed. If his Court waded into the political battle of the time forcefully—ordering Jefferson's administration to deliver the commissions—he risked being rebuffed by the president or even impeached by the Republican-controlled Congress. Marshall *could* choose not to enter the battle. He could deny Marbury's petition, thus preventing a confrontation with Jefferson and his Republicans. However, to do so might send a message that the judiciary was weak in the face of powerful political forces, which could deal a blow to its power, prestige, and independence.[56] Marshall was in a bind and he knew it. In the decision that he ultimately delivered, Marshall noted the "peculiar delicacy of this case."[57] The way in which Marshall dealt with this dilemma continues to shape the role of the Supreme Court in American political life to this day. The two questions with which he wrestled, however, have not gone away. How political is the federal judiciary? How powerful is it?

Marbury v. Madison and the Establishment of Judicial Review

Because of the changes to the Supreme Court's schedule brought about by the Judiciary Act of 1801, Marbury and his associates had to wait for nearly two years before Marshall and the Court heard their request to issue a writ of mandamus to Secretary of State Madison. Both of Marshall's apparent options in the case seemed likely to diminish the power of the branch of government that he led. Either he could order Jefferson's administration to deliver the commissions and risk being refused or ignored, or he could decide not to challenge the president and risk looking weak and timid.

Marshall chose neither option. Instead, in what remains a still-debated but tactically brilliant move, he broke the decision before him into three separate questions. First, the chief justice asked if the men were entitled to their commissions. To this first question, Marshall, in his opinion, answered "yes." The presidential signing of such commissions is the last formal act, and that had been done. Delivery of the commissions, Marshall noted, "is a practice directed by convenience, but not by law."[58] Once this part of the decision was established, Marshall considered whether or not a legal remedy involving the courts was available to Marbury and his fellow plaintiffs. To this second question, Marshall also answered in the affirmative, arguing that "the individual who considers himself [so] injured has a right to resort to the laws of the country for a remedy."[59]

So far, it seemed that Marshall was going to take on Jefferson's administration, with all of the risks that such a strategy entailed. But he did not. Instead, Marshall presented a third question for his Court to consider: Were Marbury and the other plaintiffs entitled to the remedy that they sought—the writs of mandamus? To this question, Marshall answered "no." The power to issue these kinds of writs in this particular instance, he declared, had been improperly given to the Court by a section of the Judiciary Act of 1789.[60] Though the reasoning is a bit technical, Marshall argued that when Congress granted the Court the authority "to issue writs of mandamus to public officers," it was attempting to expand the scope of the original jurisdiction of the Court, which Congress cannot do. Only the Constitution can. Therefore, the Court did not have the power to give Marbury the remedy he sought.

In stating the inability of his Court to legitimately provide the sought-after remedy, Marshall also found that the part of the Judiciary Act that tried to give his Court such power was in violation of the Constitution and, therefore, invalid: "[A] law repugnant to the Constitution is void, and that courts, as well as other departments, are bound by that instrument."[61] It may have appeared to be a tactical retreat, but it was a bold strategic move. Madison did not have to deliver the commissions. Marshall, however, had just asserted what the Constitution had failed to lay out in its brief treatment of the third branch: The Supreme Court had the power of **judicial review**, which is the authority of a court to review laws and actions of other branches and levels of government to decide if they are in conflict with the highest law of the land—in this case, the Constitution—and, if they are, to declare those laws or actions invalid.

The Implications of Marshall's Decision

In establishing the precedent for judicial review over federal laws, Marshall expanded the Court's responsibility in **constitutional interpretation**, in which the judiciary reviews laws and actions in light of the meaning of the Constitution. In exercising judicial review, according to Marshall's logic, the Court does not place itself above the other two branches; it is coequal to them, and the Constitution is supreme to all three.

Marshall did not invent the idea of judicial review; he drew on constitutional principles that were already understood.[62] Several delegates to the Constitutional Convention had referred to a similar power. In *Federalist* No. 78, Alexander Hamilton had discussed the ability of the courts to be able to "pronounce legislative acts void" as necessary to preserving a limited constitution. Hamilton also made it clear that "whenever a particular statue contravenes the constitution, it will be the duty of the judicial tribunals to adhere to the latter and disregard the former." However, Hamilton cautioned, "Nor does this conclusion by any means suppose a superiority of the judicial to the legislative power. It only supposes that the power of the people is superior to both."[63]

President Jefferson had been a student and practitioner of the law, and he clearly understood the implications of Marshall's decision. Jefferson argued that Marshall had set a dangerous precedent. In a letter to Abigail Adams in 1804, Jefferson worried, "But the opinion which gives to the judges the right to decide what laws are constitutional, and what not, not only for themselves in their own sphere of action, but for the legislature and executive also, in their spheres, would make the judiciary a despotic branch."[64]

Jefferson and the Republicans waited to see if Marshall's Court would declare the Judiciary Act of 1802—their

judicial review
the authority of the highest court in a political system to determine if a law is or is not in conflict with a government's highest law, which in the United States is the Constitution.

constitutional interpretation
the process of applying the Constitution in assessing whether or not a law, part of a law, or an action by a governmental official is or is not in conflict with that the Constitution.

Abigail Adams, wife of President John Adams and correspondent to Thomas Jefferson. Their conversations via letters outline Jefferson's fear that Marshall's decision could make the judicial branch "despotic."

Alexander Bickel on the Powers of Judicial Review

In his 1962 book, *The Least Dangerous Branch*, public law scholar Alexander Bickel explored the history of and controversies surrounding judicial review in American politics. In doing so, Bickel pointed out the often overlooked fact that there are *three* possible outcomes when the Supreme Court ascertains the degree to which a federal law, state law, state constitutional provision, or governmental action is or is not in conflict with the Constitution of the United States.

In the first possible outcome, the Court overturns a law or provision. In doing so, it risks undermining democratic principles, acting, in Bickel's words, as "a countermajoritarian force in our system."[67] The "countermajoritarian difficulty" arises from the fact that a group of unelected justices will be overturning the will of a majority of citizens that is being exercised through their elected representatives, presidents, and governors.

The second possible outcome is that the Court upholds a law, giving the law its approval. In this case, the Court again inserts itself into the democratic process. In both of these cases, Bickel notes, "the Court must act rigorously on principle, else it undermines the justification for its power."[68]

The third possible outcome occurs when the Court does not act at all and refuses to weigh in on the constitutionality of a law, state constitution, or action. To Bickel and other scholars, the act of *not acting* is an important tool in preserving judicial legitimacy. In the words of Justice Louis Brandeis, "The most important thing we do is not doing."[69] The tricky thing about refusing to hear a major constitutional case is that the Court is not required to say why it has made this decision.

WHAT DO YOU THINK?

When the Supreme Court overturns or upholds a federal or state law, it must make its case to the American people. What does it mean, however, when the Court chooses not to exercise its power? How can Americans understand the inaction of this institution of government that is tasked with such an enormous power?

attack on the Federalists' judicial efforts—unconstitutional. There was already a "case positively inviting such an opinion" on the Court's docket challenging the Federalists' reorganization of the federal judiciary.[65] Marshall and the other justices, in the tense political times, expected to be impeached by the Republican-controlled Congress.[66] However, if the Republicans were hoping for a showdown with Marshall's Court over the Judiciary Act of 1802, they would not get the chance.

Under the decades-long tenure of Marshall, the Supreme Court used the tool of judicial review to weigh in on the constitutionality of several state laws, declaring some invalid. Marshall, however, never again used the power of judicial review to strike down an act of Congress. It would be more than fifty years before the Court took such an action again, in its infamous decision in *Dred Scott v. Sanford* (1857). In this case, Justice Roger Taney and his Court overturned the Missouri Compromise, deepening national divisions over the future of slavery [70]

In the end, William Marbury and his fellow job seekers never received their commissions, and the power of judicial review and the role of the Court in constitutional interpretation remain highly debated issues to this day. Before we can explore the implications of this claimed authority, however, it is necessary to examine the structure and operation of the American judicial system.

1. In his opinion in *Marbury v. Madison* (1803), Justice John Marshall had to confront the politics of the nation.

   a. True
   b. False

2. Facing defeat after the election of 1800, the losing Federalist Party chose to _____.

   a. Accept its losses
   b. Impeach the incoming president
   c. Use judicial appointments to secure its future power
   d. Use the Supreme Court to overturn the election

3. What was John Marshall's strategy in his decision in *Marbury v. Madison*?

Answer Key: 1. a.; 2. c; 3. Answers should include his creation of judicial review without directly confronting the power of President Jefferson.

THE FEDERAL JUDICIARY AND THE AMERICAN LEGAL SYSTEM

Each of the two levels in the federalist system—the nation and the states—operates its own system of courts, with a single federal judiciary for the nation and separate state judiciaries in each of the fifty states. While the structure of American federalism defines the basic organization of the nation's legal system, the dual systems of federal and state courts share in common the tradition of the **adversarial system** of justice, in which the opposing parties present their sides of a case in the most persuasive way possible. In this system, a **plaintiff** is the party bringing a complaint and the **defendant** is the party accused of wrongdoing.[71]

Criminal and Civil Cases

Whether or not a specific court has jurisdiction over a specific case may depend on whether that court is a state or a federal court, the details of the case, or where that court lies within the overall structure of the federal or state court system. Both state and federal courts have jurisdiction over two categories of law, criminal and civil.[72] **Criminal law** covers actions determined to harm the community itself, such as committing an act of violence against another person.[73] In a criminal case, the state or federal government acts as the plaintiff and tries to prove the guilt of the defendant, the party accused of a crime. Although many acts (such as murder or assault) are considered to be criminal offences in all of the states, some acts (such as gambling or recreational use of marijuana) are legal in some states but not in others. As of 2016, for example, an adult in several states could lawfully use marijuana recreationally according to state law (subject to certain restrictions) but in doing so be in violation of federal law, presenting a tricky issue for American federalism.[74] States may also vary in the punishments handed out for those convicted of similar crimes.

Defendants in criminal cases are guaranteed a set of constitutional protections, including the right not to be forced to testify (Fifth Amendment), the right to a speedy and

---

CONNECTING TO . . .

The American Legal System

As you read about the structure of the American federal judiciary, reflect upon John Marshall's strategic action in *Marbury v. Madison* and Alexander Hamilton's arguments in *Federalist* No. 78. Consider the following:

- The power, or limitations on that power, that the framers established for the judicial branch

- How the Supreme Court might approach the decision of whether or not to hear a case on appeal

- Why the process of Senate confirmation of federal judicial nominees has become so politically charged

adversarial system
a legal structure in which two opposing sides present their case in the most persuasive way possible.

plaintiff
a person or group who brings a case in court.

defendant
a person or group against whom a case is brought in court.

criminal law
a category of law covering actions determined to harm the community itself.

Video taken by a bystander captured the beating of black motorist Rodney King by Los Angeles police officers in March 1991. The following year a jury found four white Los Angeles police officers not guilty of assault, but a federal jury found two of the officers guilty of violating King's civil rights.

Charles Steiner/Image Works/LIFE Images Collection/Getty Images.

plea bargaining
a legal process in which the plaintiff and defendant agree to an outcome prior to the handing out of a verdict.

civil law
a category of law covering cases involving private rights and relationships between individuals and groups.

public trial by an impartial jury, the right to confront witnesses, and (as the amendment has been interpreted) the right to provision of a lawyer at government expense if the defendant is unable to pay for one (Sixth Amendment).[75] If found by a jury to be "not guilty," criminal defendants are protected from being tried for the same crime again by what is called the double jeopardy clause (Fifth Amendment). This protection, however, is for crimes and not actions, and a defendant may be tried more than once for the same actions if more than one law has been broken.

In 1992 an all-white California jury found four white Los Angeles police officers not guilty of assaulting Rodney King, an African American man, during a traffic stop and arrest, much of which was captured on videotape by a witness. That verdict was quickly followed by rioting and heightened racial tensions throughout the city. The next year, a federal jury found two of the officers guilty of violating King's civil rights through the application of excessive force or a refusal to stop the exercise of excessive force during the original incident.

Being convicted under a criminal statute leads to some form of punishment, such as fines, imprisonment, or, in some cases, the death penalty.[76] Most criminal cases are resolved through the process of **plea bargaining**. In this process, a defendant in a criminal case agrees to plead guilty to a lesser charge than the one brought by the prosecutors in order to reduce his or her punishment. Plea bargaining is also used in civil cases. As is the case with defendants during the arrest and trial phases, those ultimately convicted of crimes have constitutional protections, specifically against the imposition of "cruel and unusual punishments" (Eighth Amendment). Whether or not the death penalty—or specific methods of instituting it—constitutes a violation of the Eighth Amendment's protections continues to be debated today.

Noncriminal law, commonly referred to as **civil law**, covers cases involving private rights and relationships between individuals and groups. In a civil case, the plaintiff is the party who argues that she or he has been wronged, and the defendant is the party accused of violating a person's rights or breaking an agreement. While in criminal cases a government (state or federal) is always the plaintiff, in civil cases the plaintiff may be a government or an individual. A jury or a judge might decide civil cases, though most are settled without a formal verdict either before the case goes to trial or during the proceedings.

The State Courts

While our focus is on the federal judiciary, it is important to note that state courts handle the vast majority of court cases in the United States. While states may vary in how their judicial systems are structured and organized—including how judges are selected—the state court systems share a few common traits. State judicial systems handle both criminal and civil cases. Each state has a system of trial courts that does most of the work of the state's judiciary, handles cases arising under that state's laws, and possesses original jurisdiction. More than half of the states have an intermediate system of appellate courts

FIGURE 15.1

Comparing Criminal and Civil Law

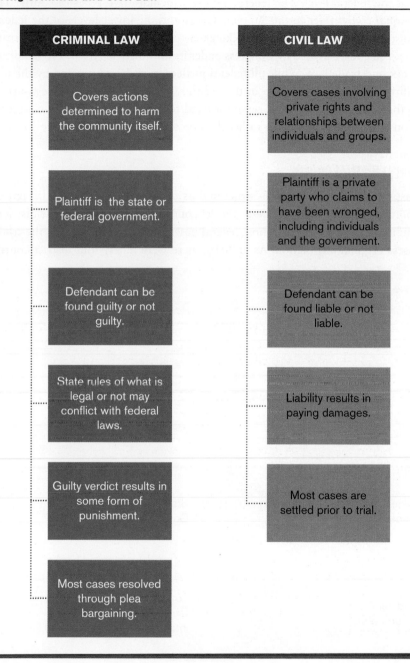

CRIMINAL LAW	CIVIL LAW
Covers actions determined to harm the community itself.	Covers cases involving private rights and relationships between individuals and groups.
Plaintiff is the state or federal government.	Plaintiff is a private party who claims to have been wronged, including individuals and the government.
Defendant can be found guilty or not guilty.	Defendant can be found liable or not liable.
State rules of what is legal or not may conflict with federal laws.	Liability results in paying damages.
Guilty verdict results in some form of punishment.	Most cases are settled prior to trial.
Most cases resolved through plea bargaining.	

that operate with appellate jurisdiction. Each state has at least one state supreme court, which acts as the highest court in that state's system and as the final level of appeal.[77] A select group of cases may proceed to the federal judiciary from the highest state court of appeals. These types of cases generally involve a question arising under the Constitution, such as a claim that an individual's constitutional rights have been violated. States also operate systems of specialized courts that typically handle issues like traffic violations, family disputes, and small claims.

The Structure of the Federal Judiciary

While the majority of cases are handled by the state courts, many of the most impactful happen at the federal level. The federal judiciary includes two types of courts. The term *constitutional courts* refer to the Supreme Court and the lower levels of the federal judiciary that the Constitution authorized Congress to create in Article III. Legislative courts are specialized courts created by Congress under its authority in Article I to handle matters such as tax and trade law. While all federal justices must be nominated by the president and confirmed by a majority vote in the Senate, justices in the legislative courts, unlike those in the constitutional courts, serve for fixed terms. Our focus in this chapter will be on the constitutional court system rather than on the specialized legislative courts.

The Federal District Courts

federal district courts
the lowest level of the federal judiciary; these courts usually possess original jurisdiction in cases that originate at the federal level.

The constitutional court system is structured as a three-layered pyramid (Figure 15.2). At the bottom are the nation's **federal district courts**. Congress created the district courts in the Judiciary Act of 1789. In most federal cases, district courts act as the trial courts and possess original jurisdiction. As of 2016, there were ninety-four district courts in the

FIGURE 15.2

The Modern Court System

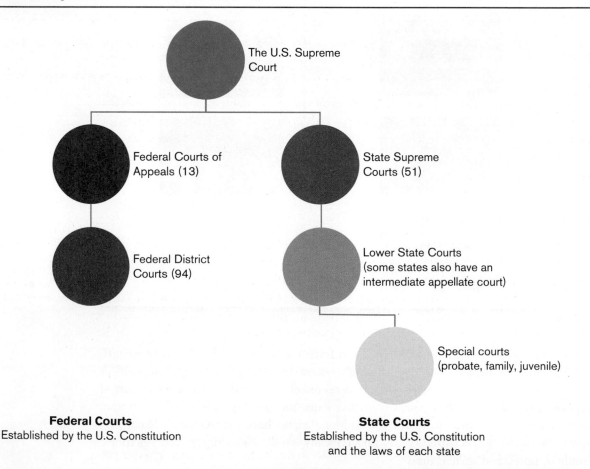

The U.S. Supreme Court

Federal Courts of Appeals (13)

State Supreme Courts (51)

Federal District Courts (94)

Lower State Courts (some states also have an intermediate appellate court)

Special courts (probate, family, juvenile)

Federal Courts
Established by the U.S. Constitution

State Courts
Established by the U.S. Constitution and the laws of each state

FIGURE 15.3

Map of the District and Appellate Courts

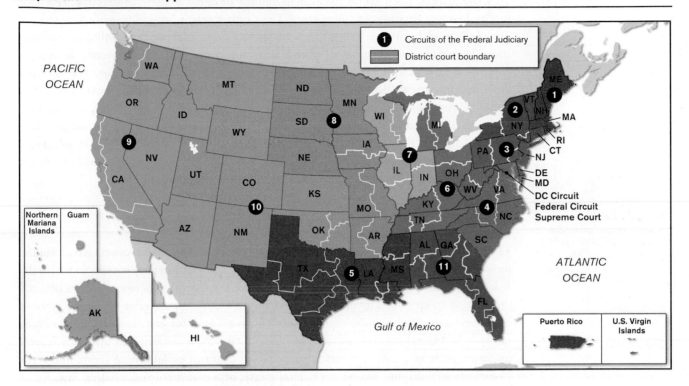

Source: United States Courts, "Geographic Boundaries of United States Courts of Appeals and United States District Courts," http://www.uscourts.gov/uscourts/images/CircuitMap.pdf.

United States, and each state had at least one. District court boundaries do not cut across state lines. The district courts handle most of the work of the federal courts, and their cases are heard by a single federal judge. Cases heard in a district court may or may not include a jury; the Constitution guarantees the right to a jury trial in all federal criminal cases (Sixth Amendment) and in some civil cases (Seventh Amendment).

The Appellate Courts

The **federal courts of appeals** occupy the middle level of the constitutional courts. There are thirteen courts of appeals; eleven have jurisdiction over regionally based "circuits," one has jurisdiction over the District of Columbia (which handles appeals involving federal agencies), and the thirteenth handles cases arising under international trade and patent law. The courts of appeals exercise appellate jurisdiction only, reviewing decisions made by the federal district courts and certain specialized federal courts (Figure 15.2). The federal appellate courts have, as their name implies, appellate jurisdiction only and are staffed with justices specifically appointed to that level of the federal judiciary.

federal courts of appeals
the middle level of the federal judiciary; these courts review and hear appeals from the federal district courts.

The Supreme Court

At the top of the federal judicial system is the United States Supreme Court, which, as the Constitution established, is the highest court in the nation. Part of the Court's intended purpose was to resolve differences between the states, which had not effectively been provided for in the government created by the Articles of Confederation. The Court also acts to resolve differing interpretations of the law in the lower federal courts. Since 1869, the Court (when no seats are vacant) has consisted of nine justices, including a chief justice and eight associate justices. Each justice has a small number of clerks to assist in selecting, researching, and issuing decisions in Court cases. The Court meets in session roughly nine months out of the year, beginning on the first Monday in October. Those cases still on the docket (the schedule of cases to be heard) when a term ends continue to the next term's docket.

Cases in which the Supreme Court exercises original jurisdiction are few and are described in Article III of the Constitution: "In all Cases affecting Ambassadors, other public Ministers and Consuls, and those in which a State shall be a Party, the supreme Court shall have original jurisdiction."[78] In all other cases in which the federal judiciary has jurisdiction, the Court possesses appellate jurisdiction only. In addition to having appellate jurisdiction over all federal cases, the Court possesses appellate jurisdiction over certain state cases, especially those involving a federal issue.

How Cases Proceed through the Federal Judiciary

Those cases that begin in the federal judiciary—in which the federal courts have original jurisdiction—must fall into one of three categories. The first category is cases in which the federal government is a party in a dispute. Second, the federal judiciary possesses original jurisdiction in civil suits involving parties from two different states in which the amount of money in question is more than $75,000. Finally—and, for our purposes, most importantly—the federal judiciary possesses original jurisdiction in cases that involve a federal question, such as a case in which a party files a claim of violations of rights under the Constitution, a dispute involving a federal treaty, or a case involving a federal law. Cases involving federal questions may be either criminal or civil cases. State cases that proceed to the Supreme Court also involve federal questions. Many of the most important federal cases in American history—and most of the cases that we consider in this book—are those involving charges of violations of constitutional rights and liberties.

As the courts of original jurisdiction in most federal cases, the federal district courts act as the trial courts, finding facts and delivering opinions on the case. Litigants who lose in a district court have an option to appeal the decision to the appellate courts, in which case the case moves up to the next level.[79] Most federal cases, however, go no farther than the district courts.

Appellate courts possess appellate jurisdiction only and review cases on appeal. Rather than finding facts, the appellate courts focus on how the decision of the district court was rendered and if that decision was appropriate in the context of the law. With cases typically heard by three-judge panels, an appellate court has several options. It may refuse to hear the appeal, in which case the decision of the district court (or specialized federal court) holds. Litigants whose appeal is refused by the appellate court may still appeal to the Supreme Court, though their odds of receiving a hearing by the Court are very small.

If it decides to hear a case, an appeals court may choose to affirm the judgment of the lower court, confirming that court's ruling. It may reverse the decision; if this is the case, it is typically based on questions of how the lower court proceeded or applied the law. Finally, it may remand the case back to the lower court for reconsideration, again often because the appellate court judges had questions about procedure or application of the law. These options are not mutually exclusive for any one case. The court could affirm part of a lower court's decision in a particular case, reverse part of it, and remand yet another part, though this is far from a common outcome. The side that loses in an

brief
legal document presented by plaintiffs, defendants, and, at times, other interested parties outlining their arguments in a case.

standing
the legal ability to bring a case in court.

certiorari
the process through which most cases reach the Supreme Court; after four justices concur that the Court should hear the case, a writ of certiorari is issued to the lower court to request the relevant case records.

appellate court has the right to appeal to the Supreme Court, but there is no guarantee that its case will be heard. If not, the decision of the appellate court stands, though it only applies to that circuit.[80]

The Supreme Court: The Decision to Take Cases on Appeal

In exercising its authority of appellate jurisdiction, the Supreme Court is confronted with two questions, the first of which actually determines the outcome of roughly 99 percent of the appeals before it. First, the Court decides whether or not to hear the case. Second, if it does decide to hear the case, it issues its decision based on the merits of the case and applicable law. The vast majority of cases heard on appeal in the Court originate with a litigant who has lost in a lower court filing a petition to have his or her case heard. Almost all such petitions are denied, however. The modern Court receives, on average, between eight thousand and nine thousand such petitions a year but hears less than 1 percent of these cases, or about seventy to eighty. In recent decades, the Court has gained a much greater degree of control over its docket.

A petitioner who wishes to have the Court accept his or her case files an argument with the Court in a written **brief**, which presents the arguments for the appeal. Not everyone can file a legitimate brief before the Court. In addition to certain other technical requirements about the facts and merits of a case, a petitioner must demonstrate that he or she has **standing**, which involves demonstrating an actual or imminent harm from a law or action in question. As we will discuss later in the chapter, the need to establish standing acts as a limitation on the power of the Court to shape national public policy. The opposing party in a case may also file a brief with the Court laying out her or his arguments.[81]

As the Constitution offers little guidance on which cases the Court does or does not take, justices have adopted the custom of the rule of four, which simply means that it will generally hear a case if four or more justices vote to do so. If it decides to hear a case, the Court issues a writ of certiorari (from the Latin "to be more informed") to the lower court for the records of the case, a process that is commonly referred to as **certiorari**, or "granting cert." As discussed earlier, very few petitions for cert are granted. In its own rules, the Court makes it clear that the hurdle for having a case heard on appeal is high: "Review on a writ of certiorari is not a matter of right, but of judicial discretion. A petition of a writ of certiorari will be granted only for compelling reasons."[82]

An image of a brief filed by the solicitor general of the United States in *Hamdi v. Rumsfeld*, the case that we explored in the chapter on the presidency.

No. 03-6696

In the Supreme Court of the United States

YASER ESAM HAMDI AND ESAM FOUAD HAMDI, AS NEXT FRIEND OF YASER ESAM HAMDI, PETITIONERS

v.

DONALD RUMSFELD, SECRETARY OF DEFENSE, ET AL.

*ON WRIT OF CERTIORARI
TO THE UNITED STATES COURT OF APPEALS
FOR THE FOURTH CIRCUIT*

BRIEF FOR THE RESPONDENTS

THEODORE B. OLSON
*Solicitor General
Counsel of Record*

PAUL D. CLEMENT
Deputy Solicitor General

GREGORY G. GARRE
*Assistant to the Solicitor
General*

JOHN A. DRENNAN
Attorney

*Department of Justice
Washington, D.C. 20530-0001
(202) 514-2217*

QUESTION PRESENTED

Whether the court of appeals erred in holding that respondents have established the legality of the military's detention of Yaser Esam Hamdi, a presumed American citizen who was captured in Afghanistan during the combat operations in late 2001, and was determined by the military to be an enemy combatant who should be detained in connection with the ongoing hostilities in Afghanistan.

The most important factor in the decision to grant or deny cert is if there is confusion about or alternate interpretations of a law or previous ruling among or between lower-level federal courts or state supreme courts. Cases presenting a federal question are also more likely to be heard. The Court does not, however, act as the corrector of all lower court mistakes in finding fact or applying the law when these errors do not present or affect important federal concerns. The Court does not, however, act as the corrector of all lower court mistakes in finding fact or applying the law when these errors do not present or affect important federal concerns.

Interested parties who are not plaintiffs or defendants may also try to signal to the Court their interest in the decision to grant cert or on the merits of the case should cert be granted. Plaintiffs and defendants are not the only parties that may file briefs. An interested party (such as an interest group) may also submit its opinions to the Court in what is called an amicus curiae brief (from the Latin, "friend of the court").[83] The volume, authorship, and content of these briefs can act as a signal to the Court about how the public or interest groups view an issue.[84] An especially important filer of amici curiae briefs is the United States **solicitor general**, who is appointed by the president to represent the federal government in the Court. An indication to the Court that the government (or the president, specifically) is interested in a case can be a powerful signal both on the question of whether or not the Court should hear a particular case and on its ruling should it decide to do so.

The preferences of the justices may also play a role in the decision to grant cert. After all, the final decision rests on the votes of the justices themselves. While scholars continue to debate the role that justices' political or policy preferences play in their decisions (which we will examine later in the chapter), a justice who supports a particular view on an issue before the Court must consider how the other justices are likely to vote on the merits of the case. Justices are well aware that the outcome of a Supreme Court case can set a **precedent**, or a judicial decision that acts as a basis for deciding similar cases in the future. An individual justice may be more or less likely to grant cert if there is a perceived likelihood that the outcome might be a precedent that the justice desires or wishes to avoid.

The Supreme Court: Considering and Deciding upon Cases

If the Supreme Court decides to grant cert to a case, it requests briefs from both sides laying out their full arguments. Court clerks will assist the justices in reviewing these briefs. The case is then scheduled for **oral argument** before the assembled justices, during which each side gets a fixed amount of time (typically half an hour) to present. In exceptional circumstances, filers of amicus curiae briefs may also be given time during oral arguments, but this is not common. During this phase, the justices are not passive but frequently interrupt and question the lawyers as they present, though some justices tend to interrupt and question more than others. Cameras are not allowed in the courtroom during oral arguments, though sketch artists and audio recordings are.

Scholars debate how influential oral arguments are in shaping justices' rulings in a case.[85] This process, however, is often of intense interest to members of the public, who analyze the content of justices' questions for clues as to how those justices will ultimately vote. As most of what follows the oral argument phase happens in secret, court watchers have few other means to try to divine the Court's decisions ahead of time. After oral argument, the case proceeds to judicial conference, in which the justices meet and vote in secret; not even their clerks are present. The process can go

solicitor general
a presidential appointee who represents the federal government in the Supreme Court.

precedent
a judicial decision that guides future courts in handling similar cases.

oral arguments
presentations made by plaintiffs and attorneys before the Supreme Court.

FIGURE 15.4

How Cases Move through the Court System

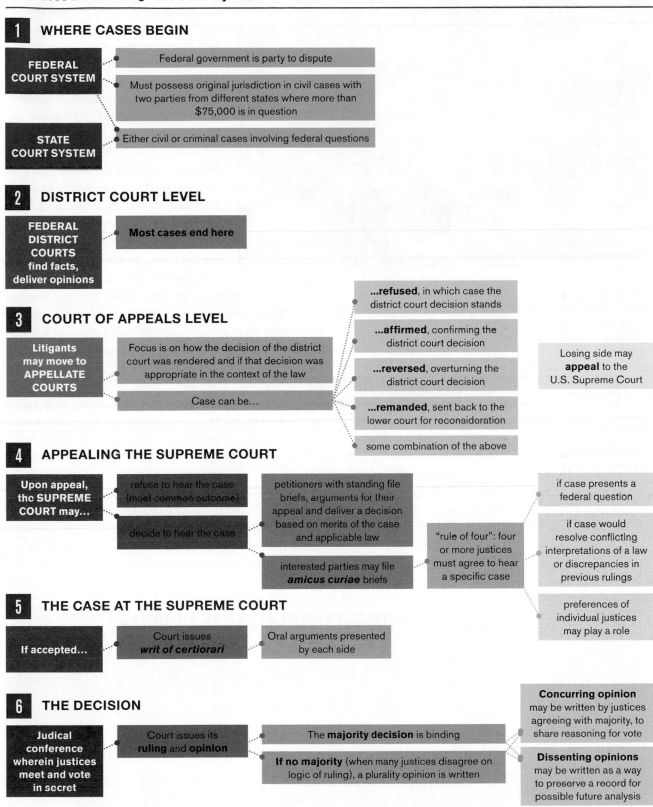

1 WHERE CASES BEGIN

FEDERAL COURT SYSTEM
- Federal government is party to dispute
- Must possess original jurisdiction in civil cases with two parties from different states where more than $75,000 is in question

STATE COURT SYSTEM
- Either civil or criminal cases involving federal questions

2 DISTRICT COURT LEVEL

FEDERAL DISTRICT COURTS find facts, deliver opinions
- **Most cases end here**

3 COURT OF APPEALS LEVEL

Litigants may move to APPELLATE COURTS

Focus is on how the decision of the district court was rendered and if that decision was appropriate in the context of the law

Case can be...
- **...refused**, in which case the district court decision stands
- **...affirmed**, confirming the district court decision
- **...reversed**, overturning the district court decision
- **...remanded**, sent back to the lower court for reconsideration
- some combination of the above

Losing side may **appeal** to the U.S. Supreme Court

4 APPEALING THE SUPREME COURT

Upon appeal, the SUPREME COURT may...
- refuse to hear the case (most common outcome)
- decide to hear the case

petitioners with standing file briefs, arguments for their appeal and deliver a decision based on merits of the case and applicable law

interested parties may file **amicus curiae** briefs

"rule of four": four or more justices must agree to hear a specific case
- if case presents a federal question
- if case would resolve conflicting interpretations of a law or discrepancies in previous rulings
- preferences of individual justices may play a role

5 THE CASE AT THE SUPREME COURT

If accepted...

Court issues **writ of certiorari**

Oral arguments presented by each side

6 THE DECISION

Judicial conference wherein justices meet and vote in secret

Court issues its **ruling** and **opinion**

- The **majority decision** is binding
- **If no majority** (when many justices disagree on logic of ruling), a plurality opinion is written

Concurring opinion may be written by justices agreeing with majority, to share reasoning for vote

Dissenting opinions may be written as a way to preserve a record for possible future analysis

In this sketch, Deputy Solicitor General Paul Clement is shown presenting his oral argument on behalf of the government before the Supreme Court on April 28, 2004, in the case of Yaser Esam Hamdi and Jose Padilla. It is not clear the extent to which oral arguments shape justices' opinions, but the questions they ask do sometimes indicate how they may vote.

on for months (on and off, of course), and individual justices can and do change their votes during this phase.

Finally, the Court issues its decision. The majority opinion consists of the ruling—and the logic behind it—of the majority of justices in the case. When it acts under appellate jurisdiction (which is most of the time), the Court has the same options as other appellate courts. It may affirm, reverse, or remand back to the lower court the case (or certain rulings within a case).[86] The decision and the majority opinion are binding and serve to guide lower courts and future Courts in handling similar cases. If the chief justice is in the majority, then he or she selects the author of the majority opinion. If not, the most senior member of the majority does so. The power to choose the author of an opinion can be a useful strategic tool as even justices who vote together may have differences in their interpretations of certain points brought up in the case. If there is no majority, which typically occurs when many justices disagree on the logic behind a ruling, then a plurality opinion will be written that expresses the views of the largest number of justices who voted together.

A justice voting with the majority may also write a concurring opinion (often called a concurrence) explaining the reasoning behind his or her particular vote. More than one justice may collaborate on a concurrence. Concurrences are more common when a justice has some differences in logic or reasoning with the other members of the majority but not enough to cause that justice to side against them. A justice who voted with the minority may write a dissenting opinion, called a dissent, also alone or with other justices. These opinions do not carry the weight of the Court behind them (since the justice writing the dissent was on the losing side). However, if a future Court should revisit a precedent with a thought to perhaps overturning it, a dissent may provide a useful record and analysis of why at least one justice thought the Court got it wrong the first time.

APPOINTMENT TO THE FEDERAL JUDICIARY

While individual states vary in how they select their judges, all federal judges must be nominated by the president and confirmed by a majority vote in the Senate. As federal judges are appointed for life—assuming "good behavior"—successfully placing individuals on the federal bench is one of the most important things that a president can do. Trying to preserve the influence of their defeated party after the election of 1800 was what drove John Adams and the Federalists to try to pack the federal judiciary with as many of their people as possible.

While most district court nominees are approved, the confirmations of appellate and Supreme Court judges have become more contentious and affected by partisan political battles in recent years, though there have been many other periods in American history where this has also been the case. Part of the reason that things tend to run more smoothly at the district court level is the custom of senatorial courtesy, in which presidents (and the high-ranking members of the Justice Department who do much of the actual work of identifying candidates) consult with senators from the state in which the vacant district judgeship is located, especially if those senators are from the president's political party.

The higher two levels of the federal judiciary often witness more direct presidential involvement in the nomination process, and these nominations are more likely to be caught up in partisan battles. While most Supreme Court nominees are confirmed, their confirmation hearings can and have often involved intense scrutiny of the nominee. In addition, recent confirmation votes in the Senate have tended to be closer than those in decades prior. As with other presidential nominees subject to Senate approval, federal judicial nominees have sometimes found their paths blocked by a filibuster or the threat of one. In November 2013, a majority of senators voted to change the filibuster rules to allow the closure of debate over executive and judicial branch nominees by a simple majority vote rather than the previous requirement of sixty votes. This change, however, was not applied to Supreme Court nominees, only lower court appointees.

Presidential Considerations in Making Nominations to the Supreme Court

Unlike presidents and members of Congress, the Constitution places no requirements on the necessary qualifications to serve in the federal judiciary; judges do not even have to be lawyers. When vacancies occur in the Supreme Court, presidents are presented with an important, though challenging, opportunity to help shape policy for years to come. When the position of chief justice is vacant, a president may nominate a sitting member of the Court for that position and fill the newly vacant position of associate justice (which is how it usually happens), or the president may nominate an individual from outside the Court to the position of chief justice directly.

Because they are such high-profile appointments, nominees to the Court have to be weighed especially carefully. When choosing Court nominees, presidents have to balance both legal and political considerations. Experience, ethical integrity, and legal accomplishment are extremely important factors and can help smooth the confirmation process. Modern Court nominees will have typically already served in the federal judiciary or a similarly high-level position.

Presidents may also strive to nominate individuals who share their judicial philosophies and approaches to constitutional interpretation. Once confirmation occurs, however, presidents have no control over the behavior of their nominees. More than one president has successfully nominated an individual only to be surprised by some of that justice's later decisions. Political calculations come into play as well. Nominees who are considered outspoken on contentious political issues are likely to face careful scrutiny and intense questioning by senators concerned about these stances. As the Court, like Congress, still does not descriptively represent the American people, presidents may also consider nominating those with diverse backgrounds to the Court to make it more closely resemble a portrait of the nation.

1. State and federal courts consider both criminal and civil cases.

    a. True
    b. False

2. The number of levels in the federal judiciary (aside from some smaller specialized courts) is
_____.

    a. 1
    b. 2
    c. 3
    d. 4

3. What considerations do Supreme Court justices take into account when deciding whether or not to grant cert?

....

Answer Key: 1. a; 2. c; 3. Answers should include whether or not the case involves a federal issue, the filing of briefs, conflict in the lower courts, and individual strategic considerations of justices.

THE "TRIAL" OF ROBERT BORK
Politics, Confirmation, and Constitutional Interpretation

In the summer of 1987, even before President Ronald Reagan named his selection to fill a pending vacant seat in the Supreme Court, the atmosphere had become politically charged. Justice Lewis F. Powell Jr. had recently announced his retirement after fifteen years on the bench. Powell had been considered a moderate, often casting the "swing vote" on important decisions. The choice of his replacement, therefore, had the potential to tilt the closely divided Court away from its liberal-moderate majority. It was also a chance for the president, struggling to enact his programs in the face of a Democratic-controlled Congress, to help cement his legacy in American political history.

As the nomination drew near, "White House officials could barely contain their glee. They had almost given up hope that any member of the Court's liberal-moderate bloc would leave the bench soon enough for Mr. Reagan to pick his successor."[87] Democrats in the Senate were wary. One Democratic senator publicly warned that in each of his two presidential campaigns Reagan had promised "to totally redo the Federal Court system, [vowing] to change its position on abortion, to make some major curtailments in free speech, [and] to change its approach on criminal matters and the rights of the accused."[88]

To complicate matters, two of the Democrats on the Senate Judiciary Committee—Joe Biden (D-DE) and Paul Simon (D-IL)—were both planning on presidential bids in 1988. Failing to try to block the president's nomination would surely haunt them in the upcoming primaries and general election.[89] When asked about the president's upcoming choice, Biden responded, in what turned out to be a moment of significant understatement, "If it's concluded that there is a desire to move to someone who has a predisposition on every one of the major issues, the social issues, and wishes to move the Court in a direction where it was 20 to 25 years ago, I think there will be some controversy."[90]

Several possible nominees emerged. Senator Orrin G. Hatch (R-UT), in spite of his stated opposition to abortion, was expected to proceed more smoothly than other conservative picks if chosen. Robert H. Bork, then serving on the Court of Appeals for the District of Columbia, provoked strong reactions at the mere mention of his potential nomination. While none questioned Bork's powerful intellect or his legal and professional qualifications, his rulings and statements in many cases involving highly charged social issues, such as abortion, sexuality, civil rights, and rights of the accused, sparked serious concern, especially since cases in many of these areas were awaiting Supreme Court action.

At the core of the controversy was Bork's view of constitutional interpretation. Bork believed that a justice should focus on the language and intent of the Constitution rather than supplying his or her own interpretation of the document—or, more significantly, inventing his or her own constitutional rights and liberties. Many, including key Democrats, were uncomfortable with the potential implications of Bork's approach. He had previously argued that the Supreme Court's decision in *Roe v. Wade* (1973), which recognized a woman's right to an abortion, was unconstitutional.[91] The death penalty, he argued, as referred to in the original text of the Constitution, was not.[92]

President Ronald Reagan with Judge Robert Bork In 1987.
Rex Features via AP Images

Democrats in the Senate geared up for a political battle. Members of certain interest groups took an even stronger stance. Kate Michelman, a leader of the National Abortion Rights Action League, promised, "We're going to wage an all-out frontal assault like you've never seen before on this nominee, assuming it's Bork."[93] Within minutes of Reagan's nomination of the controversial judge, Senator Edward M. Kennedy's (D-MA) office released a statement declaring that Bork's "rigid ideology will tip the scales of justice against the kind of country America is and ought to be."[94] Although the results of a poll conducted before the president announced his choice indicated that 49 percent of Americans felt that a nominee should be confirmed regardless of his or her political ideology, Democrats planned to "go public," and use the hearings and the media to block the nomination.[95]

As the Senate Judiciary Committee scheduled its confirmation hearings for September, its chair, Senator Joe Biden, promised civil rights leaders that "he would lead the battle against Judge Bork in the Senate."[96] A senior administration official promised that President Reagan "would 'use all his resources' to push the Bork nomination."[97] Both sides prepared their arguments "like a championship fight," according to a lobbyist helping Bork to prepare.[98]

During the hearings, a long parade of witnesses gave testimony, as the Judiciary Committee—and the nation—tried to ascertain who Bork really was.[99] American public opinion began to turn, though it still remained divided. A poll conducted during Bork's testimony found that 48 percent of Americans disapproved of his confirmation, while 44 percent approved.[100] The use of public opinion polls, political strategizing, and attempts by both sides to control the news cycle led one of the witnesses to conclude that the confirmation process might have been changed forever: "We're getting perilously close to electing a Supreme Court Justice."[101]

After twelve days of testimony by 110 witnesses, the Senate Judiciary Committee voted 9–5 against confirmation, spelling certain defeat for the nomination in the Democratic-controlled Senate. Republican senators called on the president to withdraw the nomination in order to preserve his dwindling political capital. There were also calls for Bork to withdraw on his own volition. Bork refused, not because he thought that there was a chance of a successful outcome but in protest over what he saw as an overtly political process of confirmation to the Supreme Court. In his book, *The Tempting of America: The Political Seduction of the Law*, he wrote,

> Federal judges are not appointed to decide cases according to the latest opinion polls. They are appointed to decide cases impartially according to the law. But when judicial nominees are assessed and treated like political candidates the effect will be to chill the climate

Judge Robert Bork testifies before the Senate Judiciary Committee during his hearing as a Supreme Court justice nominee on September 18, 1987, in Washington, D.C. Bork was nominated by President Reagan.

James K. W. Atherton/*The Washington Post* via Getty Images

in which judicial deliberations take place, to erode public confidence in the impartiality of our judges, and to endanger the independence of the judiciary . . .

I therefore wish to end the speculation. There should be a full debate and final Senate decision. In deciding this course, I harbor no illusions. But a crucial principle is at stake. That principle is the way in which we select the men and women who guard the liberties of all the American people. That should not be done through public campaigns of distortion. If I withdraw now, that campaign would be seen as a success and it would be mounted against future nominees.

For the sake of the federal judiciary and the American people that must not happen. The deliberative process must be restored.[102]

In the end, the Senate voted 58–42 against Bork's confirmation, the largest margin of defeat for a Court nominee in American history.[103] In the aftermath of the vote, Senator Bob Dole (R-KS) was asked to offer advice to any young lawyer contemplating one day serving on the Supreme Court. "I wouldn't write a word," the senator lamented, "I would hide in the closet until I was nominated."[104]

JUDICIAL REVIEW, CONSTITUTIONAL INTERPRETATION, AND JUDICIAL DECISION MAKING

Since its inception, the federal judiciary itself has been on trial—in the court of constitutional law, political science, and American public opinion. The chief defendant in this long and sometimes contentious history has been the Supreme Court, and the primary behavior in question has been the use of judicial review.

The first, and potentially biggest, worry in considering the power and use of judicial review arises from the fact that Supreme Court justices are not elected by the people but are appointed, and for life at that, removable only through the process of impeachment. In striking down state or federal laws, a small group of unelected justices can overturn acts passed by representatives who *were* elected. In *The Least Dangerous Branch*, legal scholar—and close friend of Robert Bork—Alexander Bickel described the countermajoritarian difficulty in the exercise of judicial review. The worry is that in striking down legislation, the Court "exercises control, not in behalf of the prevailing majority, but against it."[105] This is precisely what President Thomas Jefferson warned about when he feared the judiciary becoming a "despotic branch."[106]

Second, there is the concern that Americans may become less vigilant about who they elect, knowing that if they do a poor job in choosing their representatives, the Supreme Court will be there to bail them out. In his 1901 biography of Justice Marshall, constitutional scholar James Bradley Thayer pointed out this rarely discussed but very modern worry about the exercise of judicial review: "The people, all this while, become careless as to whom they send to the legislature; too often they cheerfully vote for men whom they would not trust with an important private affair, and when these unfit persons are found to pass foolish and bad laws, and the courts step in and disregard them, the people are glad that these few wiser gentlemen on the bench are so ready to protect them against their more immediate representatives."[107] In modern terms, this is called the problem of moral hazard. The term comes from the concept of unwanted incentives created by having insurance. When a person is insured against bad outcomes from his or her own actions, then the person may take less care in avoiding those outcomes. By acting as a safety valve against poor, factious, or tyrannical legislation, the Court might actually make unwanted legislative outcomes more, not less, likely.

> When a person is insured against bad outcomes from his or her own actions, then the person may take less care in avoiding those outcomes.

Third, the power of judicial review lies as much in its power to affirm as in its power to negate. In upholding the constitutionality of laws, the Supreme Court also exercises power over the legislative process by adding legitimacy in the minds of the American public to those laws passed by Congress.[108] In doing so, the Court risks validating laws that trample on the rights of minorities, thereby giving its stamp of approval to tyranny of the majority.

Finally, there exists the challenge inherent in interpreting and applying the Constitution to a variety of specific cases and circumstances, across time, and by individuals with their own opinions on what is or is not in accordance with the document, its language, and its intent. As James Bradley Thayer cautioned in an 1893 article, "Much which will seem unconstitutional to one man, or body of men, may reasonably not seem so to another; [and] that the constitution often admits of different interpretations."[109] In order to fully consider this issue, however, it is first necessary to explore in more detail how justices go about interpreting the Constitution and applying this highest law of the land to the cases brought before them.

Theories of Constitutional Interpretation

Trying to figure out why justices vote the way they do on any specific case is very difficult given all of the factors that likely contribute to an individual justice's vote. However, political scientists have identified several models that describe different approaches to judicial decision making. While a justice may emphasize one approach more than others, these models are best thought of as elements in the overall process and not as exclusive approaches that a given justice will only use. Justices themselves likely combine several considerations when approaching a case, especially difficult ones involving constitutional interpretation.

The Legal Model

The legal model focuses on applying the law to the facts of the case. In this model, justices rely on precedent—a previous decision on a similar case that serves as a basis for future decisions. When a justice follows precedent, he or she is said to be employing the doctrine of stare decisis (from the Latin, "to stand by things decided").[110] All justices—even the ones who emphasize their own capacity to interpret the Constitution—are bound by and employ the legal model to some extent in their decisions. There is good reason for this. It is, after all, how the legal system operates; similar cases are supposed to be decided in similar ways. To do otherwise would bring an unacceptable lack of uniformity to the legal system. There is also, however, a more strategic concern. A Supreme Court that is constantly ignoring its own precedents would likely not retain much legitimacy and authority in the eyes of the American people. While all justices employ the legal model, especially when deciding criminal cases, when it comes to those cases with significant implications for public policy—when the constitutionality of laws is at stake—other models may factor into judicial decision making as well.

Some justices applying the legal model look to the written text of the Constitution and the intent of the framers of the document for guidance rather than to their own interpretation of the document's intent. Proponents of original understanding (or originalism) argue that the process of constitutional amendment, not Supreme Court decisions, should be the primary way to make major changes in the fundamental law of the nation. A main concern of Robert Bork's detractors was how Bork, if approved to the Court, would handle the weighty responsibility of constitutional interpretation in light of his stated support of the originalist approach, especially in cases involving deeply contested issues such as abortion, sexuality, and civil rights. Given that the right to privacy—upon which the Court has relied to assert and protect individuals' choices in many of these areas—is not textually present in the document, Bork's opponents worried that his votes on cases involving privacy assertions would argue for a restriction of Americans' rights.

The Attitudinal Model

The attitudinal model describes a process through which the political and policy preferences of individual justices shape their votes on cases rather than a neutral weighing of the facts and the law.[111] This model describes an overtly political approach to judicial decision making, one very far from Alexander Hamilton's reassurances about the nonpolitical federal judiciary in *Federalist* No. 78. Much of the research in this area has focused on explaining and predicting the votes of justices based on what we know about their political ideologies.[112] For scholars who emphasize the role of the individual attitudes and political ideologies of justices, the countermajoritarian difficulty can be especially worrisome. Not only can unelected justices strike down the will of the majority but they may do so in order to advance their own political and policy agendas.

The Strategic Model

Finally, the strategic model portrays individual justices as strategic political actors who, according to political scientist Walter F. Murphy, try to make the best use of their "resources, official and personal, to achieve a particular set of policy objectives."[113] Strategic justices do more than just vote according to their individual preferences. They consider the likely behaviors of their fellow justices, understand the national political context and the system of shared powers in which their branch of government operates, and, when deciding how to act, "compute in terms of costs and revenues whether a particular choice is worth the price which is required to attain it."[114] Strategic considerations may shape whether or not a justice votes to grant cert,[115] how justices vote on cases before them, and how justices craft their opinions.[116]

Judicial Restraint and Judicial Activism

Related to the question of how justices make their decisions is the issue of how willing or reluctant they are to exercise the authority of judicial review. How eager, in other words, should the Court be to overturn the actions of the other two branches of government?

NEWS CLIP
Paul Ryan outlines the partiality of Justice Ginsburg's comments about Trump

FIGURE 15.5

Theoretical Models of Constitutional Interpretation

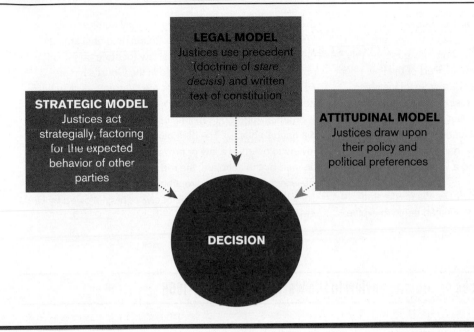

Proponents of **judicial restraint** argue that the Court should use this power rarely and whenever possible defer to the judgment of the legislative and executive branches on decisions that those branches have made. These proponents offer several justifications for their caution. First, they point to the dangers of the countermajoritarian difficulty and the potential antidemocratic consequences of unelected justices overturning the actions of elected representatives. In addition, the Supreme Court's voice in declaring a law to be unconstitutional is more authoritative when used sparingly, sending a clear signal in those times when it is employed. Finally, justices are legal and constitutional specialists; they are not policy specialists, nor are their clerks. The public policies that may be impacted by the use of judicial review may involve complex technical questions the details of which justices may not fully understand.

Proponents of **judicial activism**, on the other hand, argue that justices should be willing to step in and overturn laws when they see a need to do so. Sometimes the other two branches may make mistakes, or worse, trample on individual rights and liberties. The very power that fuels concerns about the countermajoritarian difficulty—that the Court can strike down the will of the majority—also gives it the power to protect the rights of minorities. Proponents of activism point to times when the other two branches act in ways damaging to rights and liberties; they also point to the fact that these branches often do not act at all. Free from the need to be concerned about the popularity of their actions, Supreme Court justices can place on the agenda issues that Congress and the president are unwilling to tackle.

Judicial activism and restraint are not inherently linked to political liberalism or conservatism. During the 1960s, an activist and liberal Court used the power of judicial review to strike down state laws restricting the civil rights of Americans in the areas of education and voting. In the 1930s, however, the strongest opposition to President Franklin Roosevelt's efforts to employ the power of the federal government in his New Deal came

judicial restraint
a philosophy of constitutional interpretation that asserts justices should be cautious in overturning laws.

judicial activism
a philosophy of constitutional interpretation that asserts justices should wield the power of judicial review when needed.

Judicial Review and the Political Ideologies of Justices

What role do the political ideologies of Supreme Court justices play in the willingness of justices to overturn federal or state laws? This is a very complex question that political scientists continue to debate. Part of the issue is actually measuring the political ideologies of justices as they are not required to wear a label or announce to the world their personal politics. Many presidents are unhappily surprised to find that a justice they nominated has a different judicial philosophy than expected once the justice is on the Court and serving a lifetime term.

Using data from the *Supreme Court Database*—created and shared by a group of scholars—we can begin to explore

this question. Figure A displays the total number of cases in which the Court declared as unconstitutional an act of Congress or a state or territorial law (or state constitutional provision) during a specific time in the Court's history: 1953–1968. These years cover the Warren Court, in which Earl Warren served as the chief justice. The Warren Court is often considered to be one of the most liberal Courts in the nation's history. The blue bars indicate a use of judicial review to overturn a law or provision in a liberal direction as defined by the scholars; the red bars, a use that overturned a law in a conservative direction. The largest group of these decisions involved questions of civil rights, followed by First Amendment concerns.

FIGURE A

Liberal and Conservative Uses of Judicial Review in the Warren Court, 1953-1968

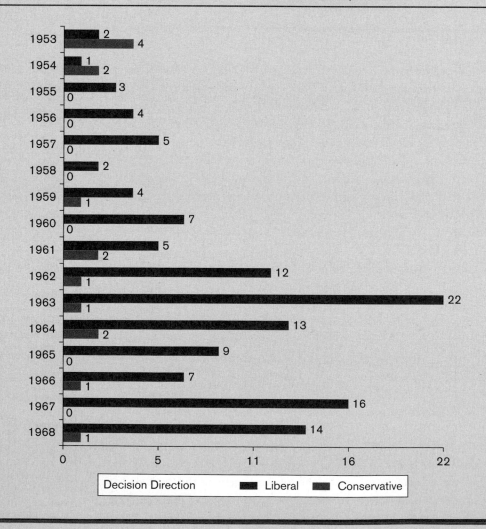

Liberal and Conservative Uses of Judicial Review in the Hughes Court, 1929-1940

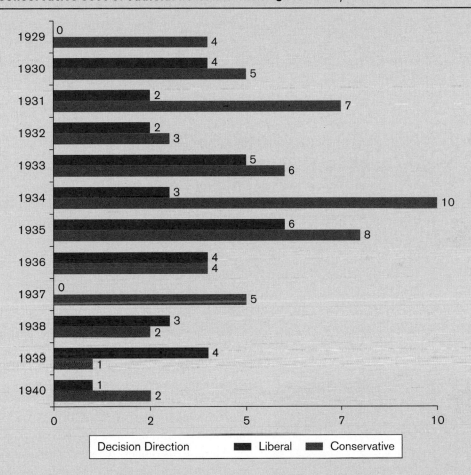

Based on Figure A, one might infer that liberal justices are more likely to overturn federal or state laws than conservative justices since nearly 90 percent of the decisions are in a liberal direction, and the Court was considered to be composed of a majority of liberal justices.

However, it is important to remember that these data are from only one Supreme Court era. Figure B presents a similar analysis; however, these data are from the tenure of Chief Justice Charles Evans Hughes, when the Court was considered to be a very conservative one.[117] In contrast to the Warren Court, the majority of uses of judicial review to overturn federal or state laws in the Hughes Court era were conservative and focused primarily on economic activity and taxation policy. In terms of federal laws, many of these uses of judicial review focused on challenging President Roosevelt's New Deal, which we discussed in Chapter 3.

The data from Figure B present a more complex picture of the connection between judicial ideology and the willingness of justices to overturn federal or state laws, especially before Roosevelt began a series of appointments (some of whom served on the Warren Court) in 1937. These data challenge the assertion that liberal justices are *necessarily* more likely to exercise judicial review to overturn federal or state laws than conservative ones. However, they do support the idea that the political ideologies of the justices *can* affect patterns of the use of judicial review. This important issue is one scholars will continue to examine.

WHAT DO YOU THINK?

To what extent do you think justices should or should not bring their own political views into the use of judicial review? What responsibility should the Senate exercise in trying to ascertain the politics of Supreme Court nominees during the confirmation proceedings?

Source: All data are from Harold J. Spaeth et al., *2016 Supreme Court Database,* http://Supremecourtdatabase.org, accessed July 11, 2016.

from an activist, conservative Supreme Court willing to use the power of judicial review to oppose the reforms enacted by the president and members of his Democratic Party.

The Supreme Court as National Policymaker

NEWS CLIP
Background on public opinions related to abortion case

No one branch of the federal government operates in a vacuum, and the federal judiciary, including the Supreme Court, is no exception. When the Court attempts to influence public policy, it does so in the face of multiple constraints on its independent use of authority, but its unique role within the system of shared powers offers it opportunities to shape policy in a way that the other two branches cannot.

Limitations on the Power of the Supreme Court

One constraint on the power of the Court is the legal process itself. A Court, no matter how activist, cannot simply declare unconstitutional a law that it does not like. It can only rule on a specific case that has been properly filed and brought before it. Only plaintiffs who can demonstrate standing can bring suit in court, which requires that they demonstrate that they have been wronged by a law or action and that the law in question covers the interests the plaintiff alleges to have been violated or denied. Even when everything works efficiently, the process of moving a case through the federal judiciary takes time. When a case begins in a state judiciary, the process can take even longer.

Missionary Samuel Worcester was arrested for residing within the limits of the Cherokee Nation without a license, thus violating a Georgia state law. The Marshall Court declared Georgia's law unconstitutional, but Georgia continued to enforce it regardless.

The legislative and executive branches may also act as a check on the power of the federal judiciary. We have discussed the role of the president in nominating justices and that of the Senate in confirming them. We have also examined the role of Congress in setting the size of the Supreme Court and establishing other federal courts. Congress and the states may collectively amend the Constitution, the results of which are not subject to judicial review. In addition, the Court lacks the tools for implementing public policy and often must turn to the other two branches to add force to its rulings. When a Court goes against the will of the president or Congress, the other branches may be less than supportive in implementing the decisions or even might ignore or defy the Court entirely.

New Echota Historical Site.

In 1832, near the end of his long term as chief justice, John Marshall once again went toe to toe with a president—this time with Andrew Jackson in *Worcester v. Georgia*. The case focused on federalism, specifically which level of government, state or federal, had authority over the treaties and laws covering Native American territories in the United States. It also had to do with money, at least with regard to the state laws under consideration. Gold had recently been discovered on Cherokee lands, and the government of Georgia sought to control prospecting on these potentially valuable lands.[118]

Samuel Worcester, a missionary, had been arrested under a Georgia law for "residing within the limits of the Cherokee Nation without a license" and was convicted and sentenced to "hard labour in the penitentiary for four years."[119] Under Marshall, the Court ruled that the federal government, not the states, had authority over these territories and declared the Georgia law to be unconstitutional. In doing so, Marshall sought to protect the rights of Native Americans secured by the treaties governing their autonomy. In the case decision, which he handwrote, Marshall claimed, "A weaker power does not surrender its independence—its right to self-government—by associating with a stronger and taking protection."[120]

President Jackson, who, according to one historian, "had almost as little regard for the Supreme Court" as he had for Native Americans, is reported to have exclaimed, "Well, John Marshall has made his decision; now let him enforce it!"[121] Whether or not the quotation is true, it does capture Jackson's hostility towards the Marshall Court. Georgia continued to enforce its laws, Jackson pursued his destructive policies towards the Cherokee Nation, and Worcester remained in prison until the following year.

Even when the other two branches do not openly defy the Supreme Court, their lack of support of its rulings can limit the Court's power in setting national policy. As we have explored, the Court's landmark ruling declaring separate educational facilities unconstitutional in *Brown v. Board of Education* (1954) was not quickly followed by progress on the ground in the nation's public schools. As political scientist Gerald Rosenberg concluded, "For ten years the Court spoke forcefully while Congress and the executive did little."[122] It was only after the executive and the legislative branches began to use their own powers in shaping American public policy that desegregation on the ground actually gained momentum (Chapter 5).

Finally, although justices are appointed for life and do not need to worry about being reelected, they do operate in the American political system, in which public opinion plays an important role. Political scientists continue to debate the degree to which Supreme Court justices attend to public opinion in crafting specific decisions; however, scholars agree that it is not something that can completely be ignored.[123] President Washington ensured that the first Court "contained judges from Massachusetts, New York, Pennsylvania, Virginia, Maryland, and South Carolina" to demonstrate to the experimental nation his commitment to ensuring representation from all parts of the country.[124] Another instance where public opinion seemed to affect the Court came shortly after the ruling in *Brown v. Board of Education* in 1954, when the Court had to decide whether or not to grant cert to a case involving interracial marriage. The Court refused to take the case. According to one report, one of the justices said, "One bombshell at a time is enough."[125]

Since the time of John Marshall, justices have had to attend to the fact that their power in exercising judicial review is tied to Americans' views of the legitimacy of their branch of government. It is no accident that of all the branches only the federal judiciary, and the Supreme Court in particular, chooses to retain its costumes, secrecy, and traditional ways of doing things, as out of time as they may seem. The drama of the Court adds to its legitimacy in the view of the American people, and all justices—whatever their own political beliefs—know that they play a key role in preserving the story of the Court and its power.

The Agenda-Setting Power of the Supreme Court

While the Supreme Court and the rest of the federal judiciary cannot act as all-powerful, unilateral makers of public policy, their particular position in the nation and the federal government does give them a unique role in American politics: that of setting the national agenda. Because they do not face elections like members of the other two branches, Supreme Court justices are able to bring up in the national conversation issues that need to be discussed. They can act in front of public opinion—perhaps not *too* far, but far enough to force debate on the national stage. Recent Court rulings on same-sex marriage and marriage equality may be perfect examples of this power. In exercising this power, the Court may not necessarily be acting against the wishes of elected representatives, or at

NEWS CLIP
Interviews on federal appellate lawsuit for same-sex marriage in Utah

least of all of them. A member of Congress or a president who may be afraid to weigh in on an important and controversial issue out of fear of the backlash from public opinion can point to a Court decision and tell the American people that they now have to act. Providing political cover for elected representatives who wish to act on an issue may be one of the most important powers of the unelected branch of government.

WHAT HAVE I LEARNED?

1. The term *countermajoritarian difficulty* refers to _____.

   a. The ability to impeach Supreme Court justices
   b. The fact that justices are not elected by the people
   c. Congressional oversight of the Supreme Court
   d. Presidential nominations of justices

2. What are some of the limitations on the power of the Supreme Court?

3. What are arguments made in support of judicial restraint? Of judicial activism?

Answer Key: 1. b; 2. Answers should include the fact that the Court decides only on cases before it, executive and legislative checks on its functioning, and that it has few tools with which to implement public policy. 3. For restraint, answers should focus on the countermajoritarian difficulty, the fact that justices may not have policy expertise, and the risk of its overuse. For activism, answers should focus on the fact that Congress may not act in areas that it needs to and the danger of tyranny of the majority.

CONCLUSION

The "Trial" of Merrick Garland?

In February 2016, Justice Antonin Scalia passed away, presenting President Barack Obama with the possibility of a third Supreme Court nomination during his tenure. While Sonia Sotomayor's confirmation had been somewhat contested, his second, that of Elena Kagan, had gone relatively smoothly. In March 2016, Obama nominated Judge Merrick Garland to fill Scalia's seat. Republicans refused even to consider the president's nominee, arguing that the nomination should be made by the next president, a gamble that a Republican might win the White House. As Scalia was one of the staunchest conservatives on the Court, Republicans knew that his replacement would have the potential to shift the ideological balance of the Court for years, if not decades.

Both Donald Trump's win in the presidential election of 2016 and the continuing Republican control of the Senate ensured that Garland would not get his "trial." As a candidate, Trump had presented his own list of possible Supreme Court nominees. Without a filibuster-proof Senate—but with the possibility that Republicans in the Senate might change the rules of the institution to prevent filibusters of Supreme Court nominees—other nominees might very well face their own trials, or, perhaps, the Senate itself.

In this chapter, we have explored two important and closely related questions: How political is the Court? And how powerful is it? In *Federalist* No. 78, Alexander Hamilton—a proponent of a strong national government—tried to reassure a skeptical confederation during the ratification debates that the Court was neither political nor powerful. History has proven Hamilton correct and incorrect on both counts.

The justices of the Supreme Court and the federal judiciary are not political in the ways that presidents, representatives, and senators are, in no small part because they do not have to worry about reelection. They must consider the facts of the case and the letter of the law when ruling on cases. Justices are, however, political people, and their personal views on issues may affect their decisions on impactful cases. They must always be strategic in understanding the role their institution plays in the system of separation of powers and in Americans' views on the legitimacy of the institution.

Theirs is a power that must be nurtured, cultivated, and protected, as John Marshall and subsequent members of the federal judiciary have had to learn. Compared to the legislative and executive branches, the power of the federal judiciary in national policymaking is much less imposing. It cannot write laws; it has no army. It has only the power of its decisions and the willingness of the people and the members of the other two branches to acquiesce to its decisions. It is not powerless; it is just different. How dangerous—or promising—this difference is continues to be a central subject of debate in American politics.

Want a better grade?

Get the tools you need to sharpen your study skills. **SAGE edge** offers a robust online environment featuring an impressive array of free tools and resources. Access practice quizzes, eFlashcards, video, and multimedia at **edge.sagepub.com/abernathy1e.**

CHAPTER REVIEW

This chapter's main ideas are reflected in the Learning Objectives below. By reviewing them here you should be able to **remember** the key points, **connect** them to the stories presented in the chapter, **think** critically about these questions, and **know** these terms that are central to the topic.

15.1 Describe the structure and powers of the federal judiciary as laid out in the Constitution.

REMEMBER...

- The Constitution contains less detail about the judiciary than about the legislative or executive branches, but it is clear that the framers intended it to be the weakest of the three and also relatively independent of the other two.

- Article III does not expressly give the judiciary the power to strike down laws that it views as being in violation of the Constitution.

- The Supreme Court is described in Article III, and it is clearly intended to be the highest court in the nation. However, the establishment of lower courts was left to Congress.

- The Constitution also clarified the jurisdiction of the courts—what authority they have to hear and decide on specific cases.

- The Judiciary Act of 1789 allowed Congress to flesh out the organization of the court system: it established the office of the attorney general, set the number of seats on the Supreme Court, and said when the Court would meet.

THINK...

- What powers does the Constitution give to the federal judiciary? What is one key power that is not fully described in the text?

- What were the debates about judicial power during the ratification process?

KNOW...

- *federal judiciary* (p. 535)

- *United States Supreme Court* (p. 535)

- *appellate jurisdiction* (p. 539)

- *original jurisdiction* (p. 539)

15.2 Summarize John Marshall's development of judicial review in the Supreme Court decision in *Marbury v. Madison*.

REMEMBER...

- In part of his ruling in *Marbury v. Madison*, Marshall found that part of the law that Marbury was basing his claim on, the Federal Judiciary Act of 1789, was unconstitutional and thus unenforceable.

- Marshall therefore asserted that the Supreme Court had the power of judicial review over federal laws, which is the power to review laws and actions of other branches and levels of government to decide if they are in conflict with the Constitution. If conflict is found, the Court may declare that law or action invalid.

CONNECT...

- Following the election of 1800, the Federalist Party was in decline. In an attempt to preserve their influence, Federalists turned to the judiciary. Before incoming president Thomas Jefferson could take office, they reorganized and expanded the federal judiciary, attempting to fill new vacancies in lower courts with Federalist candidates, and shrank the Supreme Court to block Jefferson from appointing a new justice who would be hostile to them.

- The judicial appointment of Federalist William Marbury was initiated by outgoing president John Adams and confirmed by Congress, but Marbury's commission was not delivered before Adams's departure and thus was left to the Jefferson administration. Marbury brought suit, forcing the Supreme Court to become involved in an intensely partisan battle.

- On one hand, Chief Justice John Marshall risked the displeasure of Jefferson and possible impeachment if he delivered Marbury's commission. On the other hand, to deny Marbury's commission could make the Court appear weak. In his ruling, Marshall concluded that Marbury was not entitled to the remedy that he and others sought because the court did not itself have the constitutional power to grant it. In essence, the Court found a part of the Judiciary Act of 1798 unconstitutional.

THINK...

- What challenges did Marshall face in *Marbury v. Madison*? How did he handle them?

KNOW...

- *constitutional interpretation* (p. 547)
- *judicial review* (p. 547)
- Marbury v. Madison *(1803)* (p. 545)

15.3 Be familiar with the structure of the American legal system and the federal judiciary.

REMEMBER...

- All courts in the American system are based on the adversarial system, with plaintiffs and defendants arguing their opposing sides of the case in the most persuasive way possible.

- Criminal law covers actions determined to harm the community itself whereas civil law covers cases involving private rights and relationships between individuals and groups.

- State courts handle the vast majority of cases in the United States. If not resolved at the lower court level, cases may work their way up through the state system to appeals courts, and sometimes to the highest court in the states. Some may proceed to the federal judiciary system; those cases generally involve a constitutional question.

- The federal judiciary is composed of constitutional courts and specialized legislative courts. The constitutional courts are organized into three levels: federal district courts, the federal court of appeals, and the Supreme Court.

- While individual states vary in how they select their judges, all federal judges must be nominated by the president and confirmed by a majority vote in the Senate. Most district court nominees are approved, but appellate and Supreme Court appointment processes can be more contentious.

- The Constitution places no requirements on the necessary qualifications to serve in the federal judiciary, but experience, ethical integrity, and legal accomplishment are important factors and can help smooth the confirmation process.

- Presidents tend to nominate individuals with whom they share similar philosophies and approaches to constitutional interpretation, but there is no guarantee that justice will behave as expected once confirmed.

CONNECT...

- Justice Robert Bork was nominated by President Ronald Reagan to fill a vacancy left by Justice Lewis F. Powell Jr., a moderate and frequent swing vote on the then liberal-to-moderate Court. Reagan saw an opportunity to shift the political balance of the Court towards conservatism.

- Bork's previous rulings and statements on many highly charged social issues revealed his view that justices should focus on the language and intent of the Constitution. Liberal members of Congress and other interest groups exerted pressure to reject his nomination. Bork objected that the nomination process had become overtly political. His candidacy was ultimately rejected.

THINK...

- Why was Robert Bork's nomination to the Supreme Court so controversial?

KNOW...

- *adversarial system* (p. 549)
- *civil law* (p. 550)
- *criminal law* (p. 549)
- *defendant* (p. 549)

- *federal courts of appeals* (p. 553)
- *federal district courts* (p. 552)
- *plaintiff* (p. 549)
- *plea bargaining* (p. 550)

15.4 Trace the path of most cases through the federal judiciary.

REMEMBER...

- Cases beginning at the state court level may be either civil or criminal cases; to move on to the federal level they must involve federal or constitutional questions. Most are resolved at the lower court level. If they move from the district court to the highest state court, the losing side may appeal to the Supreme Court.

- Cases beginning in the federal system must meet certain requirements and may involve either a civil or criminal case, but the federal government must be party to the dispute.

- The Supreme Court may refuse to hear a case appealed to it. Four or more justices must agree to hear a case before it is accepted. If the Court does decide to hear a case, petitioners file briefs, and other interested parties may file amicus curiae briefs.

- If the case is accepted, the Court issues a writ of certiorari and oral arguments are presented.

- In deciding the case, justices conference and vote in secret. The majority decision is binding. Concurring opinions may be written by justices agreeing with the majority to share their reasoning. Dissenting opinions may be written to preserve a record of what some justices saw as problematic about the decision.

THINK...

- How do the majority of federal cases proceed through the judiciary?

▰ 15.5 Compare theories of judicial decision making as well as arguments for or against judicial restraint and activism in constitutional review.

REMEMBER . . .

- There are a number of concerns raised by use of judicial review: (1) an unelected group of justices may overturn acts that were passed by representatives who *were* elected, (2) the American people could become lax in who they elect to office, thinking that the court could bail them out if their representatives made serious errors, (3) in validating laws that trample on the rights of minorities, the Supreme Court may give its stamp of approval to tyranny of the majority, and (4) interpreting and applying the Constitution to a variety of specific cases and circumstances across time and by individuals with their own opinions on what is or is not in accordance with the document is inherently challenging.

- There are three main models of constitutional interpretation: (1) the legal model, which is based on precedent; (2) the attitudinal model, which relies on the political and policy preferences of individual justices; and (3) the strategic model, in which justices make calculations about the behavior of other actors and take context into account in their decision. Justices do not always use the same model in their decisions, and the models may sometimes be used in combination with one another.

- Proponents of judicial restraint argue that the Court should use the power of judicial review rarely and whenever possible defer to the judgment of the legislative and executive branches on decisions that those branches have made. Proponents of judicial activism, on the other hand, argue that justices should be willing to step in and overturn laws when they see a need to do so.

- The Supreme Court may act as a national policymaker and agenda setter, but there are powerful checks on its power. The legal process itself is slow and exacting, and the other branches of government may drag their heels in implementing Court decisions or ignore or defy the Court.

CONNECT . . .

- In *Worcester v. Georgia*, the Marshall Court ruled in favor of the federal government over the state of Georgia, saying that the federal government had authority over Native American territories. Marshall's goal was to protect the rights of Native Americans secured by the treaties governing their autonomy. President Andrew Jackson and the state of Georgia both defied the Court's ruling.

THINK . . .

- How willing should the Court be to overturn federal and state laws?

KNOW . . .

- *judicial activism* (p. 565)
- *judicial restraint* (p. 565)

APPENDIX 1   ARTICLES OF CONFEDERATION

To all to whom these Presents shall come, we the undersigned Delegates of the States affixed to our Names send greeting.

Articles of Confederation and perpetual Union between the states of New Hampshire, Massachusetts-bay Rhode Island and Providence Plantations, Connecticut, New York, New Jersey, Pennsylvania, Delaware, Maryland, Virginia, North Carolina, South Carolina and Georgia.

Article I

The Stile of this Confederacy shall be **"The United States of America"**.

Article II

Each state retains its sovereignty, freedom, and independence, and every power, jurisdiction, and right, which is not by this Confederation expressly delegated to the United States, in Congress assembled.

Article III

The said States hereby severally enter into a firm league of friendship with each other, for their common defense, the security of their liberties, and their mutual and general welfare, binding themselves to assist each other, against all force offered to, or attacks made upon them, or any of them, on account of religion, sovereignty, trade, or any other pretense whatever.

Article IV

The better to secure and perpetuate mutual friendship and intercourse among the people of the different States in this Union, the free inhabitants of each of these States, paupers, vagabonds, and fugitives from justice excepted, shall be entitled to all privileges and immunities of free citizens in the several States; and the people of each State shall free ingress and regress to and from any other State, and shall enjoy therein all the privileges of trade and commerce, subject to the same duties, impositions, and restrictions as the inhabitants thereof respectively, provided that such restrictions shall not extend so far as to prevent the removal of property imported into any State, to any other State, of which the owner is an inhabitant; provided also that no imposition, duties or restriction shall be laid by any State, on the property of the United States, or either of them.

If any person guilty of, or charged with, treason, felony, or other high misdemeanor in any State, shall flee from justice, and be found in any of the United States, he shall, upon demand of the Governor or executive power of the State from which he fled, be delivered up and removed to the State having jurisdiction of his offense.

Full faith and credit shall be given in each of these States to the records, acts, and judicial proceedings of the courts and magistrates of every other State.

Article V

For the most convenient management of the general interests of the United States, delegates shall be annually appointed in such manner as the legislatures of each State shall direct, to meet in Congress on the first Monday in November, in every year, with a power reserved to each State to recall its delegates, or any of them, at any time within the year, and to send others in their stead for the remainder of the year.

No State shall be represented in Congress by less than two, nor more than seven members; and no person shall be capable of being a delegate for more than three years in any term of six years; nor shall any person, being a delegate, be capable of holding any office under the United States, for which he, or another for his benefit, receives any salary, fees or emolument of any kind.

Each State shall maintain its own delegates in a meeting of the States, and while they act as members of the committee of the States.

In determining questions in the United States in Congress assembled, each State shall have one vote.

Freedom of speech and debate in Congress shall not be impeached or questioned in any court or place out of Congress, and the members of Congress shall be protected in their persons from arrests or imprisonments, during the time of their going to and from, and attendence on Congress, except for treason, felony, or breach of the peace.

Article VI

No State, without the consent of the United States in Congress assembled, shall send any embassy to, or receive any embassy from, or enter into any conference, agreement, alliance or treaty with any King, Prince or State; nor shall any person holding any office of profit or trust under the United States, or any of them, accept any present, emolument, office or title of any kind whatever from any King, Prince or foreign State; nor shall the United States in Congress assembled, or any of them, grant any title of nobility.

No two or more States shall enter into any treaty, confederation or alliance whatever between them, without the consent of the United States in Congress assembled, specifying accurately the purposes for which the same is to be entered into, and how long it shall continue.

No State shall lay any imposts or duties, which may interfere with any stipulations in treaties, entered into by the United States in Congress assembled, with any King, Prince or State, in pursuance of any treaties already proposed by Congress, to the courts of France and Spain.

No vessel of war shall be kept up in time of peace by any State, except such number only, as shall be deemed necessary by the United States in Congress assembled, for the defense of such State, or its trade; nor shall any body of forces be kept up by any State in time of peace, except such number only, as in the judgement of the United States in Congress assembled, shall be deemed requisite to garrison the forts necessary for the defense of such State; but every State shall always keep up a well-regulated and disciplined militia, sufficiently armed and accoutered, and shall provide and constantly have ready for use, in public stores, a due number of filed pieces and tents, and a proper quantity of arms, ammunition and camp equipage.

No State shall engage in any war without the consent of the United States in Congress assembled, unless such State be actually invaded by enemies, or shall have received certain advice of a resolution being formed by some nation of Indians to invade such State, and the danger is so imminent as not to admit of a delay till the United States in Congress assembled can be consulted; nor shall any State grant commissions to any ships or vessels of war, nor letters of marque or reprisal, except it be after a declaration of war by the United States in Congress assembled, and then only against the Kingdom or State and the subjects thereof, against which war has been so declared, and under such regulations as shall be established by the United States in Congress assembled, unless such State be infested by pirates, in which case vessels of war may be fitted out for that occasion, and kept so long as the danger shall continue, or until the United States in Congress assembled shall determine otherwise.

Article VII

When land forces are raised by any State for the common defense, all officers of or under the rank of colonel, shall be appointed by the legislature of each State respectively, by whom such forces shall be raised, or in such manner as such State shall direct, and all vacancies shall be filled up by the State which first made the appointment.

Article VIII

All charges of war, and all other expenses that shall be incurred for the common defense or general welfare, and allowed by the United States in Congress assembled, shall be defrayed out of a common treasury, which shall be supplied by the several States in proportion to the value of all land within each State, granted or surveyed for any person, as such land and the buildings and improvements thereon shall be estimated according to such mode as the United States in Congress assembled, shall from time to time direct and appoint.

The taxes for paying that proportion shall be laid and levied by the authority and direction of the legislatures of the several States within the time agreed upon by the United States in Congress assembled.

Article IX

The United States in Congress assembled, shall have the sole and exclusive right and power of determining on peace and war, except in the cases mentioned in the sixth article—of sending and receiving ambassadors—entering into treaties and alliances, provided that no treaty of commerce shall be made whereby the legislative power of the respective States shall be restrained from imposing such imposts and duties on foreigners, as their own people are subjected to, or from prohibiting the exportation or importation of any species of goods or commodities whatsoever—of establishing rules for deciding in all cases, what captures on land or water shall be legal, and in what manner prizes taken by land or naval forces in the service of the United States shall be divided or appropriated—of granting letters of marque and reprisal in times of peace—appointing courts for the trial of piracies and felonies commited on the high seas and establishing courts for receiving and determining finally appeals in all cases of captures, provided that no member of Congress shall be appointed a judge of any of the said courts.

The United States in Congress assembled shall also be the last resort on appeal in all disputes and differences now subsisting or that hereafter may arise between two or more States concerning boundary, jurisdiction or any other causes whatever; which authority shall always be exercised in the manner following. Whenever the legislative or executive authority or lawful agent of any State in controversy with another shall present a petition to Congress stating the matter in question and praying for a hearing, notice thereof shall be given by order of Congress to the legislative or executive authority of the other State in controversy, and a day assigned for the appearance of the parties by their lawful agents, who shall then be directed to appoint by joint consent, commissioners or judges to constitute a court for hearing and determining the matter in question: but if they cannot agree, Congress shall name three persons out of each of the United States, and from the list of such persons each party shall alternately strike out one, the petitioners beginning, until the number shall be reduced to thirteen; and from that number not less than seven, nor more than nine names as Congress shall direct, shall in the presence of Congress be drawn out by lot, and the persons whose names shall be so drawn or any five of them, shall be commissioners or judges, to hear and finally determine the controversy, so always as a major part of the judges who shall hear the cause shall agree in the determination: and if either party shall neglect to attend at the day appointed, without showing reasons, which Congress shall judge sufficient, or being present shall refuse to strike, the Congress shall proceed to nominate three persons out of each State, and the secretary of Congress shall strike in behalf of such party absent or refusing; and the judgement and sentence of the court to be appointed, in the manner before prescribed, shall be final and conclusive; and if any of the parties shall refuse to submit to the authority of such court, or to appear or defend their claim or cause, the court shall nevertheless proceed to pronounce sentence, or judgement, which shall in like manner be final and decisive, the judgement or sentence and other proceedings being in either case transmitted to Congress, and lodged among the acts of Congress for the security of the parties concerned: provided that every commissioner, before he sits in judgement, shall take an oath to be administered by one of the judges of the supreme or superior court of the State, where the cause shall be tried, 'well and truly to hear and determine the matter in question, according to the best of his judgement, without favor, affection or hope of reward': provided also, that no State shall be deprived of territory for the benefit of the United States.

All controversies concerning the private right of soil claimed under different grants of two or more States, whose jurisdictions as they may respect such lands, and the States which passed such grants are adjusted, the said grants or either of them being at the same time claimed to have originated antecedent to such settlement of jurisdiction, shall on the petition of either party to the Congress of the United States, be finally determined as near as may be in the same manner as is before presecribed for deciding disputes respecting territorial jurisdiction between different States.

The United States in Congress assembled shall also have the sole and exclusive right and power of regulating the alloy and value of coin struck by their own authority, or by that of the respective States—fixing the standards of weights and measures throughout the United States—regulating the trade and managing all affairs with the Indians, not members of any of the States, provided that the legislative right of any State within its own limits be not infringed or violated—establishing or regulating post offices from one State to another, throughout all the United States, and exacting such postage on the papers passing through the same as may be requisite to defray the expenses of the said office—appointing all officers of the land forces, in the service of the United States, excepting regimental officers—appointing all the officers of the naval forces, and commissioning all officers whatever in the service of the United States—making rules for the government and regulation of the said land and naval forces, and directing their operations.

The United States in Congress assembled shall have authority to appoint a committee, to sit in the recess of Congress, to be denominated 'A Committee of the States', and to consist of one delegate from each State; and to appoint such other committees and civil officers as may be necessary for managing the general affairs of the United States under their direction—to appoint one of their members to preside, provided that no person be allowed to serve in the office of president more than one year in any term of three years; to ascertain the necessary sums of money to be raised for the service of the United States, and to appropriate and apply the same for defraying the public expenses—to borrow money, or emit bills on the credit of the United States, transmitting every half-year to the respective States an account of the sums of money so borrowed or emitted—to build and equip a navy—to agree upon the number of land forces, and to make requisitions from each State for its quota, in proportion to the number of white inhabitants in such State; which requisition shall be binding, and thereupon the legislature of each State shall appoint the regimental officers, raise the men and cloath, arm and equip them in a solid-like manner, at the expense of the United States; and the officers and men so cloathed, armed and equipped shall march to the place appointed, and within the time agreed on by the United States in Congress assembled. But if the United States in Congress assembled shall, on consideration of circumstances judge proper that any State should not raise men, or should raise a smaller number of men than the quota thereof, such extra number shall be raised, officered, cloathed, armed and equipped in the same manner as the quota of each State, unless the legislature of such State shall judge that such extra number cannot be safely spread out in the same, in which case they shall raise, officer, cloath, arm and equip as many of such extra number as they judge can be safely spared. And the officers and men so cloathed, armed, and equipped, shall march to the place appointed, and within the time agreed on by the United States in Congress assembled.

The United States in Congress assembled shall never engage in a war, nor grant letters of marque or reprisal in time of peace, nor enter into any treaties or alliances, nor coin money, nor regulate the value thereof, nor ascertain the sums and expenses necessary for the defense and welfare of the United States, or any of them, nor emit bills, nor borrow money on the credit of the United States, nor appropriate money, nor agree upon the number of vessels of war, to be built or purchased, or the number of land or sea forces to be raised, nor appoint a commander in chief of the army or navy, unless nine States assent to the same: nor shall a question on any other point, except for adjourning from day to day be determined, unless by the votes of the majority of the United States in Congress assembled.

The Congress of the United States shall have power to adjourn to any time within the year, and to any place within the United States, so that no period of adjournment be for a longer duration than the space of six months, and shall publish the journal of their proceedings monthly, except such parts thereof relating to treaties, alliances or military operations, as in their judgement require secrecy; and the yeas and nays of the delegates of each State on any question shall be entered on the journal, when it is desired by any delegates of a State, or any of them, at his or their request shall be furnished with a transcript of the said journal, except such parts as are above excepted, to lay before the legislatures of the several States.

Article X

The Committee of the States, or any nine of them, shall be authorized to execute, in the recess of Congress, such of the powers of Congress as the United States in Congress assembled, by the consent of the nine States, shall from time to time think expedient to vest them with; provided that no power be delegated to the said Committee, for the exercise of which, by the Articles of Confederation, the voice of nine States in the Congress of the United States assembled be requisite.

Article XI

Canada acceding to this confederation, and adjoining in the measures of the United States, shall be admitted into, and entitled to all the advantages of this Union; but no other colony shall be admitted into the same, unless such admission be agreed to by nine States.

Article XII

All bills of credit emitted, monies borrowed, and debts contracted by, or under the authority of Congress, before the assembling of the United States, in pursuance of the present confederation, shall be deemed and considered as a charge against the United States, for payment and satisfaction whereof the said United States, and the public faith are hereby solemnly pledged.

Article XIII

Every State shall abide by the determination of the United States in Congress assembled, on all questions which by this confederation are submitted to them. And the Articles of this Confederation shall be inviolably observed by every State, and the Union shall be perpetual; nor shall any alteration at any time hereafter be made in any of them; unless such alteration be agreed to in a Congress of the United States, and be afterwards confirmed by the legislatures of every State.

And Whereas it hath pleased the Great Governor of the World to incline the hearts of the legislatures we respectively represent in Congress, to approve of, and to authorize us to ratify the said Articles of Confederation and perpetual Union. Know Ye that we the undersigned delegates, by virtue of the power and authority to us given for that purpose, do by these presents, in the name and in behalf of our respective constituents, fully and entirely ratify and confirm each and every of the said Articles of Confederation and perpetual Union, and all and singular the matters and things therein contained: And we do further solemnly plight and engage the faith of our respective constituents, that they shall abide by the determinations of the United States in Congress assembled, on all questions, which by the said Confederation are submitted to them. And that the Articles thereof shall be inviolably observed by the States we respectively represent, and that the Union shall be perpetual.

In Witness whereof we have hereunto set our hands in Congress. Done at Philadelphia in the State of Pennsylvania the ninth day of July in the Year of our Lord One Thousand Seven Hundred and Seventy-Eight, and in the Third Year of the independence of America.

Agreed to by Congress 15 November 1777

In force after ratification by Maryland, 1 March 1781

APPENDIX 2   DECLARATION OF INDEPENDENCE

On June 11, 1776, the responsibility to "prepare a declaration" of independence was assigned by the Continental Congress, meeting in Philadelphia, to five members: John Adams, Benjamin Franklin, Thomas Jefferson, Robert Livingston, and Roger Sherman. Impressed by his talents as a writer, the committee asked Jefferson to compose a draft. After modifying Jefferson's draft the committee turned it over to Congress on June 28. On July 2 Congress voted to declare independence; on the evening of July 4, it approved the Declaration of Independence.

In Congress, July 4, 1776,
The Unanimous Declaration of
the Thirteen United States of America,

When in the Course of human events, it becomes necessary for one people to dissolve the political bands which have connected them with another, and to assume among the Powers of the earth, the separate and equal station to which the Laws of Nature and of Nature's God entitle them, a decent respect to the opinions of mankind requires that they should declare the causes which impel them to the separation.

We hold these truths to be self-evident, that all men are created equal, that they are endowed by their Creator with certain unalienable Rights, that among these are Life, Liberty and the pursuit of Happiness. That to secure these rights, Governments are instituted among Men, deriving their just powers from the consent of the governed. That whenever any form of Government becomes destructive of these ends, it is the Right of the People to alter or to abolish it, and to institute new Government, laying its foundation on such principles and organizing its powers in such form, as to them shall seem most likely to effect their Safety and Happiness. Prudence, indeed, will dictate that Government long established should not be changed for light and transient causes; and accordingly all experience hath shown, that mankind are more disposed to suffer, while evils are sufferable, than to right themselves by abolishing the forms to which they are accustomed. But when a long train of abuses and usurpations, pursuing invariably the same Object evinces a design to reduce them under absolute Despotism, it is their right, it is their duty, to throw off such Government, and to provide new Guards for their future security. Such has been the patient sufferance of these Colonies; and such is now the necessity which constrains them to alter their former Systems of Government. The history of the present King of Great Britain is a history of repeated injuries and usurpations, all having in direct object the establishment of an absolute Tyranny over these States. To prove this, let Facts be submitted to a candid world.

He has refused his Assent to Laws, the most wholesome and necessary for the public good.

He has forbidden his Governors to pass Laws of immediate and pressing importance, unless suspended in their operation till his Assent should be obtained; and when so suspended, he has utterly neglected to attend to them.

He has refused to pass other Laws for the accommodation of large districts of people, unless those people would relinquish the right of Representation in the Legislature, a right inestimable to them and formidable to tyrants only.

He has called together legislative bodies at places unusual, uncomfortable, and distant from the depository of their Public Records, for the sole purpose of fatiguing them into compliance with his measures.

He has dissolved Representative Houses repeatedly, for opposing with manly firmness his invasions on the rights of the people.

He has refused for a long time, after such dissolutions, to cause others to be elected; whereby the Legislative Powers, incapable of Annihilation, have returned to the People at large for their exercise; the State remaining in the mean time exposed to all the dangers of invasion from without, and convulsions within.

He has endeavored to prevent the population of these States; for that purpose obstructing the Laws of Naturalization of Foreigners; refusing to pass others to encourage their migration hither, and raising the conditions of new Appropriations of Lands.

He has obstructed the Administration of Justice, by refusing his Assent to Laws for establishing Judiciary Powers.

He has made Judges dependent on his Will alone, for the tenure of their offices, and the amount and payment of their salaries.

He has erected a multitude of New Offices, and sent hither swarms of Officers to harass our People, and eat out their substance.

He has kept among us, in times of peace, Standing Armies without the Consent of our legislature.

He has affected to render the Military independent of and superior to the Civil Power.

He has combined with others to subject us to a jurisdiction foreign to our constitution, and unacknowledged by our laws; giving his Assent to their acts of pretended legislation:

For quartering large bodies of armed troops among us:

For protecting them, by a mock Trial, from Punishment for any Murders which they should commit on the Inhabitants of these States:

For cutting off our Trade with all parts of the world:

For imposing taxes on us without our Consent:

For depriving us in many cases, of the benefits of Trial by Jury:

For transporting us beyond Seas to be tried for pretended offences:

For abolishing the free System of English Laws in a neighbouring Province, establishing therein an Arbitrary government, and enlarging its Boundaries so as to render it at once an example and fit instrument for introducing the same absolute rule into these Colonies:

For taking away our Charters, abolishing our most valuable Laws, and altering fundamentally the Forms of our Governments:

For suspending our own Legislature, and declaring themselves invested with Power to legislate for us in all cases whatsoever.

He has abdicated Government here, by declaring us out of his Protection and waging War against us.

He has plundered our seas, ravaged our Coasts, burnt our towns, and destroyed the lives of our people.

He is at this time transporting large armies of foreign mercenaries to compleat the works of death, desolation and tyranny, already begun with circumstances of Cruelty & perfidy scarcely parallel in the most barbarous ages, and totally unworthy the Head of a civilized nation.

He has constrained our fellow Citizens taken Captive on the high Seas to bear Arms against their Country, to become the executioners of their friends and Brethren, or to fall themselves by their Hands.

He has excited domestic insurrections amongst us, and has endeavoured to bring on the inhabitants of our frontiers, the merciless Indian Savages, whose known rule of warfare, is an undistinguished destruction of all ages, sexes and conditions.

In every stage of these Oppressions We have Petitioned for Redress in the most humble terms: Our repeated Petitions have been answered only by repeated injury. A Prince, whose character is thus marked by every act which may define a Tyrant, is unfit to be the ruler of a free People.

Nor have We been wanting in attention to our British brethren. We have warned them from time to time of attempts by their legislature to extend an unwarrantable jurisdiction over us. We have reminded them of the circumstances of our emigration and settlement here. We have appealed to their native justice and magnanimity, and we have conjured them by the ties of our common kindred to disavow these usurpations, which would inevitably interrupt our connections and correspondence. They too have been deaf to the voice of justice and of consanguinity. We must, therefore, acquiesce in the necessity, which denounces our Separation, and hold them, as we hold the rest of mankind, Enemies in War, in Peace Friends.

We, therefore, the Representatives of the United States of America, in General Congress, Assembled, appealing to the Supreme Judge of the world for the rectitude of our intentions, do, in the Name, and by Authority of the good People of these Colonies, solemnly publish and declare, That these United Colonies are, and of Right ought to be Free and Independent States; that they are Absolved from all Allegiance to the British Crown, and that all political connection between them and the State of Great Britain, is and ought to be totally dissolved; and that as Free and Independent States, they have full Power to levy War, conclude Peace, contract Alliances, establish Commerce, and to do all other Acts and Things which Independent States may of right do. And for the support of this Declaration, with a firm reliance on the Protection of Divine Providence, we mutually pledge to each other our Lives, our Fortunes and our sacred Honor.

John Hancock.

New Hampshire:
Josiah Bartlett,
William Whipple,
Matthew Thornton.

Massachusetts-Bay:
Samuel Adams,
John Adams,
Robert Treat Paine,
Elbridge Gerry.

Rhode Island:
Stephen Hopkins,
William Ellery.

Connecticut:
Roger Sherman,
Samuel Huntington,
William Williams,
Oliver Wolcott.

New York:
William Floyd,
Philip Livingston,
Francis Lewis,
Lewis Morris.

Pennsylvania:
Robert Morris,
Benjamin Harris,
Benjamin Franklin,
John Morton,
George Clymer,
James Smith,
George Taylor,
James Wilson,
George Ross.

Delaware:
Caesar Rodney,
George Read,
Thomas McKean.

Georgia:
Button Gwinnett,
Lyman Hall,
George Walton.

Maryland:
Samuel Chase,
William Paca,
Thomas Stone,
Charles Carroll of Carrollton.

Virginia:
George Wythe,
Richard Henry Lee,
Thomas Jefferson,
Benjamin Harrison,
Thomas Nelson Jr.,
Francis Lightfoot Lee,
Carter Braxton.

North Carolina:
William Hooper,
Joseph Hewes,
John Penn.

South Carolina:
Edward Rutledge,
Thomas Heyward Jr.,
Thomas Lynch Jr.,
Arthur Middleton.

New Jersey:
Richard Stockton,
John Witherspoon,
Francis Hopkinson,
John Hart,
Abraham Clark.

APPENDIX 3 CONSTITUTION OF THE UNITED STATES

The United States Constitution was written at a convention that Congress called on February 21, 1787, for the purpose of recommending amendments to the Articles of Confederation. Every state but Rhode Island sent delegates to Philadelphia, where the convention met that summer. The delegates decided to write an entirely new constitution, completing their labors on September 17. Nine states (the number the Constitution itself stipulated as sufficient) ratified by June 21, 1788.

The Framers of the Constitution included only six paragraphs on the Supreme Court. Article III, Section 1, created the Supreme Court and the federal system of courts. It provided that "[t]he judicial power of the United States, shall be vested in one supreme Court," and whatever inferior courts Congress "from time to time" saw fit to establish. Article III, Section 2, delineated the types of cases and controversies that should be considered by a federal—rather than a state—court. But beyond this, the Constitution left many of the particulars of the Supreme Court and the federal court system for Congress to decide in later years in judiciary acts.

We the People of the United States, in Order to form a more perfect Union, establish Justice, insure domestic Tranquillity, provide for the common defence, promote the general Welfare, and secure the Blessings of Liberty to ourselves and our Posterity, do ordain and establish this Constitution for the United States of America.

Article I

Section 1. All legislative Powers herein granted shall be vested in a Congress of the United States, which shall consist of a Senate and House of Representatives.

Section 2. The House of Representatives shall be composed of Members chosen every second Year by the People of the several States, and the Electors in each State shall have the Qualifications requisite for Electors of the most numerous Branch of the State Legislature.

No Person shall be a Representative who shall not have attained to the age of twenty five Years, and been seven Years a Citizen of the United States, and who shall not, when elected, be an Inhabitant of that State in which he shall be chosen.

[Representatives and direct Taxes shall be apportioned among the several States which may be included within this Union, according to their respective Numbers, which shall be determined by adding to the whole Number of free Persons, including those bound to Service for a Term of Years, and excluding Indians not taxed, three fifths of all other Persons.][1] The actual Enumeration shall be made within three Years after the first Meeting of the Congress of the United States, and within every subsequent Term of ten Years, in such Manner as they shall by Law direct. The Number of Representatives shall not exceed one for every thirty Thousand, but each State shall have at Least one Representative; and until such enumeration shall be made, the State of New Hampshire shall be entitled to chuse three, Massachusetts eight, Rhode-Island and Providence Plantations one, Connecticut five, New-York six, New Jersey four, Pennsylvania eight, Delaware one, Maryland six, Virginia ten, North Carolina five, South Carolina five, and Georgia three.

When vacancies happen in the Representation from any State, the Executive Authority thereof shall issue Writs of Election to fill such Vacancies.

The House of Representatives shall chuse their Speaker and other Officers; and shall have the sole Power of Impeachment.

Section 3. The Senate of the United States shall be composed of two Senators from each State, [chosen by the Legislature thereof,][2] for six Years; and each Senator shall have one Vote.

Immediately after they shall be assembled in Consequence of the first Election, they shall be divided as equally as may be into three Classes. The Seats of the Senators of the first Class shall be vacated at the

Expiration of the second Year, of the second Class at the Expiration of the fourth Year, and of the third Class at the Expiration of the sixth Year, so that one third may be chosen every second Year; [and if Vacancies happen by Resignation, or otherwise, during the Recess of the Legislature of any State, the Executive thereof may make temporary Appointments until the next Meeting of the Legislature, which shall then fill such Vacancies.][3]

No Person shall be a Senator who shall not have attained to the Age of thirty Years, and been nine Years a Citizen of the United States, and who shall not, when elected, be an Inhabitant of that State for which he shall be chosen.

The Vice President of the United States shall be President of the Senate, but shall have no Vote, unless they be equally divided.

The Senate shall chuse their other Officers, and also a President pro tempore, in the Absence of the Vice President, or when he shall exercise the Office of President of the United States.

The Senate shall have the sole Power to try all Impeachments. When sitting for that Purpose, they shall be on Oath or Affirmation. When the President of the United States is tried, the Chief Justice shall preside: And no Person shall be convicted without the Concurrence of two thirds of the Members present.

Judgment in Cases of Impeachment shall not extend further than to removal from Office, and disqualification to hold and enjoy any Office of honor, Trust or Profit under the United States: but the Party convicted shall nevertheless be liable and subject to Indictment, Trial, Judgment and Punishment, according to Law.

Section 4. The Times, Places and Manner of holding Elections for Senators and Representatives, shall be prescribed in each State by the Legislature thereof; but the Congress may at any time by Law make or alter such Regulations, except as to the Places of chusing Senators.

The Congress shall assemble at least once in every Year, and such Meeting shall [be on the first Monday in December],[4] unless they shall by Law appoint a different Day.

Section 5. Each House shall be the Judge of the Elections, Returns and Qualifications of its own Members, and a Majority of each shall constitute a Quorum to do Business; but a smaller Number may adjourn from day to day, and may be authorized to compel the Attendance of absent Members, in such Manner, and under such Penalties as each House may provide.

Each House may determine the Rules of its Proceedings, punish its Members for disorderly Behaviour, and, with the Concurrence of two thirds, expel a Member.

Each House shall keep a Journal of its Proceedings, and from time to time publish the same, excepting such Parts as may in their Judgment require Secrecy; and the Yeas and Nays of the Members of either House on any question shall, at the Desire of one fifth of those Present, be entered on the Journal.

Neither House, during the Session of Congress, shall, without the Consent of the other, adjourn for more than three days, nor to any other Place than that in which the two Houses shall be sitting.

Section 6. The Senators and Representatives shall receive a Compensation for their Services, to be ascertained by Law, and paid out of the Treasury of the United States. They shall in all Cases, except Treason, Felony and Breach of the Peace, be privileged from Arrest during their Attendance at the Session of their respective Houses, and in going to and returning from the same; and for any Speech or Debate in either House, they shall not be questioned in any other Place.

No Senator or Representative shall, during the Time for which he was elected, be appointed to any civil Office under the Authority of the United States, which shall have been created, or the Emoluments whereof shall have been encreased during such time; and no Person holding any Office under the United States, shall be a Member of either House during his Continuance in Office.

Section 7. All Bills for raising Revenue shall originate in the House of Representatives; but the Senate may propose or concur with Amendments as on other Bills.

Every Bill which shall have passed the House of Representatives and the Senate, shall, before it become a Law, be presented to the President of the United States; If he approve he shall sign it, but if not he shall return it, with his Objections to that House in which it shall have originated, who shall enter the Objections at large on their Journal, and proceed to reconsider it. If after such Reconsideration two thirds of that House shall agree to pass the Bill, it shall be sent, together with the Objections, to the other House, by which it shall likewise be reconsidered, and if approved by two thirds of that House, it shall become a Law. But in all such Cases the Votes of both Houses shall be determined by yeas and Nays, and the Names of the Persons voting for and against the Bill shall be entered on the Journal of each House respectively. If any Bill shall not be returned by the President within ten Days (Sundays excepted) after it shall have been presented to him, the Same shall be a Law, in like Manner as if he had signed it, unless the Congress by their Adjournment prevent its Return, in which Case it shall not be a Law.

Every Order, Resolution, or Vote to which the Concurrence of the Senate and House of Representatives may be necessary (except on a question of Adjournment) shall be presented to the President of the United States; and before the Same shall take Effect, shall be approved by him, or being disapproved by him, shall be repassed by two thirds of the Senate and House of Representatives, according to the Rules and Limitations prescribed in the Case of a Bill.

Section 8. The Congress shall have Power To lay and collect Taxes, Duties, Imposts and Excises, to pay the Debts and provide for the common Defence and general Welfare of the United States; but all Duties, Imposts and Excises shall be uniform throughout the United States;

To borrow Money on the credit of the United States;

To regulate Commerce with foreign Nations, and among the several States, and with the Indian Tribes;

To establish an uniform Rule of Naturalization, and uniform Laws on the subject of Bankruptcies throughout the United States;

To coin Money, regulate the Value thereof, and of foreign Coin, and fix the Standard of Weights and Measures;

To provide for the Punishment of counterfeiting the Securities and current Coin of the United States;

To establish Post Offices and post Roads;

To promote the Progress of Science and useful Arts, by securing for limited Times to Authors and Inventors the exclusive Right to their respective Writings and Discoveries;

To constitute Tribunals inferior to the supreme Court;

To define and punish Piracies and Felonies committed on the high Seas, and Offences against the Law of Nations;

To declare War, grant Letters of Marque and Reprisal, and make Rules concerning Captures on Land and Water;

To raise and support Armies, but no Appropriation of Money to that Use shall be for a longer Term than two Years;

To provide and maintain a Navy;

To make Rules for the Government and Regulation of the land and naval Forces;

To provide for calling forth the Militia to execute the Laws of the Union, suppress Insurrections and repel Invasions;

To provide for organizing, arming, and disciplining, the Militia, and for governing such Part of them as may be employed in the Service of the United States, reserving to the States respectively, the Appointment of the Officers, and the Authority of training the Militia according to the discipline prescribed by Congress;

To exercise exclusive Legislation in all Cases whatsoever, over such District (not exceeding ten Miles square) as may, by Cession of particular States, and the Acceptance of Congress, become the Seat of the Government of the United States, and to exercise like Authority over all Places purchased by the Consent of the Legislature of the State in which the Same shall be, for the Erection of Forts, Magazines, Arsenals, dock-Yards, and other needful Buildings;—And

To make all Laws which shall be necessary and proper for carrying into Execution the foregoing Powers, and all other Powers vested by this Constitution in the Government of the United States, or in any Department or Officer thereof.

Section 9. The Migration or Importation of such Persons as any of the States now existing shall think proper to admit, shall not be prohibited by the Congress prior to the Year one thousand eight hundred and eight, but a Tax or duty may be imposed on such Importation, not exceeding ten dollars for each Person.

The Privilege of the Writ of Habeas Corpus shall not be suspended, unless when in Cases of Rebellion or Invasion the public Safety may require it.

No Bill of Attainder or ex post facto Law shall be passed.

No Capitation, or other direct, Tax shall be laid, unless in Proportion to the Census or Enumeration herein before directed to be taken.[5]

No Tax or Duty shall be laid on Articles exported from any State.

No Preference shall be given by any Regulation of Commerce or Revenue to the Ports of one State over those of another; nor shall Vessels bound to, or from, one State, be obliged to enter, clear, or pay Duties in another.

No Money shall be drawn from the Treasury, but in Consequence of Appropriations made by Law; and a regular Statement and Account of the Receipts and Expenditures of all public Money shall be published from time to time.

No Title of Nobility shall be granted by the United States: And no Person holding any Office of Profit or Trust under them, shall, without the Consent of the Congress, accept of any present, Emolument, Office, or Title, of any kind whatever, from any King, Prince, or foreign State.

Section 10. No State shall enter into any Treaty, Alliance, or Confederation; grant Letters of Marque and Reprisal; coin Money; emit Bills of Credit; make any Thing but gold and silver Coin a Tender in Payment of Debts; pass any Bill of Attainder, ex post facto Law, or Law impairing the Obligation of Contracts, or grant any Title of Nobility.

No State shall, without the Consent of the Congress, lay any Imposts or Duties on Imports or Exports, except what may be absolutely necessary for executing its inspection Laws: and the net Produce of all Duties and Imposts, laid by any State on Imports or Exports, shall be for the Use of the Treasury of the United States; and all such Laws shall be subject to the Revision and Controul of the Congress.

No State shall, without the Consent of Congress, lay any Duty of Tonnage, keep Troops, or Ships of War in time of Peace, enter into any Agreement or Compact with another State, or with a foreign Power, or engage in War, unless actually invaded, or in such imminent Danger as will not admit of delay.

Article II

Section 1. The executive Power shall be vested in a President of the United States of America. He shall hold his Office during the Term of four Years, and, together with the Vice President, chosen for the same Term, be elected, as follows:

Each State shall appoint, in such Manner as the Legislature thereof may direct, a Number of Electors, equal to the whole Number of Senators and Representatives to which the State may be entitled in the Congress: but no Senator or Representative, or Person holding an Office of Trust or Profit under the United States, shall be appointed an Elector.

[The Electors shall meet in their respective States, and vote by Ballot for two Persons, of whom one at least shall not be an Inhabitant of the same State with themselves. And they shall make a List of all the Persons voted for, and of the Number of Votes for each; which List they shall sign and certify, and transmit sealed to the Seat of the Government of the United States, directed to the President of the Senate. The President of the Senate shall, in the Presence of the Senate and House of Representatives, open all the Certificates, and the Votes shall then be counted. The Person having the greatest Number of Votes shall be the President, if such Number be a Majority of the whole Number of Electors appointed; and if there be more than one who have such Majority, and have an equal Number of Votes, then the House of Representatives shall immediately chuse by Ballot one of them for President; and if no Person have a Majority, then from the five highest on the list the said House shall in like Manner chuse the President. But in chusing the President, the Votes shall be taken by States, the Representation from each State having one Vote; A quorum for this Purpose shall consist of a Member or Members from two thirds of the States, and a Majority of all the States shall be necessary to a Choice. In every Case, after the Choice of the President, the Person having the greatest Number of Votes of the Electors shall be the Vice President. But if there should remain two or more who have equal Votes, the Senate shall chuse from them by Ballot the Vice President.][6]

The Congress may determine the Time of chusing the Electors, and the Day on which they shall give their Votes; which Day shall be the same throughout the United States.

No Person except a natural born Citizen, or a Citizen of the United States, at the time of the Adoption of this Constitution, shall be eligible to the Office of President; neither shall any Person be eligible to that Office who shall not have attained to the Age of thirty five Years, and been fourteen Years a Resident within the United States.

In Case of the Removal of the President from Office, or of his Death, Resignation, or Inability to discharge the Powers and Duties of the said Office,[7] the Same shall devolve on the Vice President, and the Congress may by Law provide for the Case of Removal, Death, Resignation or Inability, both of the President and Vice President, declaring what Officer shall then act as President, and such Officer shall act accordingly, until the Disability be removed, or a President shall be elected.

The President shall, at stated Times, receive for his Services, a Compensation, which shall neither be encreased nor diminished during the Period for which he shall have been elected, and he shall not receive within that Period any other Emolument from the United States, or any of them.

Before he enter on the Execution of his Office, he shall take the following Oath or Affirmation:—"I do solemnly swear (or affirm) that I will faithfully execute the Office of President of the United States, and will to the best of my Ability, preserve, protect and defend the Constitution of the United States."

Section 2. The President shall be Commander in Chief of the Army and Navy of the United States, and of the

Militia of the several States, when called into the actual Service of the United States; he may require the Opinion, in writing, of the principal Officer in each of the executive Departments, upon any Subject relating to the Duties of their respective Offices, and he shall have Power to grant Reprieves and Pardons for Offences against the United States, except in Cases of Impeachment.

He shall have Power, by and with the Advice and Consent of the Senate, to make Treaties, provided two thirds of the Senators present concur; and he shall nominate, and by and with the Advice and Consent of the Senate, shall appoint Ambassadors, other public Ministers and Consuls, Judges of the supreme Court, and all other Officers of the United States, whose Appointments are not herein otherwise provided for, and which shall be established by Law: but the Congress may by Law vest the Appointment of such inferior Officers, as they think proper, in the President alone, in the Courts of Law, or in the Heads of Departments.

The President shall have Power to fill up all Vacancies that may happen during the Recess of the Senate, by granting Commissions which shall expire at the End of their next Session.

Section 3. He shall from time to time give to the Congress Information of the State of the Union, and recommend to their Consideration such Measures as he shall judge necessary and expedient; he may, on extraordinary Occasions, convene both Houses, or either of them, and in Case of Disagreement between them, with Respect to the Time of Adjournment, he may adjourn them to such Time as he shall think proper; he shall receive Ambassadors and other public Ministers; he shall take Care that the Laws be faithfully executed, and shall Commission all the Officers of the United States.

Section 4. The President, Vice President and all civil Officers of the United States, shall be removed from Office on Impeachment for, and Conviction of, Treason, Bribery, or other high Crimes and Misdemeanors.

Article III

Section 1. The judicial Power of the United States, shall be vested in one supreme Court, and in such inferior Courts as the Congress may from time to time ordain and establish. The Judges, both of the supreme and inferior Courts, shall hold their Offices during good Behaviour, and shall, at stated Times, receive for their Services, a Compensation, which shall not be diminished during their Continuance in Office.

Section 2. The judicial Power shall extend to all Cases, in Law and Equity, arising under this Constitution, the Laws of the United States, and Treaties made, or which shall be made, under their Authority; — to all Cases affecting Ambassadors, other public Ministers and Consuls; —to all Cases of admiralty and maritime Jurisdiction; —to Controversies to which the United States shall be a Party; —to Controversies between two or more States; —between a State and Citizens of another State;[8] —between Citizens of different States; —between Citizens of the same State claiming Lands under Grants of different States, and between a State, or the Citizens thereof, and foreign States, Citizens or Subjects.[8]

In all Cases affecting Ambassadors, other public Ministers and Consuls, and those in which a State shall be Party, the supreme Court shall have original Jurisdiction. In all the other Cases before mentioned, the supreme Court shall have appellate Jurisdiction, both as to Law and Fact, with such Exceptions, and under such Regulations as the Congress shall make.

The Trial of all Crimes, except in Cases of Impeachment, shall be by Jury; and such Trial shall be held in the State where the said Crimes shall have been committed; but when not committed within any State, the Trial shall be at such Place or Places as the Congress may by Law have directed.

Section 3. Treason against the United States, shall consist only in levying War against them, or in adhering to their Enemies, giving them Aid and Comfort. No Person shall be convicted of Treason unless on the Testimony of two Witnesses to the same overt Act, or on Confession in open Court.

The Congress shall have Power to declare the Punishment of Treason, but no Attainder of Treason shall work Corruption of Blood, or Forfeiture except during the Life of the Person attainted.

Article IV

Section 1. Full Faith and Credit shall be given in each State to the public Acts, Records, and judicial Proceedings of every other State. And the Congress may by general Laws prescribe the Manner in which such Acts, Records and Proceedings shall be proved, and the Effect thereof.

Section 2. The Citizens of each State shall be entitled to all Privileges and Immunities of Citizens in the several States.

A Person charged in any State with Treason, Felony, or other Crime, who shall flee from Justice, and be found in another State, shall on Demand of the executive Authority of the State from which he fled, be delivered up, to be removed to the State having Jurisdiction of the Crime.

[No Person held to Service or Labour in one State, under the Laws thereof, escaping into another, shall, in Consequence of any Law or Regulation therein, be discharged from such Service or Labour, but shall be delivered up on Claim of the Party to whom such Service or Labour may be due.][9]

Section 3. New States may be admitted by the Congress into this Union; but no new State shall be formed or erected within the Jurisdiction of any other State; nor any State be formed by the Junction of two or more States, or Parts of States, without the Consent of the Legislatures of the States concerned as well as of the Congress.

The Congress shall have Power to dispose of and make all needful Rules and Regulations respecting the Territory or other Property belonging to the United States; and nothing in this Constitution shall be so construed as to Prejudice any Claims of the United States, or of any particular State.

Section 4. The United States shall guarantee to every State in this Union a Republican Form of Government, and shall protect each of them against Invasion; and on Application of the Legislature, or of the Executive (when the Legislature cannot be convened) against domestic Violence.

Article V

The Congress, whenever two thirds of both Houses shall deem it necessary, shall propose Amendments to this Constitution, or, on the Application of the Legislatures of two thirds of the several States, shall call a Convention for proposing Amendments, which, in either Case, shall be valid to all Intents and Purposes, as Part of this Constitution, when ratified by the Legislatures of three fourths of the several States, or by Conventions in three fourths thereof, as the one or the other Mode of Ratification may be proposed by the Congress; Provided [that no Amendment which may be made prior to the Year One thousand eight hundred and eight shall in any Manner affect the first and fourth Clauses in the Ninth Section of the first Article; and][10] that no State, without its Consent, shall be deprived of its equal Suffrage in the Senate.

Article VI

All Debts contracted and Engagements entered into, before the Adoption of this Constitution, shall be as valid against the United States under this Constitution, as under the Confederation.

This Constitution, and the Laws of the United States which shall be made in Pursuance thereof; and all Treaties made, or which shall be made, under the Authority of the United States, shall be the supreme Law of the Land; and the Judges in every State shall be bound thereby, any Thing in the Constitution or Laws of any State to the Contrary notwithstanding.

The Senators and Representatives before mentioned, and the Members of the several State Legislatures, and all executive and judicial Officers, both of the United States and of the several States, shall be bound by Oath or Affirmation, to support this Constitution; but no religious Test shall ever be required as a Qualification to any Office or public Trust under the United States.

Article VII

The Ratification of the Conventions of nine States, shall be sufficient for the Establishment of this Constitution between the States so ratifying the Same.

Done in Convention by the Unanimous Consent of the States present the Seventeenth Day of September in the Year of our Lord one thousand seven hundred and Eighty seven and of the Independence of the United States of America the Twelfth. IN WITNESS whereof We have hereunto subscribed our Names,

George Washington, President and deputy from Virginia, and thirty-eight other delegates.

[The language of the original Constitution, not including the Amendments, was adopted by a convention of the states on September 17, 1787, and was subsequently ratified by the states on the following dates: Delaware, December 7, 1787; Pennsylvania, December 12, 1787; New Jersey, December 18, 1787; Georgia, January 2, 1788; Connecticut, January 9, 1788; Massachusetts, February 6, 1788; Maryland, April 28, 1788; South Carolina, May 23, 1788; New Hampshire, June 21, 1788.

Ratification was completed on June 21, 1788.

The Constitution subsequently was ratified by Virginia, June 25, 1788; New York, July 26, 1788; North Carolina, November 21, 1789; Rhode Island, May 29, 1790; and Vermont, January 10, 1791.]

AMENDMENTS

Amendment I

(First ten amendments ratified December 15, 1791.)

Congress shall make no law respecting an establishment of religion, or prohibiting the free exercise thereof; or abridging the freedom of speech, or of the press; or the right of the people peaceably to assemble, and to petition the Government for a redress of grievances.

Amendment II

A well regulated Militia, being necessary to the security of a free State, the right of the people to keep and bear Arms, shall not be infringed.

Amendment III

No Soldier shall, in time of peace be quartered in any house, without the consent of the Owner, nor in time of war, but in a manner to be prescribed by law.

Amendment IV

The right of the people to be secure in their persons, houses, papers, and effects, against unreasonable searches and seizures, shall not be violated, and no Warrants shall issue, but upon probable cause, supported by Oath or affirmation, and particularly describing the place to be searched, and the persons or things to be seized.

Amendment V

No person shall be held to answer for a capital, or otherwise infamous crime, unless on a presentment or indictment of a Grand Jury, except in cases arising in the land or naval forces, or in the Militia, when in actual service in time of War or public danger; nor shall any person be subject for the same offence to be twice put in jeopardy of life or limb; nor shall be compelled in any criminal case to be a witness against himself, nor be deprived of life, liberty, or property, without due process of law; nor shall private property be taken for public use, without just compensation.

Amendment VI

In all criminal prosecutions, the accused shall enjoy the right to a speedy and public trial, by an impartial jury of the State and district wherein the crime shall have been committed, which district shall have been previously ascertained by law, and to be informed of the nature and cause of the accusation; to be confronted with the witnesses against him; to have compulsory process for obtaining witnesses in his favor, and to have the Assistance of Counsel for his defence.

Amendment VII

In Suits at common law, where the value in controversy shall exceed twenty dollars, the right of trial by jury shall be preserved, and no fact tried by a jury, shall be otherwise re-examined in any Court of the United States, than according to the rules of the common law.

Amendment VIII

Excessive bail shall not be required, nor excessive fines imposed, nor cruel and unusual punishments inflicted.

Amendment IX

The enumeration in the Constitution, of certain rights, shall not be construed to deny or disparage others retained by the people.

Amendment X

The powers not delegated to the United States by the Constitution, nor prohibited by it to the States, are reserved to the States respectively, or to the people.

Amendment XI
(Ratified February 7, 1795)

The Judicial power of the United States shall not be construed to extend to any suit in law or equity, commenced or prosecuted against one of the United States by Citizens of another State, or by Citizens or Subjects of any Foreign State.

Amendment XII
(Ratified June 15, 1804)

The Electors shall meet in their respective states and vote by ballot for President and Vice-President, one of whom, at least, shall not be an inhabitant of the same state with themselves; they shall name in their ballots the person voted for as President, and in distinct ballots the person voted for as Vice-President, and they shall make distinct lists of all persons voted for as President, and of all persons voted for as Vice-President, and of the number of votes for each, which lists they shall sign and certify, and transmit sealed to the seat of the government of the United States, directed to the President of the Senate; — The President of the Senate shall, in the presence of the Senate and House of Representatives, open all the certificates and the votes shall then be counted; — The person having the greatest number of votes for President, shall be the President, if such number be a majority of the whole number of Electors appointed; and if no person have such majority, then from the persons having the highest numbers not exceeding three on the list of those voted for as President, the House of Representatives shall choose immediately, by ballot, the President. But in choosing the President, the votes shall be taken by states, the representation from each state having one vote; a quorum for this purpose shall consist of a member or members from two-thirds of the states, and a majority of all the states shall be necessary to a choice. [And if the House of Representatives shall not choose a President whenever the right of choice shall devolve upon them, before the fourth day of March next following, then the Vice-President shall act as President, as in the case of the death or other constitutional disability of the President. —][11] The person having the greatest number of votes as Vice-President, shall be the Vice-President, if such number be a majority of the whole number of Electors appointed, and if no person have a majority, then from the two highest numbers on the list, the Senate shall choose the Vice-President; a quorum for the purpose shall consist of two-thirds of the whole number of Senators, and a majority of the whole number shall be necessary to a choice. But no person constitutionally ineligible to the office of President shall be eligible to that of Vice-President of the United States.

Amendment XIII (Ratified December 6, 1865)

Section 1. Neither slavery nor involuntary servitude, except as a punishment for crime whereof the party shall have been duly convicted, shall exist within the United States, or any place subject to their jurisdiction.

Section 2. Congress shall have power to enforce this article by appropriate legislation.

Amendment XIV (Ratified July 9, 1868)

Section 1. All persons born or naturalized in the United States, and subject to the jurisdiction thereof, are citizens of the United States and of the State wherein they reside. No State shall make or enforce any law which shall abridge the privileges or immunities of citizens of the United States; nor shall any State deprive any person of life, liberty, or property, without due process of law; nor deny to any person within its jurisdiction the equal protection of the laws.

Section 2. Representatives shall be apportioned among the several States according to their respective numbers, counting the whole number of persons in each State, excluding Indians not taxed. But when the right to vote at any election for the choice of electors for President and Vice President of the United States, Representatives in Congress, the Executive and Judicial officers of a State, or the members of the Legislature thereof, is denied to any of the male inhabitants of such State, being twenty-one years of age,[12] and citizens of the United States, or in any way abridged, except for participation in rebellion, or other crime, the basis of representation therein shall be reduced in the proportion which the number of such male citizens shall bear to the whole number of male citizens twenty-one years of age in such State.

Section 3. No person shall be a Senator or Representative in Congress, or elector of President and Vice President, or hold any Office, civil or military, under the United States, or under any State, who, having previously taken an oath, as a member of Congress, or as an officer of the United States, or as a member of any State legislature, or as an executive or judicial officer of any State, to support the Constitution of the United States, shall have engaged in insurrection or rebellion against the same, or given aid or comfort to the enemies thereof. But Congress may by a vote of two-thirds of each House, remove such disability.

Section 4. The validity of the public debt of the United States, authorized by law, including debts incurred for payment of pensions and bounties for services in suppressing insurrection or rebellion, shall not be questioned. But neither the United States nor any State shall assume or pay any debt or obligation incurred in aid of insurrection or rebellion against the United States, or any claim for the loss or emancipation of any slave; but all such debts, obligations and claims shall be held illegal and void.

Section 5. The Congress shall have power to enforce, by appropriate legislation, the provisions of this article.

Amendment XV
(Ratified February 3, 1870)

Section 1. The right of citizens of the United States to vote shall not be denied or abridged by the United States or by any State on account of race, color, or previous condition of servitude.

Section 2. The Congress shall have power to enforce this article by appropriate legislation.

Amendment XVI
(Ratified February 3, 1913)

The Congress shall have power to lay and collect taxes on incomes, from whatever source derived, without apportionment among the several States, and without regard to any census or enumeration.

Amendment XVII
(Ratified April 8, 1913)

The Senate of the United States shall be composed of two Senators from each State, elected by the people thereof, for six years; and each Senator shall have one vote. The electors in each State shall have the qualifications requisite for electors of the most numerous branch of the State legislatures.

When vacancies happen in the representation of any State in the Senate, the executive authority of such State shall issue writs of election to fill such vacancies: *Provided,* That the legislature of any State may empower the executive thereof to make temporary appointments until the people fill the vacancies by election as the legislature may direct.

This amendment shall not be so construed as to affect the election or term of any Senator chosen before it becomes valid as part of the Constitution.

Amendment XVIII
(Ratified January 16, 1919)

Section 1. After one year from the ratification of this article the manufacture, sale, or transportation of intoxicating liquors within, the importation thereof into, or the exportation thereof from the United States and all

territory subject to the jurisdiction thereof for beverage purposes is hereby prohibited.

Section 2. The Congress and the several States shall have concurrent power to enforce this article by appropriate legislation.

Section 3. This article shall be inoperative unless it shall have been ratified as an amendment to the Constitution by the legislatures of the several States, as provided in the Constitution, within seven years from the date of the submission hereof to the States by the Congress.[13]

Amendment XIX
(Ratified August 18, 1920)

The right of citizens of the United States to vote shall not be denied or abridged by the United States or by any State on account of sex.

Congress shall have power to enforce this article by appropriate legislation.

Amendment XX
(Ratified January 23, 1933)

Section 1. The terms of the President and Vice President shall end at noon on the 20th day of January, and the terms of Senators and Representatives at noon on the 3d day of January, of the years in which such terms would have ended if this article had not been ratified; and the terms of their successors shall then begin.

Section 2. The Congress shall assemble at least once in every year, and such meeting shall begin at noon on the 3d day of January, unless they shall by law appoint a different day.

Section 3.[14] If, at the time fixed for the beginning of the term of the President, the President elect shall have died, the Vice President elect shall become President. If a President shall not have been chosen before the time fixed for the beginning of his term, or if the President elect shall have failed to qualify, then the Vice President elect shall act as President until a President shall have qualified; and the Congress may by law provide for the case wherein neither a President elect nor a Vice President elect shall have qualified, declaring who shall then act as President, or the manner in which one who is to act shall be selected, and such person shall act accordingly until a President or Vice President shall have qualified.

Section 4. The Congress may by law provide for the case of the death of any of the persons from whom the

House of Representatives may choose a President whenever the right of choice shall have devolved upon them, and for the case of the death of any of the persons from whom the Senate may choose a Vice President whenever the right of choice shall have devolved upon them.

Section 5. Sections **1** and **2** shall take effect on the **15th** day of October following the ratification of this article.

Section 6. This article shall be inoperative unless it shall have been ratified as an amendment to the Constitution by the legislatures of three-fourths of the several States within seven years from the date of its submission.

Amendment XXI
(Ratified December 5, 1933)

Section 1. The eighteenth article of amendment to the Constitution of the United States is hereby repealed.

Section 2. The transportation or importation into any State, Territory, or possession of the United States for delivery or use therein of intoxicating liquors, in violation of the laws thereof, is hereby prohibited.

Section 3. This article shall be inoperative unless it shall have been ratified as an amendment to the Constitution by conventions in the several States, as provided in the Constitution, within seven years from the date of the submission hereof to the States by the Congress.

Amendment XXII
(Ratified February 27, 1951)

Section 1. No person shall be elected to the office of the President more than twice, and no person who has held the office of President, or acted as President, for more than two years of a term to which some other person was elected President shall be elected to the office of the President more than once. But this Article shall not apply to any person holding the office of President when this Article was proposed by the Congress, and shall not prevent any person who may be holding the office of President, or acting as President, during the term within which this Article becomes operative from holding the office of President or acting as President during the remainder of such term.

Section 2. This article shall be inoperative unless it shall have been ratified as an amendment to the Constitution by the legislatures of three-fourths of the several States within seven years from the date of its submission to the States by the Congress.

Amendment XXIII
(Ratified March 29, 1961)

Section 1. The District constituting the seat of Government of the United States shall appoint in such manner as the Congress may direct:

A number of electors of President and Vice President equal to the whole number of Senators and Representatives in Congress to which the District would be entitled if it were a State, but in no event more than the least populous State; they shall be in addition to those appointed by the States, but they shall be considered, for the purposes of the election of President and Vice President, to be electors appointed by a State; and they shall meet in the District and perform such duties as provided by the twelfth article of amendment.

Section 2. The Congress shall have power to enforce this article by appropriate legislation.

Amendment XXIV
(Ratified January 23, 1964)

Section 1. The right of citizens of the United States to vote in any primary or other election for President or Vice President, for electors for President or Vice President, or for Senator or Representative in Congress, shall not be denied or abridged by the United States or any State by reason of failure to pay any poll tax or other tax.

Section 2. The Congress shall have power to enforce this article by appropriate legislation.

Amendment XXV
(Ratified February 10, 1967)

Section 1. In case of the removal of the President from office or of his death or resignation, the Vice President shall become President.

Section 2. Whenever there is a vacancy in the office of the Vice President, the President shall nominate a Vice President who shall take office upon confirmation by a majority vote of both Houses of Congress.

Section 3. Whenever the President transmits to the President pro tempore of the Senate and the Speaker of the House of Representatives his written declaration that he is unable to discharge the powers and duties of his office, and until he transmits to them a written declaration to the contrary, such powers and duties shall be discharged by the Vice President as Acting President.

Section 4. Whenever the Vice President and a majority of either the principal officers of the executive departments or of such other body as Congress may by law provide, transmit to the President pro tempore of the Senate and the Speaker of the House of Representatives their written declaration that the President is unable to discharge the powers and duties of his office, the Vice President shall immediately assume the powers and duties of the office as Acting President.

Thereafter, when the President transmits to the President pro tempore of the Senate and the Speaker of the House of Representatives his written declaration that no inability exists, he shall resume the powers and duties of his office unless the Vice President and a majority of either the principal officers of the executive departments or of such other body as Congress may by law provide, transmit within four days to the President pro tempore of the Senate and the Speaker of the House of Representatives their written declaration that the President is unable to discharge the powers and duties of his office. Thereupon Congress shall decide the issue, assembling within forty-eight hours for that purpose if not in session. If the Congress, within twenty-one days after receipt of the latter written declaration, or, if Congress is not in session, within twenty-one days after Congress is required to assemble, determines by two-thirds vote of both Houses that the President is unable to discharge the powers and duties of his office, the Vice President shall continue to discharge the same as Acting President; otherwise, the President shall resume the powers and duties of his office.

Amendment XXVI (Ratified July 1, 1971)

Section 1. The right of citizens of the United States, who are eighteen years of age or older, to vote shall not be denied or abridged by the United States or by any State on account of age.

Section 2. The Congress shall have power to enforce this article by appropriate legislation.

Amendment XXVII (Ratified May 7, 1992)

No law varying the compensation for the services of the Senators and Representatives shall take effect, until an election of Representatives shall have intervened.

Source: U.S. Congress, House, Committee on the Judiciary, *The Constitution of the United States of America, as Amended,* 100th Cong., 1st sess., 1987, H Doc 100–94.

Notes

1. The part in brackets was changed by section 2 of the Fourteenth Amendment.
2. The part in brackets was changed by the first paragraph of the Seventeenth Amendment.
3. The part in brackets was changed by the second paragraph of the Seventeenth Amendment.
4. The part in brackets was changed by section 2 of the Twentieth Amendment.
5. The Sixteenth Amendment gave Congress the power to tax incomes.
6. The material in brackets was superseded by the Twelfth Amendment.
7. This provision was affected by the Twenty-fifth Amendment.
8. These clauses were affected by the Eleventh Amendment.
9. This paragraph was superseded by the Thirteenth Amendment.
10. Obsolete.
11. The part in brackets was superseded by section 3 of the Twentieth Amendment.
12. See the Nineteenth and Twenty-sixth Amendments.
13. This amendment was repealed by section 1 of the Twenty-first Amendment.
14. See the Twenty-fifth Amendment.

The Same Subject Continued: The Union as a Safeguard Against Domestic Faction and Insurrection.

From the New York Packet
Friday, November 23, 1787.

Author: James Madison

To the People of the State of New York:

AMONG the numerous advantages promised by a wellconstructed Union, none deserves to be more accurately developed than its tendency to break and control the violence of faction. The friend of popular governments never finds himself so much alarmed for their character and fate, as when he contemplates their propensity to this dangerous vice. He will not fail, therefore, to set a due value on any plan which, without violating the principles to which he is attached, provides a proper cure for it. The instability, injustice, and confusion introduced into the public councils, have, in truth, been the mortal diseases under which popular governments have everywhere perished; as they continue to be the favorite and fruitful topics from which the adversaries to liberty derive their most specious declamations. The valuable improvements made by the American constitutions on the popular models, both ancient and modern, cannot certainly be too much admired; but it would be an unwarrantable partiality, to contend that they have as effectually obviated the danger on this side, as was wished and expected. Complaints are everywhere heard from our most considerate and virtuous citizens, equally the friends of public and private faith, and of public and personal liberty, that our governments are too unstable, that the public good is disregarded in the conflicts of rival parties, and that measures are too often decided, not according to the rules of justice and the rights of the minor party, but by the superior force of an interested and overbearing majority. However anxiously we may wish that these complaints had no foundation, the evidence, of known facts will not permit us to deny that they are in some degree true. It will be found, indeed, on a candid review of our situation, that some of the distresses under which we labor have been erroneously charged on the operation of our governments; but it will be found, at the same time, that other causes will not alone account for many of our heaviest misfortunes; and, particularly, for that prevailing and increasing distrust of public engagements, and alarm for private rights, which are echoed from one end of the continent to the other. These must be chiefly, if not wholly, effects of the unsteadiness and injustice with which a factious spirit has tainted our public administrations.

By a faction, I understand a number of citizens, whether amounting to a majority or a minority of the whole, who are united and actuated by some common impulse of passion, or of interest, adversed to the rights of other citizens, or to the permanent and aggregate interests of the community.

There are two methods of curing the mischiefs of faction: the one, by removing its causes; the other, by controlling its effects.

There are again two methods of removing the causes of faction: the one, by destroying the liberty which is essential to its existence; the other, by giving to every citizen the same opinions, the same passions, and the same interests.

It could never be more truly said than of the first remedy, that it was worse than the disease. Liberty is to faction what air is to fire, an aliment without which it instantly expires. But it could not be less folly to abolish liberty, which is essential to political life, because it nourishes faction, than it would be to wish the annihilation of air, which is essential to animal life, because it imparts to fire its destructive agency.

The second expedient is as impracticable as the first would be unwise. As long as the reason of man continues fallible, and he is at liberty to exercise it, different opinions will be formed. As long as the connection subsists between his reason and his self-love, his opinions and his passions will have a reciprocal influence on each other; and the former will be objects to which the latter will attach themselves. The diversity in the faculties of men, from which the rights of property originate, is not less an insuperable obstacle to a uniformity of interests. The protection of these faculties is the first object of government. From the protection of different and unequal faculties of acquiring property, the possession of different degrees and kinds of property immediately results; and from the influence of these on the sentiments and views of the respective proprietors, ensues a division of the society into different interests and parties.

The latent causes of faction are thus sown in the nature of man; and we see them everywhere brought into different degrees of activity, according to the different circumstances of civil society. A zeal for different opinions concerning religion, concerning government, and many other points, as well of speculation as of practice; an attachment to different leaders ambitiously contending for pre-eminence and power; or to persons of other descriptions whose fortunes have been interesting to the human passions, have, in turn, divided mankind into parties, inflamed them with mutual animosity, and rendered them much more disposed to vex and oppress each other than to co-operate for their common good. So strong is this propensity of mankind to fall into mutual animosities, that where no substantial occasion presents itself, the most frivolous and fanciful distinctions have been sufficient to kindle their unfriendly passions and excite their most violent conflicts. But the most common and durable source of factions has been the various and unequal distribution of property. Those who hold and those who are without property have ever formed distinct interests in society. Those who are creditors, and those who are debtors, fall under a like discrimination. A landed interest, a manufacturing interest, a mercantile interest, a moneyed interest, with many lesser interests, grow up of necessity in civilized nations, and divide them into different classes, actuated by different sentiments and views. The regulation of these various and interfering interests forms the principal task of modern legislation, and involves the spirit of party and faction in the necessary and ordinary operations of the government.

No man is allowed to be a judge in his own cause, because his interest would certainly bias his judgment, and, not improbably, corrupt his integrity. With equal, nay with greater reason, a body of men are unfit to be both judges and parties at the same time; yet what are many of the most important acts of legislation, but so many judicial determinations, not indeed concerning the rights of single persons, but concerning the rights of large bodies of citizens? And what are the different classes of legislators but advocates and parties to the causes which they determine? Is a law proposed concerning private debts? It is a question to which the creditors are parties on one side and the debtors on the other. Justice ought to hold the balance between them. Yet the parties are, and must be, themselves the judges; and the most numerous party, or, in other words, the most powerful faction must be expected to prevail. Shall domestic manufactures be encouraged, and in what degree, by restrictions on foreign manufactures? are questions which would be differently decided by the landed and the manufacturing classes, and probably by neither with a sole regard to justice and the public good. The apportionment of taxes on the various descriptions of property is an act which seems to require the most exact impartiality; yet there is, perhaps, no legislative act in which greater opportunity and temptation are given to a predominant party to trample on the rules of justice. Every shilling with which they overburden the inferior number, is a shilling saved to their own pockets.

It is in vain to say that enlightened statesmen will be able to adjust these clashing interests, and render them all subservient to the public good. Enlightened statesmen will not always be at the helm. Nor, in many cases, can such an adjustment be made at all without taking into view indirect and remote considerations, which will rarely prevail over the immediate interest which one party may find in disregarding the rights of another or the good of the whole.

The inference to which we are brought is, that the CAUSES of faction cannot be removed, and that relief is only to be sought in the means of controlling its EFFECTS.

If a faction consists of less than a majority, relief is supplied by the republican principle, which enables the majority to defeat its sinister views by regular vote. It may clog the administration, it may convulse the society; but it will be unable to execute and mask its violence under the forms of the Constitution. When a majority is included in a faction, the form of popular government, on the other hand, enables it to sacrifice to its ruling passion or interest both the public good and the rights of other citizens. To secure the public good and private rights against the danger of such a faction, and at the same time to preserve the spirit and the form of popular government, is then the great object to which our inquiries are directed. Let me add that it is the great desideratum by which this form of government can be rescued from the opprobrium under which it has so long labored, and be recommended to the esteem and adoption of mankind.

By what means is this object attainable? Evidently by one of two only. Either the existence of the same passion or interest in a majority at the same time must be prevented, or the majority, having such coexistent passion or interest, must be rendered, by their number and local situation, unable to concert and carry into effect schemes of oppression. If the impulse and the opportunity be suffered to coincide, we well know that neither moral nor religious motives can be relied on as an adequate control. They are not found to be such on the injustice and violence of individuals, and lose their efficacy in proportion to the number combined together, that is, in proportion as their efficacy becomes needful.

From this view of the subject it may be concluded that a pure democracy, by which I mean a society consisting of a small number of citizens, who assemble and administer the government in person, can admit of no cure for the mischiefs of faction. A common passion or interest will, in almost every case, be felt by a majority of the whole; a communication and concert result from the form of government itself; and there is nothing to check the inducements to sacrifice the weaker party or an obnoxious individual. Hence it is that such democracies have ever been spectacles of turbulence and contention; have ever been found incompatible with personal security or the rights of property; and have in general been as short in their lives as they have been violent in their deaths. Theoretic politicians, who have patronized this species of government, have erroneously supposed that by reducing mankind to a perfect equality in their political rights, they would, at the same time, be perfectly equalized and assimilated in their possessions, their opinions, and their passions.

A republic, by which I mean a government in which the scheme of representation takes place, opens a different prospect, and promises the cure for which we are seeking. Let us examine the points in which it varies from pure democracy, and we shall comprehend both the nature of the cure and the efficacy which it must derive from the Union.

The two great points of difference between a democracy and a republic are: first, the delegation of the government, in the latter, to a small number of citizens elected by the rest; secondly, the greater number of citizens, and greater sphere of country, over which the latter may be extended.

The effect of the first difference is, on the one hand, to refine and enlarge the public views, by passing them through the medium of a chosen body of citizens, whose wisdom may best discern the true interest of their country, and whose patriotism and love of justice will be least likely to sacrifice it to temporary or partial considerations. Under such a regulation, it may well happen that the public voice, pronounced by the representatives of the people, will be more consonant to the public good than if pronounced by the people themselves, convened for the purpose. On the other hand, the effect may be inverted. Men of factious tempers, of local prejudices, or of sinister designs, may, by intrigue, by corruption, or by other means, first obtain the suffrages, and then betray the interests, of the people. The question resulting is, whether small or extensive republics are more favorable to the election of proper guardians of the public weal; and it is clearly decided in favor of the latter by two obvious considerations:

In the first place, it is to be remarked that, however small the republic may be, the representatives must be raised to a certain number, in order to guard against the cabals of a few; and that, however large it may be, they must be limited to a certain number, in order to guard against the confusion of a multitude. Hence, the number of representatives in the two cases not being in proportion to that of the two constituents, and being proportionally greater in the small republic, it follows that, if the proportion of fit characters be not less in the large than in the small republic, the former will present a greater option, and consequently a greater probability of a fit choice.

In the next place, as each representative will be chosen by a greater number of citizens in the large than in the small republic, it will be more difficult for unworthy candidates to practice with success the vicious arts by which elections are too often carried; and the suffrages of the people being more free, will be more likely to centre in men who possess the most attractive merit and the most diffusive and established characters.

It must be confessed that in this, as in most other cases, there is a mean, on both sides of which inconveniences will be found to lie. By enlarging too much the number of electors, you render the representatives too little acquainted with all their local circumstances and lesser interests; as by reducing it too much, you render him unduly attached to these, and too little fit to comprehend and pursue great and national objects. The federal Constitution forms a happy combination in this respect;

the great and aggregate interests being referred to the national, the local and particular to the State legislatures.

The other point of difference is, the greater number of citizens and extent of territory which may be brought within the compass of republican than of democratic government; and it is this circumstance principally which renders factious combinations less to be dreaded in the former than in the latter. The smaller the society, the fewer probably will be the distinct parties and interests composing it; the fewer the distinct parties and interests, the more frequently will a majority be found of the same party; and the smaller the number of individuals composing a majority, and the smaller the compass within which they are placed, the more easily will they concert and execute their plans of oppression. Extend the sphere, and you take in a greater variety of parties and interests; you make it less probable that a majority of the whole will have a common motive to invade the rights of other citizens; or if such a common motive exists, it will be more difficult for all who feel it to discover their own strength, and to act in unison with each other. Besides other impediments, it may be remarked that, where there is a consciousness of unjust or dishonorable purposes, communication is always checked by distrust in proportion to the number whose concurrence is necessary.

Hence, it clearly appears, that the same advantage which a republic has over a democracy, in controlling the effects of faction, is enjoyed by a large over a small republic,—is enjoyed by the Union over the States composing it. Does the advantage consist in the substitution of representatives whose enlightened views and virtuous sentiments render them superior to local prejudices and schemes of injustice? It will not be denied that the representation of the Union will be most likely to possess these requisite endowments. Does it consist in the greater security afforded by a greater variety of parties, against the event of any one party being able to outnumber and oppress the rest? In an equal degree does the increased variety of parties comprised within the Union, increase this security. Does it, in fine, consist in the greater obstacles opposed to the concert and accomplishment of the secret wishes of an unjust and interested majority? Here, again, the extent of the Union gives it the most palpable advantage.

The influence of factious leaders may kindle a flame within their particular States, but will be unable to spread a general conflagration through the other States. A religious sect may degenerate into a political faction in a part of the Confederacy; but the variety of sects dispersed over the entire face of it must secure the national councils against any danger from that source. A rage for paper money, for an abolition of debts, for an equal division of property, or for any other improper or wicked project, will be less apt to pervade the whole body of the Union than a particular member of it; in the same proportion as such a malady is more likely to taint a particular county or district, than an entire State.

In the extent and proper structure of the Union, therefore, we behold a republican remedy for the diseases most incident to republican government. And according to the degree of pleasure and pride we feel in being republicans, ought to be our zeal in cherishing the spirit and supporting the character of Federalists.

PUBLIUS.

The Structure of the Government Must Furnish the Proper Checks and Balances Between the Different Departments

From the New York Packet.
Friday, February 8, 1788.

Author: James Madison

To the People of the State of New York:

TO WHAT expedient, then, shall we finally resort, for maintaining in practice the necessary partition of power among the several departments, as laid down in the Constitution? The only answer that can be given is, that as all these exterior provisions are found to be inadequate, the defect must be supplied, by so contriving the interior structure of the government as that its several constituent parts may, by their mutual relations, be the means of keeping each other in their proper places. Without presuming to undertake a full development of this important idea, I will hazard a few general observations, which may perhaps place it in a clearer light, and enable us to form a more correct judgment of the principles and structure of the government planned by the convention.

In order to lay a due foundation for that separate and distinct exercise of the different powers of government, which to a certain extent is admitted on all hands to be essential to the preservation of liberty, it is evident that each department should have a will of its own; and consequently should be so constituted that the members of each should have as little agency as possible in the appointment of the members of the others. Were this principle rigorously adhered to, it would require that all the appointments for the supreme executive, legislative, and judiciary magistracies should be drawn from the same fountain of authority, the people, through channels having no communication whatever with one another. Perhaps such a plan of constructing the several departments would be less difficult in practice than it may in contemplation appear. Some difficulties, however, and

some additional expense would attend the execution of it. Some deviations, therefore, from the principle must be admitted. In the constitution of the judiciary department in particular, it might be inexpedient to insist rigorously on the principle: first, because peculiar qualifications being essential in the members, the primary consideration ought to be to select that mode of choice which best secures these qualifications; secondly, because the permanent tenure by which the appointments are held in that department, must soon destroy all sense of dependence on the authority conferring them.

It is equally evident, that the members of each department should be as little dependent as possible on those of the others, for the emoluments annexed to their offices. Were the executive magistrate, or the judges, not independent of the legislature in this particular, their independence in every other would be merely nominal. But the great security against a gradual concentration of the several powers in the same department, consists in giving to those who administer each department the necessary constitutional means and personal motives to resist encroachments of the others. The provision for defense must in this, as in all other cases, be made commensurate to the danger of attack. Ambition must be made to counteract ambition. The interest of the man must be connected with the constitutional rights of the place. It may be a reflection on human nature, that such devices should be necessary to control the abuses of government. But what is government itself, but the greatest of all reflections on human nature? If men were angels, no government would be necessary. If angels were to govern men, neither external nor internal controls on government would be necessary. In framing a government which is to be administered by men over men, the great difficulty lies in this: you must first enable the government to control the governed; and in the next place oblige it to control itself.

A dependence on the people is, no doubt, the primary control on the government; but experience has taught mankind the necessity of auxiliary precautions.

This policy of supplying, by opposite and rival interests, the defect of better motives, might be traced through the whole system of human affairs, private as well as public. We see it particularly displayed in all the subordinate distributions of power, where the constant aim is to divide and arrange the several offices in such a manner as that each may be a check on the other that the private interest of every individual may be a sentinel over the public rights. These inventions of prudence cannot be less requisite in the distribution of the supreme powers of the State. But it is not possible to give to each department an equal power of self-defense. In republican government, the legislative authority necessarily predominates. The remedy for this inconveniency is to divide the legislature into different branches; and to render them, by different modes of election and different principles of action, as little connected with each other as the nature of their common functions and their common dependence on the society will admit. It may even be necessary to guard against dangerous encroachments by still further precautions. As the weight of the legislative authority requires that it should be thus divided, the weakness of the executive may require, on the other hand, that it should be fortified.

An absolute negative on the legislature appears, at first view, to be the natural defense with which the executive magistrate should be armed. But perhaps it would be neither altogether safe nor alone sufficient. On ordinary occasions it might not be exerted with the requisite firmness, and on extraordinary occasions it might be perfidiously abused. May not this defect of an absolute negative be supplied by some qualified connection between this weaker department and the weaker branch of the stronger department, by which the latter may be led to support the constitutional rights of the former, without being too much detached from the rights of its own department? If the principles on which these observations are founded be just, as I persuade myself they are, and they be applied as a criterion to the several State constitutions, and to the federal Constitution it will be found that if the latter does not perfectly correspond with them, the former are infinitely less able to bear such a test.

There are, moreover, two considerations particularly applicable to the federal system of America, which place that system in a very interesting point of view. First. In a single republic, all the power surrendered by the people is submitted to the administration of a single government; and the usurpations are guarded against by a division of the government into distinct and separate departments. In the compound republic of America, the power surrendered by the people is first divided between two distinct governments, and then the portion allotted to each subdivided among distinct and separate departments. Hence a double security arises to the rights of the people. The different governments will control each other, at the same time that each will be controlled by itself. Second. It is of great importance in a republic not only to guard the society against the oppression of its rulers, but to guard one part of the society against the injustice of the other part. Different interests necessarily exist in different classes of citizens. If a majority be united by a common interest, the rights of the minority will be insecure.

There are but two methods of providing against this evil: the one by creating a will in the community independent of the majority that is, of the society itself; the other, by comprehending in the society so many separate descriptions of citizens as will render an unjust combination of a majority of the whole very improbable, if not impracticable. The first method prevails in all governments possessing an hereditary or self-appointed authority. This, at best, is but a precarious security; because a power independent of the society may as well espouse the unjust views of the major, as the rightful interests of the minor party, and may possibly be turned against both parties. The second method will be exemplified in the federal republic of the United States. Whilst all authority in it will be derived from and dependent on the society, the society itself will be broken into so many parts, interests, and classes of citizens, that the rights of individuals, or of the minority, will be in little danger from interested combinations of the majority.

In a free government the security for civil rights must be the same as that for religious rights. It consists in the one case in the multiplicity of interests, and in the other in the multiplicity of sects. The degree of security in both cases will depend on the number of interests and sects; and this may be presumed to depend on the extent of country and number of people comprehended under the same government. This view of the subject must particularly recommend a proper federal system to all the sincere and considerate friends of republican government, since it shows that in exact proportion as the territory of the Union may be formed into more circumscribed Confederacies, or States oppressive combinations of a majority will be facilitated: the best security, under the republican forms, for the rights of every class of citizens, will be diminished: and consequently the stability and independence of some member of the government, the only other security, must be proportionately increased. Justice is the end of government. It is the end of civil society. It ever has been and ever will be pursued until it be obtained, or until liberty be lost in the pursuit. In a society under the forms of which the stronger faction can readily unite and oppress the weaker, anarchy may as truly be said to reign as in a state of nature, where the weaker individual is not secured against the violence of the stronger; and as, in the latter state, even the stronger individuals are prompted, by the uncertainty of their condition, to submit to a government which may protect the weak as well as themselves; so, in the former state, will the more powerful factions or parties be gradually induced, by a like motive, to wish for a government which will protect all parties, the weaker as well as the more powerful.

It can be little doubted that if the State of Rhode Island was separated from the Confederacy and left to itself, the insecurity of rights under the popular form of government within such narrow limits would be displayed by such reiterated oppressions of factious majorities that some power altogether independent of the people would soon be called for by the voice of the very factions whose misrule had proved the necessity of it. In the extended republic of the United States, and among the great variety of interests, parties, and sects which it embraces, a coalition of a majority of the whole society could seldom take place on any other principles than those of justice and the general good; whilst there being thus less danger to a minor from the will of a major party, there must be less pretext, also, to provide for the security of the former, by introducing into the government a will not dependent on the latter, or, in other words, a will independent of the society itself. It is no less certain than it is important, notwithstanding the contrary opinions which have been entertained, that the larger the society, provided it lie within a practical sphere, the more duly capable it will be of self-government. And happily for the REPUBLICAN CAUSE, the practicable sphere may be carried to a very great extent, by a judicious modification and mixture of the FEDERAL PRINCIPLE.

PUBLIUS.

APPENDIX 6 POLITICAL PARTY AFFILIATIONS IN CONGRESS AND THE PRESIDENCY, 1789-2017

Year	Congress	House Majority party	Principal minority party	Senate Majority party	Principal minority party	President
1789–1791	1st	AD-38	Op-26	AD-17	Op-9	F (Washington)
1791–1793	2nd	F-37	DR-33	F-16	DR-13	F (Washington)
1793–1795	3rd	DR-57	F-48	F-17	DR-13	F (Washington)
1795–1797	4th	F-54	DR-52	F-19	DR-13	F (Washington)
1797–1799	5th	F-58	DR-48	F-20	DR-12	F (John Adams)
1799–1801	6th	F-64	DR-42	F-19	DR-13	F (John Adams)
1801–1803	7th	DR-69	F-36	DR-18	F-13	DR (Jefferson)
1803–1805	8th	DR-102	F-39	DR-25	F-9	DR (Jefferson)
1805–1807	9th	DR-116	F-25	DR-27	F-7	DR (Jefferson)
1807–1809	10th	DR-118	F-24	DR-28	F-6	DR (Jefferson)
1809–1811	11th	DR-94	F-48	DR-28	F-6	DR (Madison)
1811–1813	12th	DR-108	F-36	DR-30	F-6	DR (Madison)
1813–1815	13th	DR-112	F-68	DR-27	F-9	DR (Madison)
1815–1817	14th	DR-117	F-65	DR-25	F-11	DR (Madison)
1817–1819	15th	DR-141	F-42	DR-34	F-10	DR (Monroe)
1819–1821	16th	DR-156	F-27	DR-35	F-7	DR (Monroe)
1821–1823	17th	DR-158	F-25	DR-44	F-4	DR (Monroe)
1823–1825	18th	DR-187	F-26	DR-44	F-4	DR (Monroe)
1825–1827	19th	AD-105	J-97	AD-26	J-20	DR (John Q. Adams)
1827–1829	20th	J-119	AD-94	J-28	AD-20	DR (John Q. Adams)
1829–1831	21st	D-139	NR-74	D-26	NR-22	DR (Jackson)
1831–1833	22nd	D-141	NR-58	D-25	NR-21	D (Jackson)
1833–1835	23rd	D-147	AM-53	D-20	NR-20	D (Jackson)
1835–1837	24th	D-145	W-98	D-27	W-25	D (Jackson)
1837–1839	25th	D-108	W-107	D-30	W-18	D (Van Buren)
1839–1841	26th	D-124	W-118	D-28	W-22	D (Van Buren)
1841–1843	27th	W-133	D-102	W-28	D-22	W (W. Harrison)
						W (Tyler)
1843–1845	28th	D-142	W-79	W-28	D-25	W (Tyler)
1845–1847	29th	D-143	W-77	D-31	W-25	D (Polk)

(Continued)

Year	Congress	House Majority party	Principal minority party	Senate Majority party	Principal minority party	President
1847–1849	30th	W-115	D-108	D-36	W-21	D (Polk)
1849–1851	31st	D-112	W-109	D-35	W-25	W (Taylor)
						W (Fillmore)
1851–1853	32nd	D-140	W-88	D-35	W-24	W (Fillmore)
1853–1855	33rd	D-159	W-71	D-38	W-22	D (Pierce)
1855–1857	34th	R-108	D-83	D-42	R-15	D (Pierce)
1857–1859	35th	D-131	R-92	D-35	R-20	D (Buchanan)
1859–1861	36th	R-113	D-101	D-38	R-26	D (Buchanan)
1861–1863	37th	R-106	D-42	R-31	D-11	R (Lincoln)
1863–1865	38th	R-103	D-80	R-39	D-12	R (Lincoln)
1865–1867[1]	39th	U-145	D-46	U-42	D-10	U (Lincoln)
						U (A. Johnson)
1867–1869	40th	R-143	D-49	R-42	D-11	R (A. Johnson)
1869–1871	41st	R-170	D-73	R-61	D-11	R (Grant)
1871–1873	42nd	R-139	D-104	R-57	D-17	R (Grant)
1873–1875	43rd	R-203	D-88	R-54	D-19	R (Grant)
1875–1877	44th	D-181	R-107	R-46	D-29	R (Grant)
1877–1879	45th	D-156	R-137	R-39	D-36	R (Hayes)
1879–1881	46th	D-150	R-128	D-43	R-33	R (Hayes)
1881–1883	47th	R-152	D-130	R-37	D-37	R (Garfield)
						R (Arthur)
1883–1885	48th	D-200	R-119	R-40	D-36	R (Arthur)
1885–1887	49th	D-182	R-140	R-41	D-34	D (Cleveland)
1887–1889	50th	D-170	R-151	R-39	D-37	D (Cleveland)
1889–1891	51st	R-173	D-159	R-37	D-37	R (B. Harrison)
1891–1893	52nd	D-231	R-88	R-47	D-39	R (B. Harrison)
1893–1895	53rd	D-220	R-126	D-44	R-38	D (Cleveland)
1895–1897	54th	R-246	D-104	R-43	D-39	D (Cleveland)
1897–1899	55th	R-206	D-134	R-46	D-34	R (McKinley)
1899–1901	56th	R-185	D-163	R-53	D-26	R (McKinley)
1901–1903	57th	R-198	D-153	R-56	D-29	R (McKinley)
						R (T. Roosevelt)
1903–1905	58th	R-207	D-178	R-58	D-32	R (T. Roosevelt)
1905–1907	59th	R-250	D-136	R-58	D-32	R (T. Roosevelt)
1907–1909	60th	R-222	D-164	R-61	D-29	R (T. Roosevelt)
1909–1911	61st	R-219	D-172	R-59	D-32	R (Taft)
1911–1913	62nd	D-228	R-162	R-49	D-42	R (Taft)
1913–1915	63rd	D-290	R-127	D-51	R-44	D (Wilson)
1915–1917	64th	D-231	R-193	D-56	R-39	D (Wilson)

Year	Congress	House Majority party	Principal minority party	Senate Majority party	Principal minority party	President
1917–1919	65th	D-216	R-210	D-53	R-42	D (Wilson)
1919–1921	66th	R-237	D-191	R-48	D-47	D (Wilson)
1921–1923	67th	R-300	D-132	R-59	D-37	R (Harding)
1923–1925	68th	R-225	D-207	R-51	D-43	R (Coolidge)
1925–1927	69th	R-247	D-183	R-54	D-40	R (Coolidge)
1927–1929	70th	R-237	D-195	R-48	D-47	R (Coolidge)
1929–1931	71st	R-267	D-163	R-56	D-39	R (Hoover)
1931–1933	72nd	D-216	R-218	R-48	D-47	R (Hoover)
1933–1935	73rd	D-313	R-117	D-59	R-36	D (F. Roosevelt)
1935–1937	74th	D-322	R-103	D-69	R-25	D (F. Roosevelt)
1937–1939	75th	D-333	R-89	D-75	R-17	D (F. Roosevelt)
1939–1941	76th	D-262	R-169	D-69	R-23	D (F. Roosevelt)
1941–1943	77th	D-267	R-162	D-66	R-28	D (F. Roosevelt)
1943–1945	78th	D-222	R-209	D-57	R-38	D (F. Roosevelt)
1945–1947	79th	D-243	R-190	D-56	R-38	D (F. Roosevelt)
						D (Truman)
1947–1949	80th	R-246	D-188	R-51	D-45	D (Truman)
1949–1951	81st	D-263	R-171	D-54	R-42	D (Truman)
1951–1953	82nd	D-234	R-199	D-48	R-47	D (Truman)
1953–1955	83rd	R-221	D-213	R-48	D-46	R (Eisenhower)
1955–1957	84th	D-234	R-201	D-48	R-47	R (Eisenhower)
1957–1959	85th	D-233	R-200	D-49	R-47	R (Eisenhower)
1959–1961	86th	D-283	R-153	D-64	R-34	R (Eisenhower)
1961–1963	87th	D-262	R-175	D-64	R-36	D (Kennedy)
1963–1965	88th	D-258	R-176	D-67	R-33	D (Kennedy)
						D (L. Johnson)
1965–1967	89th	D-295	R-140	D-68	R-32	D (L. Johnson)
1967–1969	90th	D-248	R-187	D-64	R-36	D (L. Johnson)
1969–1971	91st	D-243	R-192	D-58	R-42	R (Nixon)
1971–1973	92nd	D-255	R-180	D-54	R-44	R (Nixon)
1973–1975	93rd	D-242	R-192	D-56	R-42	R (Nixon)
						R (Ford)
1975–1977	94th	D-291	R-144	D-60	R-37	R (Ford)
1977–1979	95th	D-292	R-143	D-61	R-38	D (Carter)
1979–1981	96th	D-277	R-158	D-58	R-41	D (Carter)
1981–1983	97th	D-242	R-192	R-53	D-46	R (Reagan)
1983–1985	98th	D-269	R-166	R-54	D-46	R (Reagan)
1985–1987	99th	D-253	R-182	R-53	D-47	R (Reagan)
1987–1989	100th	D-258	R-177	D-55	R-45	R (Reagan)

(Continued)

(Continued)

Year	Congress	House Majority party	Principal minority party	Senate Majority party	Principal minority party	President
1989–1991	101st	D-260	R-175	D-55	R-45	R (G. H. W. Bush)
1991–1993	102nd	D-267	R-167	D-56	R-44	R (G. H. W. Bush)
1993–1995	103rd	D-258	R-176	D-57	R-43	D (Clinton)
1995–1997	104th	R-230	D-204	R-52	D-48	D (Clinton)
1997–1999	105th	R-226	D-207	R-55	D-45	D (Clinton)
1999–2001	106th	R-223	D-211	R-55	D-45	D (Clinton)
2001–2003	107th	R-221	D-212	D-50	R-50	R (G. W. Bush)
2003–2005	108th	R-229	D-204	R-51	D-48	R (G. W. Bush)
2005–2007	109th	R-232	D-202	R-55	D-44	R (G. W. Bush)
2007–2009	110th	D-233	R-202	D-49	R-49	R (G. W. Bush)
2009–2011	111th	D-254	R-175	D-57	R-40	D (Obama)
*2011–2013	112th	D-193	R-242	D-53	R-47	D (Obama)
2013–2015	113th	R-232	D-200	D-53	R-45	D (Obama)
2015–2017	114th	R-246	D-188	R-54	D-44	D (Obama)
2017–	115th	R-241	D-194	R-52	D-46	R (Trump)

Sources: For data through the 33rd Congress, see U.S. Bureau of the Census, *Historical Statistics of the United States, Colonial Times to 1970* (Washington, D.C.: Government Printing Office, 1975), 1083–1084; for data after the 33rd Congress, see U.S. Congress, Joint Committee on Printing, *Official Congressional Directory* (Washington, D.C.: Government Printing Office, 2008), 553–554; for 2008 election data see CQ *Politics Election 2008*, www .cqpolitics.com/wmspage.cfn?parm1=2. See also http://innovation.cq.com/ election_night08?tab2=f; for 2010 election data, see http://www.rollcall.com/politics/. For 2012 election data, see the Office of the Clerk of the U.S. House of Representatives, http://clerk.house.gov/member_info/cong.aspx.

Notes: Figures are for the beginning of the first session of each Congress. Key to abbreviations: AD–Administration; AM–Anti-Masonic;

D–Democratic; DR–Democratic-Republican; F–Federalist; J–Jacksonian; NR–National Republican; Op–Opposition; R–Republican;

U–Unionist; W–Whig.

1. The Republican Party ran under the Union Party banner in 1864.

APPENDIX 7   SUMMARY OF PRESIDENTIAL ELECTIONS, 1789-2016

Year	No. of states	Candidates		Electoral vote		Popular vote	
1789[a]	10	Fed.		Fed.		—[b]	
		George Washington		69			
1792[a]	15	Fed.		Fed.		—[b]	
		George Washington		132			
1796[a]	16	Dem.-Rep.	Fed.	Dem.-Rep.	Fed.	—[b]	
		Thomas Jefferson	John Adams	68	71		
1800[a]	16	Dem.-Rep.	Fed.	Dem.-Rep	Fed.	—[b]	
		Thomas Jefferson	John Adams	73	65		
		Aaron Burr	Charles Cotesworth Pinckney				
1804	17	Dem.-Rep.	Fed.	Dem.-Rep	Fed.	—[b]	
		Thomas Jefferson	Charles Cotesworth Pinckney	162	14		
		George Clinton	Rufus King				
1808	17	Dem.-Rep.	Fed.	Dem.-Rep	Fed.	—[b]	
		James Madison	Charles Cotesworth Pinckney	122	47		
		George Clinton	Rufus King				
1812	18	Dem.-Rep.	Fed.	Dem.-Rep	Fed.	—[b]	
		James Madison	George Clinton	128	89		
		Elbridge Gerry	Jared Ingersoll				
1816	19	Dem.-Rep.	Fed.	Dem.-Rep	Fed.	—[b]	
		James Monroe	Rufus King	183	34		
		Daniel D. Tompkins	John Howard				
1820	24	Dem.-Rep	—[c]	Dem.-Rep	—[c]	—[b]	
		James Monroe		231			
		Daniel D. Tompkins					
1824[d]	24	Dem.-Rep	Dem.-Rep	Dem.-Rep	Dem.-Rep.	Dem.-Rep	Dem.-Rep
		Andrew Jackson	John Q. Adams	99	84	151,271	113,122
		John C. Calhoun	Nathan Sanford			41.3%	30.9%
1828	24	Dem.-Rep.	Nat.-Rep.	Dem.-Rep.	Nat.-Rep.	Dem.-Rep.	Nat.-Rep.
		Andrew Jackson	John Q. Adams	178	83	642,553	500,897
		John C. Calhoun	Richard Rush			56.0%	43.6%
1832[e]	24	Dem.	Nat.-Rep.	Dem.	Nat.-Rep.	Dem.	Nat.-Rep.
		Andrew Jackson	Henry Clay	219	49	701,780	484,205
		Martin Van Buren	John Sergeant		54.2%		37.4%

(Continued)

(Continued)

Year	No. of states	Candidates		Electoral vote		Popular vote	
		Dem.	**Whig**	**Dem.**	**Whig**	**Dem.**	**Whig**
1836[f]	26	Martin Van Buren Richard M. Johnson	William H. Harrison Francis Granger	170	73	764,176 50.8%	550,816 36.6%
1840	26	Martin Van Buren Richard M. Johnson	William H. Harrison John Tyler	60	234	1,128,854 46.8%	1,275,390 52.9%
1844	26	James Polk George M. Dallas	Henry Clay Theodore Frelinghuysen	170	105	1,339,494 49.5%	1,300,004 48.1%
1848	30	Lewis Cass William O. Butler	Zachary Taylor Millard Fillmore	127	163	1,233,460 42.5%	1,361,393 47.3%
1852	31	Franklin Pierce William R. King	Winfield Scott William A. Graham	254	42	1,607,510 50.8%	1,386,942 43.9%

Year	No. of states	Candidates		Electoral vote		Popular vote	
		Dem.	**Rep.**	**Dem.**	**Rep.**	**Dem.**	**Rep.**
1856[g]	31	James Buchanan John C. Breckinridge	John C. Fremont William L. Dayton	174	114	1,836,072 45.3%	1,342,345 33.1%
1860[h]	33	Stephen A. Douglas Herschel V. Johnson	Abraham Lincoln Hannibal Hamlin	12	180	1,380,202 29.5%	1,865,908 39.8%
1864[i]	36	George B. McClellan George H. Pendleton	Abraham Lincoln Andrew Johnson	21	212	1,812,807 45.0%	2,218,388 55.0%
1868[j]	37	Horatio Seymour Francis P. Blair Jr.	Ulysses S. Grant Schuyler Colfax	80	214	2,708,744 47.3%	3,013,650 52.7%
1872[k]	37	Horace Greeley Benjamin Gratz Brown	Ulysses S. Grant Henry Wilson		286	2,834,761 43.8%	3,598,235 55.6%
1876	38	Samuel J. Tilden Thomas A. Hendricks	Rutherford B. Hayes William A. Wheeler	184	185	4,288,546 51.0%	4,034,311 47.9%
1880	38	Winfield S. Hancock William H. English	James A. Garfield Chester A. Arthur	155	214	4,444,260 48.2%	4,446,158 48.3%
1884	38	Grover Cleveland Thomas A. Hendricks	James G. Blaine John A. Logan	219	182	4,874,621 48.5%	4,848,936 48.2%
1888	38	Grover Cleveland Allen G. Thurman	Benjamin Harrison Levi P. Morton	168	233	5,534,488 48.6%	5,443,892 47.8%
1892[l]	44	Grover Cleveland Adlai E. Stevenson	Benjamin Harrison Whitelaw Reid	277	145	5,551,883 46.1%	5,179,244 43.0%
1896	45	William J. Bryan Arthur Sewall	William McKinley Garret A. Hobart	176	271	6,511,495 46.7%	7,108,480 51.0%
1900	45	William J. Bryan Adlai E. Stevenson	William McKinley Theodore Roosevelt	155	292	6,358,345 45.5%	7,218,039 51.7%
1904	45	Alton B. Parker Henry G. Davis	Theodore Roosevelt Charles W. Fairbanks	140	336	5,028,898 37.6%	7,626,593 56.4%

Year	No. of states	Candidates Dem.	Candidates Rep.	Electoral vote Dem.	Electoral vote Rep.	Popular vote Dem.	Popular vote Rep.
		John W. Kern	James S. Sherman			43.0%	51.6%
1912[m]	48	Woodrow Wilson	William H. Taft	435	8	6,293,152	3,486,333
		Thomas R. Marshall	James S. Sherman			41.8%	23.2%
1916	48	Woodrow Wilson	Charles E. Hughes	277	254	9,126,300	8,546,789
		Thomas R. Marshall	Charles W. Fairbanks			49.2%	46.1%
1920	48	James M. Cox	Warren G. Harding	127	404	9,140,884	16,133,314
		Franklin D. Roosevelt	Calvin Coolidge			34.2%	60.3%
1924[n]	48	John W. Davis	Calvin Coolidge	136	382	8,386,169	15,717,553
		Charles W. Bryant	Charles G. Dawes			28.8%	54.1%
1928	48	Alfred E. Smith	Herbert C. Hoover	87	444	15,000,185	21,411,991
		Joseph T. Robinson	Charles Curtis			40.8%	58.2%
1932	48	Franklin D. Roosevelt	Herbert C. Hoover	472	59	22,825,016	15,758,397
		John N. Garner	Charles Curtis			57.4%	39.6%
1936	48	Franklin D. Roosevelt	Alfred M. Landon	523	8	27,747,636	16,679,543
		John N. Garner	Frank Knox			60.8%	36.5%
1940	48	Franklin D. Roosevelt	Wendell L. Willkie	449	82	27,263,448	22,336,260
		Henry A. Wallace	Charles L. McNary			54.7%	44.8%
1944	48	Franklin D. Roosevelt	Thomas E. Dewey	432	99	25,611,936	22,013,372
		Harry S. Truman	John W. Bricker			53.4%	45.9%
1948[o]	48	Harry S. Truman	Thomas E. Dewey	303	189	24,105,587	21,970,017
		Alben W. Barkley	Earl Warren			49.5%	45.1%
1952	48	Adlai E. Stevenson II	Dwight D. Eisenhower	89	442	27,314,649	33,936,137
		John J. Sparkman	Richard M. Nixon			44.4%	55.1%
1956[p]	48	Adlai E. Stevenson II	Dwight D. Eisenhower	73	457	26,030,172	35,585,245
		Estes Kefauver	Richard M. Nixon			42.0%	57.4%
1960[q]	50	John F. Kennedy	Richard M. Nixon	303	219	34,221,344	34,106,671
		Lyndon B. Johnson	Henry Cabot Lodge			49.7%	49.5%
1964	50*	Lyndon B. Johnson	Barry Goldwater	486	52	43,126,584	27,177,838
		Hubert H. Humphrey	William E. Miller			61.1%	38.5%
1968[r]	50*	Hubert H. Humphrey	Richard M. Nixon	191	301	31,274,503	31,785,148
		Edmund S. Muskie	Spiro T. Agnew			42.7%	43.4%
1972[s]	50*	George McGovern	Richard M. Nixon	17	520	29,171,791	47,170,179
		Sargent Shriver	Spiro T. Agnew			37.5%	60.7%
1976[t]	50*	Jimmy Carter	Gerald R. Ford	297	240	40,830,763	39,147,793
		Walter F. Mondale	Robert Dole			50.1%	48.0%
1980	50*	Jimmy Carter	Ronald Reagan	49	489	35,483,883	43,904,153
		Walter F. Mondale	George H. W. Bush			41.0%	50.7%
1984	50*	Walter F. Mondale	Ronald Reagan	13	525	37,577,185	54,455,075
		Geraldine Ferraro	George H. W. Bush			40.6%	58.8%
1988[u]	50*	Michael S. Dukakis	George H. W. Bush	111	426	41,809,074	48,886,097
		Lloyd Bentsen	Dan Quayle			45.6%	53.4%
1992	50*	William J. Clinton	George H. W. Bush	370	168	44,909,326	39,103,882
		Albert Gore	Dan Quayle			43.0%	37.4%

(Continued)

(Continued)

Year	No. of states	Candidates Dem.	Candidates Rep.	Electoral vote Dem.	Electoral vote Rep.	Popular vote Dem.	Popular vote Rep.
		Albert Gore	Jack F. Kemp			49.2%	40.7%
2000	50*	Albert Gore	George W. Bush	266	271	50,992,335	50,455,156
		Joseph I. Lieberman	Richard B. Cheney			48.4%	47.9%
2004	50*	John Kerry	George W. Bush	252	286	59,026,013	62,025,554
		John Edwards	Richard B. Cheney			47.3%	50.7%
2008	50*	Barack Obama	John McCain	365	173	69,498,459	59,948,283
		Joe Biden	Sarah Palin			52.9%	45.6%
2012	50*	Barack Obama	Mitt Romney	332	206	62,611,250	59,134,475
		Joe Biden	Paul Ryan			51.5%	48.5%
2016**	50*	Hillary Clinton	Donald Trump	232	306	64,827,442	62,494,402
		Tim Kaine	Mike Pence			(48.2%)	(46.4%)

Sources: Harold W. Stanley and Richard G. Niemi, *Vital Statistics on American Politics, 2007–2008* (Washington, D.C.: CQ Press, 2008), 26–30; *CQ Press Guide to U.S. Elections*, 5th ed. (Washington, D.C.: CQ Press, 2006), 715–719; for the 2008 election: for presidential race electoral vote data, see *CQ Politics Election 2008*, http://innovation.cq.com/election_night08?tab2=f. For presidential race popular vote data, see the *New York Times*'s Presidential Big Board, http://elections.nytimes.com/2008/results/ president/votes.html. 2012 election data calculated from Politico, 2012 Presidential Election, http://www.politico.com/2012-election/ map/#/President/2012/.

Note: Dem.-Rep.—Democratic-Republican; Fed.—Federalist; Nat.-Rep.—National-Republican; Dem.—Democratic; Rep.—Republican.

a. Elections from 1789 through 1800 were held under rules that did not allow separate voting for president and vice president.

b. Popular vote returns are not shown before 1824 because consistent, reliable data are not available.

c. 1820: One electoral vote was cast for John Adams and Richard Stockton, who were not candidates.

d. 1824: All four candidates represented Democratic-Republican factions. William H. Crawford received 41 electoral votes and Henry Clay received 37 votes. Because no candidate received a majority, the election was decided (in Adams's favor) by the House of Representatives.

e. 1832: Two electoral votes were not cast.

f. 1836: Other Whig candidates receiving electoral votes were Hugh L. White, who received 26 votes, and Daniel Webster, who received 14 votes.

g. 1856: Millard Fillmore, Whig-American, received 8 electoral votes.

h. 1860: John C. Breckinridge, southern Democrat, received 72 electoral votes. John Bell, Constitutional Union, received 39 electoral votes.

i. 1864: Eighty-one electoral votes were not cast.

j. 1868: Twenty-three electoral votes were not cast.

k. 1872: Horace Greeley, Democrat, died after the election. In the Electoral College, Democratic electoral votes went to Thomas Hendricks, 42 votes; Benjamin Gratz Brown, 18 votes; Charles J. Jenkins, 2 votes; and David Davis, 1 vote. Seventeen electoral votes were not cast.

l. 1892: James B. Weaver, People's Party, received 22 electoral votes.

m. 1912: Theodore Roosevelt, Progressive Party, received 88 electoral votes.

n. 1924: Robert M. La Follette, Progressive Party, received 13 electoral votes.

o. 1948: J. Strom Thurmond, States' Rights Party, received 39 electoral votes.

p. 1956: Walter B. Jones, Democrat, received 1 electoral vote.

q. 1960: Harry Flood Byrd, Democrat, received 15 electoral votes.

r. 1968: George C. Wallace, American Independent Party, received 46 electoral votes.

s. 1972: John Hospers, Libertarian Party, received 1 electoral vote.

t. 1976: Ronald Reagan, Republican, received 1 electoral vote.

u. 1988: Lloyd Bentsen, the Democratic vice-presidential nominee, received 1 electoral vote for president.

* Fifty states plus the District of Columbia.

**Election data current as of November 29, 2016.

GLOSSARY

absentee ballots
votes completed and submitted by a voter prior to the day of an election.

abolitionist movement
a political struggle to end slavery and free all slaves.

achievement gap
the persistent differences in school performance of students of majority ethnicity and higher incomes versus those of minority ethnicity and lower incomes.

adversarial system
a legal structure in which two opposing sides present their case in the most persuasive way possible.

affirmative action
a policy designed to address the consequences of previous discrimination by providing advantages to individuals based upon their identities.

agency capture
a problem that occurs when a bureaucrat's own interests are more closely aligned with the targets of regulation than the mission of the agency, thus undermining effective regulation.

agency capture
when agencies tasked with regulating businesses, industries, or other interest groups are populated by individuals with close ties to the very firms that they are supposed to regulate.

agenda setting
the media's ability to highlight certain issues and bring them to the attention of the public.

aggregating
a process through which Internet and other news providers relay the news as reported by journalists and other sources.

The Alien and Sedition Acts
four separate laws passed under the administration of President John Adams that, among other things, restricted the freedom of speech and the press.

the American dream
The idea that individuals should be able to achieve prosperity through hard work, sacrifice, and their own talents.

amendment
a constitutional provision for a process by which changes may be made to the Constitution.

Albany Plan
a proposal for a union of British colonies in North America in which colonial legislatures would choose delegates to form an assembly under the leadership of a chief executive appointed by Great Britain.

American exceptionalism
the belief in the special character of the United States as a uniquely free nation based on its history and its commitment to democratic ideals and personal liberty.

American political culture
a shared set of beliefs, customs, traditions, and values that define the relationship of Americans to their government and to other American citizens.

Antifederalists
the name taken by those opposed to the proposed Constitution; the Antifederalists favored stronger state governments.

appellate jurisdiction
the authority of a court to hear and review decisions made by lower courts in that system.

apportionment
the process of determining the number of representatives for each state using census data; states are divided into congressional districts that have at least one representative each.

appropriation
the process through which congressional committees allocate funds to executive branch agencies, bureaus, and departments.

Arab Spring
a series of protests taking place across North Africa and the Middle East beginning in early 2010 that led to democratic reforms in some nations and civil war and chaos in others.

Articles of Confederation and Perpetual Union
a constituting document calling for the creation of a union of thirteen sovereign states in which the states, not the union, were supreme.

Astroturf lobbying
when a group presents the façade of grassroots support that does not exist on its own or would not exist without the "purchase" of support by the lobbying firm itself.

bail
an amount of money posted as a security to allow the charged individual to be freed while awaiting trial.

ballot roll-off
when voters do not cast votes for a set of races with which they are not familiar and for which they may not have traditional cues.

bill of rights
a list of fundamental rights and freedoms that individuals possess. The first ten amendments to the United States Constitution are referred to as the Bill of Rights.

bipolarity
a distribution of power in the international system where two states exert most of the power and influence.

block grant
a type of grant-in-aid that gives state officials more authority in the disbursement of the federal funds.

brief
legal document presented by plaintiffs, defendants, and, at times, other interested parties outlining their arguments in a case.

broadcast media
outlets for news and other content that rely on mass communications technology to bring stories directly into people's homes; these media sources are subject to stricter content regulations than cable television outlets and alternative sources of information.

Brown v. Board of Education
a landmark 1954 Supreme Court ruling that overturned _Plessy v. Ferguson_ and declared legal segregation in public education to be in conflict with the equal protection clause of the Fourteenth Amendment.

budget deficit
when the federal government takes in less money than it spends.

budget resolution
a step in the budgeting process in which Congress provides broad outlines for federal spending.

budget surplus
when the federal government takes in more money than it spends.

bureaucrat
an official employed within a government bureaucracy.

bureaucratic adjudication
when the federal bureaucracy settles disputes between parties that arise over the implementation of federal laws and presidential executive orders or determine which individuals or groups are covered under a regulation or program.

bureaucratic discretion

the power to decide how a law is implemented and, at times, what Congress actually meant when it passed a given law.

bureaucratic drift

when bureaucracies stray from their established goals and devote their energies and efforts to peripheral tasks.

business cycle

the fluctuation of economic activity around a long-term trend, with periods of expansion and contraction.

capitalist system

a way of structuring economic activity in which private firms are allowed to make most or all of the decisions involving the production and distribution of goods and services.

categorical grants

grants-in-aid provided to states with specific provisions on their use.

caucus

a process through which a state's eligible voters gather to discuss candidates and issues and select delegates to represent their preferences in later stages of the nomination process.

Central Intelligence Agency (CIA)

the federal agency charged with collecting intelligence around the world to protect national security.

certiorari

the process through which most cases reach the Supreme Court; after four justices concur that the Court should hear the case, a writ of certiorari is issued to the lower court to request the relevant case records.

challenger

a candidate for office who does not currently hold office.

charter schools

public schools that are funded only by taxpayer money and subject to many of the same regulations as traditional public schools but that are accountable primarily to their founding document (their charter) and that have greater curricular and professional autonomy.

citizen journalists

nonprofessionals who cover or document news and events or offer their own analyses of them.

civic education

the transmission of information about the political world and civic norms to learners.

civic engagement

working to improve society through political and nonpolitical action.

civil disobedience

the intentional refusal to obey a law in order to call attention to its injustice.

civil disobedience

an intentional breaking of a law for the purpose of calling attention to an injustice.

civil law

a category of law covering cases involving private rights and relationships between individuals and groups.

civil liberties

fundamental rights and freedoms of citizens the protection of which involves restricting the power of a government.

civil rights

fundamental guarantees ensuring equal treatment and protecting against discrimination under the laws of a nation.

clear and present danger test

a Supreme Court tool to evaluate whether or not forms of political expression constitute such a threat to national security as to warrant restriction.

clientele agencies

organizations that act to serve and promote the interests of their clients.

closed primary

a primary election in which only registered voters from a particular political party may vote.

cloture

a procedure through which senators can end debate on a bill and proceed to action, provided three-fifths of senators agree to it.

coattail effect

a phenomenon that occurs when a presidential candidate's increasing popularity results in increased support for congressional candidates of the same party.

Cold War

the period of time between 1945 and 1991 characterized by conflict between the United States and its allies and the Soviet Union and its allies but that did not result in full global war.

collective action

political action that occurs when individuals contribute their energy, time, or money to a larger group goal.

collective good

also called a public good; some benefit or desirable outcome that individuals can enjoy or profit from even if they do not help achieve or secure it.

command-and-control economy

a type of economic policy in which government dictates much of a nation's economic activity, including the amount of production and prices for goods.

commerce clause

a part of the Constitution that grants Congress the authority to regulate business and commercial activity.

commercial bias

the shaping of the content and focus of news based upon the desire to capture news consumers.

committee chairs

leaders of the subunits of congressional committees who have authority over the committee's agenda.

Committee on Rules (House)

a powerful committee that determines when a bill will be subject to debate and vote on the House floor, how long the debate will last, and whether amendments will be allowed on the floor.

communist system

a way of structuring economic activity in which a government exerts complete control over the production and distribution of goods and services.

concurrent powers

powers granted to both states and the federal government in the Constitution.

confederal systems

structures of governance in which the subnational governments retain the majority of the granted authority.

Congressional Budget Office (CBO)

the federal agency tasked with producing independent analyses of budgetary and economic issues to support the congressional budget process.

consideration

a combination of cognition and affect that contributes to any one answer to any one question or evaluation.

constituencies

bodies of voters in a given area who elect a representative or senator.

constitution

A document that defines and creates a people politically, sets out the fundamental principles of governance, and creates the rules and institutions through which a people choose to self-govern.

Constitutional Convention

a meeting held in Philadelphia in 1787 at which state delegates met to fix the Articles of Confederation.

constitutional interpretation

the process of applying the Constitution in assessing whether or not a law, part of a law, or an action by a governmental official is or is not in conflict with that of the Constitution.

constitutional republic

a form of government in which people vote for elected representatives to make laws and policies and in which limits on the ability of that government to restrict individual rights are placed in a constituting document that is recognized as the highest law of the land.

consumer price index (CPI)

an economic measure that is used to assess price changes associated with the cost of living.

containment
a Cold War foreign policy strategy designed to restrict expansion of Soviet ideological and military influence, using military force if necessary.

cooperative federalism
a vision of American federalism in which the states and the national government work together to shape public policy.

criminal law
a category of law covering actions determined to harm the community itself.

critical election
a major national election that signals a change either in the balance of power between two major parties or the emergence of a new party system.

Daughters of Liberty
a group of colonial-era women who participated in the boycotting of British goods.

de facto segregation
a separation of individuals based on identity that arises not by law but because of other factors, such as residential housing patterns.

defendant
a person or group against whom a case is brought in court.

deflation
when a cascading series of defaults arises because there is not enough money to pay off outstanding debt.

de jure segregation
the separation of individuals based on their characteristics, such as race, intentionally and by law.

delegates
people who act as voters' representatives at a convention to select their party's presidential nominee.

democracy
a system of government where power is held and political decisions made by the people in that society.

demographics
the grouping of individuals based on shared characteristics, such as ancestry, race, ethnicity, and gender.

Department of Defense
the executive branch department responsible for formulating and enacting American defense policy and managing the United States Armed Forces.

Department of Homeland Security
the executive branch department responsible for overseeing and implementing policies enacted to respond to national disasters, secure transit points to and within the United States, and protect the nation's borders.

Department of State
the cabinet department primarily responsible for diplomatic relationships with other nations.

deregulation
the reduction or elimination of government power in a particular industry, usually in order to create more competition within the industry.

descriptive representation
the degree to which a body of representatives in a legislature does or does not reflect the diversity of that nation's identities and lived experiences.

desegregation
the act of eliminating laws or practices that separate individuals based upon racial identity.

devolution
a national policy goal of returning more authority to state or local governments.

devolution
the transfer of power over public policy back to the states in order to shrink the size of the federal government and allow states to have more authority to determine how taxpayer dollars should be spent.

digital divide
divisions in society that are driven by access to and knowledge about technologies; these gaps often fall along the lines of partisanship, class, race, and ethnicity.

direct democracy
a political system in which citizens vote directly on public policies.

direction
the focus of an individual's opinion.

director of national intelligence
the head of all of the intelligence agencies in the United States.

discretionary spending
spending for programs and policies at the discretion of Congress and the president.

divided government
a situation that occurs when control of the presidency and one or both chambers of Congress is split between the two major parties.

domestic policy
policy designed to improve the social welfare of citizens.

double jeopardy
the prosecution of an individual more than once for the same crime.

dual federalism
a view of American federalism in which the states and the nation operate independently in their own areas of public policy.

due process clause
the clause in the Fourteenth Amendment that restricts state governments from denying their citizens the right to due process of law.

earmark
an addition to a piece of legislation that directs specific funds to projects within districts or states.

economic equality
when wealth is relatively evenly distributed across society.

economic interest groups
groups that organize to advocate on behalf of the economic interests of their members.

economic policy
the efforts of government to regulate and support the economy in order to protect and expand citizens' financial well-being and economic prospects and to support businesses in the global financial system.

economic recession
a period of decline in economic activity, typically defined by two consecutive quarters of negative GDP growth.

economy
the systems and organizations through which a society produces and distributes goods and services.

Electoral College
a process for electing the president that involves the voting population choosing a slate of electors who are pledged to vote for a nominee in the presidential election.

elites
a small number of individuals (who tend to have well-informed and well-reasoned opinions).

elitist theory
a theory of governmental influence that focuses on the advantages that certain interests have in the political process based on the unequal distribution of economic and political power.

entitlement programs
programs wherein one receives a set of benefits regardless of income provided one meets certain categorical requirements, such as age or a minimum number of years of payroll contributions.

enumerated powers
powers explicitly granted to the government via the Constitution.

equal protection clause
a clause of the Fourteenth Amendment that serves as the constitutional basis for the assault on educational segregation in the courts and for the assertion of civil rights for Americans of many different identities in many different areas of public and private life.

Equal Rights Amendment
a proposed but not ratified amendment to the Constitution that sought to guarantee equality of rights based upon sex.

Equal time rule
a regulation that requires American radio and television broadcast networks to provide equal time for political candidates to present their views on issues.

essentialism
the risks posed by linking individuals' lived experiences to policy preferences, whether by identifying those individuals by those policies or excluding them from advocating different policy objectives.

European Union (EU)
an association of European countries formed in the 1990s for the purpose of achieving political and economic integration.

exclusionary rule
a rule governing the inadmissibility of evidence obtained without a proper warrant.

executive agreement
an agreement between a president and another nation that does not have the same durability in the American system as a treaty but that may carry important foreign policy consequences.

executive branch
the branch of government charged with putting the nation's laws into effect.

executive branch
the institution responsible for carrying out laws passed by the legislative branch.

Executive Office of the President
a collection of offices within the White House organization designed primarily to provide information to the president.

executive orders
directions made by presidents to the executive branch departments that often contain nothing more than instructions to be carried out by agencies, bureaus, and departments but that may at times be considered to be acts of presidential lawmaking.

executive political appointees
employees at high levels in the federal bureaucracy who serve at the pleasure of the president and are subject to presidential removal.

executive privilege
a right claimed by presidents to keep confidential certain conversations, records, and transcripts from outside scrutiny, especially that of Congress.

exit poll
a survey conducted outside of a polling place in which individuals are asked who or what they just voted for and why.

exploratory committee
a group that helps determine whether a potential candidate should run for office and that helps lay the groundwork for the campaign.

extended republic
a republic so large and diverse, with so many factions vying for power, that no one faction is able to assert its will over all of the others.

faction
a group of self-interested people who use the government to get what they want, trampling the rights of others in the process.

fairness doctrine
a federal rule that expanded regulations for American political news coverage beyond just the provision of time for candidates to the content of the coverage itself.

faithless elector
a party elector who changes his or her mind in between the general election and the Electoral College vote.

federal bureaucracy
the organizations and suborganizations within the executive branch that are tasked with putting the laws of the nation into effect.

Federal Bureau of Investigation (FBI)
the federal agency charged with carrying out investigations for the attorney general and with safeguarding national security, primarily within the United States.

federal civil service
the permanent professional branches of government concerned with administrative functions, excluding the armed forces and political appointments.

federal courts of appeals
the middle level of the federal judiciary; these courts review and hear appeals from the federal district courts.

federal district courts
the lowest level of the federal judiciary; these courts usually possess original jurisdiction in cases that originate at the federal level.

federalism
a structure of governance that places the people's authority in two or more levels of government.

Federalist Papers
a series of eighty-five essays written by Alexander Hamilton, James Madison, and John Jay and published between 1787 and 1788 that lay out the theory behind the Constitution.

Federalists
the name taken by supporters of the proposed Constitution; the Federalists called for a strong national government.

federal judiciary
the branch of the federal government that interprets and applies the laws of the nation.

Federal Reserve System
the central bank of the United States.

federal systems
structures of governance that divide a people's sovereignty between two or more levels of government.

felon disenfranchisement
the denial of voting rights to Americans who have been convicted of felonies.

Fifteenth Amendment
an amendment to the Constitution passed in 1870 affirming the voting rights of all freedmen.

filibuster
a tactic through which an individual senator may postpone action on a piece of legislation.

fire alarm oversight
a term that describes congressional oversight procedures primarily in response to problems or complaints.

fiscal policy
a set of activities through which government tries to lower unemployment, support economic activity, and stabilize the economy by using policies of taxation and spending.

focus group
a small group of individuals assembled for a directed conversation during which one hopes to uncover patterns of thinking about issues and individuals.

foreign policy
the ways in which political actors in a nation engage others at home and abroad in order to advance their nation's interests, protect and secure national security, and support national commercial interests.

Fourteenth Amendment
an amendment to the Constitution passed in 1868 affirming the citizenship of all persons born or naturalized in the United States and, for the first time in the history of the Constitution, placing explicit restrictions on the laws of states that sought to abridge the privileges and immunities of citizens of the United States.

framing
influencing people's interpretations of news, events, or issues through the presentation of the context.

freedom of expression
a fundamental right affirmed in the First Amendment to speak, publish, and act in the political space.

free riders
individuals who enjoy collective goods without help to secure them.

free trade
a trade policy characterized by few restrictions on the flow of goods and services across national borders.

front-loading
when a state pushes its primary or caucus to a date as early in the season as possible to become more instrumental in the nomination process.

full faith and credit clause
a portion of the Constitution that generally requires states to honor licenses and judicial outcomes of other states.

gender gap
a term that refers to the fact American women are more likely to identify with and vote for Democratic Party candidates than men, who are more likely to vote for Republican Party candidates.

gerrymandering
the intentional use of redistricting to benefit a specific interest or group of voters.

get out the vote (GOTV)

efforts to mobilize voters or potential voters.

going public

a strategy through which presidents reach out directly to the American people with the hope that the people will, in turn, put pressure upon their representatives and senators to press for a president's policy goals.

government

a system of rules and institutions that defines and shapes the contours of public action.

government corporations

organizations that act as businesses within the federal government, charging fees for their services but still subject to governmental control and possible financial subsidization.

government interest groups

organizations that act to secure the interests of local, state, or foreign governments in the political process.

grand jury

a group of citizens who, based on the evidence presented to them, conclude whether or not a person is to be indicted and subsequently tried in a court of law.

grants-in-aid

federal money provided to states to implement public policy objectives.

Great Compromise

an agreement for a plan of government that drew upon both the Virginia and New Jersey Plans; it settled issues of state representation by calling for a bicameral legislature with a House of Representatives apportioned proportionately and a Senate apportioned equally.

The Great Depression

a period defined by the most significant economic crisis in American history.

gridlock

an inability to compromise and enact legislation that is driven by political polarization.

gridlock

a situation in which Congress's ability to legislate is slowed or stopped by its inability to overcome divisions, especially those based on partisanship.

gross domestic product (GDP)

a measure of the total value of goods and services produced by American economic activity.

hate speech

speech that has no other purpose but to express hatred, particularly toward members of a group identified by racial or ethnic identity, gender, or sexual orientation.

horse race phenomenon

coverage of political campaigns that focuses more on the drama of the campaign than on policy issues.

hyperinflation

extremely rapid or out of control inflation brought on by excessive printing of money and a loss of faith in a currency.

implementation

the bureaucracy's role in putting into action the laws that Congress has passed.

Implementation

the enactment of public policies on the ground.

Implied powers

powers not textually granted to a government but considered valid in order to carry out the enumerated powers.

inalienable rights

rights that exist before and above any government or its power.

incentives

inducements that leaders of a bureaucracy can offer to their employees to spur successful performance.

income-based repayment

a type of loan repayment plan in which individual student debtors could have their loan payments reduced and eventually forgiven based on their incomes and ability to pay off these significant debts.

incumbency advantage

institutional advantages held by those already in office who are trying to fend off challengers in an election.

Incumbent

a current officeholder.

incumbent

a political official who is currently in office.

independent executive agency

agencies otherwise similar to cabinet departments but existing outside of the cabinet structure and usually having a narrower focus of mission.

independent regulatory agencies

organizations that exist outside of the major cabinet departments and whose job is to monitor and regulate specific sectors of the economy.

inflation

the rise in the prices of goods and services purchased by individuals.

infotainment

a merging of information and entertainment in a way designed to attract viewers and gain market share.

inside lobbying

when lobbyists contact members of Congress or their staff directly to advocate for their group's position.

intelligence community

the collective name for all of the intelligence agencies in the United States and their members.

intensity

the strength of involvement and preference of an individual's opinion.

interagency rivalry

when two or more agencies are charged with a similar mandate, an outcome that becomes more

likely in times of budget cuts and competition for scarce or dwindling appropriations.

interest groups

voluntary associations of people who come together with an agreed-upon set of political and policy objectives and who attempt to pull the levers of political power in service of these defined goals.

interest rates

the rates paid to borrow money.

intergovernmental lobbying

efforts by state and local governments to act in Washington on behalf of their own interests.

internationalism

an approach to international affairs that emphasizes close contact and cooperation between nations.

Intolerable Acts

a term used in the American colonies to refer to a series of laws enacted by Great Britain in response to the Boston Tea Party.

investigative journalism

an approach to newsgathering in which reporters dig into stories, often looking for instances of corruption or failures to uphold the interests of citizens.

iron triangle

the coordinated (and mutually beneficial) activities of interest groups, Congress, and the bureaucracy to achieve shared policy goals, sometimes against the general interests of society or specific groups within it.

isolationism

a foreign policy orientation in which a nation attempts to stay out of foreign entanglements.

issue network

the webs of influence between interest groups, policymakers, and policy advocates.

Joint Chiefs of Staff

an advisory body reporting to the president on military operations.

judicial activism

a philosophy of constitutional interpretation that asserts justices should wield the power of judicial review when needed.

judicial branch

the institution responsible for hearing and deciding cases via a system of federal courts.

judicial restraint

a philosophy of constitutional interpretation that asserts justices should be cautious in overturning laws.

judicial review

the authority of the highest court in a political system to determine if a law is or is not in conflict with a government's highest law, which in the United States is the Constitution.

laissez-faire economics

a type of economic policy in which governments intrude as little as possible in the economic transactions between citizens and businesses.

legal segregation
the separation by law of individuals based upon their racial identities.

legislative branch
in a divided government, the institution responsible for making laws.

legislative deliberation
the considered argument and discussion of the issues by congressional representatives.

Lemon test
A three-pronged test developed by the Supreme Court to determine whether a law or action by the federal or a state government violates the establishment clause.

libel
expression in written form or similarly published media that defames a person's character.

liberty
social, political, and economic freedoms.

linked fate
a theory of group identification that describes ways in which individuals tie their own life chances to those of a group.

lobbying
interacting with government officials in order to advance a group's goals in the area of public policy.

logroll
an exchange of political favors, such as when legislators trade votes to support one another's proposed legislation.

majority
when a candidate receives more than 50 percent of the vote.

majority-minority district
a district in which voters of a minority ethnicity constitute an electoral majority within that electoral district.

majority party leader
the head of the party with the most seats in Congress, chosen by the party's members.

malapportionment
the uneven distribution of the population between legislative districts.

***Marbury v. Madison* (1803)**
a Supreme Court decision that established judicial review over federal laws.

markup
a process during which a bill is revised prior to a final vote in Congress.

Marshall Plan
a Cold War policy wherein loans and aid were made available to the nations of Western Europe; it also established organizations of economic cooperation.

masses
the majority of individuals (who tend to be less well informed).

mass media
sources of information that appeal to a wide audience, including newspapers, radio, television, and Internet outlets.

material rewards
a type of tangible benefit made available to members and contributors of a group.

media effects
the power of the news media in shaping individuals' political knowledge, preferences, and political behavior.

merit system
a system of hiring and promotion based on competitive testing results, education, and other qualifications rather than politics and personal connections.

minimalist paradigm
a theory of public opinion that emphasizes how most people fall short of what we expect them to know, think about, and pay attention to in the complicated world of politics and policy.

minority party leader
the head of the party with the second-highest number of seats in Congress, chosen by the party's members.

Miranda rights
the right not to speak and to have an attorney present during questioning; these rights must be given by police to individuals suspected of criminal activity.

mixed economy
a type of economic policy in which many economic decisions are left to individuals and businesses, but the federal government also plays a role in shaping these decisions.

monetary policy
a set of economic policy tools designed to regulate the amount of money in the economy (in circulation and in the deposits).

Monroe Doctrine
a policy that asserted American interests in and primacy over actions in the Western hemisphere.

Motor Voter Law
a law allowing Americans to register to vote when applying for or renewing their driver's licenses and making it easier for Americans with disabilities to register to vote.

national convention
a meeting where delegates officially select their party's nominee for the presidency.

national debt
the sum of all previously incurred annual federal deficits.

National Security Council
an advisory body that provides the president with intelligence, analysis, and advice on critical matters of national security.

natural rights
rights that people have inherently that are not granted by any government.

necessary and proper clause
a part of the Constitution that grants the federal government the authority to pass laws required to carry out its enumerated powers. Also called the elastic clause.

need-based assistance
social welfare programs whose benefits are allocated to individuals demonstrating specific needs.

negative campaign advertisements
campaign ads that attack an opponent or opponents and try to raise doubts in voters' minds about them.

negative freedoms
fundamental liberties the protection of which is ensured by restricting governmental action and authority.

net neutrality
a Federal Communications Commission (FCC) rule that requires Internet service providers to treat all data and content providers equally and not discriminate based upon content or bandwidth demands.

neutrality test
a Supreme Court test for examining questions of free expression that allows restrictions upon religious expression, provided that laws doing so not single out one faith, or faith over nonfaith.

The New Deal
a set of policies passed during the administration of President Franklin Roosevelt in order to combat the Great Depression.

New Jersey Plan
a plan of government that preserved many of the provisions in the Articles of Confederation, including the unicameral legislature with equal votes for each states, but that strengthened the confederal government.

news media
the variety of sources providing information and covering events, including newspapers, television, radio, the Internet, and social media.

niche journalism
media that caters to fragmented and specialized audiences.

Nineteenth Amendment
a 1920 amendment to the Constitution that prevented states from denying the right to vote based on sex.

nomination
the formal process through which parties choose their candidates for political office.

nonattitudes
a term referring to the lack of stable and coherent opinions on political issues and candidates.

North American Free Trade Agreement (NAFTA)
a regional trade agreement made between the United States, Canada, and Mexico designed to increase trade between the nations.

North Atlantic Treaty Alliance (NATO)
an alliance created during the Cold War that requires America and all other members to

come to the military aid of each other in case of attack.

obscenity and pornography
text, images, or video that depicts sexual activity in ways offensive to the broader community and that lacks any artistic merit.

Office of Management and Budget (OMB)
the executive branch office whose purpose is to assist the president in setting national spending priorities.

open primary
a primary election in which all eligible voters may vote, regardless of their partisan affiliation.

open seat election
an election in which no incumbent is seeking reelection.

oral arguments
presentations made by plaintiffs and attorneys before the Supreme Court.

original jurisdiction
the authority of a court to act as the first court to hear a case, which includes the finding of facts in the case.

outside (or grassroots) lobbying
a type of lobbying that focuses on reaching constituents and mobilizing them to pressure their representatives rather than pressuring the representatives directly.

oversight
efforts by Congress to ensure that executive branch agencies, bureaus, and cabinet departments, as well as their officials, are acting legally and in accordance with congressional goals.

partisan bias
the slanting of political news coverage in support of a particular political party or ideology.

partisan polarization
when an individual's stance on a given issue, policy, or person is more likely to be strictly defined by their identification with a particular political party (e.g., Democrat or Republican) or ideology (e.g., liberal or conservative).

partisan press
media outlets or organizations that promote a particular political ideology or support a political party.

party identification
the degree to which an individual identifies with and supports a particular political party.

party identification
an individual's attachment to a particular party.

party ideology
a set of stances shaped by an underlying philosophy about key issues and the proper role of government in society and then communicated to voters.

party platform
a set of positions and policy objectives that members of a political party agree to.

party systems
periods of stability of the composition of political parties and the issues around which they coalesce, brought on by shorter periods of intense change.

path dependence
the way in which a set of political outcomes shapes future possibilities for political action.

Pendleton Act
(or Civil Service Reform Act of 1883) created the first United States Civil Service Commission to draw up and enforce rules on hiring, promotion, and tenure of office within the civil service.

penny press
nineteenth-century American newspapers that sold for only one cent each, thus increasing the size of the audience that could afford to purchase them.

plaintiff
a person or group who brings a case in court.

plea bargaining
a legal process in which the plaintiff and defendant agree to an outcome prior to the handing out of a verdict.

Plessy v. Ferguson
a Supreme Court case in 1896 that upheld legal racial segregation.

pluralism
a theory of governmental influence that views the distribution of political power among many competing groups as serving to keep any one of them in check.

plurality
when a candidate receives more votes than any other candidate.

polarization
a sharp ideological distance between political parties.

police patrol oversight
a term that describes congressional oversight as a process of constant monitoring rather than responding to specific crises.

police powers
a category of reserved powers that includes the protection of people's health, safety, and welfare.

policy agenda
the set of issues to which government officials, voters, and the public attend.

policy diffusion
the process through which states emulate and adopt policies enacted by other states.

policy entrepreneurs
individuals in government, academic institutions, think tanks, interest groups, and other venues who try to shape the political agenda and get their solutions implemented.

policy feedback
the idea that policies, once enacted, open up and close off future policy options, especially because of the effects of policy on politics and political actors.

political action committees
organizations that raise money to support chosen candidates and defeat others.

political efficacy
a person's belief that she or he can make effective political change.

political equality
when members of a society possess the same rights under the laws of the nation.

political ideology
a set of beliefs about the desired goals and outcomes of a process of governance.

political institutions
the rules, laws, and structures that channel and shape political action.

political mobilization
efforts by members of American political parties to turn out the vote and encourage their members to get others to do so.

political participation
the different ways in which individuals take action to shape the laws and policies of a government.

political party
an organized group of candidates, officeholders, voters, and activists that work together to elect candidates to political office.

political patronage
filling administrative positions as a reward for support, rather than solely on merit.

political propaganda
attempts to shape governmental actions and laws by changing people's beliefs and opinions.

political science
the systematic study of the ways in which ideas, individuals, and institutions shape political outcomes.

political socialization
the variety of experiences and factors that shape our political values, attitudes, and behaviors.

politics
the process of influencing the actions of officials and the policies of a nation, state, locality, or community.

positive freedoms
fundamental rights and freedoms that require action by individuals to express and by governments to secure.

power elite
a group composed of the top echelons of people in the business world, government, and military.

precedent
a judicial decision that guides future courts in handling similar cases.

preemptive war
a type of war in which a state uses its military might to challenge adversaries before

they launch attacks or harbor those who might do so.

presidential pardon
the presidential authority to forgive an individual and set aside punishment for a crime.

presidential primaries
elections in which a state's voters choose delegates who support a particular candidate for nomination.

priming
shaping individuals' interpretations of news or events by highlighting certain details or contexts.

principal-agent problem
the challenge that arises when one actor, the principal, tasks another, the agent, to carry out the principal's wishes in the presence of uncertainty and unequal information.

prior restraint
the suppression of material prior to publication on the grounds that it might endanger national security.

privacy
a right not enumerated in the Constitution but affirmed by Supreme Court decisions that covers individuals' decisions in their private lives, including decisions regarding reproductive rights and sexuality.

private bureaucracies
privately owned corporations and companies that carry out specific tasks according to a prescribed set of rules and procedures.

private contractors
nongovernmental workers hired by the federal bureaucracy to provide goods and services in support of federal activity.

privatization
shifting control over the provision of certain governmental functions from the federal bureaucracy to the private sector.

probable cause
reasonable belief that a crime has been committed or that there is evidence indicating so.

procedural justice
a judicial standard requiring that fairness be applied to all participants equally.

proportional representation system
a structure of electoral representation in which parties are represented in government according to their candidates' overall share of the vote.

protectionism
restricting access by foreign producers to American markets in order to benefit specific domestic agricultural, industrial, and service providers.

protest
a public demonstration designed to call attention to the need for action or change.

proxy wars
wars in which major powers support different sides but do not directly go to war with each other.

public interest groups
groups that act on behalf of the collective interests of a broad group of individuals, many of who may not be members or contributors to the organization.

public opinion
the sum of individual attitudes about government, policies, and issues.

public opinion surveys
systematic attempts to make inferences about the opinions of large numbers of individuals by carefully sampling and asking questions of a small, randomly assigned sample of the larger population.

public policy
the intentional use of governmental power to secure the health, welfare, opportunities, and national security of citizens.

purposive benefits
rewards in the form of satisfaction from working with others to achieve a common goal or purpose.

push poll
a negative campaign tactic disguised as a survey in which a candidates' opponent or opponents are portrayed in an unfavorable way.

question order
a concern in measuring public opinion having to do with how the sequencing of questions affects responses.

question wording
a concern in measuring public opinion having to do with how the way a question is phrased affects responses.

race of interviewer effects
the shaping of survey responses due to the racial identities of respondents and interviewers.

random digit dialing
when potential survey respondents are selected by computer-generated random numbers.

random selection
how participants are selected from the population for inclusion in the study.

Reagan Doctrine
a foreign policy agenda under President Ronald Reagan offering American assistance, including military training and weaponry, to anticommunist groups.

realignment
a major shift in allegiance to the political parties that is often driven by changes in the issues that unite or divide voters.

recess appointment
occurs when Congress is not in session and the president appoints a person to fill a position that would normally require the advice and consent of the Senate. Unless the person is formally confirmed when the Senate reconvenes, the position ends at the conclusion of that session of Congress.

recruitment
the process through which political parties identify potential candidates.

redistricting
states' redrawing of the electoral district boundaries following each census.

registration requirements
the set of rules that govern who can vote and how, when, and where they vote.

representation
the act of "standing for" one's constituents in government.

representative democracy
a political system in which voters select representatives who then vote on matters of public policy.

republics
governments ruled by representatives of the people.

reserved powers
powers reserved to the states if not textually granted to the federal government.

respondents
individuals who answer a survey.

responsible party model
a proposal for party reform that emphasized cohesive party positions that presents voters with a clear set of choices and allows members' voices to be effectively incorporated into party positions on issues.

retrospective voting
reflecting back on an incumbent's past performance in an election.

revolving door phenomenon
the movement of individuals between government and lobbying positions.

roll-call vote
a recorded vote on a bill.

Roosevelt Corollary
a policy that asserted that the United States was the guarantor of political, military, and economic stability in Latin America and the Caribbean.

rulemaking
the process through which the federal bureaucracy fills in critical details of a law.

runoff election
an election that is held between the two candidates with the highest total votes if no one candidate scores a majority.

salience
the centrality of an individual's opinion in the sense of the opinion's ability to shape the individual's views on other issues or candidates.

sample
the subgroup of individuals from the larger population one wants to measure the opinions of.

sampling error
error in a statistical analysis arising from the unrepresentativeness of the sample taken.

school choice
a type of reform that allows parents and guardians to choose their students' schools and produces competition between the schools themselves to attract students.

scientific poll
when pollsters try to gain an understanding of a large group of individuals by obtaining the opinions of a carefully chosen small sample of the group, although they are aware of the limitations of the effort.

Second Continental Congress
an assembly of delegates from the thirteen British colonies in America that drafted and approved the Declaration of Independence, conducted the Revolutionary War, and created the governmental structure that followed the war.

secretary of defense
the head of the Department of Defense.

secretary of State
the head of the Department of State.

selective benefits
goods that are made available only to those who join or contribute to a group.

selective incorporation
the piecemeal process through which the Supreme Court has affirmed that almost all of the protections within the Bill of Rights also apply to state governments.

self-selected listener opinion polls (or SLOP polls)
a survey in which respondents choose to respond to a survey prompt on their own.

senatorial courtesy
a traditional norm in which presidents consult with senators from the states when considering potential nominees to the lower levels of the federal judiciary.

Senior Executive Service (SES)
federal employees with higher-level supervisory and administrative responsibilities who are paid and treated more like vice presidents of businesses than political figures.

separate but equal
the doctrine that racial segregation was constitutional so long as the facilities for blacks and whites were roughly equal.

separation of powers
a design of government that distributes powers across institutions in order to avoid making one branch too powerful on its own.

Seven Years' War
a war principally between France and Great Britain and other European nations that was fought across the globe.

Shays' Rebellion
a grassroots popular uprising against the government of Massachusetts.

signing statements
text written by presidents while signing a bill into law that usually consists of political statements or reasons for signing the bill but that might also include a president's interpretation of the law itself.

single-member plurality system
a structure of electoral representation in which a candidate and the party that he or she represents must win the most votes in a state or district in order to be represented in government.

slander
expression in spoken form that defames a person's character.

social benefits
rewards in the form of new connections or access to networks that members of a group receive through their participation.

social contract
an agreement in which people give to their governments the ability to rule over them to ensure an orderly and functioning society.

social equality
when no individual's social status is inherently higher than another's.

social insurance programs
programs such as Social Security that are financed by payroll taxes paid by individuals and that do not have income-based requirements to receive their benefits.

socialist system
a way of structuring economic activity in which private firms are allowed to operate and make decisions over production and distribution but with significant governmental involvement to ensure economic equality.

social media
forms of electronic communication that enable users to create and share content or to participate in social networking.

social movements
voluntary associations of individuals who come together to change things or keep things from changing, but they often do so by calling attention to a set of injustices or wrongs in order to get policymakers to act and to educate the public about the issue.

social welfare policies
governmental efforts designed to improve or protect the health, safety, education, and opportunities for citizens and residents.

socioeconomic status (SES)
a measure that captures an individual's wealth, income, occupation, and educational attainment.

soft news
stories that focus on celebrity and personality rather than political or economic issues.

soft power
the advancement of a nation's interests by exporting its values and culture abroad.

solicitor general
a presidential appointee who represents the federal government in the Supreme Court.

Sons of Liberty
a group initially formed of merchants and workingmen in response to the Stamp Act that resisted Great Britain and its tax policies.

Speaker of the House
the leader of the House of Representatives, chosen by an election of its members.

split-ticket voting
when a voter chooses a candidate from one party for one office and a candidate from a different party for another position on the ballot.

spoils system
the practice of cleaning house of one's opponents and installing supporters in their place following a successful election.

stability
the degree of change over time, in different contexts, or in response to differently worded survey questions of a particular opinion.

Stamp Act of 1765
a highly unpopular law designed to raise revenue by requiring the purchase of stamps for newspapers, legal papers, and other documents.

standard operating procedures
the sets of rules governing the behavior of bureaucrats.

standards-based reforms
reforms that set specific state or nationwide student achievement goals, rewards for success, and, most notably, consequences for failure.

standing
the legal ability to bring a case in court.

state and local bureaucracies
public organizations below the federal level designed to carry out specific tasks according to a prescribed set of rules and procedures.

State of the Union Address
the annual, constitutionally required transmittal of information from the president to Congress updating that branch on the state of national affairs.

state sovereignty resolutions
state legislative measures that affirm the sovereignty of states under the Tenth Amendment.

states' rights
the idea that American states have the authority to self-govern, even when in conflict with national laws.

statute
a written law established by a legislative body.

stereotype
a preconceived, often oversimplified idea about something that people apply as a filter to the world.

straw poll

an unofficial tally of opinion or support at a meeting or event.

substantive representation

the degree to which elected representatives or senators represent the interests and policy preferences of their constituents.

suffrage

the right to vote in political elections.

Sugar Act

a law passed by Great Britain in 1764 that taxed sugar and molasses and angered New England merchants.

superdelegates

members of the Democratic Party—usually elected officials or party activists—who are not pledged to any certain candidate based on the outcomes of their state's primary or caucus.

super PACs

political action committees permitted to spend unlimited amounts of money in a campaign, though these actions must not be coordinated with that campaign.

superpower

an extremely powerful state that is capable of influencing international events and the actions of other less powerful states.

supremacy clause

a part of the Constitution that establishes the Constitution and the laws of the nation passed under its authority as the highest laws of the nation.

Supreme Court

the highest level of the federal judiciary, which was established in the Constitution and serves as the highest court in the nation.

swing states

states where no one political party tends to dominate national elections.

symbolic speech

protected expression in the form of images, signs, and other symbols.

terrorism

the use of violence as a means to achieve political ends.

third party

(or minor party) a political party operating over a limited period of time in competition with two other major parties.

Thirteenth Amendment

an amendment to the Constitution passed in 1865 prohibiting slavery within the United States.

Three-fifths Compromise

an agreement reached by delegates at the Constitutional Convention that ensured that a slave would count as three-fifths of a person for a state's representation.

top-two primary system

an electoral system in which candidates, regardless of party, compete in the primary elections, with the top two vote-getters, regardless of party, advancing to the general election.

Trans-Pacific Partnership (TPP)

a regional trade agreement struck between twelve nations in the Pacific Rim, including Mexico, Australia, and East Asian and South American nations.

turf wars

when bureaucrats compete to take duties and responsibilities away from one another's departments or keep their opponents from doing so.

tyranny

the suppression of the rights of a people by those holding power.

tyranny of the majority

when a large number of citizens use the power of their majority to trample on the rights of a smaller group.

tyranny of the minority

when a small number of citizens tramples on the rights of the larger population.

unemployment rate

the percentage of the total labor force that is unemployed.

unfunded mandate

when the federal government institutes a policy that members of state governments do not feel has been properly funded.

unfunded mandates

federal regulations that must be followed by the states but whose costs must also be shouldered by the states.

unipolarity

a distribution of power in the international system where one state exerts most of the power and influence.

unitary systems

structures of governance that place the people's sovereignty in a national government, with subnational governments deriving their authority from it.

United Nations

an international organization formed in 1945 to promote international dialogue and cooperation.

unorthodox lawmaking

a term that refers to ways in which legislative activity, especially on major bills, is often more fluid than described in a traditional textbook description.

veto

the power of a president to reject a bill passed by Congress, sending it back to the originating branch with objections noted.

Virginia Plan

a plan of government calling for a strong national government with three branches of government and a bicameral legislature, with legislators elected using proportional representation.

voter turnout

the number of eligible voters who actually participate in an election versus the total number of eligible voters.

voucher program

an educational policy that distributes public funds to parents and guardians, allowing them to send their students to private and alternative schools.

War Powers Resolution

A law passed over President Nixon's veto that restricts the power of the president in committing the nation's armed forces into combat or situations of likely combat.

warrant

a writ issued by a judge authorizing some activity.

weighting

a procedure in which the observed results of a survey are adjusted according to what is known about specific proportions in the larger population.

whip

an individual in the House or Senate, chosen by his or her party members, whose job is to ensure party unity and discipline.

wire service

an organization that gathers and reports on news and then sells the stories to other outlets.

writ of habeas corpus

a statement demanding that authorities in charge of a person's detention establish the reasons for that detention.

yellow journalism

an approach to reporting employed in the nineteenth century that relied on sensational headlines and emotional language to persuade readers and sell newspapers.

NOTES

Chapter 1

1. Tony Mauro, "Bible Club vs. School Lands in High Court," *USA Today*, January 8, 1990.
2. Ibid.
3. 98 Stat. 1302, 20 U.S.C. §§ 4071-4074. Cornell University Law School, Legal Information Institute, https://www.law.cornell.edu/uscode/text/20/4071.
4. *Widmar v. Vincent*, 454 U.S. 263 (1981).
5. Nat Hentoff, "A Bible Study Club in a Public School?" *The Washington Post*, March 14, 1989.
6. Mauro, "Bible Club vs. School Lands in High Court."
7. *Board of Education of Westside Community Schools v. Mergens* by and through Mergens, 496 U.S. 226 (1990).
8. Robert K. Skolrood, "Don't Bar Bible Clubs from Schools," *USA Today*, January 10, 1990.
9. *Board of Education of Westside Community Schools v. Mergens.*
10. Ruth Marcus, "Schools Brace for Fallout from Bible-Club Ruling: Some Officials Fear Disruptive Groups Will Enter through Door Opened by Court to Religion," *The Washington Post*, June 11, 1990.
11. *Boyd County High School Gay Straight Alliance v. Board of Education of Boyd County, KY*, 258 F. Supp. 2d 667 (E.D. Ky. 2003).
12. Ibid. The ACLU had sent the letter in September, before the meeting in which the decision to deny was taken.
13. Ibid.
14. Ibid.
15. Ibid.
16. American Civil Liberties Union, "ACLU Wins Settlement for Kentucky School's Gay-Straight Alliance," February 3, 2014, https://www.aclu.org/news/aclu-wins-settlement-kentucky-schools-gay-straight-alliance.
17. National Legal Foundation, "Welcome," http://www.nlf.net.
18. American Civil Liberties Union, "ACLU Blasts KY Board of Ed's Decision to Ban All School Clubs Rather Than Allow Gay-Straight Alliance," December 20, 2002, https://www.aclu.org/news/aclu-blasts-ky-board-eds-decision-ban-all-school-clubs-rather-allow-gay-straight-alliance.
19. Philip Bump, "48 Percent of Millennials Think the American Dream Is Dead. Here's Why," *The Washington Post*, December 10, 2015, https://www.washingtonpost.com/news/the-fix/wp/2015/12/10/48-percent-of-millennials-think-the-american-dream-is-dead-heres-why/, accessed May 9, 2016. The authors obtained their data from Harvard Institute of Politics, "Harvard IOP Fall 2015 Poll: Trump, Carson Lead Republican Primary; Sanders Edging Clinton among Democrats, Harvard IOP Poll Finds," December 10, 2015, http://iop.harvard.edu/survey/details/harvard-iop-fall-2015-poll.
20. Samuel Huntington, *American Politics: The Promise of Disharmony* (Cambridge, MA: Harvard University Press, 1983); John Kingdon, *America the Unusual* (New York: St. Martin's Press, 1999).
21. John Winthrop, "A Model of Christian Charity," 1630, The Winthrop Society, http://winthropsociety.com/doc_charity.php.
22. R. B. Bernstein, *Thomas Jefferson* (New York: Oxford University Press, 2003), 32. Presumably, Jefferson wrote in the evenings, as he served during the day in the Second Continental Congress. Though he had seventeen days to write, it is unclear how long it actually took for him to write the draft; not many detailed records were kept of its creation. John Adams indicated that Jefferson produced a draft in one or two days. (Pauline Maier, *American Scripture: Making the Declaration of Independence* [New York: Alfred A. Knopf, 1997], 104.)
23. Merrill D. Peterson, *Thomas Jefferson and the New Nation* (New York: Oxford University Press, 1970), 11.
24. Maier, *American Scripture*, 149.
25. "Letter from Thomas Jefferson to Henry Lee, May 8, 1825," in Philip S. Foner, ed., *Basic Writings of Thomas Jefferson* (New York: Wiley Book Company), 802.
26. Julian P. Boyd, *The Declaration of Independence: The Evolution of the Text as Shown in Facsimiles of Various Drafts by Its Author, Thomas Jefferson* (Princeton, NJ: Princeton University Press, 1945), 20.
27. Boyd, *The Declaration of Independence*, 21.
28. Paraphrasing Eric Foner, *Give Me Liberty! An American History* (New York: W. W. Norton & Company, 2006), 36.
29. Russell Shorto, *The Island at the Center of the World: The Epic Story of Dutch Manhattan and the Forgotten Colony That Shaped America* (New York: Doubleday, 2004), 50.
30. See, for example, Gail D. MacLeitch, *Imperial Entanglements: Iroquois Change and Persistence on the Frontiers of Empire* (Philadelphia: University of Pennsylvania Press, 2011); Karim M. Tiro, *The People of Standing Stone: The Oneida Nation from the Revolution through the Era of Removal* (Amherst: University of Massachusetts Press, 2011).
31. Donald R. Wright, *African Americans in the Colonial Era: From African Origins through the American Revolution* (Arlington Heights, IL: Harlan Davidson, Inc., 1990), 19.
32. Foner, *Give Me Liberty!*, 53.
33. Ibid., 123.
34. Sylvia R. Frey, *Water from the Rock: Black Resistance in a Revolutionary Age* (Princeton, NJ: Princeton University Press, 1991), 17.
35. George Brown Tindall and David E. Shi, *America: A Narrative History*, Brief Second Edition. (New York: W. W. Norton & Company, 1989), 16.
36. Foner, *Give Me Liberty!*, 43.
37. Charles M. Andrews, *The Colonial Background of the American Revolution* (New Haven, CT: Yale University Press, 1924), 42-44.
38. Global war began in 1756, while conflict in the colonies started two years earlier. Other major European powers became involved in various theatres in the war.
39. The colonies that sent representatives were Connecticut, Maryland, Massachusetts, New Hampshire, New York, Pennsylvania, and Rhode Island.
40. Eleven of the thirteen colonies were included in Franklin's proposed plan; Georgia and Delaware were not. Virginia and Massachusetts would each have had seven of the forty-eight total seats, being the largest and wealthiest colonies.
41. Richard Hofstadter, William Miller, and Daniel Aaron, *The American Republic*, Vol. 1 (Upper Saddle River, NJ: Prentice Hall, 1970), 144.
42. Merrill Jensen, *The Founding of a Nation* (Indianapolis: Hackett, 2004), 4-5.
43. "The Revenue Act of 1764," in *English Historical Documents: Volume IX, American Colonial Documents to 1776*, ed. Merrill Jensen (New York: Oxford University Press, 1955), 644.
44. "The Stamp Act," in Jensen, *English Historical Documents*, 656.
45. Andrews, *The Colonial Background of the American Revolution*, 134.
46. Literacy rates varied significantly by gender and race.
47. Bernard Bailyn, *The Ideological Origins of the American Revolution* (Cambridge, MA: The Belknap Press of Harvard University Press, 1967), 2.
48. Philip Davidson, *Propaganda and the American Revolution, 1763-1783* (Chapel Hill: The University of North Carolina Press, 1941), xiii.

49. Eric Foner, *Tom Paine and Revolutionary America* (New York: Oxford University Press, 1976), xi.

50. Ibid., 73.

51. Ibid., 16.

52. Andrews, *The Colonial Background of the American Revolution*, 64–65.

53. Thomas Paine, *Common Sense* (New York: Buccaneer Books, Inc., 1976), 69, 63.

54. Foner, *Tom Paine and Revolutionary America*, 74.

55. Jensen, *The Founding of a Nation*, 99.

56. Pauline Maier, *From Resistance to Revolution: Colonial Radicals and the Development of American Opposition to Britain, 1765–1776* (New York: Alfred A. Knopf, 1972), 58.

57. Bernard Bailyn, *The Ordeal of Thomas Hutchinson* (Cambridge, MA: The Belknap Press of Harvard University Press, 1974), 35. According to historian Pauline Maier, due to the fact that papers were targeted, the attack on Hutchinson's house may have had been motivated "by a group of merchants who feared they had been named in a set of depositions about smuggling" rather than by protest over the Stamp Act (*From Resistance to Revolution*, 58).

58. New York, New Hampshire, Virginia, North Carolina, and Georgia did not send delegates. Support in several of these colonies was strong, but royal governors prevented them from sending delegates.

59. "Newspaper Account of the Boston Massacre," in Jensen, *English Historical Documents, 749*.

60. Andrews, *The Colonial Background of the American Revolution*, 157.

61. Jensen, *The Founding of a Nation*, 33. Citing "John Adams to Hezekiah Niles," in *The Works of John Adams,* Vol. X, ed. C. F. Adams (Boston, 1850–56), 283.

62. Jackson Turner Main, *The Social Structure of Revolutionary America* (Princeton, NJ: Princeton University Press, 1965), 221–227.

63. Ibid., 221.

64. Sylvia R. Frey, "Liberty, Equality, and Slavery: The Paradox of the American Revolution," in *The American Revolution: Its Character and Limits*, ed. Jack P. Greene (New York: New York University Press, 1987), 230. Quoting Thomas Hutchinson, *Strictures upon the Declaration of the Congress at Philadelphia* (London, 1776), 9–10.

65. Thomas J. Davis, "Emancipation Rhetoric, Natural Rights, and Revolutionary New England: A Note on Four Black Petitions in Massachusetts, 1773–1777," *The New England Quarterly* 62, no. 2 (June 1989): 248–263.

66. Ibid., 255–256. Citing Herbert Aptheker, ed., *Documentary History of the Negro People in the United States*, Vol. 1 (New York: International Publishers), 7–8.

67. Ruth Bogin, "'Liberty Further Extended': A 1776 Antislavery Manuscript by Lemuel Haynes," *The William and Mary Quarterly* 40, no. 1 (January 1983): 94.

68. Ibid., 97–98.

69. Hofstadter, Miller, and Aaron, *The American Republic*, 167.

70. The Articles of Confederation and Perpetual Union, (See Chapter 2).

71. "The Virginia Resolutions for Independence," in Jensen, *English Historical Documents, 867–868*.

72. Elaine F. Crane, "Dependence in the Era of Independence: The Role of Women in a Republican Society," in *The American Revolution: Its Character and Limits*, ed. Jack P. Greene (New York: New York University Press, 1987).

73. Gunderson, *To Be Useful to the World*, 23.

74. Mary Beth Norton, *Liberty's Daughters: The Revolutionary Experience of American Women, 1750–1800* (Boston, MA: Little, Brown and Company, 1980), 22.

75. Sara M. Evans, *Born for Liberty: A History of Women in America* (New York: The Free Press, 1989), 48.

76. Carol Berkin, *Revolutionary Mothers: Women in the Struggle for America's Independence* (New York: Alfred A. Knopf, 2005), 21.

77. Ibid., 44.

78. Ibid., 45.

79. Ibid., 46.

80. Norton, *Liberty's Daughters*, 179.

81. Esther de Berdt Reed, *The Sentiments of an American Woman*, Philadelphia, PA: 1780.

82. Jonathan S. Bass. *Blessed Are the Peacemakers: Martin Luther King, Jr., Eight White Religious Leaders, and the "Letter from Birmingham Jail"* (Baton Rouge: Louisiana State University Press, 2001), 112.

83. Taylor Branch, *Parting the Waters: America in the King Years, 1954–63* (New York: Simon and Schuster, 1988), 706.

84. Ibid., 729.

85. Godfrey Hodgson, *Martin Luther King* (Ann Arbor: The University of Michigan Press, 2009), 3.

86. Montgomery Improvement Association, "Bus Protesters Call Southern Negro Leaders Conference on Transportation and Nonviolent Integration," January 7, 1957, Montgomery, Alabama, The Martin Luther King Papers Project, http://mlk-kpp01.stanford.edu/primarydocuments/Vol4/7-Jan-1957_MIAConference.pdf.

87. Martin Luther King Jr., "Letter from Birmingham Jail," http://okra.stanford.edu/transcription/document_images/undecided/630416-019.pdf.

88. Clayborne Carson, ed., *The Autobiography of Martin Luther King, Jr.* (New York: Warner Books, 1998), 184.

89. Ibid., 187.

90. "White Clergymen Urge Local Negroes to Withdraw from Demonstrations," *The Birmingham News*, April 13, 1963, Birmingham Public Library Digital Collections, http://bplonline.cdmhost.com/cdm/singleitem/collection/p4017coll2/id/746/rec/8.

91. Parts of the letter were also written on paper later smuggled in or provided to King by his attorneys.

92. Doyle "Texas Dolly" Brunson, *Doyle Brunson's Super Strategy*, 3rd ed. (New York: Cardoza Publishing, 2002), 442.

Chapter 2

1. Robert Livingston Schuyler, *The Constitution of the United States: An Historical Survey of Its Formation* (New York, 1923), 90.

2. "Letter from James Madison to Thomas Jefferson, May 12, 1786," in *The Papers of James Madison: Vol. 9, 9 April 1786–24 May 1787*, ed. Robert A. Rutland and William M. E. Rachal (Chicago: The University of Chicago Press, 1975), 51.

3. William Lee Miller, *The Business of May Next: James Madison and the Founding* (Charlottesville: University Press of Virginia, 1992), 10.

4. Madison's two papers were titled "Notes of Ancient and Modern Confederacies," written in the spring of 1786, and "Vices of the Political System of the United States," written in the spring of 1787.

5. "Letter from James Madison to Thomas Jefferson, August 12, 1786," in Rutland and Rachal, *The Papers of James Madison*, 97.

6. Schuyler, *The Constitution of the United States*, 90.

7. "Virginia Laws for Blacks–17C & 18C," in William Waller Hening, *Laws of Virginia, 1619–1792* (1823), I-III. For more on Madison's ambivalence toward slavery, see Miller, *The Business of May Next*, 177–184.

8. Charles M. Andrews, *The Colonial Background of the American Revolution* (New Haven: Yale University Press, 1924), 26.

9. Merrill Jensen, *The Articles of Confederation: An Interpretation of the Social-Constitutional History of the American Revolution, 1774–1781* (Madison: The University of Wisconsin Press, 1948), 150.

10. Robert W. Hoffert, *A Politics of Tensions: The Articles of Confederation and American Political Ideals* (Niwot: The University Press of Colorado, 1992), 86.

11. Article II.

12. Andrews, *The Colonial Background of the American Revolution*, 44.

13. This idea of term limits is one that we continue to debate today. For a discussion of challenges of coordination under the Articles of Confederation, see Keith L. Dougherty, *Collective Action under the Articles of Confederation* (New York: Cambridge University Press, 2001).

14. Jensen, *The Articles of Confederation*, 240.

15. Gordon S. Wood, "The Origins of the Constitution," in *This Constitution: A Bicentennial Chronicle* (The American Political Science Association, 1987), available online at http://www.apsanet.org/imgtest/OriginsofConst.pdf, accessed on June 21, 2011.

16. William H. Riker, *The Strategy of Rhetoric: Campaigning for the American Constitution* (New Haven, CT: Yale University Press, 1996).

17. "We do Each one of us, acknowledge our Selves to be Inlisted . . . in colo Hazeltons Regiment of Regulators . . . for Suppressing of tyrannical government in the Massachusetts State." "Report of the Commissioners, April 27, 1787," in David P. Szatmary, *Shays' Rebellion: The Making of an Agrarian Insurrection* (Amherst: The University of Massachusetts Press, 1980), 63.

18. James MacGregor Burns, *The Vineyard of Liberty* (New York: Alfred A. Knopf, 1982), 14.

19. Szatmary, *Shays' Rebellion*.

20. Louise B. Dunbar, "A Study of 'Monarchical' Tendencies in the United States from 1776 to 1801," in Rutland and Rachal, *The Papers of James Madison*, 162.

21. Leonard L. Richards, *Shays' Rebellion: The American Revolution's Final Battle.* (Philadelphia: University of Pennsylvania Press, 2002), 16. Quoting John M. Palmer, *General von Stueben* (New Haven, CT: 1937), 339–340.

22. Richards, *Shays' Rebellion*, 2.

23. "Letter from George Washington to James Madison, November 5, 1786," in Rutland and Rachal, *The Papers of James Madison*, 162.

24. George Washington had been reluctant to be a delegate in part because the Society of the Cincinnati, an organization of former Revolutionary War officers of which he had been a president, was to meet in Philadelphia at the same time. The society was viewed with mistrust due to its potential to form a new aristocracy. See Catherine Drinker Bowen, *Miracle at Philadelphia: The Story of the Constitutional Convention, May to September 1787* (Boston: Little Brown and Company, 1966).

25. Dougherty, *Collective Action under the Articles of Confederation*, 129.

26. Dickinson of Delaware in Miller, *The Business of May Next,* 44.

27. Bowen, *Miracle at Philadelphia*, 16.

28. Ira Stoll, *Samuel Adams: A Life* (New York, NY: Free Press, 2008), 229–230.

29. Patrick Henry, "Virginia Ratifying Convention, June 4 and 5, 1788," in *The Essential Antifederalist*, 2nd ed, ed. W. B. Allen and Gordon Lloyd (New York: Rowman & Littlefield Publishers, Inc., 2002), 130.

30. Wood, "The Origins of the Constitution."

31. Max Farrand, ed., *The Records of the Federal Convention of 1787, Volume I* (New Haven, CT: Yale University Press, 1911), xi.

32. "Notes of James Madison, May 29, 1787," in Farrand, *The Records of the Federal Convention of 1787*, 15.

33. Bowen, *Miracle at Philadelphia*, 22.

34. Though Madison would state that the entire Virginia delegation was responsible for it. See Bowen, *Miracle at Philadelphia*.

35. "Notes of James Madison, May 29, 1787," 18.

36. Ibid., 18.

37. Ibid., 20.

38. "Notes of James Madison, June 9, 1787," in Farrand, *The Records of the Federal Convention of 1787*, 179.

39. Bowen, *Miracle at Philadelphia*, 116.

40. "Notes of James Madison, June 20, 1787," in Farrand, *The Records of the Federal Convention of 1787*, 339.

41. Ibid., 285.

42. Ibid., 492.

43. "Notes of Robert Yates, July 2, 1787," in Farrand, *The Records of the Federal Convention of 1787*, 519.

44. "Notes of James Madison, May 29, 1787," 531.

45. It is also known as Connecticut Compromise, after Roger Sherman, a Connecticut delegate, member of the committee, and author of the proposal. One state delegation was split.

46. For an analysis of Madison's strategic shift, see Miller, *The Business of May Next*, 78–80.

47. Bowen, *Miracle at Philadelphia*, 115.

48. Richard E. Neustadt, *Presidential Power and the Modern Presidents: The Politics of Leadership from Roosevelt to Reagan* (New York: The Free Press, 1990), 29.

49. James Madison, *Federalist* No. 51, in *The Federalist Papers*, ed. George W. Carey and James McClellan (Indianapolis, IN: Liberty Fund, 2001), 268.

50. Also called the Committee of Eleven.

51. Bruce Ackerman, *We the People: Foundations* (Cambridge, MA: Harvard University Press, 1991).

52. Native Americans not paying taxes would not count at all.

53. "Notes of James Madison, July 12, 1787," in Farrand, *The Records of the Federal Convention of 1787*, 593.

54. "Notes of James Madison, June 28, 1787," in Farrand, *The Records of the Federal Convention of 1787*, 449. Recent empirical research in political science supports this interpretation. See Jeremy C. Pope and Shawn Treier, "Reconsidering the Great Compromise at the Federal Convention of 1787: Deliberation and Agenda Effects on the Senate and Slavery," *American Journal of Political Science* 55, no. 2 (2011): 289–306. For a full discussion of slavery and logrolling at the convention, see Samuel Kernell and Gary C. Jacobson, *The Logic of American Politics,* 3rd ed. (Washington, D.C.: CQ Press, 2006), 62–63.

55. James Madison, *Federalist* No. 54, in Carey and McClellan, *The Federalist Papers*, 283.

56. "James Madison to Robert Evans, June 15, 1819," Library of Congress, https://www.loc .gov/item/mjm018592/, accessed August 5, 2016.

57. Riker, *The Strategy of Rhetoric*, 81.

58. Douglass Adair, "The Authorship of the Disputed Federalist Papers," in *Fame and the Founding Fathers: Essays by Douglass Adair*, ed. Trevor Colbourn (New York: W. W. Norton & Company, 1974), 28.

59. Ibid., 53.

60. Madison, *Federalist* No. 51, 269.

61. James Madison, *Federalist* No. 10, in Carey and McClellan, *The Federalist Papers*, 42.

62. Ibid., 44.

63. Ibid., 43.

64. Ibid., 43.

65. Ibid., 46.

66. Alexander Hamilton, *Federalist* No. 9, in Carey and McClellan, *The Federalist Papers*, 41.

67. Alexander Hamilton, *Federalist* No. 16, in Carey and McClellan, *The Federalist Papers*, 76–77.

68. James Madison, *Federalist* No. 39, in Carey and McClellan, *The Federalist Papers*, 197–199.

69. James Madison, *Federalist* No. 45, in Carey and McClellan, *The Federalist Papers*, 241.

70. Madison, *Federalist* No. 51, 271.

71. W. B. Allen and Gordon Lloyd, *The Essential Antifederalist*, 2nd ed. (New York: Rowan & Littlefield Publishers, INC., 2002), xxiii.

72. Ibid., xxiii.

73. "Centinel Letter I, October 5, 1787," in Allen and Lloyd, *The Essential Antifederalist*, 102–103. See also Herbert J. Storing, *What the Antifederalists Were For* (Chicago: The University of Chicago Press, 1981), 57.

74. "Brutus Essay V, December 13, 1787," in Allen and Lloyd, *The Essential Antifederalist*, 119.

75. "Brutus Essay I, October 18, 1787," in Allen and Lloyd, *The Essential Antifederalist*, 110.

76. Bowen, *Miracle at Philadelphia*, 246.

77. "Centinal I, October 5, 1787," in Allen and Lloyd, *The Essential Antifederalist*, 102–103.

78. See Storing, *What the Antifederalists Were For*.

79. Riker, *The Strategy of Rhetoric*.

80. Ibid., 211.

81. Charles A. Beard, *An Economic Interpretation of the Constitution of the United States* (New Brunswick, NJ: Transaction Publishers, 1998).

82. Robert A. McGuire, "Constitution Making: A Rational Choice Model of the Federal Convention of 1787," *American Journal of Political Science* 32, no. 2 (May 1988): 483–522.

83. Adair, "The Authorship of the Disputed Federalist Papers," 7.

84. Kenneth M. Dolbeare and Linda Medcalf, "The Dark Side of the Constitution," in *The Case against the Constitution from the Antifederalists to the Present*, ed. John F. Manley and Kenneth M. Dolbeare (Armonk, NY: M. E. Sharpe, 1987), 120–142;

85. "Notes of James Madison, May 31, 1787," in Farrand, *The Records of the Federal Convention of 1787*, 48.

86. Ibid., 48.

87. Douglass C. North and Barry R. Weingast, "Constitutions and Commitment: The Evolution of Institutions Governing Public Choice in Seventeenth-Century England," *The Journal of Economic History* 49, no. 4 (December 1989): 803–832.

88. Donald S. Lutz, "From Covenant to Constitution in American Political Thought," in *Covenant, Polity, and Constitutionalism*, ed. Daniel Elazar and John Kincaid (Lanham, MD: University Press of America, 1983).

89. Edward S. Corwin, "The Constitution as an Instrument and as a Symbol," *The American Political Science Review* 30, no. 6 (December 1936): 1071–1085. See also Edward S. Corwin, *The "Higher Law" Background of American Constitutional Law* (Ithaca, NY: Great Seal Books, 1928).

Chapter 3

1. Joel Roberts, "Dying Woman Loses Medical Marijuana Case," CBS News, March 14, 2007, http://www.cbsnews.com/news/dying-woman-loses-medical-marijuana-case/, accessed February 29, 2016.

2. Dan Reed, "Medicinal Pot Users Renew Legal Challenge," *San Jose Mercury News*, October 10, 2002; available from Lexis-Nexis Academic.

3. Brian Anderson, "Women File Suit for Continued Access to Marijuana," *Contra Costa Times*, October 10, 2002; available from Lexis-Nexis Academic.

4. "Declaration of Diane Monson in Support of Motion for Preliminary Injunction," *Raich v. Ashcroft*, 248 F. supp 918 (ND Cal. 2003).

5. Comprehensive Drug Abuse and Control Act of 1970, 84 Stat. 1236.

6. *Gonzales v. Raich*, 545 U.S. 1 (2005).

7. Ibid.

8. "Declaration of Diane Monson in Support of Motion for Preliminary Injunction."

9. Anderson, "Women File Suit for Continued Access to Marijuana."

10. Richard Willing, "Medical-pot Fight Goes to Justices," *USA Today*, November 26, 2004; available from Lexis-Nexis Academic.

11. Guy Ashley, "U.S. Supreme Court to Hear Medical Marijuana Lawsuit: An Oakland Patient Is Suing John Ashcroft for the Right to Use the Drug," *Contra Costa Times*, June 29, 2004; available from Lexis-Nexis Academic.

12. Richard H. Leach, *American Federalism* (New York: W. W. Norton & Company, Inc., 1970), 8.

13. Article VI.

14. Article I, Section 8.

15. Ibid.

16. Ibid.

17. Article I, Sections 2 and 4; Article II, Section 1.

18. Article V.

19. Article I, Section 10.

20. Richard E. Neustadt, *Presidential Power and the Modern Presidents: The Politics of Leadership from Roosevelt to Reagan* (New York: The Free Press, 1990), 29.

21. Daniel J. Elazar, *American Federalism: A View from the States* (New York: Thomas Y. Crowell Company, 1972), 190.

22. Howard Mintz, "Oakland Woman Battles for Medical Pot," *San Jose Mercury News* (California), November 23, 2004; available from Lexis-Nexis Academic.

23. Ibid.

24. Richard Willing, "Justices Doubtful about Medical Marijuana," *USA Today*, November 30, 2004; available from Lexis-Nexis Academic.

25. *Gonzales v. Raich*.

26. *Wickard v. Filburn*, 317 U.S. 111 (1942).

27. Paul E. Peterson, *The Price of Federalism* (Washington, D.C.: The Brookings Institution, 1995), 12.

28. *Gonzales v. Raich*.

29. *Alberto Gonzales, Attorney General, et al. v. Angel McClary Raich et al.*, 545 U.S. 1 (2005).

30. Reagan Ali and M. David, "Obama Effectively Tells Supreme Court to Legalize Marijuana," *Counter Current News*, January 17, 2016, http://countercurrentnews.com/2016/01/obama-tells-supreme-court-to-legalize/, accessed May 18, 2016.

31. Ariane de Vogue, "Obama Admin Weighs in on Legalized Marijuana at the Supreme Court," CNN.com, December 16, 2015, http://www.cnn.com/2015/12/16/politics/supreme-court-marijuana-colorado-obama/, accessed May 18, 2016.

32. *McCulloch v. Maryland*, 17 U.S. (4 Wheat.) 316 (1819).

33. *Gibbons v. Ogden*, 22 U.S. (9 Wheat.) 11 (1824).

34. Morton Grodzins, *The American System: A New View of Government in the United States* (Chicago: McNally & Company), 29.

35. *Gibbons v. Ogden*.

36. *Barron v. Mayor and City Council of Baltimore*, 32 U.S. 243 (1833).

37. This interpretation would change during the process of incorporation, which began in the twentieth century (see Chapter 4).

38. James Bryce, *The American Commonwealth*, Vol. I (New York: Macmillan and Co., 1888), 432.

39. *Tarble's Case*, 80 Wall. 397 (1871).

40. The Northwest Ordinance of 1787, for example, stated, "Religion, morality, and knowledge, being necessary to good government and the happiness of mankind, schools and the means of education shall forever be encouraged." Henry Steele Commager, ed., *Documents of American History*, 8th ed. (New York: Appleton-Century-Crofts, 1968), 131.

41. *Slaughterhouse Cases*, 83 U.S. (16 Wall.) 36 (1873).

42. Ronald M. Labbé and Jonathan Lurie, *The Slaughterhouse Cases: Regulation, Reconstruction, and the Fourteenth Amendment* (Lawrence: The University Press of Kansas, 2003), 211.

43. *Plessy v. Ferguson*, 163 U.S. 537 (1896).

44. Mark V. Tushnet, *The NAACP's Legal Strategy against Segregated Education, 1925–1950* (Chapel Hill: The University of North Carolina Press, 1987), 21.

45. Elazar, *American Federalism*, 33.

46. Ibid., 47–48.

47. See *United States v. E.C. Knight Company*, 156 U.S. 1 (1895); *Hammer v. Dagenhart*, 247 U.S. 251 (1918).

48. National Drought Mitigation Center, "Drought in the Dust Bowl Years," http://drought.unl.edu/DroughtBasics/DustBowl/DroughtintheDustBowlYears.aspx, accessed December 10, 2012.

49. John F. Bauman and Thomas H. Coode, *In the Eye of the Great Depression: New Deal Reporters and the Agony of the American People* (DeKalb: Northern Illinois University Press, 1988), 3.

50. "Farm Crisis Rises; Law Breaks Down: 'Holiday' Movement in Midwest Adds Thousands, with Temper Increasingly Ugly." *The New York Times*, January 22, 1933, N1.

51. Jean Edward Smith, *FDR* (New York: Random House, 2007), 327.

52. "Meier to Hoover, June 28, 1932" (*Hoover Papers*, Box 275). Quoted in James T. Patterson, *The New Deal and the States: Federalism in Transition* (Princeton, NJ: Princeton University Press, 1969), 31.

53. Smith, *FDR*, 301.

54. Ibid., 15.

55. The Twenty-first Amendment was ratified in December of 1933. President Roosevelt passed away in April 1945, early in his fourth term.

56. See, for example, Bruce Ackerman, *We the People: Foundations* (Cambridge, MA: The Belknap Press of Harvard University Press, 1991).

57. Arthur M. Schlesinger Jr., *The Age of Roosevelt, Vol II: The Coming of the New Deal* (Boston: Houghton Mifflin Company, 1958), 4.

58. See the Banking Act of 1933, the Federal Securities Act (1933), and the Securities Exchange Act of 1934.

59. Agricultural Adjustment Act (1933) (48 Stat. 31–54).

60. Smith, *FDR*, 318.

61. Alan Brinkley, *Franklin Delano Roosevelt* (New York: Oxford University Press, 2010), 36.

62. Farm Mortgage Refinancing Act (1934) (48 Stat. 456-65).

63. Smith, *FDR*, 319; Civilian Conservation Corps (1933) (48 Stat. 22-23).

64. Brinkley, *Franklin Delano Roosevelt*, 43–44.

65. Amity Shlaes, *The Forgotten Man: A New History of the Great Depression* (New York: HarperCollins Publishers, 2007), 150

66. Ibid., 151.

67. Ibid.

68. Schlesinger, *The Age of Roosevelt*, 121.

69. Brinkley, *Franklin Delano Roosevelt*, 52.

70. Steven Horwitz, "The Story of the Schechter Brothers," George Mason University History News Network, http://historynewsnetwork.org/blog/57574, accessed December 29, 2014.

71. The brothers were charged with violating the Code of Fair Competition for the Live Poultry Industry of the Metropolitan Area in and about the City of New York.

72. Shlaes, *The Forgotten Man*, 224.

73. Ibid., 218–219.

74. Ibid., 220.

75. Ibid., 227.

76. See also *Panama Refining Co. v. Ryan*, 293 U.S. 388 (1935).

77. Shlaes, *The Forgotten Man*, 241.

78. *Schechter Poultry Corp. v. United States* 295 U.S. 495 (1935).

79. Shlaes, *The Forgotten Man*, 239.

80. Ibid.

81. Robert Mayer, *The Supreme Court in American Life, Vol. 7: The Court and the American Crisis* (New York: Associated Faculty Press, Inc., 1987), vii.

82. *Schechter Poultry Corp. v. United States*.

83. Ibid.

84. Ibid.

85. Ibid.

86. Arthur M. Schlesinger Jr., *The Age of Roosevelt, Vol III: The Politics of Upheaval* (Boston: Houghton Mifflin Company, 1960), 278.

87. Paul E. Peterson, *The Price of Federalism* (Washington, D.C.: The Brookings Institution, 1995), 11.

88. Smith, *FDR*, 345.

89. Ibid., 345–346.

90. Shlaes, *The Forgotten Man*, 244.

91. Jeff Shesol, *Supreme Power: Franklin Roosevelt vs. the Supreme Court* (New York: W.W. Norton & Company, 2010), 2–3.

92. Pub. L. 74-271, 49 Stat 620-648 (1935). The programs were collectively called Old Age Security and Disability Insurance (OASDI), commonly referred to as Social Security. Aid to Dependent Children was later renamed Aid to Families with Dependent Children (AFDC), which was abolished in 1996 and replaced with Temporary Aid to Needy Families (TANF).

93. Brinkley, *Franklin Delano Roosevelt*, 54.

94. Jean Edward Smith, *FDR* (New York: Random House, 2007), 381.

95. Shesol, *Supreme Power*, 2.

96. Ibid., 3–4.

97. Brinkley, *Franklin Delano Roosevelt*, 56.

98. Shesol, *Supreme Power*, 6.

99. Suzanne Mettler, *Dividing Citizens: Gender and Federalism in New Deal Public Policy* (Ithaca, NY: Cornell University Press, 1998), 3.

100. Ibid., 45.

101. Ibid., xi.

102. Joseph F. Zimmerman, *Contemporary American Federalism: The Growth of National Power* (New York: Praeger, 1992), 118.

103. Ibid., 118–119.

104. Lawrence D. Brown, James W. Fossett, and Kenneth T. Palmer, *The Changing Politics of Federal Grants* (Washington, D.C.: The Brookings Institution, 1984), 6. President Johnson first took office on November 22, 1963, upon the assassination of President John F. Kennedy.

105. Brown et al., *The Changing Politics of Federal Grants*, 7.

106. Ibid., 8.

107. "Acceptance Speeches: Reagan: 'Time to Recapture Our Destiny,'" in CQ *Almanac 1980*, 36th ed. (Washington, D.C.: Congressional Quarterly, 1981), http://library .cqpress.com/cqalmanac/cqal80-860-25879-1173673, accessed January 7, 2013.

108. The Republican Party gained fifty-four seats in the House of Representatives and eight seats in the Senate.

109. John D. Nugent, *Safeguarding Federalism: How States Protect Their Interests in National Policymaking* (Norman: University of Oklahoma Press, 2009), 6.

110. James Madison, *Federalist No. 46*, in *The Federalist Papers*, ed. George W. Carey and James McClellan (Indianapolis, IN: Liberty Fund, 2001), 246.

111. Nugent, *Safeguarding Federalism*, 56.

112. Peterson, *The Price of Federalism*, 45.

113. Nugent, *Safeguarding Federalism*, 66. Quoting Bryan Schweitzer, "Montana Governor on 'REAL ID' Act," by Melissa Block (host), National Public Radio's *All Things Considered*, March 7, 2008.

114. "Angel McClary Raich," angeljustice.org, http:// angeljustice.org/angel/Angel_Raichs_Bio.html, accessed March 3, 2016.

115. Alaska, Colorado, Oregon, and Washington.

116. Office of National Drug Control Policy, "Marijuana Resource Center: State Laws Related to Marijuana," https://www.whitehouse .gov/ondcp/state-laws-related-to-marijuana, accessed March 5, 2016.

117. "Number of Legal Medical Marijuana Patients (as of March 1, 2016)," ProCon.org, March 3, 2016, http://medicalmarijuana.procon.org/ view.resource.php?resourceID=005889, accessed March 5, 2016.

118. James M. Cole, "Memorandum for All United States Attorneys," U.S. Department of Justice, August 29, 2013, https://www.justice.gov/iso/ opa/resources/3052013829132756857467 .pdf, accessed March 5, 2016.

Chapter 4

1. James Bamford, "The Most Wanted Man in the World, *Wired Magazine*, August 2014, http:// www.wired.com/2014/08/edward-snowden/, accessed March 8, 2016.

2. Glenn Greenwald, "NSA Whistleblower Edward Snowden: 'I Do Not Expect to See Home Again'," *The Guardian*, June 9, 2013; available from Lexis-Nexis Academic.

3. Ibid.

4. Bamford, "The Most Wanted Man in the World."

5. Greenwald, "NSA Whistleblower Edward Snowden."

6. Cheryl K. Chumley, "Donald Trump on Edward Snowden: Kill the 'Traitor,'" *The Washington Times*, July 2, 2013, http://www.washing tontimes.com/news/2013/jul/2/donald-trump-edward-snowden-kill-traitor/, accessed March 10, 2016.

7. Espionage Act of 1917 (amended in 1918).

8. Jonah Engel Bromwich, "Snowden Leaks Illegal but Were a 'Public Service,' Eric Holder Says," *The New York Times*, May 31, 2016, http://www.nytimes.com/2016/06/01/us/ holder-says-snowden-performed-a-public-service.html?_r=0.

9. Benjamin Wittes, "Edward Snowden: Civil Liberties Violator," *Lawfare*, July 7, 2014, https://www.lawfareblog.com/edward-snowden-civil-liberties-violator, accessed March 11, 2016.

10. Irving Brant, *The Bill of Rights: Its Origin and Meaning* (New York: The Bobbs-Merrill Company, Inc., 1965), 20.

11. Catherine Drinker Bowen, *Miracle at Philadelphia: The Story of the Constitutional Convention, May to September 1787* (Boston: Little, Brown and Company, 1985 [1966]), 244.

12. Brant, *The Bill of Rights*, 228–230.

13. Article III, Section 3.

14. Elbridge Gerry (MA) offered the motion; George Mason (VA) seconded it. Max Farrand, ed., *The Records of the Federal Convention of 1787, Volume II* (New Haven: Yale University Press, 1911), 588–589. Available at http://lcweb2.loc.gov/ammem/amlaw/lwfr .html, accessed July 22, 2014.

15. Farrand, *The Records of the Federal Convention of 1787*, 617–618.

16. Brant, *The Bill of Rights*, 39.

17. Alexander Hamilton, *Federalist No. 84*, in *The Federalist*, ed. George W. Carey and James McClellan (Indianapolis, IN: Liberty Fund, 2001), 447.

18. Ibid., 445.

19. Bowen, *Miracle at Philadelphia*, 245.

20. *Annals of Congress*, House of Representatives, 1st Cong., 1st sess. (June 8, 1789), 440–441. Available at http://memory .loc.gov/ammem/amlaw/lwac.html, accessed July 19, 2014.

21. Two of the proposed twelve did not receive enough votes to secure ratification. The first involved apportionment of seats in the House of Representatives, the second restricted Congress's ability to raise its own pay. This latter amendment was ratified, but not until 1992 (Twenty-seventh Amendment). Amendments are typically proposed including a date of expiry, but this was not the case for the two unratified, originally proposed amendments.

22. The National Council of the Left Wing, "The Left Wing Manifesto," *The Revolutionary Age: Devoted to the International Communist Struggle* 2, no. 1 (July 5, 1919): 6, 14, 15. Available at https://www.marxists.org/ history/usa/pubs/revolutionaryage/v2n01-jul-05-1919.pdf, accessed July 22, 2014.

23. Michael Hannon, "The People v. Benjamin Gitlow (1920)," University of Minnesota Law Library, May 2010, http://darrow.law.umn.edu/ trialpdfs/Gitlow_Case.pdf, accessed July 22, 2014.

24. Ibid., 10.

25. Ibid., 14.

26. *Gitlow v. New York*, 268 U.S. 652 (1925).

27. The Fifth Amendment to the Constitution includes a similar clause asserting that "No person . . . shall be deprived of life, liberty, or property, without due process of law," but the Supreme Court had interpreted the Fifth Amendment as only restricting the power of the federal government.

28. *The Slaughterhouse Cases*, 83 U.S. 36 (1873). The Court also placed limits on the privileges and immunities clause of the same amendment, stating that its protections apply only to national, not state, citizenship.

29. *Gitlow v. New York*. In *Chicago, Burlington & Quincy Railroad Company v. Chicago*, 166 U.S. 226 (1897), the Supreme Court had already applied the Fifth Amendment's due process clause to state actions in its reasoning, though ruling against the plaintiffs.

30. *Gitlow v. New York*.

31. *McDonald v. Chicago*, 561 U.S. 742 (2010).

32. Benjamin Gitlow, *I Confess: The Truth about American Communism* (New York: E. P. Dutton & Co., Inc., 1940).

33. *Annals of Congress*, House of Representatives, 449, 451.

34. "Thomas Jefferson to the Danbury Baptists, 1 January 1802," in *Church and State in American History: Key Documents, Decisions, and Commentary from the Past Three Centuries*, 3rd ed., ed. John F. Wilson and Donald L. Drakeman (Cambridge, MA: Westview Press, 2003), 74.

35. *Everson v. Board of Education*, 330 U.S. 1 (1947). The justices were closely divided, 5–4.

36. *Everson v. Board of Education*.

37. *Board of Education v. Allen*, 392 U.S. 236 (1968). The Court has been similarly divided over the issue of tax relief for tuition reimbursement. See *Committee for Public Education v. Nyquist*, 413 U.S. 756 (1973) and *Mueller v. Allen*, 463 U.S. 388 (1983). In *Zobrest v. Catalina Foothills School District*, 509 U.S. 1 (1993), the Court, again divided 5–4, ruled in favor of using taxpayer funds to provide a student in a Catholic high school with a sign language interpreter.

38. *Engle v. Vitale*, 370 U.S. 421 (1962).

39. *Abington School District v. Schempp*, 374 U.S. 203 (1963). The Pennsylvania case was considered with a similar program in Maryland.

40. *Abington School District v. Schempp*. Quoting Madison, "A Memorial and Remonstrance," in *The Constitution & Religion: Leading Supreme Court Cases on Church and State*, ed. Robert S. Alley (Amherst, MA: Prometheus Books, 1999), 30.

41. United States Department of Education, "Guidance on Constitutionally Protected Prayer in Public Elementary and Secondary Schools," February 7, 2003, http://www2

.ed.gov/policy/gen/guid/religionandschools/prayer_guidance.html, accessed July 25, 2014.

42. *Lemon v. Kurtzman*, 403 U.S. 602 (1971). In establishing the test, the Court drew on the logic of *Board of Education v. Allen* (1968) and other cases.

43. *Mueller v. Allen*, 463 U.S. 388 (1983); *Witters v. Washington Dept. of Services for the Blind*, 474 U.S. 481 (1986); *Zobrest v. Catalina Foothills School Dist.*, 509 U.S. 1 (1993).

44. *Cantwell v. Connecticut*, 310 U.S. 296 (1940).

45. *Employment Division Dept. of Human Resources of Oregon v. Smith*, 494 U.S. 872 (1990).

46. "The Sedition Act (1798)," in *Documents of American History*, 8th ed., ed. Henry Steele Commager (New York: Appleton-Century-Crofts, 1968), 177–178.

47. Paul E. Peterson, *The Price of Federalism* (Washington, D.C.: The Brookings Institution, 1995), 8.

48. *Schenck v. United States*, 249 U.S. 47 (1919).

49. *Abrams v. United States*, 250 U.S. 616 (1919).

50. Ibid.

51. Formally, the Alien Registration Act of 1940.

52. Brant, *The Bill of Rights*, 5.

53. *Brandenburg v. Ohio*, 395 U.S. 444 (1969).

54. Ibid.

55. *New York Times v. United States*, 403 U.S. 713 (1971).

56. *United States v. O'Brien*, 391 U.S. 367 (1968).

57. *Tinker v. Des Moines Independent Community School District*, 393 U.S. 503 (1969).

58. *Morse v. Frederick*, 551 U.S. 393 (2007).

59. *Texas v. Johnson*, 491 U.S. 397 (1989). See also *Spence v. Washington*, 418 U.S. 405 (1974).

60. The definitions of legal terms in this section are informed by Bryan A. Garner, ed., *Black's Law Dictionary*, 8th ed. (St. Paul, MN: Thompson/West, 2004).

61. *New York Times v. Sullivan*, 376 U.S. 254 (1964).

62. *R.A.V. v. St. Paul*, 505 U.S. 377 (1992).

63. Ibid.

64. *Chaplinsky v. State of New Hampshire*, 315 U.S. 586 (1942).

65. *Roth v. United States*, 354 U.S. 476 (1957).

66. *Miller v. California*, 413 U.S. 15 (1973).

67. *Reno v. American Civil Liberties Union et al.*, 521 U.S. 844 (1997).

68. *De Jonge v. Oregon*, 299 U.S. 353 (1937). See also *Edwards v. South Carolina*, 372 U.S. 229 (1963).

69. Noting, however, that the process of incorporating these rights has involved the Fourteenth Amendment as well.

70. National Firearms Act (1934).

71. *United States v. Miller*, 307 U.S. 174 (1939).

72. *District of Columbia v. Heller*, 554 U.S. 570 (2008).

73. *McDonald v. Chicago*. A similar law in Oak Park, a suburb of Chicago, was also overturned.

74. Article I, Section 9.

75. John Rawls, *A Theory of Justice* (Cambridge, MA: Belknap Press of Harvard University Press, 1999).

76. *Katz v. United States*, 389 U.S. 347 (1967).

77. See *Warden v. Hayden*, 387 U.S. 294 (1967).

78. *Mapp v. Ohio*, 367 U.S. 643 (1961).

79. *United States v. Sokolow*, 490 U.S. 1 (1989).

80. *Horton v. California*, 496 U.S. 128 (1990).

81. *Whren v. United States*, 517 U.S. 806 (1996).

82. *Kyllo v. United States*, 533 U.S. 27 (2001).

83. *Riley v. California*, 573 U.S. _____ (2014).

84. *Ferguson v. City of Charleston*, 532 U.S. 67 (2001).

85. *Vernonia School District v. Acton*, 515 U.S. 646 (1995).

86. *Board of Education of Independent School District No. 92 of Pottawatomie County v. Earls*, 536 U.S. 822 (2002).

87. *Miranda v. Arizona*, 384 U.S. 436 (1966). Miranda was retried without the illegally obtained evidence but was convicted based on other evidence, including identification by the victim and the testimony of his girlfriend.

88. *Kloppfer v. North Carolina*, 386 U.S. 213 (1967).

89. *Powell v. Alabama*, 287 U.S. 45 (1932).

90. *Johnson v. Zerbst*, 304 U.S. 458 (1938).

91. *Gideon v. Wainwright*, 372 U.S. 335 (1963).

92. *Wiggins v. Smith*, 539 U.S. 510 (2003).

93. The Court's decision in *Furman v. Georgia*, 408 U.S. 238 (1972) invalidated the use of the death penalty according to the state laws at the time, finding them arbitrary and discriminatory. Rewritten death penalty statutes were held constitutional in *Gregg v. Georgia*, 428 U.S. 153 (1976).

94. *Atkins v. Virginia*, 536 U.S. 304 (2002).

95. *Roper v. Simmons*, 543 U.S. 551 (2005).

96. "Let the Good Times Roll," ediewindsor.com, http://ediewindsor.com, accessed March 12, 2016.

97. *United States v. Windsor*, 570 U.S. __ (2013).

98. Justin Jones, "The Godmother of Gay Marriage: Edie Windsor's Passionate Life," The Daily Beast, March 18, 2015, http://www.thedailybeast.com/articles/2015/03/18/the-godmother-of-gay-marriage-edie-windsor-s-passionate-life.html, accessed March 121, 2016.

99. Article IV Section 1.

100. *United States v. Windsor*.

101. Ibid.

102. Ibid.

103. Jones, "The Godmother of Gay Marriage."

104. *Griswold v. Connecticut*, 381 U.S. 479 (1965).

105. Ibid.

106. *Lawrence v. Texas*, 539 U.S. 558 (2003). In its ruling, the Court overturned *Bowers v. Hardwick*, 478 U.S. 186 (1986).

107. *Lawrence v. Texas*.

108. *Roe v. Wade*, 410 U.S. 113 (1973).

109. Ibid.

110. See *Webster v. Reproductive Health Services*, 492 U.S. 490 (1989); *Planned Parenthood v. Casey*, 505 U.S. 833 (1992); *Stenberg v. Carhart*, 530 U.S. 914 (2000); *Gonzales v. Carhart*, 550 U.S. 124 (2007).

111. ALS Association, "What is ALS?," http://www.alsa.org/about-als/what-is-als.html, accessed March 12, 2016.

112. Chris Geidner, "Two Years after His Husband's Death, Jim Obergefell Is Still Fighting for the Right to Be Married," BuzzFeed.com, March 22, 2015, http://www.buzzfeed.com/chrisgeidner/his-husband-died-in-2013-but-jim-obergefell-is-still-fighting#.ldrnVM0Ag, accessed March 12, 2016.

113. *Obergefell v. Hodges*, 576 U.S. __ (2015).

114. Geidner, "Two Years after His Husband's Death."

115. Richard Wolf, "Grieving Widower Takes Lead in Major Gay Marriage Case," USA Today, April 10, 2015, http://www.usatoday.com/story/news/nation/2015/04/10/supreme-court-gay-marriage-obergefell/25512405/, accessed March 12, 2016.

116. Ibid.

Chapter 5

1. Harriet Hartman and Moshe Hartman, "How Equal Is Equal? A Comparison of Gender Equality among Israeli and American Jews," *Contemporary Jewry* 14, no. 1 (1993): 48–72.

2. Judith Heumann, "Justice for All: Advancing Dr. King's Call," *DIPNOTE, U.S Department of State Official Blog*, January 18, 2016, https://blogs.state.gov/stories/2016/01/18/justice-all-advancing-dr-king-s-call, accessed March 17, 2016.

3. Team Celebration, "Judith E. Huemann—Woman of Action," A Celebration of Women, July 24, 2012, http://acelebrationofwomen.org/2012/07/judith-e-heumann-woman-of-action/, accessed March 16, 2016.

4. Ibid.

5. "A Look Back at 'Section 504,'" The Minnesota Governor's Council on Developmental Disabilities, April 28, 2002, http://mn.gov/mnddc/ada-legacy/npr-504.html, accessed March 18, 2016. The article was drawn from the transcript of "Disability Rights, Part II," National Public Radio, April 28, 2002, http://www.npr.org/templates/story/story.php?storyId=1142485.

6. Michael Irvin, "The 25 Day Siege That Brought Us 504," Independent Living Institute, http://www.independentliving.org/docs4/ervin1986.html, accessed March 17, 2016.

7. Lanny E. Perkins, Esq. and Sara D. Perkins, Esq., "ADA Update," Multiple Sclerosis Foundation, http://msfocus.org/article-details.aspx?articleID=340, accessed March 16, 2016.

8. Otis, "Trailblazing Advocate Judy Heumann Says There's More Work to Do."

9. *City of Cleburne, Texas v. Cleburne Living Center, Inc.*, 473 U.S. 432 (1985).

10. Ibid. Quoting *University of California Regents v. Bakke*, 438 U.S. 265, 438 U.S. 303 (1978).

11. David Pfeiffer, "Eugenics and Disability Discrimination," *Disability & Society* 9, no. 4 (1994): 481–499.

12. American Civil Liberties Union, "Disability Rights—ACLU Position/Briefing Paper," no. 21 (Winter 1999), https://www.aclu.org/disability-

rights-aclu-positionbriefing-paper, accessed March 17, 2016.

13. Ibid.

14. The four states were Kansas (*Brown v. Board of Education*, 98 F. Supp. 797 [D. Kan. 1951]); South Carolina (*Briggs v. Elliot*, 103 F. Supp. 920 [E.D.S.C. 1952]); Delaware (*Gebhart v. Belton*, 33 Del. 145, 91 A.2d. 137 [1952]); and Virginia (*Davis v. County School Board of Prince Edward County, Virginia*, 103 F. Supp. 337 [E.D. Va. 1952]). The Washington, D.C., case was *Bolling v. Sharpe*, 347 U.S. 497 (1954). As the District of Columbia is not a state, the case was tried under the due process clause of the Fifth Amendment. Thurgood Marshall argued the South Carolina case before the Supreme Court. His legal team divided the oral arguments.

15. Jack Greenberg, *Crusaders in the Courts: How a Dedicated Band of Lawyers Fought for the Civil Rights Revolution* (New York: Basic Books, 1994), 167.

16. Alexander Hamilton, *Federalist No. 78*, in *The Federalist Papers*, ed. George W. Carey and James McClellan (Indianapolis, IN: Liberty Fund, 2001), 402.

17. Richard Kluger, *Simple Justice: The History of* Brown v. Board of Education *and Black America's Struggle for Equality* (New York: Vintage Books, 1977), 706.

18. *Dred Scott v. Sandford*, 60 U.S. 393 (1857).

19. See Eric Foner, *A Short History of Reconstruction, 1863–1877* (New York: Harper & Row Publishers, 1990).

20. Eric Foner, *Give Me Liberty! An American History* (New York: W. W. Norton & Company, 2006), 4.

21. W. E. B. Du Bois, *Black Reconstruction in America, 1860–1880* (New York: Anthem, 1992), 167.

22. Richard Wormser, *The Rise and Fall of Jim Crow* (New York: St. Martin's Press, 2003), 6.

23. Ibid., 9

24. Du Bois, *Black Reconstruction in America*, 123.

25. Greenberg, *Crusaders in the Courts*, 175.

26. Wormser, *The Rise and Fall of Jim Crow*, 11.

27. Francis Curtis, *The Republican Party: A History of Its Fifty Years' Existence and a Record of Its Measures and Leaders*, Vol. II (New York: The Knickerbocker Press, 1904), 51.

28. *Plessy v. Ferguson*, 163 U.S. 737 (1896).

29. *Plessy* did not deal with education. In 1899 the Supreme Court approved segregated educational facilities in *Cumming v. Board of Education*, 175 U.S. 528 (1899).

30. Mark V. Tushnet, *The NAACP's Legal Strategy against Segregated Education, 1925–1950* (Chapel Hill: The University of North Carolina Press, 1987), 21. The section on the NAACP's strategic decision-making processes draws heavily on Tushnet's analysis and Richard Kluger's historical account.

31. Tushnet, *The NAACP's Legal Strategy*, 36.

32. *State of Missouri ex rel Gaines v. Canada*, 305 U.S. 337 (1938).

33. Tushnet, *The NAACP's Legal Strategy*, 67–68.

34. *Sweatt v. Painter*, 339 U.S. 629 (1950); McLaurin v. Oklahoma State Regents for Higher Education, 339 U.S. 637 (1950).

35. Tushnet, *The NAACP's Legal Strategy*, 125.

36. Kluger, *Simple Justice*, 268.

37. Ibid., 395.

38. Ibid., 570.

39. Quoted in Kluger, *Simple Justice*, 574.

40. Kluger, *Simple Justice*, 656.

41. Ibid., 664.

42. *Brown v. Board of Education of Topeka*, 347 U.S. 483 (1954).

43. It was said that Justice Frankfurter told Justice Reed, who was most likely to dissent, that "a dissent is written for the future, but that there was no future for segregation." (Greenberg, *Crusaders in the Courts,* 198.)

44. Quoted in Jennifer Hochschild, *The New American Dilemma: Liberal Democracy and School Desegregation* (New Haven, CT: Yale University Press, 1984), 15.

45. Juan Williams, *Eyes on the Prize: America's Civil Rights Years, 1954–1965* (New York: Viking Penguin, Inc., 1987), 35.

46. Ibid., 34.

47. *Brown v. Board of Education of Topeka*.

48. Gerald N. Rosenberg, *The Hollow Hope: Can Courts Bring about Social Change?* (Chicago: The University of Chicago Press, 1991), 49.

49. Taylor Branch, *Parting the Waters: American in the King Years, 1954–63* (New York: Simon and Schuster, 1988), 129.

50. *Gayle v. Browder*, 352 U.S. 903 (1956).

51. Branch, *Parting the Waters*, 129.

52. Ibid., 139–140.

53. *Griffin v. Prince Edward County*, 375 U.S. 391 (1964).

54. *Green v. County School Board of New Kent County, Virginia*, 391 U.S. 430 (1968).

55. *Alexander v. Holmes County Board of Education*, 396 U.S. 19 (1969).

56. *Swann v. Charlotte-Mecklenburg Board of Education*, 401 U.S. 1 (1971).

57. *Milliken v. Bradley*, 418 U.S. 717 (1974).

58. *Regents of the University of California v. Bakke*, 438 U.S. 265 (1978).

59. *Gratz v. Bollinger*, 539 U.S. 244 (2003).

60. *Gunner v. Bollinger*, 539 U.S. 306 (2003).

61. Adam Liptak, " Supreme Court Upholds Affirmative Action Program at University of Texas," *The New York Times*, June 23, 2016, http://www.nytimes.com/2016/06/24/us/politics/supreme-court-affirmative-action-university-of-texas.html?_r=0.

62. See Eleanor Flexner, *Century of Struggle: The Woman's Rights Movement in the United States* (Cambridge, MA: The Belknap Press, 1959); and Edwin W. Small and Miriam R. Small, "Prudence Crandall: Champion of Negro Education," *The New England Quarterly* 17, no. 4 (December 1944): 506–529.

63. Flexner, *Century of Struggle*, 39.

64. Angelina Grimké, "An Appeal to the Women of the Nominally Free States," in Kathryn Kish Sklar, *Women's Rights Emerges within the Antislavery Movement: A Brief History with Documents* (Binghamton: State University of New York, 2000), 101–102.

65. Sklar, *Women's Rights Emerges*, 58.

66. *Woman's Rights Conventions, Seneca Falls & Rochester, 1848* (New York: Arno & The New York Times, 1969), 4.

67. Sklar, *Women's Rights Emerges*, 1.

68. Sally G. McMillen, *Seneca Falls and the Origins of the Women's Rights Movement* (New York: Oxford University Press, 2008), 119.

69. Frances Ellen Watkins Harper, "We Are All Bound Up Together," in Proceedings of the Eleventh Women's Rights Convention (New York: Robert J. Johnston, 1866). Read more at BlackPast.org, http://www.blackpast.org/1866-frances-ellen-watkins-harper-we-are-all-bound-together-0#sthash.rrwYWPvy.dpuf.

70. McMillen, *Seneca Falls*, 167.

71. See Jo Freeman, "How 'Sex' Got into Title VII: Persistent Opportunism as a Maker of Public Policy," *Law and Inequality: A Journal of Theory and Practice* 9, no. 2 (March 1991): 163–184; Rosalind Rosenberg, *Divided Lives: American Women in the Twentieth Century* (New York: Hill and Wang, 2008), 187–188.

72. Betty Friedan, *The Feminine Mystique* (New York: Dell Publishing Co., 1963), 351.

73. National Organization for Women, "National Organization for Women, N.O.W.) Statement of Purpose, 1966," http://coursesa.matrix.msu.edu/~hst306/documents/nowstate.html, accessed August 11, 2016.

74. Title IX of the Education Amendments of 1972, vol. 20, U.S.C. sec. 1681.

75. Jane J. Mansbridge, *Why We Lost the ERA* (Chicago: University of Chicago Press, 1986).

76. Mark R. Daniels and Robert E. Darcy, "As Time Goes By: The Arrested Diffusion of the Equal Rights Amendment," *Publius* 15, no. 4 (Autumn 1985): 51–60.

77. The distinction originally appeared in a footnote to Justice Harlan Fiske Stone's opinion in *United States v. Carolene Products Co.* 304 U.S. 144 (1938).

78. In Sklar, *Women's Rights Emerges*, 179–180. Many versions of Truth's speech have been presented. Some were heavily edited by newspapers of the time, which sometimes changed her words to fit racial stereotypes of the period. See Carla Peterson, *"Doers of the Word": African American Women Speakers and Writers in the North (1830–1880)* (New York: Oxford University Press, 1995), 47–55.

79. Sklar, *Women's Rights Emerges*, 10. See also Marilyn Richardson, ed., *Maria W. Stewart, America's First Black Woman Political Writer: Essays and Speeches* (Bloomington: Indiana University Press, 1987).

80. Kimberlé Crenshaw, "Demarginalizing the Intersection of Race and Sex: A Black Feminist Critique of Antidiscrimination Doctrine, Feminist Theory, and Antiracist Politics," *University of Chicago Legal Forum* 1989, no. 1, http://chicagounbound.uchicago.edu/cgi/viewcontent.cgi?article=1052&context=uclf, accessed August 11, 2016.

81. See Shirley J. Yee, *Black Women Abolitionists: A Study in Activism, 1828–1860* (Knoxville: The University of Tennessee Press, 1992).

82. "Thurgood Marshall Speaks: In Howard University Speech, Architect of Landmark Legal Victory Recalls Veterans of Struggle, Notes Dangers Ahead," *Ebony* (May 1979): 179.

83. Susan Saulny, "Census Data Presents Rise in Multiracial Population of Youths," *The New York Times*, March 24, 2011, http://www.nytimes.com/2011/03/25/us/25race.html, accessed on August 5, 2011.

84. Molefi Kete Asante, "Racing to Leave the Race: Black Postmodernists Off-Track," *The Black Scholar* 23 (Summer/Fall 1993): 50–51.

85. Marvin C. Arnold, "Testimony before the Subcommittee on Census, Statistics, and Postal Personnel of the House Committee on Post Office and Civil Service 103-7," June 30, 1993, 162.

86. "Transcript: Barack Obama's Speech on Race," National Public Radio, March 28, 2008, http://www.npr.org/templates/story/story.php?storyId=88478467, accessed August 5, 2011.

Chapter 6

1. From a protest and art installation titled *Carry That Weight: Rules of Engagement* by Columbia University student Emma Sulkowicz.

2. "Statement by Amanda Collins," Michigan State Senate, Senate Committee on Natural Resources, Environment and Great Lakes, March 22, 2012, http://senate.michigan.gov/committees/files/2012-SCT-NAT_-03-22-1-02.PDF, accessed February 15, 2016.

3. Ibid.

4. Nevada CCW permit holders were allowed to carry on university campuses but only after having received written permission from the Nevada System of Higher Education, which generally denies such requests. (Brian Vasek, "Rethinking the Nevada Campus Protection Act: Future Challenges & Reaching a Legislative Compromise," *Nevada Law Journal* 15, no. 1 [2014]: 389–430.)

5. "Statement by Amanda Collins."

6. Crimesider Staff, "Women with Guns: Is It a Solution to Rape on Campus?," CBS News, February 24, 2015, http://www.cbsnews.com/news/women-with-guns-is-the-push-for-concealed-carry-legislation-a-solution-to-rape-on-campus/, accessed February 12, 2016.

7. "CLP Activism: Strong Women," YouTube, https://www.youtube.com/watch?v=iFsdZGRWUWc, accessed February 20, 2016.

8. Alan Schwarz, "A Bid for Guns on Campus to Deter Rape," *The New York Times*, February 19, 2015; available from Lexis-Nexis Academic.

9. David Hemenway and Sara J. Solnick, "The Epidemiology of Self-Defense Gun Use: Evidence from the National Crime Victimization Surveys 2007–2011," *Preventative Medicine: Special Issue on the Epidemiology and Prevention of Gun Violence* 79 (October 2015): 22–27.

10. Ryan Parker, "Colorado Senator's Comments to Rape Victim Drawing Criticism," *San Jose Mercury News*, March 5, 2013; available from Lexis-Nexis Academic.

11. Alan Schwarz, "A Bid for Guns on Campuses to Deter Rape," *The New York Times*, February 18, 2015, http://www.nytimes.com/2015/02/19/us/in-bid-to-allow-guns-on-campus-weapons-are-linked-to-fighting-sexual-assault.html?_r=1, accessed May 12, 2016.

12. Alan Schwarz, "Advocates Push Guns as Tactic to Fight Rape on Campus," *International New York Times*, February 19, 2015; available from Lexis-Nexis Academic.

13. Crimesider Staff, "Women with Guns."

14. Landen Gambill, "Returning to College, Where I Was Raped," Refinery 29, October 23, 2014, http://www.refinery29.com/campus-rape-survivor, accessed May 13, 2016.

15. Dave Dewitt, "Sexual Assault Case Splits Campus, Prompts Federal Investigation," WUNC, March 7, 2013, http://wunc.org/post/sexual-assault-case-splits-campus-prompts-federal-investigation#stream/0, accessed May 13, 2016.

16. Landen Gambill, "Don't Vote to Allow Guns on College Campuses," Change.org, https://www.change.org/p/arizona-state-house-don-t-vote-to-allow-guns-on-college-campuses, accessed May 13, 2016.

17. Sidney Verba, Kay Lehman Schlozman, and Henry E. Brady, *Voice and Equality: Civic Voluntarism in American Politics* (Cambridge, MA: Harvard University Press, 1995), 42.

18. Sidney Verba and Norman H. Nie, *Participation in America: Political Democracy and Social Equality* (New York: Harper & Row, Publishers, 1972), 46–48.

19. Russell J. Dalton, "The Myth of the Disengaged American," *Comparative Study of Electoral Systems (CSES)*, 2005, http://www.cses.org/resources/results/POP_Oct2005_1.htm, accessed May 13, 2016.

20. BWOG Staff, "'Accessible, Prompt, and Equitable?' An Examination of Sexual Assault at Columbia," BWOG: Columbia Student News, January 23, 2014, http://bwog.com/2014/01/23/accessible-prompt-and-equitable-an-examination-of-sexual-assault-at-columbia/, accessed February 19, 2016.

21. Richard Perez-Pena and Kate Taylor, "Fight against Sex Assaults Holds Colleges to Account," *The New York Times*, May 4, 2014; available from Lexis-Nexis Academic.

22. Ibid.

23. Lucia Peters, "Columbia Student Emma Sulkowicz's 'Mattress Performance/Carry That Weight' Performance Art Piece Tackles Campus Sexual Assault Culture Head-On," Bustle, September 3, 2014, http://www.bustle.com/articles/38346-columbia-student-emma-sulkowiczs-mattress-performancecarry-that-weight-performance-art-piece-tackles-campus-sexual-assault-culture, accessed February 14, 2016.

24. Laura Krantz, "UVM Students Raise Awareness of Sexual Assault on Campus," *Brattleboro Reformer* (Vermont), October 31, 2014; available from Lexis-Nexis Academic.

25. Feminist Newswire, "Columbia University Fined Student Activists for the Carry That Weight Day of Action," Feminist Majority Foundation, November 10, 2014, https://feminist.org/blog/index.php/2014/11/10/columbia-university-fined-student-activists-for-the-carry-that-weight-day-of-action/, accessed February 20, 2016.

26. Sarah Kaplan, "No Longer Just a Mattress, but a Symbol," *The Washington Post*, November 29, 2014; available from Lexis-Nexis Academic.

27. Perez-Pena and Taylor, "Fight against Sex Assaults Holds Colleges to Account."

28. Office of United States Senator Claire McCaskill, Press Release, "Expanded Bipartisan Coalition Introduces Legislation to Prevent Sexual Assaults on College and University Campuses," February 26, 2015, http://www.mccaskill.senate.gov/media-center/news-releases/expanded-bipartisan-coalition-introduces-legislation-to-prevent-sexual-assaults-on-college-and-university-campuses, accessed February 20, 2016.

29. Office of United States Senator Claire McCaskill, "The Bipartisan Campus Accountability and Safety Act," http://www.mccaskill.senate.gov/imo/media/doc/CampusAccountabilityAndSafetyAct.pdf, accessed February 20, 2016.

30. John Lauerman, "Campus Sexual Assault Hearings Planned by Senator McCaskill," Bloomberg Business, April 22, 2014, http://www.bloomberg.com/news/articles/2014-04-22/campus-sexual-assault-hearings-planned-by-senator-mccaskill, accessed February 20, 2016.

31. Gambill, "Returning to College, Where I Was Raped."

32. Ibid.

33. Roberta Smith, "In a Mattress, a Fulcrum of Art and Political Protest," *The New York Times*, September 22, 2014; available from Lexis-Nexis Academic.

34. Kaminer, "A New Factor in Campus Assault Cases."

35. "Gillibrand Testimony before Senate Judiciary at Hearing to Examine Role of Law Enforcement in Campus Sexual Assault Cases," Plus Media Solutions, December 10, 2014; available from Lexis-Nexis Academic.

36. Jessica Glenza, "Columbia University Student at Center of Alleged Rape Calls Lawsuit 'Ridiculous'" *The Guardian*, April 24, 2015; available from Lexis-Nexis Academic.

37. Ibid.

38. Ibid.

39. Jose A. DelReal, "Voter Turnout in 2014 Was the Lowest Since WWII," *The Washington Post*, November 10, 2014, https://www.washingtonpost.com/news/post-politics/wp/2014/11/10/voter-turnout-in-2014-was-the-lowest-since-wwii/, accessed February 19, 2016.

40. Anthony Downs, *An Economic Theory of Democracy* (New York: HarperCollins: 1957), 233.

41. Raymond E. Wolfinger and Steven J. Rosenstone, *Who Votes?* (New Haven, CT: Yale University Press, 1980).

42. See Eric Plutzer, "Becoming a Habitual Voter: Inertia, Resources, and Growth in Young Adulthood," *American Political Science Review* 96, no. 1 (March 2002): 41–56.

43. Drew DeSilver, "U.S. Voter Turnout Trails Most Developed Countries," Pew Research Center, May 6, 2015, http://www.pewresearch.org/fact-tank/2015/05/06/u-s-voter-turnout-trails-most-developed-countries/, accessed February 16, 2016.

44. Christopher Uggen and Sarah Shannon, "State-Level Estimates of Felon Disenfranchisement in the United States, 2010," The Sentencing Project, July 2012, http://sentencingproject.org/doc/publications/fd_State_Level_Estimates_of_Felon_Disen_2010.pdf, accessed February 28, 2016.

45. *Symm v. United States*, 439 U.S. 1105 (1979).

46. Laura Fitzpatrick, "College Students Still Face Voting Stumbling Blocks," *Time*, October 14, 2008, http://content.time.com/time/nation/article/0,8599,1849906,00.html, accessed February 15, 2016.

47. Center for American Women and Politics, Eagleton Institute of Politics, Rutgers, the State University of New Jersey, "Fact Sheet: Gender Differences in Voter Turnout," October 2015, http://www.cawp.rutgers.edu/sites/default/files/resources/genderdiff.pdf, accessed June 10, 2016.

48. Angus Campbell et al., *The American Voter*, Midway Reprint (Chicago: The University of Chicago Press, 1960).

49. Steven J. Rosenstone and John Mark Hansen, *Mobilization, Participation, and Democracy in America* (New York: Macmillan Publishing Company, 1993).

50. USA.gov, "Voter Registration Deadlines for the General Election by State," https://www.usa.gov/voter-registration-deadlines, accessed February 17, 2016.

51. Jack Fitzpatrick, "College Students Face New Voting Barriers," Minnpost, August 16, 2012, https://www.minnpost.com/politics-policy/2012/08/college-students-face-new-voting-barriers, accessed February 19, 2016.

52. National Conference of State Legislatures, "Online Voter Registration," May 9, 2016, http://www.ncsl.org/research/elections-and-campaigns/electronic-or-online-voter-registration.aspx, accessed June 7, 2016.

53. Dorothy Edwards, "Origin of Green Dot etc.," greendot.etcetra, https://www.livethegreendot.com/gd_origins.html, accessed May 15, 2016.

54. Tyler Kingkade, "This Is Why Every College Is Talking about Bystander Intervention," *The Huffington Post*, February 8, 2016, http://www.huffingtonpost.com/entry/colleges-bystander-intervention_us_56abc134e4b0010e80ea021d, accessed May 14, 2016.

55. Ibid.

56. Collin Brennan and Kristi Cook, "Why College Students Aren't Voting (and Why It Matters)," *USA Today*, September 25, 2015, http://college.usatoday.com/2015/09/25/why-college-students-arent-voting/, accessed February 16, 2016.

57. Ibid.

58. Richard Fry, "Millennials Overtake Baby Boomers as America's Largest Generation," Pew Research Center, April 25, 2016, http://www.pewresearch.org/fact-tank/2016/04/25/millennials-overtake-baby-boomers, accessed June 7, 2016.

59. Hollie Russon Gilman and Elizabeth Stokes, "The Civic and Political Participation of Millennials," https://www.newamerica.org/downloads/The_Civic_and_Political_Participation_of_Millennials.pdf, accessed February 20, 2016.

60. Pew Research Center, "Millennials in Adulthood: Detached from Institutions, Networked with Friends," March 7, 2014, http://www.pewsocialtrends.org/2014/03/07/millennials-in-adulthood/, accessed February 20, 2016.

61. Ibid.

62. Alia Wong, "The Renaissance of Student Activism," *The Atlantic*, May 21, 2015, http://www.theatlantic.com/education/archive/2015/05/the-renaissance-of-student-activism/393749/, accessed February 18, 2016.

63. Mike Paluska, "Hundreds of Students Protest for Embattled History Teacher," CBS46.com, September 9, 2014, http://www.cbs46.com/story/26491159/hundreds-of-students-protest-for-embattled-history-teacher, accessed February 21, 2016.

64. Wong, "The Renaissance of Student Activism."

65. Institute of Politics, Harvard University, "Survey of Young Americans' Attitudes Toward Politics and Public Service: 26th Edition," October 29, 2014, http://www.iop.harvard.edu/sites/default/files_new/fall%20poll%2014%20-%20exec%20summ%20final.pdf, accessed February 28, 2016.

66. Russell J. Dalton, *The Good Citizen: How a Younger Generation Is Reshaping American Politics* (Washington, D.C.: CQ Press, 2008), 171.

Chapter 7

1. Mitch Smith, "A Year On, Ferguson Killing Is Recalled," *The New York Times*, August 8, 2015, http://www.nytimes.com/2015/08/09/us/a-year-on-ferguson-killing-is-recalled.html?_r=0.

2. "Police-Community Reform and the Two Fergusons," Editorial, *St. Louis Post-Dispatch*, December 3, 2014, http://www.stltoday.com/news/opinion/columns/the-platform/editorial-police-community-reform-and-the-two-fergusons/article_c486f098-588a-5951-af85-036d74bd6999.html.

3. Leah Thorsen, "Shooting of Teen by Ferguson Police Officer Spurs Angry Backlash," *St. Louis Post-Dispatch*, August 10, 2014; available from Lexis-Nexis Academic.

4. "Ferguson Timeline," *St. Louis Post-Dispatch*, August 2, 2015; available from Lexis-Nexis Academic.

5. Lisa Brown, "Man Shot by Police in Ferguson after He Fired at Officers, Police Say," *St. Louis Post-Dispatch*, August 10, 2014; available from Lexis-Nexis Academic.

6. Tim Barker, "Ferguson-Area Businesses Cope with Aftermath of Weekend Riot," *St. Louis Post-Dispatch*, August 12, 2014; available from Lexis-Nexis Academic.

7. Joe Holleman and Kevin Johnson, "Ferguson Notes Ferguson Police Shooting," *St. Louis Post-Dispatch*, November 22, 2014. (Lexis-Nexis Academic Universe)

8. Christine Byers, "Darren Wilson Resigns from Ferguson Police Department: 'It Is My Hope That My Resignation Will Allow the Community to Heal,'" *St. Louis Post-Dispatch*, November 30, 2014; available from Lexis-Nexis Academic.

9. Frances Robles and Michael S. Schmidt, "Shooting Accounts Differ as Holder Schedules Visit," *The New York Times*, August 20, 2014; available from Lexis-Nexis Academic.

10. Amanda Paulson, "In Ferguson's Wake, Outcries Arise about Police Shootings in Other Cities," *The Christian Science Monitor*, August 19, 2014; available from Lexis-Nexis Academic.

11. "When Does a Moment Become a Movement?," *The Washington Post*, August 24, 2014; available from Lexis-Nexis Academic.

12. Smith, "A Year On, Ferguson Killing is Recalled."

13. "Police-Community Reform and the Two Fergusons."

14. See Paul M. Sniderman, Richard A. Brody, and Philip E. Tetlock, *Reasoning and Choice: Explorations in Political Psychology* (New York: Cambridge University Press, 1991).

15. Walter Lippmann, *Public Opinion* (New York: The Macmillan Company, 1957 [1922]), 81.

16. Angus Campbell et al., *The American Voter* (Chicago: The University of Chicago Press, 1960), 151.

17. Philip E. Converse, "The Nature of Belief Systems in Mass Publics," in *Ideology and Discontent*, ed. David E Apter (London: The Free Press of Glencoe, 1964), 212.

18. Christopher H. Achen, "Mass Political Attitudes and the Survey Response," *The American Political Science Review* 69, no. 4 (1975): 1218–1231.

19. John Zaller and Stanley Feldman, "A Simple Theory of the Survey Response: Answering Questions versus Revealing Preferences," *American Journal of Political Science* 36, no. 3 (1992): 582.

20. Michael Delli Carpini and Scott Keeter, *What Americans Know about Politics and Why It Matters* (New Haven, CT: Yale University Press, 1996).

21. John Zaller, *The Nature and Origins of Mass Opinion* (New York: Cambridge University Press, 1992).

22. While Zaller also maintains the traditional distinction between elite and mass opinion, his work emphasizes the ability of masses to draw on political elites in the process of constructing opinions.

23. Samuel L. Popkin, *The Reasoning Voter: Communication and Persuasion in Political Campaigns* (Chicago: The University of Chicago Press, 1991), 212.

24. Arthur Lupia and Mathew D. McCubbins, *The Democratic Dilemma: Can Citizens Learn What They Need to Know?* (New York: Cambridge University Press, 1998).

25. Wendy M. Rahn, "The Role of Partisan Stereotypes in Information Processing about Political Candidates," *American Journal of Political Science* 37, no. 2 (1993): 472–496.

26. See James Surowiecki, *The Wisdom of Crowds* (New York: Doubleday, 2004).

27. Bernard R. Berelson, Paul F. Lazarsfeld, and William N. McPhee, *Voting: A Study of Opinion Formation in a Presidential Campaign* (Chicago: The University of Chicago Press, 1954), 312.

28. Benjamin I. Page and Robert Y. Shapiro, *The Rational Public: Fifty Years of Trends in Americans' Policy Preferences* (Chicago: The University of Chicago Press, 1992), 14.

29. Chuck Raasch, "Since Brown Shooting, It's Been Night-and-Day in the Community," *St. Louis Post-Dispatch*, August 14, 2014; available from Lexis-Nexis Academic.

30. Julie Bosman, "Bruised and Weary, Ferguson Struggles to Heal," *The New York Times*, October 7, 2014; available from Lexis-Nexis Academic.

31. Julie Hirschfeld Davis, "Calling for Calm in Ferguson, Obama Cites Need for Improved Race Relations," *The New York Times*, August 19, 2014; available from Lexis-Nexis Academic.

32. Bosman, "Bruised and Weary, Ferguson Struggles to Heal."

33. Ibid.

34. Ibid.

35. Ibid.

36. Touré, "Black America and the Burden of the Perfect Victim," *The Washington Post*, August 24, 2014; available from Lexis-Nexis Academic.

37. David Hunn, "No Charges for Wilson, Arson, Rioting Erupt in Ferguson Decision: Federal Inquiries Continue," *St. Louis Post-Dispatch*, November 25, 2014; available from Lexis-Nexis Academic.

38. "Ferguson Timeline."

39. Chuck Raasch, "Clay Says Ferguson Revealed 'Staggering Divisions' in America," *St. Louis Post-Dispatch*, June 10, 2015; available from Lexis-Nexis Academic.

40. Paulson, "In Ferguson's Wake, Outcries Arise about police Shootings in Other Cities."

41. Robert D. Behn, "What Right Do Public Managers Have to Lead?" *Public Administration Review* 58, no. 3 (1998): 209–224.

42. James M. Druckman, "The Implications of Framing Effects for Citizen Competence," *Political Behavior* 23, no. 3 (Sep. 2001): 225–256.

43. Pew Research Center, "Questionnaire Design," http://www.pewresearch.org/methodology/u-s-survey-research/questionnaire-design/.

44. Darren W. Davis and Brian D. Silver, "Stereotype Threat and Race of Interviewer Effects in a Survey on Political Knowledge," *American Journal of Political Science* 47, no. 1 (2003): 33–45.

45. Fred I. Greenstein, "The Benevolent Leader: Children's Images of Political Authority," *The American Political Science Review* 54, no. 4 (1960): 934–943; David Easton and Robert D. Hess, "The Child's Political World," *Midwest Journal of Political Science* 6, no. 3 (1962): 229–246. For a more qualified view of the effectiveness of parent-child transmission of political attitudes and values, see M. Kent Jennings and Richard G. Niemi, "The Transmission of Political Values from Parent to Child," *The American Political Science Review* 62, no. 1 (1968): 169–184.

46. Christopher H. Achen, "Parental Socialization and Rational Party Identification," *Political Behavior* 24, no. 2 (2002): 151–170.

47. See Kenneth P. Langton and M. Kent Jennings, "Political Socialization and the High School Civics Curriculum in the United States," *The American Political Science Review* 62, no. 3 (1968): 852–867.

48. David E. Campbell, *Why We Vote: How Schools and Communities Shape Our Civic Life* (Princeton, NJ: Princeton University Press, 2006).

49. Lee H. Ehman, "The American School in the Political Socialization Process," *Review of Educational Research* 50, no. 1 (1980): 99–119.

50. Lisa Brown, "Hundreds of Protesters March to Ferguson Police Department," *St. Louis Post-Dispatch*, August 21, 2014; available from Lexis-Nexis Academic.

51. Ibid.

52. Jessica Block, "Call for Paper Ballots Slows Voting," *St. Louis Post-Dispatch*, November 5, 2014; available from Lexis-Nexis Academic.

53. John R. Alford, Carolyn Funk, and John R. Hibbing, "Are Political Orientations Genetically Transmitted?" *The American Political Science Review* 99, no. 2 (2005): 153.

54. Bill McClellan, "Ferguson Police Chief Takes on a Battle of Words," *St. Louis Post-Dispatch*, August 20, 2014, http://www.stltoday.com/news/local/columns/bill-mcclellan/mcclellan-ferguson-police-chief-takes-on-a-battle-of-words/article_6073018d-35ff-5857-84bd-f21cf1130259.html.

55. "When Does a Moment Become a Movement?" *The Washington Post*, August 24, 2014; available from Lexis-Nexis Academic.

56. Robert Patrick, "Naming Officers Who Fire Shots Far from Routine in St. Louis Area," *St. Louis Post-Dispatch*, August 14, 2014; available from Lexis-Nexis Academic.

57. David Hunn, "How Computer Hackers Changed the Ferguson Protests," *St. Louis Post-Dispatch*, August 13, 2014; available from Lexis-Nexis Academic.

58. Ibid.

59. See for example, Morris P. Fiorina, *Culture War? The Myth of a Polarized America* (New York: Longman/Pearson, 2011).

60. Pew Research Center, "Stark Racial Divisions in Reactions to Ferguson Police Shooting," August 18, 2014, http://www.people-press.org/files/2014/08/8-18-14-Ferguson-Release.pdf.

61. Michael Dawson, *Black Visions: The Roots of Contemporary African American Political Ideologies* (Chicago: The University of Chicago Press, 2001).

62. Dennis Chong and Dukhong Kim, "The Experiences and Effects of Economic Status among Racial and Ethnic Minorities," *American Political Science Review* 100, no. 3 (2006): 335–351.

63. Evelyn M. Simien, "Race, Gender, and Linked Fate," *Journal of Black Studies* 35, no. 5 (2005): 529.

64. Pew Research Center, "Stark Racial Divisions in Reactions to Ferguson Police Shooting."

65. Bosman, "Bruised and Weary, Ferguson Struggles to Heal."

66. Lauren Carroll, "Rand Paul Says Federal Program Incentivizes Police Militarization," *Tampa Bay Times*, August 21, 2014; available from Lexis-Nexis Academic.

67. Patrick Jonsson, "How Current Events Might Play into America's Shift in Favor of Gun Rights," *The Christian Science Monitor*, December 11, 2014; available from Lexis-Nexis Academic.

68. Ibid.

69. Pew Research Center, "Sharp Racial Divisions in Reactions to Brown, Garner Decisions: Many Blacks Expect Police-Minority Relations to Worsen," December 8, 2014, http://www.people-press.org/2014/12/08/sharp-racial-divisions-in-reactions-to-brown-garner-decisions/.

70. "1 Person Shot, Crowd Scatters as Gunshots Ring out Late Sunday in Ferguson," *St. Louis Post-Dispatch*, August 10, 2015; available from Lexis-Nexis Academic.

71. Smith, "A Year On, Ferguson Killing Is Recalled."

72. Zeeshan Aleem, "The First Democratic Debate Proved That Black Lives Matter Is Making a Difference," Policy.Mic, October 14, 2015, http://mic.com/articles/126730/the-first-democratic-debate-proved-that-black-lives-matter-is-making-a-difference.

73. Ibid.

74. Ibid.

75. Ibid.

76. Lilly Fowler, "Members of the Congressional Black Caucus Arrive in Ferguson to Pledge Their Support," *St. Louis Post-Dispatch*, January 19, 2015; available from Lexis-Nexis Academic.

77. Ibid.

78. Jeremy Kohler, "Prominent Ferguson Protesters Publish Anti-Police Violence Policy Platform," *St. Louis Post-Dispatch*, August 22, 2015; available from Lexis-Nexis Academic.

79. Ibid.

80. Pew Research Center, "Across Racial Lines, More Say Nation Needs to Make Changes to Achieve Racial Equality," August 5, 2015, http://www.people-press.org/2015/08/05/across-racial-lines-more-say-nation-needs-to-make-changes-to-achieve-racial-equality/; Scott Clement, "A Year after Ferguson, 6 in 10 Americans Say Changes Are Needed to Give Blacks and Whites Equal Rights," *The Washington Post*, August 5, 2015, https://www.washingtonpost.com/news/the-fix/wp/2015/08/05/what-changed-since-ferguson-americans-are-far-more-worried-about-black-rights/.

81. John W. Kingdon, *Agendas, Alternatives, and Public Policies*, 2nd ed. (New York: Longman, 2003), 1.

82. Mark Trumbull, "How Differently Do Blacks and Whites View Ferguson? Here Are the Numbers," *The Christian Science Monitor*, November 21, 2104; available from Lexis-Nexis Academic.

83. Bosman, "Bruised and Weary, Ferguson Struggles to Heal."

Chapter 8

1. Mike Guzman, "I Wonder," Doonesbury.com, *The Sandbox*, October 20, 2006, http://gocomics.typepad.com/the_sandbox/2006/10/index.html, accessed May 18, 2015.

2. James Hider, "Milblogs: Telling It Like It Is on the Front Line," *The Times* (London), October 11, 2004; available from Lexis-Nexis Academic.

3. Nikki Schwab, "Blogs Chronicle War from Soldiers' Perspectives," *The Washington Post*, May 2, 2007, http://www.washingtonpost.com/wp-dyn/content/article/2007/05/02/AR2007050202253.html, accessed April 16, 2016.

4. Ibid.

5. Michelle Rosengarten, "Notes & Recent Development: All Quiet on the Middle Eastern Front? Proposed Legislation to Regulate Milblogs and Effectuate the First Amendment in the Combat Zone," Yeshiva University, *Cardozo Arts & Entertainment Law Journal*, 2007; available from Lexis-Nexis Academic.

6. Katherine C. Den Bleyker, "The First Amendment versus Operational Security: Where Should the Milblogging Balance Lie?," *Fordham Intellectual Property, Media and Entertainment Law Journal* 17, no. 2 (2006): 410.

7. Ibid., 433.

8. Chuck Haga, "The Blogs of War; The Diaries of Dan (Zeke) Gazelka, a Minnesota National Guard Sergeant Deployed in Iraq, Are a Vivid Example of How Soldiers and Their Families Are Turning Online to Express Their Hopes and Fears," *Star Tribune* (Minneapolis), March 18, 2007; available from Lexis-Nexis Academic.

9. Mark Memmott, "'Milbloggers' Are Typing Their Place in History," *USA Today*, May 12, 2005; available from Lexis-Nexis Academic.

10. "Soldiers Use Web to Share Their Lives," *The Augusta Chronicle* (Georgia), November 7, 2005; available from Lexis-Nexis Academic.

11. Chris Vaughn, "Military Increasingly Open to Bloggers in the Ranks; Soldiers Offer Perspective Mainstream Media Cannot," *The Washington Post*, October 12, 2008; available from Lexis-Nexis Academic.

12. Haga, "The Blogs of War."

13. Patrick Novotny, *The Press in American Politics, 1787–2012* (Denver, CO: Praeger, 2014), 1.

14. Ibid., 2.

15. Max Farrand, ed., *The Records of the Federal Convention of 1787, Volume II* (New Haven: Yale University Press, 1911), 334.

16. Michael Schudson, *Discovering the News: A Social History of American Newspapers* (New York: Basic Books, 1978), 15–16.

17. Ibid., 18.

18. John D. Stevens, *Sensationalism and the New York Press* (New York: Columbia University Press, 1991).

19. The Associated Press, "AP's History," http://www.ap.org/company/history/ap-history, accessed June 13, 2015.

20. David Protess, *The Journalism of Outrage: Investigative Reporting and Agenda Building in America* (New York: Guilford Press, 1991).

21. Novotny, *The Press in American Politics*, 96.

22. Jeffrey M. Berry and Sarah Sobieraj, *The Outrage Industry: Political Opinion Media and the New Incivility* (New York: Oxford University Press, 2014), 7.

23. Jules Witcover, "Brian Williams' Fib: Embellished Stories May Be the Norm in Politics, but They're a Career-Killer in Journalism," *The Baltimore Sun*, February 10, 2015; available from Lexis-Nexis Academic.

24. "The Revolution Will Be Posted," *The New York Times*, November 2, 2004; available from Lexis-Nexis Academic.

25. Garrett Hardin, "The Tragedy of the Commons," *Science* 162, no. 3859 (1968): 1243–1248.

26. *Annual Report of the Federal Radio Commission to the Congress of the United States for the Fiscal Year Ended June 30, 1927* (Washington, D.C.: U.S. Government Printing Office, 1927), 1.

27. Federal Communications Commission, "Telecommunications Act of 1996," https://transition.fcc.gov/telecom.html, accessed June 25, 2015.

28. Alex Byers, "Court Upholds Obama-backed Net Neutrality Rules," Politico, June 14, 2016, http://www.politico.com/story/2016/06/court-upholds-obama-backed-net-neutrality-rules-224309, accessed June 24, 2016.

29. Clyde Wayne Crews Jr., "Counterpoint: A Defense of Media Monopoly," *Communications Lawyer* (Fall 2003): 13–14.

30. Doris A. Graber, *Mass Media and American Politics*, 8th ed. (Washington, D.C: CQ Press, 2010), 52.

31. "Applicability of the Fairness Doctrine in the Handling of Controversial Issues of Public Importance," 29 Fed. Reg. 10426 (1964). Quoted in Kathleen Ann Ruane, *Fairness Doctrine: History and Constitutional Issues* (Washington, D.C.: Congressional Research Service, 2011), 2.

32. Graber, *Mass Media and American Politics*, 53.

33. NBC News, "Dateline Special: Operation Iraqi Freedom," March 26, 2003, http://www.nbcnews.com/nightly-news/video/dateline-special-operation-iraqi-freedom-394019395828, accessed May 20, 2015.

34. Ibid.

35. *Late Night with David Letterman*, YouTube, March 26, 2013, https://www.youtube.com/watch?v=hq6Sp5GNWHA, accessed June 2, 2015.

36. *NBC Nightly News*, "New York Rangers Fans Break Out in Applause for Veteran," YouTube, February 2, 2015. https://www.youtube.com/watch?v=0hxQ_PM_gDc. Accessed June 8, 2015.

37. Bryan Burrough, "The Inside Story of the Civil War for the Soul of NBC News," *Vanity Fair*, May 2015, http://www.vanityfair.com/news/2015/04/nbc-news-brian-williams-scandal-comcast, accessed May 20, 2015.

38. Travis J. Tritten, "In His Words: Brian Williams' Interview with *Stars and Stripes*," *Stars and Stripes*, February 9, 2015, http://www.stripes.com/news/us/in-his-words-brian-williams-interview-with-stars-and-stripes-1.328590.

39. Mary McNamara, "Brian Williams: A Brand, Now Tarnished," *Los Angeles Times*, February 9, 2015; available from Lexis-Nexis Academic.

40. Rem Reider, "Brian Williams Loses Credibility with 'Mistake'; Hard to See How Anchor Will Survive as Face of NBC News," *USA Today*, February 6, 2015; available from Lexis-Nexis Academic.

41. Paul Farhi, "NBC Remains Mum but Privately Stands behind Williams," *The Washington Post*, February 6, 2015; available from Lexis-Nexis Academic.

42. Emily Steel and Ravi Somaiya, "Williams Suspended, at Low Point in His Career," *The New York Times*, February 11, 2015; available from Lexis-Nexis Academic.

43. Brian Moylan, "That's Entertainment: Why Brian Williams Will Survive His NBC Scandal," *The Guardian*, February 9, 2015; available from Lexis-Nexis Academic.

44. Burrough, "The Inside Story of the Civil War for the Soul of NBC News."

45. Moylan, "That's Entertainment."

46. Verne Gay, "Under Fire for War Tale: Brian Williams Criticized after Retracting Rocket Story," *Newsday* (New York), February 6, 2015; available from Lexis-Nexis Academic.

47. Brad Knickerbocker, "Brian Williams Off the Air: Will He Ever Be Back?," *The Christian Science Monitor*, February 8, 2015; available from Lexis-Nexis Academic.

48. Tony Hicks, "Brian Williams Blasted after Apologizing for Iraq War Lie," *Contra Costa Times* (California), February 5, 2015; available from Lexis-Nexis Academic.

49. Ibid.

50. Burrough, "The Inside Story of the Civil War for the Soul of NBC News."

51. Ibid.

52. Manuel Roig-Franzia, Scott Higham, and Paul Farhi, "At NBC, an Intense Debate on Firing Williams," *The Washington Post*, February 12, 2015; available from Lexis-Nexis Academic.

53. Peter Lauria, "Brian Williams' Years of Courting Celebrity May Lead to His Undoing," *The Hollywood Reporter*, February 6, 2015; available from Lexis-Nexis Academic.

54. Gloria Goodale, "Brian Williams Suspended: How Big a Blow Was Dealt to Network News?," *The Christian Science Monitor*, February 10, 2015; available from Lexis-Nexis Academic.

55. Michael Parkin, "Taking Late Night Comedy Seriously: How Candidate Appearances on Late Night Television Can Engage Voters," *Political Research Quarterly* 63, no. 1 (2010): 3–15.

56. Matthew A. Baum and Angela S. Jamison, "The *Oprah* Effect: How Soft News Helps Inattentive Citizens Vote Consistently," *The Journal of Politics* 68, no. 4 (2006): 946–959.

57. Matthew A. Baum, "Sex, Lies, and War: How Soft News Brings Foreign Policy to the Inattentive Public," *The American Political Science Review* 96, no. 1 (2002): 91–109.

58. Jody Baumgartner and Jonathan S. Morris, "The *Daily Show* Effect: Candidate Evaluations, Efficacy, and American Youth," *American Politics Research* 34, no. 3 (2006): 341–367.

59. Thomas E. Patterson, "Doing Well and Doing Good," Faculty Research Working Paper Series, RWP01-001 (Cambridge, MA: John F. Kennedy School of Government, Harvard University, 2000).

60. See, for example, Bernard Goldberg, *Bias: A CBS Insider Exposes How the Media Distort the News* (New York: Perennial, 2002).

61. See, for example, William Schneider and I. A. Lewis, "Views on the News," *Public Opinion* 8, no. 4 (1985): 6–13.

62. D. Domke et al., "The Politics of Conservative Elites and the 'Liberal Media' Argument," *Journal of Communication* 49, no. 4 (1999): 35–58.

63. Frank Newport, "Brian Williams Situation Plays Out in Context of Already Low Trust in Mass Media," Gallup, February 11, 2015, http://www.gallup.com/opinion/polling-matters/181544/brian-williams-situation-plays-context-already-low-trust-mass-media.aspx?g_source=trust%20media&g_medium=search&g_campaign=tiles, accessed May 12, 2016.

64. Larry J. Sabato, *Feeding Frenzy: How Attack Journalism Has Transformed American Politics* (New York: Free Press, 1991).

65. Walter Lippmann, *Public Opinion* (New York: Harcourt Brace, 1922), 81.

66. Bernard R. Berelson, Paul F. Lazarsfeld, and William N. McPhee, *Voting: A Study of Opinion Formation in a Presidential Campaign* (Chicago: The University of Chicago Press, 1954).

67. James N. Druckman and Kjersten R. Nelson, "Framing and Deliberation: How Citizens' Conversations Limit Elite Influence," *American Journal of Political Science* 47, no. 4 (2003): 730. See also Thomas E. Nelson, Rosalee A. Clawson, and Zoe M. Oxley, "Media Framing of a Civil Liberties Conflict and Its Effect on Tolerance," *American Political Science Review* 91, no. 3 (1997): 567–583.

68. Harold Lasswell, "The Structure and Function of Communication in Society," in *Mass Communications*, ed. Wilbur Schram (Urbana: The University of Illinois Press, 1969), 103, as discussed in Graber, *Mass Media and American Politics*, 5.

69. Graber, *Mass Media and American Politics*, 5.

70. Pew Research Center, "What Americans Know: 1989–2007," April 15, 2007, http://www.people-press.org/files/legacy-pdf/319.pdf.

71. Markus Prior, *Post-Broadcast Democracy: How Media Choice Increases Inequality in Political Involvement and Polarizes Elections* (New York: Cambridge University Press, 2007).

72. Aldous Huxley, *Brave New World* (London: Chatto & Windus, 1932).

73. Prior, *Post-Broadcast Democracy*, 142.

74. Andrea Caumont, "Who's Not Online? 5 Factors Tied to the Digital Divide," Pew Research Center, November 8, 2013, http://www.pewresearch.org/fact-tank/2013/11/08/whos-not-online-5-factors-tied-to-the-digital-divide/, accessed Mary 12, 2016.

75. *The Daily Show with Jon Stewart*, "Guardians of the Veracity," February 11, 2015, http://www.cc.com/video-clips/j3ware/the-daily-show-with-jon-stewart-guardians-of-the-veracity, accessed April 16, 2016.

76. Ibid.

77. Ibid.

78. Moylan, "That's Entertainment."

79. *The Daily Show with Jon Stewart*, "Guardians of the Veracity."

80. Ibid.

81. Ibid.

82. Frazier Moore, "Jon Stewart's Exit as a Phony Newsman Is a Loss to Real News," Business Insider, February 11, 2015, http://www.businessinsider.com/jon-stewarts-exit-as-a-phony-newsman-is-a-loss-to-real-news-2015-2.

83. Jason Zinoman, "A Late-Night Host Who Seamlessly Mixed Analysis, Politics, and Humor," Critic's Notebook, *International New York Times*, February 12, 2015; available from Lexis-Nexis Academic.

Chapter 9

1. Jonathan Rauch, "The Secret to Saner Elections? Stronger State Parties," *The Los Angeles Times*, March 22, 2016, http://www.latimes.com/opinion/op-ed/la-oe-0322-rauch-state-parties-20160322-story.html.

2. Center for Responsive Politics, "Hillary Clinton (D): Top Industries, Federal Election Data," February 22, 2016, http://www.opensecrets.org/pres16/indus.php?id=N00000019&cycle=2016&type=f&src=o.

3. Michael Barone and Chuck McCutcheon, *The Almanac of American Politics 2014* (Chicago: University of Chicago Press, 2013), 1704–1705.

4. "Transcript of the Democratic Presidential Debate in Milwaukee," *The New York Times*, February 11, 2016, http://www.nytimes.com/2016/02/12/us/politics/transcript-of-the-democratic-presidential-debate-in-milwaukee.html?_r=0.

5. Eliza Gray, "Why Democrats Love Denmark," *Time*, October 14, 2015, http://time.com/4073063/why-democrats-love-denmark/.

6. Chuck McCutcheon, "Young Voters," *CQ Researcher*, October 2, 2015, http://library.cqpress.com/cqresearcher/document.php?id=cqresrre2015100203.

7. Joshua Gillin, "Bush Says Trump Was a Democrat Longer than a Republican 'in the Last Decade,'" PolitiFact, August 24, 2015, http://www.politifact.com/florida/statements/2015/aug/24/jeb-bush/bush-says-trump-was-democrat-longer-republican-las/.

8. Ibid.

9. Mitt Romney Facebook post, March 18, 2016, https://www.facebook.com/mittromney/posts/10153370698696121.

10. "'This Week' Transcript: Gov. John Kasich," ABC News, December 27, 2015, http://abcnews.go.com/Politics/week-transcript-gov-john-kasich/story?id=35959367.

11. Nicholas Confessore and Karen Yourish, "Measuring Donald Trump's Mammoth Advantage in Free Media," *The New York Times*, March 15, 2016, http://www.nytimes.com/2016/03/16/upshot/measuring-donald-trumps-mammoth-advantage-in-free-media.html.

12. Jim Rutenberg, "The Mutual Dependence of Donald Trump and the News Media," *The New York Times*, March 20 2016, http://www.nytimes.com/2016/03/21/business/media/the-mutual-dependence-of-trump-and-the-news-media.html.

13. Michael Cooper Jr., "A Message from Trump's America," *U.S. News & World Report*, March 9, 2016, http://www.usnews.com/news/the-report/articles/2016-03-09/a-message-from-trumps-america.

14. Lee Drutman, "Sanders and Trump Really Are the Candidates of Economic Pessimism," Vox.com, April 1, 2016, http://www.vox.com/polyarchy/2016/4/1/11340264/sanders-trump-economic-pessimism.

15. Jim Tankersley, "Five Myths about Trade," *The Washington Post*, April 8, 2016, https://www.washingtonpost.com/opinions/five-myths-about-trade/2016/04/08/97cc317c-fcf0-11e5-80e4-c381214de1a3_story.html.

16. Pew Research Center, "Free Trade Agreements Seen as Good for U.S., but Concerns Persist," May 27, 2015, http://www.people-press.org/files/2015/05/5-27-15-Trade-release.pdf.

17. Julia Glum, "Is Donald Trump Expanding The Republican Party? White Voters May Not Determine 2016 Election," *International Business Times*, March 16, 2016, http://www.ibtimes.com/donald-trump-expanding-republican-party-white-voters-may-not-determine-2016-election-2336070.

18. "Washington's Farewell Address," Digital History, http://www.digitalhistory.uh.edu/disp_textbook.cfm?smtID=3&psid=160.

19. American Political Science Association, "A Report of the Committee on Political Parties: Toward a More Responsible Two-Party System," *The American Political Science Review* 44, no. 3, Part 2, Supplement (September 1950).

20. Austin Ranney, "Toward a More Responsible Two-Party System: A Commentary," *The American Political Science Review* 45, no. 2 (1951): 488–499.

21. V. O. Key Jr., *Politics, Parties, and Pressure Groups*, 5th ed. (New York: Cromwell, 1964).

22. Rauch, "The Secret to Saner Elections?"

23. Ibid.

24. Ed O'Keefe, "Republicans outside of Washington Are Dropping Their Opposition to Gay Marriage. Will the National Party Follow Along?" *The Washington Post*, April 22, 2014, https://www.washingtonpost.com/news/the-fix/wp/2014/04/22/republicans-outside-of-washington-are-dropping-their-opposition-to-gay-marriage-will-the-national-party-follow-along/.

25. Zeke J. Miller, "Republican Committee Quietly Rejects Anti-Gay Marriage Resolution," *Time*, August 5, 2015, http://time.com/3986485/republican-national-committee-gay-marriage/.

26. Alexander Burns and Kenneth P. Vogel, "Steele vs. the Establishment," Politico, April 30, 2009, http://www.politico.com/story/2009/04/steele-vs-the-establishment-021966; Ralph Z. Hallow, "Exclusive: Steele Yields Powers to Foes in RNC," *The Washington Times*, May 6, 2009, http://www.washingtontimes.com/news/2009/may/06/steele-yields-powers-to-foes-in-rnc/.

27. Richard E. Cohen with James A. Barnes, *The Almanac of American Politics 2016* (Washington, D.C.: Columbia Books, 2015), 706.

28. Barone and McCutcheon, *The Almanac of American Politics 2014*, 1151.

29. Russell Berman, "What If the Parties Didn't Run Primaries?," *The Atlantic*, October 19, 2015, http://www.theatlantic.com/politics/archive/2015/10/what-if-the-parties-didnt-run-primaries/411022/.

30. Kevin J. Coleman, "The Presidential Nominating Process and the National Party Conventions, 2016: Frequently Asked Questions," Congressional Research Service, December 30, 2015, https://www.fas.org/sgp/crs/misc/R42533.pdf.

31. Michael P. McDonald, "Iowa's Caucus Turnout and What It Means from Now until November," The Huffington Post, February 2, 2016, http://www.huffingtonpost.com/michael-p-mcdonald/iowa-caucus-turnout-what-it-means_b_9141408.html.

32. Drew DeSilver, "So Far, Turnout in This Year's Primaries Rivals 2008 Record," Pew Research Center, March 8, 2016, http://www.pewresearch.org/fact-tank/2016/03/08/so-far-turnout-in-this-years-primaries-rivals-2008-record/.

33. Marty Cohen, David Karol, Hans Noel, and John Zaller, *The Party Decides: Presidential Nominations before and after Reform* (Chicago: The University of Chicago Press, 2008), 3.

34. John H. Aldrich, *Why Parties? The Origin and Transformation of Political Parties in America* (Chicago: The University of Chicago Press, 1995), 26.

35. Jeffrey M. Jones, "Democratic, Republican Identification near Historical Lows," Gallup, January 11, 2016, http://www.gallup .com/poll/188096/democratic-republican-identification-near-historical-lows.aspx?g_source=Politics&g_medium=lead&g_campaign=tiles.

36. Lydia Saad, "Government Named Top U.S. Problem for Second Straight Year," Gallup, January 11, 2016, http://www.gallup.com/poll/187979/government-named-top-problem-second-straight-year.aspx.

37. Steve Inskeep and Shankar Vedantam, "Why Compromise Is a Bad Word in Politics," NPR, March 13, 2012, http://www.npr.org/2012/03/13/148499310/why-compromise-is-terrible-politics.

38. Republican National Committee, Press Release, "RNC Statement on the ISIS-Linked Terrorist Attack in California," December 4, 2015, https://gop.com/rnc-statement-on-the-isis-linked-terrorist-attack-in-california/.

39. Jennifer Bendery, "Debbie Wasserman Schultz Campaigns against Republicans Who 'Prefer to Act Like Children,'" The Huffington Post, July 31, 2012, http://www.huffingtonpost.com/2012/07/31/debbie-wasserman-schultz-campaign_n_1726020.html.

40. Tom Price, "Polarization in America," *CQ Researcher*, February 28, 2014, http://library.cqpress.com/cqresearcher/document.php?id=cqresrre2014022800.

41. Chris Cillizza, "Ticket Splitting Reached a 92-Year Low in 2012," *The Washington Post*, April 22, 2014, https://www.washingtonpost.com/news/the-fix/wp/2014/04/22/ticket-splitting-is-the-lowest-its-been-in-92-years/.

42. Marc Fisher, "GOP Platform through the Years Shows Party's Shift from Moderate to Conservative," *The Washington Post*, August 28, 2012, https://www.washingtonpost.com/politics/gop-platform-through-the-years-shows-partys-shift-from-moderate-to-conservative/2012/08/28/09094512-ed70-11e1-b09d-07d971dee30a_story.html.

43. Mark Landler, "Pushed by Obama, Democrats Alter Platform over Jerusalem," *The New York Times*, September 5, 2012, http://www.nytimes.com/2012/09/06/us/politics/pushed-by-obama-democrats-alter-platform-over-jerusalem.html.

44. Jonah Goldberg, "The Republican Aristocracy Is Already Bending Its Knee to King Trump," *The Los Angeles Times*, May 10, 2016, http://www.latimes.com/opinion/op-ed/la-oe-0510-goldberg-trump-party-20160510-column.html, accessed May 12, 2016.

45. Republican National Committee, Growth and Opportunity Project, March 2013, http://goproject.gop.com/rnc_growth_opportunity_book_2013.pdf, accessed September 5, 2016.

46. Ibid.

47. Democratic National Committee, "Democratic Victory Task Force Final Report and Action Plan," February 2015, https://uploads.democrats.org/Downloads/DVTF_FinalReport.pdf, accessed September 5, 2016.

48. Jane Mansbridge, "Three Reasons Political Polarization Is Here to Stay," *The Washington Post*, March 11, 2016, https://www.washingtonpost.com/news/in-theory/wp/2016/03/11/three-reasons-political-polarization-is-here-to-stay/.

49. Joel Kotkin, "Farewell, Grand Old Party," *Orange County Register*, March 20, 2016, http://www.ocregister.com/articles/party-708782-trump-voters.html.

50. Ibid.

51. D. Stephen Voss, "Will Superdelegates Pick the Democratic Nominee? Here's Everything You Need to Know," *The Washington Post*, February 26, 2016, https://www.washingtonpost.com/news/monkey-cage/wp/2016/02/26/will-superdelegates-pick-the-democratic-nominee-heres-everything-you-need-to-know/.

52. Nolan D. McCaskill, "Sanders' Camp Serves DNC with Lawsuit over Voter Data," Politico, March 24, 2016, http://www.politico.com/blogs/2016-dem-primary-live-updates-and-results/2016/03/bernie-sanders-dnc-lawsuit-221216.

53. John Wagner, "Sanders Says DNC's Timing of Saturday Night's Debate Was Meant to 'Protect' Clinton," *The Washington Post*, December 20, 2015, https://www.washingtonpost.com/news/post-politics/wp/2015/12/20/sanders-says-dncs-timing-of-saturday-nights-debate-was-meant-to-protect-clinton/.

54. Jonathan Martin, "Alarmed Clinton Supporters Begin Focusing on Sanders's Socialist Edge," *The New York Times*, Jan. 19, 2016, http://www.nytimes.com/2016/01/20/us/politics/alarmed-hillary-clinton-supporters-begin-focusing-on-bernie-sanders-socialist-edge.html.

55. Amy Chozick, "After Michigan Loss, Hillary Clinton Sharpens Message on Jobs and Trade," *The New York Times*, March 9, 2016, http://www.nytimes.com/2016/03/10/us/politics/after-michigan-loss-hillary-clinton-retools-message-on-jobs-and-trade.html?_r=0.

56. Ibid.

57. Dylan Scott, "Clinton Is Moving Left on Social Security," *National Journal*, August 13, 2015, http://www.govexec.com/management/2015/08/clinton-moving-left-social-security/119093/.

58. Eliza Collins, "Priebus '100 Percent' Confident He Can Rally GOP behind Cruz or Trump," Politico, January 8, 2016, http://www.politico.com/story/2016/01/reince-priebus-ted-cruz-trump-217489.

59. Trip Gabriel, "Donald Trump Finds Ally in Delegate System, Much to GOP's Chagrin," *The New York Times*, February 29, 2016, http://www.nytimes.com/2016/03/01/us/politics/donald-trump-delegates.html.

60. Senator Ben Sasse, "An Open Letter to Trump Supporters," Facebook, February 28, 2016, https://www.facebook.com/sassefornebraska/posts/561073597391141.

61. Reid Epstein, "Ted Cruz Gains in Louisiana after Loss There to Donald Trump," *The Wall Street Journal*, March 24, 2016, http://www.wsj.com/articles/ted-cruz-gains-in-louisiana-after-loss-there-to-donald-trump-1458861959.

62. David Weigel, "Cruz: *National Enquirer* Story Is 'Garbage' from 'Donald Trump and His Henchmen,'" *The Washington Post*, March 25, 2016, http://www.washingtonpost.com/news/post-politics/wp/2016/03/25/cruz-national-enquirer-story-is-garbage-from-donald-trump-and-his-henchmen/.

63. Jennifer Agriesta, "CNN/ORC Poll: Clinton Tops Trump on Presidential Traits," CNN.com, March 24, 2016, http://www.cnn.com/2016/03/24/politics/hillary-clinton-donald-trump-cnn-poll-2016-election/index.html.

64. Dan Balz, "How the GOP Loyalty Pledge Completely Fell Apart," *The Washington Post*, March 30, 2016, https://www.washingtonpost.com/politics/the-gops-patina-of-cohesion-has-been-shattered-by-the-candidates/2016/03/30/850de0c6-f69c-11e5-a3ce-f06b5ba21f33_story.html.

65. Robert Costa, "Internal Memo Reveals Trump Campaign's Mounting Fury with Its Critics," *The Washington Post*, April 4, 2016, https://www.washingtonpost.com/news/post-politics/wp/2016/04/04/internal-memo-reveals-trump-campaigns-mounting-fury-with-its-critics/.

66. John H. Aldrich, *Why Parties? The Origin and Transformation of Political Parties in America* (Chicago: The University of Chicago Press, 1995), 261. See also V. O. Key Jr., "A Theory of Critical Elections," *The Journal of Politics* 17, no. 1 (February 1955): 3–18.

67. Amy Kittelstrom, "Ignorance, Racism and Rage," Salon, April 9, 2016, http://www.salon.com/2016/04/09/ignorance_racism_and_rage_the_gops_transformation_to_the_party_of_stupid_started_long_before_donald_trump/?utm_source=twitter&utm_medium=socialflow.

68. "Political Parties and Elections," in *CQ Press Guide to Congress*, 7th ed. (Washington, D.C.: CQ Press, 2013), 997–1000.

69. Ibid., 1002.

70. "Lyndon B. Johnson—the Campaign of 1964," Profiles of U.S. Presidents, President Profiles.com, http://www.presidentprofiles.com/Kennedy-Bush/Lyndon-B-Johnson-The-campaign-of-1964.html.

71. Nixon Presidential Library and Museum Collection, "Silent Majority," https://www.nixonlibrary.gov/forresearchers/find/subjects/silent-majority.php.

72. Chuck McCutcheon, "Ronald Reagan Remains GOP Icon," *CQ Researcher*, October 24, 2014, http://library.cqpress.com/cqresearcher/document.php?id=cqresrre2014102420#Sidebar2.

73. Napp Nazworth, "Barna: Romney Got Lowest Level of Evangelical Support since Dole," *Christian Post*, December 5, 2012, http://www.christianpost.com/news/barna-romney-got-lowest-level-of-evangelical-support-since-dole-86145/.

74. John Feehery, "Kristol Attacks Me?" *Feehery Theory*, March 18, 2016, http://www.thefeeherytheory.com/kristol-attacks-me/.

75. Vanessa Williamson, Theda Skocpol, and John Coggin, "The Tea Party and the Remaking of American Conservatism," *American Political Science Association Perspectives on Politics 9*, no. 1 (March 2011): 25–43.

76. Jon R. Bond, Richard Fleisher and Nathan Ilderton, "Was the Tea Party Responsible for the Republican Victory in the 2010 House Elections?," American Political Science Association Meeting Paper, August 19, 2011, http://papers.ssrn.com/sol3/papers.cfm?abstract_id=1912707.

77. Republican National Committee, Growth and Opportunity Project.

78. Democratic National Committee, "Democratic Victory Task Force Final Report and Action Plan."

79. Ibid.

80. Corwin D. Smidt, "Polarization and the Decline of the American Floating Voter," *American Journal of Political Science*, October 14, 2015, http://onlinelibrary.wiley.com/doi/10.1111/ajps.12218/abstract.

81. Robert Reich, "Robert Reich Sees the Future: Why America's Two-Party System May Collapse," Alternet.org, March 22, 2016, http://www.alternet.org/election-2016/robert-reich-sees-futurewhy-americas-two-party-system-may-collapse.

82. Alex Isenstadt, "Republicans Prep for Long, Ugly Nomination Fight," Politico, March 15, 2016, http://www.politico.com/story/2016/03/republicans-nomination-trump-cruz-220757.

83. This section draws upon Norm Ornstein, "The Eight Causes of Trumpism," *The Atlantic*, January 4, 2016, http://www.theatlantic.com/politics/archive/2016/01/the-eight-causes-of-trumpism/422427/, accessed May 12, 2016.

84. Robert Kagan, "Trump Is the GOP's Frankenstein Monster. Now He's Strong Enough to Destroy the Party," *The Washington Post,* February 25, 2016, https://www.washingtonpost.com/opinions/trump-is-the-gops-frankenstein-monster-now-hes-strong-enough-to-destroy-the-party/2016/02/25/3e443f28-dbc1-11e5-925f-1d10062cc82d_story.html.

85. Lindsey McPherson and Rema Rahman, "The Right Holds," *CQ Guide to the New Congress*, November 10, 2016, p. 12.

86. Mara Liasson, "The Democratic Party Got Crushed during the Obama Presidency. Here's Why," NPR, March 4, 2016, http://www.npr.org/2016/03/04/469052020/the-democratic-party-got-crushed-during-the-obama-presidency-heres-why.

87. Douglas Adams, *The Hitchhiker's Guide to the Galaxy* (New York: Pocket Books, 1979).

88. Kristina Nwazota, "Third Parties in the U.S. Political Process," PBS NewsHour, July 26, 2004, http://www.pbs.org/newshour/updates/politics-july-dec04-third_parties/.

89. "1968 Presidential Election Results," U.S.ElectionAtlas.org, http://uselectionatlas.org/RESULTS/national.php?year=1968.

90. "1980 Presidential Election Results," U.S.ElectionAtlas.org, http://uselectionatlas.org/RESULTS/national.php?year=1980.

91. "1992 Presidential Election Results," U.S.ElectionAtlas.org, http://uselectionatlas.org/RESULTS/national.php?year=1992.

92. "2000 Presidential Election Results," U.S.ElectionAtlas.org, http://uselectionatlas.org/RESULTS/national.php?year=2000.

93. Christopher J. Devine and Kyle C. Kopko, "5 things you need to know about how third-party candidates did in 2016," *The Washington Post,* November 15, 2016, https://www.washingtonpost.com/news/monkey-cage/wp/2016/11/15/5-things-you-need-to-know-about-how-third-party-candidates-did-in-2016/. Accessed November 20, 2016.

94. "Spotlight: Cambridge," FairVote.org, http://www.fairvote.org/spotlight_cambridge.

95. "Closer Look: Criticism Mounting over Ranked-Choice Voting," CBS News, November 11, 2011, http://sanfrancisco.cbslocal.com/2011/11/16/closer-look-criticism-mounting-over-ranked-choice-voting/.

96. *Attack of the Crab Monsters* (roughly 39:24 into the film), YouTube, https://www.youtube.com/watch?v=-RA12RHnYIA, accessed April 26, 2016.

Chapter 10

1. See, for example, José Calderon, "'Hispanic' and 'Latino': The Viability for Categories for Panethnic Unity, *Latin American Perspectives* 75, no. 4 (1992): 37–44.

2. The third senator of Latino heritage is Bob Menendez (D-NJ), also of Cuban descent.

3. Ashley Parker and Alan Rappeport, "Marco Rubio Announces 2016 Presidential Bid," *The New York Times*, April 13, 2015, http://www.nytimes.com/2015/04/14/us/politics/marco-rubio-2016-presidential-campaign.html?_r=0.

4. Theodore Schleifer, "Cruz Allies Tout His Latino Background as General Election Benefit," CNN.com, January 26, 2016, http://www.cnn.com/2016/01/26/politics/cruz-latino-general-election-2016/, accessed June 23, 2016.

5. Mary Jordan, "'He's Cuban. I'm Mexican.': Can Rubio and Cruz Connect with Latino Voters?," *The New York Times*, January 10, 2016, https://www.washingtonpost.com/politics/2016/01/10/32d20f8e-b4bc-11e5-a842-0feb51d1d124_story.html.

6. Marc Fisher, "The GOP's Identity-Politics Crisis: Holding Race-Card Aces but Loath to Play Them," *The Washington Post*, November 19, 2016, https://www.washingtonpost.com/politics/the-gops-identity-politics-crisis-a-diverse-field-but-an-aversion-to-tout-it/2015/11/29/48c6f040-8fad-11e5-ae1f-af46b7df8483_story.html, accessed February 23, 2016.

7. Esther Yu-Hsi Lee, "Young Latinos Are Set to Change American Elections," ThinkProgress.org, January 22, 2016, http://thinkprogress.org/immigration/2016/01/22/3741434/latino-voters-millennials/, accessed February 223, 2016.

8. Amanda Sakuma, "The Rubio-Cruz Immigration War Heats Up," MSNBC, January 15, 2016, http://www.msnbc.com/msnbc/the-rubio-cruz-immigration-war-heats, accessed January 30, 2016.

9. Ibid.

10. Eric Bradner, "Rubio Hits Cruz on Immigration, Snowden," CNN, January 10, 2016, http://www.cnn.com/2016/01/10/politics/marco-rubio-ted-cruz-immigration-edward-snowden/, accessed January 30, 2016.

11. Mary Jordan, "Liberal Hispanic Activists Assail Rubio, Cruz as 'Traitors' to Their Culture," *The Washington Post*, December 15, 2015, https://www.washingtonpost.com/politics/liberal-hispanic-activists-assail-rubio-cruz-as-traitors-to-their-culture/2015/12/15/9bcca938-a317-11e5-b53d-972e2751f433_story.html, accessed January 23, 2016.

12. Ibid.

13. Ibid.

14. Ibid.

15. Ibid.

16. Ibid.

17. Paola Luisi, "7 Things Hillary Clinton Has in Common with Your *Abuela*," HillaryClinton.com, https://www.hillaryclinton.com/feed/8-ways-hillary-clinton-just-your-abuela/?utm_medium=social&utm_source=fb&utm_campaign=20151222feed_abuela, accessed January 23, 2016.

18. Ibid.

19. Ibid.

20. Jane C. Timm, "Clinton's 'Abuela' Pitch to Latinos Prompts Twitter Backlash," http://www.nbcnews.com/politics/2016-election/clinton-s-abuela-pitch-latinos-prompts-twitter-backlash-n485166, NBC News, accessed January 23, 2016.

21. Ben Norton, "'Not My Abuela': Twitter Explodes in Outrage over Hillary Clinton's 'Hispandering,'" Salon.com, December 23, 2015, http://www.salon.com/2015/12/23/not_my_abuela_twitter_explodes_in_outrage_over_hillary_clintons_hispandering/, accessed January 23, 2016.

22. Stephanie Ewert, "U.S. Population Trends: 2000 to 2060," United States Census Bureau, October 15, 2015, http://www.ncsl.org/Portals/1/Documents/nalfo/USDemographics.pdf, accessed January 22, 2016.

23. Joshua Fletcher, "Hispanics to Outnumber Whites in Texas by 2020, State Says," MySanAntonio.com, July 9, 2015, http://www.mysanantonio.com/news/local/article/Hispanics-to-outnumber-whites-in-Texas-by-the-end-6375597.php, accessed June 23, 2016.

24. Republican National Committee, Growth and Opportunity Project, http://goproject.gop.com/rnc_growth_opportunity_book_2013.pdf, accessed June 23, 2016.

25. Nate Cohn, "Hispanic Voters Are Important for Republicans, but Not Indispensable," *The New York Times*, November 20, 2014, http://www.nytimes.com/2014/11/21/upshot/hispanic-voters-are-important-for-republicans-but-not-indispensable.html?_r=0, accessed February 24, 2016.

26. Article I, Section 4.

27. The power of states to restrict the rights of convicted felons to vote, which is called felony (or felon) disenfranchisement, is rooted in the Fourteenth Amendment's vague phrase, "or other crime."

28. Morris P. Fiorina, *Retrospective Voting in American National Elections* (New Haven, CT: Yale University Press, 1981).

29. Mark Hugo Lopez, Ana Gonzalez-Barrera, and Jens Manuel Krogstad, "Chapter 4: Top Issues

in This Year's Election for Hispanic Voters," Pew Research Center, October 29, 2014, http://www.pewhispanic.org/2014/10/29/chapter-4-top-issues-in-this-years-election-for-hispanic-voters/, accessed February 24, 2016.

30. Center for Responsive Politics, "2012 Presidential Race," OpenSecrets.org, http://www.opensecrets.org/pres12/#out, accessed January 25, 2016.

31. Tarini Parti, "FED: $7B Spent on 2012 Campaign," Politico, January 31, 2013, http://www.politico.com/story/2013/01/7-billion-spent-on-2012-campaign-fec-says-087051, accessed January 24, 2016.

32. John G. Geer, *In Defense of Negativity: Attack Ads in Presidential Campaigns* (Chicago: The University of Chicago Press, 2006), 13.

33. *Buckley v. Valeo*, 424 U.S. 1 (1976).

34. *Citizens United v. Federal Election Commission*, 558 U.S.__ (2010).

35. Pew Research Center, "Mapping the Latino Electorate by State," January 19, 2016, http://www.pewhispanic.org/interactives/mapping-the-latino-electorate-by-state/, accessed January 30, 2016.

36. Kate Linthicum, "The Latino Vote Is Growing—but It Could Be Much Bigger," *The Los Angeles Times*, September 10, 2015, http://www.latimes.com/nation/politics/la-na-latino-voters-20150910-story.html, accessed January 23, 2016.

37. Ibid.

38. Mark Hugo Lopez, Ana Gonzalez-Barrera, "Latino Support for Democrats Falls, but Democratic Advantage Remains," Pew Research Center, October 29, 2014, http://www.pewhispanic.org/2014/10/29/latino-support-for-democrats-falls-but-democratic-advantage-remains/, accessed January 30, 2016.

39. Ibid.

40. Mark Hugo Lopez et al., "Latino Voters and the 2014 Midterm Elections. Chapter 2: Latinos' Views on Selected 2014 Ballot Measure Issues," Pew Research Center, October 16, 2014, http://www.pewhispanic.org/2014/10/16/chapter-2-latinos-views-on-selected-2014-ballot-measure-issues/, accessed January 30, 2016.

41. Mark Leberfinger, "Election 2016: Snowstorm to Unfold as Thousands Gather for Iowa Caucuses," AccuWeather.com, January 30, 2016, http://www.accuweather.com/en/weather-news/election-2016-iowa-caucus-snow-central-northern-plains-monday-night/55036213, accessed January 30, 2016.

42. Iowa Farm Bureau, "Learn How to Caucus," https://www.iowafarmbureau.com/News/2016-Farmers-Caucus/Learn-how-to-caucus, accessed September 9, 2016.

43. "2016 Iowa Caucus," 2016 Election Central, http://www.uspresidentialelectionnews.com/2016-presidential-primary-schedule-calendar/2016-iowa-caucuses/, accessed January 30, 2016.

44. Nate Silver, "What Happens if Bernie Sanders Wins Iowa?," FiveThirtyEight.com, January 29, 2016, http://fivethirtyeight.com/features/what-happens-if-bernie-sanders-wins-iowa/, accessed January 30, 2016.

45. State Data Center of Iowa, "Latinos in Iowa: 2015," September 2015, http://www.iowadatacenter.org/Publications/latinos2015.pdf, accessed February 24, 2016.

46. Emily Aitkin, "Latino Voters Turned Out in Iowa in a Record Way," ThinkProgress.org, February 15, 2016, http://thinkprogress.org/politics/2016/02/15/3748919/update-iowa-latino-voter-turnout-preliminary/, accessed February 24, 2016.

47. Neil Munro, "Fox, Google Pick 1994 Illegal Immigrant to Ask Question in Iowa GOP Debate," Breitbart.com, January 27, 2016, http://www.breitbart.com/2016-presidential-race/2016/01/27/fox-google-pick-1994-illegal-immigrant-to-ask-question-in-iowa-gop-debate/, accessed January 28, 2016.

48. Dulce Candy, "My Story | Dulce Candy," YouTube, https://www.youtube.com/watch?v=CR2fIM5TjpE, accessed January 31, 2016.

49. "Digital Exclusive: The Dulce Candy Interview," Latino USA, November 17, 2015, http://latinousa.org/2015/11/17/digital-exclusive-the-dulce-candy-interview/, accessed January 31, 2016.

50. Carmen Sesin, "'Hispanicize 2015' Showcases Latino Ventures, Talent," NBC News, March 18, 2015, http://www.nbcnews.com/news/latino/hispanicize-2015-event-showcases-latino-ventures-talent-n325646, accessed January 30, 2016.

51. Maeve Reston, "Donald Trump Throws a Grand Old Party," CNN.com, January 29, 2016, http://www.cnn.com/2016/01/29/politics/donald-trump-2016-election-rally-gop-debate/index.html, accessed January 30, 2016.

52. Ibid.

53. Team Fix, "7th Republican Debate Transcript, Annotated: Who Said What and What It Meant," *The Washington Post*, January 28, 2016, https://www.washingtonpost.com/news/the-fix/wp/2016/01/28/7th-republican-debate-transcript-annotated-who-said-what-and-what-it-meant/, accessed January 29, 2016.

54. Ibid.

55. Gabriel Sanchez and Matt A. Barreto, "In Record Numbers, Latinos Voted Overwhelmingly Against Trump. We Did the Research," *The Washington Post, Monkey Cage,* November 11, 2016, https://www.washingtonpost.com/news/monkey-cage/wp/2016/11/11/in-record-numbers-latinos-voted-overwhelmingly-against-trump-we-did-the-research/. Accessed November 21, 2016.

56. Chris Good, "What's an Exploratory Committee?" *The Atlantic*, April 14, 2011, http://www.theatlantic.com/politics/archive/2011/04/whats-an-exploratory-committee/237309/, accessed January 28, 2016.

57. Chris Meagher, "Can Salud Carbajal Really Be Everything to Everyone?," *Santa Barbara Independent*, March 27, 2008, http://www.independent.com/news/2008/mar/27/can-salud-carbajal-really-be-everything-everyone/, accessed January 26, 2016.

58. "California's 24th Congressional District," Ballotpedia, https://ballotpedia.org/California%27s_24th_Congressional_District#2016, accessed January 26, 2016.

59. Oscar Flores, "Candidates Already Announce Bids or Capps' Seat," KEYT-KCOY-KKFX, April 8, 2015, http://www.keyt.com/news/local-politicians-announce-bid-for-congressional-district-seat/32264312, accessed January 26, 2016.

60. California's primary nomination system does not apply to candidates for the United States presidency and some local offices.

61. Christopher Caen, "The Consequences of California's Top-Two Primary," *The Atlantic*, December 29, 2015, http://www.theatlantic.com/politics/archive/2015/12/california-top-two-open-primary/421557/, accessed January 25, 2016.

62. Jean Merl, "No-Incumbent Races Draw Crowd; Two of the Three Such California House Seats Favor Democrats," *The Los Angeles Times*, October 25, 2015; available from Lexis-Nexis Academic.

63. "Analysis of California's Congressional Districts (January Edition)," Races and Redistricting, January 11, 2012, http://racesandredistricting.blogspot.com/2011/12/analysis-of-californias-congressional.html, accessed February 24, 2016.

64. Cristina Marcos, "Lois Capps's Daughter Won't Run for Her Mother's Seat," The Hill.com, April 28, 2015; available from Lexis-Nexis Academic.

65. Merl, "No-Incumbent Races Draw Crowd."

66. Ben Kamisar, "Pelosi Backs Ally's Pick for Successor," The Hill.com, October 7, 2015; available from Lexis-Nexis Academic.

67. Ibid.

68. Ibid.

69. "Salud Carbajal Brings in More Than $407,000 in Third Quarter," *A-Town Daily News*, October 8, 2015, http://atowndailynews.com/salud-carbajal-brings-in-more-than-407000-in-third-quarter/37321/, accessed January 30, 2016.

70. Professor Bartels attributes the term to a comment made by George Bush in 1980. Larry M. Bartels, *Presidential Primaries and the Dynamics of Public Choice* (Princeton, NJ: Princeton University Press, 1988), 27.

71. The size of the House was fixed at 435 members by the Reapportionment Act of 1929. The number rose to 437 for a time after the admission of Alaska and Hawaii as states, but it has stayed at 435 since the apportionment following the 1960 census. Washington, D.C., has three nonvoting delegates in the House.

72. "Did the California Citizens Redistricting Commission Really Create More Competitive Districts?" FairVote.org, November 26, 2013, http://www.fairvote.org/did-the-california-citizens-redistricting-commission-really-create-more-competitive-districts, accessed June 25, 2016.

73. Ibid.

74. Gary C. Jacobson, *The Politics of Congressional Elections*, 7th ed. (New York: Pearson Longman, 2009), 12.

75. Ibid., 12.

76. Ibid., 12.

77. Ibid., 23 (footnotes).

78. Ibid., 13.

79. *Wesberry v. Sanders*, 376 U.S. 1 (1964); *Reynolds v. Sims*, 377 U.S. 533 (1964).

80. *Davis v. Bandemer*, 478 U.S. 109 (1986).

81. *Vieth v. Jubelirer*, 541 U.S. 267 (2004).

82. *League of United Latin American Citizens v. Perry*, 548 U.S. 399 (2006). The Court ruled that the proposed Texas Twenty-fifth District violated the rights of Hispanic Americans protected under provisions of the Voting Rights Act of 1965.

83. *Thornburg v. Gingles*, 478 U.S. 30 (1986); the Voting Rights Act of 1965.

84. *Shaw v. Reno*, 509 U.S. 630 (1993).

85. California's voting age population was twenty-eight million in 2010 and Wyoming's was 428,000, according to the 2010 census. United States Census Bureau, *Statistical Abstract of the United States: 2012*, http://www.census.gov/compendia/statab/, accessed May 4, 2013.

86. Frances E. Lee, "Representation and Public Policy: The Consequences of Senate Apportionment for the Geographic Distribution of Federal Funds," *The Journal of Politics* 60, no. 1 (Feb. 1998): 34–62.

87. Jacobson, The Politics of Congressional Elections, 27.

88. Ibid., 27–28.

89. David R. Mayhew, *Congress: The Electoral Connection* (New Haven, CT: Yale University Press), 5. See also David R. Mayhew, "Congressional Elections: The Case of the Vanishing Marginals," *Polity* 6, no. 3 (Spring 1974): 295–317.

90. Mayhew, *Congress*, 49–77.

91. Gary C. Jacobson and Samuel Kernell, *Strategy and Choice in Congressional Elections* (New Haven, CT: Yale University Press, 1981), 32.

92. Gary W. Cox and Jonathan N. Katz, "Why Did the Incumbency Advantage in U.S. House Elections Grow?," *American Journal of Political Science* 40, no. 2 (May 1996): 483.

93. Alan I. Abramowitz, Brad Alexander, and Matthew Gunning, "Incumbency, Redistricting, and the Decline of Competition in U.S. House Elections," *The Journal of Politics* 68, no. 1 (February 2006): 82.

94. Samantha Schmidt, "A 'Silver Lining' on Election Night: First Latina Elected to U.S. Senate," *The Washington Post*, November 9, 2016, https://www.washingtonpost.com/news/morning-mix/wp/2016/11/09/a-silver-lining-on-election-night-first-latina-elected-to-u-s-senate/. Accessed November 18, 2016.

95. Cristina Marcos, "115th Congress Will Be Most Racially Diverse in History," *The Hill*, November 17, 2016, http://thehill.com/homenews/house/306480-115th-congress-will-be-most-racially-diverse-in-history. Accessed November 18, 2016.

96. Ibid.

Chapter 11

1. Chairman Ben. S. Bernanke, "The Economic Outlook," testimony before the Joint Economic Committee, United States Congress, March 28, 2007, http://www.federalreserve.gov/newsevents/testimony/bernanke20070328a.htm, accessed February 15, 2015.

2. United States Department of the Treasury, "The Financial Crisis Response in Charts," April 2012, http://www.treasury.gov/resource-center/data-chart-center/Documents/20120413_FinancialCrisisResponse.pdf, accessed February 18, 2015.

3. Helen Kennedy, "Dems Balk at Bailout. Press Help for Homeowners, Exec Pay Cuts as Part of Deal," *The New York Daily News*, September 23, 2008; available from Lexis-Nexis Academic.

4. Henry M. Paulson Jr., On the Edge: Inside the Race to Stop the Collapse of the Global Financial System (New York, NY: Business Plus, 2010), 63.

5. James Madison, *Federalist No. 10*, in *The Federalist Papers*, ed. George W. Carey and James McClellan (Indianapolis, IN: Liberty Fund, 2001), 48.

6. Alexis de Tocqueville, *Democracy in America*, trans. George Lawrence, ed. J. P. Mayer (New York, NY: Harper Perennial Modern Classics, 1966), 9.

7. Ibid., 189.

8. For a historical treatment of these ideas, see Arthur M. Schlesinger, "Biography of a Nation of Joiners," *The American Historical Review* 50, no. 1 (October 1944): 1–25.

9. Madison, *Federalist No. 10*, 44.

10. Robert A. Dahl, *Who Governs? Democracy and Power in an American City* (New Haven, CT: Yale University Press, 1961), 3.

11. C. Wright Mills, *The Power Elite* (New York: Oxford University Press, 1956), 4–5.

12. E. E. Schattschneider, *The Semisovereign People: A Realist's View of Democracy in America* (Hinsdale, IL: The Dryden Press, 1960), 32.

13. Ibid.

14. David B. Truman, The Governmental Process: Political Interests and Public Opinion (New York, NY: Alfred A. Knopf, 1962), 5.

15. Mancur Olson, *The Logic of Collective Action: Public Goods and the Theory of Groups* (Cambridge, MA: Harvard University Press, 1965), 2. Italics are the author's.

16. Paul Samuelson, "The Pure Theory of Public Expenditure," *The Review of Economics and Statistics* 36, no. 4 (November 1954): 387–389. Technically, the characteristic is called *nonexcludability*. Public goods also exhibit the characteristic of *nonrivalry*, referring to the fact that the consumption of the good by one individual does not reduce its availability to others.

17. Olson, The Logic of Collective Action, 14–15.

18. Alistair Osborne, Philip Aldrick, and James Quinn, "Lehman Collapse: The Drama of a Mad 48 Hours That Will Never Fade," *The Telegraph*, September 13, 2009, http://www.telegraph.co.uk/finance/financialcrisis/6179138/Lehman-collapse-the-drama-of-a-mad-48-hours-that-will-never-fade.html.

19. David C. King and Jack L. Walker, "The Provision of Benefits by Interest Groups in the United States," *The Journal of Politics* 54, no. 2 (May 1992): 394–426.

20. Helen Kennedy, "Economy Is Headin' for Cliff! OK Bailout Soon or Else, Says Treasury Chief," *The New York Daily News*, September 22, 2008; available from Lexis-Nexis Academic.

21. Ibid.

22. Ibid.

23. Mark Landler and Steven Lee Myers, "Buyout Plan for Wall Street Is a Hard Sell on Capitol Hill," *The New York Times*, September 23, 2008, http://www.nytimes.com/2008/09/24/business/economy/24fannie.html?_r=1&, accessed March 20, 2015.

24. Ibid.

25. Kevin G. Hall, "Is It Safe to Trust a Wall Street Veteran with a Wall Street Bailout?," *McClatchy Newspapers*, September 21, 2008; available from Lexis-Nexis Academic.

26. Suzy Jagger, "Rage Sweeps over Middle America as Wall Street Clambers on the Lifeboat," *The Times* (London), September 23, 2008; available from Lexis-Nexis Academic.

27. Wonkblog Staff, "'Enough Is Enough': Elizabeth Warren Launches Fiery Attack after Congress Weakens Wall Street Regs," *The Washington Post*, December 12, 2014, http://www.washingtonpost.com/news/wonkblog/wp/2014/12/12/enough-is-enough-elizabeth-warrens-fiery-attack-comes-after-congress-weakens-wall-street-regulations/, accessed August 7, 2015.

28. Jeffrey H. Birnbaum, "Vital Part of Housing Bill Is Brainchild of Banks," *The Washington Post*, June 25, 2008, http://www.washingtonpost.com/wp-dyn/content/article/2008/06/24/AR2008062401389.html.

29. Jenny Anderson, Vikas Bajaj, and Leslie Wayne, "Big Financiers Start to Lobby for Wider Aid," *The New York Times*, September 21, 2008, http://www.nytimes.com/2008/09/22/business/22lobby.html?_r=0.

30. Kennedy, "Dems. Balk at Bailout."

31. Ibid.

32. Suzy Jagger, "Rage Sweeps over Middle America."

33. Jerry Zremski, "Bailout Plan Hit by Backlash; Congress Expresses Outrage; Reflects Taxpayers' Mood amid Call for Quick Action," *Buffalo News* (New York), September 24, 2008; available from Lexis-Nexis Academic.

34. Kenneth R. Bazinet, "Poll: It's All Wall Street & W.'s Fault," *The New York Daily News*, September 24, 2008; available from Lexis-Nexis Academic.

35. Tony Pugh, "Groups Say Bailout Doesn't Do Enough for Struggling Homeowners," Knight Ridder Washington Bureau, September 23, 2008; available from Lexis-Nexis Academic.

36. Stephanie Gaskell and Corky Siemaszko, "Closing Bell Tolls Gloom 'Market in Sheer Panic,' Says Expert," *The New York Daily News*, September 30, 2008; available from Lexis-Nexis Academic.

37. Juan Gonzalez, "Bailout Dish Has Heaping Side of Pork," *The New York Daily News*, October 3, 2008; available from Lexis-Nexis Academic.

38. Ibid.

39. Stephen Labaton and Jackie Calmes, "Obama Proposes a First Overhaul of Finance Rules," *The New York Times*, May 14, 2009; available from Lexis-Nexis Academic.

40. Deniz Igan, Prachi Mishra, and Thierry Tressel, "A Fistful of Dollars: Lobbying and the Financial Crisis," National Bureau of Economic Research Working Paper 17076, May 2001, http://www.nber.org/papers/w17076.

41. Erika Lovely, "Wall St. Ramps Up Lobbying on Hill," Politico, June 3, 2010, http://www.politico.com/news/stories/0610/38091.html (Accessed November 27, 2014).

42. Ibid.

43. Sandy Mackenzie, 'The Impact of the Financial Crisis on Older Americans,' *Insight on the*

Issues, *AARP Public Policy Institute* 19 (December 2008): 11.

44. Anthony J. Nownes, *Total Lobbying: What Lobbyists Want (and How They Try to Get it)* (New York: Cambridge University Press, 2006), 6.

45. Center for Responsive Politics, "Lobbying Database," OpenSecrets.org, 2014, https://www.opensecrets.org/lobby/, accessed November 21, 2014. Their figures were calculated from data obtained from the Senate Office of Public Records.

46. Kay Lehman Schlozman and John T. Tierney, *Organized Interests and American Democracy* (New York: Harper & Row, Publishers, 1986), 148–157.

47. Joseph White, "Making Connections to the Appropriations Process," in *The Interest Group Connection: Electioneering, Lobbying, and Policymaking in Washington*, 2nd ed., ed. Paul S Herrnson, Ronald G. Shaiko, and Clyde Wilcox (Washington, D.C.: CQ Press, 2005), 164–188.

48. Administrative Procedure Act of 1946.

49. Scott R. Furlong, "Exploring Interest Group Participation in Executive Policymaking," in Herrnson, Shaiko, and Wilcox, *The Interest Group Connection*, 282–297.

50. Marver Bernstein, *Regulating Business by Independent Commission* (Princeton, NJ: Princeton University Press, 1955).

51. Karen O'Connor, "Lobbying the Justices or Lobbying for Justice? The Role of Organized Interests in the Judicial Process," in Herrnson, Shaiko, and Wilcox, *The Interest Group Connection*, 331.

52. Gregory A. Caldeira and John R. Wright, "Organized Interests and Agenda Setting in the U.S. Supreme Court," *The American Political Science Review* 82, no. 4 (December 1988): 1109–1127.

53. Lee Epstein and C. K. Rowland. "Debunking the Myth of Interest Group Invincibility in the Courts." *The American Political Science Review* 85, no. 1 (March 1991): 205–217.

54. Citizens United v. Federal Election Commission, 558 U.S. ___ (2010).

55. Norman J. Ornstein and Shirley Elder, *Interest Groups, Lobbying, and Policymaking* (Washington, D.C.: CQ Press, 1978), 88.

56. Ken Kollman, *Outside Lobbying: Public Opinion and Interest Group Strategies* (Princeton, NJ: Princeton University Press, 1998), 80.

57. Kenneth M. Goldstein, *Interest Groups, Lobbying, and Participation in America* (New York: Cambridge University Press, 1999), 125.

58. Grant McConnell, *Private Power & American Democracy* (New York: Alfred A. Knopf, 1966), 5.

59. Kay Lehman Schlozman, "What Accent the Heavenly Chorus? Political Equality and the American Pressure System," *The Journal of Politics* 46, no. 4 (November 1984): 1006–1032.

60. Dara Z. Strolovitch, *Affirmative Advocacy: Race, Class, and Gender in Interest Group Politics* (Chicago: The University of Chicago Press, 2007).

61. Maud Dillingham, "Top 5 Targets of Occupy Wall Street," *The Christian Science Monitor*,

October 24, 2011; available from Lexis-Nexis Academic.

62. Ibid.

63. "Economic Unrest," *Charleston Gazette*, September 26, 2011; available from Lexis-Nexis Academic.

64. Robert Mackey and Karen McVeigh, "Occupy Wall Street: Inquiries Launched as New Pepper-Spray Video Emerges," *The Guardian*, September 28, 2011; available from Lexis-Nexis Academic.

65. John Wellington Ennis, "Three Years Later, What Has Come of Occupy Wall Street?," The Huffington Post, September 17, 2014, http://www.huffingtonpost.com/john-wellington-ennis/three-years-later-what-ha_b_5833682.html, accessed April 1, 2015.

66. Occupy*Posters, Tumblr, http://owsposters.tumblr.com/post/11944143747/if-us-land-mass-were-distributed-like-us, accessed July 3, 2016.

67. Carrie Kahn, "Battle Cry: Occupy's Messaging Tactics Catch On," NPR, December 6, 2011, http://www.npr.org/2011/12/06/142999617/battle-cry-occupys-messaging-tactics-catch-on, accessed April 1, 2015.

68. Ibid.

69. "Occupy Wall Street: What Hollywood Is Saying about the Protests," *The Hollywood Reporter*, October 1, 2011; available from Lexis-Nexis Academic.

70. Ibid.

71. Ralph R. Reiland, "Occupying and Unlevel Battlefield," *Pittsburgh Tribune Review*, October 24, 2011; available from Lexis-Nexis Academic.

72. "*Real World* Seeks Occupy Wall Street Protestors," *Edmonton Journal*, October 21, 2011; available from Lexis-Nexis Academic.

73. Gina Bellafante, "Gunning for Wall Street, with Faulty Aim," *The New York Times*, September, 25, 2011; available from Lexis-Nexis Academic.

74. Ibid.

75. Harold Brubaker, "'Occupy Wall Street' Protest Movement Seeks a Philadelphia Foothold," *The Philadelphia Inquirer*, October 2, 2011; available from Lexis-Nexis Academic.

76. James C. McKinley Jr., "At the Protests, the Message Lacks a Melody," *The New York Times*, October 19, 2011; available from Lexis-Nexis Academic.

77. #Occupy Wall Street, NYC General Assembly, "Declaration of the Occupation of New York City" September 29, 2011, http://www.nycga.net/resources/documents/declaration/, accessed December 4, 2014.

78. Brad Knickerbocker, "Occupy Wall Street Protest 'about People Claiming Some Autonomy,'" *The Christian Science Monitor*, October 2, 2011; available from Lexis-Nexis Academic.

79. Jonathan Easley, "GOP: Dems Mum on Anti-Semitism from Occupy Wall Street Protestors," The Hill.com, October 20, 2011; available from Lexis-Nexis Academic.

80. Alice Speri, "Struggling to Make 'the 99%' More Representative of Reality," *The New York Times*, October 29, 2011; available from Lexis-Nexis Academic.

81. Ibid.

82. Cara Buckley and Colin Moynihan, "A Protest Reaches a Crossroads," *The New York Times*, November 6, 2011; available from Lexis-Nexis Academic.

83. Michelle Nichols, "Wall Street Demonstrators Evicted by New York Police," Reuters, November 16, 2011; available from Lexis-Nexis Academic.

84. Letter to the Editor, *The New York Times*, November 17, 2011; available from Lexis-Nexis Academic.

85. Gloria Goodale, "Occupy Wall Street: Time to Become More Overtly Political?," *The Christian Science Monitor*, November 16, 2011; available from Lexis-Nexis Academic.

86. See, for example, Dennis Chong, *Collective Action and the Civil Rights Movement* (Chicago: University of Chicago Press, 1991).

87. This section draws upon Ken Kollman, *The American Political System* (New York: W. W. Norton & Company, 2012), 378–379.

88. Christian Davenport, "How Social Movements Die–the Blog Entry (Book on the Way)," Mobilizing Ideas, The Center for the Study of Social Movements at the University of Notre Dame, December 2, 2013, https://mobilizingideas.wordpress.com/2013/12/02/how-social-movements-die-the-blog-entry-book-on-the-way/, accessed August 10, 2015.

89. Edwin Amenta, "Failure Is Not an Option," Mobilizing Ideas, The Center for the Study of Social Movements at the University of Notre Dame, December 2, 2013, https://mobilizingideas.wordpress.com/2013/12/02/failure-is-not-an-option/, accessed August 10, 2015.

90. Erik W. Johnson, "Social Movement Size, Organizational Diversity and the Making of Federal Law," *Social Forces* 86, no. 3 (2008): 967–993.

91. John W. Kingdon, *Agendas, Alternatives, and Public Policies*, updated 2nd ed. (Boston: Longman 2011).

92. David S. Meyer and Steven A. Boutcher, "Signals and Spillover: *Brown v. Board of Education* and Other Social Movements," *Perspectives on Politics* 5, no. 1 (2007): 81–93.

Chapter 12

1. Hanna Fenichel Pitkin, *The Concept of Representation* (Berkeley: University of California Press, 1972).

2. Angela Fritz, "We Hereby Name This Winter Storm 'Snowzilla,'" *The Washington Post*, January 22, 2016, https://www.washingtonpost.com/news/capital-weather-gang/wp/2016/01/21/poll-name-this-winter-storm/, accessed March 25, 2016.

3. Bridget Bowman, "Senate Women Rule as Work Begins after Blizzard," *Roll Call*, January 26, 2016, http://www.rollcall.com/wgdb/senate-women-rule-as-work-begins-after-blizzard/, accessed March 23, 2016. The original article substituted "our" for "are."

4. "The 114th Session of Congress," Ballotpedia, https://ballotpedia.org/114th_United_States_Congress#114th_Congress:_Demographics,

accessed March 21, 2016. In a discussion of one specific session of Congress, the precise number of members varies during the term (with events such as resignations and special elections transpiring over the two years of the session) and depending upon whether or not one chooses to include nonvoting delegates in the counts.

5. Jennifer E. Manning, "Membership of the 114th Congress: A Profile," Congressional Research Service, December 1, 2015, http://www.senate.gov/CRSReports/crs-publish.cfm?pid=%260BL*RLC2%0A.

6. Meredith Shiner, "Murray, Mikulski Blazing Trail for Future Female Leaders," Yahoo News, June 11, 2014, http://news.yahoo.com/murray-mikulski-blazing-trail-for-future-women-leaders-213011933.html, accessed October 1, 2015.

7. There had been a total of four women serving in the Senate at some point during the 102nd Congress. Jocelyn Burdick (D-ND) had served as an interim appointee before retiring in December 1992, and Dianne Feinstein's (D-CA) success in the election on November 3, 1992, enabled her to serve out the remainder of the term of interim appointee John F. Seymour (R-CA). The numbers for the House of Representatives do not include nonvoting delegates.

8. Debra L. Dodson et al., Voices, Views, Votes: The Impact of Women in the 103rd Congress (New Brunswick, NJ: Center for American Women and Politics, Eagleton Institute of Politics, Rutgers, 1995), 2.

9. Barbara Mikulski et al., Nine and Counting: The Women of the Senate (New York: Perennial, 2001), 14.

10. Michael X. Delli Carpini and Ester R. Fuchs, "The Year of the Woman? Candidates, Voters, and the 1992 Election," Political Science Quarterly 108, no. 1 (1993): 30.

11. [Missing]

12. James Madison, Federalist No. 62, in The Federalist, ed. George W. Carey and James McClellan (Indianapolis, IN: Liberty Fund, 2001), 321.

13. James Madison, Federalist No. 53, in Carey and McClellan, The Federalist, 279.

14. Although they are only required by the Constitution to live in the states that they represent, members of the House are, by custom, expected to maintain a residence in their electoral district.

15. James Madison, Federalist No. 52, in Carey and McClellan, The Federalist, 273.

16. James Madison, Federalist No. 63, in Carey and McClellan, The Federalist, 327.

17. The Articles of Confederation and Perpetual Union, Article V.

18. Also referred to as The Congressional Budget Control and Impoundment Act of 1974, P.L. 93-344.

19. Barbara Sinclair, Unorthodox Lawmaking: New Legislative Processes in the U.S. Congress, 2nd ed. (Washington, D.C.: CQ Press, 2000), 76.

20. Martin Frost and Tom Davis, "How to Fix What Ails Congress: Bring Back Earmarks," The Los Angeles Times, February 8, 2015, http://www.latimes.com/nation/la-oe-frost-earmark-spending-20150209-story.html, accessed July 7, 2016.

21. Mathew McCubbins and Thomas Schwartz, "Congressional Oversight Overlooked: Police Patrols versus Fire Alarms," American Journal of Political Science 28 (1984): 165–179.

22. If the president is being tried for impeachment, the chief justice of the Supreme Court presides (Article I, Section 3).

23. Clara Bingham, "Queens of the Hill: Will the Newly Empowered Women Lawmakers Clean up Congress?" Washington Monthly, January February 2007, http://www.washingtonmonthly.com/features/2007/0701.bingham.html, accessed March 29, 2013.

24. Delli Carpini and Fuchs, "The Year of the Woman?," 34–35.

25. Mikulski et al., Nine and Counting, 47.

26. Ibid., 47–48.

27. Sue Tolleson Rinehart, "The California Senate Races," in The Year of the Woman: Myths and Realities, ed. Elizabeth Adell Cook et al. (Boulder, CO: Westview Press, 1994), 30.

28. Mikulski et al., Nine and Counting, 48–49.

29. "The Year of the Woman. Then and Now: Women in U.S. Politics in 1992 and 2008," International Museum of Women, Global Fund for Women, http://exhibitions.globalfundforwomen.org/exhibitions/women-power-and-politics/elections/year-woman, accessed March 30, 2013.

30. Mikulski et al., Nine and Counting, 40.

31. Ibid., 40–41.

32. Ibid., 45.

33. Ibid., 23.

34. Andy Kroll, "Wisconsin's Tammy Baldwin Writes Her Way into the History Books," Mother Jones, November 7, 2012, http://www.motherjones.com/mojo/2012/11/wisconsin-senate-tammy-baldwin-win-tommy-thompson. Accessed October 8, 2015.

35. Gary C. Jacobson, The Politics of Congressional Elections, 8th ed. (New York: Pearson, 2012), 178.

36. Clyde Wilcox, "Why Was 1992 the 'Year of the Woman?' Explaining Women's Gains in 1992," in The Year of the Woman: Myths and Realities, ed. Elizabeth Adell Cook et al. (Boulder, CO: Westview Press, 1994), 5.

37. Linda L. Fowler and Robert D. McClure, Political Ambition: Who Decides to Run for Congress (New Haven, CT: Yale University Press, 1989), xii. See also Jennifer L. Lawless, Becoming a Candidate: Political Ambition and the Decision to Run for Office (New York: Cambridge University Press, 2012).

38. Fowler and McClure, Political Ambition, 5.

39. Isabel Wilkerson, "The 1992 Campaign: Women in the News; Storming Senate 'Club': Carol Elizabeth Moseley Braun," The New York Times, March 19, 1992, http://www.nytimes.com/1992/03/19/us/1992-campaign-woman-storming-senate-club-carol-elizabeth-moseley-braun.html.

40. Candice J. Nelson, "Women's PACs in the Year of the Woman," in Cook et al., The Year of the Woman, 183.

41. Ibid., 187–188.

42. Debra L. Dodson, "Whatever Happened to the 'Year of the Woman?'" The Public Perspective (August/September, 1996), 5.

43. Jean R. Schoedel and Bruce Snyder, "Patty Murray: The Mom in Tennis Shoes Goes to the Senate," in Cook et al., The Year of the Woman, 60–61.

44. Nelson, "Women's PACs in the Year of the Woman," 188.

45. Mikulski et al., Nine and Counting, 44.

46. Nicole Gaudino, "Longtime Sen. Barbara Mikulski to Retire," USA Today, March 2, 2015, http://www.usatoday.com/story/news/politics/elections/2015/03/02/barbara-mikulski-retires-senate/24252897/, accessed September 21, 2015.

47. Ibid.

48. Susan B. Hansen, "Lynn Yeakel versus Arlen Specter in Pennsylvania," in Cook et al., The Year of the Woman, 91.

49. Ibid., 93.

50. John M. Baer, "Arlen Backer: I'm No Boob," Philly.com (August 15, 1992), accessed May 24, 2013, http://articles.philly.com/1992-08-15/news/25992039_1_specter-campaign-manager-remark-democratic-women.

51. Dodson, "Whatever Happened to the 'Year of the Woman?,'" 5.

52. Ted G. Jelen, "Carol Moseley-Braun: The Insider as Insurgent," in Cook et al., The Year of the Woman, 71.

53. Clyde Wilcox, "Why Was 1992 the 'Year of the Woman'? Explaining Women's Gains in 1992," in Cook et al., The Year of the Woman, 2.

54. Ibid., footnote 3.

55. Wilcox, "Why Was 1992 the 'Year of the Woman'?, 20

56. George Bush: "Presidential Debate at the University of Richmond," The American Presidency Project, October 15, 1992, http://www.presidency.ucsb.edu/ws/?pid=21617, accessed March 28, 2013.

57. American Congresses are numbered consecutively, beginning with the session following each congressional election (every two years). The 1st Congress convened in 1789. Each Congress usually consists of two annual sessions, though the president has the authority to convene a special session of Congress.

58. Mikulski et al., Nine and Counting, 46.

59. "Leadership PACs," OpenSecrets.org, http://www.opensecrets.org/industries/indus.php?ind=Q03, accessed May 24, 2013.

60. Woodrow Wilson, Congressional Government: A Study in American Politics (Boston, MA: Houghton, Mifflin and Company, 1885), 79.

61. Richard F. Fenno Jr., Congressmen in Committees (Boston, MA: Little Brown, 1973).

62. Schoolhouse Rock! "I'm Just a Bill," available on YouTube at https://www.youtube.com/watch?v=tyeJ55o3El0.

63. Scott Franklin Abernathy, No Child Left Behind and the Public Schools (Ann Arbor: The University of Michigan Press, 2007), vii.

64. Sinclair, Unorthodox Lawmaking, 3.

65. Ibid., 33.

66. Ibid., 221–222.

67. Ibid., 14.

68. Ibid., 15.

69. Ibid., 52.

70. The term filibuster is generally also used to describe several other delaying tactics in the Senate.

71. Sinclair, *Unorthodox Lawmaking*, 43.

72. Ashley Parker, "Rand Paul Leads Filibuster of Brennan Nomination," *The New York Times*, March 6, 2013, http://thecaucus.blogs.nytimes.com/2013/03/06/rand-paul-filibusters-brennan-nomination/, accessed May 30, 2013.

73. Daniel Bier, @danieljbier, Twitter, March 6, 2013, https://twitter.com/danieljbier/status/309496305875554304.

74. Shane Miller, @sash_miller, #StandWithRand, Twitter, March 6, 2013, https://twitter.com/sash_miller/status/309518378664611840

75. Mark Memmott, "Nearly 13 Hours Later, Sen. Paul Ends His Filibuster; Here's the Video," NPR.org, the Two-Way, March 7, 2013, http://www.npr.org/blogs/thetwo-way/2013/03/07/173693133/nearly-13-hours-later-sen-paul-ends-his-filibuster-heres-the-video, accessed May 30, 2013.

76. Sinclair, *Unorthodox Lawmaking*, 58.

77. See Charles M. Cameron, *Veto Bargaining: Presidents and the Politics of Negative Power* (New York: Cambridge University Press, 2000).

78. Pitkin, *The Concept of Representation*.

79. Ibid., 8.

80. Richard F. Fenno, Jr., *Home Style: House Members in Their Districts* (HarperCollins Publishers, 1978).

81. John W. Kingdon, *Congressmen's Voting Decisions*, 3rd ed., (Ann Arbor: The University of Michigan Press, 1989).

82. Fenno, *Home Style*.

83. Jane Mansbridge calls the former *promissory representation* and the latter *anticipatory representation*. Jane Mansbridge, "Rethinking Representation," *American Political Science Review* 97, no. 4 (November 2003): 515–528.

84. R. Douglas Arnold, *The Logic of Congressional Action* (New Haven, CT: Yale University Press, 1990).

85. Ibid.

86. Tracy Sulkin, *Issue Politics in Congress* (New York: Cambridge University Press, 2005).

87. Richard L. Hall, *Participation in Congress* (New Haven, CT: Yale University Press, 1996).

88. "1994 Committee Supplement: Senate Judiciary," *CQ Weekly*, March 5, 1994, http://library.cqpress.com/cqweekly/wr103403788, accessed May 1, 2013.

89. Mikulski et al., *Nine and Counting*, 61.

90. Dodson et al., *Voices, Views, Votes*, 13.

91. See Morris P. Fiorina, Samuel J. Abrams, and Jeremy C. Pope, *Culture War? The Myth of a Polarized America*, 3rd ed. (New York: Longman, 2011); and Alan I. Abramowitz, *The Disappearing Center: Engaged Citizens, Polarization, and American Democracy* (New Haven, CT: Yale University Press, 2010).

92. John Adams, "Letter to John Penn," as quoted in Pitkin, *The Concept of Representation*, 60.

93. Jane Mansbridge, "Should Blacks Represent Blacks and Women Represent Women? A Contingent 'Yes,'" *The Journal of Politics* 61, no. 3 (August 1999): 628.

94. Ibid., 632.

95. Carol M. Swain, *Black Faces, Black Interests: The Representation of African Americans in Congress* (Cambridge, MA: Harvard University Press, 1995), 5.

96. Mansbridge, "Should Blacks Represent Blacks and Women Represent Women?," 637.

97. Pitkin, *The Concept of Representation*, 114.

98. Mansbridge, "Should Blacks Represent Blacks and Women Represent Women?," 634.

99. John W. Kingdon, *Agendas, Alternatives, and Public Policies*, 2nd ed., (New York: Longman, 2003).

100. Mansbridge, "Rethinking Representation," 522.

101. John Stuart Mill, *Representative Government*, as quoted in Pitkin, *The Concept of Representation*, 83.

102. Mikulski et al., *Nine and Counting*, 197.

103. Mansbridge, "Should Blacks Represent Blacks and Women Represent Women?," 647.

104. Ibid., 636.

105. Ibid.

106. Mikulski et al., *Nine and Counting*, 120.

107. Ibid., 122.

108. Ibid., 123.

109. "The Women of the Senate Discuss 'The Women of the Senate,'" *Larry King Live*, aired July 26, 2000, CNN.com, http://edition.cnn.com/TRANSCRIPTS/0007/26/lkl.00.html, accessed June 14, 2013.

110. Sheryl Gay Stolberg, "More Women than Ever in Congress, but with Less Power than Before," *The New York Times*, February 2, 2015, http://www.nytimes.com/2015/02/03/us/politics/republican-takeover-of-senate-pushes-women-out-of-powerful-committee-posts.html?_r=1, accessed September 23, 2015.

111. Ibid.

112. Ibid.

113. Daniella Diaz, "Sen. Barbara Boxer to Introduce Bill to end Electoral College," *CNN*, November 15, 2016, http://www.cnn.com/2016/11/15/politics/barbara-boxer-electoral-college-donald-trump-2016-election/. Accessed November 19, 2016.

114. Kevin Robillard and Elana Schor, "Van Hollen to Serve as DSCC chair," *Politico.com*, November 18, 2016, http://www.politico.com/story/2016/11/chris-van-hollen-dscc-chair-231621. Accessed November 19, 2016.

Chapter 13

1. Dina Temple-Rastan, "Kill and Tell: Inside the President's Terrorist Hunt," *The Washington Post*, June 17, 2012, B01; available from Lexis-Nexis Academic.

2. Mark Mazetti, Charlie Savage, and Scott Shane, "A U.S. Citizen in America's Cross Hairs," *The New York Times*, March 10, 2013, A1; available from Lexis-Nexis Academic.

3. "Details of Al-Awlaki's Death," *Yemen Times*, October 3, 2011; available from Lexis-Nexis Academic.

4. Mazetti, Savage, and Shane, "A U.S. Citizen in America's Cross Hairs."

5. Ibid.

6. Scott Shane, "Judging a Long, Deadly Reach," *The New York Times*, October 1, 2011, A1; available from Lexis-Nexis Academic.

7. Charlie Savage, "Top U.S. Security Official Says 'Rigorous Standards' Used for Drone Strikes," *The New York Times*, May 1, 2012, A8; available from Lexis-Nexis Academic.

8. Karen DeYoung and Peter Finn, "4 Americans Killed in Drone Strikes since '09," *The Washington Post*, May 23, 2013, A1; available from Lexis-Nexis Academic.

9. Mazetti, Savage, and Shane, "A U.S. Citizen in America's Cross Hairs."

10. Conor Friedersdorf, "How Team Obama Justifies the Killing of a 16-Year-Old American," *The Atlantic*, October 24, 2012. http://www.theatlantic.com/politics/archive/2012/10/how-team-obama-justifies-the-killing-of-a-16-year-old-american/264028/.

11. Scott Shane and Souad Mekhennet, "From Condemning Terror to Preaching Jihad," *The New York Times*, May 9, 2010, A1; available from Lexis-Nexis Academic.

12. Scott Shane and Mark Mazzetti, "A Newly Religious Immigrant Is Linked to a Militant Yemeni-American Cleric," *The New York Times*, May 7, 2010, A13; available from Lexis-Nexis Academic.

13. Anthony Shadid and David D. Kirkpatrick, "As the West Celebrates a Cleric's Death, the Mideast Shrugs," *The New York Times*, October 2, 2011, A14; available from Lexis-Nexis Academic.

14. Scott Shane and Robert F. Worth, "Challenge Heard on Move to Kill Qaeda-Linked Cleric," *The New York Times*, November 9, 2010, A12; available from Lexis-Nexis Academic.

15. Scott Shane, "Born in U.S., a Radical Cleric Inspires Terror against West," *The New York Times*, November 19, 2009, A1; available from Lexis-Nexis Academic.

16. Shane and Mekhennet, "From Condemning Terror to Preaching Jihad."

17. Ibid.

18. Ibid.

19. Charlie Savage, "Secret U.S. Memo Made Legal Case to Kill a Citizen," *The New York Times*, October 9, 2011, A1; available from Lexis-Nexis Academic.

20. Scott Shane, "A Legal Debate as C.I.A. Stalks a U.S. Jihadist," *The New York Times*, May 10, 2010, A1; available from Lexis-Nexis Academic.

21. Max Farrand, *The Framing of the Constitution of the United States* (New Haven, CT: Yale University Press, 1913), 21.

22. Clinton Rossiter, *The American Presidency*, 2nd ed. (Baltimore, MD: The Johns Hopkins University Press, 1987), 62.

23. Ulysses S. Grant unsuccessfully sought a third term in 1880.

24. In some states, widows with property were allowed to participate in public and political life.

25. Farrand, The Framing of the Constitution of the United States, 161.

26. Ibid., 163.

27. Many of these titles are in Rossiter, *The American Presidency*.

28. Article II, Section 1.

29. Article II, Section 1 and Article II, Section 3.

30. Article II, Section 2.

31. Article II, Sections 2 and 3.

32. Rossiter, The American Presidency, 12.

33. Article II, Section 3.

34. Charles M. Cameron, *Veto Bargaining: Presidents and the Politics of Negative Power* (New York: Cambridge University Press, 2000).

35. Article II, Section 2.

36. Rossiter, The American Presidency, 9.

37. Edward S. Corwin, *Presidential Power and the Constitution: Essays* (Ithaca, NY: Cornell University Press, 1976), 159.

38. Ibid., 163.

39. Article II, Section 2.

40. Articles I and III.

41. Article II, Section 2.

42. Article II, Section 4.

43. The chief justice presides only when presidents are impeached. Otherwise, the presiding office of the Senate would chair the proceedings.

44. Brian McGinty, *The Body of John Merryman: Abraham Lincoln and the Suspension of Habeas Corpus* (Cambridge, MA: Harvard University Press, 2011), 28.

45. "Affairs in Baltimore," *The New York Times*, May 29, 1861; available from ProQuest Historical Newspapers.

46. McGinty, The Body of John Merryman, 57.

47. Some reports suggest seven thousand casualties in twenty minutes, though there is some debate on the precise numbers as accurate figures were often difficult to obtain under the conditions.

48. Ken Burns, *The Civil War*, PBS, 1990.

49. "Startling from Baltimore: The Northern Troops Mobbed and Fired Upon," *The New York Times*, April 19, 1861; available from ProQuest Historical Newspapers.

50. "Testimony of William Lynch, September 9, 1861." Quoted in Jonathan W. White, *Abraham Lincoln and Treason in the Civil War: The Trials of John Merryman* (Baton Rouge: Louisiana State University Press, 2011), 13. The reported comments were most likely not referring to the racial identity of the soldier but used as a derogatory remark.

51. "The Battle of Baltimore: Detailed Account of the Affair," *The New York Times*, April 19, 1861; available from ProQuest Historical Newspapers.

52. "Startling From Baltimore."

53. McGinty, The Body of John Merryman, 67.

54. "Abraham Lincoln to Orville H. Browning, Washington, D.C., September 22, 1861," in *The Collected Works of Abraham Lincoln*, Vol. 4, ed. Roy P. Basler (New Brunswick, NJ: Rutgers University Press, 1953), 531.

55. Edward S. Corwin, *Presidential Power and the Constitution: Essays* (Ithaca, NY: Cornell University Press, 1976), 130.

56. *Ex parte Merryman*, 17 Fed. Cases 146 (1861).

57. Fort McHenry.

58. McGinty, The Body of John Merryman.

59. The term *habeas corpus* refers to several situations. Technically, Merryman's situation involved a writ of *habeas corpus ad subjiciendum* (McGinty, *The Body of John Merryman*, fn 4, 210–211).

60. George William Brown, *Baltimore and the Nineteenth of April 1861: A Study of the War* (Baltimore, MD: Johns Hopkins University Press, 1887), 87. Brown was present in Taney's courtroom on May 28, 1861.

61. Brown, Baltimore and the Nineteenth of April 1861, 88.

62. *Ex parte Merryman*. The legal term *ex parte* refers to a decision that affects one party only or a suit that is brought by or on behalf of one individual. Justice Taney, in standard practice at the time, also served as a circuit court judge, with Baltimore included in his circuit. Scholars continue to debate whether Taney was properly acting as chief justice of the Supreme Court (which the *Merryman* opinion so identifies him as) or in his role as circuit judge when he issued the opinion.

63. Brown, Baltimore and the Nineteenth of April 1861, 89.

64. McGinty, The Body of John Merryman, 1–2.

65. The seven states were South Carolina, Georgia, Alabama, Florida, Mississippi, Louisiana, and Texas.

66. Basler, The Collected Works of Abraham Lincoln, Vol. 4, 332.

67. Ibid. At the time, Congress was not typically in session during the entire summer. Officially, this allowed members to consult with their constituents given the lengthy travel times; however, the capitol's climate was also far from idyllic in the peak summer heat and humidity.

68. Virginia, Arkansas, North Carolina, and Tennessee.

69. "Abraham Lincoln to Winfield Scott, Washington, D.C., April 25, 1861," in Basler, *The Collected Works of Abraham Lincoln*, Vol 4, 344.

70. Article I, Section 9.

71. Ex parte Merryman.

72. Ibid.

73. Benjamin I. Page and Mark P. Petracca, *The American Presidency* (New York: McGraw-Hill Book Company, 1983), 51.

74. Habeas Corpus Suspension Act of March 3, 1863, 12 Stat 755 (1863).

75. Corwin, Presidential Power and the Constitution, 112, 158.

76. White, Abraham Lincoln and Treason in the Civil War, 115, 117.

77. Article I, Section 9.

78. "Abraham Lincoln to Erastus Corning and Others, Washington, D.C., June 12, 1863," in Basler, *The Collected Works of Abraham Lincoln*, Vol. 6, 267.

79. Page and Petracca, The American Presidency, 40.

80. "Pierce Butler to Weedon Butler, Mary Villa, May 5, 1788," in *Records of the Federal Convention of 1787*, ed. Max Farrand (New Haven, CT: Yale University Press, 1911), 302.

81. Page and Petracca, The American Presidency, 42.

82. Norman C. Thomas and Joseph A. Pika, *The Politics of the Presidency*, rev. 4th ed. (Washington, D.C.: CQ Press, 1997), 25.

83. Paul F. Boller Jr., *Presidential Anecdotes*, rev. ed. (New York: Oxford University Press, 1996), 66–67.

84. Page and Petracca, The American Presidency, 47.

85. Ibid., 54.

86. Boller, *Presidential Anecdotes*. Quoting from William F. McCombs, *Making Woodrow Wilson President* (New York: 1921), 208.

87. America formally entered the war in 1917.

88. Thomas and Pika, The Politics of the Presidency, 28.

89. The German invasion of Poland in September 1, 1939, is commonly used to mark the beginning of World War II. Formal American involvement in the war, apart from aid to Great Britain, lasted from 1941 to 1945. Japan's invasion and occupation of much of Northeast Asia in 1937 might be said to mark the beginning of the war in Asia. (Rossiter, *The American Presidency*, 11).

90. Corwin, Presidential Power and the Constitution, 165.

91. He had assumed office from the vice presidency on November 22, 1963, when President Kennedy was assassinated.

92. Joseph Kraft, "The Post-Imperial Presidency," *The New York Times Magazine*, November 2, 1980, 78; available from ProQuest Historical Newspapers.

93. Pub. L. No. 93-148, 87 Stat. 555 (November 7, 1973). Codified in 50 U.S.C. 33, Sections 1541-48 (1973). It is also called the War Powers Act, which was the title of the version of the joint resolution passed in the Senate.

94. Louis Fisher and David Gray Adler, "The War Powers Resolution: Time to Say Goodbye," *Political Science Quarterly* 113, no. 1 (1998): 1.

95. War Powers Resolution, Section 2(a).

96. War Powers Resolution, Section 2(c).

97. War Powers Resolution, Section 4(a). The president must notify both the Speaker of the House and the president of the Senate pro tempore.

98. War Powers Resolution, Section 5(b).

99. See Fisher and Adler, "The War Powers Resolution."

100. A third World Trade Center building nearby not hit by a plane, World Trade Center 7, also collapsed.

101. Congress authorized military operations in Afghanistan in Authorization for Use of Military Force, Pub. L. 107-40 (2001) and in Iraq in Authorization for Use of Military Force against Iraq Resolution of 2002, Pub. L. 107-243 (2002).

102. Authorization for Use of Military Force, Section 2(a).

103. James David Barber, *The Presidential Character: Predicting Performance in the White House*, 4th ed. (Englewood Cliffs, NJ: Prentice Hall, 1992).

104. Farrand, The Framing of the Constitution of the United States, 169.

105. Article I, Section 3.

106. Rossiter, The American Presidency, 121.

107. Boller Jr., *Presidential Anecdotes*, 300. Quoting Bill Adler, ed., *The Complete Kennedy Wit* (New York, 1967), 27–28.

108. Rossiter, The American Presidency, 123.

109. Arthur M. Schlesinger Jr., "Is the Vice Presidency Necessary?," *The Atlantic*, May 1, 1974, http://www.theatlantic.com/magazine/archive/1974/05/is-the-vice-presidency-necessary/305732/, accessed August 31, 2013.

110. The *Report of the President's Committee on Administrative Management* (1937), also known as the Brownlow Committee Report. The Reorganization Act of 1939 provided the legislative authorization for President Roosevelt's reorganization of the executive branch.

111. For a challenge to the argument that divided government necessarily leads to legislative

gridlock, see David R. Mayhew, *Divided We Govern: Party Control, Lawmaking, and Investigations, 1946–1990* (New Haven, CT: Yale University Press, 1991).

112. Rossiter, *The American Presidency*, 54, 56.

113. Page and Petracca, *The American Presidency*, 118. Quoting J. D. Richardson, ed., *Messages and Papers of the Presidents* (New York, 1879), 3.

114. Samuel Kernell, *Going Public: New Strategies of Presidential Leadership* (Washington, D.C.: CQ Press, 2007), 1–2.

115. James A. Stimson, "Public Support for American Presidents: A Cyclical Model," *The Public Opinion Quarterly* 40, no. 1 (1976): 1–21.

116. See, for example, Mark J. Rozell, "The Law: Executive Privilege: Definition and Standards of Application," *Presidential Studies Quarterly* 29, no. 4 (1999): 918–930.

117. *United States v. Nixon*, 418 U.S. 683 (1974).

118. Kenneth R. Mayer, *With the Stroke of a Pen: Executive Orders and Presidential Power* (Princeton, NJ: Princeton University Press, 2001).

119. Executive Order 9066, 7 *Federal Register* 1407 (February 19, 1942).

120. *Korematsu v. United States*, 323 U.S. 214 (1944).

121. Ibid.

122. *Youngstown Sheet & Tube Co. v. Sawyer*, 343 U.S. 579 (1952). The president's order was Executive Order No. 10340, 16 Federal Register 3503 (April 8, 1952).

123. William G. Howell, *Power without Persuasion: The Politics of Direct Presidential Action* (Princeton, NJ: Princeton University Press, 2003), 14.

124. Kenneth R. Mayer and Kevin Price, "Unilateral Presidential Powers: Significant Executive Orders, 1949–99," *Presidential Studies Quarterly* 32, no. 2 (2002): 370.

125. Executive Order No. 13223, "Ordering the Ready Reserve of the Armed Forces to Active Duty and Delegating Certain Authorities to the Secretary of Defense and the Secretary of Transportation," 66 Fed. Reg. 48201 (September 14, 2001); Executive Order No. 13224, "Blocking Property and Prohibiting Transactions with Persons Who Commit, Threaten to Commit, or Support Terrorism," 66 Fed. Reg. 49079 (September 23, 2001); Executive Order No. 13228, "Establishing the Office of Homeland Security and the Homeland Security Council," 66 Fed. Reg. 51812 (October 8, 2001). Congress later authorized the Department of Homeland Security as a cabinet-level department.

126. *Hamdi v. Rumsfeld*, 542 U.S. 507 (2002).

127. Ibid.

128. Ibid.

129. Ibid. Citing *Youngstown Sheet & Tube Co. v. Sawyer*. Justice O'Connor's opinion was of the plurality, with three other justices concurring and two joining in part.

130. See James David Barber, *The Presidential Character: Predicting Performance in the White House* (Englewood Cliffs, NJ: Prentice-Hall, Inc., 1972).

131. Richard E. Neustadt, Presidential Power and the Modern Presidents: The Politics of Leadership from Roosevelt to Reagan (New York: The Free Press, 1990), 163.

132. Ibid., 30.

133. Lester G. Seligman, "On Models of the Presidency," *Presidential Studies Quarterly* 10, no. 3 (1980): 356.

134. Alexander Hamilton, *Federalist No. 74*, in *The Federalist Papers*, ed. George W. Carey and James McClellan (Indianapolis, IN: Liberty Fund, 2001), 385.

135. James Bryce, *The American Commonwealth*, Vol. 1 (New York: Macmillan and Co., 1888), 83–84.

136. "Attorney General Eric S. Holder Jr. to Patrick J. Leahy, Chairman on the Judiciary, United States Senate," May 22, 2013, https://www.justice.gov/slideshow/AG-letter-5-22-13.pdf.

137. Mark Mazzetti, "American Drone Strike in Yemen Was Aimed at Awlaki," *The New York Times*, May 7, 2011, A11; available from Lexis-Nexis Academic.

138. Thomas E. Cronin and Michael A. Genovese, *The Paradoxes of the American Presidency*, 2nd ed. (New York: Oxford University Press, 2004).

139. Rishabh Jain, "President Trump's Drone Stance: Will He Continue Obama's Drone Policy?" *International Business Times*, November 21, 2016, http://www.ibtimes.com/president-trumps-drone-stance-will-he-continue-obamas-drone-policy-2449124. Accessed November 21, 2016.

140. Andrew Kaczynski, "Trump's Pick for National Security Advisor Once Bashed Torture, Drone Strikes, Night Raids," *CNN*, November 21, 2016, http://www.cnn.com/2016/11/21/politics/kfile-flynn-on-torture/. Accessed November 21, 2016.

141. Ibid.

Chapter 14

1. See William Safire, *Safire's Political Dictionary* (New York: Random House, 1978), 84. The term *bureau* may derive from the French *burel*, the cloth used to cover writing desks.

2. Tamara Lush, "For Forecasting Chief, No Joy in Being Right," *St. Petersburg Times*, August 30, 2005, 3A; available from Lexis-Nexis Academic.

3. Ibid.

4. Ibid.

5. The Saffir-Simpson hurricane wind scale rates hurricanes from 1 to 5 according to sustained wind speed, with 1 being the weakest. Katrina struck Florida as a Category 1 storm. Once over the Gulf, Katrina eventually strengthened to a Category 5 storm, one of the most powerful Atlantic hurricanes ever measured. It made landfall in Louisiana as a Category 3 storm.

6. Frank Cerabino, "Boca Couldn't Have Ordered a Better Storm than Katrina," *Palm Beach Post*, August 26, 2005, 1B; available from Lexis-Nexis Academic.

7. Robert P. King, "Officials State Categorically: No Hurricane Is Minimal," *Palm Beach Post*, August 27, 2005, 15A; available from Lexis-Nexis Academic.

8. Katrina officially made landfall on the Gulf Coast twice, several hours apart.

9. Deana Poole and Pat Beall, "New Orleans Emptying: Katrina on Path to Bring Disaster," *Palm Beach Post*, August 28, 2005, 1A; available from Lexis-Nexis Academic.

10. Donald F. Kettl, The Next Government of the United States: Why Our Institutions Fail Us and How to Fix Them (New York: W. W. Norton & Company, 2009), 18.

11. "Katrina Storms Ashore: 'Big One' Casts Fury at New Orleans," *The Atlanta Journal-Constitution*, August 29, 2005, 1A; available from Lexis-Nexis Academic.

12. Russell McCulley, "Governor, 'We Need to Pray: Katrina, the 'Perfect' Hurricane, to Hit Louisiana," *National Post*, August 29, 2005, A1; available from Lexis-Nexis Academic.

13. "Katrina Storms Ashore."

14. Poole and Beall, "New Orleans Emptying."

15. "Katrina Storms Ashore."

16. John Ashton, "Thousands Flee as Hurricane Nears U.S. Coast," *Birmingham Post*, August 29, 2005, 9; available from Lexis-Nexis Academic.

17. Phyllis Furman, "Wall St. Weathers Storm. Investors See Bright Spots," *New York Daily News*, August 30, 2005, 55; available from Lexis-Nexis Academic.

18. Kettl, The Next Government of the United States, 21.

19. Jed Horne, "5 Myths about Hurricane Katrina," *The Washington Post*, September 3, 2012, B04; available from Lexis-Nexis Academic.

20. Tina Hesman, "Most People Killed by Katrina Were Elderly, Researcher Finds," *St. Louis Post-Dispatch*, February 17, 2006, A5; available from Lexis-Nexis Academic.

21. Sheldon Alberts, "Big Easy Rests Easier Despite Katrina Disaster: Hurricane Falls Short of Doomsday Predictions, but Kills at Least 55 in Mississippi, Alabama," *Edmonton Journal*, August 30, 2005, A1; available from Lexis-Nexis Academic.

22. "A Call for Help; Donations Are the Quickest Way to Aid Katrina's Victims," *Sarasota Herald-Tribune*, August 30, 2005, A10; available from Lexis-Nexis Academic.

23. Anthony R. Wood, "Count of Losses Turns Grimmer; Katrina Has Killed More than Any Storm since 1972's Agnes," *Philadelphia Inquirer*, August 31, 2005, A10; available from Lexis-Nexis Academic.

24. Bryan Dean and Ryan McNeill, "Facing the Future: Hurricane Survivors Express Thanks to State," *The Oklahoman*, September 5, 2005, 1A; available from Lexis-Nexis Academic.

25. The United States Department of Transportation. The Uniform Time Act of 1966 (15 U.S.C. §§ 260-64) established the system of uniform Daylight Saving Time. States are allowed to opt out of the national daylight savings program. If they do participate, they must change the time according to a federally set schedule.

26. Max Weber, "The Permanent Character of the Bureaucratic Machine," in *From Max Weber: Essays in Sociology*, ed. H. H. Gerth and C. Wright Mills (1991 [1948]), 229.

27. Max Weber, *Economy and Society: An Outline of Interpretive Sociology*, trans. and ed.

Guenther Roth and Claus Wittich (Berkeley: University of California Press, 1978), 987. The work was first published in Germany, posthumously, in 1922.

28. Ibid., 957–958.

29. Ibid., 975.

30. Chester I. Barnard, *The Functions of the Executive* (Cambridge, MA: Harvard University Press, 1968 [1938]), 72.

31. Barnard, The Functions of the Executive, 82.

32. James Q. Wilson, Bureaucracy: What Government Agencies Do and Why They Do It (New York: Basic Books, 1989), 173.

33. Wilson calls this category of bureaucracies "coping organizations." Wilson, *Bureaucracy*, 175.

34. Public education is largely governed by the states, not the federal government; however, the illustration applies to the actions of federal bureaucrats as well.

35. See Scott F. Abernathy, *No Child Left Behind and the Public Schools* (Ann Arbor: The University of Michigan Press, 2007), 25–45.

36. James Q. Wilson, "The Rise of the Bureaucratic State," *The Public Interest* 41 (Fall 1975): 77.

37. Article II, Section 2.

38. Michael Nelson, "A Short, Ironic History of the American National Bureaucracy," *The Journal of Politics* 44, no. 3 (August 1982): 751. Quoting from Charles Thatch Jr., *The Creation of the Presidency, 1775–1789* (Baltimore, MD: Johns Hopkins University Press, 1923), 59.

39. Roughly 1,350 of 6,500 presidentially nominated officials require Senate confirmation.

40. Article II, Sections 2 and 4.

41. Leonard D. White, *The Federalists: A Study in Administrative History* (New York: The Macmillan Company, 1948), 20.

42. The use of the gendered language is intentional in this section, given the exclusion of women from political life at the time. A woman would not serve as a cabinet secretary until 1933, when President Franklin Roosevelt appointed Frances Perkins as secretary of labor.

43. David H. Rosenbloom, The Federal Service and the Constitution: The Development of the Public Employment Relationship (Ithaca, NY: Cornell University Press, 1971), 30.

44. James Madison, June 17, 1789, *Annals of Congress*, 1st Cong., 1st sess.

45. *Myers v. United States*, 272 U.S. 52 (1926).

46. White, *The Federalists*, 258. Quoting George Washington to Edward Rutledge, 21 March 1789.

47. White, *The Federalists*, 259.

48. Ibid., 222.

49. David H. Rosenbloom, Federal Service and the Constitution: The Development of the Public Employment Relationship (Ithaca, NY: Cornell University Press, 1971), 35. See also Brian J. Cook, Bureaucracy and Self-Government: Reconsidering the Role of Public Administration in American Politics (Baltimore, MD: The Johns Hopkins University Press, 1996), 45.

50. James D. Richardson, ed., *A Compilation of the Messages and Papers of the Presidents of the United States, 1789–1897*, Vol. II (Washington, D.C.: U.S. Government Printing Office, 1896), 449.

51. Wilson, "The Rise of the Bureaucratic State," 82. See also Nelson, "A Short, Ironic History of the American National Bureaucracy," 757–762.

52. The Department of Agriculture was given full cabinet status in 1889.

53. Stephen Skowronek, Building a New American State: The Expansion of National Administrative Capacities, 1877–1920 (New York: Cambridge University Press, 1982).

54. Theda Skocpol, *Protecting Soldiers and Mothers: The Political Origins of Social Policy in the United States* (Cambridge, MA: The Belknap Press of Harvard University Press, 1992). Professor Skocpol also examined the gendered aspects of American social welfare policy and how the degree to which recipients were seen as "deserving" shaped the policies themselves.

55. In *The Jungle* (1906), Upton Sinclair described unhealthy and dangerous working conditions in the meatpacking industry, which helped secure the passage of the Pure Food and Drug Act and the Meat Inspection Act.

56. George William Curtis, "The Situation: An Address Delivered at the Fifth Annual Meeting of the National Civil Service Reform League, Held at Newport, R.I., August, 4, 1886," in *Orations and Addresses of George William Curtis*, Vol. II, ed. Charles Eliot Nelson (New York: Harper & Brothers Publishers, 1894), 320.

57. Rosenbloom, *Federal Service and the Constitution*, 76. Quoting from Civil Service Rule VIII (1884).

58. The United States Supreme Court affirmed the constitutionality of restriction on political contributions by civil service workers in *Ex Parte Curtis*, 106 U.S. 371 (1882).

59. The Office of Price Administration was originally established by an executive order and later became an independent agency when Congress passed the Emergency Price Control Act.

60. The National Security Act of 1947 also reorganized the cabinet structure of the departments and agencies involved in defense.

61. Public Law 88-352 (78 Stat. 241).

62. Jody Warrick, "White House Got Early Warning on Katrina," *The Washington Post*, January 24, 2006, A02; available from Lexis-Nexis Academic.

63. Richard W. Stevenson, "After Katrina's Lesson, Bush Is Heading to Texas," *The New York Times*, September 23, 2005, A1; available from Lexis-Nexis Academic.

64. Ibid.

65. MaryAnne Borelli, *The President's Cabinet: Gender, Power, and Representation* (Boulder, CO: Lynne Rienner Publishers, 2002), 2.

66. For an examination of political executives' perspectives on politics within the federal bureaucracy, see Joel D. Aberbach and Bert A. Rockman, *In the Web of Politics: Three Decades of the U.S. Federal Executive* (Washington, D.C.: Brookings Institution, 2000).

67. President George W. Bush initially established the White House Office of Homeland Security by executive order. Congress passed Public Law 107-296 in November 2002, formally establishing it as a cabinet department. It has since undergone subsequent modifications in its organizational structure.

68. Frank J., "A Frank Guide to Homeland Security Alert Levels," *IMAO*, May 22, 2003, http://www.imao.us/archives/000651.html, accessed July 10, 2016.

69. Jed Graham, "Gov't Better Prepared for Rita; Katrina's Lessons Learned; Officials at Federal, State, City Level Move Resources Fast as Many Flee Cyclone," *Investor's Business Daily*, September 23, 2005, A01; available from Lexis-Nexis Academic.

70. White House, Office of the Press Secretary, "President Arrives in Alabama, Briefed on Hurricane Katrina," September 2, 2005, http://georgewbushwhitehouse.archives.gov/news/releases/2005/09/20050902-2.html, accessed February 28, 2014.

71. Brad Delong. "Katrina Reveals the Presidential Flaws," *Financial Times*, September 7, 2005, 13; available from Lexis-Nexis Academic.

72. Michael A. Fletcher, "Bush Praises Progress in Rebuilding Efforts: Region Closely Tracking Hurricane Rita," *The Washington Post*, September 21, 2005, A07; available from Lexis-Nexis Academic.

73. Eric Lipton, "White House Was Told Hurricane Posed Danger," *The New York Times*, January 24, 2006, A14; available from Lexis-Nexis Academic.

74. Megan O'Matz, "Fraud Cost Millions in Katrina, Rita Aid; FEMA Failed to Verify Damage in Many Cases," *The Record*, February 14, 2006, A01. Original Byline: *South Florida Sun-Sentinel*, Wire Services; available from Lexis-Nexis Academic.

75. Charles T. Goodsell, *The Case For Bureaucracy: A Public Administration Polemic*, 2nd ed. (Chatham, NJ: Chatham House Publishers, Inc., 1985), 83.

76. Richard Stillman II, *The American Bureaucracy: The Core of Modern Government*, 3rd ed. (Belmont, CA: Thomson Wadsworth, 2004), 129–130.

77. The United States Armed Forces, which are part of the executive branch, have a different organizational structure, though the secretary of defense and deputy and assistant secretaries are political appointees.

78. For a foundational study of the challenges of implementation, see Jeffrey L. Pressman and Aaron Wildavsky, *Implementation: How Great Expectations in Washington Are Dashed in Oakland; Or, Why It's Amazing That Federal Programs Work at All, This Being a Saga of the Economic Development Administration as Told by Two Sympathetic Observers Who Seek to Build Morals on a Foundation of Ruined Hopes*, 3rd ed. (Berkeley: University of California Press, 1984).

79. Herbert Kaufman, "Fear of Bureaucracy: A Raging Pandemic," *Public Administration Review* 41, no. 1 (1981): 7.

80. Ibid., 4.

81. Michael Lipsky, Street-Level Bureaucracy: Dilemmas of the Individual in Public Services (New York: Russell Sage Foundation, 1980).

82. Cornelius M. Kerwin, *Rulemaking: How Government Agencies Write Laws and Make Policy* (Washington, D.C.: CQ Press, 1994), 4.

83. Kenneth J. Meier, "Representative Bureaucracy: A Theoretical and Empirical Exposition," in *Research in Public Administration*, ed. James Perry (Greenwich, CT: JAI Press, 1993).

84. Sally Coleman Selden, The Promise of Representative Bureaucracy: Diversity and Responsiveness in a Government Agency (Armonk, NY: ME Sharpe, 1997).

85. Goodsell, The Case For Bureaucracy, 63.

86. William A. Niskanen, "The Peculiar Economics of Bureaucracy," *The American Economic Review* 58, no. 2 (May 1968): 293–305.

87. John Brehm and Scott Gates, *Working, Shirking, and Sabotage: Bureaucratic Responses to a Democratic Public* (Ann Arbor: The University of Michigan Press, 1997).

88. For a classic study of the challenges posed by outside pressures on bureaucrats and how bureaucratic agencies deal with them, see Herbert Kaufman, *The Forest Ranger: A Study in Administrative Behavior* (Washington, D.C.: Resources for the Future, 1960).

89. Joel D. Aberbach, *Keeping a Watchful Eye: The Politics of Congressional Oversight* (Washington, D.C.: The Brookings Institution, 1990), 4.

90. The legislative and judicial branches also contain bureaucratic organizations, though these are few in number and small in size compared to the departments, agencies, and bureaus in the executive branch.

91. Saul Pett, "It's No Mickey Mouse War: White House Fights Mice That Roar," *Chicago Tribune*, March 12, 1978, 4; available from ProQuest Historical Newspapers.

92. United States Government Accountability Office, "Preliminary Observations on Hurricane Response," February 1, 2006. GAO-06-365R, http://www.gao.gov/assets/100/94002.pdf.

93. Mathew D. McCubbins and Thomas Schwartz, "Congressional Oversight Overlooked: Police Patrols versus Fire Alarms," *American Journal of Political Science* 28, no. 1 (February 1984): 165–179.

94. Eric Lipton, "Chertoff Hears Harsh Criticism from Senators," *The New York Times*, February 16, 2006, A1; available from Lexis-Nexis Academic.

95. Ibid.

96. Ibid.

97. Select Bipartisan Committee to Investigate the Preparation for and Response to Hurricane Katrina, A Failure of Initiative: Final Report of the Select Bipartisan Committee to Investigate the Preparation for and Response to Hurricane Katrina (Washington, D.C.: U.S. Government Printing Office, 2006), x.

98. Ibid.

99. Leah Hodges, Written Testimony, Select Bipartisan Committee to Investigate the Preparation for and Response to Hurricane Katrina, December 6, 2005.

100. Kaufman, "Fear of Bureaucracy," 6.

101. Walter Lippmann, *The Phantom Public* (New Brunswick, NJ: Transaction Publishers, 2011 [1927]), 55.

102. William Douglas and Steven Thomas, "On Katrina Anniversary, Bush Returns to Gulf Coast," Knight Ridder Washington Bureau, August 28, 2006; available from Lexis-Nexis Academic.

103. John J. Dilulio Jr., Gerald Garvey, and Donald F. Kettl, *Improving Government Performance: An Owner's Manual* (Washington, D.C.: The Brookings Institution, 1993), 64.

104. Ibid., 4.

105. David Osborne and Ted Gaebler, Reinventing Government: How the Entrepreneurial Spirit Is Transforming the Public Sector (New York: Plume/Penguin Books, 1993), xix.

106. Wilson, *Bureaucracy*, 134–136. Professor Wilson did not necessarily condemn efforts at privatization, instead pointing out differences in mandates and structure. In the provision of services in which outputs and outcomes are difficult to measure—such as education—he pointed out that parents, and not supervisors, might be more effective at measuring the quality of the product (364).

107. Select Bipartisan Committee, *A Failure of Initiative*, 17.

108. Brad Delong, "Katrina Reveals the Presidential Flaws," *Financial Times*, September 7, 2005, 13; available from Lexis-Nexis Academic.

109. Anthony Lonetree, "From the Wreckage of Katrina to the Walls of Local Art Centers: Artwork That Survived or Was Influenced by the Hurricane Makes Its Way Here from Mississippi in Yet Another Step in the Long Recovery," *Star Tribune*, January 11, 2006, 1B; available from Lexis-Nexis Academic.

110. David Hench, "Katrina Response Brings Out the Best, Worst in People," *Portland Press Herald, Maine*, September 15, 2005; available from Lexis-Nexis Academic.

111. "See Katrina's Trail," *Gold Coast Bulletin*, December 17, 2005, 96; available from Lexis-Nexis Academic.

112. Sarah Ladislaw, "Hurricane Sandy: Evaluating the Response One Year Later," *Center for Strategic and International Studies*, November 4, 2013, https://www.csis.org/analysis/hurricane-sandy-evaluating-response-one-year-later, accessed July 10, 2016.

Chapter 15

1. The title refers to Alexander Hamilton's characterization in *Federalist* No. 78 of the federal judiciary as "least dangerous to the political rights of the Constitution." In *The Federalist Papers*, ed. George W. Carey and James McClellan (Indianapolis, IN: Liberty Fund, 2001), 402. Alexander M. Bickel also chose the phrase from the title of his critique of judicial power, *The Least Dangerous Branch: The Supreme Court at the Bar of Politics* (Indianapolis, IN: Bobbs-Merrill Educational Publishing, 1962).

2. Robert Barnes and Michael A. Fletcher, "Riskiest Choice on Obama's List Embodies His Criteria; President and Judge Cite Her Life Experience," *The Washington Post*, May 27, 2009; available from Lexis-Nexis Academic.

3. Jeffrey Rosen, "The Case against Sotomayor," *New Republic*, May 4, 2009, http://www.newrepublic.com/article/politics/the-case-against-sotomayor, accessed May 20, 2014.

4. Charlie Savage, "Conservatives Map Strategies on Court Fight," *The New York Times*, May 17, 2009; available from Lexis-Nexis Academic.

5. Ibid.

6. Sonia Sotomayor, "A Latina Judge's Voice," *Berkeley La Raza Law Journal* 13, no. 1 (Spring 2002): 87–93.

7. David S. Broder, "After Bork–and Obama; Confirmation Fights Still Echo," *The Washington Post*, June 4, 2009; available from Lexis-Nexis Academic.

8. *The Washington Post*, "GOP Senator Sums Up Sotomayor Issue," June 7, 2009; available from Lexis-Nexis Academic.

9. Kate Phillips, "Witness List for Sotomayor Has a Couple of Surprises," *The New York Times*, July 10, 2009; available from Lexis-Nexis Academic.

10. David Montgomery and Kate Kilpatrick, "For Some Latinos, Hearing Is Believing; Sotomayor's Ascension Trickles Down," *The Washington Post*, July 14, 2009; available from Lexis-Nexis Academic.

11. Peter Baker and Neil A. Lewis, "Judge Focuses on Rule of Law at the Hearings," *The New York Times*, July 14, 2009; available from Lexis-Nexis Academic.

12. Amy Goldstein, Paul Kane, and Robert Barnes, "Sotomayor Avoids Pointed Queries; Supreme Court Nominee Is Elusive about Abortion and Other Issues," *The Washington Post*, July 16, 2009; available from Lexis-Nexis Academic.

13. Robert Barnes and Michael D. Shear, "Abortion Rights Backers Get Reassurances on Nominee," *The Washington Post*, May 29, 2009; available from Lexis-Nexis Academic.

14. N. C. Aizenman, "For Latinos, Confirmation Is an Emotional Moment," *The Washington Post*, August 7, 2009; available from Lexis-Nexis Academic.

15. Forrest McDonald, *Novus Ordo Seclorum: The Intellectual Origins of the Constitution* (Lawrence: University Press of Kansas, 1985), 253.

16. The delegates did debate the need to raise judges' salaries to keep up with changes in the cost of living, but they ultimately left the issue of pay raises out of the document.

17. Article III, Section 1.

18. Article II, Section 2.

19. McDonald, *Novus Ordo Seclorum*, 254–255.

20. Article III, Section 1.

21. Article II, Section 1.

22. Article VI.

23. The term *jurisdiction* is also applied in other contexts, such as the authority of a specific law enforcement agency to investigate a case. However, we will focus only on the jurisdiction of courts in this chapter.

24. Catherine Drinker Bowen, Miracle at Philadelphia: The Story of the Constitutional Convention May to September 1787 (Boston: Little, Brown and Company, 1986), 64.

25. "Brutus," Essay VI, December 27, 1787, in *The Essential Antifederalist*, 2nd ed., eds. W. B.

Allen and Gordon Lloyd (New York: Rowman & Littlefield Publishers, Inc., 2002), 188.

26. Ibid., 188.

27. Hamilton, *Federalist* No. 78, in Carey and McClellan, *The Federalist Papers*, 402.

28. Ibid.

29. "The Judiciary Act of 1789," in *Documents of American History*, 6th ed., ed. Henry Steele Commager (New York: Appleton-Century-Crofts, Inc., 1958), 153.

30. Ibid., 155.

31. John Ferling, *Adams vs. Jefferson: The Tumultuous Election of 1800* (New York: Oxford University Press, 2004), xi.

32. Jefferson's party is often referred to as the Democratic-Republican Party, though it was more commonly called the Republican Party at the time. "Jeffersonian Republicans" is also a commonly used label today.

33. John Adams and Alexander Hamilton were not always in complete agreement. Adams and other Federalists sometimes expressed misgivings about Hamilton's ardent nationalism.

34. Jefferson's Republicans are viewed as having been better organized than the Federalists at the time.

35. Taxation and foreign policy in Adams's administration also became campaign issues.

36. Ferling, *Adams vs. Jefferson*, 18. Quoting "Abigail Adams to Thomas Jefferson, 6 June 1785," in *The Adams-Jefferson Letters: The Complete Correspondence between Thomas Jefferson and Abigail and John Adams*, Vol. 1, ed. Lester J. Cappan (Chapel Hill: University of North Carolina Press, 1961), 28.

37. Ferling, *Adams vs. Jefferson*, 151–154.

38. Article II, Section 1.

39. The Twelfth Amendment to the Constitution (ratified in 1804) changed the presidential election rules by separating the votes for president and vice president. The House would continue to settle presidential elections if there was not a majority vote for one candidate by the electors, and the Senate would choose the vice president. While no presidential election has gone to Congress since 1824 (when John Quincy Adams, son of John Adams, was selected over the popular vote winner Andrew Jackson), this process remains in place today.

40. The Twentieth Amendment to the Constitution (ratified in 1933) changed the date of the inauguration of the president to January 20 to shorten the time between the election and the transition to the next administration.

41. Ferling, *Adams vs. Jefferson*, 181.

42. "Thomas Jefferson, First Inaugural Address, 4 March 1801," in *Basic Writings of Thomas Jefferson*, ed. Philip S. Foner (New York: Wiley Book Company, 1944), 333.

43. Article III, Section 1.

44. Kathryn Turner, "Federalist Policy and the Judiciary Act of 1801," *The William and Mary Quarterly* 22, no. 1 (January 1965): 32. Turner notes that as many of the provisions in the Judiciary Act of 1801 had been introduced prior to the election, there were other reasons for these provisions, particularly a desire to strengthen the power of the national government. The electoral results, however,

45. Turner, "Federalist Policy and the Judiciary Act of 1801," 20. Quoting "Gouverneur Morris to Robert R. Livingston, 20 February 1801," in *The Life of Gouverneur Morris: With Selections from His Correspondence and Miscellaneous Papers*, Vol. III, ed. Jared Sparks (Boston: Gray & Bowen, 1832), 153–154.

46. Kathryn Turner, "The Midnight Judges," *University of Pennsylvania Law Review* 109, no. 4 (February 1961): 494. Quoting "Letter from Thomas Jefferson to John Dickinson, 19 December 1801," in *The Writings of Thomas Jefferson*, Vol. 10, ed. Andrew A. Lipscomb (The Thomas Jefferson Memorial Association, 1903), 302.

47. David Loth, *Chief Justice: John Marshall and the Growth of the Republic* (New York: W. W. Norton & Company, 1949), 176.

48. Turner, "The Midnight Judges," 494.

49. Oliver Ellsworth, the former chief justice, had retired shortly before.

50. Mark R. Killenbeck, *M'Culloch v. Maryland: Securing a Nation* (Lawrence: University Press of Kansas, 2006), 74.

51. James Bradley Thayer, *John Marshall*, rev. ed. (New York: Da Capo Press, 1974 [1901]), 12–13.

52. Killenbeck, *M'Culloch v. Maryland*, 81.

53. Turner, "The Midnight Judges," 519.

54. The four plaintiffs were William Marbury, Dennis Ramsay, Robert Townsend Hope, and William Harper.

55. *Marbury v. Madison*, 5 U.S. 137 (1803).

56. For fans of the television and film series *Star Trek*, Marshall's dilemma might be seen as one of America's first political Kobayashi Maru scenarios. In *Star Trek* lore, Captain James T. Kirk only defeated the no-win training scenario by cheating, something that several historians and scholars have accused Marshall of doing in his interpretation and reading of the Constitution and Judiciary Act of 1789.

57. *Marbury v. Madison*.

58. Ibid.

59. Ibid.

60. Section 13 of the Judiciary Act of 1789.

61. *Marbury v. Madison*.

62. Michael Stokes Paulsen, "The Irrepressible Myth of *Marbury*," *Michigan Law Review* 101, no. 8 (August 2003): 2707.

63. Hamilton, *Federalist* No. 78, in Carey and McClellan, *The Federalist Papers*, 403–405.

64. "Thomas Jefferson to Abigail Adams, Monticello, VA, 11 September 1804," in Foner, *Basic Writings of Thomas Jefferson*, 670.

65. Loth, *Chief Justice*, 194–195.

66. Ibid, 201.

67. Bickel, The Least Dangerous Branch, 16.

68. Ibid., 69.

69. Ibid., 71.

70. *Dred Scott v. Sanford*, 60 U.S. 393 (1857).

71. For cases heard on appeal, the petitioner is the party that lost in the lower court and the respondent is the other party in the case.

72. Another category of law, called procedural law, refers to proceedings and rules through which laws are enforced, such as how law enforcement officials interact with those accused of crimes.

73. Many of the definitions of legal terms in this chapter are informed by Bryan A. Garner, ed., *Black's Law Dictionary*, 8th ed. (St. Paul, MN: Thompson/West, 2004).

74. The relevant federal law is the Controlled Substances Act (1970). Under that act, marijuana, along with heroin, ecstasy, and other substances, is classified as one having a high potential for abuse and no accepted medical use.

75. As discussed in Chapter 3, the process of incorporation has resulted in the application of most of the protections of the Bill of Rights to the states as well as the federal government.

76. As of September 2016, thirty states had the death penalty. (Death Penalty Information Center, "States with and without the Death Penalty," http://www.deathpenaltyinfo.org/states-and-without-death-penalty, accessed September 18, 2016.) The United States government also has the authority to impose the death penalty for conviction under certain federal laws. In addition, the military retains the death penalty for conviction of certain offenses under the Uniform Code of Military Justice, though it has not been carried out since 1961.

77. Two states, Texas and Oklahoma, have separate state supreme courts for criminal and civil cases.

78. Article III, Section 2.

79. A small set of cases may bypass the appellate courts in this process, such as those involving voting rights and aspects of the 1964 Civil Rights Act.

80. The Supreme Court automatically hears a small set of cases on appeal—those involving voting rights and congressional redistricting. Unless overturned by the Supreme Court, appellate court decisions are binding but only within the jurisdiction of that specific court of appeals. Such jurisdictions (excepting the D.C. and federal circuits) are geographically determined.

81. The opposition files a "brief in opposition to a petition for a writ of certiorari." Briefs in opposition are only mandatory in capital cases. United States Supreme Court, *Rules of the Supreme Court of the United States*, Rule 15, http://www.supremecourt.gov/ctrules/2013RulesoftheCourt.pdf, accessed April 27, 2014.

82. Ibid., Rule 10.

83. Only attorneys admitted to the Bar of the Court may file amicus curiae briefs (*Rules of the U.S. Supreme Court*, Rule 37).

84. Gregory A. Caldiera and John R. Wright, "Amici Curiae before the Supreme Court: Who Participates, When, and How Much?," *The Journal of Politics* 52, no. 3 (August 1990): 782–806.

85. See, for example, Timothy R. Johnson, Paul J. Wahlbeck, and James F. Spriggs Jr., "The Influence of Oral Arguments on the U.S. Supreme Court," *American Political Science Review* 100, no. 1 (February 2006): 99–113.

86. Another option for the Court is to send it back to the lower court under the status of review being improvidently granted. In such a case, the Court has decided that after review it now

chooses not to give a full hearing to the case. If so, the lower ruling stands, but the Court has not officially weighed in on that ruling.

87. Steven V. Roberts, "In the Balance: Reagan Gets His Chance to Tilt the High Court," *The New York Times*, June 28, 1987; available from Lexis-Nexis Academic.

88. Ibid.

89. Irvin Molotsky, "Inside Fight Seen over Court Choice," *The New York Times*, June 28, 1987; available from Lexis-Nexis Academic.

90. David Johnston, "Reagan to Select Nominee for Court within 2 Weeks," *The New York Times*, June 29, 1987; available from Lexis-Nexis Academic.

91. *Roe v. Wade*, 410 U.S. 113 (1973).

92. Ruth Marcus, "Bork on 'Judicial Imperialism': Judges Accused of Inventing Constitutional Rights to Fit Their Views," *The Washington Post*, July 2, 1987; available from Lexis-Nexis Academic.

93. "The Bork Nomination," Editorial, *The Washington Post*, July 2, 1987; available from Lexis-Nexis Academic.

94. Linda Greenhouse, "Senators' Remarks Portend a Bitter Debate over Bork," *The New York Times*, July 2, 1987; available from Lexis-Nexis Academic.

95. "Poll Hints at Bork Support," *The New York Times*, July 8, 1987; available from Lexis-Nexis Academic; Linda Greenhouse, "Washington Talk: The Bork Nomination; In No Time at All, Both Proponents and Opponents Are Ready for Battle," *The New York Times*, July 9, 1987; available from Lexis-Nexis Academic.

96. Martha A. Miles and Caroline Rand Herron, "The Nation; Bork Opponents: N.A.A.C.P., N.E.A., and Biden, Too," *The New York Times*, July 12, 1987; available from Lexis-Nexis Academic.

97. David Hoffman, "Confirm Bork, Reagan Urges," *The Washington Post*, July 30, 1987; available from Lexis-Nexis Academic.

98. Edward Walsh and Al Kamen, "Ideological Stakes High in Bork Fight: On Eve of Hearings, Both Sides Seem Eager to Keep Calm," *The Washington Post*, September 13, 1987; available from Lexis-Nexis Academic.

99. Stuart Taylor Jr., "The Bork Hearings: A Long Parade of Witnesses, Pro and Con: Ex-Officials Praise Bork; Others See Him as a Threat," *The New York Times*, September 22, 1987; available from Lexis-Nexis Academic.

100. Edward Walsh, "Public Opposition to Bork Grows: In Shift, Plurality Objects to Confirmation, Post-ABC Poll Finds," *The Washington Post*, September 25, 1987; available from Lexis-Nexis Academic.

101. Stuart Taylor Jr., "Politics in the Bork Battle: Opinion Polls and Campaign-Style Pressure May Change Supreme Court Confirmations," *The New York Times*, September 28, 1987; available from Lexis-Nexis Academic.

102. Robert H. Bork, *The Tempting of America: The Political Seduction of the Law* (New York: The Free Press, 1990), 313–314.

103. Edward Walsh and Ruth Marcus, "Bork Rejected for High Court: Senate's 58-to-42 Vote Sets Record for Margin of Defeat," *The Washington Post*, October 24, 1987; available from Lexis-Nexis Academic.

104. Steven V. Roberts, "Washington Talk: The White House; Picking Another Nominee: Lessons from Bork," *The New York Times*, October 28, 1987; available from Lexis-Nexis Academic.

105. Bickel, The Least Dangerous Branch, 17.

106. For historical perspectives on the countermajoritarian difficulty, see Sylvia Snowiss, *Judicial Review and the Law of the Constitution* (New Haven, CT: Yale University Press, 1990) and Barry Friedman, "The History of the Countermajoritarian Difficulty, Part One: The Road to Judicial Supremacy," *New York University Law Review* 73, no. 2 (May 1998): 333–433.

107. Thayer, *John Marshall*, 104.

108. Bickel, The Least Dangerous Branch, 29–33.

109. James B. Thayer, "The Origin and Scope of the American Doctrine of Constitutional Law," *Harvard Law Review* 7, no. 3 (October 25, 1893): 144.

110. Jack Knight and Lee Epstein, "The Norm of Stare Decisis," *American Journal of Political Science* 40, no. 4 (November 1996): 1018–1035. For an analysis that challenges the use of stare decisis, especially when crafting dissenting opinions, see Jeffrey A. Segal and Harold J. Spaeth, "The Influence of Stare Decisis on the Votes of United States Supreme Court Justices," *American Journal of Political Science* 40, no. 4 (November 1996): 971–1003.

111. Glendon A. Schubert, The Judicial Mind: The Attitudes and Ideologies of Supreme Court Justices, 1946–1963 (Evanston, IL: Northwestern University Press, 1965).

112. Jeffrey A. Segal and Albert D. Cover, "Ideological Values and the Votes of U.S. Supreme Court Justices," *American Political Science Review* 83, no. 2 (June 1989): 557–565.

113. Walter F. Murphy, *Elements of Judicial Strategy* (Chicago: The University of Chicago Press, 1964), 3–4.

114. Ibid., 35–36.

115. Charles M. Cameron, et al., "Strategic Auditing in a Political Hierarchy: An Informational Model of the Supreme Court's *Certiorari* Decisions," *American Political Science Review* 94, no. 1 (March 2000): 101–116.

116. James F. Spriggs II, Forrest Maltzman, and Paul J. Wahlbeck, "Bargaining on the U.S. Supreme Court: Justices' Responses to Majority Opinion Drafts," *The Journal of Politics* 61, no. 2 (May 1999): 485–506.

117. The cases listed under the year 1929 were decided in 1930 following Hughes's confirmation as chief justice in February 1930.

118. Loth, *Chief Justice*, 358.

119. *Worcester v. Georgia*, 31 U.S. 515 (1832).

120. Ibid.

121. Loth, *Chief Justice*, 360, 367.

122. Gerald N. Rosenberg, *The Hollow Hope: Can Courts Bring about Social Change?* (Chicago: The University of Chicago Press, 1991), 49.

123. Kevin T. McGuire and James A. Stimson, "The Least Dangerous Branch Revisited: New Evidence on Supreme Court Responsiveness to Public Preferences," *The Journal of Politics* 66, no. 4 (November 2004): 1018–1035.

124. Leonard D. White, *The Federalists: A Study in Administrative History* (New York: The Macmillan Company, 1948), 259–260.

125. Murphy, Elements of Judicial Strategy, 193.

INDEX